~~~~~~~~~~~~~~~~~~~~~~~~~~~~~~~~~~~~~

A Gift for

~~~~~~~~~~~~~~~~~~~~~~~~~~~~~~~~~~~~~

From

~~~~~~~~~~~~~~~~~~~~~~~~~~~~~~~~~~~~~

Date

Bedtime
DEVOTIONS
WITH JESUS
BIBLE

A kid-friendly,
early-reader edition
of the Holy Bible,
with selections
from the

International
Children's Bible®

An Imprint of Thomas Nelson

Library of Congress Control Number: 2019947735

Editorial Direction: Jill M. Smith
Editorial Assistance: Bri Loomis
Cover and Interior Design: Kristy L. Edwards
Images copyright: Shutterstock (www.shutterstock.com)

ISBN: 978-0-7852-3022-9

Printed in China

20 21 22 23 24 25 26 27 – AMC – 8 7 6 5 4 3 2 1

❀ Table of Contents ❀

The above contents do not represent the complete list of Bible books or order found in most English Bibles. For more information, see the "Note Regarding Scripture Selections" on page xiii.

Dear Parents and Teachers,

O ur children are surrounded by negative influences. And even while growing up in a loving family, children can still struggle to find their place in that family, their school, and the church. Through this very special Bible, we hope to show your children how much God loves them. We hope that, regardless of what your kids face, they will always be able to find a place in God's family.

This is not a Bible storybook nor is it a book of devotions. It is a Bible for young children, set up in such a way as to help them connect events of the Bible with God's love for them. This Bible contains over 50 percent of the text from the International Children's Bible®. To learn more about our Scripture selections, see the "Note Regarding Scripture Selections" on page xiii. However, for clarity and to use as a memorization tool, you will find a list of all the books of the Bible on page 811.

In this Bible, we included several features to help direct your child's reading. Throughout, you will find over 100 summaries that either fill gaps between books or shed light on the passages referenced in the feature boxes. To make it easy to find the Scripture referenced in each box, we've placed a gold star near the verse or passage used. In addition to a summary, each feature box contains a devotional and a takeaway to help your child get the most out of the reading. The summaries, devotionals, and takeaways are themed toward the Father's love for us and his desire for a family.

You will also see callout verses throughout this Bible. These can be used for memorization or simply as eye-catchers to bring children into the text. And the bears—have you seen the bears? The beautiful illustrations throughout will help your children want to spend time with their Bible.

We hope we've represented the Father's love in such a way that your child will sense God's love toward them personally. Although this devotional Bible was put together with your kids in mind, we all need to be reminded of the depth of God's love for us. We hope that as you read this with your child (or sneak it away and read it on your own), you will also see the thread of our heavenly Father's great love woven throughout his word.

And I pray that you and all God's holy people will have the power to understand the greatness of Christ's love. I pray that you can understand how wide and how long and how high and how deep that love is. Christ's love is greater than any person can ever know. But I pray that you will be able to know that love. (Ephesians 3:18–19)

THOMAS NELSON BIBLES EDITORIAL TEAM

Hi, Kids!

You may already know the song that goes like this: "Jesus loves me; this I know, for the Bible tells me so." But do you really know this? Have you seen it in the Bible? The Bible you hold in your hands is a very special one. As you read it, you can *know* that Jesus loves you because you'll see it for yourself.

It starts out with Father God creating the world so his new family would have a safe and beautiful place to live. When his first kids made a huge mistake, he told them a little bit of the plan he had all along—that God himself would become a man and fix the huge mistake his people had made.

The first part of the Bible shows the Father's family growing and growing but also making lots of mistakes. Through it all, God shares more and more of his plan with them. Then, finally, it happened! The Father sent his Son—who is God as a human—who fixed the first people's huge mistake by . . . dying. What?

It is a crazy but amazing plan that actually worked! The rest of the Bible (called the New Testament) shows us how Jesus' dying and then coming back to life made it so *we* can become part of the family Father God wanted all along.

Our heavenly Father's love for each of us is bigger and greater than anything we can imagine. A long time ago, a man named Paul prayed that you **"will have the power to understand the greatness of Christ's love"** (Ephesians 3:18). From everyone who put this devotional Bible together for you, well, that's our prayer too!

HAPPY READING,
THE EDITORS

PREFACE TO THE INTERNATIONAL CHILDREN'S BIBLE®

The International Children's Bible® is not a storybook or a paraphrased Bible. It is a translation of God's word from the original Hebrew and Greek languages. It is the first translation of the Holy Scriptures prepared specifically for children. Until now children have had to learn God's truths either from Bible storybooks or adult-language Bibles. Many words and concepts, readily understood by adults, may leave children mystified or with false impressions.

Yet God intended for everyone to be able to understand his word. Earliest Scriptures were in Hebrew, ideally suited for a barely literate society because of its economy of words, acrostic literary form, and poetic parallelism. The New Testament was first written in the simple Greek of everyday life, not in the Latin of Roman courts or the classical Greek of the academies. Even Jesus, the Master Teacher, taught spiritual principles by comparing them to such familiar terms as pearls, seeds, rocks, trees, and sheep. It is for this same purpose of making the Scriptures intelligible that this translation was created.

A TRUSTWORTHY TRANSLATION

Two basic premises guided the translation process. The first concern was that the translation be faithful to the manuscripts in the original languages. A team composed of the World Bible Translation Center and twenty-one additional highly qualified and experienced Bible scholars and translators was assembled. The team included people with translation experience on such accepted versions as the New International Version, the New American Standard Bible, and the New King James Version. The most recent scholarship and the best available Hebrew and Greek texts were used, principally the third edition of the United Bible Societies' Greek text and the latest edition of *Biblia Hebraica*, along with the Septuagint.

A CLEAR TRANSLATION

The second concern was to make the language simple enough for children to read and understand it for themselves. In maintaining language simplicity, several guidelines were followed. Sentences were kept short and uncomplicated. Vocabulary choice was based upon *The Living Word Vocabulary* by Dr. Edgar

Dale and Dr. Joseph O'Rourke (Worldbook-Childcraft International, 1981), which is the standard used by the editors of *The World Book Encyclopedia* to determine appropriate vocabulary. For difficult words which have no simpler synonyms, footnotes are provided. Footnotes appear at the bottom of the page and are indicated in the text by an *n* (for "note").

Dr. Charles K. Kinzer of Peabody College of Education, Vanderbilt University, did a comparative study of this base text and four other versions commonly used by children. The results showed that the International Children's Bible® was clearly the easiest version for children to comprehend on the literal level. The word choice in this version was also judged to be the most appropriate for the youngest students. It was, in fact, the only version that could be comprehended on a third-grade instructional level (Kinzer, Ransom, and Hammond, 1983).

The International Children's Bible® aids a child's understanding by putting concepts into natural terms. Modern measurements and geographical locations have been used as much as possible. For instance, the traditional *shekels* and *cubits* have been converted to modern equivalents of weights and measures. Where geographical references are identical, the modern name has been used, such as the "Mediterranean Sea" instead of "Great Sea" or "Western Sea." Also, to minimize confusion, the most familiar name for a place is used consistently, instead of using variant names for the same place. "Lake Galilee" is used throughout rather than its variant forms, "Sea of Kinnereth," "Lake Gennesaret," and "Sea of Tiberias."

Ancient customs are often unfamiliar to modern readers. Customs such as shaving a man's beard to shame him or walking between the halves of a dead animal to seal an agreement are difficult for many readers to understand. So these are clarified either in the text or in a footnote.

Since *connotations* of words change with time, care has been taken to avoid potential misunderstandings. Instead of describing ancient citadels as forts, which for modern readers would likely conjure up pictures of wooden stockades in the Old West, the International Children's Bible® uses "strong, walled cities." Instead of using the phrase "God drove the nations out of Canaan," the phrase is translated "forced them out of Canaan."

Rhetorical questions have been worded as statements, showing the implied meaning, as in this example: "No one is equal to our God," instead of "Who is equal to our God?"

Figures of speech can easily be misunderstood as literal statements. For instance, when Canaan is described as a land "flowing with milk and honey," children might literally see milk and honey running through the streets. To clarify, the International Children's Bible® has translated the meaning of the figures, while preserving the image as much as possible.

Idiomatic expressions of the biblical languages are translated to communicate the same meaning to today's child that would have been understood by the original audience. For example, the Hebrew idiom "he rested with his fathers" is translated by its meaning—"he died."

Every attempt has been made to maintain proper English style, while simplifying concepts and communications. The beauty of the Hebrew parallelism in poetry and the wordplays have been retained. Images of the ancient languages have been captured in equivalent English images wherever possible.

OUR PRAYER

It is with great humility and prayerfulness that this Bible is presented to God's children, young and old. We acknowledge the infallibility of God's word and our own human frailty. We pray that God has worked through us as his vessels so that his precious children might learn his truth for themselves and that it might richly grow in their lives. It is to his glory that this Bible is given.

THE PUBLISHER

NOTE REGARDING SCRIPTURE SELECTIONS FOR THE ICB *BEDTIME DEVOTIONS WITH JESUS BIBLE*

The Bible you hold in your hands contains just over 50 percent of International Children's Bible® text. Although the ICB translation uses simple language so all readers can understand, some of the concepts and themes throughout the Bible are not as easy to grasp—for readers young and old. The editors of this Bible did not cherry-pick Scripture, choosing only favorite books and passages or text that supports a certain doctrine. The editors carefully chose the books and book portions that would give a good overview of God's plan throughout time yet leave out some of the more graphic elements of biblical history.

The editors are not ignoring entire topics but simply representing them in a more compact and chronological way. For example, the early Mosaic law is represented in Exodus and portions of Deuteronomy, while the book of Leviticus is not included. The first kingdoms and early kings of Israel are represented, but the multiple kingships of 2 Kings and 1 and 2 Chronicles do not appear in this Bible. The prophecies of Israel and Judah's impending destruction are represented through the use of summaries and the inclusion of the Book of Lamentations. In addition, the New Testament contains three of the four Gospels and a small representation of the letters to the church.

This is not a Bible storybook but an actual Bible, and what remains is not sugar-coated text. It is still encouraged that adults be available to children as questions arise during their reading of Scripture.

THE EDITORS

OLD TESTAMENT

Genesis

THE BEGINNING OF THE WORLD

1 In the beginning God created the sky and the earth. ²The earth was empty and had no form. Darkness covered the ocean, and God's Spirit was moving over the water.

³Then God said, "Let there be light!" And there was light. ⁴God saw that the light was good. So he divided the light from the darkness. ⁵God named the light "day" and the darkness "night." Evening passed, and morning came. This was the first day.

⁶Then God said, "Let there be something to divide the water in two!" ⁷So God made the air to divide the water in two. Some of the water was above the air, and some of the water was below it. ⁸God named the air "sky." Evening passed, and morning came. This was the second day.

⁹Then God said, "Let the water under the sky be gathered together so the dry land will appear." And it happened. ¹⁰God named the dry land "earth." He named the water that was gathered together "seas." God saw that this was good.

¹¹Then God said, "Let the earth produce plants. Some plants will make grain for seeds. Others will make fruit with seeds in it. Every seed will produce more of its own kind of plant." And it happened. ¹²The earth produced plants. Some plants had grain for seeds. The trees made fruit with seeds in it. Each seed grew its own kind of plant. God saw that all this was good. ¹³Evening passed, and morning came. This was the third day.

¹⁴Then God said, "Let there be lights in the sky to separate day from night. These lights will be used for signs, seasons, days and years. ¹⁵They will be in the sky to give light to the earth." And it happened.

¹⁶So God made the two large lights. He made the brighter light to rule the day. He made the smaller light to rule the night. He also made the stars. ¹⁷God put all these in the sky to shine on the earth. ¹⁸They are to rule over the day and over the night. He put them there to separate the light from the darkness. God saw that all these things were good. ¹⁹Evening passed, and morning came. This was the fourth day.

²⁰Then God said, "Let the water be filled with living things. And let birds fly in the air above the earth."

²¹So God created the large sea animals. He created every living thing that moves in the sea. The sea is filled with these living things. Each one produces more of its own kind. God also made every bird that flies. And each bird produces more of its own kind. God saw that this was good. ²²God blessed them and said, "Have many young ones and grow in number. Fill the water of the seas, and let the birds grow in number on the earth." ²³Evening passed, and morning came. This was the fifth day.

²⁴Then God said, "Let the earth be filled with animals. And let each produce more of its own kind. Let there be tame animals and small crawling animals and wild animals. And let each produce more of its kind." And it happened.

²⁵So God made the wild animals, the tame animals and all the small crawling animals to produce more of their own kind. God saw that this was good.

²⁶Then God said, "Let us make human beings in our image and likeness. And let them rule over the fish in the sea and the birds in the sky. Let them rule over the tame animals, over all the earth and over all the small crawling animals on the earth."

²⁷So God created human beings in his image. In the image of God he created them. He created them male

and female. ²⁸God blessed them and said, "Have many children and grow in number. Fill the earth and be its master. Rule over the fish in the sea and over the birds in the sky. Rule over every living thing that moves on the earth."

²⁹God said, "Look, I have given you all the plants that have grain for seeds. And I have given you all the trees whose fruits have seeds in them. They will be food for you. ³⁰I have given all the green plants to all the animals to eat. They will be food for every wild animal, every bird of the air and every small crawling animal." And it happened. ³¹God looked at everything he had made, and it was very good. Evening passed, and morning came. This was the sixth day.

THE SEVENTH DAY—REST

2 So the sky, the earth and all that filled them were finished. ²By the seventh day God finished the work he had been doing. So on the seventh day he rested from all his work. ³God blessed the seventh day and made it a holy day. He made it holy because on that day he rested. He rested from all the work he had done in creating the world.

THE FIRST PEOPLE

⁴This is the story of the creation of the sky and the earth. When the Lord God made the earth and the sky, ⁵there were no plants on the earth. Nothing was growing in the fields. The Lord God had not yet made it rain on the land. And there was no man to care for the

---

☆ Genesis 1

God made our entire world in one week. Each day he created something new, like the sun and moon, the oceans, and then all the animals. On the sixth day, God made the first person. After seeing his work was good, he rested on the seventh day.

Do you like to create things with Legos or Play–Doh? God likes to create things too. The Bible says that God created everything. He created light, day, night, stars, moon, water, land, trees, plants, fish, bears, lions, kangaroos, and people. Our God is an awesome Creator, but he is also a loving Father. He created people because he wanted a family. He made you because he wants to be with you now and forever!

* * * * * * * * * * * * * * * *

When you accept God's Son, Jesus, you become God's child too!

ground. [6]But a mist often rose from the earth and watered all the ground.

[7]Then the Lord God took dust from the ground and formed man from it. The Lord breathed the breath of life into the man's nose. And the man became a living person. [8]Then the Lord God planted a garden in the East, in a place called Eden. He put the man he had formed in that garden. [9]The Lord God caused every beautiful tree and every tree that was good for food to grow out of the ground. In the middle of the garden, God put the tree that gives life. And he put there the tree that gives the knowledge of good and evil.

[10]A river flowed through Eden and watered the garden. From that point the river was divided. It had four streams flowing into it. [11]The name of the first stream is Pishon. It flows around the whole land of Havilah, where there is gold. [12]That gold is good. Bdellium and onyx[n] are also there. [13]The name of the second river is Gihon. It flows around the whole land of Cush. [14]The name of the third river is Tigris. It flows out of Assyria toward the east. The fourth river is the Euphrates.

[15]The Lord God put the man in the garden of Eden to care for it and work it. [16]The Lord God commanded him, "You may eat the fruit from any tree in the garden. [17]But you must not eat the fruit from the tree which gives the knowledge of good and evil. If you ever eat fruit from that tree, you will die!"

THE FIRST WOMAN

[18]Then the Lord God said, "It is not good for the man to be alone. I will make a helper who is right for him."

[19]From the ground God formed every wild animal and every bird in the sky. He brought them to the man so the man could name them. Whatever the man called each living thing, that became its name. [20]The man gave names to all the tame animals, to the birds in the sky and to all the wild animals. But Adam[n] did not find a helper that was right for him. [21]So the Lord God caused the man to sleep very deeply. While the man was asleep, God took one of the ribs from the man's body. Then God closed the man's skin at the place where he took the rib. [22]The Lord God used the rib from the man to make a woman. Then the Lord brought the woman to the man.

[23]And the man said,

> "Now, this is someone whose bones
>   came from my bones.
>   Her body came from my body.
> I will call her 'woman,'
>   because she was taken out of man."

[24]So a man will leave his father and mother and be united with his wife. And the two people will become one body. [25]The man and his wife were naked, but they were not ashamed.

THE BEGINNING OF SIN

3 Now the snake was the most clever of all the wild animals the Lord God had made. One day the snake spoke to the woman. He said, "Did God really say that you must not eat fruit from any tree in the garden?"

[2]The woman answered the snake, "We may eat fruit from the trees in the garden. [3]But God told us, 'You must not eat fruit from the tree that is in the middle of the garden. You must not even touch it, or you will die.'"

[4]But the snake said to the woman, "You will not die. [5]God knows that if you eat the fruit from that tree, you will learn about good and evil. Then you will be like God!"

[6]The woman saw that the tree was beautiful. She saw that its fruit was good to eat and that it would make her wise. So she took some of its fruit and ate it.

2:12 **bdellium and onyx** Bdellium is an expensive, sweet-smelling resin like myrrh. And onyx is a gem.
2:20 **Adam** This is the name of the first man. It also means "humans," including men and women.

She also gave some of the fruit to her husband who was with her, and he ate it.

⁷Then, it was as if the man's and the woman's eyes were opened. They realized they were naked. So they sewed fig leaves together and made something to cover themselves.

⁸Then they heard the Lord God walking in the garden. This was during the cool part of the day. And the man and his wife hid from the Lord God among the trees in the garden. ⁹But the Lord God called to the man. The Lord said, "Where are you?"

¹⁰The man answered, "I heard you walking in the garden. I was afraid because I was naked. So I hid."

¹¹God said to the man, "Who told you that you were naked? Did you eat fruit from that tree? I commanded you not to eat from that tree."

¹²The man said, "You gave this woman to me. She gave me fruit from the tree. So I ate it."

¹³Then the Lord God said to the woman, "What have you done?"

She answered, "The snake tricked me. So I ate the fruit."

¹⁴The Lord God said to the snake,

"Because you did this,
    a curse will be put on you.
You will be cursed more than any
        tame animal or wild animal.
You will crawl on your stomach,
    and you will eat dust all the days of
        your life.
¹⁵ I will make you and the woman
        enemies to each other.
Your descendants and her descendants
    will be enemies.
Her child will crush your head.
    And you will bite his heel."

¹⁶Then God said to the woman,

"I will cause you to have much trouble
    when you are pregnant.
And when you give birth to children,
    you will have great pain.
You will greatly desire your husband,
    but he will rule over you."

¹⁷Then God said to the man, "You listened to what your wife said. And you ate fruit from the tree that I commanded you not to eat from.

"So I will put a curse on the ground.
    You will have to work very hard for
        food.
In pain you will eat its food
    all the days of your life.
¹⁸ The ground will produce thorns and
        weeds for you.
    And you will eat the plants of the
        field.
¹⁹ You will sweat and work hard
    for your food.
Later you will return to the ground.
    This is because you were taken
        from the ground.
You are dust.
    And when you die, you will return
        to the dust."

²⁰The man named his wife Eve.ⁿ This is because she is the mother of everyone who ever lived.

²¹The Lord God made clothes from animal skins for the man and his wife. And so the Lord dressed them. ²²Then the Lord God said, "Look, the man has become like one of us. He knows good and evil. And now we must keep him from eating some of the fruit from the tree of life. If he does, he will live forever." ²³So the Lord God forced the man out of the garden of Eden. He had to work the ground he was taken from.

3:20 Eve This name sounds like the Hebrew word meaning "alive."

²⁴God forced the man out of the garden. Then God put angels on the east side of the garden. He also put a sword of fire there. It flashed around in every direction. This kept people from getting to the tree of life.

THE FIRST FAMILY

4 Adam had intimate relations with his wife Eve. She became pregnant and gave birth to Cain.ⁿ Eve said, "With the Lord's help, I have given birth to a man." ²After that, Eve gave birth to Cain's brother Abel. Abel took care of sheep. Cain became a farmer.

³Later, Cain brought a gift to God. He brought some food from the ground. ⁴Abel brought the best parts of his best sheep. The Lord accepted Abel and his gift. ⁵But God did not accept Cain and his gift. Cain became very angry and looked unhappy.

⁶The Lord asked Cain, "Why are you angry? Why do you look so unhappy? ⁷If you do good, I will accept you. But if you do not do good, sin is ready to attack you. Sin wants you. But you must rule over it."

⁸Cain said to his brother Abel, "Let's go out into the field." So Cain and Abel went into the field. Then Cain attacked his brother Abel and killed him.

⁹Later, the Lord said to Cain, "Where is your brother Abel?"

Cain answered, "I don't know. Is it my job to take care of my brother?"

¹⁰Then the Lord said, "What have you done? Your brother's blood is on the ground. That blood is like a voice that tells me what happened. ¹¹And now you will be cursed in your work with the ground. It is the same ground where your brother's blood fell. Your hands killed him. ¹²You will work the ground. But it will not grow good crops for you anymore. You will wander around on the earth."

¹³Then Cain said to the Lord, "This punishment is more than I can stand! ¹⁴Look! You have forced me to stop working the ground. And now I must hide from you. I will wander around on the earth. And anyone who meets me can kill me."

¹⁵Then the Lord said to Cain, "No! If anyone kills you, I will punish that person seven times more." Then the Lord put a mark on Cain. It was a warning to anyone who met him not to kill him.

CAIN'S FAMILY

¹⁶Then Cain went away from the Lord. Cain lived in the land of Nod,ⁿ east of Eden. ¹⁷Cain had intimate relations with his wife. She became pregnant and gave birth to Enoch. At that time Cain was building a city. He named it after his son Enoch. ¹⁸Enoch had a son named Irad. Irad had a son named Mehujael. Mehujael had a son named Methushael. And Methushael had a son named Lamech.

¹⁹Lamech married two women. One wife was named Adah, and the other was Zillah. ²⁰Adah gave birth to Jabal. He was the first person to live in tents and raise cattle. ²¹Jabal's brother was Jubal. Jubal was the first person to play the harp and flute. ²²Zillah gave birth to Tubal-Cain. He made tools out of bronze and iron. The sister of Tubal-Cain was Naamah.

²³Lamech said to his wives:

"Adah and Zillah, hear my voice!
  You wives of Lamech, listen to
    what I say.
I killed a man for wounding me.
  I killed a young man for hitting me.
²⁴ Cain's killer may be punished 7 times.
  Then Lamech's killer will be
    punished 77 times."

ADAM AND EVE HAVE A NEW SON

²⁵Adam had intimate relations with his wife Eve again. And she gave birth to a son. She named him Seth.ⁿ Eve said,

---

4:1 Cain This name sounds like the Hebrew word for "I have given birth."
4:16 Nod This name sounds like the Hebrew word for "wander."
4:25 Seth This name sounds like the Hebrew word for "to give."

"God has given me another child. He will take the place of Abel, who was killed by Cain." ²⁶Seth also had a son. They named him Enosh. At that time people began to pray to the Lord.

ADAM'S FAMILY HISTORY

5 This is the family history of Adam. When God created human beings, he made them in God's likeness. ²He created them male and female. And on that day he blessed them and named them human beings.

³When Adam was 130 years old, he became the father of another son. He was in the likeness and image of Adam. Adam named him Seth. ⁴After Seth was born, Adam lived 800 years. During that time he had other sons and daughters. ⁵So Adam lived a total of 930 years. Then he died.

⁶When Seth was 105 years old, he had a son named Enosh. ⁷After Enosh was born, Seth lived 807 years. During that time he had other sons and daughters. ⁸So Seth lived a total of 912 years. Then he died.

⁹When Enosh was 90 years old, he had a son named Kenan. ¹⁰After Kenan was born, Enosh lived 815 years. During that time he had other sons and daughters. ¹¹So Enosh lived a total of 905 years. Then he died.

¹²When Kenan was 70 years old, he had a son named Mahalalel. ¹³After Mahalalel was born, Kenan lived 840 years. During that time he had other sons and daughters. ¹⁴So Kenan lived a total of 910 years. Then he died.

¹⁵When Mahalalel was 65 years old, he had a son named Jared. ¹⁶After Jared was born, Mahalalel lived 830 years. During that time he had other sons and daughters. ¹⁷So Mahalalel lived a total of 895 years. Then he died.

¹⁸When Jared was 162 years old, he had a son named Enoch. ¹⁹After Enoch was born, Jared lived 800 years. During that time he had other sons and daughters. ²⁰So Jared lived a total of 962 years. Then he died.

²¹When Enoch was 65 years old, he had a son named Methuselah. ²²After Methuselah was born, Enoch walked with God 300 years more. During that time he had other sons and daughters. ²³So Enoch lived a total of 365 years. ²⁴Enoch walked with God. One day Enoch could not be found, because God took him.

²⁵When Methuselah was 187 years old, he had a son named Lamech. ²⁶After Lamech was born, Methuselah lived 782 years. During that time he had other sons and daughters. ²⁷So Methuselah lived a total of 969 years. Then he died.

²⁸When Lamech was 182, he had a son. ²⁹Lamech named his son Noah.[n] Lamech said, "Noah will comfort us from the pain of our work. The pain is because God has cursed the ground." ³⁰After Noah was born, Lamech lived 595 years. During that time he had other sons and daughters. ³¹So Lamech lived a total of 777 years. Then he died.

³²After Noah was 500 years old, he became the father of Shem, Ham and Japheth.

THE HUMAN RACE BECOMES EVIL

6 The number of people on earth began to grow. Daughters were born to these people. ²The sons of God saw that these girls were beautiful. And they married any of them they chose. ³The Lord said, "My Spirit will not remain in human beings forever. This is because they are flesh. They will live only 120 years."

⁴The Nephilim were on the earth in those days and also later. That was when the sons of God had physical relations with the daughters of men. These women gave birth to children, who became famous. They were the mighty warriors of long ago.

⁵The Lord saw that the human beings

5:29 Noah This name sounds like the Hebrew word for "rest."

on the earth were very wicked. He also saw that their thoughts were only about evil all the time. [6]The Lord was sorry he had made human beings on the earth. His heart was filled with pain. [7]So the Lord said, "I will destroy all human beings that I made on the earth. And I will destroy every animal and everything that crawls on the earth. I will also destroy the birds of the air. This is because I am sorry that I have made them." [8]But Noah pleased the Lord.

NOAH AND THE GREAT FLOOD

[9]This is the family history of Noah. Noah was a good man. He was the most innocent man of his time. He walked with God. [10]Noah had three sons: Shem, Ham and Japheth.

[11]People on earth did what God said was evil. Violence was everywhere. [12]And God saw this evil. All people on the earth did only evil. [13]So God said to Noah, "People have made the earth full of violence. So I will destroy all people from the earth. [14]Build a boat of cypress wood for yourself. Make rooms in it and cover it inside and outside with tar. [15]This is how big I want you to build the boat: 450 feet long, 75 feet wide and 45 feet high. [16]Make an opening around the top of the boat. Make it 18 inches high from the edge of the roof down. Put a door in the side of the boat. Make an upper, middle and lower deck in it. [17]I will bring a flood of water on the earth. I will destroy all living things that live under the sky. This includes everything that has the breath of life. Everything on the earth will die. [18]But I will make an agreement with you. You, your sons, your wife and your sons' wives will all go into the boat. [19]Also, you must bring into the boat two of every living thing, male and female. Keep them alive with you. [20]There will be two of every kind of bird, animal and crawling thing. They will come to you to be kept alive.

[21]Also gather some of every kind of food. Store it on the boat as food for you and the animals."

[22]Noah did everything that God commanded him.

THE FLOOD BEGINS

7 Then the Lord said to Noah, "I have seen that you are the best man among the people of this time. So you and your family go into the boat. [2]Take with you seven pairs, each male with its female, of every kind of clean animal. And take one pair, each male with its female, of every kind of unclean animal. [3]Take seven pairs of all the birds of the sky, each male with its female. This will allow all these animals to continue living on the earth after the flood. [4]Seven days from now I will send rain on the earth. It will rain 40 days and 40 nights. I will destroy from the earth every living thing that I made."

[5]Noah did everything that the Lord commanded him.

[6]Noah was 600 years old when the flood came. [7]He and his wife and his sons and their wives went into the boat. They went in to escape the waters of the flood. [8]The clean animals, the unclean animals, the birds and everything that crawls on the ground [9]came to Noah. They went into the boat in groups of two, male and female. This was just as God had commanded Noah. [10]Seven days later the flood started.

[11]Noah was now 600 years old. The

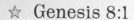

God warned Noah about a big flood that was coming. He told Noah to make a huge boat that would fit his family and two of every kind of animal on the earth. When Noah, his family, and all the animals got in the boat, God shut the door, and it started to rain. It rained for forty days and forty nights. But God didn't forget about Noah. God made the flood waters dry up so Noah, his family, and the animals could come out.

Grace loved to spend time with her dad. Her favorite thing to do with him was to go shopping on Saturday mornings. One day, as her dad looked for a new fishing rod, Grace decided to trick him and hide in the center of a clothes rack. When she finally came out, she didn't see her dad anywhere and she got very scared. Suddenly she felt a hand on her shoulder and heard a familiar voice. Little did she know, her father had never taken his eyes off of her.

. . . .

Just like God didn't forget about Noah, he will never forget you. You can always trust him!

flood started on the seventeenth day of the second month of that year. That day the underground springs split open. And the clouds in the sky poured out rain. [12]The rain fell on the earth for 40 days and 40 nights.

[13]On that same day Noah and his wife, his sons Shem, Ham and Japheth and their wives went into the boat. [14]They had every kind of wild animal and tame animal. There was every kind of animal that crawls on the earth. Every kind of bird was there. [15]They all came to Noah in the boat in groups of two. There was every creature that had the breath of life. [16]One male and one female of every living thing came. It was just as God had commanded Noah. Then the Lord closed the door behind them.

[17]Water flooded the earth for 40 days. As the water rose, it lifted the boat off the ground. [18]The water continued to rise, and the boat floated on the water above the earth. [19]The water rose so much that even the highest mountains under the sky were covered by it. [20]The water continued to rise until it was more than 20 feet above the mountains.

[21]All living things that moved on the earth died. This included all the birds, tame animals, wild animals and creatures that swarm on the earth. And

all human beings died. ²²So everything on dry land died. This means everything that had the breath of life in its nose. ²³So God destroyed from the earth every living thing that was on the land. This was every man, animal, crawling thing and bird of the sky. All that was left was Noah and what was with him in the boat. ²⁴And the waters continued to cover the earth for 150 days.

THE FLOOD ENDS

⭐ 8 But God remembered Noah and all the wild animals and tame animals with him in the boat. God made a wind blow over the earth. And the water went down. ²The underground springs stopped flowing. And the clouds in the sky stopped pouring down rain. ³⁻⁴The water that covered the earth began to go down. After 150 days the water had gone down so much that the boat touched land again. It came to rest on one of the mountains of Ararat.ⁿ This was on the seventeenth day of the seventh month. ⁵The water continued to go down. By the first day of the tenth month the tops of the mountains could be seen.

⁶Forty days later Noah opened the window he had made in the boat. ⁷He sent out a raven. It flew here and there until the water had dried up from the earth. ⁸Then Noah sent out a dove. This was to find out if the water had dried up from the ground. ⁹The dove could not find a place to land because water still covered the earth. So it came back to the boat. Noah reached out his hand and took the bird. And he brought it back into the boat.

¹⁰After seven days Noah again sent out the dove from the boat. ¹¹And that evening it came back to him with a fresh olive leaf in its mouth. Then Noah knew that the ground was almost dry. ¹²Seven days later he sent the dove out again. But this time it did not come back.

¹³Noah was now 601 years old. It was the first day of the first month of that year. The water was dried up from the land. Noah removed the covering of the boat and saw that the land was dry. ¹⁴By the twenty-seventh day of the second month the land was completely dry.

¹⁵Then God said to Noah, ¹⁶"You and your wife, your sons and their wives should go out of the boat. ¹⁷Bring every animal out of the boat with you—the birds, animals and everything that crawls on the earth. Let them have many young ones and let them grow in number."

¹⁸So Noah went out with his sons, his wife and his sons' wives. ¹⁹Every animal, everything that crawls on the earth and every bird went out of the boat. They left by families.

²⁰Then Noah built an altar to the Lord. Noah took some of all the clean birds and animals. And he burned them on the altar as offerings to God. ²¹The Lord was pleased with these sacrifices. He said to himself, "I will never again curse the ground because of human beings. Their thoughts are evil even when they are young. But I will never again destroy every living thing on the earth as I did this time.

²² "As long as the earth continues,
    there will be planting and harvest.
Cold and hot,
    summer and winter,
    day and night
    will not stop."

THE NEW BEGINNING

9 Then God blessed Noah and his sons. He said to them, "Have many children. Grow in number and fill the earth. ²Every animal on earth and every bird in the sky will respect and fear you. So will every animal that crawls on the ground and every fish in the sea respect and fear you. I have given them to you.

³"Everything that moves, everything that is alive, is yours for food. Earlier I gave you the green plants. And now I

8:3–4 **Ararat** The ancient land of Urartu, an area in Eastern Turkey.

give you everything for food. ⁴But you must not eat meat that still has blood in it, because blood gives life. ⁵I will demand your blood for your lives. That is, I will demand the life of any animal that kills a person. And I will demand the life of anyone who takes another person's life.

⁶ "Whoever kills a human being
   will be killed by a human being.
   This is because God made humans
   in his own image.

⁷"Noah, I want you and your family to have many children. Grow in number on the earth and become many."

⁸Then God said to Noah and his sons, ⁹"Now I am making my agreement with you and your people who will live after you. ¹⁰And I also make it with every living thing that is with you. It is with the birds, the tame animals and the wild animals. It is with all that came out of the boat with you. I make my agreement with every living thing on earth. ¹¹I make this agreement with you: I will never again destroy all living things by floodwaters. A flood will never again destroy the earth."

¹²And God said, "I am making an agreement between me and you and every living creature that is with you. It will continue from now on. This is the sign: ¹³I am putting my rainbow in the clouds. It is the sign of the agreement between me and the earth. ¹⁴When I bring clouds over the earth, a rainbow appears in the clouds. ¹⁵Then I will remember my agreement. It is between me and you and every living thing. Floodwaters will never again destroy all life on the earth. ¹⁶When the rainbow appears in the clouds, I will see it. Then

I will remember the agreement that continues forever. It is between me and every living thing on the earth."

¹⁷So God said to Noah, "That rainbow is a sign. It is the sign of the agreement that I made with all living things on earth."

NOAH AND HIS SONS

¹⁸The sons of Noah came out of the boat with him. They were Shem, Ham and Japheth. (Ham was the father of Canaan.) ¹⁹These three men were Noah's sons. And all the people on earth came from these three sons.

²⁰Noah became a farmer and planted a vineyard. ²¹He drank wine made from his grapes. Then he became drunk and lay naked in his tent. ²²Ham, the father of Canaan, looked at his naked father. Ham told his brothers outside. ²³Then Shem and Japheth got a coat and carried it on both their shoulders. They walked backwards into the tent and covered their father. They turned their faces away. In this way they did not see their father without clothes.

²⁴Noah was sleeping because of the wine. Later he woke up. Then he learned what his youngest son, Ham, had done to him. ²⁵So Noah said,

"May there be a curse on Canaan!
   May he be the lowest slave to his
   brothers."

²⁶Noah also said,

"May the Lord, the God of Shem, be
   praised!
   May Canaan be Shem's slave.
²⁷ May God give more land to Japheth.
   May Japheth live in Shem's tents,
   and may Canaan be their slave."

> When I bring clouds over the earth, a rainbow appears in the clouds.
> —GENESIS 9:14

28After the flood Noah lived 350 years. 29He lived a total of 950 years. Then he died.

NATIONS GROW AND SPREAD

10 This is the family history of the sons of Noah: Shem, Ham and Japheth. After the flood these three men had sons.

JAPHETH'S SONS

2The sons of Japheth were Gomer, Magog, Madai, Javan, Tubal, Meshech and Tiras.

3The sons of Gomer were Ashkenaz, Riphath and Togarmah.

4The sons of Javan were Elishah, Tarshish, Kittim[n] and Rodanim. 5Those who lived in the lands around the Mediterranean Sea came from these sons of Japheth. All the families grew and became different nations. Each nation had its own land and its own language.

HAM'S SONS

6The sons of Ham were Cush, Mizraim,[n] Put and Canaan.

7The sons of Cush were Seba, Havilah, Sabtah, Raamah and Sabteca.

The sons of Raamah were Sheba and Dedan.

8Cush also had a descendant named Nimrod. Nimrod became a very powerful man on earth. 9He was a great hunter before the Lord. That is why people say someone is "like Nimrod, a great hunter before the Lord." 10At first Nimrod's kingdom covered Babylon, Erech, Akkad and Calneh in the land of Babylonia. 11From there he went to Assyria. There he built the cities of Nineveh, Rehoboth Ir and Calah. 12He also built Resen, the great city between Nineveh and Calah.

13Mizraim was the father of the Ludites, Anamites, Lehabites, Naphtuhites, 14Pathrusites, Casluhites and the people of Crete. (The Philistines came from the Casluhites.)

15Canaan was the father of Sidon his first son and of Heth. 16Canaan was also the father of the Jebusites, Amorites, Girgashites, 17Hivites, Arkites, Sinites, 18Arvadites, Zemarites and Hamathites. The families of the Canaanites scattered. 19The land of the Canaanites reached from Sidon to Gerar as far as Gaza. And it reached to Sodom, Gomorrah, Admah and Zeboiim, as far as Lasha.

20All these people were the sons of Ham. All these families had their own languages, their own lands and their own nations.

SHEM'S SONS

21Shem, Japheth's older brother, also had sons. One of his descendants was the father of all the sons of Eber.

22The sons of Shem were Elam, Asshur, Arphaxad, Lud and Aram.

23The sons of Aram were Uz, Hul, Gether and Meshech.

24Arphaxad was the father of Shelah. Shelah was the father of Eber. 25Eber was the father of two sons. One son was named Peleg[n] because the earth was divided during his life. Eber's other son was named Joktan.

26Joktan was the father of Almodad, Sheleph, Hazarmaveth, Jerah, 27Hadoram, Uzal, Diklah, 28Obal, Abimael, Sheba, 29Ophir, Havilah and Jobab. All these people were the sons of Joktan. 30These people lived in the area between Mesha and Sephar in the hill country in the East.

31These are the people from the family of Shem. They are arranged by families, languages, countries and nations.

32This is the list of the families from the sons of Noah. They are arranged according to their nations. From these families came all the nations who spread across the earth after the flood.

10:4 **Kittim** His descendants were the people of Cyprus.
10:6 **Mizraim** This is another name for Egypt.
10:25 **Peleg** This name sounds like the Hebrew word for "divided."

THE LANGUAGES CONFUSED

11 At this time the whole world spoke one language. Everyone used the same words. ²As people moved from the East, they found a plain in the land of Babylonia. They settled there to live.

³They said to each other, "Let's make bricks and bake them to make them hard." So they used bricks instead of stones, and tar instead of mortar. ⁴Then they said to each other, "Let's build for ourselves a city and a tower. And let's make the top of the tower reach high into the sky. We will become famous. If we do this, we will not be scattered over all the earth."

⁵The Lord came down to see the city and the tower that the people had built. ⁶The Lord said, "Now, these people are united. They all speak the same language. This is only the beginning of what they will do. They will be able to do anything they want. ⁷Come, let us go down and confuse their language. Then they will not be able to understand each other."

⁸So the Lord scattered them from there over all the earth. And they stopped building the city. ⁹That is where the Lord confused the language of the whole world. So the place is called Babel." So the Lord caused them to spread out from there over all the whole world.

THE STORY OF SHEM'S FAMILY

¹⁰This is the family history of Shem. Two years after the flood, when Shem was 100 years old, his son Arphaxad was born. ¹¹After that, Shem lived 500 years and had other sons and daughters.

¹²When Arphaxad was 35 years old, his son Shelah was born. ¹³After that, Arphaxad lived 403 years and had other sons and daughters.

¹⁴When Shelah was 30 years old, his son Eber was born. ¹⁵After that, Shelah lived 403 years and had other sons and daughters.

¹⁶When Eber was 34 years old, his son Peleg was born. ¹⁷After that, Eber lived 430 years and had other sons and daughters.

¹⁸When Peleg was 30 years old, his son Reu was born. ¹⁹After that, Peleg lived 209 years and had other sons and daughters.

²⁰When Reu was 32 years old, his son Serug was born. ²¹After that, Reu lived 207 years and had other sons and daughters.

²²When Serug was 30 years old, his son Nahor was born. ²³After that, Serug lived 200 years and had other sons and daughters.

²⁴When Nahor was 29 years old, his son Terah was born. ²⁵After that, Nahor lived 119 years and had other sons and daughters.

²⁶After Terah was 70 years old, his sons Abram, Nahor and Haran were born.

THE STORY OF TERAH'S FAMILY

²⁷This is the family history of Terah. Terah was the father of Abram, Nahor and Haran. Haran was the father of Lot. ²⁸Haran died while his father, Terah, was still alive. This happened in Ur in Babylonia, where he was born. ²⁹Abram and Nahor both married. Abram's wife was named Sarai. Nahor's wife was named Milcah. She was the daughter of Haran. Haran was the father of Milcah and Iscah. ³⁰Sarai was not able to have children.

³¹Terah took his son Abram, his grandson Lot (Haran's son) and his daughter-in-law Sarai (Abram's wife). They moved out of Ur of Babylonia. They had planned to go to the land of Canaan. But when they reached the city of Haran, they settled there.

³²Terah lived to be 205 years old. Then he died in Haran.

11:9 **Babel** This name sounds like the Hebrew word for "confused."

☆ Genesis 12:1–2

God told Abram (Abraham) to pack his things and move from his home in Haran to the land of Canaan. The Lord promised Abram he would receive blessings and he would be a blessing to others.

God promised Abraham that he would have as many children— and grandchildren and great-grandchildren and so on—as there are stars! That is a lot of people! God said that he would bless all those people and make them into a great nation. Abraham was seventy-five years old. He had no children. But he believed God's promise and waited for God's word to happen. God kept his promise. Twenty-five years later, Abraham's son Isaac was born. Sometimes it is hard to wait, but God's best is worth waiting for. Remember, God is always on time. He is never late.

. . . .

God always keeps his promises to us. So don't be sad if you have to wait for them.

GOD CALLS ABRAM

☆ **12** Then the Lord said to Abram, "Leave your country, your relatives and your father's family. Go to the land I will show you.

² I will make you a great nation,
   and I will bless you.
 I will make you famous.
   And you will be a blessing to
      others.
³ I will bless those who bless you.
   I will place a curse on those who
      harm you.
 And all the people on earth
   will be blessed through you."

⁴So Abram left Haran as the Lord had told him. And Lot went with him. At this time Abram was 75 years old. ⁵Abram took his wife Sarai, his nephew Lot and everything they owned. They took all the servants they had gotten in Haran. They set out from Haran, planning to go to the land of Canaan. In time they arrived there.

⁶Abram traveled through that land. He went as far as the great tree of Moreh at Shechem. The Canaanites were living in the land at that time. ⁷The Lord appeared to Abram. The Lord said, "I will give this land to your descendants." So Abram built an altar there to the

Lord, who had appeared to him. [8]Then Abram traveled from Shechem to the mountain east of Bethel. And he set up his tent there. Bethel was to the west, and Ai was to the east. There Abram built another altar to the Lord and worshiped him. [9]After this, he traveled on toward southern Canaan.

ABRAM GOES TO EGYPT

[10]At this time there was not much food in the land. So Abram went down to Egypt to live because there was so little food. [11]Just before they arrived in Egypt, Abram said to his wife Sarai, "I know you are a very beautiful woman. [12]When the Egyptians see you, they will say, 'This woman is his wife.' Then they will kill me but let you live. [13]Tell them you are my sister. Then things will go well with me. And I may be allowed to live because of you."

[14]So Abram went into Egypt. The people of Egypt saw that Sarai was very beautiful. [15]Some of the Egyptian officers saw her also. They told the king of Egypt how beautiful she was. They took her to the king's palace. [16]The king was kind to Abram because he thought Abram was Sarai's brother. He gave Abram sheep, cattle and male and female donkeys. Abram also was given male and female servants and camels.

[17]But the Lord sent terrible diseases on the king and all the people in his house. This was because of Abram's wife Sarai. [18]So the king sent for Abram. The king said, "What have you done to me? Why didn't you tell me Sarai was your wife? [19]Why did you say, 'She is my sister'? I made her my wife. But now here is your wife. Take her and leave!" [20]Then the king commanded his men to make Abram leave Egypt. So Abram and his wife left with everything they owned.

ABRAM AND LOT SEPARATE

13 So Abram, his wife and Lot left Egypt. They took everything they owned and traveled to southern Canaan. [2]Abram was very rich in cattle, silver and gold.

[3]He left southern Canaan and went back to Bethel. He went where he had camped before, between Bethel and Ai. [4]It was the place where Abram had built an altar before. So he worshiped the Lord there.

[5]During this time Lot was traveling with Abram. Lot also had many sheep, cattle and tents. [6]Abram and Lot had so many animals that the land could not support both of them together. [7]Abram's herders and Lot's herders began to argue. The Canaanites and the Perizzites were living in the land at this time.

[8]So Abram said to Lot, "There should be no arguing between you and me. Your herders and mine should not argue either. We are brothers. [9]We should separate. The whole land is there in front of you. If you go to the left, I will go to the right. If you go to the right, I will go to the left."

[10]Lot looked all around and saw the whole Jordan Valley. He saw that there was much water there. It was like the Lord's garden, like the land of Egypt in the direction of Zoar. (This was before the Lord destroyed Sodom and Gomorrah.) [11]So Lot chose to move east and live in the Jordan Valley. In this way Abram and Lot separated. [12]Abram lived in the land of Canaan. But Lot lived among the cities in the Jordan Valley. He moved very near to Sodom. [13]Now the people of Sodom were very evil. They were always sinning against the Lord.

[14]After Lot left, the Lord said to

> The Lord appeared to Abram (and) said, "I will give this land to your descendants."
>
> –GENESIS 12:7

Abram, "Look all around you. Look north and south and east and west. [15]All this land that you see I will give to you and your descendants forever. [16]I will make your descendants as many as the dust of the earth. If anyone could count the dust on the earth, he could count your people. [17]Get up! Walk through all this land. I am now giving it to you."

[18]So Abram moved his tents. He went to live near the great trees of Mamre. This was at the city of Hebron. There he built an altar to the Lord.

LOT IS CAPTURED

14 Now Amraphel was king of Babylonia. Arioch was king of Ellasar. Kedorlaomer was king of Elam. And Tidal was king of Goiim. [2]All these kings went to war against several other kings: Bera king of Sodom, Birsha king of Gomorrah, Shinab king of Admah, Shemeber king of Zeboiim and the king of Bela. (Bela is also called Zoar.)

[3]These kings who were attacked united their armies in the Valley of Siddim. (The Valley of Siddim is now the Dead Sea.) [4]These kings had served Kedorlaomer for 12 years. But in the thirteenth year, they all turned against him. [5]Then in the fourteenth year, Kedorlaomer and the kings with him came and defeated the Rephaites in Ashteroth Karnaim. They also defeated the Zuzites in Ham and the Emites in Shaveh Kiriathaim. [6]And they defeated the Horites in the mountains of Edom to El Paran. (El Paran is near the desert.) [7]Then they turned back and went to En Mishpat (that is, Kadesh). They defeated all the Amalekites. They also defeated the Amorites who lived in Hazazon Tamar.

[8]At that time the kings of Sodom, Gomorrah, Admah, Zeboiim and Bela went out to fight in the Valley of Siddim. (Bela is called Zoar.) [9]They fought against Kedorlaomer king of Elam, Tidal king of Goiim, Amraphel king of Babylonia, and Arioch king of Ellasar. So there were four kings fighting against five. [10]There were many tar pits in the Valley of Siddim. The kings of Sodom and Gomorrah and their armies ran away. Some of the soldiers fell into the tar pits. But the others ran away to the mountains.

[11]Now Kedorlaomer and his armies took everything the people of Sodom and Gomorrah owned. They also took all their food. [12]They took Lot, Abram's nephew who was living in Sodom. The enemy also took everything he owned. Then they left. [13]One of the men who was not captured went to Abram, the Hebrew. He told Abram what had happened. At that time Abram was camped near the great trees of Mamre the Amorite. Mamre was a brother of Eshcol and a brother of Aner. And they had all made an agreement to help Abram.

ABRAM RESCUES LOT

[14]Abram learned that Lot had been captured. So he called out his 318 trained men who had been born in his camp. Abram led the men and chased the enemy all the way to the town of Dan. [15]That night he divided his men into groups. And they made a surprise attack against the enemy. They chased them all the way to Hobah, north of Damascus. [16]Then Abram brought back everything the enemy had stolen. Abram brought back the women and the other people. And he also brought back Lot and everything Lot owned.

[17]After defeating Kedorlaomer and the kings who were with him, Abram went home. As Abram was returning, the king of Sodom came out to meet him in the Valley of Shaveh. (That is now called King's Valley.)

[18]Melchizedek king of Salem also went to meet Abram. Melchizedek was a priest for God Most High. He brought bread and wine. [19]Melchizedek blessed Abram and said,

"Abram, may God Most High give you
    blessings.
God made heaven and earth.

20 And we praise God Most High.
He has helped you to defeat your
enemies."

Then Abram gave Melchizedek a tenth
of everything he had brought back from
the battle.

21 Then the king of Sodom said to
Abram, "You may keep all these things
for yourself. Just give me my people who
were captured."

22 But Abram said to the king of Sodom, "I make a promise to the Lord. He is
the God Most High, who made heaven
and earth. 23 I promise that I will not keep
anything that is yours. I will not keep
even a thread or a sandal strap. That way
you cannot say, 'I made Abram rich.' 24 I
will keep nothing but the food my young
men have eaten. But give Aner, Eshcol
and Mamre their share of what we won.
They went with me into battle."

GOD'S AGREEMENT WITH ABRAM

15 After these things happened, the
Lord spoke his word to Abram
in a vision. God said, "Abram, don't be
afraid. I will defend you. And I will give
you a great reward."

2 But Abram said, "Lord God, what
can you give me? I have no son. So my
slave Eliezer from Damascus will get
everything I own after I die." 3 Abram
said, "Look, you have given me no son.
So a slave born in my house will inherit
everything I have."

4 Then the Lord spoke his word to
Abram. He said, "That slave will not be
the one to inherit what you have. You
will have a son of your own. And your
son will inherit what you have."

5 Then God led Abram outside. God
said, "Look at the sky. There are so
many stars you cannot count them. And
your descendants will be too many to
count."

6 Abram believed the Lord. And the
Lord accepted Abram's faith, and that
faith made him right with God.

7 God said to Abram, "I am the Lord
who led you out of Ur of Babylonia. I
did that so I could give you this land to
own."

8 But Abram said, "Lord God, how can
I be sure that I will own this land?"

9 The Lord said to Abram, "Bring me
a three-year-old cow, a three-year-old
goat and a three-year-old male sheep.
Also bring me a dove and a young
pigeon."

10 Abram brought them all to God.
Then Abram killed the animals and cut
each of them into two pieces. He laid
each half opposite the other half. But
he did not cut the birds in half. 11 Later,
large birds flew down to eat the animals. But Abram chased them away.

12 As the sun was going down, Abram
fell into a deep sleep. While he was
asleep, a very terrible darkness came.
13 Then the Lord said to Abram, "You can
be sure that your descendants will be
strangers and travel in a land they don't
own. The people there will make them
slaves. And they will do cruel things to
them for 400 years. 14 But I will punish
the nation where they are slaves. Then
your descendants will leave that land,
taking great wealth with them. 15 Abram,
you will live to be very old. You will die
in peace and will be buried. 16 After your
great-great-grandchildren are born, your
people will come to this land again. It
will take that long, because the Amorites
are not yet evil enough to punish."

17 The sun went down, and it was
very dark. Suddenly a smoking firepot
and a blazing torch passed between the
halves of the dead animals.ⁿ 18 So on
that day the Lord made an agreement
with Abram. The Lord said, "I will give
this land to your descendants. I will
give them the land between the river
of Egypt and the great river Euphrates.
19 This is the land of the Kenites,
Kenizzites, Kadmonites, 20 Hittites,
Perizzites, Rephaites, 21 Amorites,
Canaanites, Girgashites and Jebusites."

15:17 passed . . . animals This showed that God sealed the agreement between himself and Abram.

HAGAR AND ISHMAEL

16 Sarai, Abram's wife, had no children. She had a slave girl from Egypt named Hagar. [2]Sarai said to Abram, "Look, the Lord has not allowed me to have children. So have physical relations with my slave girl. If she has a child, maybe I can have my own family through her."

Abram did what Sarai said. [3]This was after Abram lived ten years in Canaan. And Sarai gave Hagar to her husband Abram. (Hagar was her slave girl from Egypt.)

[4]Abram had physical relations with Hagar, and she became pregnant. When Hagar learned she was pregnant, she began to treat her mistress Sarai badly. [5]Then Sarai said to Abram, "This is your fault. I gave my slave girl to you. And when she became pregnant, she began to treat me badly. Let the Lord decide who is right—you or me."

[6]But Abram said to Sarai, "You are Hagar's mistress. Do anything you want to her." Then Sarai was hard on Hagar, and Hagar ran away.

[7]The angel of the Lord found Hagar beside a spring of water in the desert. The spring was by the road to Shur. [8]The angel said, "Hagar, you are Sarai's slave girl. Where have you come from? Where are you going?"

Hagar answered, "I am running from my mistress Sarai."

[9]The angel of the Lord said to her, "Go home to your mistress and obey her." [10]The angel of the Lord also said, "I will give you so many descendants they cannot be counted."

[11]The angel also said to her,

"You are now pregnant,
and you will have a son.
You will name him Ishmael,[n]
because the Lord has heard your cries.
[12] Ishmael will be like a wild donkey.
He will be against everyone.
And everyone will be against him.
He will attack all his brothers."

[13]The slave girl gave a name to the Lord who spoke to her. She said to him, "You are 'God who sees me.'" This is because she said to herself, "Have I really seen God who sees me?" [14]So the well there was called Beer Lahai Roi.[n] It is between Kadesh and Bered.

[15]Hagar gave birth to a son for Abram. And Abram named him Ishmael. [16]Abram was 86 years old when Hagar gave birth to Ishmael.

> God made heaven and earth. And we praise God Most High.
> —GENESIS 14:19–20

PROOF OF THE AGREEMENT

17 When Abram was 99 years old, the Lord appeared to him. The Lord said, "I am God All-Powerful. Obey me and do what is right. [2]I will make an agreement between us. I will make you the ancestor of many people."

[3]Then Abram bowed facedown on the ground. God said to him, [4]"I am making my agreement with you: I will make you the father of many nations. [5]I am changing your name from Abram[n] to Abraham.[n] This is because I am making you a father of many nations.

16:11 Ishmael The Hebrew words for "Ishmael" and "has heard" sound similar.
16:14 Beer Lahai Roi This means "the well of the Living One who sees me."
17:5 Abram This name means "honored father."
17:5 Abraham The end of the Hebrew word for "Abraham" sounds like the beginning of the Hebrew word for "many."

[6]I will give you many descendants. New nations will be born from you. Kings will come from you. [7]And I will make an agreement between me and you and all your descendants from now on: I will be your God and the God of all your descendants. [8]You live in the land of Canaan now as a stranger. But I will give you and your descendants all this land forever. And I will be the God of your descendants."

[9]Then God said to Abraham, "You and your descendants must keep this agreement from now on. [10]This is my agreement with you and all your descendants: Every male among you must be circumcised. You must obey this agreement. [11]Cut away the foreskin to show that you follow the agreement between me and you. [12]From now on when a baby boy is eight days old, you will circumcise him. This includes any boy born among your people or any who is your slave. (He would not be one of your descendants.) [13]So circumcise every baby boy. Circumcise him whether he is born in your family or bought as a slave. Your bodies will be marked. This will show that you are part of my agreement that lasts forever. [14]Any male who is not circumcised will be separated from his people. He has broken my agreement."

ISAAC—THE PROMISED SON

[15]God said to Abraham, "I will change the name of Sarai,[n] your wife. Her new name will be Sarah.[n] [16]I will bless her. I will give her a son, and you will be the father. She will be the mother of many nations. Kings of nations will come from her."

[17]Abraham bowed facedown on the ground and laughed. He said to himself, "Can a man have a child when he is 100 years old? Can Sarah give birth to a child when she is 90?" [18]Then Abraham said to God, "Please let Ishmael be the son you promised."

[19]God said, "No. Sarah your wife will have a son, and you will name him Isaac.[n] I will make my agreement with him. It will be an agreement that continues forever with all his descendants. [20]"You asked me about Ishmael, and I heard you. I will bless him. I will give him many descendants. And I will cause their numbers to grow very greatly. He will be the father of 12 great leaders. I will make him into a great nation. [21]But I will make my agreement with Isaac. He is the son whom Sarah will have at this same time next year." [22]After God finished talking with Abraham, God rose and left him.

[23]Then Abraham gathered Ishmael and all the males born in his camp. He also gathered the slaves he had bought. So that day Abraham circumcised every man and boy in his camp. This was what God had told him to do. [24]Abraham was 99 years old when he was circumcised. [25]And Ishmael, his son, was 13 years old when he was circumcised. [26]Abraham and his son were circumcised on that same day. [27]Also on that day all the men in Abraham's camp were circumcised. This included all those born in his camp and all the slaves he had bought from other nations.

THE THREE VISITORS

18 Later, the Lord again appeared to Abraham near the great trees of Mamre. At that time Abraham was sitting at the door of his tent. It was during the hottest part of the day. [2]He looked up and saw three men standing near him. When Abraham saw them, he ran from his tent to meet them. He bowed facedown on the ground before them. [3]Abraham said, "Sir, if you think well of me, please stay awhile with me, your servant. [4]I will bring some water so all of you can wash your feet. You may rest under the tree. [5]I will get some bread

---

17:15 **Sarai** An Aramaic name meaning "princess."
17:15 **Sarah** A Hebrew name meaning "princess."
17:19 **Isaac** The Hebrew words for "he laughed" (vs. 17) and "Isaac" sound the same.

for you, so you can regain your strength. Then you may continue your journey."

The three men said, "That is fine. Do as you said."

⁶Abraham hurried to the tent where Sarah was. He said to her, "Hurry, prepare 20 quarts of fine flour. Make it into loaves of bread." ⁷Then Abraham ran to his cattle. He took one of his best calves and gave it to a servant. The servant hurried to kill the calf and to prepare it for food. ⁸Abraham gave the three men the calf that had been cooked. He also gave them milk curds and milk. While the three men ate, he stood under the tree near them.

⁹The men asked Abraham, "Where is your wife Sarah?"

"There, in the tent," said Abraham.

¹⁰Then the Lord said, "I will certainly return to you about this time a year from now. At that time your wife Sarah will have a son."

Sarah was listening at the entrance of the tent which was behind him. ¹¹Abraham and Sarah were very old. Sarah was past the age when women normally have children. ¹²So she laughed to herself, "My husband and I are too old to have a baby."

¹³Then the Lord said to Abraham, "Why did Sarah laugh? Why did she say, 'I am too old to have a baby'? ¹⁴Is anything too hard for the Lord? No! I will return to you at the right time a year from now. And Sarah will have a son."

¹⁵Sarah was afraid. So she lied and said, "I didn't laugh."

But the Lord said, "No. You did laugh."

¹⁶Then the men got up to leave and started out toward Sodom. Abraham walked along with them a short time to send them on their way.

ABRAHAM'S BARGAIN WITH GOD

¹⁷The Lord said, "Should I tell Abraham what I am going to do now? ¹⁸Abraham's children will certainly become a great and powerful nation. And all nations on earth will be blessed through him. ¹⁹I

have chosen him so he would command his children and his descendants to live the way the Lord wants them to. I did this so they would live right and be fair. Then I, the Lord, will give Abraham what I promised him."

²⁰Then the Lord said, "I have heard many things against the people of Sodom and Gomorrah. They are very evil. ²¹So I will go down and see if they are as bad as I have heard."

²²So the men turned and went toward Sodom. But Abraham stood there before the Lord. ²³Then Abraham approached the Lord. Abraham asked, "Lord, do you plan to destroy the good persons along with the evil persons? ²⁴What if there are 50 good people in that city? Will you still destroy it? Surely you will save the city for the 50 good people living there. ²⁵Surely you will not destroy the good people along with the evil people. Then the good people and the evil people would be treated the same. You are the judge of all the earth. Won't you do what is right?"

²⁶Then the Lord said, "If I find 50 good people in the city of Sodom, I will save the whole city because of them."

²⁷Then Abraham said, "I am only dust and ashes. Yet I have been brave to speak to the Lord. ²⁸What if there are only 45 good people in the city? Will you destroy the whole city for the lack of 5 good people?"

The Lord said, "If I find 45 good people there, I will not destroy the city."

²⁹Again Abraham said to the Lord, "If you find only 40 good people there, will you destroy the city?"

The Lord said, "If I find 40 good people, I will not destroy the city."

³⁰Then Abraham said, "Lord, please don't be angry with me. Let me ask you this. If you find only 30 good people in the city, will you destroy it?"

The Lord said, "If I find 30 good people there, I will not destroy the city."

³¹Then Abraham said, "I have been brave to speak to the Lord. But what if there are 20 good people in the city?"

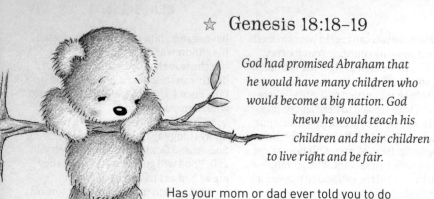

✫ Genesis 18:18–19

God had promised Abraham that he would have many children who would become a big nation. God knew he would teach his children and their children to live right and be fair.

Has your mom or dad ever told you to do something but then you did not do it? Everybody has. God chose your parents to teach you and to help you grow up. Did you know God chose Abraham for the same reason? God knew that Abraham would teach his kids how to follow God. That would make God's family grow bigger and bigger. Your parents do the same thing. They tell you certain things to keep you safe. They want the best for you just like God does. When we obey our parents, we are also obeying God.

. . . .

When you have Jesus in your heart, he helps you obey your parents. He never leaves you to do things alone.

The Lord answered, "If I find 20 good people there, I will not destroy the city." ³²Then Abraham said, "Lord, please don't be angry with me. Let me bother you this one last time. What if you find 10 good people there?"

The Lord said, "If I find 10 good people there, I will not destroy it."

³³When the Lord finished speaking to Abraham, he left. And Abraham returned home.

LOT'S VISITORS

19 The two angels came to Sodom in the evening. Lot was sitting near the city gate and saw them. He got up and went to them and bowed facedown on the ground. ²Lot said, "Sirs, please come to my house and spend the night. There you can wash your feet. Then tomorrow you may continue your journey."

The angels answered, "No, we will spend the night in the city's public square."

³But Lot begged them to come to his house. So they agreed and went to his house. Then Lot prepared a meal for them. He baked bread without yeast, and they ate it.

⁴Before bedtime, all the men of the city surrounded Lot's house. These men were both young and old and came from every part of Sodom. ⁵They called

to Lot, "Where are the two men who came to you tonight? Bring them out to us. We want to force them to have physical relations with us."

⁶Lot went outside to them, closing the door behind him. ⁷He said, "No, my brothers! Do not do this evil thing. ⁸Look! I have two daughters. They have never slept with a man. I will give them to you. You may do anything you want with them. But please don't do anything to these men. They have come to my house, and I must protect them."

⁹The men around the house answered, "Move out of the way!" Then they said to each other, "This man Lot came to our city as a stranger. Now he wants to tell us what to do!" They said to Lot, "We will do worse things to you than to them." So they started pushing Lot back. They were ready to break down the door.

¹⁰But the two men staying with Lot opened the door and pulled him back inside the house. Then they closed the door. ¹¹The two men struck the men outside the door with blindness. So these men, both young and old, could not find the door.

¹²The two men said to Lot, "Do you have any other relatives in this city? Do you have any sons-in-law, sons, daughters or any other relatives? If you do, tell them to leave now. ¹³We are about to destroy this city. The Lord has heard of all the evil that is here. So he has sent us to destroy it."

¹⁴So Lot went out and spoke to his future sons-in-law. They were pledged to marry his daughters. Lot said, "Hurry and leave this city! The Lord is about to destroy it!" But they thought Lot was joking.

¹⁵At dawn the next morning, the angels begged Lot to hurry. They said, "Go! Take your wife and your two daughters with you. Then you will not be destroyed when the city is punished."

¹⁶But Lot delayed. So the two men took the hands of Lot, his wife and his two daughters. The men led them safely out of the city. So the Lord was merciful to Lot and his family. ¹⁷The two men brought Lot and his family out of the city. Then one of the men said, "Run for your lives! Don't look back or stop anywhere in the valley. Run to the mountains or you will be destroyed."

¹⁸But Lot said to one of them, "Sir, please don't force me to go so far! ¹⁹You have been merciful and kind to me. You have saved my life. But I can't run to the mountains. The disaster will catch me, and I will die. ²⁰Look, that little town over there is not too far away. Let me run there. It's really just a little town. I'll be safe there."

²¹The angel said to Lot, "Very well, I will allow you to do this also. I will not destroy that town. ²²But run there fast. I cannot destroy Sodom until you are safely in that town." (That town is named Zoar,ⁿ because it is little.)

SODOM AND GOMORRAH DESTROYED

²³The sun had already come up when Lot entered Zoar. ²⁴The Lord sent a rain of burning sulfur down from the sky on Sodom and Gomorrah. ²⁵So the Lord destroyed those cities. He also destroyed the whole Jordan Valley, everyone living in the cities and even all the plants.

²⁶At that point Lot's wife looked back. When she did, she became a pillar of salt.

²⁷Early the next morning, Abraham got up and went to the place where he had stood before the Lord. ²⁸Abraham looked down toward Sodom and Gomorrah and all the Jordan Valley. He saw smoke rising from the land. It was like smoke from a furnace.

²⁹God destroyed the cities in the valley. But he remembered what Abraham had asked. So God saved Lot's life. But he destroyed the city where Lot had lived.

19:22 **Zoar** This name sounds like the Hebrew word for "little."

LOT AND HIS DAUGHTERS

³⁰Lot was afraid to continue living in Zoar. So he and his two daughters went to live in the mountains. They lived in a cave there. ³¹One day the older daughter said to the younger, "Our father is old. Everywhere on the earth women and men marry. But there are no men around here for us to marry. ³²Let's get our father drunk. Then we can have physical relations with him. We can use our father to have children. That way we can continue our family."

³³That night the two girls got their father drunk. Then the older daughter went and had physical relations with him. But Lot did not know when she lay down or when she got up.

³⁴The next day the older daughter said to the younger, "Last night I had physical relations with my father. Let's get him drunk again tonight. Then you can go and have physical relations with him, too. In this way we can use our father to have children to continue our family." ³⁵So that night they got their father drunk again. Then the younger daughter went and had physical relations with him. Again, Lot did not know when she lay down or when she got up.

³⁶So both of Lot's daughters became pregnant by their father. ³⁷The older daughter gave birth to a son. She named him Moab. Moab is the ancestor of all the Moabite people who are still living today. ³⁸The younger daughter also gave birth to a son. She named him Ben-Ammi. He is the father of all the Ammonite people who are still living today.

ABRAHAM AND ABIMELECH

20 Abraham left Hebron and traveled to southern Canaan. He stayed awhile between Kadesh and Shur. Then he moved to Gerar. ²Abraham told people that his wife Sarah was his sister. Abimelech king of Gerar heard this. So he sent some servants to take her. ³But one night God spoke to Abimelech in a dream. God said, "You will die. That woman you took is married."

⁴But Abimelech had not slept with Sarah. So he said, "Lord, would you destroy an innocent nation? ⁵Abraham himself told me, 'This woman is my sister.' And she also said, 'He is my brother.' I am innocent. I did not know I was doing anything wrong."

⁶Then God said to Abimelech in the dream, "Yes, I know that you did not realize what you were doing. So I did not allow you to sin against me. I did not allow you to sleep with her. ⁷Give Abraham his wife back. He is a prophet. He will pray for you, and you will not die. But if you do not give Sarah back, you will die. And all your family will surely die."

⁸So early the next morning, Abimelech called all his officers. He told them everything that had happened in the dream. They were very much afraid. ⁹Then Abimelech called Abraham to him. Abimelech said, "What have you done to us? What wrong did I do against you? Why did you bring this trouble to my kingdom? You should not have done these things to me. ¹⁰What were you thinking that caused you to do this?"

¹¹Then Abraham answered, "I thought no one in this place respected God. I thought someone would kill me to get Sarah. ¹²And it is true that she is my sister. She is the daughter of my father. But she is not the daughter of my mother. ¹³God told me to leave my father's house and wander in many different places. When that happened, I told Sarah, 'You must do a special favor for me. Everywhere we go tell people I am your brother.'"

¹⁴Then Abimelech gave Abraham some sheep, cattle and male and female slaves. Abimelech also gave Sarah, his wife, back to him. ¹⁵And Abimelech said, "Look around you at my land. You may live anywhere you want."

¹⁶Abimelech said to Sarah, "I gave your brother Abraham 25 pounds of silver. I did this to make up for any

wrong that people may think about you. I want everyone to know that you are innocent."

[17]Then Abraham prayed to God. And God healed Abimelech, his wife and his servant girls. Now they could have children. [18]The Lord had kept all the women in Abimelech's house from having children. This was God's punishment on Abimelech for taking Abraham's wife Sarah.

A BABY FOR SARAH

21 The Lord cared for Sarah as he had said. He did for her what he had promised. [2]Sarah became pregnant. And she gave birth to a son for Abraham in his old age. Everything happened at the time God had said it would. [3]Abraham named his son Isaac. Sarah gave birth to this son of Abraham. [4]Abraham circumcised Isaac when he was eight days old as God had commanded.

[5]Abraham was 100 years old when his son Isaac was born. [6]And Sarah said, "God has made me laugh.[n] Everyone who hears about this will laugh with me. [7]No one thought that I would be able to have Abraham's child. But I have given Abraham a son while he is old."

HAGAR AND ISHMAEL

[8]Isaac grew and became old enough to eat food. At that time Abraham gave a great feast. [9]But Sarah saw Ishmael making fun of Isaac. (Ishmael was the son of Abraham by Hagar, Sarah's Egyptian slave.) [10]So Sarah said to Abraham, "Throw out this slave woman and her son. When we die, our son Isaac will inherit everything we have. I don't want her son to inherit any of our things."

[11]This troubled Abraham very much because Ishmael was also his son. [12]But God said to Abraham, "Don't be troubled about the boy and the slave woman. Do whatever Sarah tells you. The descendants I promised you will be from Isaac. [13]I will also make the descendants of Ishmael into a great nation. I will do this because he is your son, too."

[14]Early the next morning Abraham took some food and a leather bag full of water. He gave them to Hagar and sent her away. Hagar carried these things and her son. She went and wandered in the desert of Beersheba.

[15]Later, all the water was gone from the bag. So Hagar put her son under a bush. [16]Then she went away a short distance and sat down. Hagar thought, "My son will die. I cannot watch this happen." She sat there and began to cry.

[17]God heard the boy crying. And God's angel called to Hagar from heaven. He said, "What is wrong, Hagar? Don't be afraid! God has heard the boy crying there. [18]Help the boy up. Take him by the hand. I will make his descendants into a great nation."

[19]Then God showed Hagar a well of water. So she went to the well and filled her bag with water. Then she gave the boy a drink.

[20]God was with the boy as he grew up. Ishmael lived in the desert. He learned to shoot with a bow very well. [21]He lived in the Desert of Paran. His mother found a wife for him in Egypt.

ABRAHAM'S BARGAIN WITH ABIMELECH

[22]Then Abimelech came with Phicol, the commander of Abimelech's army.

> God
> has made
> me laugh.
> Everyone who
> hears about
> this will laugh
> with me.
> —GENESIS 21:6

21:6 laugh The Hebrew words for "he laughed" and "Isaac" sound the same.

They said to Abraham, "God is with you in everything you do. [23]So make a promise to me here before God. Promise that you will be fair with me and my children and my descendants. Be kind to me and to this land where you have lived as a stranger. Be as kind to me as I have been to you."

[24]And Abraham said, "I promise." [25]Then Abraham complained to Abimelech about Abimelech's servants. They had captured a well of water.

[26]But Abimelech said, "I don't know who did this. You never told me about this before today."

[27]Then Abraham gave Abimelech some sheep and cattle. And they made an agreement. [28]Abraham also put seven female lambs in front of Abimelech.

[29]Abimelech asked Abraham, "Why did you put these seven female lambs by themselves?"

[30]Abraham answered, "Accept these lambs from me. That will prove that you believe I dug this well."

[31]So that place was called Beersheba[n] because they made a promise to each other there.

[32]So Abraham and Abimelech made an agreement at Beersheba. Then Abimelech and Phicol, the commander of his army, went back to the land of the Philistines.

[33]Abraham planted a tamarisk tree at Beersheba. There Abraham prayed to the Lord, the God who lives forever. [34]And Abraham lived as a stranger in the land of the Philistines for a long time.

GOD TESTS ABRAHAM

22 After these things God tested Abraham's faith. God said to him, "Abraham!"

And he answered, "Here I am."

[2]Then God said, "Take your only son, Isaac, the son you love. Go to the land of Moriah. There kill him and offer him as a whole burnt offering. Do this on one of the mountains there. I will tell you which one."

[3]Early in the morning Abraham got up and saddled his donkey. He took Isaac and two servants with him. He cut the wood for the sacrifice. Then they went to the place God had told them to go. [4]On the third day Abraham looked up and saw the place in the distance. [5]He said to his servants, "Stay here with the donkey. My son and I will go over there and worship. Then we will come back to you."

[6]Abraham took the wood for the sacrifice and gave it to his son to carry. Abraham took the knife and the fire. So Abraham and his son went on together.

[7]Isaac said to his father Abraham, "Father!"

Abraham answered, "Yes, my son."

Isaac said, "We have the fire and the wood. But where is the lamb we will burn as a sacrifice?"

[8]Abraham answered, "God will give us the lamb for the sacrifice, my son."

So Abraham and his son went on together. [9]They came to the place God had told him about. There, Abraham built an altar. He laid the wood on it. Then he tied up his son Isaac. And he laid Isaac on the wood on the altar. [10]Then Abraham took his knife and was about to kill his son.

[11]But the angel of the Lord called to him from heaven. The angel said, "Abraham! Abraham!"

Abraham answered, "Yes."

[12]The angel said, "Don't kill your son or hurt him in any way. Now I can see that you respect God. I see that you have not kept your son, your only son, from me."

[13]Then Abraham looked up and saw a male sheep. Its horns were caught in a bush. So Abraham went and took the sheep and killed it. He offered it as a whole burnt offering to God. Abraham's son was saved. [14]So Abraham named that place The Lord Gives. Even today people say, "On the mountain of the Lord it will be given."

21:31 **Beersheba** This name means "well of the promise" or "well of seven."

[15]The angel of the Lord called to Abraham from heaven a second time. [16]The angel said, "The Lord says, 'You did not keep back your son, your only son, from me. Because you did this, I make you this promise by my own name: [17]I will surely bless you and give you many descendants. They will be as many as the stars in the sky and the sand on the seashore. And they will capture the cities of their enemies. [18]Through your descendants all the nations on the earth will be blessed. This is because you obeyed me.'"

[19]Then Abraham returned to his servants. They all traveled back to Beersheba, and Abraham stayed there.

[20]After these things happened, someone told Abraham: "Your brother Nahor and his wife Milcah have children now. [21]The first son is Uz. The second son is Buz. The third son is Kemuel (the father of Aram). [22]Then there are Kesed, Hazo, Pildash, Jidlaph and Bethuel." [23]Bethuel became the father of Rebekah. Milcah was the mother of these eight sons, and Nahor was the father. Nahor was Abraham's brother. [24]Also Nahor had four other sons by his slave woman Reumah. Their names were Tebah, Gaham, Tahash and Maacah.

SARAH DIES

23 Sarah lived to be 127 years old. [2]She died in Kiriath Arba (that is, Hebron) in the land of Canaan. Abraham was very sad and cried because of her. [3]After a while Abraham got up from the side of his wife's body. And he went to talk to the Hittites. He said, [4]"I am only a stranger and a foreigner here. Sell me some of your land so that I can bury my dead wife."

[5]The Hittites answered Abraham, [6]"Sir, you are a great leader among us. You may have the best place we have to bury your dead. You may have any of our burying places that you want. None of us will stop you from burying your dead wife."

[7]Abraham rose and bowed to the people of the land, the Hittites. [8]Abraham said to them, "If you truly want to help me bury my dead wife here, speak to Ephron for me. He is the son of Zohar. [9]Ask him to sell me the cave of Machpelah. It is at the edge of his field. I will pay him the full price. You can be the witnesses that I am buying it as a burial place."

[10]Ephron was sitting among the Hittites at the city gate. Ephron answered Abraham, [11]"No, sir. I will give you the land and the cave that is in it. I will give it to you with these people as witnesses. Bury your dead wife."

[12]Then Abraham bowed down before the Hittites. [13]He said to Ephron before all the people, "Please let me pay you the full price for the field. Accept my money, and I will bury my dead there."

[14]Ephron answered Abraham, [15]"Sir, the land is worth ten pounds of silver. But I won't argue with you over the price. Take the land, and bury your dead wife."

[16]Abraham agreed and paid Ephron in front of the Hittite witnesses. Abraham weighed out the full price: ten pounds of silver. They counted the weight as the traders normally did.

[17-18]So Ephron's field in Machpelah, east of Mamre, was sold. Abraham became the owner of the field, the cave in it and all the trees that were in the field. The sale was made at the city gate, with the Hittites as witnesses. [19]After this, Abraham buried his wife Sarah in the cave. It was in that field of Machpelah, near Mamre. (Mamre was later called Hebron in the land of Canaan.) [20]Abraham bought the field and the cave on it from the Hittites. He used it as a burying place.

A WIFE FOR ISAAC

24 Abraham was now very old. The Lord had blessed him in every way. [2]Abraham's oldest servant was in charge of everything Abraham owned. Abraham called that servant to him and said, "Put your hand under my leg." [3] Make a promise to me before the Lord, the God of heaven and earth. Don't get a wife for my son from the Canaanite girls who live around here. [4] Instead, go back to my country, to the land of my relatives. Get a wife for my son Isaac from there."

[5] The servant said to him, "What if this woman does not want to return with me to this land? Then, should I take your son with me back to your homeland?"

[6] Abraham said to him, "No! Don't take my son back there. [7] The Lord is the God of heaven. He brought me from the home of my father and the land of my relatives. But the Lord promised me, 'I will give this land to your descendants.' The Lord will send his angel before you. The angel will help you get a wife for my son there. [8] But if the girl won't come back with you, you will be free from this promise. But you must not take my son back there."

[9] So the servant put his hand under his master's leg. He made a promise to Abraham about this.

[10] The servant took ten of Abraham's camels and left. He carried with him many different kinds of beautiful gifts. He went to Northwest Mesopotamia to Nahor's city. [11] He made the camels kneel down at the well outside the city. It was in the evening when the women come out to get water.

[12] The servant said, "Lord, you are the God of my master Abraham. Allow me to find a wife for his son today. Please show this kindness to my master Abraham. [13] Here I am, standing by the spring of water. The girls from the city are coming out to get water. [14] I will say to one of the girls, 'Please put your jar

down so I can drink.' Then let her say, 'Drink, and I will also give water to your camels.' If that happens, I will know she is the right one for your servant Isaac. And I will know that you have shown kindness to my master."

[15] Before the servant had finished praying, Rebekah came out of the city. She was the daughter of Bethuel. (Bethuel was the son of Milcah and Nahor, Abraham's brother.) Rebekah was carrying her water jar on her shoulder. [16] She was very pretty. She was a virgin; she had never had physical relations with a man. She went down to the spring and filled her jar. Then she came back up. [17] The servant ran to her and said, "Please give me a little water from your jar."

[18] Rebekah said, "Drink, sir." She quickly lowered the jar from her shoulder and gave him a drink. [19] After he finished drinking, Rebekah said, "I will also pour some water for your camels." [20] So she quickly poured all the water from her jar into the drinking trough for the camels. Then she kept running to the well until she had given all the camels enough to drink.

[21] The servant quietly watched her. He wanted to be sure the Lord had made his trip successful. [22] After the camels had finished drinking, he gave Rebekah a gold ring weighing one-fifth of an ounce. He also gave her two gold arm bracelets weighing about four ounces each. [23] The servant asked, "Who is your father? Is there a place in his house for me and my men to spend the night?"

[24] Rebekah answered, "My father is Bethuel. He is the son of Milcah and Nahor." [25] Then she said, "And, yes, we

> Blessed is the Lord . . . The Lord has been kind and truthful.
> —GENESIS 24:27

24:2 **Put . . . leg.** This showed that a person would keep the promise.

have straw for your camels. We have a place for you to spend the night."

²⁶The servant bowed and worshiped the Lord. ²⁷He said, "Blessed is the Lord, the God of my master Abraham. The Lord has been kind and truthful to him. He has led me to my master's relatives."

²⁸Then Rebekah ran and told her mother's family about all these things. ²⁹She had a brother named Laban. He ran out to Abraham's servant, who was still at the spring. ³⁰Laban had heard what she had said. And he had seen the ring and the bracelets on his sister's arms. So he ran out to the well. And there was the man standing by the camels at the spring. ³¹Laban said, "Sir, you are welcome to come in. You don't have to stand outside. I have prepared the house for you and also a place for your camels."

³²So Abraham's servant went into the house. Laban unloaded the camels and gave them straw and food. Then Laban gave water to Abraham's servant so he and the men with him could wash their feet. ³³Then Laban gave the servant food. But the servant said, "I will not eat until I have told you why I came."

So Laban said, "Then tell us."

³⁴He said, "I am Abraham's servant. ³⁵The Lord has greatly blessed my master in everything. My master has become a rich man. The Lord has given him many flocks of sheep and herds of cattle. He has given Abraham silver and gold, male and female servants, camels and horses. ³⁶Sarah, my master's wife, gave birth to a son when she was old. My master has given everything he owns to that son. ³⁷My master had me make a promise to him. He said, 'Don't get a wife for my son from the Canaanite girls who live around here. ³⁸Instead you must go to my father's people and to my family. There you must get a wife for my son.' ³⁹I said to my master, 'What if the woman will not come back with me?' ⁴⁰But he said, 'I serve the Lord. He will send his angel with you and will help you. You will get

a wife for my son from my family and my father's people. ⁴¹Then you will be free from the promise. Or if they will not give you a wife for my son, you will be free from this promise.'

⁴²"Today I came to this spring. I said, 'Lord, God of my master Abraham, please make my trip successful. ⁴³Look, I am standing by this spring of water. I will wait for a young woman to come out to get water. Then I will say, "Please give me water from your jar to drink." ⁴⁴Then let her say, "Drink this water. I will also get water for your camels." By this I will know the Lord has chosen her for my master's son.'

⁴⁵"Before I finished my silent prayer, Rebekah came out of the city. She had her water jar on her shoulder. She went down to the spring and got water. I said to her, 'Please give me a drink.' ⁴⁶She quickly lowered the jar from her shoulder. She said, 'Drink this. I will also get water for your camels.' So I drank, and she gave water to my camels also. ⁴⁷Then I asked her, 'Who is your father?' She answered, 'My father is Bethuel son of Milcah and Nahor.' Then I put the ring in her nose and the bracelets on her arms. ⁴⁸At that time I bowed my head and thanked the Lord. I praised the Lord, the God of my master Abraham. I thanked him because he led me on the right road to get the granddaughter of my master's brother for his son. ⁴⁹Now, tell me, will you be kind and truthful to my master? And if not, tell me so. Then I will know what I should do."

⁵⁰Laban and Bethuel answered, "This is clearly from the Lord. We cannot change what must happen. ⁵¹Rebekah is yours. Take her and go. Let her marry your master's son as the Lord has commanded."

⁵²When Abraham's servant heard these words, he bowed facedown on the ground before the Lord. ⁵³Then the servant gave Rebekah gold and silver jewelry and clothes. He also gave expensive gifts to her brother and mother. ⁵⁴The

servant and the men with him ate and drank. And they spent the night there. When they got up the next morning, the servant said, "Now let me go back to my master."

⁵⁵Rebekah's mother and her brother said, "Let Rebekah stay with us at least ten days. After that she may go."

⁵⁶But the servant said to them, "Do not make me wait. The Lord has made my trip successful. Now let me go back to my master."

⁵⁷Rebekah's brother and mother said, "We will call Rebekah and ask her what she wants to do." ⁵⁸They called her and asked her, "Do you want to go with this man now?"

She said, "Yes, I do."

⁵⁹So they allowed Rebekah and her nurse to go with Abraham's servant and his men. ⁶⁰They blessed Rebekah and said,

> "Our sister, may you be the mother of
>   thousands of people.
> And may your descendants capture
>   the cities of their enemies."

⁶¹Then Rebekah and her servant girls got on the camels and followed the servant and his men. So the servant took Rebekah and left.

⁶²At this time Isaac had left Beer Lahai Roi. He was living in southern Canaan. ⁶³One evening he went out to the field to think. As he looked up, he saw camels coming. ⁶⁴Rebekah looked and saw Isaac. Then she jumped down from the camel. ⁶⁵She asked the servant, "Who is that man walking in the field to meet us?"

The servant answered, "That is my master." So Rebekah covered her face with her veil.

⁶⁶The servant told Isaac everything that had happened. ⁶⁷Then Isaac brought Rebekah into the tent of Sarah, his mother. And she became his wife. Isaac loved her very much. So he was comforted after his mother's death.

ABRAHAM'S FAMILY

25 Abraham married again. His new wife was Keturah. ²She gave birth to Zimran, Jokshan, Medan, Midian, Ishbak and Shuah. ³Jokshan was the father of Sheba and Dedan. Dedan's descendants were the people of Assyria, Letush and Leum. ⁴The sons of Midian were Ephah, Epher, Hanoch, Abida and Eldaah. All these were descendants of Keturah. ⁵Abraham left everything he owned to Isaac. ⁶But before Abraham died, he did give gifts to the sons of his other wives. Abraham sent them to the East to be away from Isaac.

⁷Abraham lived to be 175 years old. ⁸He breathed his last breath and died at an old age. He had lived a long and satisfying life. ⁹His sons Isaac and Ishmael buried him in the cave of Machpelah. This cave is in the field of Ephron east of Mamre. Ephron was the son of Zohar the Hittite. ¹⁰This is the same field that Abraham had bought from the Hittites. Abraham was buried there with his wife Sarah. ¹¹After Abraham died, God blessed his son Isaac. Isaac was now living at Beer Lahai Roi.

¹²This is the family history of Ishmael, Abraham's son. (Hagar, Sarah's Egyptian servant, was Ishmael's mother.) ¹³These are the names of Ishmael's sons in the order they were born. The first son was Nebaioth. Then came Kedar, Adbeel, Mibsam, ¹⁴Mishma, Dumah, Massa, ¹⁵Hadad, Tema, Jetur, Naphish and Kedemah. ¹⁶These were Ishmael's sons. And these are the names of the tribal leaders. They are listed according to their settlements and camps. ¹⁷Ishmael lived 137 years. Then he breathed his last breath and died. ¹⁸Ishmael's descendants lived from Havilah to Shur. This is east of Egypt stretching toward Assyria. Ishmael's descendants often attacked the descendants of his brothers.

ISAAC'S FAMILY

¹⁹This is the family history of Isaac. Abraham had a son named Isaac.

²⁰When Isaac was 40 years old, he married Rebekah. Rebekah was from Northwest Mesopotamia. She was Bethuel's daughter and the sister of Laban the Aramean. ²¹Isaac's wife could not have children. So Isaac prayed to the Lord for her. The Lord heard Isaac's prayer, and Rebekah became pregnant.

²²While she was pregnant, the babies struggled inside her. She asked, "Why is this happening to me?" Then she went to get an answer from the Lord.

²³The Lord said to her,

"Two nations are in your body.
    Two groups of people will be taken
      from you.
    One group will be stronger than the
      other.
    The older will serve the younger."

²⁴And when the time came, Rebekah gave birth to twins. ²⁵The first baby was born red. His skin was like a hairy robe. So he was named Esau.ⁿ ²⁶When the second baby was born, he was holding on to Esau's heel. So that baby was named Jacob.ⁿ Isaac was 60 years old when they were born.

²⁷When the boys grew up, Esau became a skilled hunter. He loved to be out in the fields. But Jacob was a quiet man. He stayed among the tents. ²⁸Isaac loved Esau. Esau hunted the wild animals that Isaac enjoyed eating. But Rebekah loved Jacob.

²⁹One day Jacob was boiling a pot of vegetable soup. Esau came in from hunting in the fields. He was weak from hunger. ³⁰So Esau said to Jacob, "Let me eat some of that red soup. I am weak with hunger." (That is why people call him Edom.ⁿ)

³¹But Jacob said, "You must sell me your rights as the firstborn son."ⁿ

³²Esau said, "I am almost dead from hunger. If I die, all of my father's wealth will not help me."

³³But Jacob said, "First, promise me that you will give it to me." So Esau made a promise to Jacob. In this way he sold his part of their father's wealth to Jacob. ³⁴Then Jacob gave Esau bread and vegetable soup. Esau ate and drank and then left. So Esau showed how little he cared about his rights as the firstborn son.

ISAAC LIES TO ABIMELECH

26 Once there was a time of hunger in the land. This was besides the time of hunger that happened during Abraham's life. So Isaac went to the town of Gerar. He went to see Abimelech king of the Philistines. ²The Lord appeared to Isaac and said, "Don't go down to Egypt. Live in the land where I tell you to live. ³Stay in this land, and I will be with you. I will bless you. I will give you and your descendants all these lands. I will keep the agreement I made to Abraham your father. ⁴I will give you many descendants. They will be as hard to count as the stars in the sky. And I will give them all these lands. Through your descendants all the nations on the earth will be blessed. ⁵I will do this because your father Abraham obeyed me. He did what I said. He obeyed my commands, my teachings and my rules."

⁶So Isaac stayed in Gerar. ⁷Isaac's wife Rebekah was very beautiful. The men of that place asked Isaac about her. Isaac said, "She is my sister." He was afraid to tell them she was his wife. He thought they might kill him so they could have her.

⁸Isaac lived there a long time. One day as Abimelech king of the Philistines looked out his window, he saw Isaac. Isaac was holding his wife Rebekah tenderly. ⁹Abimelech called for Isaac and

---

25:25 **Esau** This name may mean "hairy."
25:26 **Jacob** This name sounds like the Hebrew word for "heel." "Grabbing someone's heel" is a Hebrew saying for tricking someone.
25:30 **Edom** This name sounds like the Hebrew word for "red."
25:31 **rights . . . son** Usually the firstborn son had a high rank in the family. The firstborn son usually became the new head of the family.

said, "This woman is your wife. Why did you say she was your sister?"

Isaac said to him, "I was afraid you would kill me so you could have her."

[10]Abimelech said, "What have you done to us? One of our men might have had physical relations with your wife. Then we would have been guilty of a great sin."

[11]So Abimelech warned everyone. He said, "Anyone who touches this man or his wife will be put to death."

ISAAC BECOMES RICH

[12]Isaac planted seed in that land. And that year he gathered a great harvest. The Lord blessed him very much. [13]Isaac became rich. He gathered more wealth until he became a very rich man. [14]He had many slaves and many flocks and herds. The Philistines envied him. [15]So they stopped up all the wells the servants of Isaac's father Abraham had dug. (They had dug them when Abraham was alive.) The Philistines filled those wells with dirt. [16]And Abimelech said to Isaac, "Leave our country. You have become much more powerful than we are."

[17]So Isaac left that place. He camped in the Valley of Gerar and lived there. [18]Long before this time Abraham had dug many wells. After Abraham died, the Philistines filled them with dirt. So Isaac dug those wells again. He gave them the same names his father had given them. [19]Isaac's servants dug a well in the valley. From it a spring of water flowed. [20]But the men who herded sheep in Gerar argued with Isaac's servants. They said, "This water is ours." So Isaac named that well Argue because they argued with him. [21]Then Isaac's servants dug another

well. The people also argued about it. So Isaac named that well Fight. [22]Isaac moved from there and dug another well. No one argued about this one. So he named that well Room Enough. Isaac said, "Now the Lord has made room for us. We will be successful in this land."

[23]From there Isaac went to Beersheba. [24]The Lord appeared to Isaac that night. The Lord said, "I am the God of your father Abraham. Don't be afraid because I am with you. I will bless you and give you many descendants. I will do this because of my servant Abraham." [25]So Isaac built an altar and worshiped the Lord there. He made a camp there, and his servants dug a well.

[26]Abimelech came from Gerar to see Isaac. Abimelech brought with him Ahuzzath, who advised him, and Phicol, the commander of his army. [27]Isaac asked them, "Why have you come to see me? You were my enemy. You forced me to leave your country."

[28]They answered, "Now we know that the Lord is with you. We will make a promise to you. And we would like you to make one to us. We would like to make an agreement with you. [29]We did not hurt you. So promise you will not hurt us. And we were good to you, and we sent you away in peace. Now the Lord has blessed you."

[30]So Isaac prepared food for them, and they all ate and drank. [31]Early the next morning the men made a promise to each other. Then Isaac sent them away, and they left in peace.

[32]That day Isaac's servants came and told him about the well they had dug. They said, "We found water in that well." [33]So Isaac named it Shibah[n] and

> Through your descendants all the nations on the earth will be blessed.
>
> —GENESIS 26:4

26:33 Shibah This name sounds like the Hebrew words for "seven" and "promise."

that city is still called Beersheba even now.

[34] When Esau was 40 years old, he married two Hittite women. One was Judith daughter of Beeri. The other was Basemath daughter of Elon. [35] These women brought much sorrow to Isaac and Rebekah.

JACOB TRICKS ISAAC

27 When Isaac was old, his eyes were not good. He could not see clearly. One day he called his older son Esau to him. Isaac said, "Son."

Esau answered, "Here I am."

[2] Isaac said, "I am old. I don't know when I might die. [3] So take your bow and arrows, and go hunting in the field. Kill an animal for me to eat. [4] Prepare the tasty food that I love. Bring it to me, and I will eat. Then I will bless you before I die." [5] So Esau went out in the field to hunt.

Rebekah was listening as Isaac said this to his son Esau. [6] Rebekah said to her son Jacob, "Listen, I heard your father talking to your brother Esau. [7] Your father said, 'Kill an animal. Prepare some tasty food for me to eat. Then I will bless you before the Lord before I die.' [8] So obey me, my son. Do what I tell you. [9] Go out to our goats and bring me two young ones. I will prepare them just the way your father likes them. [10] Then you will take the food to your father. And he will bless you before he dies."

[11] But Jacob said to his mother Rebekah, "My brother Esau is a hairy man. I am smooth! [12] If my father touches me, he will know I am not Esau. Then he will not bless me. He will place a curse on me because I tried to trick him."

[13] So Rebekah said to him, "If your father puts a curse on you, I will accept the blame. Just do what I said. Go and get the goats for me."

[14] So Jacob went out and got two goats and brought them to his mother. Then she cooked them in the special way Isaac enjoyed. [15] She took the best clothes of her older son Esau that were in the house. She put them on the younger son Jacob. [16] She took the skins of the goats. And she put them on Jacob's hands and neck. [17] Then she gave Jacob the tasty food and the bread she had made.

[18] Jacob went in to his father and said, "Father."

And his father said, "Yes, my son. Who are you?"

[19] Jacob said to him, "I am Esau, your first son. I have done what you told me. Now sit up and eat some meat of the animal I hunted for you. Then bless me."

[20] But Isaac asked his son, "How did you find and kill the animal so quickly?"

Jacob answered, "Because the Lord your God led me to find it."

[21] Then Isaac said to Jacob, "Come near so I can touch you, my son. If I can touch you, I will know if you are really my son Esau."

[22] So Jacob came near to Isaac his father. Isaac touched him and said, "Your voice sounds like Jacob's voice. But your hands are hairy like the hands of Esau." [23] Isaac did not know it was Jacob, because his hands were hairy like Esau's hands. So Isaac blessed Jacob. [24] Isaac asked, "Are you really my son Esau?"

Jacob answered, "Yes, I am."

[25] Then Isaac said, "Bring me the food. I will eat it and bless you." So Jacob gave him the food, and Isaac ate. Jacob gave him wine, and he drank. [26] Then Isaac said to him, "My son, come near and kiss me." [27] So Jacob went to his father and kissed him. Isaac smelled Esau's clothes and blessed him. Isaac said,

"The smell of my son
　　is like the smell of the field
　　that the Lord has blessed.
[28] May God give you plenty of rain
　　and good soil.
　　Then you will have plenty of grain
　　and wine.

[29] May nations serve you.
  May peoples bow down to you.
  May you be master over your brothers.
    May your mother's sons bow down
      to you.
  May everyone who curses you be
    cursed.
      And may everyone who blesses you
        be blessed."

[30]Isaac finished blessing Jacob. Then, just as Jacob left his father Isaac, Esau came in from hunting. [31]Esau also prepared some tasty food and brought it to his father. He said, "Father, rise and eat the food that your son killed for you. Then bless me."

[32]Isaac asked, "Who are you?"

He answered, "I am your son—your firstborn son—Esau."

[33]Then Isaac trembled greatly. He said, "Then who was it that hunted the animals and brought me food before you came? I ate it, and I blessed him. And it is too late now to take back my blessing."

[34]When Esau heard the words of his father, he let out a loud and bitter cry. He said to his father, "Bless me—me, too, my father!"

[35]But Isaac said, "Your brother came and tricked me. He has taken your blessing."

[36]Esau said, "Jacob[n] is the right name for him. He has tricked me these two times. He took away my share of everything you own. And now he has taken away my blessing." Then Esau asked, "Haven't you saved a blessing for me?"

[37]Isaac answered, "I gave Jacob the power to be master over you. And all his brothers will be his servants. And I kept him strong with grain and wine. There is nothing left to give you, my son."

[38]But Esau continued, "Do you have only one blessing, Father? Bless me, too, Father!" Then Esau began to cry out loud.

[39]Isaac said to him,

"You will live far away from the best
    land,
  far from the rain.
[40] You will live by using your sword
  and be a slave to your brother.
But when you struggle,
  you will break free from him."

[41]After that Esau hated Jacob because of the blessing from Isaac. Esau thought to himself, "My father will soon die, and I will be sad for him. After that I will kill Jacob."

[42]Rebekah heard about Esau's plan to kill Jacob. So she sent for Jacob. She said to him, "Listen, your brother Esau is comforting himself by planning to kill you. [43]So, son, do what I say. My brother Laban is living in Haran. Go to him at once! [44]Stay with him for a while, until your brother is not so angry. [45]In time, your brother will not be angry. He will forget what you did to him. Then I will send a servant to bring you back. I don't want to lose both of my sons on the same day."

[46]Then Rebekah said to Isaac, "I am tired of Hittite women. If Jacob marries one of these Hittite women here in this land, I want to die."

JACOB SEARCHES FOR A WIFE

28 Isaac called Jacob and blessed him. Then Isaac commanded him, "You must not marry a Canaanite woman. [2]Go to the house of Bethuel, your mother's father, in Northwest Mesopotamia. Laban, your mother's brother, lives there. Marry one of his daughters. [3]May God All-Powerful bless you and give you many children. May you become the father of many peoples. [4]May the Lord give you and your descendants the blessing of Abraham. Then you may own the land where you are now living as a stranger. This is the land God gave to Abraham." [5]So Isaac sent Jacob to Northwest Mesopotamia. Jacob

---

27:36 Jacob This name sounds like the Hebrew word for "heel." "Grabbing someone's heel" is a Hebrew saying for tricking someone.

☆ Genesis 28:13–15

Jacob left home and traveled to a far place. In a dream one night, he saw a ladder that reached from earth to heaven. God stood at the top of the ladder and spoke to Jacob. He promised to bring Jacob back to the land he had given him. He also promised to protect him wherever he went.

Nyla told her friends, "If Daddy said he is coming to get me, then he will." Nyla knew she could trust her daddy to keep his promises. But Nyla's daddy was late, and she started to worry. When her dad showed up an hour late, he wrapped Nyla up in a bear hug and said he was sorry. "I knew you would come," Nyla said. Parents are people, and all people make mistakes. But God never makes mistakes. If God says he will do something, then he will do it.

. . . .

We can trust our heavenly Father to always keep his promises.

went to Laban, the brother of Rebekah. Bethuel, the Aramean, was the father of Laban and Rebekah. And Rebekah was the mother of Jacob and Esau.

⁶Esau learned that Isaac had blessed Jacob and sent him to Northwest Mesopotamia. Jacob went to find a wife there. Esau also learned that Isaac had commanded Jacob not to marry a Canaanite woman. ⁷And Esau learned that Jacob had obeyed his father and mother. He had gone to Northwest Mesopotamia. ⁸So Esau saw that his father Isaac did not want his sons to marry Canaanite women. ⁹Now Esau already had wives. But he went to Ishmael son of Abraham. And he married Mahalath, Ishmael's daughter. Mahalath was the sister of Nebaioth.

JACOB'S DREAM AT BETHEL

¹⁰Jacob left Beersheba and set out for Haran. ¹¹He came to a place and spent the night there because the sun had set. He found a stone there and laid his head on it to go to sleep. ¹²Jacob dreamed that there was a ladder resting on the earth and reaching up into heaven. And he saw angels of God going up and coming down the ladder. ¹³And then Jacob saw the Lord standing above the ladder. The Lord said, "I am the Lord, the God of Abraham, your grandfather. And I am the God of Isaac. I will give you and your descendants the land on which you are now sleeping. ¹⁴Your descendants will be as many as the dust of the earth. They will spread west and east, north and south. All the families of the earth will be blessed through you and your descendants. ¹⁵I am with you, and I will protect you everywhere you go. And I will bring you back to this land. I will not leave you until I have done what I have promised you."

¹⁶Then Jacob woke from his sleep.

He said, "Surely the Lord is in this place. But I did not know it." [17]Jacob was afraid. He said, "This place frightens me! It is surely the house of God and the gate of heaven."

[18]Jacob rose early in the morning. He took the stone he had slept on and set it up on its end. Then he poured olive oil on the top of it. [19]At first, the name of that city was Luz. But Jacob named it Bethel.[n]

[20]Then Jacob made a promise. He said, "I want God to be with me and protect me on this journey. I want God to give me food to eat and clothes to wear. [21]Then I will be able to return in peace to my father's house. If the Lord does these things, he will be my God. [22]This stone which I have set up on its end will be the house of God. And I will give God one-tenth of all he gives me."

JACOB ARRIVES IN NORTHWEST MESOPOTAMIA

29 Then Jacob continued his journey. He came to the land of the people of the East. [2]He looked and saw a well in the field. Three flocks of sheep were lying nearby, because they drank water from this well. A large stone covered the mouth of the well. [3]All the flocks would gather there. The shepherds would roll the stone away from the well and water the sheep. Then they would put the stone back in its place.

[4]Jacob said to the shepherds there, "My brothers, where are you from?"

They answered, "We are from Haran."

[5]Then Jacob asked, "Do you know Laban grandson of Nahor?"

They answered, "We know him."

[6]Then Jacob asked, "How is he?"

They answered, "He is well. Look, his daughter Rachel is coming now with his sheep."

[7]Jacob said, "But look, it is still the middle part of the day. It is not time for the sheep to be gathered for the night. So give them water and let them go back into the pasture."

[8]But they said, "We cannot do that until all the flocks are gathered. Then we will roll away the stone from the mouth of the well and water the sheep."

[9]While Jacob was talking with the shepherds, Rachel came with her father's sheep. It was her job to take care of the sheep. [10]Then Jacob saw Laban's daughter Rachel and Laban's sheep. So he went to the well and rolled the stone from its mouth. Then he watered Laban's sheep. Now Laban was the brother of Rebekah, Jacob's mother. [11]Then Jacob kissed Rachel and cried. [12]He told her that he was from her father's family. He said that he was the son of Rebekah. So Rachel ran home and told her father.

[13]When Laban heard the news about his sister's son Jacob, Laban ran to meet him. Laban hugged him and kissed him and brought him to his house. Jacob told Laban everything that had happened.

[14]Then Laban said, "You are my own flesh and blood."

JACOB IS TRICKED

So Jacob stayed there a month. [15]Then Laban said to Jacob, "You are my relative. But it is not right for you to keep on working for me without pay. What would you like me to pay you?"

[16]Now Laban had two daughters. The older was Leah, and the younger was Rachel. [17]Leah had weak eyes, but Rachel was very beautiful. [18]Jacob loved Rachel. So he said to Laban, "Let me marry your younger daughter Rachel. If you will, I will work seven years for you."

[19]Laban said, "It would be better for her to marry you than someone else. So stay here with me." [20]So Jacob worked for Laban seven years so he could marry Rachel. But they seemed to him like just a few days. This was because he loved Rachel very much.

28:19 **Bethel** This name means "house of God."

²¹After seven years Jacob said to Laban, "Give me Rachel so that I may marry her. The time I promised to work for you is over."

²²So Laban gave a feast for all the people there. ²³That evening Laban brought his daughter Leah to Jacob. Jacob and Leah had intimate relations together. ²⁴(Laban gave his slave girl Zilpah to his daughter to be her servant.) ²⁵In the morning Jacob saw that he had had intimate relations with Leah! He said to Laban, "What have you done to me? I worked hard for you so that I could marry Rachel! Why did you trick me?"

²⁶Laban said, "In our country we do not allow the younger daughter to marry before the older daughter. ²⁷But complete the full week of the marriage ceremony with Leah. I will give you Rachel to marry also. But you must serve me another seven years."

²⁸So Jacob did this and completed the week with Leah. Then Laban gave him his daughter Rachel as a wife. ²⁹(Laban gave his slave girl Bilhah to his daughter Rachel to be her servant.) ³⁰So Jacob had intimate relations with Rachel also. And Jacob loved Rachel more than Leah. Jacob worked for Laban for another seven years.

JACOB'S FAMILY GROWS

³¹The Lord saw that Jacob loved Rachel more than Leah. So the Lord made it possible for Leah to have children. But Rachel did not have any children. ³²Leah became pregnant and gave birth to a son. She named him Reuben,ⁿ because she said, "The Lord has seen my troubles. Surely now my husband will love me."

³³Leah became pregnant again and gave birth to another son. She named

him Simeon.ⁿ She said, "The Lord has heard that I am not loved. So he gave me this son."

³⁴Leah became pregnant again and gave birth to another son. She named him Levi.ⁿ Leah said, "Now, surely my husband will be close to me. I have given him three sons."

³⁵Then Leah gave birth to another son. She named him Judah.ⁿ Leah named him this because she said, "Now I will praise the Lord." Then Leah stopped having children.

30

Rachel saw that she was not giving birth to children for Jacob. So she envied her sister Leah. Rachel said to Jacob, "Give me children, or I'll die!"

²Jacob became angry with her. He said, "Can I do what only God can do? He is the one who has kept you from having children."

³Then Rachel said, "Here is my slave girl Bilhah. Have physical relations with her so she can give birth to a child for me. Then I can have my own family through her."

⁴So Rachel gave Bilhah, her slave girl, to Jacob as a wife. And he had physical relations with her. ⁵She became pregnant and gave Jacob a son. ⁶Rachel said, "God has declared me innocent. He has listened to my prayer and has given me a son." So Rachel named this son Dan.ⁿ

⁷Bilhah became pregnant again and gave Jacob a second son. ⁸Rachel said, "I have struggled hard with my sister. And I have won." So she named that son Naphtali.ⁿ

⁹Leah saw that she had stopped having children. So she gave her slave girl Zilpah to Jacob as a wife. ¹⁰Then Zilpah had a son. ¹¹Leah said, "I am lucky." So she named her son Gad.ⁿ ¹²Zilpah gave

---

29:32 **Reuben** This name sounds like the Hebrew word for "he has seen my troubles."
29:33 **Simeon** This name sounds like the Hebrew word for "has heard."
29:34 **Levi** This name sounds like the Hebrew word for "be close to."
29:35 **Judah** This name sounds like the Hebrew word for "praise."
30:6 **Dan** This name means "he has declared innocent."
30:8 **Naphtali** This name sounds like the Hebrew word for "my struggle."
30:11 **Gad** This name may mean "lucky."

birth to another son. [13]Leah said, "I am very happy! Now women will call me happy." So she named that son Asher.[n]

[14]During the wheat harvest Reuben went into the field and found some mandrake[n] plants. He brought them to his mother Leah. But Rachel said to Leah, "Please give me some of your son's mandrakes."

[15]Leah answered, "You have already taken away my husband. Now you are trying to take away my son's mandrakes."

But Rachel answered, "If you will give me your son's mandrakes, you may sleep with Jacob tonight."

[16]When Jacob came in from the field that night, Leah went out to meet him. She said, "You will have intimate relations with me tonight. I have paid for you with my son's mandrakes." So Jacob slept with her that night.

[17]Then God answered Leah's prayer, and she became pregnant again. She gave birth to a fifth son. [18]Leah said, "God has given me what I paid for, because I gave my slave girl to my husband." So Leah named her son Issachar.[n]

[19]Leah became pregnant again and gave birth to a sixth son. [20]She said, "God has given me a fine gift. Now surely Jacob will honor me, because I have given him six sons." So Leah named the son Zebulun.[n]

[21]Later Leah gave birth to a daughter. She named her Dinah.

[22]Then God remembered Rachel and answered her prayer. God made it possible for her to have children. [23]She became pregnant and gave birth to a son. She said, "God has taken away my shame." [24]She named him Joseph.[n] Rachel said, "I wish the Lord would give me another son."

JACOB TRICKS LABAN

[25]After the birth of Joseph, Jacob said to Laban, "Now let me go to my own home and country. [26]Give me my wives and my children, and let me go. I have earned them by working for you. You know that I served you well."

[27]Laban said to him, "If I have pleased you, please stay. I know the Lord has blessed me because of you. [28]Tell me what I should pay you, and I will give it to you."

[29]Jacob answered, "You know that I have worked hard for you. Your flocks have grown while I cared for them. [30]When I came, you had little. Now you have much. Every time I did something for you, the Lord blessed you. But when will I be able to do something for my own family?"

[31]Laban asked, "Then what should I give you?"

Jacob answered, "I don't want you to give me anything. Just do this one thing. Then I will come back and take care of your flocks. [32]Today let me go through all your flocks of white sheep and black goats. I will take every spotted or speckled lamb. I will take every black lamb and every spotted or speckled goat. That will be my pay. [33]In the future you can easily see if I am honest. You can come to look at my flocks. If I have any goat that isn't speckled or

> The Lord said to Jacob, "Go back to the land . . . I will be with you."
> —GENESIS 31:3

30:13 **Asher** This name may mean "happy."
30:14 **mandrake** A plant which was believed to cause a woman to become pregnant.
30:18 **Issachar** This name sounds like the Hebrew word for "paid for."
30:20 **Zebulun** This name sounds like the Hebrew word for "honor."
30:24 **Joseph** This name sounds like the Hebrew word for "he adds."

spotted or any sheep that isn't black, you will know I stole it."

³⁴Laban answered, "Agreed! We will do what you ask." ³⁵But that day Laban took away all the male goats that had streaks or spots. And he took all the speckled and spotted female goats (all those that had white on them). And he took all the black sheep. He told his sons to watch over them. ³⁶Laban took these animals to a place that was three days' journey away from Jacob. Jacob took care of all the animals that were left.

³⁷So Jacob cut green branches from poplar, almond and plane trees. He peeled off some of the bark so that the branches had white stripes on them. ³⁸He put the branches in front of the flocks at the watering places. When the animals came to drink, they also mated there. ³⁹So the goats mated in front of the branches. Then the young that were born were streaked, speckled or spotted. ⁴⁰Jacob separated the young animals from the others. And he made them face the streaked and dark animals in Laban's flock. Jacob kept his animals separate from Laban's. ⁴¹When the stronger animals in the flock were mating, Jacob put the branches before their eyes. This was so the animals would mate near the branches. ⁴²But when the weaker animals mated, Jacob did not put the branches there. So the animals born from the weaker animals were Laban's. And the animals born from the stronger animals were Jacob's. ⁴³In this way Jacob became very rich. He had large flocks, many male and female servants, camels and donkeys.

JACOB RUNS AWAY

31 One day Jacob heard Laban's sons talking. They said, "Jacob has taken everything our father owned. Jacob has become rich in this way." ²Then Jacob noticed that Laban was not as friendly as he had been before. ³The Lord said to Jacob, "Go back to the land where your ancestors lived. I will be with you."

⁴So Jacob told Rachel and Leah to meet him in the field where he kept his flocks. ⁵He said to them, "I have seen that your father is not as friendly with me as he used to be. But the God of my father has been with me. ⁶You both know that I have worked as hard as I could for your father. ⁷But he cheated me. He has changed my pay ten times. But God has not allowed your father to harm me. ⁸At one time Laban said, 'You can have all the speckled goats as your pay.' After that, all the animals gave birth to speckled young ones. But then Laban said, 'You can have all the streaked goats as your pay.' After that, all the animals gave birth to streaked babies. ⁹So God has taken the animals away from your father. And God has given them to me.

¹⁰"I had a dream during the season when the animals were mating. I saw that the only male goats who were mating were streaked, speckled or spotted. ¹¹The angel of God spoke to me in that dream. He said, 'Jacob!' I answered, 'Yes!' ¹²The angel said, 'Look! Only the streaked, speckled or spotted goats are mating. I have seen all the wrong things Laban does to you. ¹³I am the God who appeared to you at Bethel. There you poured olive oil on the stone you set up on end. There you made a promise to me. Now I want you to leave here. Go back to the land where you were born.'"

¹⁴Rachel and Leah answered Jacob, "Our father has nothing to give us when he dies. ¹⁵He has treated us like strangers. He sold us to you, and then he spent all of the money you paid for us. ¹⁶God took all this wealth from our father, and now it belongs to us and our children. So you do whatever God told you to do."

¹⁷So Jacob put his children and his wives on camels. ¹⁸Then they began their journey back to Isaac, his father. He lived in the land of Canaan. All the flocks of animals that Jacob owned walked ahead of them. He carried everything with him that he had gotten while he lived in Northwest Mesopotamia. ¹⁹Laban was gone to cut the wool

from his sheep. While he was gone, Rachel stole the idols of false gods that belonged to him. ²⁰And Jacob tricked Laban the Aramean. He did not tell Laban he was leaving. ²¹Jacob and his family left quickly. They crossed the Euphrates River and traveled toward the mountains of Gilead.

²²Three days later Laban learned that Jacob had run away. ²³So Laban gathered his relatives and began to chase Jacob. After seven days Laban found him in the mountains of Gilead. ²⁴That night God came to Laban the Aramean in a dream. The Lord said, "Be careful! Do not say anything to Jacob, good or bad."

THE SEARCH FOR THE STOLEN IDOLS

²⁵So Laban caught up with Jacob. Now Jacob had made his camp in the mountains. So Laban and his relatives set up their camp in the mountains of Gilead. ²⁶Laban said to Jacob, "What have you done? Why did you trick me? You took my daughters as if you had captured them in a war. ²⁷Why did you run away without telling me? Why did you trick me? Why didn't you tell me? Then I could send you away with joy and singing. There would be the music of tambourines and harps. ²⁸You did not even let me kiss my grandchildren and my daughters good-bye. You were very foolish to do this! ²⁹I have the power to harm you. But last night the God of your father spoke to me. He warned me not to say anything to you, good or bad. ³⁰I know you want to go back to your home. But why did you steal my idols?"

³¹Jacob answered Laban, "I left without telling you, because I was afraid! I thought you would take your daughters away from me. ³²If you find anyone here who has taken your idols, he will be killed! Your relatives will be my witnesses. You may look for anything that belongs to you. Take anything that is yours." (Now Jacob did not know that Rachel had stolen Laban's idols.)

³³So Laban looked in Jacob's tent and in Leah's tent. He looked in the tent where the two slave women stayed. But he did not find his idols. When he left Leah's tent, he went into Rachel's tent. ³⁴Rachel had hidden the idols inside her camel's saddle. And she was sitting on them. Laban looked through the whole tent, but he did not find them.

³⁵Rachel said to her father, "Father, don't be angry with me. I am not able to stand up before you. I am having my monthly period." So Laban looked through the camp, but he did not find his idols.

³⁶Then Jacob became very angry. He said, "What wrong have I done? What law have I broken to cause you to chase me? ³⁷You have looked through everything I own. But you have found nothing that belongs to you. If you have found anything, show it to everyone. Put it in front of your relatives and my relatives. Then let them decide which one of us is right. ³⁸I have worked for you now for 20 years. During all that time none of the lambs and kids died during birth. And I have not eaten any of the male sheep from your flocks. ³⁹Any time a sheep was killed by wild animals, I did not bring it to you. I made up for the loss myself. You made me pay for any animal that was stolen during the day or night. ⁴⁰In the daytime the sun took away my strength. At night I was cold and could not sleep. ⁴¹I worked like a slave for you for 20 years. For the first 14 years I worked to get your two daughters. The last 6 years I worked to earn your animals. And during that time you changed my pay ten times. ⁴²But the God of my father was with me. He is the God of Abraham and the God of Isaac. If God had not been with me, you would have sent me away with nothing. But he saw the trouble I had and the hard work I did. And last night God corrected you."

JACOB AND LABAN'S AGREEMENT

⁴³Laban said to Jacob, "These girls are my daughters. Their children belong

to me, and these animals are mine. Everything you see here belongs to me. But I can do nothing to keep my daughters and their children. [44]Let us make an agreement. Let us set up a pile of stones to remind us of our agreement."

[45]So Jacob took a large rock and set it up on its end. [46]He told his relatives to gather rocks. So they took the rocks and piled them up. Then they ate beside the pile of rocks. [47]Laban named that place in his language A Pile to Remind Us. And Jacob gave the place the same name in Hebrew.

[48]Laban said to Jacob, "This pile of rocks will remind us of the agreement between us." That is why the place was called A Pile to Remind Us. [49]It was also called Mizpah.[n] This was because Laban said, "Let the Lord watch over us while we are separated from each other. [50]Remember that God is our witness. This is true even if no one else is around us. He will know if you harm my daughters or marry other women. [51]Here is the pile of rocks that I have put between us. And here is the rock I set up on end. [52]This pile of rocks and this rock set on end will remind us of our agreement. I will never go past this pile to hurt you. And you must never come to my side of them to hurt me. [53]The God of Abraham is the God of Nahor and the God of their ancestors. Let God punish either of us if we break this agreement."

So Jacob made a promise in the name of God. This was the God of his father Isaac. [54]Then Jacob killed an animal and offered it as a sacrifice on the mountain. And he invited his relatives to share in the meal. After they finished eating, they spent the night on the mountain. [55]Early the next morning Laban kissed his grandchildren and his daughters. He blessed them, and then he left to return home.

JACOB MEETS ESAU

32 When Jacob also went his way, the angels of God met him. [2]When Jacob saw them, he said, "This is the camp of God!" So Jacob named that place Mahanaim.[n]

[3]Jacob's brother Esau was living in the area called Seir in the country of Edom. Jacob sent messengers to Esau. [4]Jacob told the messengers, "Give this message to my master Esau: 'This is what Jacob, your servant, says: I have lived with Laban and have remained there until now. [5]I have cattle, donkeys, flocks, and male and female servants. I send this message to you and ask you to accept us.'"

[6]The messengers returned to Jacob and said, "We went to your brother Esau. He is coming to meet you. And he has 400 men with him."

[7]Then Jacob was very afraid and worried. He divided the people who were with him into two camps. He also divided all the flocks, herds and camels into two camps. [8]Jacob thought, "Esau might come and destroy one camp. But the other camp can run away and be saved."

[9]Jacob said, "God of my father Abraham! God of my father Isaac! Lord, you told me to return to my country and my family. You said that you would do good to me. [10]I am not worthy of the kindness and continual goodness you have shown me. The first time I traveled across the Jordan River, I had only my walking stick. But now I own enough to have two camps. [11]Please save me from my brother Esau. I am afraid he will come and kill all of us, even the mothers with the children. [12]You said to me, 'I will do good to you. I will make your children as many as the sand of the seashore. There will be too many to count.'"

[13]Jacob stayed there for the night.

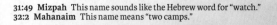

31:49 **Mizpah** This name sounds like the Hebrew word for "watch."
32:2 **Mahanaim** This name means "two camps."

He prepared a gift for Esau from what he had with him. [14]It was 200 female goats and 20 male goats, 200 female sheep and 20 male sheep. [15]There were 30 female camels and their young, 40 cows and 10 bulls, 20 female donkeys and 10 male donkeys. [16]Jacob gave each separate flock of animals to one of his servants. Then he said to them, "Go ahead of me and keep some space between each herd." [17]Jacob gave them their orders. To the servant with the first group of animals he said, "My brother Esau will come to you. He will ask you, 'Whose servant are you? Where are you going? Whose animals are these?' [18]Then you will answer, 'These animals belong to your servant Jacob. He sent them as a gift to you my master, Esau. And Jacob also is coming behind us.'"

[19]Jacob ordered the second servant, the third servant and all the other servants to do the same thing. He said, "Say the same thing to Esau when you meet him. [20]Say, 'Your servant Jacob is coming behind us.'" Jacob thought, "If I send this gift ahead of me, maybe Esau will forgive me. Then when I see him, perhaps he will accept me." [21]So Jacob sent the gift to Esau. But Jacob stayed that night in the camp.

JACOB WRESTLES WITH GOD

[22]During the night Jacob rose and crossed the Jabbok River at the crossing. He took his 2 wives, his 2 slave girls and his 11 sons with him. [23]He sent his family and everything he had across the river. [24]But Jacob stayed behind alone. And a man came and wrestled with him until the sun came up. [25]The man saw that he could not defeat Jacob. So he struck Jacob's hip and put it out of joint. [26]Then the man said to Jacob, "Let me go. The sun is coming up."

But Jacob said, "I will let you go if you will bless me."

[27]The man said to him, "What is your name?"

And he answered, "Jacob."

[28]Then the man said, "Your name will no longer be Jacob. Your name will now be Israel,[n] because you have wrestled with God and with men. And you have won."

[29]Then Jacob asked him, "Please tell me your name."

But the man said, "Why do you ask my name?" Then he blessed Jacob there.

[30]So Jacob named that place Peniel.[n] He said, "I have seen God face to face. But my life was saved." [31]Then the sun rose as he was leaving that place. Jacob was limping because of his leg. [32]So even today the people of Israel do not eat the muscle that is on the hip joint of animals. This is because Jacob was touched there.

JACOB SHOWS HIS BRAVERY

33 Jacob looked up and saw Esau coming. With him were 400 men. So Jacob divided his children among Leah, Rachel and the two slave girls. [2]Jacob put the slave girls with their children first. Then he put Leah and her children behind them. And he put Rachel and Joseph last. [3]Jacob himself went out in front of them. He bowed down flat on the ground seven times as he was walking toward his brother.

[4]But Esau ran to meet Jacob. Esau put his arms around him and hugged him. Then Esau kissed him, and they both cried. [5]Esau looked up and saw the women and children. He asked, "Who are these people with you?"

Jacob answered, "These are the children God has given me. God has been good to me, your servant."

[6]Then the two slave girls and their children came up to Esau. They bowed down flat on the earth before him. [7]Then Leah and her children came up to Esau. They also bowed down flat on the earth.

32:28 **Israel** This name means "he wrestles with God."
32:30 **Peniel** This name means "the face of God."

Last of all, Joseph and Rachel came up to Esau. And they, too, bowed down flat before him.

[8]Esau said, "I saw many herds as I was coming here. Why did you bring them?"

Jacob answered, "They were to please you, my master."

[9]But Esau said, "I already have enough, my brother. Keep what you have."

[10]Jacob said, "No! Please! If I have pleased you, then please accept the gift I give you. I am very happy to see your face again. It is like seeing the face of God because you have accepted me. [11]So I beg you to accept the gift I give you. God has been very good to me. And I have more than I need." And because Jacob begged, Esau accepted the gift.

[12]Then Esau said, "Let us get going. I will travel with you."

[13]But Jacob said to him, "My master, you know that the children are weak. And I must be careful with my flocks and their young ones. If I force them to go too far in one day, all the animals will die. [14]So, my master, you go on ahead of me, your servant. I will follow you slowly. I will let the animals and the children set the speed at which we travel. I will meet you, my master, in Edom."

[15]So Esau said, "Then let me leave some of my men with you."

"No, thank you," said Jacob. "I only want to please you, my master." [16]So that day Esau started back to Edom. [17]But Jacob went to Succoth. There he built a house for himself. And he made shelters for his animals. That is why the place was named Succoth.[n]

[18]Jacob left Northwest Mesopotamia.

And he arrived safely at the city of Shechem in the land of Canaan. He camped east of the city. [19]He bought a part of the field where he had camped. He bought it from the sons of Hamor father of Shechem for 100 pieces of silver. [20]He built an altar there and named it after God, the God of Israel.

DINAH IS ATTACKED

34 Dinah was the daughter of Leah and Jacob. At this time Dinah went out to visit the women of that land. [2]Shechem son of Hamor the Hivite, the ruler of that land, saw Dinah. He took her and raped her. [3]Shechem fell in love with Dinah, and he spoke kindly to her. [4]He told his father, Hamor, "Please get this girl for me so I can marry her."

[5]Jacob learned how Shechem had disgraced his daughter. But Jacob's sons were out in the field with the cattle. So Jacob said nothing until they came home. [6]And Hamor father of Shechem went to talk with Jacob.

[7]When Jacob's sons heard what had happened, they came in from the field. They were very angry, because Shechem had done such a wicked thing to Israel. It was wrong for him to have raped Jacob's daughter. A thing like this should not be done.

[8]But Hamor talked to the brothers of Dinah. He said, "My son Shechem is deeply in love with Dinah. Please let him marry her. [9]Marry our people. Give your women to our men as wives. And take our women for your men as wives. [10]You can live in the same land with us. You will be free to own land and to trade here."

[11]Shechem also talked to Jacob and

> These are the children God has given me. God has been good to me.
> —GENESIS 33:5

33:17 **Succoth** This name means "shelters."

to Dinah's brothers. He said, "Please accept my offer. I will give anything you ask. [12]Ask as much as you want for the payment for the bride. I will give it to you. Just let me marry Dinah."

[13]The sons of Jacob answered Shechem and his father with lies. They were angry because Shechem had disgraced their sister Dinah. [14]The brothers said to them, "We cannot allow you to marry our sister. You are not circumcised. That would be a disgrace to us. [15]But we will allow you to marry her if you do this one thing: Every man in your town must be circumcised like us. [16]Then your men can marry our women, and our men can marry your women. Then we will live in your land and become one people. [17]If you refuse to be circumcised, we will take Dinah and leave."

[18]What they asked seemed fair to Hamor and Shechem. [19]So Shechem went quickly to be circumcised because he loved Jacob's daughter.

Now Shechem was the most respected man in his family. [20]So Hamor and Shechem went to the gate of their city. They spoke to the men of their city. They said, [21]"These people want to be friends with us. So let them live in our land and trade here. There is enough land for all of us. Let us marry their women. And we can let them marry our women. [22]But our men must agree to one thing. All our men must agree to be circumcised as they are. Then they will agree to live in our land. And we will be one people. [23]If we do this, their cattle and their animals will belong to us. Let us do what they say, and they will stay in our land." [24]All the men who had come to the city gate heard this. And they agreed with Hamor and Shechem. And every man was circumcised.

[25]Three days later the men who were circumcised were still in pain. Two of Jacob's sons, Simeon and Levi (Dinah's brothers), took their swords. They made a surprise attack on the city. And they killed all the men there. [26]Simeon and Levi killed Hamor and his son Shechem. Then they took Dinah out of Shechem's house and left. [27]Jacob's sons went among the dead bodies and stole everything that was in the city. This was to pay them back for what Shechem had done to their sister. [28]So the brothers took the flocks, herds and donkeys. And they took everything in the city and in the fields. [29]They took every valuable thing those people owned. They even took the wives and children and everything that was in the houses.

[30]Then Jacob said to Simeon and Levi, "You have caused me a lot of trouble. Now the Canaanites and the Perizzites who live in the land will hate me. There are only a few of us. If they join together to attack us, my people and I will be destroyed."

[31]But the brothers said, "We will not allow our sister to be treated like a prostitute."

JACOB IN BETHEL

35 God said to Jacob, "Go to the city of Bethel and live there. Make an altar to the God who appeared to you there. This was when you were running away from your brother Esau."

[2]So Jacob said to his family and to all who were with him, "Put away the foreign gods you have. Make yourselves clean, and change your clothes. [3]We will leave here and go to Bethel. There I will build an altar to God. He has helped me during my time of trouble. He has been with me everywhere I have gone." [4]So they gave Jacob all the foreign gods they had. And they gave him the earrings they were wearing. He hid them under the great tree near the town of Shechem. [5]Then Jacob and his sons left there. But God caused the people in the nearby cities to be afraid. So they did not follow the sons of Jacob. [6]And Jacob and all the people who were with him went to Luz. It is now called Bethel. It is in the land of Canaan. [7]There Jacob built an

altar. He named the place Bethel, after God, because God had appeared to him there. That was when he was running from his brother.

⁸Deborah, Rebekah's nurse, died and was buried under the oak tree at Bethel. They named that place Oak of Crying.

JACOB'S NEW NAME

⁹When Jacob came back from Northwest Mesopotamia, God appeared to him again. And God blessed him. ¹⁰God said to him, "Your name is Jacob. But you will not be called Jacob any longer. Your new name will be Israel." So he called him Israel. ¹¹God said to him, "I am God All-Powerful. Have many children and grow in number as a nation. You will be the ancestor of many nations and kings. ¹²I gave Abraham and Isaac land. I will give that same land to you and your descendants." ¹³Then God left him. ¹⁴Jacob set up a stone on edge in that place where God had talked to him. And he poured a drink offering and olive oil on it to make it special for God. ¹⁵And Jacob named the place Bethel.

RACHEL DIES GIVING BIRTH

¹⁶Jacob and his group left Bethel. Before they came to Ephrath, Rachel began giving birth to her baby. ¹⁷But she was having much trouble with this birth. When Rachel's nurse saw this, she said, "Don't be afraid, Rachel. You are giving birth to another son." ¹⁸Rachel gave birth to the son, but she died. As she lay dying, she named the boy Son of My Suffering. But Jacob called him Benjamin.ⁿ

¹⁹Rachel was buried on the road to Ephrath, a district of Bethlehem. ²⁰And Jacob set up a rock on her grave to honor her. That rock is still there today. ²¹Then Israel, also called Jacob, continued his journey. He camped just south of Migdal Eder.

²²While Israel was in that land Reuben had physical relations with Israel's slave woman Bilhah. And Israel heard about it.

THE FAMILY OF ISRAEL

Jacob had 12 sons. ²³He had 6 sons by his wife Leah. Reuben was his first son. Then Leah had Simeon, Levi, Judah, Issachar and Zebulun.

²⁴He had 2 sons by his wife Rachel: Joseph and Benjamin.

²⁵He had 2 sons by Rachel's slave girl Bilhah: Dan and Naphtali.

²⁶And he had 2 sons by Leah's slave girl Zilpah: Gad and Asher.

These are Jacob's sons who were born in Northwest Mesopotamia.

²⁷Jacob went to his father Isaac at Mamre near Hebron. This is where Abraham and Isaac had lived. ²⁸Isaac lived 180 years. ²⁹So Isaac breathed his last breath and died when he was very old. And his sons Esau and Jacob buried him.

ESAU'S FAMILY

36 This is the family history of Esau (also called Edom).

²Esau married women from the land of Canaan. He married Adah daughter of Elon the Hittite. And he married Oholibamah daughter of Anah. Anah was the son of Zibeon the Hivite. And he married ³Basemath, Ishmael's daughter, the sister of Nebaioth.

⁴Adah gave Esau one son, Eliphaz. Basemath gave Esau Reuel. ⁵And Oholibamah gave Esau Jeush, Jalam and Korah. These were Esau's sons who were born in the land of Canaan.

⁶Esau took his wives, his sons, his daughters and all the people who lived with him. He took his herds and other animals. And he took all the belongings he had gotten in Canaan. And he went to a land away from his brother Jacob. ⁷Esau and Jacob's belongings were becoming too many for them to live in the same land. The land where they had lived could not support both of them.

35:18 **Benjamin** This name means "right-hand son" or "favorite son."

They had too many herds. ⁸So Esau lived in the mountains of Edom. (Esau is also named Edom.)

⁹This is the family history of Esau. He is the ancestor of the Edomites, who live in the mountains of Edom.

¹⁰Esau's sons were Eliphaz son of Adah and Esau, and Reuel son of Basemath and Esau.

¹¹Eliphaz had five sons: Teman, Omar, Zepho, Gatam and Kenaz. ¹²Eliphaz also had a slave woman named Timna. Timna and Eliphaz gave birth to Amalek. These were Esau's grandsons by his wife Adah.

¹³Reuel had four sons: Nahath, Zerah, Shammah and Mizzah. These were Esau's grandsons by his wife Basemath.

¹⁴Esau's third wife was Oholibamah. She was the daughter of Anah. (Anah was the son of Zibeon.) Esau and Oholibamah gave birth to Jeush, Jalam and Korah.

¹⁵These were the leaders that came from Esau. Esau's first son was Eliphaz. From him came these leaders: Teman, Omar, Zepho, Kenaz, ¹⁶Korah, Gatam and Amalek. These were the leaders that came from Eliphaz in the land of Edom. They were the grandsons of Adah.

¹⁷Esau's son Reuel was the father of these leaders: Nahath, Zerah, Shammah and Mizzah. These were the leaders that came from Reuel in the land of Edom. They were the grandsons of Esau's wife Basemath.

¹⁸Esau's wife Oholibamah gave birth to these leaders: Jeush, Jalam and Korah. These are the leaders that came from Esau's wife Oholibamah. She was the daughter of Anah. ¹⁹These were the sons of Esau (also called Edom), and these were their leaders.

²⁰These were the sons of Seir the Horite, who were living in the land: Lotan, Shobal, Zibeon, Anah, ²¹Dishon, Ezer and Dishan. These sons of Seir were the leaders of the Horites in Edom.

²²The sons of Lotan were Hori and Homam. (Timna was Lotan's sister.)

²³The sons of Shobal were Alvan, Manahath, Ebal, Shepho and Onam.

²⁴The sons of Zibeon were Aiah and Anah. Anah is the man who found the hot springs in the desert. He found them while he was caring for his father's donkeys.

²⁵The children of Anah were Dishon and Oholibamah daughter of Anah.

²⁶The sons of Dishon were Hemdan, Eshban, Ithran and Keran.

²⁷The sons of Ezer were Bilhan, Zaavan and Akan.

²⁸The sons of Dishan were Uz and Aran.

²⁹These were the names of the Horite leaders: Lotan, Shobal, Zibeon, Anah, ³⁰Dishon, Ezer and Dishan.

These men were the leaders of the Horite families. They lived in the land of Edom.

³¹These are the kings who ruled in the land of Edom before the Israelites ever had a king.

³²Bela son of Beor was the king of Edom. He came from the city of Dinhabah.

³³When Bela died, Jobab son of Zerah became king. Jobab was from Bozrah.

³⁴When Jobab died, Husham became king. He was from the land of the Temanites.

³⁵When Husham died, Hadad son of Bedad became king. Hadad had defeated Midian in the country of Moab. Hadad was from the city of Avith.

³⁶When Hadad died, Samlah became king. He was from Masrekah.

³⁷When Samlah died, Shaul became king. He was from Rehoboth on the Euphrates River.

³⁸When Shaul died, Baal-Hanan son of Acbor became king.

³⁹When Baal-Hanan son of Acbor died, Hadad became king. He was from the city of Pau. His wife's name was Mehetabel daughter of Matred. Matred was the daughter of Me-Zahab.

⁴⁰These Edomite leaders came from Esau. They are listed by their families and regions. Their names were

Timna, Alvah, Jetheth, ⁴¹Oholibamah, Elah, Pinon, ⁴²Kenaz, Teman, Mibzar, ⁴³Magdiel and Iram. These were the leaders of Edom. (Esau was the father of the Edomites.) The area where each of these families lived was named after that family.

JOSEPH THE DREAMER

37 Jacob lived in the land of Canaan, where his father had lived. ²This is the family history of Jacob.

Joseph was a young man, 17 years old. He and his brothers cared for the flocks. His brothers were the sons of Bilhah and Zilpah, his father's wives. Joseph gave his father bad reports about his brothers. ³Joseph was born when his father Israel, also called Jacob, was old. So Israel loved Joseph more than his other sons. He made Joseph a special robe with long sleeves. ⁴Joseph's brothers saw that their father loved Joseph more than he loved them. So they hated their brother and could not speak to him politely.

⁵One time Joseph had a dream. When he told his brothers about it, they hated him even more. ⁶Joseph said, "Listen to the dream I had. ⁷We were in the field tying bundles of wheat together. My bundle stood up, and your bundles of wheat gathered around mine. Your bundles bowed down to mine."

⁸His brothers said, "Do you really think you will be king over us? Do you truly think you will rule over us?" His brothers hated him even more now. They hated him because of his dreams and what he had said.

⁹Then Joseph had another dream. He told his brothers about it also. He said, "Listen, I had another dream. I saw the sun, moon and 11 stars bowing down to me."

¹⁰Joseph also told his father about this dream. But his father scolded him, saying, "What kind of dream is this? Do you really believe that your mother, your brothers and I will bow down to you?" ¹¹Joseph's brothers were jealous of him. But his father thought about what all these things could mean.

¹²One day Joseph's brothers went to Shechem to herd their father's sheep. ¹³Jacob said to Joseph, "Go to Shechem. Your brothers are there herding the sheep."

Joseph answered, "I will go."

¹⁴His father said, "Go and see if your brothers and the sheep are all right. Then come back and tell me." So Joseph's father sent him from the Valley of Hebron.

When Joseph came to Shechem, ¹⁵a man found him wandering in the field. He asked Joseph, "What are you looking for?"

¹⁶Joseph answered, "I am looking for my brothers. Can you tell me where they are herding the sheep?"

¹⁷The man said, "They have already gone. I heard them say they were going to Dothan." So Joseph went to look for his brothers and found them in Dothan.

JOSEPH SOLD INTO SLAVERY

¹⁸Joseph's brothers saw him coming from far away. Before he reached them, they made a plan to kill him. ¹⁹They said to each other, "Here comes that dreamer. ²⁰Let's kill him and throw his body into one of the wells. We can tell our father that a wild animal killed him. Then we will see what will become of his dreams."

²¹But Reuben heard their plan and saved Joseph. He said, "Let's not kill him. ²²Don't spill any blood. Throw him into this well here in the desert. But don't hurt him!" Reuben planned to save Joseph later and send him back to his father. ²³So when Joseph came to his brothers, they pulled off his robe with long sleeves. ²⁴Then they threw him into the well. It was empty. There was no water in it.

²⁵While Joseph was in the well, the brothers sat down to eat. When they looked up, they saw a group of

Ishmaelites. They were traveling from Gilead to Egypt. Their camels were carrying spices, balm and myrrh.

²⁶Then Judah said to his brothers, "What will we gain if we kill our brother and hide his death? ²⁷Let's sell him to these Ishmaelites. Then we will not be guilty of killing our own brother. After all, he is our brother, our own flesh and blood." And the other brothers agreed. ²⁸So when the Midianite traders came by, the brothers took Joseph out of the well. They sold him to the Ishmaelites for eight ounces of silver. And the Ishmaelites took him to Egypt.

²⁹Reuben was not with his brothers when they sold Joseph to the Ishmaelites. When Reuben came back to the well, Joseph was not there. Reuben tore his clothes to show he was sad. ³⁰Then he went back to his brothers and said, "The boy is not there! What will I do?" ³¹The brothers killed a goat and dipped Joseph's long-sleeved robe in its blood. ³²Then they brought the robe to their father. They said, "We found this robe. Look it over carefully. See if it is your son's robe."

³³Jacob looked it over and said, "It is my son's robe! Some savage animal has eaten him. My son Joseph has been torn to pieces!" ³⁴Then Jacob tore his clothes and put on rough cloth to show that he was sad. He continued to be sad about his son for a long time. ³⁵All of Jacob's sons and daughters tried to comfort him. But he could not be comforted. Jacob said, "I will be sad about my son until the day I die." So Jacob cried for his son Joseph.

³⁶Meanwhile the Midianites who had bought Joseph had taken him to Egypt. There they sold him to Potiphar. Potiphar was an officer to the king of Egypt and captain of the palace guard.

JUDAH AND TAMAR

38 About that time, Judah left his brothers. He went to stay with a man named Hirah. Hirah was from the town of Adullam. ²Judah met a Canaanite girl there and married her. Her father was named Shua. And Judah had intimate relations with her. ³She became pregnant and gave birth to a son. Judah named him Er. ⁴Later she gave birth to another son. She named him Onan. ⁵Later she had another son. She named him Shelah. She was at Kezib when this third son was born.

⁶Judah chose a girl named Tamar to be the wife of his first son Er. ⁷Er was Judah's oldest son. But he did what the Lord said was evil. So the Lord killed him. ⁸Then Judah said to Er's brother Onan, "Go and have physical relations with your dead brother's wife.ⁿ It is your duty to provide children for your brother in this way."

⁹But Onan knew that the children would not belong to him. Onan was supposed to have physical relations with Tamar. But he did not complete the physical act. This made it impossible for Tamar to become pregnant. So Er could not have descendants. ¹⁰The Lord was displeased by this wicked thing Onan had done. So the Lord killed Onan also. ¹¹Then Judah said to his daughter-in-law Tamar, "Go back to live in your father's house. And don't marry until my young son Shelah grows up." Judah was afraid that Shelah also would die like his

> (Joseph was) sold . . . for eight ounces of silver. And the Ishmaelites took him to Egypt.
> —GENESIS 37:28

38:8 Go . . . wife. It was a custom in Israel that if a man died without children, one of his brothers would marry the widow. If a child was born, it would be considered the dead man's child.

brothers. So Tamar returned to her father's home.

¹²After a long time Judah's wife, the daughter of Shua, died. After Judah had gotten over his sorrow, he went to Timnah. He went to his men who were cutting the wool from his sheep. His friend Hirah from Adullam went with him. ¹³Tamar learned that Judah, her father-in-law, was going to Timnah to cut the wool from his sheep. ¹⁴So she took off the clothes that showed she was a widow. Then she covered her face with a veil to hide who she was. She sat down by the gate of Enaim. It was on the road to Timnah. She did this because Judah's younger son Shelah had grown up. But Judah had not made plans for her to marry him.

¹⁵When Judah saw her, he thought she was a prostitute. This was because she had covered her face with a veil. ¹⁶So Judah went to her and said, "Let me have physical relations with you." He did not know that she was Tamar, his daughter-in-law.

She asked, "What will you give me if I let you have physical relations with me?"

¹⁷Judah answered, "I will send you a young goat from my flock."

She answered, "First give me something to keep as a deposit until you send the goat."

¹⁸Judah asked, "What do you want me to give you as a deposit?"

Tamar answered, "Give me your seal and its cord,ⁿ and give me your walking stick." So Judah gave these things to her. Then Judah and Tamar had physical relations, and Tamar became pregnant. ¹⁹Tamar went home. She took off the veil that covered her face. And she put on the clothes that showed she was a widow.

²⁰Judah sent his friend Hirah with the young goat. Judah told Hirah to find the woman and get back his seal and the walking stick he had given her. But Hirah could not find her. ²¹Hirah asked some of the men at the town of Enaim, "Where is the prostitute who was here by the road?"

The men answered, "There has never been a prostitute here."

²²So he went back to Judah and said, "I could not find the woman. The men who lived there said, 'There has never been a prostitute here.'"

²³Judah said, "Let her keep the things. I don't want people to laugh at us. I sent her the goat as I promised. But you could not find her."

²⁴About three months later someone told Judah, "Tamar, your daughter-in-law, is guilty of acting like a prostitute. Now she is pregnant."

Then Judah said, "Bring her out and let her be burned to death."

²⁵When the men went to bring Tamar out, she sent a message to her father-in-law. She said, "The man who owns these things has made me pregnant. Look at this seal and its cord and this walking stick. Tell me whose they are."

²⁶Judah recognized them. He said, "She is more in the right than I. She did this because I did not give her to my son Shelah as I promised." And Judah did not have physical relations with her again.

²⁷When time came for Tamar to give birth, there were twins in her body. ²⁸While she was giving birth, one baby put his hand out. The nurse tied a red string on his hand. She said, "This baby came out first." ²⁹But he pulled his hand back in. So the other baby was born first. The nurse said, "So you are able to break out first." And they named him Perez.ⁿ ³⁰After this, the baby with the red string on his hand was born. They named him Zerah.

JOSEPH IS SOLD TO POTIPHAR

39 Now Joseph had been taken down to Egypt. An Egyptian named Potiphar was an officer to the

---

38:18 seal...cord A seal was used like a rubber stamp. People ran a string through it to tie around the neck. They wrote a contract, folded it, put wax or clay on the contract, and pressed the seal onto it as a signature.

38:29 Perez This name means "breaking out."

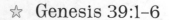

☆ Genesis 39:1-6

*Joseph was sold into slavery by his own brothers.
He was taken to Egypt and worked for a man
named Potiphar. But the Lord was with Joseph
and made him a successful man.*

Joseph's life was not an easy one. His father had been very kind to him and loved Joseph very much. But his brothers were not always kind to him. Joseph's brothers sold him to some people going to Egypt. They told Joseph's father that he had been killed by a wild animal. This made Joseph's father very sad.

While Joseph was in Egypt, God protected him and kept him from harm. God even blessed Joseph by giving him a place of honor in a very important Egyptian home. Joseph's story reminds us that God is always with us even when things around us look bad. He will never leave us alone. He can take what seems to be a bad thing and use it for our good.

. . . .

*Just like God was with Joseph when things were bad, he
will be with you too. God will never leave us.*

king of Egypt. He was the captain of the palace guard. He bought Joseph from the Ishmaelites who had brought him down there. ²The Lord was with Joseph, and he became a successful man. He lived in the house of his master, Potiphar the Egyptian.

³Potiphar saw that the Lord was with Joseph. He saw that the Lord made Joseph successful in everything he did. ⁴So Potiphar was very happy with Joseph. He allowed Joseph to be his personal servant. He put Joseph in charge of the house. Joseph was trusted with everything Potiphar

owned. ⁵So Joseph was put in charge of the house. He was put in charge of everything Potiphar owned. Then the Lord blessed the people in Potiphar's house because of Joseph. And the Lord blessed everything that belonged to Potiphar, both in the house and in the field. ⁶So Potiphar put Joseph in charge of everything he owned. Potiphar was not concerned about anything, except the food he ate.

JOSEPH IS PUT INTO PRISON
Now Joseph was well built and handsome. ⁷After some time the wife of

Joseph's master began to desire Joseph. One day she said to him, "Have physical relations with me."

[8]But Joseph refused. He said to her, "My master trusts me with everything in his house. He has put me in charge of everything he owns. [9]There is no one in his house greater than I. He has not kept anything from me, except you. And that is because you are his wife. How can I do such an evil thing? It is a sin against God."

[10]The woman talked to Joseph every day, but he refused to have physical relations with her or even spend time with her.

[11]One day Joseph went into the house to do his work as usual. He was the only man in the house at that time. [12]His master's wife grabbed his coat. She said to him, "Come and have physical relations with me." But Joseph left his coat in her hand and ran out of the house.

[13]She saw what Joseph had done. He had left his coat in her hands and had run outside. [14]So she called to the servants in her house. She said, "Look! This Hebrew slave was brought here to shame us. He came in and tried to have physical relations with me. But I screamed. [15]My scream scared him, and he ran away. But he left his coat with me." [16]She kept his coat until her husband came home. [17]And she told her husband the same story. She said, "This Hebrew slave you brought here came in to shame me! [18]When he came near me, I screamed. He ran away, but he left his coat."

[19]When Joseph's master heard what his wife said Joseph had done, he became very angry. [20]So Potiphar arrested Joseph and put him into prison. This prison was where the king's prisoners were put. And Joseph stayed there in the prison.

[21]But the Lord was with Joseph and showed him kindness. The Lord caused the prison warden to like Joseph. [22]The prison warden chose Joseph to take care of all the prisoners. He was responsible for whatever was done in the prison. [23]The warden paid no attention to anything that was in Joseph's care. This was because the Lord was with Joseph. The Lord made Joseph successful in everything he did.

JOSEPH INTERPRETS TWO DREAMS

40 After these things happened, two of the king's officers displeased the king. These officers were the man who served wine to the king and the king's baker. [2]The king became angry with his officer who served him wine and his baker. [3]So he put them in the prison of the captain of the guard. This was the same prison where Joseph was kept. [4]The captain of the guard put the two prisoners in Joseph's care. They stayed in prison for some time.

[5]One night both the king's officer who served him wine and the baker had a dream. Each had his own dream with its own meaning. [6]When Joseph came to them the next morning, he saw they were worried. [7]Joseph asked the king's officers who were with him, "Why do you look so unhappy today?"

[8]The two men answered, "We both had dreams last night. But no one can explain the meaning of them to us."

Joseph said to them, "God is the only One who can explain the meaning of dreams. So tell me your dreams."

[9]So the man who served wine to the king told Joseph his dream. He said, "I dreamed I saw a vine. [10]On the vine there were three branches. I watched the branches bud and blossom, and then the grapes ripened. [11]I was holding the king's cup. So I took the grapes and squeezed the juice into the cup. Then I gave it to the king."

[12]Then Joseph said, "I will explain the dream to you. The three branches stand for three days. [13]Before the end of three days the king will free you. He will allow you to return to your work. You will serve the king his wine just as you did before. [14]But when you are free,

remember me. Be kind to me. Tell the king about me so that I can get out of this prison. [15]I was taken by force from the land of the Hebrews. And I have done nothing here to deserve being put in prison."

[16]The baker saw that Joseph's explanation of the dream was good. So he said to Joseph, "I also had a dream. I dreamed there were three bread baskets on my head. [17]In the top basket there were all kinds of baked food for the king. But the birds were eating this food out of the basket on my head."

[18]Joseph answered, "I will tell you what the dream means. The three baskets stand for three days. [19]Before the end of three days, the king will cut off your head! He will hang your body on a pole. And the birds will eat your flesh."

[20]Three days later it was the king's birthday. So he gave a feast for all his officers. In front of his officers, he let the chief officer who served his wine and the chief baker out of prison. [21]The king gave his chief officer who served wine his old position. Once again he put the king's cup of wine into the king's hand. [22]But the king hanged the baker on a pole. Everything happened just as Joseph had said it would. [23]But the officer who served wine did not remember Joseph. He forgot all about him.

THE KING'S DREAMS

41 Two years later the king had a dream. He dreamed he was standing on the bank of the Nile River. [2]He saw seven fat and beautiful cows come up out of the river. They stood there, eating the grass. [3]Then seven more cows came up out of the river. But they were thin and ugly. They stood beside the seven beautiful cows on the bank of the Nile. [4]The seven thin and ugly cows ate the seven beautiful fat cows. Then the king woke up. [5]The king slept again and dreamed a second time. In his dream he saw seven full and good heads of grain growing on one stalk. [6]After that, seven more heads

of grain sprang up. But they were thin and burned by the hot east wind. [7]The thin heads of grain ate the seven full and good heads. Then the king woke up again. And he realized it was only a dream. [8]The next morning the king was troubled about these dreams. So he sent for all the magicians and wise men of Egypt. The king told them his dreams. But no one could explain their meaning to him.

[9]Then the chief officer who served wine to the king said to him, "I remember something I promised to do. But I had forgotten about it. [10]There was a time when you were angry with me and the baker. You put us in prison in the house of the captain of the guard. [11]In prison we each had a dream on the same night. Each dream had a different meaning. [12]A young Hebrew man was in the prison with us. He was a servant of the captain of the guard. We told him our dreams, and he explained their meanings to us. He told each man the meaning of his dream. [13]Things happened exactly as he said they would: I was given back my old position, and the baker was hanged."

[14]So the king called for Joseph. The guards quickly brought him out of the prison. He shaved, put on clean clothes and went before the king.

[15]The king said to Joseph, "I have had a dream. But no one can explain its meaning to me. I have heard that you can explain a dream when someone tells it to you."

[16]Joseph answered the king, "I am not able to explain the meaning of dreams. God will do this for the king."

[17]Then the king said to Joseph, "In my dream I was standing on the bank of the Nile River. [18]I saw seven fat and beautiful cows. They came up out of the river and ate the grass. [19]Then I saw seven more cows come out of the river. They were thin and lean and ugly. They were the worst looking cows I have seen in all the land of Egypt. [20]And these thin and ugly cows ate the first seven

fat cows. [21]But after they had eaten the seven cows, no one could tell they had eaten them. They just looked as thin and ugly as they did in the beginning. Then I woke up.

[22]"I had another dream. I saw seven full and good heads of grain growing on one stalk. [23]Then seven more heads of grain sprang up after them. But these heads were thin and ugly. They were burned by the hot east wind. [24]Then the thin heads ate the seven good heads. I told this dream to the magicians. But no one could explain its meaning to me."

JOSEPH TELLS THE DREAMS' MEANING

[25]Then Joseph said to the king, "Both of these dreams mean the same thing. God is telling you what he is about to do. [26]The seven good cows stand for seven years. And the seven good heads of grain stand for seven years. Both dreams mean the same thing. [27]The seven thin and ugly cows stand for seven years. And the seven thin heads of grain burned by the hot east wind stand for seven years of hunger. [28]This will happen as I told you. God is showing the king what he is about to do. [29]You will have seven years of good crops and plenty to eat in all the land of Egypt. [30]But after those seven years, there will come seven years of hunger. All the food that grew in the land of Egypt will be forgotten. The time of hunger will eat up the land. [31]People will forget what it was like to have plenty of food. This is because the hunger that follows will be so great. [32]You had two dreams which mean the same thing. This shows that God has firmly decided that this will happen. And he will make it happen soon.

[33]"So let the king choose a man who is very wise and understanding. Let the king set him over the land of Egypt. [34]And let the king also appoint officers over the land. They should take one-fifth of all the food that is grown during the seven good years. [35]They should gather all the food that is produced during the good years that are coming. Under the king's authority they should store the grain in the cities and guard it. [36]That food should be saved for later. It will be used during the seven years of hunger that will come on the land of Egypt. Then the people in Egypt will not die during the seven years of hunger."

> This will happen as I told you. God is showing the king what he is about to do.
> –GENESIS 41:28

JOSEPH IS MADE RULER OVER EGYPT

[37]This seemed like a very good idea to the king. All his officers agreed. [38]And the king asked them, "Can we find a better man than Joseph to take this job? God's spirit is truly in him!"

[39]So the king said to Joseph, "God has shown you all this. There is no one as wise and understanding as you are. [40]I will put you in charge of my palace. All the people will obey your orders. Only I will be greater than you."

[41]Then the king said to Joseph, "Look! I have put you in charge of all the land of Egypt." [42]Then the king took off from his own finger his ring with the royal seal on it. And he put it on Joseph's finger. He gave Joseph fine linen clothes to wear. And he put a gold chain around Joseph's neck. [43]The king had Joseph ride in the second royal chariot. Men walked ahead of his chariot calling, "Bow down!" By doing these things, the king put Joseph in charge of all of Egypt.

[44]The king said to him, "I am the king. And I say that no one in all the land of Egypt may lift a hand or a foot

unless you say he may." [45]The king gave Joseph the name Zaphenath-Paneah. He also gave Joseph a wife named Asenath. She was the daughter of Potiphera, priest of On. So Joseph traveled through all the land of Egypt.

[46]Joseph was 30 years old when he began serving the king of Egypt. And he left the king's court and traveled through all the land of Egypt. [47]During the seven good years, the crops in the land grew well. [48]And Joseph gathered all the food produced in Egypt during those seven years of good crops. He stored the food in the cities. In every city he stored grain that had been grown in the fields around that city. [49]Joseph stored much grain, as much as the sand of the seashore. He stored so much grain that he could not measure it.

[50]Joseph's wife was Asenath daughter of Potiphera, the priest of On. Before the years of hunger came, Joseph and Asenath had two sons. [51]Joseph named the first son Manasseh.[n] Joseph said, "God has made me forget all the troubles I have had and all my father's family." [52]Joseph named the second son Ephraim.[n] Joseph said, "God has given me children in the land of my troubles."

[53]The seven years of good crops came to an end in the land of Egypt. [54]Then the seven years of hunger began, just as Joseph had said. In all the lands people had nothing to eat. But in Egypt there was food. [55]The time of hunger became terrible in all of Egypt. The people cried to the king for food. He said to all the Egyptians, "Go to Joseph. Do whatever he tells you to do."

[56]The hunger was everywhere in that part of the world. And Joseph opened the storehouses and sold grain to the people of Egypt. This was because the time of hunger became terrible in Egypt. [57]And all the people in that part of the world came to Joseph in Egypt to buy grain. This was because the hunger was terrible everywhere in that part of the world.

THE DREAMS COME TRUE

42 Jacob learned that there was grain in Egypt. So he said to his sons, "Why are you just sitting here looking at one another? [2]I have heard that there is grain in Egypt. Go down there and buy grain for us to eat. Then we will live and not die."

[3]So ten of Joseph's brothers went down to buy grain from Egypt. [4]But Jacob did not send Benjamin, Joseph's brother, with them. Jacob was afraid that something terrible might happen to Benjamin. [5]Along with many other people, the sons of Jacob, also called Israel, went to Egypt to buy grain. This was because the people in the land of Canaan were hungry also.

[6]Now Joseph was governor over Egypt. He was the one who sold the grain to people who came to buy it. So Joseph's brothers came to him. They bowed facedown on the ground before him. [7]When Joseph saw his brothers, he knew who they were. But he acted as if he didn't know them. He asked unkindly, "Where do you come from?"

They answered, "We have come from the land of Canaan to buy food."

[8]Joseph knew they were his brothers. But they did not know who he was. [9]And Joseph remembered his dreams about his brothers bowing to him. He said to them, "You are spies! You came to learn where the nation is weak!"

[10]But his brothers said to him, "No, my master. We come as your servants just to

---

41:51 **Manasseh** This name sounds like the Hebrew word for "made me forget."
41:52 **Ephraim** This name sounds like the Hebrew word for "given me children."

buy food. ¹¹We are all sons of the same father. We are honest men, not spies."

¹²Then Joseph said to them, "No! You have come to learn where this nation is weak!"

¹³And they said, "We are 10 of 12 brothers. We are sons of the same father. We live in the land of Canaan. Our youngest brother is there with our father right now. And our other brother is gone."

¹⁴But Joseph said to them, "I can see I was right! You are spies! ¹⁵But I will give you a way to prove you are telling the truth. As surely as the king lives, you will not leave this place until your youngest brother comes here. ¹⁶One of you must go and get your brother. The rest of you will stay here in prison. We will see if you are telling the truth. If not, as surely as the king lives, you are spies." ¹⁷Then Joseph put them all in prison for three days.

¹⁸On the third day Joseph said to them, "I am a God-fearing man. Do this thing, and I will let you live: ¹⁹If you are honest men, let one of your brothers stay here in prison. The rest of you go and carry grain back to feed your hungry families. ²⁰Then bring your youngest brother back here to me. If you do this, I will know you are telling the truth. Then you will not die."

The brothers agreed to this. ²¹They said to each other, "We are being punished for what we did to our brother. We saw his trouble. He begged us to save him, but we refused to listen. That is why we are in this trouble now."

²²Then Reuben said to them, "I told you not to harm the boy. But you refused to listen to me. So now we are being punished for what we did to him."

²³When Joseph talked to his brothers, he used an interpreter. So they did not know that Joseph understood what they were saying. ²⁴Then Joseph left them and cried. After a short time he went back and spoke to them. He took Simeon and tied him up while the other brothers watched. ²⁵Joseph told his servants to fill his brothers' bags with grain. They were to put the money the brothers had paid for the grain back in their bags. They were to give them things they would need for their trip back home. And the servants did this.

²⁶So the brothers put the grain on their donkeys and left. ²⁷When they stopped for the night, one of the brothers opened his sack. He was going to get food for his donkey. Then he saw his money in the top of the sack. ²⁸He said to the other brothers, "The money I paid for the grain has been put back. Here it is in my sack!"

The brothers were very frightened. They said to each other, "What has God done to us?"

THE BROTHERS RETURN TO JACOB

²⁹The brothers went to their father Jacob in the land of Canaan. They told him everything that had happened. ³⁰They said, "The master of that land spoke unkindly to us. He accused us of spying on his country. ³¹But we told him that we were honest men, not spies. ³²We told him that we were 10 of 12 brothers—sons of one father. We said that 1 of our brothers was gone. And we said that our youngest brother was with our father in Canaan.

³³"Then the master of the land said to us, 'Here is a way I can know you are honest men: Leave 1 of your brothers with me. Take back grain to feed your hungry families, and go. ³⁴And bring your youngest brother to me. Then I will know that you are not spies but honest men. And I will give you back your brother whom you leave with me. And you can move about freely in our land.'"

³⁵Then the brothers emptied their sacks. And each of them found his money in his sack. When they and their father saw it, they were afraid.

³⁶Their father Jacob said to them, "You are robbing me of all my children. Joseph is gone. Simeon is gone. And

now you want to take Benjamin away, too. Everything is against me."

³⁷Then Reuben said to his father, "You may put my 2 sons to death if I don't bring Benjamin back to you. Trust him to my care. I will bring him back to you."

³⁸But Jacob said, "I will not allow Benjamin to go with you. His brother is dead. He is the only son left from my wife Rachel. I am afraid something terrible might happen to him during the trip to Egypt. Then I would be sad until the day I die."

THE BROTHERS GO BACK TO EGYPT

43 Still no food grew in the land of Canaan. ²Jacob's family had eaten all the grain they had brought from Egypt. So Jacob said to them, "Go to Egypt again. Buy a little more grain for us to eat."

³But Judah said to Jacob, "The governor of that country strongly warned us. He said, 'Bring your brother back with you. If you don't, you will not be allowed to see me.' ⁴If you will send Benjamin with us, we will go down and buy food for you. ⁵But if you refuse to send Benjamin, we will not go. The governor of that country warned us. He said we would not see him if we didn't bring Benjamin with us."

⁶Jacob, also called Israel, said, "Why did you tell the man you had another brother? You have caused me a lot of trouble."

⁷The brothers answered, "He questioned us carefully about ourselves and our family. He asked us, 'Is your father still alive? Do you have another brother?' We just answered his questions. How could we know he would ask us to bring our other brother to him?"

⁸Then Judah said to his father Jacob, "Send Benjamin with me. Then we will go at once. Do this so that we, you and our children may live and not die. ⁹I will guarantee you that he will be safe. I will be personally responsible for him.

If I don't bring him back to you, you can blame me all my life. ¹⁰If we had not wasted all this time, we could have already made two trips."

¹¹Then their father Jacob said to them, "If it has to be that way, then do this: Take some of the best foods in our land in your packs. Give them to the man as a gift: some balm, some honey, spices, myrrh, pistachio nuts and almonds. ¹²Take twice as much money with you this time. Take back the money that was returned to you in your sacks last time. Maybe it was a mistake. ¹³And take Benjamin with you. Now leave and go to the man. ¹⁴I pray that God All-Powerful will cause the governor to be merciful to you. I pray that he will allow Simeon and Benjamin to come back with you. If I am robbed of my children, then I am robbed of them!"

¹⁵So the brothers took the gifts. They also took twice as much money as they had taken the first time. And they took Benjamin. They hurried down to Egypt and stood before Joseph.

¹⁶In Egypt Joseph saw Benjamin with them. Joseph said to the servant in charge of his house, "Bring those men into my house. Kill an animal and prepare a meal. Those men will eat with me today at noon." ¹⁷The servant did as Joseph told him. He brought the men to Joseph's house.

¹⁸The brothers were afraid when they were brought to Joseph's house. They thought, "We were brought here because of the money that was put in our sacks on the first trip. He wants to attack us, make us slaves and take our donkeys." ¹⁹So the brothers went to the servant in charge of Joseph's house. They spoke to him at the door of the house. ²⁰They said, "Sir, we came here once before to buy food. ²¹While we were going home, we stopped for the night and opened our sacks. Each of us found all his money in his sack. We brought that money with us to give it back to you. ²²And we have brought more money. It is to pay for the food we

want to buy this time. We don't know who put that money in our sacks."

²³But the servant answered, "It's all right. Don't be afraid. Your God, the God of your father, must have put the money in your sacks. I got the money you paid me for the grain last time." Then the servant brought Simeon out to them.

²⁴The servant led the men into Joseph's house. He gave them water, and they washed their feet. Then he gave their donkeys food to eat. ²⁵The men prepared their gift to give to Joseph when he arrived at noon. They had heard they were going to eat with him there.

²⁶When Joseph came home, the brothers gave him the gift they had brought into the house. Then they bowed down to the ground to him. ²⁷Joseph asked them how they were doing. He said, "How is your aged father you told me about? Is he still alive?"

²⁸The brothers answered, "Your servant, our father, is well. He is still alive." And they bowed low before Joseph to show him respect.

²⁹Then Joseph saw his brother Benjamin, who had the same mother as he. Joseph asked, "Is this your youngest brother you told me about?" Then Joseph said to Benjamin, "God be good to you, my son!" ³⁰Then Joseph hurried off. He had to hold back the tears when he saw his brother Benjamin. So Joseph went into his room and cried there. ³¹Then he washed his face and came out. He controlled himself and said, "Serve the meal."

³²So they served Joseph at one table. They served his brothers at another table. And they served the Egyptians who ate with him at another table. This was because Egyptians did not like Hebrews and never ate with them. ³³Joseph's brothers were seated in front of him. They were in order of their ages, from oldest to youngest. And they looked at each other because they were so amazed. ³⁴Food from Joseph's table was taken to them. But Benjamin was given five times more food than the others. Joseph's brothers drank with him until they were very drunk.

JOSEPH SETS A TRAP

44 Then Joseph gave a command to the servant in charge of his house. Joseph said, "Fill the men's sacks with as much grain as they can carry. And put each man's money into his sack with the grain. ²Put my silver cup in the sack of the youngest brother. Also put his money for the grain in that sack." The servant did what Joseph told him.

³At dawn the brothers were sent away with their donkeys. ⁴They were not far from the city when Joseph said to the servant in charge of his house, "Go after the men. When you catch up with them, say, 'Why have you paid back evil for good? ⁵The cup you have stolen is the one my master uses for drinking. And he uses it for explaining dreams. You have done a very wicked thing!'"

⁶So the servant caught up with the brothers. He said to them what Joseph had told him to say.

⁷But the brothers said to the servant, "Why do you say these things? We would not do anything like that! ⁸We brought back to you the money we found in our sacks. We brought it back from the land of Canaan. So surely we would not steal silver or gold from your master's house. ⁹If you find that silver cup in the sack of one of us, then let him die. And we will be your slaves."

¹⁰The servant said, "We will do as you say. But only the man who has taken the cup will become my slave. The rest of you may go free."

¹¹Then every brother quickly lowered his sack to the ground and opened it. ¹²The servant searched the sacks, going from the oldest brother to the youngest. He found the cup in Benjamin's sack. ¹³The brothers tore their clothes to show they were sad. Then they put their sacks back on the donkeys. And they returned to the city.

¹⁴When Judah and his brothers went

back to Joseph's house, Joseph was still there. The brothers bowed facedown on the ground before him. ¹⁵Joseph said to them, "What have you done? Didn't you know that a man like me can learn things by signs and dreams?"

¹⁶Judah said, "Sir, what can we say? And how can we show we are not guilty? God has uncovered our guilt. So all of us will be your slaves, not just Benjamin."

¹⁷But Joseph said, "I will not make you all slaves! Only the man who stole the cup will be my slave. The rest of you may go back safely to your father."

¹⁸Then Judah went to Joseph and said, "Sir, please let me speak plainly to you. Please don't be angry with me. I know that you are as powerful as the king of Egypt himself. ¹⁹When we were here before, you asked us, 'Do you have a father or a brother?' ²⁰And we answered you, 'We have an old father. And we have a younger brother. He was born when our father was old. This youngest son's brother is dead. So he is the only one of his mother's children left alive. And our father loves him very much.' ²¹Then you said to us, 'Bring that brother to me. I want to see him.' ²²And we said to you, 'That young boy cannot leave his father. If he leaves him, his father would die.' ²³But you said to us, 'You must bring your youngest brother. If you don't, you will not be allowed to see me again.' ²⁴So we went back to our father and told him what you had said.

²⁵"Later, our father said, 'Go again. Buy us a little more food.' ²⁶We said to our father, 'We cannot go without our youngest brother. Without our youngest brother, we will not be allowed to see the governor.' ²⁷Then my father said to us, 'You know that my wife Rachel gave me

two sons. ²⁸One son left me. I thought, "Surely he has been torn apart by a wild animal." And I haven't seen him since. ²⁹Now you want to take this son away from me also. But something terrible might happen to him. Then I would be sad until the day I die.' ³⁰Now what will happen if we go home to our father without our youngest brother? He is the most important thing in our father's life. ³¹When our father sees that the young boy is not with us, he will die. And it will be our fault. We will cause the great sorrow that kills our father.

³²"I gave my father a guarantee that the young boy would be safe. I said to my father, 'If I don't bring him back to you, you can blame me all my life.' ³³So now, please allow me to stay here and be your slave. And let the young boy go back home with his brothers. ³⁴I cannot go back to my father if the boy is not with me. I couldn't stand to see my father that sad."

> God sent me here ahead of you . . . to keep you alive in an amazing way.
> –GENESIS 45:7–8

JOSEPH REVEALS WHO HE IS

45 Joseph could not control himself in front of his servants any longer. He cried out, "Have everyone leave me." When only the brothers were left with Joseph, he told them who he was. ²Joseph cried so loudly that the Egyptians heard him. And the people in the king's palace heard about it. ³He said to his brothers, "I am Joseph. Is my father still alive?" But the brothers could not answer him, because they were very afraid of him.

⁴So Joseph said to them, "Come close to me." So the brothers came close to him. And he said to them, "I am your brother Joseph. You sold me as a slave to go to Egypt. ⁵Now don't be worried. Don't be angry with yourselves because you sold me here. God sent me here

ahead of you to save people's lives. ⁶No food has grown on the land for two years now. And there will be five more years without planting or harvest. ⁷So God sent me here ahead of you. This was to make sure you have some descendants left on earth. And it was to keep you alive in an amazing way. ⁸So it was not you who sent me here, but God. God has made me the highest officer of the king of Egypt. I am in charge of his palace. I am the master of all the land of Egypt.

⁹"So leave quickly and go to my father. Tell him, 'Your son Joseph says: God has made me master over all Egypt. Come down to me quickly. ¹⁰Live in the land of Goshen. You will be near me. Also your children, your grandchildren, your flocks and herds and all that you have will be near me. ¹¹I will care for you during the next five years of hunger. In this way, you and your family and all that you have will not starve.'

¹²"Now you can see for yourselves. The one speaking to you is really Joseph. And my brother Benjamin can see this. ¹³So tell my father about how powerful I have become in Egypt. Tell him about everything you have seen. Now hurry and bring him back to me."

¹⁴Then Joseph hugged his brother Benjamin and cried. And Benjamin cried also. ¹⁵Then Joseph kissed all his brothers. He cried as he hugged them. After this, his brothers talked with him.

¹⁶The king of Egypt and his officers learned that Joseph's brothers had come. And they were very happy about this. ¹⁷So the king said to Joseph, "Tell your brothers to load their animals and go back to the land of Canaan. ¹⁸Tell them to bring their father and their families back here to me. I will give them the best land in Egypt. And they will eat the best food we have here. ¹⁹Tell them to take some wagons from Egypt for their children and their wives. And tell them to bring their father back also. ²⁰Tell them not to worry about bringing any of their things with them.

We will give them the best of what we have in Egypt."

²¹So the sons of Israel did this. Joseph gave them wagons as the king had ordered. And he gave them food for their trip. ²²He gave each brother a change of clothes. But he gave Benjamin five changes of clothes. And Joseph gave him about seven and one-half pounds of silver. ²³Joseph also sent his father ten donkeys loaded with the best things from Egypt. And he sent ten female donkeys. They were loaded with grain, bread and other food for his father on his trip back. ²⁴Then Joseph told his brothers to go. As they were leaving, he said to them, "Don't quarrel on the way home."

²⁵So the brothers left Egypt and went to their father Jacob in the land of Canaan. ²⁶They told him, "Joseph is still alive. He is the ruler over all the land of Egypt." Their father was shocked and did not believe them. ²⁷But the brothers told him everything Joseph had said. Then Jacob saw the wagons that Joseph had sent to carry him back to Egypt. Now Jacob felt better. ²⁸Jacob, also called Israel, said, "Now I believe you. My son Joseph is still alive. I will go and see him before I die."

JACOB GOES TO EGYPT

46 So Jacob, also called Israel, took all he had and started his trip. He went to Beersheba. There he offered sacrifices to the God of his father Isaac. ²During the night God spoke to Israel in a vision. He said, "Jacob, Jacob."

And Jacob answered, "Here I am."

³Then God said, "I am God, the God of your father. Don't be afraid to go to Egypt. I will make your descendants a great nation there. ⁴I will go to Egypt with you. And I will bring you out of Egypt again. Joseph's own hands will close your eyes when you die."

⁵Then Jacob left Beersheba. The sons of Israel loaded their father, their children and their wives. They put

them in the wagons the king of Egypt had sent. ⁶They also took their farm animals and everything they had gotten in Canaan. So Jacob went to Egypt with all his descendants. ⁷He took his sons and grandsons, his daughters and granddaughters. He took all his family to Egypt with him.

JACOB'S FAMILY

⁸Now these are the names of the children of Israel who went into Egypt. (They are Jacob and his descendants.)

Reuben was Jacob's first son. ⁹Reuben's sons were Hanoch, Pallu, Hezron and Carmi.

¹⁰Simeon's sons were Jemuel, Jamin, Ohad, Jakin, Zohar and Shaul. (Shaul was Simeon's son by a Canaanite woman.)

¹¹Levi's sons were Gershon, Kohath and Merari.

¹²Judah's sons were Er, Onan, Shelah, Perez and Zerah. (But Er and Onan had died in the land of Canaan.) Perez's sons were Hezron and Hamul.

¹³Issachar's sons were Tola, Puah, Jashub and Shimron.

¹⁴Zebulun's sons were Sered, Elon and Jahleel.

¹⁵These are the sons of Leah and Jacob born in Northwest Mesopotamia. His daughter Dinah was also born there. There were 33 persons in this part of Jacob's family.

¹⁶Gad's sons were Zephon, Haggi, Shuni, Ezbon, Eri, Arodi and Areli.

¹⁷Asher's sons were Imnah, Ishvah, Ishvi and Beriah. Their sister was Serah. Beriah's sons were Heber and Malkiel.

¹⁸These are Jacob's sons by Zilpah. She was the slave girl whom Laban gave to his daughter Leah. There were 16 persons in this part of Jacob's family.

¹⁹The sons of Jacob's wife Rachel were Joseph and Benjamin. ²⁰In Egypt, Joseph became the father of Manasseh and Ephraim by his wife Asenath. She was the daughter of Potiphera, priest of On.

²¹Benjamin's sons were Bela, Beker, Ashbel, Gera, Naaman, Ehi, Rosh, Muppim, Huppim and Ard.

²²These are the sons of Jacob by his wife Rachel. There were 14 persons in this part of Jacob's family.

²³Dan's son was Hushim.

²⁴Naphtali's sons were Jahziel, Guni, Jezer and Shillem.

²⁵These are Jacob's sons by Bilhah. She was the slave girl whom Laban gave to his daughter Rachel. There were 7 persons in this part of Jacob's family.

²⁶So the total number of Jacob's direct descendants who went to Egypt was 66. (The wives of Jacob's sons were not counted in this number.) ²⁷Joseph had 2 sons born in Egypt. So the total number in the family of Jacob in Egypt was 70.

JACOB ARRIVES IN EGYPT

²⁸Jacob sent Judah ahead of him to see Joseph in Goshen. Then Jacob and his people came into the land of Goshen. ²⁹Joseph prepared his chariot and went to meet his father Israel in Goshen. As soon as Joseph saw his father, he hugged his neck. And he cried there for a long time.

³⁰Then Israel said to Joseph, "Now I am ready to die. I have seen your face. And I know that you are still alive."

³¹Joseph said to his brothers and his father's family, "I will go and tell the king you are here. I will say, 'My brothers and my father's family have left the land of Canaan. They have come here to me. ³²They are shepherds and take care of farm animals. And they have brought their flocks and their herds and everything they own with them.' ³³When the king calls you, he will ask, 'What work do you do?' ³⁴This is what you should tell him: 'We, your servants, have taken care of farm animals all our lives. Our ancestors did the same thing.' Then the king will allow you to settle in the land of Goshen. This is away from the Egyptians. They don't like to be near shepherds."

JACOB SETTLES IN GOSHEN

47 Joseph went in to the king and said, "My father and my brothers have arrived from Canaan. They have their flocks and herds and everything they own with them. They are now in the land of Goshen." ²Joseph chose five of his brothers to introduce to the king.

³The king said to the brothers, "What work do you do?"

And they said to him, "We, your servants, are shepherds. Our ancestors were also shepherds." ⁴They said to the king, "We have come to live in this land. There is no grass in the land of Canaan for our animals to eat. The hunger is very terrible there. So please allow us to live in the land of Goshen."

⁵Then the king said to Joseph, "Your father and your brothers have come to you. ⁶You may choose any place in Egypt for them to live. Give your father and your brothers the best land. Let them live in the land of Goshen. And if any of them are skilled shepherds, put them in charge of my sheep and cattle."

⁷Then Joseph brought in his father Jacob and introduced him to the king. And Jacob blessed the king. ⁸Then the king said to Jacob, "How old are you?"

⁹Jacob said to him, "My life has been spent wandering from place to place. It has been short, filled with trouble. I have lived only 130 years. My ancestors lived much longer than I." ¹⁰Then Jacob blessed the king and left.

¹¹Joseph obeyed the king. He gave his father and brothers the best land in Egypt. It was near the city of Rameses. ¹²And Joseph gave his father, his brothers and everyone who lived with them the food they needed.

JOSEPH BUYS LAND FOR THE KING

¹³The hunger became worse, and there was no food anywhere in the land. The land of Egypt and the land of Canaan became very poor because of this. ¹⁴Joseph collected all the money that was to be found in Egypt and Canaan. People paid him this money for the grain they were buying. He brought that money to the king's palace. ¹⁵After some time, the people in Egypt and Canaan had no money left. So they went to Joseph and said, "Please give us food. Our money is gone. If we don't eat, we will die here in front of you."

¹⁶Joseph answered, "Since you have no money, give me your farm animals. I will give you food in return." ¹⁷So people brought their farm animals to Joseph. And he gave them food in exchange for their horses, sheep, cattle and donkeys. So he kept them alive by trading food for their farm animals that year.

¹⁸The next year the people came to Joseph and said, "You know we have no money left. And all our animals belong to you. We have nothing left except our bodies and our land. ¹⁹Surely both we and our land will die here in front of you. Buy us and our land in exchange for food. And we will be slaves to the king, together with our land. Give us seed to plant. Then we will live and not die. And the land will not become a desert."

²⁰So Joseph bought all the land in Egypt for the king. Every Egyptian sold Joseph his field, because the hunger was very great. So the land became the king's. ²¹And Joseph made the people slaves from one end of Egypt to the other. ²²The only land he did not buy was the land the priests owned. They

> Then God said, "I am God, the God of your father. Don't be afraid."
>
> —GENESIS 46:3

did not need to sell their land because the king paid them for their work. So they had money to buy food.

²³Joseph said to the people, "Now I have bought you and your land for the king. So I will give you seed. And you can plant your fields. ²⁴At harvest time you must give one-fifth to the king. You may keep four-fifths for yourselves. Use it as seed for the field and as food for yourselves, your families and your children."

²⁵The people said, "You have saved our lives. If you like, we will become slaves of the king."

²⁶So Joseph made a law in Egypt, which continues today: One-fifth of everything from the land belongs to the king. The only land the king did not get was the priests' land.

"DON'T BURY ME IN EGYPT"

²⁷The Israelites continued to live in the land of Goshen in Egypt. There they got possessions. They had many children and grew in number.

²⁸Jacob, also called Israel, lived in Egypt 17 years. So he lived to be 147 years old. ²⁹Israel knew he soon would die. So he called his son Joseph to him. He said to Joseph, "If you love me, put your hand under my leg.ⁿ Promise me you will not bury me in Egypt. ³⁰When I die, carry me out of Egypt. Bury me where my ancestors are buried."

Joseph answered, "I will do as you say."

³¹Then Jacob said, "Promise me." And Joseph promised him that he would do this. Then Israel worshiped as he leaned on the top of his walking stick.

BLESSINGS FOR MANASSEH AND EPHRAIM

48 Some time later Joseph learned that his father was very sick. So he took his two sons Manasseh and Ephraim and went to his father. ²When Joseph arrived, someone told Jacob, also called Israel, "Your son Joseph has come to see you." Jacob was weak. So he used all his strength and sat up on his bed.

³Then Jacob said to Joseph, "God All-Powerful appeared to me at Luz in the land of Canaan. God blessed me there. ⁴He said to me, 'I will give you many children. I will make you the father of many peoples. And I will give your descendants this land forever.' ⁵Your two sons were born here in Egypt before I came. They will be counted as my own sons. Ephraim and Manasseh will be my sons just as Reuben and Simeon are my sons. ⁶But if you have other children, they will be your own. But their land will be part of the land given to Ephraim and Manasseh. ⁷When I came from Northwest Mesopotamia, Rachel died in the land of Canaan. We were traveling toward Ephrath. This made me very sad. I buried her there beside the road to Ephrath." (Today Ephrath is Bethlehem.)

⁸Then Israel saw Joseph's sons. He said, "Who are these boys?"

⁹Joseph said to his father, "They are my sons. God has given them to me here in Egypt."

Israel said, "Bring your sons to me so I may bless them."

¹⁰At this time Israel's eyesight was bad because he was old. So Joseph brought the boys close to him. Israel kissed the boys and put his arms around them. ¹¹He said to Joseph, "I thought I would never see you alive again. And now God has let me see you and also your children." ¹²Then Joseph moved his sons off Israel's lap. Joseph bowed face-down to the ground. ¹³He put Ephraim on his right side and Manasseh on his left. (So Ephraim was near Israel's left hand, and Manasseh was near Israel's right hand.) Joseph brought the boys close to Israel. ¹⁴But Israel crossed his arms. He put his right hand on the head of Ephraim, who was younger. He put his left hand on the head of Manasseh.

47:29 put . . . leg This showed that a person would keep a promise.

But he was the firstborn son. ¹⁵And Israel blessed Joseph and said,

> "My ancestors Abraham and Isaac
>   served our God.
>   And like a shepherd God has led me
>   all my life.
> ¹⁶ He was the Angel who saved me from
>   all my troubles.
>   Now I pray that he will bless these
>   boys.
> May my name be known through
>   these boys.
>   And may the names of my
>   ancestors Abraham and Isaac be
>   known through them.
> May they have many descendants on
>   the earth."

¹⁷Joseph saw that his father put his right hand on Ephraim's head. Joseph didn't like it. So he took hold of his father's hand. He wanted to move it from Ephraim's head to Manasseh's head. ¹⁸Joseph said to his father, "You are doing it wrong, Father. Manasseh is the firstborn son. Put your right hand on his head."

¹⁹But his father refused and said, "I know, my son, I know. Manasseh will be great and have many descendants. But his younger brother will be greater. And his descendants will be enough to make a nation."

²⁰So Israel blessed them that day. He said,

> "When a blessing is given in Israel,
>   they will say:
>   'May God make you like Ephraim
>   and Manasseh.'"

In this way he made Ephraim greater than Manasseh.

²¹Then Israel said to Joseph, "Look at me. I am about to die. But God will be with you. He will take you back to the land of your fathers. ²²I have given you something that I did not give your brothers. I have given you the land of Shechem that I took from the Amorite

people. I took it with my sword and my bow."

JACOB BLESSES HIS SONS

49 Then Jacob called his sons to him. He said, "Come here to me. I will tell you what will happen to you in the future.

² "Come together and listen, sons of
    Jacob.
    Listen to Israel, your father.

³ "Reuben, my first son, you are my
    strength.
    Your birth showed I could be a
    father.
You have the highest position among
    my sons.
    You are the most powerful.
⁴ But you are uncontrolled like water.
    So you will no longer lead your
    brothers.
This is because you got into your
    father's bed.
    You shamed me by having physical
    relations with my slave girl.

⁵ "Simeon and Levi are brothers.
    They used their swords to do
    violence.
⁶ I will not join their secret talks.
    I will not meet with them to plan
    evil.
They killed men because they were
    angry.
    And they crippled oxen just for fun.
⁷ May their anger be cursed, because it
    is too violent.
    May their violence be cursed,
    because it is too cruel.
I will divide them up among the
    tribes of Jacob.
    I will scatter them through all the
    tribes of Israel.

⁸ "Judah, your brothers will praise
    you.
    You will grab
    your enemies
    by the neck.

Your brothers will bow down to
you.
⁹ Judah is like a young lion.
You have returned from killing, my
son.
Like a lion, he stretches out and lies
down to rest.
No one is brave enough to wake
him.
¹⁰ Men from Judah's family will be
kings.
Someone from Judah will always be
on the throne.
Judah will rule until the real king
comes.
And the nations will obey him.
¹¹ He ties his donkey to a grapevine.
He ties his young donkey to the
best branch.
He can afford to use wine to wash his
clothes.
He even uses grape juice to wash
his robes.
¹² His eyes are bright from drinking
wine.
His teeth are white from drinking
milk.

¹³ "Zebulun will live near the sea.
His shore will be a safe place for
ships.
His land will reach as far as Sidon.

¹⁴ "Issachar is like a strong donkey.
He lies down while carrying his
load.
¹⁵ He will see his resting place is good.
He will see how pleasant his
land is.
Then he will put his back to the load.
He will become a slave.

¹⁶ "Dan will rule his own people
like the other tribes in Israel.
¹⁷ Dan will be like a snake by the side of
the road.
He will be like a dangerous snake
lying near the path.
That snake bites a horse's leg.
And the rider is thrown off
backward.

¹⁸ "Lord, I wait for your salvation.

¹⁹ "Robbers will attack Gad.
But he will defeat them and drive
them away.

²⁰ "Asher's land will grow much good
food.
He will grow food fit for a king.

²¹ "Naphtali is like a female deer that
runs free.
She has beautiful fawns.

²² "Joseph is like a grapevine that
produces much fruit.
He is like a healthy vine watered by
a spring.
He is like a vine whose branches
grow over the wall.
²³ Men attack him violently with
arrows.
They shoot at him angrily.
²⁴ But he aims his bow well.
His arms are made strong.
He gets his power from the Mighty
God of Jacob.
He gets his strength from the
Shepherd, the Rock of Israel.
²⁵ Your father's God helps you.
God All-Powerful blesses you.
He blesses you with rain from
above.
He blesses you with water from
springs below.
He blesses you with many babies
born to your wives.
He blesses you with many
young ones born to your
animals.
²⁶ The blessings of your father are
greater
than the blessings of the oldest
mountains.
They are greater than the good
things of the long-lasting hills.
May these blessings rest on the head
of Joseph.
May they rest on the forehead of
the one who was separated from
his brothers.

²⁷ "Benjamin is like a hungry wolf.
In the morning he eats what he has
caught.
In the evening he divides what he
has taken."

²⁸These are the 12 tribes of Israel.
And this is what their father said to
them. He gave each son the blessing
that was right for him. ²⁹Then Israel
gave them a command. He said, "I am
about to die. Bury me with my ancestors in the cave in the field of Ephron
the Hittite. ³⁰That cave is in the field
of Machpelah east of Mamre. It is in
the land of Canaan. Abraham
bought that field from
Ephron the Hittite for a
burying place. ³¹Abraham
and Sarah his wife are
buried there. Isaac and
Rebekah his wife are
buried there. I buried
my wife Leah there.
³²The field and the cave
in it were bought from
the Hittite people."
³³After Jacob finished
talking to his sons, he
lay down. He put his feet
back on the bed, took his
last breath and died.

> Judah will rule until the real king comes. And the nations will obey him.
>
> –GENESIS 49:10

JACOB'S BURIAL

50 When Jacob died, Joseph
hugged his father and cried
over him and kissed him. ²He commanded the doctors who served him to
prepare his father's body. So the doctors prepared Jacob's body to be buried.
³It took the doctors 40 days to prepare
his body. This was the usual time it
took. And the Egyptians had a time of
sorrow for Jacob. It lasted 70 days.

⁴When this time of sorrow had
ended, Joseph spoke to the king's officers. He said, "If you think well of me,
please tell this to the king: ⁵'When my
father was near death, I made a promise
to him. I promised I would bury him in
a cave in the land of Canaan. This is a

burial place that he cut out for himself.
So please let me go and bury my father.
Then I will return.'"

⁶The king answered, "Keep your
promise. Go and bury your father."

⁷So Joseph went to bury his father.
All the king's officers, the elders of his
court and all the elders of Egypt went
with Joseph. ⁸Everyone who lived with
Joseph and his brothers went with him.
And everyone who lived with his father
also went. They left only their children,
their flocks and their herds in the land
of Goshen. ⁹Men in chariots and on
horses also went with Joseph. It was a
very large group.

¹⁰They went to the threshing floor of Atad, east of the
Jordan River. There they
cried loudly and bitterly
for Jacob, also called
Israel. Joseph's time
of sorrow continued
for seven days. ¹¹The
people that lived in
Canaan saw the sad-
ness at the threshing
floor of Atad. They said,
"Those Egyptians are
showing great sorrow!"
So now that place is named
Sorrow of the Egyptians.

¹²So Jacob's sons did what
their father commanded. ¹³They
carried his body to the land of Canaan.
They buried it in the cave in the field
of Machpelah near Mamre. Abraham
had bought this cave and field from
Ephron the Hittite. He bought the cave
to use as a burial place. ¹⁴After Joseph
buried his father, he returned to
Egypt. His brothers and everyone who
had gone with him to bury his father
also returned.

THE BROTHERS FEAR JOSEPH

¹⁵After Jacob died, Joseph's brothers
said, "What if Joseph is still angry with
us? We did many wrong things to him.
What if he plans to pay us back?" ¹⁶So
they sent a message to Joseph. It said,

"Your father gave this command before he died. [17]He said to us, 'You have done wrong. You have sinned and done evil to Joseph. Tell Joseph to forgive you, his brothers.' So now, Joseph, we beg you to forgive our wrong. We are the servants of the God of your father." When Joseph received the message, he cried.

[18]And his brothers went to him and bowed low before him. They said, "We are your slaves."

[19]Then Joseph said to them, "Don't be afraid. Can I do what only God can do? [20]You meant to hurt me. But God turned your evil into good. It was to save the lives of many people. And it is being done. [21]So don't be afraid. I will take care of you and your children." So Joseph comforted his brothers and spoke kind words to them.

[22]Joseph continued to live in Egypt with all his father's family. He died when he was 110 years old. [23]During Joseph's life Ephraim had children and grandchildren. And Joseph's son Manasseh had a son named Makir. Joseph accepted Makir's children as his own.

THE DEATH OF JOSEPH

[24]Joseph said to his brothers, "I am about to die. But God will take care of you. He will lead you out of this land. He will lead you to the land he promised to Abraham, Isaac and Jacob." [25]Then Joseph had the sons of Israel make a promise. He said, "Promise me that you will carry my bones with you out of Egypt."

[26]Joseph died when he was 110 years old. Doctors prepared his body for burial. Then they put him in a coffin in Egypt.

Exodus

JACOB'S FAMILY IN EGYPT

1 When Jacob, also called Israel, went to Egypt, he took his sons. And each son took his own family with him. These are the names of the sons of Israel: ²Reuben, Simeon, Levi, Judah, ³Issachar, Zebulun, Benjamin, ⁴Dan, Naphtali, Gad and Asher. ⁵There was a total of 70 people who were descendants of Jacob. Jacob's son Joseph was already in Egypt.

⁶By some time later, Joseph and his brothers had died, along with all the people who had lived at that same time. ⁷But the people of Israel had many children, and their number grew greatly. They became very strong, and the country of Egypt was filled with them.

TROUBLE FOR THE PEOPLE OF ISRAEL

⁸Then a new king began to rule Egypt. He did not know who Joseph was. ⁹This king said to his people, "Look! The people of Israel are too many! And they are too strong for us to handle! ¹⁰We must make plans against them. If we don't, the number of their people will grow even more. Then if there is a war, they might join our enemies. Then they could fight us and escape from the country!"

¹¹So the Egyptians made life hard for the people of Israel. They put slave masters over the Israelites. The slave masters forced the Israelites to build the cities Pithom and Rameses for the king. These cities were supply centers in which the Egyptians stored things. ¹²The Egyptians forced the Israelites to work even harder. But this made the Israelites grow in number and spread more. So the Egyptians became more afraid of them. ¹³They forced the Israelites to work even harder. ¹⁴The Egyptians made life hard for the Israelites. They forced the Israelites

to work very hard making bricks and mortar. They also forced them to do all kinds of hard work in the fields. The Egyptians were not merciful to them in all their hard work.

¹⁵There were two Hebrew nurses named Shiphrah and Puah. These nurses helped the Israelite women give birth to their babies. The king of Egypt said to the nurses, ¹⁶"When you are helping the Hebrew women give birth to their babies, watch! If the baby is a girl, let the baby live. But if it is a boy, kill it!" ¹⁷But the nurses feared God. So they did not do as the king told them. They let all the boy babies live. ¹⁸Then the king of Egypt sent for the nurses. He said, "Why did you do this? Why did you let the boys live?"

¹⁹The nurses said to him, "The Hebrew women are much stronger than the Egyptian women. They give birth to their babies before we can get there." ²⁰God was good to the nurses. And the Hebrew people continued to grow in number. So they became even stronger. ²¹Because the nurses feared God, he gave them families of their own.

²²So the king commanded all his people: "Every time a boy is born to the Hebrews, you must throw him into the Nile River. But let all the girl babies live."

BABY MOSES

2 There was a man from the family of Levi. He married a woman who was also from the family of Levi. ²She became pregnant and gave birth to a son. She saw how wonderful the baby was, and she hid him for three months. ³But after three months, she was not able to hide the baby any longer. So she got a basket made of reeds and covered it with tar so that it would float. She put the baby in the basket. Then she put the basket among the tall grass at the edge of the Nile River. ⁴The baby's sister stood a

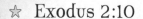

Before Moses was born, there was an evil king in Egypt. He made a rule that all Hebrew baby boys were to be killed! When Moses was born, his mom hid him for three months. Then she put him in a basket and set it in the river. The king's daughter found the baby and adopted him. She named him Moses, which means "to pull out" because she pulled him from the river.

Do you know what your name means? In the Bible, many babies were given names because of what happened in the past or what will happen in the future. Do you know what the name *Jesus* means? It means "salvation" and "he will save." And that's exactly what he did! He came to the earth and healed people to save them from their sicknesses. And then he died and rose again to save us from our sins.

· ·

Just like God saved Moses when he was pulled out of the river, he can save you from trouble. When you are sick or scared, call on Jesus. He saves!

---

short distance away. She wanted to see what would happen to him.

⁵Then the daughter of the king of Egypt came to the river. She was going to take a bath. Her servant girls were walking beside the river. She saw the basket in the tall grass. So she sent her slave girl to get it. ⁶The king's daughter opened the basket and saw the baby boy. He was crying, and she felt sorry for him. She said, "This is one of the Hebrew babies."

⁷Then the baby's sister asked the king's daughter, "Would you like me to find a Hebrew woman to nurse the baby for you?"

⁸The king's daughter said, "Yes,

please." So the girl went and got the baby's own mother.

⁹The king's daughter said to the woman, "Take this baby and nurse him for me. I will pay you." So the woman took her baby and nursed him. ¹⁰After the child had grown older, the woman took him to the king's daughter. She adopted the baby as her own son. The king's daughter named him Moses,ⁿ because she had pulled him out of the water.

MOSES HELPS HIS PEOPLE
¹¹Moses grew and became a man. One day he visited his people, the Hebrews.

2:10 **Moses** The name Moses sounds like the Hebrew word for "to pull out."

He saw that they were forced to work very hard. He saw an Egyptian beating a Hebrew man, one of Moses' own people. [12]Moses looked all around and saw that no one was watching. So he killed the Egyptian and hid his body in the sand.

[13]The next day Moses returned and saw two Hebrew men fighting each other. He saw that one man was in the wrong. Moses said to that man, "Why are you hitting one of your own people?"

[14]The man answered, "Who made you our ruler and judge? Are you going to kill me as you killed the Egyptian?"

Then Moses was afraid. He thought, "Now everyone knows what I did."

[15]When the king heard about what Moses had done, he tried to kill Moses. But Moses ran away from the king and went to live in the land of Midian. There he sat down near a well.

MOSES IN MIDIAN

[16]There was a priest in Midian who had seven daughters. His daughters went to that well to get water for their father's sheep. They were trying to fill the water troughs for their father's sheep. [17]But some shepherds came and chased the girls away. Then Moses defended the girls and watered their sheep.

[18]Then they went back to their father, Reuel, also called Jethro. He asked them, "Why have you come home early today?"

[19]The girls answered, "The shepherds chased us away. But an Egyptian defended us. He got water for us and watered our sheep."

[20]He asked his daughters, "Where is this man? Why did you leave him? Invite him to eat with us."

[21]Moses agreed to stay with Jethro. And he gave his daughter Zipporah to Moses to be his wife. [22]Zipporah gave birth to a son, and Moses named him Gershom.[n] Moses named him this because Moses was a stranger in a land that was not his own.

[23]After a long time, the king of Egypt died. The people of Israel groaned because they were forced to work very hard. They cried for help. And God heard them. [24]God heard their cries, and he remembered the agreement he had made with Abraham, Isaac and Jacob. [25]God saw the troubles of the people of Israel, and he was concerned about them.

THE BURNING BUSH

3 One day Moses was taking care of Jethro's sheep. Jethro was the priest of Midian and also Moses' father-in-law. Moses led the sheep to the west side of the desert. He came to Sinai, the mountain of God. [2]There the angel of the Lord appeared to Moses in flames of fire coming out of a bush. Moses saw that the bush was on fire, but it was not burning up. [3]So Moses said, "I will go closer to this strange thing. How can a bush continue burning without burning up?"

[4]The Lord saw Moses was coming to look at the bush. So God called to him from the bush, "Moses, Moses!"

And Moses said, "Here I am."

[5]Then God said, "Do not come any closer. Take off your sandals. You are standing on holy ground. [6]I am the God of your ancestors. I am the God of Abraham, the God of Isaac and the God of Jacob." Moses covered his face because he was afraid to look at God.

[7]The Lord said, "I have seen the troubles my people have suffered in Egypt. And I have heard their cries when the Egyptian slave masters hurt them. I am concerned about their pain. [8]I have come down to save them from the Egyptians. I will bring them out of that land. I will lead them to a good land with lots of room. This is a land where much food grows. This is the land of these people: the Canaanites, Hittites, Amorites, Perizzites, Hivites and Jebusites. [9]I have heard the cries of

---

2:22 **Gershom** This name sounds like the Hebrew word meaning "a stranger there."

the people of Israel. I have seen the way the Egyptians have made life hard for them. [10]So now I am sending you to the king of Egypt. Go! Bring my people, the Israelites, out of Egypt!"

[11]But Moses said to God, "I am not a great man! Why should I be the one to go to the king and lead the Israelites out of Egypt?"

[12]God said, "I will be with you. This will be the proof that I am sending you: You will lead the people out of Egypt. Then all of you will worship me on this mountain."

[13]Moses said to God, "When I go to the Israelites, I will say to them, 'The God of your ancestors sent me to you.' What if the people say, 'What is his name?' What should I tell them?"

[14]Then God said to Moses, "I AM WHO I AM."[n] When you go to the people of Israel, tell them, 'I AM sent me to you.'"

[15]God also said to Moses, "This is what you should tell the people: 'The Lord is the God of your ancestors. He is the God of Abraham, the God of Isaac and the God of Jacob. And he sent me to you.' This will always be my name. That is how people from now on will know me.

[16]"Go and gather the elders and tell them this: 'The Lord, the God of your ancestors, has appeared to me. The God of Abraham, Isaac and Jacob spoke to me. He says: I care about you, and I have seen what has happened to you in Egypt. [17]I have decided that I will take you away from the troubles you are suffering in Egypt. I will lead you to the land of the Canaanites, Hittites, Amorites, Perizzites, Hivites and Jebusites. This land grows much food.'

[18]"The elders will listen to you. And then you and the elders of Israel will go to the king of Egypt. You will tell him, 'The Lord, the God of the Hebrews, appeared to us. Let us travel three days into the desert. There we must offer sacrifices to the Lord our God.'

[19]"But I know that the king of Egypt will not let you go. Only a great power will force him to let you go. [20]So I will use my great power against Egypt. I will make miracles happen in that land. After I do this, he will let you go. [21]And I will cause the Egyptian people to think well of the people of Israel. So when you leave, they will give gifts to your people. [22]Each Hebrew woman will ask her Egyptian neighbor and any Egyptian woman living in her house for gifts. Ask for silver, gold and clothing. You will put those gifts on your children when you leave Egypt. In this way you will take with you the riches of the Egyptians."

> Then God said to Moses, "I AM WHO I AM."
>
> –EXODUS 3:14

PROOF FOR MOSES

4 Then Moses answered, "What if the people of Israel do not believe me or listen to me? What if they say, 'The Lord did not appear to you'?"

[2]The Lord said to him, "What is that in your hand?"

Moses answered, "It is my walking stick."

[3]The Lord said, "Throw it on the ground."

So Moses threw it on the ground. And it became a snake. Moses ran from the snake. [4]But the Lord said to him, "Reach out and grab the snake by its

---

3:14 I...I AM The Hebrew words are like the name "YAHWEH." This Hebrew name for God, usually called "Lord," shows that God always lives and is always with his people.

tail." So Moses reached out and took hold of the snake. When he did this, it again became a stick in his hand. ⁵The Lord said, "When this happens, the Israelites will believe that the Lord appeared to you. I am the God of their ancestors. I am the God of Abraham, the God of Isaac and the God of Jacob."

⁶Then the Lord said to Moses, "Put your hand inside your coat." So Moses put his hand inside his coat. When he took his hand out, it was white with a harmful skin disease.

⁷Then the Lord said, "Now put your hand inside your coat again." So Moses put his hand inside his coat again. When he took it out, his hand was healthy again. It was like the rest of his skin.

⁸Then the Lord said, "The people may not believe you or be convinced by the first miracle. They may believe you when you show them this second miracle. ⁹After these two miracles they still may not believe or listen to you. Then take some water from the Nile River. Pour it on the dry ground. The water will become blood when it touches the ground."

¹⁰But Moses said to the Lord, "But Lord, I am not a skilled speaker. I have never been able to speak well. And now, even after talking to you, I am not a good speaker. I speak slowly and can't find the best words."

¹¹Then the Lord said to him, "Who made man's mouth? And who makes him deaf or not able to speak? Or who gives a man sight or makes him blind? It is I, the Lord. ¹²Now go! I will help you speak. I will tell you what to say."

¹³But Moses said, "Please, Lord, send someone else."

¹⁴The Lord became angry with Moses. He said, "Your brother Aaron, from the family of Levi, is a skilled speaker. He is already coming to meet you. And he will be happy when he sees you. ¹⁵I will tell you what to say. Then you will tell Aaron. I will help both of you know what to say and do.

¹⁶And Aaron will speak to the people for you. You will tell him what God says. And he will speak for you. ¹⁷Take your walking stick with you. Use it to do the miracles."

MOSES RETURNS TO EGYPT

¹⁸Then Moses went back to Jethro, his father-in-law. Moses said to him, "Let me go back to my people in Egypt. I want to see if they are still alive."

Jethro said to Moses, "You may go. Have a safe trip."

¹⁹While Moses was still in Midian, the Lord said to him, "Go back to Egypt. The men who wanted to kill you are dead now."

²⁰So Moses took his wife and his sons and put them on a donkey. Then he started back to Egypt. He took with him the walking stick of God.

²¹The Lord said to Moses, "When you get back to Egypt, do all the miracles. I have given you the power to do them. Show them to the king of Egypt. But I will make the king very stubborn. He will not let the people go. ²²Then say to the king: 'This is what the Lord says: Israel is my firstborn son. ²³And I told you to let my son go. Let him go so he may worship me. But you refused to let Israel go. So I will kill your firstborn son.'"

²⁴As Moses was on his way to Egypt, he stopped at a resting place for the night. The Lord met him there and tried to kill him. ²⁵But Zipporah took a flint knife and circumcised her son. She took the skin and touched Moses' feet with it. Then she said to him, "You are a bridegroom of blood to me." ²⁶Zipporah said this because she had to circumcise her son. So the Lord did not kill Moses.

²⁷Meanwhile the Lord said to Aaron, "Go out into the desert to meet Moses." When Aaron went, he met Moses at Sinai, the mountain of God, and kissed him. ²⁸Moses told Aaron everything the Lord had said to him when he sent him to Egypt. And Moses told him about the

miracles which the Lord had commanded him to do.

²⁹So Moses and Aaron gathered all the elders of the Israelites. ³⁰Aaron told them everything that the Lord had told Moses. Then Moses did the miracles for all the people to see. ³¹So the Israelites believed. They heard that the Lord was concerned about them and had seen their troubles. Then they bowed down and worshiped him.

MOSES AND AARON BEFORE THE KING

5 After Moses and Aaron talked to the people, they went to the king of Egypt. They said, "This is what the Lord, the God of Israel says: 'Let my people go so they may hold a feast for me in the desert.'"

²But the king of Egypt said, "Who is the Lord? Why should I obey him and let Israel go? I do not know the Lord. And I will not let Israel go."

³Then Aaron and Moses said, "The God of the Hebrews has talked with us. Now let us travel three days into the desert. There we will offer sacrifices to the Lord our God. If we don't do this, he may kill us with a disease or in war."

⁴But the king said to them, "Moses and Aaron, why are you taking the people away from their work? Go back to your hard work! ⁵There are very many Hebrews. And now you want them to quit their hard work!"

⁶That same day the king gave a command to the slave masters and foremen. ⁷He said, "Don't give the people straw to make bricks as you used to do. Let them gather their own straw. ⁸But they must still make the same number of bricks as they did before. Do not accept fewer. They have become lazy. That is why they are asking me, 'Let us go to offer sacrifices to our God.' ⁹Make these people work harder. Keep them busy. Then they will not have time to listen to the lies of Moses."

¹⁰So the slave masters and foremen went to the Israelites and said, "This is what the king says: I will no longer give you straw. ¹¹Go and get your own straw wherever you can find it. But you must make as many bricks as you made before." ¹²So the people went everywhere in Egypt looking for dry stalks to use for straw. ¹³The slave masters kept forcing the people to work harder. They said, "You must make just as many bricks as you did when you were given straw." ¹⁴The king's slave masters had chosen the Israelite foremen. They had made them responsible for the work the people did. The Egyptian slave masters beat these men and asked them, "Why aren't you making as many bricks as you made in the past?"

¹⁵Then the Israelite foremen went to the king. They complained and said, "Why are you treating us, your servants, this way? ¹⁶You give us no straw. But we are commanded to make bricks. Our slave masters beat us. But it is your own people's fault."

¹⁷The king answered, "You are lazy! You don't want to work! That is why you ask to leave here and make sacrifices to the Lord. ¹⁸Now, go back to work! We will not give you any straw. But you must make just as many bricks as you did before."

¹⁹The Israelite foremen knew they were in trouble. This was because the king had told them: "You must make just as many bricks each day as you did before." ²⁰As they were leaving the meeting with the king, they met Moses and Aaron. Moses and Aaron were waiting for them. ²¹So they said to Moses and Aaron, "May the Lord punish you. You caused the king and his officers to hate us. You have given them an excuse to kill us."

MOSES COMPLAINS TO GOD

²²Then Moses returned to the Lord and said, "Lord, why have you brought this trouble on your people? Is this why you sent me here? ²³I went to the king and said what you told me to say. But ever since that time he has made the people

suffer. And you have done nothing to save them."

6 Then the Lord said to Moses, "Now you will see what I will do to the king of Egypt. I will use my great power against him, and he will let my people go. Because of my power, he will force them out of his country."

²Then God said to Moses, "I am the Lord. ³I appeared to Abraham, Isaac and Jacob by the name, God All-Powerful. But they did not know me by my name, the Lord. ⁴I also made my agreement with them to give them the land of Canaan. They lived in that land, but it was not their own land. ⁵Now I have heard the cries of the Israelites. The Egyptians are treating them as slaves. And I remember my agreement. ⁶So tell the people of Israel that I say to them, 'I am the Lord. I will save you from the hard work the Egyptians force you to do. I will make you free. You will not be slaves to the Egyptians. I will free you by my great power. And I will punish the Egyptians terribly. ⁷I will make you my own people, and I will be your God. You will know that I am the Lord your God. I am the One who saves you from the hard work the Egyptians force you to do. ⁸I will lead you to the land that I promised to Abraham, Isaac and Jacob. I will give you that land to own. I am the Lord.'"

⁹So Moses told this to the people of Israel. But they would not listen to him. They were discouraged, and their slavery was hard.

¹⁰Then the Lord said to Moses, ¹¹"Go tell the king of Egypt that he must let the Israelites leave his land."

¹²But Moses answered, "The Israelites will not listen to me. So surely the king will not listen to me, either. I am not a good speaker."

¹³But the Lord told Moses and Aaron to talk to the king. He commanded them to lead the Israelites out of Egypt.

FAMILIES OF ISRAEL

¹⁴These are the leaders of the families of Israel:

Israel's first son, Reuben, had four sons. They were Hanoch, Pallu, Hezron and Carmi. These are the family groups of Reuben.

¹⁵Simeon's sons were Jemuel, Jamin, Ohad, Jakin, Zohar and Shaul. Shaul was the son of a Canaanite woman. These are the family groups of Simeon.

¹⁶Levi lived 137 years. These are the names of his sons according to their family history: Gershon, Kohath and Merari.

¹⁷Gershon had two sons, Libni and Shimei, with their families.

¹⁸Kohath lived 133 years. The sons of Kohath were Amram, Izhar, Hebron and Uzziel.

¹⁹The sons of Merari were Mahli and Mushi.

These are the family groups of Levi, according to their family history.

²⁰Amram married his father's sister Jochebed. Jochebed gave birth to Aaron and Moses. Amram lived 137 years.

²¹Izhar's sons were Korah, Nepheg and Zicri.

²²Uzziel's sons were Mishael, Elzaphan and Sithri.

²³Aaron married Elisheba. She was the daughter of Amminadab and the sister of Nahshon. Elisheba gave birth to Nadab, Abihu, Eleazar and Ithamar.

²⁴The sons of Korah were Assir, Elkanah and Abiasaph. These are the family groups of the Korahites.

²⁵Eleazar son of Aaron married a daughter of Putiel. And she gave birth to Phinehas.

These are the leaders of the family groups of the Levites.

²⁶This was the Aaron and Moses to whom the Lord spoke. He said, "Lead my people out of Israel in their divisions." ²⁷Aaron and Moses are the ones who talked to the king of Egypt. They told him to let the people of Israel leave Egypt.

GOD REPEATS HIS CALL TO MOSES

²⁸The Lord spoke to Moses in the land of Egypt. ²⁹He said, "I am the Lord. Tell the king of Egypt everything I tell you."

³⁰But Moses answered, "I am not a good speaker. The king will not listen to me."

7 The Lord said to Moses, "I have made you like God to the king of Egypt. And your brother Aaron will be like a prophet for you. ²Tell Aaron your brother everything that I command you. Then let him tell the king of Egypt to let the Israelites leave his country. ³But I will make the king stubborn. Then I will do many miracles in Egypt. ⁴But he will still refuse to listen. So then I will punish Egypt terribly. And I will lead my divisions, my people the Israelites, out of that land. ⁵I will punish Egypt with my power. And I will bring the Israelites out of that land. Then they will know I am the Lord."

⁶Moses and Aaron did just as the Lord had commanded them. ⁷Moses was 80 years old, and Aaron was 83, when they spoke to the king.

AARON'S WALKING STICK BECOMES A SNAKE

⁸The Lord said to Moses and Aaron, ⁹"The king will ask you to do a miracle. When he does, Moses, you tell Aaron to throw his walking stick down in front of the king. It will become a snake."

¹⁰So Moses and Aaron went to the king as the Lord had commanded. Aaron threw his walking stick down in front of the king and his officers. And it became a snake.

¹¹So the king called in his wise men and his magicians. With their tricks the Egyptian magicians were able to do the same thing. ¹²They threw their walking sticks on the ground, and their sticks became snakes. But then Aaron's stick swallowed theirs. ¹³But the king was stubborn. He refused to listen to Moses and Aaron, just as the Lord had said.

THE WATER BECOMES BLOOD

¹⁴Then the Lord said to Moses, "The king is being stubborn. He refuses to let the people go. ¹⁵In the morning the king will go out to the Nile River. Go meet him by the edge of the river. Take with you the walking stick that became a snake. ¹⁶Tell him this: The Lord, the God of the Hebrews, sent me to you. He said, 'Let my people go worship me in the desert.' Until now you have not listened. ¹⁷This is what the Lord says: 'This is how you will know that I am the Lord. I will strike the water of the Nile River with this stick in my hand. And the water will change into blood. ¹⁸Then the fish in the Nile will die, and the river will begin to stink. And the Egyptians will not be able to drink the water from the Nile.'"

¹⁹The Lord said to Moses, "Tell Aaron to stretch the walking stick in his hand over the rivers, canals, ponds and pools in Egypt. The water will become blood everywhere in Egypt. There even will be blood in the wooden buckets and stone jars."

²⁰So Moses and Aaron did just as the Lord had commanded. Aaron raised his walking stick and struck the water in the Nile River. He did this in front of the king and his officers. So all the water in the Nile changed into blood. ²¹The fish in the Nile died, and the river began to stink. So the Egyptians could not drink water from it. Blood was everywhere in the land of Egypt.

²²Using their tricks, their magicians of Egypt did the same thing. So the king was stubborn and refused to listen to Moses and Aaron. This happened just as the Lord had said. ²³The king turned and went into his palace. He ignored what Moses and Aaron had done. ²⁴The Egyptians could not drink the water from the Nile. So all of them dug along the bank of the river. They were looking for water to drink.

THE FROGS

²⁵Seven days passed after the Lord changed the Nile River.

8 Then the Lord told Moses, "Go to the king of Egypt and tell him, 'This is what the Lord says: Let my people go to worship me. ²If you refuse,

then I will punish Egypt with frogs. ³The Nile River will be filled with frogs. They will come from the river and enter your palace. They will be in your bedroom and your bed. The frogs will enter the houses of your officers and your people. They will enter your ovens and your baking pans. ⁴The frogs will jump up all over you, your people and your officers.'"

⁵Then the Lord said to Moses, "Tell Aaron to hold his walking stick in his hand over the rivers, canals and ponds. Make frogs come up out of the water onto the land of Egypt."

⁶So Aaron held his hand over all the waters of Egypt. The frogs came up out of the water and covered the land of Egypt. ⁷The magicians used their tricks to do the same thing. So even more frogs came up onto the land of Egypt.

⁸So the king called for Moses and Aaron. He said, "Pray to the Lord to take the frogs away from me and my people. I will let your people go to offer sacrifices to the Lord."

⁹Moses said to the king, "Please set the time that I should pray for you, your people and your officers. Then the frogs will leave you and your houses. They will remain only in the Nile."

¹⁰The king answered, "Tomorrow."

Moses said, "What you want will happen. By this you will know that there is no one like the Lord our God. ¹¹The frogs will leave you, your houses, your officers and your people. They will remain only in the Nile."

¹²Moses and Aaron left the king. Moses asked the Lord about the frogs he had sent to the king. ¹³And the Lord did as Moses asked. The frogs died in the houses, in the yards and in the fields. ¹⁴The Egyptians put them in piles. The whole country began to stink. ¹⁵When the king saw that they were free of the frogs, he became stubborn again. He did not listen to Moses and Aaron, just as the Lord had said.

THE GNATS

¹⁶Then the Lord said to Moses, "Tell Aaron to raise his walking stick and strike the dust on the ground. Then everywhere in Egypt the dust will change into gnats." ¹⁷They did this. Aaron raised the walking stick that was in his hand and struck the dust on the ground. Then everywhere in Egypt the dust changed into gnats. The gnats got on the people and animals. ¹⁸Using their tricks, the magicians tried to do the same thing. But they could not make the dust change into gnats. The gnats remained on the people and animals. ¹⁹So the magicians told the king that the power of God had done this. But the king was stubborn and refused to listen to them. This happened just as the Lord had said.

THE FLIES

²⁰The Lord told Moses, "Get up early in the morning. Meet the king of Egypt as he goes out to the river. Tell him, 'This is what the Lord says: Let my people go so they can worship me. ²¹If you don't let them go, I will send swarms of flies. I will send them into your houses. The flies will be on you, your officers and your people. The houses of Egypt will be full of flies. And they will be all over the ground, too. ²²But I will not treat the people of Israel the same as the Egyptian people. There will not be any flies in the land of Goshen, where my people live. By this you will know that I, the Lord, am in this land. ²³I will treat

Moses and Aaron did just as the Lord had commanded them.

–EXODUS 7:6

my people differently from your people. This miracle will happen tomorrow.'"

²⁴So the Lord did as he had said. Great swarms of flies came into the king's palace and his officers' houses. All over Egypt flies were ruining the land. ²⁵The king called for Moses and Aaron. He told them, "Offer sacrifices to your God here in this country."

²⁶But Moses said, "It wouldn't be right to do that. The Egyptians hate the sacrifices we offer to the Lord our God. They will see us offer sacrifices they hate. Then they will throw stones at us and kill us. ²⁷Let us make a three-day journey into the desert. We must offer sacrifices to the Lord our God there. This is what the Lord told us to do."

²⁸The king said, "I will let you go. Then you may offer sacrifices to the Lord your God in the desert. But you must not go very far away. Now go and pray for me."

²⁹Moses said, "I will leave and pray to the Lord. He will take the flies away from you, your officers and your people tomorrow. But do not try to trick us again. Do not stop the people from going to offer sacrifices to the Lord."

³⁰So Moses left the king and prayed to the Lord. ³¹And the Lord did as Moses asked. He removed the flies from the king, his officers and his people. Not one fly was left. ³²But the king became stubborn again and did not let the people go.

THE DISEASE ON THE FARM ANIMALS

9 Then the Lord told Moses, "Go to the king of Egypt. Tell him, 'This is what the Lord, the God of the Hebrews, says: Let my people go to worship me. ²You might refuse to let them go and continue to hold them. ³Then the Lord will punish you. He will send a terrible disease on all your farm animals. He will cause all of your horses, donkeys, camels, cattle and sheep to become sick. ⁴But the Lord will treat Israel's animals differently from the animals of Egypt.

None of the animals that belong to the Israelites will die. ⁵The Lord has set tomorrow as the time he will do this in the land.'" ⁶The next day the Lord did as he promised. All the farm animals in Egypt died. But none of the animals belonging to Israelites died. ⁷The king sent people to see what had happened to the animals of Israel. They found that not one of them had died. But the king was still stubborn. He did not let the people go.

THE BOILS

⁸The Lord said to Moses and Aaron, "Fill your hands with the ashes from a furnace. Moses, throw the ashes into the air in front of the king of Egypt. ⁹The ashes will spread like dust through all the land of Egypt. The dust will cause boils to break out and become sores on the skin. These sores will be on people and animals everywhere in the land."

¹⁰So Moses and Aaron took ashes from a furnace. Then they went and stood before the king. Moses threw ashes into the air. It caused boils to break out and become sores on people and animals. ¹¹The magicians could not stand before Moses. This was because all the Egyptians had boils, even the magicians. ¹²But the Lord made the king stubborn. So he refused to listen to Moses and Aaron. This happened just as the Lord had said.

THE HAIL

¹³Then the Lord said to Moses, "Get up early in the morning and go to the king of Egypt. Tell him, 'This is what the Lord, the God of the Hebrews, says: Let my people go to worship me. ¹⁴If you do not do this, this time I will punish you with all my power. I will punish you, your officers and your

people. Then you will know that there is no one in the whole land like me. [15]By now I could have used my power and caused a bad disease. It would have destroyed you and your people from the earth. [16]But I have let you live for this reason: to show you my power. In this way my name will be talked about in all the earth. [17]You are still against my people. You do not want to let them go. [18]So at this time tomorrow, I will send a terrible hailstorm. It will be the worst in Egypt since it became a nation. [19]Now send for your animals and whatever you have in the fields. Bring them into a safe place. The hail will fall on every person or animal that is still in the fields. If they have not been brought in, they will die.'" [20]Some of the king's officers respected the word of the Lord. They hurried to bring their slaves and animals inside. [21]But others ignored the Lord's message. They left their slaves and animals in the fields.

[22]The Lord told Moses, "Raise your hand toward the sky. Then the hail will start falling over all the land of Egypt. It will fall on people, animals and on everything that grows in the fields of Egypt." [23]So Moses raised his walking stick toward the sky. And the Lord sent thunder and hail. And lightning flashed down to the earth. So he caused hail to fall upon the land of Egypt. [24]There was hail, and there was lightning flashing as it hailed. This was the worst hailstorm in Egypt since it had become a nation. [25]The hail destroyed everything that was in the fields in all the land of Egypt. The hail destroyed both people and animals. It also destroyed everything that grew in the fields. It broke all the trees in the fields. [26]The only place it did not hail was in the land of Goshen. The people of Israel lived there.

[27]The king sent for Moses and Aaron. He told them, "This time I have sinned. The Lord is in the right. And I and my people are in the wrong. [28]Pray to the Lord. We have had enough of God's thunder and hail. I will let you go. You do not have to stay here any longer."

[29]Moses told the king, "When I leave the city, I will raise my hands to the Lord in prayer. And the thunder and hail will stop. Then you will know that the earth belongs to the Lord. [30]But I know that you and your officers do not yet fear the Lord God."

[31]The flax was in bloom, and the barley had ripened. So these crops were destroyed. [32]But both wheat crops ripen later. So they were not destroyed.

[33]Moses left the king and went outside the city. He raised his hands to the Lord. And the thunder and hail stopped. The rain also stopped falling to the ground. [34]The king saw that the rain, hail and thunder had stopped. Then he sinned again. He and his officers became stubborn again. [35]The king became stubborn and refused to let the Israelites go. This happened just as the Lord had said through Moses.

THE LOCUSTS

10 The Lord said to Moses, "Go to the king of Egypt. I have made him and his officers stubborn. I did this so I could show them my powerful miracles. [2]I also did this so you could tell your children and your grandchildren. Tell them how I made fools of the Egyptians. Tell them about the miracles I did among them. Then all of you will know that I am the Lord."

[3]So Moses and Aaron went to the king. They told him, "This is what the Lord, the God of the Hebrews, says: 'How long will you refuse to be sorry for what you have done? Let my people go to worship me. [4]If you refuse to let my people go, tomorrow I will bring locusts into your country. [5]They will cover the land, and no one will be able to see the ground. They will eat anything that was left from the hailstorm. They will eat the leaves from every tree growing in the field. [6]They will fill your palaces and all your officers' houses. They will fill the houses of all the Egyptian people. There

will be more locusts than your fathers or ancestors have ever seen. There will be more locusts than there have been since people began living in Egypt.'" Then Moses turned and walked away from the king.

⁷The king's officers asked him, "How long will this man make trouble for us? Let the Israelite men go to worship the Lord their God. Don't you know that Egypt is ruined?"

⁸So Moses and Aaron were brought back to the king. He said to them, "Go and worship the Lord your God. But tell me, just who is going?"

⁹Moses answered, "We will go with our young and our old people, our sons and daughters and sheep and cattle. This is because we are going to have a feast to honor the Lord."

¹⁰The king said to them, "The Lord really will have to be with you if ever I let you and all of your children leave Egypt. See, you are planning something evil. ¹¹No! Only the men may go and worship the Lord. That is what you have been asking for." Then the king forced Moses and Aaron out of his palace.

¹²The Lord told Moses, "Raise your hand over the land of Egypt, and the locusts will come. They will spread all over the land of Egypt. They will eat all the plants that the hail did not destroy."

¹³So Moses raised his walking stick over the land of Egypt. And the Lord caused a strong wind to blow from the east. It blew across the land all that day and night. When morning came, the east wind had brought the locusts. ¹⁴Swarms of locusts covered all the land of Egypt and settled everywhere. There were more locusts than ever before or after. ¹⁵The locusts covered the whole land so that it was black. They ate everything that was left after the hail. They ate every plant in the field and all the fruit on the trees. Nothing green was left on any tree or plant anywhere in Egypt.

¹⁶The king quickly called for Moses and Aaron. He said, "I have sinned against the Lord your God and against

you. ¹⁷Now forgive my sin this time. Pray to the Lord your God. Ask him to stop this punishment that kills."

¹⁸Moses left the king and prayed to the Lord. ¹⁹So the Lord changed the wind. He made a very strong wind to blow from the west. It blew the locusts away into the Red Sea. Not one locust was left anywhere in Egypt. ²⁰But the Lord caused the king to be stubborn again. And he did not let the people of Israel go.

THE DARKNESS

²¹Then the Lord told Moses, "Raise your hand toward the sky, and darkness will cover the land of Egypt. It will be so dark you will be able to feel it." ²²So Moses raised his hand toward the sky. Then total darkness was everywhere in Egypt for three days. ²³No one could see anyone else. And no one could go anywhere for three days. But the Israelites had light where they lived.

²⁴Again the king of Egypt called for Moses. He said, "All of you may go and worship the Lord. You may take your women and children with you. But you must leave your sheep and cattle here."

²⁵Moses said, "You must let us have animals to use as sacrifices and burnt offerings. We have to offer them to the Lord our God. ²⁶So we must take our animals with us. Not a hoof will be left behind. We have to use some of the animals to worship the Lord our God. We do not yet know exactly what we will need to worship the Lord. We will know when we get there."

²⁷But the Lord made the king stubborn again. So he refused to let them go. ²⁸Then he told Moses, "Get out of here! Don't come here again! The next time you see me, you will die."

²⁹Then Moses told the king, "I'll do what you say. I will not come to see you again."

THE DEATH OF THE FIRSTBORN

11 Now the Lord had told Moses, "I have one more way to punish the king and the people of Egypt. After this,

the king will send all of you away from Egypt. When he does, he will force you to leave completely. ²Tell the men and women of Israel to ask their neighbors for things made of silver and gold."

³The Lord had caused the Egyptians to respect the Israelites. The king's officers and the Egyptian people already considered Moses to be a great man.

⁴So Moses said to the king, "This is what the Lord says: 'About midnight tonight I will go through all Egypt. ⁵Every firstborn son in the land of Egypt will die. The firstborn son of the king, who sits on his throne, will die. Even the firstborn of the slave girl grinding grain will die. Also the firstborn farm animals will die. ⁶There will be loud crying everywhere in Egypt. It will be worse than any time before or after this. ⁷But not even a dog will bark at the Israelites or their animals.' Then you will know that the Lord treats Israel differently from Egypt. ⁸Then all your officers will come to me. They will bow facedown to the ground before me. They will say, 'Leave and take all your people with you.' After that, I will leave." Then Moses very angrily left the king.

⁹The Lord had told Moses, "The king will not listen to you and Aaron. This is so that I may do many miracles in the land of Egypt." ¹⁰Moses and Aaron did all these great miracles in front of the king. But the Lord made him stubborn. And the king would not let the people of Israel leave his country.

PASSOVER

12 The Lord spoke to Moses and Aaron in the land of Egypt: ²"This month will be the first month of the year for you. ³Both of you are to tell the whole community of Israel: On the tenth day of this month each man must get one lamb. It is for the people in his house. ⁴There may not be enough people in his house to eat a whole lamb. Then he must share it with his closest neighbor. There must be enough lamb for everyone to eat. ⁵The lamb must be a one-year-old male. It must have nothing wrong with it. This animal can be either a young sheep or a young goat. ⁶Keep the animal with you to take care of it until the fourteenth day of the month. On that day all the people of the community of Israel will kill these animals. They will do this as soon as the sun goes down. ⁷The people must take some of the blood. They must put it on the sides and tops of the doorframes. These are the doorframes of the houses where they eat the lambs. ⁸On this night they must roast the lamb over a fire. Then they must eat it with bitter herbs and bread made without yeast. ⁹Do not eat the lamb raw or boiled in water. Roast the whole lamb over a fire—with its head, legs and inner organs. ¹⁰You must not leave any of it until morning. But if any of it is left over until morning, you must burn it with fire.

¹¹"This is the way you must eat it: You must be fully dressed as if you were going on a trip. You must have your sandals on, and you must have your walking stick in your hand. You must eat it in a hurry. This is the Lord's Passover.

¹²"That night I will go through the land of Egypt. I will kill all the firstborn of animals and people in the land of Egypt. I will punish all the gods of Egypt. I am the Lord. ¹³But the blood will be a sign on the houses where you are. When I see the blood, I will pass over you. Nothing terrible will hurt you when I punish the land of Egypt.

¹⁴"You are always to remember this day. Celebrate it with a feast to the Lord. Your descendants are to honor the Lord with this feast from now on. ¹⁵For this feast you must eat bread made without yeast for seven days. On the first day of this feast, you are to remove all the yeast from your houses. No one should eat any yeast for the full seven days of the feast. If anyone eats yeast, then that person will be separated from Israel. ¹⁶You are to have holy meetings on the first and last days of the feast. You

must not do any work on these days. The only work you may do on these days is to prepare your meals. ¹⁷You must celebrate the Feast of Unleavened Bread. Do this because on this very day I brought your divisions of people out of Egypt. So all of your descendants must celebrate this day. This is a law that will last from now on. ¹⁸You are to eat bread made without yeast. Start this on the evening of the fourteenth day of the first month of your year. Eat this until the evening of the twenty-first day. ¹⁹For seven days there must not be any yeast in your houses. Anybody who eats yeast during this time must be separated from the community of Israel. This includes Israelites and non-Israelites. ²⁰During this feast you must not eat yeast. You must eat bread made without yeast wherever you live."

²¹Then Moses called all the elders of Israel together. He told them, "Get the animals for your families. Kill the animals for the Passover. ²²Take a branch of the hyssop plant and dip it into the bowl filled with blood. Wipe the blood on the sides and tops of the doorframes. No one may leave his house until morning. ²³The Lord will go through Egypt to kill the Egyptians. He will see the blood on the sides and tops of the doorframes. Then the Lord will pass over that house. He will not let the one who brings death come into your houses and kill you.

²⁴"You must keep this command. This law is for you and your descendants from now on. ²⁵Do this when you go to the land the Lord has promised to give to you. ²⁶When your children ask you, 'Why are we doing these things?' ²⁷you will say, 'This is the Passover sacrifice to honor the Lord. When we were in Egypt, the Lord passed over the houses of Israel. The Lord killed the Egyptians, but he saved our homes.'" So now the people bowed down and worshiped the Lord. ²⁸They did just as the Lord commanded Moses and Aaron.

²⁹At midnight the Lord killed all the firstborn sons in the land of Egypt. The firstborn of the king, who sat on the throne, died. Even the firstborn of the prisoner in jail died. Also all the firstborn farm animals died. ³⁰The king, his officers and all the Egyptians got up during the night. Someone had died in every house. So there was loud crying everywhere in Egypt.

ISRAEL LEAVES EGYPT

³¹During the night the king called for Moses and Aaron. He said to them, "Get up and leave my people. You and your people may do as you have asked. Go and worship the Lord. ³²Take all of your sheep and cattle as you have asked. Go. And also bless me." ³³The Egyptians also asked the Israelites to hurry and leave. They said, "If you don't leave, we will all die!"

³⁴The people of Israel took their dough before the yeast was added. They wrapped the bowls for making dough in clothing and carried them on their shoulders. ³⁵The people of Israel did what Moses told them to do. They asked their Egyptian neighbors for things made of silver and gold and for clothing. ³⁶The Lord caused the Egyptians to think well of the Israelites. So the Israelites took rich gifts from the Egyptians.

³⁷The Israelites traveled from Rameses to Succoth. There were about 600,000 men walking. This does not include the women and children. ³⁸Many other people who were not Israelites went with them. A large number of sheep, goats and cattle went with them. ³⁹The Israelites used the dough they had brought out of Egypt. They baked loaves of bread without yeast. The dough had no yeast in it because they had been rushed out of Egypt. So they had no time to get food ready for their trip.

⁴⁰The people of Israel had lived in Egypt for 430 years. ⁴¹On the day the 430 years ended, the Lord's divisions of people left Egypt. ⁴²That night the Lord kept watch to bring them out of Egypt. So on this same night the Israelites are

to keep watch. They are to do this to honor the Lord from now on.

⁴³The Lord told Moses and Aaron, "Here are the rules for Passover: No foreigner is to eat the Passover. ⁴⁴Suppose a person buys a slave and circumcises him. Then the slave may eat the Passover. ⁴⁵But no one who lives for a short time in your country may eat it. No hired worker may eat it.

⁴⁶"The meal must be eaten inside the house. None of the meat is to be taken outside the house. Don't break any of the bones. ⁴⁷The whole community of Israel must take part in this feast. ⁴⁸A foreigner who lives with you may share in the Lord's Passover. But first all the males in his house must be circumcised. Then, since he will be like a citizen of Israel, he may share in the meal. But a man who is not circumcised may not eat the Passover meal. ⁴⁹The same rules apply to an Israelite born in the country. And they apply to a foreigner living there."

⁵⁰So all the Israelites did just as the Lord had commanded Moses and Aaron. ⁵¹Then on that same day, the Lord led the Israelites out of Egypt. The people left by divisions.

THE LAW OF THE FIRSTBORN

13 Then the Lord said to Moses, ²"Give every firstborn male to me. Every firstborn male among the Israelites belongs to me, whether human or animal."

³Moses said to the people, "Remember this day, the day you left Egypt. You were slaves in that land. The Lord with his great power brought you out of it. You must not eat bread made with yeast. ⁴Today, in the month of Abib, you are leaving Egypt. ⁵The Lord made a promise to your ancestors. The Lord promised to give you the land of these people: the Canaanites, Hittites, Amorites, Hivites and Jebusites. The Lord will lead you to this land where much food grows. There you must celebrate this feast during the first month of every year. ⁶For seven days you must eat bread made without yeast. On the seventh day there will be a feast to honor the Lord. ⁷So for seven days you must not eat any bread made with yeast. There must be no bread made with yeast anywhere in your land. ⁸On that day you should tell your son: 'We are having this feast because of what the Lord did for me when I came out of Egypt.' ⁹This feast will help you remember. It will be like a mark on your hand. It will be like a reminder on your forehead. This feast will remind you to speak the Lord's teachings. This is because the Lord used his great power to bring you out of Egypt. ¹⁰So celebrate this feast every year at the right time.

¹¹"The Lord will take you into the land of the Canaanites. He promised to give this land to you and your ancestors. ¹²Then you must give him every firstborn male. And every firstborn male animal must be given to the Lord. ¹³Buy back every firstborn donkey by offering a lamb. If you don't want to buy the donkey back, then break its neck. You must buy back from the Lord every firstborn of your sons.

¹⁴"From now on your son will ask you: 'What does this mean?' You will answer, 'With his great power, the Lord brought us out of Egypt. We were slaves in that land. ¹⁵In Egypt the king was stubborn. He refused to let us leave. But the Lord killed every firstborn male in Egypt, both human and animal. That is

> This feast will remind you to speak the Lord's teachings.
>
> –EXODUS 13:9

why I sacrifice every firstborn male animal to the Lord. And that is why I buy back each of my firstborn sons from the Lord.' [16]This feast is like a mark on your hand. And it is like a reminder on your forehead. It will help you remember that the Lord brought us out of Egypt with his great power."

THE WAY OUT OF EGYPT

[17]The king sent the people out of Egypt. God did not lead them on the road through the Philistine country. That road is the shortest way. But God said, "They might think they will have to fight. Then they might change their minds and go back to Egypt." [18]So God led them through the desert toward the Red Sea. The Israelites were dressed for fighting when they left the land of Egypt.

[19]Moses carried the bones of Joseph with him. Before Joseph died, he had made the sons of Israel promise to do this. He had said, "When God saves you, remember to carry my bones with you out of Egypt."

[20]The people of Israel left Succoth and camped at Etham. Etham was on the edge of the desert. [21]The Lord showed them the way. During the day he went ahead of them in a pillar of cloud. And during the night the Lord was in a pillar of fire to give them light. They could travel during the day or night. [22]The pillar of cloud was always with them during the day. And the pillar of fire was always with them at night.

14 Then the Lord said to Moses, [2]"Tell the Israelites to turn back to Pi Hahiroth. Tell them to camp for the night between Migdol and the Red Sea. This is near Baal Zephon. [3]The king will think, 'The Israelites are lost, trapped by the desert.' [4]I will make the king stubborn again so he will chase after them. But I will defeat the king and his army. This will bring honor to me. Then the people of Egypt will know that I am the Lord." The people of Israel did just as they were told.

THE KING CHASES THE ISRAELITES

[5]The king of Egypt was told that the people of Israel had already left. Then he and his officers changed their minds about them. They said, "What have we done? We have let the people of Israel leave. We have lost our slaves!" [6]So the king prepared his war chariot and took his army with him. [7]He took 600 of his best chariots. He also took all the other chariots of Egypt. Each chariot had an officer in it. [8]The Lord made the king of Egypt stubborn. So he chased the Israelites, who were leaving victoriously. [9]The king of Egypt came with his horses, chariot drivers and army. And they chased the Israelites. They caught up with the Israelites while they were camped by the Red Sea. This was near Pi Hahiroth and Baal Zephon.

[10]The Israelites saw the king and his army coming after them. They were very frightened and cried to the Lord for help. [11]They said to Moses, "What have you done to us? Why did you bring us out of Egypt to die in the desert? There were plenty of graves for us in Egypt. [12]We told you in Egypt, 'Let us alone! Let us stay and serve the Egyptians.' Now we will die in the desert."

[13]But Moses answered, "Don't be afraid! Stand still and see the Lord save

you today. You will never see these Egyptians again after today. [14]You will only need to remain calm. The Lord will fight for you."

[15]Then the Lord said to Moses, "Why are you crying out to me? Command the people of Israel to start moving. [16]Raise your walking stick and hold it over the sea. The sea will split. Then the people can cross the sea on dry land. [17]I have made the Egyptians stubborn so they will chase the Israelites. But I will be honored when I defeat the king and all of his chariot drivers and chariots. [18]I will defeat the king, his chariot drivers and chariots. Then Egypt will know that I am the Lord."

[19]The angel of God usually traveled in front of Israel's army. Now the angel of God moved behind them. Also, the pillar of cloud moved from in front of the people and stood behind them. [20]So the cloud came between the Egyptians and the people of Israel. The cloud made it dark for the Egyptians. But it gave light to the Israelites. So the cloud kept the two armies apart all night.

[21]Moses held his hand over the sea. All that night the Lord drove back the sea with a strong east wind. And so he made the sea become dry ground. The water was split. [22]And the Israelites went through the sea on dry land. A wall of water was on both sides.

[23]Then all the king's horses, chariots and chariot drivers followed them into the sea. [24]Between two and six o'clock in the morning, the Lord looked down from the pillar of cloud and fire at the Egyptian army. He made them panic. [25]He kept the wheels of the chariots from turning. This made it hard to drive the chariots. The Egyptians shouted, "Let's get away from the Israelites! The Lord is fighting for them and against us Egyptians."

[26]Then the Lord told Moses, "Hold your hand over the sea. Then the water will come back over the Egyptians, their chariots and chariot drivers." [27]So Moses raised his hand over the sea. And at dawn the water became deep again. The Egyptians were trying to run from it. But the Lord swept them away into the sea. [28]The water became deep again. It covered the chariots and chariot drivers. So all the king's army that had followed the Israelites into the sea was covered. Not one of them survived.

[29]But the people of Israel crossed the sea on dry land. There was a wall of water on their right and on their left. [30]So that day the Lord saved the Israelites from the Egyptians. And the Israelites saw the Egyptians lying dead on the seashore. [31]When the people of Israel saw the great power that the Lord had used against the Egyptians, they feared the Lord. And they trusted the Lord and his servant Moses.

THE SONG OF MOSES

15 Then Moses and the Israelites sang this song to the Lord:

"I will sing to the Lord
　because he is worthy of great
　　honor.
He has thrown the horse and its rider
　into the sea.
[2] The Lord gives me strength and
　　makes me sing.
　He has saved me.
He is my God,
　and I will praise him.
He is the God of my ancestors,
　and I will honor him.
[3] The Lord is a great warrior.
　The Lord is his name.
[4] The chariots and soldiers of the king
　　of Egypt
　he has thrown into the sea.
　The king's best officers
　are drowned in the Red Sea.
[5] The deep waters covered them.
　They sank to the bottom like a
　　rock.
[6] Your right hand, Lord,
　is amazingly strong.
Lord, your right hand
　broke the enemy into pieces.
[7] In your great victory

☆ Exodus 14:29–30

When the Israelites were being chased by the Egyptians, God told Moses to raise his walking stick over the Red Sea. Moses obeyed God and a wind started to blow. God pushed all the water aside and split the Red Sea wide open. The Israelites crossed the sea on dry land with walls of water on their right and left. The Israelites were Abraham's descendants. God kept his promise to Abraham on the day he saved the Israelites from the Egyptians.

Everything that happens in life is not always good. There are bad people who do bad things. Things do not always go the way you want them to. The good news is God has a plan for your life. God has a purpose for you. Because he loves you, he works everything together for your good. Nothing can stop his plan.

. . . .

God split open a whole ocean to keep his promise to Abraham's family. He will do whatever he can to make his plan for your life work out.

you destroyed those who were
   against you.
Your anger destroyed them,
   like fire burning straw.
⁸ Just a blast of your breath,
   and the waters were blown back.
The moving water stood up like a
   wall.
   And the deep waters became solid
     in the middle of the sea.

⁹ "The enemy bragged,
   'I'll chase them and catch them.
I'll take all their riches.
   I'll take all I want.
I'll pull out my sword,

   and my hand will destroy them.'
¹⁰ But you blew on them with your
   breath
   and covered them with the sea.
They sank like lead
   in the powerful water.

¹¹ "Are there any gods like you, Lord?
   No! There are no gods like you.
   You are wonderfully holy.
   You are amazingly powerful.
   You do great miracles.
¹² You reached out with your right
   hand,
   and the earth swallowed our
     enemies.

¹³ You keep your loving promise.
   You lead the people you have
      saved.
   With your strength you will guide
      them
      to your holy land.

¹⁴ "The other nations will hear this and
      tremble with fear.
   Terror will take hold of the
      Philistines.
¹⁵ The leaders of the tribes of Edom will
      be very frightened.
   The powerful men of Moab will
      shake with fear.
   The people of Canaan will lose all
      their courage.
¹⁶ Those people will be filled with fear.
   When they see your strength,
      they will be as still as a rock.
   They will be still until your people
      pass by, Lord.
   They will be still until the people
      you have bought from slavery
      pass by.
¹⁷ You will lead your people and place
      them
      on your very own mountain.
   Lord, that is the place that you made
      for yourself to live.
   Lord, that is the temple that your
      hands have made.
¹⁸ The Lord will rule forever!"

¹⁹The horses, chariot drivers and
chariots of the king of Egypt went
into the sea. And the Lord covered
them with water from the sea. But the
Israelites walked through the sea on dry
land. ²⁰Then Aaron's sister Miriam, who
was a prophetess, took a tambourine
in her hand. All the women followed
her, playing tambourines and dancing.
²¹Miriam told them:

   "Sing to the Lord
      because he is worthy of great honor.
   He has thrown the horse and its rider
      into the sea."

THE BITTER WATER

²²Moses led the people of Israel away
from the Red Sea. The people went
into the Desert of Shur. They traveled for three days in the desert but
found no water. ²³Then they came to
Marah, where there was water. But
they could not drink it because it was
too bitter. That is why the place was
named Marah." ²⁴The people grumbled
to Moses. They asked, "What will we
drink?"

²⁵Moses cried out to the Lord. So the
Lord showed him a tree. Moses threw
the tree into the water. And the water
became good to drink.

There the Lord gave the people a
rule and a law to live by. There he also
tested their loyalty to him. ²⁶He said,
"You must obey the Lord, your God.
You must do what the Lord said is right.
You must obey all his laws and keep his
rules. If you do these things, I will not
give you any of the sicknesses I gave the
Egyptians. I am the Lord. I am the Lord
who heals you."

²⁷Then the people traveled to Elim.
At Elim there were 12 springs of water
and 70 palm trees. So the people
camped there near the water.

THE PEOPLE DEMAND FOOD

16 Then the whole Israelite community left Elim. They came
to the Desert of Sin. This place was
between Elim and Sinai. They came to
this place on the fifteenth day of the
second month after they had left Egypt.
²Then the whole Israelite community
grumbled to Moses and Aaron in the
desert. ³The Israelites said to them, "It
would have been better if the Lord had
killed us in the land of Egypt. There we
had meat to eat. We had all the food we
wanted. But you have brought us into
this desert. You will starve us to death
here."

⁴Then the Lord said to Moses, "I will
cause food to fall like rain from the sky.

15:23 **Marah** This name means "bitter."

This food will be for all of you. Every day the people must go out and gather what they need for that day. I will do this to see if the people will do what I teach them. ⁵On the sixth day of each week, they are to gather twice as much as they gather on other days. Then they are to prepare it."

⁶So Moses and Aaron said to all the Israelites: "This evening you will know that the Lord is the one who brought you out of Egypt. ⁷Tomorrow morning you will see the greatness of the Lord.

He has heard you grumble against him. We are nothing. You are not grumbling against us, but against the Lord." ⁸And Moses said, "Each evening the Lord will give you meat to eat. And every morning he will give you all the bread you want. He will do this because he has heard you grumble against him. You are not grumbling against Aaron and me. You are grumbling against the Lord."

⁹Then Moses said to Aaron, "Speak to the whole community of the Israelites.

☆ Exodus 16:3-14

The people of Israel were hungry and complained. They said God did not care about them. But God did care. He told them he would make food fall like rain from the sky. He sent huge clouds of quail that night. He sent manna in the dew the next morning. He never let them go hungry.

Sometimes, people can act like the Israelites did. God had rescued them from a bad king. He saved their lives. But instead of being thankful, they complained. God took care of the Israelites in a very special way: he provided food that fell from the sky! Sometimes we are grumpy and unthankful too. Sometimes we forget that God wants to take care of us. He promised Abraham that he would take care of his children—the Israelites. He makes us promises too.

. . . .

God always keeps his promises. We can trust him!

Say to them, 'Meet together in front of the Lord because he has heard your grumblings.'"

¹⁰So Aaron spoke to the whole community of the Israelites. While he was speaking, they looked toward the desert. There the greatness of the Lord appeared in a cloud.

¹¹The Lord said to Moses, ¹²"I have heard the grumblings of the people of Israel. So tell them, 'At twilight you will eat meat. And every morning you will eat all the bread you want. Then you will know I am the Lord, your God.'"

¹³That evening, quail came and covered the camp. And in the morning dew lay around the camp. ¹⁴When the dew was gone, thin flakes like frost were on the desert ground. ¹⁵When the Israelites saw it, they asked each other, "What is that?" They asked this question because they did not know what it was.

So Moses told them, "This is the bread the Lord has given you to eat. ¹⁶The Lord has commanded, 'Each one of you must gather what he needs. Gather about two quarts for every person in your family.'"

¹⁷So the people of Israel did this. Some people gathered much, and some gathered little. ¹⁸Then they measured it. The person who gathered more did not have too much. The person who gathered less did not have too little. Each person gathered just as much as he needed.

¹⁹Moses said to them, "Don't keep any of it to eat the next day." ²⁰But some of the people did not listen to Moses. They kept part of it to eat the next morning. But it became full of worms and began to stink. So Moses was angry with these people.

²¹Every morning each person gathered as much food as he needed. But when the sun became hot, it melted away.

²²On the sixth day the people gathered twice as much food. They gathered four quarts for every person. So all the leaders of the community came and told this to Moses. ²³Moses said to them, "This is what the Lord commanded. Tomorrow is the Sabbath, the Lord's holy day of rest. Bake what you want to bake, and boil what you want to boil today. But save the rest of the food until tomorrow morning."

²⁴So the people saved it until the next morning, as Moses had commanded. And none of it began to stink or have worms in it. ²⁵Moses told the people, "Eat the food you gathered yesterday. Today is a Sabbath, the Lord's day of rest. So you will not find any out in the field today. ²⁶You should gather the food for six days. But the seventh day is a Sabbath day. On that day there will not be any food on the ground."

²⁷On the seventh day some of the people went out to gather food, but they couldn't find any. ²⁸Then the Lord said to Moses, "How long will all you people refuse to obey my commands and teachings? ²⁹Look, the Lord has made the Sabbath a day of rest for all of you. So on the sixth day he will give you enough food for two days. But on the Sabbath each of you must stay where you are. Do not leave your house." ³⁰So the people rested on the Sabbath.

³¹The people of Israel called the food manna. The manna was like small white seeds. It tasted like wafers made with honey.

³²Then Moses said, "The Lord said, 'Save two quarts of this food for your descendants. Then they can see the food that I gave you to eat. I did this in the desert when I brought you out of Egypt.'"

³³Moses told Aaron, "Take a jar and fill it with two quarts of manna. And save this manna for your descendants." ³⁴So Aaron did what the Lord had commanded Moses. Aaron put the jar of manna in front of the Ark of the Covenant. He did this so it could be kept. ³⁵The Israelites ate manna for 40 years. They ate it until they came to

the land where they settled. They ate manna until they came to the edge of the land of Canaan. [36] The measure they used for the manna was two quarts. It was one-tenth of an ephah.[n]

WATER FROM A ROCK

17 The whole Israelite community left the Desert of Sin. They traveled from place to place as the Lord commanded. They camped at Rephidim. But there was no water there for the people to drink. [2] So they quarreled with Moses. They said, "Give us water to drink."

But Moses said to them, "Why do you quarrel with me? Why are you testing the Lord?"

[3] But the people were very thirsty for water. So they grumbled against Moses. They said, "Why did you bring us out of Egypt? Was it to kill us, our children and our farm animals with thirst?"

[4] So Moses cried to the Lord, "What can I do with these people? They are almost ready to kill me with stones."

[5] The Lord said to Moses, "Go ahead of the people of Israel. And take some of the elders of Israel with you. Carry with you the walking stick that you used to strike the Nile River. Now go! [6] I will stand in front of you on a rock at Mount Sinai. Hit that rock with the stick, and water will come out of it. Then the people can drink." Moses did these things as the elders of Israel watched. [7] Moses named that place Massah[n] because the Israelites tested the Lord. They asked, "Is the Lord with us or not?" He also named it Meribah[n] because they quarreled.

THE AMALEKITES FIGHT ISRAEL

[8] At Rephidim the Amalekites came and fought the Israelites. [9] So Moses said to Joshua, "Choose some men and go and fight the Amalekites. Tomorrow I will stand on the top of the hill. I will hold the stick God gave me to carry."

[10] Joshua obeyed Moses and went to fight the Amalekites. At the same time Moses, Aaron and Hur went to the top of the hill. [11] As long as Moses held his hands up, the Israelites would win the fight. But when Moses put his hands down, the Amalekites would win. [12] Later, Moses' arms became tired. So the men put a large rock under Moses, and he sat on it. Then Aaron and Hur held up Moses' hands. Aaron was on one side of Moses, and Hur was on the other side. They held his hands up like this until the sun went down. [13] So Joshua defeated the Amalekites in this battle.

[14] Then the Lord said to Moses, "Write about this battle in a book so people will remember. And be sure to tell Joshua. Tell him because I will completely destroy the Amalekites from the earth."

[15] Then Moses built an altar. He named it The Lord is my Banner. [16] Moses said, "I lifted my hands toward the Lord's throne. The Lord will fight against the Amalekites forever."

> The God of my father is my help. He saved me.
> –EXODUS 18:4

JETHRO VISITS MOSES

18 Jethro, Moses' father-in-law, was the priest of Midian. He heard about everything that God had done for Moses and his people, the Israelites. Jethro heard how the Lord had led the

---

16:36 **ephah** An ephah was a measure that equaled 20 quarts.
17:7 **Massah** This name sounds like the Hebrew word for "testing."
17:7 **Meribah** This name sounds like the Hebrew word for "quarreled."

Israelites out of Egypt. [2]Moses had sent his wife Zipporah to Jethro, his father-in-law. [3]Moses had also sent his two sons. The first son was named Gershom.[n] When he was born, Moses said, "I am a stranger in a foreign country." [4]The other son was named Eliezer.[n] When he was born, Moses said, "The God of my father is my help. He saved me from the king of Egypt."

[5]So Jethro, Moses' father-in-law, went to Moses. Moses was camped in the desert near Sinai, the mountain of God. Moses' wife and his two sons came with Jethro. [6]Jethro had sent a message ahead to Moses. He said, "I am Jethro, your father-in-law. I am coming to you with your wife and her two sons."

[7]So Moses went out to meet his father-in-law. Moses bowed down and then kissed him. The two men asked about each other's health. Then they went into Moses' tent. [8]Moses told his father-in-law everything the Lord had done to the king and the Egyptians. The Lord had done these things to help Israel. Moses told about all the problems they had faced along the way. And Moses told him how the Lord had saved them.

[9]Jethro was very happy when he heard all the good things the Lord had done for Israel. He was happy because the Lord had saved them from the Egyptians. [10]Jethro said, "Praise the Lord. He has saved all of you from the Egyptians and their king. He has saved the people from the power of the Egyptians. [11]Now I know the Lord is greater than all gods. He did this to those who looked down on Israel."

[12]Then Jethro, Moses' father-in-law, gave a whole burnt offering and other sacrifices to God. Aaron and all the elders of Israel came to Moses' father-in-law. They ate the holy meal together before God.

[13]The next day Moses solved disagreements among the people. So the people stood around Moses from morning until night. [14]Moses' father-in-law saw all that Moses was doing for the people. He asked, "What is all this you are doing for the people? Why are you the only one to solve disagreements? All the people are standing around you from morning until night!"

[15]Then Moses said to his father-in-law, "It is because the people come to me for God's help in solving their disagreements. [16]When people have a disagreement, they come to me. I decide who is right. And I tell them God's laws and teachings."

[17]Moses' father-in-law said to him, "You are not doing this right. [18]You and the people who come to you will get too tired. This is too much work for you. You can't do it by yourself. [19]Now listen to me. I will give you some advice. I want God to be with you. You must talk to God for the people. You must tell him about their disagreements. [20]You should tell them the laws and teachings. Tell them the right way to live and what they should do. [21]But choose some capable men from among the people. Choose men who respect God and who can be trusted. They will not change their decisions for money. Make these men officers over groups of 1,000, 100, 50 and 10 people. [22]Let these officers solve the disagreements among the people all the time. They can bring the hard cases to you. But they can decide the simple cases themselves. That will make it easier for you. These men will share the work with you. [23]Do this if it is what God commands. Then you will be able to do your job. And all the people will go home with their disagreements solved."

[24]So Moses listened to his father-in-law and did everything he said. [25]He chose capable men from all the Israelites. He made them leaders over the people. They were officers over

---

18:3 Gershom This name sounds like the Hebrew word for "a stranger there."
18:4 Eliezer This name sounds like the Hebrew word for "my help."

groups of 1,000, 100, 50 and 10 people. ²⁶These officers solved disagreements among the people all the time. They brought the hard cases to Moses. But they decided the simple cases themselves.

²⁷Then Moses let his father-in-law leave. And Jethro went back to his own home.

ISRAEL AT SINAI

19 Exactly three months after the Israelites had left Egypt, they reached the Desert of Sinai. ²They had left Rephidim and had come to the Desert of Sinai. The Israelites camped in the desert in front of Mount Sinai. ³Then Moses went up on the mountain to God. The Lord called to him from the mountain. The Lord said, "Say this to the family of Jacob. And tell this to the people of Israel: ⁴'Every one of you has seen what I did to the people of Egypt. You saw how I carried you out of Egypt. I did it as an eagle carries her young on her wings. And I brought you here to me. ⁵So now obey me and keep my agreement. Do this, and you will be my own possession, chosen from all nations. Even though the whole earth is mine, ⁶you will be my kingdom of priests. You will be a nation that belongs to me alone.' You must tell the Israelites these words."

⁷So Moses went down and called the elders of the people together. He told them all the words the Lord had commanded him to say. ⁸And all the people answered together, "We will do everything he has said." Then Moses took their answer back to the Lord.

⁹And the Lord said to Moses, "I will come to you in a thick cloud. I will speak to you. The people will hear me talking to you. I will do this so the people will always trust you." Then Moses told the Lord what the people had said.

¹⁰The Lord said to Moses, "Go to the people and have them spend today and tomorrow preparing themselves. They must wash their clothes ¹¹and be ready by the day after tomorrow. On that day I, the Lord, will come down on Mount Sinai. And all the people will see me. ¹²But you must set a limit around the mountain. The people are not to cross it. Tell the people not to go up on the mountain. Tell them not to touch the foot of it. Anyone who touches the mountain must be put to death. ¹³He must be put to death with stones or shot with arrows. No one is allowed to touch him. Whether it is a person or an animal, he will not live. But the trumpet will make a long blast. Only then may the people go up on the mountain."

¹⁴So Moses went down from the mountain to the people. He made them prepare themselves for service to God. And the people washed their clothes. ¹⁵Then Moses said to the people, "Be ready in three days. Do not have physical relations during this time."

¹⁶It was the morning of the third day. There was thunder and lightning with a thick cloud on the mountain. And there was a very loud blast from a trumpet. All the people in the camp were frightened. ¹⁷Then Moses led the people out of the camp to meet God. They stood at the foot of the mountain. ¹⁸Mount Sinai was covered with smoke. This happened because the Lord came down on it in fire. The smoke rose from the mountain like smoke from a furnace. And the whole mountain shook wildly. ¹⁹The sound from the trumpet became louder. Then Moses spoke, and the voice of God answered him.

²⁰So the Lord came down on the top of Mount Sinai. Then he called Moses to come up to the top of the mountain. So Moses went up. ²¹The Lord said to Moses, "Go down and warn the people. They must not force their way through to see me. If they do, many of them will die. ²²Even the priests, who may come near me, must first prepare themselves. If they don't, I, the Lord, will punish them."

²³Moses told the Lord, "The people

cannot come up Mount Sinai. You yourself told us to set a limit around the mountain. We made it holy."

²⁴The Lord said to him, "Go down and bring Aaron with you. But don't allow the priests or the people to force their way through. They must not come up to the Lord. If they do, I will punish them."

²⁵So Moses went down to the people and told them these things.

THE TEN COMMANDMENTS

20 Then God spoke all these words:

²"I am the Lord your God. I brought you out of the land of Egypt where you were slaves.

³"You must not have any other gods except me.

⁴"You must not make for yourselves any idols. Don't make something that looks like anything in the sky above or on the earth below or in the water below the land. ⁵You must not worship or serve any idol. This is because I, the Lord your God, am a jealous God. A person may sin against me and hate me. I will punish his children, even his grandchildren and great-grandchildren. ⁶But I will be very kind to thousands who love me and obey my commands.

⁷"You must not use the name of the Lord your God thoughtlessly. The Lord will punish anyone who is guilty and misuses his name.

⁸"Remember to keep the Sabbath as a holy day. ⁹You may work and get everything done during six days each week. ¹⁰But the seventh day is a day of rest to honor the Lord your God. On that day no one may do any work: not you, your son or daughter, or your men or women slaves. Neither your animals nor the foreigners living in your cities may work. ¹¹The reason is that in six days the Lord made everything. He made the sky, earth, sea and everything in them. And on the seventh day, he rested. So the Lord blessed the Sabbath day and made it holy.

¹²"Honor your father and your mother. Then you will live a long time in the land. The Lord your God is going to give you this land.

¹³"You must not murder anyone.

¹⁴"You must not be guilty of adultery.

¹⁵"You must not steal.

¹⁶"You must not tell lies about your neighbor in court.

¹⁷"You must not want to take your neighbor's house. You must not want his wife or his men or women slaves. You must not want his ox or his donkey. You must not want to take anything that belongs to your neighbor."

¹⁸The people heard the thunder and the trumpet. They saw the lightning on the mountain and smoke rising from the mountain. They shook with fear and stood far away from the mountain. ¹⁹Then they said to Moses, "Speak to us yourself. Then we will listen. But don't let God speak to us, or we will die."

²⁰Then Moses said to the people, "Don't be afraid. God has come to test you. He wants you to respect him so you will not sin."

²¹The people stood far away from the mountain while Moses went near the dark cloud where God was. ²²Then the Lord told Moses to say these things to the Israelites: "You yourselves have seen that I talked with you from heaven. ²³You must not use gold or silver to make idols for yourselves. You must not worship these false gods in addition to me.

²⁴"Make an altar of dirt for me. Offer your whole burnt offerings and fellowship offerings on this altar as a sacrifice to me. Use your sheep and your cattle to do this. Worship me in every place that I choose. Then I will come and bless you. ²⁵You may use stones to make an altar for me. But don't use stones that you have made smooth with tools. You must not use any tools on the stones. If you do, you make them unsuitable for use in worship. ²⁶And you must not make steps leading up to my altar. If you go up steps, people will be able to see under your clothes."

LAWS FOR LIVING

21 Then God said to Moses, "These are the laws for living that you will give to the Israelites:

²"If you buy a Hebrew slave, he will serve you for six years. In the seventh year you are to set him free. And he will have to pay nothing. ³He might not be married when he becomes your slave. Then he must leave without a wife. The man might be married when he becomes your slave. Then he may take his wife with him. ⁴The slave's master might give him a wife, and she might give birth to sons or daughters. Then the woman and her children will belong to the master. When the slave is set free, only he may leave.

⁵"But the slave might say, 'I love my master, my wife and my children. I don't want to go free.' ⁶Then the slave's master will take him to God. The master will take him to a door or doorframe. And he will punch a hole through the slave's ear using a sharp tool. Then the slave will serve that master all his life.

⁷"A man might sell his daughter as a slave. There are rules for setting her free. They are different from the rules for setting the men slaves free. ⁸Maybe the master wanted to marry her but then decided he was not pleased with her. He must let one of her close relatives buy her back. He has no right to sell her to foreigners. This is because he has treated her unfairly. ⁹The man who bought her might promise to let the woman marry his son. Then he must treat her as a daughter. ¹⁰The man who bought her might marry another woman. Then he must not keep his slave woman from having food or clothing or physical relations. ¹¹If he does not give her these three things, she may go free. She owes him no money.

INJURIES

¹²"Anyone who hits a person and kills him must be put to death. ¹³But if a person kills someone accidentally, God allowed that to happen. So the person must go to a place I will choose. ¹⁴A person might plan and murder another person on purpose. Put him to death, even if he has run to my altar for safety.

¹⁵"Anyone who hits his father or his mother must be put to death.

¹⁶"A person might kidnap someone. Then he either sells him as a slave or still has him when he is caught. That person must be put to death.

¹⁷"Anyone who says cruel things to his father or mother must be put to death.

¹⁸"Two men might argue. And one might hit the other with a rock or with his fist. The hurt man might not be killed. But he might have to stay in bed. ¹⁹Later he might be able to get up. And he might be able to walk around outside with his walking stick. Then the one who hit him is not to be punished. But he must pay the injured man for the loss of his time. And he must support the injured man until he is completely healed.

²⁰"A man might beat his male or female slave with a stick. And the slave might die on the spot. Then the owner must be punished. ²¹But the slave might get well after a day or two. Then that owner will not be punished since the slave belongs to him.

²²"Two men might be fighting, and they might hit a pregnant woman so that the baby comes out. But there is no further injury. Then the man who caused the injury must pay money. He must pay what the woman's husband says and the court allows. ²³But if there is further injury, then the punishment is that life must be paid for life, ²⁴eye for eye, tooth for tooth. It is also hand for hand, foot for foot, ²⁵burn for burn, wound for wound and bruise for bruise.

²⁶"A man might hit his male or female slave in the eye. And the eye might be blinded. Then the man is to free the slave to pay for the eye. ²⁷A master might knock out a tooth of his male or

female slave. Then the man is to free the slave to pay for the tooth.

²⁸"A man's bull might kill a man or woman. Then you must kill that bull with stones. You should not eat the bull. But the owner of the bull is not guilty. ²⁹But the bull might have hurt people in the past. The owner might have been warned. If he did not keep it in a pen and then it kills a man or woman, the bull must be killed with stones. And the owner must also be put to death. ³⁰But the family of the dead man might accept money. Then the man who owned the bull may buy back his life. But he must pay whatever is demanded. ³¹Use this same law if the bull kills a person's son or daughter. ³²But the bull might kill a male or female slave. Then the owner must pay the master the price for a new slave. That is 12 ounces of silver. And the bull must also be killed with stones.

³³"A man might take the cover off a pit. Or he might dig one and not cover it. Another man's ox or donkey might come and fall into it. ³⁴The owner of the pit must pay the owner of the animal for his loss. The dead animal will belong to the one who pays.

³⁵"One man's bull might kill another man's bull. Then they must sell the bull that is alive. Both men get half of the money. And both men will also get half of the bull that was killed. ³⁶A man's bull might have hurt other animals in the past. But the owner might not have kept it in a pen. Then that owner must pay bull for bull. And the dead animal is his.

PROPERTY LAWS

22 "A man might steal a bull or a sheep and kill or sell it. Then he must pay back five bulls for the one bull he stole. Or he must pay back four sheep for the one sheep he stole.

²⁻⁴"The robber who is caught must pay back what he stole. He might own nothing. Then he must be sold as a slave to pay for what he stole. The stolen animal might be found alive with the robber. Then he must give the owner two animals for every animal he stole. He must pay, whether he stole a bull, donkey or sheep.

"A thief might be killed while breaking into a house at night. Then the one who killed him is not guilty of murder. But if this happens during the day, he is guilty of murder.

⁵"A person might let his farm animal graze in his field or vineyard. And it might wander into another person's field or vineyard. Then the owner of the animal must pay back the loss. The payment must come from the best of his crop.

⁶"A man might start a fire that spreads through the thornbushes to his neighbor's field. The fire might burn his neighbor's growing grain or grain that has been stacked. Or it might burn his whole field. Then the person who started the fire must pay for what was burned.

⁷"A man might give his neighbor money or other things to keep for him. Those things might be stolen from the neighbor's house. And the thief might be caught. Then he must pay back twice as much as he stole. ⁸But maybe the thief is never found. Then the owner of the house must make a promise before God. He must promise that he has not stolen his neighbor's things.

⁹"Two men might disagree about who owns something. It might be an ox, donkey, sheep or clothing. Or it might be something else that is lost. Each says, 'This is mine.' Each man must bring his case to God. God's judges will decide who is guilty. Then he must pay the other man twice as much as the thing is worth.

¹⁰"A man might ask his neighbor to keep his animal for him. This animal might be a donkey, ox, sheep or some other animal. And that animal might die, be hurt or be taken away. And no one saw what happened. ¹¹That neighbor must promise before the Lord that

he did not harm or kill the other man's animal. The owner of the animal must accept his promise made before God. The neighbor does not have to pay the owner for the animal. ¹²But the animal might have been stolen from the neighbor. Then he must pay the owner for it. ¹³Wild animals might have killed the animal. Then the neighbor must bring the body as proof. He will not have to pay for the animal that was killed.

¹⁴"A man might borrow an animal from his neighbor. It might get hurt or die while the owner is not there. Then the one who borrowed it must pay the owner for the animal. ¹⁵The owner might be with the animal. Then the one who borrowed it does not have to pay. If the animal was rented, the rental price covers the loss.

LAWS AND RELATIONSHIPS

¹⁶"A man might find a woman who is not pledged to be married. She has never had physical relations with a man. He might trick her into having physical relations with him. Then he must give her family the payment to marry her. And she will be his wife. ¹⁷But her father might refuse to allow his daughter to marry him. Then the man must still give the payment for a bride. He must pay the usual charge for a woman who is a virgin.

¹⁸"Put to death any woman who does evil magic.

¹⁹"Put to death anyone who has unnatural physical relations with an animal.

²⁰"Destroy completely any person who makes a sacrifice to any god except the Lord.

²¹"Do not cheat or hurt a foreigner. Remember that you were foreigners in the land of Egypt.

²²"Do not cheat a widow or an orphan. ²³If you do, they will cry out to me for help. I certainly will hear their cry. ²⁴And I will be very angry and kill you in war. Then your wives will become widows, and your children will become orphans.

²⁵"You might lend money to one of my people who is poor. Then do not treat him as a moneylender would. Charge him nothing for using your money. ²⁶Your neighbor might give you his coat as a promise. He is promising to pay you the money he owes you. But you must give it back to him by sunset. ²⁷That coat is the only cover to keep his body warm. He has nothing else to sleep in. If he cries out to me for help, I will listen because I am merciful.

²⁸"You must not speak against God. You must not curse a leader of your people. ²⁹"Do not hold back your offering from the first of your harvest. Give me the first grain that you harvest. Give me the first wine that you make. Also, you must give me your firstborn sons. ³⁰You must do the same with your bulls and your sheep. Let the firstborn males stay with their mothers for seven days. On the eighth day you must give them to me.

³¹"You are to be my holy people. You must not eat the meat of any animal that has been killed by wild animals. Instead, give it to the dogs.

> You are to be my holy people.
>
> —EXODUS 22:31

LAWS ABOUT FAIRNESS

23 "You must not tell lies. You might be a witness in court. Don't help a bad person by telling lies.

2"You must not do wrong just because everyone else is doing it. You might be a witness in court. Then you must not ruin a fair trial. You must not tell lies just because everyone else is. ³A poor man might be in court. You must not take his side just because he is poor.

4"You might see your enemy's ox or donkey wandering away. Then you must return it to him. ⁵You might see that your enemy's donkey has fallen because its load is too heavy. You must not leave it there. You must help your enemy get the donkey back on its feet.

6"You must not be unfair to a poor man when he is in court. ⁷You must not lie when you accuse someone in court. Never allow an innocent or honest person to be put to death as punishment. This is because I will not treat guilty people as if they were innocent.

8"You must not accept money from a person who wants you to lie in court. Such money will not let you see what is right. Such money makes good people tell lies.

9"You must not mistreat a foreigner. You know how it feels to be a foreigner. You were foreigners in Egypt.

LAWS FOR THE SABBATH

10"For six years you are to plant and harvest crops on your land. ¹¹Then during the seventh year, do not plow or plant your land. If any food grows there, allow the poor people to have it. And let the wild animals eat what is left. You should do the same with your vineyards and your orchards of olive trees.

12"You should work six days a week. But on the seventh day you must rest. This lets your ox and your donkey rest. This also lets the slave born in your house and the foreigner be refreshed.

13"Be sure to do all that I have said to you. You must not even say the names of other gods. The names of those gods must not come out of your mouth.

THREE YEARLY FEASTS

14"Three times each year you must hold a feast to honor me. ¹⁵You must celebrate the Feast of Unleavened Bread. Do this in the way I commanded you. For seven days you must eat bread that is made without yeast. You must do this at the set time during the month of Abib. This is the month when you came out of Egypt. No one is to come to worship me without bringing an offering.

16"You must celebrate the Feast of Harvest. Offer to God the first things you harvest. These are from the crops you planted in your fields.

"You must celebrate the Feast of Tents in the fall. Do this when you gather all the crops from your fields.

17"So three times during every year all men must come to worship the Lord God.

18"You must not offer animal blood along with anything that has yeast in it.

"You must not save any of the fat from the sacrifice for the next day.

19"You must bring the best of the firstfruits of your land. Bring them to the Holy Tent^n of the Lord your God.

"You must not cook a young goat in its mother's milk.

PROMISES

20"I am sending an angel ahead of you. He will protect you as you travel. He will lead you to the place I have prepared. ²¹Pay attention to the angel and obey him. Do not turn against him. He will not forgive such turning against him because my power is in him. ²²You must listen carefully to all he says. You must do everything that I tell you. If you do this, I will be an enemy to your enemies. I will fight all who fight against you. ²³My angel will go ahead of you. He will take you into the land of these people: the Amorites, Hittites, Perizzites, Canaanites, Hivites and Jebusites. And I will destroy them.

23:19 Holy Tent Literally, "house of the Lord your God." See Exodus 25:9.

24"You must not bow down to their gods or worship those gods. You must not live the way those people live. You must destroy their idols. And you must break into pieces stone pillars they use in worship. 25You must worship the Lord your God. If you do, I will bless your bread and your water. I will take away sickness from you. 26None of your women will have her baby die before it is born. All women will have children. I will allow you to live long lives.

27"I will make your enemies afraid of me. I will confuse any people you fight against. I will make all your enemies run away from you. 28I will send something like hornets ahead of you. They will force the Hivites, Canaanites and Hittites out of your way. 29But I will not force all those people out in only one year. If I did, the land would become a desert. Then the wild animals would become too many for you. 30Instead, I will force those people out of your land very slowly. I will wait until there are enough of you to take over the land.

31"I will give you the land from the Gulf of Aqaba to the Mediterranean Sea. And I will give you the land between the desert and the Euphrates River. I will give you power over the people who now live in the land. You will force them out ahead of you. 32You must not make an agreement with those people or with their gods. 33You must not let them live in your land. If they live there, they will make you sin against me. If you worship their gods, you will be like someone caught in a trap."

GOD AND ISRAEL MAKE THEIR AGREEMENT

24 The Lord told Moses, "You, Aaron, Nadab, Abihu and 70 of the elders of Israel must come up to me. You must worship me from a distance. 2Then Moses alone must come near me. The other men must not come near. And the rest of the people must not come up the mountain with Moses."

3So Moses told the people all the Lord's words and laws for living. Then all of the people answered out loud together. They said, "We will do all the things that the Lord has said." 4So Moses wrote down all the words of the Lord. And he got up early the next morning. He built an altar near the bottom of the mountain. He set up 12 stones, 1 stone for each of the 12 tribes of Israel. 5Then Moses sent young Israelite men to offer whole burnt offerings. They also sacrificed young bulls as fellowship offerings to the Lord. 6Moses took the blood of these animals. He put half of it in bowls. And he sprinkled the other half of the blood on the altar. 7Then Moses took the book with the agreement written in it. He read it so the people could hear him. And they said, "We will do everything that the Lord has said. We will obey."

8Then Moses took the blood from the bowls. He sprinkled it on the people. He said, "This is the blood that begins the agreement. This is the agreement which the Lord has made with you about all these things."

9Moses, Aaron, Nadab, Abihu and 70 of the elders of Israel went up the mountain. 10They saw the God of Israel. Under his feet was a surface. It looked as if it were paved with blue sapphire stones. And it was as clear as the sky! 11These leaders of the Israelites saw God. But God did not destroy them. Then they ate and drank together.

MOSES GETS THE STONE TABLETS

12The Lord said to Moses, "Come up the mountain to me. Wait there, and I will give you two stone tablets. On these are the teachings and the commandments. I have written these to teach the people."

13So Moses and his helper Joshua set out. Moses went up Sinai, the mountain of God. 14Moses said to the elders, "Wait

☆ Exodus 24:12–13

In order for God to give Moses the Ten Commandments, Moses needed to climb up Mount Sinai. It was a long way up and a hard climb, but Joshua was his helper. He went with Moses and helped him up the mountain.

Have you thought about what you want to be when you grow up? Maybe you will be a police officer or a school teacher. You may even become a pastor or a missionary in a country far away. No matter what you decide to be, God has a special job for you. He wants you to tell others about Jesus and how much he loves them. Even now, you can help others and share Jesus' love with your friends and family.

. . . .

Just like Joshua had a special job helping Moses, you can help your family and friends. One way you can help is to remind them that Jesus loves them.

here for us until we come back to you. Aaron and Hur are with you. Anyone who has a disagreement with others can take it to them."

MOSES MEETS WITH GOD

¹⁵When Moses went up on the mountain, the cloud covered it. ¹⁶The greatness of the Lord came down on Mount Sinai. The cloud covered the mountain for six days. On the seventh day the Lord called to Moses from inside the cloud. ¹⁷The Israelites could see the greatness of the Lord. It looked like a fire burning on top of the mountain. ¹⁸Then Moses went into the cloud and went higher up the mountain. Moses was on the mountain for 40 days and 40 nights.

GIFTS FOR THE LORD

25 The Lord said to Moses, ²"Tell the Israelites to bring me gifts. Receive for me the gifts each man wants to give. ³These are the gifts that you should receive from them: gold, silver, bronze, ⁴blue, purple and red thread, and fine linen. Receive cloth made of goat hair. ⁵Receive the male sheep skins that are dyed red. Receive fine leather, acacia wood ⁶and olive oil to burn in the lamps. And receive spices for sweet-smelling incense and the special olive oil poured on a person's head to make him a priest. ⁷Also accept onyx stones and other jewels to be put on the holy vest and the chest covering.

⁸"The people must build a holy place for me. Then I can live among them.

⁹Build this Holy Tent and everything in it by the plan I will show you.

THE ARK OF THE COVENANT

¹⁰"Use acacia wood and build an Ark. It must be 45 inches long, 27 inches wide and 27 inches high. ¹¹Cover the Ark of the Covenant inside and out with pure gold. And put a gold strip all around it. ¹²Make four gold rings for the Ark of the Covenant. Attach the gold rings to its four feet, two rings on each side. ¹³Then make poles from acacia wood and cover them with gold. ¹⁴Put the poles through the rings on the sides of the Ark. Use these poles to carry the Ark of the Covenant. ¹⁵These poles must always stay in the rings of the Ark of the Covenant. Do not take the poles out. ¹⁶Then put the two flat stones in the Ark of the Covenant. I will give you these stones on which the commands are written.

¹⁷"Then make a lid of pure gold for the Ark of the Covenant. This lid is the mercy seat. Make it 45 inches long and 27 inches wide. ¹⁸Then hammer gold to make two creatures with wings. Put one on each end of the lid. ¹⁹Put one creature with wings on one end of the lid. And put the other creature with wings on the other end. Attach the creatures with wings to the lid so that they will all be one piece. ²⁰The creatures' wings should be spread out over the lid. The creatures are to face each other across the lid. ²¹Put this lid on top of the Ark of the Covenant. Also put in this Ark of the Covenant the agreement which I will make with you. ²²I will meet with you there, above the lid between the two creatures with wings. These are on the Ark of the Covenant. There I will give you all my commands for the Israelites.

THE TABLE

²³"Make a table out of acacia wood. It must be 36 inches long, 18 inches wide and 27 inches high. ²⁴Cover it with pure gold. Put a gold strip around it. ²⁵Then make a frame three inches high that stands up all around the edge. Put a gold strip around the frame. ²⁶Then make four gold rings. Attach them to the four corners of the table where the four legs are. ²⁷Put the rings close to the frame around the top of the table. These rings will hold the poles for carrying the table. ²⁸Make the poles out of acacia wood and cover them with gold. Carry the table with these poles. ²⁹Make the plates and bowls for the table out of pure gold. Make the jars and cups out of pure gold. They will be used for pouring out the drink offerings. ³⁰On this table put the bread that shows you are in my presence. It must always be there in front of me.

THE LAMPSTAND

³¹"Hammer pure gold to make a lampstand. Its base, stand, flower-like cups, buds and petals must all be joined together in one piece. ³²The lampstand must have three branches on one side and three branches on the other. ³³Each branch must have three cups shaped like almond flowers on it. Each cup must have a bud and a petal. ³⁴And there must be four more cups made like almond flowers on the lampstand itself. These cups must also have buds and petals. ³⁵Put a bud under each pair of branches that goes out from the lampstand. ³⁶The branches, buds and lampstand must be one piece of pure, hammered gold.

³⁷"Then make seven small oil lamps and put them on the lampstand. They will give light to the area in front of the

> Build this Holy Tent and everything in it by the plan I will show you.
> –EXODUS 25:9

lampstand. ³⁸The wick trimmers and trays must be made of pure gold. ³⁹Use 75 pounds of pure gold to make the lampstand and everything with it. ⁴⁰Be very careful to make them by the plan I showed you on the mountain.

THE HOLY TENT

26 "Make the Holy Tent with ten pieces of cloth. These pieces must be made of fine linen and blue, purple and red thread. Have a skilled craftsman sew designs of creatures with wings on the pieces of cloth. ²Make each piece the same size. Each piece should be 42 feet long and 6 feet wide. ³Sew five pieces of cloth together for one set. Sew the other pieces together for the second set. ⁴Make loops of blue cloth down the edge of the end piece of each set. ⁵Make 50 loops on the end piece of the first set. And make 50 loops on the end piece of the second set. These loops must be opposite each other. ⁶And make 50 gold hooks. Use these to join the two sets of cloth. This will make the Holy Tent one piece.

⁷"Then make another tent that will cover the Holy Tent. Make this tent of 11 pieces of cloth made from goat hair. ⁸All these pieces of cloth must be the same size. They must be 45 feet long and 6 feet wide. ⁹Sew five of the pieces together into one set. Then sew the other six pieces together into the second set. Fold the sixth piece double over the front of the Tent. ¹⁰Make 50 loops down the edge of the end piece of one set. Do the same for the end piece of the other set. ¹¹Then make 50 bronze hooks. Put these in the loops to join the two sets of cloth. This will make the covering one piece. ¹²Let the extra half piece of cloth hang over the back of the Holy Tent. ¹³There will be 18 inches hanging over the sides of the Holy Tent. This will protect the Tent. ¹⁴Make two more coverings for the Holy Tent. One should be made from male sheep skins colored red. The outer covering should be from fine leather.

¹⁵"Use acacia wood to make upright frames for the Holy Tent. ¹⁶Each frame must be 15 feet long and 27 inches wide. ¹⁷Every frame must be made the same way. There must be two pegs side by side in each frame. ¹⁸Make 20 frames for the south side of the Holy Tent. ¹⁹Each frame must have 2 silver bases to go under it. A peg fits into each silver base. You must make 40 silver bases for the frames. ²⁰Make 20 more frames for the north side of the Holy Tent. ²¹Make 40 silver bases for them. Make 2 bases for each frame. ²²You must make 6 frames for the rear or west end of the Holy Tent. ²³Make 2 frames for each corner at the rear. ²⁴The 2 frames at each corner are to be joined together. Hold them together from bottom to top with a metal ring. Both corner frames must be made this way. ²⁵So there will be a total of 8 frames at the rear of the Tent. And there will be 16 silver bases—2 bases under each frame.

²⁶"Make crossbars of acacia wood to connect the upright frames of the Holy Tent. Make five crossbars to hold the frames together on one side. ²⁷Also make five crossbars to hold the frames together on the other side. And make crossbars to hold the frames together on the west end, at the rear. ²⁸The middle crossbar is to be set halfway up the frames. It is to run along the entire length of each side and rear. ²⁹Make gold rings on the sides of the frames. Pass the crossbars through the rings. Cover the frames and the crossbars with gold. ³⁰Set up the Holy Tent by the plan shown to you on the mountain.

³¹"Make a curtain of fine linen and blue, purple and red thread. Have a skilled craftsman sew designs of creatures with wings on the curtain. ³²Hang the curtain by gold hooks on four posts of acacia wood. Cover these posts with gold and set them in four silver bases. ³³Hang the curtain from the hooks in the roof. Put the Ark of the Covenant containing the two

flat stones behind the curtain. This curtain will separate the Holy Place from the Most Holy Place. ³⁴Put the lid on the Ark of the Covenant in the Most Holy Place.

³⁵"Outside the curtain, put the table on the north side of the Holy Tent. And put the lampstand on the south side of the Holy Tent. This will be across from the table.

THE ENTRANCE OF THE HOLY TENT

³⁶"Then make a curtain for the entrance of the Tent. Make it with fine linen and blue, purple and red thread. Someone who can sew well is to sew designs on it. ³⁷Make five posts of acacia wood covered with gold. Make five gold hooks on which to hang the curtain from the posts. And make five bronze bases for the five posts.

THE ALTAR

27 "Make an altar for burnt offerings out of acacia wood. Make it 4½ feet high. It should be square: 7½ feet long and 7½ feet wide. ²Make each of the four corners of the altar stick out like a horn. The corners with their horns must be all one piece. Then cover the whole altar with bronze.

³"Use bronze to make all the tools and dishes that will be used on the altar. Make pots to remove the ashes. Make shovels, bowls for sprinkling blood, meat forks and pans for carrying the burning wood.

⁴"Make a large, bronze screen to hold the burning wood. And put a bronze ring at each of the four corners of the screen. ⁵Put the screen inside the altar, under its rim, halfway up from the bottom.

⁶"Make poles of acacia wood for the altar. And cover them with bronze. ⁷Put the poles through the rings on both sides of the altar to carry it. ⁸Make the altar out of boards and leave the inside hollow. Make it as you were shown on the mountain.

THE COURTYARD OF THE HOLY TENT

⁹"Make a wall of curtains to form a courtyard around the Holy Tent. The south side should have a wall of fine linen curtains 150 feet long. ¹⁰Hang the curtain with silver hooks and bands. Put these on 20 bronze posts on 20 bronze bases. ¹¹The north side must also be 150 feet long. Hang its curtains on silver hooks and bands. Put these on 20 bronze posts on 20 bronze bases.

¹²"The west end of the courtyard must have a wall of curtains 75 feet long. It must have 10 posts and 10 bases on that wall. ¹³The east end of the courtyard must also be 75 feet long. ¹⁴On one side of the entry, there is to be a wall of curtains. It is to be 22½ feet long. It is to be held up by 3 posts on 3 bases. ¹⁵On the other side of the entry, there is to be a wall of curtains. It is to be 22½ feet long. It is to be held up by 3 posts on 3 bases.

¹⁶"The entry to the courtyard is to be a curtain 30 feet wide. It is to be made of fine linen with blue, purple and red thread. Someone who can sew well is to sew designs on it. It is to be held up by 4 posts on 4 bases. ¹⁷All the posts around the courtyard must have silver bands and hooks and bronze bases. ¹⁸The courtyard must be 150 feet long and 75 feet wide. The wall of curtains around it should be 7½ feet high. They must be made of fine linen. The bases in which the posts are set must be bronze. ¹⁹All the things used in the Holy Tent must be made of bronze. And all the tent pegs for the Holy Tent and the wall around the courtyard must be made of bronze.

OIL FOR THE LAMP

²⁰"Command the people of Israel to bring you pure olive oil. It is to be made from pressed olives. This is to keep the lamps on the lampstand burning. ²¹Aaron and his sons must keep the lamps burning before the Lord from evening till morning. This will be in the Meeting Tent. It is outside the

curtain which is in front of the Ark of the Covenant. The Israelites and their descendants must obey this rule from now on.

CLOTHES FOR THE PRIESTS

28 "Tell your brother Aaron to come to you. His sons Nadab, Abihu, Eleazar and Ithamar must come with him. Separate them from the other Israelites. These men must serve as priests. ²Make holy clothes for your brother Aaron to give him honor and beauty. ³Speak to all the people to whom I have given the ability to make clothes. Tell these skilled craftsmen to make the clothes for Aaron. Use these clothes to make him belong to me. Then he may serve me as a priest. ⁴These are the clothes they must make: a chest covering, a holy vest, an outer robe, a woven inner robe, a turban and a cloth belt. The craftsmen must make these holy clothes. They are for your brother Aaron and his sons. Then Aaron and his sons may serve me as priests. ⁵The craftsmen must use gold and blue, purple and red thread, and fine linen.

THE HOLY VEST

⁶"Use gold and blue, purple and red thread, and fine linen to make the holy vest. The craftsmen are to make this holy vest. ⁷At each top corner of this holy vest there will be a pair of shoulder straps. These are to be tied together over each shoulder.

⁸"The craftsmen will very carefully weave a belt on the holy vest. Make the belt with gold and blue, purple and red thread, and fine linen.

⁹"Take two onyx stones. Write the name of the 12 sons of Israel on these jewels. ¹⁰Write 6 names on one stone and 6 names on the other stone. Write the names in order, from the oldest son to the youngest. ¹¹Carve the names of the sons of Israel on these stones. Do this the same way a person carves words and designs on the seals. Put gold around the stones to hold them on the holy vest. ¹²Put the two stones on the two straps of the holy vest. These stones are reminders of the 12 sons of Israel. Aaron is to wear their names on his shoulders. They are before the Lord as reminders of the sons of Israel. ¹³Make two gold pieces to hold the stones. ¹⁴Then make two chains of pure gold. Twist them together like a rope. Attach the chains to the two gold pieces that hold the stones.

THE CHEST COVERING

¹⁵"Make a chest covering to help in making decisions. The craftsmen should make it as they made the holy vest. They must use gold and blue, purple and red thread, and fine linen. ¹⁶The chest covering must be square. It should be nine inches long and nine inches wide. Fold it double to make a pocket. ¹⁷Put four rows of beautiful gems on the chest covering. The first row of jewels must have a ruby, topaz and yellow quartz. ¹⁸The second row must have turquoise, a sapphire and an emerald. ¹⁹The third row must have a jacinth, an agate and an amethyst. ²⁰The fourth row must have a chrysolite, an onyx and a jasper. Put gold around these jewels to attach them to the chest covering. ²¹There must be 12 jewels on the chest covering. That is 1 jewel for each of the names of the sons of Israel. Carve the name of one of the 12 tribes on each of the stones. Carve them as you would carve a seal.

²²"Make chains of pure gold for the chest covering. Twist them together like rope. ²³Make two gold rings. Put them on the two upper corners of the chest covering. ²⁴Attach the two gold chains to the two rings. These are at the upper corners of the chest covering. ²⁵Attach the other ends of the two chains to the two gold pieces on the shoulder straps. This will tie the chains to the shoulder straps in the front of the holy vest.

²⁶"Make two more gold rings. Put them at the two lower corners of the

chest covering. Put them on the inside edge of the chest covering next to the holy vest. ²⁷Make two more gold rings. Attach them to the bottom of the shoulder straps in the front of the holy vest. Put the gold rings close to the seam above the woven belt of the holy vest. ²⁸Join the rings of the chest covering to the rings of the holy vest with blue ribbon. This will connect it to the woven belt. In this way the chest covering will not swing out from the holy vest.

²⁹"When Aaron enters the Holy Place, he will wear the names of the sons of Israel over his heart. These names are on the chest covering that helps in making decisions. This will be a continual reminder before the Lord. ³⁰And put the Urim and Thummim inside the chest covering. These things will be on Aaron's heart when he goes before the Lord. They will help in making decisions for the Israelites. So Aaron will always carry them with him when he is before the Lord.

³¹"Make the outer robe to be worn under the holy vest, using only blue cloth. ³²Make a hole in the center for Aaron's head. And there must be a woven collar around the hole so it will not tear. ³³Make balls like pomegranates of blue, purple and red thread. Hang these pomegranate balls around the bottom of the outer robe. And hang gold bells between them. ³⁴So all around the bottom of the outer robe there should be a gold bell and a pomegranate ball, a gold bell and a pomegranate ball. ³⁵Aaron must wear this robe when he serves as priest. The ringing of the bells will be heard. They will ring when he enters and leaves the Holy Place before the Lord. This way Aaron will not be killed.

³⁶"Make a strip of pure gold. Carve these words on the gold strip as you would carve on a seal: 'Holy to the Lord.' ³⁷Use blue ribbon to tie a strip of gold to the turban. Put it on the front of the turban. ³⁸Aaron must wear this on his forehead. In this way, he will be blamed

if anything is wrong with the gifts of the Israelites. Aaron must always wear this on his head so the Lord will accept the gifts of the people.

³⁹"Make the woven inner robe of fine linen. Make the turban of fine linen, also. Make the cloth belt with designs sewn on it. ⁴⁰Also make woven inner robes, cloth belts and headbands for Aaron's sons. This will give them honor and beauty. ⁴¹Put these clothes on your brother Aaron and his sons. Then pour olive oil on their heads to appoint them as priests. Make them belong to me so they may serve me as priests.

⁴²"Make for them linen underclothes to cover them from the waist to the upper parts of the legs. ⁴³Aaron and his sons must wear these underclothes when they enter the Meeting Tent. And they must wear these clothes anytime they come near the altar to serve as priests in the Holy Place. If they do not wear these clothes, they will be guilty of wrong. And they will be killed. This will be a law that will last from now on for Aaron and all his descendants.

APPOINTING THE PRIESTS

29 "This is what you must do to appoint Aaron and his sons. Then they may serve me as priests. Take one young bull and two male sheep that have nothing wrong with them. ²Use fine wheat flour without yeast to make bread and cakes mixed with olive oil. Also use wheat flour without yeast to make wafers brushed with olive oil. ³Put these in one basket. Bring them in the basket along with the bull and two male sheep. ⁴Bring Aaron and his sons to the entrance of the Meeting Tent. Then wash them with water. ⁵Take the clothes. Dress Aaron in the inner robe and the outer robe of the holy vest. Then put on him the holy vest and the chest covering. Then tie the holy vest on him with its skillfully woven belt. ⁶Put the turban on his head. Put the holy crown, the strip of gold, on the turban. ⁷Take the special olive oil and pour it on his head to make him a priest.

⁸"Then bring his sons and put the inner robes on them. ⁹Put the headbands on their heads. Then tie cloth belts around their waists. Aaron and his descendants will be priests in Israel. This is by a rule that will continue from now on. This is how you will appoint Aaron and his sons as priests.

¹⁰"Bring the bull to the front of the Meeting Tent. Aaron and his sons must put their hands on the bull's head. ¹¹Then kill the bull before the Lord at the entrance to the Meeting Tent. ¹²Take some of the bull's blood and go to the altar. Use your finger to put some blood on the corners of the altar. Pour the blood that is left at the bottom of the altar. ¹³Then take all the fat that covers the inner organs. Take the best part of the liver, and take both kidneys and the fat around them. Burn these on the altar. ¹⁴Take the bull's meat, skin and intestines. Burn these things outside the camp. This is an offering to take away sin.

¹⁵"Take one of the male sheep. Have Aaron and his sons put their hands on its head. ¹⁶Then kill that male sheep. Take its blood and sprinkle it on all four sides of the altar. ¹⁷Then cut the male sheep into pieces. Wash its inner organs and its legs. Put them with its head and its other pieces. ¹⁸Burn the whole male sheep on the altar. It is a burnt offering made by fire to the Lord. Its smell is pleasing to the Lord.

¹⁹"Take the other male sheep. Have Aaron and his sons put their hands on its head. ²⁰Kill that male sheep and take some of its blood. Put it on the bottom of the right ears of Aaron and his sons. Also put it on the thumbs of their right hands. And put it on the big toes of their right feet. Then sprinkle the rest of the blood against all four sides of the altar. ²¹Then take some of the blood from the altar. Mix it with the special oil used in appointing priests. Sprinkle this on Aaron and his clothes. And sprinkle this on his sons and their clothes. This will show that Aaron and his sons and their clothes are given to my service.

²²"Then take the fat from the male sheep. Take the fat tail and the fat that covers the inner organs. Take the best part of the liver. Take both kidneys and the fat around them and the right thigh. This is the male sheep to be used in appointing priests.

²³"Then take the basket of bread that you made without yeast. This is the basket you put before the Lord. From it take a loaf of bread, a cake made with olive oil and a wafer. ²⁴Put these in the hands of Aaron and his sons. Tell them to present these things in their hands before the Lord. This will be an offering presented to the Lord. ²⁵Then take them from their hands. Burn them on the altar with the whole burnt offering. This is an offering made by fire to the Lord. Its smell is pleasing to the Lord. ²⁶Then take the breast of the male sheep used to appoint Aaron as priest. Present the breast of the male sheep before the Lord. It is an offering presented to the Lord. This part of the animal will be your share. ²⁷Then give to the service of the Lord the parts of the male sheep used to appoint them as priests. They belong to Aaron and his sons. They are the breast and the right thigh. These were presented to the Lord. ²⁸This is to be the regular share which the Israelites will always give to Aaron and his sons. This is the gift the Israelites must give to the Lord from their fellowship offerings.

> Aaron and his descendants will be priests in Israel.
> —EXODUS 29:9

[29] "The holy clothes made for Aaron will belong to his descendants. They must wear these clothes when they are appointed as priests. [30] Aaron's son will become high priest after Aaron. He will come to the Meeting Tent to serve in the Holy Place. He is to wear these clothes for seven days.

[31] "Take the male sheep used to appoint priests. Boil its meat in a place made holy for serving me. [32] Then Aaron and his sons must eat the meat of the male sheep. They must do that at the entrance of the Meeting Tent. And they must also eat the bread that is in the basket. [33] These offerings were used to remove their sins when they were made priests so they would belong to God. Now they should eat these offerings. But no one else is to eat these things because they are holy. [34] If any of the meat from that male sheep or any of the bread is left the next morning, it must be burned. It shall not be eaten because it is holy.

[35] "Do all these things that I commanded you to do to Aaron and his sons. You are to spend seven days appointing them. [36] Each day for seven days you are to offer a bull. This will remove the sins of Aaron and his sons so they will be given for service to the Lord. Make the altar ready for service to the Lord. Pour oil on it to make it holy. [37] Spend seven days making the altar ready for service to God and making it holy. Then the altar will become very holy. Anything that touches it must be holy.

THE DAILY SACRIFICES

[38] "Every day from now on, offer on the altar two lambs that are one year old. [39] Offer one lamb in the morning and the other in the evening. [40] In the morning, when you offer the first lamb, offer also two quarts of fine flour. Mix it with one quart of oil from pressed olives. Pour out a quart of wine as a drink offering. [41] Offer the second lamb in the evening. Also offer the same grain offering and drink offering as you did in the morning. This is an offering by fire to the Lord. And its smell is pleasing to the Lord.

[42] "You must burn these things as an offering to the Lord every day. Do this at the entrance of the Meeting Tent before the Lord from now on. When you make the offering, I, the Lord, will meet you there and speak to you. [43] I will meet with the people of Israel there. And that place will be holy because of my greatness.

[44] "So I will make the Meeting Tent and the altar holy. And I will make Aaron and his sons holy so they may serve me as priests. [45] I will live with the people of Israel. I will be their God. [46] And they will know that I am the Lord their God. They will know that I am the one who led them out of Egypt. I did this so I could live with them. I am the Lord their God.

THE ALTAR FOR BURNING INCENSE

30 "Make an altar out of acacia wood for burning incense. [2] Make it square—18 inches long and 18 inches wide. It must be 36 inches high. Make the corners stick out like horns. These must be one piece with the altar. [3] Cover its top, its sides and its corners with pure gold. And put a gold strip all around the altar. [4] Make two gold rings beneath the gold strip on opposite sides of the altar. Slide poles through these gold rings to carry the altar. [5] Make the poles from acacia wood and cover them with gold. [6] Put the altar of incense in front of the curtain. This curtain is in front of the Ark of the Covenant. Put the altar in front of the lid that covers that Ark of the Covenant. There I will meet with you.

[7] "Aaron must burn sweet-smelling incense on the altar every morning. He will do this when he comes to take care of the oil lamps. [8] He must burn incense again in the evening when he lights the lamps. So incense will burn

before the Lord every day from now on. ⁹Do not use this altar for offering any other incense or burnt offering. Do not use this altar to offer any kind of grain offering or drink offering. ¹⁰Once a year Aaron must make the altar ready for service to God. He will do it by putting blood on its corners. This is blood of the animal offered to remove sins. He is to do this once a year from now on. This altar belongs completely to God's service."

THE TAX FOR THE MEETING TENT

¹¹The Lord said to Moses, ¹²"Count the people of Israel. At that time every person must pay to buy back his life from the Lord. Then no terrible things will happen to the people when you number them. ¹³Every person who is counted must pay one-fifth of an ounce of silver. This is set by the Holy Place measure, which weighs two-fifths of an ounce. This amount is a gift to the Lord. ¹⁴Every person who is counted and is 20 years old or older must give this amount to the Lord. ¹⁵A rich person must not give more than one-fifth of an ounce. And a poor person must not give less than one-fifth of an ounce. You are paying this to the Lord to buy back your lives. ¹⁶Gather from the people of Israel this money paid to buy back their lives. Spend it to buy things for the service in the Meeting Tent. This payment will remind the Lord that the Israelites' lives have been bought back."

THE BRONZE BOWL

¹⁷The Lord said to Moses, ¹⁸"Make a bronze bowl for washing. Build it on a bronze stand. Put the bowl and stand between the Meeting Tent and the altar. Put water in the bowl. ¹⁹Aaron and his sons must wash their hands and feet with the water from this bowl. ²⁰Each time, before they enter the Meeting Tent, they must wash with water. This way they will not die. They approach the altar to serve as priests. They offer a sacrifice to the Lord by fire. ²¹Each

time they do this, they must wash their hands and their feet so they will not die. This is a rule which Aaron and his descendants are to keep from now on."

OIL FOR APPOINTING

²²Then the Lord said to Moses, ²³"Take the finest spices: 12 pounds of liquid myrrh, half that amount (that is, 6 pounds) of sweet-smelling cinnamon, 6 pounds of sweet-smelling cane ²⁴and 12 pounds of cassia. Weigh all these by the Holy Place measure. Also take 4 quarts of olive oil. ²⁵Mix all these things like a perfume to make a holy olive oil. This special oil must be put on people and things. Do this to make them ready for service to God. ²⁶Put this oil on the Meeting Tent and the Ark of the Covenant with my laws in it. ²⁷Put this oil on the table and all its dishes. And put this oil on the lampstand and all its tools. Put the oil on the incense altar. ²⁸Also, put the oil on the altar for burning offerings and all its tools. Put this oil on the bowl and the stand under the bowl. Put oil on all these things to prepare them for service to God. ²⁹You will give these things for service to God. They will be very holy. Anything that touches these things must also be holy.

³⁰"Put the oil on Aaron and his sons to make them priests. Give them for service to me. Then they may serve me as priests. ³¹Tell the Israelites, 'This is to be my holy olive oil from now on. It is to be put on people and things to make them ready for service to God. ³²Do not pour it on the bodies of ordinary people. Do not make perfume the same way you make this oil. It is holy, and you must treat it as holy. ³³Someone might make perfume like it. Or he might put it on someone who is not a priest. Then that person must be separated from his people.'"

INCENSE

³⁴Then the Lord said to Moses, "Take these sweet-smelling spices: resin, onycha, galbanum and pure frankincense. Be sure that you have equal amounts

of each. ³⁵You must make incense as a man who makes perfume would do. Add salt to it to keep it pure and holy. ³⁶Beat some of the incense into a fine powder. Put some of it in front of the Ark of the Covenant in the Meeting Tent. There I will meet with you. You must use this incense powder only for its very special purpose. ³⁷Do not make incense for yourselves the same way you make this incense. Treat it as holy to the Lord. ³⁸Whoever makes incense like this to use as perfume must be separated from his people."

BEZALEL AND OHOLIAB

31 Then the Lord said to Moses, ²"See, I have chosen Bezalel son of Uri from the tribe of Judah. Uri was the son of Hur. ³I have filled Bezalel with the Spirit of God. I have given him the skill, ability and knowledge to do all kinds of work. ⁴He is able to design pieces to be made from gold, silver and bronze. ⁵He is able to cut jewels and put them in metal. And he can carve wood. Bezalel can do all kinds of work. ⁶I have also chosen Oholiab son of Ahisamach from the tribe of Dan. Oholiab will work with Bezalel. I have given skills to all skilled craftsmen. They will be able to make all these things I have commanded you: ⁷the Meeting Tent, the Ark of the Covenant, the lid that covers the Ark of the Covenant and everything in the Tent. ⁸This includes the table and everything on it, the pure gold lampstand and everything with it and the altar of incense. ⁹It also includes the altar for burnt offerings and everything used with it, the bowl and the stand under it. ¹⁰They will make the woven clothes and the holy clothes for Aaron and the clothes for his sons to wear when they serve as priests. ¹¹They will also make the special olive oil used in appointing people and things to the service of the Lord, and the sweet-smelling incense for the Holy Place.

"These workers will make all these things just as I have commanded you."

THE DAY OF REST

¹²Then the Lord said to Moses, ¹³"Tell the Israelites, 'You must keep the rules about my Sabbaths. This is because they will be a sign between you and me from now on. In this way you will know that I, the Lord, am making you holy. ¹⁴"'Make the Sabbath a holy day. If anyone treats the Sabbath like any other day, that person must be put to death. Anyone who works on the Sabbath day must be separated from his people. ¹⁵There are six days for working. But the seventh day is a day of rest. It is a day holy for the Lord. Anyone who works during the Sabbath day must be put to death. ¹⁶The Israelites must remember the Sabbath day. It is an agreement between them and me that will continue from now on. ¹⁷The Sabbath day will be a sign between me and the Israelites forever. This is because in six days I, the Lord, made the sky and the earth. And on the seventh day I did not work. I rested.'"

¹⁸So the Lord finished speaking to Moses on Mount Sinai. Then the Lord gave him the two stone tablets with the agreement written on them. The finger of God wrote the commands on the stones.

THE PEOPLE MAKE A GOLD CALF

32 The people saw that a long time had passed. And Moses had not come down from the mountain. So they gathered around Aaron.

> I have given him the skill, ability and knowledge to do all kinds of work.
>
> –EXODUS 31:3

They said to him, "Moses led us out of Egypt. But we don't know what has happened to him. So make us gods who will lead us."

2Aaron said to the people, "Take off the gold earrings that your wives, sons and daughters are wearing. Bring them to me." 3So all the people took their gold earrings and brought them to Aaron. 4Aaron took the gold from the people. Then he melted it and made a statue of a calf. He finished it with a tool. Then the people said, "Israel! These are your gods who brought you out of the land of Egypt!"

5Aaron saw all this, and he built an altar before the calf. Then he made an announcement. He said, "Tomorrow there will be a special feast to honor the Lord." 6The people got up early the next morning. They offered whole burnt offerings and fellowship offerings. First the people sat down to eat and drink. Then they got up and had wild parties.

7And the Lord said to Moses, "Go down from this mountain. Your people, the people you brought out of the land of Egypt, have done a terrible sin. 8They have quickly turned away from the things I commanded them to do. They have made for themselves a calf of melted gold. They have worshiped that calf and offered sacrifices to it. The people have said, 'Israel, these are your gods who brought you out of Egypt.'"

9The Lord said to Moses, "I have seen these people. I know that they are very stubborn people. 10So now do not stop me. I am so angry with them that I am going to destroy them. Then I will make you and your descendants a great nation."

11But Moses begged the Lord his God. Moses said, "Lord, don't let your anger destroy your people. You brought these people out of Egypt with your great power and strength. 12Don't let the people of Egypt say, 'The Lord brought the Israelites out of Egypt. But he planned to kill them in the mountains and destroy them from the earth.' So

stop being angry. Don't destroy your people. 13Remember the men who served you—Abraham, Isaac and Israel. You promised with an oath to them. You said, 'I will make your descendants as many as the stars in the sky. I will give your descendants all this land that I have promised them. It will be theirs forever.'" 14So the Lord changed his mind. He did not destroy the people as he had said he might.

15Then Moses went down the mountain. In his hands he had the two stone tablets with the agreement on them. The commands were written on both sides of each stone, front and back. 16God himself had made the stones. And God himself had written the commands on the stones.

17Then Joshua heard the noise of the people shouting. He said to Moses, "It sounds like war down in the camp."

18Moses answered:

"It is not an army's shout of victory.
   It is not an army's cry of defeat.
   It is the sound of singing that I
      hear."

19When Moses came close to the camp, he saw the gold calf and the dancing. He became very angry. He threw down the stone tablets which he was carrying. He broke them at the bottom of the mountain. 20Then he took the calf that the people had made. He melted it in the fire. And he ground the gold until it became powder. He threw the powder into the water. And he forced the Israelites to drink that water.

21Moses said to Aaron, "What did these people do to you? Why did you cause them to do such a terrible sin?"

22Aaron answered, "Don't be angry, master. You know that these people are always ready to do wrong. 23The people said to me, 'Moses led us out of Egypt. But we don't know what has happened to him. So make us gods who will lead us.' 24So I told the people, 'Take off your gold jewelry.' So they gave me the gold. I threw it into the fire and out came this calf!"

²⁵Moses saw that the people were acting wildly. He saw that Aaron had let them get out of control. Their enemies would laugh at them. ²⁶So Moses stood at the entrance to the camp. He said, "Let anyone who wants to follow the Lord come to me." And all the people from the family of Levi gathered around Moses.

²⁷Then Moses said to them, "The Lord, the God of Israel, says this: 'Every man must put on his sword and go through the camp from one end to the other. Each man must kill his brother, his friend and his neighbor.'" ²⁸The people from the family of Levi obeyed Moses. That day about 3,000 of the people of Israel died. ²⁹Then Moses said, "Today you have been given for service to the Lord. You were willing to kill your own sons and brothers. And God has blessed you for this."

³⁰The next day Moses told the people, "You have done a terrible sin. But now I will go up to the Lord. Maybe I can do something so your sins will be removed. Then you will belong to God again." ³¹So Moses went back to the Lord and said, "How terrible it is! These people have sinned horribly. They have made for themselves gods from gold. ³²Now, forgive them of this sin. If you will not, then erase my name. Erase it from the book in which you have written the names of your people."

³³But the Lord told Moses, "I will erase from my book the names of the people who sin against me. ³⁴So now, go. Lead the people where I have told you. My angel will lead you. When the time comes to punish, I will punish them for their sin."

³⁵So the Lord caused terrible things to happen to the people. He did this because of what they did with the calf Aaron had made.

33 Then the Lord said to Moses, "You and the people you

brought out of Egypt must leave this place. Go to the land that I promised with an oath to give to Abraham, Isaac and Jacob. I said, 'I will give that land to your descendants.' ²I will send an angel to lead you. And I will force these people out of the land: the Canaanites, Amorites, Hittites, Perizzites, Hivites and Jebusites. ³Go up to the land where much food grows. But I will not go with you. This is because I might destroy you on the way. You are such a stubborn people."

⁴The people heard this bad news, and they became very sad. None of them put on jewelry. ⁵This was because the Lord had said to Moses, "Tell the Israelites, 'You are a stubborn people. If I were to go with you even for a moment, I would destroy you. So take off all your jewelry. Then I will decide what to do with you.'" ⁶So the people of Israel took off their jewelry at Mount Sinai.

THE MEETING TENT

⁷Moses used to take a tent and set it up a long way outside the camp. Moses called it the "Meeting Tent." A person might want to ask the Lord about something. Then he would go to the Meeting Tent outside the camp. ⁸Anytime Moses went out to the Tent, all the people would rise. They stood at the entrances of their tents and watched Moses until he entered the Meeting Tent. ⁹When Moses went into the Tent, the pillar of cloud would always come down. It would stay at the entrance of the Tent while the Lord spoke with Moses. ¹⁰The people saw the pillar of cloud at the entrance of the Tent. Then they stood and worshiped, each person at the entrance of his own tent.

¹¹The Lord spoke to Moses face to face as a man speaks with his friend. Then Moses would return to the camp. But Moses' young helper, Joshua son of Nun, did not leave the Tent.

¹²Moses said to the Lord, "You have told me to lead these people. But you did not say whom you would send with me.

You have said to me, 'I know you very well. I am pleased with you.' ¹³If I have truly pleased you, show me your plans. Then I may know you and continue to please you. Remember that this nation is your people."

¹⁴The Lord answered, "I myself will go with you. And I will give you victory."

¹⁵Then Moses said to him, "If you yourself don't go with us, then don't send us away from this place. ¹⁶If you don't go with us, no one will know that you are pleased with me and your people. These people and I would be no different from any other people on earth."

¹⁷Then the Lord said to Moses, "I will do what you ask. This is because I know you very well, and I am pleased with you."

MOSES AND GOD'S GREATNESS

¹⁸Then Moses said, "Now, please show me your greatness."

¹⁹The Lord answered, "I will cause all my goodness to pass in front of you. I will announce my name, the Lord, so you can hear it. I will show kindness to anyone I want to show kindness. I will show mercy to anyone I want to show mercy. ²⁰But you cannot see my face. No one can see me and stay alive.

²¹"There is a place near me where you may stand on a rock. ²²My greatness will pass that place. I will put you in a large crack in that rock. And I will cover you with my hand until I have passed by. ²³Then I will take away my hand, and you will see my back. But my face must not be seen."

MOSES GETS NEW TABLETS

34 The Lord said to Moses, "Cut two more stone tablets like the first two. I will write the same words on them that were on the first two stones which you broke. ²Be ready tomorrow morning. Then come up on Mount Sinai. Stand before me there on the top of the mountain. ³No one may come with you. No one should even be seen any place on the mountain. Not even the sheep or cattle may eat grass near that mountain."

⁴So Moses cut two stone tablets like the first ones. Then early the next morning he went up Mount Sinai. He did this just as the Lord had commanded him. Moses carried the two stone tablets with him. ⁵Then the Lord came down in the cloud and stood there with Moses. And the Lord called out his name, the Lord.

⁶The Lord passed in front of Moses and said, "I am the Lord. The Lord is a God who shows mercy and is kind. The Lord doesn't become angry quickly. The Lord has great love and faithfulness. ⁷The Lord is kind to thousands of people. The Lord forgives people for wrong and sin and turning against him. But the Lord does not forget to punish guilty people. The Lord will punish not only the guilty people. He will also punish their children, their grandchildren, their great-grandchildren and their great-great-grandchildren."

⁸Then Moses quickly bowed to the ground and worshiped. ⁹Moses said, "Lord, if you are pleased with me, please go with us. I know that these are stubborn people. But forgive our evil and our sin. Take us as your own people."

¹⁰Then the Lord said, "I am making this agreement with you. I will do miracles in front of all your people. These things have never before been done for any other nation on earth. The people with you will see my work. I, the Lord, will do wonderful things for you. ¹¹Obey the things I command you today, and I will force your enemies to leave your land. I will force out the Amorites, Canaanites, Hittites, Perizzites, Hivites and Jebusites ahead of you. ¹²Be careful. Don't make any agreement with the people who live in the land where you are going. It will bring you trouble. ¹³But destroy their altars. Break their stone pillars. Cut down their Asherah idols. ¹⁴Don't worship any other god. This is because I, the Lord, the Jealous One, am a jealous God.

¹⁵"Be careful. Don't make any agreements with the people who live in that land. They will worship their false gods. And they will invite you to join them. Then you will join them, and you will eat their sacrifices. ¹⁶You might choose some of their daughters as wives for your sons. Those daughters worship false gods. They might lead your sons to do the same thing.

¹⁷"Do not make gods of melted metal.

¹⁸"Celebrate the Feast of Unleavened Bread. For seven days you must eat bread made without yeast as I commanded you. Do this during the month I have chosen, the month of Abib. This is because in that month you came out of Egypt.

¹⁹"Every firstborn cow or sheep that is born to each animal belongs to me. ²⁰You may buy back a donkey by paying for it with a lamb. But if you don't want to buy back a donkey, you must break its neck. You must buy back all your firstborn sons.

"No one is to come before me without a gift.

²¹"You must work for six days. But on the seventh day you must rest. You must do this even during the planting season and harvest season.

²²"Celebrate the Feast of Weeks when you gather the first grain of the wheat harvest. And celebrate the Feast of Harvest in the fall.

²³"Three times each year all your men must come before the Master, the Lord, the God of Israel. ²⁴I will force out nations ahead of you. I will expand the borders of your land. You will go before the Lord your God three times each year. And at that time no one will try to take your land from you.

²⁵"Do not offer the blood of a sacrifice to me with anything containing yeast. And do not leave any of the sacrifice of the Feast of Passover. It must not be left until the next morning.

²⁶"Bring the best first crops that you harvest from your ground. Bring those things to the Tent of the Lord your God.

"You must not cook a young goat in its mother's milk."

²⁷Then the Lord said to Moses, "Write down these words. This is because with these words I have made an agreement with you and Israel."

²⁸Moses stayed there with the Lord 40 days and 40 nights. During that time he did not eat food or drink water. And Moses wrote the words of the agreement—the Ten Commandments—on the stone tablets.

THE FACE OF MOSES SHINES

²⁹Then Moses came down from Mount Sinai. In his hands he was carrying the two stone tablets of the agreement. But Moses did not know that his face was shining because he had talked with the Lord. ³⁰Aaron and all the people of Israel saw that Moses' face was shining. So they were afraid to go near him. ³¹But Moses called to them. So Aaron and all the leaders of the people returned to Moses. Moses talked with them. ³²After that, all the people of Israel came near him. And he gave them all the commands that the Lord had given him on Mount Sinai.

³³When Moses finished speaking to the people, he put a covering over his face. ³⁴Anytime Moses went before the Lord to speak with him, Moses took off the covering until he came out. Then Moses would come out and tell the people of Israel the things the Lord had commanded. ³⁵The Israelites would see that Moses' face was shining. So he would cover his face again. He did this until the next time he went in to speak with the Lord.

RULES ABOUT THE SABBATH

35 Moses gathered all the Israelite community together. He said to them, "These are the things the Lord has commanded you to do. ²You are to work for six days. But the seventh day will be a holy day, a Sabbath of rest to honor the Lord. Anyone who works on that day must be put to death. ³On the Sabbath day you must not light a fire in any of your houses."

⁴Moses said to all the Israelites, "This is what the Lord has commanded: ⁵From what you have, take an offering for the Lord. Let everyone who is willing bring this offering to the Lord: gold, silver, bronze, ⁶blue, purple and red thread, and fine linen, goat hair ⁷and male sheep skins, colored red. And they may bring fine leather and acacia wood. ⁸They may also bring olive oil for the lamps, spices for the special olive oil used for appointing priests and for the sweet-smelling incense. ⁹And they may bring onyx stones and other jewels to be put on the holy vest and chest covering of the priests.

¹⁰"Let all the skilled workers come and make everything the Lord commanded: ¹¹the Holy Tent, its outer tent and its covering, the hooks, frames, cross-bars, posts and bases; ¹²the Ark of the Covenant, its poles, lid and the curtain in front of it; ¹³the table and its poles, all the things that go with the table and the bread that shows we are in God's presence; ¹⁴the lampstand for the light and all the things that go with it, the lamps and olive oil for the light; ¹⁵the altar of incense and its poles, the special oil and the sweet-smelling incense, the curtain for the entrance of the Meeting Tent; ¹⁶the altar of burnt offering and its bronze screen, its poles and all its tools, the bronze bowl and its base; ¹⁷the curtains around the courtyard, their posts and bases, and the curtain at the entry to the courtyard; ¹⁸the pegs of the Holy Tent and of the courtyard and their ropes; ¹⁹the special clothes that the priest will wear in the Holy Place. These

are the holy clothes for Aaron the priest and his sons to wear when they serve as priests."

²⁰Then all the people of Israel went away from Moses. ²¹Everyone who wanted to give came and brought a gift to the Lord. These gifts were used for making the Meeting Tent, all the things in the Tent and the special clothes. ²²All the men and women who wanted to give brought gold jewelry of all kinds. They brought pins, earrings, rings and bracelets. They all presented their gold to the Lord. ²³Everyone who had blue, purple and red thread, and fine linen came and gave it to the Lord. Anyone who had goat hair or male sheep skins colored red or fine leather brought them to the Lord. ²⁴Everyone who could give silver or bronze brought that as a gift to the Lord. Everyone who had acacia wood to be used in the work brought it. ²⁵Every skilled woman used her hands to make the blue, purple and red thread and fine linen. And they brought what they had made. ²⁶All the women who were skilled and wanted to help made thread of the goat hair. ²⁷The leaders brought onyx stones and other jewels. These stones and jewels were put on the holy vest and chest covering for the priest. ²⁸They also brought spices and olive oil. These were used for the sweet-smelling incense, the special oil and the oil to burn in the lamps. ²⁹All the men and women of Israel who wanted to help brought gifts to the Lord. They were used for all the work the Lord had commanded Moses and the people to do.

³⁰Then Moses said to the people of Israel, "Look, the Lord has chosen Bezalel. He is the son of Uri the son of Hur, from the tribe of Judah. ³¹The Lord has

> Everyone who wanted to give came and brought a gift to the Lord.
>
> –EXODUS 35:21

filled Bezalel with the Spirit of God. The Lord has given Bezalel the skill, ability and knowledge to do all kinds of work. ³²He is able to design pieces to be made of gold, silver and bronze. ³³He is able to cut stones and jewels and put them in metal. Bezalel can carve wood and do all kinds of work. ³⁴The Lord has given Bezalel and Oholiab the ability to teach others. Oholiab is the son of Ahisamach from the tribe of Dan. ³⁵The Lord has given them the skill to do all kinds of work. They are able to cut designs in metal and stone. They can plan and sew designs in the fine linen with the blue, purple and red thread. And they are also able to weave things.

36 "So Bezalel, Oholiab and every skilled person will do the work the Lord has commanded. The Lord gave these people the wisdom and understanding to do all the skilled work needed to build the Holy Tent."

²Then Moses called Bezalel, Oholiab and all the other skilled people to whom the Lord had given skills. And they came because they wanted to help with the work. ³They received from Moses everything the people of Israel had brought as gifts to build the Holy Tent. The people continued to bring gifts each morning because they wanted to. ⁴So all the skilled workers left the work they were doing on the Holy Tent. And they went to speak to Moses. They said, ⁵"The people are bringing more than we need to do the work the Lord commanded."

⁶Then Moses sent this command throughout the camp: "No man or woman should make anything else as a gift for the Holy Tent." So the people were kept from giving more. ⁷What they had was already more than enough to do all the work.

THE HOLY TENT

⁸Then the skilled workers made the Holy Tent. They made the ten pieces of blue, purple and red cloth. And they sewed designs of creatures with wings on the pieces. ⁹Each piece was the same size. It was 42 feet long and 6 feet wide. ¹⁰Five of the pieces were fastened together to make one set. The other five were fastened together to make another set. ¹¹Then they made loops of blue cloth along the edge of the end piece on the first set of five. They did the same thing with the other set of five. ¹²There were 50 loops on one piece and 50 loops on the other piece. The loops were opposite each other. ¹³Then they made 50 gold hooks to join the two pieces together. So the Holy Tent was joined together as one piece.

¹⁴Then the workers made another tent of 11 pieces of cloth made of goat hair. This was to put over the Holy Tent. ¹⁵All 11 pieces were the same size. They were 45 feet long and 6 feet wide. ¹⁶The workers sewed five pieces together into one set. Then they sewed six together into another set. ¹⁷They made 50 loops along the edge of the outside piece of one set. And they made 50 loops along the edge of the outside piece of the other set. ¹⁸Then they made 50 bronze rings to join the two sets of cloth together and make the tent one piece. ¹⁹Then they made two more coverings for the outer tent. One covering was made of male sheep skin colored red. The other covering was made of fine leather.

²⁰Then they made upright frames of acacia wood. ²¹Each board was 15 feet tall and 27 inches wide. ²²There were two pegs side by side on each frame. Every frame of the Holy Tent was made this same way. ²³They made 20 frames for the south side of the Tent. ²⁴Then they made 40 silver bases that went under the 20 frames. There were two bases for every frame—one for each peg of each board. ²⁵They also made 20 frames for the north side of the Holy Tent. ²⁶They made 40 silver bases—2 to go under each frame. ²⁷They made 6 frames for the rear or west end of the Holy Tent ²⁸and 2 frames for the corners at the rear of the Holy Tent. ²⁹These 2 frames were joined together

from the bottom to the top with a metal ring. They did this for each of these corners. ³⁰So there were 8 frames and 16 silver bases—2 bases under each frame.

³¹Then they made crossbars of acacia wood to connect the upright frames of the Holy Tent. Five crossbars held the frames together on one side of the Tent. ³²Five crossbars held the frames together on the other side. And five crossbars held the frames together on the west end, at the rear of the Tent. ³³They made the crossbar run along the entire length of each side and rear of the Tent. It was set halfway up the frames. ³⁴They made gold rings on the sides of the frames. They passed the crossbars through the rings. They covered the frames and the crossbars with gold.

³⁵Then they made the curtain with blue, purple and red thread, and fine linen. A skilled craftsman sewed designs of creatures with wings on it. ³⁶They made four posts of acacia wood and covered them with gold. Then they made gold hooks for the posts. And they made four silver bases in which to set the posts. ³⁷Then they made a curtain for the entrance to the Tent. They used blue, purple and red thread, and fine linen. A person who sewed well sewed designs on it. ³⁸Then they made five posts and hooks for it. They covered the tops of the posts and their bands with gold. And they made five bronze bases for the posts.

THE ARK OF THE COVENANT

37 Bezalel made the Ark of the Covenant of acacia wood. The Ark of the Covenant was 45 inches long, 27 inches wide and 27 inches high. ²He covered the inside and outside of the Ark of the Covenant with pure gold. Then he put a gold strip around it. ³He made four gold rings for it and attached them to its four feet. There were two rings on each side. ⁴Then he made poles of acacia wood and covered them with gold. ⁵He put the poles through the rings on each side of the Ark of the

Covenant to carry it. ⁶Then he made a lid of pure gold. It was 45 inches long and 27 inches wide. ⁷Then Bezalel hammered gold to make two creatures with wings. He attached them to each end of the lid. ⁸He made one creature with wings on one end of the lid. He made the other creature with wings on the other end. He attached them to the lid so that it would be one piece. ⁹The creatures' wings were spread out over the lid. The creatures faced each other across the lid.

THE TABLE

¹⁰Then he made the table of acacia wood. The table was 36 inches long, 18 inches wide and 27 inches high. ¹¹He covered the table with pure gold. He put a gold strip around it. ¹²Then he made a frame 3 inches high that stood up all around the edge. He put a gold strip around the frame. ¹³Then he made four gold rings for the table. He attached them to the four corners of the table, where the four legs were. ¹⁴The rings were put close to the frame around the top of the table. The rings held the poles that were used to carry the table. ¹⁵The poles for carrying the table were made of acacia wood. They were covered with gold. ¹⁶Then he made of pure gold all the things that were used on the table: the plates, bowls, cups and jars used for pouring the drink offerings.

THE LAMPSTAND

¹⁷Then he made the lampstand of pure gold. He hammered out its base and stand. Its flower-like cups, buds and petals were joined together in one piece with the base and stand. ¹⁸There were three branches on one side of the lampstand and three branches on the other. ¹⁹Each branch had three cups shaped like almond flowers. Each cup had a bud and a petal. ²⁰There were four more cups shaped like almond flowers on the lampstand itself. Each cup had its buds and petals. ²¹Three pairs of branches went out from the lampstand. A bud was

under the place where each pair was attached to the lampstand. ²²The buds, branches and lampstand were all one piece of pure, hammered gold. ²³He made seven pure gold lamps for this lampstand. Then he made pure gold wick trimmers and trays. ²⁴He used about 75 pounds of pure gold to make the lampstand and all the things that go with it.

THE ALTAR FOR BURNING INCENSE

²⁵Then he made the altar of incense of acacia wood. The altar was square. It was 18 inches long, 18 inches wide and 36 inches high. Each corner stuck out like a horn. Each corner was joined into one piece with the altar. ²⁶He covered the top and all the sides and the corners with pure gold. Then he put gold trim around the altar. ²⁷He made two gold rings and put them below the trim on opposite sides of the altar. These rings held the poles for carrying the altar. ²⁸He made the poles of acacia wood and covered them with gold.

²⁹Then he made the holy olive oil for appointing the priests. He also made the pure, sweet-smelling incense. He made them like a person who mixes perfumes.

THE ALTAR

38 Then he built the altar for burning offerings. He made the altar of acacia wood. The altar was square. It was 7½ feet long, 7½ feet wide and 4½ feet high. ²He made each corner stick out like a horn. The horns and the altar were joined together in one piece. Then he covered the altar with bronze. ³He made all the tools of bronze to use on the altar: the pots, shovels, bowls for sprinkling blood, meat forks and pans for carrying the fire. ⁴He made a large bronze screen to hold the burning wood for the altar. He put the screen inside the altar, under its rim, halfway up from the bottom. ⁵He made bronze rings for holding the poles for carrying the altar. He put the rings at the four corners of the screen. ⁶Then he made poles of acacia wood and covered them with bronze. ⁷He put the poles through the rings on both sides of the altar. They were used for carrying the altar. He made the altar of boards and left the inside hollow.

THE BRONZE BOWL

⁸He made the bronze bowl for washing. He built it on a bronze stand. He used the bronze of mirrors. These mirrors belonged to the women who served at the entrance to the Meeting Tent.

THE COURTYARD OF THE HOLY TENT

⁹Then he made a wall of curtains to form a courtyard around the Holy Tent. On the south side the curtains were 150 feet long and were made of fine linen. ¹⁰The curtains hung on silver hooks and bands. These were on 20 bronze posts on 20 bronze bases. ¹¹On the north side the wall of curtains was also 150 feet long. It hung on silver hooks and bands on 20 posts with 20 bronze bases.

¹²On the west side of the courtyard, the wall of curtains was 75 feet long. It was held up by silver hooks and bands on 10 posts and 10 bases. ¹³The east side was 75 feet wide. ¹⁴On one side of the entry there was a wall of curtains that was 22½ feet long. It was held up by 3 posts and 3 bases. ¹⁵On the other side of the entry there was a wall of curtains 22½ feet long. It was held up by 3 posts and 3 bases. ¹⁶All the curtains around the courtyard were made of fine linen. ¹⁷The bases for the posts were made of bronze. The hooks and the bands on the posts were made of silver. The tops of the posts were covered with silver also. All the posts in the courtyard had silver bands.

¹⁸The curtain for the entry of the courtyard was made of blue, purple and red thread, and fine linen. It was sewn by a person who could sew well. The curtain was 30 feet long and 7½ feet high. It was the same height as the

curtains around the courtyard. [19]The curtain was held up by 4 posts and 4 bronze bases. The hooks and bands on the posts were made of silver. The tops on the posts were covered with silver. [20]All the tent pegs for the Holy Tent and for the curtains around the courtyard were made of bronze.

[21]This is a list of the metals used to make the Holy Tent. This is where the two flat stones with the Ten Commandments are kept. Moses ordered the Levites to make this list. Ithamar son of Aaron was in charge of keeping the list. [22]Bezalel son of Uri made everything the Lord commanded Moses. Uri was the son of Hur of the tribe of Judah. [23]Oholiab son of Ahisamach of the tribe of Dan helped him. Oholiab could cut designs into metal and stone. He was a designer. He was also skilled at sewing the blue, purple and red thread, and fine linen.

[24]The total amount of gold used to build the Holy Tent was presented to the Lord. It weighed over 2,000 pounds, as set by the Holy Place measure.

[25]The silver was given by the members of the community who were counted. It weighed 7,550 pounds, as set by the Holy Place measure. [26]All the men 20 years old or older were counted. There were 603,550 men, and each man had to pay 1/5 ounce of silver. This is the weight as set by the Holy Place measure. [27]Of this silver, 7,500 pounds was used to make the 100 bases. These bases were for the Holy Tent and for the curtain. There was 75 pounds of silver in each base. [28]The other 50 pounds of silver was used to make the hooks for the posts. It was also used to cover the tops of the posts and to make the bands on the posts.

[29]The bronze which was presented to the Lord weighed about 5,000 pounds. [30]They used the bronze to make the bases at the entrance of the Meeting Tent. They also used the bronze to make the altar and the bronze screen. And this bronze was used to make all the tools for the altar. [31]This bronze was also used to make bases for the wall of curtains around the courtyard. It was used for the bases for the curtains at the entry to the courtyard. And this bronze was used to make the tent pegs for the Holy Tent and curtains that surrounded the courtyard.

CLOTHES FOR THE PRIESTS

39 They used blue, purple and red thread to make woven clothes for the priests. They were to wear these when they served in the Holy Place. They also made the holy clothes for Aaron as the Lord had commanded Moses.

[2]They made the holy vest of gold and blue, purple and red thread, and fine linen. [3]They hammered the gold into sheets. Then they cut the gold into long, thin strips. They worked the gold into the blue, purple and red thread, and fine linen. This was done by a skilled craftsman. [4]They made the shoulder straps for the holy vest. These straps were attached to the top corners of the vest. Then the shoulder straps were tied together over each shoulder. [5]The skillfully woven belt was made in the same way. It was joined to the holy vest as one piece. It was made of gold and blue, purple and red thread, and fine linen. It was made the way the Lord commanded Moses.

[6]They put gold around the onyx stones. Then they wrote the names of the sons of Israel on these gems. They did that as a person carves words and designs on a seal. [7]Then they attached the gems on the shoulder straps of the holy vest. These gems are reminders of the 12 sons of Israel. This was done the way the Lord had commanded Moses.

[8]The skilled craftsmen made the chest covering. It was made like the holy vest. It was made of gold and blue, purple and red thread, and fine linen. [9]The chest covering was square, nine inches long and nine inches wide. It was folded double to make a pocket.

¹⁰Then they put four rows of beautiful jewels on it. In the first row there was a ruby, a topaz and a yellow quartz. ¹¹In the second row there was a turquoise, a sapphire and an emerald. ¹²In the third row there was a jacinth, an agate and an amethyst. ¹³In the fourth row there was a chrysolite, an onyx and a jasper. Gold was put around these jewels to attach them to the chest covering. ¹⁴The names of the sons of Israel were carved on these 12 jewels as a person carves a seal. Each jewel had the name of 1 of the 12 tribes of Israel.

¹⁵They made chains of pure gold for the chest covering. They were twisted together like a rope. ¹⁶The workers made two gold pieces and two gold rings. They put the two gold rings on the two upper corners of the chest covering. ¹⁷Then they put two gold chains in the two rings. These are at the ends of the chest covering. ¹⁸They fastened the other two ends of the chains to the two gold pieces. Then they attached these gold pieces to the two shoulder straps in the front of the holy vest. ¹⁹They made two more gold rings and put them at the lower corners of the chest covering. They put them on the inside edge next to the holy vest. ²⁰Then they made two more gold rings on the bottom of the shoulder straps in front of the holy vest. These rings were near the seam, just above the woven belt of the holy vest. ²¹They used a blue ribbon and tied the rings of the chest covering to the rings of the holy vest. This connected it to the woven belt. In this way the chest covering would not swing out from the holy vest. They did all these things the way the Lord commanded.

²²Then they made the outer robe to be worn under the holy vest. It was woven of blue cloth. ²³They made a hole in the center of the outer robe. A woven collar was sewn around this hole so it would not tear. ²⁴Then they made balls like pomegranates of blue, purple and red thread, and fine linen. They hung them around the bottom of the outer robe. ²⁵They also made bells of pure gold. They hung these around the bottom of the outer robe between the balls. ²⁶So around the bottom of the outer robe there was a bell and a pomegranate ball, a bell and a pomegranate ball. The priest wore this outer robe when he served as priest, just as the Lord had commanded Moses.

²⁷They wove inner robes of fine linen for Aaron and his sons. ²⁸And they made turbans and underclothes of fine linen. ²⁹Then they made the cloth belt of fine linen and blue, purple and red thread. Designs were sewn onto the cloth. These things were made as the Lord had commanded Moses.

³⁰They made a strip of pure gold, which is the holy crown. They carved these words in the gold: "Holy to the Lord." They did it as one might carve on a seal. ³¹Then they tied this flat piece to the turban with a blue ribbon. This was done as the Lord had commanded Moses.

³²So all the work on the Meeting Tent was finished. The Israelites did everything just as the Lord had commanded Moses. ³³Then they brought the Holy Tent to Moses: the Tent and all its furniture, hooks, frames, crossbars, posts and bases; ³⁴the covering made of male sheep skins colored red, the covering made of fine leather and the curtain that covered the entrance to the Most Holy Place; ³⁵the Ark of the Covenant, its poles and lid; ³⁶the table, all its containers and the bread that showed they were in God's presence; ³⁷the pure gold lampstand with its lamps in a row, all its tools and the olive oil for the light; ³⁸the gold altar, the special olive oil used for appointing priests, the sweet-smelling incense, and the curtain that covered the entrance to the Tent; ³⁹the bronze altar and its screen, its poles and all its tools, the bowl and its stand; ⁴⁰the curtains for the courtyard with their posts and bases, the curtain that covered the entry to the courtyard, the cords, pegs and all the things in the Meeting

Tent. ⁴¹They brought the clothes for the priests to wear when they served in the Holy Tent: the holy clothes for Aaron the priest and the clothes for his sons. They wore these when they served as priests.

⁴²The Israelites had done all this work just as the Lord had commanded Moses. ⁴³Moses looked closely at all the work. He saw they had done it just as the Lord had commanded. So Moses blessed them.

SETTING UP THE HOLY TENT

40 Then the Lord said this to Moses: ²"On the first day of the first month, set up the Holy Tent, which is the Meeting Tent. ³Put the Ark of the Covenant in the Meeting Tent. Hang the curtain in front of the Ark of the Covenant. ⁴Then bring in the table. Arrange everything on the table that should be there. Then bring in the lampstand and set up its lamps. ⁵Put the gold altar for burning incense in front of the Ark of the Covenant. Then put the curtain at the entrance to the Holy Tent.

⁶"Put the altar of burnt offerings in front of the entrance of the Holy Tent, the Meeting Tent. ⁷Put the bowl between the Meeting Tent and the altar. Put water in the bowl. ⁸Set up the courtyard around the Holy Tent. Then put the curtain at the entry to the courtyard.

⁹"Use the special olive oil and pour it on the Holy Tent and everything in it. Give the Tent and all that is in it for service to the Lord. They will be holy. ¹⁰Pour the special oil on the altar for burning offerings. Pour it on all its tools. Give the altar for service to God. It will be very holy. ¹¹Then pour the special olive oil on the bowl and the base under it. When you do this, they will be given for service to God.

¹²"Bring Aaron and his sons to the entrance of the Meeting Tent. Wash them with water. ¹³Then put the holy clothes on Aaron. Pour the special oil on him, and give him for service to God. Then he may serve me as a priest. ¹⁴Bring Aaron's sons and put the inner robes on them. ¹⁵Pour the special oil on them to make them priests. Do this the same way that you appointed their father as priest. Then they may also serve me as priests. Pouring oil on them will make them a family of priests. They and their descendants will be priests from now on."

¹⁶Moses did everything that the Lord commanded him.

¹⁷So the Holy Tent was set up. It was the first day of the first month during the second year after they left Egypt. ¹⁸When Moses set up the Holy Tent, he put the bases in place. Then he put the frames on the bases. Next he put the crossbars through the rings of the frames and set up the posts. ¹⁹After that, Moses spread the cloth over the Holy Tent. Then he put the covering over the Tent. He did these things just as the Lord commanded.

²⁰Moses put the flat stones into the Ark of the Covenant. These had God's law written on them. Moses put the poles through the rings of the Ark of the Covenant. Then he put the lid on it. ²¹Next Moses brought the Ark of the Covenant into the Tent. He hung the curtain to cover the Ark of the Covenant. Moses did these things just as the Lord commanded him.

²²Moses put the table in the Meeting Tent. He put it on the north side of the Holy Tent in front of the curtain. ²³Then he put the bread on the table before the Lord. He did this just as the

> Moses did everything that the Lord commanded him.
>
> –EXODUS 40:16

Lord commanded him. [24]Moses put the lampstand in the Meeting Tent. He put it on the south side of the Holy Tent across from the table. [25]Then he put the lamps on the lampstand before the Lord. He did this just as the Lord commanded him.

[26]Moses put the gold altar for burning incense in the Meeting Tent. He put it in front of the curtain. [27]Then he burned sweet-smelling incense on it, just as the Lord commanded him. [28]Then he hung the curtain at the entrance to the Holy Tent.

[29]He put the altar for burning sacrifices at the entrance to the Holy Tent, the Meeting Tent. Then Moses offered a whole burnt offering and grain offerings on that altar. He did these things just as the Lord commanded him. [30]Moses put the bowl between the Meeting Tent and the altar for burning sacrifices. Moses put water in the bowl for washing. [31]Moses, Aaron and Aaron's sons used this water to wash their hands and feet. [32]They washed themselves every time they entered the Meeting Tent. They also washed themselves every time they went near the altar for burning sacrifices. They did these things just as the Lord commanded Moses.

★ Exodus 40:36–38

God's goodness filled the Holy Tent, and Moses couldn't go in. A cloud covered the tent, and at night a fire lit up the cloud so the Israelites could always see it—even in the dark. The Israelites only traveled when the cloud began to move away.

Have you ever played Follow the Leader? One person is in charge, and whatever he or she does, you do it too. Jesus is our leader. We should learn about Jesus and do what he does. The best way to know Jesus is to read God's word, the Bible. Then you will know how to follow him. The more you know about Jesus, the more you can be like him.

The people of Israel followed God by following his cloud. Now we have the Bible to show us how to live. It's like a handbook for the family of God!

³³Then Moses set up the courtyard around the Holy Tent. He put the altar for burning sacrifices in the courtyard. Then he put up the curtain at the entry to the courtyard. So Moses finished the work.

THE CLOUD OVER THE HOLY TENT

³⁴Then the cloud covered the Meeting Tent. The greatness of the Lord filled the Holy Tent. ³⁵Moses could not enter the Meeting Tent. This was because the cloud had settled on it. And this was because the greatness of the Lord filled the Holy Tent.

³⁶When the cloud rose from the Holy Tent, the Israelites would begin to travel. ³⁷But as long as the cloud stayed on the Holy Tent, the people did not travel. They stayed in that place until the cloud rose. ³⁸So the cloud of the Lord was over the Holy Tent during the day. And there was a fire in the cloud at night. So all the Israelites could see the cloud while they traveled.

Numbers

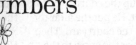

THE PRIESTS' BLESSINGS

6 ²²The Lord said to Moses, ²³"Tell Aaron and his sons, 'This is how you should bless the Israelites. Say to them:

²⁴ "May the Lord bless you and keep you.
²⁵ May the Lord show you his kindness. May he have mercy on you.
²⁶ May the Lord watch over you and give you peace."'

²⁷"So Aaron and his sons will bless the Israelites with my name. And I will bless them."

THE HOLY TENT

7 When Moses finished setting up the Holy Tent, he gave it for service to the Lord. Moses poured olive oil on the Tent and on everything used in the Tent. He also poured oil on the altar and all its tools. In this way he prepared them for service to the Lord. ²Then the leaders of Israel made offerings. These were the heads of the families and leaders of each tribe. They were the men who counted the people. ³They brought to the Lord 6 covered carts and 12 oxen. Each leader gave an ox. Every two leaders gave a cart. They gave these to the Holy Tent.

⁴The Lord said to Moses, ⁵"Accept these gifts from the leaders. Use them in the work of the Meeting Tent. Give them to the Levites as they need them."

⁶So Moses accepted the carts and the oxen. He gave them to the Levites. ⁷He gave 2 carts and 4 oxen to the Gershonites. This is what they needed for their work. ⁸Then Moses gave 4 carts and 8 oxen to the Merarites. This is what they needed for their work. Ithamar son of Aaron, the priest, directed the work of all of them. ⁹Moses did not give any oxen or carts to the Kohathites. They were to carry the holy things on their shoulders. This was their job.

¹⁰The oil was poured on the altar. Then the leaders brought their offerings to it to give to the Lord's service. ¹¹The Lord had already told Moses, "Each day one leader must bring his gift. The gifts will make the altar ready for service to me."

¹²⁻⁸³Each of the 12 leaders brought these gifts. Each leader brought 1 silver plate that weighed about 3¼ pounds. And each one brought 1 silver bowl that weighed about 1¾ pounds. These weights were set by the Holy Place measure. Each bowl and plate were filled with fine flour mixed with oil. This was for a grain offering. Each leader also brought a large gold dish that weighed about 4 ounces. It was filled with incense.

Each leader also brought 1 young bull, 1 male sheep and 1 male lamb a year old. These were for a burnt offering. Each leader also brought 1 male goat for a sin offering. Each leader brought 2 oxen, 5 male sheep, 5 male goats and 5 male lambs a year old. All of these were sacrificed for a fellowship offering.

On the first day Nahshon son of Amminadab brought his gifts. He was the leader of the tribe of Judah.

On the second day Nethanel son of Zuar brought his gifts. He was the leader of the tribe of Issachar.

On the third day Eliab son of Helon brought his gifts. He was the leader of the tribe of Zebulun.

On the fourth day Elizur son of Shedeur brought his gifts. He was the leader of the tribe of Reuben.

On the fifth day Shelumiel son of Zurishaddai brought his gifts. He was the leader of the tribe of Simeon.

On the sixth day Eliasaph son of Deuel brought his gifts. He was the leader of the tribe of Gad.

As the Israelites learned how to be a nation that follows the Lord, God had some very important plans for them. One plan was to set priests into place. These priests would work in the Holy Tent—which was like our church building—every day. They would always be there to show the people the way to God. Moses told the new priests what they should say to the people. The words they used were very important to God. The way they spoke God's blessing over his family needed to be just right because it was like it was coming straight from God himself.

Blessings! We say them before our meals. Sometimes we even sing them. But a blessing is much more than simply thanking God for our food. We can bless God, but did you know that God wants to bless you? He wants to give you a happiness that bubbles up from inside. And he wants to meet every need you have! God wants to pour out his blessings on you. And his greatest blessing to you is Jesus. The Bible says that "God has given us every spiritual blessing in heaven" (Ephesians 1:3). But that blessing is in Jesus—or, as the Bibles says, "in Christ."

∙ ∙

When you know God's Son, Jesus, you are blessed with everything you'll ever want or need.

On the seventh day Elishama son of Ammihud brought his gifts. He was the leader of the tribe of Ephraim.

On the eighth day Gamaliel son of Pedahzur brought his gifts. He was the leader of the tribe of Manasseh.

On the ninth day Abidan son of Gideoni brought his gifts. He was the leader of the tribe of Benjamin.

On the tenth day Ahiezer son of Ammishaddai brought his gifts. He was the leader of the tribe of Dan.

On the eleventh day Pagiel son of Ocran brought his gifts. He was the leader of the tribe of Asher.

On the twelfth day Ahira son of Enan brought his gifts. He was the leader of the tribe of Naphtali.

⁸⁴So these were the gifts from the Israelite leaders. Moses poured oil on

the altar. And they brought their gifts to give the altar for service to the Lord. They brought 12 silver plates, 12 silver bowls and 12 gold dishes. ⁸⁵Each silver plate weighed about 3¼ pounds. And each bowl weighed about 1¾ pounds. All the silver plates and silver bowls together weighed about 60 pounds. This weight was set by the Holy Place measure. ⁸⁶The 12 gold dishes filled with incense weighed 4 ounces each. Together the gold dishes weighed about 3 pounds. ⁸⁷The total number of animals for the burnt offering was 12 bulls, 12 male sheep and 12 male lambs a year old. There was also a grain offering. And there were 12 male goats for a sin offering. ⁸⁸The total number of animals for the fellowship offering was 24 bulls, 60 male sheep, 60 male goats and 60 male lambs a year old. All these offerings were for giving the altar to the service of the Lord. This was after Moses had poured oil on it.

⁸⁹Moses went into the Meeting Tent to speak with the Lord. He heard the Lord speaking to him. The voice was coming from between the two gold creatures with wings. They were above the lid of the Ark of the Covenant. And the Lord spoke with him.

THE LAMPSTAND

8 The Lord said to Moses, ²"Speak to Aaron. Tell him, 'Put the seven lamps where they can light the area in front of the lampstand.'"

³Aaron did this. He put the lamps so they lighted the area in front of the lampstand. He obeyed the command the Lord gave Moses. ⁴The lampstand was made from hammered gold. It was gold from its base to the flowers. It was made exactly the way the Lord had showed Moses.

THE LEVITES

⁵The Lord said to Moses, ⁶"Take the Levites away from the other Israelites and make them clean. ⁷This is what you should do to make them clean. Sprinkle the cleansing water on them. Have them shave their bodies and wash their clothes. Then they will be clean. ⁸They must take a young bull and the grain offering that goes with it. The grain offering will be flour mixed with oil. Then take another young bull for a sin offering. ⁹Bring the Levites to the front of the Meeting Tent. And gather all the Israelites around. ¹⁰Bring the Levites before the Lord. Then the Israelites should put their hands on them.ⁿ ¹¹Aaron will present the Levites before the Lord. They will be like an offering presented from the Israelites. Then the Levites will be ready to do the work of the Lord.

¹²"The Levites will put their hands on the bulls' heads. One bull will be a sin offering to the Lord. The other will be a burnt offering. This will remove the sins of the Levites so they will belong to God. ¹³Make the Levites stand in front of Aaron and his sons. Then present the Levites as an offering to the Lord. ¹⁴In this way you must set apart the Levites from the other Israelites. The Levites will be mine.

¹⁵"So make the Levites pure. And present them as an offering. Then they may come to work at the Meeting Tent. ¹⁶They will be given to me from the Israelites. I have taken them for myself. They are mine instead of the firstborn son of every Israelite woman. ¹⁷Every firstborn male in Israel—man or animal—is mine. I killed all the firstborn in Egypt. So now I set them aside for myself. ¹⁸I have taken the Levites instead of all the firstborn sons in Israel. ¹⁹I have chosen the Levites from all the Israelites. And I have given them to Aaron and his sons. They will serve all the Israelites at the Meeting Tent. They will help remove the Israelites' sins so they will belong to God. Then no disaster will strike the Israelites when they approach the Holy Place."

8:10 put...them This showed that the people had a part in giving the Levites their special work.

²⁰So Moses, Aaron and all the Israelites obeyed the Lord. They did with the Levites what the Lord commanded Moses. ²¹The Levites made themselves clean and washed their clothes. Then Aaron presented them as an offering to the Lord. Aaron also removed their sins so they would be pure for the Lord. ²²After that, the Levites came to the Meeting Tent to work. Aaron and his sons told them what to do. They did with the Levites what the Lord commanded Moses.

²³The Lord said to Moses, ²⁴"This command is for the Levites. Every man 25 years old or older must come to the Meeting Tent. They all have a job to do in the work there. ²⁵At the age of 50, he must retire from his job. He doesn't have to work again. ²⁶He may help his fellow Levites with their work at the Meeting Tent. But he must not do the work himself. This is the way you are to give the Levites their jobs."

THE PASSOVER

9 The Lord spoke to Moses in the Desert of Sinai. This was in the first month of the second year after the Israelites left Egypt. He said, ²"Tell the Israelites to celebrate the Passover at the appointed time. ³That appointed time is the fourteenth day of this month. They should celebrate it at twilight. They must obey all the rules about it."

⁴So Moses told the Israelites to celebrate the Passover. ⁵And so they did. It was in the Desert of Sinai at twilight. This was on the fourteenth day of the first month. The Israelites did everything just as the Lord commanded Moses.

⁶But some of the people could not celebrate the Passover on that day. They were unclean because of a dead body. So they went to Moses and Aaron that day. ⁷They said to Moses, "We are unclean because of a dead body. But why should we be kept from offering gifts to the Lord at this appointed time? Why can't we join the other Israelites?"

⁸Moses said to them, "Wait. I will find out what the Lord says about you."

⁹Then the Lord said to Moses, ¹⁰"Tell the Israelites this: 'You or your descendants might become unclean because of a dead body. Or, you might be away on a trip during the Passover. Still celebrate the Lord's Passover. ¹¹But celebrate it at twilight on the fourteenth day of the second month. Eat the lamb with bitter herbs and bread made without yeast. ¹²Don't leave any of it until the next morning. Don't break any of its bones. When you celebrate the Passover, follow all the rules. ¹³Anyone who is clean and is not away on a trip must eat the Passover. If he doesn't, he must be separated from his people. He did not give an offering to the Lord at the appointed time. He must be punished for his sin.

¹⁴"'A foreigner among you may celebrate the Lord's Passover. But he must follow all the rules. You must have the same rules for foreigners as you have for yourselves.'"

THE CLOUD ABOVE THE TENT

¹⁵On the day the Holy Tent was set up, a cloud covered it. (The Holy Tent was also called the Tent of the Agreement.) From dusk until dawn the cloud above the Tent looked like fire. ¹⁶The cloud stayed above the Tent. At night it looked like fire. ¹⁷When the cloud moved from its place over the Tent, the Israelites moved. Wherever the cloud stopped, the Israelites camped. ¹⁸So the Israelites moved at the Lord's

> Moses went into the Meeting Tent to speak with the Lord . . . And the Lord spoke with him.
> –NUMBERS 7:89

command. And they camped at his command. While the cloud stayed over the Tent, they stayed in place. [19]Sometimes the cloud stayed over the Tent for a long time. The Israelites obeyed the Lord and did not move. [20]Sometimes the cloud was over it only a few days. At the Lord's command the people camped. And at his command they moved. [21]Sometimes the cloud stayed only from dusk until dawn. When the cloud lifted the next morning, the people moved. When the cloud lifted, day or night, the people moved. [22]The cloud might stay over the Tent for two days, a month or a year. As long as it stayed, the people would camp. But when the cloud lifted, they moved. [23]At the Lord's command the people camped. And at his command they moved. They obeyed the Lord's order that he commanded through Moses.

THE SILVER TRUMPETS

10 The Lord said to Moses, [2]"Make two trumpets of hammered silver. Use them to call the people together and to march out of camp. [3]When both trumpets are blown, the people should gather. They should gather before you at the entrance to the Meeting Tent. [4]If you blow only one trumpet, the leaders should meet before you. [5]When you blow the trumpets once, the tribes camping on the east should move. [6]When you blow them again, the tribes camping on the south should move. The sound will tell them to move. [7]When you want to gather the people, blow the trumpets. But don't blow them the same way.

[8]"Aaron's sons, the priests, should blow the trumpets. This is a law for you and your descendants from now on. [9]You might be fighting an enemy who attacks you in your own land. Blow the trumpets. The Lord your God will remember you. He will save you from your enemies. [10]Also blow your trumpets at happy times. Blow them during your feasts and at New Moon festivals.

Blow them over your burnt offerings and fellowship offerings. They will help you remember your God. I am the Lord your God."

THE ISRAELITES MOVE CAMP

[11]The cloud lifted from the Tent of the Agreement. This was on the twentieth day of the second month of the second year. [12]So the Israelites moved from the Desert of Sinai. They moved until the cloud stopped in the Desert of Paran. [13]This was their first time to move. They did it as the Lord had commanded Moses.

[14]The divisions from the camp of Judah moved first under their flag. Nahshon son of Amminadab was the commander. [15]Nethanel son of Zuar was over the division of the tribe of Issachar. [16]Eliab son of Helon was over the division of the tribe of Zebulun. [17]Then the Meeting Tent was taken down. The Gershonites and Merarites, who carried it, moved next.

[18]Then came the divisions from the camp of Reuben under their flag. Elizur son of Shedeur was the commander. [19]Shelumiel son of Zurishaddai was over the division of the tribe of Simeon. [20]Eliasaph son of Deuel was over the division of the tribe of Gad. [21]Then came the Kohathites. They carried the holy things. The Holy Tent was to be set up before they arrived.

[22]Next came the divisions from the camp of Ephraim under their flag. Elishama son of Ammihud was the commander. [23]Gamaliel son of Pedahzur was over the division of the tribe of Manasseh. [24]Abidan son of Gideoni was over the division of the tribe of Benjamin.

[25]The last ones were the rear guard for all the tribes. These were the divisions from the camp of Dan under their flag. Ahiezer son of Ammishaddai was the commander. [26]Pagiel son of Ocran was over the division of the tribe of Asher. [27]Ahira son of Enan was over the division of the tribe of Naphtali. [28]This

was the order the Israelite divisions marched in when they moved.

²⁹Hobab was the son of Reuel the Midianite. Reuel, who is also called Jethro, was Moses' father-in-law. Moses said to Hobab, "We are moving to the land God promised to give us. Come with us. We will be good to you. The Lord has promised good things to Israel."

³⁰But Hobab answered, "No, I will not go. I will go back to my own land where I was born."

³¹But Moses said, "Please don't leave us. You know where we can camp in the desert. You can be our guide. ³²Come with us. We will share with you all the good things the Lord gives us." ³³So they left the mountain of the Lord. The Ark of the Lord's Covenant went in front of the people. For three days they looked for a place to camp. ³⁴The Lord's cloud was over them during the day when they left their camp.

³⁵When the Ark of the Covenant left the camp, Moses always said,

> "Rise up, Lord!
>   Scatter your enemies.
>   Make those who are against you
>   run from you."

³⁶And when the Ark of the Covenant was set down, Moses always said,

> "Return, Lord,
>   to the thousands of people of
>   Israel."

FIRE FROM THE LORD

11 The people complained to the Lord about their troubles. When he heard them, he became angry. Fire from the Lord burned among the people. It burned the edge of the camp. ²So the people cried out to Moses. He prayed to the Lord, and the fire stopped burning. ³So that place was called Taberah.ⁿ The people named it

that because the Lord's fire had burned among them.

THE 70 OLDER LEADERS

⁴Some troublemakers among them wanted better food. Soon all the Israelites began complaining. They said, "We want meat! ⁵We remember the fish we ate for free in Egypt. We also had cucumbers, melons, leeks, onions and garlic. ⁶But now we have lost our appetite. We never see anything but this manna!"

⁷The manna was like small white seeds. ⁸The people would go to gather it. Then they ground it in handmills. Or they crushed it between stones. They cooked it in a pot or made cakes with it. It tasted like bread baked with olive oil. ⁹When the dew fell on the camp each night, so did the manna.

¹⁰Moses heard every family crying. They stood in the entrances of their tents. The Lord became very angry. And Moses got upset. ¹¹He asked the Lord, "Why have you brought me this trouble? I'm your servant. What have I done wrong? Why did you make me responsible for all these people? ¹²I am not the father of all these people. I didn't give birth to them. Why do you make me carry them to the land you promised to our ancestors? Must I carry them in my arms as a nurse carries a baby? ¹³Where can I get meat for all these people? They keep crying to me, 'We want meat!' ¹⁴I can't take care of all these people alone. It is too much for me. ¹⁵If you are going to continue doing this to me, then kill me now. If you like me, put me to death. Then I won't have any more troubles."

¹⁶The Lord said to Moses, "Bring me 70 of Israel's elders. Pick men you know are leaders among the people. Bring them to the Meeting Tent. Have them stand there with you. ¹⁷I will come down and speak with you there. I will take some of the Spirit that is in you.

11:3 **Taberah** This name means "burning."

And I will give it to them. They will help you care for the people. Then you will not have to care for them alone.

[18]"Tell the people this: 'Make yourselves holy. Tomorrow you will eat meat. The Lord heard you cry, "We want meat! We were better off in Egypt!" So now the Lord will give you meat to eat. [19]You will not eat it for just 1, 2, 5, 10 or even 20 days. [20]You will eat that meat for a whole month. You will eat it until it comes out your nose. You will hate it. This is because you have rejected the Lord. He is here with you. But you have cried to him. You said, "Why did we ever leave Egypt?"'"

[21]Moses said, "Lord, here are 600,000 men standing around me. And you say, 'I will give them enough meat to eat for a month!' [22]If we killed all the sheep and cattle, that would not be enough. If we caught all the fish in the sea, that would not be enough."

[23]But the Lord said to Moses, "Do you think I'm weak? You will see if I can do what I say."

[24]So Moses went out to the people. He told them what the Lord had said. Moses gathered 70 of the elders together. He had them stand around the Tent. [25]Then the Lord came down in the cloud and spoke to Moses. The Lord took some of the Spirit Moses had. And he gave it to the 70 leaders. With the Spirit in them, they prophesied, but just that one time.

[26]Two men named Eldad and Medad were also listed as leaders. But they did not go to the Tent. They stayed in the camp. The Spirit was given to them. So they prophesied in the camp. [27]A young man ran to Moses. He said, "Eldad and Medad are prophesying in the camp."

[28]Joshua son of Nun said, "Moses, my master, stop them!" (Since he was a young boy, Joshua had been Moses' assistant.)

[29]But Moses answered, "Are you afraid for me? I wish all the Lord's people could prophesy. I wish the Lord would give his Spirit to all of them!" [30]Then Moses and the leaders of Israel went back to the camp.

THE QUAIL COME

[31]The Lord sent a strong wind from the sea. It blew quail into the area all around the camp. The quail were about three feet above the ground. There were quail a day's walk in any direction. [32]The people went out and gathered quail. They gathered all that day, that night and the next day. Everyone gathered at least 60 bushels. Then they spread them around the camp. [33]But the Lord became very angry. He gave the people a terrible sickness. This came while the meat was still in their mouths. [34]So the people named that place Kibroth Hattaavah.[n] They named it that because there they buried those who wanted other food.

[35]From Kibroth Hattaavah the people went to stay at Hazeroth.

MIRIAM AND AARON SPEAK AGAINST MOSES' WIFE

12 Miriam and Aaron began to talk against Moses, who had married a Cushite. [2]They said to themselves, "Is Moses the only one the Lord speaks through? Doesn't he speak through us?" And the Lord heard this.

[3](Now Moses was very humble. He was the least proud person on earth.) [4]So the Lord suddenly spoke to

> I speak face to face with [Moses]. I speak clearly, not with hidden meanings.
>
> –NUMBERS 12:8

11:34 **Kibroth Hattaavah** This name in Hebrew means "graves of craving."

Moses, Aaron and Miriam. He said, "All three of you come to the Meeting Tent now." So they went. ⁵The Lord came down in a pillar of cloud. He stood at the entrance to the Tent. He called to Aaron and Miriam, and they both came near. ⁶He said, "Listen to my words:

When a prophet is among you,
  I, the Lord, will show myself to him
    in visions.
  I will speak to him in dreams.
⁷ But this is not true with my servant
    Moses.
  I trust him to lead all my people.
⁸ I speak face to face with him.
  I speak clearly, not with hidden
    meanings.
  He has even seen the form of the
    Lord.
You should be afraid
  to speak against my servant
    Moses."

⁹The Lord was very angry with them, but he left.

¹⁰The cloud lifted from the Tent. Then Aaron turned toward Miriam. She was as white as snow. She had a harmful skin disease. ¹¹Aaron said to Moses, "Please, my master, forgive us for our foolish sin. ¹²Don't let her be like a baby who is born dead. (Sometimes a baby is born with half of its flesh eaten away.)"

¹³So Moses cried out to the Lord, "God, please heal her!"

¹⁴The Lord answered Moses, "If her father had spit in her face, she would have been shamed for seven days. So put her outside the camp for seven days. After that, she may come back." ¹⁵So Miriam was shut outside of the camp for seven days. And the people did not move on until she came back.

¹⁶After that, the people left Hazeroth. And they camped in the Desert of Paran.

THE SPIES EXPLORE CANAAN

13 The Lord said to Moses, ²"Send men to explore the land of Canaan. I will give that land to the Israelites. Send one leader from each tribe."

³So Moses obeyed the Lord's command. He sent the Israelite leaders out from the Desert of Paran. ⁴These are their names: from the tribe of Reuben, Shammua son of Zaccur; ⁵from the tribe of Simeon, Shaphat son of Hori; ⁶from the tribe of Judah, Caleb son of Jephunneh; ⁷from the tribe of Issachar, Igal son of Joseph; ⁸from the tribe of Ephraim, Hoshea son of Nun; ⁹from the tribe of Benjamin, Palti son of Raphu; ¹⁰from the tribe of Zebulun, Gaddiel son of Sodi; ¹¹from the tribe of Manasseh (a tribe of Joseph), Gaddi son of Susi; ¹²from the tribe of Dan, Ammiel son of Gamalli; ¹³from the tribe of Asher, Sethur son of Michael; ¹⁴from the tribe of Naphtali, Nahbi son of Vophsi; ¹⁵from the tribe of Gad, Geuel son of Maki.

¹⁶These are the names of the men Moses sent to explore the land. (Moses gave Hoshea son of Nun the new name Joshua.)

¹⁷Moses sent them to explore Canaan. He said, "Go through southern Canaan and then into the mountains. ¹⁸See what the land looks like. Are the people who live there strong or weak? Are there a few or many? ¹⁹What kind of land do they live in? Is it good or bad? What about the towns they live in—do they have walls, or are they open like camps? ²⁰What about the soil? Is it fertile or poor? Are there trees there? Try to bring back some of the fruit from that land." (It was the season for the first grapes.)

²¹So they went up and explored the land. They went from the Desert of Zin all the way to Rehob by Lebo Hamath. ²²They went through the southern area to Hebron. That is where Ahiman, Sheshai and Talmai lived. They were the descendants of Anak. (The city of Hebron had been built seven years before Zoan in Egypt.) ²³In the Valley of Eshcol, they cut off a branch of a grapevine. It had one bunch of grapes

☆ Numbers 13:30

God told Moses to send some men to explore the land of Canaan. This was the land God said he would give to Abraham's descendants. When the men came back, they told everyone that the land was great. But the people who lived there were stronger than they were. They wouldn't be able to fight them. Caleb quieted the men and said God was strong. He would help them win the land.

Who is the strongest person you know? Is it Dad? Is it Mom? Is it a friend? God is the strongest person in the entire world. He is stronger than everyone else. There is no one like God. He is so strong that he protects you all the time. He is so strong that he takes care of you every day. Remember this and you can be brave all the time. Be strong!

. . . .

Remember, because God is so strong, you can be bold like Caleb. God is always with you.

---

on it. They carried that branch on a pole between two of them. They also got some pomegranates and figs. ²⁴They call that place the Valley of Eshcol.ⁿ That is because the Israelites cut off the bunch of grapes there. ²⁵After 40 days of exploring the land, the men returned to the camp.

²⁶They came back to Moses and Aaron and all the Israelites at Kadesh. This was in the Desert of Paran. The men reported to them and showed everybody the fruit from the land. ²⁷They told Moses, "We went to the land where you sent us. It is a land where much food grows! Here is some of its fruit. ²⁸But the people who live

there are strong. Their cities are walled and large. We even saw some Anakites there. ²⁹The Amalekites live in the southern area. The Hittites, Jebusites and Amorites live in the mountains. The Canaanites live near the sea and along the Jordan River."

³⁰Then Caleb told the people near Moses to be quiet. Caleb said, "We should go up and take the land for ourselves. We can do it."

³¹But the men who had gone with him said, "We can't attack those people. They are stronger than we are." ³²And those men gave the Israelites a bad report about the land they explored. They said, "The land would eat us up.

13:24 **Eshcol** This name in Hebrew means "bunch."

All the people we saw are very tall.
[33] We saw the Nephilim people there.
(The Anakites come from the Nephilim people.) We felt like grasshoppers. And we looked like grasshoppers to them."

THE PEOPLE COMPLAIN AGAIN

14 That night all the people in the camp began crying loudly. [2] All the Israelites complained against Moses and Aaron. All the people said to them, "We should have died in Egypt. Or we should have died in the desert. [3] Why is the Lord bringing us to this land? We will be killed with swords. Our wives and children will be taken away. We would be better off going back to Egypt." [4] They said to each other, "Let's get a leader and go back to Egypt."

[5] Then Moses and Aaron bowed facedown in front of all the Israelites gathered there. [6] Joshua son of Nun and Caleb son of Jephunneh were among those who had explored the land. They tore their clothes. [7] They said to all of the Israelites, "The land we went to explore is very good. [8] If the Lord is pleased with us, he will lead us into that land. He will give us that land where much food grows. [9] Don't turn against the Lord! Don't be afraid of the people in that land! We will chew them up. They have no protection, but we have the Lord. So don't be afraid of them."

[10] Then all the people talked about killing them with stones. But the glory of the Lord appeared at the Meeting Tent to the Israelites. [11] The Lord said to Moses, "How long will these people ignore me? How long will it be before they believe me? I have done miracles among them. [12] I will give them a terrible sickness. I will destroy them. But I will make you into a great nation. It will be stronger than they are."

[13] Then Moses said to the Lord, "The Egyptians will hear about it! You brought these people from there by your great power. [14] And the Egyptians will tell this to those who live in this land. They have already heard about

you, Lord. They know that you are with your people. And they know you were seen face to face. They know your cloud stays over your people. They know you lead your people with that cloud during the day and with fire at night. [15] The nations have heard about your power. If you put to death your people all at once, the nations will talk. They will say, [16] 'The Lord was not able to bring them into the land he promised them. So he killed them in the desert.'

[17] "So show your strength now, my Lord. Do what you said. You said: [18] 'The Lord doesn't become angry quickly. The Lord has great love. The Lord forgives sin and law breaking. He has great mercy. But the Lord does not forget to punish guilty people. When parents sin, he will also punish their children. He will punish their grandchildren, great-grandchildren and great-great-grandchildren.' [19] Show your great love. Forgive these people's sin. Forgive them as you have from the time they left Egypt until now."

[20] The Lord answered, "I have forgiven them as you asked. [21] But, as surely as I live, I make this promise. As surely as my glory fills the whole earth, I make this promise. [22] All these men saw my glory. They saw the miracles I did in Egypt and in the desert. But they disobeyed me and tested me 10 times. [23] So not one will see the land I promised to their ancestors. No one who angered me will see that land. [24] But my servant Caleb has a different spirit. He follows me completely. So I will bring him into the land he has already seen. And his children will own that land. [25] The Amalekites and the Canaanites are living in the valleys. So leave tomorrow and go back. Follow the desert road toward the Gulf of Aqaba."

THE LORD PUNISHES THE PEOPLE

[26] The Lord said to Moses and Aaron, [27] "How long will these evil people complain about me? I have heard these Israelites' grumbling and complaining.

²⁸So tell them, 'This is what the Lord says. I heard what you said. As surely as I live, I will do those things to you. ²⁹You will die in this desert. Every one of you who is 20 years old or older and who was counted with the people will die. You complained against me, the Lord. ³⁰Not one of you will enter and live in the land I promised to you. Only Caleb son of Jephunneh and Joshua son of Nun will go in. ³¹You said that your children would be taken away. But I will bring them into the land. They will enjoy what you refused. ³²As for you, you will die in this desert. ³³Your children will be shepherds here for 40 years. They will suffer because you were not loyal. They will suffer until you lie dead in the desert. ³⁴For 40 years you will suffer for your sins. That is a year for each of the 40 days you explored the land. You will know me as your enemy.' ³⁵I, the Lord, have spoken. I will certainly do these things to all these evil people. They have come together against me. So they will all die here in this desert."

³⁶The men Moses had sent to explore the land had returned. They had spread complaints among all the Israelites.

They had given a bad report about the land. ³⁷They were responsible for the bad report. So the Lord killed them with a terrible sickness. ³⁸Only two of the men did not die. They were Joshua son of Nun and Caleb son of Jephunneh.

³⁹When Moses told these things to the Israelites, they were very sad. ⁴⁰Early the next morning they started to go toward the beginning of the mountains. They said, "We have sinned. We will go where the Lord told us."

⁴¹But Moses said, "Why are you disobeying the Lord's command? You will not win! ⁴²Don't go. The Lord is not with you. You will be beaten by your enemies. ⁴³You will run into the Amalekites and Canaanites. They will kill you with swords. You have turned away from the Lord. He will not be with you."

⁴⁴But they were proud. They went toward the beginning of the mountains. But Moses and the Ark of the Covenant with the Lord did not leave the camp. ⁴⁵The Amalekites and the Canaanites who lived in those mountains came down. And they attacked the Israelites. They beat them back all the way to Hormah.

Deuteronomy

THE LAW WRITTEN ON STONES

27 Moses and the elders of Israel commanded the people. They said, "Keep all the commands I have given you today. ²Soon you will cross the Jordan River. You will go into the land the Lord your God is giving you. On that day set up some large stones. Cover them with plaster. ³When you cross over, write all the words of these teachings on them. Then you may enter the land the Lord your God is giving you. It is a land where much food grows. It is just as the Lord, the God of your ancestors, promised. ⁴After you have crossed the Jordan River, set up these stones. Set them on Mount Ebal as I command you today. And cover them with plaster. ⁵Build an altar of stones there to the Lord your God. But don't use any iron tool to cut the stones. ⁶Build the altar of the Lord your God with stones from the field. Offer burnt offerings on it to the Lord your God. ⁷Offer fellowship offerings there. Eat them and rejoice before the Lord your God. ⁸Then write clearly all the words of these teachings on the stones."

CURSES OF THE LAW

⁹Then Moses and the Levites, who are the priests, spoke to all Israel. They said, "Be quiet, Israel. Listen! Today you have become the people of the Lord your God. ¹⁰Obey the Lord your God. Keep his commands and laws that I give you today."

BLESSINGS FOR OBEYING

28 You must completely obey the Lord your God. And you must carefully follow all his commands I am giving you today. Then the Lord your God will make you greater than any other nation on earth. ²Obey the Lord your God. Then all these blessings will come and stay with you:

³You will be blessed in the city. You will be blessed in the country.

⁴Your children will be blessed. Your crops will be blessed. Your cattle will be blessed with calves and your sheep with lambs.

⁵Your basket and your kitchen will be blessed.

⁶You will be blessed when you come in and when you go out.

⁷The Lord will let you defeat the enemies that come to fight you. They will attack you from one direction. But they will run from you in seven directions.

⁸The Lord your God will bless you with full barns. He will bless everything you do. He will bless the land he is giving you.

⁹The Lord will make you his holy people, as he promised. But you must obey his commands. You must do what he wants you to do. ¹⁰Then everyone on earth will see that you are the Lord's people. They will be afraid of you. ¹¹The Lord will make you rich. You will have many children. Your cattle will have many calves. Your land will give good crops. It is the land that the Lord promised your ancestors he would give to you.

¹²The Lord will open up his storehouse. The skies will send rain on your land at the right time. And he will bless everything you do. You will lend to other nations. But you will not need to borrow from them. ¹³The Lord will make you like the head and not like the tail. You will be on top and not on bottom. But you must obey the commands of the Lord your God that I am giving you today. Be careful to keep them. ¹⁴Do not disobey anything I command you today. Do exactly as I command. Do not follow other gods or serve them.

CURSES FOR DISOBEYING

¹⁵But you might not obey the Lord your God. You might not carefully follow all

☆ Deuteronomy 28:3–14

God made some rules for the Israelites so they could be happy, healthy, and safe. Moses told them all about God's promised blessings when they obeyed God's law.

Have you ever gone to get ice cream and your parents got you an extra scoop? Chocolate and vanilla! Yum! You did not need both scoops, but they sure did taste good. Sometimes parents like to surprise their kids with treats. God is your heavenly Father, and he enjoys surprising you too! He gives you everything you need and more. His blessings overflow in your life if you look for them.

. . . .

The Bible says that every good gift comes from our heavenly Father (James 1:17). Just keep watching for his blessings. You will find them.

his commands and laws I am giving you today. Then all these curses will come upon you and stay:

¹⁶You will be cursed in the city. You will be cursed in the country.

¹⁷Your basket and your kitchen will be cursed.

¹⁸Your children will be cursed. Your crops will be cursed. The calves of your cattle will be cursed. And the lambs of your flocks will be cursed.

¹⁹You will be cursed when you go in and when you go out.

²⁰The Lord will send you curses, confusion and punishment in everything you do. You will be destroyed. You will suddenly be ruined. You did wrong when you left him. ²¹The Lord will give you terrible diseases. He will destroy you from the land you are going to take. ²²The Lord will punish you with disease, fever, swelling, heat, no rain, plant diseases and mildew. Then you will die. ²³The sky above will look like bronze. And the ground below will be like iron. ²⁴The Lord will turn the rain into dust and sand. It will fall from the skies until you are destroyed.

²⁵The Lord will let your enemies defeat you. You will attack them from one direction. But you will run from them in seven directions. And you will become a thing of horror among all the kingdoms on earth. ²⁶Your dead bodies will be food for all the birds and wild animals. There will be no one to scare them away. ²⁷The Lord will punish you with boils like those the Egyptians had. You will have bad growths, sores and itches that can't be cured. ²⁸The Lord will give you madness, blindness and a confused mind. ²⁹You will have to feel around in the daylight like a blind man. You will fail in everything you do. People

will hurt you and steal from you every day. There will be no one to save you.

³⁰You will be engaged to a woman. But another man will rape her. You will build a house. But you will not live in it. You will plant a vineyard. But you will not get its grapes. ³¹Your ox will be killed before your eyes. But you will not eat any of it. Your donkey will be taken away from you. And it will not be brought back. Your sheep will be given to your enemies. And no one will rescue them. ³²Your sons and daughters will be given to another nation. You will grow tired looking for them every day. But there is nothing you can do. ³³People you don't know will eat the crops your land and hard work have produced. You will be mistreated and abused all your life. ³⁴The things you see will cause you to go mad. ³⁵The Lord will give you sore boils on your knees and legs. They cannot be cured. They will go from the soles of your feet to the tops of your heads.

³⁶The Lord will send you and your king away to a nation you do not know. There you will serve other gods made of wood and stone. ³⁷You will become a hated thing to the nations where the Lord sends you. They will laugh at you and make fun of you.

³⁸You will plant much seed in your field. But your harvest will be small. Locusts will eat the crop. ³⁹You will plant vineyards and work hard in them. But you will not pick the grapes or drink the wine. The worms will eat them. ⁴⁰You will have olive trees in all your land. But you will not get any olive oil. The olives will drop off the trees. ⁴¹You will have sons and daughters. But you will not be able to keep them. They will be taken captive. ⁴²Locusts will destroy all your trees and crops.

⁴³The foreigners who live among you will get stronger and stronger. And you will get weaker and weaker. ⁴⁴Foreigners will lend money to you. But you will not be able to lend to them. They will be like the head. And you will be like the tail.

⁴⁵All these curses will come upon you. They will chase you and catch you and destroy you. This will happen because you did not obey the Lord your God. You did not keep the commands and laws he gave you. ⁴⁶The curses will be signs and miracles to you and your descendants forever. ⁴⁷You had plenty of everything. But you did not serve the Lord your God with joy and a pure heart. ⁴⁸So you will serve the enemies the Lord sends against you. You will be hungry, thirsty, naked and poor. The Lord will put a load on you until he has destroyed you.

THE CURSE OF AN ENEMY NATION

⁴⁹The Lord will bring a nation against you from far away. It will be from the end of the world. The nation will swoop down like an eagle. You won't understand their language. ⁵⁰They will look mean. They will not respect old people or feel sorry for the young. ⁵¹They will eat the calves from your cattle and the harvest of your field. And you will be destroyed. They will not leave you any grain, new wine or oil. They will not leave you any calves from your herds or lambs from your flocks. You will be ruined. ⁵²That nation will surround and attack all your cities. You trust in your high, strong walls. But they will fall down. That nation will surround all your cities everywhere in the land the Lord your God is giving you.

⁵³Your enemy will surround you. Those people will make you starve. You will eat your own babies. You will eat the bodies of the sons and daughters the Lord gave you. ⁵⁴Even the most gentle and kind man among you will become cruel. He will be cruel to his brother, his wife whom he loves and his children who are still alive. ⁵⁵He will not even give them any of the flesh of his children he is eating. It will be all he has left. Your enemy will surround you. Those people will make you starve in all your cities. ⁵⁶The most gentle and kind woman among you will become cruel. She is so gentle and kind she would

hardly even walk on the ground. But she will be cruel to her husband whom she loves. And she will be cruel to her son and daughter. [57]She will give birth to a baby. But she will plan to eat the baby and what comes after the birth itself. She will eat them while the enemy surrounds the city. Those people will make you starve in all your cities.

[58]Be careful to obey everything in these teachings. They are written in this book. You must respect the glorious and wonderful name of the Lord your God. [59]The Lord will give terrible diseases to you and your descendants. You will have long and serious diseases. You will have long and miserable sicknesses. [60]And the Lord will give you all the diseases of Egypt that you dread. And the diseases will stay with you. [61]The Lord will also give you every disease and sickness not written in this Book of the Teachings. Then you will be destroyed. [62]You people may have outnumbered the stars. But only a few of you will be left. You did not obey the Lord your God. [63]Once the Lord was happy with you. He gave you good things. He made you grow in number. But now the Lord will be happy to ruin and destroy you. You will be removed from the land you are entering to own.

[64]Then the Lord will scatter you among the nations. He will scatter you from one end of the earth to the other. There you will serve other gods of wood and stone. They are gods that neither you nor your ancestors have known. [65]You will have no rest among those nations. You will have no place that is yours. The Lord will make your mind worried, your sight weak and your soul sad. [66]You will live with danger. You will be afraid night and day. You will not be sure that you will live. [67]In the morning you will say, "I wish it were evening." And in the evening you will say, "I wish it were morning." Terror will be in your heart because of the things you have seen. [68]The Lord will send you back to Egypt in ships. I, Moses, said you would never go back to Egypt. And there you will try to sell yourselves as slaves to your enemies. But no one will buy you.

THE AGREEMENT IN MOAB

29 The Lord commanded Moses to make an agreement with the Israelites in Moab. This agreement was in addition to the agreement he had made with them at Mount Sinai.

[2]Moses called all the Israelites together. And he said to them:

You have seen everything the Lord did to the king of Egypt. You saw what he did to the king's leaders and to the whole country. [3]With your own eyes you saw the great troubles, signs and miracles. [4]But to this day the Lord has not given you a mind that understands. You don't really understand what you see with your eyes or hear with your ears. [5]The Lord led you through the desert for 40 years. During that time neither your clothes nor sandals wore out. [6]You ate no bread. You drank no wine or beer. This was so you would understand that he is the Lord your God.

[7]You came to this place. Then Sihon king of Heshbon and Og king of Bashan came out to fight us. But we defeated them. [8]We captured their land. And we gave it to the Reubenites, the Gadites and the eastern half-tribe of Manasseh to own.

[9]You must carefully obey everything in this agreement. Then you will succeed in everything you do. [10]Today you are all standing here before the Lord your God. Here are your leaders and important men. Your elders, officers and all the other men of Israel are here. [11]Here are your wives and children and the foreigners who live among you. They chop your wood and carry your water. [12]You are all here to enter into an agreement and a promise with the Lord your God. The Lord is making this agreement with you today. [13]This will make you today the Lord's own people. He will be your God. This is what he told you. He promised it to your ancestors Abraham, Isaac and Jacob. [14]But the

Lord is not just making this agreement and its promises with you. ¹⁵You are standing here before the Lord your God today. But he is also making it with those who are not here today.

¹⁶You know how we lived in Egypt. You know how we passed through the countries when we came here. ¹⁷You saw their hated idols made of wood, stone, silver and gold. ¹⁸Make sure no man, woman, family group or tribe among you leaves the Lord. Don't let them go and serve the gods of those nations. That would be like a plant that grows bitter, poisonous fruit.

¹⁹That kind of person might hear these curses. But he blesses himself. And he thinks, "I will be safe. I will continue doing what I want to do." That person might destroy all of your land, both wet and dry. ²⁰The Lord will not forgive that person. His anger will be like a burning fire against that man. All the curses written in this book will come on him. And the Lord will destroy any memory of him on the earth. ²¹The Lord will separate him from all the tribes of Israel for punishment. All the curses of the agreement will happen to him. They are written in this Book of the Teachings.

²²Your children who will come after you will see this. And foreigners from faraway lands will see this. They will see the disasters that come to this land. And they will see the diseases the Lord will send on it. They will say, ²³"The land is nothing but burning cinders and salt. Nothing is planted. Nothing grows. Nothing blooms. It is like Sodom and Gomorrah, and Admah and Zeboiim. The Lord destroyed them because he was very angry." ²⁴All the other nations will ask, "Why has the Lord done this to the land? Why is he so angry?"

²⁵And the answer will be, "It is because the people broke the agreement of the Lord, the God of their ancestors. He made it with them when he brought them out of Egypt. ²⁶They went and served other gods. They bowed down to gods they did not even know. The Lord

did not allow that. ²⁷So the Lord became very angry at the land. And he brought all the curses on it that are written in this book. ²⁸The Lord became angry and furious with them. So he took them out of their land. And he put them in another land where they are today."

²⁹There are some things the Lord our God has kept secret. But there are some things he has let us know. These things belong to us and our children forever. It is so we will do everything in these teachings.

THE ISRAELITES WILL RETURN

30

All these blessings and curses I have said will happen to you. The Lord your God will send you away to other nations. There you will think about these things. ²Then you and your children will return to the Lord your God. And you will obey him with your whole being. You will obey everything I command you today. ³Then the Lord your God will give you back your riches. He will feel sorry for you. And he will bring you back again from the nations where he sent you. ⁴He may send you to the ends of the earth. But he will gather you. He will bring you back from there. ⁵He will bring you back to the land that belonged to your ancestors. It will be yours. He will give you success. And there will be more of you than there were of your ancestors. ⁶The Lord your God will prepare you and your descendants to serve him. You will love him with your whole being. Then you will live. ⁷The Lord your God will put all these curses on your enemies. They hate you and are cruel to you. ⁸And you will again obey the Lord. You will keep all his commands that I give you today. ⁹The Lord your God will make you successful in everything you do. You will have many children. Your cattle will have many calves. Your fields will produce good crops. He will again be happy with you, just as he was with your ancestors. ¹⁰But you must obey the Lord your God. You must obey his commands and rules that are written in this Book of the Teachings. You must follow the Lord your God with your whole being.

LIFE OR DEATH

[11]This command I give you today is not too hard for you. It is not beyond what you can do. [12]It is not up in heaven. You do not have to ask, "Who will go up to heaven and get it for us? Then we can obey it and keep it." [13]It is not on the other side of the sea. You do not have to ask, "Who will go across the sea and get it? Who will tell it to us? Then we can keep it." [14]No, the word is very near you. It is in your mouth and in your heart. So, you may obey it.

[15]Look, today I offer you life and success, death and destruction. [16]I command you today to love the Lord your God. Do what he wants you to do. Keep his commands, his rules and his laws. Then you will live and grow in number. And the Lord your God will bless you in the land you are going to take as your own.

[17]But you might turn away from the Lord. You might not obey him. You might be led to bowing down and serving other gods. [18]I tell you today that you will be destroyed. And you will not live long in the land you are crossing the Jordan River to enter and own.

[19]Today I ask heaven and earth to be witnesses. I am offering you life or death, blessings or curses. Now, choose life! Then you and your children may live. [20]Love the Lord your God. Obey him. Stay close to him. He is your life. And he will let you live many years in the land. This is the land he promised to give your ancestors Abraham, Isaac and Jacob.

JOSHUA TAKES MOSES' PLACE

31 Then Moses went and spoke these words to all the Israelites: [2]"I am now 120 years old. I cannot lead you anymore. The Lord told me I would not cross the Jordan River. [3]The Lord your God will lead you across himself. He will destroy those nations for you. You will take over their land. Joshua will also lead you across. This is what the Lord has said. [4]The Lord will do to these nations what he did to Sihon and Og. They were the kings of the Amorites. He destroyed them and their land. [5]The Lord will give those nations to you. Do to them everything I told you. [6]Be strong and brave. Don't be afraid of them. Don't be frightened. The Lord your God will go with you. He will not leave you or forget you."

[7]Then Moses called Joshua and spoke to him in front of the people. Moses said, "Be strong and brave. Lead these people into the land the Lord promised to give their ancestors. Help the people take it as their own. [8]The Lord himself will go before you. He will be with you. He will not leave you or forget you. Don't be afraid. Don't worry."

MOSES WRITES THE TEACHINGS

[9]So Moses wrote down the teachings. He gave them to the priests and all the elders of Israel. The priests are the sons of Levi. They carried the Ark of the Covenant with the Lord. [10-11]Then Moses commanded them: "Read these teachings for all Israel to hear. Do it at the end of every seven years. That is the year to forget what people owe. Do it during the Feast of Shelters. All the Israelites will come to appear before the Lord your God. They will stand at the place the Lord will choose. [12]Gather all the people: the men, women, children and foreigners living in your towns. Then they can listen and learn to respect the Lord your God. Then they can carefully obey everything in this law. [13]Their children do not know this law. They must hear it. They must learn to respect the Lord your God for as long as they live in the land. It is the land you are crossing the Jordan River to own."

THE LORD CALLS MOSES AND JOSHUA

[14]The Lord said to Moses, "Soon you will die. Get Joshua and come to the Meeting Tent. I will command him." So

Moses and Joshua went to the Meeting Tent.

15 The Lord appeared at the Meeting Tent in a cloud. The cloud stood over the entrance of the Tent. 16 And the Lord said to Moses, "You will soon die. Then these people will not be loyal to me. They will worship the foreign gods of the land they are entering. They will leave me. And they will break the agreement I made with them. 17 Then I will become very angry at them. I will leave them. I will turn away from them. And they will be destroyed. Many terrible things will happen to them. Then they will say, 'God is not with us. That is why these terrible things are happening.' 18 I will turn away from them then. They have done wrong. They have turned to other gods.

19 "Now write down this song. And teach it to the Israelites. Then have them sing it. It will testify against them. 20 I will bring them into the land I promised to their ancestors. It is a land where much food grows. They will eat as much as they want and get fat. But then they will turn to other gods and serve them. They will reject me and break my agreement. 21 Then many troubles and terrible things will happen to them.

☆ Deuteronomy 31:6–8

Moses was old and would not lead the Israelites much longer. He made his helper, Joshua, the new leader. Moses told Joshua and the people to be strong and brave. They would win the land God promised them. Moses reminded them that the Lord was with them.

God promises to keep us safe. Sometimes we are scared because of a real danger, and sometimes we are scared because of something we made up. Everyone feels scared at times. But God promises that when we are afraid, he will be with us. No matter what you fear, Jesus is bigger and stronger than anything that makes you scared. He will never leave you alone. God is always there. You do not have to be afraid because he is with you!

. . . .

Remember those promises God made to Abraham and then to Jacob? God said their kids would be a big nation and live in the land of Canaan. Hundreds of years later, that's exactly what happened. God always keeps his promises. He never leaves us!

And this song will testify against them. The song will not be forgotten by their descendants. I know what they plan to do, even before I take them into the land I promised them." ²²So Moses wrote down the song that day. And he taught it to the Israelites.

²³Then the Lord gave this command to Joshua son of Nun: "Be strong and brave. Lead the people of Israel to the land I promised them. And I will be with you."

²⁴Moses wrote all the words of the teachings in a book. ²⁵Then he gave a command to the Levites. They carried the Ark of the Covenant with the Lord. ²⁶He said, "Take this Book of the Teachings. Put it beside the Ark of the Covenant with the Lord your God. It must stay there as a witness against you. ²⁷I know how stubborn and disobedient you are. You have disobeyed the Lord while I am alive and with you. You will disobey even more after I die! ²⁸Gather all the older leaders of your tribes and all your officers. I will say these things for them to hear. And I will ask heaven and earth to testify against them. ²⁹I know that after I die you will become completely evil. You will turn away from the commands I have given you. Then terrible things will happen to you in the future. You will do what the Lord says is evil. You will make him angry with the idols you have made."

MOSES' SONG

³⁰And Moses spoke this whole song for all the people of Israel to hear:

32 Hear, heavens, and I will speak.
  Listen, earth, to what I say.
² My teaching will drop like rain.
  My words will fall like dew.
  They will be like showers on the grass.
  They will pour down like rain on young plants.
³ I will announce the name of the Lord.
  Praise God because he is great!
⁴ He is like a rock. What he does is perfect.
  He is always fair.
  He is a faithful God who does no wrong.
  He is right and fair.
⁵ They have done evil against him.
  To their shame they are no longer his children.
  They are an evil and lying people.
⁶ This is not the way to repay the Lord.
  You are foolish and unwise.
  He is your Father and Maker.
  He made you and formed you.

⁷ Remember the old days.
  Think of the years already passed.
  Ask your father. He will tell you.
  Ask your elders. They will inform you.
⁸ The Most High God gave the nations their lands.
  He divided up the human race.
  He set up borders for the people.
  He even numbered the Israelites.
⁹ The Lord took his people as his share.
  The people of Jacob were his very own.

¹⁰ He found them in a desert.
  It was a windy, empty land.
  He surrounded them and brought them up.
  He guarded them as those he loved very much.
¹¹ He was like an eagle building its nest.
  It flutters over its young.
  It spreads its wings to catch them.
  It carries them on its feathers.
¹² The Lord alone led them.
  There were no foreign gods among them.

¹³ The Lord brought them to the heights of the land.
  He fed them the fruit of the fields.
  He gave them honey from the rocks.
  He brought oil from the solid rock.
¹⁴ There were milk curds from the cows and milk from the sheep.
  There were fat sheep and goats.
  There were sheep and goats from Bashan.

There was the best of the wheat.
You drank the juice of grapes.

¹⁵ Israel grew fat and kicked.
They were fat and full and firm.
They left the God who made them.
They rejected the Rock who saved
them.
¹⁶ They made God jealous with foreign
gods.
They made him angry with hated
idols.
¹⁷ They made sacrifices to demons, not
God.
They were gods they had never
known.
They were new gods from nearby.
Your ancestors did not fear them.
¹⁸ You left God who is the Rock, your
Father.
You forgot the God who gave you
birth.

¹⁹ The Lord saw this and rejected them.
His sons and daughters had made
him angry.
²⁰ He said, "I will turn away from them.
I will see what will happen to them.
They are evil people.
They are unfaithful children.
²¹ They used things that are not gods to
make me jealous.
They used worthless idols to make
me angry.
So I will use those who are not a
nation to make them jealous.
I will use a nation that does not
understand to make them angry.
²² My anger has started a fire.
It burns down to where the dead are.
It will burn up the ground and its crops.
And it will set fire to the mountains.

²³ "I will pile troubles upon them.
I will shoot my arrows at them.
²⁴ They will be starved and sick.
They will be destroyed by terrible
diseases.
I will send them vicious animals
and gliding, poisonous snakes.
²⁵ In the streets the sword will kill.

In their homes there will be terror.
Young men and women will die.
So will babies and gray-haired men.
²⁶ I will scatter them as I said.
And no one will remember them.
²⁷ But I didn't want their enemy to brag.
Their enemy might misunderstand.
They might say, 'We have won!
The Lord has done none of this.'"

²⁸ Israel has no sense.
They do not understand.
²⁹ I wish they were wise and
understood this.
I wish they could see what will
happen to them.
³⁰ One person cannot chase 1,000 people.
And 2 people cannot fight 10,000.
This only happens if the Lord has
sold them.
Their Rock would have to give
them up.
³¹ The rock of these people is not like
our Rock.
Our enemies agree to that.
³² Their vine comes from Sodom.
Their fields are like Gomorrah.
Their grapes are full of poison.
Their bunches of grapes are bitter.
³³ Their wine is like snake poison,
like the deadly poison of cobras.

³⁴ "I have been saving this.
I have it locked in my storehouses.
³⁵ I will punish those who do wrong. I
will repay them.
Sometime their foot will slip.
Their day of trouble is near.
And their punishment will come
quickly."

³⁶ The Lord will defend his people.
He will have mercy on his servants.
He will see that their strength is gone.
He will see that nobody is left,
slaves or free.
³⁷ Then he will say, "Where are their gods?
Where is the rock they trusted?
³⁸ Who ate the fat from their sacrifices?
Who drank the wine of their drink
offering?

Let those gods come to help you!
Let them protect you!

39 "Now you will see that I am the one God!
There is no god but me.
I send life and death.
I can hurt, and I can heal.
No one can escape from me.
40 I raise my hand toward heaven and make this promise:
As surely as I live forever,
41 I will sharpen my flashing sword.
And I will take it in my hand to judge.
I will punish my enemies.
I will pay back those who hate me.
42 My arrows will be covered with their blood.
My sword will eat their flesh.
The blood will flow from those who are killed and the captives.
The heads of the enemy leaders will be cut off."

43 Be happy, nations, with his people.
He will repay you for the blood of his servants.
He will punish his enemies.
And he will remove the sin of his land and people.

44 Moses came with Joshua son of Nun. And they spoke all the words of this song for the people to hear. 45 When Moses finished speaking these words to all Israel, 46 he said to them: "Pay attention to all the words I have said to you today. Command your children to obey carefully everything in these teachings. 47 These should not be unimportant words for you. They mean life for you! By these words you will live a long time in the land you are crossing the Jordan River to own."

MOSES GOES UP TO MOUNT NEBO

48 The Lord spoke to Moses again that same day. He said, 49 "Go up the Abarim Mountains. Go to Mount Nebo in the country of Moab. It is across from Jericho. Look at the land of Canaan. I am giving it to the Israelites to own. 50 You will die on that mountain that you climb. This is how your brother Aaron died on Mount Hor. 51 You both sinned against me at the waters of Meribah Kadesh. That is in the Desert of Zin. You did not honor me as holy there among the Israelites. 52 So now you will only look at the land from far away. You will not enter the land I am giving the people of Israel."

MOSES BLESSES THE PEOPLE

33 Moses, the man of God, gave this blessing to the Israelites before he died. 2 He said:

"The Lord came from Mount Sinai.
He rose like the sun from Edom.
He showed his greatness from Mount Paran.
He came with thousands of angels.
He came from the southern mountains.
3 The Lord surely loves his people.
He takes care of all those who belong to him.
They bow down at his feet.
And they are taught by him.
4 Moses gave us the teachings.
They belong to the people of Jacob.
5 The Lord became king of Israel.
The leaders of the people gathered then.
The tribes of Israel came together.

6 "Let the people of Reuben live and not die.
But let the people be few."

> These should not be unimportant words for you. They mean life for you!
> – DEUTERONOMY 32:47

⁷Moses said this about the people of Judah:

"Lord, listen to Judah's prayer.
  Bring them back to their people.
They defend themselves with their
    hands.
  Help them fight their enemies!"

⁸Moses said this about the people of Levi:

"Lord, your Thummim and Urim
    belong
  to Levi whom you love.
Lord, you tested him at Massah.
  You argued with him at the waters
    of Meribah.
⁹ He said about his father and mother,
  'I don't care about them.'
He did not recognize his brothers.
  He did not know his children.
But he protected your word.
  And he guarded your agreement.
¹⁰ He teaches your laws to the people of
    Jacob
  and your teachings to the people
    of Israel.
He burns incense before you.
  And he makes whole burnt
    offerings on your altar.
¹¹ Lord, make them strong.
  Be pleased with the work they do.
Defeat those who attack them.
  Don't let their enemies rise up again."

¹²Moses said this about the people of Benjamin:

"The Lord's loved ones will lie down
    in safety.
  The Lord protects them all day long.
The ones the Lord loves rest with
    him."

¹³Moses said this about the people of Joseph:

"May the Lord bless their land with
    the best fruits.
  Send rain from heaven above.
And bring the water from the
    springs below.
¹⁴ Let the sun produce the best fruits.
  Let each month bring its best fruits.
¹⁵ Let the old mountains give the finest
    crops.
  And let the everlasting hills give
    the best fruits.
¹⁶ Let the full earth give the best fruits.
  Let the Lord who lived in the
    burning bush be pleased.
May these blessings rest on the head
    of Joseph.
  May they rest on the forehead of
    the one who was separated from
    his brothers.
¹⁷ Joseph has the majesty of a firstborn
    bull.
  He is as strong as a wild ox.
He will stab other nations,
  even those nations far away.
These are the ten thousands of
    Ephraim.
  And these are the thousands of
    Manasseh."

¹⁸Moses said this about the people of Zebulun:

"Be happy when you go out, Zebulun.
  And be happy in your tents, Issachar.
¹⁹ They will call the people to the
    mountain.
  And there they will offer the right
    sacrifices.
They will do well from all that is in
    the sea.
  And they will do well from the
    treasures hidden in the sand on
    the shore."

²⁰Moses said this about the people of Gad:

"Praise God who gives Gad more land!
  Gad lives there like a lion.
  He tears off arms and heads.
²¹ They chose the best land for
    themselves.
  They received a large share, like
    that given to an officer.

When the leaders of the people
gathered,
the people of Gad did what the
Lord said was right.
And they judged Israel fairly."

²²Moses said this about the people of
Dan:

"Dan is like a lion's cub,
who jumps out of Bashan."

²³Moses said this about the people of
Naphtali:

"Naphtali enjoys the Lord's special
kindnesses.
They are full of his blessings.
Their land goes south to Lake
Galilee."

²⁴Moses said this about the people of
Asher:

"Asher is the most blessed of the sons.
He should be his brothers' favorite.
Let him bathe his feet in olive oil.
²⁵ Your gates will have locks of iron and
bronze.
You will be strong as long as you
live.
²⁶ "There is no one like the God of Israel.
He rides through the skies to help
you.
He rides on the clouds in his
majesty.
²⁷ The everlasting God is your place of
safety.
His arms will hold you up forever.
He will force your enemy out ahead
of you.
He will say, 'Destroy the enemy!'
²⁸ The people of Israel will lie down in
safety.
Jacob's spring is theirs alone.
Theirs is a land full of grain and wine.
There the skies drop their dew.
²⁹ Israel, you are blessed!
No one else is like you.

You are a people saved by the Lord.
He is your shield and helper.
He is your glorious sword.
Your enemies will be afraid of you.
You will walk all over their holy
places."

MOSES DIES

34 Then Moses climbed up Mount
Nebo. He went from the plains
of Moab to the top of Mount Pisgah. It is
across from Jericho. From there the Lord
showed him all the land. He could see
from Gilead to Dan. ²He could see all of
Naphtali and the lands of Ephraim and
Manasseh. He could see all the land of
Judah as far as the Mediterranean Sea.
³He could see the southern desert and
the whole Valley of Jericho up to Zoar.
Jericho is called the city of palm trees.
⁴Then the Lord said to Moses, "This is
the land I promised to Abraham, Isaac
and Jacob. I said to them, 'I will give this
land to your descendants.' I have let you
look at it, Moses. But you will not cross
over there."

⁵Then Moses, the servant of the Lord,
died there in Moab. It was as the Lord
had said. ⁶The Lord buried Moses in
Moab in the valley opposite Beth Peor.
But even today no one knows where his
grave is. ⁷Moses was 120 years old when
he died. His eyes were not weak. And he
was still strong. ⁸The Israelites cried for
Moses for 30 days. They stayed in the
plains of Moab until the time of sadness
was over.

⁹Joshua son of Nun was then filled
with wisdom. Moses had put his hands
on Joshua. So the Israelites listened to
Joshua. And they did what the Lord had
commanded Moses.

¹⁰There has never been another
prophet like Moses. The Lord knew
Moses face to face. ¹¹The Lord sent
Moses to do signs and miracles in Egypt.
He did them to the king, to all his officers
and to the whole land of Egypt. ¹²Moses
had great power. He did wonderful
things for all the Israelites to see.

Joshua

GOD'S COMMAND TO JOSHUA

1 Moses was the servant of the Lord. Joshua son of Nun was Moses' assistant. After Moses died, the Lord said to Joshua: ²"My servant Moses is dead. Now you and all these people go across the Jordan River. Go into the land I am giving to the people of Israel. ³I promised Moses I would give you this land. So I will give you every place you go in the land. ⁴All the land from the desert in the south to Lebanon in the north will be yours. All the land from the great river, the Euphrates, in the east, to the Mediterranean Sea in the west will be yours. This includes the land of the Hittites. ⁵Just as I was with Moses, so I will be with you. No one will be able to stop you all your life. I will not leave you. I will never leave you alone.

⁶"Joshua, be strong and brave! You must lead these people so they can take

---

☆ Joshua 1:8

After Moses died, God commanded Joshua to lead the Israelites across the Jordan River and into the land he had promised them. The Lord told Joshua to read and study his teachings as often as possible. By studying them, Joshua would become wise.

God says it is important to obey him. We know what God wants us to do when we read the Bible. If we ask for help to know what is right and wrong, then we will know how he wants us to live. People who do not follow God's word end up doing the wrong things and getting into trouble. God can only speak the truth. So what he tells us in the Bible is right and true. When we listen to his word and do what it says, we are obeying God. He says that when we know him and follow him, we will be happy.

. . . .

When you read the Bible, you put God's words in your heart. And just like Joshua, you will become wise and know what to do.

their land. This is the land I promised their fathers I would give them. ⁷Be strong and brave. Be sure to obey all the teachings my servant Moses gave you. If you follow them exactly, you will be successful in everything you do. ⁸Always remember what is written in the Book of the Teachings. Study it day and night. Then you will be sure to obey everything that is written there. If you do this, you will be wise and successful in everything. ⁹Remember that I commanded you to be strong and brave. So don't be afraid. The Lord your God will be with you everywhere you go."

JOSHUA'S ORDERS TO THE PEOPLE

¹⁰So Joshua gave orders to the officers of the people. He said, ¹¹"Go through the camp and tell the people, 'Get your supplies ready. Three days from now you will cross the Jordan River. You will go and take the land the Lord your God is giving you.'"

¹²Then Joshua spoke to the people of Reuben, Gad and the eastern half-tribe of Manasseh. Joshua said, ¹³"Remember what Moses, the servant of the Lord, told you. He said the Lord your God would give you rest. And he said the Lord would give you this land. ¹⁴Now the Lord has given you this land east of the Jordan River. Your wives, your children and your animals may stay here. But your fighting men must dress for war and cross the Jordan River ahead of your brothers. You must help your brothers. ¹⁵The Lord has given you a place to rest. He will do the same for your brothers. But you must help them until they take the land. This is the land the Lord their God is giving them. Then you may return to your own land east of the Jordan River. That is the land that Moses, the servant of the Lord, gave you."

¹⁶Then the people answered Joshua, "Anything you command us to do, we will do. Any place you send us, we will go. ¹⁷Just as we fully obeyed Moses, we will obey you. We ask only that the Lord your God be with you just as he was with Moses. ¹⁸Then, if anyone refuses to obey your commands or turns against you, he will be put to death. Just be strong and brave!"

SPIES SENT TO JERICHO

2 Joshua son of Nun secretly sent out two spies from Acacia. Joshua said to them, "Go and look at the land. Look closely at the city of Jericho."

So the men went to Jericho. They went to the house of a prostitute and stayed there. This woman's name was Rahab.

²Someone told the king of Jericho, "Some men from Israel have come here tonight. They are spying out the land."

³So the king of Jericho sent this message to Rahab: "Bring out the men who came to you and entered your house. They have come to spy out our whole land."

⁴Now the woman had hidden the two men. She said, "They did come here. But I didn't know where they came from. ⁵In the evening, when it was time to close the city gate, they left. I don't know where they went. Go quickly. Maybe you can catch them." ⁶(But the woman had taken the men up to the roof.ⁿ She had hidden them there under stalks of flax. She had spread the flax out there to dry.) ⁷So the king's men went out looking for the spies from Israel. They went to the places where people cross the Jordan River. The city gate was closed just after the king's men left the city.

⁸The spies were ready to sleep for the night. So Rahab went to the roof and talked to them. ⁹She said, "I know the Lord has given this land to your people. You frighten us very much. Everyone living in this land is terribly afraid of you. ¹⁰We are afraid because

---

2:6 roof In Bible times houses were built with flat roofs. The roof was used for drying things such as flax and fruit. And it was used as an extra room, as a place for worship and as a place to sleep in the summer.

we have heard how the Lord helped you. We heard how he dried up the Red Sea when you came out of Egypt. We heard how you destroyed Sihon and Og. They were the two Amorite kings who lived east of the Jordan. ¹¹When we heard this, we became very frightened. Now our men are afraid to fight you. This is because the Lord your God rules the heavens above and the earth below! ¹²So now, make me a promise before the Lord. Promise that you will show kindness to my family just as I showed you kindness. Give me some proof that you will do this. ¹³Promise me you will allow my family to live. Save my father, mother, brothers, sisters and all of their families from death."

¹⁴The men agreed. They said, "We will trade our lives for your lives. Don't tell anyone what we are doing. When the Lord gives us our land, we will be kind to you. You may trust us."

¹⁵The house Rahab lived in was built on the city wall. So she used a rope to let the men down through a window. ¹⁶She said to them, "Go into the hills. The king's men will not find you there. Hide there for three days. After the king's men return, you may go on your way."

¹⁷The men said to her, "You must do as we say. If not, we cannot be responsible for keeping our promise. ¹⁸You are using a red rope to help us escape. When we return to this land, you must tie it in the window through which you let us down. Bring your father, mother, brothers and all your family into your house. ¹⁹We can keep everyone safe who stays in this house. If anyone in your house is hurt, we will be responsible. If anyone goes out of your house and is killed, it is his own fault. We cannot be responsible for him. ²⁰But you must not tell anyone about this agreement. If you do, we are free from it."

²¹Rahab answered, "I agree to this." So she sent them away, and they left. Then she tied the red rope in the window.

²²The men left and went into the hills. There they stayed for three days. The king's men looked for them all along the road. But after three days, the king's men returned to the city without finding them. ²³Then the two men started back to Joshua. They left the hills and crossed the river. They went to Joshua son of Nun and told him everything that had happened to them. ²⁴They said to Joshua, "The Lord surely has given us all of the land. All the people in that land are terribly afraid of us."

CROSSING THE JORDAN

3 Early the next morning Joshua and all the people of Israel left Acacia. They traveled to the Jordan River and camped there before crossing it. ²After three days the officers went through the camp. ³They gave orders to the people. They said, "You will see the priests and Levites carrying the Ark of the Covenant with the Lord your God. Then you should leave where you are and follow it. ⁴That way you will know which way to go. You have never traveled this way before. But do not follow too closely. Stay about a thousand yards behind the Ark of the Covenant."

⁵Then Joshua told the people, "Make yourselves holy for the Lord. Tomorrow the Lord will do amazing things among you."

⁶Joshua said to the priests, "Take the Ark of the Covenant. Cross over the river ahead of the people." So the priests lifted the Ark of the Covenant and carried it ahead of the people.

⁷Then the Lord said to Joshua, "Today I will begin to make you a great man to all the Israelites. So the people will know I am with you just as I was with Moses. ⁸The priests will carry the Ark of the Covenant. Tell them this: 'Go to the edge of the Jordan River and stand in the water.'"

⁹Then Joshua said to the people of Israel, "Come here. Listen to the words of the Lord your God. ¹⁰Here is proof that the living God is with you.

Here is proof that he will drive out the Canaanites, Hittites, Hivites, Perizzites, Girgashites, Amorites and the Jebusites. [11] This is the proof: The Ark of the Covenant will go ahead of you into the Jordan River. It is the Agreement with the Lord of the whole world. [12] Now choose 12 men from among you. Choose 1 from each of the 12 tribes of Israel. [13] The priests will carry the Ark of the Covenant of the Lord, the Master of the whole world. They will carry it into the Jordan ahead of you. When they enter the water, the river will stop flowing. The water will be stopped. It will stand up in a heap as if a dam were there."

[14] So the priests carried the Ark of the Covenant. And the people left the place where they had camped. Then they started across the Jordan River. [15] During harvest the Jordan is flooded. So the river was at its fullest. The priests who were carrying the Ark of the Covenant came to the edge of the river. And they stepped into the water. [16] Just at that moment, the water stopped flowing. It stood up in a heap a great distance away at Adam. This is a town near Zarethan. The water flowing down to the Sea of Arabah (the Dead Sea) was completely cut off. So the people crossed the river near Jericho. [17] The ground there became dry. The priests carried the Ark of the Covenant with the Lord to the middle of the river and stopped. They waited there while all the people of Israel walked across. They crossed the Jordan River on dry land.

ROCKS TO REMIND THE PEOPLE

4 All the people finished crossing the Jordan. Then the Lord said to Joshua, [2] "Choose 12 men from among the people. Choose 1 from each tribe. [3] Tell the men to get 12 large rocks from the middle of the river. Take them from where the priests stood. Carry the rocks and put them down where you stay tonight."

[4] So Joshua chose 1 man from each tribe. Then he called the 12 men together. [5] He said to them, "Go out into the river where the Ark of the Covenant of the Lord your God is. Each of you should find 1 large rock. There will be 1 rock for each tribe of Israel. Carry the rock on your shoulder. [6] They will be a sign among you. In the future your children will ask you, 'What do these rocks mean?' [7] Tell them the Lord stopped the water from flowing in the Jordan. When the Ark of the Covenant with the Lord crossed the river, the water was stopped. These rocks will help the Israelites remember this forever."

[8] So the Israelites obeyed Joshua. They carried 12 rocks from the middle of the Jordan River. There was 1 rock for each of the 12 tribes of Israel. They did this the way the Lord had commanded Joshua. They carried the rocks with them. And they put them down where they made their camp. [9] Joshua also put 12 rocks in the middle of the Jordan River. He put them where the priests had stood while carrying the Ark of the Covenant of the Lord. These rocks are still there today.

[10] The Lord had commanded Joshua to tell the people what to do. It was what Moses had said Joshua must do. So the priests carrying the Ark of the Covenant continued standing in the middle of the river until everything was done. And the people hurried across the river. [11] The people finished crossing the river. Then the priests carried the Ark of the Covenant of the Lord to the

> The Ark of the Covenant will go ahead of you into the Jordan River.
>
> –JOSHUA 3:11

other side. As they carried it, the people watched. ¹²The men from the tribes of Reuben, Gad and the eastern half-tribe of Manasseh obeyed what Moses had told them. They were prepared for war. So they crossed the river ahead of the other people. ¹³About 40,000 soldiers were prepared for war. They passed before the Lord as they marched across the river. Then they went toward the plains of Jericho to go to war.

¹⁴That day the Lord made Joshua a great man to all the Israelites. They respected Joshua all his life, just as they had respected Moses.

¹⁵Then the Lord spoke to Joshua. ¹⁶He said, "Command the priests to bring the Ark of the Covenant out of the river."

¹⁷So Joshua commanded the priests, "Come up out of the Jordan."

¹⁸So the priests carried the Ark of the Covenant with the Lord out of the river. As soon as their feet touched dry land, the water began flowing again. The river again overflowed its banks. It was just as it had been before they crossed.

¹⁹The people crossed the Jordan on the tenth day of the first month. They camped at Gilgal, east of Jericho. ²⁰They carried with them the 12 rocks taken from the Jordan. And Joshua set them up at Gilgal. ²¹Then he spoke to the Israelites. He said, "In the future your children will ask you, 'What do these rocks mean?' ²²Tell them, 'Israel crossed the Jordan River on dry land. ²³The Lord your God caused the water to stop flowing. The river was dry until the people finished crossing it. The Lord did the same thing for us at the Jordan that he did for the people at the Red Sea. Remember that he stopped the water at the Red Sea so we could cross. ²⁴The Lord did this so all people would know he has great power. Then they will always respect the Lord your God.'"

5 So the Lord dried up the Jordan River until the Israelites had crossed it. Now all the kings of the Amorites west of the Jordan heard about it. And the Canaanite kings living by the Mediterranean Sea heard about it. They were very scared. After that they were too afraid to face the Israelites.

THE ISRAELITES ARE CIRCUMCISED

²At that time the Lord spoke to Joshua. He said, "Make knives from flint stones. Circumcise the Israelites again." ³So Joshua made knives from flint stones. Then he circumcised the Israelites at Gibeath Haaraloth.

⁴This is why Joshua circumcised the men: After the Israelites left Egypt, all the men old enough to serve in the army died. They died in the desert on the way out of Egypt. ⁵The men who had come out of Egypt had been circumcised. But many were born in the desert on the trip from Egypt. They had not been circumcised. ⁶The Israelites had moved about in the desert for 40 years. During that time all the fighting men who had left Egypt had died. This was because they had not obeyed the Lord. So the Lord swore they would not see the land. This was the land he had promised their ancestors to give them. It was a land where much food grows. ⁷So their sons took their places. But none of the sons born on the trip from Egypt had been circumcised. So Joshua circumcised them. ⁸After all the Israelites had been circumcised, they stayed in camp until they were healed.

⁹Then the Lord said to Joshua, "As slaves in Egypt you were ashamed. But today I have removed that shame." So Joshua named that place Gilgal. And it is still named Gilgal today.

¹⁰The people of Israel were still camped at Gilgal on the plains of Jericho. It was there, on the evening of the fourteenth day of the month, they celebrated the Passover Feast. ¹¹The next day after the Passover, the people ate some of the food grown on that land: bread made without yeast and roasted grain. ¹²The day they ate this food, the manna stopped coming. The

Israelites no longer got the manna from heaven. They ate the food grown in the land of Canaan that year.

¹³Joshua was near Jericho. He looked up and saw a man standing in front of him. The man had a sword in his hand. Joshua went to him and asked, "Are you a friend or an enemy?"

¹⁴The man answered, "I am neither one. I have come as the commander of the Lord's army."

Then Joshua bowed facedown on the ground. He asked, "Does my master have a command for me, his servant?"

¹⁵The commander of the Lord's army answered, "Take off your sandals. The place where you are standing is holy." So Joshua did.

THE FALL OF JERICHO

6 Now the people of Jericho were afraid because the Israelites were near. So they closed the city gates and guarded them. No one went into the city. And no one came out.

²Then the Lord spoke to Joshua. He said, "Look, I have given you Jericho, its king and all its fighting men. ³March around the city with your army one time every day. Do this for six days. ⁴Have seven priests carry trumpets made from horns of male sheep. Tell them to march in front of the Ark of the Covenant. On the seventh day march around the city seven times. On that day tell the priests to blow the trumpets as they march. ⁵They will make one long blast on the trumpets. When you hear that sound, have all the people give a loud shout. Then the walls of the city will fall. And the people will go straight into the city."

⁶So Joshua son of Nun called the priests together. He said to them, "Carry the Ark of the Covenant with the Lord. Tell seven priests to carry trumpets and march in front of it." ⁷Then Joshua ordered the people, "Now go! March around the city. The soldiers with weapons should march in front of the Ark of the Covenant with the Lord."

⁸So Joshua finished speaking to the people. Then the seven priests began marching before the Lord. They carried the seven trumpets and blew them as they marched. The priests carrying the Ark of the Covenant with the Lord followed them. ⁹The soldiers with weapons marched in front of the priests. And armed men walked behind the Ark of the Covenant. They were blowing their trumpets. ¹⁰But Joshua had told the people not to give a war cry. He said, "Don't shout. Don't say a word until the day I tell you. Then shout!" ¹¹So Joshua had the Ark of the Covenant of the Lord carried around the city one time. Then they went back to camp for the night.

¹²Early the next morning Joshua got up. And the priests carried the Ark of the Covenant of the Lord again. ¹³The seven priests carried the seven trumpets. They marched in front of the Ark of the Covenant of the Lord, blowing their trumpets. The soldiers with weapons marched in front of them. Other soldiers walked behind the Ark of the Covenant of the Lord. All this time the priests were blowing their trumpets. ¹⁴So on the second day they marched around the city one time. Then they went back to camp. They did this every day for six days.

¹⁵On the seventh day they got up at dawn. They marched around the city seven times. They marched just as they had on the days before. But on that day they marched around the city seven times. ¹⁶The seventh time around the priests blew their trumpets. Then Joshua gave the command: "Now, shout! The Lord has given you this city! ¹⁷The city and everything in it are to be destroyed as an offering to the Lord. Only Rahab the prostitute and everyone in her house should remain alive. They must not be killed. This is because Rahab hid the two spies we sent out. ¹⁸Don't take any of the things that are to be destroyed as an offering to the Lord. If you take them and bring them into our camp, then you yourselves will be destroyed. You will

also bring trouble to all of Israel. ¹⁹All the silver and gold and things made from bronze and iron belong to the Lord. They must be saved for him."

²⁰When the priests blew the trumpets, the people shouted. At the sound of the trumpets and the people's shout, the walls fell. And everyone ran straight into the city. So the Israelites defeated that city. ²¹They completely destroyed every living thing in the city. They killed men and women, young and old. They killed cattle, sheep and donkeys.

²²Joshua spoke to the two men who had spied out the land. Joshua said, "Go into the prostitute's house. Bring her out. And bring out all the people who are with her. Do this because of the promise you made to her." ²³So the two men went into the house and brought out Rahab. They also brought out her father, mother, brothers and all those with her. They put all of her family in a safe place outside the camp of Israel.

²⁴Then Israel burned the whole city and everything in it. But they did not burn the things made from silver, gold, bronze and iron. These were saved for the Lord. ²⁵Joshua saved Rahab the prostitute, her family and all who were with her. He let them live. This was because Rahab had helped the men he had sent to spy out Jericho. Rahab still lives among the Israelites today.

²⁶Then Joshua made this important promise. He said:

"Anyone who tries to rebuild this city
   of Jericho
   will be punished by a curse from
      the Lord.
The man who lays the foundation of
      this city
   will lose his oldest son.
The man who sets up the gates
   will lose his youngest son."

²⁷So the Lord was with Joshua. And Joshua became famous through all the land.

THE SIN OF ACHAN

7 But the people of Israel did not obey the Lord. There was a man from the tribe of Judah named Achan. (He was the son of Carmi and grandson of Zimri. And Zimri was the son of Zerah.) Achan kept some of the things that were to be given to the Lord. So the Lord became very angry at the Israelites.

²Joshua sent some men from Jericho to Ai. (Ai was near Beth Aven, east of Bethel.) He told them, "Go to Ai and spy out the area." So the men went to spy on Ai.

³Later they came back to Joshua. They said, "There are only a few men in Ai to fight against us. So we will not need all our people to defeat them. Send 2,000 or 3,000 men to fight there. There is no need to send all of our people." ⁴So about 3,000 men went to Ai. But the people of Ai beat them badly. ⁵The people of Ai chased the Israelites. They chased them from the city gate all the way to where stones were cut from the ground. They killed about 36 Israelites as they went down the hill. When the Israelites saw this, they became very afraid.

⁶Then Joshua tore his clothes to show how upset he was. He bowed facedown on the ground before the Ark of the Covenant. And he stayed there until evening. The leaders of Israel did the same thing. They also threw dirt on their heads to show they were upset. ⁷Then Joshua said, "Lord God, you brought our people across the Jordan River. Why did you bring us this far and then let the Amorites destroy us? We should have been happy to stay on the other side of the Jordan. ⁸Lord, there is nothing I can say now. Israel has been beaten by the enemy. ⁹The Canaanites and all the other people in this country will hear about this. They will surround and kill all of us! Then what will you do for your own great name?"

¹⁰The Lord said to Joshua, "Stand up! Why are you down on your face? ¹¹The Israelites have sinned. They have

broken the agreement I commanded them to obey. They took some of the things I commanded them to destroy. They have stolen from me. They have lied. They have taken those things for themselves. [12]That is why the Israelites cannot face their enemies. They turn away from the fight and run. I have commanded that they be destroyed. You must destroy everything I commanded you to destroy. I will not help you anymore unless you do this.

[13]"Now go! Have the people make themselves holy for me. Tell them, 'Set yourselves apart to the Lord for tomorrow. The Lord, the God of Israel, says some of you are keeping things he commanded you to destroy. You will never defeat your enemies until you throw away those things.

[14]"'Tomorrow morning you must all stand before the Lord. All the tribes will stand before him. The Lord will choose one tribe. And that tribe must stand alone before him. Then the Lord will choose one family group from that tribe. And that family group must stand alone before him. Then the Lord will choose one family from that family group. And it must stand alone before him. Then the Lord will look at that family man by man. [15]The man who is keeping what should have been destroyed will himself be destroyed by fire. And everything he owns will be destroyed with him. He has broken the agreement with the Lord. He has done a disgraceful thing among the people of Israel!'"

[16]Early the next morning Joshua led all of Israel before the Lord. All of the tribes stood before him. And the Lord chose the tribe of Judah. [17]So all the family groups of Judah stood before the Lord. The Lord then chose the family group of Zerah. And all the families of Zerah stood before the Lord. Then the family of Zimri was chosen. [18]And Joshua told all the men in that family to come before the Lord. The Lord chose Achan son of Carmi. (Carmi was the son of Zimri. And Zimri was the son of Zerah.)

[19]Then Joshua said to Achan, "My son, you should tell the truth. Confess to the Lord, the God of Israel. Tell me what you did. Don't try to hide anything from me."

[20]Achan answered, "It is true! I have sinned against the Lord, the God of Israel. This is what I did: [21]Among the things I saw was a beautiful coat from Babylonia. And I saw about five pounds of silver and more than one and one-quarter pounds of gold. I wanted these things very much for myself. So I took them. You will find them buried in the ground under my tent. The silver is under the coat."

[22]So Joshua sent some men to the tent. They ran to the tent and found the things hidden there. The silver was under the coat. [23]The men brought them out of the tent. Then they took them to Joshua and all the Israelites. They spread them out on the ground before the Lord. [24]Then Joshua and all the people led Achan son of Zerah to the Valley of Trouble. They also took the silver, the coat and the gold. They took Achan's sons, daughters, cattle, donkeys, sheep, tent and everything he owned. [25]Joshua said, "I don't know why you caused so much trouble for us. But now the Lord will bring trouble to you." Then all the people threw stones at Achan until he died. They also killed his family with stones. Then the people burned them. [26]They piled rocks over Achan's body. And those rocks are still there today. That is why it is called the Valley of Trouble. After this the Lord was no longer angry.

AI IS DESTROYED

8 Then the Lord said to Joshua, "Don't be afraid. Don't give up. Lead all your fighting men to Ai. I will help you defeat the king of Ai. I am giving you his people, his city and his land. [2]You will do to Ai and its king what you did to Jericho and its king. Only this time you may take all the wealth. You may keep it for yourselves.

Now tell some of your soldiers to set up an ambush behind the city."

³So Joshua led his whole army toward Ai. Then he chose 30,000 of his best fighting men. He sent these men out at night. ⁴Joshua gave them these orders: "Listen carefully. You must set up an ambush behind the city. Don't go far from it. Continue to watch and be ready. ⁵I and the men who are with me will march toward the city. The men in the city will come out to fight us. Then we will turn and run away from them as we did before. ⁶They will chase us away from the city. They will think we are running away from them as we did before. When we run away, ⁷come out from your ambush and take the city. The Lord your God will give you the power to win. ⁸After you take the city, burn it. See to it! You have your orders."

⁹Then Joshua sent them to their place of ambush to wait. They went to a place between Bethel and Ai, to the west of Ai. But Joshua stayed the night with his people.

¹⁰Early the next morning Joshua gathered his men together. He and the older leaders of Israel led them to Ai. ¹¹All of the soldiers who were with Joshua marched to Ai. They stopped in front of the city and made camp north of Ai. There was a valley between them and the city. ¹²Then Joshua chose about 5,000 men. He set them in ambush in the area west of the city between Bethel and Ai. ¹³So the people took their positions. The main camp was north of the city. The other men were hiding to the west. That night Joshua went down into the valley.

¹⁴Now the king of Ai saw the army of Israel. So he and his people got up early the next morning and hurried out to fight them. They went out to a place east of the city. The king did not know soldiers were waiting in ambush behind the city. ¹⁵Joshua and all the men of Israel let the army of Ai push them back. Then they ran east toward the desert. ¹⁶The men in Ai were called to chase Joshua and his men. So they left the city and went after them. ¹⁷All the men of Ai and Bethel chased the army of Israel. The city was left open. Not a man stayed to protect it.

¹⁸Then the Lord said to Joshua, "Hold your spear toward Ai. I will give you that city." So Joshua held his spear toward the city of Ai. ¹⁹The men of Israel who were in ambush saw this. They quickly came out of their hiding place and hurried toward the city. They entered the city and took control of it. Then they quickly set it on fire.

²⁰When the men of Ai looked back, they saw smoke rising from their city. At the same time the men of Israel stopped running. They turned against the men of Ai. The men of Ai could not escape in any direction. ²¹Joshua and all his men saw that the army had taken control of the city. They saw the smoke rising from it. So they stopped running and turned to fight the men of Ai. ²²The men who were in ambush also came out of the city to help with the fight. The men of Ai were caught between the armies of Israel. The Israelites fought until not one of the men of Ai was left alive. None of the enemy escaped. ²³But the king of Ai was left alive. And Joshua's men brought him to Joshua.

A REVIEW OF THE FIGHTING

²⁴During the fighting the army of Israel chased the men of Ai into the fields and desert. So the Israelites killed all

> Then the Lord said to Joshua, "Don't be afraid. Don't give up."
>
> —JOSHUA 8:1

of them in the fields and desert. Then they went back to Ai and killed everyone there. ²⁵All the people of Ai died that day, 12,000 men and women. ²⁶Joshua had held his spear toward Ai. It was a sign to his people to destroy the city. And Joshua held out his spear until all the people of Ai were destroyed. ²⁷The people of Israel kept the animals for themselves. They also kept the other things the people of Ai had owned. This is what the Lord told them to do when he gave Joshua the commands.

²⁸Then Joshua burned the city of Ai. It became an empty pile of ruins. And it is still like that today. ²⁹Joshua hung the king of Ai on a tree. He left him hanging there until evening. At sunset Joshua told his men to take the king's body down from the tree. He told them to throw it down at the city gate. Then they covered it with rocks. That pile of rocks is still there today.

³⁰Then Joshua built an altar for the Lord, the God of Israel. He built it on Mount Ebal, as ³¹Moses, the Lord's servant, had commanded. Joshua built the altar as it was explained in the Book of the Teachings of Moses. The altar was made from stones that were not cut. No tool was ever used on them. The Israelites offered burnt offerings to the Lord on that altar. They also offered fellowship offerings. ³²There Joshua wrote the teachings of Moses on stones. He did this for all the people of Israel to see. ³³The elders, officers, judges and all the Israelites were there. They were standing around the Ark of the Covenant with the Lord. They stood before the priests, the Levites who had carried the Ark of the Covenant. Israelites and non-Israelites were all standing there. Half of the people stood in front of Mount Ebal. The other half stood in front of Mount Gerizim. This was the way the Lord's servant Moses had earlier commanded the people to be blessed.

³⁴Then Joshua read all the words of the teachings. He read the blessings and the curses. He read it exactly as they were written in the Book of the Teachings. ³⁵All the Israelites were gathered together. All the women and children were there. All the non-Israelites living with the Israelites were there. Joshua read every command that Moses had given.

THE GIBEONITE TRICKERY

9 All the kings west of the Jordan River heard about these things. These were the kings of the Hittites, Amorites, Canaanites, Perizzites, Hivites and Jebusites. They lived in the mountains and on the western mountain slopes. They also lived along the whole Mediterranean Sea coast. ²All these kings gathered to fight Joshua and the Israelites.

³The people of Gibeon heard how Joshua had defeated Jericho and Ai. ⁴So they decided to trick the Israelites. They gathered old leather wine bags that were cracked and mended. They put them on the backs of their donkeys. They also put old sacks on their donkeys. ⁵The men put old sandals on their feet and wore old clothes. They took some dry, moldy bread. ⁶Then they went to Joshua in the camp near Gilgal.

The men spoke to Joshua and the men of Israel. They said, "We have traveled from a faraway country. Make a peace agreement with us."

⁷The men of Israel said to these Hivites, "Maybe you live near us. How can we make a peace agreement with you?"

⁸The Hivites said to Joshua, "We are your servants."

But Joshua asked, "Who are you? Where do you come from?"

⁹The men answered, "We are your servants. We have come from a far country. We came because we heard of the fame of the Lord your God. We heard about what he has done. We heard about everything he did in Egypt. ¹⁰We heard that he defeated the two

kings of the Amorites. They were from the east side of the Jordan River: Sihon king of Heshbon and Og king of Bashan who was king in Ashtaroth. [11]So our elders and our people spoke to us. They said, 'Take food for your journey. Go and meet the Israelites. Tell them, "We are your servants. Make a peace agreement with us."'

[12]"Look at our bread. When we left home it was warm and fresh. But now it is dry and moldy. [13]Look at our leather winebags. When we left home they were new and filled with wine. Now they are cracked and old. Look at our clothes and sandals. The long journey has almost destroyed them."

[14]The men of Israel tasted the bread. But they did not ask the Lord what to do. [15]So Joshua agreed to make peace with the Gibeonites. He agreed to let them live. The leaders of the Israelites made a promise to keep the agreement.

[16]Three days later the Israelites learned that the Gibeonites lived nearby. [17]So the Israelites went to where they lived. On the third day the Israelites came to their cities. The cities were Gibeon, Kephirah, Beeroth and Kiriath Jearim. [18]But the Israelites did not attack those cities. They had made a promise to them before the Lord, the God of Israel.

All the Israelites grumbled against the leaders who had made the agreement. [19]But the leaders answered, "We have given our promise before the Lord, the God of Israel. We cannot attack them now. [20]This is what we must do. We must let them live. We cannot hurt them, or God's anger will be against us. We would be breaking the promise we made to them. [21]So let them live. But they will cut wood and carry water for our people." So the leaders kept their promise of peace to them.

[22]Joshua called for the Gibeonites. He said, "Why did you lie to us? Your land was near our camp. But you told us you were from a far country. [23]Now, you will be placed under a curse. You will be our slaves. You will have to cut wood and carry water for the people of the house of God."

[24]The Gibeonites answered Joshua, "We lied to you because we were afraid you would kill us. We heard that God commanded his servant Moses to give you all of this land. And God told you to kill all the people who lived in the land. That is why we did this. [25]Now you can decide what to do with us. You can do anything to us that you think is right."

[26]So Joshua saved their lives. He did not allow the Israelites to kill them. [27]But Joshua made the Gibeonites slaves to the Israelites. They cut wood and carried water for the Israelites. And they did it for the altar of the Lord—wherever he chose it to be. They are still doing this today.

THE SUN STANDS STILL

10 At this time Adoni-Zedek was the king of Jerusalem. He heard that Joshua had defeated Ai and completely destroyed it. He learned that Joshua had done the same thing to Jericho and its king. The king also learned that the Gibeonites had made a peace agreement with Israel. And they lived very near Jerusalem. [2]So Adoni-Zedek and his people were very afraid because of this. Gibeon was not a little town like Ai. It was a large city. It was as big as a city that had a king. All its men were good fighters. [3]So Adoni-Zedek king of Jerusalem sent a message to Hoham king of Hebron. He also sent it to Piram king of Jarmuth, Japhia king of Lachish, and Debir king of Eglon. The king of Jerusalem begged these men, [4]"Come with me and help me attack Gibeon. Gibeon has made a peace agreement with Joshua and the Israelites."

[5]Then these five Amorite kings joined their armies. They were the kings of Jerusalem, Hebron, Jarmuth, Lachish and Eglon. These armies went to Gibeon, surrounded it and attacked it.

⁶The Gibeonites sent a message to Joshua in his camp at Gilgal. The message said: "We are your servants. Don't let us be destroyed. Come quickly and help us! Save us! All the Amorite kings from the mountains have joined their armies. They are fighting against us."

⁷So Joshua marched out of Gilgal with his whole army. His best fighting men were with him. ⁸The Lord said to Joshua, "Don't be afraid of those armies. I will allow you to defeat them. None of them will be able to defeat you."

⁹Joshua and his army marched all night to Gibeon. So Joshua surprised them when he attacked. ¹⁰The Lord confused those armies when Israel attacked. So Israel defeated them in a great victory. They chased them from Gibeon on the road going to Beth Horon. The army of Israel killed men all the way to Azekah and Makkedah. ¹¹They chased the enemy down the road from Beth Horon to Azekah. While they were chasing them, the Lord threw large hailstones on them from the sky. Many of the enemy were killed by the hailstones. More men were killed by the hailstones than the Israelites killed with their swords.

¹²That day the Lord allowed the Israelites to defeat the Amorites. And that day Joshua stood before all the people of Israel and said to the Lord:

"Sun, stand still over Gibeon.
    Moon, stand still over the Valley of
    Aijalon."
¹³ So the sun stood still.
    And the moon stopped
    until the people defeated their
    enemies.

These words are written in the Book of Jashar.

The sun stopped in the middle of the sky. It waited to go down for a full day. ¹⁴That has never happened at any time before that day or since. That was the day the Lord listened to a man. Truly the Lord was fighting for Israel!

¹⁵After this, Joshua and his army went back to the camp at Gilgal.

¹⁶During the fight the five kings ran away. They hid in a cave near Makkedah. ¹⁷But someone found them hiding in the cave and told Joshua. ¹⁸So he said, "Cover the opening to the cave with large rocks. Put some men there to guard it. ¹⁹But don't stay there yourselves. Continue chasing the enemy. Continue attacking them from behind. Don't let them get to their cities safely. The Lord your God has given you the victory over them."

²⁰So Joshua and the Israelites killed the enemy. But a few were able to get back to their strong, walled cities. ²¹After the fighting, Joshua's men came back safely to him at Makkedah. No one was brave enough to say a word against the Israelites.

²²Joshua said, "Move the rocks that are covering the opening to the cave. Bring those five kings out to me." ²³So Joshua's men brought the five kings out of the cave. They were the kings of Jerusalem, Hebron, Jarmuth, Lachish and Eglon. ²⁴They brought the five kings out to Joshua. He called all his men to come to that place. He said to the commanders of his army, "Come here! Put your feet on the necks of these kings." So they came close and put their feet on their necks.

²⁵Then Joshua said to his men, "Be strong and brave! Don't be afraid. I will

> The sun stopped in the middle of the sky. It waited to go down for a full day.
> –JOSHUA 10:13

show you what the Lord will do to the enemies you will fight in the future."

²⁶Then Joshua killed the five kings. He hung their bodies on five trees. And he left them hanging on the trees until evening.

²⁷At sunset Joshua told his men to take the bodies down from the trees. Then they threw their bodies into the same cave where they had been hiding. They covered the opening to the cave with large rocks. They are still there today.

²⁸That day Joshua defeated Makkedah. He killed the king and completely destroyed all the people in that city. He killed them as an offering to the Lord. There was no one left alive. He did the same thing to the king of Makkedah as he had done to the king of Jericho.

DEFEATING SOUTHERN CITIES

²⁹Then Joshua and all the Israelites traveled from Makkedah. They went to Libnah and attacked it. ³⁰The Lord allowed them to defeat it and its king. They killed every person in the city. No one was left alive. And they did the same thing to that king as they had done to the king of Jericho.

³¹Then Joshua and all the Israelites left Libnah and went to Lachish. They camped around Lachish and attacked it. ³²The Lord allowed them to defeat Lachish. On the second day Joshua defeated it. The Israelites killed everyone in that city. This was the same thing they had done to Libnah. ³³During this same time Horam king of Gezer came to help Lachish. But Joshua also defeated him and his army. There was no one left alive.

³⁴Then Joshua and all the Israelites went from Lachish to Eglon. They camped around Eglon and attacked it. ³⁵That day they captured Eglon. They killed all its people and completely destroyed everything in it as an offering to the Lord. This is the same thing they had done to Lachish.

³⁶Then Joshua and the Israelites went from Eglon to Hebron and attacked it. ³⁷They captured it and all the little towns near it. The Israelites killed everyone in Hebron. No one was left alive there. This was the same thing they had done to Eglon. They completely destroyed the city and all its people as an offering to the Lord.

³⁸Then Joshua and the Israelites went back to Debir and attacked it. ³⁹They captured that city, its king and all the little towns near it. They completely destroyed everyone in Debir as an offering to the Lord. No one was left alive there. Israel did to Debir and its king the same thing they had done to Libnah and its king. This was what they had done to Hebron.

⁴⁰So Joshua defeated all the kings of the cities of these areas: the mountains, southern Canaan, the western mountain slopes and the eastern mountain slopes. The Lord, the God of Israel, had told Joshua to completely destroy all the people as an offering to the Lord. So he left no one alive in those places. ⁴¹Joshua captured all the cities from Kadesh Barnea to Gaza. And he captured all the cities from Goshen to Gibeon. ⁴²He captured all these cities and their kings on one trip. He did it because the Lord, the God of Israel, was fighting for Israel.

⁴³Then Joshua and all the Israelites returned to their camp at Gilgal.

DEFEATING NORTHERN KINGS

11 Jabin king of Hazor heard about all that had happened. He sent messages to Jobab king of Madon, to the king of Shimron and to the king of Acshaph. ²He sent one to the kings in the northern mountains. Jabin also sent a message to the kings in the Jordan Valley south of Lake Galilee and in the western mountain slopes. He sent a message to the king of Naphoth Dor in the west. ³Jabin also sent one to the kings of the Canaanites in the east and in the west. He sent messages to the Amorites, Hittites, Perizzites and

Jebusites in the mountains. Jabin also sent one to the Hivites. They lived below Mount Hermon in the area of Mizpah. ⁴So the armies of all these kings came together. There were many fighting men, horses and chariots. It was a huge army. It looked like there were as many men as grains of sand on the seashore.

⁵All of these kings met together at the Waters of Merom. They joined their armies together into one camp. They made plans to fight against the Israelites.

⁶Then the Lord said to Joshua, "Don't be afraid of them. At this time tomorrow I will allow you to defeat them. You will kill all of them. You will cripple their horses and burn all their chariots."

⁷So Joshua and his whole army surprised the enemy. They attacked them at the Waters of Merom. ⁸The Lord allowed Israel to defeat them. They chased them to Greater Sidon, Misrephoth Maim and the Valley of Mizpah in the east. Israel fought until none of the enemy was left alive. ⁹Joshua did what the Lord said to do. He cut the legs of their horses and burned their chariots.

¹⁰Then Joshua went back and captured the city of Hazor. He killed the king of Hazor. (Hazor had been the leader of all the kingdoms that fought against Israel.) ¹¹Israel killed everyone in Hazor. They completely destroyed them. There was nothing left alive. Then they burned Hazor itself.

¹²Joshua captured all of these cities. He killed all of their kings. He completely destroyed everything in these cities. He did this the way Moses, the servant of the Lord, had commanded. ¹³But the Israelites did not burn any cities that were built on their hills, except Hazor. That city alone was burned by Joshua. ¹⁴The people of Israel kept for themselves everything they found in the cities. They kept all the animals they found. But they killed all the people there. They did not leave anyone

alive. ¹⁵Long ago the Lord had commanded his servant Moses to do this. Then Moses had commanded Joshua to do it. So Joshua obeyed God. He did everything the Lord had commanded Moses.

¹⁶So Joshua defeated all the people in the land. He had control of the mountains and the area of southern Canaan. He controlled all the areas of Goshen, the western mountain slopes and the Jordan Valley. He controlled the mountains of Israel and all the hills near them. ¹⁷Joshua controlled all the land from Mount Halak near Edom to Baal Gad. Baal Gad was in the Valley of Lebanon, below Mount Hermon. Joshua captured all the kings in the land and killed them. ¹⁸He fought against them for many years. ¹⁹The people of only one city in all the land had made a peace agreement with Israel. They were the Hivites living in Gibeon. All the other cities were defeated in war. ²⁰The Lord made those people stubborn so they would fight against Israel. This way he could completely destroy them without mercy. This is what the Lord had commanded Moses to do.

²¹Now Joshua fought the Anakites who lived in the mountains of Hebron, Debir, Anab, Judah and Israel. And he completely destroyed them and their towns. ²²There were no Anakites left living in the land of the Israelites. Only a few Anakites were left in Gaza, Gath and Ashdod. ²³Joshua took control of all the land of Israel. This was what the Lord had told Moses to do long ago. He gave the land to Israel because he had promised it to them. Then Joshua divided the land among the tribes of Israel. The fighting had finally ended. And there was peace in the land.

KINGS DEFEATED BY ISRAEL

12 The Israelites took control of the land east of the Jordan River. They now had all the land from the Arnon Ravine to Mount Hermon. And they had all the land along the eastern side of the Jordan Valley. Here are all the kings the Israelites defeated to take this land:

²Sihon was the king of the Amorites. He lived in the city of Heshbon. He ruled the land from Aroer at the Arnon Ravine to the Jabbok River. His land started in the middle of the ravine. This was their border with the Ammonites. Sihon ruled over half the land of Gilead. ³He also ruled over the eastern side of the Jordan Valley from Lake Galilee to the Dead Sea. And he ruled from Beth Jeshimoth south to the hills of Pisgah.

⁴Og king of Bashan was one of the last of the Rephaites. He ruled the land in Ashtaroth and Edrei. ⁵He ruled over Mount Hermon, Salecah and all the area of Bashan. His land ended where the people of Geshur and Maacah lived. Og also ruled half the land of Gilead. It stopped at the border of Sihon king of Heshbon.

⁶The Lord's servant Moses and the Israelites defeated all these kings. And Moses gave that land to the tribes of Reuben and Gad and to the eastern half-tribe of Manasseh. This land was to be their own.

⁷The Israelites also defeated kings in the land that was west of the Jordan River. Joshua led the people in this land. He gave the people this land and divided it among the 12 tribes. This was the land that was promised to them. It was between Baal Gad in the Valley of Lebanon and Mount Halak near Edom. ⁸This included the mountains, the western mountain slopes and the Jordan Valley. It also included the eastern mountain slopes, the desert and southern Canaan. This was the land where the Hittites, Amorites, Canaanites, Perizzites, Hivites and Jebusites had lived. The people of Israel defeated the king of each of the following cities: ⁹Jericho, Ai (near Bethel), ¹⁰Jerusalem, Hebron, ¹¹Jarmuth, Lachish, ¹²Eglon, Gezer, ¹³Debir, Geder, ¹⁴Hormah, Arad, ¹⁵Libnah, Adullam, ¹⁶Makkedah, Bethel, ¹⁷Tappuah, Hepher, ¹⁸Aphek, Lasharon, ¹⁹Madon, Hazor, ²⁰Shimron Meron, Acshaph, ²¹Taanach, Megiddo, ²²Kedesh, Jokneam in Carmel, ²³Dor (in Naphoth Dor), Goyim in Gilgal, and ²⁴Tirzah.

The total number of kings was 31.

LAND STILL TO BE TAKEN

13 When Joshua was very old, the Lord spoke to him. He said, "Joshua, you have grown old. But there is still much land for you to take. ²You have not yet taken the land of Geshur and the land of the Philistines. ³You have not yet taken the area from the Shihor River at the border of Egypt to Ekron in the north. That belongs to the Canaanites. You must still defeat the five Philistine leaders. They are at Gaza, Ashdod, Ashkelon, Gath and Ekron. You must also defeat the Avvites. ⁴They live south of the Canaanite land. ⁵You have not yet defeated the Gebalites. And there is also the area of Lebanon east of Baal Gad below Mount Hermon to Lebo Hamath.

⁶"The Sidonians are living in the hill country from Lebanon to Misrephoth Maim. But I will force out all of them ahead of the Israelites. Be sure to remember this land when you divide the land among the Israelites. Do this as I told you.

⁷"Now divide the land among the nine tribes and the western half-tribe of Manasseh."

DIVIDING THE LAND

⁸The eastern half-tribe of Manasseh and the tribes of Reuben and Gad had received their land. The Lord's servant Moses gave them the land east of the Jordan River. ⁹Their land started at Aroer at the Arnon Ravine. It continued to the town in the middle of the ravine. And it included the whole plain from Medeba to Dibon. ¹⁰All the towns that Sihon king of the Amorites ruled were in that land. He ruled in the city of Heshbon. The land continued to

the area where the Ammonites lived. ¹¹Gilead was also there. And the area where the people of Geshur and Maacah lived was in that land. All of Mount Hermon and all of Bashan as far as Salecah was included. ¹²All the kingdom of Og king of Bashan was in the land. In the past he ruled in Ashtaroth and Edrei. Og was one of the last of the Rephaites. In the past Moses had defeated them and had taken their land. ¹³The Israelites did not force out the people of Geshur and Maacah. They still live among the Israelites today.

¹⁴The tribe of Levi was the only one that did not get any land. Instead, they were to be given all the burned sacrifices made to the Lord, the God of Israel. That is what the Lord had promised them.

¹⁵Moses had given each family group from the tribe of Reuben some land. This is the land they were given: ¹⁶It was the land from Aroer near the Arnon Ravine to the town of Medeba. This included the whole plain and the town in the middle of the ravine. ¹⁷The land continued to Heshbon. It included all the towns on the plain. These towns were Dibon, Bamoth Baal and Beth Baal Meon. ¹⁸They included Jahaz, Kedemoth, Mephaath, ¹⁹Kiriathaim, Sibmah and Zereth Shahar on the hill in the valley. ²⁰They also included Beth Peor, the hills of Pisgah and Beth Jeshimoth. ²¹So that land included all the towns on the plain and all the area that Sihon the king of the Amorites had ruled. He ruled from the town of Heshbon. But Moses had defeated him and the leaders of the Midianites. Those leaders included Evi, Rekem, Zur, Hur and Reba. All these leaders fought together with Sihon. And they lived in that country. ²²The Israelites killed many people during the fighting. They also killed Balaam of Beor. He tried to use magic to tell the future. ²³The land given to Reuben stopped at the shore of the Jordan River. So the land given to the family groups of Reuben included

all these towns and their fields that were listed.

²⁴This is the land Moses gave to the tribe of Gad. He gave it to all the family groups: ²⁵He gave them the land of Jazar and all the towns of Gilead. He also gave them half the land of the Ammonites. It went as far as Aroer near Rabbah. ²⁶It included the area from Heshbon to Ramath Mizpah and Betonim. It included the area from Mahanaim to the land of Debir. ²⁷The land included the valley, Beth Haram, Beth Nimrah, Succoth and Zaphon. All the other land Sihon king of Heshbon had ruled was also included in it. This is the land on the east side of the Jordan River. It continued to the end of Lake Galilee. ²⁸All this is the land Moses gave to the tribe of Gad. It included all the towns that were listed. Moses gave it to all the family groups.

²⁹This is the land Moses had given to the eastern half-tribe of Manasseh. Half of all the family groups in the tribe of Manasseh were given this land: ³⁰The land started at Mahanaim. It included all of Bashan and the land ruled by Og king of Bashan. It also included all the Towns of Jair in Bashan. There were 60 cities in all. ³¹It also included half of Gilead, Ashtaroth and Edrei. (These were the cities where Og king of Bashan had ruled.) All this land had been given to the family of Makir son of Manasseh. Half of all his sons had been given this land.

³²Moses had given this land to these tribes on the plains of Moab. It was across the Jordan River east of Jericho. ³³But Moses had given no land to the tribe of Levi. The Lord, the God of Israel, promised that he himself would be the gift for the Levites.

14 Eleazar the priest, Joshua son of Nun and the leaders of all the tribes of Israel decided what land to give to the people. ²The Lord had commanded Moses long ago how he wanted the people to choose their land. The people of the nine-and-a-half

Caleb remembered what Moses had promised him before he died. Caleb would inherit a piece of land called Hebron. Caleb got his land and his children and grandchildren and great-grandchildren lived in Hebron for many years.

Caleb, Joshua, and ten other men had been sent by Moses to explore the land God had promised to give to Israel (Numbers 13). When they got there, they saw that it was a wonderful place. It was full of all kinds of food. The clusters of grapes had to be carried by two men! It would be a great place to live, but there was a huge problem. There were giants already living in the land. When everybody else was afraid, Caleb and Joshua trusted in God. Caleb believed God would defeat the giants and Israel would get their land. Caleb believed God. He had faith.

· ·

When you read your Bible, you learn what God's promises are. Then you can believe and have faith like Caleb.

tribes threw lots to decide which land they would receive. ³Moses had already given the two-and-a-half tribes their land east of the Jordan River. But the tribe of Levi was not given any land like the others. ⁴The sons of Joseph had divided into two tribes—Manasseh and Ephraim. The tribe of Levi was not given any land. It was given only some towns in which to live. It was also given pastures for its animals. ⁵The Lord had told Moses how to give the land to the tribes of Israel. The Israelites divided the land as the Lord had commanded.

CALEB'S LAND

⁶One day some men from the tribe of Judah went to Joshua at Gilgal. One of those men was Caleb son of Jephunneh the Kenizzite. He said to Joshua, "You remember what the Lord said at Kadesh Barnea. He was speaking to the prophet Moses about you and me. ⁷Moses, the Lord's servant, sent me to look at the land where we were going. I was 40 years old then. When I came back, I told Moses what I thought about the land. ⁸The other men who went with me told the people things that made them afraid. But I fully believed the Lord would allow us to take the land. ⁹So that day Moses promised me, 'The land where you went will become your land. Your children will own it forever. I will give you that land because you fully believed in the Lord, my God.'

[10]"Now then, the Lord has kept his promise. He has kept me alive for 45 years from the time he said this to Moses. During that time we all wandered in the desert. Now here I am, 85 years old. [11]I am still as strong today as I was the day Moses sent me out. I am just as ready to fight now as I was then. [12]So give me the mountain country the Lord promised me that day long ago. Back then you heard that the Anakite people lived there. And the cities were large and well protected. But now with the Lord helping me, I will force them out, just as the Lord said."

[13]Joshua blessed Caleb son of Jephunneh. He gave him the city of Hebron as his own. [14]And Hebron still belongs to the family of Caleb son of Jephunneh the Kenizzite. It still belongs to his people because he had faith. He obeyed the Lord, the God of Israel. [15](In the past it was called Kiriath Arba. It was named for the greatest man among the Anakites. He was named Arba.)

After this there was peace in the land.

LAND FOR JUDAH

15 The land that was given to the tribe of Judah was divided among all the family groups. It went all the way to the Desert of Zin in the far south, at the border of Edom.

[2]The southern border of Judah's land started at the south end of the Dead Sea. [3]It went south of Scorpion Pass to Zin. From there it passed to the south of Kadesh Barnea. It continued past Hezron to Addar. From Addar it turned and went to Karka. [4]It continued to Azmon, the brook of Egypt and then to the Mediterranean Sea. This was the southern border.

[5]The eastern border was the shore of the Dead Sea. It went as far as the area where the Jordan River flowed into the sea.

The northern border started at the area where the Jordan River flowed into the Dead Sea. [6]Then it went to Beth Hoglah and continued north of Beth Arabah. It continued to the stone of Bohan. Bohan was the son of Reuben. [7]Then the northern border went through the Valley of Achor to Debir. There it turned toward the north and went to Gilgal. Gilgal is across from the road that goes through the mountain of Adummim. It is on the south side of the ravine. The border continued along the waters of En Shemesh. It stopped at En Rogel. [8]Then it went through the Valley of Ben Hinnom. This is next to the southern side of the Jebusite city. (That city was called Jerusalem.) There the border went to the top of the hill on the west side of Hinnom Valley. This was at the northern end of the Valley of Giants. [9]From there it went to the spring of the Waters of Nephtoah. Then it went to the cities near Mount Ephron. There it turned and went toward Baalah. (Baalah is also called Kiriath Jearim.) [10]At Baalah the border turned west and went toward Mount Edom. It continued along the north side of Mount Jearim (also called Kesalon) and came to Beth Shemesh. From there it went past Timnah. [11]Then it went to the hill north of Ekron. From there it turned toward Shikkeron and went past Mount Baalah. It continued on to Jabneel and ended at the sea.

[12]The Mediterranean Sea was the western border. Inside these borders lived the family groups of Judah.

[13]The Lord had commanded Joshua to give Caleb son of Jephunneh part of the land in Judah. So he gave Caleb the land God had commanded. He gave him the town of Kiriath Arba, also called Hebron. (Arba was the father of Anak.) [14]Caleb forced out the three Anakite families living in Hebron. Those families were Sheshai, Ahiman and Talmai. They were descendants of Anak. [15]Then he fought against the people living in Debir. (In the past Debir had been called Kiriath Sepher.) [16]Caleb said, "I want a man to attack and capture Kiriath Sepher. I will give him Acsah,

my daughter, as a wife." ¹⁷Othniel son of Kenaz defeated the city. So Caleb gave his daughter Acsah to Othniel to be his wife. ¹⁸Acsah wanted Othniel to ask her father Caleb for more land.

So Acsah went to her father. When she got off her donkey, Caleb asked her, "What do you want?"

¹⁹Acsah answered, "I would like a special favor. The land you gave me is very dry. So also give me land with springs of water on it."

So Caleb gave her land with springs of water on the upper and lower part of it.

²⁰The tribe of Judah got the land God had promised them. Each family group got part of the land.

²¹The tribe of Judah got all the towns in the southern part of Canaan. These towns were near the border of Edom. Here is a list of the towns: Kabzeel, Eder, Jagur, ²²Kinah, Dimonah, Adadah, ²³Kedesh, Hazor and Ithnan; ²⁴Ziph, Telem, Bealoth, ²⁵Hazor Hadattah and Kerioth Hezron (also called Hazor); ²⁶Amam, Shema, Moladah, ²⁷Hazar Gaddah, Heshmon and Beth Pelet; ²⁸Hazar Shual, Beersheba, Biziothiah, ²⁹Baalah, Iim, Ezem, ³⁰Eltolad, Kesil and Hormah; ³¹Ziklag, Madmannah, Sansannah, ³²Lebaoth, Shilhim, Ain and Rimmon. There were 29 towns and all their fields.

³³The tribe of Judah got these towns in the western mountain slopes: Eshtaol, Zorah, Ashnah, ³⁴Zanoah, En Gannim, Tappuah and Enam; ³⁵Jarmuth, Adullam, Socoh, Azekah, ³⁶Shaaraim, Adithaim and Gederah (also called Gederothaim). There were 14 towns and all their fields.

³⁷Judah was also given these towns in the western mountain slopes: Zenan, Hadashah, Migdal Gad, ³⁸Dilean, Mizpah, Joktheel, ³⁹Lachish, Bozkath and Eglon; ⁴⁰Cabbon, Lahmas, Kitlish, ⁴¹Gederoth, Beth Dagon, Naamah and Makkedah. There were 16 towns and all their fields.

⁴²Judah was also given these towns in the western mountain slopes: Libnah, Ether, Ashan, ⁴³Iphtah, Ashnah, Nezib, ⁴⁴Keilah, Aczib and Mareshah. There were nine towns and all their fields.

⁴⁵The tribe of Judah also got the town of Ekron and all the small towns and fields near it. ⁴⁶They also got the area west of Ekron and all the fields and towns near Ashdod. ⁴⁷Ashdod and all the small towns around it were part of the land of Judah. They also got the fields and towns around Gaza. Their land continued to the brook of Egypt. And it went on along the coast of the Mediterranean Sea.

⁴⁸The tribe of Judah was also given these towns in the mountains: Shamir, Jattir, Socoh, ⁴⁹Dannah and Kiriath Sannah (also called Debir); ⁵⁰Anab, Eshtemoh, Anim, ⁵¹Goshen, Holon and Giloh. There were 11 towns and all their fields.

⁵²They were also given these towns in the mountains: Arab, Dumah, Eshan, ⁵³Janim, Beth Tappuah and Aphekah; ⁵⁴Humtah, Kiriath Arba (also called Hebron) and Zior. There were 9 towns and all their fields.

⁵⁵Judah was also given these towns in the mountains: Maon, Carmel, Ziph, Juttah, ⁵⁶Jezreel, Jokdeam, Zanoah, ⁵⁷Kain, Gibeah and Timnah. There were 10 towns and all their fields.

⁵⁸They were also given these towns in the mountains: Halhul, Beth Zur, Gedor, ⁵⁹Maarath, Beth Anoth and Eltekon. There were 6 towns and all their fields.

⁶⁰The people of Judah were also given the 2 towns of Rabbah and Kiriath Baal (also called Kiriath Jearim).

⁶¹Judah was given towns in the desert. Here are those towns: Beth Arabah, Middin, Secacah, ⁶²Nibshan, the City of Salt and En Gedi. There were 6 towns and all their fields.

⁶³The army of Judah was not able to force out the Jebusites living in Jerusalem. So the Jebusites still live among the people of Judah in Jerusalem to this day.

LAND FOR EPHRAIM AND MANASSEH

16 This is the land the tribe of Joseph received. It started at the Jordan River near Jericho. It continued to the waters of Jericho, just east of the city. The border went up from Jericho to the mountains of Bethel. ²Then it continued from Bethel (also called Luz) to the Arkite border at Ataroth. ³From there it went west to the border of the Japhletites. It continued to the area of the Lower Beth Horon. Then it went to Gezer and ended at the sea.

⁴So Manasseh and Ephraim received their land. They were sons of Joseph.

⁵This is the land that was given to the family groups of Ephraim: Their border started at Ataroth Addar in the east. It went to Upper Beth Horon ⁶and then to the sea. From Micmethath it turned eastward toward Taanath Shiloh and continued eastward to Janoah. ⁷Then it went down from Janoah to Ataroth and to Naarah. It continued until it touched Jericho and stopped at the Jordan River. ⁸The border went from Tappuah west to Kanah Ravine and went to the sea. This is all the land that was given to the Ephraimites. Each family group in the tribe got a part of this land. ⁹Many of the border towns of Ephraim were actually within Manasseh's borders. But the people of Ephraim got those towns and their fields. ¹⁰The Ephraimites could not force the Canaanites to leave Gezer. So the Canaanites still live among the Ephraimites today. But they became slaves of the Ephraimites.

17 Then land was given to the tribe of Manasseh. He was Joseph's first son. Manasseh's first son was Makir, the father of Gilead. Makir was a great soldier. So the lands of Gilead and Bashan were given to his family. ²Land was also given to the other family groups of Manasseh. They were Abiezer, Helek, Asriel, Shechem, Hepher and Shemida. These were all the other sons of Manasseh son of Joseph.

³Zelophehad was the son of Hepher. Hepher was the son of Gilead. Gilead was the son of Makir, and Makir was the son of Manasseh. But Zelophehad had no sons. He had five daughters. The daughters were named Mahlah, Noah, Hoglah, Milcah and Tirzah. ⁴The daughters went to Eleazar the priest. They also went to Joshua son of Nun and all the leaders. They said, "The Lord told Moses to give us land like the men received." So Eleazar obeyed the Lord and gave the daughters some land. These daughters received land just as the brothers of their father did. ⁵So the tribe of Manasseh had ten sections of land west of the Jordan River. They also had two more sections, Gilead and Bashan. These sections were on the other side of the Jordan River. ⁶The daughters of Manasseh got land just as the sons did. Gilead was given to the rest of the families of Manasseh.

⁷The lands of Manasseh were in the area between Asher and Micmethath. This is near Shechem. The border went south to the En Tappuah area. ⁸The land of Tappuah belonged to Manasseh. But the town of Tappuah did not. It was along the border of Manasseh's land and belonged to the sons of Ephraim. ⁹The border of Manasseh continued south to Kanah Ravine. The cities in this area of Manasseh belonged to Ephraim. Manasseh's border was on the north side of the ravine and went to the sea. ¹⁰The land to the south belonged to Ephraim. And the land to the north belonged to Manasseh. The Mediterranean Sea was the western border. The border touched Asher's land on the north. And it touched Issachar's land on the east.

¹¹In the areas of Issachar and Asher, the people of Manasseh owned Beth Shan and its small towns. They also owned Ibleam and its small towns. And they owned all the people who lived in Dor and its small towns. They owned the people in Naphoth Dor and its small towns. And they owned all the

people who lived in Taanach and its small towns. Manasseh also owned the people in Megiddo and its small towns. [12]Manasseh was not able to defeat those cities. So the Canaanites continued to live there. [13]But the Israelites grew strong. When this happened, they forced the Canaanites to work for them. But they did not force them to leave the land.

[14]The people from the tribes of Joseph spoke to Joshua. They said, "You gave us only one area of land. But we are many people. Why did you give us only one part of all the land the Lord gave his people?"

[15]And Joshua answered them, "You have many people. Go up to the forest. Make a place for yourselves to live there. This is in the land of the Perizzites and the Rephaites. The mountain country of Ephraim is too small for you."

[16]The people of Joseph said, "It is true. The mountain country of Ephraim is not enough for us. But the land where the Canaanites live is dangerous. They are skilled fighters. They have powerful weapons in Beth Shan and all the small towns in that area. And they are also in the Valley of Jezreel."

[17]Then Joshua spoke to the people of Joseph—to Ephraim and to Manasseh. He said, "But there are many of you. And you have great power. You should be given more than one share of land. [18]You also will have the mountain country. It is a forest. But you can cut down the trees and make it a good place to live. And you will own all of it. You will force the Canaanites to leave the land. You can defeat them even though they have powerful weapons and are strong."

THE REST OF THE LAND DIVIDED

18 All of the Israelites gathered together at Shiloh. There they set up the Meeting Tent. The Israelites controlled that country. They had defeated all the enemies there. [2]But there were still seven tribes of Israel that had not yet received the land God had promised them.

[3]So Joshua said to the Israelites: "Why do you wait so long to take your land? The Lord, the God of your fathers, has given this land to you. [4]So each tribe should choose three men. I will send them out to study the land. They will describe in writing the land their tribe wants as its share. Then they will come back to me. [5]They will divide the land into seven parts. The people of Judah will keep their land in the south. The people of Joseph will keep their land in the north. [6]But you should divide the land into seven parts. Describe the seven parts in writing. Then bring what you have written to me. We will let the Lord our God decide which tribe will get which land. [7]But the Levites do not get any part of these lands. They are priests, and their work is to serve the Lord. Gad, Reuben and the eastern half-tribe of Manasseh have received the land promised to them. They are on the east side of the Jordan River. Moses, the servant of the Lord, gave it to them."

[8]So the men who were chosen started into the land. Their plan was to describe it in writing and take it back to Joshua. Joshua told them, "Go and study the land. Describe it in writing. Then come back to me. Then I will ask the Lord to choose the land you should get. We will do this here in Shiloh." [9]So the men left and went into the land. They studied it and described

> The Lord, the God of your fathers, has given this land to you.
>
> –JOSHUA 18:3

it in writing for Joshua. They studied each town. They saw that the land had seven parts. They described it in writing and then came back to Joshua. He was still at the camp at Shiloh. [10]Then Joshua asked the Lord to help. He threw lots to choose the lands that should be given to each tribe.

LAND FOR BENJAMIN

[11]The first part of the land was given to the tribe of Benjamin. Each family group in the tribe of Benjamin received some land. They were given the land between the land of Judah and the land of Joseph. This is the land chosen for Benjamin:

[12]The northern border started at the Jordan River. It went along the northern edge of Jericho. Then it went west into the mountains. That boundary continued until it was just east of Beth Aven. [13]From there it went south to Luz (also called Bethel). Then it went down to Ataroth Addar. Ataroth Addar is on the hill south of Lower Beth Horon.

[14]There is a hill to the south of Beth Horon. At this hill the border turned and went south near the western side of the hill. It went to Kiriath Baal (also called Kiriath Jearim). This is a town where people of Judah lived. It was the western border.

[15]The southern border started near Kiriath Jearim and went to the Waters of Nephtoah. [16]Then it went down to the bottom of the hill. This was near the Valley of Ben Hinnom. It was the north side of the Valley of Rephaim. The border continued down the Hinnom Valley just south of the Jebusite city to En Rogel. [17]There it turned north and went to En Shemesh. It continued to Geliloth near the Adummim Pass in the mountains. Then it went down to the great Stone of Bohan. Bohan was the son of Reuben. [18]The border continued to the northern part of Beth Arabah. Then it went down into the Jordan Valley. [19]From there it went to the northern part of Beth Hoglah. It ended at the north shore of the Dead Sea. This is where the Jordan River flows into the sea. This was the southern border.

[20]The Jordan River was the border on the eastern side. So this was the land given to the family groups of Benjamin. These were the borders on all sides.

[21]Each family group of Benjamin received some of this land. And these are the cities they owned: Jericho, Beth Hoglah, Emek Keziz, [22]Beth Arabah, Zemaraim and Bethel; [23]Avvim, Parah, Ophrah, [24]Kephar Ammoni, Ophni and Geba. There were 12 towns and all their villages.

[25]The tribe of Benjamin also owned Gibeon, Ramah and Beeroth. [26]They owned Mizpah, Kephirah, Mozah, [27]Rekem, Irpeel and Taralah. [28]They also owned Zelah, Haeleph, the Jebusite city (Jerusalem), Gibeah and Kiriath. There were 14 towns and all their villages. All these areas are the lands the tribe of Benjamin was given.

LAND FOR SIMEON

19 The second part of the land was given to the tribe of Simeon. Each family group received some of the land. It was inside the area of Judah. [2]They received Beersheba (also called Sheba), Moladah, [3]Hazar Shual, Balah, Ezem, [4]Eltolad, Bethul and Hormah. [5]They also received Ziklag, Beth Marcaboth, Hazar Susah, [6]Beth Lebaoth and Sharuhen. There were 13 towns and all their fields.

[7]They also received the towns of Ain, Rimmon, Ether and Ashan. There were 4 towns and all their fields. [8]They also received all the very small areas with people living in them as far as Baalath Beer. (This is the same as Ramah in southern Canaan.) So these were the lands given to the tribe of Simeon. Each family group received some of the land. [9]The land of the Simeonites was taken from part of the land of Judah. Judah had much more land than they needed. So the Simeonites received part of their land.

LAND FOR ZEBULUN

¹⁰The third part of the land was given to the tribe of Zebulun. Each family group of Zebulun received some of the land. The border of Zebulun went as far as Sarid. ¹¹Then it went west to Maralah and came near Dabbesheth. Then it went near Jokneam. ¹²Then it turned to the east. It went from Sarid to the area of Kisloth Tabor. From there it went on to Daberath and to Japhia. ¹³It continued eastward to Gath Hepher and Eth Kazin. Then it ended at Rimmon. Then the border turned and went toward Neah. ¹⁴At Neah it turned again and went to the north. It went to Hannathon and continued to the Valley of Iphtah El. ¹⁵Inside this border were the cities of Kattath, Nahalal, Shimron, Idalah and Bethlehem. There were 12 towns and all their fields.

¹⁶So these are the towns and the areas that were given to Zebulun. Each family group received some of the land.

LAND FOR ISSACHAR

¹⁷The fourth part of the land was given to the tribe of Issachar. Each family group of Issachar received some of the land. ¹⁸Their land included Jezreel, Kesulloth, Shunem, ¹⁹Hapharaim, Shion and Anaharath; ²⁰Rabbith, Kishion, Ebez, ²¹Remeth, En Gannim, En Haddah and Beth Pazzez.

²²The border of their land touched the area called Tabor, Shahazumah and Beth Shemesh. It stopped at the Jordan River. There were 16 towns and their fields.

²³These cities and towns were part of the land that was given to the tribe of Issachar. Each family group received part of this land.

LAND FOR ASHER

²⁴The fifth part of the land was given to the tribe of Asher. Each family group of Asher received some of the land. ²⁵Their land included Helkath, Hali, Beten, Acshaph, ²⁶Allammelech, Amad and Mishal.

The western border touched Mount Carmel and Shihor Libnath. ²⁷Then it turned toward the east. It went to Beth Dagon. It touched Zebulun and the Valley of Iphtah El. Then it went north of Beth Emek and Neiel. It passed north to Cabul. ²⁸Then it went to Abdon, Rehob, Hammon and Kanah. It continued to Greater Sidon. ²⁹Then the border went back south toward Ramah. It continued to the strong, walled city of Tyre. Then it turned and went toward Hosah. It ended at the sea. This was in the area of Aczib, ³⁰Ummah, Aphek and Rehob. There were 22 towns and their fields.

³¹These cities and their fields were part of the land that was given to the tribe of Asher. Each family group in that tribe received some of this land.

LAND FOR NAPHTALI

³²The sixth part of the land was given to the tribe of Naphtali. Each family group of Naphtali received some of the land. ³³The border of their land started at the large tree in the area of Zaanannim. This is near Heleph. Then it went through Adami Nekeb and Jabneel. It continued to the area of Lakkum and ended at the Jordan River. ³⁴Then it went to the west through Aznoth Tabor. It stopped at Hukkok. It went to the area of Zebulun on the south. And it went to the area of Asher on the west. It went to Judah, at the Jordan River, on the east. ³⁵There were some strong, walled cities inside these borders. Those cities were Ziddim, Zer, Hammath, Rakkath and Kinnereth; ³⁶Adamah, Ramah, Hazor, ³⁷Kedesh, Edrei and En Hazor; ³⁸Iron, Migdal El, Horem, Beth Anath and Beth Shemesh. There were 19 towns and all their fields.

³⁹The cities and the towns around them were in the land that was given to the tribe of Naphtali. Each family group in that tribe got some of this land.

LAND FOR DAN

⁴⁰The seventh part of the land was given to the tribe of Dan. Each family

group of Dan received some of the land.
⁴¹Their land included Zorah, Eshtaol,
Ir Shemesh, ⁴²Shaalabbin, Aijalon
and Ithlah; ⁴³Elon, Timnah, Ekron,
⁴⁴Eltekeh, Gibbethon, Baalath, ⁴⁵Jehud,
Bene Berak and Gath Rimmon; ⁴⁶Me
Jarkon, Rakkon and the area near Joppa.

⁴⁷(But the Danites had trouble taking
their land. There were strong enemies
there. And the Danites could not easily
defeat them. So the Danites went and
fought against Leshem. They defeated
Leshem and killed the people who lived
there. So the Danites lived in the town
of Leshem. They changed its name to
Dan because he was the father
of their tribe.) ⁴⁸All of these
cities and towns were given
to the tribe of Dan. Each
family group got part of
this land.

LAND FOR JOSHUA

⁴⁹So the Israelite lead-
ers finished dividing
the land and giving it
to the different tribes.
After they finished, all
the Israelites decided to
give Joshua son of Nun
some land, too. This was
land that had been prom-
ised to him. ⁵⁰The Lord had
commanded that he be given
this land. So they gave Joshua the town
of Timnath Serah in the mountains
of Ephraim. This was the town that
Joshua told them he wanted. So he built
up the town and lived there.

⁵¹So all of these lands were given to
the different tribes of Israel. Eleazar the
priest, Joshua son of Nun and the leaders
of each tribe worked together. They
divided up the land while they were at
Shiloh. They met before the Lord at the
entrance to the Meeting Tent to do this.
Now they had finished dividing the land.

CITIES OF SAFETY

20 Then the Lord said to Joshua:
²"Tell the Israelites to choose

the special cities of safety. This is what
I had Moses command you to do. ³A
person might kill someone accidentally
and without meaning to kill him. He
may go to a city of safety to hide. There
he will be safe from the relative who
has the duty of punishing a murderer.

⁴"This is what he must do. When he
runs to one of those cities, he must stop
at the entrance gate. He must stand
there and tell the leaders of the people
what happened. Then they will allow
him to enter the city. They will give him
a place to live among them. ⁵But the
one who is chasing him might follow
him to that city. If this happens,
the leaders of the city must
not give him up. They must
protect the person who
came to them for safety.
They must protect him
because he killed that
person accidentally.
He was not angry and
did not decide ahead of
time to kill the person.
⁶He should stay in the
city until he has been
judged by the court
there. And he should stay
until the high priest dies.
Then he may go back to his
own home in the town from
which he ran away."

⁷So the Israelites chose some cities
to be cities of safety. These cities were:
Kedesh in Galilee in the mountains of
Naphtali; Shechem in the mountains
of Ephraim; Kiriath Arba (also called
Hebron) in the mountains of Judah;
⁸Bezer on the east side of the Jordan
River near Jericho in the desert in the
land of Reuben; Ramoth in Gilead in
the land of Gad; and Golan in Bashan in
the land of Manasseh. ⁹Any Israelite or
anyone living among them who killed
someone accidentally was included. He
was to be allowed to run to one of these
cities of safety. Then he could be safe
there and would not be killed by the
relative who had the duty of punishing

> All the
> Israelites
> decided to
> give Joshua son
> of Nun some
> land, too.
>
> —JOSHUA 19:49

a murderer. He would be judged by the court in that city.

TOWNS FOR THE LEVITES

21 The heads of the Levite families went to talk to Eleazar the priest. They also talked to Joshua son of Nun and to the heads of the families of all the tribes of Israel. ²This happened at the town of Shiloh in the land of Canaan. The heads of the Levite families said to them, "The Lord commanded Moses that you give us towns where we may live. And he commanded that you give us pastures." ³So the Israelites obeyed this commandment of the Lord. They gave the Levite people these towns and pastures: ⁴The Kohath family groups were part of the tribe of Levi. Some of the Levites in the Kohath family groups were from the family of Aaron the priest. To these Levites were given 13 towns. These towns were in the areas that belonged to Judah, Simeon and Benjamin. ⁵The other family groups of Kohath were given 10 towns. These 10 towns were in the areas of Ephraim, Dan and West Manasseh.

⁶The people from the Gershon groups were given 13 towns. They were in the land that belonged to Issachar, Asher, Naphtali and the eastern half-tribe of Manasseh in Bashan.

⁷The family groups of Merari were given 12 towns. These 12 towns were in the area that belonged to Reuben, Gad and Zebulun.

⁸So the Israelites gave the Levites these towns and the pastures around them. They did this to obey the commandment that the Lord had given Moses.

⁹These are the names of the towns that came from the lands of Judah and Simeon. ¹⁰The first choice of towns was given to the Kohath family groups of the Levites. ¹¹They gave them Kiriath Arba (also called Hebron) and all its pastures. This was in the mountains of Judah. (Arba was the father of Anak.) ¹²But the fields and the small towns around the city of Kiriath Arba had been given to Caleb son of Jephunneh.

¹³So they gave the city of Hebron to the descendants of Aaron. (Hebron was a city of safety.) They also gave them these towns: Libnah, ¹⁴Jattir, Eshtemoa, ¹⁵Holon, Debir, ¹⁶Ain, Juttah and Beth Shemesh. They also gave them all the pastures that were around these towns. There were 9 towns given to these two groups.

¹⁷They also gave the people of Aaron cities that belonged to the tribe of Benjamin. These cities were Gibeon, Geba, ¹⁸Anathoth and Almon. They gave them these 4 towns and all the pastures around them.

¹⁹So these towns were given to the priests. These priests were from the family of Aaron. The total number of towns with their pastures was 13.

²⁰The other Kohathite family groups of the Levites were given these towns from the tribe of Ephraim: ²¹They gave them the city of Shechem from the mountains of Ephraim. (Shechem was a city of safety.) They also gave them Gezer, ²²Kibzaim and Beth Horon. There were 4 towns and their pastures.

²³The tribe of Dan gave them Eltekeh, Gibbethon, ²⁴Aijalon and Gath Rimmon. There were 4 towns and their pastures.

²⁵The western half-tribe of Manasseh gave them Taanach and Gath Rimmon. They were also given all the pastures around these 2 towns.

²⁶So this was 10 more towns and all the pastures around the towns. These were given to the rest of the Kohathite family groups.

²⁷The Gershonite family groups of the Levite tribe were given these towns: The eastern half-tribe of Manasseh gave them Golan in Bashan. (Golan was a city of safety.) Manasseh also gave them Be Eshtarah. All the pastures around these two towns were also given to the Gershonites.

²⁸The tribe of Issachar gave them Kishion, Daberath, ²⁹Jarmuth and En

Gannim. Issachar also gave them all the pastures around these 4 towns.

[30] The tribe of Asher gave them Mishal, Abdon, [31] Helkath and Rehob. All the pastures around these 4 towns were also given to them.

[32] The tribe of Naphtali gave them Kedesh in Galilee. (Kedesh was a city of safety.) Naphtali also gave them Hammoth Dor and Kartan. All the pastures around these 2 towns were also given to the Gershonites.

[33] So the Gershonite family groups received 13 towns. They also received all the pastures around these towns.

[34] The Merarite family groups (the rest of the Levites) were given these towns: The tribe of Zebulun gave them Jokneam, Kartah, [35] Dimnah and Nahalal. All the pastures around these 4 towns were also given to the Merarites.

[36] The tribe of Reuben gave them Bezer, Jahaz, [37] Kedemoth and Mephaath. All the pastures around these 4 towns were also given to the Merarites.

[38] The tribe of Gad gave them Ramoth in Gilead. (Ramoth was a city of safety.) They also gave them Mahanaim, [39] Heshbon and Jazer. Gad also gave them all the pastures around these 4 towns.

[40] So the total number of towns given to the Merarite family groups was 12.

[41] A total of 48 towns with their pastures were given to the Levites. All these towns were in the land controlled by the Israelites. [42] Each town had pastures around it.

[43] So the Lord kept the promise he had made to the Israelites. He gave the people all the land he had promised. The people took the land and lived there. [44] The Lord allowed them to have peace on all sides of their land. This is what he had promised to their people who lived long ago. None of their enemies defeated them. The Lord allowed the Israelites to defeat every enemy. [45] He kept every promise he had made to the Israelites. No promises failed. Each one came true.

THREE TRIBES GO HOME

22 Then Joshua called a meeting of all the people from the tribes of Reuben, Gad and the eastern half-tribe of Manasseh. [2] He said to them, "You have obeyed everything Moses told you to do. He was a servant of the Lord. And also, you have obeyed all my commands. [3] All this time you have supported all the other Israelites. You have been careful to obey all the commands the Lord your God gave you. [4] The Lord your God promised to give the Israelites peace. Now he has kept his promise. Now you may go back to your homes. You may go to the land that Moses, the Lord's servant, gave you. It is the land on the east side of the Jordan River. [5] But continue to obey the teachings Moses gave you. That law is to love the Lord your God and obey his commands. Continue to follow him and serve him the very best you can."

[6] Then Joshua said good-bye to them, and they left. They went away to their homes. [7] Moses had given the land of Bashan to the eastern half-tribe of Manasseh. Joshua gave land on the west side of the Jordan River to the western half-tribe of Manasseh. And he sent them to their homes. He blessed them. [8] He said, "Go back to your homes and your riches. You have many animals, silver, gold, bronze and iron. And you have many beautiful clothes. Also, you have taken many things from your enemies. You should divide these among yourselves."

[9] So the people from the tribes of Reuben, Gad and the eastern half-tribe of Manasseh left the other Israelites. They left Shiloh in Canaan and went back towards Gilead. This was their own land. Moses gave it to them as the Lord had commanded.

[10] The people of Reuben, Gad and the eastern half-tribe of Manasseh traveled to Geliloth. This was near the Jordan

River in the land of Canaan. There they built a beautiful altar. ¹¹But the other Israelites still at Shiloh heard about the altar these three tribes had built. They heard that the altar was at the border of Canaan at Geliloth. It was near the Jordan River on Israel's side. ¹²All the Israelites became very angry at these three tribes. They met together and decided to fight them.

¹³So the Israelites sent some men to talk to the people of Reuben, Gad and the eastern half-tribe of Manasseh. The leader of these men was Phinehas son of Eleazar the priest. ¹⁴They also sent one leader of each of the ten tribes at Shiloh. Each of these men was a leader of his family group of Israelites.

¹⁵So these men went to Gilead. They went to talk to the people of Reuben, Gad and the eastern half-tribe of Manasseh. The men said to them: ¹⁶"All the Israelites ask you: 'Why did you turn against the God of Israel? Why did you build an altar for yourselves? You know that this is against God's law. ¹⁷Remember what happened at Peor? We still suffer today because of that sin. Because of it, God caused many of the Israelites to become very sick. ¹⁸And now are you doing the same thing? Are you turning against the Lord? Will you refuse to follow the Lord?

"'If you don't stop what you're doing, the Lord will be angry with everyone in Israel. ¹⁹Your land may not be a good enough place to worship. If not, come over into our land. The Lord's Tent is in our land. You may have some of our land and live there. But don't turn against the Lord by building another altar. We already have the altar of the Lord our God. ²⁰Remember Achan son of Zerah. He refused to obey the command about what must be completely destroyed. That one man broke God's law, but all the Israelites were punished. Achan died because of his sin. But many other people also died.'"

²¹The people from Reuben, Gad and the eastern half-tribe of Manasseh answered them. They said: ²²"The Lord is our God! Again we say that the Lord is our God! God knows why we did this. We want you to know also. You can judge what we did. If you believe we have done something wrong, you may kill us. ²³If we broke God's law, we ask the Lord himself to punish us. Do you think we built this altar to offer burnt offerings? And did we build it to use for offerings of grain and fellowship?

²⁴"No! We did not build it for that reason. We feared that some day your people would not accept us as part of your nation. Then they might say, 'You cannot worship the Lord, the God of Israel. ²⁵God gave you land on the other side of the Jordan River. It separates us from you people of Reuben and Gad. You cannot worship the Lord.' So we feared that your children might make our children stop worshiping the Lord.

²⁶"So we decided to build this altar. But we did not plan to use it for burning sacrifices and making offerings. ²⁷It was really to show our people that we worship the same God as you. This altar is proof to you and us. And it will prove to all our children who will come after us that we worship the Lord. We give our whole burnt offerings, grain and fellowship offerings to the Lord. This was to keep your children from saying that our children could not worship the Lord.

²⁸"In the future your children might say that we do not belong to Israel. Then our children could say, 'Look! Our fathers who lived before us made an altar. It is exactly like the Lord's altar. We do not use it for sacrifices. This altar shows that we are part of Israel.'

²⁹"Truly, we don't want to be against the Lord. We don't want to stop following him. We know the only true altar is the one in front of the Holy Tent. It belongs to the Lord our God."

³⁰Phinehas the priest and the ten leaders heard these things. They listened to the people of Reuben, Gad and Manasseh. And they were pleased. ³¹So Phinehas, son of Eleazar the priest,

spoke. He said, "Now we know the Lord is with us. And we know you didn't turn against him. We're happy that the Israelites will not be punished by the Lord."

³²Then Phinehas and the leaders went home. They left the people of Reuben and Gad in Gilead. And they went back to Canaan. There they told the Israelites what had happened. ³³They were also pleased. They were happy and thanked God. And they decided not to fight against the people of Reuben and Gad. They decided not to destroy those lands.

³⁴And the people of Reuben and Gad gave the altar a name. They called it Proof that We Believe that the Lord Is God.

JOSHUA SAYS GOOD-BYE

23 The Lord gave Israel peace from their enemies around them. He made Israel safe. Many years passed, and Joshua became very old. ²So he called a meeting of all the elders, heads of families, judges and officers of the Israelites. He said, "I am now very old. ³You have seen what the Lord has done to our enemies. He did it to help us. The Lord your God fought for you. ⁴Remember that your people have been given their land. It's the land between the Jordan River and the Mediterranean Sea in the west. It's the land I promised to give you. But you don't control that land yet. ⁵The Lord your God will make the people living there leave. You will enter the land. And the Lord will force them out ahead of you. He has promised you this.

⁶"Be strong. You must be careful to obey everything the Lord has commanded. Obey everything written in the Book of the Teachings of Moses. Do exactly as it says. ⁷There are still some people living among us who are not Israelites. They worship their own gods. Don't become friends with them. Don't serve or worship their gods. ⁸You must continue to follow the Lord your God.

You have done this in the past. And you must continue to do it.

⁹"The Lord has helped you defeat many great and powerful nations. He has forced them to leave ahead of you. No nation has been able to defeat you. ¹⁰With his help, one Israelite could defeat a thousand enemies. This is because the Lord your God fights for you, as he promised to do. ¹¹So you must be careful to love the Lord your God.

¹²"Don't turn away from the way of the Lord. Don't become friends with these people who are not part of Israel. Don't marry them. If you do become their friends, ¹³the Lord your God will not help you defeat your enemies. So they will become like traps for you. They will cause you pain like a whip on your back and thorns in your eyes. And none of you will be left in this good land the Lord your God has given you.

¹⁴"It's almost time for me to die. You know and fully believe that the Lord has done great things for you. You know that he has not failed in any of his promises. He has kept every promise he has given. ¹⁵Every good promise that the Lord your God made has come true. And in the same way, his other promises will come true. He promised that evil will come to you. He will destroy you from this good land that he gave you. ¹⁶This will happen if you don't keep your agreement with the Lord your God. You will lose this land if you go and serve other gods. You must not worship them. If you do, the Lord will become very angry with you. Then none of you will be left in this good land he has given you."

24 Then all the tribes of Israel met together at Shechem. Joshua called them all together there. Then he called the elders, heads of families, judges and officers of Israel. These men stood before God.

²Then Joshua spoke to all the people. He said, "Here's what the Lord, the God of Israel, says to you: 'A long time ago your ancestors lived on the other side of the Euphrates River. I am talking about

men like Terah, the father of Abraham and Nahor. They worshiped other gods. ³But I, the Lord, took your ancestor Abraham out of the land on the other side of the river. I led him through the land of Canaan. And I gave him many children. I gave him his son Isaac. ⁴And I gave Isaac two sons named Jacob and Esau. I gave the land around the mountains of Edom to Esau. But Jacob and his sons went down to Egypt. ⁵Then I sent Moses and Aaron to Egypt. I caused many terrible things to happen to the Egyptians. Then I brought you people out. ⁶When I brought your fathers out of Egypt, they came to the Red Sea. And the Egyptians chased them. There were chariots and men on horses. ⁷So the people asked me, the Lord, for help. And I caused great trouble to come to the Egyptians. I caused the sea to cover them. You yourselves saw what I did to the army of Egypt. After that, you lived in the desert for a long time.

⁸"Then I brought you to the land of the Amorites. This was east of the

☆ Joshua 24:15

When Joshua was old, he reminded the people of Israel about God's rules that would keep them safe. The people promised to do everything God told them to do. But Joshua was sad. He knew the people would not be able to keep that promise. Still, Joshua wanted them to try. He showed them that they had to make a choice to follow God. Joshua said that he and his whole family would serve the Lord.

One of God's gifts to us is our family. We have family who live with us, a family of friends, and a family at church. God wants you and all your family to know him and to help other people. Can you think of something your whole family can do to help others? Maybe you can all collect food to give to people who are hungry. Maybe you can work together at a shelter where people live who do not have homes of their own. When we serve other people, we are acting like Jesus. You can serve the Lord by helping somebody today.

· ·

When we help people, we are serving the Lord. Look around you and see if there is something you can do to help others.

Jordan River. They fought against you, but I gave you the power to defeat them. I destroyed them before you. Then you took control of that land. ⁹But the king of Moab, Balak son of Zippor, prepared to fight against the Israelites. The king sent for Balaam son of Beor to curse you. ¹⁰But I, the Lord, refused to listen to Balaam. So he asked for good things to happen to you! He blessed you many times. I saved you and brought you out of his power.

¹¹"Then you traveled across the Jordan River and came to Jericho. The people in the city of Jericho fought against you. Also, the Amorites, Perizzites, Canaanites, Hittites, Girgashites, Hivites and Jebusites fought against you. But I allowed you to defeat them all. ¹²While your army traveled forward, I sent hornets ahead of them. These hornets made the people leave before you came. So you took the land without using your swords and bows. ¹³It was I, the Lord, who gave you that land. I gave you land where you did not have to work. I gave you cities that you did not have to build. And now you live in that land and in those cities. You eat from

vineyards and olive trees. But you did not have to plant them.'"

¹⁴Then Joshua spoke to the people. He said, "Now you have heard the Lord's words. So you must respect the Lord and serve him fully and sincerely. Throw away the false gods that your people worshiped. That happened on the other side of the Euphrates River and in Egypt. Now you must serve the Lord. ¹⁵But maybe you don't want to serve the Lord. You must choose for yourselves today. You must decide whom you will serve. You may serve the gods that your people worshiped when they lived on the other side of the Euphrates River. Or you may serve the gods of the Amorites who lived in this land. As for me and my family, we will serve the Lord."

¹⁶Then the people answered, "No! We will never stop following the Lord. We will never serve other gods! ¹⁷We know it was the Lord our God who brought our people out of Egypt. We were slaves in that land. But the Lord did great things for us there. He brought us out. He protected us while we traveled through other lands. ¹⁸Then he helped us defeat the people living in these lands. He helped us defeat the Amorites who lived here. So we will continue to serve the Lord because he is our God."

¹⁹Then Joshua said, "You will not be able to serve the Lord well enough. He is a holy God. And he is a jealous God. If you turn against him and sin, he will not forgive you. ²⁰If you leave the Lord and serve other gods, he will cause great trouble to come to you. The Lord has been good to you. But if you turn against him, he will destroy you."

²¹But the people said to Joshua, "No! We will serve the Lord."

[22] Then Joshua said, "Look around at yourselves and the people with you here. Do you all know and agree that you have chosen to serve the Lord? Are you all witnesses to this?"

The people answered, "Yes, it's true! We all see that we have chosen to serve the Lord."

[23] Then Joshua said, "Now throw away the false gods that you have among you. Love the Lord, the God of Israel, with all your heart."

[24] Then the people said to Joshua, "We will serve the Lord our God. We will obey him."

[25] On that day Joshua made an agreement for the people. He made the agreement a law for them to follow. This happened at Shechem. [26] Joshua wrote these things in the Book of the Teachings of God. Then he found a large stone. He put the stone under the oak tree near the Lord's Holy Tent.

[27] Then Joshua said to all the people, "See this stone! It will help you remember what we did today. It was here when the Lord was speaking to us today. It will help you remember what happened. It will stop you from turning against your God."

JOSHUA DIES

[28] Then Joshua told the people to go back to their homes. And everyone went back to his own land.

[29] After that, Joshua son of Nun died. He was 110 years old. [30] And they buried him in his own land at Timnath Serah. This was in the mountains of Ephraim, north of Mount Gaash.

[31] The Israelites had served the Lord during the time Joshua was living. And after he died, they continued to serve the Lord. They continued to serve him while their elders were still alive. These were the leaders who had seen what the Lord had done for the Israelites.

JOSEPH COMES HOME

[32] When the Israelites left Egypt, they carried the bones of Joseph with them. They buried them at Shechem, in the land Jacob had bought from the sons of Hamor. (Hamor was the father of Shechem.) Jacob had bought the land for 100 pieces of silver. This land belonged to Joseph's children.

[33] And Eleazar son of Aaron died. He was buried at Gibeah in the mountains of Ephraim. Gibeah had been given to Eleazar's son Phinehas.

ISRAEL FORGETS TO FOLLOW THE LORD

At that time the Israelites did
not have a king. So everyone did
what he thought was right.
JUDGES 17:6

In those days the Israelites did
not have a king. Everyone did
what he thought was right.
JUDGES 21:25

God started his chosen family when he gave Abraham
and Sarah their son, Isaac. Isaac and his wife had two
sons, and one was named Jacob. Jacob got married and
had twelve sons! God changed Jacob's name to Israel. The
nation of Israel was born. Those twelve sons had so many
descendants, they almost outnumbered the people of
Egypt where they were living.

But Egypt wasn't the place God planned for them
to live forever. So he made Moses the leader, and God
led Israel out of Egypt and kept them safe. After Moses,
Joshua became the leader and helped Israel start taking
over the land God had promised them.

The people were used to someone leading them. But
after Joshua died, they didn't know what to do. They had
promised Joshua that they would follow God, but then they
forgot how.

In the Bible, there is a book called Judges. It tells
the stories of the different people God raised up to help
lead Israel. But because there was no main leader, the
Bible says "everyone did what he thought was right." They
did not follow the laws that would keep them safe. Other

nations took things from them, and many of the people suffered.

God was not surprised his people forgot to follow his rules. He always knew it would be too hard for them. But he had a plan. One day he would send the ultimate leader. He would send himself! He would create a man who would be both his Son and God himself. This leader would change everything. He would turn Israel and the world into a true family.

Until then, God continued to watch over the Israelites. He helped them when they got themselves in trouble. Sometimes they followed him and sometimes they didn't. God never stopped loving his people.

Ruth

THE STORY OF A GIRL FROM MOAB

1 ¹⁻²Long ago the judges[n] ruled Israel. During their rule, there was a time in the land when there was not enough food to eat. A man named Elimelech left Bethlehem in Judah and moved to the country of Moab. He took his wife and his two sons with him. His wife was named Naomi, and his two sons were named Mahlon and Kilion. These people were from the Ephrathah district around Bethlehem in Judah. The family traveled to Moab and lived there.

³Later, Naomi's husband, Elimelech, died. So only Naomi and her two sons were left. ⁴These sons married women from Moab. The name of one wife was Orpah. The name of the other wife was Ruth. Naomi and her sons lived in Moab about ten years. ⁵Then Mahlon and Kilion also died. So Naomi was left alone without her husband or her two sons.

⁶While Naomi was in Moab, she heard that the Lord had taken care of his people. He had given food to them in Judah. So Naomi got ready to leave Moab and go back home. The wives of Naomi's sons also got ready to go with her. ⁷So they left the place where they had lived. And they started back on the way to the land of Judah. ⁸But Naomi said to her two daughters-in-law, "Go back home. Each of you go to your own mother's house. You have been very kind to me and to my sons who are now dead. I hope the Lord will also be kind to you in the same way. ⁹I hope the Lord will give you another home and a new husband."

Then Naomi kissed the women. And they began to cry out loud. ¹⁰Her daughters-in-law said to her, "No. We will go with you to your people."

¹¹But Naomi said, "My daughters, go back to your own homes. Why do you want to go with me? I cannot give birth to more sons to give you new husbands. ¹²So go back to your own homes. I am too old to have another husband. But even if I had another husband tonight and if I had more sons, it wouldn't help! ¹³Would you wait until the babies were grown into men? Would you live for so many years without husbands? Don't do this thing. My life is much too sad for you to share. This is because the Lord is against me!"

¹⁴The women cried together again. Then Orpah kissed Naomi good-bye, but Ruth held on to her.

¹⁵Naomi said, "Look, your sister-in-law is going back to her own people and her own gods. Go back with her."

RUTH STAYS WITH NAOMI

¹⁶But Ruth said, "Don't ask me to leave you! Don't beg me not to follow you! Every place you go, I will go. Every place you live, I will live. Your people will be my people. Your God will be my God. ¹⁷And where you die, I will die. And there I will be buried. I ask the Lord to punish me terribly if I do not keep this promise: Only death will separate us."

¹⁸Naomi saw that Ruth had made up her mind to go with her. So Naomi stopped arguing with her. ¹⁹Naomi and Ruth went on until they came to the town of Bethlehem. When the two women entered Bethlehem, all the people became very excited. The women of the town said, "Is this Naomi?"

²⁰But Naomi told the people, "Don't call me Naomi.[n] Call me Mara,[n] because God All-Powerful has made my life very sad. ²¹When I left, I had all I wanted. But now, the Lord has brought me home with nothing. So why should you call me

1:1–2 **judges** They were not judges in courts of law, but leaders of the people in times of emergency.
1:20 **Naomi** This name means "happy" or "pleasant."
1:20 **Mara** This name means "bitter" or "sad."

☆ Ruth 1:16

Ruth was from a nation called Moab, but she married a man from Israel. Ruth loved her new family, especially her mother-in-law, Naomi. But Naomi's husband died and then her sons died too. One of the sons was Ruth's husband. Naomi was so sad, and she felt alone. She told Ruth to go back to her family in Moab. Ruth said she would not go. Naomi was Ruth's family now. Israel was her nation. And God was now her God.

Who are the people you look up to? Maybe it is your mom and dad, your Sunday school teacher, your grandparents, or a favorite teacher at school. Do those people have faith and patience? God tells us in the Bible to look up to those who love him. Make sure the people you choose to look up to love Jesus. People who love Jesus show faith, love, patience, and gentleness.

. . . .

God puts people in your life who love you and love Jesus. A person like that is another one of his many gifts to you.

Naomi when the Lord has spoken against me? God All-Powerful has given me much trouble."

²²So Naomi and her daughter-in-law Ruth, the woman from Moab, came back from Moab. They came to Bethlehem at the beginning of the barley harvest.

RUTH MEETS BOAZ

2 Now there was a rich man living in Bethlehem whose name was Boaz. Boaz was one of Naomi's close relatives from Elimelech's family.

²One day Ruth, the woman from Moab, said to Naomi, "Let me go to the fields. Maybe someone will be kind and let me gather the grain he leaves in his field."

Naomi said, "Go, my daughter."

³So Ruth went to the fields. She followed the workers who were cutting the grain. And she gathered the grain that they had left. It just so happened that the field belonged to Boaz. He was a close relative from Elimelech's family.

⁴When Boaz came from Bethlehem,

he spoke to his workers: "The Lord be with you!"

And the workers answered, "May the Lord bless you!"

⁵Then Boaz spoke to his servant who was in charge of the workers. He asked, "Whose girl is that?"

⁶The servant answered, "She is the Moabite woman who came with Naomi from the country of Moab. ⁷She said, 'Please let me follow the workers and gather the grain that they leave on the ground.' She came and has remained here. From morning until just now, she has stopped only a few moments to rest in the shelter."

⁸Then Boaz said to Ruth, "Listen, my daughter. Stay here in my field to gather grain for yourself. Do not go to any other person's field. Continue following behind my women workers. ⁹Watch to see which fields they go to and follow them. I have warned the young men not to bother you. When you are thirsty, you may go and drink. Take water from the water jugs that the servants have filled."

¹⁰Then Ruth bowed low with her face to the ground. She said to Boaz, "I am a stranger. Why have you been so kind to notice me?"

¹¹Boaz answered her, "I know about all the help you have given to Naomi, your mother-in-law. You helped her even after your husband died. You left your father and mother and your own country. You came to this nation where you did not know anyone. ¹²The Lord will reward you for all you have done. You will be paid in full by the Lord, the God of Israel. You have come to him as a little bird finds shelter under the wings of its mother."

¹³Then Ruth said, "You are very kind to me, sir. You have said kind words to me, your servant. You have given me hope. And I am not even good enough to be one of your servants."

¹⁴At mealtime Boaz told Ruth, "Come here! Eat some of our bread. Here, dip your bread in our vinegar."

So Ruth sat down with the workers. Boaz gave her some roasted grain. Ruth ate until she was full, and there was some food left over. ¹⁵Ruth rose and went back to work. Then Boaz told his servants, "Let her gather even around the bundles of grain. Don't tell her to go away. ¹⁶Drop some full heads of grain for her. Let her gather that grain, and don't tell her to stop."

¹⁷So Ruth gathered grain in the field until evening. Then she separated the grain from the chaff. There was about one-half bushel of barley. ¹⁸Ruth carried the grain into town. And her mother-in-law saw what she had gathered. Ruth also gave her the food that was left over from lunch.

¹⁹Naomi asked her, "Where did you gather all this grain today? Where did you work? Blessed be the man who noticed you!"

Ruth told her about whose field she had worked in. She said, "The man I worked with today is named Boaz."

²⁰Naomi told her daughter-in-law, "The Lord bless him! The Lord still continues to be kind to all people—the living and the dead!" Then Naomi told Ruth, "Boaz is one of our close relatives," one who will take care of us."

²¹Then Ruth said, "Boaz also told me to come back and continue working. He said, 'Keep close by my servants until they have finished the harvest.'"

²²Then Naomi said to her daughter-in-law Ruth, "It is good for you to continue working with his women servants. If you work in another field, someone might hurt you." ²³So Ruth continued working closely with the women servants of Boaz. She gathered grain until the barley harvest was finished. She also worked there through the end of the wheat harvest. And Ruth

---

2:20 close relatives In Bible times the closest relative could marry a widow without children so she could have children. He would care for this family, but they and their property would not belong to him. They would belong to the dead husband.

continued to live with Naomi, her mother-in-law.

NAOMI'S PLAN

3 Then Naomi, Ruth's mother-in-law, said to her, "My daughter, I must find a suitable home for you. That would be good for you. [2]Now Boaz is our close relative.[n] You worked with his women servants. Tonight he will be working at the threshing floor. [3]Go wash yourself and put on perfume. Change your clothes, and go down to the threshing floor. But don't let him see you until he has finished eating and drinking. [4]Then he will lie down. Watch him so you will know the place where he lies down. Go there and lift the cover off his feet[n] and lie down. He will tell you what you should do."

[5]Then Ruth answered, "I will do everything you say."

[6]So Ruth went down to the threshing floor. She did all her mother-in-law told her to do. [7]After eating and drinking, Boaz was feeling good. He went to lie down beside the pile of grain. Then Ruth went to him quietly. She lifted the cover from his feet and lay down.

[8]About midnight Boaz woke up suddenly and rolled over. He was startled! There was a woman lying near his feet! [9]Boaz asked, "Who are you?"

She said, "I am Ruth, your servant girl. Spread your cover over me because you are the one who is to take care of me."

[10]Then Boaz said, "The Lord bless you, my daughter. Your kindness to me is greater than the kindness you showed to Naomi in the beginning. You didn't look for a young man to marry, either rich or poor. [11]Now, my daughter, don't be afraid. I will do everything you ask. All the people in our town know you are a very good woman. [12]And it is true, I am a relative who is to take care of you. But there is a man who is a closer relative to you than I. [13]But stay here tonight. In the morning we will see if he will take care of you. If he decides to take care of you, that is fine. If he refuses to take care of you, I myself will marry you. Then I will buy back Elimelech's land for you. As surely as the Lord lives, I promise to do this. So lie here until morning."

[14]So Ruth lay near his feet until the morning. She rose while it was still too dark to be recognized. Boaz said to his servants, "Don't tell anyone that the woman came here to the threshing floor." [15]Then Boaz said to Ruth, "Bring me your shawl. Now, hold it open."

So Ruth held her shawl open, and Boaz poured six portions of barley into it. Boaz then put it on her back, and she went to the city.

[16]Ruth went to the home of her mother-in-law. And Naomi asked, "How did you do, my daughter?"

So Ruth told Naomi everything that Boaz did for her. [17]She said, "Boaz gave me these six portions of barley. He said, 'You must not go home without a gift for your mother-in-law.'"

[18]Naomi answered, "Ruth, my daughter, wait until you hear what happens. Boaz will not rest until he has finished doing what he should do this day."

> You have come to [God] as a little bird finds shelter under the wings of its mother.
>
> –RUTH 2:12

3:2 **close relative** In Bible times the closest relative could marry a widow without children so she could have children. He would care for this family, but they and their property would not belong to him. They would belong to the dead husband.
3:4 **lift . . . feet** This showed Ruth was asking him to be her husband.

BOAZ MARRIES RUTH

4 Boaz went to the city gate. He sat there until the close relative he had mentioned passed by. Boaz called to him, "Come here, friend! Sit down here!" So the man came over and sat down. ²Boaz gathered ten of the old men who were leaders of the city. He told them, "Sit down here!" So they sat down.

³Then Boaz spoke to the close relative. He said, "Naomi has come back from the country of Moab. She wants to sell the piece of land that belonged to our relative Elimelech. ⁴So I decided to say this to you: If you want to buy back the land, then buy it! Buy it in front of the people who live here and in front of the elders of my people. If you don't want to buy it, tell me. I am the only person after you who can buy back the land. If you don't buy it back, I will."

And the close relative said, "I will buy back the land."

⁵Then Boaz said, "When you buy the land from Naomi, you must marry Ruth, the dead man's wife. She is the woman from Moab. That way, the land will stay in her dead husband's family."

⁶The close relative answered, "Then I can't buy back the land. If I did, I might lose what I can pass on to my own sons. I cannot buy the land back. So you buy it yourself."

⁷Long ago in Israel when people traded or bought back something, one person took off his sandal and gave it to the other person. This was their proof of purchase.

⁸So the close relative said, "Buy the land yourself." And then he took off his sandal.

⁹Then Boaz spoke to the elders and to all the people. He said, "You are witnesses today of what I am buying from Naomi. I am buying everything that belonged to Elimelech and Kilion and Mahlon. ¹⁰I am also taking Ruth as my wife. She is the Moabite who was the wife of Mahlon. I am doing this so her dead husband's property will stay with his family. This way, his name will not be separated from his family and his land. You are witnesses this day."

¹¹So all the people and elders who were at the city gate said, "We are witnesses. This woman will be coming into your home. We hope the Lord will make her like Rachel and Leah. They had many children. So the people of Israel grew in number. May you become powerful in the district of Ephrathah. May you become famous in Bethlehem! ¹²Tamar gave birth to Judah's son Perez.[n] In the same way, may the Lord give you many children through Ruth. And may your family be great like his."

¹³So Boaz took Ruth and married her. The Lord let her become pregnant, and she gave birth to a son. ¹⁴The women told Naomi, "Praise the Lord who gave you this grandson. And may he become famous in Israel. ¹⁵He will give you new life. And he will take care of you in your old age. This happened because of your daughter-in-law. She loves you. And she is better for you than seven sons. She has given birth to your grandson."

¹⁶Naomi took the boy, held him in her arms and cared for him. ¹⁷The neighbors gave the boy his name. These women said, "This boy was born for Naomi." The neighbors named him Obed. Obed was Jesse's father. And Jesse was the father of David.

¹⁸This is the family history of Perez. Perez was the father of Hezron. ¹⁹Hezron was the father of Ram. Ram was the father of Amminadab. ²⁰Amminadab was the father of Nahshon. Nahshon was the father of Salmon. ²¹Salmon was the father of Boaz. Boaz was the father of Obed. ²²Obed was the father of Jesse, and Jesse was the father of David.

4:12 Perez One of Boaz's ancestors.

First Samuel

SAMUEL'S BIRTH

1 There was a man named Elkanah son of Jeroham. He was from Ramathaim in the mountains of Ephraim. Elkanah was from the family of Zuph. (Jeroham was Elihu's son. Elihu was Tohu's son. And Tohu was the son of Zuph from the family group of Ephraim.) [2]Elkanah had two wives. One was named Hannah, and the other was named Peninnah. Peninnah had children, but Hannah had none.

[3]Every year Elkanah left his town Ramah and went up to Shiloh. There he worshiped the Lord of heaven's armies and offered sacrifices to him. Shiloh was where Hophni and Phinehas served as priests of the Lord. They were the sons of Eli. [4]When Elkanah offered sacrifices, he always gave a share of the meat to his wife Peninnah. He also gave shares of the meat to her sons and daughters. [5]But Elkanah always gave a special share of the meat to Hannah. He did this because he loved Hannah and because the Lord had made Hannah unable to have children. [6]Peninnah would upset Hannah and make her feel bad. She did this because the Lord had made Hannah unable to have children. [7]This happened every year when they went up to the Tent of the Lord at Shiloh. Peninnah would upset Hannah until Hannah would cry and not eat anything. [8]Her husband Elkanah would say to her, "Hannah, why are you crying? Why won't you eat? Why are you sad? Don't I mean more to you than ten sons?"

[9]Once, after they had eaten their meal in Shiloh, Hannah got up. Now Eli the priest was sitting on a chair near the entrance to the Lord's Holy Tent. [10]Hannah was very sad. She cried much and prayed to the Lord. [11]She made a promise. She said, "Lord of heaven's armies, see how bad I feel. Remember me! Don't forget me. If you will give me a son, I will give him back to you all his life. And no one will ever use a razor to cut his hair." [n]

[12]While Hannah kept praying, Eli watched her mouth. [13]She was praying in her heart. Her lips moved, but her voice was not heard. So Eli thought she was drunk. [14]He said to her, "Stop getting drunk! Throw away your wine!"

[15]Hannah answered, "No, master, I have not drunk any wine or beer. I am a woman who is deeply troubled. I was telling the Lord about all my problems. [16]Don't think of me as an evil woman. I have been praying because of my many troubles and much sadness."

[17]Eli answered, "Go in peace. May the God of Israel give you what you asked of him."

[18]Hannah said, "I want to be pleasing to you always." Then she left and ate something. She was not sad anymore.

[19]Early the next morning Elkanah's family got up and worshiped the Lord. Then they went back home to Ramah. Elkanah had intimate relations with his wife Hannah. And the Lord remembered her. [20]So Hannah became pregnant, and in time she gave birth to a son. She named him Samuel. [n] She said, "His name is Samuel because I asked the Lord for him."

HANNAH GIVES SAMUEL TO GOD

[21]Every year Elkanah went to Shiloh to offer sacrifices. He went to keep the promise he had made to God. He brought his whole family with him. So once again he went up to Shiloh. [22]But Hannah did not go with him. She told

1:11 **And...hair** People who made special promises not to cut their hair or to drink wine or beer were called Nazirites. These people gave their lives to the Lord. See Numbers 6:1–5.
1:20 **Samuel** This name sounds like the Hebrew word for "God heard."

him, "When the boy is old enough to eat solid food, I will take him to Shiloh. Then I will give him to the Lord. He will become a Nazirite. He will always live there at Shiloh."

23Elkanah, Hannah's husband, said to her, "Do what you think is best. You may stay home until the boy is old enough to eat. May the Lord do what you have said." So Hannah stayed at home to nurse her son until he was old enough to eat.

24When Samuel was old enough to eat, Hannah took him to the Tent of the Lord at Shiloh. She also took a three-year-old bull, one-half bushel of flour and a leather bag filled with wine. 25They killed the bull for the sacrifice. Then Hannah brought Samuel to Eli. 26She said to Eli, "As surely as you live, my master, I am the same woman who stood near you praying to the Lord. 27I prayed for this child. The Lord answered my prayer and gave him to me. 28Now I give him back to the Lord. He will belong to the Lord all his life." And he worshiped the Lord there.

HANNAH GIVES THANKS

2 Hannah said:

"The Lord has filled my heart with
    joy.
  I feel very strong in the Lord.
I can laugh at my enemies.
  I am glad because you have helped
    me!

2 "There is no one holy like
    the Lord.
  There is no God but you.
  There is no Rock like our God.

3 "Don't continue bragging.
  Don't speak proud words.
The Lord is a God who knows
    everything.
  He judges what people do.

4 "The bows of warriors break,
    but weak people become strong.

5 Those who once had plenty of food
    now must work for food.
  But people who once were hungry
    now grow fat on food.
The woman who was unable to have
    children now has had seven.
  But the woman who had many sons
    now is sad.

6 "The Lord causes people to die,
    and he causes them to live.
  He brings people down to where the
    dead are,
    and he raises them to life again.
7 The Lord makes people poor,
    and he makes people rich.
  He makes people humble,
    and he makes people great.
8 The Lord raises the poor up from the
    dust.
  And he picks needy people up from
    the ashes.
  He lets the poor sit with princes.
    He lets them sit on a throne of honor.

"The foundations of the earth belong
    to the Lord.
  The Lord set the world upon them.
9 He protects his holy people.
  But those who do evil will be
    silenced in darkness.
  Their power will not help them win.
10 The Lord destroys his enemies.
  He will thunder in heaven against
    them.
The Lord will judge all the earth.
  He will give power to his king.
  He will make his appointed king
    strong."

ELI'S EVIL SONS

11Then Elkanah went home to Ramah. But the boy continued to serve the Lord under Eli the priest.

12Now Eli's sons were evil men. They did not care about the Lord. 13This is what the priests would do to the people: Every time someone brought a sacrifice, the meat would be cooked in a pot. The priest's servant would then come with a fork in his hand.

The fork had three prongs. ¹⁴He would plunge the fork into the pot or the kettle. Whatever the fork brought out of the pot belonged to the priest. This is how they treated all the Israelites who came to Shiloh to offer sacrifices. ¹⁵But even before the fat was burned, the priest's servant would come to the person offering sacrifices. The servant would say, "Give the priest some meat to roast. The priest won't accept boiled meat from you. He will only accept raw meat."

¹⁶But the man who offered the sacrifice might say, "Let the fat be burned up first as usual. Then you may take anything you want."

If so, the priest's servant would answer, "No, give me the meat now. If you don't, I'll take it by force."

¹⁷The Lord saw that the sin of the servants was very great. They did not show respect for the offerings made to the Lord.

SAMUEL GROWS UP

¹⁸But Samuel obeyed the Lord. He wore a linen holy vest. ¹⁹Every year Samuel's mother would make a little coat for him. She would take it to him when she went to Shiloh. She went there with her husband for the sacrifice. ²⁰Eli would bless Elkanah and his wife. Eli would say, "May the Lord repay you with children through Hannah. They will take the place of the boy Hannah prayed for and gave back to the Lord." Then Elkanah and Hannah would go home. ²¹The Lord was kind to Hannah. She became the mother of three sons and two daughters. And the boy Samuel grew up serving the Lord.

²²Now Eli was very old. He heard about everything his sons were doing to all the Israelites. He also heard about how his sons had physical relations with the women who served at the entrance to the Meeting Tent. ²³Eli said to his sons, "The people here tell me about the evil you do. Why do you do these evil things? ²⁴No, my sons. The Lord's people are saying bad things about you. ²⁵If someone sins against another person, God can help him. But if he sins against the Lord himself, no one can help him!" But Eli's sons would not listen to him. This was because the Lord had decided to put them to death.

²⁶The boy Samuel kept growing. He pleased God and the people.

²⁷A man of God came to Eli. He said, "This is what the Lord says: 'I clearly showed myself to the family of your ancestor Aaron. This was when they were slaves to the king of Egypt. ²⁸I chose them from all the tribes of Israel to be my priests. I wanted them to go up to my altar, to burn incense and to wear the holy vest. I also let the family of your ancestor have part of all the offerings sacrificed by the Israelites.' ²⁹So why don't you respect the sacrifices and gifts? You honor your sons more than me. You become fat on the best parts of the meat the Israelites bring to me.'

³⁰"Here's what the Lord, the God of Israel, says: 'I promised that your family and your ancestor's family would serve me forever.' But now the Lord says this: 'That will never be! I will honor those who honor me. But I will take honor away from those who do not honor me. ³¹The time is coming when I will destroy the descendants of both you and your ancestors. No man will grow old in your family. ³²You will see trouble in my house. Good things will be done to Israel. But there will never be an old man in your family. ³³I will save one man to serve as priest at my altar. He will wear

> There is no one holy like the Lord . . . There is no Rock like our God.
> –1 SAMUEL 2:2

out his eyes and use up his strength. The rest of your descendants will die by the sword.

³⁴"I will give you a sign. Both your sons, Hophni and Phinehas, will die on the same day. ³⁵I will choose a loyal priest for myself. He will listen to me and do what I want. I will make his family strong. He will always serve before my appointed king. ³⁶Then everyone left in your family will come and bow down before him. They will beg for a little money or a little food. They will say, 'Please give me a job as priest so I can have food to eat.'"

GOD CALLS SAMUEL

3 The boy Samuel served the Lord under Eli. In those days the Lord did not speak directly to people very often. There were very few visions.

²Eli's eyes were so weak he was almost blind. One night he was lying in bed. ³Samuel was also in bed in the Lord's Holy Tent. The Ark of the Covenant was in the Holy Tent. God's lamp was still burning.

⁴Then the Lord called Samuel. Samuel answered, "I am here!" ⁵He ran to Eli and said, "I am here. You called me."

☆ 1 Samuel 3:6

When Samuel was a boy, he lived in "the Lord's Holy Tent" and helped Eli the priest. Samuel was sleeping one night when he heard someone call his name. He thought it was Eli, but Eli said he didn't call Samuel. This happened two more times. Finally Eli realized God was calling Samuel. He told Samuel to answer God the next time the Lord said his name. When Samuel heard his name again, he knew that God was talking to him.

"Jesus loves me, this I know, for the Bible tells me so." This song can remind you that Jesus always loves you. He never leaves you. He knows your name. The Bible says he even knows the number of hairs on your head! He loves you so much! You can feel safe knowing that God will be with you wherever you go. When you feel scared, remember that God loves you. And he calls you by name.

. . . .

Samuel heard God's voice in his ears. But we hear God in our hearts. Listen closely for his voice. You might even hear him say your name.

But Eli said, "I didn't call you. Go back to bed." So Samuel went back to bed.

⁶The Lord called again, "Samuel!"

Samuel again went to Eli and said, "I am here. You called me."

Again Eli said, "I didn't call you. Go back to bed."

⁷Samuel did not yet know the Lord. The Lord had not spoken directly to him yet.

⁸The Lord called Samuel for the third time. Samuel got up and went to Eli. He said, "I am here. You called me."

Then Eli realized the Lord was calling the boy. ⁹So he told Samuel, "Go to bed. If he calls you again, say, 'Speak, Lord. I am your servant, and I am listening.'" So Samuel went and lay down in bed.

¹⁰The Lord came and stood there. He called as he had before. He said, "Samuel, Samuel!"

Samuel said, "Speak, Lord. I am your servant, and I am listening."

¹¹The Lord said to Samuel, "See, I am going to do something in Israel. It will shock those who hear about it. ¹²At that time I will do to Eli and his family everything I promised. I will not stop until I have finished. ¹³I told Eli I would punish his family forever. I will do it because Eli knew his sons were evil. They spoke against me, but he did not control them. ¹⁴So here is what I promised Eli's family: 'Your guilt will never be removed by sacrifice or offering.'"

¹⁵Samuel lay down until morning. Then he opened the doors of the Tent of the Lord. He was afraid to tell Eli about the vision. ¹⁶But Eli said to him, "Samuel, my son!"

Samuel answered, "I am here."

¹⁷Eli asked, "What did the Lord say to you? Don't hide it from me. May God punish you terribly if you hide from me anything he said to you." ¹⁸So Samuel told Eli everything. He did not hide anything from him. Then Eli said, "He is the Lord. Let him do what he thinks is best."

¹⁹The Lord was with Samuel as he grew up. He did not let any of Samuel's messages fail to come true. ²⁰Then all Israel, from Dan to Beersheba,ⁿ knew Samuel was a prophet of the Lord. ²¹And the Lord continued to show himself to Samuel at Shiloh. He also showed himself to Samuel through his word.

4 News about Samuel spread through all of Israel.

THE PHILISTINES CAPTURE THE ARK OF THE COVENANT

At that time the Israelites went out to fight the Philistines. The Israelites camped at Ebenezer, and the Philistines camped at Aphek. ²The Philistines went to meet the Israelites in battle. And as the battle spread, the Philistines defeated the Israelites. They killed about 4,000 soldiers of the Israelite army. ³Then some Israelite soldiers went back to their camp. The elders of Israel asked, "Why did the Lord let the Philistines defeat us? Let's bring the Ark of the Covenant with the Lord here from Shiloh. In this way God will go with us into battle. He will save us from our enemies."

⁴So the people sent men to Shiloh. They brought back the Ark of the Covenant with the Lord of heaven's armies. Eli's two sons, Hophni and Phinehas, were there with the Ark of the Covenant.

⁵The Ark of the Covenant with the Lord came into the camp. And all the Israelites gave a great shout of joy. It made the ground shake. ⁶The Philistines heard Israel's shout. They asked, "What's all this shouting in the Hebrew camp?"

Then the Philistines found out that the Ark of the Covenant of the Lord had come into the Hebrew camp.

3:20 Dan to Beersheba Dan was the city farthest north in Israel. Beersheba was the city farthest south. So this means all the people of Israel.

7They were afraid and said, "A god has come into the Hebrew camp! We're in trouble! This has never happened before! 8How terrible it will be for us! Who can save us from these powerful gods? They are the ones who struck the Egyptians with all kinds of disasters in the desert. 9Be brave, Philistines! Fight like men! In the past they were our slaves. So fight like men, or you will become their slaves."

10So the Philistines fought hard and defeated the Israelites. Every Israelite soldier ran away to his own home. It was a great defeat for Israel, because 30,000 Israelite soldiers were killed. 11The Ark of the Covenant of God was taken by the Philistines. And Eli's two sons, Hophni and Phinehas, were killed.

12That same day a man from the tribe of Benjamin ran from the battle. He tore his clothes and put dust on his head to show his great sadness. 13When he arrived in Shiloh, Eli was by the side of the road. Eli was sitting there in a chair, watching. He was worried about the Ark of the Covenant of God. When the Benjaminite entered Shiloh, he told the bad news. Then all the people in town cried loudly. 14Eli heard the crying and asked, "What's all this noise?"

The Benjaminite ran to Eli and told him what had happened. 15Eli was now 98 years old, and he was blind. 16The Benjaminite told him, "I have come from the battle. I ran all the way here today."

Eli asked, "What happened, my son?"

17The Benjaminite answered, "Israel ran away from the Philistines. The Israelite army has lost many soldiers. Your two sons are both dead. And the Philistines have taken the Ark of the Covenant of God."

18When he mentioned the Ark of the Covenant of God, Eli fell backward off his chair. He fell beside the gate and broke his neck, because he was old and fat. And Eli died. He had led Israel for 40 years.

THE GLORY IS GONE

19Eli's daughter-in-law, the wife of Phinehas, was pregnant. It was nearly time for her baby to be born. She heard the news that the Ark of the Covenant of God had been taken. She heard also that Eli, her father-in-law, and Phinehas, her husband, were both dead. So she began to give birth to her child. The child was born, but the mother had much trouble in giving birth. 20As she was dying, the women who helped her give birth said, "Don't worry! You've given birth to a son!" But she did not answer or pay attention. She named the baby Ichabod.[n] 21She named him Ichabod and said, "Israel's glory is gone." She said this because the Ark of the Covenant of God had been taken. It was also because her father-in-law and husband were dead. 22She said, "Israel's glory is gone, because the Ark of the Covenant of God has been taken away."

TROUBLE FOR THE PHILISTINES

5 After the Philistines had captured the Ark of the Covenant of God, they took it from Ebenezer to Ashdod. 2They carried it into Dagon's temple and put it next to Dagon. 3The people of Ashdod rose early the next morning. They found that Dagon had fallen on his face on the ground. He was lying before the Ark of the Covenant of the Lord. So the people of Ashdod put Dagon back in his place. 4The next morning the people of Ashdod rose from sleep. And again they found Dagon on the ground! He had fallen down before the Ark of the Covenant of the Lord. His head and hands had broken off and were lying in the doorway. Only his body was still in one piece. 5So, even today, Dagon's priests and others who enter his temple at Ashdod refuse to step on the doorsill.

6The Lord punished the people of Ashdod and their neighbors. He gave them much trouble. He gave them

---

4:20 **Ichabod** This name means "Where is the glory?"

growths on their skin. ⁷The people of Ashdod saw what was happening. They said, "The Ark of the Covenant of the God of Israel can't stay with us. God is punishing us and Dagon our god." ⁸The people of Ashdod called all five Philistine kings together. They asked them, "What should we do with the Ark of the Covenant of the God of Israel?"

The rulers answered, "Move the Ark of the Covenant of the God of Israel to Gath." So the Philistines moved it to Gath.

⁹But after they had moved it to Gath, the Lord punished that city also. He made the people very afraid. God troubled both old and young people in Gath. He caused them to have growths on their skin. ¹⁰Then the Philistines sent the Ark of the Covenant of God to Ekron.

But when it came into Ekron, the people of Ekron yelled. They said, "Why are you bringing the Ark of the Covenant of the God of Israel to our city? Do you want to kill us and our people?" ¹¹The people of Ekron called all the kings of the Philistines together. They said to the kings, "Send the Ark of the Covenant of the God of Israel back to its place. Do it before it kills us and our people!" They were very afraid. God's punishment was very terrible there. ¹²The people who did not die were troubled with growths on their skin. So the people of Ekron cried loudly to heaven.

THE ARK OF THE COVENANT OF GOD IS SENT HOME

6 The Philistines kept the Ark of the Covenant of God in their land seven months. ²Then they called for their priests and magicians. They said, "What should we do with the Ark of the

Covenant of the Lord? Tell us how to send it back home!"

³The priests and magicians answered them. They said, "If you send back the Ark of the Covenant of the God of Israel, don't send it away empty. You must offer a penalty offering so the God of Israel will forgive your sins. Then you will be healed. When God has forgiven you, he will stop punishing you."

⁴The Philistines asked, "What kind of penalty offering should we send to Israel's God?"

The priests and magicians answered, "Make five gold models of the growths on your skin. Also make five gold models of rats. The number of models must be the same as the number of Philistine kings. This is because the same sickness has come on you and your kings. ⁵Make models of the growths and the rats that are ruining the country. Give them to Israel's God and honor him. Then maybe Israel's God will stop punishing you, your gods and your land. ⁶Don't be stubborn like the king of Egypt and the Egyptians. God punished them terribly. That is why the Egyptians let the Israelites leave Egypt.

⁷"You must build a new cart. And get two cows that have just had calves. These must be cows that have never had yokes on their necks. Then hitch the cows to the cart. Take the calves home. Don't let them follow their mothers. ⁸Put the Ark of the Covenant of the Lord on the cart. And put the gold models in a box beside the Ark of the Covenant. They are your penalty offerings for God to forgive your sins. Send the cart straight on its way. ⁹Watch the cart. It may go toward Beth Shemesh in Israel's own land. If so, the Lord has given us this great sickness.

> Israel's glory is gone, because the Ark of the Covenant of God has been taken away.
>
> –1 SAMUEL 4:22

But it may not go toward Beth Shemesh. Then we will know that Israel's God has not punished us. We will know that our sickness just happened by chance."

¹⁰The Philistines did what the priests and magicians said. They took two cows that had just had calves. They hitched them to the cart. But they kept their calves at home. ¹¹They put the Ark of the Covenant of the Lord on the cart. And they put the box with the gold rats and models of growths on the cart. ¹²Then the cows went straight toward Beth Shemesh. They stayed on the road, mooing all the way. They did not turn right or left. The Philistine kings followed the cows as far as the border of Beth Shemesh.

¹³Now the people of Beth Shemesh were harvesting their wheat in the valley. They looked up and saw the Ark of the Covenant of the Lord. They were very happy to see it again. ¹⁴The cart came to the field belonging to Joshua of Beth Shemesh. The cart stopped in this field near a large rock. The people of Beth Shemesh chopped up the wood of the cart. Then they killed the cows and sacrificed them to the Lord. ¹⁵The Levites took down the Ark of the Covenant of the Lord. They also took down the box that had the gold models. They put both on the large rock. That day the people of Beth Shemesh offered whole burnt offerings and made sacrifices to the Lord. ¹⁶The five Philistine kings watched them do all these things. Then they went back to Ekron the same day.

¹⁷The Philistines sent these gold models of the growths. They were penalty offerings to the Lord for their sins. They sent one model for each Philistine town. These towns were Ashdod, Gaza, Ashkelon, Gath and Ekron. ¹⁸And the Philistines also sent gold models of rats. The number of rats was the same as the number of towns belonging to the Philistine kings. These towns included strong, walled cities and country villages. The large rock on which they put the Ark of the Covenant of the Lord is still there. It is in the field of Joshua of Beth Shemesh.

¹⁹But some of the men of Beth Shemesh looked into the Ark of the Covenant of the Lord. So God killed 70 of them. The people of Beth Shemesh cried because the Lord had punished them so terribly. ²⁰They said, "Who can stand before the Lord, this holy God? Where can the Ark of the Covenant go from here?"

²¹Then they sent messengers to the people of Kiriath Jearim. The messengers said, "The Philistines have brought back the Ark of the Covenant of the Lord. Come down and take it to your city."

7 The men of Kiriath Jearim came and took the Ark of the Covenant of the Lord. They took it to Abinadab's house on a hill. There they made Abinadab's son Eleazar holy for the Lord so he could guard the Ark of the Covenant.

THE LORD SAVES THE ISRAELITES

²The Ark of the Covenant stayed at Kiriath Jearim a long time—20 years in all. And the people of Israel began to follow the Lord again. ³Samuel spoke to the whole group of Israel. He said, "If you're turning back to the Lord with all your hearts, you must remove your foreign gods. You must remove your idols of Ashtoreth. You must give yourselves fully to the Lord and serve only him. Then he will save you from the Philistines."

⁴So the Israelites put away their idols of Baal and Ashtoreth. And they served only the Lord.

⁵Samuel said, "All Israel must meet at Mizpah. I will pray to the Lord for you." ⁶So the Israelites met together at Mizpah. They drew water from the ground and poured it out before the Lord. They did not eat that day. They confessed, "We have sinned against the Lord." And Samuel served as judge of Israel at Mizpah.

⁷The Philistines heard the Israelites were meeting at Mizpah. So the

Philistine kings came up to attack them. When the Israelites heard they were coming, they were afraid. ⁸They said to Samuel, "Don't stop praying to the Lord our God for us! Ask the Lord to save us from the Philistines!" ⁹Then Samuel took a baby lamb. He offered the lamb to the Lord as a whole burnt offering. He called to the Lord for Israel's sake. And the Lord answered him.

¹⁰While Samuel was burning the offering, the Philistines came near. They were going to attack Israel. But the Lord thundered against the Philistines with loud thunder. They were so frightened they became confused. So the Israelites defeated the Philistines in battle. ¹¹The men of Israel ran out of Mizpah and chased the Philistines. They went almost to Beth Car, killing the Philistines along the way.

PEACE COMES TO ISRAEL

¹²After this happened Samuel took a stone. He set it up between Mizpah and Shen. He named the stone Ebenezer.ⁿ Samuel said, "The Lord has helped us to this point." ¹³So the Philistines

7:12 Ebenezer This name means "stone of help."

☆ 1 Samuel 8:5, 19

Samuel grew up and became a great leader for Israel. He helped the people follow the Lord like Moses and Joshua had. The people were worried about who would be the next leader when Samuel got too old. They wanted to be like all the other nations around them. They wanted to have a king.

The people of Israel asked Samuel to find a king for them. This made Samuel sad. He knew Israel was a special nation. They had God himself as their king. They did not need a man to be their king. Samuel told the people that it was a bad idea. Kings can become very bossy. The people did not listen, so Samuel made Saul the first king of Israel. Saul tried to be a good king, but he did not follow God closely. He made many mistakes. And the people of Israel were not as happy as they thought they would be.

· ·

Sometimes we think other people have better things than we do. And sometimes we want to be like them. But God knows what is best for you. You can always trust him.

were defeated. They did not enter the Israelites' land again.

The Lord was against the Philistines all Samuel's life. [14]Earlier the Philistines had taken towns from the Israelites. But the Israelites won them back, from Ekron to Gath. They also took back from the Philistines the neighboring lands of these towns. There was peace also between Israel and the Amorites.

[15]Samuel continued as judge of Israel all his life. [16]Every year he went from Bethel to Gilgal to Mizpah. He judged the Israelites in all these towns. [17]But Samuel always went back to Ramah, where his home was. He also judged Israel there. And there he built an altar to the Lord.

ISRAEL ASKS FOR A KING

8 When Samuel became old, he made his sons judges for Israel. [2]His first son was named Joel, and his second son was named Abijah. Joel and Abijah were judges in Beersheba. [3]But Samuel's sons did not live as he did. They tried to get money dishonestly. They took money secretly to be dishonest in their judging.

[4]So all the elders came together and met Samuel at Ramah. [5]They said to him, "You're old, and your sons don't live as you do. Give us a king to rule over us like all the other nations."

[6]When the elders said that, Samuel was not pleased. He prayed to the Lord. [7]The Lord told Samuel, "Listen to whatever the people say to you. They have not rejected you. They have rejected me from being their king. [8]They are doing as they have always done. When I took them out of Egypt, they left me. They served other gods. They are doing the same to you. [9]Now listen to the people. But give them a warning. Tell them what the king who rules over them will do."

[10]Samuel answered those who had asked him for a king. He told them all the words of the Lord. [11]Samuel said, "If you have a king ruling over you, this is what he will do: He will take your sons. He will make them serve with his chariots and his horses. They will run in front of the king's chariot. [12]The king will make some of your sons commanders over 1,000 men or over 50 men. He will make some of your other sons plow his ground and reap his harvest. He will take others to make weapons of war and equipment for his chariots. [13]This king will take your daughters. Some of your daughters will make perfume. Others will cook and bake for him. [14]He will take your best fields, vineyards and olive groves. He will give them to his servants. [15]He will take one-tenth of your grain and grapes and give it to his officers and servants. [16]He will take your men servants and girl servants. He will take your best cattle and your donkeys. He will use them all for his own work. [17]He will take one-tenth of your flocks. And you yourselves will become his slaves. [18]When that time comes, you will cry out because of the king you chose. The Lord will not answer you then."

[19]But the people would not listen to Samuel. They said, "No! We want a king to rule over us. [20]Then we will be the same as all the other nations. Our king will judge us. He will go with us and fight our battles."

[21]Samuel heard all that the people said. Then he repeated all their words to the Lord. [22]The Lord answered, "You must listen to them. Give them a king."

Then Samuel told the people of Israel, "Everyone go back to his town."

SAUL LOOKS FOR HIS FATHER'S DONKEYS

9 Kish son of Abiel was from the tribe of Benjamin. He was an important man. (Abiel was the son of Zeror. And Zeror was the son of Becorath. He was the son of Aphiah of Benjamin.) [2]Kish had a son named Saul. Saul was a fine young man. There was no Israelite better than he. Saul stood a head taller than any other man in Israel.

[3]Now the donkeys of Saul's father,

Kish, were lost. So Kish said to Saul, his son, "Take one of the servants. Go and look for the donkeys." ⁴Saul went through the mountains of Ephraim. And he went through the land of Shalisha. But he and the servant could not find the donkeys. They went into the land of Shaalim, but the donkeys were not there. They went through the land of Benjamin. But they still did not find the donkeys. ⁵They arrived in the area of Zuph. Saul said to his servant, "Let's go back. My father will stop thinking about the donkeys. He will start worrying about us."

⁶But the servant answered, "A man of God is in this town. People respect him because everything he says comes true. Let's go into the town now. Maybe he can tell us something about the journey we have taken."

⁷Saul said to his servant, "If we go into the town, what can we give him? The food in our bags is gone. We have no gift to give him. Do we have anything at all to give him?"

⁸Again the servant answered Saul. "Look, I have one-tenth of an ounce of silver. Give it to the man of God. Then he will tell us about our journey." ⁹(In the past, someone in Israel might want to ask something from God. If so, he would say, "Let's go to the seer." We call the person a man of God today. But in the past he was called a "seer.")

¹⁰Saul said to his servant, "That is a good idea. Come, let's go." So they went toward the town where the man of God was.

¹¹Saul and the servant were going up the hill to the town. On the way they met some young women coming out to get water. Saul and the servant asked them, "Is the seer here?"

¹²The young women answered, "Yes, he's here. He's ahead of you. Hurry now. He has just come to our town today. This is because the people will offer a sacrifice at the place of worship. ¹³When you enter the town, you will find him. He will be there before he goes up to the place of worship to eat. The people will not begin eating until the seer comes. He must bless the sacrifice. After that, the guests will eat. Go now, and you should find him."

SAUL MEETS SAMUEL

¹⁴Saul and the servant went up to the town. Just as they entered the town, they saw Samuel. He was on his way up to the place of worship. So he was coming out of the city toward them.

¹⁵The day before Saul came, the Lord had told Samuel: ¹⁶"About this time tomorrow I will send you a man. He will be from Benjamin. You must appoint him as leader over my people Israel. He will save my people from the Philistines. I have seen the suffering of my people. I have listened to their cry."

¹⁷When Samuel first saw Saul, the Lord spoke to Samuel. He said, "This is the man I told you about. He will rule my people."

¹⁸Saul came near Samuel at the gate. Saul said, "Please tell me where the seer's house is."

¹⁹Samuel answered, "I am the seer. Go ahead of me to the place of worship. Today you and your servant are to eat with me. Tomorrow morning I will send you home. And I will answer all your questions. ²⁰Don't worry about the donkeys you lost three days ago. They have been found. Israel now wants you and all your father's family."

²¹Saul answered, "But I am from the tribe of Benjamin. It's the smallest tribe in Israel. And my family group is the smallest in the tribe of Benjamin. Why do you say Israel wants me?"

²²Then Samuel took Saul and his servant into a large room. He gave them a chief place at the table. About 30 guests were there. ²³Samuel said to the cook, "Bring the meat I gave you. It's the portion I told you to set aside."

²⁴So the cook took the thigh and put it on the table in front of Saul. Samuel said, "This is the meat saved for you. Eat it because it was set aside for you

for this special time. As I said, 'I have invited the people.'" So Saul ate with Samuel that day.

²⁵After they finished eating, they came down from the place of worship. They went to the town. Then Samuel talked with Saul on the roof[n] of his house. ²⁶At dawn they got up, and Samuel called to Saul on the roof. He said, "Get up, and I will send you on your way." So Saul got up. He went out of the house with Samuel. ²⁷Saul, his servant and Samuel were getting near the edge of the city. Samuel said to Saul, "Tell the servant to go on ahead of us. I have a message from God for you."

SAMUEL APPOINTS SAUL

10 Samuel took a jar of olive oil. He poured the oil on Saul's head. He kissed Saul and said, "The Lord has appointed you to be leader of his people Israel. You will rule over the people of the Lord. You will save them from their enemies all around. This will be the sign that the Lord has appointed you as leader of his people. ²After you leave me today, you will meet two men. They will be near Rachel's tomb on the border of Benjamin at Zelzah. They will say to you, 'The donkeys you were looking for have been found. But now your father has stopped thinking about his donkeys. He is worrying about you. He is asking, "What will I do about my son?"'

³"Then you will go on until you reach the great tree at Tabor. There three men will meet you. They will be on their way to worship God at Bethel. One man will be carrying three young goats. The second man will be carrying three loaves of bread. And the third one will have a leather bag full of wine. ⁴They will greet you and offer you two loaves of bread. You will accept the bread from them. ⁵Then you will go to Gibeah of God. There is a Philistine camp there. When you come near this town, a group of prophets will come out. They will be coming from the place of worship. And they will be playing harps, tambourines, flutes and lyres. And they will be prophesying. ⁶The Spirit of the Lord will enter you with power. You will prophesy with these prophets. You will be changed into a different man. ⁷After these signs happen, do whatever you find to do. God will help you.

⁸"Go ahead of me to Gilgal. I will come down to you. Then I will offer whole burnt offerings and fellowship offerings. But you must wait seven days. Then I will come and tell you what to do."

SAUL MADE KING

⁹When Saul turned to leave Samuel, God changed Saul's heart. All these signs came true that day. ¹⁰When Saul and his servant arrived at Gibeah, Saul met a group of prophets. The Spirit of God entered him. And he prophesied with the prophets. ¹¹People who had known Saul before saw him prophesying with the prophets. They asked each other, "What has happened to Kish's son? Is even Saul one of the prophets?" ¹²A man who lived there said, "Who is the father of these prophets?" This became a famous saying: "Is even Saul one of the prophets?" ¹³When Saul finished prophesying, he went to the place of worship.

¹⁴Saul's uncle asked him and his servant, "Where have you been?"

Saul said, "We were looking for the donkeys. When we couldn't find them, we went to talk to Samuel."

¹⁵Saul's uncle asked, "Please tell me. What did Samuel say to you?"

¹⁶Saul answered, "He told us the donkeys had already been found." But Saul did not tell his uncle what Samuel had said about his becoming king.

¹⁷Samuel called all the people of Israel to meet with the Lord at Mizpah. ¹⁸He

---

9:25 roof In Bible times houses were built with flat roofs. The roof was used for drying things such as flax and fruit. And it was used as an extra room, as a place for worship and as a place to sleep in the summer.

said, "This is what the Lord, the God of Israel, says: 'I led Israel out of Egypt. I saved you from Egypt's control. And I saved you from other kingdoms that were troubling you.' [19]But now you have rejected your God. He saves you from all your troubles and problems. But you said, 'No! We want a king to rule over us.' Now come, stand before the Lord in your tribes and family groups."

[20]Samuel brought all the tribes of Israel near. And the tribe of Benjamin was chosen. [21]Samuel had them pass by in family groups, and Matri's family was chosen. Then he had each man of Matri's family pass by. And Saul son of Kish was chosen. But when they looked for Saul, they could not find him. [22]Then they asked the Lord, "Has Saul come here yet?"

The Lord said, "Yes. He's hiding behind the baggage."

[23]So they ran and brought him out. When Saul stood among the people, he was a head taller than anyone else. [24]Then Samuel said to the people, "See the man the Lord has chosen. There is no one like him among all the people."

Then the people shouted, "Long live the king!"

[25]Samuel explained the rights and duties of the king. He wrote the rules in a book and put the book before the Lord. Then he told the people to go to their homes.

[26]Saul also went to his home in Gibeah. God touched the hearts of certain brave men who went along with him. [27]But some troublemakers said, "How can this man save us?" They hated Saul and refused to bring gifts to him. But Saul kept quiet.

NAHASH TROUBLES JABESH GILEAD

11 About a month later Nahash the Ammonite and his army surrounded the city of Jabesh in Gilead. All the people of Jabesh said to Nahash, "Make a treaty with us. And we will serve you."

[2]But he answered, "I will make a treaty with you. But I will only do it if I'm allowed to tear out the right eye of each of you. Then all Israel will be ashamed!"

[3]The elders of Jabesh said to Nahash, "Let us have seven days. We will send messengers through all Israel. If no one comes to help us, we will give ourselves up to you."

[4]The messengers came to Gibeah where Saul lived. When they told the people the news, the people cried loudly. [5]Saul had finished plowing in the fields with his oxen. He was coming home when he heard the people crying. He asked, "What's wrong with the people? Why are they crying?" Then they told Saul what the messengers from Jabesh had said. [6]When Saul heard their words, God's Spirit entered him with power. Saul became very angry. [7]So he took a pair of oxen and cut them into pieces. Then he gave the pieces of the oxen to messengers. He ordered them to carry the pieces through all the land of Israel.

The messengers made an announcement to the people. They said, "This is what will happen to the oxen of anyone who does not follow Saul and Samuel." So the people became very afraid of the Lord. They all came together as if they were one person. [8]Saul gathered the people together at Bezek. There were 300,000 men from Israel and 30,000 men from Judah.

[9]They spoke to the messengers who had come. They said, "Tell the people at Jabesh Gilead this: 'Before the day becomes hot tomorrow, you will be saved.'" So the messengers went and reported this to the people at Jabesh. They were very happy. [10]The people said to Nahash the Ammonite, "Tomorrow we will give ourselves up to you. Then you can do anything you want to us."

[11]The next morning Saul divided his soldiers into three groups. At dawn they entered the Ammonite camp. And they

defeated the Ammonites before the heat of the day. The Ammonites who were left alive were scattered. Not even two of them were still together.

¹²Then the people said to Samuel, "Who was it that didn't want Saul as king? Bring them here, and we will kill them!"

¹³But Saul said, "No! No one will be put to death today. The Lord has saved Israel today!"

¹⁴Then Samuel said to the people, "Come, let's go to Gilgal. At Gilgal we will again promise to obey the king." ¹⁵All the people went to Gilgal. And there, before the Lord, the people made Saul king. They offered fellowship offerings to the Lord. Saul and all the Israelites had a great celebration.

SAMUEL'S FAREWELL SPEECH

12 Samuel said to all Israel, "I have done everything you wanted me to do. I have put a king over you. ²Now you have a king to lead you. I am old and gray, and my sons are here with you. I have been your leader since I was young. ³Here I am. If I have done anything wrong, you must testify against me. Do this before the Lord and his appointed king. Did I steal anyone's ox or donkey? Did I hurt or cheat anyone? Did I ever secretly take money to pretend not to see something wrong? If I did any of these things, I will make it right."

⁴The Israelites answered, "You have not cheated us. You have not hurt us. You have not taken anything unfairly from anyone."

⁵Samuel said to them, "The Lord is a witness to what you have said. His appointed king is also a witness today. They are both witnesses that you did not find anything wrong in me."

"He is our witness," they said.

⁶Then Samuel said to the people, "The Lord is our witness. He chose Moses and Aaron. He brought your

ancestors out of Egypt. ⁷Now, stand there. And I will talk with you about all the good things the Lord did for you and your ancestors.

⁸"After Jacob entered Egypt, his descendants cried to the Lord for help. So the Lord sent Moses and Aaron. They took your ancestors out of Egypt and brought them to live in this place.

⁹"But they forgot the Lord their God. So he let them become the slaves of Sisera. He was the commander of the army of Hazor. The Lord let them become the slaves of the Philistines and the king of Moab. They all fought against your ancestors. ¹⁰Then your ancestors cried to the Lord. They said, 'We have sinned. We have left the Lord. We served the Baals and the Ashtoreths. But now save us from our enemies, and we will serve you.' ¹¹The Lord sent Gideon, who is also called Jerub-Baal. And he sent Barak, Jephthah and Samuel. Then he saved you from your enemies around you. And you lived in safety. ¹²But then you saw Nahash king of the Ammonites coming against you. You said, 'No! We want a king to rule over us!' ¹³Now here is the king you chose. The Lord has put him over you. ¹⁴You must honor the Lord and serve him. You must obey his commands. Both you and the king ruling over you must follow the Lord your God. If you do, it will be well with you. ¹⁵But if you don't obey the Lord, and if you fight against his commands, he will be against you. He will do to you what he did to your ancestors.

¹⁶"Now stand still and see the great thing the Lord will do before your eyes. ¹⁷It is now the time of the wheat harvest.ⁿ I will pray for the Lord to send thunder and rain. Then you will know what an evil thing you did against the Lord when you asked for a king."

¹⁸Then Samuel prayed to the Lord. That same day the Lord sent thunder and rain. And the people became very afraid of the Lord and Samuel. ¹⁹They

---

12:17 **time . . . harvest** This was a dry time in the summer when no rains fell.

said to Samuel, "Pray to the Lord your God for us, your servants! Don't let us die! We've added to all our sins the evil of asking for a king."

²⁰Samuel answered, "Don't be afraid. It's true that you did wrong. But don't turn away from the Lord. Serve the Lord with all your heart. ²¹Idols are of no use. So don't worship them. They can't help you or save you. They are useless! ²²For his own sake, the Lord won't leave his people. Instead, he was pleased to make you his own people. ²³I will surely not stop praying for you. If I did, I would be sinning against the Lord. I will teach you what is good and right. ²⁴But you must honor the Lord. You must always serve him with all your heart. Remember the wonderful things he did for you! ²⁵But if you are stubborn and do evil, God will sweep you and your king away."

13 Saul was 30 years old when he became king. He was king over Israel 42 years.ⁿ ²Saul chose 3,000 men from Israel. There were 2,000 men who stayed with him at Micmash in the mountains of Bethel. And 1,000 men stayed with Jonathan at Gibeah in Benjamin. Saul sent the other men in the army back home.

³Jonathan attacked the Philistine camp in Geba. And the other Philistines heard about it. Saul said, "Let the Hebrew people hear what happened." So he told the men to blow trumpets through all the land of Israel. ⁴All the Israelites heard the news. The men said, "Saul has defeated the Philistine camp. Now the Philistines really hate us!" Then the Israelites were called to join Saul at Gilgal.

⁵The Philistines gathered to fight Israel. They had 3,000ⁿ chariots and 6,000 men to ride in the chariots. Their soldiers were many in number, like the grains of sand on the seashore. The Philistines went and camped at Micmash which is east of Beth Aven. ⁶The Israelites saw that they were in trouble. So they went to hide in caves and bushes. They also hid among the rocks and in pits and wells. ⁷Some Hebrews even went across the Jordan River to the land of Gad and Gilead.

But Saul stayed at Gilgal. All the men in his army were shaking with fear. ⁸Saul waited seven days, because Samuel had said he would meet him then. But Samuel did not come to Gilgal. And the soldiers began to leave.

⁹So Saul said, "Bring me the whole burnt offering and the fellowship offerings." Then Saul offered the whole burnt offering. ¹⁰Just as he finished, Samuel arrived. Saul went to meet him.

¹¹Samuel asked, "What have you done?"

Saul answered, "I saw the soldiers leaving me, and you were not here. The Philistines were gathering at Micmash. ¹²Then I thought, 'The Philistines will come against me at Gilgal. And I haven't asked for the Lord's approval.' So I forced myself to offer the whole burnt offering."

¹³Samuel said, "You acted foolishly! You haven't obeyed God's command. If you had obeyed him, God would make your kingdom continue in Israel forever. ¹⁴But now your kingdom will not continue. The Lord has looked for the kind of man he wants. The Lord has appointed him to become ruler of

> The Lord won't leave his people . . . Remember the wonderful things he did for you!
>
> –1 SAMUEL 12:22, 24

13:1 Saul . . . years. This is how the verse is worded in some early Greek copies. The Hebrew is not clear here.
13:5 3,000 Some Greek copies say 3,000. The Hebrew copies say 30,000.

his people. He is doing this because you haven't obeyed his command."

15 Then Samuel left Gilgal and went to Gibeah in Benjamin. The rest of the army followed Saul into battle. Saul counted the men still with him, and there were about 600.

HARD TIMES FOR ISRAEL

16 Saul and his son Jonathan stayed in Geba in the land of Benjamin. The soldiers with them also stayed there. The Philistines made their camp at Micmash. 17 Three groups went out from their camp to attack. One group went on the Ophrah road in the land of Shual. 18 The second group went on the Beth Horon road. And the third group went on the border road. It overlooked the Valley of Zeboim toward the desert.

19 The whole land of Israel had no blacksmith. This is because the Philistines had said, "The Hebrews might make swords and spears." 20 So all the Israelites went down to the Philistines. They went to have their plows, hoes, axes and sickles sharpened. 21 The Philistine blacksmiths charged about one-fourth of an ounce of silver for sharpening plows and hoes. And they charged one-eighth of an ounce of silver for sharpening picks, axes and the sticks used to guide oxen.

22 So when the battle came, the soldiers with Saul and Jonathan had no swords or spears. Only Saul and his son Jonathan had them.

ISRAEL DEFEATS THE PHILISTINES

23 A group from the Philistine army had gone out to the mountain pass at Micmash.

14 One day Jonathan, Saul's son, spoke to the officer who carried his armor. Jonathan said, "Come, let's go over to the Philistine camp on the other side." But Jonathan did not tell his father.

2 Saul was sitting under a pomegranate tree at the threshing floor near Gibeah. He had about 600 men with him. 3 One man was Ahijah, who was a son of Ichabod's brother Ahitub. Ichabod was the son of Phinehas, Eli's son. Eli was the Lord's priest in Shiloh. He wore the holy vest. No one knew Jonathan had left.

4 There was a steep slope on each side of the pass. Jonathan planned to go through the pass to the Philistine camp. The cliff on one side was named Bozez. The other cliff was named Seneh. 5 One cliff faced north toward Micmash. The other faced south toward Geba.

6 Jonathan said to his officer who carried his armor, "Come. Let's go to the camp of those men who are not circumcised. Maybe the Lord will help us. It doesn't matter if we have many people, or just a few. Nothing can keep the Lord from giving us victory."

7 The officer who carried Jonathan's armor said to him, "Do whatever you think is best. Go ahead. I'm with you."

8 Jonathan said, "Then come. We will cross over to the Philistines. We will let them see us. 9 They may say to us, 'Stay there until we come to you.' If they do, we will stay where we are. We won't go up to them. 10 But they may say, 'Come up to us.' If so, we will climb up. And the Lord will allow us to defeat them. This will be the sign for us."

11 Both Jonathan and his officer let the Philistines see them. The Philistines said, "Look! The Hebrews are crawling out of the holes they were hiding in!"

12 The Philistines in the camp shouted to Jonathan and his officer, "Come up to us. We'll teach you a lesson!"

Jonathan said to his officer, "Climb up behind me. The Lord has given the Philistines to Israel!" 13 So Jonathan climbed up, using his hands and feet. His officer climbed just behind him. Jonathan cut down the Philistines as he went. And his officer killed them as he followed behind Jonathan. 14 In that first fight Jonathan and his officer killed about 20 Philistines.

15 All the Philistine soldiers panicked.

Those in the camp and those in the raiding party were frightened. The ground itself shook! God caused the panic.

[16]Saul's guards were at Gibeah in the land of Benjamin. They saw the Philistine soldiers running in every direction. [17]Saul said to his army, "Check and find who has left our camp." When they checked, they learned that Jonathan and his officer were gone.

[18]So Saul said to Ahijah the priest, "Bring the Ark of the Covenant of God." (At that time it was with the Israelites.) [19]While Saul was talking to the priest, the confusion in the Philistine camp was growing. Then Saul said to Ahijah, "Stop. There's not time to pray now!"

[20]Then Saul and the army with him gathered and entered the battle. They found the Philistines confused, even striking each other with their swords! [21]Earlier, there were Hebrews who had served the Philistines and had stayed in their camp. They now joined the Israelites with Saul and Jonathan. [22]All the Israelites hidden in the mountains of Ephraim heard that the Philistine soldiers were running away. They too joined the battle and chased the Philistines. [23]So the Lord saved the Israelites that day. And the battle moved on past Beth Aven.

SAUL MAKES ANOTHER MISTAKE

[24]The men of Israel were miserable that day. This was because Saul had made an oath for all of them. He had said, "No one should eat food before evening and before I finish defeating my enemies. If he does, he will be cursed!" So no Israelite soldier ate food.

[25]Now the army went into the woods. There was some honey on the ground. [26]They came to where the honey was. But no one took any because they were afraid of the oath. [27]But Jonathan had not heard the oath Saul had put on the people. So Jonathan dipped the end of his stick into the honey. He pulled out the honey and ate it. Then he felt better. [28]So one of the soldiers told Jonathan, "Your father made an oath for all the soldiers. He said any man who eats today will be cursed! That's why they are weak."

[29]Jonathan said, "My father has made trouble for the land! See how much better I feel after just tasting a little of this honey! [30]It would have been much better for the men to eat the food they took from their enemies today. We could have killed many more Philistines!"

[31]That day the Israelites defeated the Philistines from Micmash to Aijalon. After they did this, they were very tired. [32]They had taken sheep, cattle and calves from the Philistines. Now they were so hungry they killed the animals on the ground and ate them. But the blood was still in the animals! [33]Someone said to Saul, "Look! The men are sinning against the Lord. They're eating meat that still has blood in it!"

Saul said, "You have sinned! Roll a large stone over here now!" [34]Then he said, "Go to the men. Tell them that each person must bring his ox and sheep to me. They must kill and eat their ox and sheep here. Don't sin against the Lord. Don't eat meat with the blood still in it."

That night everyone brought his animals and killed them there. [35]Then Saul built an altar to the Lord. It was the first altar Saul had built to the Lord.

[36]Saul said, "Let's go after the Philistines tonight. Let's take what they own. We won't let any of them live!"

The men answered, "Do whatever you think is best."

But the priest said, "Let's ask God."

[37]So Saul asked God, "Should I chase the Philistines? Will you let us defeat them?" But that day God did not answer Saul. [38]That is why Saul said to all the leaders of his army, "Come here. Let's find what sin has been done today. [39]As surely as the Lord lives, even if my son

Jonathan did the sin, he must die." But no one in the army answered.

⁴⁰Then Saul said to all the Israelites, "You stand on this side. I and my son Jonathan will stand on the other side."

The men answered, "Do whatever you think is best."

⁴¹Then Saul prayed to the Lord, the God of Israel, "Give me the right answer."

And Saul and Jonathan were chosen by throwing lots. The other men went free. ⁴²Saul said, "Throw the lot. It will show if it is I or Jonathan my son who is guilty." And Jonathan was chosen.

⁴³Saul said to Jonathan, "Tell me what you have done."

So Jonathan told Saul, "I only tasted a little honey from the end of my stick. And must I die now?"

⁴⁴Saul said, "Jonathan, if you don't die, may God punish me terribly."

⁴⁵But the soldiers said to Saul, "Must Jonathan die? Never! He is responsible for saving Israel today! As surely as the Lord lives, not even a hair of his head will fall to the ground! Today Jonathan fought against the Philistines with God's help!" So the army saved Jonathan, and he did not die.

⁴⁶Then Saul stopped chasing the Philistines. And they went back to their own land.

SAUL FIGHTS ISRAEL'S ENEMIES

⁴⁷When Saul became king over Israel, he fought against Israel's enemies all around. He fought Moab, the Ammonites, Edom, the king of Zobah and the Philistines. Everywhere Saul went he defeated Israel's enemies. ⁴⁸He became strong. He fought bravely and defeated the Amalekites. He saved Israel from the enemies who had taken what the Israelites owned.

⁴⁹Saul's sons were Jonathan, Ishvi and Malki-Shua. His older daughter was named Merab. His younger daughter was named Michal. ⁵⁰Saul's wife was Ahinoam daughter of Ahimaaz. The commander of his army was Abner son of Ner. Ner was Saul's uncle. ⁵¹Saul's father Kish and Abner's father Ner were sons of Abiel.

⁵²All Saul's life he fought hard against the Philistines. When he saw strong or brave men, he took them into his army.

SAUL REJECTED AS KING

15 Samuel said to Saul, "The Lord sent me to appoint you king over Israel. Now listen to his message. ²This is what the Lord of heaven's armies says: 'The Israelites came out of Egypt. But the Amalekites tried to stop them from going to Canaan. I saw what they did. ³Now go, attack the Amalekites. Destroy everything that belongs to them as an offering to the Lord. Don't let anything live. Put to death men and women, children and small babies. Kill the cattle and sheep, camels and donkeys.'"

⁴So Saul called the army together at Telaim. There were 200,000 soldiers and 10,000 men from Judah. ⁵Then Saul went to the city of Amalek and set up an ambush in the ravine. ⁶He said to the Kenites, "Go away. Leave the Amalekites so that I won't destroy you with them. You showed kindness to the Israelites when they came out of Egypt." So the Kenites moved away from the Amalekites.

⁷Then Saul defeated the Amalekites. He fought them all the way from Havilah to Shur, at the border of Egypt. ⁸He took Agag king of the Amalekites alive. But he killed all of Agag's army

> The Lord spoke . . . "Saul has stopped following me. And I am sorry I made him king."
>
> –1 SAMUEL 15:10–11

with the sword. ⁹But Saul and the army let Agag live. They also let the best sheep, fat cattle and lambs live. They let every good animal live. They did not want to destroy them. But when they found an animal that was weak or useless, they killed it.

¹⁰Then the Lord spoke his word to Samuel: ¹¹"Saul has stopped following me. And I am sorry I made him king. He has not obeyed my commands." Samuel was upset, and he cried out to the Lord all night long.

¹²Early the next morning Samuel got up and went to meet Saul. But the people told Samuel, "Saul has gone to Carmel. He has put up a monument in his own honor. Now he has gone down to Gilgal."

¹³Then Samuel came to Saul. And Saul said, "May the Lord bless you! I have obeyed the Lord's commands."

¹⁴But Samuel said, "Then why do I hear cattle mooing and sheep bleating?"

¹⁵Saul answered, "The soldiers took them from the Amalekites. They saved the best sheep and cattle to offer as sacrifices to the Lord your God. But we destroyed all the other animals."

¹⁶Samuel said to Saul, "Stop! Let me tell you what the Lord said to me last night."

Saul answered, "Tell me."

¹⁷Samuel said, "Once you didn't think much of yourself. But now you have become the leader of the tribes of Israel. The Lord appointed you to be king over Israel. ¹⁸And he told you to do something. He said, 'Go and destroy those evil people, the Amalekites. Make war on them until all of them are dead.' ¹⁹Why didn't you obey the Lord? Why did you take the best things? Why did you do what the Lord said was wrong?"

²⁰Saul said, "But I did obey the Lord. I did what the Lord told me to do. I destroyed all the Amalekites. And I brought back Agag their king. ²¹The soldiers took the best sheep and cattle to sacrifice to the Lord your God at Gilgal."

²²But Samuel answered,

"What pleases the Lord more:
    burnt offerings and sacrifices or
        obedience?
It is better to obey God than to offer a
    sacrifice.
    It is better to listen to God than to
        offer the fat of male sheep.
²³ Refusing to obey is as bad as the sin
        of sorcery.
    Being stubborn is as bad as the sin
        of worshiping idols.
You have rejected the Lord's
        command.
    For this reason, he now rejects you
        as king."

²⁴Then Saul said to Samuel, "I have sinned. I didn't obey the Lord's commands. I didn't do what you told me. I was afraid of the people, and I did what they said. ²⁵Now I beg you, forgive my sin. Come back with me so I may worship the Lord."

²⁶But Samuel said to Saul, "I won't go back with you. You refused the Lord's command. And now he rejects you as king of Israel."

²⁷As Samuel turned to leave, Saul caught his robe, and it tore. ²⁸Samuel said to him, "The Lord has torn the kingdom of Israel from you today. He has given it to one of your neighbors. He has given it to one better than you. ²⁹The Lord is the Eternal One of Israel. He does not lie or change his mind. He is not a man. So he does not change his mind as men do."

³⁰Saul answered, "I have sinned. But please honor me in front of my people's elders. Please honor me in front of the Israelites. Come back with me so that I may worship the Lord your God." ³¹So Samuel went back with Saul, and Saul worshiped the Lord.

³²Then Samuel said, "Bring me Agag king of the Amalekites."

Agag came to Samuel in chains. Yet Agag thought, "Surely the threat of death has passed."

33 Samuel said to him, "Your sword caused mothers to be without their children. Now your mother will have no children." And Samuel cut Agag to pieces before the Lord at Gilgal.

34 Then Samuel left and went to Ramah. But Saul went up to his home in Gibeah. 35 And Samuel never saw Saul again all the rest of his life. But he was sorry for Saul. And the Lord was very sorry he had made Saul king of Israel.

SAMUEL GOES TO BETHLEHEM

16 The Lord said to Samuel, "How long will you continue to feel sorry for Saul? I have rejected him as king of Israel. Fill your container with olive oil and go. I am sending you to Jesse who lives in Bethlehem. I have chosen one of his sons to be king."

2 But Samuel said, "If I go, Saul will hear the news. And he will try to kill me."

The Lord said, "Take a young calf with you. Say, 'I have come to offer a sacrifice to the Lord.' 3 Invite Jesse to the sacrifice. Then I will show you what to do. You must appoint the one I show you."

4 Samuel did what the Lord told him to do. When he arrived at Bethlehem, the elders of Bethlehem shook with

☆ 1 Samuel 16:7

Things did not work out well for Israel when Saul was king. He did not follow God with his whole heart. God had someone else in mind to be king. Samuel went to Bethlehem to meet Jesse and his sons. Samuel saw that Jesse's oldest son was big and strong. Samuel knew this must be the new king. But he was wrong. God sees deep into the heart of a person.

David was not the tallest. He was not the strongest. In fact, he was the youngest of seven brothers! No one thought he could be someone important. But God saw that young David had a pure heart. David loved God. He loved others. He worked hard at his job of being a shepherd. God chose David to be king of Israel.

. . . .

You may not be the biggest, smartest, or tallest, but that is okay. God is much more interested in what's in your heart. He chooses people like you to do great things for him!

fear. They met him and asked, "Are you coming in peace?"

⁵Samuel answered, "Yes, I come in peace. I have come to make a sacrifice to the Lord. Make yourselves holy for the Lord and come to the sacrifice with me." Then he made Jesse and his sons holy for the Lord. And he invited them to come to the sacrifice.

⁶When they arrived, Samuel saw Eliab. Samuel thought, "Surely the Lord has appointed this person standing here before him."

⁷But the Lord said to Samuel, "Don't look at how handsome Eliab is. Don't look at how tall he is. I have not chosen him. God does not see the same way people see. People look at the outside of a person, but the Lord looks at the heart."

⁸Then Jesse called Abinadab and told him to pass by Samuel. But Samuel said, "The Lord has not chosen this man either." ⁹Then Jesse had Shammah pass by. But Samuel said, "No, the Lord has not chosen this one." ¹⁰Jesse had seven of his sons pass by Samuel. But Samuel said to him, "The Lord has not chosen any of these."

¹¹Then he asked Jesse, "Are these all the sons you have?"

Jesse answered, "I still have the youngest son. He is out taking care of the sheep."

Samuel said, "Send for him. We will not sit down to eat until he arrives."

¹²So Jesse sent and had his youngest son brought in. He was a fine boy, tanned and handsome.

The Lord said to Samuel, "Go! Appoint him. He is the one."

¹³So Samuel took the container of olive oil. Then he poured oil on Jesse's youngest son to appoint him in front of his brothers. From that day on, the Lord's Spirit entered David with power. Samuel then went back to Ramah.

DAVID SERVES SAUL

¹⁴But the Lord's Spirit had gone out of Saul. And an evil spirit from the Lord troubled him.

¹⁵Saul's servants said to him, "See, an evil spirit from God is troubling you. ¹⁶Give us the command. We will look for someone who can play the harp. When the evil spirit from the Lord enters you, he will play. Then the evil spirit will leave you alone. And you will feel better."

¹⁷So Saul said to his servants, "Find someone. If he plays well, bring him to me."

¹⁸One of the servants said, "Jesse of Bethlehem has a son who plays the harp. I have seen him play it. He is a brave man and fights well. He is a good speaker and handsome. And the Lord is with him."

¹⁹Then Saul sent messengers to Jesse. The message said, "Send me your son David, who is with the sheep." ²⁰So Jesse loaded a donkey with bread and a leather bag full of wine. He also took a young goat. He sent them all with his son David to Saul.

²¹When David came to Saul, he began to serve him. Saul loved David very much. And David became the officer who carried Saul's armor. ²²Saul sent a message to Jesse. He said, "Let David stay and serve me. I like him."

²³When the evil spirit from God entered Saul, David would take his harp and play. Then the evil spirit would go out of him. And Saul would feel relief. He would feel better again.

DAVID AND GOLIATH

17 The Philistines gathered their armies for war. They met at Socoh in Judah. Their camp was at Ephes Dammim between Socoh and Azekah. ²Saul and the Israelites gathered in the Valley of Elah. And they camped there. They took their positions to fight the Philistines. ³The Philistines controlled one hill. The Israelites controlled another. The valley was between them.

⁴The Philistines had a champion fighter named Goliath. He was from Gath. He was about nine feet

four inches tall. He came out of the Philistine camp. ⁵He had a bronze helmet on his head. And he wore a coat of scale armor. It was made of bronze and weighed about 125 pounds. ⁶He wore bronze protectors on his legs. And he had a small spear of bronze tied on his back. ⁷The wooden part of his larger spear was like a weaver's rod. And its blade weighed about 15 pounds. The officer who carried his shield walked in front of him.

⁸Goliath stood and shouted to the Israelite soldiers, "Why have you taken positions for battle? I am a Philistine, and you are Saul's servants! Choose a man and send him to fight me. ⁹If he can fight and kill me, we will become your servants. But if I defeat and kill him, you will become our servants." ¹⁰Then he said, "Today I stand and dare the army of Israel! Send one of your men to fight me!" ¹¹When Saul and the Israelites heard the Philistine's words, they were very afraid.

¹²Now David was the son of Jesse, an Ephrathite. Jesse was from Bethlehem in Judah. He had eight sons. In Saul's time Jesse was an old man. ¹³His three oldest sons followed Saul to the war. The first son was Eliab. The second son was Abinadab. And the third son was Shammah. ¹⁴David was the youngest son. Jesse's three oldest sons followed Saul. ¹⁵But David went back and forth from Saul to Bethlehem. There he took care of his father's sheep.

¹⁶The Philistine Goliath came out every morning and evening. He stood before the Israelite army. This continued for 40 days.

¹⁷Now Jesse said to his son David, "Take this half bushel of cooked grain. And take ten loaves of bread. Take them to your brothers in the camp. ¹⁸Also take ten pieces of cheese. Give them to the commander of your brothers' group of 1,000 soldiers. See how your brothers are. Bring back something to show me they are all right. ¹⁹Your brothers are with Saul and the army in the Valley of Elah. They are fighting against the Philistines."

²⁰Early in the morning David left the sheep with another shepherd. He took the food and left as Jesse had told him. When David arrived at the camp, the army was leaving. They were going out to their battle positions. The soldiers were shouting their war cry. ²¹The Israelites and Philistines were lining up their men to face each other in battle.

²²David left the food with the man who kept the supplies. Then he ran to the battle line and talked to his brothers. ²³While he was talking with them, Goliath came out. He was the Philistine champion from Gath. He shouted things against Israel as usual, and David heard it. ²⁴When the Israelites saw Goliath, they were very much afraid and ran away.

²⁵They said, "Look at this man Goliath. He keeps coming out to speak against Israel. The king will give much money to the man who kills Goliath. He will also give his daughter in marriage to whoever kills him. And his father's family will not have to pay taxes in Israel."

²⁶David asked the men who stood near him, "What will be done to reward the man who kills this Philistine? What will be done for whoever takes away the shame from Israel? Goliath is a Philistine. He is not circumcised. Why does he think he can speak against the armies of the living God?"

²⁷The Israelites told David what they had been saying. They said, "This is what will be done for the man who kills Goliath."

²⁸David's oldest brother Eliab heard David talking with the soldiers. He became angry with David. He asked David, "Why did you come here? Who's taking care of those few sheep of yours in the desert? I know you are proud. Your attitude is very bad. You came down here just to watch the battle!"

²⁹David asked, "Now what have I done wrong? Can't I even talk?" ³⁰He

then turned to other people and asked the same questions. And they gave him the same answer as before. ³¹Some men heard what David said and told Saul. Then Saul ordered David to be sent to him.

³²David said to Saul, "Don't let anyone be discouraged. I, your servant, will go and fight this Philistine!"

³³Saul answered, "You can't go out against this Philistine and fight him. You're only a boy. Goliath has been a warrior since he was a young man."

³⁴But David said to Saul, "I, your servant, have been keeping my father's sheep. When a lion or bear came and took a sheep from the flock, ³⁵I would chase it. I would attack it and save the sheep from its mouth. When it attacked me, I caught it by its fur. I would hit it and kill it. ³⁶I, your servant, have killed both a lion and a bear! Goliath, the Philistine who is not circumcised, will be like the lion or bear I killed. He will die because he has stood against the armies of the living God. ³⁷The Lord saved me from a lion and a bear. He will also save me from this Philistine."

Saul said to David, "Go, and may the Lord be with you." ³⁸Saul put his own clothes on David. He put a bronze helmet on David's head and armor on his body. ³⁹David put on Saul's sword and tried to walk around. But he was not used to all the armor Saul had put on him.

He said to Saul, "I can't go in this. I'm not used to it." Then David took it all off. ⁴⁰He took his stick in his hand. And he chose five smooth stones from a stream. He put them in his pouch and held his sling in his hand. Then he went to meet Goliath.

⁴¹At the same time, the Philistine was coming closer to David. The man who held his shield walked in front of him. ⁴²Goliath looked at David. He saw that David was only a boy, tanned and handsome. He looked down at David with disgust. ⁴³He said, "Do you think I am a dog, that you come at me with a stick?" He used his gods' names to curse David. ⁴⁴He said to David, "Come here. I'll feed your body to the birds of the air and the wild animals!"

⁴⁵But David said to him, "You come to me using a sword, a large spear and a small spear. But I come to you in the name of the Lord of heaven's armies. He's the God of the armies of Israel! You have spoken out against him. ⁴⁶Today the Lord will give you to me. I'll kill you, and I'll cut off your head. Today I'll feed the bodies of the Philistine soldiers to the birds of the air and the wild animals. Then all the world will know there is a God in Israel! ⁴⁷Everyone gathered here will know the Lord does not need swords or spears to save people. The battle belongs to him! And he will help us defeat all of you."

⁴⁸As Goliath came near to attack him, David ran quickly to meet him. ⁴⁹He took a stone from his pouch. He put it into his sling and slung it. The stone hit the Philistine on his forehead and sank into it. Goliath fell facedown on the ground.

⁵⁰So David defeated the Philistine with only a sling and a stone! He hit him and killed him. He did not even have a sword in his hand. ⁵¹David ran and stood beside the Philistine. He took Goliath's sword out of its holder and killed him. Then he cut off Goliath's head.

When the Philistines saw that their champion was dead, they turned and ran. ⁵²The men of Israel and Judah

> I come to you in the name of the Lord of heaven's armies. He's the God of the armies of Israel!
>
> –1 SAMUEL 17:45

shouted and started chasing the Philistines. They chased them all the way to the entrance to the city of Gath. And they chased them to the gates of Ekron.

Many of the Philistines died. Their bodies lay on the Shaaraim road as far as Gath and Ekron. ⁵³The Israelites returned after chasing the Philistines. Then they took many things from the Philistine camp. ⁵⁴David took Goliath's head to Jerusalem. He also put Goliath's weapons in his own tent.

⁵⁵Saul had watched David go out to meet Goliath. Saul spoke to Abner, commander of the army. He said, "Abner, who is that young man's father?"

Abner answered, "As surely as you live, my king, I don't know."

⁵⁶The king said, "Find out whose son he is."

⁵⁷When David came back from killing Goliath, Abner brought him to Saul. David still held Goliath's head.

⁵⁸Saul asked him, "Young man, who is your father?"

David answered, "I am the son of your servant Jesse of Bethlehem."

SAUL FEARS DAVID

18 When David finished talking with Saul, Jonathan felt very close to David. He loved David as much as he loved himself. ²Saul kept David with him from that day on. He did not let David go home to his father's house. ³Jonathan made an agreement with David. He did this because he loved David as much as himself. ⁴He took off his coat and gave it to David. He also gave David his uniform, including his sword, bow and belt.

⁵Saul sent David to fight in different battles. And David was very successful. Then Saul put David over the soldiers. When he did this, Saul's officers and all the other people were pleased.

⁶After David had killed the Philistine, he and the men returned home. Women came out from all the towns of Israel to meet King Saul. They sang songs of joy, danced and played tambourines and stringed instruments. ⁷As they played, they sang,

"Saul has killed thousands of his enemies.
But David has killed tens of thousands!"

⁸The women's song upset Saul, and he became very angry. He thought, "The women say David has killed tens of thousands of enemies. But they say I killed only thousands of enemies. The only thing left for him to have is the kingdom!" ⁹So Saul watched David closely from then on. He was jealous of him.

¹⁰The next day an evil spirit from God entered Saul with power. And he prophesied in his house. David was playing the harp as he usually did. But Saul had a spear in his hand. ¹¹He raised the spear and thought, "I'll pin David to the wall." But David got away from him two times.

¹²The Lord was with David but had left Saul. So Saul was afraid of David. ¹³He sent David away from him. He made David commander of 1,000 soldiers. So David led them in battle. ¹⁴He had great success in everything he did because the Lord was with him. ¹⁵Saul saw that David was very successful. And he became even more afraid of David. ¹⁶But all the people of Israel and Judah loved David. This was because he led them well in battle.

SAUL'S DAUGHTER AND DAVID

¹⁷Saul said to David, "You're a brave soldier. And you fight the Lord's battles. Here is my older daughter Merab. I will let you marry her." Saul had decided, "I won't have to kill David. The Philistines will do that!"

¹⁸But David said, "I am not good enough for this honor. And my family is not important enough for me to become the king's son-in-law." ¹⁹So when the time came for Saul's daughter Merab to marry David, Saul gave her instead to Adriel of Meholah.

²⁰Now Saul's other daughter Michal loved David. When they told Saul about Michal loving David, he was pleased. ²¹He thought, "I will let Michal marry David. Then she will become a trap for him. And the Philistines will defeat him." So Saul said to David a second time, "You may become my son-in-law."

²²And Saul gave an order to his servants. He told them, "Speak to David in private. Say, 'Look, the king is pleased with you. His servants like you. You should become his son-in-law.'"

²³Saul's servants said these words to David. But David answered, "Do you think it is easy to become the king's son-in-law? I'm only a poor man. Nobody knows me."

²⁴Then Saul's servants told him what David had said. ²⁵Saul said, "Say to David, 'The king doesn't want you to pay a large price for the bride. All he wants is 100 Philistine foreskins. Then he will be even with his enemies.'" Saul planned to let the Philistines kill David.

²⁶Saul's servants told David these words. David was pleased that he could become the king's son-in-law. ²⁷So he and his men went out and killed 200 Philistines. David took all their foreskins and brought them to Saul. He wanted to become the king's son-in-law. Then Saul gave him his daughter Michal for his wife. ²⁸Saul saw that the Lord was with David. He also saw that his daughter Michal loved David. ²⁹So he became even more afraid of David. And he was David's enemy all his life.

³⁰The Philistine commanders continued to go out to fight the Israelites. But every time, David defeated them. He had more success than Saul's officers. And he became famous.

SAUL PLANS TO KILL DAVID

19 Saul told his son Jonathan and all his servants to kill David. But Jonathan cared very much for David. ²So he warned David, "My father Saul is looking for a chance to kill you. Watch out in the morning. Hide in a secret place. ³I will go out and stand with my father in the field where you are hiding. I'll talk to him about you. Then I'll let you know what I find out."

⁴Jonathan talked to Saul his father. He said good things about David. Jonathan said, "You are the king. Don't do wrong to your servant David. He did nothing wrong to you. What he did has helped you greatly. ⁵David risked his life when he killed Goliath the Philistine. The Lord won a great victory for all Israel. You saw it, and you were happy. Why would you do wrong against David? He's innocent. There's no reason to kill him!"

⁶Saul listened to Jonathan. Then he made this promise: "As surely as the Lord lives, David won't be put to death."

⁷So Jonathan called to David. He told David everything that had been said. And he brought David to Saul. So David was with Saul as before.

⁸When war broke out again, David went out to fight the Philistines. He defeated them, and they ran away from him.

⁹But once again an evil spirit from the Lord entered Saul. He was sitting in his house, and he had his spear in his hand. David was playing the harp. ¹⁰Saul tried to pin David to the wall with his spear. But David moved away from him. So Saul's spear went into the wall. And David ran away that night.

¹¹Saul sent men to David's house. They watched it, wanting to kill him in the morning. But Michal, David's wife, warned him. She said, "Tonight you must run away to save your own life. If you don't, you will be killed tomorrow morning." ¹²Then she let David down out of a window. So he ran away and escaped. ¹³Then Michal took an idol and laid it on the bed. She covered it with clothes and put goats' hair at its head.

¹⁴Saul sent messengers to take David prisoner. But Michal said, "He is sick."

¹⁵The men went and told Saul, but he sent them back to see David. He told

them, "Bring him to me on his bed so I can kill him."

¹⁶But when the messengers entered David's house, they found it was just an idol on the bed. Its hair was goats' hair.

¹⁷Saul said to Michal, "Why did you trick me this way? You let my enemy go. He has run away!"

Michal answered Saul, "David told me if I did not help him escape, he would kill me."

¹⁸After David had escaped from Saul, he went to Samuel at Ramah. He told Samuel everything Saul had done to him. Then David and Samuel went to Naioth and stayed there.

¹⁹Saul heard that David was in Naioth at Ramah. ²⁰So he sent men to capture him. But they met a group of prophets prophesying. Samuel was leading this group and was standing there. The Spirit of God entered Saul's men, and they also prophesied.

²¹Saul heard the news. So he sent other men, but they also prophesied. Then he sent men a third time, but they also prophesied. ²²Finally, Saul himself went to Ramah. He came to the well at Secu. He asked, "Where are Samuel and David?"

The people answered, "In Naioth at Ramah."

²³Then Saul went to Naioth at Ramah. But the Spirit of God also entered him. And he walked on, prophesying until he came to Naioth at Ramah. ²⁴He took off his robes and prophesied in front of Samuel. He lay that way all day and all night. That is why people ask, "Is even Saul one of the prophets?"

DAVID AND JONATHAN

20 Then David ran away from Naioth in Ramah. He went to Jonathan and asked, "What have I done? What is my crime? How have I sinned against your father so that he's trying to kill me?"

²Jonathan answered, "No! You won't die! See, my father doesn't do anything without first telling me. It doesn't matter if it is very important or just a small thing. Why would he refuse to tell me he wants to kill you? No, it's not true!"

³But David took an oath. He said, "Your father knows very well that I'm your friend. He has said to himself, 'Jonathan must not know about it. If he knows, he will tell David.' But as surely as the Lord lives and as you live, I am very close to death!"

⁴Jonathan said to David, "I'll do anything you want me to do."

⁵So David said, "Look, tomorrow is the New Moon festival. I am supposed to eat with the king. But let me hide in the field until the third evening. ⁶Your father may notice I am gone. If he does, tell him, 'David begged me to let him go to his hometown of Bethlehem. Every year at this time, his family group offers a sacrifice.' ⁷If your father says, 'Fine,' I am safe. But if he becomes angry, you can believe he wants to hurt me. ⁸Jonathan, be kind to me, your servant. You have made an agreement with me before the Lord. If I am guilty, you may kill me yourself! Why hand me over to your father?"

⁹Jonathan answered, "No, never! If I learn that my father plans to harm you, I will warn you!"

¹⁰David asked, "Who will let me know if your father answers you unkindly?"

¹¹Then Jonathan said, "Come, let's go out into the field." So Jonathan and David went together into the field.

¹²Jonathan said to David, "I promise this before the Lord, the God of Israel:

> Jonathan said to David . . . "You must not stop showing your kindness to my family."
>
> –1 SAMUEL 20:12, 15

At this same time day after tomorrow, I will find out how my father feels. If he feels good toward you, I'll send word to you. I'll let you know. ¹³But my father may mean to hurt you. If so, I will let you know and send you away safely. May the Lord punish me terribly if I don't do this. And may the Lord be with you as he has been with my father. ¹⁴But show me the kindness of the Lord as long as I live. Do this so that I may not die. ¹⁵You must not stop showing your kindness to my family. Don't do this, even when the Lord has destroyed all your enemies from the earth."

¹⁶So Jonathan made an agreement with David. He said, "May the Lord punish David's enemies." ¹⁷And Jonathan asked David to repeat his promise of love for him. He did this because he loved David as much as he loved himself.

¹⁸Jonathan said to David, "Tomorrow is the New Moon festival. Your seat will be empty. So my father will notice you're gone. ¹⁹On the third day go to the place where you hid when this trouble began. Wait by the rock Ezel. ²⁰On the third day I will shoot three arrows to the side of the rock. I will shoot as if I am shooting at a target. ²¹Then I will send a boy and tell him to go find the arrows. I may say to him, 'Look, the arrows are on this side of you. Bring them here.' If so, you may come out of hiding. You may do this as surely as the Lord lives because you are safe. There is no danger. ²²But I may say to the boy, 'Look, the arrows are beyond you.' If I do, you must go, because the Lord has sent you away. ²³Remember what we talked about. The Lord is a witness between you and me forever."

²⁴So David hid in the field. And when the New Moon festival came, the king sat down to eat. ²⁵He sat where he always sat, near the wall. Jonathan sat across from him, and Abner sat next to him. But David's place was empty. ²⁶That day Saul said nothing. He thought, "Maybe something has happened to David so that he is unclean."

²⁷But the next day was the second day of the month. And David's place was empty again. So Saul said to Jonathan, "Why hasn't the son of Jesse come to the festival yesterday or today?"

²⁸Jonathan answered, "David begged me to let him go to Bethlehem. ²⁹He said, 'Let me go, because our family has a sacrifice in the town. And my brother has ordered me to be there. Now if I am your friend, please let me go and see my brothers.' That is why he has not come to the king's table."

³⁰Then Saul became very angry with Jonathan. He said, "You son of an evil and disobedient woman! I know you are on the side of David son of Jesse! You bring shame on yourself and on your mother who gave birth to you. ³¹As long as Jesse's son lives, you'll never be king or have a kingdom. Now send for David and bring him to me. He must die!"

³²Jonathan asked his father, "Why should David be killed? What wrong has he done?" ³³Then Saul threw his spear at Jonathan, trying to kill him. So Jonathan knew that his father really wanted to kill David. ³⁴Jonathan was very angry and left the table. That second day of the month he refused to eat. He was upset about what his father wanted to do to David.

³⁵The next morning Jonathan went out to the field. He went to meet David as they had agreed. He had a young boy with him. ³⁶Jonathan said to the boy, "Run and find the arrows I shoot." When he ran, Jonathan shot an arrow beyond him. ³⁷The boy ran to the place where Jonathan's arrow fell. But Jonathan called, "The arrow is beyond you!" ³⁸Then he shouted, "Hurry! Go quickly! Don't stop!" The boy picked up the arrow and brought it back to his master. ³⁹(The boy knew nothing about what this meant. Only Jonathan and David knew.) ⁴⁰Then Jonathan gave his weapons to the boy. He told him, "Go back to town."

⁴¹When the boy left, David came out from the south side of the rock. He bowed facedown on the ground before

Jonathan. He did this three times. Then David and Jonathan kissed each other. They cried together, but David cried the most.

⁴²Jonathan said to David, "Go in peace. We have promised by the Lord that we will be friends. We said, 'The Lord will be a witness between you and me, and between our descendants forever.'" Then David left, and Jonathan went back to town.

DAVID GOES TO SEE AHIMELECH

21 David went to Nob to see Ahimelech the priest. Ahimelech shook with fear when he saw David. He asked David, "Why are you alone? Why is no one with you?"

²David answered him, "The king gave me a special order. He told me, 'No one must know about the work I am sending you to do. And no one must know what I told you to do.' I told my men where to meet me. ³Now, what food do you have with you? Give me five loaves of bread or anything you find."

⁴The priest said to David, "I don't have any plain bread here. But I do have some holy bread*ⁿ* here. You may eat it if your men have kept themselves from women."

⁵David answered, "Women have been kept from us. My men always keep their bodies holy, even when we do ordinary work. And this is especially true when the work is holy."

⁶There was no bread except the bread made holy for the Lord. So the priest gave David the bread that showed the people were in the presence of God. This was the bread the priests had taken from the holy table before the Lord. Each day they took this bread away and put hot bread in its place.

⁷Now one of Saul's servants was there that day. He had been held there before the Lord. He was Doeg the Edomite, the chief of Saul's shepherds.

⁸David asked Ahimelech, "Do you have a spear or sword here? The king's business was very important. I had to leave quickly, and I didn't bring my sword or any other weapon."

⁹The priest answered, "The sword of Goliath the Philistine is here. He is the one you killed in the Valley of Elah. His sword is wrapped in a cloth. It is behind the holy vest. If you want it, you may take it. There's no other sword here but that one."

David said, "There is no other sword like Goliath's. Give it to me."

DAVID GOES TO GATH

¹⁰That day David ran away from Saul. He went to Achish king of Gath. ¹¹But the servants of Achish said to him, "This is David king of the Israelites. He's the man the Israelite women sing about when they dance. They sing:

'Saul has killed thousands of his
        enemies.
    But David has killed tens of
        thousands.'"

¹²David paid attention to these words. And he was very much afraid of Achish king of Gath. ¹³So he pretended to be insane in front of Achish and his servants. While he was with them, he acted like a madman. He made marks on the doors of the gate. He let spit run down his beard.

¹⁴Achish said to his servants, "Look at the man! He's insane! Why do you bring him to me? ¹⁵I have enough madmen. I don't need you to bring him here to act like this in front of me! Don't leave him in my house!"

DAVID AT ADULLAM AND MIZPAH

22 David left Gath and escaped to the cave of Adullam. His brothers and other relatives heard that he was there. And they went to see

---

21:4 holy bread This was the bread that showed the people were in the presence of God. Normally only the priests should eat this bread.

him. ²Many people joined David. All those who were in trouble, who owed money or who were unsatisfied gathered around him. And he became their leader. He had about 400 men with him.

³From there David went to Mizpah in Moab. He spoke to the king of Moab. He said, "Please let my father and mother come and stay with you. Let them stay until I learn what God is going to do for me." ⁴So he left them with the king of Moab. And they stayed with the king as long as David was hiding in the protected place.

⁵But the prophet Gad said to David, "Don't stay in the protected place. Go to the land of Judah." So David left and went to the forest of Hereth.

SAUL DESTROYS AHIMELECH'S FAMILY

⁶Saul heard that David and his men had been seen. He sat under the tamarisk tree on the hill at Gibeah. All his officers were standing around him. He had a spear in his hand. ⁷Saul said to them, "Listen, men of Benjamin! Do you think the son of Jesse will give all of you fields and vineyards? Will David make you commanders over thousands of men or hundreds of men? ⁸You have all made plans against me! No one tells me when my son makes an agreement with the son of Jesse! No one cares about me! No one tells me my son has encouraged my servant to ambush me! And David is doing this now!"

⁹Doeg the Edomite was standing there with Saul's officers. He said, "I saw the son of Jesse. He came to see Ahimelech son of Ahitub at Nob. ¹⁰Ahimelech prayed to the Lord for David. He also gave him food. And he gave him the sword of Goliath the Philistine."

¹¹Then the king sent for the priest Ahimelech son of Ahitub. He sent for all of Ahimelech's relatives who were priests at Nob. And they all came to the king. ¹²Saul said to Ahimelech, "Listen now, son of Ahitub."

Ahimelech answered, "Yes, master."

¹³Saul said, "Why have you and Jesse's son made plans against me? You gave him bread and a sword! You prayed to God for him. David is waiting to attack me. He is doing this now!"

¹⁴Ahimelech answered, "David is very loyal to you. You have no other servant who is as loyal as David. He is your own son-in-law and captain of your bodyguards. All the people in your house respect him. ¹⁵That was not the first time I prayed to God for David. Not at all! Don't blame me or any of my relatives. We are your servants. I know nothing about what is going on."

¹⁶But the king said, "Ahimelech, you and all your relatives must die!" ¹⁷Then he told the guards at his side, "Go and kill the priests of the Lord. Do this because they are on David's side. They knew he was running away, but they didn't tell me!"

But the king's officers refused to hurt the priests of the Lord.

¹⁸Then the king ordered Doeg, "Go and kill the priests." So Doeg the Edomite went and killed the priests. That day he killed 85 men who wore the linen holy vest. ¹⁹He also killed the people of Nob, the city of the priests. With the sword he killed men, women, children and small babies. And he killed cattle, donkeys and sheep.

²⁰But Abiathar escaped. He was a son of Ahimelech, who was the son of Ahitub. Abiathar ran away and joined David. ²¹He told David that Saul had killed the Lord's priests. ²²Then David told him, "Doeg the Edomite was there at Nob that day. I knew he would surely tell Saul. So I am responsible for the death of all your father's family. ²³The man who wants to kill you also wants to kill me. Stay with me. Don't be afraid. You will be safe with me."

DAVID AT KEILAH

23 Someone told David, "Look, the Philistines are fighting against Keilah. They are robbing grain from the threshing floors."

²David asked the Lord, "Should I go and fight these Philistines?"

The Lord answered him, "Go. Attack them, and save Keilah."

³But David's men said to him, "We're afraid here in Judah. We will be much more afraid if we go to Keilah where the Philistine army is."

⁴David again asked the Lord. And the Lord answered, "Go down to Keilah. I will help you defeat the Philistines." ⁵So David and his men went to Keilah. They fought the Philistines and took their cattle. David killed many Philistines and saved the people of Keilah. ⁶(Now Abiathar son of Ahimelech had brought the holy vest with him. He brought it when he came to David at Keilah.)

SAUL CHASES DAVID

⁷Someone told Saul that David was now at Keilah. Saul said, "God has given David to me! He has trapped himself because he has entered a town with gates and bars." ⁸Saul called all his army together for battle. They prepared to go down to Keilah to attack David and his men.

⁹David learned Saul was making evil plans against him. So he said to Abiathar the priest, "Bring the holy vest." ¹⁰David prayed, "Lord, God of Israel, I have heard about Saul's plans. He is coming to Keilah to destroy the town because of me. ¹¹Will the people of Keilah give me to Saul? Will Saul come to Keilah, as I heard? Lord, God of Israel, tell me, your servant!"

The Lord answered, "Saul will come down."

¹²Again David asked, "Will the people of Keilah give me and my men to Saul?"

The Lord answered, "They will."

¹³So David and his men left Keilah. There were about 600 men who went with him. And they kept moving from place to place. When Saul found that David had escaped from Keilah, he did not go there.

¹⁴David stayed in the protected places in the desert. He also stayed in the hills of the Desert of Ziph. Every day Saul looked for David. But the Lord did not let him take David.

¹⁵David was at Horesh in the Desert of Ziph. He was afraid because Saul was coming to kill him. ¹⁶But Saul's son Jonathan went to David at Horesh. He helped David have stronger faith in God. ¹⁷Jonathan told him, "Don't be afraid. My father won't touch you. You will become king of Israel, and I will be second to you. Even my father Saul knows this." ¹⁸The two of them made an agreement before the Lord. Then Jonathan went home. But David stayed at Horesh.

¹⁹The people from Ziph went to Saul at Gibeah. They told him, "David is hiding in our land. He's at the protected places of Horesh. They are on the hill of Hakilah, south of Jeshimon. ²⁰Now, our king, come down anytime you want. It's our duty to give David to you."

²¹Saul answered, "The Lord bless you for helping me. ²²Go and learn more about him. Find out where he is staying. Find out who has seen him there. I have heard that he is clever. ²³Find all the hiding places he uses. And come back and tell me everything. Then I'll go with you. If David is in the area, I will find him. I will track him down among all the families in Judah."

²⁴So they went back to Ziph ahead of Saul. David and his men were in the Desert of Maon.ⁿ This was in the desert area south of Jeshimon. ²⁵Saul and his men went to look for David. But people warned David that Saul was looking for him. David then went down to a rock and stayed in the Desert of Maon. Saul heard that David had gone there. So he went after him into the Desert of Maon.

²⁶Saul was going along one side of the mountain. David and his men were on the other side. They were hurrying to get away from Saul. Saul and

23:24 **Maon** Some early Greek copies say "Maon." The Hebrew copies say "Paran."

☆ 1 Samuel 24

Saul was still king, but he knew God had picked David to be king instead. He became jealous of David and even tried to kill him—many times. David took some friends and ran away from Saul. But Saul chased David all over Israel. It was a very scary time for David. Even though he had friends, sometimes he felt alone. But he trusted God. He knew God was with him.

Have you ever had to walk somewhere kind of scary, like a street that was sort of dark? David wrote a song that said, "The Lord is my shepherd. I have everything I need" (Psalm 23:1). When he wrote that, he was facing a scary time. But he knew that God would provide exactly what he needed. God would help David stay strong and show him where he needed to go.

. . . .

Maybe you are a little afraid of something. That is okay. Just remember that God is always right beside you, even in the scariest times.

his soldiers were closing in on David and his men. ²⁷But a messenger came to Saul. He said, "Come quickly! The Philistines are attacking our land!" ²⁸So Saul stopped chasing David and went to fight the Philistines. That is why people call this place Rock of Parting. ²⁹David left the Desert of Maon and lived in the protected places of En Gedi.

DAVID SHAMES SAUL

24 Now Saul had chased the Philistines away. Then he was told, "David is in the Desert of En Gedi." ²So he chose 3,000 men from all Israel. He took these men and began looking for David and his men. They looked near the Rocks of the Wild Goats.

³Saul came to the sheep pens beside the road. A cave was there, and he went in to relieve himself. Now David and his men were hiding far back in the cave. ⁴The men said to David, "Today is the day the Lord talked about! The Lord told you, 'I will give your enemy to you. You can do anything you want with him.'"

Then David crawled near Saul. He cut off a corner of Saul's robe. But Saul did not notice him. ⁵Later David felt guilty because he had cut off a corner of Saul's robe. ⁶He said to his men, "May the Lord keep me from doing such a thing to my master! Saul is the Lord's appointed king. I should not do anything against him, because he is the Lord's appointed king!" [7]David used these words to stop his men. He did not let them attack Saul. Then Saul left the cave and went his way.

[8]When David came out of the cave, he shouted to Saul, "My master and king!" Saul looked back, and David bowed facedown on the ground. [9]He said to Saul, "Why do you listen when people say, 'David plans to harm you'? [10]You have seen something with your own eyes today. You have seen how the Lord put you in my power in the cave. But I refused to kill you. I was merciful to you. I said, 'I won't harm my master, because he is the Lord's appointed king.' [11]My father, look at this piece of your robe in my hand! I cut off the corner of your robe, but I didn't kill you. Now understand and know I am not planning any evil against you. I did nothing wrong to you, but you are hunting me to kill me. [12]May the Lord judge between us. And may he punish you for the wrong you have done to me! But I won't fight you. [13]There is an old saying: 'Evil things come from evil people.' So I won't hurt you. [14]Whom is the king of Israel coming out against? Whom are you chasing? You're not chasing someone who will hurt you! It's as if you are chasing a dead dog or a flea. [15]May the Lord be our judge and decide between you and me. May the Lord support me and show that I am right. May he save me from you!"

[16]David finished saying these words. Then Saul asked, "Is that your voice, David my son?" And he cried loudly. [17]He said, "You are right, and I am wrong. You have been good to me. But I have done wrong to you. [18]You told me what good things you did. The Lord brought me to you, but you did not kill me. [19]If a man finds his enemy, he won't send him away with goodness, will he? May the Lord reward you because you were good to me today. [20]I know you will surely be king. You will rule the kingdom of Israel. [21]Now make a promise to me. Promise in the name of the Lord that you will not kill my descendants. Promise me that you won't wipe out my name from my father's family."

[22]So David made the promise to Saul. Then Saul went back home. David and his men went up to the protected place.

DAVID AND NABAL

25 Now Samuel died. All the Israelites met and had a time of sadness for him. They buried him at his home in Ramah.

Then David moved to the Desert of Maon.[n] [2]A man in Maon who had land at Carmel was very rich. He had 3,000 sheep and 1,000 goats. He was cutting the wool off his sheep at Carmel. [3]His name was Nabal, and he was a descendant of Caleb. His wife was named Abigail. She was a wise and beautiful woman. But Nabal was cruel and mean.

[4]David was in the desert. He heard that Nabal was cutting the wool from his sheep. [5]So he sent ten young men. He told them, "Go to Nabal at Carmel. Greet him for me. [6]Say to Nabal, 'May you and your family have good health! And may all who belong to you have good health. [7]I have heard that you are cutting the wool from your sheep. When your shepherds were with us, we did nothing wrong to them. All the time your shepherds were at Carmel, we stole nothing from them. [8]Ask your servants, and they will tell you. We come at a happy time. So for this reason, be kind to my young men. Please give them anything you can find for them. Please do this for your son David.'"

[9]When the men arrived, they gave the message to Nabal. But Nabal insulted them. [10]He answered them, "Who is David? Who is this son of Jesse? Many slaves are running away from their masters today! [11]I have bread

and water. And I have meat that I killed for my servants who cut the wool. But I won't give it to men I don't know."

¹²David's men went back and told him all Nabal had said. ¹³Then David said to them, "Put on your swords!" So they put on their swords, and David put on his also. About 400 men went with David. But 200 men stayed with the supplies.

¹⁴One of Nabal's servants spoke to Abigail, Nabal's wife. He said, "David sent messengers from the desert to greet our master. But Nabal insulted them. ¹⁵These men were very good to us. They did nothing wrong to us. They stole nothing from us during all the time we were out in the field with them. ¹⁶Night and day they protected us. They were like a wall around us while we were with them caring for the sheep. ¹⁷Now think about it, and decide what you can do. Terrible trouble is coming to our master and all his family. Nabal is such a wicked man that no one can even talk to him."

¹⁸Abigail hurried. She took 200 loaves of bread, 2 leather bags full of wine and 5 cooked sheep. She took about a bushel of cooked grain, 100 cakes of raisins and 200 cakes of pressed figs. She put all these on donkeys. ¹⁹Then she told her servants, "Go on. I'll follow you." But she did not tell her husband.

²⁰Abigail rode her donkey and came down into the mountain ravine. There she met David and his men coming down toward her. ²¹David had just said, "It's been useless! I watched over Nabal's property in the desert. I made sure none of his sheep were missing. I did good to him, but he has paid me back with evil. ²²May God punish me terribly if I let just one of Nabal's family live until tomorrow."

²³When Abigail saw David, she quickly got off her donkey. She bowed facedown on the ground before David. ²⁴She lay at David's feet. She said, "My master, let the blame be on me! Please let me talk to you! Listen to what I say.

²⁵My master, don't pay attention to this worthless man Nabal. He is the same as his name. His name means 'fool,' and he is truly foolish. But I, your servant, didn't see the men you sent. ²⁶The Lord has kept you from killing and punishing people yourself. As surely as the Lord lives and as surely as you live, may your enemies become like Nabal! ²⁷I have brought a gift to you. Please give it to the men who follow you. ²⁸Please forgive my wrong. The Lord will certainly let your family have many kings. He will do this because you fight his battles. As long as you live, people will find nothing bad in you. ²⁹A man might chase you to kill you. But the Lord your God will keep you alive. He will throw away your enemies' lives as he would throw a stone from a sling. ³⁰The Lord will keep all his promises about good things for you. He will make you leader over Israel. ³¹Then you won't feel guilty. You won't have problems about killing innocent people and punishing them yourself. Please remember me when the Lord brings you success."

³²David answered Abigail, "Praise the Lord, the God of Israel. He sent you to meet me. ³³May you be blessed for your wisdom. You have kept me from killing or punishing people today. ³⁴As surely as the Lord, the God of Israel, lives, he has kept me from hurting you. If you hadn't come quickly to meet me, no one belonging to Nabal would have lived until tomorrow."

³⁵Then David accepted Abigail's gifts. He told her, "Go home in peace. I have heard your words, and I will do what you have asked."

NABAL'S DEATH

³⁶When Abigail went back to Nabal, he was in the house. He was eating like a king. He was very drunk and in a good mood. So she told him nothing until the next morning. ³⁷In the morning he was not drunk. Then his wife told him everything. His heart failed him, and he

became like a stone. ³⁸About ten days later the Lord struck Nabal and caused him to die.

³⁹When David heard that Nabal was dead, he said, "Praise the Lord! Nabal insulted me, but the Lord has supported me! He has kept me from doing wrong. And the Lord caused Nabal to die because he did wrong."

Then David sent a message to Abigail. He asked her to become his wife. ⁴⁰His servants went to Carmel and spoke to Abigail. They said, "David sent us to take you so you can become his wife."

⁴¹Abigail bowed facedown on the ground. She said, "I am your servant. I'm ready to serve you. I'm ready to wash the feet of my master's servants." ⁴²Abigail quickly got on a donkey and went with David's messengers. She had five maids following her. And she became David's wife.

⁴³David also had married Ahinoam of Jezreel. So they were both David's wives. ⁴⁴Saul's daughter Michal was also David's wife. But Saul had given her to Paltiel son of Laish. Paltiel was from Gallim.

DAVID SHAMES SAUL AGAIN

26 The people of Ziph went to see Saul at Gibeah. They said to him, "David is hiding on the hill of Hakilah opposite Jeshimon."

²So Saul went down to the Desert of Ziph. His 3,000 chosen men of Israel went with him. They looked for David in the Desert of Ziph. ³Saul made his camp on the hill of Hakilah, beside the road opposite Jeshimon. But David stayed in the desert. He heard Saul had followed him. ⁴So David sent out spies and learned that Saul had come to Hakilah.

⁵Then David went to the place where Saul had camped. He saw where Saul and Abner son of Ner were sleeping. Abner was the commander of Saul's army. Saul was sleeping in the middle of the camp with all the army around him.

⁶David talked to Ahimelech the Hittite and Abishai son of Zeruiah. Abishai was Joab's brother. He asked them, "Who will go down into Saul's camp with me?"

Abishai answered, "I'll go with you."

⁷So that night David and Abishai went into Saul's camp. Saul was asleep in the middle of the camp. His spear was stuck in the ground near his head. Abner and the army were sleeping around Saul. ⁸Abishai said to David, "Today God has let you defeat your enemy! Let me pin Saul to the ground with the spear. I'll only do it once! I won't hit him twice."

⁹But David said to Abishai, "Don't kill Saul! No one can harm the Lord's appointed king and still be innocent! ¹⁰As surely as the Lord lives, the Lord himself will punish Saul. Maybe Saul will die naturally. Or maybe he will go into battle and be killed. ¹¹But may the Lord keep me from harming his appointed king! Now pick up the spear and water jug that are near Saul's head. Then let's go."

¹²So David took the spear and water jug that were near Saul's head. They left, and no one saw them. No one knew about it or woke up. The Lord had made them stay asleep.

¹³David crossed over to the other side of the hill. He stood on top of the mountain far from Saul's camp. David's and Saul's camps were far apart. ¹⁴David shouted to the army and to Abner son of Ner, "Answer me, Abner!"

> The Lord will keep all his promises about good things for you.
>
> –1 SAMUEL 25:30

Abner answered, "Who is calling for the king? Who are you?"

15David said, "You're the greatest man in Israel. Isn't that true? Then why didn't you guard your master the king? Someone came into your camp to kill your master the king! 16What you have done is not good. As surely as the Lord lives, you and your men should die. You haven't guarded your master, the Lord's appointed king. Look! Where are the king's spear and water jug that were near his head?"

17Saul knew David's voice. He said, "Is that your voice, David my son?"

David answered, "Yes, it is, my master and king." 18David also said, "Why are you chasing me, my master? What wrong have I done? What evil am I guilty of? 19My master and king, listen to me. If the Lord caused you to be angry with me, let him accept an offering. But if men caused you to be angry with me, let the Lord curse them! They have made me leave the land the Lord gave me. They have told me, 'Go and serve other gods.' 20Now don't let me die far away from the Lord's presence. The king of Israel has come out looking for a flea! You're like a man hunting a partridge bird in the mountains!"

21Then Saul said, "I have sinned. Come back, David my son. Today you respected my life. So I will not try to hurt you. I have acted foolishly. I have made a big mistake."

22David answered, "Here is your spear. Let one of your young men come here and get it. 23The Lord rewards every man for the things he does right and for his loyalty to him. The Lord put you into my power today. But I wouldn't harm the Lord's appointed king. 24I respected your life today. Surely, in the same way, the Lord will respect my life. Surely he will save me from all trouble."

25Then Saul said to David, "You are blessed, my son David. You will do great things and succeed."

So David went on his way, and Saul went back home.

DAVID AND THE PHILISTINES

27 But David thought to himself, "Saul will catch me someday. The best thing I can do is escape to the land of the Philistines. Then he will give up looking for me in Israel. That way I can get away from him."

2So David and his 600 men left Israel. They went to Achish son of Maoch. Achish was king of Gath. 3David, his men and their families made their home in Gath with Achish. David had his two wives with him. Their names were Ahinoam of Jezreel and Abigail of Carmel. Abigail was the widow of Nabal. 4Now Saul was told that David had run away to Gath. So he stopped looking for him.

5Then David said to Achish, "If you are pleased with me, give me a place in one of the country towns. I can live there. I don't need to live in the royal city with you."

6That day Achish gave David the town of Ziklag. That is why Ziklag has belonged to the kings of Judah ever since. 7David lived in the Philistine land a year and four months.

8David and his men went to raid the people of Geshur, Girzi and Amalek. (These people had lived for a long time in the land that reached to Shur and Egypt.) 9When David fought them, he killed all the men and women. He took sheep, cattle, donkeys, camels and clothes. Then he returned to Achish.

10Many times Achish would ask David, "Where did you go raiding today?" And David would tell him that he had gone to the southern part of Judah. Or he would say he had gone to the territory of the Jerahmeelites or of the Kenites. 11David never brought a man or woman alive to Gath. He thought, "If we bring anyone alive, he may tell Achish, 'This is what David really did.'" David did this all the time he lived in the Philistine land. 12Achish trusted David. He said to himself, "David's own people, the Israelites, now hate David very much. So David will serve me forever."

SAUL AND THE MEDIUM OF ENDOR

28 Later, the Philistines gathered their armies to fight against Israel. Achish said to David, "You understand that you and your men must join with me in my army."

²David answered, "Certainly! Then you can see for yourself what I, your servant, can do!"

Achish said, "Fine, I'll make you my bodyguard for life."

³Now Samuel was dead, and all the Israelites had shown their sadness for him. They had buried Samuel in his hometown of Ramah.

And Saul had forced out the mediums and fortune-tellers from the land of Israel.

⁴The Philistines came together and made camp at Shunem. Saul gathered all the Israelites and made camp at Gilboa. ⁵When he saw the Philistine army, he was afraid. His heart pounded with fear. ⁶He prayed to the Lord, but the Lord did not answer him through dreams, Urim or prophets. ⁷Then Saul said to his servants, "Find me a woman who is a medium. I'll go and ask her what will happen."

His servants answered, "There is a medium in Endor."

⁸Then Saul put on other clothes so no one would know who he was. At night Saul and two of his men went to see the woman. Saul said to her, "Talk to a spirit for me. Call up the person I name."

⁹But the woman said to him, "Surely you know what Saul has done. He has forced the mediums and fortune-tellers out from the land of Israel. You are trying to trap me and kill me."

¹⁰Saul made a promise to the woman in the name of the Lord. He said, "As surely as the Lord lives, you won't be punished for doing this."

¹¹The woman asked, "Whom do you want me to bring up for you?"

He answered, "Bring up Samuel."

¹²When the woman saw Samuel, she screamed loudly. She said, "Why have you tricked me? You are Saul!"

¹³The king said to the woman, "Don't be afraid! What do you see?"

The woman said, "I see a spirit coming up out of the ground."

¹⁴Saul asked, "What does he look like?"

The woman answered, "An old man wearing a coat is coming up."

Then Saul knew it was Samuel, and he bowed facedown on the ground.

¹⁵Samuel asked Saul, "Why have you disturbed me by bringing me up?"

Saul said, "I am greatly troubled. The Philistines are fighting against me. God has left me. He won't answer me anymore, either by prophets or in dreams. That's why I called you. I want you to tell me what to do."

¹⁶Samuel said, "The Lord has left you. He has become your enemy. So why do you call on me? ¹⁷He has done what he said he would do. He said these things through me. He has torn the kingdom out of your hands. He has given it to one of your neighbors, David. ¹⁸You did not obey the Lord. You did not show the Amalekites how angry he was with them. That's why he has done this to you today. ¹⁹The Lord will give both Israel and you to the Philistines. Tomorrow you and your sons will be with me. The Lord will let the Philistines defeat the army of Israel."

²⁰Saul quickly fell to the ground and lay there. He was afraid because of what Samuel had said. He was also very weak because he had eaten nothing all that day and night.

²¹Then the woman came to Saul. She saw that he was really frightened. She said, "Look, I, your servant, have obeyed you. I have risked my life and done what you told me to do. ²²Now please listen to me. Let me give you

some food. Then you may eat and have enough strength to go on your way."

²³But Saul refused. He said, "I won't eat."

His servants joined the woman in asking him to eat. And he listened to them. So he got up from the ground and sat on the bed.

²⁴The woman had a fat calf at the house. She quickly killed it. She took some flour and mixed dough with her hands. Then she baked some bread without yeast. ²⁵She put the food before them, and they ate. Then that same night they got up and left.

DAVID GOES BACK TO ZIKLAG

29 The Philistines gathered all their soldiers at Aphek. Israel camped by the spring at Jezreel. ²The Philistine kings were marching with their groups of 100 and 1,000 men. David and his men were marching at the back with Achish. ³The Philistine commanders asked, "What are these Hebrews doing here?"

Achish told them, "This is David. He was an officer to Saul king of Israel. But he has been with me for over a year now. I have found nothing wrong in David since the time he left Saul and came to me."

⁴But the Philistine commanders were angry with Achish. They said, "Send David back! He must go back to the city you gave him. He can't go with us into battle. If he's here, we'll have an enemy in our own camp. He would please his king by killing our own men. ⁵David is the one the Israelites sing about in their dances:

'Saul has killed thousands of his enemies.
    But David has killed tens of thousands.'"

⁶So Achish called David. He said to him, "As surely as the Lord lives, you are loyal. I would be pleased to have you serve in my army. Since the day you came to me, I have found no wrong in you. But the Philistine kings don't trust you. ⁷Go back in peace. Don't do anything to displease the Philistine kings."

⁸David asked, "What wrong have I done? What evil have you found in me from the day I came to you until now? Why won't you allow me to fight your enemies, my lord and king?"

⁹Achish answered, "I know you are as pleasing to me as an angel from God. But the Philistine commanders have said, 'David can't go with us into battle.' ¹⁰Early in the morning you and your master's servants, the Israelites, should go back. Go back to the city I gave you. Leave as soon as the sun comes up."

¹¹So David and his men got up early in the morning. They went back to the country of the Philistines. And the Philistines went up to Jezreel.

DAVID'S WAR WITH THE AMALEKITES

30 On the third day David and his men arrived at Ziklag. The Amalekites had raided southern Judah and Ziklag. They had attacked Ziklag and burned it. ²They took the women and everyone in Ziklag as prisoners, both young and old. But they did not kill any of the people. They only took them away.

³When David and his men came to Ziklag, they found the town had been burned. Their wives, sons and daughters had been taken as prisoners. ⁴Then David and his army cried loudly until they were too weak to cry anymore. ⁵David's two wives had also been taken. They were Ahinoam of Jezreel and Abigail the widow of Nabal from Carmel. ⁶The men in the army were threatening to kill David with stones. This upset David very much. Each man was sad and angry because his sons and daughters had been taken as prisoners. But David found strength in the Lord his God. ⁷David said to Abiathar the priest, "Bring me the holy vest."

[8]Then David prayed to the Lord. He said, "Should I chase the people who took our families? Will I catch them?"

The Lord answered, "Chase them. You will catch them. You will succeed in saving your families."

[9]David and the 600 men with him came to the Besor Ravine. Some of the men stayed there. [10]David and 400 men kept up the chase. The other 200 men stayed behind because they were too tired and weak to cross the ravine.

[11]David's men found an Egyptian in a field. They took him to David. They gave the Egyptian some water to drink and some food to eat. [12]They gave him a piece of a fig cake and two clusters of raisins. He felt better after eating. He had not eaten any food or drunk any water for three days and nights.

[13]David asked him, "Who is your master? Where do you come from?"

He answered, "I'm an Egyptian. I'm the slave of an Amalekite. Three days ago my master left me, because I became sick. [14]We attacked the southern area of the Kerethites. We attacked the land of Judah and the southern area belonging to Caleb. We burned Ziklag, as well.

[15]David asked him, "Will you lead me to the people who took our families?"

He answered, "Yes, if you will make a promise to me before God. Promise that you won't kill me or give me back to my master. Then I will take you to them."

[16]So the Egyptian led David to the Amalekites. They were lying around on the ground, eating and drinking. They were celebrating with the things they had taken from the land of the Philistines and from Judah. [17]David fought them from sunset until evening the next day. None of them escaped, except 400 young men who rode off on their camels. [18]David got his two wives back. He also got back everything the Amalekites had taken. [19]Nothing was missing. David brought back everything: the young and old people, the sons and daughters, the valuable things and everything the Amalekites had taken. [20]David took all the sheep and cattle. His men made these animals go in front. They said, "They are David's prize."

[21]Then David came to the 200 men who had been too tired and weak to follow him. He had made them stay at the Besor Ravine. They came out to meet David and the army with him. When he came near, the men at the ravine greeted David and his army.

[22]But there were evil men and troublemakers in the group that followed David. They said, "These 200 men didn't go with us. So we won't give them any of the things we took. But each man may take his wife and children and go."

[23]David answered, "No, my brothers. Don't do that after what the Lord has given us. He has given us the enemy who attacked us. [24]Who will listen to what you say? The share will be the same for the man who stayed with the supplies as for the man who went into battle. All will share alike." [25]David made this an order and rule for Israel. This order and rule continues even today.

[26]David arrived in Ziklag. Then he sent some of the things he had taken from the Amalekites to his friends, the leaders of Judah. He said, "Here is a present for you from the things we took from the Lord's enemies."

[27]David sent some things from the Amalekites to the leaders in Bethel, Ramoth in the southern part of Judah, Jattir, [28]Aroer, Siphmoth, Eshtemoa [29]and Racal. He also sent some to the leaders of the cities of the Jerahmeelites and the Kenites, [30]to Hormah, Bor Ashan, Athach [31]and Hebron. He sent some things to the people in all the other places where he and his men had been.

THE DEATH OF SAUL

31 The Philistines fought against Israel, and the Israelites ran away from them. Many Israelites were killed at Mount Gilboa. [2]The Philistines fought hard against Saul and his sons. They killed his sons Jonathan, Abinadab and Malki-Shua. ³The fighting became bad around Saul. When the archers shot at him, he was badly wounded. ⁴He said to the officer who carried his armor, "Pull out your sword and kill me. Then those uncircumcised men won't make fun of me and kill me." But Saul's officer refused, because he was afraid. So Saul took his own sword and threw himself on it. ⁵The officer saw that Saul was dead. So he threw himself on his own sword. And he died with Saul. ⁶So Saul, his three sons and the officer who carried his armor died together that day.

⁷Now there were Israelites who lived on the other side of Jezreel Valley. And some lived across the Jordan River. They saw how the Israelite army had run away. And they saw that Saul and his sons were dead. So they left their cities and ran away. Then the Philistines came and lived there.

⁸The next day the Philistines came to take all the valuable things from the dead soldiers. They found Saul and his three sons dead on Mount Gilboa. ⁹They cut off Saul's head and took off his armor. Then they sent men to tell the news through all the land of the Philistines. They told it in the temple of their idols and to their people. ¹⁰They put Saul's armor in the temple of the Ashtoreths. They also hung his body on the wall of Beth Shan.

¹¹The people living in Jabesh Gilead heard what the Philistines had done to Saul. ¹²So the brave soldiers of Jabesh marched all night and came to Beth Shan. They took the bodies of Saul and his sons off the wall of Beth Shan. Then they took them to Jabesh. There the people of Jabesh burned the bodies. ¹³They took their bones and buried them under the tamarisk tree in Jabesh. Then the people of Jabesh gave up eating for seven days.

FROM KING SAUL TO KING DAVID

While Saul was still king, David worked for him. He was a soldier in Saul's army. He was best friends with Saul's son Jonathan. David even married Saul's daughter. Saul's family loved David, and the people of Israel loved David. But Saul did not. In fact, sometimes he hated David.

Samuel told Saul that God would not let him be king for much longer. But back in those days, if a new man became king, that meant the old king was dead. And Saul did not want to die. His plan was to kill David instead, so Saul could stay king.

The Bible tells the story of when David and Saul ended up hiding in the same cave (1 Samuel 24). David and his men were hiding way in the back of the huge cave. Without knowing they were there, Saul went inside to rest. David crawled up behind Saul and cut off a piece of his robe. David didn't hurt Saul, but he felt guilty. Saul was still his king and his father-in-law. After Saul left the cave, David ran out and showed him what he had done. He told Saul that he would never hurt him. Saul said he was wrong to try to kill David. He asked David to promise that he would not hurt Saul's family when David became king of Israel.

Saul and his sons eventually went to war against another country. The fighting was heavy, and Saul and his sons died in battle. It was now time for a new king.

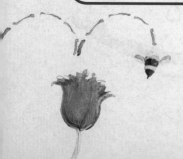

Second Samuel

DAVID LEARNS ABOUT SAUL'S DEATH

1 Now Saul was dead. And after David had defeated the Amalekites, he returned to Ziklag. He stayed there two days. ²On the third day a young man came to Ziklag. He came from Saul's camp. To show his sadness his clothes were torn, and he had dirt on his head. He came and bowed facedown on the ground before David.

³David asked him, "Where did you come from?"

The man answered him, "I escaped from the Israelite camp."

⁴David asked him, "What happened? Please tell me!"

The man answered, "The people have run away from the battle. Many of them have fallen dead. Saul and his son Jonathan are dead also."

⁵David said to him, "How do you know Saul and his son Jonathan are dead?"

⁶The young man answered, "I happened to be on Mount Gilboa. There I saw Saul leaning on his spear. The Philistine chariots and the men riding in them were coming closer to Saul. ⁷When he looked back and saw me, he called to me. I answered him, 'Here I am!'

⁸"Then Saul asked me, 'Who are you?'

"I told him, 'I am an Amalekite.'

⁹"Then Saul said to me, 'Please come here and kill me. I am badly hurt and am almost dead already.'

¹⁰"So I went over and killed him. He had been hurt so badly I knew he couldn't live. Then I took the crown from his head and the bracelet from his arm. I have brought them here to you, my master."

¹¹Then David tore his clothes to show his sorrow. And all the men with him did also. ¹²They were very sad and cried. They did not eat until evening. They cried for Saul and his son Jonathan. And they cried for the Israelites who had been killed with swords.

DAVID ORDERS THE AMALEKITE KILLED

¹³David asked the young man who brought the report, "Where are you from?"

The young man answered, "I am the son of a foreigner. I am an Amalekite."

¹⁴David asked him, "Why were you not afraid to kill the Lord's appointed king?"

¹⁵Then David called one of his men. David told him, "Go! Kill the Amalekite!" So the Israelite killed the Amalekite. ¹⁶David had said to the Amalekite, "You are responsible for your own death. You have spoken against yourself! You said, 'I have killed the Lord's appointed king.'"

DAVID'S SONG ABOUT SAUL AND JONATHAN

¹⁷David sang a funeral song about Saul and his son Jonathan. ¹⁸David ordered that the people of Judah be taught this song. It is called "The Bow." This song is written in the Book of Jashar:

¹⁹ "Israel, your leaders have been killed on the hills.
   How the mighty men have fallen in battle!
²⁰ Don't tell it in Gath.
   Don't announce it in the streets of Ashkelon.
   If you do, the daughters of the Philistines will be happy.
   The daughters of the Philistines will rejoice.

²¹ "May there be no dew or rain on the mountains of Gilboa.
   May their fields produce no grain.
   This is because there the mighty warrior's shield was dishonored.

Saul's shield was no longer rubbed
with oil.
22 Jonathan's bow killed its share of
enemies.
And Saul's sword killed its share,
too.
Their weapons are stained with the
blood of dead men.
Their weapons have stabbed the
flesh of strong men.

23 "We loved Saul and Jonathan.
We enjoyed them while they lived.
Saul and Jonathan are together
even in death.
They were faster than eagles.
They were stronger than lions.

24 "You daughters of Israel, cry for Saul.
Saul clothed you with red dresses.
He put gold decorations on your
dresses.

25 "How the mighty men have fallen in
battle!
Jonathan is dead on Gilboa's hills.
26 I cry for you, my brother Jonathan.
I enjoyed your friendship so much.
Your love to me was wonderful,
more wonderful than the love of
women.

27 "How the mighty men have fallen in
battle!
The weapons of war are gone."

☆ 2 Samuel 2:4; 5:2-3

*Way back when David was still a boy, God chose him to be the next king
of Israel. After Saul died, the people of Israel accepted God's new choice.
First David was made king over his "tribe," Judah. Then all the people got
excited and made him king of the whole nation of
Israel.*

Have you ever told someone something
that wasn't true? The Bible calls that a lie
and we know that everyone has lied before.
Sometimes we make promises that we cannot
keep and that is lying as well. The awesome
thing about God is that he does what he says he
will do and keeps all his promises. God never
lies. And that is awesome! Jesus fulfilled the
promises of God, and now he keeps on keeping
all the promises from the Bible. God never lies.
He cares for each of us so much.

* *

God never lies. What he says he will do, he will do.

DAVID IS MADE KING OF JUDAH

2 Later, David prayed to the Lord. David said, "Should I go up to any of the cities of Judah?"

The Lord said to David, "Go."

David asked, "Where should I go?"

The Lord answered, "To Hebron." ²So David went up to Hebron with his two wives. One was Ahinoam from Jezreel. The other was Abigail, the widow of Nabal in Carmel. ³David also brought his men and their families. They all made their homes in the cities of Hebron. ⁴Then the men of Judah came to Hebron. They appointed David king over Judah.

They told David that the men of Jabesh Gilead had buried Saul. ⁵So David sent messengers to the men of Jabesh Gilead. They told David's message to the men in Jabesh: "The Lord bless you. You have shown kindness to your master Saul by burying him. ⁶May the Lord now be kind and true to you. I will also be kind to you because you have done this. ⁷Now be strong and brave. Saul your master is dead. The people of Judah have appointed me their king."

WAR BETWEEN JUDAH AND ISRAEL

⁸Now Abner son of Ner was the commander of Saul's army. Abner took Saul's son Ish-Bosheth to Mahanaim. ⁹There Abner made him king of Gilead, Ashuri, Jezreel, Ephraim, Benjamin and all Israel. ¹⁰Saul's son Ish-Bosheth was 40 years old when he became king over Israel. He ruled two years. But the people of Judah followed David. ¹¹David was king in Hebron for seven years and six months.

¹²Abner son of Ner and the servants of Ish-Bosheth son of Saul left Mahanaim. They went to Gibeon. ¹³Joab son of Zeruiah and David's men also went there. They met Abner and Ish-Bosheth's men at the pool of Gibeon. Abner's group sat on one side of the pool. Joab's group sat on the other side. ¹⁴Abner said to Joab, "Let's have the

young men get up and have a contest here."

Joab said, "Yes, let them have a contest."

¹⁵Then the young men got up. The two groups counted their men for the contest. Twelve men were chosen from the people of Benjamin for Ish-Bosheth son of Saul. Twelve men were chosen from David's men. ¹⁶Each man grabbed his enemy's head. Then he stabbed his enemy's side with a knife. And the men fell down together. So that place in Gibeon is called The Field of the Sharp Knives. ¹⁷That day the contest became a terrible battle. And David's men defeated Abner and the Israelites.

ABNER KILLS ASAHEL

¹⁸Zeruiah's three sons, Joab, Abishai and Asahel, were there. Now Asahel was a fast runner. He was as fast as a deer in the field. ¹⁹Asahel chased Abner, going straight toward him. ²⁰Abner looked back and asked, "Are you Asahel?"

Asahel said, "Yes, I am."

²¹Then Abner said to Asahel, "Turn to your right or left. Catch one of the young men and take his armor." But Asahel refused to stop chasing him.

²²Abner again said to Asahel, "Stop chasing me! If you don't stop, I'll have to kill you! Then I won't be able to face your brother Joab again!"

²³But Asahel refused to stop chasing Abner. So Abner used the back end of his spear. He stabbed it into Asahel's stomach, and the spear came out of his back. Asahel died right there. Everyone stopped when they came to the place where Asahel's body lay.

²⁴But Joab and Abishai continued chasing Abner. The sun was going down when they arrived at the hill of Ammah. This is near Giah on the way to the empty land near Gibeon. ²⁵The men of Benjamin came to Abner. They all stood together at the top of the hill.

²⁶Abner shouted to Joab, "Must the sword kill forever? Surely you must

know this will only end in sadness! Tell the people to stop chasing their own brothers!"

²⁷Then Joab said, "If you had not said anything, the people would have chased their brothers until morning. This is as sure as God is alive." ²⁸Then Joab blew a trumpet, and his people stopped chasing the Israelites. They did not try to fight them anymore.

²⁹Abner and his men marched all night through the Jordan Valley. They crossed the Jordan River. After marching all day, they arrived at Mahanaim.

³⁰Joab came back after he had stopped chasing Abner. Then Joab gathered the people together. Asahel and 19 of David's men were missing. ³¹But David's men had killed 360 Benjaminites who had followed Abner. ³²David's men took Asahel and buried him. They put him in the tomb of his father at Bethlehem. Then Joab and his men marched all night. The sun came up as they reached Hebron.

3 There was a long war between the people who supported Saul's family and those who supported David's family. The supporters of David's family became stronger and stronger. And the supporters of Saul's family became weaker and weaker.

DAVID'S SONS

²Sons were born to David at Hebron. The first son was Amnon. Amnon's mother was Ahinoam from Jezreel. ³The second son was Kileab. Kileab's mother was Abigail, the widow of Nabal from Carmel. The third son was Absalom. Absalom's mother was Maacah daughter of Talmai. Talmai was king of Geshur. ⁴The fourth son was Adonijah. His mother was Haggith. The fifth son was Shephatiah. His mother was Abital. ⁵The sixth son was Ithream. His mother was Eglah, David's wife. These sons were born to David at Hebron.

ABNER JOINS DAVID

⁶Abner made himself a main leader among the supporters of Saul. He did this during the war between the supporters of Saul's family and the supporters of David's family.

⁷Now Saul had once had a slave woman named Rizpah. She was the daughter of Aiah. Ish-Bosheth said to Abner, "Why did you have physical relations with my father's slave woman?"

⁸Abner was very angry because of what Ish-Bosheth said. Abner said, "I have been loyal to Saul and his family and friends! I didn't hand you over to David. I am not a traitor working for Judah! But now you are saying I did something wrong with this woman! ⁹May God punish me terribly if I don't help David. I will make sure that what God promised does happen! ¹⁰I will take the kingdom from the family of Saul. I will make David king of Israel and Judah! He will rule from Dan to Beersheba." ⁿ

¹¹Ish-Bosheth couldn't say anything to Abner. He was too afraid of Abner.

¹²Then Abner sent messengers to David. Abner said, "Who is going to rule the land? Make an agreement with me, and I will help you become the king of all Israel."

¹³David answered, "Good! I will make an agreement with you. But I ask you one thing. I will not meet with you unless you bring Saul's daughter Michal to me." ¹⁴Then David sent messengers to Saul's son Ish-Bosheth. David said, "Give me my wife Michal. She was promised to me. I killed 100 Philistines to get her."

¹⁵So Ish-Bosheth sent men to take Michal from her husband. He was Paltiel son of Laish. ¹⁶Michal's husband went with her, crying as he followed her to Bahurim. But Abner said to Paltiel, "Go back home." So he went home.

¹⁷Abner sent a message to the elders

3:10 Dan to Beersheba Dan was the city farthest north in Israel. Beersheba was the city farthest south. So this means all the people of Israel.

of Israel. He said, "You have been wanting to make David your king. ¹⁸Now do it! The Lord has spoken about David. The Lord said, 'I will save my people the Israelites. I will save them from the Philistines and all their enemies. I will do this through my servant David.'"

¹⁹Abner also said these things to the people of Benjamin. He then went to Hebron to tell David what the Benjaminites and Israel wanted to do. ²⁰Abner came with 20 men to David at Hebron. There David prepared a feast for them. ²¹Then Abner said to David, "My master and king, I will go and bring all the Israelites to you. Then they will make an agreement with you. You will rule over all Israel as you wanted." So David let Abner go, and he left in peace.

ABNER'S DEATH

²²Just then Joab and David's men came from a battle. They had many valuable things they had taken from the enemy. David had let Abner leave in peace. So he was not with David at Hebron. ²³Joab and all his army arrived at Hebron. The army said to Joab, "Abner son of Ner came to King David. And David let him leave in peace."

²⁴Joab came to the king and said, "What have you done? Abner came to you. Why did you let him go? Now he's gone. ²⁵You know Abner son of Ner! He came to trick you! He came to learn about everything you are doing!"

²⁶Then Joab left David and sent messengers after Abner. They brought Abner back from the well of Sirah. But David did not know this. ²⁷When Abner arrived at Hebron, Joab took him aside into the gateway. Joab acted as though he wanted to talk with him in private. But Joab stabbed Abner in the stomach, and Abner died. Abner had killed Joab's

brother Asahel. So Joab killed Abner to pay him back.

²⁸Later David heard the news. He said, "My kingdom and I are innocent forever. We did not kill Abner son of Ner. The Lord knows this. ²⁹Joab and his family are responsible for this. I hope many troubles will come to his family. May his family always have someone with sores or with a harmful skin disease. May they always have someone who must lean on a crutch. May some of his family be killed in war. May they always have someone without food to eat."

³⁰(Joab and his brother Abishai had killed Abner, because he had killed their brother Asahel. This was in the battle at Gibeon.)

³¹Then David spoke to Joab and to all the people with Joab. He said, "Tear your clothes and put on rough cloth to show how sad you are. Cry for Abner." King David himself followed behind the body of Abner. ³²So they buried Abner in Hebron. David and all the people cried at Abner's grave.

³³King David sang this funeral song for Abner.

"Did Abner die like a foolish man?
³⁴ His hands were not tied.
   His feet were not in chains.
He fell as a person falls before evil
   men."

Then all the people cried again for Abner. ³⁵They came to encourage David to eat while it was still day. But he made a promise. He said, "May God punish me terribly if I eat bread or any other food before the sun sets!"

³⁶All the people saw what happened. They agreed with what the king was doing. ³⁷That day all the people of

> There was a long war between the people who supported Saul's family and those who supported David's family.
>
> –2 SAMUEL 3:1

Judah and all the Israelites understood. They knew it was not David who had killed Abner son of Ner.

[38] David said to his officers, "You know that a very important leader died today in Israel. [39] Even though I am the appointed king, I am weak today. These sons of Zeruiah are too strong for me. May the Lord give them the punishment they should have."

ISH-BOSHETH'S DEATH

4 Ish-Bosheth son of Saul heard that Abner had died at Hebron. Then Ish-Bosheth and all Israel became very frightened. [2] Two men who were captains in Saul's army came to Ish-Bosheth. One man was named Baanah, and the other was named Recab. They were the sons of Rimmon of Beeroth, who was a Benjaminite. (The town Beeroth belonged to the tribe of Benjamin.) [3] The people of Beeroth ran away to Gittaim. And they still live there today.

[4] (Now Jonathan son of Saul had a son who was crippled in both feet. His name was Mephibosheth. He was five years old when the news came from Jezreel that Saul and Jonathan were dead. Mephibosheth's nurse picked him up and ran away. But as she hurried to leave, he fell and became crippled.)

[5] Recab and Baanah, sons of Rimmon, were from Beeroth. They went to Ish-Bosheth's house at noon. [6-7] They came into the middle of the house. Recab and Baanah came as if they were going to get some wheat. Ish-Bosheth was lying on his bed in his bedroom. Recab and Baanah stabbed him in the stomach. Then they cut off his head and took it with them. They traveled all night through the Jordan Valley. [8] When they arrived at Hebron, they gave his head to David. They said to the king, "Here is the head of Ish-Bosheth son of Saul. He was your enemy. He tried to kill you! Today the Lord has paid back Saul and his family for what they did to you!"

[9] David answered Recab and his brother Baanah sons of Rimmon of Beeroth. David said, "As surely as the Lord lives, he has saved me from all trouble! [10] Once a man thought he was bringing me good news. He told me, 'Look! Saul is dead!' But I took hold of him and killed him at Ziklag. That was the reward I gave him for his news! [11] So even more I must require your death. This is because evil men have killed an innocent man. And he was on his own bed in his own house!"

[12] So David commanded his men to kill Recab and Baanah. Then they cut off the hands and feet of Recab and Baanah. They hung their hands and feet over the pool of Hebron. Then they took Ish-Bosheth's head and buried it in Abner's tomb at Hebron.

DAVID IS MADE KING OF ISRAEL

5 Then all the tribes of Israel came to David at Hebron. They said to him, "Look, we are your own family. [2] In the past Saul was king over us. But you were the one leading us in battle for Israel. The Lord said to you, 'You will be like a shepherd for my people, the Israelites. You will become their ruler.'"

[3] All the elders of Israel came to King David at Hebron. Then he made an agreement with them in Hebron in front of the Lord. Then they poured oil on David to make him king over Israel.

[4] David was 30 years old when he became king. He ruled 40 years. [5] He was king over Judah in Hebron for 7 years and 6 months. And he was king over all Israel and Judah in Jerusalem for 33 years.

[6] The king and his men went to Jerusalem to attack the Jebusites who lived there. The Jebusites said to David, "You can't come into our city. Even our people who are blind and crippled can stop you." They said this because they thought David could not enter their city. [7] But David did take the city of Jerusalem with its strong walls. It became the City of David.

[8] That day David said to his men,

"To defeat the Jebusites you must go through the water tunnel. Then you can reach those 'crippled' and 'blind' enemies. This is why people say, 'The blind and the crippled cannot enter the palace.'"

9So David lived in the city with its strong walls. He called it the City of David. David built more buildings around it. He began where the land was filled in on the east side of the city. He also built more buildings inside the city. 10He became stronger and stronger, because the Lord of heaven's armies was with him.

11Hiram king of the city of Tyre sent messengers to David. He also sent cedar logs, carpenters and men to cut stone. They built a palace for David. 12Then David knew the Lord really had made him king of Israel. And he knew the Lord had made his kingdom very important. This was because the Lord loved his people, the Israelites.

13In Jerusalem David took for himself more slave women and wives. This was after he moved there from Hebron. More sons and daughters were born to David. 14These are the names of the sons born to David in Jerusalem: Shammua, Shobab, Nathan, Solomon, 15Ibhar, Elishua, Nepheg, Japhia, 16Elishama, Eliada and Eliphelet.

DAVID DEFEATS THE PHILISTINES

17Now the Philistines heard that David had been made king over Israel. So all the Philistines went to look for him. But when David heard the news, he went down to a safe place. 18So the Philistines came and camped in the Valley of Rephaim. David asked the Lord, "Should I attack the Philistines? Will you help me defeat them?"

19The Lord said to David, "Go! I will certainly help you defeat them."

20So David went to Baal Perazim and defeated the Philistines there. David said, "Like a flood of water, the Lord has broken through my enemies." So David named the place Baal Perazim.[n] 21The Philistines left their idols behind at Baal Perazim. And David and his men carried these idols away.

22Once again the Philistines came and camped at the Valley of Rephaim. 23David prayed to the Lord. This time the Lord told David, "Don't attack the Philistines from the front. Instead, go around them. Attack them opposite the balsam trees. 24You will hear the sound of marching in the tops of the balsam trees. Then you must act quickly. I, the Lord, will have gone ahead of you and defeated the Philistine army." 25So David did what the Lord commanded. He defeated the Philistines and chased them all the way from Gibeon to Gezer.

THE ARK OF THE COVENANT IS BROUGHT TO JERUSALEM

6 David again gathered all the chosen men of Israel. There were 30,000 of them. 2Then David and all his people went to Baalah in Judah.[n] They took the Ark of the Covenant of God from Baalah in Judah and moved it to Jerusalem. The Ark of the Covenant is called by the Name, the name of the Lord of heaven's armies. His throne is between the gold creatures with wings that are on the Ark of the Covenant. 3David's men put the Ark of the Covenant of God on a new cart. Then they brought the Ark of the Covenant out of Abinadab's house on the hill. Uzzah and Ahio, sons of Abinadab, led the new cart. 4This cart had the Ark of the Covenant of God on it. Ahio was walking in front of it. 5David and all the Israelites were playing all kinds of musical instruments before the Lord. They were made of pine wood. There were lyres, harps, tambourines, rattles and cymbals.

6When David's men came to the

5:20 **Baal Perazim** This name means "the Lord breaks through."
6:2 **Baalah in Judah** Another name for Kiriath Jearim.

threshing floor of Nacon, the oxen stumbled. The Ark of the Covenant of God began to fall off the cart. So Uzzah reached out and took hold of it. [7]The Lord was angry with Uzzah and killed him. Uzzah had not honored God when he touched the Ark of the Covenant. So Uzzah died there beside it. [8]David was angry because the Lord had killed Uzzah. So that place is called The Punishment of Uzzah even today.

[9]David was afraid of the Lord that day. He said, "How can the Ark of the Covenant of the Lord come to me now?" [10]So David would not move the Ark of the Covenant of the Lord to be with him in Jerusalem. Instead, he took it to the house of Obed-Edom, a man from Gath. [11]The Ark of the Covenant of the Lord stayed in Obed-Edom's house for three months. And the Lord blessed Obed-Edom and all his family.

[12]The people told David, "The Lord has blessed the family of Obed-Edom. And all his things are blessed. This is because the Ark of the Covenant of God is there." So David went and brought it up from Obed-Edom's house to Jerusalem with joy. [13]When the men carrying the Ark of the Covenant of the Lord had walked six steps, David sacrificed a bull and a fat calf. [14]Then David danced with all his might before the Lord. He had on a holy linen vest. [15]David and all the Israelites shouted with joy. They blew the trumpets as they brought the Ark of the Covenant of the Lord to the city.

[16]Saul's daughter Michal was looking out the window. She watched as the Ark of the Covenant of the Lord came into the city. When she saw David jumping and dancing before the Lord, she hated him.

> They blew the trumpets as they brought the Ark of the Covenant of the Lord to the city.
> —2 SAMUEL 6:15

[17]David put up a tent for the Ark of the Covenant. Then the Israelites put it in its place inside the tent. David offered whole burnt offerings and fellowship offerings before the Lord. [18]When David finished offering the whole burnt offerings and the fellowship offerings, he blessed the people in the name of the Lord of heaven's armies. [19]David gave a loaf of bread, a cake of dates and a cake of raisins to everyone. He gave them to all the Israelites, both men and women. Then all the people went home.

[20]David went back to bless the people in his home. But Saul's daughter Michal came out to meet him. She said, "The king of Israel did not honor himself today! You took off your clothes in front of the servant girls of your officers. You were like a foolish man who takes off his clothes without shame!"

[21]Then David said to Michal, "I did it before the Lord. The Lord chose me, not your father. He didn't choose anyone from Saul's family. The Lord appointed me to be leader of his people, the Israelites. So I will celebrate in front of the Lord. [22]Maybe I will lose even more honor. And you may think little of me. But the girls you talk about will honor me!"

[23]And Saul's daughter Michal had no children to the day she died.

DAVID WANTS TO BUILD A TEMPLE

7 King David was living in his palace. And the Lord gave him peace from all his enemies around him. [2]David said to Nathan the prophet, "Look, I am living in a palace made of cedar wood. But the Ark of the Covenant of God is still kept in a tent!"

[3]Nathan said to the king, "Go and do

what you really want to do. The Lord is with you."

⁴But that night the Lord spoke his word to Nathan. The Lord said, ⁵"Go and tell my servant David, 'This is what the Lord says: You are not the person to build a house for me to live in. ⁶I did not live in a house when I brought the Israelites out of Egypt. I have been moving around all this time with a tent as my home. ⁷I have continued to move with the tribes of Israel. But I have never asked their leaders who take care of them to build me a house of cedar wood.'

⁸"You must tell my servant David, 'This is what the Lord of heaven's armies says: I took you from the pasture when you were following the sheep. I took you to become leader of my people, the Israelites. ⁹I have been with you everywhere you have gone. I have defeated your enemies for you. I will make you as famous as any of the great men on the earth. ¹⁰Also I will choose a place for my people, the Israelites. I will plant them so they can live in their own home. They will not be bothered anymore. Wicked people will no longer make them suffer as they have in the past. ¹¹Wicked people continued to do this even when I appointed judges. But I will give you peace from all your enemies. I also tell you that I will make your descendants kings of Israel after you.

¹²"'Your days will come to an end, and you will die. At that time I will make one of your sons the next king. ¹³He will build a temple for me. I will make his kingdom strong forever. ¹⁴I will be his father, and he will be my son. When he sins, I will use other people to punish him. They will be my whips. ¹⁵But I will not stop loving him. I took away my love and kindness from Saul. I removed Saul when I turned to you. ¹⁶But your family and your kingdom will continue forever before me. Your rule will last forever.'"

¹⁷Nathan told David everything he had heard.

DAVID PRAYS TO GOD

¹⁸Then King David went in the tent and sat in front of the Lord. David said, "Lord God, why have you made me so important to you? Why have you made my family important? ¹⁹But that was not enough for you, Lord God. You have also said these kind things about my future family. I am your servant. Lord God, this is not the usual way you talk to people.

²⁰"What more can I say to you? Lord God, you love me, your servant, so much! ²¹You have done this wonderful thing because you said you would. You have done it because you wanted to. And you have decided to let me know all these great things. ²²This is why you are great, Lord God! There is no one like you. There is no God except you. We have heard all this ourselves! ²³And there are no others like your people, the Israelites. They are the one nation on earth that God chose to be his people. You used them to make your name well-known. You did great and wonderful miracles for them. You went ahead of them and forced other nations and their gods out of the land. You freed your people from slavery in Egypt. ²⁴You made the people of Israel your very own people forever. And, Lord, you became their God.

²⁵"Now, Lord God, keep the promise you made about my family and me, your servant. Do what you have promised. ²⁶Then you will be honored forever. And people will say, 'The Lord of heaven's armies is God over Israel!' And the family of your servant David will continue before you.

²⁷"Lord of heaven's armies, the God of Israel, you have shown things to me. You have said, 'I will make your family great.' So I, your servant, am brave enough to pray to you. ²⁸Lord God, you are God, and your words are true. And you have promised these good things to me, your servant. ²⁹Please, bless my family. Let it continue before you forever. Lord God, you have said these

wonderful things. With your blessing let my family be blessed forever."

DAVID WINS MANY WARS

8 Later, David defeated the Philistines. And he took control of their capital city.

²He also defeated the people of Moab. He forced them to lie on the ground. Then he used a rope to measure them. When two men were measured, David ordered them killed. But every third man was allowed to live. So the people of Moab became servants of David. They gave him the payments he demanded.

³As David went to take control again at the Euphrates River, he defeated Hadadezer. Hadadezer son of Rehob was king of Zobah. ⁴David took from Hadadezer 1,700 men who rode in his chariots. He also captured 20,000 foot soldiers. David crippled all but 100 of the chariot horses. He saved those horses to pull chariots.

⁵Arameans from Damascus came to help Hadadezer king of Zobah. But David defeated those 22,000 Arameans. ⁶Then David put groups of soldiers in Damascus in Aram. The Arameans became David's servants and gave him the payments he demanded. The Lord gave David victory everywhere he went.

⁷David took the shields of gold that had belonged to Hadadezer's officers. He brought them to Jerusalem. ⁸David also took many things made of bronze from Tebah and Berothai. (They were cities that had belonged to Hadadezer.)

⁹Toi king of Hamath heard that David had defeated all the army of Hadadezer. ¹⁰So Toi sent his son Joram to greet and congratulate King David. Joram congratulated David for defeating Hadadezer. (Hadadezer had fought wars against Toi before.) Joram brought things made of silver, gold and bronze. ¹¹David took these things and gave them to the Lord. He also had given other silver and gold to the Lord. He had taken it from the nations he had defeated. ¹²These nations were Edom, Moab, Ammon, Philistia and Amalek. David also defeated the king of Zobah who was Hadadezer son of Rehob.

¹³David was famous after he returned from the Valley of Salt. There he had defeated 18,000 Arameans. ¹⁴David put groups of soldiers through all the land of Edom. All the people of Edom became servants for him. The Lord gave David victory everywhere he went.

¹⁵David was king over all Israel. His decisions were fair and right for all his people. ¹⁶Joab son of Zeruiah was commander over the army. Jehoshaphat son of Ahilud was the recorder. ¹⁷Zadok son of Ahitub and Ahimelech son of Abiathar were priests. Seraiah was the royal assistant. ¹⁸Benaiah son of Jehoiada was over the Kerethites and Pelethites, the king's bodyguards. And David's sons were important leaders.

DAVID HELPS SAUL'S FAMILY

9 David asked, "Is there anyone still left in Saul's family? I want to show kindness to this person for Jonathan's sake!"

²Now there was a servant named Ziba from Saul's family. So David's servants called Ziba to him. King David said to him, "Are you Ziba?"

He answered, "Yes, I am Ziba, your servant."

³The king asked, "Is there anyone left in Saul's family? I want to show God's kindness to this person."

Ziba answered the king, "Jonathan has a son still living. He is crippled in both feet."

⁴The king asked Ziba, "Where is this son?"

Ziba answered, "He is at the house of Makir son of Ammiel in Lo Debar."

⁵Then King David had servants bring Jonathan's son from the house of Makir son of Ammiel in Lo Debar. ⁶Mephibosheth, Jonathan's son, came before David and bowed facedown on the floor.

David had promised that he would not hurt Saul's family. And he was very sad when Saul and his sons died in battle. King David wanted to show kindness to Saul's family. When he found out that Saul's grandson Mephibosheth was alive, he took him in and cared for him.

Long ago, new kings did not like old kings. They did not like their families either. But David was different. He wanted to do something good for Saul's family. He found out that Jonathan's son, Mephibosheth, was alive. David invited Jonathan's son, Saul's grandson, into his home and made him a part of his family. King David wanted to show goodness to Mephibosheth because God was always good to David. And by doing this for Mephibosheth, David showed everyone the love God has for each of us.

. . . .

Just like David, when we do good things for others, we show God's love.

David said, "Mephibosheth!"

Mephibosheth said, "I am your servant."

⁷David said to him, "Don't be afraid. I will be kind to you for your father Jonathan's sake. I will give you back all the land of your grandfather Saul. And you will always be able to eat at my table."

⁸Mephibosheth bowed to David again. Mephibosheth said, "You are being very kind to me, your servant! And I am no better than a dead dog!"

⁹Then King David called Saul's servant Ziba. David said to him, "I have given your master's grandson everything that belonged to Saul and his family. ¹⁰You, your sons and your servants will farm the land for Mephibosheth. You will harvest the crops. Then your master's grandson will have food to eat. But Mephibosheth, your master's grandson, will always be able to eat at my table."

(Now Ziba had 15 sons and 20 servants.) ¹¹Ziba said to King David, "I am your servant. I will do everything my master, the king, commands me."

So Mephibosheth ate at David's table as if he were one of the king's sons. ¹²Mephibosheth had a young son named Mica. Everyone in Ziba's family became Mephibosheth's servants. ¹³Mephibosheth was crippled in both feet. He lived in Jerusalem and always ate at the king's table.

WAR WITH AMMONITES AND ARAMEANS

10 Later Nahash king of the Ammonites died. His son Hanun became king after him. [2]David said, "Nahash was kind to me. So I will be kind to his son Hanun." So David sent his officers to comfort Hanun about his father's death.

David's servants went to the land of the Ammonites. [3]But the important men of Ammon spoke to Hanun, their master. They said, "Do you think David wants to honor your father by sending men to comfort you? No! David sent them to study the city and to spy it out. They plan to capture it!" [4]So Hanun took David's officers and shaved off half their beards to shame them. He cut their clothes off at the hips to insult them. Then he sent them away.

[5]When the people told David, he sent messengers to meet his officers. He did this because these men were very ashamed. King David said, "Wait at Jericho until your beards have grown out. Then come back to Jerusalem."

[6]Now the Ammonites saw that they had become David's enemies. So they hired 20,000 Aramean foot soldiers from Beth Rehob and Zobah. They also hired the king of Maacah with 1,000 men. And they hired 12,000 men from Tob.

[7]David heard about this. So he sent Joab with the whole army of warriors. [8]The Ammonites came out and got ready for the battle. They stood at the city gate. The Arameans from Zobah and Rehob and the men from Tob and Maacah were out in the field. They were standing away from the Ammonites.

[9]Joab saw that there were enemies both in front of him and behind him. So he chose some of the best men from the Israelites. He got them ready for battle against the Arameans. [10]Then Joab gave the other men to his brother Abishai to lead against the Ammonites. [11]Joab said to Abishai, "If the Arameans are too strong for me, come help me. If the Ammonites are too strong for you, I will come and help you. [12]Be strong. Let us fight bravely for our people and for the cities of our God. The Lord will do what he decides is right."

[13]Then Joab and his men attacked the Arameans, and they ran away. [14]The Ammonites saw that the Arameans were running away. So they ran away from Abishai and went back to their city. So Joab returned from the battle with the Ammonites and came to Jerusalem.

[15]The Arameans saw that the Israelites had defeated them. So they came together into one big army. [16]Hadadezer sent messengers to bring the Arameans who lived on the other side of the Euphrates River. These Arameans went to Helam. Their leader was Shobach, the commander of Hadadezer's army.

[17]When David heard about this, he gathered all the Israelites together. They crossed over the Jordan River and went to Helam. There the Arameans prepared for battle and attacked. [18]But David defeated the Arameans, and they ran away from the Israelites. David killed 700 Aramean chariot drivers and 40,000 Aramean horsemen. He also killed Shobach, the commander of the Aramean army.

[19]The kings who served Hadadezer saw that the Israelites had defeated them. So they made peace with the Israelites and served them. And the Arameans were afraid to help the Ammonites again.

DAVID AND BATHSHEBA

11 In the spring the kings would go out to war. So in the spring David sent out Joab, his servants and all the Israelites. They destroyed the Ammonites and attacked the city of Rabbah. But David stayed in Jerusalem. [2]One evening David got up from his bed. He walked around on the roof[n] of

---

11:2 **roof** In Bible times houses were built with flat roofs. The roof was used for drying things such as flax and fruit. And it was used as an extra room, as a place for worship and as a place to sleep in the summer.

his palace. While he was on the roof, he saw a woman bathing. She was very beautiful. [3]So David sent his servants to find out who she was. A servant answered, "That woman is Bathsheba daughter of Eliam. She is the wife of Uriah the Hittite." [4]David sent messengers to bring Bathsheba to him. When she came to him, he had physical relations with her. (Now Bathsheba had purified herself from her monthly period.) Then she went back to her house. [5]But Bathsheba became pregnant. She sent word to David, saying, "I am pregnant."

[6]So David sent this message to Joab: "Send Uriah the Hittite to me." So Joab sent Uriah to David. [7]Uriah came to David. And David asked him how Joab was, how the soldiers were and how the war was going. [8]Then David said to Uriah, "Go home and rest."

So Uriah left the palace. The king also sent a gift to him. [9]But Uriah did not go home. He slept outside the door of the palace. He slept there as all the king's officers did.

[10]The officers told David, "Uriah did not go home."

Then David said to Uriah, "You came from a long trip. Why didn't you go home?"

[11]Uriah said to him, "The Ark of the Covenant and the soldiers of Israel and Judah are staying in tents. My master Joab and his officers are camping out in the fields. It isn't right for me to go home to eat and drink and have intimate relations with my wife!"

[12]David said to Uriah, "Stay here today. Tomorrow I'll send you back to the battle." So Uriah stayed in Jerusalem that day and the next. [13]Then David called Uriah to come to see him. Uriah ate and drank with David. David made Uriah drunk, but he still did not go home. That evening Uriah went to sleep with the king's officers outside the king's door.

[14]The next morning David wrote a letter to Joab and sent it by Uriah. [15]In the letter David wrote, "Put Uriah on the front lines where the fighting is worst. Then leave him there alone. Let him be killed in battle."

[16]Joab watched the city and saw where its strongest defenders were. He put Uriah there. [17]The men of the city came out to fight against Joab. Some of David's men were killed. And Uriah the Hittite was one of them.

[18]Then Joab sent a report to David about everything that had happened in the war. [19]Joab told the messenger, "Tell King David what happened in the war. [20]After you finish, the king may become angry. He may ask you, 'Why did you go so near the city to fight? Didn't you know they would shoot arrows from the city wall? [21]Do you remember who killed Abimelech son of Jerub-Besheth?[n] It was a woman on the city wall. She threw a large stone for grinding grain on Abimelech. She killed him there in Thebez. Why did you go so near the wall?' If King David asks that, you must answer, 'Your servant Uriah the Hittite also died.'"

[22]The messenger went in and told David everything Joab had told him to say. [23]The messenger told David, "The men of Ammon were winning. They came out and attacked us in the field. But we fought them back to the city gate. [24]The men on the city wall shot arrows at your servants. Some of your men were killed. Your servant Uriah the Hittite also died."

[25]David said to the messenger, "Say this to Joab: 'Don't be upset about this. The sword kills everyone the same. Make a stronger attack against the city and capture it.' Encourage Joab with these words."

[26]When Bathsheba heard that her husband was dead, she cried for him. [27]After she finished her time of sadness, David sent servants to bring her to his house. She became David's wife and

---

11:21 Jerub-Besheth Another name for Gideon.

gave birth to his son. But the Lord did not like what David had done.

DAVID'S SON DIES

12 The Lord sent Nathan to David. When Nathan came to David, Nathan said, "There were two men in a city. One man was rich, but the other was poor. ²The rich man had very many sheep and cattle. ³But the poor man had nothing except one little female lamb he had bought. The poor man fed the lamb. It grew up with him and his children. It shared his food and drank from his cup. It slept in his arms. The lamb was like a daughter to him.

⁴"Then a traveler stopped to visit the rich man. The rich man wanted to give food to the traveler. But he didn't want to take one of his own sheep or cattle to feed the traveler. Instead, he took the lamb from the poor man. The rich man killed the lamb and cooked it for his visitor."

⁵David became very angry at the rich man. He said to Nathan, "As surely as the Lord lives, the man who did this should die! ⁶He must pay for the lamb four times for doing such a thing. He had no mercy!"

⁷Then Nathan said to David, "You are the man! This is what the Lord, the God of Israel, says: 'I appointed you king of Israel. I saved you from Saul. ⁸I gave you his kingdom and his wives. And I made you king of Israel and Judah. And if that had not been enough, I would have given you even more. ⁹So why did you ignore the Lord's command? Why did you do what he says is wrong? You killed Uriah the Hittite with the sword of the Ammonites! And you took his wife to become your wife! ¹⁰So there will always be people in your family who will be killed by a sword. This is because you showed that you did not respect me! And you took the wife of Uriah the Hittite!'

¹¹"This is what the Lord says: 'I am bringing trouble to you from your own family. While you watch, I will take your wives from you. And I will give them to someone who is very close to you. He will have physical relations with your wives, and everyone will know it. ¹²You had physical relations with Bathsheba in secret. But I will do this so all the people of Israel can see it.'"

¹³Then David said to Nathan, "I have sinned against the Lord."

Nathan answered, "The Lord has taken away your sin. You will not die. ¹⁴But what you did caused the Lord's enemies to lose all respect for him. For this reason the son who was born to you will die."

¹⁵Then Nathan went home. And the Lord caused the son of David and Bathsheba, Uriah's widow, to become very sick. ¹⁶David prayed to God for the baby. David refused to eat or drink. He went into his house and stayed there. He lay on the ground all night. ¹⁷The elders of David's family came to him. They tried to pull him up from the ground. But he refused to get up. And he refused to eat food with them.

¹⁸On the seventh day the baby died. David's servants were afraid to tell him that the baby was dead. They said, "Look, we tried to talk to David while the baby was alive. But he refused to listen to us. If we tell him the baby is dead, he may harm himself."

¹⁹But David saw his servants whispering. Then he understood that the baby was dead. So he asked them, "Is the baby dead?"

They answered, "Yes, he is dead."

²⁰Then David got up from the floor. He washed himself, put lotions on himself and changed his clothes. Then he went into the Lord's house to worship. After that, he went home and asked for something to eat. His servants gave him some food, and he ate.

²¹David's servants said to him, "Why are you doing this? When the baby was still alive, you refused to eat. You cried. But when the baby died, you got up and ate food."

²²David said, "While the baby was still alive, I refused to eat, and I cried. I

thought, 'Who knows? Maybe the Lord will feel sorry for me and let the baby live.' ²³But now the baby is dead. So why should I go without food? I can't bring him back to life. Some day I will go to him. But he cannot come back to me."

²⁴Then David comforted Bathsheba his wife. He slept with her and had intimate relations with her. She became pregnant again and had another son. David named the boy Solomon. The Lord loved Solomon. ²⁵The Lord sent word through Nathan the prophet to name the baby Jedidiah.ⁿ This was because the Lord loved the child.

DAVID CAPTURES RABBAH

²⁶Now Joab fought against Rabbah, a city of the Ammonites. And he was about to capture the royal city. ²⁷Joab sent messengers to David and said, "I have fought against Rabbah. I have captured its water supply. ²⁸Now bring the other soldiers together and attack this city. Capture it before I capture it myself. If I capture this city, it will be called by my name!"

²⁹So David gathered all the army and went to Rabbah. He fought against Rabbah and captured it. ³⁰David took the crown off their king's head. It was gold and weighed about 75 pounds. It also had gems in it. They put the crown on David's head. And David took many valuable things out of the city. ³¹He also brought out the people of the city. He made them work with saws, iron picks and axes. He also forced them to build with bricks. David did this to all the Ammonite cities. Then David and all his army went back to Jerusalem.

AMNON AND TAMAR

13 Now David had a son named Absalom and a son named Amnon. Absalom had a beautiful sister named Tamar. And Amnon loved her. ²Tamar was a virgin. Amnon did not think he should do anything bad to her. But he wanted her very much. He made himself sick just thinking about her.

³Amnon had a friend named Jonadab son of Shimeah. (Shimeah was David's brother.) Jonadab was a very clever man. ⁴He asked Amnon, "Why do you look so sad day after day? You are the king's son! Tell me what's wrong!"

Amnon told him, "I love Tamar. But she is the sister of my half-brother Absalom."

⁵Jonadab said to Amnon, "Go to bed. Act as if you are sick. Then your father will come to see you. Tell him, 'Please let my sister Tamar come in and give me food to eat. Let her make the food in front of me. Then I will see it and eat it from her hand.'"

⁶So Amnon lay down in bed and acted as if he were sick. King David came in to see him. Amnon said to him, "Please let my sister Tamar come in. Let her make two of her special cakes for me while I watch. Then I will eat them from her hands."

⁷David sent messengers to Tamar in the palace. They told her, "Go to your brother Amnon's house and make some food for him." ⁸So Tamar went to her brother Amnon's house. He was in bed. Tamar took some dough and pressed it together with her hands. She made some special cakes while Amnon watched. Then she baked them. ⁹Next she took the pan and took out the cakes for Amnon. But he refused to eat.

He said to his servants, "All of you, leave me alone!" So all his servants left the room. ¹⁰Amnon said to Tamar, "Bring the food into the inner room. Then I'll eat from your hand."

Tamar took the cakes she had made. And she brought them to her brother Amnon in the inner room. ¹¹She went to him so he could eat from her hands. But Amnon grabbed her. He said, "Sister, come and have physical relations with me."

12:25 Jedidiah This name means "loved by the Lord."

¹²Tamar said to him, "No, brother! Don't force me! This should never be done in Israel! Don't do this shameful thing! ¹³I could never get rid of my shame! And you will become like the shameful fools in Israel! Please talk with the king. He will let you marry me."

¹⁴But Amnon refused to listen to her. He was stronger than she was. So he raped her. ¹⁵After that, Amnon hated Tamar. He hated her much more than he had loved her before. Amnon said to her, "Get up and leave!"

¹⁶Tamar said to him, "No! Sending me away would be an even greater evil. That would be worse than what you've already done!"

But he refused to listen to her. ¹⁷He called his young servant back in. Amnon said, "Get this girl out of here right now! Lock the door after her." ¹⁸So his servant led her out of the room. And he bolted the door after her.

Now Tamar was wearing a special robe with long sleeves. The king's virgin daughters wore this kind of robe. ¹⁹To show how upset she was Tamar took ashes and put them on her head. She tore her special robe. And she put her hand on her head. Then she went away, crying loudly.

²⁰Absalom, Tamar's brother, said to her, "Has Amnon, that brother of yours, violated you? He is your brother. So for now, sister, be quiet. Don't let this upset you so much!" So Tamar lived in her brother Absalom's house. She was sad and lonely.

²¹When King David heard the news, he was very angry. ²²Absalom did not say a word, good or bad, to Amnon. He hated Amnon for violating his sister Tamar.

David said, "As surely as the Lord lives, no one will hurt your son."
–2 SAMUEL 14:11

ABSALOM'S REVENGE

²³Two years later Absalom had some men come to Baal Hazor, near Ephraim. They were to cut the wool from his sheep. Absalom invited all the king's sons to come also. ²⁴Absalom went to the king and said, "I have men coming to cut the wool. Please come with your officers and join me."

²⁵King David said to Absalom, "No, my son. We won't all go. It would be too much trouble for you." Absalom begged David to go. David did not go, but he did give his blessing.

²⁶Absalom said, "If you don't want to go, then please let my brother Amnon go with me."

King David asked Absalom, "Why should he go with you?"

²⁷Absalom kept begging David. Finally, David let Amnon and all the king's sons go with Absalom.

²⁸Then Absalom gave a command to his servants. He said, "Watch Amnon. When he is drunk, I will tell you, 'Kill Amnon.' Right then, kill him! Don't be afraid. I have commanded you! Be strong and brave!" ²⁹So Absalom's young men killed Amnon as Absalom commanded. But all of David's other sons got on their mules and escaped.

³⁰While the king's sons were on their way, the news came to David. The message was, "Absalom has killed all of the king's sons! Not one of them is left alive!" ³¹King David tore his clothes and lay on the ground to show his sadness. All his servants standing nearby tore their clothes also.

³²Jonadab was the son of Shimeah, David's brother. Jonadab said to David, "Don't think all the young men, your sons, are killed. No, only Amnon is dead! Absalom planned this because

Amnon raped his sister Tamar. [33]"My master and king, don't think that all of the king's sons are dead. Only Amnon is dead!"

[34]In the meantime Absalom had run away.

There was a guard standing on the city wall. He saw many people coming from the other side of the hill. [35]So Jonadab said to King David, "Look, I was right! The king's sons are coming!"

[36]As soon as Jonadab had said this, the king's sons arrived. They were crying loudly. David and all his servants began crying also. They all cried very much. [37]David cried for his son every day.

But Absalom ran away to Talmai[n] son of Ammihud. Talmai was king of Geshur. [38]After Absalom ran away to Geshur, he stayed there for three years. [39]When King David got over Amnon's death, he missed Absalom greatly.

JOAB SENDS A WISE WOMAN TO DAVID

14 Joab son of Zeruiah knew that King David missed Absalom very much. [2]So Joab sent messengers to Tekoa to bring a wise woman from there. Joab said to her, "Please pretend to be very sad for someone. Put on clothes to show your sadness. Don't put lotion on yourself. Act like a woman who has been crying many days for someone who died. [3]Go to the king. Talk to him using the words that I tell you." Then Joab told the wise woman what to say.

[4]So the woman from Tekoa talked to the king. She bowed facedown on the ground to show respect. She said, "My king, help me!"

[5]King David asked her, "What is the matter?"

The woman said, "I am a widow. My husband is dead. [6]I had two sons. They were out in the field fighting. No one was there to stop them. So one son killed the other son. [7]Now all the family group is

against me. They said to me, 'Bring the son who killed his brother. Then we will kill him for killing his brother. That way we will also get rid of the one who would receive what belonged to his father.' My son is like the last spark of a fire. He is all I have left. If they kill him, my husband's name and property will be gone from the earth."

[8]Then the king said to the woman, "Go home. I will take care of this for you."

[9]The woman of Tekoa said to him, "Let the blame be on me. My father's family and I are to blame, my master and king. But you and your throne are innocent."

[10]King David said, "Bring me anyone who says anything bad to you. Then he won't bother you again."

[11]The woman said, "Please promise in the name of the Lord your God. Then my relative who has the duty of punishing a murderer won't add to the destruction. And he won't kill my son."

David said, "As surely as the Lord lives, no one will hurt your son. Not even one hair from your son's head will fall to the ground."

[12]The woman said, "Let me say something to you, my master and king."

The king said, "Speak."

[13]Then the woman said, "Why have you planned this? It is against the people of God. When you say this, you show that you are guilty. You have not brought back your son whom you forced to leave home. [14]We will all die some day. We're like water spilled on the ground. No one can gather it back. But God doesn't take away life. Instead, he plans ways that those who have been sent away will not have to stay away from him! [15]My master and king, I came to say this to you because the people have made me afraid! I thought, 'Let me talk to the king. Maybe he will do what I ask. [16]Maybe he will listen. Perhaps he will save me from the man who wants to kill both me and my

13:37 **Talmai** He was Absalom's grandfather.

son. That man is trying to keep us from getting what God gave us.'

[17]"Now I say, 'May the words of my master the king give me rest. Like an angel of God, you know what is good and what is bad. May the Lord your God be with you!'"

[18]Then King David said, "You must answer the question I will ask you."

The woman said, "My master the king, please ask your question."

[19]The king said, "Did Joab tell you to say all these things?"

The woman answered, "As you live, my master the king, you are right. Your servant Joab did tell me to say these things. [20]Joab did it so you would see things differently. My master, you are wise like an angel of God. You know everything that happens on earth."

ABSALOM RETURNS TO JERUSALEM

[21]The king said to Joab, "Look, I will do what I promised. Now please bring back the young man Absalom."

[22]Joab bowed facedown on the ground. He blessed the king. Then he said, "Today I know you are pleased with me. I know because you have done what I asked."

[23]Then Joab got up and went to Geshur. And he brought Absalom back to Jerusalem. [24]But King David said, "Absalom must go to his own house. He may not come to see me." So Absalom went to his own house. He did not go to see the king.

[25]Now Absalom was greatly praised for his handsome appearance. No man in Israel was as handsome as Absalom. No blemish was on him from his head to his foot. [26]At the end of every year, Absalom would cut the hair on his head. He cut it because it became too heavy. He would weigh it, and it would weigh about five pounds by the royal measure.

[27]Absalom had three sons and one daughter. His daughter's name was Tamar. She was a beautiful woman.

[28]So Absalom lived in Jerusalem for two full years without seeing King David. [29]Then Absalom sent for Joab. Absalom wanted to send Joab to the king. But Joab would not come. Absalom sent a message a second time. But Joab still refused to come. [30]Then Absalom said to his servants, "Look, Joab's field is next to mine. He has barley growing there. Go burn it." So Absalom's servants set fire to Joab's field.

[31]Then Joab went to Absalom's house. Joab said to him, "Why did your servants burn my field?"

[32]Absalom said to Joab, "I sent a message to you, asking you to come here. I wanted to send you to the king. I wanted you to ask him why he brought me home from Geshur. It would have been better for me to stay there! Now let me see the king. If I have sinned, he can kill me!"

[33]So Joab went to the king and told him Absalom's words. The king called for Absalom, and Absalom came. He bowed facedown on the ground before the king. And the king kissed him.

ABSALOM PLANS TO TAKE DAVID'S KINGDOM

15 After this, Absalom got a chariot and horses for himself. He got 50 men to run before him. [2]Absalom would get up early and stand near the city gate.[n] If anyone had a problem he wanted the king to settle, he would come here. When he came, Absalom would call to the man. Absalom would say, "What city are you from?"

The man would answer, "I'm from one of the tribes of Israel."

[3]Then Absalom would say to him, "Look, your claims are right. But the king has no one to listen to you." [4]Absalom would also say, "I wish someone would make me judge in this land! Then I could help everyone who comes

---

15:2 city gate People came here to conduct business. Public meetings and court cases were also held here.

with a problem. I could help him get a fair decision for his problem!"

[5]People would come near Absalom to bow to him. When they did, Absalom would reach out his hand and take hold of them. Then he would kiss them. [6]Absalom did that to all the Israelites who came to King David for decisions. In this way, Absalom won the hearts of all Israel.

[7]After four years Absalom said to King David, "Please let me go to Hebron. I want to carry out my promise that I made to the Lord. [8]I made it while I was living in Geshur in Aram. I said, 'If the Lord takes me back to Jerusalem, I will worship him in Hebron.'"

[9]The king said, "Go in peace."

So Absalom went to Hebron. [10]But he sent secret messengers through all the tribes of Israel. They told the people, "When you hear the trumpets, say this: 'Absalom has become the king at Hebron!'"

[11]Absalom had invited 200 men to go with him. So they went from Jerusalem with him. But they didn't know what he was planning. [12]Ahithophel was one of the people who advised David. He was from the town of Giloh. While Absalom was offering sacrifices, he called Ahithophel to come from his hometown of Giloh. So Absalom's plans were working very well. More and more people began to support him.

[13]A man came in to tell the news to David. The man said, "The Israelites are beginning to follow Absalom."

[14]Then David spoke to all his officers who were with him in Jerusalem. He said, "We must leave quickly! If we don't, we won't be able to get away from Absalom. We must hurry before he catches us. He would destroy us and kill the people of Jerusalem."

[15]The king's officers said to him, "We will do anything you say."

[16]The king set out with everyone in his house. But he left ten slave women to take care of the palace. [17]The king left with all his people following him. They stopped at the last house. [18]All the king's servants passed by him. All the Kerethites and Pelethites, the king's bodyguards, passed by him. All those from Gath, the 600 men who had followed him, passed by him.

[19]The king spoke to Ittai, a man from Gath. He said, "Why are you also going with us? Turn back and stay with King Absalom. You are a foreigner. This is not your homeland. [20]Only a short time ago you came to join me. Today should I make you go with us to other places? I don't even know where I'm going. Turn back, and take your brothers with you. May kindness and loyalty be shown to you."

[21]But Ittai said to the king, "As surely as the Lord lives and as you live, I will stay with you. I'll be with you wherever you are. I'll be with you whether it means life or death."

[22]David said to Ittai, "Go, march on." So Ittai from Gath and all his people with their children marched on. [23]All the people cried loudly as everyone passed by. King David also crossed the Kidron Valley. Then all the people went on to the desert. [24]Zadok and all the Levites with him were carrying the Ark of the Covenant with God. They set down the Ark of the Covenant. And Abiathar offered sacrifices until all the people had left the city.

[25]The king said to Zadok, "Take the Ark of the Covenant of God back into the city. If the Lord is pleased with me, he will bring me back. He will let me see both it and Jerusalem again. [26]But if the Lord says he is not pleased with me, I am ready. He can do what he wants with me."

[27]The king also said to Zadok the priest, "You are a seer. Go back to the city in peace. Take your son Ahimaaz and Abiathar's son Jonathan with you. [28]I will wait near the crossings into the desert until I hear from you." [29]So Zadok and Abiathar took the Ark of the Covenant of God back to Jerusalem and stayed there.

³⁰David went up the Mount of Olives crying as he went. He covered his head and went barefoot. All the people with David covered their heads also. And they were crying as they went. ³¹Someone told David, "Ahithophel is one of the people with Absalom who made secret plans against you."

So David prayed, "Lord, please make Ahithophel's advice foolish."

³²David came to the top of the mountain. This was where he used to worship God. Hushai the Arkite came to meet him. Hushai's coat was torn, and there was dirt on his head to show how sad he was. ³³David said to Hushai, "If you go with me, you will be just one more person to take care of. ³⁴But if you return to the city, you can make Ahithophel's advice useless. Tell Absalom, 'I am your servant, my king. In the past I served your father. But now I will serve you.' ³⁵The priests Zadok and Abiathar will be with you. You must tell them everything you hear in the king's palace. ³⁶Zadok's son Ahimaaz and Abiathar's son Jonathan are with them. Send them to tell me everything you hear."

³⁷So David's friend Hushai entered Jerusalem. About that time, Absalom also arrived there.

ZIBA MEETS DAVID

16 David passed a short way over the top of the Mount of Olives. There Ziba, Mephibosheth's servant, met David. Ziba had two donkeys with saddles on them. They carried 200 loaves of bread, 100 cakes of raisins and 100 cakes of figs. They also carried leather bags full of wine. ²The king asked Ziba, "What are these things for?"

Ziba answered, "The donkeys are for your family to ride. The bread and cakes of figs are for the servants to eat. And the wine is for anyone to drink who becomes weak in the desert."

³The king asked, "Where is Mephibosheth?"

Ziba answered him, "Mephibosheth is staying in Jerusalem. He thinks, 'Today the Israelites will give my father's kingdom back to me!'"

⁴Then the king said to Ziba, "All right. Everything that belonged to Mephibosheth, I now give to you!"

Ziba said, "I bow to you. I hope I will always be able to please you."

SHIMEI CURSES DAVID

⁵As King David came to Bahurim, a man came out from there. He was from Saul's family group. His name was Shimei son of Gera. Shimei came out, cursing David as he came. ⁶He began throwing stones at David and his officers. But the people and soldiers gathered all around David. ⁷Shimei cursed David. He said, "Get out, get out, you murderer, you troublemaker. ⁸The Lord is punishing you for the people in Saul's family you killed! You took Saul's place as king! But now the Lord has given the kingdom to your son Absalom! Now you are ruined because you are a murderer!"

⁹Abishai son of Zeruiah said to the king, "Why should this dead dog curse you, the king? Let me go over and cut off his head!"

¹⁰But the king answered, "This does not concern you, sons of Zeruiah! If he is cursing me because the Lord told him to, who can question him?"

¹¹David also said to Abishai and all his officers, "My own son is trying to kill me! This man is a Benjaminite and has more right to kill me! Leave him alone. Let him curse me. The Lord told him to do this. ¹²Maybe the Lord will see my misery. Then maybe he will repay me with something good for the curses Shimei says today!"

¹³So David and his men went on down the road. But Shimei kept following David. Shimei walked on the hillside on the other side of the road. He kept cursing David and throwing stones and dirt at him. ¹⁴The king and all his people arrived at the Jordan. They were very tired. So they rested there.

[15]Meanwhile, Absalom, Ahithophel and all the men of Israel arrived at Jerusalem. [16]David's friend Hushai the Arkite came to Absalom. He said to Absalom, "Long live the king! Long live the king!"

[17]Absalom asked, "Why are you not loyal to your friend David? Why didn't you leave Jerusalem with your friend?"

[18]Hushai said, "I belong to the one chosen by the Lord and by these people and all the men of Israel. I will stay with you. [19]In the past I served your father. So whom should I serve now? David's son! I will serve you."

AHITHOPHEL'S ADVICE

[20]Absalom said to Ahithophel, "Please tell us what we should do."

[21]Ahithophel said, "Your father left behind some of his slave women who give birth to his children. He left them here to take care of the palace. Have physical relations with them. Then all the Israelites will hear that your father is your enemy. And all your people will be encouraged to give you more support." [22]So they put up a tent for Absalom on the flat roof[n] of the palace. Everyone in Israel could see it. And Absalom had physical relations with his father's slave women.

[23]At that time people thought Ahithophel's advice was as reliable as God's own word. Both David and Absalom thought it was that reliable.

17 Ahithophel said to Absalom, "Let me choose 12,000 men. I'll chase David tonight. [2]I'll catch him while he is tired and weak. I'll frighten him so all his people will run away. But

I'll kill only King David. [3]Then I'll bring everyone back to you. If the man you are looking for is dead, everyone else will return safely." [4]This plan seemed good to Absalom and to all the leaders of Israel.

[5]But Absalom said, "Now call Hushai the Arkite. I also want to hear what he says." [6]So Hushai came to Absalom. Absalom said to him, "This is the plan Ahithophel gave. Should we follow it? If not, tell us."

[7]Hushai said to Absalom, "Ahithophel's advice is not good this time."

[8]Hushai added, "You know your father and his men are strong. They are as angry as a bear that is robbed of its babies. Your father is a skilled fighter. He won't stay all night with the people. [9]He is probably already hiding in a cave or some other place. If your father attacks your men first, people will hear the news. And they will think, 'Absalom's followers are losing!' [10]Then even the men who are as brave as a lion will become frightened. This is because all the Israelites know your father is a fighter. They know his men are brave!

[11]"This is what I suggest: Gather all the Israelites from Dan to Beersheba.[n] There will be as many people as grains of sand by the sea. Then yourself must go into the battle. [12]We will catch David where he is hiding. We will fall on him as dew falls on the ground. We will kill him and all of his men. No one will be left alive. [13]What if David escapes into a city? Then all the Israelites will bring ropes to that city. We'll pull that city into the valley.

> Maybe the Lord will see my misery. Then maybe he will repay me with something good.
> —2 SAMUEL 16:12

16:22 roof In Bible times houses were built with flat roofs. The roof was used for drying things such as flax and fruit. And it was used as an extra room, as a place for worship and as a place to sleep in the summer.

17:11 Dan to Beersheba Dan was the city farthest north in Israel. Beersheba was the city farthest south. So this means all the people of Israel.

There won't be even a small stone left there!"

[14]Absalom and all the Israelites said, "The advice of Hushai the Arkite is better than that of Ahithophel." They said this because the Lord had planned to destroy the good advice of Ahithophel. In this way the Lord could bring disaster on Absalom.

[15]Hushai told these things to Zadok and Abiathar, the priests. He told them what Ahithophel had suggested to Absalom and the elders of Israel. He also reported to them what he himself had suggested. Hushai said, [16]"Quickly! Send a message to David. Tell him not to stay tonight at the crossings into the desert. Tell him to cross over the Jordan River at once. If he crosses the river, he and all his people won't be caught."

[17]Jonathan and Ahimaaz were waiting at En Rogel. They did not want to be seen going into the town. So a servant girl would go out to them and give them messages. Then Jonathan and Ahimaaz would go and tell King David.

[18]But a boy saw Jonathan and Ahimaaz and told Absalom. So Jonathan and Ahimaaz ran away quickly. They went to a man's house in Bahurim. He had a well in his courtyard, and they climbed down into it. [19]The man's wife spread a sheet over the opening of the well. Then she covered it with grain. No one could tell that Jonathan and Ahimaaz were hiding there.

[20]Absalom's servants came to the woman at the house. They asked, "Where are Ahimaaz and Jonathan?"

She said to them, "They have already crossed the brook."

Absalom's servants then went to look for Jonathan and Ahimaaz. But they could not find them. So they went back to Jerusalem.

[21]After Absalom's servants had left, Jonathan and Ahimaaz climbed out of the well. Then they went to tell King David. They said, "Hurry, cross over the river! Ahithophel has said these things against you!" [22]So David and all his people crossed the Jordan River. By dawn, everyone had crossed the Jordan.

[23]Now Ahithophel saw that the Israelites did not accept his advice. So he saddled his donkey and went to his hometown. He gave orders for his family and property. Then he hung himself. After Ahithophel died, he was buried in his father's tomb.

WAR BETWEEN DAVID AND ABSALOM

[24]David arrived at Mahanaim. And Absalom and all his Israelites crossed over the Jordan River. [25]Now Absalom had made Amasa captain of the army instead of Joab. Amasa was the son of a man named Jether the Ishmaelite. Amasa's mother was Abigail daughter of Nahash and sister of Zeruiah. Zeruiah was Joab's mother. [26]Absalom and the Israelites camped in the land of Gilead.

[27]Shobi, Makir and Barzillai were at Mahanaim when David arrived. Shobi son of Nahash was from the Ammonite town of Rabbah. Makir son of Ammiel was from Lo Debar. And Barzillai was from Rogelim in Gilead. [28]They brought beds, bowls and clay pots. They brought wheat, barley, flour, roasted grain, beans and small peas. [29]They also brought honey and milk curds, sheep, and cheese made from cows' milk. They brought these things for David and his people. They had said, "The people have become hungry and tired and thirsty in the desert."

18 David counted his men. He chose commanders over groups of 1,000 and commanders over groups of 100. [2]He sent the troops in three groups. Joab commanded one-third of the men. Joab's brother Abishai son of Zeruiah commanded another third. And Ittai from Gath commanded the last third. King David said to them, "I will also go with you."

[3]But the men said, "No! You must not go with us! If we run away in the battle,

Absalom's men won't care. Even if half of us are killed, Absalom's men won't care. But you're worth 10,000 of us! It is better for you to stay in the city. Then, if we need help, you can send it."

⁴The king said to his people, "I will do what you think is best." So the king stood at the side of the gate as the army went out. They went out in groups of 100 and 1,000.

⁵The king gave a command to Joab, Abishai and Ittai. He said, "Be gentle with young Absalom for my sake." Everyone heard the king's orders about Absalom to the commanders.

⁶David's army went out into the field against Absalom's Israelites. They fought in the forest of Ephraim. ⁷There David's army defeated the Israelites. Many died that day—20,000 men. ⁸The battle spread through all the country. But that day more men died in the forest than in the fighting.

ABSALOM DIES

⁹Then Absalom happened to meet David's troops. As Absalom was riding his mule, it went under a large oak tree. The branches were thick, and Absalom's head got caught in the tree. His mule ran out from under him. So Absalom was left hanging above the ground.

¹⁰When one of the men saw it happen, he told Joab. He said, "I saw Absalom hanging in an oak tree!"

¹¹Joab said to him, "You saw him? Why didn't you kill him and let him fall to the ground? I would have given you a belt and four ounces of silver!"

¹²The man answered, "I wouldn't try to hurt the king's son. I wouldn't even if you gave me 25 pounds of silver. We heard the king's command to you, Abishai and Ittai. The king said, 'Be careful not to hurt young Absalom.' ¹³If I had killed him, the king would have found out. And you would not have protected me!"

¹⁴Joab said, "I won't waste time here with you!" Now Absalom was still alive

in the oak tree. So Joab took three spears and stabbed him in the heart. ¹⁵Ten young men who carried Joab's armor also gathered around Absalom. They struck him and killed him.

¹⁶Then Joab blew the trumpet. So the troops stopped chasing Absalom's Israelites. ¹⁷Then Joab's men took Absalom's body. They threw it into a large pit in the forest. Then they filled the pit with many stones. All the Israelites who followed Absalom ran away and went home.

¹⁸When Absalom was alive, he had put up a pillar in the King's Valley. It was a monument to himself. He said, "I have no son to keep my name alive." So he named the pillar after himself. That pillar is called Absalom's Monument even today.

¹⁹Ahimaaz son of Zadok spoke to Joab. He said, "Let me run and take the news to King David. I'll tell him the Lord has destroyed the enemy for him."

²⁰Joab answered Ahimaaz, "No, you are not the one to take the news today. You may do it another time. But do not take it today, because the king's son is dead."

²¹Then Joab said to a man from Cush, "Go. Tell the king what you have seen." The Cushite bowed to Joab and ran to tell David.

²²But Ahimaaz son of Zadok begged Joab again. He said, "No matter what happens, please let me go, along with the Cushite!"

Joab said, "Son, why do you want to carry the news? You won't get any reward for the news you bring!"

²³Ahimaaz answered, "No matter what happens, I will run."

So Joab said to Ahimaaz, "Run!" Then Ahimaaz ran by way of the Jordan Valley and passed the Cushite.

²⁴Now David was sitting between the inner and outer gates of the city. The watchman went up to the roof by the gate walls. As he looked up, he saw a man running alone. ²⁵He shouted to tell King David.

The king said, "If he is alone, he is bringing good news!"

The man came nearer and nearer to the city. 26 Then the watchman saw another man running. The watchman called to the gatekeeper, "Look! Another man is running alone!"

The king said, "He is also bringing good news!"

27 The watchman said, "I think the first man runs like Ahimaaz son of Zadok."

The king said, "Ahimaaz is a good man. He must be bringing good news!"

28 Then Ahimaaz called a greeting to the king. He bowed facedown on the ground to the king. He said, "Praise the Lord your God! The Lord has defeated the men who were against you, my king."

29 The king asked, "Is young Absalom all right?"

Ahimaaz answered, "When Joab sent me, I saw some great excitement. But I don't know what it was."

30 Then the king said, "Step over here and wait." So Ahimaaz stepped aside and stood there.

31 Then the Cushite arrived. He said, "Master and king, hear the good news! Today the Lord has punished the people who were against you!"

32 The king asked the Cushite, "Is young Absalom all right?"

The Cushite answered, "May your enemies be like that young man. May all who come to hurt you be like that young man!"

33 Then the king knew Absalom was dead. He was very upset. He went to the room over the city gate and cried. As he went, he cried out, "My son Absalom, my son Absalom! I wish I had died for you. Absalom, my son, my son!"

JOAB SCOLDS DAVID

19 People told Joab, "Look, the king is crying. He is very sad because of Absalom." 2 David's army had won the battle that day. But it became a very sad day for all the people. This was because they heard, "The king is very sad for his son." 3 The people came into the city quietly. They were like people who had been defeated in battle and had run away. 4 The king covered his face and cried loudly, "My son Absalom! Absalom, my son, my son!"

5 Then Joab went into the king's house. He said to the king, "Today you have shamed all your men. They saved your life today! They saved the lives of your sons, daughters, wives and slave women. 6 You have shamed them because you love those who hate you. And you hate those people who love you. Today you've made it clear that your commanders and men mean nothing to you. What if Absalom had lived and all of us were dead? I can see you would be very pleased. 7 Now go out and encourage your servants. I swear by the Lord that if you don't go out, no man will be left with you by tonight! That will be worse than all the troubles you have had from your youth until today."

8 So the king went to the city gate.[n] The news spread that the king was at the gate. So everyone came to see him.

DAVID GOES BACK TO JERUSALEM

All the Israelites who had followed Absalom had run away to their homes.

> Ahimaaz answered, "No matter what happens, I will run." So Joab said . . . "Run!"
>
> –2 SAMUEL 18:23

19:8 **city gate** People came here to conduct business. Public meetings and court cases were also held here.

⁹People in all the tribes of Israel began to argue. They said, "The king saved us from the Philistines and our other enemies. But he left the country because of Absalom. ¹⁰We appointed Absalom to rule us, but now he has died in battle. We should make David the king again."

¹¹King David sent a message to Zadok and Abiathar, the priests. David said, "Speak to the elders of Judah. Say, 'Even in my house I have heard what all the Israelites are saying. So why are you the last tribe to bring the king back to his palace? ¹²You are my brothers, my own family. Then why are you the last tribe to bring back the king?' ¹³And say to Amasa, 'You are part of my own family. May God punish me terribly if I don't make you commander of the army in Joab's place!'"

¹⁴David touched the hearts of all the people of Judah. They agreed as if they were one man. They sent a message to the king. They said, "Return with all your men." ¹⁵Then the king returned as far as the Jordan River. The men of Judah came to Gilgal to meet him. They wanted to bring the king across the Jordan River.

¹⁶Shimei son of Gera was a Benjaminite. He lived in Bahurim. He hurried down with the men of Judah to meet King David. ¹⁷With Shimei came 1,000 Benjaminites. Ziba, the servant from Saul's family, also came. He brought his 15 sons and 20 servants with him. They all hurried to the Jordan River to meet the king. ¹⁸The people went across the Jordan River to help bring the king's family back to Judah. They did whatever the king wanted. As the king was about to cross the river, Shimei son of Gera came to him. Shimei bowed facedown on the ground in front of the king. ¹⁹He said to the king, "My master, don't hold me guilty. Don't remember the wrong things I did when you left Jerusalem! Don't hold it against me. ²⁰I know I have sinned. That is why I am the first person from Joseph's family to come down and meet you today, my master and king!"

²¹But Abishai son of Zeruiah said, "Shimei should die. He cursed you, the Lord's appointed king!"

²²David said, "This does not concern you, sons of Zeruiah! Today you're against me! No one will be put to death in Israel today. Today I know I am king over Israel!" ²³Then the king said to Shimei, "You won't die." The king made this promise to Shimei.

²⁴Mephibosheth, Saul's grandson, also went down to meet King David. Mephibosheth had not cared for his feet, cut his beard or washed his clothes while David was gone. He had not done this from the time the king had left Jerusalem until he returned safely. ²⁵Mephibosheth came from Jerusalem to meet the king. The king asked him, "Mephibosheth, why didn't you go with me?"

²⁶He answered, "My master, my servant Ziba tricked me! I said to Ziba, 'I am crippled. So saddle a donkey. Then I will ride it so I can go with the king.' ²⁷But he lied about me to you. You, my master and king, are like an angel from God. Do what you think is good. ²⁸You could have killed all my grandfather's family. Instead, you put me with the people who eat at your own table. So I don't have a right to ask anything more from the king!"

²⁹The king said to him, "Don't say anything more. I have decided that you and Ziba may divide the land."

³⁰Mephibosheth said to the king, "Let Ziba take all the land. I'm just happy that my master the king has arrived in peace at his own house."

³¹Barzillai of Gilead came down from Rogelim to cross the Jordan River with the king. ³²Now Barzillai was a very old man. He was 80 years old. He had taken care of the king when David was staying at Mahanaim. Barzillai could do this, because he was a very rich man. ³³David said to Barzillai, "Cross the river with me. Come with me to Jerusalem, and I will take care of you."

34But Barzillai answered the king, "Do you know how old I am? Do you think I can go with you to Jerusalem? 35I am 80 years old! I am too old to taste what I eat or drink. I am too old to hear the voices of men and women singers. Why should you be bothered with me? 36I am not worthy of a reward from you. But I will cross the Jordan River with you. 37Then please let me go back so I may die in my own city. Let me die near the grave of my father and mother. But here is Kimham. Let him go with you, my master and king. Do with him whatever you want."

38The king answered, "Kimham will go with me. I will do for him anything you wish. And I will do anything for you that you wish." 39The king kissed Barzillai and blessed him. Then Barzillai returned home. And the king and all the people crossed the Jordan.

40When the king crossed the Jordan to Gilgal, Kimham went with him. All the troops of Judah and half the troops of Israel led David across the river.

41Soon all the men of Israel came to the king. They said to him, "Our brothers, the men of Judah, stole you away. They brought you and your family across the Jordan River with your men! Why did they do this?"

42All the men of Judah answered the Israelites, "We did this because the king is our close relative. Why are you angry about it? We have not eaten food at the king's expense! He did not give us any gifts!"

43The men of Israel answered the people of Judah, "We have ten tribes in the kingdom. So we have more right to David than you do! But you ignored us! We were the first ones to talk about bringing our king back!"

But the men of Judah spoke even more unkindly than the men of Israel.

SHEBA LEADS ISRAEL AWAY FROM DAVID

20 It happened that a trouble-maker named Sheba son of Bicri was there. Sheba was from the tribe of Benjamin. He blew the trumpet and said:

> "We have no share in David!
> We have no part in the son of Jesse!
> People of Israel, let's go to our own homes!"

2So all the Israelites left David and followed Sheba son of Bicri. But the men of Judah stayed with their king all the way from the Jordan River to Jerusalem.

3David came to his palace in Jerusalem. Earlier he had left there ten of his slave women who gave birth to his children. He had left them there to take care of the palace. Now he put them in a house where they would be guarded. They were kept there for the rest of their lives. David gave them food, but he did not have physical relations with them. They lived like widows until they died.

4The king said to Amasa, "Tell the men of Judah to meet with me in three days. And you must also be here." 5So Amasa went to call the men of Judah together. But he took longer than the time the king had told him.

6David said to Abishai, "Sheba son of Bicri is more dangerous to us than Absalom was. Take my men and chase him. Hurry before he finds strong, walled cities. If he gets there, he will escape from us." 7So Joab's men, the Kerethites and the Pelethites, who were the king's bodyguards, and all the soldiers went with Abishai. They went out from Jerusalem to chase Sheba son of Bicri.

8When Joab and the army came to the great rock at Gibeon, Amasa came out to meet them. Joab was wearing his uniform. At his waist he wore a belt. It held his sword in its case. As Joab stepped forward, his sword fell out of its case. 9Joab asked Amasa, "Brother, is everything all right with you?" Then with his right hand he took Amasa by the beard to kiss him. 10Amasa did not guard against the sword that was in

Joab's hand. So Joab pushed the sword into Amasa's stomach. This caused Amasa's insides to spill on the ground. Joab did not have to stab Amasa again. He was already dead. Then Joab and his brother Abishai continued to chase Sheba son of Bicri.

¹¹One of Joab's young men stood by Amasa's body. The young man said, "Everyone who is for Joab and David should follow Joab!" ¹²Amasa lay in the middle of the road, covered with his own blood. The young man saw that everyone was stopping to look at the body. So he dragged Amasa's body from the road and laid it in a field. Then he put a cloth over it. ¹³After Amasa's body was taken off the road, all the men followed Joab. They went with him to chase Sheba son of Bicri.

¹⁴Sheba went through all the tribes of Israel to Abel Beth Maacah. All the Berites also came together and followed him. ¹⁵So Joab and his men came to Abel Beth Maacah and surrounded it. They piled dirt up against the city wall so they could attack it. And they began digging under the city walls to make them fall down.

¹⁶But a wise woman shouted out from the city. She said, "Listen! Listen! Tell Joab to come here. I want to talk to him!"

¹⁷So Joab came near her. She asked him, "Are you Joab?"

He answered, "Yes, I am."

Then she said, "Listen to what I say!"

Joab said, "I'm listening."

¹⁸Then the woman said, "In the past people would say, 'Ask for advice at Abel.' Then the problem would be solved. ¹⁹I am one of the peaceful, loyal people of Israel. You are trying to destroy an important city of Israel. Why must you destroy what belongs to the Lord?"

²⁰Joab answered, "May I not destroy or ruin anything. ²¹That is not what I want. But there is a man here from the mountains of Ephraim. He is named Sheba son of Bicri. He has turned against King David. If you will bring him to me, I will leave the city alone."

The woman said to Joab, "His head will be thrown over the wall to you."

²²Then the woman spoke very wisely to all the people of the city. They cut off the head of Sheba son of Bicri. Then they threw it over the wall to Joab. So he blew the trumpet, and the army left the city. Every man returned home. And Joab went back to the king in Jerusalem.

²³Joab was commander of all the army of Israel. Benaiah son of Jehoiada led the Kerethites and Pelethites, the king's bodyguards. ²⁴Adoniram led the men who were forced to do hard work. Jehoshaphat son of Ahilud was the recorder. ²⁵Sheba was the royal assistant. Zadok and Abiathar were the priests. ²⁶And Ira the Jairite was David's priest.

THE GIBEONITES PUNISH SAUL'S FAMILY

21 During the time David was king, there was a time of hunger. It continued for three years. So David prayed to the Lord.

The Lord answered, "Saul and his family of murderers are the reason for this time of hunger. It has come because Saul killed the Gibeonites." ²(Now the Gibeonites were not Israelites. They were a group of Amorites who were left alive. The Israelites had promised not to hurt the Gibeonites. But Saul was very eager to help the people of Israel and Judah. So he tried to kill all the Gibeonites.)

King David called the Gibeonites together and talked to them. ³He asked them, "What can I do for you? What can I do to take away Israel's sin so you can bless the Lord's people?"

⁴The Gibeonites said to David, "Saul and his family don't have enough silver and gold to pay for what they did! And we don't have the right to kill anyone in Israel."

Then David asked, "What do you want me to do for you?"

⁵The Gibeonites said to him, "Saul made plans against us. He tried to destroy all our people who are left in the land of Israel. ⁶Saul was the Lord's chosen king. So bring seven of his sons to us. Then we will kill them and hang them on stakes. We will put them in front of the Lord at Gibeah, Saul's hometown."

The king said, "I will give them to you." ⁷But the king protected Jonathan's son Mephibosheth. (Jonathan was Saul's son.) David did this because of the promise he had made to Jonathan in the Lord's name. So the king did not let them hurt Mephibosheth. ⁸But the king did take Armoni and Mephibosheth,ⁿ sons of Rizpah and Saul. (Rizpah was the daughter of Aiah.) And the king took the five sons of Saul's daughter Merab. Adriel was the father of Merab's five sons. (Adriel was the son of Barzillai the Meholathite.) ⁹David gave these seven sons to the Gibeonites. Then the Gibeonites killed them and hung them on stakes on a hill before the Lord. All seven sons died together. They were put to death during the first days of the harvest season. (The barley harvest was just beginning.)

¹⁰Aiah's daughter Rizpah took the rough cloth that was worn to show sadness. Then she put it on a rock for herself. She stayed there from the beginning of the harvest until the rain fell on her sons' bodies. During the day she did not let the birds of the sky touch her sons' bodies. At night she did not let the wild animals touch them.

¹¹People told David what Aiah's daughter Rizpah, Saul's slave woman, was doing. ¹²Then David took the bones of Saul and Jonathan from the men of Jabesh Gilead. (They had taken these bones secretly from the public square of Beth Shan. The Philistines had hung the bodies of Saul and Jonathan there after they had killed Saul at Gilboa.) ¹³David brought the bones of Saul and his son Jonathan from Gilead. Then the people gathered the bodies of Saul's seven sons who were hanged on stakes. ¹⁴The people buried the bones of Saul and his son Jonathan at Zela in Benjamin. They buried them in the tomb of Saul's father Kish. The people did everything the king commanded.

Then God answered the prayers of the people in the land.

WARS WITH THE PHILISTINES

¹⁵Again there was war between the Philistines and Israel. David and his men went out to fight the Philistines. But David became tired and weak. ¹⁶Ishbi-Benob was one of the sons of Rapha. His bronze spearhead weighed about seven and a half pounds. Ishbi-Benob had a new sword, and he planned to kill David. ¹⁷But Abishai son of Zeruiah killed the Philistine. So he saved David's life.

Then David's men made a promise to David. They said, "Never again will you go out with us to battle. If you were killed, Israel would lose its greatest leader."

¹⁸Later, at Gob, there was another battle with the Philistines. Sibbecai the Hushathite killed Saph, another one of the sons of Rapha.

¹⁹Later, there was another battle at Gob with the Philistines. Elhanan son of Jaare-Oregim from Bethlehem killed Goliathⁿ from Gath. Goliath's spear was as large as a weaver's rod.

²⁰At Gath another battle took place. A very large man was there. He had 6 fingers on each hand. And he had 6 toes on each foot. He had 24 fingers and toes in all. This man also was one of the sons of Rapha. ²¹When he challenged Israel, Jonathan killed him. Jonathan was the son of Shimeah, David's brother.

²²These four men were sons of Rapha from Gath. They all were killed by David and his men.

21:8 **Mephibosheth** This is not Jonathan's son but another man with the same name.
21:19 **Goliath** In 1 Chronicles 20:5 he is called Lahmi brother of Goliath.

☆ 2 Samuel 22:2-3

David wrote and sang songs to God all his life. David sang when he was happy. He sang when he was sad. And David sang when he was scared. This was how David prayed, but it is also how he praised God. David praised God for always keeping him safe.

Do you ever feel scared? Did you know that God is strong enough to help you? The Bible is full of stories about God helping people who were afraid. David was a soldier and then a king, and even he got scared at times. But God was always there to help him feel safe. God loves you and wants to protect you. He sent his Son, Jesus, to save you and to keep you safe now and forever. So, when you feel scared, you can pray to Jesus. He cares for you and is ready to help you whenever you ask.

. . . .

David knew where to go for help. He went to God.
When you need help, you can do the same!

DAVID'S SONG OF PRAISE

22 David sang this song to the Lord. He sang it when the Lord had saved him from Saul and all his other enemies. ²He said:

"The Lord is my rock, my place of safety, my Savior.
³ My God is my rock.
I can run to him for safety.
He is my shield and my saving strength.
The Lord is my high tower and my place of safety.
The Lord saves me from those who want to harm me.

⁴ I will call to the Lord.
He is worthy of praise.
And I will be saved from my enemies.

⁵ "The waves of death came around me.
The deadly rivers overwhelmed me.
⁶ The ropes of death wrapped around me.
The traps of death were before me.
⁷ In my trouble I called to the Lord.
I cried out to my God.
From his temple he heard my voice.
My call for help reached his ears.

8 "The earth trembled and shook.
   The foundations of heaven began
      to shake.
   They shook because the Lord was
      angry.
9 Smoke came out of his nose.
   Burning fire came out of his mouth.
   Burning coals went before him.
10 He tore open the sky and came down.
   Dark clouds were under his feet.
11 He rode a creature with wings and
      flew.
   He flew on the wings of the wind.
12 He made darkness his shelter around
      him,
   surrounded by fog and clouds.
13 Out of the brightness of his presence
      came flashes of lightning.
14 The Lord thundered from heaven.
   The Most High God raised his voice.
15 He shot his arrows and scattered his
      enemies.
   His bolts of lightning confused
      them with fear.
16 The Lord spoke strongly.
   The wind blew from his nose.
   The valleys of the sea appeared.
   The foundations of the earth were
      seen.

17 "The Lord reached down from above
      and took me.
   He pulled me from the deep water.
18 He saved me from my powerful
      enemies.
   Those who hated me were too
      strong for me.
19 They attacked me at my time of
      trouble.
   But the Lord supported me.
20 He took me to a safe place.
   Because he delights in me, he saved
      me.

21 "The Lord spared me because I did
      what was right.
   Because I have not done evil, he
      has rescued me.
22 I have followed the ways of the Lord.
   I have not done evil by turning
      from my God.

23 I remember all his laws.
   I have not broken his rules.
24 I have kept myself innocent before
      him.
   I have kept myself from doing evil.
25 The Lord rescued me because I did
      what was right.
   I did what the Lord said was right.

26 "Lord, you are loyal to those who are
      loyal.
   You are good to those who are good.
27 You are pure to those who are pure.
   But you are against those who are
      bad.
28 You save those who are not proud.
   But you make humble those who
      are proud.
29 Lord, you give light to my lamp.
   The Lord brightens the darkness
      around me.
30 With your help, I can attack an army.
   With God's help, I can jump over a
      wall.

31 "The ways of God are without fault.
   The Lord's words are pure.
   He is a shield to those who trust him.
32 Who is God? Only the Lord.
   Who is the Rock? Only our God.
33 God is my protection.
   He makes my way free from fault.
34 He makes me like a deer, which does
      not stumble.
   He helps me stand on the steep
      mountains.
35 He trains my hands for battle.
   So my arms can bend a bronze bow.
36 You protect me with your saving
      shield.
   You have stooped to make me great.
37 You give me a better way to live.
   So I live as you want me to.
38 I chased my enemies and destroyed
      them.
   I did not quit till they were
      destroyed.
39 I destroyed and crushed them,
   so they couldn't rise up again.
   They fell beneath my feet.
40 You gave me strength in battle.

You made my enemies bow before
me.
⁴¹ You made my enemies turn back.
I destroyed those who hated me.
⁴² They called for help,
but no one came to save them.
They called to the Lord,
but he did not answer them.
⁴³ I beat my enemies into pieces.
They were like dust on the ground.
I pounded them out and walked on
them
like mud in the streets.

⁴⁴ "You saved me when my people
attacked me.
You kept me as the leader of
nations.
People I never knew serve me.
⁴⁵ Foreigners obey me.
As soon as they hear me, they obey
me.
⁴⁶ They all become afraid.
They tremble in their hiding places.

⁴⁷ "The Lord lives!
May my Rock be praised!
Praise God, the Rock, who saves me!
⁴⁸ God gives me victory over my
enemies.
He brings people under my rule.
⁴⁹ He frees me from my enemies.

"You set me over those who hate
me.
You saved me from cruel men.
⁵⁰ So I will praise you, Lord, among the
nations.
I will sing praises to your name.
⁵¹ The Lord gives great victories to his
king.
He is loyal to his appointed king,
to David and his descendants
forever."

DAVID'S LAST WORDS

23 These are the last words of
David.

This is the message of David son of
Jesse.

The man made great by the Most
High God speaks.
He is the appointed king of the God
of Jacob.
He is the sweet singer of Israel.

² "The Lord's Spirit spoke through me.
His word was on my tongue.
³ The God of Israel spoke.
The Rock of Israel said to me:
'The person who rules fairly over
people,
the person who rules with respect
for God,
⁴ he is like the morning light at dawn.
He is like a morning without
clouds.
He is like sunshine after a rain.
The sunshine makes the tender
grass grow out of the ground.'

⁵ "This is how God has cared for my
family.
God made a lasting agreement
with me,
good in every way and strong.
This agreement is my salvation.
This agreement is all I want.
Truly, the Lord will make it grow.

⁶ "But all evil people will be thrown
away like thorns.
People cannot hold on to thorns.

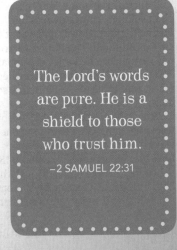

The Lord's words
are pure. He is a
shield to those
who trust him.

–2 SAMUEL 22:31

7 Anyone who touches them
uses a tool of iron or a spear.
They will be thrown in the fire and
burned where they lie."

DAVID'S ARMY

[8] These are the names of David's warriors:

Josheb-Basshebeth, the Tahkemonite, was head of the Three.[n] He killed 800 men at one time.

[9] Next there was Eleazar son of Dodai the Ahohite. Eleazar was one of the three soldiers who were with David when they challenged the Philistines. The Philistines were gathered for battle, and the Israelites drew back. [10] But Eleazar stayed where he was. He fought the Philistines until he was so tired he could not let go of his sword. The Lord gave a great victory for the Israelites that day. The people came back after Eleazar had won the battle. But they came only to take weapons and armor from the enemy.

[11] Next there was Shammah son of Agee the Hararite. The Philistines came together to fight. They stood where there was a field full of small peas. Israel's troops ran away from the Philistines. [12] But Shammah stood in the middle of the field. He fought for the field and killed the Philistines. And the Lord gave a great victory.

[13] Once, three of the Thirty, David's chief soldiers, came down to him during harvest. Now David was at the cave of Adullam. The Philistine army had camped in the Valley of Rephaim. [14] At that time David was in a protected place. And some of the Philistine soldiers were in Bethlehem. [15] David had a strong desire for some water. He said, "Oh, I wish someone would get me water from the well near the city gate of Bethlehem!" [16] So the three warriors broke through the Philistine army. They took water out of the well near the city gate of Bethlehem.

Then they took it to David. But he refused to drink it. He poured it out on the ground before the Lord. [17] David said, "Lord, I can't drink this! It would be like drinking the blood of the men who risked their lives!" So David refused to drink the water. These were the brave things that the three warriors did.

[18] Abishai was the brother of Joab son of Zeruiah. He was captain of the Three. Abishai used his spear against 300 enemies and killed them. He became as famous as the Three. [19] Abishai received even more honor than the Three. He became their commander. But he was not a member of them.

[20] Benaiah son of Jehoiada was a brave fighter from Kabzeel. He did many brave things. He killed two of the best soldiers from Moab. He also went down into a pit when it was snowing. There he killed a lion. [21] Benaiah killed a big Egyptian. The Egyptian had a spear in his hand. But Benaiah only had a club. Benaiah grabbed the spear from the Egyptian's hand. Then Benaiah killed him with his own spear. [22] These were the brave things that Benaiah son of Jehoiada did. He was as famous as the Three. [23] He received more honor than the Thirty. But he did not become a member of the Three. David made him leader of his bodyguard.

THE THIRTY CHIEF SOLDIERS

[24] The following men were among the Thirty:

Asahel the brother of Joab;
Elhanan son of Dodo from Bethlehem;
[25] Shammah the Harodite;
Elika the Harodite;
[26] Helez the Paltite;
Ira son of Ikkesh (from Tekoa);
[27] Abiezer the Anathothite;
Mebunnai the Hushathite;
[28] Zalmon the Ahohite;
Maharai the Netophathite;
[29] Heled son of Baanah the Netophathite;

23:8 Three These were David's most powerful soldiers. See 1 Chronicles 11:11.

Ithai son of Ribai from Gibeah of the land of Benjamin;

30 Benaiah the Pirathonite;
Hiddai from the ravines of Gaash;

31 Abi-Albon the Arbathite;
Azmaveth the Barhumite;

32 Eliahba the Shaalbonite;
the sons of Jashen;
Jonathan 33son of Shammah the Hararite;
Ahiam son of Sharar the Hararite;

34 Eliphelet son of Ahasbai the Maacathite;
Eliam son of Ahithophel the Gilonite;

35 Hezro the Carmelite;
Paarai the Arbite;

36 Igal son of Nathan of Zobah;
the son of Hagri;

37 Zelek the Ammonite;
Naharai the Beerothite, who carried the armor of Joab son of Zeruiah;

38 Ira the Ithrite;
Gareb the Ithrite

39 and Uriah the Hittite.

There were 37 in all.

DAVID COUNTS HIS ARMY

24 The Lord was angry with Israel again. He caused David to turn against the Israelites. David said, "Go, count the people of Israel and Judah."

2King David spoke to Joab, the commander of the army. David said, "Go through all the tribes of Israel. Go from Dan to Beersheba[n] and count the people. Then I will know how many there are."

3But Joab said to the king, "May the Lord your God give you 100 times more people. And may you live to see this happen. But why do you want to do this?"

4But the king very strongly commanded Joab and the commanders of the army. So they left the king to count the people of Israel.

5After crossing the Jordan River, they camped near Aroer. They camped on the south side of the city in the ravine. They went through Gad and on to Jazer. 6Then they went to Gilead and the land of Tahtim Hodshi. Next they went to Dan Jaan and around to Sidon. 7They went to the strong, walled city of Tyre. They also went to all the cities of the Hivites and Canaanites. Finally, they went to southern Judah, to Beersheba. 8After 9 months and 20 days, they had gone through all the land. Then they came back to Jerusalem.

9Joab gave the list of the people to the king. There were 800,000 men in Israel who could use the sword. And there were 500,000 men in Judah.

10David felt ashamed after he had counted the people. He said to the Lord, "I have sinned greatly in what I have done! Lord, I beg you, forgive my sin! I have been very foolish."

11Before David got up in the morning, the Lord spoke his word to Gad. He was a prophet and David's seer. 12The Lord told Gad, "Go and tell David, 'This is what the Lord says: I offer you three choices. Choose one for me to do to you.'"

13Gad went to David and told him. Gad said, "Choose one of these three things. Should three years of hunger come to you and your land? Or should your enemies chase you for three months? Or should there be three days of disease in your country? Think about it. Then decide which of these things I should tell the Lord who sent me."

14David said to Gad, "I am really in trouble. But the Lord is very merciful. So let the Lord punish us. Don't let my punishment come from people!"

15So the Lord sent disease on Israel. It began in the morning. And it continued until the chosen time to stop. From Dan to Beersheba 70,000 people died. 16The angel raised his arm toward Jerusalem to destroy it also. But the Lord felt very

---

24:2 Dan to Beersheba Dan was the city farthest north in Israel. Beersheba was the city farthest south. So this means all the people of Israel.

sorry about the terrible things that had happened. He said to the angel who was destroying the people, "That's enough! Put down your arm!" At this time the angel of the Lord was by the threshing floor of Araunah the Jebusite.

17David saw the angel that killed the people. Then he said to the Lord, "I've sinned! I've done wrong! But these people only followed me like sheep! They did nothing wrong! Please let your punishment be against me and my father's family!"

18That day Gad came to David. Gad told him, "Go and build an altar to the Lord. Build it on the threshing floor of Araunah the Jebusite." 19So David did what Gad told him to do. He obeyed the Lord's command and went to see Araunah.

20Araunah looked and saw the king and his servants coming to him. So he went out and bowed facedown on the ground. 21He said, "Why has my master the king come to me?"

David answered, "To buy the threshing floor from you. I want to build an altar to the Lord. Then the disease will stop."

22Araunah said to David, "My master and king, you may take anything you want for a sacrifice. Here are some oxen for the whole burnt offering. Here are the threshing boards and the yokes for the wood! 23My king, I give everything to you!" Araunah also said to the king, "May the Lord your God be pleased with you!"

24But the king answered Araunah, "No. I will pay you for the land. I won't offer to the Lord my God burnt offerings which cost me nothing!"

So David bought the threshing floor and the oxen for one and one-fourth pounds of silver. 25Then he built an altar to the Lord there. And he offered whole burnt offerings and fellowship offerings. Then the Lord answered his prayer for the country. And the disease in Israel stopped.

First Kings

ADONIJAH TRIES TO BECOME KING

1 At this time King David was very old. His servants covered him with blankets, but he could not keep warm. [2] So they said to him, "We will find a young woman to care for you. She will lie close to you and keep you warm." [3] So the king's servants looked everywhere in Israel for a beautiful young woman. They found a girl named Abishag from the Shunammite people. They brought her to the king. [4] The girl was very beautiful. She cared for the king and served him. But King David did not have physical relations with her.

[5-6] Adonijah was King David and Haggith's son. He was born next after Absalom. He was a very handsome man. He said, "I will be the king." So he got chariots and horses for himself. And he got 50 men to run ahead of him. Now David had never interfered with him by questioning what he did.

[7] Adonijah talked with Joab son of Zeruiah. He also talked with Abiathar the priest. They told him they would help him. [8] But several men did not join Adonijah. These men were Zadok the priest, Benaiah son of Jehoiada, Nathan the prophet, Shimei, Rei and King David's special guard.

[9] Then Adonijah killed some sheep, cows and fat calves for sacrifices. He made these sacrifices at the Stone of Zoheleth near the spring, En Rogel. He invited all his brothers, the other sons of King David, to come. He invited all the rulers and leaders of Judah also. [10] But Adonijah did not invite Nathan the prophet, Benaiah, his father's special guard or his brother Solomon.

[11] When Nathan heard about this, he went to Bathsheba. She was the mother of Solomon. Nathan asked her, "Have you heard what Adonijah, Haggith's son, is doing? He has made himself king. And our real king, David, does not know it. [12] Your life and the life of your son Solomon may be in danger. But I will tell you how to save yourselves. [13] Go to King David and say to him, 'My master and king, you made a promise to me. You promised that my son Solomon would be the king after you. You said he would rule on your throne. So why has Adonijah become king?' [14] While you are still talking to him, I will come in. I will tell the king that what you have said about Adonijah is true."

[15] So Bathsheba went in to see the king in his bedroom. He was now very old. Abishag, the girl from Shunam, was caring for him there. [16] Bathsheba bowed down before the king.

He asked, "What do you want?"

[17] She answered, "My master, you made a promise to me in the name of the Lord your God. You said, 'Your son Solomon will become king after me. He will rule on my throne.' [18] But now Adonijah has become king. And you did not know it. [19] Adonijah has killed many cows, fat calves and sheep for sacrifices. And he has invited all your sons. He also has invited Abiathar the priest and Joab the commander of your army. But he did not invite Solomon, your son who serves you. [20] My master and king, all the people of Israel are watching you. They are waiting for you to decide who will be king after you. [21] As soon as you die, Solomon and I will be treated as criminals."

[22] While Bathsheba was still talking with the king, Nathan the prophet arrived. [23] The servants told the king, "Nathan the prophet is here." So Nathan went to the king and bowed facedown on the ground before him.

King David knew how to keep his promises. He knew how because God showed him. God had kept all his promises to David. Even though David had many sons, he knew Solomon would be the best king. So when David was old, he kept his promise and made Solomon king of Israel.

T.R.O.U.B.L.E. Have you ever been in trouble? Have you ever been in trouble at school? What about at home? Sometimes we bring trouble on ourselves. Sometimes trouble finds us. Trouble comes in all shapes and sizes. Trouble happens to all people.

Do you know that friends, brothers, sisters, and even moms and dads go through trouble? Do you know that even people like presidents and kings go through trouble? King David said that the Lord helped him with all trouble. Jesus promised that we would all go through trouble. But Jesus is bigger than the biggest trouble. Jesus wants to hear about your trouble. Tell Jesus about your trouble and trust him to help you.

. . . .

Jesus is never troubled by your trouble—no matter how big or small.

²⁴Then Nathan said, "My master and king, have you said that Adonijah will be the king after you? Have you decided he will rule on your throne after you? ²⁵Today he has sacrificed many cows, fat calves and sheep. And he has invited all your other sons, the commanders of the army and Abiathar the priest. Right now they are eating and drinking with him. They are saying, 'Long live King Adonijah!' ²⁶But he did not invite me, Zadok the priest, Benaiah son of Jehoiada or your son Solomon. ²⁷Did you do this? We are your servants. Why didn't you tell us whom you chose to be the king after you?"

DAVID MAKES SOLOMON KING
²⁸Then King David said, "Tell Bathsheba to come in!" So she came in and stood before the king.

²⁹Then the king said, "The Lord has saved me from all trouble. As surely as he lives, I make this promise to you. ³⁰Today

I will do what I promised you in the past. I made that promise in the name of the Lord, the God of Israel. I promised that your son Solomon would be king after me. I promised he would rule on my throne after me."

³¹Then Bathsheba bowed facedown on the ground before the king. She said, "Long live my master King David!"

³²Then King David said, "Tell Zadok the priest, Nathan the prophet and Benaiah son of Jehoiada to come in here." So they came before the king. ³³Then the king said to them, "Take my servants with you and put my son Solomon on my own mule. Take him down to the spring called Gihon. ³⁴There Zadok the priest and Nathan the prophet should pour olive oil on him and make him king over Israel. Blow the trumpet and shout, 'Long live King Solomon!' ³⁵Then come back here with him. He will sit on my throne and rule in my place. I have chosen him to be the ruler over Israel and Judah."

³⁶Benaiah son of Jehoiada answered the king, "This is good! And may your God make it happen. ³⁷The Lord has always helped you, our king. Let the Lord also help Solomon. And let King Solomon be an even greater king than you."

³⁸So Zadok the priest, Nathan the prophet and Benaiah son of Jehoiada went down. The Kerethites and Pelethites, the king's bodyguards, went with them. They put Solomon on King David's mule and went with him to the spring called Gihon. ³⁹Zadok the priest took with him the container of olive oil from the Holy Tent. He poured the olive oil on Solomon's head to show he was the king. Then they blew the trumpet. And all the people shouted, "Long live King Solomon!" ⁴⁰All the people followed Solomon into the city. They were playing flutes and shouting for joy. They made so much noise the ground shook.

⁴¹At this time Adonijah and all the guests with him were finishing their meal. They heard the sound from the trumpet. Joab asked, "What does all that noise from the city mean?"

⁴²While Joab was speaking, Jonathan son of Abiathar the priest arrived. Adonijah said, "Come in! You are an important man. So you must be bringing good news."

⁴³But Jonathan answered, "No! Our master King David has made Solomon the new king. ⁴⁴King David sent Zadok the priest, Nathan the prophet, Benaiah son of Jehoiada and all the king's bodyguards with him. They put Solomon on the king's own mule. ⁴⁵And Zadok the priest and Nathan the prophet poured olive oil on Solomon at Gihon to make him king. Then they went into the city, shouting with joy. Now the whole city is excited. That is the noise you hear. ⁴⁶Solomon has now become the king. ⁴⁷All the king's officers have come to tell King David that he has done a good thing. They are saying, 'May your God make Solomon even more famous than you. And may your God make Solomon an even greater king than you.'" Jonathan continued, "And King David bowed down on his bed to worship God. ⁴⁸He said, 'Praise the Lord, the God of Israel. Today he has made one of my sons the king and allowed me to see it.'"

⁴⁹Then all of Adonijah's guests were afraid, and they left quickly. ⁵⁰Adonijah was also afraid of Solomon. So he went and took hold of the corners of the altar.ⁿ ⁵¹Then someone told Solomon, "Adonijah is afraid of you. He is at the altar, holding on to its corners. He says, 'Tell King Solomon to promise me today that he will not kill me.'"

⁵²So Solomon answered, "Adonijah must show that he is a man of honor. If he does, I promise that he will not lose even a hair from his head. But if he does anything wrong, he will die." ⁵³Then King Solomon sent some men to get

---

1:50 corners of the altar If a person were innocent of a crime, he could run into the Holy Place. If he held on to the corners of the altar there, he would not be punished. The corners looked like horns.

Adonijah. They brought him to King Solomon. So Adonijah came before King Solomon and bowed down. Then Solomon said, "Go home."

THE DEATH OF DAVID

2 It was almost time for David to die. So he talked to Solomon and gave him his last commands. ²David said, "My time to die is near. Be a good and strong leader. ³Obey everything that the Lord commands. Follow the commands he has given us. Obey all his laws, and do what he told us. Obey what is written in the teachings of Moses. If you do these things, you will be successful in all you do and wherever you go. ⁴And if you obey the Lord, he will keep the promise he made to me. He promised: 'Your descendants must live as I tell them. They must have complete faith in me. If they do this, then a man from your family will always be king over the people of Israel.'

⁵"Also, you remember what Joab son of Zeruiah did to me. He killed the two commanders of Israel's armies. He killed Abner son of Ner and Amasa son of Jether. He killed them as if he and they were at war. But this was in a time of peace. He killed innocent men. And their blood got on his belt and sandals. ⁶You should punish him in the way you think is wisest. (But do not let him die peacefully of old age.)

⁷"Be kind to the children of Barzillai of Gilead. Allow them to eat at your table. They helped me when I ran away from your brother Absalom.

⁸"And remember, Shimei son of Gera is here with you. He is from the people of Benjamin in Bahurim. Remember he cursed me the day I went to Mahanaim. Then he came down to meet me at the Jordan River. I promised him before the Lord, 'Shimei, I will not kill you.' ⁹But you should not leave him unpunished. You are a wise man. You will know what to do to him. But you must be sure he is killed."

¹⁰Then David died and was buried with his ancestors in Jerusalem. ¹¹He had ruled over Israel 40 years. Seven years were in Hebron, and 33 years were in Jerusalem.

SOLOMON TAKES CONTROL AS KING

¹²Now Solomon became king after David, his father. And he was in control of his kingdom.

¹³At this time Adonijah son of Haggith went to Bathsheba, Solomon's mother. Bathsheba asked, "Do you come in peace?"

Adonijah answered, "Yes. This is a peaceful visit. ¹⁴I have something to say to you."

"You may speak," she said.

> Then David died and was buried . . . He had ruled over Israel 40 years.
> –1 KINGS 2:10–11

¹⁵Adonijah said, "You remember that at one time the kingdom was mine. All the people of Israel thought I was their king. But things changed. Now my brother is the king because the Lord chose him. ¹⁶So now I have one thing to ask you. Please do not refuse me."

Bathsheba answered, "What do you want?"

¹⁷Adonijah said, "I know King Solomon will do anything you ask him. So please ask him to give me Abishag the Shunammite woman to be my wife."

¹⁸"Very well," she answered. "I will speak to the king for you."

¹⁹So Bathsheba went to King Solomon to talk to him for Adonijah. When Solomon saw her, he stood up to meet her. Then he bowed down to

her and sat on the throne. He told some servants to bring another throne for his mother. Then she sat down at his right side.

²⁰Bathsheba said to him, "I have one small thing to ask you. Please do not refuse me."

The king answered, "Ask, mother. I will not refuse you."

²¹So she said, "Allow Abishag the Shunammite woman to marry your brother Adonijah."

²²King Solomon answered his mother, "Why do you ask me to give him Abishag? Why don't you ask for him to become the king also since he is my older brother? Abiathar the priest and Joab son of Zeruiah will support him!"

²³Then King Solomon made a promise in the name of the Lord. He said, "I promise Adonijah will pay for asking me this! May God punish me terribly if it doesn't cost Adonijah his life! ²⁴The Lord has given me the throne that belonged to my father David. The Lord has kept his promise and given the kingdom to me and my people. As surely as the Lord lives, Adonijah will die today!" ²⁵So King Solomon gave orders to Benaiah son of Jehoiada. And he went out and killed Adonijah.

²⁶Then King Solomon said to Abiathar the priest, "I should kill you. But I will allow you to go back to your home in Anathoth. I will not kill you now because you helped to carry the Ark of the Covenant of the Lord God while marching with my father David. And I know you shared in all of the hard times with my father." ²⁷So Solomon removed Abiathar from being a priest to the Lord. This happened as the Lord had said it would. He had said this about the priest Eli and his family in Shiloh.

²⁸When Joab heard about this, he was afraid. He had supported Adonijah, but not Absalom. So Joab ran to the Tent of the Lord and took hold of the corners of the altar." ²⁹Someone told King Solomon that Joab had run to the Tent of the Lord and was beside the altar. So Solomon ordered Benaiah to go and kill him.

³⁰Benaiah went into the Tent of the Lord and said to Joab, "The king says, 'Come out!'"

But Joab answered, "No, I will die here."

So Benaiah went back to the king and told him what Joab had said. ³¹Then the king commanded Benaiah, "Do as he says! Kill him there and bury him. Then my family and I will be free of the guilt of Joab. Joab is guilty of killing innocent people. ³²He killed two men who were much better than he was. They were Abner son of Ner and Amasa son of Jether. Abner was the commander of Israel's army, and Amasa was the commander of Judah's army. My father David did not know that he killed them. So the Lord will pay him back for those men he killed. ³³He and his family will be forever guilty for their deaths. But there will be peace from God for David, his descendants, his family and his rule forever."

³⁴So Benaiah son of Jehoiada killed Joab. And he was buried near his home in the desert. ³⁵Solomon then made Benaiah son of Jehoiada commander of the army in Joab's place. Solomon also made Zadok the new high priest in Abiathar's place.

³⁶Next the king sent for Shimei. The king said to him, "Build a house for yourself here in Jerusalem. Live in the house, and don't leave the city. ³⁷If you leave and go past Kidron Valley, someone will kill you. And it will be your own fault."

³⁸So Shimei answered the king, "What you have said is good. I will obey you, my master and king." So Shimei lived in Jerusalem for a long time.

2:28 **corners of the altar** If a person were innocent of a crime, he could run into the Holy Place. If he held on to the corners of the altar there, he would not be punished. The corners looked like horns.

³⁹But three years later two of Shimei's slaves ran away. They went to Achish king of Gath. He was the son of Maacah. Shimei heard that his slaves were in Gath. ⁴⁰So he put his saddle on his donkey and left. He went to Achish at Gath to find his slaves. When he found them there, he brought them back to his home.

⁴¹Someone told Solomon that Shimei had gone from Jerusalem to Gath and had returned. ⁴²So Solomon sent for Shimei. Solomon said, "I made you promise in the name of the Lord not to leave Jerusalem. I warned you that if you went anywhere else you would die. And you agreed to what I said. You said you would obey me. ⁴³Why did you break your promise to the Lord? Why did you not obey my command? ⁴⁴You know the many wrong things you did against my father David. Now the Lord will punish you for those wrongs. ⁴⁵But the Lord will bless me. He will make the rule of David safe before the Lord forever."

⁴⁶Then the king ordered Benaiah to kill Shimei, and he did. Now Solomon was in full control of his kingdom.

SOLOMON ASKS FOR WISDOM

3 Solomon made an agreement with the king of Egypt by marrying his daughter. Solomon brought her to Jerusalem. At this time Solomon was still building his palace and the Temple of the Lord. He was also building a wall around Jerusalem. ²The Temple had not yet been finished. So people were still offering animal sacrifices at altars

---

⭐ 1 Kings 3:9

King Solomon asked God for wisdom because he wanted to be a good king. Wisdom would help him know the difference between right and wrong. Solomon knew that without wisdom he would not be a very good king. And because Solomon asked for wisdom, God gave it to him.

What is wisdom and why do you need it? Wisdom is understanding the world the way God wants you to. When you look for God and want his wisdom, he promises to give it to you. That is why reading your Bible, going to church, and learning about God from others is so important. God loves when people want to know him and what he says.

. . . .

If you ask God to help you learn more about him each day, he promises to answer.

in many places of worship. ³Solomon showed that he loved the Lord. He did this by following the commands his father David had given him. But Solomon still used the many places of worship to offer sacrifices and to burn incense.

⁴King Solomon went to Gibeon to offer a sacrifice. He went there because it was the most important place of worship. He offered 1,000 burnt offerings on that altar. ⁵While he was at Gibeon, the Lord came to him in a dream during the night. God said, "Ask for anything you want. I will give it to you."

⁶Solomon answered, "You were very kind to your servant, my father David. He obeyed you. He was honest and lived right. And you showed great kindness to him when you allowed his son to be king after him. ⁷Lord my God, you have allowed me to be king in my father's place. But I am like a little child. I do not have the wisdom I need to do what I must do. ⁸I, your servant, am here among your chosen people. There are too many of them to count. ⁹So I ask that you give me wisdom. Then I can rule the people in the right way. Then I will know the difference between right and wrong. Without wisdom, it is impossible to rule this great people of yours."

¹⁰The Lord was pleased that Solomon had asked him for this. ¹¹So God said to him, "You did not ask for a long life. And you did not ask for riches for yourself. You did not ask for the death of your enemies. Since you asked for wisdom to make the right decisions, ¹²I will give you what you asked. I will give you wisdom and understanding. Your wisdom will be greater than anyone has had in the past. And there will never be anyone in the future like you. ¹³Also, I will give you what you did not ask for. You will have riches and honor. During your life no other king will be as great as you. ¹⁴I ask you to follow me and obey my laws and commands. Do this as your father

David did. If you do, I will also give you a long life."

¹⁵Then Solomon woke up. He knew that God had talked to him in the dream. Then he went to Jerusalem and stood before the Ark of the Covenant with the Lord. There he gave burnt offerings and fellowship offerings to the Lord. After that, he gave a feast for all of his leaders and officers.

SOLOMON MAKES A WISE DECISION

¹⁶One day two women who were prostitutes came to Solomon. They stood before him. ¹⁷One of the women said, "My master, this woman and I live in the same house. I gave birth to a baby while she was there with me. ¹⁸Three days later this woman also gave birth to a baby. No one else was in the house with us. There were only the two of us. ¹⁹One night this woman rolled over on her baby, and it died. ²⁰So during the night she took my son from my bed while I was asleep. She carried him to her bed. Then she put the dead baby in my bed. ²¹The next morning I got up to feed my baby. But I saw that he was dead! Then I looked at him more closely. I saw that he was not my son."

²²But the other woman said, "No! The living baby is my son. The dead baby is yours!"

But the first woman said, "No! The dead baby is yours, and the living one is mine!" So the two women argued before the king.

²³Then King Solomon said, "Each of you says the living baby is your own. And each of you says the dead baby belongs to the other woman."

²⁴Then King Solomon sent his servants to get a sword. When they brought it to him, ²⁵he said, "Cut the living baby into two pieces. Give each woman half of the baby."

²⁶The real mother of the living child was full of love for her son. She said to the king, "Please, my master, don't kill him! Give the baby to her!"

But the other woman said, "Neither of us will have him. Cut him into two pieces!"

²⁷Then King Solomon said, "Give the baby to the first woman. Don't kill him. She is the real mother."

²⁸When the people of Israel heard about King Solomon's decision, they respected him very much. They saw he had wisdom from God to make the right decisions.

SOLOMON'S OFFICERS

4 King Solomon ruled over all Israel. ²These are the names of his leading officers:

Azariah son of Zadok was the priest;

³Elihoreph and Ahijah, sons of Shisha, recorded what happened in the courts;

Jehoshaphat son of Ahilud recorded the history of the people;

⁴Benaiah son of Jehoiada was commander of the army;

Zadok and Abiathar were priests;

⁵Azariah son of Nathan was in charge of the district governors;

Zabud son of Nathan was a priest and adviser to the king;

⁶Ahishar was responsible for everything in the palace;

Adoniram son of Abda was in charge of the slaves.

⁷Solomon placed 12 governors over the districts of Israel. They had to gather food from their districts. Then they were to give it to the king and his family. Each governor was responsible for giving food to the king one month of each year. ⁸These are the names of the 12 governors:

Ben-Hur was governor over the mountain country of Ephraim.

⁹Ben-Deker was governor over Makaz, Shaalbim, Beth Shemesh and Elon Bethhanan.

¹⁰Ben-Hesed was governor over Arubboth, Socoh and Hepher.

¹¹Ben-Abinadab was governor over Naphoth Dor. (He was married to Taphath daughter of Solomon.)

¹²Baana son of Ahilud was governor over Taanach, Megiddo and all of Beth Shan next to Zarethan. (This was below Jezreel from Beth Shan to Abel Meholah across Jokmeam.)

¹³Ben-Geber was governor over Ramoth in Gilead. (He was governor over all the Towns of Jair in Gilead. Jair was the son of Manasseh. Ben-Geber was also over the district of Argob in Bashan. It had 60 large, walled cities with bronze bars on their gates.)

¹⁴Ahinadab son of Iddo was governor over Mahanaim.

¹⁵Ahimaaz was governor over Naphtali. (He was married to Basemath daughter of Solomon.)

¹⁶Baana son of Hushai was governor over Asher and Aloth.

¹⁷Jehoshaphat son of Paruah was governor over Issachar.

¹⁸Shimei son of Ela was governor over Benjamin.

¹⁹Geber son of Uri was governor over Gilead. (Gilead was the country where Sihon king of the Amorite people lived. Og king of Bashan also lived there.) But Geber was the only governor over the district.

SOLOMON'S KINGDOM

²⁰There were many people in Judah and Israel. There were as many people as there were grains of sand on the seashore. The people ate, drank and were happy. ²¹Solomon ruled over all the kingdoms from the Euphrates River to the land of the Philistine people. His kingdom went as far as the border of Egypt. These countries brought Solomon the payments he demanded. And they obeyed him all his life.

²²Solomon needed much food each day to feed himself and all the people who ate at his table. It took 185 bushels of fine flour and 375 bushels of meal. ²³It also took 10 cows that were fed good grain, 20 cows that were raised in the fields and 100 sheep. And it took 3 different kinds of deer and fat birds. ²⁴Solomon ruled over all the

countries west of the Euphrates River. This was the land from Tiphsah to Gaza. And Solomon had peace on all sides of his kingdom. ²⁵During Solomon's life Judah and Israel, from Dan to Beersheba,ⁿ lived in peace. Each man was able to sit under his own fig trees and grapevines.

²⁶Solomon had 4,000 stalls for his chariot horses. And he had 12,000 chariot soldiers. ²⁷Each month one of the district governors gave King Solomon all the food he needed. This was enough for every person who ate at the king's table. The governors made sure he had everything he needed. ²⁸They also gave the king enough barley and straw for the chariot and work horses. Each person brought this grain to the required places.

SOLOMON'S WISDOM

²⁹God gave great wisdom to Solomon. Solomon could understand many things. His wisdom was as hard to measure as the sand on the seashore. ³⁰His wisdom was greater than the wisdom of all the men in the East. And his wisdom was greater than all the wisdom of the men in Egypt. ³¹He was wiser than any other man on earth. He was even wiser than Ethan the Ezrahite. He was wiser than Heman, Calcol and Darda. They were the sons of Mahol. King Solomon became famous in all the countries around Israel and Judah. ³²During his life King Solomon spoke 3,000 wise teachings. He also knew 1,005 songs. ³³He taught about many different kinds of plants. He taught about everything from the great cedar trees of Lebanon to the hyssop that grows out of the walls. He also taught about animals, birds, crawling things and fish. ³⁴People from all nations came to listen to King Solomon's wisdom. The kings of all nations sent them to listen to him. These kings had heard of Solomon's wisdom.

SOLOMON PREPARES TO BUILD THE TEMPLE

5 Now King Hiram was the king of Tyre. He had always been a friend of David. Hiram heard that Solomon had been made king in David's place. So he sent his messengers to Solomon. ²Then Solomon sent this message back to King Hiram: ³"You remember that my father David had to fight many wars with the countries around him. So he was never able to build a temple for worship to the Lord his God. David was waiting until the Lord allowed him to defeat all his enemies. ⁴But now the Lord my God has given me peace. There is peace on all sides of my country. I have no enemies now. My people are in no danger. ⁵"The Lord made a promise to my father David. The Lord said, 'I will make your son king after you. And he will build a temple for worship to me.' Now, I plan to build that temple for worship to the Lord my God. ⁶And so I ask for your help. Send your men to cut down cedar trees for me from Lebanon. My servants will work with yours. I will pay your servants whatever wages you decide. We don't have anyone who can cut down trees as well as the people of Sidon can."

⁷When Hiram heard what Solomon asked, he was very happy. He said, "I

> God gave great wisdom to Solomon. Solomon could understand many things.
>
> –1 KINGS 4:29

4:25 **Dan to Beersheba** Dan was the city farthest north in Israel. Beersheba was the city farthest south. So this means all the people of Israel.

thank the Lord today! He has given David a wise son to rule over this great nation!" ⁸Then Hiram sent back this message to Solomon: "I received the message you sent. I will give you all the cedar and pine trees you want. ⁹My servants will bring them down from Lebanon to the sea. There I will tie them together. Then I will float them down the shore to the place you choose. There I will separate the logs, and you can take them away. In return you will give food to all those who live with me." ¹⁰So Hiram gave Solomon as much cedar and pine as he wanted. ¹¹And Solomon gave Hiram about 125,000 bushels of wheat each year. It was to feed all those who lived with Hiram. And Solomon gave him about 115,000 gallons of pure olive oil every year.

¹²The Lord gave wisdom to Solomon as he had promised. And there was peace between Hiram and Solomon. These two kings made a treaty between themselves.

¹³King Solomon forced 30,000 men of Israel to help in this work. ¹⁴He put a man named Adoniram over them. Solomon sent a group of 10,000 men each month to Lebanon. So each group worked in Lebanon one month. Then it went home for two months. ¹⁵Solomon forced 80,000 men to work in the hill country, cutting stone. And he had 70,000 men to carry the stones. ¹⁶There were also 3,300 men who directed the workers. ¹⁷King Solomon commanded them to cut large blocks of fine stone. These were to be used for the foundation of the Temple. ¹⁸Solomon's and Hiram's builders and the men from Byblos carved the stones. They prepared the stones and the logs for building the Temple.

SOLOMON BUILDS THE TEMPLE

6 So Solomon began to build the Temple. This was 480 years after the people of Israel had left Egypt. (This was the fourth year of King Solomon's rule over Israel.) It was the second month, the month of Ziv.

²The Temple was 90 feet long and 30 feet wide. It was 45 feet high. ³The porch in front of the main room of the Temple was 15 feet deep and 30 feet wide. The room ran along the front of the Temple itself. Its width was equal to the width of the Temple. ⁴There were narrow windows in the Temple. These windows were narrow on the outside and larger on the inside. ⁵Then Solomon built some side rooms against the walls of the main room of the Temple. These rooms were built on top of each other. ⁶The rooms on the bottom floor were 7½ feet wide. The rooms on the middle floor were 9 feet wide. The rooms above that were 10½ feet wide. The Temple wall which made the side of each room was thinner than the wall in the room below. The rooms were pushed against the wall but did not have their main beams built into the wall.

⁷The stones were prepared at the same place they were cut from the ground. Only these stones were used to build the Temple. So there was no noise of hammers, axes or any other iron tools at the Temple.

⁸The entrance to the bottom rooms built beside the Temple was on the south side. From there, stairs went up to the second floor rooms. And from there, they went on to the third floor rooms. ⁹Solomon put a roof made from beams and cedar boards on the Temple. So he finished building the Temple. ¹⁰He also finished building the bottom floor that was beside the Temple. It was 7½ feet high. It was attached to the Temple by cedar beams.

¹¹The Lord spoke his word to Solomon: ¹²"Obey all my laws and commands. If you do, I will do for you what I promised your father David. ¹³And I will live among the children of Israel in this Temple you are building. I will never leave the people of Israel."

¹⁴So Solomon finished building the

Temple. ¹⁵The inside walls were covered from floor to ceiling with cedar boards. The floor was made from pine boards. ¹⁶A room 30 feet long was built in the back part of the Temple. It was divided from the rest of the Temple by cedar boards reaching from floor to ceiling. It was called the Most Holy Place. ¹⁷The main room, the room in front of the Most Holy Place, was 60 feet long. ¹⁸Inside the Temple was cedar. It was carved with pictures of flowers and plants. Everything inside was covered with cedar. So a person could not see the stones of the wall.

¹⁹He prepared the inner room at the back of the Temple to keep the Ark of the Covenant with the Lord. ²⁰This inner room was 30 feet long, 30 feet wide and 30 feet high. Solomon covered this room with pure gold. He built an altar of cedar and covered it also. ²¹He covered the inside of the Temple with pure gold. And he placed gold chains across the front of the inner room. It was covered with gold. ²²So all the inside of the Temple was covered with gold. Also the altar in the Most Holy Place was covered with gold.

²³Solomon made two creatures with wings from olive wood. Each creature was 15 feet tall. They were put in the Most Holy Place. ²⁴Each creature had two wings. Each wing was 7½ feet long. So it was 15 feet from the end of one wing to the end of the other wing. ²⁵The creatures were the same size and shape. ²⁶And each was 15 feet tall. ²⁷These creatures were put beside each other in the Most Holy Place. Their wings were spread out. So one creature's wing touched one wall. The other creature's wing touched the other wall. And their wings touched each other in the middle of the room. ²⁸The two creatures were covered with gold.

²⁹All the walls around the Temple were carved. They were carved with pictures of creatures with wings, palm trees and flowers. This was true for both the main room and the inner room. ³⁰The floors of both rooms were covered with gold.

³¹Doors made from olive wood were put at the entrance to the Most Holy Place. The doors were made to fit into an area with five sides. ³²Creatures with wings, palm trees and flowers were carved on the two olive wood doors. Then the doors were covered with gold. And the creatures and the palm trees were covered with gold. ³³At the entrance to the main room there was a door frame. It was square and was made of olive wood. ³⁴Two doors were made from pine. Each door had two parts so that the doors folded. ³⁵The doors were covered with pictures of creatures with wings, palm trees and flowers. And all of the carvings were covered with gold. The gold was smoothed over the carvings.

³⁶The inner courtyard was built and enclosed with walls. The walls were made of three rows of cut stones and one row of cedar boards.

³⁷Work began on the Temple in Ziv, the second month. This was during the fourth year Solomon ruled over Israel. ³⁸The Temple was finished during the eleventh year Solomon ruled. It was finished in the eighth month, the month of Bul. It was finished exactly as it was planned. Solomon had worked seven years to build the Temple.

SOLOMON'S PALACE

7 King Solomon also built a palace for himself. It took him 13 years to finish building it. ²He built the Palace of the Forest of Lebanon. It was 150 feet long, 75 feet wide and 45 feet high. It had four rows of cedar columns. They supported the cedar beams. ³The ceiling was covered with cedar above the beams. There were 45 beams on the roof, with 15 beams in each row. ⁴Windows were placed in three rows facing each other. ⁵All the doors were square. The three doors at each end faced each other.

⁶Solomon also built the porch of

pillars. It was 75 feet long and 45 feet wide. Along the front of the porch, there was a covering supported by pillars.

⁷Solomon also built a throne room where he judged people. He called this the Hall of Justice. The room was covered with cedar from the floor to the ceiling. ⁸The palace where Solomon was to live was behind the Hall of Justice. And it was built like the Hall of Justice. Solomon also built the same kind of palace for his wife. She was the daughter of the king of Egypt.

⁹All these buildings were made with blocks of carefully cut fine stone. Then they were trimmed with a saw in the front and back. These fine stones went from the foundations of the buildings to the top of the walls. Even the courtyard was made with blocks of stone. ¹⁰The foundations were made with large blocks of fine stone. Some of the stones were 15 feet long. Others were 12 feet long. ¹¹On top of those stones there were other cut blocks of fine stone and cedar beams. ¹²The palace courtyard, the courtyard inside the Temple and the porch to the Temple were surrounded by walls. All of these walls had three rows of cut stone blocks and one row of cedar beams.

THE TEMPLE IS COMPLETED INSIDE

¹³King Solomon sent to Tyre and had Huram brought to him. ¹⁴Huram's mother was a widow from the tribe of Naphtali. His father was from Tyre and had been skilled in making things from bronze. Huram was also very skilled and experienced in bronze work. So he came to King Solomon. And he did all the bronze work Solomon wanted.

¹⁵He made two bronze pillars. Each one was 27 feet tall and 18 feet around. ¹⁶He also made two bronze capitals that were 7½ feet tall. He put them on top of the pillars. ¹⁷Then he made a net of seven chains for each capital. They covered the capitals on top of the two pillars. ¹⁸Then he made two rows of bronze pomegranates to go on the nets. They were to cover the capitals at the top of the pillars. ¹⁹The capitals on top of the pillars in the porch were shaped like lilies. They were 6 feet tall. ²⁰The capitals were on top of both pillars. They were above the bowl-shaped section and next to the nets. At that place there were 200 pomegranates in rows all around the capitals. ²¹Huram put these two bronze pillars at the porch of the Temple. He named the south pillar He Establishes. And he named the north pillar In Him Is Strength. ²²The capitals on top of the pillars were shaped like lilies. So the work on the pillars was finished.

²³Then Huram made a large round bowl from bronze, which was called the Sea. It was 45 feet around. It was 15 feet across and 7½ feet deep. ²⁴There was a rim around the outer edge of the bowl. Under this rim there were two rows of bronze plants surrounding the bowl. There were ten plants in every 18 inches. They were made in one piece with the bowl. ²⁵The bowl rested on the backs of 12 bronze bulls. They faced outward from the center of the bowl. Three bulls faced north, 3 faced east, 3 faced south and 3 faced west. ²⁶The sides of the bowl were 4 inches thick. The rim was like the rim of a cup or like a lily blossom. The bowl held about 11,000 gallons.

²⁷Then Huram made ten bronze stands. Each one was 6 feet long, 6 feet wide and 4½ feet high. ²⁸The stands were made from square sides, which were put on frames. ²⁹On the sides were bronze lions, bulls and creatures with wings. On the frames above and below the lions and bulls there were designs of flowers hammered into the bronze. ³⁰Each stand had four bronze wheels with bronze axles. At the corners there were bronze supports for a large bowl. The supports had designs of flowers. ³¹There was a frame on top of the bowls. It was 18 inches high

above the bowls. The opening of the bowl was round, 27 inches deep. There were designs carved into the bronze on the frame. The frame was square, not round. 32 The four wheels were under the frame. They were 27 inches high. The axles between the wheels were made as one piece with the stand. 33 The wheels were like a chariot's wheels. Everything on the wheels was made of bronze. The axles, rims, spokes and hubs were made of bronze.

34 The four supports were on the four corners of each stand. They were made as one piece with the stand. 35 There was a strip of bronze around the top of each stand. It was 9 inches deep. It was made as one piece with the stand. 36 The sides of the stand and the frames were totally covered with carvings. They were carved with pictures of creatures with wings, lions and palm trees. There were also flowers carved all around. 37 So this is the way Huram made the ten stands. The bronze for each stand was melted and poured into a mold. So all of the stands were the same size and shape.

38 Huram also made ten bronze bowls. There was one bowl for each of the ten stands. Each bowl was six feet across and could hold about 230 gallons. 39 Huram put five of the stands on the south side of the Temple. And he put the other five stands on the north side. He put the large bowl in the southeast corner of the Temple. 40 Huram also made bowls, shovels and small bowls.

So Huram finished making everything King Solomon wanted him to make. Here is a list of what Huram made for the Temple of the Lord:

41 two pillars;
  two large bowls for the capitals on top of the pillars;
  two nets to cover the two large bowls for the capitals on top of the pillars;
42 400 pomegranates for the two nets (there were two rows of pomegranates for each net

covering the bowls for the capitals on top of the pillars);
43 ten stands with a bowl on each stand;
44 the large bowl with 12 bulls under it;
45 the pots, shovels, small bowls and all the dishes for the Temple of the Lord.

Huram made everything King Solomon wanted. They were all made from polished bronze. 46 The king ordered these things to be made near the Jordan River between Succoth and Zarethan. They were made by melting and pouring bronze into clay molds. 47 Solomon never weighed the bronze used to make these things. There was too much to weigh. So the total weight of all the bronze was never known.

48 Solomon also commanded that many things be made of gold for the Temple:

the golden altar;
the golden table which held the bread that shows God's people are in his presence;
49 the lampstands of pure gold (five on the right side and five on the left side in front of the Most Holy Place);
the gold flowers, lamps and tongs;
50 the pure gold bowls, wick trimmers, small bowls, pans and dishes used to carry coals;
the hinges for the doors of the Most Holy Place and the main room of the Temple.

51 So the work King Solomon did for the Temple of the Lord was finished. David, Solomon's father, had saved silver, gold and other articles for the Temple. So Solomon brought these things into the Temple. And he put them into the treasuries of the Temple of the Lord.

THE ARK OF THE COVENANT IS BROUGHT INTO THE TEMPLE

8 Then King Solomon called for all the leaders of Israel to come to him

in Jerusalem. He called for the elders, the heads of the tribes and the leaders of the families. He wanted them to bring the Ark of the Covenant with the Lord from the older part of the city. ²So all the men of Israel came together with King Solomon. This was during a festival in the month of Ethanim. That is the seventh month.

³All of the elders of Israel arrived. Then the priests took up the Ark of the Covenant. ⁴They carried the Ark of the Covenant of the Lord, the Meeting Tent and the holy things in it. The Levites helped the priests carry these things. ⁵King Solomon and all the people of Israel gathered before the Ark of the Covenant. They sacrificed so many sheep and cattle no one could count them all. ⁶Then the priests put the Ark of the Covenant with the Lord in its right place. This was inside the Most Holy Place in the Temple. The Ark of the Covenant was put under the wings of the golden creatures. ⁷The wings of the creatures were spread out over the place of the Ark of the Covenant. So they covered it and its carrying poles. ⁸The carrying poles were very long. Anyone standing in the Holy Place in front of the Most Holy Place could see the ends of the poles. But no one could see them from outside the Holy Place. The poles are still there today. ⁹The only things inside the Ark of the Covenant were two stone tablets.ⁿ Moses had put them in the Ark of the Covenant at Mount Sinai. That was where the Lord made his agreement with the Israelites after they came out of Egypt.

¹⁰When the priests left the Holy Place, the cloud filled the Temple of the Lord.

¹¹The priests could not continue their work. This was because the Temple was filled with the glory of the Lord.

SOLOMON SPEAKS TO THE PEOPLE

¹²Then Solomon said, "The Lord said he would live in a dark cloud. ¹³Lord, I have truly built a wonderful Temple for you. It is a place for you to live forever."

¹⁴While all the people of Israel were standing there, King Solomon turned to them and blessed them.

¹⁵Then he prayed: "Praise the Lord, the God of Israel. He himself has done what he promised to my father David. The Lord told my father, ¹⁶'I brought my people Israel out of Egypt. But I have not yet chosen a city in any tribe of Israel where a temple will be built for worshiping me. But I have chosen David to rule over my people Israel.' ¹⁷'My father David wanted to build a temple for worshiping the Lord, the God of Israel. ¹⁸But the Lord said to my father David, 'I know you want to build a temple for worshiping me. And this is good. ¹⁹But you are not the one to build the temple. It will be your son, who comes from your own body. He is the one who will build my temple.'

²⁰"So the Lord has kept the promise that he gave. I am the king now in place of David my father. Now I rule Israel as the Lord promised. And I have built the Temple for worshiping the Lord, the God of Israel. ²¹I have made a place in the Temple for the Ark of the Covenant. Inside that Ark is the agreement the Lord made with our ancestors. He made that agreement when he brought them out of Egypt."

> Praise the Lord, the God of Israel. He himself has done what he promised.
>
> –1 KINGS 8:15

8:9 stone tablets They were the two tablets on which God wrote the Ten Commandments.

SOLOMON'S PRAYER

²²Then Solomon stood facing the Lord's altar. All of the people of Israel were standing behind him. He spread out his hands and looked toward the sky. ²³He said:

"Lord, God of Israel, there is no god like you. There is no god like you in heaven above or on the earth below. You make agreements with your people because you love them. And you keep your agreements with those who truly follow you. ²⁴You have kept the promise you made to your servant David, my father. You made that promise with your own mouth. And with your great power you have made it come true today. ²⁵Now Lord, God of Israel, keep the other promises you made to your servant David, my father. You said, 'Your sons must be careful to obey me as you have obeyed me. If they do this, there will always be someone from your family ruling Israel.' ²⁶Again, Lord, God of Israel, I ask you. Please continue to keep that promise you made to my father.

²⁷"But, God, can you really live here on the earth? Even the sky and the highest place in heaven cannot contain you. Certainly this house which I have built cannot contain you either. ²⁸But please listen to my prayer and my request. I am your servant, and you are the Lord my God. Hear this prayer I am praying to you today. ²⁹In the past you said, 'I will be worshiped there.' So please watch over this Temple night and day. Hear the prayer I pray to you here. ³⁰Hear my prayers and the prayers of your people Israel. Please hear us when we pray facing this place. Hear us from your home in heaven. And when you hear us, forgive us.

³¹"If a person does something wrong against someone else, he will be brought to the altar in this Temple. If he swears an oath that he is not guilty, ³²then hear in heaven. Judge the man. Punish the guilty person for what he has done. And declare that the innocent person is not guilty.

³³"Sometimes your people of Israel will sin against you. Because of this their enemies will defeat them. Then the people will come back to you and praise you. They will pray to you in this Temple. ³⁴Please hear them in heaven. Forgive the sins of your people Israel. Allow them to have their land again. This is the land you gave to their ancestors.

³⁵"Sometimes when they sin against you, you will stop the rain from falling on their land. Then they will pray, facing this place. They will praise you. They will stop sinning when you make them suffer. ³⁶When this happens, please hear their prayer in heaven. Then forgive the sins of your servant. And forgive the sins of the people of Israel. Teach them to do what is right. Then please send rain to this land you gave them.

³⁷"At times the land will become so dry that no food will grow. Or, a great sickness will spread among the people. Sometimes all the crops will be destroyed by locusts or grasshoppers. Your people will be attacked in their cities by their enemies. Your people will become sick. ³⁸When any of these things happen, the people will become truly sorry. If anyone of your people Israel spreads his hands in prayer toward this Temple, ³⁹please hear his prayer. Hear it from your home in heaven. Then forgive the people and help them. Only you know what people are really thinking. So judge each person, and do to him what is right. ⁴⁰Do this so your people will respect you all the time they live in this land. This is the land you gave to our ancestors.

⁴¹⁻⁴²"People who are not Israelites, who come from other lands, will hear about your greatness and power. They will come from far away to pray at this Temple. ⁴³Please hear their prayers from your home in heaven. Please do whatever they ask you. Then people everywhere will know you and respect you, as your people in Israel do. Then

everyone will know I built this Temple for worship to you.

⁴⁴"Sometimes you will command your people to go and fight against their enemies. Then your people will pray to you facing this city which you have chosen. They will pray facing the Temple I have built for your worship. ⁴⁵When they pray, hear their prayers from your home in heaven. Then help them.

⁴⁶"Everyone sins. So your people will also sin against you. And you will become angry with your people. You will let their enemies defeat them. Their enemies will make them prisoners and carry them away to their own countries. ⁴⁷Your people might be sorry for their sins when they are held as prisoners in another country. Perhaps they will be sorry and pray to you in the land where they are held as prisoners. They might say, 'We have sinned and done wrong.' ⁴⁸They may truly turn back to you in the land of their enemies. Perhaps they will pray to you, facing this land you gave their fathers. They may pray to you, facing this city you have chosen. They may face this Temple I have built for your worship. ⁴⁹If they do, then please hear them from your home in heaven. Hear their prayers and do what is right. ⁵⁰Forgive your people of all their sins. And forgive them for turning against you. Make those who have taken them as prisoners show them mercy. ⁵¹Remember that they are your people. Remember that you brought them out of Egypt. It was as if you pulled them out of a blazing furnace!

⁵²"Please give your attention to my prayers. And please give your attention to the prayers of your people Israel. Listen to their prayers anytime they ask you for help. ⁵³You chose them from all the nations on earth to be your very own people. This is what you promised through Moses your servant. You promised it when you brought our ancestors out of Egypt, Lord God."

⁵⁴Solomon prayed this prayer to the Lord. He had been kneeling in front of the altar. And his arms had been raised toward heaven. When Solomon finished praying, he stood up. ⁵⁵Then, in a loud voice, he blessed all the people of Israel. Solomon said: ⁵⁶"Praise the Lord! He promised he would give rest to his people Israel. And he has given us rest! The Lord has kept all the good promises he gave through his servant Moses. ⁵⁷I ask that the Lord our God be with us. May he be with us as he was with our ancestors. May he never leave us. ⁵⁸May he cause us to turn to him and follow him. May we obey all the laws and commands he gave our ancestors. ⁵⁹I ask that the Lord our God always remember this prayer. I pray that he will help his servant and his people Israel. I pray he will help us every day as we need it. ⁶⁰Then all the people of the world will know the Lord is the only true God. ⁶¹So you must fully obey the Lord our God. You must follow all his laws and commands. You must continue to obey in the future as you do now."

SACRIFICES ARE OFFERED

⁶²Then King Solomon and all Israel with him offered sacrifices to the Lord. ⁶³Solomon killed 22,000 cattle and 120,000 sheep. These were fellowship offerings. In this way the king and the Israelites showed they had given the Temple to the Lord.

⁶⁴Also that day King Solomon made the courtyard before the Temple holy. He offered whole burnt sacrifices and grain offerings. He also offered the fat from the fellowship offerings. He had to make these offerings in the courtyard. This was because the bronze altar before the Lord was too small. It could not hold all the offerings.

⁶⁵So King Solomon and all the people of Israel also celebrated the other festival that came at that time. People came from as far away as Lebo Hamath in the north. And they came from as far as the brook of Egypt in the south. A great many people were there. They ate, drank and rejoiced before the Lord for a total of 14 days. ⁶⁶On the following

day Solomon sent the people home. So they blessed the king and went home. They were happy because of all the good things the Lord had done for his servant David and for his people, Israel.

THE LORD APPEARS TO SOLOMON AGAIN

9 So Solomon finished building the Temple of the Lord and his royal palace. Solomon finished building everything he wanted to build. ²Then the Lord appeared to him again. This was just as he had done before, in Gibeon. ³The Lord said to him: "I have heard your prayer. I have heard what you asked me to do. You built this Temple. And I have made it a holy place. So I will be worshiped there forever. I will watch over it and protect it always.

⁴"But you must serve me as your father David did. He was fair and sincere. You must obey my laws and do everything I command. ⁵If you do these things, I will allow your family to rule Israel forever. I made this promise to your father David. I told him that someone from his family would always be king over Israel.

⁶"But you and your children must follow me. You must obey the laws and commands I have given you. You must not go off to serve or worship other gods. ⁷If you do, I will force Israel to leave the land I have given them. I made the Temple holy for people to worship me there. But if you don't obey me, I will tear it down. Then Israel will become a bad example, a joke, to other people. ⁸If the Temple is destroyed, everyone who sees it will be shocked. They will make fun of you and ask, 'Why did the Lord do this? Why did he do this terrible

thing to this land and this Temple?' ⁹Other people will answer, 'This happened because they left the Lord their God. He brought their ancestors out of Egypt. But they decided to follow other gods. They worshiped and served those gods. That is why the Lord brought all this disaster to them.'"

SOLOMON'S OTHER ACTIVITIES

¹⁰By the end of 20 years, King Solomon had built the Temple of the Lord. And he had built the royal palace. ¹¹At that time King Solomon gave 20 towns in Galilee to Hiram king of Tyre. Solomon did this because Hiram had helped with the buildings. Hiram had given him all the cedar, pine and gold he wanted. ¹²So Hiram traveled from Tyre to see the towns Solomon had given him. When Hiram saw them, he was not pleased. ¹³He asked, "What are these towns you have given me, my brother?" So he named that land the Land of Cabul.ⁿ And it is still called that today. ¹⁴Hiram had sent to King Solomon about 9,000 pounds of gold.

¹⁵King Solomon had forced slaves to build the Temple and the palace. Then he had them fill in the land on the east side of the city. And he had them build the wall around Jerusalem. He also had them rebuild the cities of Hazor, Megiddo and Gezer. ¹⁶(In the past the king of Egypt had attacked Gezer and captured it. He had burned it and killed the Canaanites who lived there. Then he gave it to his daughter as a wedding present. His daughter married Solomon. ¹⁷So Solomon rebuilt it.) He also built the cities of Lower Beth Horon, ¹⁸Baalath and Tadmor, which is in the Judean

> They were happy because of all the good things the Lord had done . . . for his people, Israel
>
> –1 KINGS 8:66

9:13 **Cabul** This name sounds like the Hebrew word for "worthless."

desert. ¹⁹King Solomon also built cities where he could store grain and supplies. And he built cities for his chariots and chariot soldiers. Solomon built whatever he wanted in Jerusalem, Lebanon and everywhere he ruled.

²⁰There were people in the land who were not Israelites. There were some Amorites, Hittites, Perizzites, Hivites and Jebusites. ²¹The Israelites had not been able to destroy them from the land. So Solomon forced them to work for him as slaves. And they are still slaves today. ²²But Solomon did not force any Israelites to be his slaves. The Israelites were his soldiers, government leaders, officers, captains and chariot commanders and drivers.

²³There were 550 supervisors over Solomon's projects. They were supervisors over the men who did the work.

²⁴The daughter of the king of Egypt moved from the old part of Jerusalem to the palace. This was the palace Solomon had built for her. Then Solomon filled in the land on the east side of the city.

²⁵Three times each year Solomon offered whole burnt offerings and fellowship offerings on the altar. This is the altar he had built for the Lord. Solomon also burned incense before the Lord. So he finished the work on the Temple.

²⁶Solomon also built ships at Ezion Geber. This town is near Elath. It is on the shore of the Gulf of Aqaba, in the land of Edom. ²⁷King Hiram had sailors who knew much about the sea. So he sent them to serve in Solomon's ships with Solomon's men. ²⁸Solomon's ships sailed to Ophir. From there they brought back about 32,000 pounds of gold to King Solomon.

THE QUEEN OF SHEBA VISITS SOLOMON

10 Now the queen of Sheba heard about Solomon's fame. So she came to test him with hard questions. ²She traveled to Jerusalem with a very large group of servants. There were many camels carrying spices, jewels and much gold. She came to Solomon and talked with him about all that she had in mind. ³Solomon answered all her questions. Nothing was too hard for him to explain to her. ⁴The queen of Sheba learned that Solomon was very wise. She saw the palace he had built. ⁵She saw his many officers and the food on his table. She saw the palace servants and their good clothes. She was shown the servants who served him at feasts. And she was shown the whole burnt offerings he made in the Temple of the Lord. All these things amazed her.

⁶So she said to King Solomon, "I heard in my own country about your achievements and wisdom. And all of it is true. ⁷I could not believe it then. But now I have come and seen it with my own eyes. I was not told even half of it! Your wisdom and wealth are much greater than I had heard. ⁸Your men and officers are very lucky! In always serving you, they are able to hear your wisdom! ⁹Praise the Lord your God! He was pleased to make you king of Israel. The Lord has constant love for Israel. So he made you king to keep justice and to rule fairly."

¹⁰Then the queen of Sheba gave the king about 9,000 pounds of gold. She also gave him many spices and jewels. No one since that time has brought more spices into Israel than the queen of Sheba gave King Solomon.

¹¹(Hiram's ships brought gold from Ophir. They also brought from there very much juniper wood and jewels. ¹²Solomon used the juniper wood to build supports for the Temple of the Lord and the palace. He also used it to make harps and lyres for the musicians. Such fine juniper wood has not been brought in or seen since that time.)

¹³King Solomon gave the queen of Sheba many gifts. He gave her gifts that a king would give to another ruler. Then he gave her whatever else she wanted

and asked for. After this, she and her servants went back to her own country.

SOLOMON'S WEALTH

[14]Every year King Solomon received about 50,000 pounds of gold. [15]Besides that he also received gold from the traders and merchants. And he received gold from the kings of Arabia and governors of the land.

[16]King Solomon made 200 large shields of hammered gold. Each shield contained about seven and one-half pounds of gold. [17]He also made 300 smaller shields of hammered gold. They each contained about three and three-fourths pounds of gold. The king put them in the Palace of the Forest of Lebanon.

[18]Then King Solomon built a large throne of ivory. And he covered it with pure gold. [19]There were six steps leading up to the throne. The back of the throne was round at the top. There were armrests on both sides of the chair. And beside each armrest was a statue of a lion. [20]Twelve lions stood on the six steps. There was one lion at each end of each step. Nothing like this had ever been made for any other kingdom. [21]All of Solomon's drinking cups were made of gold. All of the dishes in the Palace of the Forest of Lebanon were pure gold. Nothing was made from silver. In Solomon's time people did not think silver was valuable.

[22]King Solomon also had many trading ships at sea, along with Hiram's ships. Every three years the ships returned. They brought back gold, silver, ivory, apes and baboons.

[23]So Solomon had more riches and wisdom than all the other kings on earth. [24]People everywhere wanted to see King Solomon. They wanted to hear the wisdom God had given him. [25]Every year everyone who came brought a gift. They brought things made of gold and silver, along with clothes, weapons, spices, horses and mules.

[26]So Solomon had many chariots and horses. He had 1,400 chariots and 12,000 chariot soldiers. He kept some in special cities for the chariots. And he kept some with him in Jerusalem. [27]In Jerusalem silver was as common as stones while Solomon was king. Cedar trees were as common as the fig trees growing on the mountain slopes. [28]Solomon brought in horses from Egypt and Kue. His traders bought them in Kue and brought them to Israel. [29]A chariot from Egypt cost about 15 pounds of silver. And a horse cost about 3¾ pounds of silver. The traders also sold horses and chariots to the kings of the Hittites and the Arameans.

SOLOMON'S MANY WIVES

11 But King Solomon loved many women who were not from Israel. He loved the daughter of the king of Egypt. He also loved women of the Moabites, Ammonites, Edomites, Sidonians and Hittites. [2]The Lord had told the Israelites, "You must not marry people of other nations. If you do, they will cause you to follow their gods." But Solomon fell in love with these women. [3]He had 700 wives who were from royal families. He also had 300 slave women who gave birth to his children. His wives caused him to turn away from God. [4]As Solomon grew old, his wives caused him to follow other gods. He did not follow the Lord completely as his father David had done. [5]Solomon worshiped Ashtoreth, the goddess of the people of Sidon. And he worshiped Molech, the hated god of the Ammonites. [6]So Solomon did what the Lord said was wrong. He did not follow the Lord completely as his father David had done.

[7]On a hill east of Jerusalem, Solomon built two places for worship. He built a place to worship Chemosh, the hated god of the Moabites. And he built a place to worship Molech, the hated god of the Ammonites. [8]Solomon did the same thing for all of his foreign wives.

So they burned incense and gave sacrifices to their gods.

⁹The Lord had appeared to Solomon twice. But Solomon turned away from following the Lord, the God of Israel. So the Lord was angry with him. ¹⁰The Lord had commanded Solomon not to follow other gods. But Solomon did not obey the Lord's command. ¹¹So the Lord said to Solomon, "You have chosen to break your agreement with me. You have not obeyed my commands. So I promise I will tear your kingdom away from you. I will give it to one of your officers. ¹²But I will not take it away while you are alive. This is because of my love for your father David. I will tear it away from your son when he becomes king. ¹³But I will not tear away all the kingdom from him. I will leave him one tribe to rule. I will do this because of David, my servant. And I will do it because of Jerusalem, the city I have chosen."

SOLOMON'S ENEMIES

¹⁴Now Hadad was a member of the family of the king of Edom. And the Lord caused Hadad the Edomite to become Solomon's enemy. ¹⁵Earlier, David had defeated Edom. Joab, the commander of David's army, went into Edom to bury the dead. While he was there, he killed all the males. ¹⁶Joab and all the Israelites stayed in Edom for six months. During that time they killed every male in Edom. ¹⁷But at that time Hadad was only a young boy. So he ran away to Egypt with some of his father's officers. ¹⁸They left Midian and went to Paran. In Paran other men joined them. Then they all went to Egypt to see the king. He gave Hadad a house, some land and food to eat. ¹⁹The king liked Hadad so much he gave Hadad a wife. She was the sister of

Tahpenes, the king's wife. ²⁰They had a son named Genubath. Queen Tahpenes allowed him to grow up in the royal palace. So he grew up with the king's own children.

²¹While he was in Egypt, Hadad heard that David had died. He also heard that Joab, the commander of the army, was dead. So Hadad said to the king, "Let me go home. Let me return to my own country."

²²But the king said, "Why do you want to go back to your own country? What haven't I given you here?"

Hadad answered, "Nothing. But please, let me go."

²³God also caused another man to be an enemy to Solomon. This man was Rezon son of Eliada. Rezon had run away from his master, Hadadezer king of Zobah. ²⁴After David defeated the army of Zobah, Rezon gathered some men. He became the leader of a small army. They went to Damascus and settled there. And Rezon became king of Damascus. ²⁵Rezon ruled Aram, and he hated Israel. So he was an enemy of Israel all the time Solomon was alive. Rezon and Hadad caused some trouble for Israel.

²⁶Jeroboam son of Nebat was one of Solomon's officers. Jeroboam was one of the Ephraimite people. He was from the town of Zeredah. His mother was a widow named Zeruah. He turned against the king.

²⁷This is the story of how Jeroboam turned against the king. Solomon was filling in the land on the east side of Jerusalem. He was also repairing the wall of Jerusalem. It was the city of David, his ancestor. ²⁸Jeroboam was a capable man. Solomon saw that this young man was a good worker. So

> Solomon turned away from following the Lord, the God of Israel.
>
> –1 KINGS 11:9

Solomon put him over all the workers from the tribes of Ephraim and Manasseh.

²⁹One day Jeroboam was leaving Jerusalem. Ahijah, the prophet from Shiloh, met him on the road. Ahijah was wearing a new coat. The two men were alone out in the country. ³⁰Ahijah took his new coat and tore it into 12 pieces. ³¹Then he said to Jeroboam, "Take 10 pieces of this coat for yourself. The Lord, the God of Israel, says: 'I will tear the kingdom away from Solomon. Then I will give you 10 tribes. ³²But I will allow the family of David to control 1 tribe. I will do this for my servant David and for Jerusalem. Jerusalem is the city I have chosen from all the tribes of Israel. ³³I will do this because Solomon has stopped following me. He worships the Sidonian god Ashtoreth and the Moabite god Chemosh. He also worships Molech, the Ammonite god. Solomon has not obeyed me. He has not done what I said is right. He has not obeyed my laws and commands. He is not living the way his father David lived.

³⁴"'But I will not take all the kingdom away from Solomon. I will let him rule all his life. I will do this because of my servant David. I chose David, and he obeyed all my commands and laws. ³⁵But I will take the kingdom away from his son. Jeroboam, I will allow you to rule over the 10 tribes. ³⁶I will allow Solomon's son to continue to rule over 1 tribe. I will do this so that David, my servant, will always have a king before me in Jerusalem. It is the city where I chose to be worshiped. ³⁷But I will make you rule over everything you want. You will rule over all of Israel. ³⁸I will always be with you if you do what I say is right. You must obey all my commands. If you obey my laws and commands as David did, I will be with you. I will make your family a family of kings, as I did for David. I will give Israel to you. ³⁹I will punish David's children because of this. But I will not punish them forever.'"

SOLOMON'S DEATH

⁴⁰Solomon tried to kill Jeroboam. But Jeroboam ran away to Egypt. He went to Shishak king of Egypt. And Jeroboam stayed there until Solomon died.

⁴¹Everything else Solomon did is written down. He showed much wisdom. It is written in the book of the history of Solomon. ⁴²Solomon ruled in Jerusalem over all Israel for 40 years. ⁴³Then he died and was buried in Jerusalem, the city of David, his father. And his son Rehoboam became king after him.

ISRAEL TURNS AGAINST REHOBOAM

12 Rehoboam went to Shechem because all the Israelites had gone there to make him king. ²Jeroboam son of Nebat was still in Egypt. He had gone there to escape from Solomon. When Jeroboam heard about Rehoboam being made king, Jeroboam returned from Egypt. ³So the people sent for him. Then he and the people went to Rehoboam. They said to Rehoboam, ⁴"Your father forced us to work very hard. Now, make it easier for us. Don't make us work as hard as your father did. Then we will serve you."

⁵Rehoboam answered, "Come back to me in three days. Then I will answer you." So the people left.

⁶Some of the elders had helped Solomon make decisions during his lifetime. So King Rehoboam asked them what he should do. He said, "How do you think I should answer these people?"

⁷They answered, "You should be like a servant to them today. Serve them, and give them a kind answer. If you do, they will serve you always."

⁸But Rehoboam did not listen to this advice. He asked the young men who had grown up with him. They advised him in making decisions. ⁹Rehoboam said, "The people said, 'Don't make us work as hard as your father did.' How do you think I should answer them? What is your advice?"

☆ 1 Kings 12:6, 8

Solomon's son Rehoboam became king of Israel next. The Israelites had worked hard to build God's temple, and they were tired. When Rehoboam became king, the Israelites asked him if they could rest. King Rehoboam went to some of the older men for advice. They gave King Rehoboam good advice. They told him to give the people rest, and the people would love him. But he didn't listen to them. Instead, he asked some of his young friends. They told King Rehoboam to work the people even harder! The Israelites were angry, and many decided to find a new king.

A wise person is someone who knows the difference between good and bad and chooses to be good. Your parents want to help you make good choices. God gave them to you so you can learn from them. Have you ever played the game Follow the Leader—where you copy what the leader does? You should listen to what your parents have to say and follow their lead. Jesus did what his Father, God, asked him to do. You can follow Jesus' example and follow God and your dad.

• •

Older people like your dad, mom, grandparents, or teachers can be very wise. They can help you listen to God and make good decisions.

---

[10]The young men answered, "Those people came to you and said, 'Your father forced us to work very hard. Now make our work easier.' So you should tell them, 'My little finger is bigger than my father's whole body. [11]My father forced you to work hard. But I will make you work even harder! My father beat you with whips. But I will beat you with whips that have sharp points.'"

[12]Rehoboam had told the people, "Come back to me in three days." So after three days all the people returned to Rehoboam. [13]At that time King Rehoboam spoke cruel words to them. He did not listen to the advice that the elders had given him. [14]He did what the young men had told him to do. Rehoboam said, "My father forced you to work hard. So I will give you even more work. My father beat you with whips. But I will beat you with whips that have sharp points." [15]So the king did not do what the people wanted. The Lord caused this to happen. He did this to keep the promise he had

made to Jeroboam son of Nebat. He had made this promise through Ahijah, the prophet from Shiloh.

¹⁶All the people of Israel saw that the new king refused to listen to them. So they said to the king,

"We have no share in David!
  We have no part in the son of Jesse!
People of Israel, let's go to our own
    homes!
  Let David's son rule his own
    people!"

So the Israelites went home. ¹⁷But Rehoboam still ruled over the Israelites who lived in the towns of Judah.

¹⁸Adoniram was in charge of the people who were forced to work. King Rehoboam sent him to the people. But they threw stones at him until he died. But King Rehoboam ran to his chariot and escaped to Jerusalem. ¹⁹Since then, Israel has been against the family of David.

²⁰All the Israelites heard that Jeroboam had returned. So they called him to a meeting. And they made him king over all Israel. But the tribe of Judah continued to follow the family of David.

²¹When Rehoboam arrived in Jerusalem, he gathered the tribes of Judah and Benjamin. This was an army of 180,000 men. Rehoboam wanted to fight against the people of Israel. He wanted to take back his kingdom.

²²But God spoke his word to Shemaiah, a man of God. The Lord said, ²³"Talk to Solomon's son Rehoboam, the king of Judah. Talk also to all the people of Judah and Benjamin and to the rest of the people. ²⁴Say to them, 'The Lord says you must not go to war against your brothers, the Israelites. Every one of you should go home. I made all these things happen!'" So the men in Rehoboam's army obeyed the Lord's command. They all went home as the Lord had commanded.

²⁵Then Jeroboam made Shechem a very strong city. It is in the mountains of Ephraim. And Jeroboam lived there. He also went to the city of Peniel and made it stronger.

JEROBOAM BUILDS GOLDEN CALVES

²⁶Jeroboam said to himself, "The kingdom will probably go back to David's family. ²⁷The people will continue going to the Temple of the Lord in Jerusalem. If they do, they will want to be ruled again by Rehoboam. Then they will kill me and follow Rehoboam king of Judah."

²⁸King Jeroboam asked his men for advice. So he made two golden calves. He said to the people, "It is too hard for you to go to Jerusalem to worship. Israel, here are your gods who brought you out of Egypt." ²⁹King Jeroboam put one golden calf in the city of Bethel. And he put the other in the city of Dan. ³⁰And this became a very great sin. The people traveled as far as Dan to worship the calf there.

³¹Jeroboam built temples on the places of worship. He chose priests from all the people. (He did not choose priests only from the tribe of Levi.) ³²And he started a new festival. It was the fifteenth day of the eighth month. This was like the festival in Judah. During that time the king offered sacrifices on the altar. He offered sacrifices to the calves in Bethel he had made. He also chose priests in Bethel to serve at the places of worship he had made. ³³So Jeroboam chose his own time for a festival for the Israelites. It was the fifteenth day of the eighth month. During that time he offered sacrifices on the altar he had built in Bethel. So he set up a festival for the Israelites. And he offered sacrifices on the altar.

THE MAN OF GOD SPEAKS AGAINST BETHEL

13 The Lord commanded a man of God from Judah to go to Bethel. When he arrived, Jeroboam was

standing by the altar to offer a sacrifice. ²The Lord had commanded the man of God to speak against the altar. The man said, "Altar, the Lord says to you: 'David's family will have a son named Josiah. He will kill the priests of the places of worship. They now make their sacrifices on you. But Josiah will sacrifice those priests on you. Human bones will be burned on you.'" ³The man of God gave proof that these things would happen. He said, "This is God's sign that this will happen. This altar will break apart. And the ashes on it will fall onto the ground."

⁴King Jeroboam heard what the man of God said about the altar in Bethel. So Jeroboam raised his hand from the altar and pointed at the man. "Capture him!" he said. But when the king said this, his arm became paralyzed. He could not move it. ⁵Also, the altar broke into pieces. All its ashes fell onto the ground. This was the sign the Lord had told the man of God to give.

⁶Then the king said to the man of God, "Please pray to the Lord your God for me. Ask him to heal my arm."

So the man of God prayed to the Lord. And the king's arm was healed. It became as it was before.

⁷Then the king said to the man of God, "Please come home and eat with me. I will give you a gift."

⁸But the man of God answered the king, "I will not go home with you! Even if you gave me half of your kingdom, I would not go! I will not eat or drink anything in this place. ⁹The Lord commanded me not to eat or drink anything. He also commanded me not to return on the same road by which I came." ¹⁰So he traveled on a different road. He did not return on the same road by which he had come to Bethel.

¹¹Now there was an old prophet living in Bethel. His sons came and told him what the man of God had done there that day. They told their father what he had said to King Jeroboam. ¹²The father asked, "Which road did he use

when he left?" So his sons showed him which road the man of God from Judah had taken. ¹³The prophet told his sons to put a saddle on his donkey. So they saddled the donkey, and he left.

¹⁴He went after the man of God. He found the man sitting under an oak tree. The prophet asked, "Are you the man of God who came from Judah?"

The man answered, "Yes, I am."

¹⁵So the prophet said, "Please come home and eat with me."

¹⁶But the man of God answered, "I can't go home with you. I can't eat or drink with you in this place. ¹⁷The Lord said to me, 'You must not eat or drink anything there. And you must not return on the same road by which you came.'"

¹⁸Then the old prophet said, "But I also am a prophet like you." Then he told a lie. He said, "An angel from the Lord came to me. He told me to bring you to my home. He said you should eat and drink with me." ¹⁹So the man of God went to the old prophet's house. And he ate and drank with him there.

²⁰While they were sitting at the table, the Lord spoke his word to the old prophet. ²¹The old prophet cried out to the man of God from Judah. He said, "The Lord said you did not obey him! He said you did not do what the Lord your God commanded you. ²²The Lord commanded you not to eat or drink anything in this place. But you came back and ate and drank. So your body will not be buried in your family grave."

²³The man of God finished eating. Then the prophet put a saddle on his donkey for him. And the man left. ²⁴As he was traveling on the road home, a lion attacked and killed him. His body lay on the road. The donkey and the lion stood near it. ²⁵Some men were traveling on that road. They saw the body and the lion standing near it. So they went to the city where the old prophet lived. And they told what they had seen.

²⁶The old prophet who had brought the man of God back heard about what

had happened. He said, "It is the man of God who did not obey the Lord's command. So the Lord sent a lion to kill him. The Lord said he would do this."

²⁷Then the prophet said to his sons, "Put a saddle on my donkey." So they did. ²⁸The old prophet went out and found the body lying on the road. The donkey and the lion were still standing near it. The lion had not eaten the body. And it had not hurt the donkey. ²⁹So the prophet put the body on his donkey. And he carried it back to the city. There he would have a time of sadness for him and bury him. ³⁰The prophet buried the body in his own family grave. And he was sad for the man of God. He said, "Oh, my brother."

³¹So the prophet buried the body. Then he said to his sons, "When I die, bury me in this same grave. Put my bones next to his. ³²Through him the Lord spoke against the altar at Bethel. And he spoke against the places of worship in the towns of Samaria. And what the Lord spoke through him will certainly come true."

³³But King Jeroboam did not stop doing evil things. He continued to choose priests for the places of worship from all the people. Anyone who wanted to be a priest for the places of worship was allowed. ³⁴In this way the kingdom of Jeroboam sinned. And that sin caused its ruin and destruction from the earth.

JEROBOAM'S SON DIES

14 At that time Jeroboam's son Abijah became very sick. ²So Jeroboam said to his wife, "Go to Shiloh. Go to see the prophet Ahijah. He is the one who said I would become king of Israel. But dress yourself so people won't know you are my wife. ³Give the prophet ten loaves of bread, some cakes and a jar of honey. Then ask him what will happen to our son. And he will tell you." ⁴So the king's wife did as he said. She went to Ahijah's home in Shiloh. Now Ahijah was very old and had

become blind. ⁵But the Lord had said to him, "Jeroboam's son is sick. So Jeroboam's wife is coming to ask you about him. When she arrives, she will pretend to be someone else." Then the Lord told Ahijah what to say.

⁶When Ahijah heard her walking to the door, he said, "Come in, wife of Jeroboam. Why are you pretending to be someone else? I have bad news for you. ⁷Go back and tell Jeroboam that this is what the Lord, the God of Israel, says: 'Jeroboam, I chose you from among all the people of Israel. I made you the leader of my people. ⁸I took the kingdom away from David's family. And I gave it to you. But you are not like my servant David. He always obeyed my commands. He followed me with all his heart. He did only the things I said were right. ⁹But you have done more evil things than anyone who ruled before you. You have quit following me. You have made other gods and idols of metal. This has made me very angry. ¹⁰So I will bring disaster to the family of Jeroboam. I will kill all of the men in your family, both slaves and free men. I will destroy your family as completely as fire burns up manure. ¹¹Anyone from your family who dies in the city will be eaten by dogs. And anyone from your family who dies in the fields will be eaten by the birds. The Lord has spoken!'"

¹²Then Ahijah said to Jeroboam's wife, "Now go home. When you enter your city gate, your son will die. ¹³All Israel will be sad for him and bury him. He will be the only one of Jeroboam's family who will be buried. This is because he is the only one in Jeroboam's family who pleased the Lord, the God of Israel.

¹⁴"The Lord will put a new king over Israel. That king will destroy Jeroboam's family. This will happen soon. ¹⁵Then the Lord will punish Israel. The people of Israel will be like grass moving in the water. The Lord will pull up Israel from this good land.

This is the land he gave their ancestors. But he will scatter Israel beyond the Euphrates River. This will happen because the Lord is angry with the people. They made him angry when they made idols to worship Asherah. [16]Jeroboam sinned, and then he made the people of Israel sin. So the Lord will let the people of Israel be defeated."

[17]Then Jeroboam's wife traveled back to Tirzah. When she entered her home, the boy died. [18]They buried him. And all Israel had a time of sadness for him. This happened as the Lord said it would. The Lord had said these things through his servant, the prophet Ahijah.

[19]Everything else Jeroboam did is written down. He fought wars and continued to rule the people. It is all written in the book of the history of the kings of Israel. [20]Jeroboam ruled as king for 22 years. Then he died, and his son Nadab became king in his place.

THE DEATH OF REHOBOAM

[21]Solomon's son Rehoboam was 41 years old when he became king of Judah. His mother was Naamah from the land of Ammon. Rehoboam ruled in Jerusalem for 17 years. (The Lord had chosen that city from all the land of Israel. He chose to be worshiped there.)

[22]The people of Judah did what the Lord said was wrong. The people's sins made the Lord very angry at them. They made the Lord even more angry than their ancestors had done. [23]The people built stone pillars and places to worship false gods and Asherah idols. They built them on every high hill and under every green tree. [24]There were even male prostitutes at the places of worship to the gods. The people who had lived in the land before the Israelites had done many evil things. And God had taken the land away from them. Now the people of Judah were doing the same evil things.

[25]During the fifth year Rehoboam was king, Shishak attacked Jerusalem. Shishak was king of Egypt. [26]He took the treasures from the Temple of the Lord and the king's palace. He took everything, even the gold shields Solomon had made. [27]So King Rehoboam made bronze shields to put in their place. He gave them to the men who were guarding the palace gates. [28]Whenever the king went to the Temple of the Lord, the guards carried the shields. After they were finished, they put the shields back in the guardroom.

[29]Everything else King Rehoboam did is written down. It is in the book of the history of the kings of Judah. [30]Rehoboam and Jeroboam were always fighting a war with each other. [31]Rehoboam died and was buried with his ancestors in Jerusalem. His mother was Naamah from Ammon. And Rehoboam's son Abijam[n] became king in his place.

ABIJAM KING OF JUDAH

15 Abijam became king of Judah. This was during the eighteenth year Jeroboam son of Nebat ruled Israel. [2]And Abijam ruled in Jerusalem for three years. His mother was Maacah daughter of Abishalom. [3]He did all the same sins his father before him had done. Abijam was not faithful to the Lord his God. In this way he was not like David, his great-grandfather. [4]Because the Lord had loved David, the Lord gave Abijam a kingdom in Jerusalem. And the Lord allowed him to have a son to be king after him. The Lord also kept Jerusalem safe. [5]David had always done what the Lord said was right. All his life he had always obeyed the Lord's commands. There was only one time David did not obey the Lord. This was when he sinned against Uriah the Hittite.

[6]Now there was war between Abijam

14:31 **Abijam** A negative name for Abijah. See 2 Chronicles 13.

and Jeroboam during Abijam's lifetime. [7]Everything else Abijam did is written down. It is in the book of the history of the kings of Judah. During the time Abijam ruled, there was war between Abijam and Jeroboam. [8]And Abijam died and was buried in Jerusalem. Abijam's son Asa became king in his place.

ASA KING OF JUDAH

[9]During the twentieth year Jeroboam was king of Israel, Asa became king of Judah. [10]Asa ruled in Jerusalem for 41 years. His grandmother's name was Maacah. She was the daughter of Abishalom.

[11]Asa did what the Lord said was right. This was as his ancestor David had done. [12]There were male prostitutes at the places where false gods were worshiped. Asa forced them to leave the country. He also took away the idols that his ancestors had made. [13]His grandmother Maacah had made a terrible Asherah idol. So Asa removed her from being queen. He cut down this idol and burned it in the Kidron Valley. [14]Asa was faithful to the Lord all his life. But he did not destroy the places where false gods were worshiped. [15]Asa and his father had given some things to God. They had given gifts of gold, silver and other objects. Asa put all these things in the Temple.

[16]There was war between Asa and Baasha king of Israel. [17]Baasha fought against Judah. He wanted to stop people from leaving or entering Asa's country, Judah. So he made the city of Ramah very strong.

[18]Then Asa took all the silver and gold from the treasuries of the Temple of the Lord and his own palace. He gave it to his officers. And he sent them to Ben-Hadad king of Aram. (Ben-Hadad was the son of Tabrimmon. And he was the son of Hezion.) Ben-Hadad was ruling in the city of Damascus. [19]Asa sent this message: "My father and your father had a peace agreement. I am sending you a gift of gold and silver. Break your treaty with Baasha king of Israel so that he will leave my land."

[20]Ben-Hadad agreed with King Asa. So he sent his army to fight against the towns of Israel. He defeated the towns of Ijon, Dan and Abel Bethmaacah. And he defeated all the land near Lake Galilee and the area of Naphtali. [21]Baasha heard about these attacks. So he stopped building up Ramah and returned to Tirzah. [22]Then King Asa gave an order to all the people of Judah. Everyone had to help. They carried away all the stones and wood Baasha had been using in Ramah. King Asa used those things to build up Geba and Mizpah. (Geba was in the land of Benjamin.)

[23]Everything else Asa did is written down. His victories and the cities he built are written down. They are in the book of the history of the kings of Judah. When he became old, he got a disease in his feet. [24]Then Asa died. And he was buried with his ancestors in Jerusalem. It was the city of David, his ancestor. Then Jehoshaphat, Asa's son, became king in his place.

NADAB KING OF ISRAEL

[25]Nadab son of Jeroboam became king of Israel. This was during the second year Asa was king of Judah. And Nadab was king of Israel for two years. [26]He did what the Lord said was wrong. Jeroboam had caused the people of Israel to sin. Nadab sinned in the same way his father Jeroboam had sinned.

> (King) Asa did what the Lord said was right. This was as his ancestor David had done.
> —1 KINGS 15:11

²⁷Baasha son of Ahijah was from the tribe of Issachar. He made plans to kill Nadab. Nadab and all Israel were attacking the Philistine town of Gibbethon. So Baasha killed Nadab there. ²⁸This happened during Asa's third year as king of Judah. And Baasha became the next king of Israel.

BAASHA KING OF ISRAEL

²⁹As soon as Baasha became king, he killed all of Jeroboam's family. He left no one in Jeroboam's family alive. This happened as the Lord had said it would. The Lord had said this through his servant Ahijah from Shiloh. ³⁰This happened because King Jeroboam had sinned very much. And he had caused the people of Israel to sin. Jeroboam had made the Lord, the God of Israel, very angry.

³¹Everything else Nadab did is written down. It is in the book of the history of the kings of Israel. ³²There was war between Asa king of Judah and Baasha king of Israel all the time they were kings.

³³Baasha son of Ahijah became king of Israel. This was during Asa's third year as king of Judah. And Baasha ruled in Tirzah for 24 years. ³⁴But Baasha did what the Lord said was wrong. Jeroboam had caused the people of Israel to sin. And Baasha sinned in the same way Jeroboam had sinned.

16 Then Jehu son of Hanani spoke the word of the Lord against King Baasha. ²The Lord said, "You were nothing. Then I took you and made you a leader over my people Israel. But you have followed the ways of Jeroboam. You have caused my people Israel to sin. Their sins have made me angry. ³So, Baasha, I will destroy you and your family. I will do to you what I did to the family of Jeroboam son of Nebat. ⁴Anyone from your family who dies in the city will be eaten by dogs. And anyone from your family who dies in the fields will be eaten by birds."

⁵Everything else Baasha did and all his victories are written down. They are in the book of the history of the kings of Israel. ⁶So Baasha died and was buried in Tirzah. His son Elah became king in his place.

⁷The Lord spoke his word through the prophet Jehu son of Hanani. The Lord's message was against Baasha and his family. Baasha had done many things the Lord said were wrong. This made the Lord very angry. Baasha did the same things that Jeroboam's family had done before him. The Lord was also angry because Baasha killed all of Jeroboam's family.

ELAH KING OF ISRAEL

⁸Elah son of Baasha became king of Israel. This was during Asa's twenty-sixth year as king of Judah. And Elah ruled in Tirzah for two years.

⁹Zimri was one of Elah's officers. He commanded half of Elah's chariots. But Zimri made plans against Elah. Elah was in Tirzah, getting drunk at Arza's home. (Arza was the man in charge of the palace at Tirzah.) ¹⁰So Zimri went into Arza's house and killed Elah. This was during Asa's twenty-seventh year as king of Judah. Then Zimri became king of Israel in Elah's place.

ZIMRI KING OF ISRAEL

¹¹As soon as Zimri became king, he killed all of Baasha's family. He did not let any man of Baasha's family or friends live. ¹²So Zimri destroyed all of

> (King Baasha and his son) sinned and caused the people of Israel to sin.
> —1 KINGS 16:13

Baasha's family. This happened as the Lord had said it would. The Lord had spoken this against Baasha through the prophet Jehu. ¹³This happened because of all the sins of Baasha and his son Elah. They sinned and caused the people of Israel to sin. They also made the Lord, the God of Israel, angry because they had made worthless idols.

¹⁴Everything else Elah did is written down. It is in the book of the history of the kings of Israel.

¹⁵So Zimri became king of Israel. This was during Asa's twenty-seventh year as king of Judah. Zimri ruled in Tirzah seven days. This is what happened:

The army of Israel was camped near Gibbethon, a Philistine town. ¹⁶The men in the camp heard that Zimri had made secret plans against the king. And they heard that Zimri had killed him. So that day in the camp they made Omri king over Israel. (Omri was commander of the army.) ¹⁷So Omri and all the Israelites left Gibbethon and attacked Tirzah. ¹⁸Zimri saw that the city had been captured. So he went into the palace and set it on fire. He burned the palace and himself with it. ¹⁹So Zimri died because he had sinned. He did what the Lord said was wrong. Jeroboam had caused the people of Israel to sin. And Zimri sinned in the same way Jeroboam had sinned.

²⁰Everything else Zimri did is written down. It is in the book of the history of the kings of Israel. The story of how Zimri turned against King Elah is also written there.

OMRI KING OF ISRAEL

²¹The people of Israel were divided into two groups. Half of the people wanted Tibni to be king. He was the son of Ginath. The other half of the people wanted Omri. ²²But Omri's followers were stronger than the followers of Tibni son of Ginath. So Tibni died, and Omri became king.

²³Omri became king of Israel. This was during the thirty-first year Asa was king of Judah. And Omri ruled Israel for 12 years. Six of those years he ruled in the town of Tirzah. ²⁴Omri bought the hill of Samaria from Shemer. He paid about 150 pounds of silver for it. Omri built a city on that hill. And he called it Samaria after the name of its earlier owner, Shemer.

²⁵But Omri did what the Lord said was wrong. He did more evil than all the kings who were before him. ²⁶Jeroboam son of Nebat had caused the people of Israel to sin. And Omri sinned in the same way Jeroboam had sinned. So the Israelites made the Lord, the God of Israel, very angry. He was angry because they worshiped worthless idols.

²⁷Everything else Omri did and all his successes are written down. They are all in the book of the history of the kings of Israel. ²⁸So Omri died and was buried in Samaria. His son Ahab became king in his place.

AHAB KING OF ISRAEL

²⁹So Ahab son of Omri became king of Israel. This was during Asa's thirty-eighth year as king of Judah. Ahab ruled Israel in the town of Samaria for 22 years. ³⁰Ahab did many things that the Lord said were wrong. He did more evil than any of the kings before him. ³¹He sinned in the same ways that Jeroboam son of Nebat had sinned. But he did even worse things. He married Jezebel daughter of Ethbaal. (Ethbaal was king of the city of Sidon.) Then Ahab began to serve Baal and worship him. ³²He built a temple in Samaria for worshiping Baal. And he put an altar there for Baal. ³³Ahab also made an idol for worshiping Asherah. He did more things to make the Lord, the God of Israel, angry than all the other kings before him.

³⁴During the time of Ahab, Hiel from Bethel rebuilt the town of Jericho. It cost Hiel the life of Abiram, his oldest son, to begin work on the city. And it cost the life of Segub, his youngest son, to build the city gates. The Lord had

said, through Joshua, that this would happen.ⁿ (Joshua was the son of Nun.)

ELIJAH STOPS THE RAIN

17 Now Elijah was a prophet from the town of Tishbe in Gilead. Elijah said to King Ahab, "I serve the Lord, the God of Israel. As surely as the Lord lives, I tell you the truth. No rain or dew will fall during the next few years unless I command it."

²Then the Lord spoke his word to Elijah: ³"Leave this place. Go east and hide near Kerith Ravine. It is east of the Jordan River. ⁴You may drink from the brook. And I have commanded ravens to bring you food there." ⁵So Elijah did what the Lord told him to do. He went to Kerith Ravine, east of the Jordan, and lived there. ⁶The birds brought Elijah bread and meat every morning and every evening. And he drank water from the brook.

⁷After a while the brook dried up because there was no rain. ⁸Then the Lord spoke his word to Elijah, ⁹"Go to Zarephath in Sidon. Live there. I have commanded a widow there to take care of you."

¹⁰So Elijah went to Zarephath. When he reached the town gate, he saw a widow there. She was gathering wood for a fire. Elijah asked her, "Would you bring me a little water in a cup? I would like to have a drink." ¹¹As she was going to get his water, Elijah said, "Please bring me a piece of bread, too."

¹²The woman answered, "As surely as the Lord your God lives, I tell you the truth. I have no bread. I have only a handful of flour in a jar. And I have only a little olive oil in a jug. I came here to gather some wood. I will take it home and cook our last meal. My son and I will eat it and then die from hunger."

¹³Elijah said to her, "Don't worry. Go home and cook your food as you have said. But first make a small loaf of bread from the flour you have. Bring it to me. Then cook something for yourself and your son. ¹⁴The Lord, the God of Israel, says, 'That jar of flour will never become empty. The jug will always have oil in it. This will continue until the day the Lord sends rain to the land.'"

¹⁵So the woman went home. And she did what Elijah told her to do. So Elijah, the woman and her son had enough food every day. ¹⁶The jar of flour and the jug of oil were never empty. This happened just as the Lord, through Elijah, said it would.

ELIJAH BRINGS A BOY BACK TO LIFE

¹⁷Some time later the son of the woman who owned the house became sick. He grew worse and worse. Finally he stopped breathing. ¹⁸So the woman said to Elijah, "You are a man of God. What have you done to me? Did you come here to remind me of my sin? Did you come here to kill my son?"

¹⁹Elijah said to her, "Give me your son." So Elijah took the boy from her and carried him upstairs. Elijah laid the boy on the bed in the room where he was staying. ²⁰Then he prayed to the Lord. He said, "Lord my God, this widow is letting me stay in her house. Why have you done this terrible thing to her? Why have you caused her son to die?" ²¹Then Elijah lay on top of the boy three times. Elijah prayed to the Lord, "Lord my God, let this boy live again!"

²²The Lord answered Elijah's prayer. The boy began breathing again, and he was alive. ²³Elijah carried the boy downstairs. He gave the boy to his mother and said, "See! Your son is alive!"

²⁴The woman said to Elijah, "Now I know you really are a man from God. I know that the Lord truly speaks through you!"

16:34 The Lord . . . happen. When Joshua destroyed Jericho, he said whoever rebuilt the city would lose his oldest and youngest sons. See Joshua 6:26.

ELIJAH AND THE PROPHETS OF BAAL

18 During the third year without rain, the Lord spoke his word to Elijah. The Lord said, "Go and meet King Ahab. I will soon send rain." ²So Elijah went to meet Ahab.

By this time there was no food in Samaria. ³So King Ahab sent for Obadiah. Obadiah was in charge of the king's palace. (Obadiah was a true follower of the Lord. ⁴One time Jezebel was killing all the Lord's prophets. So Obadiah took 100 of them and hid them in two caves. He put 50 in one cave and 50 in another cave. And he brought them food and water.) ⁵King Ahab said to Obadiah, "Let's look at every spring and valley in the land. Maybe we can find enough grass to keep our horses and mules alive. Then we will not have to kill our animals." ⁶So each one chose a part of the country to search. Ahab went in one direction. Obadiah went in another direction.

⁷While Obadiah was walking along, Elijah met him. Obadiah knew who Elijah was. So he bowed down to the ground before Elijah. He said, "Elijah? Is it really you, master?"

⁸Elijah answered, "Yes. Go tell your master the king that I am here."

⁹Then Obadiah said, "If I tell Ahab that, he will kill me! I have done nothing wrong that I should be killed! ¹⁰As surely as the Lord your God lives, the king has looked everywhere for you! He has sent people to every country to look for you. If the ruler said you were not there, that was not enough. Ahab then forced the ruler to swear you could not be found in his country. ¹¹Now you want me to go to my master and tell him, 'Elijah is here'? ¹²The Spirit of the Lord may carry you to some other place after I leave. If I go tell King Ahab you are here, he will come. If he doesn't find you, he will kill me! I have followed the Lord since I was a boy. ¹³Haven't you heard what I did? When Jezebel was killing the Lord's prophets, I hid 100 of them. I put 50 prophets in one cave and 50 prophets in another cave. I brought them food and water. ¹⁴Now you want me to go and tell the king you are here. He will kill me!"

¹⁵Elijah answered, "I serve the Lord of heaven's armies. As surely as the Lord lives, I will stand before Ahab today."

¹⁶So Obadiah went to Ahab and told him where Elijah was. Then Ahab went to meet Elijah.

¹⁷When he saw Elijah, he said, "Is it you—the biggest troublemaker in Israel?"

¹⁸Elijah answered, "I have not caused trouble in Israel. You and your father's family have caused all this trouble. You have not obeyed the Lord's commands. You have followed the Baals. ¹⁹Now tell all Israel to meet me at Mount Carmel. Also bring the 450 prophets of Baal there. And bring the 400 prophets of Asherah, who eat at Jezebel's table."

²⁰So Ahab called all the Israelites and those prophets to Mount Carmel. ²¹Elijah stood before the people. He said, "How long will you try to serve both Baal and the Lord? If the Lord is the true God, follow him. But if Baal is the true God, follow him!"

But the people said nothing.

²²Elijah said, "I am the only prophet of the Lord here. But there are 450 prophets of Baal. ²³So bring two bulls. Let the prophets of Baal choose one bull. Let them kill it and cut it into pieces. Then let them put the meat on the wood. But they are not to set fire to it. Then I will do the same with the other bull. And I will put it on the wood. But I will not set fire to it. ²⁴You prophets of Baal, pray to your god. And I will pray to the Lord. The god who answers the prayer will set fire to his wood. He is the true God."

All the people agreed that this was a good idea.

²⁵Then Elijah said to the prophets of Baal, "There are many of you. So you go first. Choose a bull and prepare it. Pray to your god, but don't start the fire."

²⁶So they took the bull that was given to them and prepared it. They prayed to Baal from morning until noon. They shouted, "Baal, answer us!" But there was no sound. No one answered. They danced around the altar they had built.

²⁷At noon Elijah began to make fun of them. He said, "Pray louder! If Baal really is a god, maybe he is thinking. Or maybe he is busy or traveling! Maybe he is sleeping so you will have to wake him!" ²⁸So the prophets prayed louder. They cut themselves with swords and spears until their blood flowed. (This was the way they worshiped.) ²⁹The afternoon passed, and the prophets continued to act wildly. They continued until it was time for the evening sacrifice. But no voice was heard. Baal did not answer. No one paid attention.

³⁰Then Elijah said to all the people, "Now come to me." So they gathered around him. Elijah rebuilt the altar of the Lord because it had been torn down. ³¹He took 12 stones. He took 1 stone for each of the 12 tribes. These 12 tribes were named for the 12 sons of Jacob. (Jacob was the man the Lord had called Israel.) ³²Elijah used these stones to rebuild the altar in honor of the Lord. Then he dug a small ditch around it. It was big enough to hold about 13 quarts of seed. ³³Elijah put the wood on the altar. He cut the bull into pieces and laid them on the wood. Then he said, "Fill four jars with water. Put the water on the meat and on the wood."

³⁴Then Elijah said, "Do it again." And they did it again.

Then he said, "Do it a third time." And they did it the third time. ³⁵So the water ran off of the altar and filled the ditch.

³⁶It was time for the evening sacrifice. So the prophet Elijah went near the altar. He prayed, "Lord, you are the God of Abraham, Isaac and Israel. I ask you now to prove that you are the God of Israel. And prove that I am your servant. Show these people that you commanded me to do all these things. ³⁷Lord, answer my prayer. Show these people that you, Lord, are God. Then the people will know that you are bringing them back to you."

³⁸Then fire from the Lord came down. It burned the sacrifice, the wood, the stones and the ground around the altar. It also dried up the water in the ditch. ³⁹When all the people saw this, they fell down to the ground. They cried, "The Lord is God! The Lord is God!"

⁴⁰Then Elijah said, "Capture the prophets of Baal! Don't let any of them run away!" So the people captured all the prophets. Then Elijah led them down to Kishon Valley. There he killed all the prophets.

THE RAIN COMES AGAIN

⁴¹Then Elijah said to Ahab, "Now, go, eat and drink. A heavy rain is coming." ⁴²So King Ahab went to eat and drink. At the same time Elijah climbed to the top of Mount Carmel. There he bent down to the ground with his head between his knees.

⁴³Then Elijah said to his servant, "Go and look toward the sea."

The servant went and looked. He said, "I see nothing."

Elijah told him to go and look again. This happened seven times. ⁴⁴The seventh time, the servant said, "I see a small cloud. It's the size of a man's fist. It's coming from the sea."

Elijah told the servant, "Go to Ahab. Tell him to get his chariot ready and to go home now. If he doesn't leave now, the rain will stop him."

⁴⁵After a short time the sky was covered with dark clouds. The wind began to blow. Then a heavy rain began to fall. Ahab got in his chariot and started back to Jezreel. ⁴⁶The Lord gave his power to Elijah. Elijah tightened his clothes around him. Then he ran ahead of King Ahab all the way to Jezreel.

ELIJAH AT MOUNT SINAI

19 King Ahab told Jezebel everything Elijah had done. Ahab told her how Elijah had killed all the prophets with a sword. ²So Jezebel sent a messenger to Elijah. Jezebel said, "By this time tomorrow I will kill you. I will kill you as you killed those prophets. If I don't succeed, may the gods punish me terribly."

³When Elijah heard this, he was afraid. So he ran away to save his life. He took his servant with him. When they came to Beersheba in Judah, Elijah left his servant there. ⁴Then Elijah walked for a whole day into the desert. He sat down under a bush and asked to die. Elijah prayed, "I have had enough, Lord. Let me die. I am no better than my ancestors." ⁵Then Elijah lay down under the tree and slept.

Suddenly an angel came to him and touched him. The angel said, "Get up and eat." ⁶Elijah saw near his head a loaf baked over coals and a jar of water. So he ate and drank. Then he went back to sleep.

⁷Later the Lord's angel came to him a second time. The angel touched him and said, "Get up and eat. If you don't, the journey will be too hard for you." ⁸So Elijah got up and ate and drank. The food made him strong enough to walk for 40 days and nights. He walked to Mount Sinai, the mountain of God. ⁹There Elijah went into a cave and stayed all night.

Then the Lord spoke his word to him: "Elijah! Why are you here?"

¹⁰Elijah answered, "Lord, God of heaven's armies, I have always served you the best I could. But the people of Israel have broken their agreement with you. They have destroyed your altars. They have killed your prophets with swords. I am the only prophet left. And now they are trying to kill me, too!"

¹¹Then the Lord said to Elijah, "Go. Stand in front of me on the mountain. I will pass by you." Then a very strong wind blew. It caused the mountains to break apart. It broke apart large rocks in front of the Lord. But the Lord was not in the wind. After the wind, there was an earthquake. But the Lord was not in the earthquake. ¹²After the earthquake, there was a fire. But the Lord was not in the fire. After the fire, there was a quiet, gentle voice.

¹³When Elijah heard it, he covered his face with his coat. He went out and stood at the entrance to the cave.

Then a voice said to him, "Elijah! Why are you here?"

¹⁴Elijah answered, "Lord, God of heaven's armies, I have always served you the best I could. But the people of Israel have broken their agreement with you. They have destroyed your altars. They have killed your prophets with swords. I am the only prophet left. And now they are trying to kill me, too."

¹⁵The Lord said to him, "Go back on the road that leads to the desert around Damascus. Enter that city. There pour olive oil on Hazael to make him king over Aram. ¹⁶Then pour oil on Jehu son of Nimshi to make him king over Israel. Next, pour oil on Elisha son of Shaphat from Abel Meholah. He will be a prophet in your place. ¹⁷Jehu will kill anyone who escapes from Hazael's sword. And Elisha will kill anyone who escapes from Jehu's sword. ¹⁸But I have left 7,000 people living in Israel. Those 7,000 have never bowed down before Baal. Their mouths have never kissed his idol."

> Lord, God of heaven's armies, I have always served you the best I could.
>
> –1 KINGS 19:14

ELISHA BECOMES A PROPHET

¹⁹So Elijah left there and found Elisha son of Shaphat. He was plowing a field with a team of oxen. There were 11 teams ahead of him. Elisha was plowing with the twelfth team of oxen. Elijah came up to Elisha. Elijah took off his coat and put it on Elisha. ²⁰Then Elisha left his oxen and ran to follow Elijah. Elisha said, "Let me kiss my father and my mother good-bye. Then I will go with you."

Elijah answered, "That is fine. Go back. I won't stop you."

²¹So Elisha went back. He took his pair of oxen and killed them. He used the wooden yoke for the fire. Then he cooked the meat and gave it to the people. And they ate it. Then Elisha went and followed Elijah and became his helper.

BEN-HADAD AND AHAB GO TO WAR

20 Now Ben-Hadad was king of Aram. He gathered together all his army. There were 32 kings with their horses and chariots. They went with him and surrounded Samaria and attacked it. ²The king sent messengers into the city to Ahab king of Israel. ³This was his message: "Ben-Hadad says, 'You must give me your silver and gold and the best of your wives and children.'"

⁴Ahab king of Israel answered, "My master and king, I agree to what you say. I and everything I have belongs to you."

⁵Then the messengers came to Ahab again. They said, "Ben-Hadad says, 'I told you before that you must give me your silver and gold, your wives and your children. ⁶About this time tomorrow I am going to send my men to you. They are to search everywhere in your palace. And they are to search the homes of the men who rule under you. My men will take anything they want.'"

⁷So Ahab called a meeting of all the elders of his country. He said, "Ben-Hadad is looking for trouble. First he said I had to give him my wives, my children, my silver and my gold. I agreed to that."

⁸But the elders and all the people said, "Pay no attention to him. Don't do what he says."

⁹So Ahab said to Ben-Hadad's messengers, "Tell my master the king this: 'I will do what you said at first. But I will not obey your second command.'" So King Ben-Hadad's men carried the message back to him.

¹⁰Then Ben-Hadad sent another message to Ahab: "I will completely destroy Samaria. There won't be even enough left for each of my men to get a handful of dust. May the gods punish me terribly if I don't do this!"

¹¹Ahab answered, "Tell Ben-Hadad this: 'The man who puts on his armor should not brag too soon. It's the man who lives long enough to take it off who has the right to brag.'"

¹²Now Ben-Hadad was drinking in his tent with the other rulers. The messengers came and gave him the message from Ahab. Ben-Hadad commanded his men to prepare to attack the city. So they moved into their places for the battle.

¹³At the same time a prophet came to Ahab, king of Israel. The prophet said, "Ahab, the Lord says to you, 'Do you see that big army? I will let you defeat it today. Then you will know I am the Lord.'"

¹⁴Ahab said, "Who will you use to defeat them?"

The prophet answered, "The Lord says, 'The young officers of the district governors will defeat them.'"

Then the king asked, "Who will command the main army?"

The prophet answered, "You will."

¹⁵So Ahab gathered the young officers of the district governors. There were 232 of them. Then he called together the army of Israel. There were 7,000 of them.

¹⁶At noon Ben-Hadad and the 32 rulers helping him were getting drunk in their tents. At this time Ahab attacked

them. ¹⁷The young officers of the district governors attacked first.

Ben-Hadad's scouts told him that soldiers were coming from Samaria. ¹⁸So Ben-Hadad said, "They may be coming to fight. Or they may be coming to ask for peace. In either case capture them alive."

¹⁹The young officers of the district governors led the attack. The army of Israel followed them. ²⁰Then each officer of Israel killed the man who came against him. So the men from Aram ran away as Israel chased them. But Ben-Hadad king of Aram escaped on a horse with some of his horsemen. ²¹Ahab king of Israel led the army. He captured the Arameans' horses and chariots. So King Ahab caused a great defeat of the Aramean army.

²²Then the prophet went to Ahab king of Israel and said, "The king of Aram will attack you again next spring. So you should go home now and make your army stronger. Make plans to defend yourself."

²³The officers of Ben-Hadad king of Aram said to him, "The gods of Israel are mountain gods. Since we fought in a mountain area, Israel won. So let's fight them on the flat land. Then we will win. ²⁴This is what you should do. Don't allow the 32 rulers to command the armies. Put commanders in their places. ²⁵Gather an army like the one that was destroyed. Gather as many horses and chariots as it had. We will fight the Israelites on flat land. Then we will win." Ben-Hadad agreed with their advice and did what they said.

²⁶The next spring Ben-Hadad gathered the people of Aram. He went to Aphek to fight against Israel.

²⁷The Israelites also prepared for war. They marched out to meet the Arameans and camped opposite them. They looked like two small groups of goats. But the Arameans covered the area.

²⁸A man of God came to the king of Israel with this message: "The Lord says, 'The people of Aram say that I, the Lord, am a god of the mountains. They think I am not a god of the valleys. So I will allow you to defeat this big army. Then you will know I am the Lord.'"

²⁹The armies were camped across from each other for seven days. On the seventh day the battle began. The Israelites killed 100,000 Aramean soldiers in one day. ³⁰The rest of them ran away to the city of Aphek. There a city wall fell on 27,000 of them. Ben-Hadad also ran away to the city and hid in a room.

³¹His officers said to him, "We have heard that the kings of Israel are merciful. Let's dress in rough cloth to show our sadness. And let's wear ropes on our heads as a sign of surrender. Then let's go to the king of Israel. Maybe he will let you live."

³²So they dressed in rough cloth and wore ropes on their heads. Then they went to the king of Israel. They said, "Your servant Ben-Hadad says, 'Please let me live.'"

Ahab answered, "Is he still alive? He is my brother."

³³Now Ben-Hadad's men had wanted a sign from Ahab. They wanted to know he would not kill Ben-Hadad. So when Ahab called Ben-Hadad his brother, they quickly said, "Yes! Ben-Hadad is your brother."

Ahab said, "Bring him to me." When Ben-Hadad came, Ahab asked him to join him in the chariot.

³⁴Ben-Hadad said to him, "Ahab, I will give you back the towns my father took from your father. And you may put shops in Damascus, as my father did in Samaria."

Ahab said, "If you agree to this, I will allow you to go free." So the two kings made a peace agreement. Then Ahab let Ben-Hadad go free.

A PROPHET SPEAKS AGAINST AHAB

³⁵One of the prophets told another prophet, "Hit me!" He told him to do

this because the Lord had commanded it. But the other prophet refused. ³⁶So the first prophet said, "You did not obey the Lord's command. So a lion will kill you as soon as you leave me." When the second prophet left, a lion found him and killed him.

³⁷The first prophet went to another man and said, "Hit me, please!" So the man hit him and hurt him. ³⁸Then the prophet wrapped his face in a cloth. This way no one could tell who he was. Then he went and waited by the road for the king. ³⁹As Ahab king of Israel passed by, the prophet called out to him. The prophet said, "I went to fight in the battle. One of our men brought an enemy soldier to me. Our man said, 'Guard this man. If he runs away, you will have to give your life in his place. Or, you will have to pay a fine of 75 pounds of silver.' ⁴⁰But I became busy doing other things. So the man ran away."

The king of Israel answered, "You have said what the punishment is. You must do what the man said."

⁴¹Then the prophet quickly took the cloth from his face. When the king of Israel saw him, he knew he was one of the prophets. ⁴²Then the prophet said to the king, "This is what the Lord says: 'You set free the man I said should die. So your life will be taken in his place. And the lives of your people will be taken in place of the lives of his people.'"

⁴³Then the king went back to his palace in Samaria. He was angry and upset.

NABOTH'S VINEYARD

21 A man named Naboth owned a vineyard. It was in Jezreel, near the palace of Ahab king of Israel. ²One day Ahab said to Naboth, "Give me your vineyard. It is near my palace. I want to make it into a vegetable garden. I will give you a better vineyard in its place. Or, if you prefer, I will pay you what it is worth."

³Naboth answered, "May the Lord keep me from ever giving my land to you. It belongs to my family."

⁴So Ahab went home, angry and upset. He did not like what Naboth from Jezreel had said. (Naboth had said, "I will not give you my family's land.") So Ahab lay down on his bed. He turned his face to the wall and refused to eat.

⁵His wife, Jezebel, came in. She asked him, "Why are you upset? Why do you refuse to eat?"

⁶Ahab answered, "I talked to Naboth, the man from Jezreel. I said, 'Sell me your vineyard. Or, if you prefer, I will give you another vineyard for it.' But Naboth refused."

⁷Jezebel answered, "Is this how you rule as king over Israel? Get out of bed. Eat something. Cheer up. I will get Naboth's vineyard for you."

⁸So Jezebel wrote some letters and signed Ahab's name to them. And she used his own seal to seal them. Then she sent them to the elders and important men who lived in Naboth's town. ⁹The letter she wrote said: "Declare a day during which the people are to give up eating. Call the people together. And give Naboth a place of honor among them. ¹⁰Seat two troublemakers across from him. Have them say they heard Naboth speak against God and the king. Then take Naboth out of the city and kill him with stones."

¹¹So the elders and important men of Jezreel obeyed Jezebel's command. ¹²They declared a special day. On that day the people were to give up eating. They called the people together. And they put Naboth in a place of honor

before the people. ¹³Then two trouble-makers sat across from Naboth. They said they had heard Naboth speak against God and the king. So the people carried Naboth out of the city. And they killed him with stones. ¹⁴Then the leaders sent a message to Jezebel. It said, "Naboth has been killed."

¹⁵When Jezebel heard that Naboth had been killed, she told Ahab. She said, "Naboth of Jezreel is dead. Now you may go and take for yourself his vineyard you wanted." ¹⁶When Ahab heard that Naboth was dead, he left. He went to the vineyard to take it for his own.

¹⁷At this time the Lord spoke his word to Elijah. (Elijah was the prophet from Tishbe.) The Lord said, ¹⁸"Go to Ahab king of Israel, who rules in Samaria. He is at Naboth's vineyard to take it as his own. ¹⁹Tell Ahab that I, the Lord, say to him, 'Ahab! You have murdered Naboth and have taken his land. So I tell you this! In the same place that Naboth died, you will also die. The dogs that licked up Naboth's blood will lick up your blood in the same place!'"

²⁰When Ahab saw Elijah, he said, "So you have found me, my enemy!"

Elijah answered, "Yes, I have found you. You have always chosen to do what the Lord says is wrong. ²¹So the Lord says to you, 'I will destroy you. I will kill you and every male in your family, both slave and free. ²²Your family will be like the family of King Jeroboam son of Nebat. And it will be like the family of King Baasha son of Ahijah. Both of these families were completely destroyed. I will do this to you because you have made me angry. And you have caused the people of Israel to sin.'

²³"And the Lord also says, 'Dogs will eat the body of Jezebel in the city of Jezreel.'

²⁴"Anyone in your family who dies in the city will be eaten by dogs. Anyone who dies in the fields will be eaten by birds."

²⁵There was no one like Ahab. No one had so often chosen to do what the Lord said was wrong. His wife Jezebel influenced him to do evil. ²⁶Ahab sinned terribly by worshiping idols. This was the same thing the Amorite people did. So the Lord took their land away from them. And he gave it to the people of Israel.

²⁷After Elijah finished speaking, Ahab tore his clothes. He put on rough cloth and refused to eat. He even slept in the rough cloth. He did this to show how sad and upset he was.

²⁸The Lord spoke his word to Elijah from Tishbe: ²⁹"I see that Ahab is now sorry for what he has done. So I will not cause the trouble to come to him during his life. I will wait until his son is king. Then I will bring this trouble to Ahab's family."

THE DEATH OF AHAB

22 For three years there was peace between Israel and Aram. ²During the third year Jehoshaphat king of Judah went to visit Ahab king of Israel.

³At this same time Ahab asked his officers, "Remember that the king of Aram took Ramoth in Gilead from us? Why have we done nothing to get it back?" ⁴So Ahab asked King Jehoshaphat, "Will you go with us? Will you fight against the army of Aram at Ramoth in Gilead?"

Jehoshaphat answered, "I will go with you. My soldiers and my horses are ready to join with your army. ⁵But first we should ask the Lord to guide us."

⁶So Ahab called the prophets together. There were about 400 men. He asked them, "Should I go to war against the army of Aram at Ramoth in Gilead? Or should I wait?"

The prophets answered, "Go, because the Lord will let you defeat them."

⁷But Jehoshaphat asked, "Isn't there a prophet of the Lord here? Let's ask him what we should do."

⁸King Ahab answered, "There is one other prophet. We could ask the Lord through him. But I hate him. When

he prophesies, he never says anything good about me. He always says something bad. He is Micaiah, Imlah's son."

Jehoshaphat said, "King Ahab, you shouldn't say that!"

⁹So Ahab king of Israel told one of his officers to bring Micaiah to him at once.

¹⁰Ahab king of Israel and Jehoshaphat king of Judah had on their royal robes. They were sitting on their thrones at the threshing floor. This was near the entrance to the gate of Samaria. All the prophets were standing before them, speaking messages from the Lord. ¹¹One of the prophets was Zedekiah son of Kenaanah. He had made some iron horns. He said to Ahab, "This is what the Lord says, 'You will use these horns to fight the Arameans. And you will destroy them.'"

¹²All the other prophets said the same thing. They said, "Attack Ramoth in Gilead and win. The Lord will let you defeat the Arameans."

¹³The messenger who had gone to get Micaiah found him. He said to Micaiah, "All the other prophets are saying the king will succeed. You should agree with them. Give the king a good answer."

¹⁴But Micaiah answered, "As surely as the Lord lives, I can tell him only what the Lord tells me."

¹⁵Then Micaiah came to Ahab. The king asked him, "Micaiah, should we attack Ramoth in Gilead or not?"

Micaiah answered, "Attack and win! The Lord will let you defeat them."

¹⁶But Ahab said to Micaiah, "Tell me only the truth in the name of the Lord. How many times do I have to tell you this?"

¹⁷So Micaiah answered, "I saw the army of Israel. They were scattered over the hills like sheep without a shepherd. The Lord said, 'They have no leader. They should go home and not fight.'"

¹⁸Then Ahab king of Israel said to Jehoshaphat, "I told you! This prophet never says anything good about me. He only says bad things about me."

¹⁹But Micaiah continued to speak. He said, "Hear the message from the Lord: I saw the Lord sitting on his throne. His heavenly army was standing near him on his right and on his left. ²⁰The Lord said, 'Who will trick Ahab into attacking Ramoth in Gilead? Do this so he will go and be killed.'

"The spirits did not agree about what they should do. ²¹Then one spirit came and stood before the Lord. He said, 'I will trick him.'

²²"The Lord asked, 'How will you trick Ahab?'

"The spirit answered, 'I will go to Ahab's prophets. I will make them tell lies.'

"So the Lord said, 'You will succeed in tricking him. Go and do it.'"

²³Micaiah said, "Ahab, this has now happened. The Lord has caused your prophets to lie to you. The Lord has decided that great trouble should come to you."

²⁴Then Zedekiah son of Kenaanah went up to Micaiah. And he hit Micaiah in the face. Zedekiah said, "Do you really believe the Lord's spirit has left me and is now speaking through you?"

²⁵Micaiah answered, "You will find out on the day you go to hide in an inside room."

²⁶Then Ahab king of Israel ordered, "Take Micaiah. Send him to Amon, the governor of the city, and to Joash, the king's son. ²⁷Tell them I said to put Micaiah in prison. Give him only bread and water for food. Keep him there until I come home from the battle."

²⁸Micaiah said, "Ahab, if you come back safely from battle, the Lord has not spoken through me. Remember my words, all you people."

²⁹So Ahab king of Israel and Jehoshaphat king of Judah went to Ramoth in Gilead. ³⁰Ahab said to Jehoshaphat, "I will go into battle. But I will change my appearance so that no one will recognize me. But you wear your royal clothes." So Ahab changed his appearance and went into battle.

³¹The king of Aram had 32 chariot commanders. He ordered them, "Don't fight with anyone but the king of Israel. It doesn't matter if they are important or unimportant." ³²When these commanders saw Jehoshaphat, they thought he was the king of Israel. So they turned to attack him. But Jehoshaphat began shouting. ³³Then the commanders saw he was not Ahab. So they stopped chasing him. ³⁴A soldier shot an arrow without aiming at anyone. But he hit Ahab king of Israel. The arrow hit him in a place not covered by his armor. King Ahab said to his chariot driver, "Turn the chariot around. Take me out of the battle. I am hurt!" ³⁵The battle continued all day. King Ahab was in his chariot, leaning against it to hold himself up. He was facing the Arameans. His blood flowed down and covered the bottom of the chariot. That evening he died. ³⁶Near sunset a cry went out through the army of Israel: "Each man go back to his own country and city."

³⁷So in that way King Ahab died. His body was carried to Samaria and buried there. ³⁸The men cleaned Ahab's chariot at a pool in Samaria. This was a pool where prostitutes bathed. And the dogs licked King Ahab's blood from the chariot. These things happened as the Lord had said they would.

³⁹Everything else Ahab did is written down. It is in the book of the history of the kings of Israel. That book also tells about the palace Ahab built and decorated with ivory. And it tells about the cities he built. ⁴⁰So Ahab died, and his son Ahaziah became king in his place.

JEHOSHAPHAT KING OF JUDAH

⁴¹Jehoshaphat son of Asa became king of Judah. This was during Ahab's fourth year as king over Israel. ⁴²Jehoshaphat was 35 years old when he became king. And he ruled in Jerusalem for 25 years. His mother was the daughter of Shilhi. She was named Azubah. ⁴³Jehoshaphat was good like his father before him. He did what the Lord said was right. But Jehoshaphat did not destroy the places where false gods were worshiped. So the people continued offering sacrifices and burning incense there. ⁴⁴Jehoshaphat was at peace with the king of Israel. ⁴⁵Jehoshaphat fought many wars. These wars and his successes are written down. They are in the book of the history of the kings of Judah. ⁴⁶There were prostitutes in the places where false gods were worshiped. Jehoshaphat's father, Asa, had not forced all of them out. But Jehoshaphat forced the rest of them to leave.

⁴⁷During this time the land of Edom had no king. It was ruled by a governor.

⁴⁸King Jehoshaphat built trading ships to sail to Ophir for gold. But the ships were destroyed at Ezion Geber. So they never set sail. ⁴⁹Ahaziah son of Ahab went to help Jehoshaphat. Ahaziah said he would give Jehoshaphat some men to sail with his men. But Jehoshaphat refused.

⁵⁰Jehoshaphat died and was buried with his ancestors. He was buried in Jerusalem, the city of David, his ancestor. And his son Jehoram became king.

AHAZIAH KING OF ISRAEL

⁵¹Ahaziah son of Ahab became king of Israel in Samaria. This was during Jehoshaphat's seventeenth year as king over Judah. Ahaziah ruled Israel for two years. ⁵²Ahaziah did what the Lord said was wrong. He did the same things his father Ahab, his mother Jezebel and Jeroboam son of Nebat had done. All these rulers led the people of Israel into more sin. ⁵³Ahaziah worshiped and served the god Baal. So Ahaziah made the Lord, the God of Israel, very angry. In these ways Ahaziah did what his father had done.

SINGING SONGS TO JESUS

Have you ever sung the song "Row, Row, Row Your Boat"? Or "Mary Had a Little Lamb"? How about "Baby Shark"? You probably know these and can name a lot more songs that you sing at home or at school. We sing songs because they can be fun, and they can help us remember things. Sometimes when we are sad, a happy song can bring us right up out of that sadness.

The word *psalm* is another word for "song." The Bible has a whole book full of psalms. The people who wrote the Psalms probably sang them, but they can be read like poems too. The Book of Psalms has poems or songs that are happy and some that are sad. There are psalms that beg God for protection. And others praise God for the amazing things he does. There are even psalms that tell us about Jesus—written hundreds of years before he was even born!

The Bible has other books full of poetry, such as Proverbs, Ecclesiastes (that's a big word!), Song of Songs, and Lamentations. In this Bible, you can read some of Psalms, all of Proverbs, and Lamentations (which is full of sad poems—it shows up later).

Psalms

BOOK 1
Psalms 1—41

PSALM 1

TWO WAYS TO LIVE

¹ Happy is the person who doesn't
listen to the wicked.
He doesn't go where sinners go.
He doesn't do what bad people do.
² He loves the Lord's teachings.
He thinks about those teachings
day and night.
³ He is strong, like a tree planted by
a river.
It produces fruit in season.
Its leaves don't die.
Everything he does will
succeed.

⁴ But wicked people are not like that.
They are like useless chaff
that the wind blows away.
⁵ So the wicked will not escape God's
punishment.
Sinners will not worship God with
good people.
⁶ This is because the Lord protects
good people.
But the wicked will be
destroyed.

PSALM 2

GOD'S CHOSEN KING

¹ Why are the nations so angry?
Why are the people making useless
plans?
² The kings of the earth prepare to
fight.
Their leaders make plans together
against the Lord
and his appointed king.
³ "Let's break the chains that hold us
prisoners.

Let's throw off the ropes that tie
us," the nations say.

⁴ But the Lord in heaven laughs.
He makes fun of them.
⁵ Then the Lord warns them.
He frightens them with his anger.
⁶ He says, "I have appointed my own
king!
He will rule in Jerusalem on my
holy mountain."

⁷ Now I will tell you what the Lord has
declared:
He said to me, "You are my son.
Today I have become your father.
⁸ If you ask me, I will give you the
nations.
All the people on earth will be
yours.
⁹ You will make them obey you by
punishing them with an iron rod.
You will break them into pieces like
pottery."

¹⁰ So, kings, be wise.
Rulers, learn this lesson.
¹¹ Obey the Lord with great fear.
Be happy, but tremble.
¹² Show that you are loyal to his son.
Otherwise you will be destroyed.
He can quickly become angry.
But happy are those who trust him
for protection.

PSALM 3

A MORNING PRAYER
David sang this when he ran away
from his son Absalom.

¹ Lord, I have many enemies!
Many people have turned
against me.
² Many people are talking about me.
They say, "God won't rescue him."
Selah

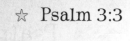

☆ Psalm 3:3

King David was loved by so many people in Israel. But even though he had lots of friends, he also had many enemies. One time, David had to run away from his son Absalom because Absalom wanted to be king. David sang this song about God being his protecting shield when he was running away from his son.

Have you ever played dodgeball? There was one boy who always used the ball like a shield. Whenever someone threw a ball his way, he would block it. But sometimes his shield let him down, and he got knocked out by the other team. But that shield was only a ball. And dodgeball is just a game. In real life, God is the best shield! He protects us perfectly, and we never have to worry about being let down. He is wonderful in everything he does. We can have courage in everything we face because God promises to keep us in his care.

• •

King David called God his shield. God will protect you and give you courage just like he did for David.

³ But, Lord, you are my shield.
  You are my wonderful God who
    gives me courage.
⁴ I will pray to the Lord.
  And he will answer me from his
    holy mountain.   *Selah*

⁵ I can lie down and go to sleep.
  And I will wake up again
    because the Lord protects me.
⁶ Thousands of enemies may
    surround me.
  But I am not afraid.

⁷ Lord, rise up!
  My God, come save me!

You have hit my enemies on the cheek.
  You have broken the teeth of the
    wicked.
⁸ The Lord can save his people.
  Lord, bless your people.   *Selah*

PSALM 4

AN EVENING PRAYER
For the director of music.
With stringed instruments.
A song of David.

¹ Answer me when I pray to you,
    my God who does what is right.

Lift the load that I carry.
Be kind to me and hear my prayer.

2 People, how long will you turn my
honor into shame?
You love what is false, and you look
for new lies. *Selah*
3 You know that the Lord has chosen
for himself those who are loyal
to him.
The Lord listens when I pray to him.
4 When you are angry, do not sin.
Think about these things quietly
as you go to bed. *Selah*
5 Do what is right as a sacrifice to the
Lord.
And trust the Lord.

6 Many people ask,
"Who will give us anything good?
Lord, be kind to us."
7 But you have made me very happy.
I am happier than they are,
even with all their grain and wine.
8 I go to bed and sleep in peace.
Lord, only you keep me safe.

PSALM 5

A MORNING PRAYER
FOR PROTECTION

For the director of music. For flutes.
A song of David.

1 Lord, listen to my words.
Understand what I am thinking.
2 Listen to my cry for help.
My king and my God, I pray to you.
3 Lord, every morning you hear my voice.
Every morning, I tell you what I
need.
And I wait for your answer.

4 You are not a God who is pleased
with what is wicked.
You do not live with those who do
evil.
5 Those people who make fun of you
cannot stand before you.
You hate all those who do wrong.

6 You destroy liars.
The Lord hates those who kill and
trick others.

7 Because of your great love,
I can come into your Temple.
Because I fear and respect you,
I can worship in your holy Temple.
8 Lord, since I have many enemies,
show me the right thing to do.
Show me clearly how you want me
to live.

9 With their mouths my enemies do
not tell the truth.
In their hearts they want to destroy
people.
Their throats are like open graves.
They use their tongues for telling
lies.
10 God, declare them guilty!
Let them fall into their own traps.
Send them away because their sins
are many.
They have turned against you.

11 But let everyone who trusts you be
happy.
Let them sing glad songs forever.
Protect those who love you.
They are happy because of you.
12 Lord, you bless those who do what is
right.
You protect them like a soldier's
shield.

PSALM 6

A PRAYER FOR MERCY
IN TROUBLED TIMES

For the director of music. With stringed
instruments. By the sheminith.
A song of David.

1 Lord, don't correct me when you are
angry.
Don't punish me when you are very
angry.
2 Lord, be kind to me because I am
weak.

Heal me, Lord, because my bones
ache.
³ I am very upset.
Lord, how long will it be?

⁴ Lord, return and save me.
Save me because of your kindness.
⁵ Dead people don't remember you.
Those in the grave don't praise you.

⁶ I am tired of crying to you.
Every night my bed is wet with
tears.
My bed is soaked from my crying.
⁷ My eyes are weak from so much
crying.
They are weak from crying about
my enemies.

⁸ Get away from me, all you who do
evil.
The Lord has heard my crying.
⁹ The Lord has heard my cry for help.
The Lord will answer my
prayer.
¹⁰ All my enemies will be ashamed and
troubled.
They will turn and suddenly leave
in shame.

PSALM 7

A PRAYER FOR FAIRNESS

A shiggaion of David which he sang to the
Lord about Cush, from the tribe of Benjamin.

¹ Lord my God, I trust in you for
protection.
Save me and rescue me
from those who are chasing me.
² Otherwise, they will tear me apart
like a lion.
They will rip me to pieces, and no
one can save me.

³ Lord my God, what have I done?
Have my hands done something
wrong?
⁴ Have I done wrong to my friend?
Have I stolen from my enemy?

⁵ If I have, let my enemy chase me and
capture me.
Let him trample me into the dust.
Let him bury me in the ground.

Selah

⁶ Lord, rise up in your anger.
Stand up against my enemies'
anger.
Get up and demand fairness.
⁷ Gather the nations around you,
and rule them from above.
⁸ Lord, judge the people.
Lord, defend me.
Prove that I am right.
Show that I have done no wrong,
God Most High.
⁹ God, you do what is right.
You know our thoughts and
feelings.
Stop those wicked actions done by
evil people.
And help those who do what is
right.

¹⁰ God Most High protects me like a
shield.
He saves those whose hearts are
right.
¹¹ God judges by what is right.
And God is always ready to punish
the wicked.
¹² If they do not change their lives,

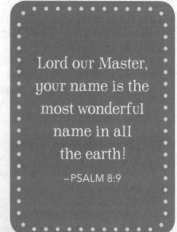

Lord our Master,
your name is the
most wonderful
name in all
the earth!

–PSALM 8:9

God will sharpen his sword.
He will string his bow and take aim.
¹³ He has prepared his deadly weapons.
He has made his flaming arrows.

¹⁴ There are people who think up evil.
They plan trouble and tell lies.
¹⁵ They dig a hole to trap other people.
But they will fall into it themselves.
¹⁶ They themselves will get into trouble.
The violence they cause will hurt
only themselves.

¹⁷ I praise the Lord because he does
what is right.
I sing praises to the name of the
Lord Most High.

PSALM 8

GOD'S GREATNESS AND
MAN'S WORTH

For the director of music. By the
gittith. A song of David.

¹ Lord our Master,
your name is the most wonderful
name in all the earth!
It brings you praise in heaven
above.
² You have taught children and babies
to sing praises to you.
This is because of your enemies.
And so you silence your enemies
and destroy those who try to get
even.

³ I look at the heavens,
which you made with your hands.
I see the moon and stars,
which you created.
⁴ But why is man important to you?
Why do you take care of human
beings?
⁵ You made man a little lower than the
angels.
And you crowned him with glory
and honor.
⁶ You put him in charge of everything
you made.

You put all things under his
control:
⁷ all the sheep, the cattle
and the wild animals,
⁸ the birds in the sky,
the fish in the sea,
and everything that lives under
water.

⁹ Lord our Master,
your name is the most wonderful
name in all the earth!

PSALM 9

THANKSGIVING FOR VICTORY

For the director of music. To the tune of
"The Death of the Son."
A song of David.

¹ I will praise you, Lord, with all my
heart.
I will tell all the miracles you have
done.
² I will be happy because of you.
God Most High, I will sing praises
to your name.

³ My enemies turn back.
They are overwhelmed and die
because of you.
⁴ You have heard what I complained to
you about.
You sat on your throne and judged
by what was right.
⁵ You spoke strongly against the
foreign nations
and destroyed the wicked people.
You wiped out their names forever
and ever.
⁶ The enemy is gone forever.
You destroyed their cities.
No one even remembers them.

⁷ But the Lord rules forever.
He sits on his throne to judge.
⁸ The Lord will judge the world by
what is right.
He will decide what is fair for the
nations.

⁹The Lord defends those who suffer.
He protects them in times of trouble.
¹⁰ Those who know the Lord trust him.
He will not leave those who come
to him.

¹¹ Sing praises to the Lord who is king
on Mount Zion.
Tell the nations what he has done.
¹² He remembers who the murderers are.
He will not forget the cries of those
who suffer.
¹³ Lord, be kind to me.
See how my enemies hurt me.
Do not let me go through the gates
of death.
¹⁴ Then, at the gates of Jerusalem, I will
praise you.
I will rejoice because you saved me.

¹⁵ The nations have fallen into the pit
they dug.
Their feet are caught in the nets
they laid.
¹⁶ The Lord has made himself known
by his fair decisions.
The wicked get trapped by what
they do.   Higgaion. *Selah*

¹⁷ Wicked people will go to the grave.
So will all those who forget God.
¹⁸ Those who have troubles will not be
forgotten.
The hopes of the poor will not die.

¹⁹ Lord, rise up and judge the nations.
Don't let humans think they are
strong.
²⁰ Teach them to fear you, Lord.
The nations must learn that they
are only human.   *Selah*

PSALM 10

A COMPLAINT ABOUT
EVIL PEOPLE

¹ Lord, why are you so far away?
Why do you hide when there is
trouble?

² Proudly the wicked chase down
those who suffer.
The wicked set traps to catch them.
³ They brag about the things they want.
They bless the greedy but hate the
Lord.
⁴ The wicked people are too proud.
They do not look for God.
There is no room for God in their
thoughts.
⁵ They always succeed.
They are far from keeping your laws.
They make fun of their enemies.
⁶ They say to themselves, "Nothing
bad will ever happen to me.
I will never be ruined."
⁷ Their mouths are full of curses, lies
and threats.
They use their tongues for sin and
evil.
⁸ They hide near the villages.
They look for innocent people to kill.
They watch in secret for the
helpless.
⁹ They wait in hiding like a lion.
They wait to catch poor people.
They catch the poor in nets.
¹⁰ The poor are thrown down and
crushed.
They are defeated because the
others are stronger.
¹¹ The wicked think,
"God has forgotten us.
He doesn't see what is happening."

¹² Lord, rise up and punish the wicked.
Don't forget those who need help.
¹³ Why do wicked people hate God?
They say to themselves, "God won't
punish us."
¹⁴ Lord, surely you see these cruel and
evil things.
Look at them and do something.
People in trouble look to you for help.
You are the one who helps the
orphans.
¹⁵ Break the power of wicked men.
Punish them for the evil they have
done.

¹⁶ The Lord is King forever and ever.

Remove from your land those
    nations that do not worship you.
¹⁷ Lord, you have heard what the poor
    people want.
    Do what they ask. Listen to them.
¹⁸ Protect the orphans. Put an end to
    suffering.
    Then they will no longer be afraid
    of evil people.

PSALM 11

A STATEMENT ABOUT TRUST IN GOD

For the director of music. Of David.

¹ I trust in the Lord for protection.
    So why do you say to me,
    "Fly like a bird to your mountain.
² Like hunters, the wicked string their
    bows.
    They set their arrows on the
    bowstrings.
They shoot from dark places
    at those who are honest.
³ When all that is good falls apart,
    what can good people do?"

⁴ The Lord is in his holy temple.
    The Lord sits on his throne in
    heaven.
And he sees what people do.
    He keeps his eye on them.
⁵ The Lord tests those who do right.
    But he hates the wicked and those
    who love to hurt others.
⁶ He will send hot coals on the wicked.
    Burning sulfur and a whirlwind is
    what they will get.
⁷ The Lord does what is right, and he
    loves justice.
    So honest people will see his face.

PSALM 12

A PRAYER AGAINST LIARS

For the director of music. By the
sheminith. A song of David.

¹ Save me, Lord, because the good
    people are all gone.
    No true believers are left on earth.
² Everyone lies to his neighbors.
    They say one thing and mean
    another.

³ The Lord will stop those lying lips.
    He will cut off those bragging
    tongues.
⁴ They say, "Our tongues will help us
    win.
    We can say what we wish. No one is
    our master."

⁵ But the Lord says,
    "I will now rise up
    because the poor are being hurt.
    Because of the moans of the helpless,
    I will give them the help they
    want."
⁶ The Lord's words are pure.
    They are like silver purified by fire,
    like silver purified seven times
    over.

⁷ Lord, keep us safe.
    Always protect us from such
    people.
⁸ The wicked are all around us.
    Everyone loves what is wrong.

PSALM 13

A PRAYER FOR GOD TO BE NEAR

For the director of music.
A song of David.

¹ How long will you forget me, Lord?
    How long will you hide from me?
    Forever?
² How long must I worry?
    How long must I feel sad in my
    heart?

How long will my enemy win over
me?

3 Lord, look at me.
Answer me, my God.
Tell me, or I will die.
4 Otherwise my enemy will say, "I have
won!"
Those against me will rejoice that
I've been defeated.

5 I trust in your love.
My heart is happy because you
saved me.
6 I sing to the Lord
because he has taken care of me.

PSALM 14

THE UNBELIEVING FOOL
For the director of music. Of David.

1 A wicked fool says to himself,
"There is no God."
Fools are evil. They do terrible things.
None of them does anything good.

2 The Lord looked down from heaven
at all the people.
He looked to see if anyone was wise,
if anyone was looking to God for
help.
3 But all have turned away.
Together, everyone has become
evil.
None of them does anything good.

4 Don't the wicked understand?
They destroy my people as if they
were eating bread.
They do not ask the Lord for help.
5 But the wicked are filled with terror
because God is with those who do
what is right.
6 The wicked upset the plans of the
poor.
But the Lord will protect the poor.

7 I pray that victory will come to Israel
from Mount Zion!

May the Lord give them back their
riches.
Then the people of Jacob will rejoice.
And the people of Israel will be
glad.

PSALM 15

WHAT GOD DEMANDS
A song of David.

1 Lord, who may enter your Holy Tent?
Who may live on your holy
mountain?

2 Only a person who is innocent
and who does what is right.
He must speak the truth from his
heart.
3 He must not tell lies about others.
He must do no wrong to his
neighbors.
He must not gossip.
4 He must not respect hateful people.
He must honor those who honor
the Lord.
He must keep his promises to his
neighbor,
even when it hurts.
5 He must not charge interest on
money he lends.
And he must not take money to
hurt innocent people.

Whoever does all these things will
never be destroyed.

PSALM 16

THE LORD TAKES CARE
OF HIS PEOPLE
A miktam of David.

1 Protect me, God,
because I trust in you.
2 I said to the Lord, "You are my Lord.
Every good thing I have comes
from you."
3 There are godly people in the world.

I enjoy them.
⁴ But those who turn to idols will have
   much pain.
   I will not offer blood to those idols.
   I won't even speak their names.

⁵ No, the Lord is all I need.
   He takes care of me.
⁶ My share in life has been pleasant.
   My part has been beautiful.

⁷ I praise the Lord because he guides
   me.
   Even at night, I feel his leading.
⁸ I keep the Lord before me always.
   Because he is close by my side
   I will not be hurt.
⁹ So I rejoice, and I am glad.
   Even my body has hope.
¹⁰ This is because you will not leave me
   in the grave.
   You will not let your holy one rot.
¹¹ You will teach me God's way to live.
   Being with you will fill me with joy.
   At your right hand I will find
   pleasure forever.

PSALM 17

A PRAYER FOR PROTECTION
A prayer of David.

¹ Lord, hear me begging for fairness.
   Listen to my cry for help.
   Pay attention to my prayer.
   I speak the truth.
² You will judge that I am right.
   Your eyes can see what is true.
³ You have examined my heart.
   You have tested me all night.
   You questioned me without finding
   anything wrong.
   I did not plan any evil.
⁴ I have obeyed your commands.
   I have not done what evil people
   do.
⁵ I have done what you told me to do.
   I have not failed.

⁶ I call to you, God,

and you answer me.
   Listen to me now.
   Hear what I say.
⁷ Your love is wonderful.
   By your power you save
   from their enemies those who
   trust you.
⁸ Protect me as you would protect your
   own eye.
   Protect me as a bird hides her
   young under her wings.
⁹ Keep me from the wicked who attack
   me.
   Protect me from my enemies who
   surround me.
¹⁰ They are selfish.
   They brag about themselves.
¹¹ They have chased me.
   Now they surround me.
   They plan to throw me to the
   ground.
¹² They are like lions ready to kill.
   Like lions, they sit in hiding.

¹³ Lord, rise up and face the enemy.
   Throw them down.
   Save me from the wicked
   with your sword.
¹⁴ Lord, save me from them by your
   power.
   Their reward is in this life.
   They have plenty of food.

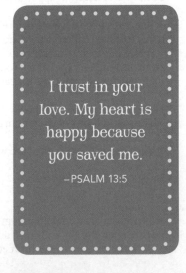

I trust in your love. My heart is happy because you saved me.

–PSALM 13:5

They have many sons.
They leave money to their children.

15 Because I have lived right, I will see
your face.
When I wake up, I will see your
likeness and be satisfied.

PSALM 18

A SONG OF VICTORY

For the director of music. By the Lord's
servant, David. David sang this song to the
Lord. He sang it when the Lord had saved
him from Saul and all his other enemies.

1 I love you, Lord. You are my strength.
2 The Lord is my rock, my protection,
my Savior.
My God is my rock.
I can run to him for safety.
He is my shield and my saving
strength, my high tower.
3 I will call to the Lord.
He is worthy of praise.
And I will be saved from my
enemies.

4 The ropes of death bound me.
The deadly rivers overwhelmed
me.
5 The ropes of death wrapped around
me.
The traps of death were before me.
6 In my trouble I called to the Lord.
I cried out to my God for help.
From his temple he heard my voice.
My call for help reached his ears.

7 The earth trembled and shook.
The foundations of the mountains
began to shake.
They shook because the Lord was
angry.
8 Smoke came out of his nose.
Burning fire came out of his
mouth.
Burning coals went before him.
9 He tore open the sky and came down.
Dark clouds were under his feet.

10 He rode a creature with wings and
flew.
He flew on the wings of the wind.
11 He made darkness his covering, his
shelter around him,
surrounded by fog and clouds.
12 Out of the brightness of his presence
came clouds.
They came with hail and lightning.
13 The Lord thundered from heaven.
God Most High raised his voice.
And there was hail and lightning.
14 He shot his arrows and scattered his
enemies.
His many bolts of lightning
confused them with fear.
15 Lord, you spoke strongly.
The wind blew from your nose.
The valleys of the sea appeared.
The foundations of the earth were
seen.

16 The Lord reached down from above
and took me.
He pulled me from the deep
water.
17 He saved me from my powerful
enemies.
Those who hated me were too
strong for me.
18 They attacked me at my time of
trouble.
But the Lord supported me.
19 He took me to a safe place.
Because he delights in me, he saved
me.

20 The Lord spared me because I did
what was right.
Because I have not done evil, he
has rewarded me.
21 I have followed the ways of the Lord.
I have not done evil by turning
away from my God.
22 I remember all his laws.
I have not broken his rules.
23 I am innocent before him.
I have kept myself from doing evil.
24 The Lord rewarded me because I did
what was right.
I did what the Lord said was right.

²⁵ Lord, you are loyal to those who are
loyal.
  You are good to those who are good.
²⁶ You are pure to those who are pure.
  But you are against those who are
  bad.
²⁷ You save those who are not proud.
  But you make humble those who
  are proud.
²⁸ Lord, you give light to my lamp.
  My God brightens the darkness
  around me.
²⁹ With your help I can attack an army.
  With God's help I can jump over a
  wall.

³⁰ The ways of God are without fault.
  The Lord's words are pure.
He is a shield to those who trust him.
³¹ Who is God? Only the Lord.
  Who is the Rock? Only our God.
³² God is my protection.
  He makes my way free from fault.
³³ He makes me like a deer, which does
  not stumble.
  He helps me stand on the steep
  mountains.
³⁴ He trains my hands for battle.
  So my arms can bend a bronze bow.
³⁵ You protect me with your saving
  shield.
  You support me with your right
  hand.
  You have stooped to make me
  great.
³⁶ You give me a wide path on which to
  walk.
  My feet have not slipped.
³⁷ I chased my enemies and caught
  them.
  I did not quit till they were
  destroyed.
³⁸ I crushed them so they couldn't rise
  up again.
  They fell beneath my feet.
³⁹ You gave me strength in battle.
  You made my enemies bow before
  me.
⁴⁰ You made my enemies turn back.
  I destroyed those who hated me.
⁴¹ They called for help,

but no one came to save them.
They called to the Lord,
  but he did not answer them.
⁴² I beat my enemies into pieces.
  They were like dust in the wind.
  I poured them out like mud in the
  streets.

⁴³ You saved me when the people
  attacked me.
  You made me the leader of nations.
  People I never knew serve me.
⁴⁴ As soon as they hear me, they obey
  me.
  Foreigners obey me.
⁴⁵ They all become afraid.
  They tremble in their hiding
  places.

⁴⁶ The Lord lives!
  May my Rock be praised.
  Praise the God who saves me!
⁴⁷ God gives me victory over my
  enemies.
  He brings people under my rule.
⁴⁸ He saves me from my enemies.

You set me over those who hate me.
  You saved me from cruel men.
⁴⁹ So I will praise you, Lord, among the
  nations.
  I will sing praises to your name.
⁵⁰ The Lord gives great victories to his
  king.
  He is loyal to his appointed king,
  to David and his descendants
  forever.

PSALM 19

GOD'S WORKS AND WORD

For the director of music.
A song of David.

¹ The heavens tell the glory of God.
  And the skies announce what his
  hands have made.
² Day after day they tell the story.
  Night after night they tell it again.
³ They have no speech or words.

They don't make any sound to be heard.
⁴ But their message goes out through all the world.
It goes everywhere on earth.
The sky is like a home for the sun.
⁵ The sun comes out like a bridegroom from his bedroom.
It rejoices like an athlete eager to run a race.
⁶ The sun rises at one end of the sky, and it follows its path to the other end.
Nothing hides from its heat.

⁷ The Lord's teachings are perfect.
They give new strength.
The Lord's rules can be trusted.
They make plain people wise.
⁸ The Lord's orders are right.
They make people happy.
The Lord's commands are pure.
They light up the way.
⁹ It is good to respect the Lord.
That respect will last forever.
The Lord's judgments are true.
They are completely right.
¹⁰ They are worth more than gold, even the purest gold.
They are sweeter than honey, even the finest honey.
¹¹ They tell your servant what to do.

> The heavens tell the glory of God. And the skies announce what his hands have made.
>
> —PSALM 19:1

Keeping them brings great reward.

¹² No one can see all his own mistakes.
Forgive me for my secret sins.
¹³ Keep me from the sins that I want to do.
Don't let them rule me.
Then I can be pure and free from the greatest of sins.

¹⁴ I hope my words and thoughts please you.
Lord, you are my Rock, the one who saves me.

PSALM 20

A PRAYER FOR THE KING

For the director of music.
A song of David.

¹ May the Lord answer you in times of trouble.
May the God of Jacob protect you.
² May he send you help from his Temple.
May he support you from Mount Zion.
³ May he remember all your offerings.
May he accept all your sacrifices.
Selah
⁴ May he give you what you want.
May all your plans succeed.
⁵ We will shout for joy when you succeed.
We will raise a flag in the name of our God.
May the Lord give you all that you ask for.

⁶ Now I know the Lord helps his appointed king.
He answers him from his holy heaven.
He saves him with his strong right hand.
⁷ Some trust in chariots, others in horses.
But we trust the Lord our God.
⁸ They are overwhelmed and defeated.

But we march forward and win.
⁹ Lord, save the king!
  Answer us when we call for help.

PSALM 21

THANKSGIVING FOR THE KING

For the director of music.
A song of David.

¹ Lord, the king rejoices because of
    your strength.
  He is so happy when you save him!
² You gave the king what he wanted.
  You did not refuse what he asked
    for.   *Selah*
³ You put good things before him.
  You placed a gold crown on his
    head.
⁴ He asked you for life.
  And you gave it to him.
  His years go on and on.
⁵ He has great glory because you gave
    him victories.
  You gave him honor and
    praise.
⁶ You always gave him blessings.
  You made him glad because you
    were with him.
⁷ The king truly trusts the Lord.
  Because God Most High always
    loves him,
  he will not be overwhelmed.
⁸ Your hand is against all your
    enemies.
  Those who hate you will feel your
    power.
⁹ When you appear, you will burn
    them like wood in a furnace.
  In your anger you will eat them up.
  Your fire will burn them up.
¹⁰ You will destroy their families from
    the earth.
  Their children will not live.
¹¹ They made evil plans against you.
  But their traps won't work.
¹² You will make them turn their backs
    when you aim your arrows at them.
¹³ Be supreme, Lord, in your power.
  We sing and praise your greatness.

PSALM 22

THE PRAYER OF A SUFFERING MAN

For the director of music. To the tune of
"The Doe of Dawn."
A song of David.

¹ My God, my God, why have you left
    me alone?
  You are too far away to save me.
  You are too far away to hear my
    moans.
² My God, I call to you during the day.
  But you do not answer.
  And I call at night.
  I am not silent.

³ You sit as the Holy One.
  The praises of Israel are your
    throne.
⁴ Our ancestors trusted you.
  They trusted you, and you saved
    them.
⁵ They called to you for help.
  And they were rescued.
  They trusted you.
  And they were not disappointed.

⁶ But I am like a worm instead of a man.
  Men make fun of me.
  They look down on me.
⁷ Everyone who looks at me laughs.
  They stick out their tongues.
  They shake their heads.
⁸ They say, "Turn to the Lord for help.
  Maybe he will save you.
  If he likes you,
    maybe he will rescue you."

⁹ You had my mother give birth to me.
  You made me trust you
    while I was just a baby.
¹⁰ I have leaned on you since the day I
    was born.
  You have been my God since my
    mother gave birth to me.
¹¹ So don't be far away from me.
  Now trouble is near,
    and there is no one to help.
¹² Men have surrounded me like angry
    bulls.

The strong bulls of Bashan are on
every side.
[13] Like hungry, roaring lions
they open their jaws at me.
[14] My strength is gone
like water poured out onto the
ground.
All my bones are out of joint.
My heart is like wax.
It has melted inside me.
[15] My strength has dried up like a piece
of a broken pot.
My tongue sticks to the top of my
mouth.
You laid me in the dust of death.
[16] Evil men have surrounded me.
Like dogs they have trapped me.
They have bitten my arms and legs.
[17] I can count all my bones.
People look and stare at me.
[18] They divided my clothes among them,
and they threw lots for my
clothing.

[19] But, Lord, don't be far away.
You are my power. Hurry to help
me.
[20] Save me from the sword.
Save my life from the dogs.
[21] Rescue me from the lion's mouth.
Save me from the horns of the
bulls.

[22] Then I will tell my brothers and
sisters about you.
I will praise you when your people
meet to worship you.
[23] Praise the Lord, all you who worship
him.
All you descendants of Jacob,
honor him.
Fear him, all you Israelites.
[24] The Lord does not ignore
the one who is in trouble.
He doesn't hide from him.
He listens when the one in trouble
calls out to him.
[25] Lord, I praise you in the great
meeting of your people.

These worshipers will see me do
what I promised.
[26] Poor people will eat until they are
full.
Those who look to the Lord will
praise him.
May your hearts live forever!
[27] People everywhere will remember
and will turn to the Lord.
All the families of the nations
will worship him.
[28] This is because the Lord is King.
He rules the nations.

[29] All the powerful people on earth will
eat and worship.
Everyone will bow down to him.
[30] The people in the future will serve
him.
They will always be told about the
Lord.
[31] They will tell that he does what is
right.
People who are not yet born
will hear what God has done.

PSALM 23

THE LORD THE SHEPHERD

A song of David.

[1] The Lord is my shepherd.
I have everything I need.
[2] He gives me rest in green pastures.
He leads me to calm water.
[3] He gives me new strength.
For the good of his name,
he leads me on paths that are right.
[4] Even if I walk
through a very dark valley,
I will not be afraid
because you are with me.
Your rod and your shepherd's staff
comfort me.

[5] You prepare a meal for me
in front of my enemies.
You pour oil of blessing on my head.[n]

23:5 pour oil...head This can mean that God gave him great wealth and blessed him.

You give me more than I can hold.
⁶ Surely your goodness and love will be
with me
all my life.
And I will live in the house of the
Lord forever.

PSALM 24

A WELCOME FOR GOD
INTO THE TEMPLE
A song of David.

¹ The earth and everything in it belong
to the Lord.
The world and all its people belong
to him.
² He built it on the waters.
He set it on the rivers.

³ Who may go up on the mountain of
the Lord?
Who may stand in his holy Temple?
⁴ Only those with clean hands and
pure hearts.
They must not have worshiped
idols.
They must not have made promises
in the name of a false god.
⁵ It is they who will receive a blessing
from the Lord.
The God who saves them will
declare them right.
⁶ They try to follow God.
They look to the God of Jacob for
help.   *Selah*

⁷ Open up, you gates.
Open wide, you aged doors.
Then the glorious king will
come in.
⁸ Who is this glorious king?
The Lord, strong and mighty.
The Lord, the powerful
warrior.
⁹ Open up, you gates.
Open wide, you aged doors.
Then the glorious king will
come in.
¹⁰ Who is this glorious king?

The Lord of heaven's armies—
he is the glorious king.   *Selah*

PSALM 25

A PRAYER FOR GOD TO GUIDE
Of David.

¹ Lord, I give myself to you.
² My God, I trust you.
Do not let me be disgraced.
Do not let my enemies laugh
at me.
³ No one who trusts you will be
disgraced.
But those who sin without excuse
will be disgraced.

⁴ Lord, tell me your ways.
Show me how to live.
⁵ Guide me in your truth.
Teach me, my God, my Savior.
I trust you all day long.
⁶ Lord, remember your mercy and love.
You have shown them since long
ago.
⁷ Do not remember the sins
and wrong things I did when I was
young.
But remember to love me always
because you are good, Lord.

⁸ The Lord is good and right.
He points sinners to the right way.
⁹ He shows those who are not proud
how to do right.
He teaches them his ways.
¹⁰ All the Lord's ways are loving and
true
for those who follow the demands
of his agreement.
¹¹ For the sake of your name, Lord,
forgive my many sins.
¹² Is there someone who worships the
Lord?
The Lord will point him to the best
way.
¹³ He will enjoy a good life.
His children will inherit
the land.

14 The Lord tells his secrets to those
who respect him.
He tells them about his agreement.
15 My eyes are always looking to the
Lord for help.
He will keep me from any
traps.
16 Turn to me and be kind to me.
I am lonely and hurting.
17 My troubles have grown larger.
Free me from my problems.
18 Look at my suffering and troubles.
Take away all my sins.
19 Look at how many enemies
I have!
See how much they hate me!
20 Protect me and save me.
I trust you.
Do not let me be disgraced.
21 My hope is in you.
So may goodness and honesty
guard me.
22 God, save Israel from all their
troubles!

☆ Psalm 25:4-5

David knew where to get help when he needed it. In this song, he asked God to show him how to live. David knew God was the best teacher ever and would help David grow and become a better person. David trusted God for everything.

Food is good for you. And it can taste very yummy! We need food to help our bodies grow and stay healthy. We need Jesus the same way. The Bible teaches us about Jesus and tells us how we should live. Learning about God's word will make you wise and help you grow strong in Jesus.

. . . .

Just like David asked God to teach him and help him grow, you can do the same. When you read your Bible, ask God to be your teacher. He loves to help you grow.

PSALM 26

THE PRAYER OF AN INNOCENT MAN

Of David.

¹ Lord, defend me.
  I have lived an innocent life.
  I trusted the Lord and never doubted.
² Lord, try me and test me.
  Look closely into my heart and mind.
³ I see your love.
  I live by your truth.
⁴ I do not spend time with liars.
  I do not make friends with people
    who hide their sin.
⁵ I hate the company of evil people.
  I won't sit with the wicked.
⁶ I wash my hands to show I am
    innocent.
  I come to your altar, Lord.
⁷ I raise my voice in praise.
  I tell of all the miracles you have
    done.
⁸ Lord, I love the Temple where you live.
  It is where your greatness is.
⁹ Do not kill me with those sinners.
  Do not take my life with those
    murderers.
¹⁰ Evil is in their hands.
  They do wrong for money.
¹¹ But I have lived an innocent life.
  So save me and be kind to me.
¹² I stand in a safe place.
  Lord, I praise you in the great
    meeting.

PSALM 27

A SONG OF TRUST IN GOD

Of David.

¹ The Lord is my light and the one who
    saves me.
  So why should I fear anyone?
  The Lord protects my life.
  So why should I be afraid?
² Evil people may try to destroy my
    body.
  My enemies and those who hate me
    attack me.

But they are overwhelmed and
    defeated.
³ If an army surrounds me,
  I will not be afraid.
If war breaks out,
  I will trust the Lord.

⁴ I ask only one thing from the Lord.
  This is what I want:
Let me live in the Lord's house
  all my life.
Let me see the Lord's beauty.
  Let me look around in his Temple.
⁵ During danger he will keep me safe
    in his shelter.
  He will hide me in his Holy Tent.
  Or he will keep me safe on a high
    mountain.
⁶ My head is higher
  than my enemies around me.
I will offer joyful sacrifices in his
    Holy Tent.
  I will sing and praise the Lord.

⁷ Lord, hear me when I call.
  Be kind and answer me.
⁸ My heart said of you, "Go, worship
    him."
  So I come to worship you, Lord.
⁹ Do not turn away from me.
  Do not turn your servant away in
    anger.
  You have helped me.
Do not push me away or leave me
    alone,
  God, my Savior.
¹⁰ If my father and mother leave me,
  the Lord will take me in.
¹¹ Lord, teach me your ways.
  Guide me to do what is right
  because I have enemies.
¹² Do not let my enemies defeat me.
  They tell lies about me.
  They say they will hurt me.

¹³ I truly believe
  I will live to see the Lord's
    goodness.
¹⁴ Wait for the Lord's help.
  Be strong and brave
  and wait for the Lord's help.

PSALM 28

A PRAYER IN TROUBLED TIMES
Of David.

¹ Lord, my Rock, I call out to you for
help.
  Do not be deaf to me.
If you are silent,
  I will be like those in the grave.
² Hear the sound of my prayer,
  when I cry out to you for help.
I raise my hands
  toward your Most Holy Place.
³ Don't drag me away with the wicked,
  with those who do evil.
They say, "Peace" to their neighbors.
  But evil is in their hearts.
⁴ Pay them back for what they have
done.
  They have done evil.
Pay them back for what they have done.
  Give them their reward.
⁵ They don't understand what the Lord
has done
  or what he has made.
So he will knock them down
  and not lift them up.

⁶ Praise the Lord.
  He heard my prayer for help.
⁷ The Lord is my strength and shield.
  I trust him, and he helps me.
I am very happy.
  And I praise him with my song.
⁸ The Lord is powerful.
  He gives power and victory to his
chosen one.
⁹ Save your people.
  Bless those who are your own.
Be their shepherd and carry them
forever.

PSALM 29

GOD IN THE THUNDERSTORM
A song of David.

¹ Praise the Lord, you angels.
  Praise the Lord's glory and power.

² Praise the Lord for the glory of his
name.
  Worship the Lord because he is
holy.

³ The Lord's voice is heard over the
sea.
  The glorious God thunders.
  The Lord thunders over the great
ocean.
⁴ The Lord's voice is powerful.
  The Lord's voice is majestic.
⁵ The Lord's voice breaks the trees.
  The Lord breaks the cedars of
Lebanon.
⁶ He makes the land of Lebanon dance
like a calf.
  He makes Mount Hermon jump
like a baby bull.
⁷ The Lord's voice makes the lightning
flash.
⁸ The Lord's voice shakes the desert.
  The Lord shakes the Desert of
Kadesh.
⁹ The Lord's voice shakes the oaks.
  The leaves fall off the trees.
In his Temple everyone says, "Glory
to God!"

¹⁰ The Lord controls the flood.
  The Lord will be King forever.
¹¹ The Lord gives strength to his
people.

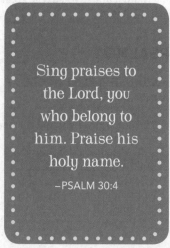

Sing praises to
the Lord, you
who belong to
him. Praise his
holy name.

–PSALM 30:4

The Lord blesses his people with peace.

PSALM 30

THANKSGIVING FOR ESCAPING DEATH

A song of David. A song for giving the Temple to the Lord.

1 I will praise you, Lord,
    because you rescued me.
    You did not let my enemies laugh
        at me.
2 Lord, my God, I prayed to you.
    And you healed me.
3 You lifted me out of the grave.
    You spared me from going down
        where the dead are.

4 Sing praises to the Lord, you who
        belong to him.
    Praise his holy name.
5 His anger lasts only a moment.
    But his kindness lasts for a lifetime.
    Crying may last for a night.
    But joy comes in the morning.

6 When I felt safe, I said,
    "I will never fail."
7 Lord, in your kindness you made my
        mountain safe.
    But when you turned away, I was
        frightened.

8 I called to you, Lord.
    I asked you to have mercy on me.
9 I said, "What good will it do if I die
    or if I go down to the grave?
    Dust cannot praise you.
    It cannot speak about your truth.
10 Lord, hear me and be merciful
        to me.
    Lord, help me."

11 You changed my sorrow into dancing.
    You took away my rough cloth,
        which shows sadness, and
        clothed me in happiness.
12 I will sing to you and not be silent.

Lord, my God, I will praise you
    forever.

PSALM 31

A PRAYER OF FAITH IN TROUBLED TIMES

For the director of music.
A song of David.

1 Lord, I trust in you.
    Let me never be disgraced.
    Save me because you do what is
        right.
2 Listen to me.
    Save me quickly.
  Be my rock of protection,
    a strong city to save me.
3 You are my rock and my protection.
    For the good of your name, lead me
        and guide me.
4 Set me free from the trap they set for
        me.
    You are my protection.
5 I give you my life.
    Save me, Lord, God of truth.

6 I hate those who worship false gods.
    I trust only in the Lord.
7 I will be glad because of your love.
    You saw my suffering.
    You knew my troubles.
8 You have not let my enemies defeat
        me.
    You have set me in a safe place.

9 Lord, have mercy. I am in misery.
    My eyes are weak from so much
        crying.
    My whole being is tired from grief.
10 My life is ending in sadness.
    My years are spent in crying.
    My troubles are using up my
        strength.
    My bones are getting weaker.
11 Because of all my troubles, my
        enemies hate me.
    Even my neighbors look down on me.
    When my friends see me,
        they are afraid and run.

¹² I am like a piece of a broken pot.
I am forgotten as if I were dead.
¹³ I have heard many insults.
Terror is all around me.
They make plans against me.
They want to kill me.

¹⁴ Lord, I trust you.
I have said, "You are my God."
¹⁵ My life is in your hands.
Save me from my enemies' grasp.
Save me from those who are
chasing me.
¹⁶ Show your kindness to me, your
servant.
Save me because of your love.
¹⁷ Lord, I called to you.
So do not let me be disgraced.
Let the wicked be disgraced.
Let them lie silent in the grave.
¹⁸ With pride and hatred
they speak against the
righteous.
So shut their lying lips.

¹⁹ How great is your goodness!
You have stored it up for those who
fear you.
You do good things for those who
trust you.
You do this for all to see.
²⁰ You protect them by your presence
from what people plan against
them.
You keep them safe in your shelter
from evil words.
²¹ Praise the Lord.
His love to me was wonderful
when my city was attacked.
²² In my distress, I said,
"God cannot see me!"
But you heard my prayer
when I cried out to you for help.
²³ Love the Lord, all you who belong to
him.
The Lord protects those who truly
believe.
But he punishes the proud as much
as they have sinned.
²⁴ All you who put your hope in the Lord
be strong and brave.

PSALM 32

IT IS BETTER TO CONFESS SIN
A maskil of David.

¹ Happy is the person
whose sins are forgiven,
whose wrongs are pardoned.
² Happy is the person
whom the Lord does not consider
guilty.
In that person there is nothing
false.

³ When I kept things to myself,
I felt weak deep inside me.
I moaned all day long.
⁴ Day and night
you punished me.
My strength was gone
as in the summer heat.   *Selah*
⁵ Then I confessed my sins to you.
I didn't hide my guilt.
I said, "I will confess my sins to the
Lord."
And you forgave my guilt.   *Selah*

⁶ For this reason, all who obey you
should pray to you while they still
can.
When troubles rise like a flood,
they will not reach them.
⁷ You are my hiding place.
You protect me from my troubles.
You fill me with songs of salvation.
Selah

⁸ The Lord says, "I will make you wise.
I will show you where to go.
I will guide you and watch over you.
⁹ So don't be like a horse or donkey.
They don't understand.
They must be led with bits and reins,
or they will not come near you."

¹⁰ Wicked people have many troubles.
But the Lord's love surrounds those
who trust him.
¹¹ Good people, rejoice and be happy in
the Lord.
All you whose hearts are right, sing.

PSALM 33

PRAISE GOD WHO CREATES AND SAVES

¹ Sing to the Lord, you who do what is
    right.
    Honest people should praise him.
² Praise the Lord on the harp.
    Make music for him on the
    ten-stringed lyre.
³ Sing a new song to him.
    Play well and joyfully.

⁴ God's word is true.
    Everything he does is right.
⁵ He loves what is right and fair.
    The Lord's love fills the earth.

⁶ The sky was made at the Lord's
    command.
    By the breath from his mouth, he
    made all the stars.
⁷ He gathered the water in the sea into
    a heap.
    He made the great ocean stay in its
    place.
⁸ All the earth should worship the Lord.
    The whole world should fear him.
⁹ He spoke, and it happened.
    He commanded, and it appeared.
¹⁰ The Lord upsets the plans of nations.
    He ruins all their plans.
¹¹ But the Lord's plans will stand
    forever.
    His ideas will last from now on.
¹² Happy is the nation whose God is the
    Lord.
    Happy are the people he chose for
    his very own.
¹³ The Lord looks down from heaven.
    He sees every person.
¹⁴ From his throne he watches
    everyone who lives on earth.
¹⁵ He made their hearts.
    He understands everything they do.
¹⁶ No king is saved by his great army.
    No warrior escapes by his great
    strength.
¹⁷ Horses can't bring victory.
    They can't save by their strength.

¹⁸ But the Lord looks after those who
    fear him.
    He watches over those who put
    their hope in his love.
¹⁹ He saves them from death.
    He spares their lives in times of
    hunger.
²⁰ So our hope is in the Lord.
    He is our help, our shield to protect
    us.
²¹ We rejoice in him.
    We trust his holy name.
²² Lord, show your love to us
    as we put our hope in you.

PSALM 34

PRAISE GOD WHO JUDGES AND SAVES

David's song from the time he acted crazy
so Abimelech would send him away.
And David did leave.

¹ I will praise the Lord at all times.
    His praise is always on my lips.
² My whole being praises the Lord.
    The poor will hear and be glad.
³ Tell the greatness of the Lord
    with me.
    Let us praise his name together.

⁴ I asked the Lord for help, and he
    answered me.
    He saved me from all that I feared.
⁵ Those who go to him for help are
    happy.
    They are never disgraced.
⁶ This poor man called, and the Lord
    heard him.
    The Lord saved him from all his
    troubles.
⁷ The Lord saves those who fear him.
    His angel camps around them.

⁸ Examine and see how good the
    Lord is.
    Happy is the person who trusts the
    Lord.
⁹ People who belong to the Lord, fear
    him!

Those who fear him will have
everything they need.
¹⁰ Even lions may become weak and
hungry.
But those people who go to the
Lord for help will have every
good thing.
¹¹ Children, come and listen to me.
I will teach you to worship the Lord.
¹² You must do these things
to enjoy life and have many happy
days.
¹³ You must not say evil things.
You must not tell lies.
¹⁴ Stop doing evil and do good.
Look for peace and work for it.

¹⁵ The Lord sees the good people.
He listens to their prayers.
¹⁶ But the Lord is against those who
do evil.
He makes the world forget them.
¹⁷ The Lord hears good people when
they cry out to him.
He saves them from all their
troubles.
¹⁸ The Lord is close to the
brokenhearted.
He saves those whose spirits have
been crushed.

¹⁹ People who do what is right may have
many problems.
But the Lord will solve them all.
²⁰ He will protect their very bones.
Not one of them will be broken.
²¹ Evil will kill the wicked people.
Those who hate good people will
be judged guilty.
²² But the Lord saves his servants' lives.
No one who trusts him will be
judged guilty.

PSALM 35

A PRAYER FOR HELP
Of David.

¹ Lord, battle with those who battle
with me.

Fight against those who fight
against me.
² Pick up the shield and armor.
Rise up and help me.
³ Lift up your spears, both large and
small,
against those who chase me.
Tell me, "I will save you."

⁴ Make those who want to kill me
be ashamed and disgraced.
Make those who plan to harm me
turn back and run away.
⁵ Make them like chaff blown by the
wind.
Let the angel of the Lord chase
them away.
⁶ Let their road be dark and slippery
as the angel of the Lord chases
them.
⁷ For no reason they spread out their
net to trap me.
For no reason they dug a pit for me.
⁸ So let ruin strike them suddenly.
Let them be caught in their own
nets.
Let them fall into the pit and die.
⁹ Then I will rejoice in the Lord.
I will be happy when he saves me.
¹⁰ Even my bones will say,
"Lord, who is like you?
You save the weak from the strong.
You save the weak and poor from
robbers."

¹¹ Men without mercy stand up to testify.
They ask me things I do not know.
¹² They repay me with evil for the good
I have done.
They make me very sad.
¹³ Yet when they were sick, I put on
rough cloth to show my sadness.
I showed my sorrow by going
without food.
But my prayers were not answered.
¹⁴ I acted as if they were my friends or
brothers.
I bowed in sadness as if I were crying
for my mother.
¹⁵ But when I was in trouble, they
gathered and laughed.

They gathered to attack before I
   knew it.
They insulted me without
   stopping.
¹⁶ They made fun of me and were cruel
   to me.
   They ground their teeth at me in
      anger.

¹⁷ Lord, how long will you watch this
   happen?
   Save my life from their attacks.
   Save me from these people who are
      like lions.
¹⁸ I will praise you in the great meeting.
   I will praise you among crowds of
      people.
¹⁹ Do not let my enemies laugh at me.
   They hate me for no reason.
   Do not let them make fun of me.
   They have no reason to
      hate me.
²⁰ Their words are not friendly.
   They think up lies about
      peace-loving people.
²¹ They speak against me.
   They say, "Aha! We saw what you
      did!"

²² Lord, you have been watching. Do
   not keep quiet.
   Lord, do not leave me alone.
²³ Wake up! Come and defend me!
   My God and Lord, fight for me!
²⁴ Lord my God, defend me with your
   justice.
   Don't let them laugh at me.
²⁵ Don't let them think, "Aha! We got
   what we wanted!"
   Don't let them say, "We destroyed
      him."
²⁶ Let them be ashamed and
   embarrassed.
   They were happy when I hurt.
   Cover them with shame and disgrace.
   They thought they were better
      than I was.
²⁷ May my friends sing and shout for
   joy.
   May they always say, "Praise the
      greatness of the Lord.

He loves to see his servants do
   well."
²⁸ I will tell of your goodness.
   I will praise you every day.

PSALM 36

WICKED MEN AND A GOOD GOD

For the director of music. Of David,
the servant of the Lord.

¹ Sin speaks to the wicked man in his
   heart.
   He has no fear of or respect for
      God.
² He thinks too much of himself.
   He doesn't see his sin and hate it.
³ His words are wicked lies.
   He is no longer wise or good.
⁴ At night he makes evil plans.
   What he does leads to nothing
      good.
   He doesn't refuse things that are
      evil.

⁵ Lord, your love reaches to the
   heavens.
   Your loyalty goes to the skies.
⁶ Your goodness is as high as the
   mountains.

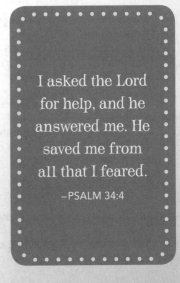

I asked the Lord
for help, and he
answered me. He
saved me from
all that I feared.

–PSALM 34:4

☆ Psalm 37:5

David wrote a lot of songs when he was by himself. But he probably knew that other people would read them someday (like us!). So some of his songs, like Psalm 37, were written to help others trust God like David did.

When you were a baby, you had to depend on your parents for everything. They changed your diapers, fed you, carried you, and protected you from bad things. They did that because they love you! But as you grew, you got more independent. You probably said things like, "I can do it myself." It's fun to learn and to try things for the first time. But we still need to trust our parents. You can depend on them because they want to take care of you. Our heavenly Father is the same way. He protects us because he loves us.

. . . .

We can depend on God and trust him in everything. He loves to take care of us.

Your justice is as deep as the great ocean.
Lord, you protect both men and animals.
⁷ God, your love is so precious!
You protect people as a bird protects her young under her wings.
⁸ They eat the rich food in your house.
You let them drink from your river of pleasure.
⁹ You are the giver of life.
Your light lets us enjoy life.

¹⁰ Continue to love those who know you.
And continue to do good to those who are good.

¹¹ Don't let proud people attack me.
Don't let the wicked force me away.
¹² Those who do evil have been defeated.
They are overwhelmed; they cannot do evil any longer.

PSALM 37

GOD WILL REWARD FAIRLY
Of David.

¹ Don't be upset because of evil people.
Don't be jealous of those who do wrong.
² Like the grass, they will soon dry up.

Like green plants, they will soon
die away.

3 Trust the Lord and do good.
Live in the land and enjoy its
safety.
4 Enjoy serving the Lord.
And he will give you what you
want.
5 Depend on the Lord.
Trust him, and he will take care of
you.
6 Then your goodness will shine like
the sun.
Your fairness will shine like the
noonday sun.

7 Wait and trust the Lord.
Don't be upset when others get rich
or when someone else's plans
succeed.
8 Don't get angry.
Don't be upset; it only leads to
trouble.
9 Evil people will be sent away.
But people who trust the Lord will
inherit the land.
10 In a little while there will be no more
wicked people.
You may look for them, but they
will be gone.
11 People who are not proud will inherit
the land.
They will enjoy complete peace.

12 The wicked make evil plans against
good people.
They grind their teeth at them in
anger.
13 But the Lord laughs at the wicked.
He sees that their day is coming.
14 The wicked draw their swords.
They bend their bows.
They try to kill the poor and helpless.
They want to kill those who are
honest.
15 But their swords will stab their own
hearts.
Their bows will break.

16 It's better to have little and be right

than to have much and be wrong.
17 The power of the wicked will be
broken.
But the Lord supports those who
do right.
18 The Lord watches over the lives of
the innocent.
Their reward will last forever.
19 They will not be ashamed when
trouble comes.
They will be full in times of hunger.
20 But the wicked will die.
The Lord's enemies will be like the
flowers of the fields.
They will disappear like smoke.
21 The wicked people borrow but don't
pay back.
But those who do right give freely
to others.
22 Those people the Lord blesses will
inherit the land.
But those he curses will be sent
away.

23 When a man's steps follow the Lord,
God is pleased with his ways.
24 If he stumbles, he will not fall,
because the Lord holds his hand.

25 I was young, and now I am old.
But I have never seen the Lord
leave good people helpless.
I have never seen their children
begging for food.
26 Good people always lend freely to
others.
And their children are a blessing.

27 Stop doing evil and do good.
Then you will live forever.
28 The Lord loves justice.
He will not leave those who
worship him.
He will always protect them.
But the children of the wicked will
die.
29 Good people will inherit the land.
They will live in it forever.

30 A good person speaks with wisdom.
He says what is fair.

³¹ The teachings of his God are in his
heart.
He does not fail to keep them.
³² The wicked watch for good people.
They want to kill them.
³³ The Lord will not take away his
protection.
He will not judge good people
guilty.

³⁴ Wait for the Lord's help
and follow him.
He will honor you and give you the
land.
And you will see the wicked people
sent away.

³⁵ I saw a wicked and cruel man.
He looked strong like a healthy tree
in good soil.
³⁶ But he died and was gone.
I looked for him, but he couldn't be
found.

³⁷ Think of the innocent person.
Watch the honest one.
The man who has peace
will have children to live after him.
³⁸ But sinners will be destroyed.
In the end the wicked will die.

³⁹ The Lord saves good people.
He is their strong city in times of
trouble.
⁴⁰ The Lord helps them and saves them.
He saves them from the wicked
because they trust in him for
protection.

PSALM 38

A PRAYER IN TIME OF SICKNESS
A song of David to remember.

¹ Lord, don't correct me when you are
angry.
Don't punish me when you are very
angry.
² Your arrows have wounded me.
Your hand has come down on me.

³ My body is sick from your
punishment.
Even my bones are not healthy
because of my sin.
⁴ My guilt has overwhelmed me.
Like a load it weighs me down.

⁵ My sores stink and become infected
because I was foolish.
⁶ I am bent over and bowed down.
I am sad all day long.
⁷ I am burning with fever.
My whole body is sore.
⁸ I am weak and faint.
I moan from the pain I feel.

⁹ Lord, you know everything I want.
My cries are not hidden from you.
¹⁰ My heart pounds, and my strength is
gone.
I am losing my sight.
¹¹ Because of my wounds, my friends
and neighbors leave me alone.
My relatives stay far away.
¹² Some people set traps to kill me.
Those who want to hurt me plan
trouble.
All day long they think up lies.

¹³ I am like a deaf man; I cannot hear.
Like a mute, I cannot speak.
¹⁴ I am like a person who does not hear.

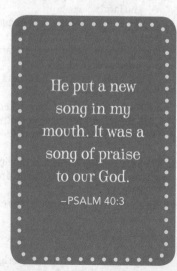

He put a new
song in my
mouth. It was a
song of praise
to our God.

−PSALM 40:3

I have no answer to give.
¹⁵ I trust you, Lord.
    You will answer, my God and Lord.
¹⁶ I said, "Don't let them laugh at me.
    Don't let them brag when I am
        defeated."
¹⁷ I am about to die.
    I cannot forget my pain.
¹⁸ I confess my guilt.
    I am troubled by my sin.
¹⁹ My enemies are strong and healthy.
    Many people hate me for no reason.
²⁰ They repay me with evil for the good
      I did.
    They lie about me because I try to
      do good.

²¹ Lord, don't leave me.
    My God, don't go away.
²² Quickly come and help me,
    my Lord and Savior.

PSALM 39

LIFE IS SHORT

For the director of music. For Jeduthun.
A song of David.

¹ I said, "I will be careful how I act.
    I will not sin by what I say.
  I will be careful what I say
    around wicked people."
² So I kept very quiet.
    I didn't even say anything good.
  But I became even more upset.
³ I became very angry inside.
    And the more I thought about it,
      the angrier I became.
  So I spoke:
⁴ "Lord, tell me when the end will
      come.
    How long will I live?
  Let me know how long I have.
⁵ You have given me only a short life.
    My lifetime is like nothing to you.
  Everyone's life is only a breath.
                Selah
⁶ A person is like a shadow moving
      about.
    All his work is for nothing.

He collects things, but he doesn't
    know who will get them.

⁷ "So, Lord, what hope do I have?
    You are my hope.
⁸ Save me from all my sins.
    Don't let wicked fools make fun
      of me.
⁹ I am quiet. I do not open my mouth.
    You are the one who has done this.
¹⁰ Quit punishing me.
    Your beating is about to kill me.
¹¹ You correct and punish people for
      their sins.
    Like a moth, you destroy what they
      love.
    Everyone's life is only a breath.
                Selah
¹² "Lord, hear my prayer.
    Listen to my cry.
    Do not ignore my tears.
  I am like a visitor with you.
    Like my ancestors, I'm only here a
      short time.
¹³ Leave me alone so I can be happy.
    Soon I will leave and be no more."

PSALM 40

PRAISE AND PRAYER FOR HELP

For the director of music.
A song of David.

¹ I waited patiently for the Lord.
    He turned to me and heard my cry.
² He lifted me out of the pit of
      destruction,
    out of the sticky mud.
  He stood me on a rock.
    He made my feet steady.
³ He put a new song in my mouth.
    It was a song of praise to our God.
  Many people will see this and
      worship him.
    Then they will trust the Lord.

⁴ Happy is the person
    who trusts the Lord.
  He doesn't turn to those who are
      proud,

to those who worship false gods.
⁵ Lord our God, you have done many
    miracles.
    Your plans for us are many.
  If I tried to tell them all,
    there would be too many to count.

⁶ You do not want sacrifices and
    offerings.
    But you have made a hole in my ear
    to show that my body and life are
    yours.
  You do not ask for burnt offerings
    and offerings to take away sins.
⁷ Then I said, "Look, I have come.
    It is written about me in the book.
⁸ My God, I want to do what you want.
    Your teachings are in my heart."

⁹ I will tell about your goodness in the
    great meeting of your people.
    Lord, you know my lips are not
    silent.
¹⁰ I do not hide your goodness in my
    heart.
    I speak about your loyalty and
    salvation.
  I do not hide your love and truth
    from the people in the great
    meeting.

¹¹ Lord, do not hold back your mercy
    from me.
    Let your love and truth always
    protect me.
¹² Troubles have gathered around me.
    There are too many to count.
  My sins have caught me.
    I cannot see a way to escape.
  I have more sins than hairs on my
    head.
    I have lost my courage.
¹³ Please, Lord, save me.
    Hurry, Lord, to help me.
¹⁴ People are trying to kill me.
    Shame them and disgrace them.
  People want to hurt me.
    Let them run away in disgrace.
¹⁵ People are making fun of me.
    Let them be shamed into silence.
¹⁶ But let those who follow you

    be happy and glad.
  They love you for saving them.
    May they always say, "Praise the
    Lord!"

¹⁷ Lord, I am poor and helpless.
    But please remember me.
  You are my helper and savior.
    My God, do not wait.

PSALM 41

A PRAYER IN TIME OF SICKNESS

For the director of music.
A song of David.

¹ Happy is the person who thinks
    about the poor.
    When trouble comes, the Lord will
    save him.
² The Lord will protect him and spare
    his life.
    The Lord will bless him in the land.
    The Lord will not let his enemies
    take him.
³ The Lord will give him strength
    when he is sick.
    The Lord will make him well again.

⁴ I said, "Lord, be kind to me.
    Heal me because I have sinned
    against you."
⁵ My enemies are saying bad things
    about me.
    They say, "When will he die and be
    forgotten?"
⁶ Some people come to see me.
    But they lie.
  They just come to get bad news.
    Then they go and gossip.
⁷ All my enemies whisper about me.
    They think the worst about me.
⁸ They say, "He has a terrible disease.
    He will never get out of bed again."
⁹ My best and truest friend ate at my
    table.
    Now even he has turned against
    me.

¹⁰ Lord, have mercy on me.

Give me strength so I can pay them
   back.
[11] My enemies do not defeat me.
   That's how I know you are pleased
      with me.
[12] Because I am innocent, you support
      me.
   You will let me be with you forever.

[13] Praise the Lord, the God of Israel.
   He has always been,
   and he will always be.
         Amen and amen.

BOOK 4
Psalms 90—106

PSALM 90

GOD IS ETERNAL, AND
WE ARE NOT
A prayer of Moses, the man of God.

[1] Lord, you have been our home
   since the beginning.
[2] Before the mountains were born,
   and before you created the earth
      and the world,
   you are God.
      You have always been, and you will
         always be.

[3] You turn people back into dust.
   You say, "Go back into dust, human
      beings."
[4] To you, a thousand years
   is like the passing of a day.
   It passes like an hour in the night.
[5] While people sleep, you take their
      lives.
   They are like weeds that grow in
      the morning.
[6] In the morning they are fresh and new.
   But by evening they dry up and die.

[7] We are destroyed by your anger.
   We are terrified by your hot anger.
[8] You have put the evil we have done
      right in front of you.
   You clearly see our secret sins.

[9] All our days pass while you are angry.
   Our years end with a moan.
[10] Our lifetime is 70 years.
   If we are strong, we may live to
      be 80.
   But the years are full of hard work
      and pain.
      They pass quickly, and then we are
         gone.

[11] Who knows the full power of your
      anger?
   Your anger is as great as our fear of
      you should be.
[12] Teach us how short our lives really are
   so that we may be wise.

[13] Lord, how long before you return
   and show kindness to your
      servants?
[14] Fill us with your love every morning.
   Then we will sing and rejoice all
      our lives.
[15] We have seen years of trouble.
   Now give us joy as you gave us
      sorrow.
[16] Show your servants the wonderful
      things you do.
   Show your greatness to their
      children.
[17] Lord our God, be pleased with us.
   Give us success in what we do.
   Yes, give us success in what we do.

PSALM 91

SAFE IN THE LORD

[1] Those who go to God Most High for
      safety
   will be protected by God
      All-Powerful.
[2] I will say to the Lord, "You are my
      place of safety and protection.
   You are my God, and I trust you."

[3] God will save you from hidden traps
   and from deadly diseases.
[4] He will protect you like a bird
   spreading its wings over its young.

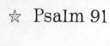

☆ Psalm 91

The person who wrote Psalm 91 knew that others would read it. The psalmist wanted us to know that God protects us. He watches over us just like a mother bird wraps her wings around her baby chicks.

When a mother bird has little baby birds, she takes care of them. The mother bird does not let anyone or anything hurt the baby birds. God does the same for you. When God protects you, He keeps you safe. He takes care of you in every way. God protects you every day in ways that you do not even know. God is protecting you all the time.

. . . .

Whenever you feel scared, read Psalm 91 out loud. Trust God that he means what he says: He will protect you!

His truth will be like your armor
 and shield.
5 You will not fear any danger by night
 or an arrow during the day.
6 You will not be afraid of diseases that
 come in the dark
 or sickness that strikes at noon.
7 At your side 1,000 people may die,
 or even 10,000 right beside you.
 But you will not be hurt.
8 You will only watch what happens.
 You will see the wicked punished.

9 The Lord is your protection.
 You have made God Most High
 your place of safety.
10 Nothing bad will happen to you.
 No disaster will come to your
 home.
11 He has put his angels in charge of you.
 They will watch over you wherever
 you go.
12 They will catch you with their hands.
 And you will not hit your foot on
 a rock.

13 You will walk on lions and cobras.
 You will step on strong lions and
 snakes.

14 The Lord says, "If someone loves me,
 I will save him.
 I will protect those who
 know me.
15 They will call to me, and I will
 answer them.
 I will be with them in trouble.
 I will rescue them and honor
 them.
16 I will give them a long, full life.
 They will see how I can save."

PSALM 92

THANKSGIVING FOR GOD'S GOODNESS

A song for the Sabbath day.

1 It is good to praise the Lord,
 to sing praises to God Most High.

² It is good to tell of your love in the morning
and of your loyalty at night.
³ It is good to praise you with the ten-stringed lyre
and with the soft-sounding harp.

⁴ Lord, you have made me happy by what you have done.
I will sing for joy about what your hands have done.
⁵ Lord, you have done such great things!
How deep are your thoughts!
⁶ Stupid people don't know these things.
Fools don't understand.
⁷ Wicked people grow like the grass.
Evil people seem to do well.
But they will be destroyed forever.
⁸ But, Lord, you will be honored forever.

⁹ Lord, surely your enemies,
surely your enemies will be destroyed.
All who do evil will be scattered.
¹⁰ But you have made me as strong as a wild ox.
You have poured fine oils on me.
¹¹ When I looked, I saw my enemies.
I heard the cries of those who are against me.

¹² But good people will grow like palm trees.
They will be tall like the cedar trees of Lebanon.
¹³ They will be like trees planted in the courtyards of the Lord.
They will grow strong in the courtyards of our God.
¹⁴ When they are old, they will still produce fruit.
They will be healthy and fresh.
¹⁵ They will say that the Lord is good.
He is my Rock, and there is no wrong in him.

PSALM 93

THE MAJESTY OF GOD

¹ The Lord is king. He is clothed with majesty.
The Lord is clothed in majesty
and armed with strength.
The world is set,
and it cannot be moved.
² Lord, your kingdom was set up long ago.
You are everlasting.

³ Lord, the seas rise up.
The seas raise their voice.
The seas lift up their pounding waves.
⁴ The sound of the water is loud.
The ocean waves are powerful.
But the Lord above is much greater.

⁵ Lord, your laws will stand forever.
Your Temple will be holy forevermore.

PSALM 94

GOD WILL PAY BACK HIS ENEMIES

¹ The Lord is a God who gives people what they should get.
God, show your greatness and punish!
² Rise up, Judge of the earth.
Give the proud what they should get.
³ How long will the wicked be happy?
How long, Lord?

⁴ They are full of proud words.
Those who do evil brag about what they have done.
⁵ Lord, they crush your people.
They make your children suffer.
⁶ They kill widows and foreigners.
They murder orphans.
⁷ They say, "The Lord doesn't see.
The God of Jacob doesn't notice."

8 You stupid ones among the people,
   pay attention.
      You fools, when will you
         understand?
9 Can't the creator of ears hear?
      Can't the maker of eyes see?
10 Won't the one who corrects nations
      punish you?
      Doesn't the teacher of men know
         everything?
11 The Lord knows what people think.
      He knows they are just a puff of
         wind.

12 Lord, those you correct are happy.
      You give them your teachings.
13 You give them rest from times of
      trouble
      until a grave is dug for the wicked.
14 The Lord won't leave his people.
      He will not give up his children.
15 Judgment will again be fair.
      And all who are honest will
         follow it.

16 Who will help me fight against the
      wicked?
      Who will stand with me against
         those who do evil?
17 If the Lord had not helped me,
      I would have died soon.
18 I said, "I am about to be
      overwhelmed."
      But, Lord, your love kept me safe.
19 I was very worried.
      But you comforted me and made
         me happy.

20 Crooked leaders cannot be your
      friends.
      They use the law to cause suffering.
21 They join forces against people who
      do right.
      They sentence to death the
         innocent.
22 But the Lord protects me like a
      strong, walled city.
      My God is the rock of my protection.
23 God will pay them back for their sins.
      He will destroy them for their evil.
      The Lord our God will destroy them.

PSALM 95

A CALL TO PRAISE AND OBEDIENCE

1 Come, let's sing for joy to the Lord.
      Let's shout praises to the Rock who
         saves us.
2 Let's come to him with thanksgiving.
      Let's sing songs to him.
3 The Lord is the great God.
      He is the great King over all gods.
4 The deepest places on earth are his.
      And the highest mountains belong
         to him.
5 The sea is his because he made it.
      He created the land with his own
         hands.

6 Come, let's bow down and worship
      him.
      Let's kneel before the Lord who
         made us.
7 He is our God.
      And we are the people he takes
         care of
      and the sheep that he tends.

   Today listen to what he says:
8   "Do not be stubborn, as your
         ancestors were at Meribah,
      as they were that day at Massah in
         the desert.
9 There your ancestors tested me.
      They put me to the test even
         though they saw what I did.
10 I was angry with those people for 40
      years.
      I said, 'They are not loyal to me.
      They have not understood my ways.'
11 I was angry and made a promise,
      'They will never enter my land of
         rest.'"

PSALM 96

PRAISE FOR GOD'S GLORY

1 Sing to the Lord a new song.
      Sing to the Lord, all the earth.
2 Sing to the Lord and praise his name.

Every day tell how he saves us.
³ Tell the nations of his glory.
Tell all peoples the miracles he does.

⁴ The Lord is great; he should be praised.
He should be honored more than all the gods.
⁵ All the gods of the nations are only idols.
But the Lord made the skies.
⁶ The Lord has glory and majesty.
He has power and beauty in his Temple.

⁷ Praise the Lord, all nations on earth.
Praise the Lord's glory and power.
⁸ Praise the glory of the Lord's name.
Bring an offering and come into his Temple courtyards.
⁹ Worship the Lord because he is holy.
The whole earth should tremble before the Lord.
¹⁰ Tell the nations, "The Lord is king."
The earth is set, and it cannot be moved.
He will judge the people fairly.
¹¹ Let the skies rejoice and the earth be glad.
Let the sea and everything in it shout.
¹² Let the fields and everything in them show their joy.
Then all the trees of the forest will sing for joy.
¹³ They will sing before the Lord because he is coming.
He is coming to judge the world.
He will judge the world with fairness and the nations with truth.

PSALM 97

A HYMN ABOUT GOD'S POWER

¹ The Lord is king. Let the earth rejoice.
Faraway lands should be glad.

² Thick, dark clouds surround him.
His kingdom is built on what is right and fair.
³ A fire goes before him
and burns up his enemies all around.
⁴ His lightning flashes in the sky.
When the people see it, they tremble.
⁵ The mountains melt like wax before the Lord.
He is Lord of all the earth.
⁶ The skies tell about his goodness.
And all the people see his glory.

⁷ Those who worship idols should be ashamed.
They brag about their false gods.
All the gods should worship the Lord.
⁸ When Jerusalem hears this, she is glad.
The towns of Judah rejoice.
They are happy because of your judgments, Lord.
⁹ You are the Lord Most High over all the earth.
You are supreme over all gods.

¹⁰ People who love the Lord should hate evil.

Let the fields and everything in them show their joy. Then all the trees of the forest will sing for joy.

–PSALM 96:12

The Lord watches over those who
follow him.
He frees them from the power of
the wicked.
11 Light shines on those who do right.
Joy belongs to those who are honest.
12 Rejoice in the Lord, you who do right.
Praise his holy name.

PSALM 98

THE GOD OF POWER AND JUSTICE
A song.

1 Sing to the Lord a new song
because he has done miracles.
By his right hand and holy arm
he has won the victory.
2 The Lord has told about his power
to save.
He has shown the other nations his
victory for his people.
3 He has remembered his love
and his loyalty to the people of
Israel.
All the ends of the earth have seen
God's power to save.

4 Shout with joy to the Lord, all the
earth.
Burst into songs and praise.
5 Make music to the Lord with harps,
with harps and the sound of
singing.
6 Blow the trumpets and the sheep's
horns.
Shout for joy to the Lord the King.

7 Let the sea and everything in it shout.
Let the world and everyone on it
sing.
8 Let the rivers clap their hands.
Let the mountains sing together
for joy.
9 Let them sing before the Lord
because he is coming to judge the
world.
He will judge the world fairly.
He will judge the nations with
fairness.

PSALM 99

GOD THE FAIR AND HOLY KING

1 The Lord is king.
Let the nations shake with fear.
He sits between the gold creatures
with wings.
Let the earth shake.
2 The Lord in Jerusalem is great.
He is supreme over all the nations.
3 Let them praise your name.
It is great, holy and to be feared.

4 The King is powerful and loves justice.
Lord, you made things fair.
You have done what is fair and right
for the people of Jacob.
5 Praise the Lord our God.
Worship at the Temple, his footstool.
He is holy.

6 Moses and Aaron were among his
priests.
And Samuel was among his
worshipers.
They called to the Lord,
and he answered them.
7 He spoke to them from the pillar of
cloud.
They kept the rules and laws he
gave them.

8 Lord our God, you answered them.
You showed them that you are a
forgiving God.
But you punished them for their
wrongs.
9 Praise the Lord our God.
Worship at his holy mountain.
The Lord our God is holy.

PSALM 100

A CALL TO PRAISE GOD
A song of thanks.

1 Shout to the Lord, all the earth.
2 Serve the Lord with joy.
Come before him with singing.

☆ Psalm 100

This song praises God. It encourages all of us to come to God with a joyful and thankful heart.

Have you ever seen someone who just seems sad all the time? If you ask them how they are doing, they always tell you about a problem they have. We all have problems sometimes. But God does not want us, his children, to be sad all the time. God wants us to be full of joy. And we can be joyful when we think about all the good things he does for us. When we think about the good things, we become thankful and joyful. It can be fun!

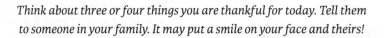

Think about three or four things you are thankful for today. Tell them to someone in your family. It may put a smile on your face and theirs!

³ Know that the Lord is God.
    He made us, and we belong to him.
    We are his people, the sheep he
        tends.

⁴ Come into his city with songs of
        thanksgiving.
    Come into his courtyards with
        songs of praise.
    Thank him, and praise his name.
⁵ The Lord is good. His love continues
        forever.
    His loyalty continues from now on.

PSALM 101

A PROMISE TO RULE WELL
A song of David.

¹ I will sing of love and fairness.
    Lord, I will sing praises to you.
² I will be careful to live an innocent
        life.
    When will you come to me?

    I will live an innocent life in my house.
³   I will not look at anything wicked.
    I hate those who turn against you.
        They will not be found near me.
⁴ Let those who want to do wrong stay
        away from me.
    I will have nothing to do with evil.
⁵ If anyone secretly says things against
        his neighbor,
    I will stop him.
    I will not allow people
        to be proud and look down on
        others.

⁶ I will look for trustworthy people
    so I can live with them in the land.

Only those who live innocent lives
  will be my servants.
7 No one who is dishonest will live in
    my house.
  No liars will stay around me.
8 Every morning I will destroy
    the wicked in the land.
  I will rid the Lord's city
    of people who do evil.

PSALM 102

A CRY FOR HELP

A prayer of a person who is suffering when he is
discouraged and tells the Lord his complaints.

1 Lord, listen to my prayer.
  Let my cry for help come to you.
2 Do not hide from me
    in my time of trouble.
  Pay attention to me.
    When I cry for help, answer me
      quickly.

3 My life is passing away like smoke.
  My bones are burned up with fire.
4 My heart is like grass
    that has been cut and dried.
  I forget to eat.
5 Because of my grief,
    my skin hangs on my bones.
6 I am like a desert owl.
  I am like an owl living among the
    ruins.
7 I lie awake.
  I am like a lonely bird on a
    housetop.
8 All day long enemies insult me.
  Those who make fun of me use my
    name as a curse.
9 I eat ashes as my food.
  My tears fall into my drinks.
10 Because of your great anger,
    you have picked me up and thrown
      me away.
11 My days are like a passing shadow.
  I am like dried grass.

12 But, Lord, you rule forever.
  Your fame continues from now on.

13 You will come and have mercy on
    Jerusalem.
  The time has now come to be kind
    to her.
14 Your servants love even her stones.
  They even care about her dust.
15 Nations will fear the name of the
    Lord.
  All the kings on earth will honor
    him.
16 The Lord will rebuild Jerusalem.
  There his glory will be seen.
17 He will answer the prayers of the
    needy.
  He will not reject their prayers.

18 Write these things for the future.
  Then people who are not yet born
    will praise the Lord.
19 The Lord looked down from his holy
    place above.
  From heaven he looked down at
    the earth.
20 He heard the moans of the prisoners.
  And he freed those sentenced to
    die.
21 The name of the Lord will be heard
    in Jerusalem.
  His praise will be heard in
    Jerusalem.
22 People will come together.
  Kingdoms will serve the Lord.

> Write these
> things for the
> future. Then
> people who are
> not yet born will
> praise the Lord.
>
> –PSALM 102:18

23 God has made me tired of living.
  He has cut short my life.
24 So I said, "My God, do not take me in
    the middle of my life.
  Your years go on and on.
25 In the beginning you made the earth.
  And your hands made the skies.
26 They will be destroyed, but you will
    remain.
  They will all wear out like clothes.
  And, like clothes, you will change
    them.
  And they will be thrown away.
27 But you never change.
  And your life will never end.
28 Our children will live in your
    presence.
  And their children will remain
    with you."

PSALM 103

PRAISE TO THE GOD OF LOVE

Of David.

1 All that I am, praise the Lord.
  Everything in me, praise his holy
    name.
2 My whole being, praise the Lord.
  Do not forget all his kindnesses.
3 The Lord forgives me for all my sins.
  He heals all my diseases.
4 He saves my life from the grave.
  He loads me with love and mercy.
5 He satisfies me with good things.
  He makes me young again, like the
    eagle.

6 The Lord does what is right and fair
  for all who are wronged by others.
7 He showed his ways to Moses
  and his miracles to the people of
    Israel.
8 The Lord shows mercy and is kind.
  He does not become angry quickly,
  and he has great love.
9 He will not always scold us.
  He will not be angry forever.
10 He has not punished us as our sins
    should be punished.

He has not repaid us for the evil we
  have done.
11 As high as the sky is above the earth,
  so great is his love for those who
    respect him.
12 He has taken our sins away from us
  as far as the east is from west.
13 The Lord has mercy on those who
    fear him,
  as a father has mercy on his children.
14 He knows how we were made.
  He remembers that we are dust.

15 Human life is like grass.
  We grow like a flower in the field.
16 After the wind blows, the flower is
    gone.
  There is no sign of where it was.
17 But the Lord's love for those who fear
    him
  continues forever and ever.
  And his goodness continues to
    their grandchildren
18 and to those who keep his agreement
  and who remember to obey his
    orders.

19 The Lord has set his throne in
    heaven.
  And his kingdom rules over
    everything.
20 You who are his angels, praise the Lord.
  You are the mighty warriors who
    do what he says.
  Listen to what he says.
21 You, his armies, praise the Lord.
  You are his servants who do what
    he wants.
22 Everything the Lord has made
  should praise him in all the places
    he rules.
  My whole being, praise the Lord.

PSALM 104

PRAISE TO GOD WHO
MADE THE WORLD

1 My whole being, praise the Lord.
  Lord my God, you are very great.

You are clothed with glory and majesty.

2 You wear light like a robe.
You stretch out the skies like a tent.

3 You build your room above the clouds.
You make the clouds your chariot.
You ride on the wings of the wind.

4 You make the winds your messengers.
Flames of fire are your servants.

5 You built the earth on its foundations.
So it can never be moved.

6 You covered the earth with oceans.
The water was above the mountains.

7 But at your command, the water rushed away.
When you gave your orders like thunder, it hurried away.

8 The mountains rose.
The valleys sank.
The water went to the places you made for it.

9 You set borders for the seas that they cannot cross.
The water will never cover the earth again.

10 You make springs pour into the ravines.
They flow between the mountains.

11 They water all the wild animals.
The wild donkeys come there to drink.

12 Wild birds make nests by the water.
They sing among the tree branches.

13 You water the mountains from above.
The earth is full of the things you made.

14 You make the grass for cattle
and vegetables for the use of man.
You make food grow from the earth.

15 You give us wine that makes happy hearts.
And you give us olive oil that makes our faces shine.
You give us bread that gives us strength.

16 The Lord's trees have plenty of water.
They are the cedar trees of Lebanon, which he planted.

17 The birds make their nests there.
The stork's home is in the fir trees.

18 The high mountains belong to the wild goats.
The rocks are hiding places for the badgers.

19 You made the moon to mark the seasons.
And the sun always knows when to set.

20 You make it dark, and it becomes night.
Then all the wild animals creep around.

21 The lions roar as they attack.
They look to God for food.

22 When the sun rises, they leave.
They go back to their dens to lie down.

23 Then people go to work.
And they work until evening.

24 Lord, you have made many things.
With your wisdom you made them all.
The earth is full of your riches.

25 Look at the sea, so big and wide.
Its creatures large and small cannot be counted.

26 Ships travel over the ocean.
And there is the sea monster Leviathan,
which you made to play there.

27 All these things depend on you
to give them their food at the right time.

28 When you give it to them,
they gather it up.
When you open your hand, they are filled with good food.

29 When you turn away from them,
they become frightened.

When you take away their breath,
they die and turn into dust.
³⁰ When you breathe on them,
they are created.
You make the land new again.

³¹ May the glory of the Lord be forever.
May the Lord enjoy what he has
made.
³² He just looks at the earth, and it
shakes.
He touches the mountains, and
they smoke.

³³ I will sing to the Lord all my life.
I will sing praises to my God as
long as I live.
³⁴ May my thoughts please him.
I am happy in the Lord.
³⁵ Let sinners be destroyed from the
earth.
Let the wicked people live no
longer.

My whole being, praise the Lord.
Praise the Lord.

PSALM 105

GOD'S LOVE FOR ISRAEL

¹ Give thanks to the Lord and pray to
him.
Tell the nations what he has done.
² Sing to him. Sing praises to him.
Tell about all the wonderful things
he has done.
³ Be glad that you are his.
Let those who ask the Lord for help
be happy.
⁴ Depend on the Lord and his strength.
Always go to him for help.
⁵ Remember the wonderful things he
has done.
Remember his miracles and his
decisions.
⁶ You are descendants of his servant
Abraham,
the children of Jacob, his chosen
people.

⁷ He is the Lord our God.
His laws are for all the world.

⁸ He will keep his agreement forever.
He will keep his promises always.
⁹ He will keep his agreement he made
with Abraham.
He will keep the promise he made
to Isaac.
¹⁰ He made it a law for the people of
Jacob.
He made it an agreement with
Israel to last forever.
¹¹ The Lord said, "I will give you the
land of Canaan.
The promised land will belong to
you."

¹² Then God's people were few in
number.
They were strangers in the land.
¹³ They went from one nation to
another.
They went from one kingdom to
another.
¹⁴ But the Lord did not let anyone hurt
them.
He warned kings not to harm them.
¹⁵ He said, "Don't hurt my chosen
people.
Don't harm my prophets."

¹⁶ God ordered a time of hunger in the
land.
And he destroyed all the food.
¹⁷ Then he sent a man ahead of them.
It was Joseph, who was sold as a
slave.
¹⁸ They put chains around his feet
and an iron ring around his neck.
¹⁹ Then the time he had spoken of
came.
The Lord's words proved that
Joseph was right.
²⁰ The king of Egypt sent for Joseph and
freed him.
The ruler of the people set him
free.
²¹ He made him the master of his
house.
Joseph was in charge of his riches.

22 He could order the princes as he
wished.
He taught the older men to be wise.
23 Then his father Israel came to Egypt.
Jacob, also called Israel, lived in
Egypt.[n]
24 The Lord made his people grow in
number.
He made them stronger than their
enemies.
25 And he caused the Egyptians to hate
his people.
They made plans against the Lord's
servants.
26 Then he sent his servant Moses,
and Aaron, whom he had chosen.
27 They did many signs among the
Egyptians.
They worked miracles in Egypt.
28 The Lord sent darkness and made the
land dark.
But the Egyptians turned against
what he said.
29 So he changed their water into
blood
and made their fish die.
30 Then their country was filled with
frogs.
They were even in the bedrooms of
their rulers.
31 The Lord spoke, and flies came.
Gnats were everywhere in the
country.
32 He made hail fall like rain.
And he sent lightning through
their land.
33 He struck down their grapevines and
fig trees.
He destroyed every tree in the
country.
34 He spoke, and grasshoppers came.
The locusts were too many to
count.
35 They ate all the plants in the land.
They ate what the earth produced.
36 The Lord also killed all the firstborn
sons in the land,
the oldest son of each family.

37 Then he brought his people out,
and they carried with them silver
and gold.
Not one of his people stumbled.
38 The Egyptians were glad when they
left
because the Egyptians were afraid
of them.
39 The Lord covered them with a cloud
and lit up the night with fire.
40 When they asked, he brought them
quail.
He filled them with bread from
heaven.
41 God split the rock, and water flowed
out.
It ran like a river through the
desert.
42 He remembered his holy promise
to his servant Abraham.

43 So God brought his people out with
joy.
He brought out his chosen ones
with singing.
44 He gave them lands that belonged to
other nations.
They received what others had
worked for.
45 This was so they would keep his
orders
and obey his teachings.

Praise the Lord!

PSALM 106

ISRAEL'S FAILURE TO TRUST GOD

1 Praise the Lord!
Thank the Lord because he is good.
His love continues forever.
2 No one can tell all the mighty things
the Lord has done.
No one can speak all his praise.
3 Happy are those people who are fair,
who do what is right at all times.

105:23 **Egypt** Literally, "the land of Ham." Also in verse 27. The people in Egypt were descendants of Ham, one of
Noah's sons. See Genesis 10:6.

4 Lord, remember me when you are
    kind to your people.
  Help me when you save them.
5 Let me see the good things you do for
    your chosen people.
  Let me be happy along with your
    happy nation.
  Let me join your own people in
    praising you.

6 We have sinned just as our ancestors
    did.
  We have done wrong. We have
    done evil.

7 Our ancestors in Egypt
    did not learn from your
    miracles.
  They did not remember all your
    kindnesses.
    So they turned against you at the
    Red Sea.
8 But the Lord saved them for his own
    sake,
  to show his great power.
9 He commanded the Red Sea, and it
    dried up.
  He led them through the deep sea
    as if it were a desert.

☆ Psalm 106:1

*We are encouraged to thank the Lord because he is so good. The psalmist
even shouts to us to "Praise the Lord!"*

Has someone ever thanked you for something nice that you did?
It feels good, doesn't it? Well, it also feels good to say thank you
to others, especially God. The Bible says that God is good, and
everything he does is good. We can thank him for all the wonderful
things in our lives. We can tell him thank you for our warm beds
and for the yummy food we eat. We can
thank him for our toys and the things
we play with. And we can thank
him for loving us and watching
over us.

. . . .

*You know what would be fun?
Right now, right where you are,
shout, "Thank you Jesus!" (Maybe
don't do this in a library or during
quiet reading time at school!)*

¹⁰ He saved them from those who hated
them.
He saved them from their enemies.
¹¹ And the water covered their enemies.
Not one of them escaped.
¹² Then the people believed what the
Lord said.
They sang praises to him.

¹³ But they quickly forgot what he had
done.
They did not wait for his advice.
¹⁴ They became greedy for food in the
desert.
And they tested God there.
¹⁵ So he gave them what they wanted.
But he also sent a terrible disease
among them.

¹⁶ The people in the camp became
jealous of Moses
and of Aaron, the holy priest of the
Lord.
¹⁷ Then the ground opened up and
swallowed Dathan.
It closed over Abiram's group.
¹⁸ Then a fire burned among their
followers.
Flames burned up the wicked
people.

¹⁹ The people made a gold calf at Mount
Sinai.
They worshiped a metal statue.
²⁰ They exchanged their glorious God
for a statue of a bull, which eats
grass.
²¹ They forgot the God who saved them,
who had done great things in
Egypt.
²² He did miracles in Egypt.ⁿ
He did amazing things by the Red
Sea.
²³ So God said he would destroy them.
But Moses, his chosen one, stood
before him.
He stopped God's anger from
destroying them.

²⁴ Then they refused to go into the
beautiful land of Canaan.
They did not believe what God
promised.
²⁵ They grumbled in their tents
and did not obey the Lord.
²⁶ So he swore to them
that they would die in the desert.
²⁷ He said their children would be killed
by other nations
and that they would be
scattered among other
countries.

²⁸ They joined in worshiping Baal at
Peor.
They ate meat that had been
sacrificed to lifeless statues.
²⁹ They made the Lord angry by what
they did.
So many people became sick with a
terrible disease.
³⁰ But Phinehas prayed to the Lord,
and the disease stopped.
³¹ The Lord will remember that
Phinehas did what was right.
And God will remember this from
now on.

³² The people also made the Lord angry
at Meribah.
And Moses was in trouble because
of them.
³³ The people turned against the Spirit
of God.
So Moses spoke without stopping
to think.

³⁴ The people did not destroy the other
nations
as the Lord had told them to do.
³⁵ Instead, they mixed with the other
nations.
And they learned their customs.
³⁶ They worshiped other nations'
idols.
And they were trapped
by them.

106:22 Egypt Literally, "the land of Ham." The people in Egypt were descendants of Ham, one of Noah's sons. See
Genesis 10:6.

³⁷ They even killed their sons and
daughters
as sacrifices to demons.
³⁸ They killed innocent people.
They killed their own sons and
daughters
as sacrifices to the idols of Canaan.
So the land was made unholy by
their blood.
³⁹ The people became unholy by their
sins.
They were unfaithful to God in
what they did.

⁴⁰ So the Lord became angry with his
people.
He hated his own children.
⁴¹ He let other nations defeat them.
He let their enemies rule over
them.
⁴² Their enemies were cruel to them.
Their enemies kept them under
their power.
⁴³ The Lord saved his people many
times.
But they continued to turn against
him.
So they became even more
wicked.

⁴⁴ But God saw their misery.
He heard their cry.
⁴⁵ He remembered his agreement with
them.
And he felt sorry for them because
of his great love.
⁴⁶ He caused them to be pitied
by those who held them captive.

⁴⁷ Lord our God, save us.
Bring us back from other
nations.
Then we will thank you.
Then we will gladly praise you.

⁴⁸ Praise the Lord, the God of Israel.
He always was and always
will be.
Let all the people say, "Amen!"

Praise the Lord!

BOOK 5
Psalms 107—150

PSALM 107

GOD SAVES FROM MANY DANGERS

¹ Thank the Lord because he is good.
His love continues forever.
² That is what the people the Lord has
saved should say.
They are the ones he has saved
from the enemy.
³ He has gathered them from other
lands,
from east and west, north and
south.

⁴ Some people had wandered in the
desert lands.
They found no city to live in.
⁵ They were hungry and thirsty.
They were discouraged.
⁶ In their misery they cried out to the
Lord.
And he saved them from their
troubles.
⁷ He led them on a straight road
to a city where they could live.
⁸ Let them give thanks to the Lord for
his love

Thank the Lord because he is good. His love continues forever.
–PSALM 107:1

and for the miracles he does for
people.

⁹ He satisfies the thirsty.
He fills up the hungry.

¹⁰ Some sat in gloom and darkness.
They were prisoners suffering in
chains.

¹¹ They had turned against the words of
God.
They had refused the advice of God
Most High.

¹² So he broke their pride by hard work.
They stumbled, and no one
helped.

¹³ In their misery they cried out to the
Lord.
And he saved them from their
troubles.

¹⁴ He brought them out of their gloom
and darkness.
He broke their chains.

¹⁵ Let them give thanks to the Lord for
his love
and for the miracles he does for
people.

¹⁶ He breaks down bronze gates.
And he cuts apart iron bars.

¹⁷ Some became fools who turned
against God.
They suffered for the evil they did.

¹⁸ They refused to eat anything.
So they almost died.

¹⁹ In their misery they cried out to the
Lord.
And he saved them from their
troubles.

²⁰ God gave the command and healed
them.
So they were saved from dying.

²¹ Let them give thanks to the Lord for
his love
and for the miracles he does for
people.

²² Let them offer sacrifices to thank
him.
With joy they should tell what he
has done.

²³ Others went out to sea in ships.

They did business on the great
oceans.

²⁴ They saw what the Lord could do.
They saw the miracles he did.

²⁵ He spoke, and a storm came up.
It blew up high waves.

²⁶ The ships tossed as high as the sky
and fell low in the waves.
The storm was so bad the men lost
their courage.

²⁷ They stumbled and fell like men who
were drunk.
They did not know what to do.

²⁸ In their misery they cried out to the
Lord.
And he saved them from their
troubles.

²⁹ He made the storm be still.
He calmed the waves.

³⁰ They were happy that it was quiet.
And God guided them to the port
they wanted.

³¹ Let them give thanks to the Lord for
his love
and for the miracles he does for
people.

³² Let them praise his greatness in the
meeting of the people.
They should praise him in the
meeting of the elders.

³³ He changed rivers into a desert,
and springs of water into dry
ground.

³⁴ He made fertile land salty
because the people there did evil.

³⁵ He changed the desert into pools of
water
and dry ground into springs of
water.

³⁶ He had the hungry settle there.
They built a city to live in.

³⁷ They planted seeds in the fields and
vineyards.
And they had a good harvest.

³⁸ God blessed them, and they grew in
number.
Their cattle did not become fewer.

³⁹ Because of disaster, troubles and
sadness,

their families grew smaller and weaker.

⁴⁰ He showed he was displeased with their important men.
He made them wander in a pathless desert.

⁴¹ But he lifted the poor out of their suffering.
And he made their families grow like flocks of sheep.

⁴² Good people see this and are happy.
But the wicked say nothing.

⁴³ Whoever is wise will remember these things.
He will think about the love of the Lord.

PSALM 108

A PRAYER FOR VICTORY

A song of David.

¹ God, my heart is right.
I will sing and praise you with all my being.

² Wake up, harp and lyre!
I will wake up the dawn.

³ Lord, I will praise you among the nations.
I will sing songs of praise about you to all the nations.

⁴ Your love is so great that it is higher than the skies.
Your truth reaches to the clouds.

⁵ God, you are supreme over the skies.
Let your glory be over all the earth.

⁶ Answer us and save us by your power.
Then the people you love will be rescued.

⁷ God has said from his Temple,
"When I win, I will divide Shechem and cut up the Valley of Succoth.

⁸ Gilead and Manasseh are mine.
Ephraim is like my helmet.
Judah holds my royal scepter.

⁹ Moab is like my washbowl.
I throw my sandals at Edom.

I shout at Philistia."

¹⁰ Who will bring me to the strong, walled city?
Who will lead me to Edom?

¹¹ God, surely you have rejected us.
You do not go out with our armies.

¹² Help us fight the enemy.
Human help is useless.

¹³ But we can win with God's help.
He will defeat our enemies.

PSALM 109

A PRAYER AGAINST AN ENEMY

For the director of music.
A song of David.

¹ God, I praise you.
Do not be silent.

² Wicked people and liars have spoken against me.
They have told lies about me.

³ They have said hateful things about me.
They attack me for no reason.

⁴ They attacked me, even though I loved them
and prayed for them.

⁵ I was good to them, but they repay me with evil.
I loved them, but they hate me in return.

⁶ They say about me, "Have the Evil One work against him.
Let the devil accuse him.

⁷ When he is judged, let him be found guilty.
Let even his prayers show that he is guilty.

⁸ Let his life be cut short.
Let another man replace him as leader.

⁹ Let his children become orphans.
Let his wife become a widow.

¹⁰ Make his children wander around, begging for food.
Let them be forced out of the ruins they live in.

¹¹ Let the people he owes money to take everything he owns.
Let strangers steal everything he has worked for.
¹² Let no one show him love.
Let no one have mercy on his children.
¹³ Let all his descendants die.
Let him be forgotten by people who live after him.
¹⁴ Let the Lord remember how wicked his ancestors were.
Don't let the sins of his mother be wiped out.
¹⁵ Let the Lord always remember their sins.
Then he will make people forget about them completely.

¹⁶ "He did not remember to be loving.
He hurt the poor, the needy and those who were sad
until they were nearly dead.
¹⁷ He loved to put curses on others.
So let those same curses fall on him.
He did not like to bless others.
So do not let good things happen to him.
¹⁸ He cursed others as often as he wore clothes.
Cursing others filled his body and his life,
like drinking water and using olive oil.
¹⁹ So let curses cover him like clothes.
Let them wrap around him like a belt."
²⁰ May the Lord do these things to those who accuse me,
to those who speak evil against me.

²¹ But you, Lord God,
be kind to me so others will know you are good.
Because your love is good, save me.
²² I am poor and helpless.
And I am very sad.
²³ I am dying like an evening shadow.
I am shaken off like a locust.
²⁴ My knees are weak from hunger.
I have become thin.
²⁵ My enemies insult me.
They look at me and shake their heads.

²⁶ Lord my God, help me.
Because you are loving, save me.
²⁷ Then they will know that you have saved me.
They will know it was your power, Lord.
²⁸ They may curse me, but you bless me.
They may attack me, but they will be disgraced.
Then I, your servant, will be glad.
²⁹ Let those who accuse me be disgraced.
Let them be covered with shame like a coat.

³⁰ I will thank the Lord very much.
I will praise him in front of many people.
³¹ He defends the helpless.
He saved me from those who accuse me.

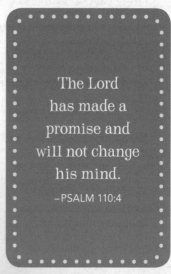

The Lord has made a promise and will not change his mind.

–PSALM 110:4

PSALM 110

THE LORD APPOINTS A KING

A song of David.

¹ The Lord said to my Master,
  "Sit by me at my right side
    until I put your enemies under your
    control."
² The Lord will make you king in
    Jerusalem over all nations.
  And you will rule your enemies in
    their own countries.
³ Your people will join you on the day
    you come to power.
  You have been dressed in holiness
    from birth.
  You have the freshness of a child.

⁴ The Lord has made a promise
    and will not change his mind.
  He said, "You are a priest forever,
    a priest like Melchizedek."

⁵ The Lord is beside you to help you.
    When he becomes angry, he will
    crush kings.
⁶ He will judge those nations, filling
    them with dead bodies.
  He will defeat rulers all over the
    world.
⁷ The king will drink from the brook
    on the way.
  Then he will be strengthened and
    win the battle.

PSALM 111

PRAISE FOR GOD'S GOODNESS

¹ Praise the Lord!

  I will thank the Lord with all my
    heart
    in the meeting of his good people.
² The Lord does great things.
    Those people who love them think
    about them.
³ What he does is glorious and
    splendid.

  His goodness continues forever.
⁴ His miracles are unforgettable.
  The Lord is kind and merciful.
⁵ He gives food to those who fear him.
  He remembers his agreement
    forever.
⁶ He has shown his people his power
    when he gave them the lands of
    other nations.

⁷ Everything he does is good and fair.
  All his orders can be trusted.
⁸ They will continue forever.
  They were made true and right.
⁹ He sets his people free.
  He made his agreement everlasting.
  He is holy and wonderful.

¹⁰ Wisdom begins with respect for the
    Lord.
  Those who obey his orders have
    good understanding.
  He should be praised forever.

PSALM 112

HONEST PEOPLE ARE BLESSED

¹ Praise the Lord!

  Happy is the person who fears the
    Lord.
  He loves what the Lord commands.
² His descendants will be powerful in
    the land.
  The children of honest people will
    be blessed.
³ His house will be full of wealth and
    riches.
  His goodness will continue forever.

⁴ A light shines in the dark for honest
    people.
  It shines for those who are good
    and kind and merciful.
⁵ It is good to be kind and generous.
  Whoever is fair in his business
⁶ will never be defeated.
  A good person will be remembered
    from now on.

⁷ He won't be afraid of bad news.
  He is safe because he trusts the
    Lord.
⁸ That person is confident. He will not
    be afraid.
  He will look down on his enemies.
⁹ He gives freely to the poor.
  The things he does are right and
    will continue forever.
  He will be given great honor.

¹⁰ The wicked will see this and become
    angry.
  They will grind their teeth in anger
    and then disappear.
  The wishes of the wicked will come
    to nothing.

PSALM 113

PRAISE FOR GOD'S KINDNESS

¹ Praise the Lord!

  Praise him, you servants of the Lord.
    Praise the name of the Lord.
² The Lord's name should be praised
    now and forever.
³ The Lord's name should be praised
    from where the sun rises to where
    it sets.
⁴ The Lord is supreme over all the
    nations.
  His glory reaches to the skies.

⁵ No one is like the Lord our God.
  He rules from heaven.
⁶ He bends down to look
    at the skies and the earth.
⁷ The Lord lifts the poor from
    the dirt.
  He takes the helpless from the
    ashes.
⁸ And he seats them with princes,
    the princes of his people.
⁹ He gives children to the woman who
    has none.
  He makes her a happy mother.

  Praise the Lord!

PSALM 114

GOD BROUGHT ISRAEL FROM EGYPT

¹ The Israelites went out of Egypt.
  The people of Jacob left that
    foreign country.
² Then Judah became God's holy place.
  Israel became the land he ruled.

³ The Red Sea looked and ran away.
  The Jordan River turned back.
⁴ The mountains danced like sheep
    and the hills like little lambs.
⁵ Sea, why did you run away?
  Jordan, why did you turn back?
⁶ Mountains, why did you dance like
    sheep?
  Hills, why did you dance like little
    lambs?

⁷ Earth, shake with fear before the Lord.
  Tremble in the presence of the God
    of Jacob.
⁸ He turned a rock into a pool of water.
  He changed a hard rock into a
    spring of water.

PSALM 115

THE ONE TRUE GOD

¹ It does not belong to us, Lord.
  The praise belongs to you
    because of your love and loyalty.

² Why do the nations ask,
  "Where is their God?"
³ Our God is in heaven.
  He does what he wants.
⁴ Their idols are made of silver and
    gold.
  They are made by human hands.
⁵ They have mouths, but they cannot
    speak.
  They have eyes, but they cannot
    see.
⁶ They have ears, but they cannot hear.
  They have noses, but they cannot
    smell.

7 They have hands, but they cannot
 feel.
 They have feet, but they cannot
 walk.
 And no sounds come from their
 throats.
8 The people who make idols and trust
 them
 are all like them.

9 Family of Israel, trust the Lord.
 He is your helper and your
 protection.
10 Family of Aaron, trust the Lord.
 He is your helper and your
 protection.
11 You people who fear the Lord should
 trust him.
 He is your helper and your
 protection.

12 The Lord remembers us and will
 bless us.
 He will bless the family of Israel.
 He will bless the family of Aaron.
13 The Lord will bless those who fear
 him,
 from the smallest to the greatest.

14 May the Lord give you many children.
 And may he give them children also.
15 May the Lord bless you.
 He made heaven and earth.

16 Heaven belongs to the Lord.
 But he gave the earth to people.
17 Dead people do not praise the Lord.
 Those in the grave are silent.
18 But we will praise the Lord
 now and forever.

 Praise the Lord!

PSALM 116

THANKSGIVING FOR ESCAPING DEATH

1 I love the Lord because he listens
 to my prayers for help.

2 He paid attention to me.
 So I will call to him for help as long
 as I live.
3 The ropes of death bound me.
 The fear of death took hold of me.
 I was troubled and sad.
4 Then I called out the name of the
 Lord.
 I said, "Please, Lord, save me!"

5 The Lord is kind and does what is
 right.
 Our God is merciful.
6 The Lord watches over the
 foolish.
 When I was helpless, he saved me.
7 I said to myself, "Relax,
 because the Lord takes care of
 you."
8 Lord, you have saved me from death.
 You have stopped my eyes from
 crying.
 You have kept me from being
 defeated.
9 So I will walk with the Lord
 in the land of the living.
10 I believed, so I said,
 "I am completely ruined."
11 In my distress I said,
 "All people are liars."

12 What can I give the Lord
 for all the good things he has given
 to me?
13 I will give him a drink offering for
 saving me.
 And I will pray to the Lord.
14 In front of all his people,
 I will give the Lord what I
 promised.

15 The death of one that belongs to him
 is precious to the Lord.
16 Lord, I am your servant.
 I am your servant and the son of
 your female servant.
 You have freed me from my chains.
17 I will give an offering to show thanks
 to you.
 And I will worship the Lord.
18 In front of all his people,

I will give the Lord what I
promised.
19 I will do this in the Temple
courtyards
in Jerusalem.

Praise the Lord!

PSALM 117

A HYMN OF PRAISE

1 All you nations, praise the Lord.
All you people, praise him.
2 The Lord loves us very much.
His truth is everlasting.

Praise the Lord!

PSALM 118

THANKSGIVING FOR VICTORY

1 Thank the Lord because he is good.
His love continues forever.
2 Let the people of Israel say,
"His love continues forever."
3 Let the family of Aaron say,
"His love continues forever."
4 Let those who fear the Lord say,
"His love continues forever."

5 I was in trouble. So I called to the
Lord.
The Lord answered me and set me
free.
6 I will not be afraid because the Lord
is with me.
People can't do anything to me.
7 The Lord is with me to help me.
I will see my enemies defeated.
8 It is better to trust the Lord
than to trust people.
9 It is better to trust the Lord
than to trust princes.

10 All the nations surrounded me.
But I defeated them in the name of
the Lord.

11 They surrounded me on every side.
But with the Lord's power, I
defeated them.
12 They surrounded me like a swarm of
bees.
But they died as quickly as thorns
burn.
By the Lord's power, I defeated
them.
13 They chased me until I was almost
defeated.
But the Lord helped me.
14 The Lord gives me strength and
makes me sing.
He has saved me.

15 Shouts of joy and victory
come from the tents of those who
do right:
"The Lord has done powerful things."
16 The power of the Lord has won the
victory.
With his power the Lord has done
mighty things.

17 I will not die, but live.
And I will tell what the Lord has
done.
18 The Lord has taught me a hard
lesson.
But he did not let me die.

19 Open for me the Temple gates.
Then I will come in and thank the
Lord.
20 This is the Lord's gate.
Only those who are good may enter
it.
21 Lord, I thank you for answering me.
You have saved me.

22 The stone that the builders did not
want
became the cornerstone.
23 The Lord did this,
and it is wonderful to us.
24 This is the day that the Lord has
made.
Let us rejoice and be glad today!

25 Please, Lord, save us.

Please, Lord, give us success.
²⁶ God bless the one who comes in the
name of the Lord.
We bless all of you from the Temple
of the Lord.
²⁷ The Lord is God.
And he has shown kindness to us.
With branches in your hands, join
the feast.
Come to the corners of the altar.

²⁸ You are my God, and I will thank you.
You are my God, and I will praise
your greatness.

²⁹ Thank the Lord because he is good.
His love continues forever.

PSALM 119

THE WORD OF GOD

¹ Happy are the people who live pure
lives.
They follow the Lord's teachings.
² Happy are the people who keep his
rules.
They ask him for help with their
whole heart.
³ They don't do what is wrong.
They follow his ways.
⁴ Lord, you gave your orders
to be followed completely.
⁵ I wish I were more loyal
in meeting your demands.
⁶ Then I would not be ashamed
when I think of your commands.
⁷ When I learned that your laws are
fair,
I praised you with an honest heart.
⁸ I will meet your demands.
So please don't ever leave me.

⁹ How can a young person live a pure
life?
He can do it by obeying your word.
¹⁰ With all my heart I try to obey you,
God.
Don't let me break your commands.
¹¹ I have taken your words to heart
so I would not sin against you.

¹² Lord, you should be praised.
Teach me your demands.
¹³ My lips will tell about
all the laws you have spoken.
¹⁴ I enjoy living by your rules
as people enjoy great riches.
¹⁵ I think about your orders
and study your ways.
¹⁶ I enjoy obeying your demands.
And I will not forget your word.

¹⁷ Do good to me, your servant, so I can
live,
so I can obey your word.
¹⁸ Open my eyes to see the wonderful
things
in your teachings.
¹⁹ I am a stranger on earth.
Do not hide your commands from
me.
²⁰ I want to study
your laws all the time.
²¹ You scold proud people.
Those who ignore your commands
are cursed.
²² Don't let me be insulted and hated
because I obey your rules.
²³ Even if princes speak against me,
I, your servant, will think about
your demands.
²⁴ Your rules give me pleasure.
They give me good advice.

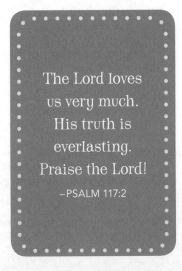

The Lord loves
us very much.
His truth is
everlasting.
Praise the Lord!

–PSALM 117:2

25 I am about to die.
   Give me life, as you have promised.
26 I told you about my life, and you
      answered me.
   Teach me your demands.
27 Help me understand your orders.
   Then I will think about your
      miracles.
28 I am sad and tired.
   Make me strong again as you have
      promised.
29 Don't let me be dishonest.
   Be kind to me by helping me obey
      your teachings.
30 I have chosen to obey you.
   I have obeyed your laws.
31 I hold on to your rules.
   Lord, do not let me be disgraced.
32 I will obey your commands
      because you have made me happy.

33 Lord, teach me your demands.
   Then I will obey them until the
      end.
34 Help me understand, so I can obey
      your teachings.
   I will obey them with all my heart.
35 Help me obey your commands
      because that makes me happy.
36 Help me want to obey your rules
      instead of selfishly wanting riches.
37 Keep me from looking at worthless
      things.
   Let me live by your word.
38 Keep your promise to me, your
      servant,
   so you will be feared.
39 Take away the shame I fear.
   Your laws are good.
40 How I want to follow your orders.
   Give me life because of your
      goodness.

41 Lord, show me your love.
   Save me as you have promised.
42 Then I will have an answer for people
      who insult me.
   I trust what you say.
43 Never keep me from speaking your
      truth.
   I depend on your fair laws.

44 I will obey your teachings
      forever and ever.
45 So I will live in freedom
      because I want to follow your
         orders.
46 I will discuss your rules with kings.
   And I will not be ashamed.
47 I enjoy obeying your commands.
   I love them.
48 I praise your commands, which I
      love.
   And I think about your demands.

49 Remember your promise to me, your
      servant.
   It gives me hope.
50 When I suffer, this comforts me:
   Your promise gives me life.
51 Proud people make fun of me all the
      time.
   But I do not reject your teachings.
52 I remember your laws from long ago.
   They comfort me, Lord.
53 I become angry with wicked people.
   They have not kept your
      teachings.
54 I sing about your demands
      wherever I live.
55 Lord, I remember you at night.
   I will obey your teachings.
56 This is what I do:
   I follow your orders.

57 Lord, you are my share in life.
   I have promised to obey your
      words.
58 I prayed to you with all my heart.
   Be kind to me as you have
      promised.
59 I thought about my life,
      and I decided to obey your rules.
60 I hurried and did not wait
      to obey your commands.
61 Wicked people have surrounded me.
   But I have not forgotten your
      teachings.
62 In the middle of the night, I get up to
      thank you
   because your laws are right.
63 I am a friend to everyone who fears
      you.

I am a friend to anyone who follows
your orders.
⁶⁴ Lord, your love fills the earth.
Teach me your demands.

⁶⁵ You have done good things for me,
your servant,
as you have promised, Lord.
⁶⁶ Teach me wisdom and knowledge
because I trust your commands.
⁶⁷ Before I suffered, I did wrong.
But now I obey your word.
⁶⁸ You are good, and you do what is
good.
Teach me your demands.
⁶⁹ Proud people have made up lies
about me.
But I will follow your orders with
all my heart.
⁷⁰ Those people have no feelings,
but I love your teachings.
⁷¹ It was good for me to suffer
so I would learn your demands.
⁷² Your teachings are worth more
to me
than thousands of pieces of gold
and silver.

⁷³ You made me and formed me with
your hands.
Give me understanding so I can
learn your commands.
⁷⁴ Let those who fear you rejoice when
they see me
because I put my hope in your
word.
⁷⁵ Lord, I know that your laws are right.
And it was right for you to punish
me.
⁷⁶ Comfort me with your love,
as you promised me, your servant.
⁷⁷ Have mercy on me so that I may live.
I love your teachings.
⁷⁸ Make the proud people ashamed
because they lied about me.
But I will think about your orders.
⁷⁹ Let those who fear you come to me.
They know your rules.
⁸⁰ Let me obey your demands
perfectly.
Then I will not be ashamed.

⁸¹ I am weak from waiting for you to
save me.
But I trust your word.
⁸² My eyes are tired from looking for
your promise.
When will you comfort me?
⁸³ Even though I am like a leather wine
bag going up in smoke,
I do not forget your demands.
⁸⁴ How long will I live?
When will you judge those who are
hurting me?
⁸⁵ Proud people have dug pits to trap me.
They have nothing to do with your
teachings.
⁸⁶ All of your commands can be trusted.
Liars are hurting me. Help me!
⁸⁷ They have almost put me in the
grave.
But I have not rejected your orders.
⁸⁸ Give me life by your love
so I can obey your rules.

⁸⁹ Lord, your word is everlasting.
It continues forever in heaven.
⁹⁰ Your loyalty will continue from now
on.
You made the earth, and it still
stands.
⁹¹ All things continue to this day
because of your laws.
All things serve you.
⁹² If I had not loved your teachings,
I would have died from my
sufferings.
⁹³ I will never forget your orders
because you have given me life by
them.
⁹⁴ I am yours. Save me.
I have wanted to know your orders.
⁹⁵ Wicked people are waiting to destroy
me.
But I will think about your rules.
⁹⁶ Everything I see has its limits.
But your commands have none.

⁹⁷ How I love your teachings!
I think about them all day long.
⁹⁸ Your commands make me wiser than
my enemies
because they are mine forever.

99 I am wiser than all my teachers
  because I think about your rules.
100 I have more understanding than the
    elders
  because I follow your orders.
101 I have avoided every evil way
  so I could obey your word.
102 I haven't stopped obeying your laws
  because you yourself are my
    teacher.
103 Your promises are so sweet to me.
  They are like honey to my mouth!
104 Your orders give me understanding.
  So I hate lying ways.

105 Your word is like a lamp for my feet
  and a light for my way.
106 I will do what I have promised
  and obey your fair laws.
107 I have suffered for a long time.
  Lord, give me life by your word.
108 Lord, accept my willing praise.
  And teach me your laws.
109 My life is always in danger.
  But I haven't forgotten your
    teachings.
110 Wicked people have set a trap for me.
  But I haven't disobeyed your
    orders.

☆ Psalm 119:105

The Bible is more than a collection of words. It contains words from God himself. His words are so important that they can even act like a very bright lamp. They can help us see where we should go.

We've all done it before: We get up in the middle of the night. It is pitch black. And we stub a toe on the corner of some furniture. Or worse, we run into a wall! When it is dark in a room, it can be hard to see your way around. You can bump into things, trip, or even fall. But when you turn on a light—ahh— you can finally see. The Bible is like that. Just like your bedroom light, a lamp, or even a flashlight, God's word can help you find your way. The word of God, the Bible, will help you to see what steps to take in life. It will help you know what directions to follow. And this will keep you from falling.

Shining the light of God's word is as simple as opening up your Bible and reading. Trust him to show you what will help you in life.

¹¹¹ I will follow your rules forever.
They make me happy.
¹¹² I will try to do what you demand
forever, until the end.
¹¹³ I hate people who are not completely
loyal to you.
But I love your teachings.
¹¹⁴ You are my hiding place and my
shield.
I trust your word.
¹¹⁵ Get away from me, you people who
do evil,
so I can keep my God's commands.
¹¹⁶ Support me as you promised so I can
live.
Don't let me be embarrassed
because of my hopes.
¹¹⁷ Help me, and I will be saved.
I will always respect your demands.
¹¹⁸ You reject everyone who ignores your
demands.
Their lies mislead them.
¹¹⁹ You throw away the wicked of the
world like trash.
So I will love your rules.
¹²⁰ I shake in fear of you.
I fear your laws.

¹²¹ I have done what is fair and
right.
Don't leave me to my enemies.
¹²² Promise that you will help me, your
servant.
Don't let proud people hurt me.
¹²³ My eyes are tired from looking for
your salvation
and for your good promise.
¹²⁴ Show your love to me, your servant.
Teach me your demands.
¹²⁵ I am your servant. Give me wisdom
so I can understand your rules.
¹²⁶ Lord, it is time for you to do
something.
People have disobeyed your
teachings.
¹²⁷ I love your commands
more than the purest gold.
¹²⁸ I respect all your orders.
So I hate lying ways.

¹²⁹ Your rules are wonderful.
That is why I obey them.
¹³⁰ Learning your words gives wisdom
and understanding for the foolish.
¹³¹ I want to learn your commands.
I am like a person breathing hard
and waiting impatiently.
¹³² Look at me and have mercy on me
as you do for those who love you.
¹³³ Guide my steps as you promised.
Don't let any sin control me.
¹³⁴ Save me from harmful people.
Then I will obey your orders.
¹³⁵ Show your kindness to me, your
servant.
Teach me your demands.
¹³⁶ Tears stream from my eyes
because people do not obey your
teachings.

¹³⁷ Lord, you do what is right.
And your laws are fair.
¹³⁸ The rules you commanded are right
and completely trustworthy.
¹³⁹ I am so upset I am worn out.
This is because my enemies have
forgotten your words.
¹⁴⁰ Your promises are proven.
I, your servant, love them.
¹⁴¹ I am unimportant and hated.
But I have not forgotten your
orders.
¹⁴² Your goodness continues forever.
And your teachings are true.
¹⁴³ I have had troubles and misery.
But I love your commands.
¹⁴⁴ Your rules are good forever.
Help me understand so I can live.

¹⁴⁵ Lord, I call to you with all my heart.
Answer me,
and I will keep your demands.
¹⁴⁶ I call to you. Save me
so I can obey your rules.
¹⁴⁷ I wake up early in the morning and
cry out.
I trust your word.
¹⁴⁸ I stay awake all night
so I can think about your promises.
¹⁴⁹ Listen to me because of your love.
Lord, give me life by your laws.
¹⁵⁰ Those who love evil are near.

They are far from your teachings.
¹⁵¹ But, Lord, you are also near.
And all your commands are true.
¹⁵² Long ago I learned from your rules
that you made them to continue
forever.

¹⁵³ See my suffering and save me
because I have not forgotten your
teachings.
¹⁵⁴ Argue my case and save me.
Let me live by your promises.
¹⁵⁵ Wicked people are far from being
saved
because they do not want to obey
your demands.
¹⁵⁶ Lord, you are very kind.
Give me life by your laws.
¹⁵⁷ Many enemies are after me.
But I have not rejected your rules.
¹⁵⁸ I see those traitors, and I hate them
because they do not obey what you
say.
¹⁵⁹ See how I love your orders.
Lord, give me life by your love.
¹⁶⁰ Your words are true from the start.
And all your laws will be fair
forever.

¹⁶¹ Leaders attack me for no reason.
But I fear your law in my heart.
¹⁶² I am as happy over your promises
as if I had found a great treasure.
¹⁶³ I hate and despise lies.
But I love your teachings.
¹⁶⁴ Seven times a day I praise you
for your fair laws.
¹⁶⁵ Those who love your teachings will
find true peace.
Nothing will defeat them.
¹⁶⁶ I am waiting for you to save me, Lord.
I will obey your commands.
¹⁶⁷ I keep your rules.
I love them very much.
¹⁶⁸ I keep your orders and rules.
You know everything I do.

¹⁶⁹ Hear my cry to you, Lord.
Let your word help me understand.
¹⁷⁰ Listen to my prayer.
Save me as you promised.

¹⁷¹ Let me speak your praise.
You have taught me your demands.
¹⁷² Let me sing about your promises.
All your commands are fair.
¹⁷³ Always be ready to help me
because I have chosen to obey your
commands.
¹⁷⁴ I want you to save me, Lord.
I love your teachings.
¹⁷⁵ Let me live so I can praise you.
Your laws will help me.
¹⁷⁶ I have wandered like a lost sheep.
Look for your servant because
I have not forgotten your
commands.

PSALM 120

A PRAYER OF SOMEONE
FAR FROM HOME

A song for going up to worship.

¹ When I was in trouble, I called to the
Lord.
And he answered me.
² Lord, save me from liars
and from those who plan evil.

³ You who plan evil, what will God do
to you?
How will he punish you?

The Lord guards
you. The Lord
protects you
as the shade
protects you
from the sun.

–PSALM 121:5

4 He will punish you with the sharp
arrows of a warrior
and with burning coals of wood.

5 How terrible it is to live in the land of
Meshech.
I have to live among the people of
Kedar.
6 I have lived too long
with people who hate peace.
7 I want peace and try to talk peace,
but they want war.

PSALM 121

THE LORD GUARDS HIS PEOPLE

A song for going up to worship.

1 I look up to the hills.
But where does my help come from?
2 My help comes from the Lord.
He made heaven and earth.

3 He will not let you be defeated.
He who guards you never sleeps.
4 He who guards Israel
never rests or sleeps.
5 The Lord guards you.
The Lord protects you as the shade
protects you from the sun.
6 The sun cannot hurt you during the
day.
And the moon cannot hurt you at
night.
7 The Lord will guard you from all
dangers.
He will guard your life.
8 The Lord will guard you as you come
and go,
both now and forever.

PSALM 122

HAPPY PEOPLE IN JERUSALEM

A song for going up to worship.
Of David.

1 I was happy when they said to me,
"Let's go to the Temple of the Lord."

2 Jerusalem, we are standing
at your gates.

3 Jerusalem is built as a city
where friends can come
together.
4 The people from the tribes go up
there.
The tribes belong to the Lord.
It is the rule to praise
the Lord at Jerusalem.
5 There the descendants of David
set their thrones to judge the
people.

6 Pray for peace in Jerusalem:
"May those who love her be
safe.
7 May there be peace within
her walls
and safety within her strong
towers."
8 To help my relatives and friends,
I repeat, "Let Jerusalem have
peace."
9 For the sake of the Temple of the
Lord our God,
I wish good for her.

PSALM 123

A PRAYER FOR MERCY

A song for going up to worship.

1 Lord, I look up to you.
You live in heaven.
2 Slaves depend on their masters.
And a female servant depends on
her mistress.
In the same way, we depend on our
God.
We wait for him to show us
mercy.

3 Be kind to us, Lord. Be kind to us
because we have been insulted.
4 We have suffered many insults from
lazy people
and much cruelty from
the proud.

PSALM 124

THE LORD SAVES HIS PEOPLE

A song for going up to worship.
Of David.

1 What if the Lord had not been on our
side?
(Let Israel repeat this.)
2 What if the Lord had not been on our
side
when men attacked us?
3 When they were angry with us,
they would have swallowed us
alive.
4 They would have been like a flood
drowning us.
They would have poured over us
like a river.
5 They would have swept us away
like a mighty stream.

6 Praise the Lord.
He did not let them chew us up.
7 We have escaped like a bird
from the hunter's trap.
The trap has been broken,
and we have escaped.
8 Our help comes from the Lord,
who made heaven and earth.

PSALM 125

GOD PROTECTS THOSE WHO TRUST HIM

A song for going up to worship.

1 Those who trust the Lord are like
Mount Zion.
It sits unmoved forever.
2 The mountains surround Jerusalem.
And the Lord surrounds his
people
now and forever.

3 The wicked will not rule
over those who do right.
If they did, the people who do right
might use their power to do
evil.

4 Lord, be good to those who are good,
whose hearts are honest.
5 But, Lord, when you punish those
who do evil,
also punish those who stop
following you.

Let there be peace in Israel.

PSALM 126

LORD, GIVE OUR RICHES BACK

A song for going up to worship.

1 When the Lord gave the riches back
to Jerusalem,
it seemed as if we were dreaming.
2 Then we were filled with laughter,
and we sang happy songs.
Then the other nations said,
"The Lord has done great things for
them."
3 The Lord has done great things for us,
and we are very glad.

4 Lord, give us back our riches again.
Do this as you bring streams to the
desert.
5 Those who cry as they plant crops
will sing at harvesttime.
6 Those who cry
as they carry out the seeds
will return singing
and carrying bundles of grain.

PSALM 127

ALL GOOD THINGS COME FROM GOD

A song for going up to worship.
Of Solomon.

1 If the Lord doesn't build the house,
the builders are working for
nothing.
If the Lord doesn't guard the city,
the guards are watching for nothing.
2 It is no use for you to get up early
and stay up late,
working for a living.

The Lord gives sleep to those he
loves.
3 Children are a gift from the Lord.
Babies are a reward.
4 Sons who are born to a young man
are like arrows in the hand of a
warrior.
5 Happy is the man
who has his bag full of arrows.
They will not be defeated
when they fight their enemies in
court.

PSALM 128

THE HAPPY HOME
A song for going up to worship.

1 Happy are those who respect the Lord
and obey him.
2 You will enjoy what you work for.
You will be blessed with good
things.
3 Your wife will give you many
children.
She will be like a vine that
produces a lot of fruit.
Your children will bring you much
good.
They will be like olive branches
that produce many olives.
4 This is how the man who respects
the Lord
will be blessed.
5 May the Lord bless you from Mount
Zion.
May you enjoy the good things of
Jerusalem all your life.
6 May you see your grandchildren.

Let there be peace in Israel.

PSALM 129

A PRAYER AGAINST THE ENEMIES
A song for going up to worship.

1 They have treated me badly all my
life.

(Let Israel repeat this.)
2 They have treated me badly all my life.
But they have not defeated me.
3 Like farmers plowing, they plowed
over my back,
making long wounds.
4 But the Lord does what is right.
He has set me free from those
wicked people.

5 Let those who hate Jerusalem
be turned back in shame.
6 Let them be like the grass on the roof.
It dries up before it has grown.
7 There is not enough of it to fill a
man's hand
or to make into a bundle to fill his
arms.
8 Let those who pass by them not say,
"May the Lord bless you.
We bless you by the power of the
Lord."

PSALM 130

A PRAYER FOR MERCY
A song for going up to worship.

1 Lord, I am in great trouble.
So I call out to you for help.
2 Lord, hear my voice.
Listen to my prayer for help.
3 Lord, if you punished people for all
their sins,
no one would be left.
4 But you forgive us.
So you are respected.

5 I wait for the Lord to help me.
I trust his word.
6 I wait for the Lord to help me
more than night watchmen wait
for the dawn,
more than night watchmen wait
for the dawn.

7 People of Israel, put your hope in the
Lord
because he is loving
and able to save.

☆ Psalm 130:2

This verse from Psalm 130 is a prayer. It shows us that when we talk to God, he listens to us. And he helps us.

There are a lot of people in this world. And it seems like they are all busy. Sometimes you might talk to your mom, but it seems like she does not even hear you. You might try to talk to your dad, but he is too busy to listen to you. Sometimes it may seem like what you have to say isn't important enough for grown-ups to hear you. But God is not like that. Adults gets busy, but God is always close to you. He is never too busy to hear you. He always thinks what you say is important.

You can pray to God from anywhere and at any time.
No matter where you are, he hears you.

---

⁸ He will save Israel
 from all their sins.

PSALM 131

CHILDLIKE TRUST IN GOD
A song for going up to worship.
Of David.

¹ Lord, my heart is not proud.
 I don't look down on others.
 I don't do great things,
 and I can't do miracles.
² But I am calm and quiet.
 I am like a baby with its mother.
 I am at peace, like a baby with its
 mother.

³ People of Israel, put your hope in the
 Lord
 now and forever.

PSALM 132

IN PRAISE OF THE TEMPLE
A song for going up to worship.

¹ Lord, remember David and all his
 suffering.
² He made a promise to the Lord.
 He made a promise to the Mighty
 God of Jacob.
³ He said, "I will not go home to my
 house.
 I will not lie down on my bed.

⁴ I will not close my eyes
or let myself sleep
⁵ until I find a place for the Lord.
I want to provide a home for the
Mighty God of Jacob."

⁶ We heard about the Ark of the
Covenant in Bethlehem.
We found it at Kiriath Jearim.
⁷ Let's go to the Lord's house.
Let's worship at his footstool.
⁸ Rise, Lord, and come to your resting
place.
Come with the Ark of the
Covenant that shows your
strength.
⁹ May your priests do what is right.
May your people sing for joy.

¹⁰ For the sake of your servant David,
do not reject your appointed
king.
¹¹ The Lord made a promise to David.
It was a sure promise that he will
not take back.
He promised, "I will make one of
your descendants
rule as king after you.
¹² But your sons must keep my
agreement
and the rules that I teach them.
Then their sons after them will rule
on your throne forever and ever."

¹³ The Lord has chosen Jerusalem.
He wants it for his home.
¹⁴ He says, "This is my resting place
forever.
Here is where I want to stay.
¹⁵ I will bless her with plenty of food.
I will fill her poor with food.
¹⁶ I will let her priests receive salvation.
And those who worship me will
really sing for joy.

¹⁷ "I will make a king come from the
family of David.
I will provide my appointed one
descendants to rule after him.
¹⁸ I will cover his enemies with shame.
But his crown will shine."

PSALM 133

THE LOVE OF GOD'S PEOPLE

A song for going up to worship.
Of David.

¹ It is good and pleasant
when God's people live together in
peace!
² It is like having perfumed oil poured
on the priest's head
and running down his beard.
It ran down Aaron's beard
and on to the collar of his robes.
³ It is like the dew of Mount Hermon
falling on the hills of Jerusalem.
There the Lord gives his blessing
of life forever.

PSALM 134

TEMPLE GUARDS, PRAISE THE LORD

A song for going up to worship.

¹ Praise the Lord, all you servants of
the Lord.
You serve at night in the Temple of
the Lord.
² Raise your hands in the Temple
and praise the Lord.

³ May the Lord bless you from Mount
Zion.
He made heaven and earth.

PSALM 135

GOD SAVES, IDOLS DO NOT

¹ Praise the Lord!

Praise the name of the Lord.
Praise him, you servants of the
Lord.
² Praise him, you who stand in the
Lord's Temple
and in the Temple courtyards.
³ Praise the Lord, because he is good.

Sing praises to him, because it is
pleasant.

4 The Lord has chosen the people of
Jacob for himself.
He has chosen the people of Israel
for his very own.
5 I know that the Lord is great.
Our Lord is greater than all the
gods.
6 The Lord does what he wants,
in heaven and on earth,
in the seas and the deep oceans.
7 He brings the clouds from the ends
of the earth.
He sends the lightning with the
rain.
He brings out the wind from his
storehouses.

8 He destroyed the firstborn sons in
Egypt,
the firstborn of both men and
animals.
9 He did many signs and miracles in
Egypt.
He did amazing things to the king
and his servants.
10 He defeated many nations
and killed powerful kings:
11 Sihon king of the Amorites,
Og king of Bashan
and all the kings of Canaan.
12 Then he gave their land as a gift.
It was a gift to his people, the
Israelites.

13 Lord, your name is everlasting.
Lord, you will be remembered from
now on.
14 You defend your people.
You have mercy on your servants.

15 The idols of other nations are made
of silver and gold.
They are made by human hands.
16 They have mouths, but they cannot
speak.
They have eyes, but they cannot
see.
17 They have ears, but they cannot hear.

They have no breath in their
mouths.
18 The people who make idols and trust
them
are all like them.

19 Family of Israel, praise the Lord.
Family of Aaron, praise the Lord.
20 Family of Levi, praise the Lord.
You people who fear the Lord
should praise him.
21 You people of Jerusalem, praise the
Lord on Mount Zion.

Praise the Lord!

PSALM 136

GOD'S LOVE CONTINUES FOREVER

1 Give thanks to the Lord because he
is good.
His love continues forever.
2 Give thanks to the God over
all gods.
His love continues forever.
3 Give thanks to the Lord of all lords.
His love continues forever.

4 Only he can do great miracles.
His love continues forever.
5 With his wisdom he made the skies.
His love continues forever.
6 He spread out the earth on the seas.
His love continues forever.
7 He made the sun and the moon.
His love continues forever.
8 He made the sun to rule the day.
His love continues forever.
9 He made the moon and stars to rule
the night.
His love continues forever.

10 He killed the firstborn sons of the
Egyptians.
His love continues forever.
11 He brought the people of Israel out
of Egypt.
His love continues forever.
12 He did it with his great power and
strength.

His love continues forever.
¹³ He parted the water of the Red Sea.
His love continues forever.
¹⁴ He brought the Israelites through the
middle of it.
His love continues forever.
¹⁵ But the king of Egypt and his army
drowned in the Red Sea.
His love continues forever.

¹⁶ He led his people through the desert.
His love continues forever.
¹⁷ He defeated great kings.
His love continues forever.
¹⁸ He killed powerful kings.
His love continues forever.
¹⁹ He defeated Sihon king of the
Amorites.
His love continues forever.
²⁰ He defeated Og king of Bashan.
His love continues forever.
²¹ He gave their land as a gift.
His love continues forever.
²² It was a gift to his servants, the
Israelites.
His love continues forever.

²³ He remembered us when we were in
trouble.
His love continues forever.
²⁴ He freed us from our enemies.
His love continues forever.
²⁵ He gives food to every living
creature.
His love continues forever.

²⁶ Give thanks to the God of heaven.
His love continues forever.

PSALM 137

ISRAELITES IN CAPTIVITY

¹ By the rivers in Babylon we sat and
cried
when we remembered Jerusalem.
² On the poplar trees nearby
we hung our harps.
³ Those who captured us asked us to
sing.

Our enemies wanted happy songs.
They said, "Sing us a Temple song
from Jerusalem!"

⁴ But we cannot sing songs about the
Lord
while we are in this foreign
country!
⁵ Jerusalem, if I forget you,
let my right hand lose its skill.
⁶ Let my tongue stick to the roof of my
mouth
if I do not remember you.
Let these things happen if I do not
think about Jerusalem
as my greatest joy.

⁷ Lord, remember what the Edomites
did
on the day Jerusalem fell.
They said, "Tear it down!
Tear it down to its foundations!"

⁸ People of Babylon, you will be
destroyed.
The people who pay you back will
be happy.
They will punish you for what you
did to us.
⁹ They will grab your babies
and throw them against the rocks.

PSALM 138

A HYMN OF THANKSGIVING
A song of David.

¹ Lord, I will thank you with all my
heart.
I will sing to you before the false
gods.
² I will bow down facing your holy
Temple.
And I will thank you for your love
and loyalty.
You have made your name and your
word
greater than anything.
³ On the day I called to you, you
answered me.

You made me strong and brave.

4 Lord, let all the kings of the earth
praise you.
They have heard the words you
speak.
5 They will sing about what the Lord
has done
because the Lord's glory is great.

6 Though the Lord is supreme
he takes care of those who are not
proud.
But he stays away from those who
are proud.
7 Lord, even when I have trouble all
around me,
you will keep me alive.
When my enemies are angry,
you will reach down and save me
by your power.
8 Lord, you do everything for me.
Lord, your love continues
forever.
You made us. Do not leave us.

PSALM 139

GOD KNOWS EVERYTHING

For the director of music.
A song of David.

1 Lord, you have examined me.
You know all about me.
2 You know when I sit down and when
I get up.
You know my thoughts before I
think them.
3 You know where I go and where I lie
down.
You know well everything I do.
4 Lord, even before I say a word,
you already know what I am going
to say.
5 You are all around me—in front and
in back.
You have put your hand on me.
6 Your knowledge is amazing to me.
It is more than I can
understand.

7 Where can I go to get away from your
Spirit?
Where can I run from you?
8 If I go up to the skies, you are there.
If I lie down where the dead are,
you are there.
9 If I rise with the sun in the east,
and settle in the west beyond the
sea,
10 even there you would guide me.
With your right hand you would
hold me.

11 I could say, "The darkness will hide
me.
The light around me will turn into
night."
12 But even the darkness is not dark to
you.
The night is as light as the day.
Darkness and light are the same to
you.

13 You made my whole being.
You formed me in my mother's
body.
14 I praise you because you made me in
an amazing and wonderful way.
What you have done is wonderful.
I know this very well.
15 You saw my bones being formed
as I took shape in my mother's
body.
When I was put together there,
16 you saw my body as it was formed.
All the days planned for me
were written in your book
before I was one day old.

17 God, your thoughts are precious to
me.
They are so many!
18 If I could count them,
they would be more than all the
grains of sand.
When I wake up,
I am still with you.

19 God, I wish you would kill the
wicked!
Get away from me, you murderers!

20 These men say evil things about you.
　　Your enemies use your name
　　　thoughtlessly.
21 Lord, I hate those who hate you.
　　I hate those who rise up against
　　　you.
22 I feel only hate for them.
　　They are my enemies.

23 God, examine me and know my
　　　heart.
　　Test me and know my thoughts.
24 See if there is any bad thing in me.
　　Lead me in the way you set long
　　　ago.

PSALM 140

A PRAYER FOR PROTECTION
For the director of music.
A song of David.

1 Lord, rescue me from evil people.
　　Save me from cruel men.
2 They make evil plans.
　　They always start fights.
3 They make their tongues sharp as a
　　　snake's.
　　Their words are like snake poison.
　　　　　　　　　　　　Selah

4 Lord, guard me from the power of
　　　wicked people.
　　Save me from cruel men
　　who plan to trip me up.
5 Proud men have hidden a trap
　　　for me.
　　They have spread out a net beside
　　　the road.
　　They have set traps for me.　*Selah*

6 I said to the Lord, "You are my
　　　God."
　　Lord, listen to my prayer for help.
7 Lord God, my mighty savior,
　　you protect me in battle.
8 Lord, do not give the wicked what
　　　they want.
　　Don't let their plans succeed,
　　or they will become proud.　*Selah*

9 Those around me have planned
　　　trouble.
　　Now let it come to them.
10 Let burning coals fall on them.
　　Throw them into the fire
　　or into pits from which they
　　　cannot escape.
11 Don't let liars settle in the land.
　　Let evil quickly hunt down cruel
　　　men.

12 I know the Lord will get justice for
　　　the poor.
　　He will defend the needy in court.
13 Good people will praise his name.
　　Honest people will live in his
　　　presence.

PSALM 141

A PRAYER NOT TO SIN
A song of David.

1 Lord, I call to you. Come quickly.
　　Listen to me when I call to you.
2 Let my prayer be like incense placed
　　　before you.
　　Let my praise be like the evening
　　　sacrifice.

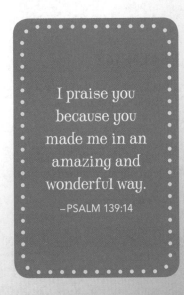

I praise you
because you
made me in an
amazing and
wonderful way.

–PSALM 139:14

³ Lord, help me control my tongue.
  Help me be careful about what I
    say.
⁴ Don't let me want to do evil
  or join others in doing wrong.
Don't let me eat
  with those who do evil.

⁵ If a good man punished me, that
    would be kind.
  If he corrected me,
  that would be like having
    perfumed oil on my head.
  I shouldn't refuse it.
But I pray against those who do evil.
⁶   Let their leaders be thrown down
      the cliffs.
    Then people will know that I have
      spoken the truth:
⁷ "The ground is plowed and broken
    up.
  In the same way, our bones have
    been scattered at the grave."

⁸ Lord God, I look to you for help.
  I trust in you. Don't let me die.
⁹ Protect me from the traps they set
    for me
  and from the net evil people have
    spread.
¹⁰ Let the wicked fall into their own
    pits.
  And let me pass by safely.

PSALM 142

A PRAYER FOR SAFETY
A maskil of David when he was
in the cave. A prayer.

¹ I cry out to the Lord.
  I pray to the Lord for mercy.
² I pour out my problems to him.
  I tell him my troubles.
³ When I am afraid,
  you, Lord, know the way out.
In the path where I walk,
  a trap is hidden for me.
⁴ Look around me and see.
  No one cares about me.

I have no place of safety.
  No one cares if I live.

⁵ Lord, I cry out to you.
  I say, "You are my protection.
  You are all I want in this life."
⁶ Listen to my cry
  because I am helpless.
Save me from those who are chasing
    me.
  They are too strong for me.
⁷ Free me from my prison.
  Then I will praise your name.
Then the good people will
    surround me
  because you have taken care of me.

PSALM 143

A PRAYER NOT TO BE KILLED
A song of David.

¹ Lord, hear my prayer.
  Listen to my cry for mercy.
Come to help me
  because you are loyal and
    good.
² Don't judge me, your servant,
  because no one alive is right before
    you.
³ My enemies are chasing me.
  They have crushed me to the
    ground.
They have made me live in darkness
  like those who are long dead.
⁴ I am afraid.
  My courage is gone.

⁵ I remember what happened long ago.
  I recall everything you have done.
  I think about all you have
    made.
⁶ I lift my hands to you in prayer.
  As a dry land needs rain, I thirst for
    you.   *Selah*

⁷ Lord, answer me quickly.
  I am getting weak.
Don't turn away from me,
  or I will be like those who are dead.

8 Tell me in the morning about your
   love.
   I trust you.
   Show me what I should do
   because my prayers go up to you.
9 Lord, save me from my enemies.
   I come to you for safety.
10 Teach me to do what you want,
   because you are my God.
   Let your good Spirit
   lead me on level ground.

11 Lord, let me live
   so people will praise you.
   In your goodness
   save me from my troubles.
12 In your love defeat my enemies.
   Destroy all those who trouble me
   because I am your servant.

PSALM 144

A PRAYER FOR VICTORY
Of David.

1 Praise the Lord, my Rock.
   He trains me for war.
   He trains me for battle.
2 He gives me love and protects me like
   a strong, walled city.
   He is my place of safety and my
   Savior.
   He is my shield and my protection.
   He helps me rule my people.

3 Lord, why is man important to you?
   Why do you even think about a
   human being?
4 A man is like a breath.
   His life is like a passing shadow.

5 Lord, tear open the sky and come
   down.
   Touch the mountains so they will
   smoke.
6 Send the lightning and scatter my
   enemies.
   Shoot your arrows and force them
   away.
7 Reach down from above.

Pull me out of this sea of enemies.
   Rescue me from these foreigners.
8 They are liars.
   They are dishonest.

9 God, I will sing a new song to you.
   I will play to you on the
   ten-stringed harp.
10 You give victory to kings.
   You save your servant David from
   cruel swords.
11 Save me, rescue me from these
   foreigners.
   They are liars.
   They are dishonest.

12 Let our sons in their youth
   grow like strong trees.
   Let our daughters be
   like the decorated stones in the
   Temple.
13 Let our barns be filled
   with crops of all kinds.
   Let our sheep in the fields have
   thousands and thousands of
   lambs.
14 Let our cattle be strong.
   Let no one break in.
   Let there be no war.
   Let there be no screams in our
   streets.

15 Happy are those who are like this.
   Happy are the people whose God is
   the Lord.

PSALM 145

PRAISE TO GOD THE KING
A song of praise. Of David.

1 I praise your greatness, my God the
   King.
   I will praise you forever and ever.
2 I will praise you every day.
   I will praise you forever and ever.
3 The Lord is great. He is worthy of our
   praise.
   No one can understand how great
   he is.

⁴ Parents will tell their children what
  you have done.
  They will retell your mighty acts,
⁵ wonderful majesty and glory.
  And I will think about your
  miracles.
⁶ They will tell about the amazing
  things you do.
  I will tell how great you are.
⁷ They will remember your great
  goodness.
  They will sing about your fairness.

⁸ The Lord is kind and shows mercy.
  He does not become angry quickly
  but is full of love.

⁹ The Lord is good to everyone.
  He is merciful to all he has made.
¹⁰ Lord, everything you have made will
  praise you.
  Those who belong to you will bless
  you.
¹¹ They will tell about the glory of your
  kingdom.
  They will speak about your power.
¹² Then everyone will know what
  powerful things you do.
  They will know about the glory and
  majesty of your kingdom.
¹³ Your kingdom will continue forever.
  And you will be King from
  now on.

☆ Psalm 144:15

David was in a fight, and he needed help. He prayed to God and asked him for victory. But even in that scary time, he knew that he could be happy by following the Lord.

What makes you happy? How do you show that you are happy? Is it with a smile or a shout, or do you clap your hands? Our parents, our friends, and our favorite things can all make us happy. God says that people who love him are happy. Even when bad things happen, we can be happy because we know that God is always with us. He loves us and takes care of us. It makes us happy to know that God loves us and is our friend.

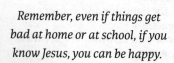

Remember, even if things get bad at home or at school, if you know Jesus, you can be happy.

The Lord will keep his promises.
  With love he takes care of all he
      has made.
¹⁴ The Lord helps those who have been
      defeated.
  He takes care of those who are in
      trouble.
¹⁵ All living things look to you for food.
  And you give it to them at the right
      time.
¹⁶ You open your hand,
  and you satisfy all living things.

¹⁷ Everything the Lord does is right.
  With love he takes care of all he
      has made.
¹⁸ The Lord is close to everyone who
      prays to him,
  to all who truly pray to him.
¹⁹ He gives those who fear him what
      they want.
  He listens when they cry, and he
      saves them.
²⁰ The Lord protects everyone who
      loves him.
  But he will destroy the wicked.

²¹ I will praise the Lord.
  Let everyone praise his holy name
      forever.

PSALM 146

PRAISE GOD WHO HELPS THE WEAK

¹ Praise the Lord!
  My whole being, praise the Lord.
² I will praise the Lord all my life.
  I will sing praises to my God as
      long as I live.

³ Do not put your trust in princes
  or other people, who cannot save
      you.
⁴ When people die, they are buried.
  Then all of their plans come to an
      end.
⁵ Happy are those who are helped by
      the God of Jacob.
  Their hope is in the Lord their God.

⁶ He made heaven and earth,
  the sea and everything in it.
  He remains loyal forever.
⁷ The Lord does what is fair for those
      who have been wronged.
  He gives food to the hungry.
  The Lord sets the prisoners free.
⁸   The Lord gives sight to the blind.
  The Lord lifts up people who are in
      trouble.
  The Lord loves those who do right.
⁹ The Lord protects the foreigners.
  He defends the orphans and
      widows.
  But he overthrows the wicked.

¹⁰ The Lord will be King forever.
  Jerusalem, your God is everlasting.

Praise the Lord!

PSALM 147

PRAISE GOD WHO HELPS HIS PEOPLE

¹ Praise the Lord!

  It is good to sing praises to our God.
  It is good and pleasant to praise
      him.
² The Lord rebuilds Jerusalem.
  He brings back the scattered
      Israelites who were taken
      captive.
³ He heals the brokenhearted.
  He bandages their wounds.

⁴ He counts the stars
  and names each one.
⁵ Our Lord is great and very powerful.
  There is no limit to what he knows.
⁶ The Lord defends those who are not
      proud.
  But he throws the wicked to the
      ground.

⁷ Sing praises to the Lord.
  Praise our God with harps.
⁸ He fills the sky with clouds.

He sends rain to the earth.
He makes grass grow on the hills.
⁹ He gives food to cattle
and to the little birds that call.

¹⁰ He is not pleased by the strength of a
horse
or the power of a man.
¹¹ The Lord is pleased with those who
fear him,
with those who trust his love.

¹² Jerusalem, praise the Lord.
Jerusalem, praise your God.
¹³ He makes your city gates strong.
He blesses the people inside.
¹⁴ He brings peace to your country.
He fills you with the finest grain.

¹⁵ He gives a command to the earth,
and it quickly obeys him.
¹⁶ He spreads the snow like wool.
He scatters the frost like ashes.
¹⁷ He throws down hail like rocks.
No one can stand the cold he
sends.
¹⁸ Then he gives a command, and it
melts.
He sends the breezes, and the
waters flow.

¹⁹ He gave his word to Jacob.
He gave his laws and demands to
Israel.
²⁰ He didn't do this for any other
nation.
They don't know his laws.

Praise the Lord!

PSALM 148

THE WORLD SHOULD PRAISE
THE LORD

¹ Praise the Lord!

Praise the Lord from the heavens.
Praise him high above the earth.
² Praise him, all you angels.
Praise him, all you armies of
heaven.
³ Praise him, sun and moon.
Praise him, all you shining stars.
⁴ Praise him, highest heavens
and you waters above the sky.
⁵ Let them praise the Lord
because they were created by his
command.
⁶ He set them in place forever and ever.
He made a law that will never end.

⁷ Praise the Lord from the earth.
Praise him, you large sea animals
and all the oceans.
⁸ Praise him, lightning and hail, snow
and clouds,
and stormy winds that obey him.
⁹ Praise him, mountains and all hills,
fruit trees and all cedar trees.
¹⁰ Praise him, you wild animals and all
cattle,
small crawling animals and birds.
¹¹ Praise him, you kings of the earth
and all nations,
princes and all rulers of the earth.
¹² Praise him, you young men and
women,
old people and children.

¹³ Praise the Lord.
He alone is great.
He is greater than heaven and
earth.
¹⁴ God has given his people a king.
He should be praised by all who
belong to him.
He should be praised by the
Israelites, the people closest to
his heart.

Praise the Lord!

PSALM 149

PRAISE THE GOD OF ISRAEL

¹ Praise the Lord!

Sing a new song to the Lord.

Sing his praise in the meeting of
his people.

² Let the Israelites be happy because of
God, their Maker.
Let the people of Jerusalem rejoice
because of their King.
³ They should praise him with
dancing.
They should praise him with
tambourines and harps.

⁴ The Lord is pleased with his people.
He saves those who are not proud.
⁵ Let those who worship him rejoice in
his glory.
Let them sing for joy even in bed!

⁶ Let them shout his praise
with their two-edged swords in
their hands.
⁷ They will punish the nations.
They will defeat the people.

☆ Psalm 150:6

*The last song in the Book of Psalms is all about praising the Lord. It lists
all kinds of very loud musical instruments that we can use to praise
God. But you don't have to have a band instrument to praise him. The
Bible says that if you have breath in your lungs you can praise the Lord.
Are you breathing? Well then, that means you!*

Think of ways that God has been good to you. Are you able to run
and play? Do you have great toys and books? Do you have a family?
Do you have friends at church or at school? Have you
gone somewhere fun lately? If so, you have a
reason to thank God. The Bible shows us
that thanking God is praising him. We
can praise him loudly or quietly. We
can praise him with drums or with
jingling Christmas bells. The
only rule is that you have to be
breathing. Are you? Then you
can praise the Lord!

* * * * * * * * * * * * * * * * * * *

*Stop what you are doing and
praise God in whatever
way you know how.*

⁸ They will put those kings in chains
and those important men in iron
bands.
⁹ They will punish them as God has
written.
God is honored by all who worship
him.

Praise the Lord!

PSALM 150

PRAISE THE LORD WITH MUSIC

¹ Praise the Lord!

Praise God in his Temple.
Praise him in his mighty heaven.
² Praise him for his strength.
Praise him for his greatness.
³ Praise him with trumpet blasts.
Praise him with harps and lyres.
⁴ Praise him with tambourines and
dancing.
Praise him with stringed
instruments and flutes.
⁵ Praise him with loud cymbals.
Praise him with crashing cymbals.
⁶ Let everything that breathes praise
the Lord.

Praise the Lord!

Proverbs

WHY PROVERBS IS IMPORTANT

1 These are the wise words of Solomon son of David. Solomon was king of Israel.

2 They teach wisdom and self-control.
They give understanding.
3 They will teach you how to be wise
and self-controlled.
They will teach you what is honest
and fair and right.
4 They give the ability to think to those
with little knowledge.
They give knowledge and good
sense to the young.
5 Wise people should also listen to
them and learn even more.
Even they can find good advice in
these words.
6 Then they will be able to understand
wise words and stories.
They will understand the words of
wise men and their riddles.

7 Knowledge begins with respect for
the Lord.
But foolish people hate wisdom
and discipline.

WARNINGS AGAINST EVIL

8 My child, listen to your father's
teaching.
And do not forget your mother's
advice.
9 Their teaching will beautify your life.
It will be like flowers in your hair
or a chain around your neck.

10 My child, sinners will try to lead you
into sin.
But do not follow them.
11 They might say, "Come with us.
Let's ambush and kill someone.
Let's attack some harmless person
just for fun.

12 Let's swallow them alive, as death
does.
Let's swallow them whole, as the
grave does.
13 We will take all kinds of valuable
things.
We will fill our houses with what
we steal.
14 Come join us,
and we will share with you what we
steal."
15 My child, do not go along with them.
Do not do what they do.
16 They run to do evil.
They are quick to kill.
17 It is useless to spread out a net
right where the birds can see it!
18 These men are setting their own trap.
They will only catch themselves!
19 All greedy people end up this way.
Greed takes away the life of the
greedy person.

WISDOM SPEAKS

20 Wisdom is like a good woman who
shouts in the street.
She raises her voice in the city
squares.
21 She cries out in the noisy street.
She makes her speech at the city
gates:
22 "You foolish people! How long do you
want to stay foolish?
How long will you make fun of
wisdom?
How long will you hate knowledge?
23 Listen when I correct you.
I will tell you what's in my
heart.
I will tell you what I am thinking.
24 I called, but you refused to listen.
I held out my hand, but you paid no
attention.
25 You did not follow my advice.
You did not want me to correct you.

26 So I will laugh when you are in
trouble.
I will make fun when disaster
happens to you.
27 Disaster will come over you like a
storm.
Trouble will strike you like a
whirlwind.
Pain and trouble will overwhelm
you.

28 "Then you will call out to me.
But I will not answer.
You will look for me.
But you will not find me.
29 You rejected knowledge.
You did not choose to respect the
Lord.
30 You did not accept my advice.
You rejected my correction.
31 So you will get what you deserve.
You will get what you planned for
others.
32 Fools wander away and get killed.
They are destroyed because they
do not care.
33 But those who listen to me will live in
safety.
They will be safe, without fear of
being hurt."

REWARDS OF WISDOM

2 My child, believe what I say.
And remember what I command
you.
2 Listen to wisdom.
Try with all your heart to gain
understanding.
3 Cry out for wisdom.
Beg for understanding.
4 Search for it as you would for silver.
Hunt for it like hidden treasure.
5 Then you will understand what it
means to respect the Lord.
Then you will begin to know
God.
6 Only the Lord gives wisdom.
Knowledge and understanding
come from him.
7 He stores up wisdom for those who
are honest.

Like a shield he protects those who
are innocent.
8 He guards those who are fair to
others.
He protects those who are loyal to
him.

9 Then you will understand what is
honest and fair and right.
You will understand what is good
to do.
10 You will have wisdom in your heart.
And knowledge will be pleasing to
you.
11 Good sense will protect you.
Understanding will guard you.
12 It will keep you from doing evil.
It will save you from people whose
words are bad.
13 Such people do not do what is right.
They do what is evil.
14 They enjoy doing wrong.
They are happy to do what is
crooked and evil.
15 What they do is wrong.
Their ways are dishonest.

16 It will save you from the unfaithful
wife
who tries to lead you into adultery
with pleasing words.
17 Such women leave the husbands
they married when they were
young.
They forget the promise they made
before God.
18 If you go to her house, you are on
your way to death.
What she does leads to death.
19 No one who goes to her comes back.
He will not continue to live.

20 But wisdom will help you be a good
person.
It will help you do what is right.
21 Those who are honest will stay in the
land.
Those who are innocent will
remain in it.
22 But evil people will be removed from
the land.

The unfaithful will be thrown out
of it.

ADVICE TO CHILDREN

3 My child, do not forget my teaching.
Keep my commands in mind.
² Then you will live a long time.
And your life will be successful.

³ Don't ever stop being kind and
truthful.
Let kindness and truth show in all
you do.
Write them down in your mind as
if on a tablet.

⁴ Then you will be respected
and pleasing to both God and men.

⁵ Trust the Lord with all your heart.
Don't depend on your own
understanding.
⁶ Remember the Lord in everything
you do.
And he will give you success.

⁷ Don't depend on your own wisdom.
Respect the Lord and refuse to do
wrong.
⁸ Then your body will be healthy.
And your bones will be strong.

☆ Proverbs 3:13

*The Book of Proverbs is full of God's wisdom. And this verse tells us that if
you are a person who gets wisdom and understanding from God, you can
be happy.*

How do you use the word happy? Do you say, "Happy Birthday,"
"Happy Easter," or "Happy Thanksgiving"? What about
"Happy Friday!"? Or better yet—Happy Meal! Is the
word happy only used for special days, or can you
be happy any day of the week? You can always
find something that makes you happy. Even on
your saddest day, the Bible shows you how
you can be happy. God says that when you
listen to his words, you will be happy. You
listen to God when you read or hear the
Bible. You make God happy and he makes
you happy. It's a happy friendship!

· · · · · · · · · · · · · · · · · · · ·

*Learning about God will help you be
happy on both good and bad days.*

9 Honor the Lord by giving him part of
your wealth.
Give him the firstfruits from all
your crops.
10 Then your barns will be full.
And your wine barrels will
overflow with new wine.

11 My child, do not reject the Lord's
discipline.
And don't become angry when he
corrects you.
12 The Lord corrects those he loves,
just as a father corrects the child
that he likes.

 13 Happy is the person who finds
wisdom.
And happy is the person who gets
understanding.
14 Wisdom is worth more than silver.
It brings more profit than gold.
15 Wisdom is more precious than
rubies.
Nothing you want is equal to it.
16 With her right hand wisdom offers
you a long life.
With her left hand she gives you
riches and honor.
17 Wisdom will make your life pleasant.
It will bring you peace.
18 As a tree makes fruit, wisdom gives
life to those who use it.
Everyone who uses wisdom will be
happy.

19 Using his wisdom, the Lord made the
earth.
Using his understanding, he set the
sky in place.
20 Using his knowledge, he made rivers
flow from underground springs.
And he made the clouds drop rain
on the earth.

21 My child, hold on to wisdom and
reason.
Don't let them out of your sight!
22 They will give you life.
Like a necklace, they will beautify
your life.

23 Then you will go on your way in
safety.
And you will not get hurt.
24 You won't need to be afraid when you
lie down.
When you lie down, your sleep will
be peaceful.
25 You won't need to be afraid of trouble
coming suddenly.
You won't need to fear the ruin that
comes to the wicked.
26 The Lord will keep you safe.
He will keep you from being
trapped.

27 Whenever you are able,
do good to people who need help.
28 If you have what your neighbor asks
for,
don't say to him,
"Come back later. I will give it to
you tomorrow."
29 Don't make plans to hurt your
neighbor.
He lives nearby and trusts you.
30 Don't accuse a man for no good
reason.
Don't accuse him if he has not
harmed you.

31 Don't be jealous of men who use
violence.
And don't choose to be like them.
32 The Lord hates those who do wrong.
But he is a friend to those who are
honest.
33 The Lord will put a curse on the evil
person's house.
But he will bless the home of
people who do what is right.
34 The Lord laughs at those who laugh
at him.
But he is kind to those who are not
proud.
35 Wise people will receive honor.
But foolish people will be
disgraced.

WISDOM IS IMPORTANT

4 My children, listen to your father's
teaching.

Pay attention so you will
understand.

² What I am telling you is good.
Do not forget what I teach you.

³ I was once a young boy in my father's
house.
I was like an only child to my
mother.

⁴ And my father taught me and said,
"Hold on to my words with all your
heart.
Keep my commands and you will
live.

⁵ Get wisdom and understanding.
Don't forget or ignore my words.

⁶ Use wisdom, and it will take care of
you.
Love wisdom, and it will keep you
safe.

⁷ Wisdom is the most important thing.
So get wisdom.
If it costs everything you have, get
understanding.

⁸ Believe in the value of wisdom, and it
will make you great.
Use it, and it will bring honor to you.

⁹ Like flowers in your hair, it will
beautify your life.
Like a crown, it will make you look
beautiful."

¹⁰ My child, listen and accept what I
say.
Then you will have a long life.

¹¹ I am guiding you in wisdom.
And I am leading you to do what is
right.

¹² Nothing will hold you back.
You will not be overwhelmed.

¹³ Always remember what you have
been taught.
Don't let go of it.
Keep safe all that you have learned.
It is the most important thing in
your life.

¹⁴ Don't follow the ways of the wicked.
Don't do what evil people do.

¹⁵ Avoid their ways. Don't go near what
they do.
Stay away from them and keep on
going.

¹⁶ They cannot sleep until they do evil.
They cannot rest until they hurt
someone.

¹⁷ They fill themselves with wickedness
and cruelty
as if they were eating bread and
drinking wine.

¹⁸ The way of the good person is like
the light of dawn.
It grows brighter and brighter until
it is full daylight.

¹⁹ But the wicked are like those who
stumble in the dark.
They can't even see what has hurt
them.

²⁰ My child, pay attention to my words.
Listen closely to what I say.

²¹ Don't ever forget my words.
Keep them deep within your heart.

²² These words are the secret to life for
those who find them.
They bring health to the whole
body.

²³ Be very careful about what you think.
Your thoughts run your life.

²⁴ Don't use your mouth to tell lies.
Don't ever say things that are not
true.

²⁵ Keep your eyes focused on what is
right.

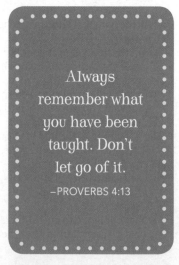

Always remember what you have been taught. Don't let go of it.

–PROVERBS 4:13

Keep looking straight ahead to
what is good.
26 Be careful what you do.
Always do what is right.
27 Do not do anything unless it is right.
Stay away from evil.

WARNING ABOUT ADULTERY

5 My son, pay attention to my
wisdom.
Listen to my words of
understanding.
2 Be careful to use good sense.
Watch what you say.
3 The words of another man's wife may
seem sweet as honey.
Her words may be as pleasant as
olive oil.
4 But in the end she will bring you
sorrow.
She will cause you pain like a
two-edged sword.
5 She is on the way to death.
Her steps are headed straight to
the grave.
6 She gives no thought to life.
She does not know that her ways
are wrong.

7 Now, my sons, listen to me.
Don't ignore what I say.
8 Stay away from such a woman.
Don't even go near the door of her
house.
9 If you do, you will give your riches to
others.
And the best years of your life
will be given to someone who is
cruel.
10 Strangers will enjoy your wealth.
And what you worked so hard for
will go to someone else.
11 You will groan at the end of your life.
Then your health will be gone.
12 Then you will say, "I hated
self-control!
I would not listen when I was
corrected!
13 I would not listen to my teachers.
I paid no attention to what they
taught me.

14 I have come very close to being
completely ruined
in front of a whole group of people."

15 Be faithful to your own wife.
She is like your own well of water
from which you drink.
16 You wouldn't drink from streams
flowing in the city streets or
squares.
So be satisfied with your wife,
not those outside your home.
17 These things are yours alone.
Don't share them with strangers.
18 Be happy with the wife
you married when you were young.
She gives you joys
as your fountain gives you water.
19 She is as lovely and graceful as a deer.
Let her love always make you
happy.
Let her love always hold you
captive.
20 My son, don't be held captive by
a woman who takes part in
adultery.
Don't hold another man's wife.

21 The Lord sees everything you do.
He watches where you go.
22 An evil man will be caught in his evil
ways.
He will be tied up by his sins as if
they were ropes.
23 He will die because he does not
control himself.
He will be held captive by his own
foolishness.

DANGERS OF BEING FOOLISH

6 My child, be careful about giving a
guarantee for somebody else.
Be careful about promising to pay
what someone else owes.
2 You might get trapped by what you
say.
You might be caught by your own
words.
3 My child, you might do this and be
under somebody's control.
Then here is how to get free.

Go to your neighbor and don't be
  proud.
  Beg him to free you from your
  promise.
⁴ Don't go to sleep.
  Don't even rest your eyes.
⁵ But free yourself like a deer running
  from a hunter.
  Free yourself like a bird flying away
  from a trapper.

⁶ Go watch the ants, you lazy person.
  Watch what they do and be wise.
⁷ Ants have no commander.
  They have no leader or ruler.
⁸ But they store up food in the summer.
  They gather their supplies at
  harvest.
⁹ How long will you lie there, you lazy
  person?
  When will you get up from
  sleeping?
¹⁰ You sleep a little; you take a nap.
  You fold your hands and rest.
¹¹ So you will be as poor as if you had
  been robbed.
  You will have as little as if you had
  been held up.

¹² Some people are wicked and no good.
  They go around telling lies.
¹³ They wink with their eyes and signal
  with their feet.
  They make signs with their fingers.
¹⁴ They make evil plans in their hearts.
  They are always causing trouble.
¹⁵ So trouble will strike them in an
  instant.
  Suddenly they will be hurt beyond
  cure.

¹⁶ There are six things the Lord hates.
  There are seven things he cannot
  stand:
¹⁷   a proud look,
  a lying tongue,
  hands that kill innocent people,
¹⁸   a mind that thinks up
    evil plans,
  feet that are quick to do evil,
¹⁹   a witness who tells lies

and a man who causes trouble
  among brothers.

WARNING ABOUT ADULTERY

²⁰ My son, keep your father's
  commands.
  Don't forget your mother's
  teaching.
²¹ Remember their words forever.
  Let it be as if they were tied around
  your neck.
²² They will guide you when you walk.
  They will guard you while you
  sleep.
  They will speak to you when you
  are awake.
²³ Their commands are like a lamp.
  Their teaching is like a light.
  And the correction that comes from
  them
  helps you have life.
²⁴ Such teaching will keep you from
  sinful women
  and from the pleasing words of
  another man's unfaithful wife.
²⁵ Don't want her because she is
  beautiful.
  Don't let her capture you by the
  way she looks at you.
²⁶ A prostitute may leave you with only
  a loaf of bread.
  And a woman who takes part in
  adultery may cost you your life.
²⁷ You cannot carry hot coals against
  your chest
  without burning your clothes.
²⁸ And you cannot walk on hot coals
  without burning your feet.
²⁹ The same thing happens if you
  commit adultery with another
  man's wife.
  Anyone who does so will be
  punished.

³⁰ People do not hate a thief
  when he steals because he is
  hungry.
³¹ But if he is caught, he must pay back
  seven times what he stole.
  It may cost him everything
  he owns.

³² A man who takes part in adultery
    doesn't have any sense.
    He will destroy himself.
³³ He will be beaten up and disgraced.
    And his shame will never go away.
³⁴ Jealousy makes a husband very
    angry.
    He will have no mercy when he
    gets even.
³⁵ He will accept no payment for the
    wrong.
    He will take no money, no matter
    how much it is.

THE WOMAN OF ADULTERY

7 My son, remember what I say.
    Treasure my commands.
² Obey my commands, and you will
    live.
    Protect my teachings as you would
    your own eyes.
³ Remind yourself of them.
    Write them down in your mind as
    if on a tablet.
⁴ Be good to wisdom as if she were
    your sister.
    Make understanding your closest
    friend.
⁵ Wisdom and understanding will keep
    you away from adultery.
    They will keep you away from the
    unfaithful wife and her pleasing
    words.

⁶ I once was standing at the window of
    my house.
    I looked out through the shutters.
⁷ I saw some foolish, young men.
    I noticed one of them who had no
    wisdom.
⁸ He was walking down the street near
    the corner.
    He was on the road leading to her
    house.
⁹ It was the twilight of the evening.
    The darkness of the night was just
    beginning.
¹⁰ Then the woman approached him.
    She was dressed like a prostitute
    and was planning to trick him.
¹¹ She was a loud and stubborn woman.

    She never stayed at home.
¹² She was always out in the streets or
    in the city squares.
    She was always waiting around on
    the street corners.
¹³ She grabbed him and kissed him.
    Without shame she said to him,
¹⁴ "I made my fellowship offering and
    have the meat at home.
    I have kept my special promises.
¹⁵ So I have come out to meet you.
    I have been looking for you and
    have found you!
¹⁶ I have covered my bed
    with colored sheets from Egypt.
¹⁷ I have made my bed smell sweet
    with myrrh, aloes and cinnamon.
¹⁸ Come, let's make love until morning.
    Let's enjoy each other's love!
¹⁹ My husband is not home.
    He has gone on a long trip.
²⁰ He took a lot of money with him.
    And he won't be home for weeks."
²¹ By her clever words she made him
    give in.
    By her pleasing words she led him
    into doing wrong.
²² All at once he followed her.
    He was like an ox being led to the
    butcher.
    He was like a deer caught in a trap.

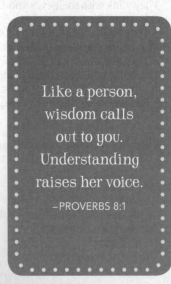

Like a person,
wisdom calls
out to you.
Understanding
raises her voice.

–PROVERBS 8:1

23 But quickly an arrow shot through
his liver.
He was like a bird caught in a trap.
He didn't know what he did would
kill him.

24 Now, my sons, listen to me.
Pay attention to what I say.
25 Don't let yourself be tricked by the
woman who is guilty of adultery.
Don't join her in her evil actions.
26 She has ruined many good men.
Many have died because of her.
27 Going to her house is like taking the
road to death.
That road leads down to where the
dead are.

LISTEN TO WISDOM

8 Like a person, wisdom calls out to
you.
Understanding raises her voice.
2 On the hilltops along the road
and at the crossroads, she stands
calling.
3 She stands beside the city gates.
At the entrances into the city, she
calls out:
4 "People, I'm calling out to you.
I am shouting to all people.
5 You who do not know better, get the
ability to think.
You who are foolish, get
understanding.
6 Listen. I have important things
to say.
What I tell you is right.
7 What I say is true.
I hate it when people speak evil.
8 Everything I say is honest.
Nothing I say is crooked or false.
9 People with good sense know that
what I say is true.
People with knowledge know that
my words are right.
10 Choose my teachings instead of
silver.
Choose knowledge rather than the
finest gold.
11 Wisdom is more precious than rubies.
Nothing you want is equal to it.

12 "I am wisdom, and I have the ability
to think.
I also have knowledge and good
sense.
13 If you respect the Lord, you also will
hate evil.
It is wise to hate pride and bragging,
evil ways and lies.
14 I have good sense and advice.
I have understanding and power.
15 Kings use me to govern.
And rulers use me to make fair laws.
16 Princes use me to lead.
So do important men and all good
judges.
17 I love those who love me.
Those who want me find me.
18 Riches and honor are mine.
So are wealth and lasting success.
19 What I give is better than the finest
gold.
What I give is better than pure
silver.
20 I do what is right.
I do what is fair.
21 I give wealth to those who love me.
I fill them with treasures.

22 "I, wisdom, was with God when he
began his work.
This was before he made anything
else long ago.
23 I was appointed in the very
beginning,
even before the world began.
24 I began before there were oceans.
There were no springs overflowing
with water.
25 I began before the hills were there.
The mountains had not even been
put in place.
26 God still had not made the earth or
fields.
He had not even made the first dust
of the earth.
27 I was there when God put the skies in
place,
when he stretched the horizon over
the oceans.
28 I was there when he made the clouds
above.

I was there when he put the
fountains in the oceans.
²⁹ I was there when he ordered the sea
not to go beyond the borders he
had set for it.
I was there when he laid the earth's
foundation.
³⁰ I was like a child by his side.
I was happy every day
and enjoyed being in his presence.
³¹ I enjoyed the whole world.
And I was happy with all its people.

³² "Now, my children, listen to me.
Those who follow my ways are
happy.
³³ Listen to my teaching, and you will
be wise.
Do not ignore it.
³⁴ Those who listen to me are happy.
They stand watching at my door
every day.
They are at my open doorway,
wanting to be with me.
³⁵ Whoever finds me finds life.
And the Lord will be pleased with
him.
³⁶ Whoever does not find me hurts
himself.
Those who hate me love death."

BEING WISE OR FOOLISH

9 Wisdom has built her house.
She has made its seven columns.
² She has prepared her food and wine.
She has set her table.
³ She has sent out her servant girls.
She calls out from the highest place
in the city.
⁴ She says to those who are not wise,
"Come in here, you foolish people!
⁵ Come and eat my food.
And drink the wine I have
prepared.
⁶ Stop your foolish ways, and you will
live.
Be a person of understanding.

⁷ "If you correct someone who makes
fun of wisdom, you will get
insulted.

If you correct an evil person, you
will get hurt.
⁸ Do not correct someone who makes
fun of wisdom, or he will hate
you.
But correct a wise man, and he will
love you.
⁹ Teach a wise man, and he will
become even wiser.
Teach a good man, and he will
learn even more.

¹⁰ "Wisdom begins with respect for the
Lord.
And understanding begins with
knowing God, the Holy One.
¹¹ If you live wisely, you will live a long
time.
Wisdom will add years to your
life.
¹² The wise person is rewarded by his
wisdom.
But a person who makes fun of
wisdom will suffer for it."

¹³ Foolishness is like a loud woman.
She does not have wisdom or
knowledge.
¹⁴ She sits at the door of her house.
It is at the highest place in the city.
¹⁵ She calls out to those who are
passing by.
They are minding their own
business.
¹⁶ She says to those who are not wise,
"Come in here, you foolish
people!
¹⁷ Stolen water is sweeter.
Stolen food tastes better."
¹⁸ But these people don't know that
everyone dies who goes there.
They don't realize that her guests
are deep in the grave.

THE PROVERBS OF SOLOMON

10 These are the wise words of
Solomon:

A wise son makes his father happy.
But a foolish son makes his mother
sad.

2 Riches gotten by doing wrong have
    no value.
    But right living will save you from
    death.

3 The Lord does not let people who live
    right go hungry.
    But he does not let evil people get
    what they hunger for.

4 A lazy person will end up poor.
    But a hard worker will become rich.

5 A son who gathers crops when they
    are ready is wise.
    But the son who sleeps through the
    harvest is a disgrace.

6 People who do what is right will have
    rich blessings.
    But the wicked will be
    overwhelmed by violence.

7 Good people will be remembered as a
    blessing.
    But evil people will soon be
    forgotten.

8 A wise person does what he is told.
    But a talkative fool will be ruined.

9 The honest person will live safely.
    But the one who is dishonest will
    be caught.

10 A wink may get you into trouble.
    And foolish talk will lead to your
    ruin.

11 Like a fountain of water, the words of
    a good person give life.
    But the words of the wicked
    contain nothing but violence.

12 Hatred stirs up trouble.
    But love forgives all wrongs.

13 You can expect wise people to speak
    with understanding.
    But people without wisdom can
    expect to be punished.

14 Wise people don't tell everything
    they know.
    But a foolish person talks too much
    and is ruined.

15 Having lots of money protects the
    rich.
    But having no money destroys the
    poor.

16 Good people are rewarded with life.
    But evil people are paid back with
    punishment.

17 The person who accepts correction is
    on the way to life.
    But the person who ignores
    correction will be ruined.

18 Whoever hides his hate is a liar.
    Whoever tells lies is a fool.

19 If you talk a lot, you are sure to sin.
    If you are wise, you will keep quiet.

20 The words of a good person are like
    pure silver.
    But an evil person's thoughts are
    worth little.

21 A good person's words will help many
    others.
    But a foolish person dies because
    he doesn't have wisdom.

22 The Lord's blessing brings wealth.
    And with it comes no sorrow.

23 A foolish person enjoys doing
    wrong.
    But a person with understanding
    enjoys doing what is wise.

24 An evil person will get what he fears
    most.
    But a good person will receive what
    he wants most.

25 A storm will blow the evil person
    away.
    But a good person will always be
    safe.

☆ Proverbs 11:3

This chapter in Proverbs has a lot of warnings about lying. It tells us that honesty can help guide us. But dishonesty hurts people.

Good people believe being honest is important. Has anyone ever lied to you? Was it hard to trust the person who lied? What if that person has lied over and over? Does it make trusting them even harder? Most people trust others who tell the truth and make good choices. God always tells the truth. He wants us to be like him, so we should be honest and keep promises.

. . . .

Just like God always tells the truth, we can do the same. He will help us when we ask him.

---

²⁶ A lazy person brings trouble to the one he works for.
  He bothers others like vinegar on the teeth or smoke in the eyes.

²⁷ Whoever respects the Lord will have a long life.
  But an evil person will have his life cut short.

²⁸ A good person can look forward to happiness.
  But an evil person can expect nothing.

²⁹ The Lord will protect good people.
  But he will ruin those who do evil.

³⁰ Good people will always be safe.
  But evil people will not remain in the land.

³¹ A good person says wise things.
  But a liar's tongue will be stopped.

³² Good people say the right thing.
  But the wicked tell lies.

11 The Lord hates dishonest scales.
  But he is pleased with correct weights.

² Pride leads only to shame.
  It is wise not to be proud.

³ Good people will be guided by honesty.
  But dishonesty will destroy those who are not trustworthy.

4 Riches will not help when it's time to
    die.
      But doing what is right will save
      you from dying too soon.

5 The goodness of an innocent person
    makes his life easier.
      But a wicked person will be
      destroyed by his wickedness.

6 Doing what is right brings freedom to
    honest people.
      But those who are not trustworthy
      will be caught by their own
      desires.

7 When a wicked person dies, his hope
    is gone.
      The hopes he placed in his riches
      will come to nothing.

8 The good man is saved from trouble.
      It comes to the wicked instead.

9 By his words an evil person can
    destroy his neighbor.
      But a good person will escape by
      being smart.

10 When good people succeed, the city
    is happy.
      When evil people die, there are
      shouts of joy.

11 The influence of good people makes a
    city great.
      But the wicked can destroy it with
      their words.

12 A person without good sense finds
    fault with his neighbor.
      But a person with understanding
      keeps quiet.

13 A person who gossips can't keep
    secrets.
      But a trustworthy person can keep
      a secret.

14 Without leadership a nation will be
    defeated.

      But when many people give advice,
      it will be safe.

15 Whoever guarantees to pay what
    somebody else owes will suffer.
      It is safer to avoid such promises.

16 A kind woman is respected.
      But cruel men get wealth.

17 A kind person is doing himself a
    favor.
      But a cruel person brings trouble
      on himself.

18 An evil person really gains nothing
    from what he earns.
      But a good person will surely be
      rewarded.

19 Those who are truly good will live.
      But those who chase after evil will
      die.

20 The Lord hates those with evil
    hearts.
      But he is pleased with those who
      are innocent.

21 You can be sure that evil people will
    be punished.
      But those who do what is right will
      not be punished.

22 A beautiful woman without good
    sense
      is like a gold ring in a pig's snout.

23 The wishes of those who do right will
    come true.
      But the hopes of the wicked will be
      defeated by God's anger.

24 Some people give much but get back
    even more.
      But others don't give what they
      should, and they end up poor.

25 A person who gives to others will get
    richer.
      Whoever helps others will himself
      be helped.

²⁶ People curse someone who keeps all
the grain for himself.
But they bless a person who is
willing to sell it.

²⁷ Whoever looks for good will find
kindness.
But whoever looks for evil will find
trouble.

²⁸ Those who trust in riches will be
ruined.
But a good person will be as
healthy as a green leaf.

²⁹ Whoever brings trouble to his family
will be left with nothing but the
wind.
And a foolish person will become a
servant to the wise.

³⁰ As a tree makes fruit, a good person
gives life to others.
The wise person shows others how
to be wise.

³¹ Good people will be rewarded on earth.
So the wicked and the sinners will
also be punished.

12 Anyone who loves learning
accepts being corrected.
But a person who hates being
corrected is stupid.

² The Lord is pleased with a good person.
But he will punish anyone who
plans evil.

³ Doing evil brings a person no safety
at all.
But a good person has safety and
security.

⁴ A good wife is like a crown for her
husband.
But a disgraceful wife is like a
disease in his bones.

⁵ The plans that good people make are
fair.
But the advice of the wicked will
trick you.

⁶ The wicked talk of killing people.
But the words of good people will
save them.

⁷ Wicked people die and leave nothing
behind.
But a good man's family goes on.

⁸ A wise person is praised.
But a stupid person is not
respected.

⁹ A person might not be important but
still have a servant.
He is better off than someone
who acts important but has
no food.

¹⁰ A good man takes care of his
animals.
But even the kindest acts of the
wicked are cruel.

¹¹ The person who works his land will
have plenty of food.
But the one who chases useless
dreams isn't wise.

¹² Evil people want what other evil
people have stolen.
But good people want to give to
others.

¹³ Evil people are trapped by their evil
talk.
But good people stay out of trouble.

¹⁴ A person will be rewarded for what
he says.
And he will also be rewarded for
what he does.

¹⁵ A foolish person thinks he is doing
right.
But a wise person listens to advice.

¹⁶ A foolish person quickly shows that
he is upset.

But a wise person ignores an insult.

17 An honest witness tells the truth.
But a dishonest witness tells lies.

18 Careless words stab like a sword.
But wise words bring healing.

19 Truth will last forever.
But lies last only a moment.

20 Those who plan evil mean to lie.
But those who plan peace will be
happy.

21 No harm comes to a good person.
But an evil person's life is full of
trouble.

22 The Lord hates those who tell lies.
But he is pleased with those who do
what they promise.

23 A wise person keeps what he knows
to himself.
But a foolish person shows how
foolish he is.

24 Hard workers will become leaders.
But those who are lazy will be
slaves.

25 Worry makes a person feel as if he is
carrying a heavy load.
But a kind word cheers up a person.

26 A good person takes advice from his
friends.
But an evil person is easily led to do
wrong.

27 A lazy person catches no food to cook.
But a hard worker will have great
wealth.

28 Doing what is right is the way to life.
But there is another way that leads
to death.

13 A wise son takes his father's
advice.
But a person who makes fun
of wisdom won't listen to
correction.

2 A person will be rewarded for what
he says.
But those who can't be trusted
want only violence.

3 Whoever is careful about what he
says protects his life.
But anyone who speaks
without thinking will be
ruined.

4 The lazy person will not get what he
wants.
But a hard worker gets everything
he wants.

5 Good people hate what is false.
But wicked people do shameful and
disgraceful things.

6 Doing what is right protects the
honest person.
But evil ruins the sinner.

7 Some people pretend to be rich but
really have nothing.
Other people pretend to be poor
but really are wealthy.

8 A rich man may have to pay a ransom
for his life.
But a poor person will never have
to face such a danger.

9 Good people will live long like bright
flames.
But the wicked will die like a flame
going out.

10 Pride leads to arguments.
But those who take advice are
wise.

11 Money that comes easily disappears
quickly.
But money that is gathered little by
little will slowly grow.

¹² It is sad when you don't get what you
hoped for.
But when wishes come true, it's like
eating fruit from the tree of life.

¹³ Whoever rejects what he is taught
will pay for it.
But whoever does what he is told
will be rewarded.

¹⁴ The teaching of a wise person gives
life.
It is like a fountain of water that
can save people from death.

¹⁵ People with good understanding will
be liked.
But the lives of those who are not
trustworthy are hard.

¹⁶ Every wise person acts with good
sense.
But a foolish person shows how
foolish he is.

¹⁷ A wicked messenger brings nothing
but trouble.
But a trustworthy one makes
everything right.

¹⁸ A person who refuses correction will
end up poor and disgraced.
But a person who accepts
correction will be honored.

¹⁹ It is so good when wishes come true.
But foolish people still refuse to
stop doing evil.

²⁰ Whoever spends time with wise
people will become wise.
But whoever makes friends with
fools will suffer.

²¹ Trouble always comes to sinners.
But good people enjoy success.

²² Good people's wealth will be
inherited by their grandchildren.
And a sinner's wealth will be saved
for good people.

²³ A poor man's field might have plenty
of food.
But unfair people steal it from him.

²⁴ If a person does not punish his
children, he does not love them.
But the person who loves his
children is careful to correct
them.

²⁵ Good people have enough to eat.
But the wicked will go hungry.

14 A wise woman strengthens her
family.
But a foolish woman destroys hers
by what she does.

² People who live good lives show
respect for the Lord.
But those who live evil lives show
no respect for him.

³ A foolish person will be punished for
his proud words.
But a wise person's words will
protect him.

⁴ When there are no oxen, there is no
food in the barn.
But with the strength of an ox,
much grain can be grown.

⁵ A truthful witness does not lie.
But a false witness tells nothing
but lies.

⁶ Those who make fun of wisdom look
for it but do not find it.
But the person with understanding
easily finds knowledge.

⁷ Stay away from a foolish person.
You won't learn anything from him.

⁸ What makes a person wise is
understanding what to do.
But what makes a person foolish is
dishonesty.

⁹ Foolish people don't care if they sin.

But honest people work at being right with others.

¹⁰ No one else can know your sadness.
Strangers cannot share your joy.

¹¹ The wicked person's house will be destroyed.
But a good person's tent will still be standing.

¹² Some people think they are doing what's right.
But what they are doing will really kill them.

¹³ When someone is laughing, he may be sad inside.
And when the laughter is over, there is sorrow.

¹⁴ Evil people will be paid back for their evil ways.
And good people will be rewarded for their good ones.

¹⁵ A foolish person will believe anything.
But a wise person thinks about what he does.

¹⁶ A wise person is careful and stays out of trouble.
But a foolish person is quick to act and careless.

¹⁷ A person who quickly loses his temper does foolish things.
But a person with understanding remains calm.

¹⁸ Foolish people get nothing for their work but more foolishness.
But wise people are rewarded with knowledge.

¹⁹ Evil people will have to bow down to good people.
The wicked will bow down at the door of those who do right.

²⁰ The poor are rejected, even by their neighbors.
But rich people have many friends.

²¹ It is a sin to hate your neighbor.
But being kind to the needy brings happiness.

²² Those who make evil plans will be ruined.
But people love and trust those who plan to do good.

²³ Those who work hard make a profit.
But those who only talk will be poor.

²⁴ Wise people are rewarded with wealth.
But foolish people will only be rewarded with more foolishness.

²⁵ A truthful witness saves lives.
But a false witness is a traitor.

²⁶ A person who respects the Lord will have security.
And his children will be protected.

²⁷ Respect for the Lord gives life.
It is like a fountain of water that can save people from death.

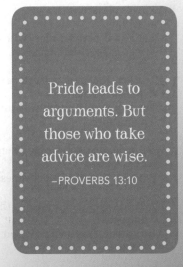

Pride leads to arguments. But those who take advice are wise.

–PROVERBS 13:10

28 A king is honored when he has many
people to rule.
But a prince is ruined if he has
none.

29 A person who does not quickly
get angry shows that he has
understanding.
But a person who quickly loses his
temper shows his foolishness.

30 Peace of mind means a healthy body.
But jealousy will rot your bones.

31 Whoever is cruel to the poor insults
their Maker.
But anyone who is kind to the
needy honors God.

32 The wicked are ruined by their own
evil.
But those who do what is right are
protected by their honesty.

33 The person who has understanding
has wisdom.
And even fools recognize it.

34 Doing what is right makes a nation
great.
But sin will bring disgrace to any
people.

35 A king is pleased with a wise
servant.
But he will become angry with one
who causes him shame.

15 A gentle answer will calm a
person's anger.
But an unkind answer will cause
more anger.

2 Wise people use knowledge when
they speak.
But fools speak only foolishness.

3 The Lord's eyes see everything that
happens.
He watches both evil and good
people.

4 As a tree gives us fruit, healing words
give us life.
But evil words crush the spirit.

5 A foolish person rejects his father's
correction.
But anyone who accepts correction
is wise.

6 There is much wealth in the houses
of good people.
But evil people are paid only with
trouble.

7 With their words wise people spread
knowledge.
But there is no knowledge in the
thoughts of the foolish.

8 The Lord hates the sacrifice that the
wicked person offers.
But he is pleased with an honest
person's prayer.

9 The Lord hates what evil people do.
But he loves those who do what is
right.

10 The person who quits doing what is
right will really be punished.
The one who hates to be corrected
will die.

11 The Lord knows what is happening
where the dead people are.
So he can surely know what living
people are thinking.

12 A person who laughs at wisdom does
not like to be corrected.
He will not ask advice from the
wise.

13 Happiness makes a person smile.
But sadness breaks a person's spirit.

14 Smart people want more knowledge.
But a foolish person just wants
more foolishness.

15 Every day is hard for those who suffer.

But a happy heart makes it like a continual feast.

16 It is better to be poor and respect the Lord
than to be wealthy and have much trouble.

17 It is better to eat vegetables with those who love you
than to eat meat with those who hate you.

18 A person who quickly gets angry causes trouble.
But a person who controls his temper stops a quarrel.

19 A lazy person's life is as difficult as walking through a patch of thorns.
But an honest person's life is as easy as walking down a smooth highway.

20 A wise son makes his father happy.
But a foolish person hates his mother.

21 A man without wisdom enjoys being foolish.
But a man with understanding does what is right.

22 Plans fail without good advice.
But plans succeed when you get advice from many others.

23 People enjoy giving good answers!
Saying the right word at the right time is so pleasing!

24 A wise person does things that will make his life better.
He avoids whatever would cause his death.

25 The Lord will tear down the proud person's house.
But he will protect the property of a widow.

26 The Lord hates evil thoughts.
But he is pleased with kind words.

27 A greedy person brings trouble to his family.
But the person who can't be paid to do wrong will live.

28 Good people think before they answer.
But the wicked simply give evil answers.

29 The Lord does not listen to the wicked.
But he hears the prayers of those who do right.

30 Good news makes you feel better.
Your happiness will show in your eyes.

31 A wise person pays attention to correction
that will improve his life.

32 A person who refuses correction hates himself.
But a person who accepts correction gains understanding.

33 Respect for the Lord will teach you wisdom.
If you want to be honored, you must not be proud.

16 People make plans in their hearts.
But only the Lord can make those plans come true.

2 A person may believe he is doing right.
But the Lord will judge his reasons.

3 Depend on the Lord in whatever you do.
Then your plans will succeed.

4 The Lord makes everything work the way he wants it.
He even has a day of disaster for evil people.

⁵ The Lord hates those who are proud.
  You can be sure that they will be
  punished.

⁶ Love and truth bring forgiveness of
  sin.
  By respecting the Lord you will
  avoid evil.

⁷ A person should live so that he
  pleases the Lord.
  If he does, even his enemies will
  make peace with him.

⁸ It is better to be poor and do what is
  right
  than to be wealthy and be unfair.

⁹ A person may think up plans.
  But the Lord decides what he will
  do.

¹⁰ The words of a king are like a
  message from God.
  So his decisions should be fair.

¹¹ The Lord wants honest balances and
  scales to be used.
  He wants all weights to be honest.

¹² Kings hate those who do wrong
  because governments only last if
  they are fair.

¹³ Kings are pleased with those who
  speak honest words.
  They value a person who speaks
  the truth.

¹⁴ If a king becomes angry, he may put
  someone to death.
  So a wise man will try to keep
  peace.

¹⁵ A king's kindness can give people life.
  His kindness is like a spring
  shower.

¹⁶ It is better to get wisdom than gold.
  It is better to choose
  understanding than silver!

¹⁷ A good person stays away from evil.
  A person who watches what he
  does protects his life.

¹⁸ Pride leads to destruction.
  A proud attitude brings ruin.

¹⁹ It is better not to be proud and to be
  with those who suffer
  than to share stolen property with
  proud people.

²⁰ Whoever pays attention to what he is
  taught will succeed.
  And whoever trusts the Lord will
  be happy.

²¹ A wise person is known for his
  understanding.
  He wins people to his side with
  pleasant words.

²² Understanding is like a fountain of
  water which gives life to those
  who use it.
  But foolishness will cause foolish
  people to be punished.

²³ A wise person's mind tells him what
  to say.
  This helps him to teach others
  better.

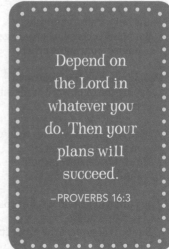

Depend on
the Lord in
whatever you
do. Then your
plans will
succeed.

—PROVERBS 16:3

²⁴ Pleasant words are like a honeycomb.
   They make a person happy and
      healthy.

²⁵ Some people think they are doing
      what's right.
   But in the end it causes them to die.

²⁶ The worker's hunger helps him.
   His desire to eat makes him work.

²⁷ An evil person makes evil plans.
   And his words are like a burning
      fire.

²⁸ An evil person causes trouble.
   And a person who gossips ruins
      friendships.

²⁹ A cruel man tricks his neighbor.
   He leads him to do wrong.

³⁰ Someone who winks at you is
      planning evil.
   And the one who grins at you is
      about to do something wrong.

³¹ Gray hair is like a crown of honor.
   You earn it by living a good life.

³² Patience is better than strength.
   Controlling your temper is better
      than capturing a city.

³³ People throw lots to make a decision.
   But the answer comes from the
      Lord.

17

It is better to eat a dry crust of
   bread in peace
than to have a feast where there is
   quarreling.

² A wise servant will rule over his
      master's disgraceful son.
   And he will even inherit a share of
      what the master leaves his sons.

³ A hot furnace tests silver and gold.
   In the same way, the Lord tests a
      person's heart.

⁴ An evil person listens to evil words.
   A liar pays attention to cruel
      words.

⁵ If you make fun of the poor,
   you insult God, who made them.
   If you laugh at someone's trouble,
      you will be punished.

⁶ Grandchildren are the reward of old
      people.
   And children are proud of their
      parents.

⁷ Foolish people should not be proud.
   And rulers should not be liars!

⁸ A person might think he can pay
      people and they will do anything
      he asks.
   He thinks it will succeed every time.

⁹ Whoever forgives someone's sin
      makes a friend.
   But the one who tells about the sin
      breaks up friendships.

¹⁰ A wise man will learn more from a
      warning
   than a foolish person will learn
      from 100 lashings.

¹¹ A disobedient person is only looking
      for trouble.
   So a cruel messenger will be sent
      against him.

¹² It is better to meet a bear robbed of
      her cubs
   than to meet a foolish person doing
      foolish things.

¹³ If a person gives evil in return for
      good,
   his house will always be full of
      trouble.

¹⁴ Starting a quarrel is like a leak in a
      dam.
   So stop the quarrel before a fight
      breaks out.

15 The Lord hates both these things:
  letting guilty people go free and
    punishing those who are not
    guilty.

16 It won't do a fool any good to try to
    buy wisdom.
  He doesn't really want to be wise.

17 A friend loves you all the time.
  A brother is always there to help
    you.

18 It is not wise to promise
  to pay what your neighbor owes.

19 Whoever loves to quarrel loves
    to sin.
  Whoever is proud is asking for
    trouble.

20 A person with an evil heart will find
    no success.
  And the person whose words are
    evil will get into trouble.

21 It is sad to have a foolish son.
  There is no joy in being the father
    of a fool.

22 A happy heart is like good medicine.
  But a broken spirit drains your
    strength.

23 A wicked person secretly accepts
    money to do wrong.
  Then there will be no fairness.

24 The person with understanding
    looks for wisdom.
  But a foolish person lets his mind
    wander everywhere.

25 A foolish son makes his father sad.
  And he causes his mother great
    sorrow.

26 It is not good to punish those who
    have done what is right.
  Nor is it good to punish leaders for
    being honest.

27 The person who has knowledge says
    very little.
  And a person with understanding
    stays calm.

28 Even a foolish person seems to be
    wise if he keeps quiet.
  He appears to have understanding
    if he doesn't speak.

18 An unfriendly person cares only
    about himself.
  He makes fun of all wisdom.

2 A foolish person does not want to
    understand anything.
  He only enjoys telling others what
    he thinks.

3 Do something evil, and people won't
    like you.
  Do something shameful, and they
    will make fun of you.

4 Understanding people's words is as
    hard as getting water out of a
    deep well.
  But understanding wisdom is as
    easy as getting water from a
    flowing stream.

5 It is not good to honor the wicked.
  Nor is it good to be unfair to the
    innocent.

6 A fool's words start quarrels.
  They make people want to give him
    a beating.

7 A fool's words will ruin him.
  He will be trapped by his own words.

8 The words of a gossip are like tasty
    bits of food.
  People take them all in.

9 A person who doesn't work hard
  is just like a person who destroys
    things.

10 The Lord is like a strong tower.

Those who do what is right can run
to him for safety.

11 Rich people trust their wealth to
protect them.
They think it is like the high walls
of a city.

12 People who are proud will be ruined.
But those who are not proud will be
honored.

13 A person who answers without
listening
is foolish and disgraceful.

14 The will to live can get you through
sickness.
But no one can live with a broken
spirit.

15 The mind of a smart person is ready
to get knowledge.
The wise person listens to learn
more.

16 Taking a gift to an important person
will help get you in to see him.

17 The first person to tell his side of a
story seems right.
But that may change when
somebody comes and asks him
questions.

18 Throwing lots settles arguments.
It keeps the two sides from fighting.

19 A brother who has been insulted is
harder to win back than a walled
city.
And arguments separate people
like the barred gates of a palace.

20 What you say affects how you live.
You will be rewarded by how you
speak.

21 What you say can mean life or death.
Those who love to talk will be
rewarded for what they say.

22 A man who finds a wife finds
something good.
She shows that the Lord is pleased
with him.

23 Poor people beg for mercy.
Rich people give rude answers.

24 Some friends may ruin you.
But a real friend will be more loyal
than a brother.

19 It is better to be poor and honest
than to be foolish and tell lies.
2 Enthusiasm without knowledge is
not good.
If you act too quickly, you might
make a mistake.

3 A person's own foolishness ruins his
life.
But in his mind he blames the Lord
for it.

4 Wealthy people are always finding
more friends.
But the poor lose their friends.

5 A witness who lies will be punished.
An untruthful person will not be
left unpunished.

6 Many people want to please a leader.
And everyone is friends with those
who give gifts.

7 A poor person's relatives avoid him.
Even his friends stay far away!
He runs after them, begging.
But they are gone.

8 The person who gets wisdom is good
to himself.
And the one who has
understanding will succeed.

9 A witness who lies will be punished.
An untruthful person will die.

10 No foolish person should live in
luxury.

No slave should rule over princes!

11 A wise person is patient.
He will be honored if he ignores a
wrong done against him.

12 A king's anger scares people like the
roar of a lion.
But his kindness is as pleasant as
the dew on the grass.

13 A foolish son will ruin his father.
And a quarreling wife is as
bothersome as dripping water.

14 Houses and wealth are inherited
from parents.
But a wise wife is a gift from the
Lord.

15 Lazy people sleep a lot.
Idle people will go hungry.

16 Whoever obeys the commands
protects his life.
Whoever is careless in what he
does will die.

☆ 17 Being kind to the poor is like lending
to the Lord.
The Lord will reward you for what
you have done.

18 Correct your son while there is still
hope.
Do not help him destroy himself.

19 A person who is always getting angry
will pay for it.
If you help him, you will have to do
it again and again.

20 Listen to advice and accept correction.
Then in the end you will be wise.

21 People can make many different
plans.
But only the Lord's plan will
happen.

22 People want others to be loyal.

So it is better to be poor than to be
a liar.

23 Those who respect the Lord will live
and be content, unbothered by
trouble.

24 The lazy person may put his hand in
the dish,
but he won't lift the food to his
mouth!

25 Whip a person who makes fun of
wisdom, and then foolish people
will learn how to think.
Just correct a smart man, and he
will gain knowledge.

26 A son who robs his father and sends
away his mother
brings shame and disgrace on
himself.

27 Don't stop listening to correction,
my child.
If you do, you will not obey what
you have already learned.

28 An evil witness makes fun of
fairness.
And wicked people love what
is evil.

29 People who make fun of wisdom will
be punished.
And the backs of foolish people
will be beaten.

20 Wine and beer make people
loud and uncontrolled.
It is not wise to get drunk on them.

2 A king's anger is like the roar of a
lion.
Making him angry may cost you
your life.

3 Foolish people are always getting
into quarrels.
But avoiding quarrels will bring
you honor.

☆ Proverbs 19:17

This chapter of Proverbs has wisdom that will help us in every area of our lives. Verse 17 tells us that when we are kind to those who are poor, it is like we are giving to God himself.

The Bible says it is a blessing to give to the poor. It teaches that one day Jesus will tell those who gave to the poor, "I was hungry, and you gave me food. I was thirsty, and you gave me something to drink" (Matthew 25:35). That means when you give to the poor it is just like giving to the Lord himself. And the Bible says that God will reward you. When you see someone who is poor, and you help them, remember it is like giving to God.

. . . .

If you see someone in need, ask God how you can help them.

---

⁴ A lazy farmer doesn't plow when he should.
　　So at harvest time he has no crop.

⁵ Understanding a person's thoughts is as hard as getting water from a deep well.
　　But someone with understanding can find the wisdom there.

⁶ Many people claim to be loyal.
　　But it is hard to find someone who really can be trusted.

⁷ The good person who lives an honest life
　　is a blessing to his children.

⁸ A king sits on his throne and judges people.
　　He knows evil when he sees it.

⁹ No one can say, "I am innocent.
　　I have never done anything wrong."

¹⁰ The Lord hates both these things:
　　dishonest weights and dishonest measures.

¹¹ Even a child is known by his behavior.
　　His actions show if he is innocent and good.

¹² The Lord has made both these things:

Ears that can hear and eyes that
can see.

13 If you love to sleep, you will be poor.
If you stay awake, you will have
plenty of food.

14 The buyer says, "This is bad. It's no
good."
Then he goes away and brags about
what he bought.

15 There is plenty of gold, and there are
many rubies.
But there are only a few people who
speak with knowledge.

16 Take the coat of someone who
promises to pay what a stranger
owes.
Keep it until he pays the stranger's
bills.

17 When a person gets food dishonestly,
it may taste sweet at first.
But later he will feel as if he has a
mouth full of gravel.

18 Get advice if you want your plans to
work.
If you go to war, get the advice of
others.

19 Gossips can't keep secrets.
So avoid people who talk too
much.

20 Whoever curses his father or mother
will die like a light going out in
darkness.

21 Wealth that is gotten quickly in the
beginning
will do you no good in the end.

22 Don't say, "I'll pay you back for the
evil you did."
Wait for the Lord. He will make
things right.

23 The Lord hates dishonest weights.

And dishonest scales do not please
him.

24 The Lord decides what a person does.
So no one can understand what his
life is all about.

25 It's dangerous to promise something
to God too quickly.
After you've thought about it, it
may be too late.

26 A wise king finds out who the evil
people are.
Then he punishes them.

27 The Lord looks into a person's
feelings.
He searches through a person's
thoughts.

28 Loyalty and truth keep a king in
power.
He continues to rule if he is loyal.

29 Young men are admired for their
strength.
Old men are honored for their
experience.

30 Hard punishment will get rid of evil.
Whippings can change the evil
person's heart.

21 The Lord can control a king's
mind as easily as he controls a
river.
He can direct it as he pleases.

2 A person may believe he is doing right.
But the Lord judges his reasons.

3 Do what is right and fair.
That is more important to the Lord
than animal sacrifices.

4 Proud looks, proud thoughts
and evil actions are sin.

5 Those who plan and work hard earn
a profit.

But those who act too quickly
become poor.

6 Wealth that comes from telling lies
vanishes like a mist and leads to
death.

7 The violence of the wicked will
destroy them
because they refuse to do what is
right.

8 Guilty people live dishonest lives.
But honest people do what is right.

9 It is better to live in a corner on the
roof[n]
than inside the house with a
quarreling wife.

10 An evil person only wants to harm
others.
His neighbor will get no mercy
from him.

11 Punish a person who makes fun of
wisdom, and he will become wise.
But just teach a wise person, and he
will get knowledge.

12 God, who is always right, sees the
house of the wicked.
And he brings about the ruin of
every evil person.

13 If you ignore the poor when they cry
for help,
you also will cry for help and not
be answered.

14 A gift given secretly will calm an
angry man.
A present given in secrecy will
calm even great anger.

15 When things are done fairly, good
people are happy,
but evil people are frightened.

16 A person who does not use
understanding
will join the dead.

17 Whoever loves pleasure will become
poor.
Whoever loves wine and rich food
will never be wealthy.

18 Wicked people will suffer instead of
good people.
And those who cannot be trusted
will suffer instead of those who
can.

19 It is better to live alone in the desert
than with a quarreling and
complaining wife.

20 Wise people store up the best foods
and olive oil.
But a foolish person eats up
everything he has.

21 A person who tries to live right and
be loyal
finds life, success and honor.

22 A wise person can defeat a city full of
strong men.
He can tear down the defenses
they trust.

23 A person who is careful about what
he says
keeps himself out of trouble.

24 People who act with stubborn
pride
are called "proud" and "bragger."

25 The lazy person's desire for sleep will
kill him
because he refuses to work.
26 All day long the lazy person wishes
for more.
But the good person gives without
holding back.

21:9 roof In Bible times houses were built with flat roofs. The roof was used for drying things such as flax and
fruit. And it was used as an extra room, as a place for worship and as a place to sleep in the summer.

²⁷ The Lord hates sacrifices made by
   evil people,
   particularly when they make them
   for the wrong reasons.

²⁸ The words of a lying witness will die.
   But the words of an obedient man
   will always be remembered.

²⁹ A wicked person is stubborn.
   But an honest person thinks
   carefully about what he does.

³⁰ There is no wisdom, understanding
   or advice
   that can succeed against the Lord.

³¹ You can get the horses ready for
   battle.
   But it is the Lord who gives the
   victory.

22 Being respected is more
   important than having great
   riches.
   To be well thought of is better than
   owning silver or gold.

² The rich and the poor are alike
   in that the Lord made them all.

³ When a wise person sees danger
   ahead, he avoids it.
   But a foolish person keeps going
   and gets into trouble.

⁴ Respecting the Lord and not being
   proud
   will bring you wealth, honor and
   life.

⁵ The lives of evil people are like paths
   covered with thorns and traps.
   People who protect themselves
   don't have such problems.

⁶ Train a child how to live the right way.
   Then even when he is old, he will
   still live that way.

⁷ The rich rule over the poor.

And borrowers become servants to
   those who lend.

⁸ A person who does evil things will
   receive trouble in return.
   Then he won't be cruel to others
   any longer.

⁹ A generous person will be blessed
   because he shares his food with the
   poor.

¹⁰ Get rid of the person who makes fun
   of wisdom.
   Then fighting, quarrels and insults
   will stop.

¹¹ A person who loves innocent
   thoughts and kind words
   will have even the king as a friend.

¹² The Lord protects knowledge from
   being lost.
   But he destroys false words.

¹³ The lazy person says, "There's a lion
   outside!
   I might get killed out in the street!"

¹⁴ The words of an unfaithful wife are
   like a deep trap.
   Those who make the Lord angry
   will get caught by them.

¹⁵ Every child is full of foolishness.
   But punishment can get rid of it.

¹⁶ The one who gets rich by being cruel
   to the poor will become poor.
   And so will the one who gives
   presents to the wealthy.

OTHER WISE SAYINGS

¹⁷ Pay attention and listen to what wise
   people say.
   Remember what I am teaching
   you.
¹⁸ It will be good to keep these things in
   mind.
   Be prepared to repeat them.
¹⁹ I am teaching them to you now

so that you will put your trust in the Lord.

²⁰ I have written down 30 sayings for you.
They give knowledge and good advice.

²¹ I am teaching you true and reliable words.
Then you can give true answers to anyone who asks.

²² Do not abuse poor people because they are poor.
And do not take away the rights of the needy in court.

²³ The Lord will defend them in court.
And he will take the life of those who take away their rights.

²⁴ Don't make friends with someone who easily gets angry.
Don't spend time with someone who has a bad temper.

²⁵ If you do, you may learn to be like him.
Then you will be in real danger.

²⁶ Don't promise to pay what someone else owes.
And don't give guarantees that you will pay what he owes.

²⁷ If you cannot pay what he owes, your own bed will be taken and sold.

²⁸ Don't move an old stone that shows where a person's land is.
These stones were set up by your ancestors.

²⁹ Do you see a man skilled in his work?
That man will work for kings.
He won't have to work for ordinary people.

23 If you sit down to eat with a ruler,
notice the food that is in front of you.

² Control yourself
if you have a big appetite.

³ Don't be greedy for his fine foods.
He might use that rich food to trick you.

⁴ Don't wear yourself out trying to get rich.
Be wise enough to control yourself.

⁵ Wealth can vanish in the wink of an eye.
It seems to grow wings
and fly away like an eagle in the sky.

⁶ Don't eat the food of a selfish person.
Don't be greedy for his fine foods.

⁷ A selfish person is always worrying about how much the food costs.
He tells you, "Eat and drink."
But he doesn't really mean it.

⁸ So you will feel like throwing up the little bit you have eaten.
And you will have wasted your kind words.

⁹ Don't speak to a foolish person.
He will only ignore your wise words.

¹⁰ Don't move an old stone that shows where somebody's land is.
And don't take fields that belong to orphans.

¹¹ God, their defender, is strong.

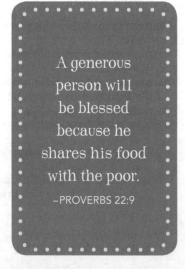

A generous person will be blessed because he shares his food with the poor.

–PROVERBS 22:9

He will take their side against you.

12 Remember what you are taught.
And listen carefully to words of
knowledge.

13 Don't fail to punish a child.
If you spank him, you will keep
him from dying.
14 If you punish him with a spanking,
you will save him from a fool's
death.

15 My child, if you are wise,
then I will be happy.
16 I will be so pleased
if you speak what is right.

17 Don't envy sinners.
But always respect the Lord.
18 If you do, you will have hope for the
future.
Your wishes will come true.

19 Listen, my child, and be wise.
Keep your mind on what is right.
20 Don't be one of those who drink too
much wine
or who eat too much food.
21 Those who drink too much and eat
too much become poor.
They sleep too much and end up
wearing rags.

22 Listen to your father, who gave you
life.
And do not forget your mother
when she is old.
23 Learn the truth and never reject it.
Get wisdom, self-control and
understanding.
24 The father of a good child is very
happy.
The person who has a wise son is
glad because of him.
25 Make your father and mother happy.
Give your mother a reason to be
glad.

26 My son, pay attention to me.
And watch closely what I do.

27 A prostitute is as dangerous as a deep
pit.
And an unfaithful wife is like a
narrow well.
28 They ambush you like robbers.
And they cause many men to be
unfaithful to their wives.

29-30 Some people drink too much wine.
They try out all the different kinds
of drinks.
So they have trouble. They are sad.
They fight. They complain.
They have unnecessary bruises.
They have bloodshot eyes.
31 Don't stare at the wine's pretty, red
color.
It may sparkle in the cup.
It may go down your throat
smoothly.
32 But later it bites like a snake.
Like a snake, it poisons you.
33 Your eyes will see strange sights.
And your mind will be confused.
34 You will feel dizzy, as if you're out on
the stormy ocean.
You will feel as if you're on top of a
ship's sails.
35 You will think, "They hit me, but I'm
not hurt!
They have beaten me up, but I don't
remember it.
I wish I could wake up.
Then I would get another drink."

24 Don't envy evil people.
Don't try to be friends with
them.
2 In their minds they plan cruel things.
And they always talk about making
trouble.

3 It takes wisdom to have a good family.
It takes understanding to make it
strong.
4 It takes knowledge to fill a home
with rare and beautiful treasures.

5 A wise man has great power.
And a man who has knowledge is
very strong.

⁶ So you need the advice of others
   when you go to war.
   If you have many people to give
   advice, you will win.

⁷ A foolish person cannot understand
   wisdom.
   He has nothing to say in court.

⁸ Whoever makes evil plans
   will be known as a troublemaker.
⁹ Making foolish plans is sinful.
   And making fun of others is
   hateful.

¹⁰ If you give up when trouble comes,
   it shows that you have very little
   strength.

¹¹ Save those who are being led to their
   death.
   Rescue those who are about to be
   killed.
¹² You may say, "We don't know
   anything about this."
   But God knows what is in your
   mind, and he will notice.
   He is watching you, and he will know.
   He will pay each person back for
   what he has done.

¹³ My child, eat honey because it is good.
   Honey from the honeycomb tastes
   sweet.
¹⁴ In the same way, wisdom is pleasing
   to you.
   If you find it, you have hope for the
   future.
   Your wishes will come true.

¹⁵ Don't be like the wicked and attack a
   good man's house.
   Don't rob the place where he lives.
¹⁶ A good man may be bothered by
   trouble seven times, but he does
   not give up.
   But the wicked are overwhelmed
   by trouble.

¹⁷ Don't be happy when your enemy is
   defeated.
   Don't be glad when he is
   overwhelmed.
¹⁸ The Lord will notice and be
   displeased.
   Then the Lord may not be angry
   with him anymore.

¹⁹ Don't envy evil people.
   And don't be jealous of the wicked.
²⁰ An evil person has nothing to hope
   for.
   The wicked will die like a flame
   that is put out.

²¹ My child, respect the Lord and the
   king.
   Don't join those people who refuse
   to obey them.
²² The Lord and the king will quickly
   destroy such people.
   Those two can cause great trouble!

MORE WORDS OF WISDOM

²³ These are also wise sayings:

   It is not good to take sides when you
   are the judge.
²⁴ Don't say that the wicked have done
   right.
   People will curse you, and nations
   will hate you.
²⁵ But things will go well for judges who
   punish the guilty.
   And they will receive good things
   from God.

²⁶ An honest answer is as pleasing
   as a kiss on the lips.

²⁷ First, you should work outside
   and prepare your fields.
   After that, you can start having your
   family.

²⁸ Don't testify against your neighbor
   for no good reason.
   Don't say things that are false.
²⁹ Don't say, "I'll get even with that man.
   I'll do to him what he did to me."

³⁰ I passed by a lazy person's field.

I went by the vineyard of a man
who had no sense.
³¹ Thorns had grown up everywhere.
The ground was covered with
weeds.
And the stone walls had fallen
down.
³² I thought about what I had seen.
I learned this lesson from what I
saw.
³³ You sleep a little; you take a nap.
You fold your hands and rest.
³⁴ Soon you will be poor, as if you had
been robbed.
You will have as little as if you had
been held up.

MORE WISE SAYINGS OF SOLOMON

25 These are more wise sayings of
Solomon. They were copied by
the men of Hezekiah king of Judah.

² God is honored for what he keeps
secret.
Kings are honored for what they
can discover.

³ No one can measure the height of the
skies or the depth of the earth.
So also no one can understand the
mind of a king.

⁴ Remove the scum from the silver.
Then the silver can be used by the
silversmith.
⁵ Remove wicked people from the
king's presence.
Then his government will be
honest and last a long time.

⁶ Don't brag to the king.
Don't act as if you are a great man.
⁷ It is better for him to promote you to
a higher job
than to give you a less important
position.

Because of something you have seen,
⁸   do not quickly take someone to
court.

What will you do later
when your neighbor proves you are
wrong?

⁹ If you have an argument with your
neighbor,
don't tell other people what was
said.
¹⁰ Whoever hears it might say bad
things about you.
And you might not ever be
respected again.

¹¹ The right word spoken at the right
time
is as beautiful as gold apples in a
silver bowl.

¹² The warning of a wise person is
valuable to someone who will
listen.
It is worth as much as gold earrings
or fine gold jewelry.

¹³ A trustworthy messenger refreshes
those who send him.
He is like the coolness of snow in
the summertime.

¹⁴ People who brag about gifts they
never give
are like clouds and wind that give
no rain.

¹⁵ With patience you can convince a
ruler.
And a gentle word can get through
to the hard-headed.

¹⁶ If you find honey, don't eat too
much.
Too much of it will make you
sick.
¹⁷ Don't go to your neighbor's house
too often.
Too much of you will make him
hate you.

¹⁸ Anyone who lies about his neighbor
hurts him as a club, a sword or a
sharp arrow would.

¹⁹ Don't trust unfaithful people when
   you are in trouble.
   It's like eating with a broken
   tooth or walking with a
   crippled foot.

²⁰ Don't sing songs to someone who is
   sad.
   It's like taking off a coat on a cold
   day
   or pouring vinegar on soda.

²¹ If your enemy is hungry, feed him.

   If he is thirsty, give him a drink.
²² Doing this will be like pouring
   burning coals on his head.
   And the Lord will reward you.

²³ The north wind brings rain.
   In the same way, telling gossip
   brings angry looks.

²⁴ It is better to live in a corner on the
   roof[n]
   than inside the house with a
   quarreling wife.

25:24 roof In Bible times houses were built with flat roofs. The roof was used for drying things such as flax and
fruit. And it was used as an extra room, as a place for worship and as a place to sleep in the summer.

☆ Proverbs 25:18

The Bible says a lie is like a sword, a club, or an arrow. It can hurt people
inside like a weapon can hurt them on the outside.

There was once a little boy who had a neighbor named Cooper.
They were best friends. Cooper had a really cool tree
house. And the two friends loved to climb up the
ladder and slide down the slide. One day, the little
boy got impatient and shoved Cooper down the
slide. When Cooper got hurt, the boy realized
it was his own fault. This made him very sad.
It's not fun to hurt a friend. The Bible teaches
us that when we tell lies, we hurt people
we love. It's not a physical hurt like falling
down a slide. But it hurts them inside.

Sometimes telling the truth can be hard,
   but it is always the right thing to do.

²⁵ Hearing good news from a faraway
place
is like having a cool drink when
you are tired.

²⁶ A good person who gives in to evil
is like a muddy spring or a dirty well.

²⁷ It is not good to eat too much honey.
In the same way, it is not good to
brag about yourself.

²⁸ A person who does not control
himself
is like a city whose walls have been
broken down.

26 It shouldn't snow in summer or
rain at harvest.
Neither should a foolish person
ever be honored.

² Curses will not harm someone who is
innocent.
They are like sparrows or
swallows that fly around and
never land.

³ A whip is used to guide a horse, and a
harness is used for a donkey.
In the same way, a paddle is used
on a foolish person to guide him.

⁴ Don't give a foolish person a foolish
answer.
If you do, you will be just like him.

⁵ But answer a foolish person as he
should be answered.
If you don't, he will think he is
really wise.

⁶ Don't send a message by a foolish
person.
That would be like cutting off your
feet or drinking poison.

⁷ A wise saying spoken by a fool does
no good.
It is like the legs of a crippled
person.

⁸ Giving honor to a foolish person does
no good.
It is like tying a stone in a slingshot.

⁹ A wise saying spoken by a fool
is like a thorn stuck in the hand of
a drunk.

¹⁰ Someone might employ a foolish
person or anyone just passing by.
That employer is like an archer
who shoots at anything he sees.

¹¹ A dog eats what it throws up.
And a foolish person repeats his
foolishness.

¹² Some people think they are wise.
There is more hope for a foolish
person than for them.

¹³ The lazy person says, "There's a lion
in the road.
There's a lion in the streets!"

¹⁴ The lazy person is like a door that
turns back and forth on its hinges.
He stays in bed and turns over and
over.

¹⁵ The lazy person may put his hand in
the dish.
But he's too tired to lift the food to
his mouth.

¹⁶ The lazy person thinks he is wiser
than seven people who give
sensible answers.

¹⁷ To grab a dog by the ears is asking for
trouble.
So is interfering in someone else's
quarrel if you're just passing by.

¹⁸⁻¹⁹ A person shouldn't trick his
neighbor
and then say, "I was just joking!"
That is like a madman shooting
deadly, burning arrows.

²⁰ Without wood, a fire will go out.

And without gossip, quarreling will
stop.

21 Charcoal and wood keep a fire going.
In the same way, a quarrelsome
person keeps an argument
going.

22 The words of a gossip are like tasty
bits of food.
People take them all in.

23 Kind words from a wicked mind
are like a shiny coating on a clay
pot.

24 A person who hates you may fool you
with his words.
But in his mind he is planning evil.
25 His words are kind, but don't believe
him.
His mind is full of evil thoughts.
26 He hides his hate with lies.
But his evil will be plain to everyone.

27 Whoever digs a deep trap for others
will fall into it himself.
Whoever tries to roll a boulder over
others will be crushed by it.

28 A liar hates the people he hurts.
And false praise can ruin others.

27 Don't brag about what will
happen tomorrow.
You don't really know what will
happen then.

2 Don't praise yourself. Let someone
else do it.
Let the praise come from a stranger
and not from your own mouth.

3 Stone is heavy, and sand is hard to
carry.
But the complaining of a foolish
person causes more trouble than
either.

4 Anger is cruel. It destroys like a flood.
But who can put up with jealousy!

5 It is better to correct someone openly
than to love him and not show it.

6 The slap of a friend can be trusted to
help you.
But the kisses of an enemy are
nothing but lies.

7 When someone is full, not even
honey tastes good.
But when he is hungry, even
something bitter tastes sweet.

8 A man who leaves his home
is like a bird that leaves its nest.

9 Perfume and oils make you happy.
And good advice from a friend is
sweet.

10 Don't forget your friend or your
father's friend.
Don't always go to your brother for
help when trouble comes.
A neighbor close by is better than a
brother far away.

11 Be wise, my child, and you will make
me happy.
Then I can respond to any insult.

12 When a wise person sees danger
ahead, he avoids it.
But a foolish person keeps going
and gets into trouble.

13 Take the coat of someone who
promises to pay what a stranger
owes.
Keep it until he pays the stranger's
bills.

14 Don't greet your neighbor loudly
early in the morning.
He will think of it as a curse.

15 A quarreling wife is as bothersome
as a continual dripping on a rainy
day.
16 Stopping her is like stopping the
wind.

It's like trying to grab oil in your hand.

¹⁷ Iron can sharpen iron.
In the same way, people can help each other.

¹⁸ The person who tends a fig tree will eat its fruit.
And the person who takes care of his master will be honored.

¹⁹ As water shows you your face,
so your mind shows you what kind of person you are.

²⁰ People will never stop dying and being destroyed.
In the same way, people will never stop wanting more than they have.

²¹ A hot furnace tests silver and gold.
And people are tested by the praise they receive.

²² Even if you ground up a foolish person like grain in a bowl,
you couldn't remove his foolishness.

²³ Be sure you know how your sheep are doing.
Pay close attention to the condition of your cattle.
²⁴ Riches will not continue forever.
Nor do governments continue forever.
²⁵ Bring in the hay. Let the new grass appear.
Gather the grass from the hills.
²⁶ Make clothes from the lambs' wool.
Sell some goats to buy a field.
²⁷ There will be plenty of goat milk to feed you and your family.
It will make your servant girls healthy.

28 Evil people run even though no one is chasing them.
But good people are as brave as a lion.

² When a country is disobedient, it has one ruler after another.
But when it is led by a man with understanding and knowledge, it continues strong.

³ Rulers who are cruel to the poor
are like a hard rain that destroys the crops.

⁴ People who disobey what they have been taught praise the wicked.
But those who obey what they have been taught are against the wicked.

⁵ Evil people do not understand fairness.
But those who follow the Lord understand it completely.

⁶ It is better to be poor and innocent
than to be rich and wicked.

⁷ The son who obeys what he has been taught
shows he is wise.
But the son who makes friends with those who have no self-control disgraces his father.

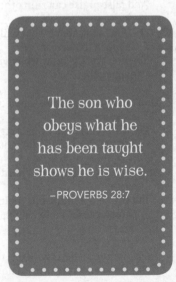

The son who obeys what he has been taught shows he is wise.

–PROVERBS 28:7

⁸ Some people get rich by overcharging
others.
But their wealth will be given to
those who are kind to the poor.

⁹ If you refuse to obey what you have
been taught,
your prayers will not be heard.

¹⁰ Those who lead honest people to do
wrong
will be ruined by their own evil.
But the innocent will be rewarded
with good things.

¹¹ A rich man may think he is wise.
But a poor man who has
understanding knows the rich
man is wrong.

¹² When good people win, there is great
happiness.
But when the wicked get power,
everybody hides.

¹³ If you hide your sins, you will not
succeed.
If you confess and reject them, you
will receive mercy.

¹⁴ Those who always respect the Lord
will be happy.
But those who are stubborn will get
into trouble.

¹⁵ A wicked ruler is as dangerous to
poor people
as a roaring lion or a charging bear.

¹⁶ A ruler who is cruel does not have
wisdom.
But the one who hates money taken
dishonestly will live a long time.

¹⁷ A man who is guilty of murder
will run until he dies.
So do not stop him.

¹⁸ Innocent people will be kept safe.
But those who are dishonest will
suddenly be ruined.

¹⁹ The person who works his land will
have plenty of food.
But the one who chases useless
dreams instead will end up very
poor.

²⁰ A truthful man will have many
blessings.
But those eager to get rich will be
punished.

²¹ It is not good for a judge to take
sides.
But some will sin for just a piece of
bread.

²² A selfish person is in a hurry to get
rich.
He does not realize his selfishness
will make him poor.

²³ Those who correct others will later
be liked
more than those who give false
praise.

²⁴ Some people rob their fathers or
mothers
and say, "It's not wrong."
Such people are just like those who
destroy things.

²⁵ A greedy person causes trouble.
But the one who trusts the Lord
will succeed.

²⁶ The person who trusts in himself is
foolish.
But the person who lives wisely
will be kept safe.

²⁷ The person who gives to the poor will
have everything he needs.
But the one who ignores the poor
will have many curses put on
him.

²⁸ When the wicked get power,
everybody hides.
But when the wicked die, the good
people do well.

29 Some people are still stubborn after they have been corrected many times.
But they will suddenly be hurt beyond cure.

2 When good people do well, everyone is happy.
But when evil people rule, everyone groans.

3 Whoever loves wisdom makes his father happy.
But the one who makes friends with prostitutes wastes his money.

4 If a king is fair, he makes his country strong.
But if he takes money dishonestly, he tears his country down.

5 Anyone who gives false praise to his neighbor
is setting a trap for him.

6 An evil person is trapped by his own sin.
But a good person can sing and be happy.

7 Good people are concerned that the poor are treated fairly.
But the wicked don't care.

8 People who make fun of others cause trouble in a city.
But wise people calm anger down.

9 A wise man should not take a foolish person to court.
The fool will only shout or laugh at him. There will be no peace.

10 Murderers hate honest people.
But those who do right try to protect them.

11 A foolish person loses his temper.
But a wise person controls his anger.

12 If a ruler pays attention to lies, then all his officers will become wicked.

13 The poor person and the cruel person are alike in this way:
The Lord gave eyes to both of them.

14 A king should judge poor people fairly.
Then his government will continue forever.

15 Punishment and correction make a child wise.
If he is left to do as he pleases, he will disgrace his mother.

16 When there are many wicked people, there is much sin.
But those who do right will see them destroyed.

17 Correct your child, and you will be proud of him.
He will give you pleasure.

18 Where there is no word from God, people are uncontrolled.
But those who obey what they have been taught are happy.

19 Words alone cannot correct a servant.
Even if he understands, he won't respond.

20 Sometimes you see people who speak too quickly.
There is more hope for a foolish person than for them.

21 Don't spoil your servant when he is young.
If you do, he will bring you grief later on.

22 An angry person causes trouble.
A person who easily gets angry sins a lot.

23 A man's pride will ruin him.
But a person who is humble will be honored.

²⁴ The partner of a thief is his own worst enemy.
> He has to testify in court, but he is afraid to say anything.

²⁵ Being afraid of people can get you into trouble.
> But if you trust the Lord, you will be safe.

²⁶ Many people want to be heard by a ruler.
> But fairness comes from the Lord.

²⁷ Good people hate those who are dishonest.
> And the wicked hate those who are honest.

WISE WORDS FROM AGUR

30 These are the words of Agur son of Jakeh.
This is his message to Ithiel and Ucal:

² "I am the most stupid person there is.
> I have no understanding.
³ I have not learned to be wise.
> And I don't know much about God, the Holy One.
⁴ Who has gone up to heaven and come back down?
> Who can hold the wind in his hand?
Who can gather up the waters in his coat?
> Who has decided where the ends of the earth will be?
What is his name? And what is his son's name?
> Surely, you know!

⁵ "Every word of God can be trusted.
> He protects those who come to him for safety.
⁶ Do not add to his words.
> If you do, he will correct you and prove that you are a liar.

⁷ "I ask two things from you, Lord.
> Don't refuse me before I die.
⁸ Keep me from lying and being dishonest.
And don't make me either rich or poor.
> Just give me enough food for each day.
⁹ If I have too much, I might reject you.
> I might say, 'I don't know the Lord.'
If I am poor, I might steal.
> Then I would disgrace the name of my God.

¹⁰ "Do not say bad things about a servant to his master.
> If you do, he will curse you, and you will suffer for it.

¹¹ "Some people curse their fathers.
> And they do not bless their mothers.
¹² Some people think they are pure.
> But they are not really free from evil.
¹³ Some people have such a proud look!
> They look down on others.
¹⁴ Some people have teeth like swords.
> It is as if their jaws are full of knives.
They want to remove the poor people from the earth.
> They want to get rid of the needy.

¹⁵ "Greed has two daughters.
> Their names are 'Give me. Give me.'
There are three things that are never satisfied.
> There are really four that never say, 'I've had enough!'
¹⁶ These things are the cemetery, the childless mother,
> the land that never gets enough rain,
> and fire that never says, 'I've had enough!'

¹⁷ "Don't make fun of your father.
> Don't refuse to obey your mother.
If you do, your eye will be pecked out by the birds of the valley.
> You will be eaten by hawks.

¹⁸ "There are three things that are too hard for me.

There are really four that I don't
understand:
19 the way an eagle flies in the sky,
the way a snake slides over a rock,
the way a ship sails on the sea
and the way a man acts with a girl.

20 "This is the way a woman who takes
part in adultery acts:
She sins and doesn't care.
She says, 'I haven't done anything
wrong.'

21 "There are three things that make
the earth tremble.
There are really four that it cannot
stand:
22 a servant who becomes a king,
a foolish person who has plenty to
eat,
23 a hateful woman who gets married
and a maid who replaces her
mistress.

24 "There are four things on earth that
are small.
But they are very wise:
25 Ants are not very strong.
But they store up food in the
summer.
26 Rock badgers are not powerful
animals.
But they can live among the rocks.
27 Locusts have no king.
But they all go out in formation.
28 And lizards can be caught in the
hand.
But they are found even in kings'
palaces.

29 "There are three things that strut
proudly.
There are really four that walk as if
they are important:
30 Lions are the proudest animals.
They are strong and run from
nothing.
31 Roosters and male goats strut
proudly.
And so does a king when his army
is around him.

32 "You may have been foolish and
proud.
If you planned evil, cover your
mouth.
33 Stirring milk makes butter.
Twisting noses makes them bleed.
And stirring up anger makes
trouble."

WISE WORDS OF KING LEMUEL

31 These are the words of King
Lemuel. This is the message his
mother taught him:

2 "My son, I gave birth to you.
You are the son I prayed for.
3 Don't waste your strength on women.
Don't waste your time on those
who ruin kings.

4 "Kings should not drink wine,
Lemuel.
Rulers should not desire beer.
5 If they drink, they might forget the
law.
They might keep the needy from
getting their rights.
6 Give beer to people who are dying.
And give wine to those who are sad.
7 Let them drink and forget their need.
Then they won't remember their
misery anymore.

8 "Speak up for those who cannot
speak for themselves.
Defend the rights of all those who
have nothing.
9 Speak up and judge fairly.
Defend the rights of the poor and
needy."

THE GOOD WIFE

10 It is hard to find an excellent wife.
She is worth more than rubies.
11 Her husband trusts her completely.
With her, he has everything he
needs.
12 She does him good and not harm
for as long as she lives.
13 She looks for wool and linen.
She likes to work with her hands.

¹⁴ She is like a trader's ship.
    She goes far to get food.
¹⁵ She gets up while it is still dark.
    She prepares food for her family.
    She also feeds her servant girls.
¹⁶ She looks at a field and buys it.
    With money she has earned, she
    plants a vineyard.
¹⁷ She does her work with energy.
    Her arms are strong.
¹⁸ She makes sure that what she makes
    is good.
    She works by her lamp late into the
    night.
¹⁹ She makes thread with her hands
    and weaves her own cloth.
²⁰ She welcomes the poor.
    She helps the needy.
²¹ She does not worry about her family
    when it snows.
    They all have fine clothes to keep
    them warm.
²² She makes coverings for her bed.
    Her clothes are made of linen and
    other expensive material.
²³ Her husband is recognized at the city
    meetings.

He makes decisions as one of the
    leaders of the land.
²⁴ She makes linen clothes and sells
    them.
    She provides belts to the
    merchants.
²⁵ She is strong and is respected by the
    people.
    She looks forward to the future
    with joy.
²⁶ She speaks wise words.
    And she teaches others to be kind.
²⁷ She watches over her family.
    And she is always busy.
²⁸ Her children bless her.
    Her husband also praises her.
²⁹ He says, "There are many excellent
    wives,
    but you are better than all of
    them."
³⁰ Charm can fool you, and beauty can
    trick you.
    But a woman who respects the
    Lord should be praised.
³¹ Give her the reward she has earned.
    She should be openly praised for
    what she has done.

ISRAEL DIVIDED

When King David's grandson (Rehoboam) followed the bad advice of his young friends, over half the people of Israel left him and found a new king. The big nation of Israel was now split in two: Israel and Judah. A new king ruled Israel. But King David's family ruled the new nation of Judah.

For many years, Israel and Judah lived side by side. Sometimes they fought like they were enemies, and sometimes they were friends. Both nations had good kings and bad kings. And sometimes the bad kings were very, very bad. Both Israel and Judah forgot how to follow God. They did bad things and acted like God did not exist.

God was sad to see his family ignore him. But he was even more sad to see them get hurt. You see, there were some evil people who lived around Israel and Judah. They hurt God's people many times. Every time the people of Israel or Judah asked God for help, he helped them. But once the people were safe, they ignored God again.

Finally, a larger nation captured both Israel and Judah and made the people move far away. The land that God had promised to Abraham and his descendants was stolen by people who did not know God.

But God never forgot his promise to Abraham—Abraham's family would be a big nation. And he never forgot the promise he made to King David that one of David's descendants would always be a king. So even after the people of Israel and Judah were forced to move to another country, some people moved back to the Promised Land. God was getting the land ready for a son of Abraham who was also a son of David—who would become the Son of God.

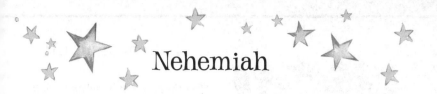

Nehemiah

NEHEMIAH'S PRAYER

1 These are the words of Nehemiah son of Hacaliah.

I, Nehemiah, was in the capital city of Susa. It was in the month of Kislev. This was in the twentieth year.[n] ²One of my brothers named Hanani came from Judah. Some other men were with him. I asked them about the Jews who lived through the captivity. And I also asked about Jerusalem.

³They answered, "Nehemiah, those who are left from the captivity are back in the area of Judah. But they are in much trouble and are full of shame. The wall around Jerusalem is broken down. And its gates have been burned."

⁴When I heard these things, I sat down and cried for several days. I was sad and did not eat food. I prayed to the God of heaven. ⁵I said, "Lord, God of heaven, you are the great God who is to be respected. You keep your agreement of love with those who love you and obey your commands. ⁶Listen carefully. Look at me. Hear the prayer your servant is praying to you day and night. I am praying for your servants, the people of Israel. I confess the sins we Israelites have done against you. My father's family and I have sinned against you. ⁷We have been wicked toward you. We have not obeyed the commands, rules and laws you gave your servant Moses.

⁸"Remember what you taught your servant Moses. You said, 'If you are unfaithful, I will scatter you among the nations. ⁹But if you come back to me and obey my commands, I will gather your people. I will gather them from the far ends of the earth. And I will bring them from captivity to where I have chosen to be worshiped.'

¹⁰"They are your servants and your people. You have saved them with your great strength and power. ¹¹Lord, listen carefully to my prayer. I am your servant. And listen to the prayers of your servants who love to honor you. Give me, your servant, success today. Allow this king to show kindness to me."

I was the one who served wine to the king.

NEHEMIAH IS SENT TO JERUSALEM

2 It was the month of Nisan. It was in the twentieth year King Artaxerxes was king. He wanted some wine. So I took some and gave it to the king. I had not been sad in his presence before. ²So the king said, "Why does your face look sad? You are not sick. Your heart must be sad."

Then I was very afraid. ³I said to the king, "May the king live forever! My face is sad because the city where my ancestors are buried lies in ruins. And its gates have been destroyed by fire."

⁴Then the king said to me, "What do you want?"

First I prayed to the God of heaven. ⁵Then I answered the king, "Send me to the city in Judah where my ancestors are buried. I will rebuild it. Do this if you are willing and if I have pleased you."

⁶The queen was sitting next to the king. He asked me, "How long will your trip take? When will you get back?" It pleased the king to send me. So I set a time.

⁷I also said to him, "If you are willing, give me letters for the governors west of the Euphrates River. Tell them to let me pass safely through their lands on my way to Judah. ⁸And may I have a letter for Asaph? He is the keeper of the king's forest. Tell him to give me timber. I will need it to make boards for the gates

---

1:1 **twentieth year** This is probably referring to the twentieth year King Artaxerxes I ruled Persia.

✭ Nehemiah 1:11

After the people of Israel and Judah left their land, they became known as Jews (from the name Judah). Nehemiah was a Jew who lived in Persia and served its king. He heard that Jerusalem was in trouble, and the walls around the city were broken down. This left the Jews living there unprotected during a very dangerous time. This made Nehemiah sad. He decided to ask the king if he could go back to Jerusalem to rebuild the wall. But first, he talked to God.

Nehemiah's brother gave him some bad news about their hometown. Nehemiah was so sad that he sat down and cried. You know, sometimes sad things happen in life. But notice what Nehemiah did. He prayed to God. No matter what happens to you, God wants you to know you can talk to him—about anything. He will listen. You may not be able to talk to the president, a famous athlete, or a movie star. But you can talk to the most important person in the universe: God!

• •

The next time you're sad and you need help, talk to God. He will listen!

of the palace. It is by the Temple. The wood is also for the city wall and the house I will live in." So the king gave me the letters. This was because God was showing kindness to me. ⁹So I went to the governors west of the Euphrates River. I gave them the king's letters. The king had also sent army officers and soldiers on horses with me.

¹⁰Sanballat the Horonite and Tobiah the Ammonite leader heard about this. They were upset that someone had come to help the Israelites.

NEHEMIAH INSPECTS JERUSALEM

¹¹I went to Jerusalem and stayed there three days. ¹²Then at night I started out with a few men. I had not told anyone what God had caused me to do for Jerusalem. There were no animals with me except the one I was riding.

¹³It was night. I went out through the Valley Gate. I rode toward the Dragon Well and the Trash Gate. I was inspecting the walls of Jerusalem. They had been broken down. And the gates had

been destroyed by fire. [14]Then I rode on toward the Fountain Gate and the King's Pool. But there was not enough room for the animal I was riding to get through. [15]So I went up the valley at night. I was inspecting the wall. Finally, I turned and went back in through the Valley Gate. [16]The officers did not know where I had gone or what I was doing. I had not yet said anything to the Jews, the priests, the important men or the officers. I had not said anything to any of the others who would do the work.

[17]Then I said to them, "You can see the trouble we have here. Jerusalem is a pile of ruins. And its gates have been burned. Come, let's rebuild the wall of Jerusalem. Then we won't be full of shame any longer." [18]I also told them how God had been kind to me. And I told them what the king had said to me.

Then they answered, "Let's start rebuilding." So they began to work hard.

[19]But Sanballat the Horonite, Tobiah the Ammonite leader and Geshem the Arab heard about it. They made fun of us and laughed at us. They said, "What are you doing? Are you turning against the king?"

[20]But I answered them, "The God of heaven will give us success. We are God's servants. We will start rebuilding. But you have no share in Jerusalem. You have no claim or past right to it."

BUILDERS OF THE WALL

3 Eliashib the high priest and his fellow priests went to work. They rebuilt the Sheep Gate. They gave it to the Lord's service and set its doors in place. They worked as far as the Tower of the Hundred, and they gave it to the Lord's service. Then they went on to the Tower of Hananel. [2]The men of Jericho built the part of the wall next to the priests. And Zaccur son of Imri built next to them.

[3]The sons of Hassenaah rebuilt the Fish Gate. They set the boards in place. And they put its doors, bolts and bars in place. [4]Meremoth son of Uriah made repairs next to them. (Uriah was the son of Hakkoz.) Meshullam son of Berekiah worked next to Meremoth. (Berekiah was the son of Meshezabel.) And Zadok son of Baana worked next to Meshullam. [5]The men from Tekoa made repairs next to them. But the leading men of Tekoa would not work under their supervisors.

[6]Joiada son of Paseah and Meshullam son of Besodeiah repaired the Old Gate. They set its boards in place. And they put its doors, bolts and bars in place. [7]Next to them, men from Gibeon and Mizpah made repairs. Melatiah was from Gibeon, and Jadon was from Meronoth. These places were ruled by the governor west of the Euphrates River. [8]Next to them, Uzziel son of Harhaiah made repairs. He was a goldsmith. And next to him, Hananiah made repairs. He was one of the people who made perfume. These men rebuilt Jerusalem as far as the Broad Wall. [9]The next part of the wall was repaired by Rephaiah son of Hur. He was ruler of half of the district of Jerusalem. [10]Next to him, Jedaiah son of Harumaph made repairs. He worked opposite his own house. And next to him, Hattush son of Hashabneiah made repairs. [11]Malkijah son of Harim and Hasshub son of Pahath-Moab repaired another part of the wall. And they repaired the Tower of the Ovens. [12]Next to them, Shallum son of Hallohesh made repairs. He was ruler of half of the district of Jerusalem. His daughters helped him.

[13]Hanun and the people of Zanoah repaired the Valley Gate. They rebuilt it and put its doors, bolts and bars in place. They also repaired the 500 yards of the wall to the Trash Gate.

[14]Malkijah son of Recab repaired the Trash Gate. He was ruler of the district of Beth Hakkerem. He rebuilt that gate and put its doors, bolts and bars in place.

[15]Shallun son of Col-Hozeh repaired the Fountain Gate. He was ruler of the

district of Mizpah. He rebuilt it and put a roof over it. And he put its doors, bolts and bars in place. He also repaired the wall of the Pool of Siloam. It is next to the King's Garden. He repaired the wall all the way to the steps. They went down from the older part of the city. [16]Next to Shallun, Nehemiah[n] son of Azbuk made repairs. He was ruler of half of the district of Beth Zur. He made repairs up to a place opposite the tombs of David. He made repairs as far as the man-made pool and the House of the Heroes.

[17]Next to him, the Levites made repairs. Some worked under Rehum son of Bani. Next to him, Hashabiah made repairs for his district. He was ruler of half of the district of Keilah. [18]Next to him, Binnui son of Henadad and his relatives made repairs. Binnui was the ruler of the other half of the district of Keilah. [19]Next to them, Ezer son of Jeshua worked. He was ruler of Mizpah. He repaired another part of the wall. He worked across from the way up to the storehouse for weapons. And he worked to the place where the wall turns. [20]Next to him, Baruch son of Zabbai worked very hard to repair another part of the wall. It went from the place where the wall turns to the entrance of the house of Eliashib. He was the high priest. [21]Next to him, Meremoth son of Uriah worked. (Uriah was the son of Hakkoz.) He repaired another part of the wall. It went from the entrance to Eliashib's house to the far end of it.

[22]Next to him worked the priests from the surrounding area. [23]Next to them, Benjamin and Hasshub made repairs in front of their own house.

Next to them, Azariah son of Maaseiah made repairs beside his own house. (Maaseiah was the son of Ananiah.) [24]Next to him, Binnui son of Henadad repaired another part of the wall. It went from Azariah's house to the place where the wall turned. And it went to the corner. [25]Palal son of Uzai worked across from the place where the wall turned. And he worked by the tower on the upper palace. That is near the courtyard of the king's guard. Next to Palal, Pedaiah son of Parosh made repairs. [26]The Temple servants lived on the hill of Ophel. They made repairs as far as a point opposite the Water Gate. They worked toward the east and the tower that extends from the palace. [27]Next to them, the men of Tekoa made repairs. They worked on the wall from the great tower that extends from the palace to the wall of Ophel.

[28]The priests made repairs above the Horse Gate. Each worked in front of his own house. [29]Next to them, Zadok son of Immer made repairs across from his own house. Next to him, Shemaiah son of Shecaniah made repairs. He was the guard of the East Gate. [30]Next to him, Hananiah son of Shelemiah and Hanun, the sixth son of Zalaph, made repairs. They worked on another part of the wall. Next to them, Meshullam son of Berekiah made repairs. It was across from where he lived. [31]Next to him, Malkijah made repairs. He was one of the goldsmiths. He worked as far as the house of the Temple servants and the traders. That is across from the Inspection Gate. And he worked as far as the room above the corner of the wall. [32]The goldsmiths

> I said, "Don't be afraid of them. Remember the Lord. He is great."
>
> –NEHEMIAH 4:14

3:16 Nehemiah This is a different Nehemiah than the one who wrote this book.

and the traders made repairs on another part of the wall. It was between the room above the corner of the wall and the Sheep Gate.

THOSE AGAINST THE REBUILDING

4 Sanballat heard we were rebuilding the wall. He was very angry, even furious. He made fun of the Jews. [2]He said to his friends and the army of Samaria, "What are these weak Jews doing? They think they can rebuild the wall. They think they will offer sacrifices. Maybe they think they can finish rebuilding it in only one day. They can't bring stones back to life. These are piles of trash and ashes."

[3]Tobiah the Ammonite was next to Sanballat. Tobiah said, "A fox could climb up on what they are building. Even it could break down their stone wall."

[4]I prayed, "Hear us, our God. We are hated. Turn the insults of Sanballat and Tobiah back on their own heads. Let them be captured and taken away like valuables that are stolen. [5]Do not hide their guilt. Do not take away their sins so you can't see them. The builders have seen them make you angry."

[6]So we rebuilt the wall until all of it went halfway up. The people were willing to work hard.

[7]But Sanballat, Tobiah, the Arabs, the Ammonites and the men from Ashdod were very angry. They heard that the repairs to Jerusalem's walls were continuing. And they heard that the holes in the wall were being closed. [8]So they all made plans against Jerusalem. They planned to come and fight and stir up trouble. [9]But we prayed to our God. And we appointed guards to watch for them day and night.

[10]The people of Judah said, "The workers are getting tired. There is too much dirt and trash. We cannot rebuild the wall."

[11]And our enemies said, "The Jews won't know it or see us. But we will come among them and kill them. We will stop the work."

[12]Then the Jews who lived near our enemies came. They told us ten times, "Everywhere you turn, the enemy will attack us." [13]So I put some of the people behind the lowest places along the wall. And I put some at the open places. I put families together with their swords, spears and bows. [14]Then I looked around. I stood up and spoke to the important men, the leaders and the rest of the people. I said, "Don't be afraid of them. Remember the Lord. He is great and others are afraid of him. And fight for your brothers, your sons and daughters, your wives and your homes."

[15]Then our enemies heard that we knew about their plans. God had ruined their plans. So we all went back to the wall. Each person went back to his own work.

[16]From that day on, half my men worked on the wall. The other half was ready with spears, shields, bows and armor. The officers stood in back of the people of Judah [17]who were building the wall. Those who carried materials did their work with one hand. They carried a weapon in the other hand. [18]Each builder wore his sword at his side as he worked. The man who blew the trumpet to warn the people stayed next to me.

[19]Then I spoke to the important men, the leaders and the rest of the people. I said, "This is a very big job. We are spreading out along the wall. We are far apart. [20]So wherever you hear the sound of the trumpet, assemble there. Our God will fight for us."

[21]So we continued to work. Half the men held spears. We worked from sunrise till the stars came out. [22]At that time I also said to the people, "Let every man and his helper stay inside Jerusalem at night. They can be our guards at night. And they can be workmen during the day." [23]Neither I, my brothers, my men nor the guards with me ever took off our clothes. Each person carried his weapon even when he went for water.

NEHEMIAH HELPS POOR PEOPLE

5 The men and their wives complained loudly against their fellow Jews. ²Some of them were saying, "We have many sons and daughters in our families. To eat and stay alive, we need grain."

³Others were saying, "We are borrowing money to get grain. There is not much food. We might not be able to pay back the money we've borrowed. Then we will have to pay with our fields, vineyards and homes."

⁴And still others were saying, "We are having to borrow money. We have to pay the king's tax on our fields and vineyards. ⁵We are just like our fellow Jews. Our sons are like their sons. But we have to sell our sons and daughters as slaves. Some of our daughters have already been sold. But there is nothing we can do. Our fields and vineyards already belong to other people."

⁶When I heard their complaints about these things, I was very angry. ⁷I thought about it. Then I accused the important people and the leaders. I told them, "You are charging your own brothers too much interest." So I called a large meeting to deal with them. ⁸I said to them, "Our fellow Jews had been sold to non-Jewish nations. But, as much as possible, we have bought them back. Now you are making your fellow Jews sell themselves to us!" The leaders were quiet. They had nothing to say.

⁹Then I said, "What you are doing is not right. You should live in fear of God. Don't let our non-Jewish enemies shame us. ¹⁰I, my brothers and my men are also lending money and grain to the people. But stop charging them too much for this! ¹¹Give back their fields, vineyards, olive trees and houses right now. Also give them back the extra amount you charged them. That is the hundredth part of the money, grain, new wine and oil."

¹²They said, "We will give it back. And we will not demand anything more from them. We will do as you say."

Then I called for the priests. And I made the important men and leaders promise to do what they had said. ¹³Also I shook out the folds of my robe. I said, "In this way may God shake out every man who does not keep his promise. May God shake him out of his house. And may he shake him out of the things that are his. Let that man be shaken out and emptied!"

Then the whole group said, "Amen." And they praised the Lord. So the people did what they had promised.

¹⁴I was appointed governor in the land of Judah. This was in the twentieth year of King Artaxerxes' rule. I was governor till his thirty-second year. So I was governor of Judah for 12 years. During that time neither my brothers nor I ate the food that was allowed for the governor. ¹⁵But the governors before me placed a heavy load on the people. They took about one pound of silver from each person. And they took food and wine. The governors' helpers before me also controlled the people. But I did not do that because I feared God. ¹⁶I worked on the wall. So did all my men who were gathered there. We did not buy any fields.

¹⁷Also, I fed 150 Jews and officers at my table. And I fed those who came from the nations around us. ¹⁸This is what was prepared every day for me and those who ate with me: one ox, six good sheep, and birds. And every ten days there were all kinds of wine. But I never demanded the food that was allowed for the governor. This was because the people were already working very hard.

¹⁹Remember, my God, to be kind to me. Remember all the good I have done for these people.

MORE PROBLEMS FOR NEHEMIAH

6 Then Sanballat, Tobiah, Geshem the Arab and our other enemies heard that I had rebuilt the wall. There was not one gap in it. But I had not yet set the doors in the gates. ²So Sanballat and Geshem sent me this message: "Come, Nehemiah, let's meet together in Kephirim on the plain of Ono."

But they were planning to harm me. ³So I sent messengers to them with this answer: "I am doing a great work. I can't come down. I don't want the work to stop while I leave to meet you." ⁴Sanballat and Geshem sent the same message to me four times. And I sent back the same answer each time.

⁵The fifth time Sanballat sent his helper to me with the message. And in his hand was an unsealed letter. ⁶This is what was written:

A report is going around to all the nations. And Geshem says it is true. It says you and the Jews are planning to turn against the king. That's why you are rebuilding the wall. They say you are going to be their king. ⁷They say you have appointed prophets to announce in Jerusalem: "There is a king of Judah!" The king will hear about this. So come, let's discuss this together.

⁸So I sent him back this answer: "Nothing you are saying is really happening. You are just making it up in your own mind."

⁹Our enemies were trying to scare us. They were thinking, "They will get too weak to work. Then the wall will not be finished."

But I prayed, "God, make me strong."

¹⁰One day I went to the house of Shemaiah son of Delaiah. Delaiah was the son of Mehetabel. Shemaiah had to stay at home. He said, "Nehemiah, let's meet in the Temple of God. Let's go inside the Temple and close the doors. Men are coming at night to kill you."

¹¹But I said, "Should a man like me run away? Should I run into the Temple to save my life? I will not go." ¹²I knew that God had not sent him. Tobiah and Sanballat had paid him to prophesy against me. ¹³They paid him to frighten me so I would do this and sin. Then they could give me a bad name to shame me.

¹⁴I prayed, "Remember Tobiah and Sanballat, my God. Remember what they have done. Also remember the prophetess Noadiah and the other prophets who have been trying to frighten me."

THE WALL IS FINISHED

¹⁵So the wall of Jerusalem was completed. It was on the twenty-fifth day of the month of Elul. It took 52 days to rebuild. ¹⁶Then all our enemies heard about it. And all the nations around us saw it. So they were shamed. They understood that the work had been done with the help of our God.

¹⁷Also in those days the important men of Judah sent many letters to Tobiah. And Tobiah answered them. ¹⁸Many Jews had promised to be faithful to Tobiah. This was because Tobiah was the son-in-law of Shecaniah son of Arah. And Tobiah's son Jehohanan had married the daughter of Meshullam son of Berekiah. ¹⁹Those important men kept telling me about the good things Tobiah was doing. Then they would tell Tobiah what I said about him. So Tobiah sent letters to frighten me.

7 After the wall had been rebuilt, I had set the doors in place. Then the gatekeepers, singers and Levites were chosen. ²I put my brother Hanani, along with Hananiah, in charge of Jerusalem. Hananiah was commander of the palace. He was honest, and he feared God more than most men. ³I said to them, "The gates of Jerusalem should not be opened until the sun is hot. While the gatekeepers are still on duty, have them shut and bolt the doors. Appoint people who live in Jerusalem as guards. Put some at guard posts and some near their own houses."

THE CAPTIVES WHO RETURNED

⁴The city was large and full of room. But there were few people in it. And the houses had not yet been rebuilt. ⁵So my

God caused me to gather the people. I gathered the important men, the leaders and the common people. This was so I could register them by families. I found the family history of those who had returned first. This is what I found written there:

⁶These are the people of the area who returned from captivity. Nebuchadnezzar king of Babylon had taken them captive. Now they returned to Jerusalem and Judah. Each one went back to his own town. ⁷These people returned with Zerubbabel, Jeshua, Nehemiah, Azariah, Raamiah, Nahamani, Mordecai, Bilshan, Mispereth, Bigvai, Nehum and Baanah.

These are the men from Israel: ⁸the descendants of Parosh—2,172; ⁹the descendants of Shephatiah—372; ¹⁰the descendants of Arah—652; ¹¹the descendants of Pahath-Moab (through the family of Jeshua and Joab)—2,818; ¹²the descendants of Elam—1,254; ¹³the descendants of Zattu—845; ¹⁴the descendants of Zaccai—760; ¹⁵the descendants of Binnui—648; ¹⁶the descendants of Bebai—628; ¹⁷the descendants of Azgad—2,322; ¹⁸the descendants of Adonikam—667; ¹⁹the descendants of Bigvai—2,067; ²⁰the descendants of Adin—655; ²¹the descendants of Ater (through Hezekiah)—98; ²²the descendants of Hashum—328; ²³the descendants of Bezai—324; ²⁴the descendants of Hariph—112; ²⁵the descendants of Gibeon—95.

²⁶These are the men from the towns of Bethlehem and Netophah—188; ²⁷the men from Anathoth—128; ²⁸the men from Beth Azmaveth—42; ²⁹the men from Kiriath Jearim, Kephirah and Beeroth—743; ³⁰the men from Ramah and Geba—621; ³¹the men from Micmash—122; ³²the men from Bethel and Ai—123; ³³the men from the other Nebo—52; ³⁴the men from the other Elam—1,254; ³⁵the men from Harim—320; ³⁶the men from Jericho—345; ³⁷the men from Lod, Hadid and Ono—721; ³⁸the men from Senaah—3,930.

³⁹These are the priests: the descendants of Jedaiah (through the family of Jeshua)—973; ⁴⁰the descendants of Immer—1,052; ⁴¹the descendants of Pashhur—1,247; ⁴²the descendants of Harim—1,017.

⁴³These are the Levites: the descendants of Jeshua (through Kadmiel through the family of Hodaviah)—74.

⁴⁴These are the singers: the descendants of Asaph—148.

⁴⁵These are the gatekeepers: the descendants of Shallum, Ater, Talmon, Akkub, Hatita and Shobai—138.

⁴⁶These are the Temple servants: the descendants of Ziha, Hasupha, Tabbaoth, ⁴⁷Keros, Sia, Padon, ⁴⁸Lebana, Hagaba, Shalmai, ⁴⁹Hanan, Giddel, Gahar, ⁵⁰Reaiah, Rezin, Nekoda, ⁵¹Gazzam, Uzza, Paseah, ⁵²Besai, Meunim, Nephusim, ⁵³Bakbuk, Hakupha, Harhur, ⁵⁴Bazluth, Mehida, Harsha, ⁵⁵Barkos, Sisera, Temah, ⁵⁶Neziah and Hatipha.

⁵⁷These are the descendants of the servants of Solomon: the descendants of Sotai, Sophereth, Perida, ⁵⁸Jaala, Darkon, Giddel, ⁵⁹Shephatiah, Hattil, Pokereth-Hazzebaim and Amon.

⁶⁰The Temple servants and the descendants of the servants of Solomon totaled 392 people.

⁶¹Some people came to Jerusalem from these towns: Tel Melah, Tel Harsha, Kerub, Addon and Immer. But they could not prove that their families came from the family of Israel. Here are their names and their number: ⁶²the descendants of Delaiah, Tobiah and Nekoda—642.

⁶³And these priests could not prove that their families came from Israel: the descendants of Hobaiah, Hakkoz and Barzillai. (He had married a daughter of Barzillai from Gilead and was called by her family name.)

⁶⁴These people searched for their family records. But they could not find them. So they could not be priests

because they were thought to be unclean. ⁶⁵So the governor ordered them not to eat any of the food offered to God. First a priest had to settle this matter by using the Urim and Thummim.

⁶⁶The total number of those who returned was 42,360. ⁶⁷This is not counting their 7,337 male and female servants. They also had 245 men and women singers with them. ⁶⁸They had 736 horses, 245 mules, ⁶⁹435 camels and 6,720 donkeys.

⁷⁰Some of the family leaders gave to the work. The governor gave to the treasury about 19 pounds of gold. He also gave 50 bowls and 530 pieces of clothing for the priests. ⁷¹Some of the family leaders gave about 375 pounds of gold to the treasury for the work. They also gave about 2,660 pounds of silver. ⁷²This is the total of what the other people gave: about 375 pounds of gold, about 2,250 pounds of silver and 67 pieces of clothing for the priests. ⁷³So these people all settled in their own towns: the priests, the Levites, the gatekeepers, the singers, the Temple servants and all the other people of Israel.

EZRA READS THE TEACHINGS

By the seventh month the Israelites were settled in their own towns.

8 All the people of Israel gathered together in the square by the Water Gate. They asked Ezra the teacher to bring out the Book of the Teachings of Moses. These are the Teachings the Lord had given to Israel.

²So Ezra the priest brought out the Teachings for the crowd. This was on the first day of the seventh month. Men, women and all who could listen and understand had gathered. ³Ezra read the Teachings out loud. He read from early morning until noon. He was facing the square by the Water Gate. He read to the men, women and everyone who could listen and understand. All the people listened carefully to the Book of the Teachings.

⁴Ezra the teacher stood on a high wooden platform. It had been built just for this time. On his right were Mattithiah, Shema, Anaiah, Uriah, Hilkiah and Maaseiah. And on his left were Pedaiah, Mishael, Malkijah, Hashum, Hashbaddanah, Zechariah and Meshullam.

⁵Ezra opened the book. All the people could see him because he was above them. As he opened it, all the people stood up. ⁶Ezra praised the Lord, the great God. And all the people held up their hands and said, "Amen! Amen!" Then they bowed down and worshiped the Lord with their faces to the ground.

⁷These Levites taught the people the Teachings as they stood there: Jeshua, Bani, Sherebiah, Jamin, Akkub, Shabbethai, Hodiah, Maaseiah, Kelita, Azariah, Jozabad, Hanan and Pelaiah. ⁸They read the Book of the Teachings of God. They read so the people could understand. And they explained what it meant. Then the people understood what was being read.

⁹Then Nehemiah the governor and Ezra the priest and teacher spoke up. And the Levites who were teaching spoke up. They said to all the people, "This is a holy day to the Lord your God. Don't be sad or cry." All the people had been crying as they listened to the words of the Teachings.

¹⁰Nehemiah said, "Go and enjoy good food and sweet drinks. Send some to people who have none. Today is a holy

> Ezra praised the Lord, the great God. And all the people . . . worshiped the Lord.
>
> –NEHEMIAH 8:6

☆ Nehemiah 8:10

Nehemiah and some friends went back to Jerusalem to rebuild the wall. Once it was safe to live there again, Jews started moving back. One day, a priest named Ezra read from the Book of the Teachings of God. When the people realized they had forgotten all about God, they cried. Nehemiah and the priests told them to treat that day like a holiday. Eat and drink and give food to others. They were told to be joyful because when they have joy, they actually have God's strength.

A young girl was on stage about to sing in front of a big crowd of people. She was so nervous and started to feel sick. She didn't feel like she could do it. But then she saw her mom and dad sitting on the front row. Suddenly, she felt brave. She smiled and sang her song with joy. When you have someone who loves and supports you, you can feel confident and strong. Did you know that God is always with you? Knowing God is around can give you joy. And when you have joy from God, you also have his strength.

• •

The next time you feel bad, remember that God is with you. His joy will make you strong!

---

day to the Lord. Don't be sad. The joy of the Lord will make you strong."

¹¹The Levites helped calm the people. They said, "Be quiet. This is a holy day. Don't be sad."

¹²Then all the people went away to eat and drink. They sent some of their food to others. And they celebrated with great joy. They finally understood what they had been taught.

¹³On the second day of the month, the leaders of all the families met with Ezra the teacher. The priests and Levites also met with him. They gathered to study the words of the Teachings. ¹⁴This is what they found written in the Teachings: The Lord had commanded through Moses that the people of Israel were to live in shelters. This was during the feast of the seventh month. ¹⁵The people were supposed to preach this message. They were to spread it through all of their towns and in Jerusalem: "Go out into the

mountains. Bring back branches from olive and wild olive trees, myrtle trees, palms and shade trees. Make shelters with them. It is written in the Law."

[16]So the people went out and got tree branches. They built shelters on their roofs[n] and in their courtyards. They built shelters in the courtyards of the Temple. And they built them in the square by the Water Gate and the square next to the Gate of Ephraim. [17]The whole group that had come back from captivity built shelters. And they lived in them. The Israelites had not done this since the time of Joshua son of Nun. And they were very happy.

[18]Ezra read to them from the Book of the Teachings. He read every day, from the first day to the last. The people of Israel celebrated the feast for seven days. Then on the eighth day the people gathered as the law said.

ISRAEL CONFESSES SINS

9 It was on the twenty-fourth day of that same month. The people of Israel gathered together. They did not eat. And they put on rough cloth and put dust on their heads. This was to show their sadness. [2]Those people whose ancestors were from Israel had separated themselves from all foreigners. They stood and confessed their sins and their ancestors' sins. [3]For a fourth of the day they stood where they were. And they read from the Book of the Teachings of the Lord their God. Then they spent another fourth of the day confessing their sins. And they worshiped the Lord their God. [4]These Levites were standing on the stairs: Jeshua, Bani, Kadmiel, Shebaniah, Bunni, Sherebiah, Bani and Kanani. They called out to the Lord their God with loud voices. [5]And these Levites spoke: Jeshua, Kadmiel, Bani, Hashabneiah, Sherebiah, Hodiah, Shebaniah and Pethahiah. They said,

"Stand up and praise the Lord your God. He lives forever and ever."

THE PEOPLE'S PRAYER

"Blessed be your wonderful name.
   It is more wonderful than all
      blessing and praise.
[6] You are the only Lord.
   You made the heavens, even the
      highest heavens.
   You made all the stars.
You made the earth and everything
      that is on it.
   You made the seas and everything
      that is in them.
   You give life to everything.
   The heavenly army worships you.

[7] "You are the Lord God.
   You chose Abram.
You brought him out of Ur of the
      Babylonians.
   You named him Abraham.
[8] You found that he was faithful to you.
   So you made an agreement with
      him.
You promised to give his descendants
      the land of the Canaanites,
      Hittites, Amorites,
      Perizzites, Jebusites and
      Girgashites.
   You have kept your promise.
   You are fair.

[9] "You saw our ancestors suffering in
      Egypt.
   You heard them cry out at the Red
      Sea.
[10] You did signs and miracles against
      the king of Egypt.
   And you did them against all his
      officers and all the people of
      Egypt.
   You knew how proud they were.
   You made everyone know your name.
   And it is still known today.
[11] You divided the sea in front of our
      ancestors.

8:16 roofs In Bible times houses were built with flat roofs. The roof was used for drying things such as flax and fruit. And it was used as an extra room, as a place for worship and as a place to sleep in the summer.

They walked through it on dry
ground.
But you threw the people chasing
them into the deep water.
They were like a stone being
thrown into mighty waters.
¹² You led our ancestors with a pillar of
cloud in the daytime.
And you led them with a pillar of
fire at night.
It lit the way
they were supposed to go.
¹³ You came down to Mount Sinai.
You talked to our ancestors from
heaven.
You gave them fair rules and true
teachings.
You gave them good orders and
commands.
¹⁴ You told them about your holy
Sabbath.
You gave commands, orders and
teachings to them
through your servant Moses.
¹⁵ When they were hungry, you gave
them bread from heaven.
When they were thirsty, you
brought them water from the
rock.
You told them to go into the land and
take it over.
You had promised to give it to them.

¹⁶ "But our ancestors were proud and
stubborn.
They did not obey your commands.
¹⁷ They refused to listen.
They forgot the miracles you did
for them.
They became stubborn and turned
against you.
They chose a leader to lead them
back to their slavery.
But you are a forgiving God.
You are kind and full of mercy.
You do not become angry quickly.
And you have great love.
So you did not leave them.
¹⁸ Our ancestors even made an idol of a
calf for themselves.
They said, 'This is your god, Israel.

It brought you up out of Egypt.'
They spoke against you.

¹⁹ "You have great mercy.
So you did not leave them in the
desert.
During the day the pillar of cloud
guided them on their way.
And the pillar of fire led them at
night.
It lit the way they were supposed
to go.
²⁰ You gave your good Spirit to teach
them.
You gave them manna to eat.
And you gave them water when
they were thirsty.
²¹ You took care of them for 40 years in
the desert.
They needed nothing.
Their clothes did not wear out.
And their feet did not swell.

²² "You gave them kingdoms and
nations.
You gave them more land.
They took over the country of Sihon
king of Heshbon.
And they took over the country of
Og king of Bashan.
²³ You made their children as many as
the stars in the sky.
And you brought them into the
land.
This was where you had told their
ancestors to enter and take
over.
²⁴ So their children went into the land
and took over.
The Canaanites lived there.
But you defeated them for our
ancestors.
You handed over to them the
Canaanites, their kings and the
people of the land.
Our ancestors could do what they
wanted with them.
²⁵ Our ancestors captured strong,
walled cities and fertile land.
They took over houses full of good
things.

They took over wells that were
　　already dug.
　They took vineyards, olive trees
　　and many fruit trees.
They ate until they were full and
　　became fat.
　They enjoyed your great goodness.

26 "But they were disobedient and
　　turned against you.
　They ignored your teachings.
Your prophets warned them to come
　　back to you.
　But they killed those prophets.
　And they spoke against you.
27 So you allowed their enemies to
　　defeat them.
　Their enemies treated them badly.
But in this time of trouble our
　　ancestors cried out to you.
　And you heard from heaven.
You had great mercy.
　You gave them saviors who saved
　　them from the power of their
　　enemies.
28 But as soon as they had rest,
　　they again did what was evil.
So you left them to their enemies
　　who ruled over them.
But they cried out to you again.
　And you heard from heaven.
　Because of your mercy, you saved
　　them again and again.
29 You warned them to return to
　　obeying your teachings.
　But they were proud. They did not
　　obey your commands.
If a man obeys your laws, he will live.
　But they sinned against your laws.
They were stubborn and disobedient.
　They would not listen.
30 You were patient with them for many
　　years.
　You warned them by your Spirit
　　through the prophets.
But they did not pay attention.
　So you allowed them to be defeated
　　by other countries.
31 But because your mercy is great, you
　　did not kill them all.
　You did not leave them.

You are a kind and merciful God.

32 "And so, our God, you are the great
　　and mighty and wonderful God.
　You keep your agreement of love.
Do not let all our trouble seem
　　unimportant in your eyes.
This trouble has come to us, to our
　　kings and to our leaders.
　It has come to our priests and
　　prophets.
　It has come to our ancestors and all
　　your people.
This trouble has come to us since the
　　days of the kings of Assyria.
　And it has lasted until today.
33 You have been fair in everything that
　　has happened to us.
　You have been loyal, but we have
　　been wicked.
34 Our kings, leaders, priests and
　　ancestors did not obey your
　　teachings.
　They did not pay attention to the
　　commands and warnings you
　　gave them.
35 Even when our ancestors were living
　　in their kingdom,
　　they did not serve you.
They were enjoying all the good
　　things you had given them.
　They were enjoying the land that
　　was fertile and full of room.
　But they did not stop their evil ways.

36 "Look, we are slaves today
　　in the land you gave our
　　ancestors.
　They were to enjoy its fruit and its
　　good things.
　But look, we are slaves here.
37 The land's great harvest belongs to
　　the kings you have put over us.
　This is because of our sins.
Those kings rule over us and our
　　cattle as they please.
　And we are in much trouble.

THE PEOPLE'S AGREEMENT

38 "Because of all this, we are making
an agreement in writing. Our leaders,

Levites and priests are putting their seals on it."

10 These are the men who sealed the agreement:

Nehemiah the governor, son of Hacaliah, sealed it.

These men also sealed it: Zedekiah, [2]Seraiah, Azariah, Jeremiah, [3]Pashhur, Amariah, Malkijah, [4]Hattush, Shebaniah, Malluch, [5]Harim, Meremoth, Obadiah, [6]Daniel, Ginnethon, Baruch, [7]Meshullam, Abijah, Mijamin, [8]Maaziah, Bilgai and Shemaiah. These are the priests.

[9]These are the Levites who sealed it: Jeshua son of Azaniah, Binnui of the sons of Henadad, Kadmiel, [10]and their fellow Levites: Shebaniah, Hodiah, Kelita, Pelaiah, Hanan, [11]Mica, Rehob, Hashabiah, [12]Zaccur, Sherebiah, Shebaniah, [13]Hodiah, Bani and Beninu.

[14]These are the leaders of the people who sealed the agreement: Parosh, Pahath-Moab, Elam, Zattu, Bani, [15]Bunni, Azgad, Bebai, [16]Adonijah, Bigvai, Adin, [17]Ater, Hezekiah, Azzur, [18]Hodiah, Hashum, Bezai, [19]Hariph, Anathoth, Nebai, [20]Magpiash, Meshullam, Hezir, [21]Meshezabel, Zadok, Jaddua, [22]Pelatiah, Hanan, Anaiah, [23]Hoshea, Hananiah, Hasshub, [24]Hallohesh, Pilha, Shobek, [25]Rehum, Hashabnah, Maaseiah, [26]Ahiah, Hanan, Anan, [27]Malluch, Harim and Baanah.

[28]The rest of the people took an oath. They were the priests, Levites, gate-keepers, singers and Temple servants. And they were all those who separated themselves from foreigners to keep the Teachings of God. It was also their wives and their sons and daughters who could understand. [29]They joined their fellow Israelites and their leading men. They took an oath, which was tied to a curse in case they broke the oath. They promised to follow the Teachings of God, which they had been given through Moses the servant of God. These people also promised to obey all the commands, rules and laws of the Lord our Master.

[30]They said:

We promise not to let our daughters marry foreigners. And we promise not to let our sons marry their daughters. [31]The foreigners might bring goods or grain to sell on the Sabbath. But we will not buy on the Sabbath day or any holy day. Every seventh year we will not plant. And that year we will forget all that people owe us.

[32]We will be responsible for obeying the commands. We will pay for the service of the Temple of our God. We will give an eighth of an ounce of silver each year. [33]It is to pay for the bread that is set out on the table. It is to pay for the regular grain offerings and burnt offerings. It is for the offerings on the Sabbaths, New Moon festivals and special feasts. It is for the holy offerings. And it is for the offerings to remove the sins of the Israelites so they will belong to God. It is for the work of the Temple of our God.

[34]We are the priests, the Levites and the people. We have thrown lots to decide when each family must bring wood to the Temple. This is to be done at certain times each year. The wood is for burning on the altar of the Lord our God. We will do this as it is written in the Teachings.

[35]We also will bring the first fruits from our crops. And we will bring the first fruits of every tree to the Temple each year.

[36]We will bring our firstborn sons

> They promised to follow the Teachings of God, which they had been given through Moses.
>
> –NEHEMIAH 10:29

and cattle to the Temple. We will bring the firstborn of our herds and flocks. We will do this as it is written in the Teachings. We will bring them to the priests who are serving in the Temple.

37 We will bring things to the priests at the storerooms of the Temple. We will bring the first of our ground meal, our offerings, the fruit from all our trees and our new wine and oil. And we will bring a tenth of our crops to the Levites. The Levites will collect these things in all the towns where we work. 38 A priest of Aaron's family must be with the Levites when they receive the tenth of the people's crops. The Levites must bring a tenth of all they receive to the Temple of our God. Then they will put it in the storerooms of the treasury. 39 The people of Israel and the Levites are to bring their gifts to the storerooms. These are the gifts of grain, new wine and oil. The things for the Temple are kept in the storerooms. It is also where the priests, who are serving, the gatekeepers and singers stay.

We will not ignore the Temple of our God.

NEW PEOPLE MOVE INTO JERUSALEM

11 The leaders of Israel lived in Jerusalem. The rest of the people threw lots. One person out of every ten was to come and live in Jerusalem. It was the holy city. The other nine could stay in their own cities. 2 The people blessed those who volunteered to live in Jerusalem.

3 These are the area leaders who lived in Jerusalem. (Some people lived on their own land in the cities of Judah. These included Israelites, priests, Levites, Temple servants and descendants of Solomon's servants. 4 Others from the families of Judah and Benjamin lived in Jerusalem.)

These are descendants of Judah who moved into Jerusalem. There was Athaiah son of Uzziah. (Uzziah was the son of Zechariah, who was the son of Amariah. Amariah was the son of Shephatiah, who was the son of Mahalalel. Mahalalel was a descendant of Perez.) 5 There was also Maaseiah son of Baruch. (Baruch was the son of Col-Hozeh, who was the son of Hazaiah. Hazaiah was the son of Adaiah, who was the son of Joiarib. Joiarib was the son of Zechariah, who was a descendant of Shelah.) 6 All the descendants of Perez who lived in Jerusalem totaled 468 men. They were soldiers.

7 These are descendants of Benjamin who moved into Jerusalem. There was Sallu son of Meshullam. (Meshullam was the son of Joed, who was the son of Pedaiah. Pedaiah was the son of Kolaiah. Kolaiah was the son of Maaseiah. Maaseiah was the son of Ithiel, who was the son of Jeshaiah.) 8 Following him were Gabbai and Sallai. All together there were 928 men. 9 Joel son of Zicri was appointed over them. And Judah son of Hassenuah was second in charge of the new area of the city.

10 These are the priests who moved into Jerusalem. There was Jedaiah son of Joiarib, Jakin 11 and Seraiah son of Hilkiah. (Hilkiah was the son of Meshullam, who was the son of Zadok. Zadok was the son of Meraioth, who was the son of Ahitub. Seraiah was the supervisor in the Temple.) 12 And there were others with them who did the work for the Temple. All together there were 822 men. Also there was Adaiah son of Jeroham. (Jeroham was the son of Pelaliah, who was the son of Amzi. Amzi was the son of Zechariah, who was the son of Pashhur. Pashhur was the son of Malkijah.) 13 And there were family heads with him. All together there were 242 men. Also there was Amashsai son of Azarel. (Azarel was the son of Ahzai, who was the son of Meshillemoth. Meshillemoth was the son of Immer.) 14 And there were brave men with Amashsai. All together there were 128 men. Zabdiel son of Haggedolim was appointed over them.

¹⁵These are the Levites who moved into Jerusalem. There was Shemaiah son of Hasshub. (Hasshub was the son of Azrikam, who was the son of Hashabiah. Hashabiah was the son of Bunni.) ¹⁶And there were Shabbethai and Jozabad. They were two of the leaders of the Levites. They were in charge of the work outside the Temple. ¹⁷There was Mattaniah son of Mica. (Mica was the son of Zabdi, who was the son of Asaph.) Mattaniah was the director. He led the people in thanksgiving and prayer. There was Bakbukiah, who was second in charge over his fellow Levites. And there was Abda son of Shammua. (Shammua was the son of Galal, who was the son of Jeduthun.) ¹⁸All together 284 Levites lived in the holy city of Jerusalem.

¹⁹These are the gatekeepers who moved into Jerusalem. There were Akkub, Talmon and others with them. There was a total of 172 men. They guarded the city gates.

²⁰The other Israelites, priests and Levites lived on their own land. They were in all the cities of Judah.

²¹The Temple servants lived on the hill of Ophel. Ziha and Gishpa were in charge of them.

²²Uzzi son of Bani was appointed over the Levites in Jerusalem. (Bani was the son of Hashabiah, who was the son of Mattaniah. Mattaniah was the son of Mica.) Uzzi was one of Asaph's descendants. They were the singers. They were responsible for the service of the Temple. ²³The singers took orders from the king. Those orders told the singers what to do each day.

²⁴Pethahiah son of Meshezabel was the king's spokesman. Meshezabel was a descendant of Zerah, the son of Judah.

²⁵Some of the people of Judah lived in villages with their surrounding fields. Some lived in Kiriath Arba and its surroundings. Some lived in Dibon and its surroundings. Some lived in Jekabzeel and its surroundings. ²⁶Others lived in Jeshua, Moladah, Beth Pelet, ²⁷Hazar Shual, Beersheba and its surroundings. ²⁸Others were in Ziklag and Meconah and its surroundings. ²⁹Some people lived in En Rimmon, Zorah, Jarmuth, ³⁰Zanoah, Adullam and their villages. Some were in Lachish and the fields around it. Some lived in Azekah and its surroundings. So they settled from Beersheba all the way to the Valley of Hinnom.

³¹The descendants of the Benjaminites from Geba lived in Micmash, Aija, Bethel and its surroundings. ³²They lived in Anathoth, Nob, Ananiah, ³³Hazor, Ramah and Gittaim. ³⁴They lived in Hadid, Zeboim, Neballat, ³⁵Lod, Ono and in the Valley of the Craftsmen.

³⁶Some groups of the Levites from Judah settled in the land of Benjamin.

PRIESTS AND LEVITES

12 These are the priests and Levites who returned with Zerubbabel son of Shealtiel and with Jeshua. There were Seraiah, Jeremiah, Ezra, ²Amariah, Malluch, Hattush, ³Shecaniah, Rehum, Meremoth, ⁴Iddo, Ginnethon, Abijah, ⁵Mijamin, Moadiah, Bilgah, ⁶Shemaiah, Joiarib, Jedaiah, ⁷Sallu, Amok, Hilkiah and Jedaiah. They were the leaders of the priests and their relatives. This was in the days of Jeshua.

⁸The Levites were Jeshua, Binnui, Kadmiel, Sherebiah, Judah and also Mattaniah. He and his relatives were in charge of the songs of thanksgiving. ⁹Bakbukiah and Unni, their relatives, stood across from them in the services.

¹⁰Jeshua was the father of Joiakim. Joiakim was the father of Eliashib. Eliashib was the father of Joiada. ¹¹Joiada was the father of Jonathan. And Jonathan was the father of Jaddua.

¹²In the days of Joiakim, these priests were the leaders of the families of priests. Meraiah was over Seraiah's family. Hananiah was over Jeremiah's family. ¹³Meshullam was over Ezra's family. Jehohanan was over Amariah's family. ¹⁴Jonathan was over Malluch's family. Joseph was over Shecaniah's family.

¹⁵Adna was over Harim's family. Helkai was over Meremoth's family. ¹⁶Zechariah was over Iddo's family. Meshullam was over Ginneton's family. ¹⁷Zicri was over Abijah's family. Piltai was over Miniamin's and Moadiah's families. ¹⁸Shammua was over Bilgah's family. Jehonathan was over Shemaiah's family. ¹⁹Mattenai was over Joiarib's family. Uzzi was over Jedaiah's family. ²⁰Kallai was over Sallu's family. Eber was over Amok's family. ²¹Hashabiah was over Hilkiah's family. Nethanel was over Jedaiah's family.

²²The leaders of the families of the Levites and the priests were written down. This was in the days of Eliashib, Joiada, Johanan and Jaddua. They were written down while Darius the Persian was king. ²³The family leaders among the Levites were written down in the history book. These were only up to the time of Johanan son of Eliashib. ²⁴The leaders of the Levites were Hashabiah, Sherebiah, Jeshua son of Kadmiel and their relatives. Their relatives stood across from them. They gave praise and thanksgiving to God. One group answered the other group. That is what David, the man of God, had commanded.

²⁵These were the gatekeepers who guarded the storerooms next to the gates: Mattaniah, Bakbukiah, Obadiah, Meshullam, Talmon and Akkub. ²⁶They served in the days of Joiakim son of Jeshua. (Jeshua was the son of Jozadak.) They also served in the days of Nehemiah the governor and Ezra the priest and teacher.

GIVING OF THE WALL OF JERUSALEM

²⁷The wall of Jerusalem was offered as a gift to God. The Levites were found in the places where they lived. And they were brought to Jerusalem to celebrate with joy the giving of the wall. They were to celebrate with songs of thanksgiving and with the music of cymbals, harps and lyres. ²⁸They also brought together singers. They came from all around Jerusalem and from the Netophathite villages. ²⁹They came from Beth Gilgal and the areas of Geba and Azmaveth. The singers had built villages for themselves around Jerusalem. ³⁰The priests and Levites made themselves pure. They also made the people, the gates and the wall of Jerusalem pure.

³¹I had the leaders of Judah go up on top of the wall. I appointed two large choruses to give thanks. One chorus went to the right on top of the wall. This was toward the Trash Gate. ³²Behind them went Hoshaiah and half the leaders of Judah. ³³Azariah, Ezra, Meshullam, ³⁴Judah, Benjamin, Shemaiah and Jeremiah also went. ³⁵Some priests with trumpets also went, along with Zechariah son of Jonathan. (Jonathan was the son of Shemaiah, who was the son of Mattaniah. Mattaniah was the son of Micaiah, who was the son of Zaccur. Zaccur was the son of Asaph.) ³⁶Zechariah's relatives also went. They were Shemaiah, Azarel, Milalai, Gilalai, Maai, Nethanel, Judah and Hanani. These men played the musical instruments of David, the man of God. Ezra the teacher walked in front of them. ³⁷They went from the Fountain Gate straight up the steps to the older part of the city. They went on to the slope of the wall. They went above the house of David to the Water Gate on the east.

³⁸The second chorus went to the left. I followed them on top of the wall. Half the people were with me. We went from the Tower of the Ovens to the Broad Wall. ³⁹We went over the Gate of Ephraim to the Old Gate and the Fish Gate. We went to the Tower of Hananel and the Tower of the Hundred. We went as far as the Sheep Gate. We stopped at the Gate of the Guard.

⁴⁰The two choruses took their places at the Temple. Half of the leaders and I did also. ⁴¹These priests were there with their trumpets: Eliakim,

Maaseiah, Miniamin, Micaiah, Elioenai, Zechariah and Hananiah. ⁴²These people were also there: Maaseiah, Shemaiah, Eleazar, Uzzi, Jehohanan, Malkijah, Elam and Ezer. The choruses sang, led by Jezrahiah. ⁴³The people offered many sacrifices that day. They were happy because God made them very happy. The women and children were happy. The sound of happiness in Jerusalem could be heard far away.

⁴⁴At that time the leaders appointed men to be in charge of the storerooms. These rooms were for the gifts, the first fruits and a tenth of what the people gained. The Teachings said they should bring a share for the priests and Levites. These were to come from the fields around the towns. The people of Judah were happy to do this for the priests and Levites who served. ⁴⁵They performed the service of their God. They had the service of purifying things. The singers and gatekeepers also did their jobs as David had commanded his son Solomon. ⁴⁶Earlier, in the time of David and Asaph, there was a leader of the singers. There were songs of praise and thanksgiving to God. ⁴⁷So it was in the days of Zerubbabel and Nehemiah. All the people of Israel gave something to the singers and gatekeepers. They also set aside things for the Levites. The Levites set aside things for the descendants of Aaron.

FOREIGN PEOPLE ARE SENT AWAY

13 On that day they read the Book of Moses to the people. They found that it said no Ammonite or Moabite should ever be allowed in the meeting to worship. ²The Ammonites and Moabites had not welcomed the Israelites with food and water. Instead, they hired Balaam to put a curse on Israel. (But our God turned the curse into a blessing.) ³The people heard this teaching. So they separated all foreigners from Israel.

NEHEMIAH RETURNS TO JERUSALEM

⁴Before that happened, Eliashib the priest was in charge of the Temple storerooms. He was friendly with Tobiah. ⁵Eliashib let Tobiah use one of the large storerooms. That storeroom had been used for grain offerings, incense and other things for the Temple. It was also used for the tenth offerings of grain, new wine and olive oil. These belonged to the Levites, singers and gatekeepers. It had also been used for gifts for the priests.

⁶I was not in Jerusalem when this happened. I had gone back to Artaxerxes king of Babylon. I went back in the thirty-second year he was king. Finally I asked the king to let me leave. ⁷I came to Jerusalem. Then I found out the evil thing Eliashib had done. He had let Tobiah have a room in the Temple courtyard. ⁸I was very upset at this. I threw all of Tobiah's goods out of the room. ⁹I ordered the rooms to be purified. And I brought back the things for God's Temple, the grain offerings and the incense.

¹⁰Then I found out the people were not giving the Levites their shares. So the Levites and singers who served had gone to their own farms. ¹¹So I argued with the officers. I said, "Why haven't you taken care of the Temple?" Then I gathered the Levites and singers. I put them back at their places.

¹²Then all the people of Judah brought a tenth of what they had gained in grain, new wine and olive oil. And they brought it to the storerooms. ¹³I put these men in charge of the storerooms: Shelemiah the priest, Zadok the teacher and Pedaiah a Levite. I made Hanan son of Zaccur their helper. (Zaccur was the son of Mattaniah.) Everyone knew they were honest men. They gave out the portions that went to their relatives.

¹⁴Remember me, my God, for this. Do not ignore my love for the Temple and its service.

¹⁵In those days I saw people in Judah working in the winepresses on the Sabbath day. People were bringing in grain and loading it on donkeys on the Sabbath day. People were bringing loads of wine, grapes and figs into Jerusalem on the Sabbath day. I warned them about selling food on that day. ¹⁶Men from the city of Tyre were living in Jerusalem. They brought in fish and other things. They sold them in Jerusalem on the Sabbath day to the people of Judah. ¹⁷I argued with the important men of Judah. I said to them, "What is this evil thing you are doing? You are ruining the Sabbath day. ¹⁸This is just what your ancestors did. So our God did terrible things to us and this city. Now you are making him even more angry at Israel. You are ruining the Sabbath day."

¹⁹So I ordered the doors shut at sunset before the Sabbath. The gates were not to be opened until the Sabbath was over. I put my servants at the gates. So no load could come in on the Sabbath. ²⁰Once or twice traders and sellers of all kinds of goods spent the night outside Jerusalem. ²¹So I warned them. I said, "Why are you spending the night by the wall? If you do it again, I will force you away." After that, they did not come back on the Sabbath. ²²Then I ordered the Levites to purify themselves. I told them to go and guard the city gates. They were to make sure the Sabbath remained holy.

Remember me, my God, for this. Have mercy on me because of your great love.

> Remember me, my God, for this. Have mercy on me because of your great love.
>
> –NEHEMIAH 13:22

²³In those days I saw men of Judah who had married women from Ashdod, Ammon and Moab. ²⁴Half their children were speaking the language of Ashdod or some other place. They couldn't speak the language of Judah. ²⁵I argued with those people. I put curses on them. I hit some of them and pulled out their hair. I forced them to make a promise to God. I said, "Do not let your daughters marry the sons of foreigners. Do not take the daughters of foreigners as wives for your sons or yourselves. ²⁶Foreign women made King Solomon of Israel sin. There was never a king like him in any of the nations. God loved Solomon. God made him king over all Israel. But foreign women made Solomon sin.

²⁷And now you are not obedient when you do this evil thing. You are unfaithful to our God when you marry foreign wives."

²⁸Joiada was the son of Eliashib the high priest. One of Joiada's sons married a daughter of Sanballat the Horonite, who was not a Jew. So I forced Joiada's son away from me.

²⁹Remember them, my God. They made the priesthood unclean. They made the agreement of the priests and Levites unclean.

³⁰So I purified them of everything that was foreign. I appointed duties for the priests and Levites. Each man had his own job. ³¹I also made sure wood was brought for the altar at regular times. And I made sure the first fruits were brought.

Remember, my God, to be kind to me.

Esther

QUEEN VASHTI DISOBEYS THE KING

1 This is what happened during the time of King Xerxes. He was the king who ruled the 127 areas from India to Cush. ²In those days King Xerxes ruled from his capital city of Susa. ³In the third year of his rule, he gave a banquet. It was for all his important men and royal officers. The army leaders from the countries of Persia and Media were there. And the important men from all Xerxes' empire were there.

⁴The banquet lasted 180 days. All during that time King Xerxes was showing off the great wealth of his kingdom. And he was showing his own honor and greatness. ⁵When the 180 days were over, the king gave another banquet. It was held in the courtyard of the palace garden for 7 days. It was for everybody in the palace at Susa, from the greatest to the least important. ⁶The courtyard had fine white curtains and purple drapes. These were tied to silver rings on marble pillars by white and purple cords. And there were gold and silver couches. These were on a floor set with tiles of white marble, shells and gems. ⁷Wine was served in gold cups of various kinds. And there was plenty of the king's wine because he was very generous. ⁸The king commanded that each guest be permitted to drink as much as he wished. He had told the wine servers to serve each man what he wanted.

⁹Queen Vashti also gave a banquet. It was for the women in the royal palace of King Xerxes.

¹⁰On the seventh day of the banquet, King Xerxes was very happy because he had been drinking much wine. He gave a command to the seven eunuchs who served him. They were Mehuman, Biztha, Harbona, Bigtha, Abagtha, Zethar and Carcas. ¹¹He commanded them to bring him Queen Vashti, wearing her royal crown. She was to come to show her beauty to the people and important men. She was very beautiful. ¹²The eunuchs told Queen Vashti about the king's command. But she refused to come. Then the king became very angry. His anger was like a burning fire.

¹³It was a custom for the king to ask advice from experts about law and order. So King Xerxes spoke with the wise men. They would know the right thing to do. ¹⁴The wise men the king usually talked to were Carshena, Shethar, Admatha, Tarshish, Meres, Marsena and Memucan. They were seven of the important men of Persia and Media. These seven had special privileges to see the king. They had the highest rank in the kingdom.

¹⁵The king asked those men, "What does the law say must be done to Queen Vashti? She has not obeyed the command of King Xerxes, which the eunuchs took to her."

¹⁶Then Memucan spoke to the king and the other important men. He said, "Queen Vashti has not done wrong to the king alone. She has also done wrong to all the important men and all the people in all the empire of King Xerxes. ¹⁷All the wives of the important men of Persia and Media will hear about the queen's actions. Then they will no longer honor their husbands. They will say, 'King Xerxes commanded Queen Vashti to be brought to him. But she refused to come.' ¹⁸Today the wives of the important men of Persia and Media have heard about the queen's actions. And they will speak in the same way to their husbands. And there will be no end to disrespect and anger.

¹⁹"So, our king, if it pleases you, give a royal order. And let it be written in the laws of Persia and Media, which cannot be changed. The law should say Vashti

is never again to enter the presence of King Xerxes. Also let the king give her place as queen to someone who is better than she is. ²⁰And let the king's order be announced everywhere in his large kingdom. Then all the women will respect their husbands, from the greatest to the least important."

²¹The king and his important men were happy with this advice. So King Xerxes did as Memucan suggested. ²²He sent letters to all the areas of the kingdom. A letter was sent to each area, written in its own form of writing. And a letter was sent to each group of people, written in their own language. These letters announced that each man was to be the ruler of his own family. Also, each family was to speak the language of the man.

ESTHER IS MADE QUEEN

2 Later, King Xerxes was not so angry. Then he remembered Vashti and what she had done. And he remembered his order about her. ²Then the king's personal servants had a suggestion. They said, "Let a search be made for beautiful young virgins for the king. ³Let the king choose supervisors in every area of his kingdom. Let them bring every beautiful young virgin to the palace at Susa. These women should be taken to the women's quarters and put under the care of Hegai. He is the king's eunuch in charge of the women. And let beauty treatments be given to them. ⁴Then let the girl who most pleases the king become queen in place of Vashti." The king liked this advice. So he did as they said.

⁵Now there was a Jewish man in the palace of Susa. His name was Mordecai son of Jair. Jair was the son of Shimei. And Shimei was the son of Kish. Mordecai was from the tribe of Benjamin. ⁶Mordecai had been taken captive from Jerusalem by Nebuchadnezzar king of Babylon. Mordecai was part of the group taken into captivity with Jehoiachin king of Judah. ⁷Mordecai had a cousin named Hadassah, who had no father or mother. So Mordecai took care of her. Hadassah was also called Esther, and she had a very pretty figure and face. Mordecai had adopted her as his own daughter when her father and mother died.

⁸The king's command and order had been heard. And many girls had been brought to the palace in Susa. They had been put under the care of Hegai. When this happened, Esther was also taken to the king's palace. She was put into the care of Hegai, who was in charge of the women. ⁹Esther pleased Hegai, and he liked her. So Hegai quickly began giving Esther her beauty treatments and special food. He gave her seven servant girls chosen from the king's palace. Then Hegai moved Esther and her seven servant girls to the best part of the women's quarters.

¹⁰Esther did not tell anyone about her family or who her people were. Mordecai had told her not to. ¹¹Every day Mordecai walked back and forth near the courtyard. This was where the king's women lived. He wanted to find out how Esther was and what was happening to her.

¹²Before a girl could take her turn with King Xerxes, she had to complete 12 months of beauty treatments. These were ordered for the women. For 6 months she was treated with oil and myrrh. And she spent 6 months with perfumes and cosmetics. ¹³Then she was ready to go to the king. Anything she asked for was given to her. She could take it with her from the women's quarters to the king's palace. ¹⁴In the evening she would go to the king's palace. And in the morning she would return to another part of the women's quarters. There she would be placed under the care of a man named Shaashgaz. Shaashgaz was the king's eunuch in charge of the slave women. The girl would not go back to the king again unless he was pleased with her.

Then he would call her by name to come back to him.

[15]Esther daughter of Abihail, Mordecai's uncle, had been adopted by Mordecai. The time came for Esther to go to the king. She asked for only what Hegai suggested she should take. (Hegai was the king's eunuch who was in charge of the women.) And everyone who saw Esther liked her. [16]So Esther was taken to King Xerxes in the royal palace. This happened in the tenth month, the month of Tebeth. It was in Xerxes' seventh year as king.

[17]And the king was pleased with Esther more than with any of the other virgins. And he liked her more than any of the others. So King Xerxes put a royal crown on Esther's head. And he made her queen in place of Vashti. [18]Then the king gave a great banquet for Esther. He invited all his important men and royal officers. He announced a holiday in all the empire. And he was generous and gave everyone a gift.

MORDECAI DISCOVERS AN EVIL PLAN

[19]Now Mordecai was sitting at the king's gate. This was when the virgins were gathered the second time. [20]And Esther had still not told anyone about her family or who her people were. That is what Mordecai had told her to do. She still obeyed Mordecai just as she had done when he was bringing her up.

[21]Now Bigthana and Teresh were two of the king's officers who guarded the doorway. While Mordecai was sitting at the king's gate, Bigthana and Teresh became angry at the king. And they began to make plans to kill King Xerxes. [22]But Mordecai found out about their plans and told Queen Esther. Then Queen Esther told the king. She also told him that Mordecai had found out about the evil plan. [23]When the report was investigated, it was found to be true. The two officers who had planned to kill the king were hanged. And all this was written down

in the daily court record in the king's presence.

HAMAN PLANS TO DESTROY THE JEWS

3 After these things happened, King Xerxes honored Haman son of Hammedatha the Agagite. He gave Haman a new rank that was higher than all the important men. [2]And all the royal officers at the king's gate would bow down and kneel before Haman. This was what the king had ordered. But Mordecai would not bow down, and he did not kneel.

[3]Then the royal officers at the king's gate asked Mordecai, "Why don't you obey the king's command?" [4]And they said this to him every day. When he did not listen to them, they told Haman about it. They wanted to see if Haman would accept Mordecai's behavior because Mordecai had told them that he was a Jew.

[5]Then Haman saw that Mordecai would not bow down to him or kneel before him. And he became very angry. [6]He had been told who the people of Mordecai were. And he thought of himself as too important to try to kill only Mordecai. So he looked for a way to destroy all of Mordecai's people, the Jews, in all of Xerxes' kingdom.

[7]It was in the first month of the twelfth year of King Xerxes' rule. That is the month of Nisan. Pur (that is, the lot) was thrown before Haman. The lot was used to choose a day and a month. So the twelfth month, the month of Adar, was chosen.

[8]Then Haman said to King Xerxes, "There is a certain group of people in all the areas of your kingdom. They are scattered among the other people. They keep themselves separate. Their customs are different from those of all the other people. And they do not obey the king's laws. It is not right for you to allow them to continue living in your kingdom. [9]If it pleases the king, let an order be given to destroy those people.

Then I will pay 375 tons of silver to those who do the king's business. They will put it into the royal treasury."

[10]So the king took his signet ring off and gave it to Haman. Haman son of Hammedatha, the Agagite, was the enemy of the Jews. [11]Then the king said to Haman, "The money and the people are yours. Do with them as you please."

[12]On the thirteenth day of the first month, the royal secretaries were called. They wrote out all of Haman's orders. They wrote to the king's governors and to the captains of the soldiers in each area. And they wrote to the important men of each group of people. The orders were written to each area in its own form of writing. And they were written to each group of people in their own language. They were written in the name of King Xerxes and sealed with his signet ring. [13]Letters were sent by messengers to all the king's empire. They stated the king's order to destroy, kill and completely wipe out all the Jews. That meant young and old, women and little children, too. The order said to kill all the Jews on a single day. That was to be the thirteenth day of the twelfth month, which was Adar. And it said to take all the things that belonged to the Jews. [14]A copy of the order was to be given out as a law in every area. It was to be made known to all the people so that they would be ready for that day.

[15]The messengers set out, hurried by the king's command. At the same time the order was given in the palace at Susa. And the king and Haman sat down to drink. But the city of Susa was in confusion.

MORDECAI ASKS ESTHER TO HELP

4 Now Mordecai heard about all that had been done. To show how upset he was, he tore his clothes. Then he put on rough cloth and ashes. And he went out into the city crying loudly and very sadly. [2]But Mordecai went only as far as the king's gate. This was because no one was allowed to enter that gate dressed in rough cloth. [3]The king's order reached every area. And there was great sadness and loud crying among the Jews. They gave up eating and cried out loudly. Many Jews lay down on rough cloth and ashes to show how sad they were.

[4]Esther's servant girls and eunuchs came to her and told her about Mordecai. Esther was very upset and afraid. She sent clothes for Mordecai to put on instead of the rough cloth. But he would not wear them. [5]Then Esther called for Hathach. He was one of the king's eunuchs chosen by the king to serve her. Esther ordered him to find out what was bothering Mordecai and why.

[6]So Hathach went to Mordecai. Mordecai was in the city square in front of the king's gate. [7]Then Mordecai told Hathach everything that had happened to him. And he told Hathach about the amount of money Haman had promised to pay into the king's treasury for the killing of the Jews. [8]Mordecai also gave him a copy of the order to kill the Jews, which had been given in Susa. He wanted Hathach to show it to Esther and to tell her about it. And Mordecai told him to order Esther to go into the king's presence. He wanted her to beg for mercy and to plead with him for her people.

[9]Hathach went back and reported to Esther everything Mordecai had said. [10]Then Esther told Hathach to say to Mordecai, [11]"All the royal officers and people of the royal areas know this: No man or woman may go to the king

> King Xerxes put a royal crown on Esther's head. And he made her queen.
> —ESTHER 2:17

☆ Esther 4:14

After the death of her parents, a young Jewish girl named Esther was raised by her relative, Mordecai. Even though they lived in a nation that did not worship God, Mordecai taught Esther to love and obey God. When the king was looking for a wife, God made Esther stand out above all the women in the land. The king chose her, and Esther became queen. When Mordecai found out about a wicked plan to kill the Jews, he urged Esther to beg the king for mercy. Esther was afraid because no one visited the king without being invited. But Mordecai knew that God chose Esther for this very time—so God could save their people.

Anya felt weird being the only person in her school who could speak German. Her parents were born in Germany and taught Anya their language and English. Some of Anya's friends told her she sounded funny even when she spoke in English. Anya felt embarrassed that she did not talk like the other kids. She asked God why he made her this way. One day, Anya's teacher introduced her to a new boy named Ben. Ben said, "Hallo." Anya gasped—German! Ben just moved from Germany and did not speak English. He needed help. Anya thought of her prayer and smiled. God showed her why he made her that way. It was exactly for a day like this.

• •

If you ever feel out of place, ask God to show you why he has you there. You might be there for a very special reason.

in the inner courtyard without being called. There is only one law about this. Anyone who enters must be put to death. But if the king holds out his gold scepter, that person may live. And I have not been called to go to the king for 30 days."

[12] And Esther's message was given to Mordecai. [13] Then Mordecai gave orders to say to Esther: "Just because you live in the king's palace, don't think that out of all the Jews you alone will escape. [14] You might keep quiet at this time. Then someone else will help and

save the Jews. But you and your father's family will all die. And who knows, you may have been chosen queen for just such a time as this."

¹⁵Then Esther sent this answer to Mordecai: ¹⁶"Go and get all the Jews in Susa together. For my sake, give up eating. Do not eat or drink for three days, night and day. I and my servant girls will also give up eating. Then I will go to the king, even though it is against the law. And if I die, I die."

¹⁷So Mordecai went away. He did everything Esther had told him to do.

ESTHER SPEAKS TO THE KING

5 On the third day Esther put on her royal robes. Then she stood in the inner courtyard of the king's palace, facing the king's hall. The king was sitting on his royal throne in the hall, facing the doorway. ²The king saw Queen Esther standing in the courtyard. When he saw her, he was very pleased. He held out to her the gold scepter that was in his hand. So Esther went up to him and touched the end of the scepter.

³Then the king asked, "What is it, Queen Esther? What do you want to ask me? I will give you as much as half of my kingdom."

⁴Esther answered, "My king, if it pleases you, come today with Haman to a banquet. I have prepared it for you."

⁵Then the king said, "Bring Haman quickly so we may do what Esther asks."

So the king and Haman went to the banquet Esther had prepared for them. ⁶As they were drinking wine, the king said to Esther, "Now, Esther, what are you asking for? I will give it to you. What is it you want? I will give you as much as half of my kingdom."

⁷Esther answered, "This is what I want and ask for. ⁸My king, I hope you are pleased with me. If it pleases you, give me what I ask for and do what I want. Come with Haman tomorrow to the banquet I will prepare for you. Then I will answer your question about what I want."

HAMAN'S PLANS AGAINST MORDECAI

⁹Haman left the king's palace that day happy and content. Then he saw Mordecai at the king's gate. And he saw that Mordecai did not stand up nor did he tremble with fear before him. So Haman became very angry with Mordecai. ¹⁰But he controlled his anger and went home.

Then Haman called his friends and Zeresh, his wife, together. ¹¹And he told them about how wealthy he was and how many sons he had. He also told them about all the ways the king had honored him. And he told them how the king had placed him higher than his important men and his royal officers. ¹²"And that's not all," Haman added. "I'm the only person Queen Esther invited to come with the king to the banquet she gave. And tomorrow also the queen has asked me to be her guest with the king. ¹³But all this does not really make me happy. I'm not happy as long as I see that Jew Mordecai sitting at the king's gate."

¹⁴Then Haman's wife Zeresh and all his friends said, "Have a platform built to hang someone. Build it 75 feet high. And in the morning ask the king to have Mordecai hanged on it. Then go to the banquet with the king and be happy." Haman liked this suggestion. So he ordered the platform to be built.

MORDECAI IS HONORED

6 That same night the king could not sleep. So he gave an order for the daily court record to be brought in and read to him. ²And it was found recorded that Mordecai had warned the king about Bigthana and Teresh. These men had planned to kill the king. They were two of the king's officers who guarded the doorway.

³Then the king asked, "What honor and reward have been given to Mordecai for this?"

The king's personal servants answered, "Nothing has been done for Mordecai."

[4]The king said, "Who is in the courtyard?" Now Haman had just entered the outer court of the king's palace. He had come to ask the king about hanging Mordecai on the platform he had prepared.

[5]The king's personal servants said, "Haman is standing in the courtyard."

So the king said, "Bring him in."

[6]So Haman came in. And the king asked him, "What should be done for a man that the king wants very much to honor?"

And Haman thought to himself, "Whom would the king want to honor more than me?" [7]So he answered the king, "This is what you could do for the man you want very much to honor. [8]Have the servants bring a royal robe that the king himself has worn. And also bring a horse with a royal crown on its head. The horse should be one the king himself has ridden. [9]Then let the robe and the horse be given to one of the king's most important men. Let the servants put the robe on the man the king wants very much to honor. And let them lead him on the horse through the city streets. As they are leading him, let them announce: 'This is what is done for the man the king wants very much to honor!'"

[10]The king commanded Haman, "Go quickly. Take the robe and the horse just as you have said. And do all this for Mordecai the Jew who sits at the king's gate. Do not leave out anything that you have suggested."

[11]So Haman took the robe and the horse. And he put the robe on Mordecai. Then he led him on horseback through the city streets. Haman announced before Mordecai: "This is what is done for the man the king wants very much to honor!"

[12]Then Mordecai went back to the king's gate. But Haman hurried home with his head covered. He was embarrassed and ashamed. [13]He told his wife Zeresh and all his friends everything that had happened to him.

Haman's wife and the men who gave him advice said, "You are starting to lose power to Mordecai. Since he is a Jew, you cannot win against him. You will surely be ruined." [14]While they were still talking, the king's eunuchs came to Haman's house. They made Haman hurry to the banquet Esther had prepared.

HAMAN IS HANGED

7 So the king and Haman went in to eat with Queen Esther. [2]They were drinking wine. And the king said to Esther on this second day also, "What are you asking for? I will give it to you. What is it you want? I will give you as much as half of my kingdom."

[3]Then Queen Esther answered, "My king, I hope you are pleased with me. If it pleases you, let me live. This is what I ask. And let my people live, too. This is what I want. [4]I ask this because my people and I have been sold to be destroyed. We are to be killed and completely wiped out. If we had been sold as male and female slaves, I would have kept quiet. That would not be enough of a problem to bother the king."

[5]Then King Xerxes asked Queen Esther, "Who is he? Where is he? Who has done such a thing?"

[6]Esther said, "A man who is against us! Our enemy is this wicked Haman!"

Then Haman was filled with terror before the king and queen. [7]The king was very angry. He got up, left his wine and went out into the palace garden. But Haman stayed inside to beg Queen Esther to save his life. He could see that the king had already decided to kill him.

[8]The king came back from the palace garden to the banquet hall. And he saw Haman falling on the couch where Esther was lying. The king said, "Will he even attack the queen while I am in the house?"

As soon as the king said that, servants came in and covered Haman's face. [9]Harbona was one of the eunuchs there serving the king. He said, "Look, a platform for hanging people stands near Haman's house. It is 75 feet high. This is the one Haman had prepared for Mordecai, who gave the warning that saved the king."

The king said, "Hang Haman on it!" [10]So they hanged Haman on the platform he had prepared for Mordecai. Then the king was not so angry anymore.

THE KING HELPS THE JEWS

8 That same day King Xerxes gave Queen Esther everything Haman had left when he died. Haman had been the enemy of the Jews. And Mordecai came in to see the king. He came because Esther had told the king how he was related to her. [2]Then the king took off his signet ring, which he had taken back from Haman. And he gave it to Mordecai. Then Esther put Mordecai in charge of everything Haman had left when he died.

[3]Once again Esther spoke to the king. She fell at the king's feet and cried. She begged the king to stop the evil plan of Haman the Agagite. Haman had thought up the plan against the Jews. [4]The king held out the gold scepter to Esther. Esther got up and stood in front of the king.

[5]She said, "My king, I hope you are pleased with me. And maybe it will please you to do this. You might think it is the right thing to do. And maybe you are happy with me. If so, let an order be written to cancel the letters Haman wrote. [6]I could not stand to see that terrible thing happen to my people. I could not stand to see my family killed."

[7]King Xerxes answered Queen Esther and Mordecai the Jew. He said, "Because Haman was against the Jews, I have given his things to Esther. And my soldiers have hanged him. [8]Now write another order in the king's name. Write it to the Jews as it seems best to you. Then seal the order with the king's signet ring. No letter written in the king's name and sealed with his signet ring can be canceled."

[9]At that time the king's secretaries were called. This was done on the twenty-third day of the third month, which is Sivan. The secretaries wrote out all of Mordecai's orders. They wrote to the Jews and to the governors and to the captains of the soldiers in each area. And they wrote to the important men of the 127 areas which reached from India to Cush. They wrote to each area in its own form of writing. And they wrote to each group of people in their own language. They also wrote to the Jews in their own form of writing and their own language. [10]Mordecai wrote orders in the name of King Xerxes. And he sealed the letters with the king's signet ring. Then he sent the king's orders by messengers on horses. The messengers rode fast horses, which were raised just for the king.

[11]These were the king's orders: The Jews in every city have the right to gather together to protect themselves. They have the right to destroy, kill and completely wipe out the army of any area or people who attack them. And they are to do the same to the women and children of that army. The Jews also have the right to take by force the property of the enemies. [12]The one day set for the Jews to do this was the thirteenth day of the twelfth month. This was the month of Adar. They were allowed to do this in all the empire of King Xerxes. [13]A copy of the king's order was to be sent out as a law in every area. It was to be made known to the people of every nation living in the kingdom. This was so the Jews would be ready on that set day. The Jews would be allowed to pay back their enemies.

[14]The messengers hurried out, riding on the royal horses. The king commanded those messengers to hurry. And the order was also given in the palace at Susa.

[15]Mordecai left the king's presence wearing royal clothes. They were blue

and white. And he had on a large gold crown. He also had a purple robe made of the best linen. And the people of Susa shouted for joy. ¹⁶It was a time of happiness, joy, gladness and honor for the Jews. ¹⁷The king's order went to every area and city. And there was joy and gladness among the Jews. This happened in every area and city to which the king's order went. The Jews were having feasts and celebrating. And many people through all the empire became Jews. They did that because they were afraid of the Jews.

VICTORY FOR THE JEWS

9 The order the king had commanded was to be done on the thirteenth day of the twelfth month. That was the month of Adar. That was the day the enemies of the Jews had hoped to defeat them. But that was changed. So the Jews themselves defeated those who hated them. ²The Jews met in their cities in all the empire of King Xerxes. They met in order to attack those who wanted to harm them. And no one was strong enough to fight against them. This was because all the other people living in the empire were afraid of the Jews. ³And all the important men of the areas, the governors, captains of the soldiers, and the king's officers helped the Jews. They helped because they were afraid of Mordecai. ⁴Mordecai was very important in the king's palace. He was famous in all the empire. This was because he was becoming a leader of more and more people.

⁵And, with their swords, the Jews defeated all their enemies, killing and destroying them. And the Jews did what they wanted with those people who hated them. ⁶In the palace at Susa, they killed and destroyed 500 men. ⁷They also killed these men: Parshandatha, Dalphon, Aspatha, ⁸Poratha, Adalia, Aridatha, ⁹Parmashta, Arisai, Aridai and Vaizatha. ¹⁰They were the ten sons of Haman, son of Hammedatha, the

enemy of the Jews. But the Jews did not take their belongings.

¹¹And on that day the number of the men killed in the palace at Susa was reported to the king. ¹²The king said to Queen Esther, "The Jews have killed and destroyed 500 men in the palace at Susa. And they have also killed Haman's ten sons. What have they done in the rest of the king's empire! Now what else are you asking? I will do it! And what else do you want? It will be done."

¹³Esther answered, "If it pleases the king, give the Jews who are in Susa permission to do this. Let them do again tomorrow what the king ordered for today. And let the bodies of Haman's ten sons be hanged on the platform built for hanging people to death."

¹⁴So the king ordered that it be done. A law was given in Susa, and the bodies of the ten sons of Haman were hanged. ¹⁵The Jews in Susa came together. It was on the fourteenth day of the month of Adar. And they killed 300 men in Susa. But they did not take their belongings.

¹⁶At that same time, the other Jews in the king's empire also met. They met in order to protect themselves and get rid of their enemies. And they killed 75,000 of those who hated them. But they did not take their belongings. ¹⁷This happened on the thirteenth day of the month of Adar. And on the fourteenth day the Jews rested. They made it a day of joyful feasting.

THE FEAST OF PURIM

¹⁸But the Jews in Susa met on the thirteenth and fourteenth days of the month of Adar. Then they rested on the fifteenth day. They made it a day of joyful feasting.

¹⁹This is why the Jews who live in the country and small villages celebrate on the fourteenth day. They keep the fourteenth day of the month of Adar as a day of joyful feasting. And it is also a day for giving presents to each other.

²⁰Mordecai wrote down everything that had happened. Then he sent letters

to all the Jews in all the empire of King Xerxes. He sent letters to places far and near. ²¹Mordecai did this to have the Jews celebrate every year. They were to celebrate on the fourteenth and fifteenth days of the month of Adar. ²²It was to celebrate a time when the Jews got rid of their enemies. They were also to celebrate it as the month their sadness was turned to joy. It was the month when their crying for the dead was turned into celebration. Mordecai wrote letters to all the Jews. He wrote to tell them to celebrate those days as days of joyful feasting. It was to be a time of giving food to each other. And it was a time of giving presents to the poor.

²³So the Jews agreed to do what Mordecai had written to them. And they agreed to hold the celebration every year. ²⁴Haman son of Hammedatha, the Agagite, was the enemy of all the Jews. He had made an evil plan against the Jews to destroy them. And Haman had thrown the pur (that is, the lot) to choose a day to ruin and destroy the Jews. ²⁵But when the king learned of the evil plan, he sent out written orders. This was so the evil plans Haman had made against the Jews would be used against him. And those orders said that Haman and his sons should be hanged on the platform for hanging. ²⁶So these days were called Purim. The name Purim comes from the word "pur" (the lot). ²⁷And so the Jews set up this custom. They and their

☆ Esther 10:3

Mordecai became very important in the land. The other Jews respected and liked him. He was kind and worked hard for his people all the days of his life.

It is important to God that we are kind. He wants us to be kind, and He also wants us to teach others to be kind. If you see boys or girls being mean to someone or not playing with that person, you should be kind and be their friend. The other kids will see how important it is to be nice. You can be the one who is kind, and others will watch you and act the same.

. . . .

Remember that God is always kind to us. Knowing this helps us to be kind to others.

descendants would celebrate these two days every year. The Jews and all those who join them are to celebrate these two days. They should do it without fail every year. They should do it in the right way and at the time Mordecai had ordered them in the letter. ²⁸These two days should be remembered and celebrated from now on in every family. And they must be celebrated in every area and every city. These days of Purim should never stop being celebrated by the Jews. And the descendants of the Jews should always remember to celebrate these two days of Purim.

²⁹So Queen Esther daughter of Abihail, along with Mordecai the Jew, wrote this second letter about Purim. Using the power they had, they wrote to prove the first letter was true. ³⁰And Mordecai sent letters to all the Jews in the 127 areas of the kingdom of Xerxes. Mordecai wrote a message of peace and truth. ³¹He wrote to set up these days of Purim. They are to be celebrated at their chosen times. Mordecai the Jew and Queen Esther had sent out the order for the Jews. They had set up

for themselves and their descendants these two days. They set them up so the Jews would give up eating and cry loudly. ³²Esther's letter showed that these practices about Purim were correct. They were written down in the records.

THE GREATNESS OF MORDECAI

10 King Xerxes made people pay taxes. Even the cities far away on the seacoast had to pay taxes. ²And all the great things that Xerxes did are written down. They tell of his power and strength. They are written in the record books of the kings of Media and Persia. Also written in those record books are all the things that Mordecai did. The king had made Mordecai a great man. ³Mordecai the Jew was second in importance to King Xerxes. He was the most important man among the Jews. And his fellow Jews respected him very much. They respected Mordecai because he worked for the good of his people. And they respected him because he spoke up for the safety of all the Jews.

Daniel

DANIEL TAKEN TO BABYLON

1 Nebuchadnezzar king of Babylon came to Jerusalem and surrounded it with his army. This happened during the third year that Jehoiakim was king of Judah. ²The Lord allowed Nebuchadnezzar to capture Jehoiakim king of Judah. Nebuchadnezzar also took some of the things from the Temple of God. He carried them to Babylonia and put them in the temple of his gods.

³Then King Nebuchadnezzar gave an order to Ashpenaz, his chief officer. He told Ashpenaz to bring some of the men from Judah into his house. He wanted them to be from important families. And he wanted those who were from the family of the king of Judah. ⁴King Nebuchadnezzar wanted only healthy, young, Israelite men. These men were not to have anything wrong with their bodies. They were to be handsome and well educated. They were to be able to learn and understand things. He wanted those who were able to serve in his palace. Ashpenaz was to teach them the language and writings of the Babylonians. ⁵The king gave the young men a certain amount of food and wine every day. That was the same kind of food that the king ate. They were to be trained for three years. Then the young men would become servants of the king of Babylon. ⁶Among those young men were some from the people of Judah. These were Daniel, Hananiah, Mishael and Azariah.

⁷Then Ashpenaz, the chief officer, gave them Babylonian names. Daniel's new name was Belteshazzar. Hananiah's was Shadrach. Mishael's was Meshach. And Azariah's new name was Abednego.

⁸Daniel decided not to eat the king's food and wine because that would make him unclean. So he asked Ashpenaz for permission not to make himself unclean in this way.

⁹God made Ashpenaz want to be kind and merciful to Daniel. ¹⁰But Ashpenaz said to Daniel, "I am afraid of my master, the king. He ordered me to give you this food and drink. If you don't eat this food, you will begin to look worse than other young men your age. The king will see this. And he will cut off my head because of you."

¹¹Ashpenaz had ordered a guard to watch Daniel, Hananiah, Mishael and Azariah. ¹²Daniel said to the guard, "Please give us this test for ten days: Don't give us anything but vegetables to eat and water to drink. ¹³Then after ten days compare us with the other young men who eat the king's food. See for yourself who looks healthier. Then you judge for yourself how you want to treat us, your servants."

¹⁴So the guard agreed to test them for ten days. ¹⁵After ten days they looked very healthy. They looked better than all of the young men who ate the king's food. ¹⁶So the guard took away the king's special food and wine. He gave Daniel, Hananiah, Mishael and Azariah vegetables instead.

¹⁷God gave these four men wisdom and the ability to learn. They learned many kinds of things people had written and studied. Daniel could also understand all kinds of visions and dreams.

¹⁸The end of the three years came. And Ashpenaz brought all of the young men to King Nebuchadnezzar. ¹⁹The king talked to them. He found that none of the young men were as good as Daniel, Hananiah, Mishael and Azariah. So those four young men became the king's servants. ²⁰Every time the king asked them about something important, they showed much wisdom and understanding. He found they were ten

times better than all the fortune-tellers and magicians in his kingdom. ²¹So Daniel continued to be the king's servant until the first year Cyrus was king.

NEBUCHADNEZZAR'S DREAM

2 During Nebuchadnezzar's second year as king, he had some dreams. Those dreams bothered him, and he could not sleep. ²So the king called for his fortune-tellers, magicians, wizards and wise men. The king wanted those men to tell him what he had dreamed. So they came in and stood in front of the king.

³Then the king said to them, "I had a dream that bothers me. I want to know what the dream means."

⁴Then the wise men answered the king in the Aramaic language. They said, "Our king, live forever! We are your servants. Please tell us your dream. Then we will tell you what it means."

⁵Then King Nebuchadnezzar said to them, "No! You must tell me the dream. And then you must tell me what it means. If you don't do these things, I will have you torn apart. And I will turn your houses into piles of stones. ⁶But if you tell me my dream and its meaning, I will reward you. I will give you gifts and great honor. So tell me the dream, and tell me what it means."

⁷Again the wise men said to the king, "Please, tell us the dream. And we will tell you what it means."

⁸King Nebuchadnezzar answered, "Now I know that you are trying to get more time. You know that I meant what I said. ⁹If you don't tell me my dream, you will be punished. You have all agreed to tell me lies and wicked things. You are hoping things will change. Now, tell me the dream. Then I will know you can tell me what it really means!"

¹⁰The wise men answered the king. They said, "No one on earth can do what the king asks! Not even a great and powerful king has ever asked the fortune-tellers, magicians or wise men to do this. ¹¹The king is asking something that is too hard. Only the gods could tell the king this. But the gods do not live among people."

¹²When the king heard that, he became very angry. He gave an order for all the wise men of Babylon to be killed. ¹³So King Nebuchadnezzar's order was announced. All the wise men were to be put to death. Men were sent to look for Daniel and his friends to kill them.

¹⁴Arioch was the commander of the king's guards. He was going to put to death the wise men of Babylon. But Daniel spoke to him with wisdom and skill. ¹⁵Daniel asked, "Why did the king order such a terrible punishment?" Then Arioch explained everything to Daniel. ¹⁶When Daniel heard the story, he went to King Nebuchadnezzar. Daniel asked him to give him some more time. Then he would tell the king what he had dreamed and what it meant.

¹⁷So Daniel went to his house. He explained the whole story to his friends Hananiah, Mishael and Azariah. ¹⁸Daniel asked his friends to pray to the God of heaven. Daniel asked them to pray that God would show them mercy and help them understand this secret. Then Daniel and his friends would not be put to death with the other wise men of Babylon.

¹⁹During the night God explained the secret to Daniel in a vision. Then Daniel praised the God of heaven. ²⁰Daniel said:

"Praise God forever and ever.
  He has wisdom and power.
²¹ He changes the times and seasons of
    the year.
  He takes away the power of kings.
  And he gives their power to new
    kings.
He gives wisdom to people so they
    become wise.
  And he helps people learn and
    know things.
²² He makes known secrets that are
    deep and hidden.

He knows what is hidden in
darkness,
and light lives with him.

²³ I thank you and praise you, God of
my ancestors.
You have given me wisdom and
power.
You told me what we asked of you.
You told us about the king's
dream."

THE MEANING OF THE DREAM

²⁴Then Daniel went to Arioch. King
Nebuchadnezzar had chosen Arioch to
put to death the wise men of Babylon.
Daniel said to Arioch, "Don't put
the wise men of Babylon to
death. Take me to the king.
I will tell him what his
dream means."

²⁵So very quickly
Arioch took Daniel to
the king. Arioch said to
the king, "I have found
a man among the cap-
tives from Judah. He
can tell the king what
his dream means."

²⁶The king asked
Daniel (also called
Belteshazzar) a question.
He asked, "Are you able to
tell me what I dreamed and
what it means?"

²⁷Daniel answered, "No person can
explain to the king the secret he has
asked about. No wise man, magician
or fortune-teller can do this. ²⁸But
there is a God in heaven who explains
secret things. God has shown King
Nebuchadnezzar what will happen at a
later time. This is your dream. This is
the vision you saw while lying on your
bed: ²⁹My king, as you were lying there,
you thought about things to come. God,
who can tell people about secret things,
showed you what is going to happen.
³⁰God also told this secret to me. It is
not because I have greater wisdom than
other men. It is so that you, my king,
may know what it means. In that way

you will understand what went through
your mind.

³¹"My king, in your dream you saw a
large statue in front of you. It was huge,
shiny and frightening. ³²The head of
the statue was made of pure gold. Its
chest and arms were made of silver. Its
middle and the upper part of its legs
were made of bronze. ³³The lower part
of the legs were made of iron. Its feet
were made partly of iron and partly of
baked clay. ³⁴While you were looking at
the statue, you saw a rock cut free. But
no human being touched the rock. It hit
the statue on its feet of iron and clay
and smashed them. ³⁵Then the
iron, clay, bronze, silver and
gold broke to pieces at the
same time. They became
like chaff on a threshing
floor in the summer-
time. The wind blew
them away, and there
was nothing left. Then
the rock that hit the
statue became a very
large mountain. It filled
the whole earth.

³⁶"That was your
dream. Now we will tell
the king what it means.
³⁷My king, you are the
greatest king. God of heaven
has given you a kingdom. He has
given you power, strength and glory.
³⁸God has given you power over people,
wild animals and birds. Wherever they
live, God has made you ruler over them
all. King Nebuchadnezzar, you are the
head of gold on that statue.

³⁹"Another kingdom will come after
you. But that kingdom will not be as
great as yours. Next a third kingdom
will rule over the earth. That is the
bronze part. ⁴⁰Then there will be a
fourth kingdom, strong as iron. Iron
crushes and smashes things to pieces.
In the same way the fourth kingdom
will smash and crush all the other
kingdoms.

⁴¹"You saw that the statue's feet and

> [God]
> gives
> wisdom to
> people so they
> become wise. And
> he helps people
> learn and know
> things.
> –DANIEL 2:21

toes were partly baked clay and partly iron. That means the fourth kingdom will be a divided kingdom. It will have some of the strength of iron in it. As you saw, iron was mixed with clay. [42]The toes of the statue were partly iron and partly clay. So the fourth kingdom will be partly strong like iron and partly breakable like clay. [43]You saw the iron mixed with clay. But iron and clay don't mix completely together. In the same way the people of the fourth kingdom will be a mixture. Those people will not be united as one people.

[44]"During the time of those kings, the God of heaven will set up another kingdom. It will never be destroyed. And it will not be given to another group of people. This kingdom will crush all the other kingdoms. It will bring them to an end. But that kingdom itself will continue forever.

[45]"King Nebuchadnezzar, you saw a rock cut from a mountain. But no human being touched it. The rock broke the iron, bronze, clay, silver and gold to pieces. In this way the great God showed you what will happen. The dream is true, and you can trust this explanation."

[46]Then King Nebuchadnezzar fell facedown on the ground in front of Daniel. The king honored him. He ordered that an offering and incense be presented to Daniel. [47]Then the king said to Daniel, "Truly I know your God is the greatest of all gods. And he is the Lord of all the kings. He tells people about things they cannot know. I know this is true. You were able to tell these secret things to me."

[48]Then the king gave Daniel an important position in his kingdom. And he gave many gifts to Daniel. Nebuchadnezzar made him ruler over the whole area of Babylon. And he put Daniel in charge of all the wise men of Babylon. [49]Daniel asked the king to make Shadrach, Meshach and Abednego important leaders over the area of Babylon. And the king did as Daniel asked. Daniel himself became one of the important people who stayed at the royal court.

THE GOLD IDOL AND BLAZING FURNACE

3 Now King Nebuchadnezzar had a gold statue made. That statue was 90 feet high and 9 feet wide. He set up the statue on the plain of Dura in the area of Babylon. [2]Then the king called the important leaders: the governors, assistant governors, captains of the soldiers, people who advised the king, keepers of the treasury, judges, rulers and all other officers in his kingdom. He wanted these men to come to the special service for the statue he had set up. [3]So they all came for the special service. And they stood in front of the statue that King Nebuchadnezzar had set up. [4]Then the man who made announcements for the king spoke in a loud voice. He said, "People, nations and men of every language, this is what you are commanded to do: [5]You will hear the sound of the horns, flutes, lyres, zithers,[n] harps, pipes and all the other musical instruments. When this happens, you must bow down and worship the gold statue. This is the one King Nebuchadnezzar has set up. [6]Everyone must bow down and worship this gold statue. Anyone who doesn't will be quickly thrown into a blazing furnace."

[7]Now people, nations and men who spoke every language were there. And they heard the sound of the horns, flutes, lyres, zithers, pipes and all the other musical instruments. So they bowed down and worshiped the gold statue that King Nebuchadnezzar had set up.

[8]Then some Babylonians came up to the king. They began speaking against the men of Judah. [9]They said to King Nebuchadnezzar, "Our king, live forever!

3:5 **zithers** Musical instruments with 30 to 40 strings.

¹⁰Our king, you gave a command. You said that everyone would hear the horns, lyres, zithers, harps, pipes and all the other musical instruments. Then they would have to bow down and worship the gold statue. ¹¹Anyone who wouldn't do this was to be thrown into a blazing furnace. ¹²Our king, there are some men of Judah who did not pay attention to your order. You made them important officers in the area of Babylon. Their names are Shadrach, Meshach and Abednego. They do not serve your gods. And they do not worship the gold statue you have set up."

¹³Nebuchadnezzar became very angry. He called for Shadrach, Meshach and Abednego. So those men were brought to the king. ¹⁴And Nebuchadnezzar said, "Shadrach, Meshach and Abednego, is it true that you do not serve my gods? And is it true that you did not worship the gold statue I have set up? ¹⁵Now, you will hear the sound of the horns, flutes, lyres, zithers, harps, pipes and all the other musical instruments. And you must be ready to bow down and worship the statue I made. That will be good. But if you do not worship it, you will be thrown quickly into the blazing furnace. Then no god will be able to save you from my power!"

¹⁶Shadrach, Meshach and Abednego answered the king. They said, "Nebuchadnezzar, we do not need to defend ourselves to you. ¹⁷You can throw us into the blazing furnace. The God we serve is able to save us from the furnace and your power. If he does this, it is good. ¹⁸But even if God does not save us, we want you, our king, to know this: We will not serve your gods. We will not worship the gold statue you have set up."

¹⁹Then Nebuchadnezzar was furious with Shadrach, Meshach and Abednego. He ordered the furnace to be heated seven times hotter than usual. ²⁰Then he commanded some of the strongest soldiers in his army to tie up Shadrach, Meshach and Abednego. The king told the soldiers to throw them into the blazing furnace.

²¹So Shadrach, Meshach and Abednego were tied up and thrown into the blazing furnace. They were still wearing their robes, trousers, turbans and other clothes. ²²The king was very angry when he gave the command. And the furnace was made very hot. The fire was so hot that the flames killed the strong soldiers who took Shadrach, Meshach and Abednego there. ²³Firmly tied, Shadrach, Meshach and Abednego fell into the blazing furnace.

²⁴Then King Nebuchadnezzar was very surprised and jumped to his feet. He asked the men who advised him, "Didn't we tie up only three men? Didn't we throw them into the fire?"

They answered, "Yes, our king."

²⁵The king said, "Look! I see four men. They are walking around in the fire. They are not tied up, and they are not burned. The fourth man looks like a son of the gods."

²⁶Then Nebuchadnezzar went to the opening of the blazing furnace. He shouted, "Shadrach, Meshach and Abednego, come out! Servants of the Most High God, come here!"

So Shadrach, Meshach and Abednego came out of the fire. ²⁷When they came out, the princes, assistant governors, governors and royal advisers crowded around them. They saw that the fire had not harmed their bodies. Their hair was not burned. Their robes were not burned. And they didn't even smell like smoke.

²⁸Then Nebuchadnezzar said, "Praise the God of Shadrach, Meshach and Abednego. Their God has sent his angel and saved his servants from the fire! These three men trusted their God. They refused to obey my command. And they were willing to die rather than serve or worship any god other than their own. ²⁹So I now make this law: The people of any nation or language must not say anything against the God

of Shadrach, Meshach and Abednego. Anyone who does will be torn apart. And his house will be turned into a pile of stones. No other god can save his people like this." ³⁰Then the king promoted Shadrach, Meshach and Abednego in the area of Babylon.

NEBUCHADNEZZAR'S DREAM OF A TREE

4 King Nebuchadnezzar sent a letter. It went to the people, nations and those who speak every language in all the world. The letter said:

I wish you great wealth!

²The Most High God has done miracles and wonderful things for me. I am happy to tell you about these things.

³ The things he has
done are great.
His miracles are
mighty.
His kingdom
continues forever.
His rule will continue
for all time.

⁴I, Nebuchadnezzar, was at my palace. I was happy and successful. ⁵I had a dream that made me afraid. As I was lying on my bed, I saw pictures and visions in my mind. Those things made me very afraid. ⁶So I gave an order. All the wise men of Babylon were to be brought to me. I wanted them to tell me what my dream meant. ⁷The fortune-tellers, magicians and wise men came. I told them about the dream. But those men could not tell me what it meant. ⁸Finally, Daniel came to me. (I called him Belteshazzar to honor my god. The spirit of the holy gods is in him.) I told my dream to Daniel. ⁹I said, "Belteshazzar, you are the most important of all the fortune-tellers. I know that the spirit of the holy gods is in you. I know there is no secret that is too hard for you to understand. This was what I dreamed. Tell me what it means. ¹⁰These are the visions I saw while I was lying in my bed: I looked, and there in front of me was a tree. It was standing in the middle of the earth. The tree was very tall. ¹¹The tree grew large and strong. The top of the tree touched the sky. It could be seen from anywhere on earth. ¹²The leaves of the tree were beautiful. It had plenty of good fruit on it. On the tree was food for everyone. The wild animals found shelter under the tree. And the birds lived in its branches. Every animal ate from it.

¹³"I was looking at those things in the vision while lying on my bed. And then I saw a holy angel coming down from heaven. ¹⁴He spoke very loudly. He said, 'Cut down the tree, and cut off its branches. Strip off its leaves. Scatter its fruit around. Let the animals that are under the tree run away. Let the birds that were in its branches fly away. ¹⁵But let the stump and its roots stay in the ground. Put a band of iron and bronze around it. Let it stay in the field with the grass around it.

"'Let the man become wet with dew. Let him live among the animals and plants of the earth. ¹⁶Let him not think like a man any longer. Let him have the mind of an animal for seven years.

¹⁷"'Messengers gave this command. The holy ones declared the sentence. This is so all the people may know that the Most High God rules over the kingdoms of men. God gives those kingdoms to anyone he

> The Most High God has done miracles and wonderful things for me.
> –DANIEL 4:2

wants. And he chooses people to rule them who are not proud.'

18"That is what I, King Nebuchadnezzar, dreamed. Now Daniel, called Belteshazzar, tell me what the dream means. None of the wise men in my kingdom can explain it to me. But you can, because the spirit of the holy gods is in you."

DANIEL EXPLAINS THE DREAM

19Then Daniel (also called Belteshazzar) was very quiet for a while. His thoughts made him afraid. So the king said, "Belteshazzar, do not let the dream or its meaning make you afraid."

Then Daniel, called Belteshazzar, answered the king. He said, "My master, I wish the dream were about your enemies. And I wish its meaning were for those who are against you! 20You saw a tree in your dream. The tree grew large and strong. Its top touched the sky. It could be seen from all over the earth. 21Its leaves were beautiful, and it had plenty of fruit. The fruit gave food for everyone. It was a home for the wild animals. And its branches were nesting places for the birds. That is the tree you saw. 22My king, you are that tree! You have become great and powerful. You are like the tall tree that touched the sky. And your power reaches to the far parts of the earth.

23"My king, you saw a holy angel coming down from heaven. He said, 'Cut down the tree and destroy it. But leave the stump and its roots in the ground. Put a band of iron and bronze around it. Leave it in the field with the grass. Let him become wet with dew. He will live like a wild animal for seven years.'

24"This is the meaning of the dream, my king. The Most High God has commanded these things to happen to my master the king: 25You will be forced away from people. You will live among the wild animals. People will feed you grass like an ox. And dew from the sky will make you wet. Seven years will pass, and then you will learn this lesson: The Most High God is ruler over the kingdoms of men. And the Most High God gives those kingdoms to anyone he wants.

26"The stump of the tree and its roots were to be left in the ground. This means your kingdom will be given back to you. This will happen when you learn that heaven rules your kingdom. 27So, my king, please accept my advice. I advise you to stop sinning and do what is right. Stop doing wicked things and be kind to poor people. Then you might continue to be successful."

THE KING'S DREAM COMES TRUE

28All these things happened to King Nebuchadnezzar. 29Twelve months after the dream, King Nebuchadnezzar was walking on the roof[n] of his palace in Babylon. 30And he said, "Look at Babylon. I built this great city. It is my palace. I built this great place by my power to show how great I am."

31The words were still in his mouth when a voice came from heaven. The voice said, "King Nebuchadnezzar, these things will happen to you: Your royal power has been taken away from you. 32You will be forced away from people. You will live with the wild animals. You will be fed grass like an ox. Seven years will pass before you learn this lesson: The Most High God rules over the kingdoms of men. And the Most High God gives those kingdoms to anyone he wants."

33Those things happened quickly. Nebuchadnezzar was forced to go away from people. He began eating

---

4:29 roof In Bible times houses were built with flat roofs. The roof was used for drying things such as flax and fruit. And it was used as an extra room, as a place for worship and as a place to sleep in the summer.

grass like an ox. He became wet from dew. His hair grew long like the feathers of an eagle. And his nails grew long like the claws of a bird.

³⁴Then at the end of that time, I, Nebuchadnezzar, looked up toward heaven. And I could think correctly again. Then I gave praise to the Most High God. I gave honor and glory to him who lives forever.

God's rule is forever.
His kingdom continues for all time.
³⁵ People on earth
are not truly important.
God does what he wants
with the powers of heaven
and the people on earth.
No one can stop his powerful hand.
No one can question the things he does.

³⁶So, at that time I could think correctly again. And God gave back my great honor and power as king. The people who advise me and the royal family came to me for help again. I became king again. And I became even greater and more powerful than before. ³⁷Now I, Nebuchadnezzar, give praise and honor and glory to the King of heaven. Everything he does is right. He is always fair. And he is able to make proud people humble.

THE WRITING ON THE WALL

5 King Belshazzar gave a big banquet for 1,000 royal guests. And he drank wine with them. ²As Belshazzar was drinking his wine, he gave an order to his servants. He told them to bring the gold and silver cups that his ancestor Nebuchadnezzar had taken from the Temple in Jerusalem. King Belshazzar wanted his royal guests to drink from those cups. He also wanted his wives and his slave women to drink from them. ³So they brought the gold cups. They had been taken from the Temple of God in Jerusalem. And the king and his royal guests, his wives and his slave women drank from them. ⁴As they were drinking, they praised their gods. Those gods were made from gold, silver, bronze, iron, wood and stone.

⁵Then suddenly a person's hand appeared. The fingers wrote words on the plaster on the wall. This was near the lampstand in the royal palace. The king watched the hand as it wrote.

⁶King Belshazzar was very frightened. His face turned white, and his knees knocked together. He could not stand up because his legs were too weak. ⁷The king called for the magicians and wise men to be brought to him. He said to the wise men of Babylon, "I will give a reward to anyone who can read this writing and explain it. I will give him purple clothes fit for a king. I will put a gold chain around his neck. And I will make him the third highest ruler in the kingdom."

⁸So all the king's wise men came in. But they could not read the writing. And they could not tell the king what it meant. ⁹King Belshazzar became even more afraid. His face became even whiter. His royal guests were confused.

¹⁰Then the king's mother came into the banquet room. She had heard the voices of the king and his royal guests. She said, "My king, live forever! Don't be afraid! Don't let your face be white with fear! ¹¹There is a man in your kingdom who has the spirit of the holy gods in him. In the days of your father, this man showed understanding, knowledge and wisdom. He was like the gods in these things. Your father, King Nebuchadnezzar, put this man in charge of all the wise men. He ruled over all the fortune-tellers, magicians and wise men. ¹²The man I am talking about is named Daniel. The king gave him the name Belteshazzar. He was very wise, and he had knowledge and understanding. He could explain dreams and secrets. He could answer very hard problems. Call for Daniel. He will tell you what the writing on the wall means."

¹³So they brought Daniel to the king. The king said to him, "Is your name Daniel? Are you one of the captives my father the king brought from Judah? ¹⁴I have heard that the spirit of the gods is in you. And I have heard that you are very wise and have knowledge and understanding. ¹⁵The wise men and magicians were brought to me to read this writing on the wall. I wanted those men to explain to me what it means. But they could not explain it. ¹⁶I have heard that you are able to explain what things mean. And you can find the answers to hard problems. Read this writing on the wall and explain it to me. If you can, I will give you purple clothes fit for a king. And I will put a gold chain around your neck. And you will become the third highest ruler in the kingdom."

¹⁷Then Daniel answered the king, "You may keep your gifts for yourself. Or you may give those rewards to someone else. I will read the writing on the wall for you. And I will explain to you what it means.

¹⁸"My king, the Most High God made your father Nebuchadnezzar a great, important and powerful king. ¹⁹God made him very important. So all the people, nations and those who spoke every language were very afraid of Nebuchadnezzar. If he wanted a person to die, he put that person to death. And if he wanted a person to live, he let that person live. If he wanted to promote a person, he promoted him. And if he wanted a person to be unimportant, he made him unimportant.

²⁰"But Nebuchadnezzar became too proud and stubborn. So he was taken off his royal throne. His glory was taken away. ²¹Then Nebuchadnezzar was forced away from people. His mind became like the mind of an animal. He lived with the wild donkeys and was fed grass like an ox. He became wet with dew. These things happened to him until he learned his lesson: The Most High God rules over the kingdoms of men. And the Most High God sets anyone he wants over those kingdoms.

²²"But, Belshazzar, you already knew these things. You are a descendant of Nebuchadnezzar. But still you have not been sorry for what you have done. ²³Instead, you have turned against the Lord of heaven. You ordered the drinking cups from the Temple of the Lord to be brought to you. Then you and your royal guests drank wine from them. Your wives and your slave women also drank wine from them. You praised the gods of silver, gold, bronze, iron, wood and stone. They are not really gods. They cannot see or hear or understand anything. But you did not honor God. He is the One who has power over your life and everything you do. ²⁴So God sent the hand that wrote on the wall.

²⁵"These are the words that were written on the wall: 'Mene, mene, tekel, parsin.'

²⁶"This is what these words mean: Mene: God has counted the days until your kingdom will end. ²⁷Tekel: You have been weighed on the scales and found not good enough. ²⁸Parsin: Your kingdom is being divided. It will be given to the Medes and the Persians."

²⁹Then Belshazzar gave an order for Daniel to be dressed in purple clothes. A gold chain was put around his neck. And he was announced to be the third highest ruler in the kingdom. ³⁰That very same night Belshazzar, king of the Babylonian people, was killed. ³¹A man named Darius the Mede became the new king. Darius was 62 years old.

DANIEL AND THE LIONS

6 Darius thought it would be a good idea to choose 120 governors. They would rule through all of his kingdom. ²And he chose three men as supervisors over those 120 governors. Daniel was one of these three supervisors. The king set up these men so that he would not be cheated. ³Daniel showed that he could do the work better than the other supervisors and the governors. Because

☆ Daniel 6

Daniel was a Jew who lived in a foreign country. He was a good man, and God showed him a lot of favor. The king of Babylon saw how smart Daniel was and gave him a very important job. Even the kings who came after the first king liked Daniel. But there were some men who hated Daniel. And they began to look for a way to have him killed.

Daniel loved God greatly and prayed to him three times every day. But some wicked men convinced King Darius to make a new law that said people could only pray to the king and not to God—for a whole month. The punishment for breaking the law? That person would be put in a den of lions!

Do you know what Daniel did? He still prayed three times a day. The men saw him and told the king what Daniel was doing. The king put Daniel in the lions' den. Daniel stayed there all night. The next morning, the king yelled, "Daniel, are you alive?" Daniel said, "Yes, God protected me!" God had sent an angel to shut the lions' mouths. Then the king brought Daniel out of the lion's den and said there is no God like Daniel's God.

• •

God protected Daniel from the lions and the wicked men. He will protect you from harm, too, because you are his kid!

of this, the king planned to put Daniel in charge of the whole kingdom. ⁴So the other supervisors and the governors tried to find reasons to accuse Daniel. But he went on doing the business of the government. And they could not find anything wrong with him. So they could not accuse him of doing anything wrong. Daniel was trustworthy. He was not lazy and did not cheat the king. ⁵Finally these men said, "We will never find any reason to accuse Daniel. But we must find something to complain about. It will have to be about the law of his God."

⁶So the supervisors and the governors went as a group to the king. They said: "King Darius, live forever!

7 The supervisors, assistant governors, governors, the people who advise you and the captains of the soldiers have all agreed on something. We think the king should make this law that everyone would have to obey: No one should pray to any god or man except to you, our king. This should be done for the next 30 days. Anyone who doesn't obey will be thrown into the lions' den. 8 Now, our king, make the law. Write it down so it cannot be changed. The laws of the Medes and Persians cannot be canceled." 9 So King Darius made the law and had it written.

10 When Daniel heard that the new law had been written, he went to his house. He went to his upstairs room. The windows of that room opened toward Jerusalem. Three times each day Daniel got down on his knees and prayed. He prayed and thanked God, just as he always had done.

11 Then those men went as a group and found Daniel. They saw him praying and asking God for help. 12 So they went to the king. They talked to him about the law he had made. They said, "Didn't you write a law that says no one may pray to any god or man except you, our king? Doesn't it say that anyone who disobeys during the next 30 days will be thrown into the lions' den?"

The king answered, "Yes, I wrote that law. And the laws of the Medes and Persians cannot be canceled."

13 Then those men spoke to the king. They said, "Daniel is one of the captives from Judah. And he is not paying attention to the law you wrote. Daniel still prays to his God three times every day." 14 The king became very upset when he heard this. He decided he had to save Daniel. He worked until sunset trying to think of a way to save him.

15 Then those men went as a group to the king. They said, "Remember, our king, the law of the Medes and Persians. It says that no law or command given by the king can be changed."

16 So King Darius gave the order. They brought Daniel and threw him into the lions' den. The king said to Daniel, "May the God you serve all the time save you!" 17 A big stone was brought. It was put over the opening of the lions' den. Then the king used his signet ring to put his special seal on the rock. And he used the rings of his royal officers to put their seals on the rock also. This showed that no one could move that rock and bring Daniel out. 18 Then King Darius went back to his palace. He did not eat that night. He did not have any entertainment brought to entertain him. And he could not sleep.

19 The next morning King Darius got up at dawn. He hurried to the lions' den. 20 As he came near the den, he was worried. He called out to Daniel. He said, "Daniel, servant of the living God! Has your God that you always worship been able to save you from the lions?"

21 Daniel answered, "My king, live forever! 22 My God sent his angel to close the lions' mouths. They have not hurt me, because my God knows I am innocent. I never did anything wrong to you, my king."

23 King Darius was very happy. He told his servants to lift Daniel out of the lions' den. So they lifted him out and did not find any injury on him. This was because Daniel had trusted in his God.

24 Then the king gave a command. The men who had accused Daniel were brought to the lions' den and thrown into it. Their wives and children were also thrown into it. The lions grabbed them before they hit the floor of the den. And the lions crushed their bones.

25 Then King Darius wrote a letter. It was to all people and all nations, to those who spoke every language in the world:

I wish you great wealth.

26 I am making a new law. This law is for people in every part of my kingdom. All of you must fear and respect the God of Daniel.

Daniel's God is the living God.
He lives forever.
His kingdom will never be destroyed.
His rule will never end.
27 God rescues and saves people.
God does mighty miracles
in heaven and on earth.
God saved Daniel
from the power of the lions.

28 So Daniel was successful during the time that Darius was king. This was also the time that Cyrus the Persian was king.

DANIEL'S DREAM ABOUT FOUR ANIMALS

7 In Belshazzar's first year as king of Babylon, Daniel had a dream. He saw visions as he was lying on his bed. Daniel wrote down what he had dreamed.

2 Daniel said: "I saw my vision at night. In the vision the wind was blowing from all four directions. These winds made the sea very rough. 3 I saw four huge animals come up from the sea. Each animal was different from the others.

4 "The first animal looked like a lion. But it had wings like an eagle. I watched this animal until its wings were torn off. It was lifted from the ground so that it stood up on two feet like a man. And it was given the mind of a man.

5 "And then I saw a second animal before me. It looked like a bear. It was raised up on one of its sides. And it had three ribs in its mouth between its teeth. It was told, 'Get up and eat all the meat you want!'

6 "After that, I looked, and there before me was another animal. This animal looked like a leopard. And the leopard had four wings on its back. The wings looked like a bird's wings. This animal had four heads. It was given power to rule.

7 "After that, in my vision at night I continued looking. There in front of me was a fourth animal. This animal looked cruel and terrible and very strong. It had large iron teeth. It crushed and ate what it killed. Then it walked on whatever was left. This fourth animal was different from all the animals I had seen before it. It had ten horns.

8 "While I was thinking about the horns, another horn grew up among them. It was a little horn. It had eyes like a person's eyes. It also had a mouth. And the mouth was bragging. The little horn pulled out three of the other horns.

9 "As I looked,
thrones were put in their places.
And God, the Eternal One, sat on
his throne.
His clothes were white like
snow.
And the hair on his head was white
like wool.
His throne was made from fire.
And the wheels of his throne were
blazing with fire.
10 A river of fire was flowing
from in front of him.
Many thousands of angels were
serving him.
Millions of angels stood before
him.
Court was ready to begin.
And the books were opened.

11 "I kept on looking because the little horn was bragging. I kept watching until finally the fourth animal was killed. Its body was destroyed, and it was thrown into the burning fire. 12 (The power and rule of the other animals had been taken from them. But they were permitted to live for a certain period of time.)

13 "In my vision at night I looked. There in front of me was someone who looked like a human being. He was coming with clouds in the sky. He came near God, who has been alive forever. And he was led to God. 14 The one who looked like a human being was given

the power to rule. He was also given glory and royal power. All peoples, nations and men who spoke every language will serve him. His rule will last forever. His kingdom will never be destroyed.

THE MEANING OF THE DREAM

[15]"I, Daniel, was worried. The visions that went through my mind frightened me. [16]I came near one of those standing there. I asked him what all this meant.

"So he told me. He explained to me what these things meant. [17]He said, 'The four great animals are four kingdoms. Those four kingdoms will come from the earth. [18]But the people who belong to the Most High God will receive the power to rule. And they will have the power to rule forever. They will have it from now on.'

[19]"Then I wanted to know what the fourth animal meant. It was different from all the other animals. It was very terrible. It had iron teeth and bronze claws. It was the animal that crushed and ate what it killed. And it walked on whatever was left. [20]I also wanted to know about the ten horns on its head. And I wanted to know about the little horn that grew there. It had pulled out three of the other ten horns. It looked greater than the others. And it had eyes and a mouth that kept bragging. [21]As I watched, the little horn began making war against God's people. And the horn kept killing them [22]until God, who has been alive forever, came. He judged in favor of the people who belong to the Most High God. And the time came for them to receive the power to rule.

[23]"And he explained this to me: 'The fourth animal is a fourth kingdom that will come on the earth. It will be different from all the other kingdoms. It will destroy people all over the world. It will walk on and crush the whole earth. [24]The ten horns are ten kings who will come from this fourth kingdom. After those ten kings are gone, another king will come. He will be different from the kings who ruled before him. He will defeat three of the other kings. [25]This king will say things against the Most High God. And he will hurt and kill God's people. He will try to change times and laws that have already been set. The people that belong to God will be in that king's power for three and one-half years.

[26]"'But the court will decide what should happen. And the power of the king will be taken away. His kingdom will be completely destroyed. [27]Then the people who belong to the Most High God will have the power to rule. They will rule over all the kingdoms under heaven with power and greatness. Their power to rule will last forever. And people from all the other kingdoms will respect and serve them.'

[28]"And that was the end of the dream. I, Daniel, was very afraid. My face became very white from fear. But I kept everything to myself."

DANIEL'S VISION

8 During the third year Belshazzar was king, I saw this vision. This was after the other one. [2]In this vision I saw myself in the capital city of Susa. Susa is in the area of Elam. I was standing by the Ulai River. [3]I looked up, and I saw a male sheep standing beside the river. It had two long horns. But one horn was longer than the other. The long horn was newer than the other horn. [4]I watched the male sheep charge to the west. He also charged to the

> God rescues and saves people. God does mighty miracles in heaven and on earth.
>
> –DANIEL 6:27

north and the south. No animal could stand before him. And none could save another animal from his power. He did whatever he wanted. And he became very powerful.

⁵While I was thinking about this, I saw a male goat come from the west. This goat had one large horn that was easy to see. It was between his eyes. He crossed over the whole earth. But his feet did not touch the ground.

⁶That goat charged the male sheep with the two horns. This was the male sheep I had seen standing by the river. The goat was very angry. ⁷I watched the goat attack the male sheep. It broke the sheep's two horns. The sheep could not stop it. The goat knocked the sheep to the ground. Then the goat walked all over him. No one was able to save the sheep from the goat. ⁸So the male goat became very great. But when he was strong, his big horn broke off. Then four horns grew in place of the one big horn. Those four horns were easy to see. They pointed in four different directions.

⁹Then a little horn grew from one of those four horns. It became very big. It grew to the south and the east and toward the beautiful land of Judah. ¹⁰That little horn grew until it reached to the sky. It even threw some of the army of heaven to the ground. And it walked on them. ¹¹That little horn became very strong against God, the commander of heaven's armies. It stopped the daily sacrifices that were offered to the commander. The place where people worshiped the commander was pulled down. ¹²There was a turning away from God. Because of this the people stopped the daily sacrifices. It was like throwing truth down to the ground. The horn was successful in everything it did.

¹³Then I heard one angel speaking. Another angel asked the first one, "How long will the things in this vision last? The vision is about the daily sacrifices. It is about the turning away from God that brings destruction. It is about the

Temple being pulled down. It is about the army of heaven being walked on."

¹⁴He said to me, "This will happen for 2,300 evenings and mornings. Then the holy place will be repaired."

¹⁵I, Daniel, saw this vision. And I tried to understand what it meant. Then someone who looked like a man suddenly stood before me. ¹⁶And I heard a man's voice calling from the Ulai River: "Gabriel, explain the vision to this man."

¹⁷Gabriel came to where I was standing. When he came close to me, I was very afraid. I bowed facedown on the ground. But Gabriel said to me, "Human being, understand that this vision is about the time of the end."

¹⁸While Gabriel was speaking, I fell into a deep sleep. My face was on the ground. Then he touched me and lifted me to my feet. ¹⁹He said, "Now, I will explain the vision to you. I will tell you what will happen later, in the time of God's anger. Your vision was about the set time of the end.

²⁰"You saw a male sheep with two horns. Those horns are the kings of Media and Persia. ²¹The male goat is the king of Greece. The big horn between its eyes is the first king. ²²After that horn broke, four horns grew in its place. Those four horns are four kingdoms. Those four kingdoms will come from the nation of the first king. But they will not be as strong as the first king.

²³"When the end comes near for those kingdoms, a bold and cruel king will come. This king will tell lies. This will happen when many people have turned against God. ²⁴This king will be very powerful. But his power will not come from himself. He will cause terrible destruction. He will be successful in everything he does. He will destroy powerful people and even God's people. ²⁵This king will use his wisdom to make lies successful. He will think that he is very important. He will destroy many people without warning. He will try to fight even God, the Prince

of princes! But that cruel king will be destroyed. And it will not be human power that destroys him.

²⁶"The vision that has been shown to you about those times is true. But seal up the vision. Those things won't happen for a long time."

²⁷I, Daniel, became very weak. I was sick for several days after that vision. Then I got up and went back to work for the king. But I was very upset about the vision. I didn't understand what it meant.

DANIEL'S PRAYER

9 These things happened during the first year Darius son of Xerxes was king. He was a descendant of the Medes. ²During Darius' first year as king, I, Daniel, was reading the Scriptures. In them I saw what the Lord told Jeremiah. He said Jerusalem would be an empty desert for 70 years.

³Then I turned to the Lord God. I prayed to him and asked him for help. I did not eat any food. To show how sad I was I put on rough cloth and sat in ashes. ⁴I prayed to the Lord my God. I told him about all of my sins. I said, "Lord, you are a great God. You cause fear and wonder. You keep your agreement of love with all who love you and obey your commands.

⁵"But we have sinned and done wrong. We have been wicked and turned against you. We have not obeyed your commands and laws. ⁶We did not listen to your servants, the prophets. They spoke for you to our kings, our leaders and our ancestors. They spoke to all the people of the land.

⁷"Lord, you are good and right. But we are full of shame today. The people of Judah and Jerusalem and all the people of Israel are ashamed. People near and far whom you scattered among many nations are ashamed. We were not loyal to you. ⁸Lord, we are all ashamed. Our kings and leaders and our fathers are ashamed. This is because we have sinned against you.

⁹"But, Lord our God, you show us mercy. You forgive us even though we have turned against you. ¹⁰We have not obeyed the Lord our God. We have not obeyed the teachings he gave us through his servants, the prophets. ¹¹All the people of Israel have disobeyed your teachings. They all have turned away and refused to obey you. So you brought on us the curses and promises of punishment written in the Teachings of Moses, the servant of God. These things have happened to us because we sinned against you.

¹²"God said these things would happen to us and our leaders. And he made them happen. You brought on us a great disaster. Nothing has ever been done here on earth like what was done to Jerusalem. ¹³All this disaster came to us just as it is written in the Teachings of Moses. But we still have not stopped sinning. We still do not pay attention to your truth. ¹⁴The Lord was ready to bring the disaster on us. This is because he is right in everything he does. But we still have not obeyed him.

¹⁵"Lord our God, you used your power and brought us out of Egypt. Because of that, your name is known even today. Lord, we have sinned. We have done wrong. ¹⁶Lord, you do the right things. So do not be angry with Jerusalem. Jerusalem is your city on your holy hill. All this has happened because of our sins and the evil things done by our ancestors. So now people all around insult and make fun of Jerusalem and your people.

¹⁷"Now, our God, hear my prayers. I am your servant. Listen to my prayer for help. Do good things for your holy place that is in ruins. Do this for your sake. ¹⁸My God, pay attention and hear me. Open your eyes and see all the terrible things that have happened to us. See what has happened to the city that is called by your name. We do not ask these things because we are good. We ask because of your mercy. ¹⁹Lord, listen! Lord, forgive! Lord, hear us and do

something! For your sake, don't wait! Your city and your people are called by your name."

GABRIEL'S EXPLANATION

20I was saying those things in my prayer to the Lord, my God. I was confessing my sins and the sins of the people of Israel. I was praying for God's holy hill. 21While I was still praying, Gabriel came to me. Gabriel was the person I had seen in my last vision. He came flying quickly to me about the time of the evening sacrifice. 22Gabriel said to me, "Daniel, I have come to give you wisdom and to help you understand. 23When you first started praying, an answer was given. And I came to tell you, because God loves you very much. So think about the message and understand the vision.

24"God has ordered 490 years for your people and your holy city. These years are ordered for these reasons: to stop people from turning against God; to put an end to sin; to take away evil; to bring in goodness that continues forever; to make the vision and prophecy come true; and to appoint a most holy place.

25"Learn and understand these things. A command will come to rebuild Jerusalem. The time from this command until the appointed leader comes will be 49 years and 434 years. Jerusalem will be rebuilt with streets and a trench around it. But it will be built in times of trouble. 26After the 434 years the appointed leader will be killed. He will have nothing. The people of the leader who is to come will destroy the city. They will also destroy the holy place. That end will come like a flood. War will continue until the end. God has ordered that place to be

completely destroyed. 27That leader will make an agreement with many people for 7 years. He will put a stop to offerings and sacrifices after 3½ years. And the horrible thing that destroys will be placed on the highest point of the Temple. But God has ordered him to be destroyed!"

DANIEL'S VISION OF A MAN

10 During Cyrus' third year as king of Persia, Daniel learned about these things. (Daniel's other name is Belteshazzar.) The message was true. It was about a great war. But Daniel understood it, because it was explained to him in a vision.

2At that time I, Daniel, was very sad for three weeks. 3I did not eat any fancy food. I did not eat any meat or drink any wine. I did not use any perfumed oil. I did not do any of these things for three weeks.

4On the twenty-fourth day of the first month, I was standing beside the great Tigris River. 5While standing there, I looked up. And I saw a man dressed in linen clothes. A belt made of fine gold was wrapped around his waist. 6His body was like shiny yellow quartz. His face was bright like lightning, and his eyes were like fire. His arms and legs were shiny like polished bronze. His voice sounded like the roar of a crowd.

7I, Daniel, was the only person who saw the vision. The men with me did not see it. But they were badly frightened. They were so afraid they ran away and hid. 8So I was left alone, watching this great vision. I lost my strength. My face turned white like a dead person, and I was helpless. 9Then I heard the man in the vision speaking. As I listened, I fell into a deep sleep. My face was on the ground.

> When you first started praying, an answer was given . . . because God loves you very much.
>
> –DANIEL 9:23

¹⁰Then a hand touched me and set me on my hands and knees. I was so afraid that I was shaking. ¹¹The man in the vision said to me, "Daniel, God loves you very much. Think very carefully about the words I will speak to you. Stand up because I have been sent to you." And when he said this, I stood up. I was still shaking.

¹²Then the man said to me, "Daniel, do not be afraid. Some time ago you decided to try to get understanding. You wanted to be humble before God. Since that time God has listened to you. And I came to you because you have been praying. ¹³But the prince of Persia has been fighting against me for 21 days. Then Michael, one of the most important angels, came to help me. He came because I had been left there with the king of Persia. ¹⁴Now I have come to you, Daniel. I will explain to you what will happen to your people. The vision is about a time in the future."

¹⁵While he was speaking to me, I bowed facedown. I could not speak. ¹⁶Then one who looked like a man touched my lips. I opened my mouth and started to speak. I said to the one standing in front of me, "Master, I am upset and afraid. It is because of what I saw in the vision. I feel helpless. ¹⁷Master, I am Daniel your servant. How can I talk with you! My strength is gone, and it is hard for me to breathe."

¹⁸The one who looked like a man touched me again. And he gave me strength. ¹⁹He said, "Daniel, don't be afraid. God loves you very much. Peace be with you. Be strong now, be strong."

When he spoke to me, I became stronger. Then I said, "Master, speak, since you have given me strength."

²⁰So then he said, "Daniel, do you know why I have come to you? Soon I must go back to fight against the prince of Persia. When I go, the prince of Greece will come. ²¹But before I go, I must first tell you what is written in the Book of Truth. No one stands with me against them except Michael. He is the angel ruling over your people.

11 "In the first year Darius the Mede was king, I stood up to support Michael. I supported him in his fight against the prince of Persia.

KINGDOMS OF THE SOUTH AND NORTH

²"Now then, Daniel, I tell you the truth: Three more kings will rule in Persia. Then a fourth king will come. He will be much richer than all the kings of Persia before him. He will use his riches to get power. And he will stir up everyone against the kingdom of Greece. ³Then a mighty king will come. He will rule with great power. He will do anything he wants. ⁴After that king has come, his kingdom will be broken up. It will be divided out toward the four parts of the world. His kingdom will not go to his descendants. And it will not have the power that he had. This is because his kingdom will be pulled up and given to other people.

⁵"The king of the South will become strong. But one of his commanders will become even stronger. He will begin to rule his own kingdom with great power. ⁶Then after a few years, the king of the South and the commander will become friends. The daughter of the king of the South will marry the king of the North. She will do this to bring peace. But she will not keep her power. And his family will not last. She, her husband, her child and those who brought her to that country will be killed.

⁷"But a person from her family will become king of the South. He will attack the armies of the king of the North. He will go into that king's strong, walled city. He will fight and win. ⁸He will take their gods and their metal idols. He will also take their valuable things made of silver and gold. He will take those things to Egypt. Then he will not bother the king of the North for a few years. ⁹Next, the king of the North will attack the king of the South.

But he will be beaten back to his own country.

¹⁰"The sons of the king of the North will prepare for war. They will get a large army together. That army will move through the land very quickly, like a powerful flood. Later, that army will come back and fight. They will fight all the way to the strong, walled city of the king of the South. ¹¹Then the king of the South will become very angry. He will march out to fight against the king of the North. The king of the North will have a large army. But he will lose the battle. ¹²The soldiers will be carried away. So the king of the South will be very proud. And he will kill thousands of soldiers from the northern army. But he will not continue to be successful. ¹³The king of the North will gather another army. That army will be larger than the first one. After several years he will attack. That army will be very large, and it will have plenty of weapons.

¹⁴"In those times many people will be against the king of the South. Some of your own people who love to fight will turn against the king of the South. They will think it is time for God's promises to come true. But it will not be the time yet. And they will fail. ¹⁵Then the king of the North will come. He will build dirt roads to the tops of the city walls. And he will capture a strong, walled city. The southern army will not have the power to fight back. Even their best soldiers will not be strong enough to stop the northern army. ¹⁶The king of the North will do whatever he wants. No one will be able to stand against him. He will gain power and control in the beautiful land of Israel. And he will have the power to destroy it. ¹⁷The king of the North will decide to use all his power to fight against the king of the South. He will make an agreement with the king of the South. The king of the North will give one of his daughters as a wife to the king of the South. He will do that so he can defeat the king of the South. But those plans will not succeed or help him. ¹⁸Then the king of the North will turn his attention to other places. He will take many cities along the coast of the Mediterranean Sea. But a commander will put an end to the pride of the king of the North. The commander will turn that pride back on him. ¹⁹After that happens the king of the North will go back to the strong, walled cities of his own country. But he will lose his power. That will be the end of him.

²⁰"The next king of the North will send out a tax collector. He will then have plenty of money. In a few years that ruler will be killed. But he will not die in anger or in a battle.

²¹"That ruler will be followed by a very cruel and hated man. He will not have the honor of being from a king's family. He will attack the kingdom when the people feel safe. He will take power by lying to the people. ²²He will sweep away in defeat large and powerful armies. He will even defeat a prince who made an agreement. ²³Many nations will make agreements with that cruel and hated ruler. But he will lie to them. He will gain much power. But only a few people will support him. ²⁴The richest areas will feel safe. But that cruel and hated ruler will attack them. And he will succeed where his ancestors did not. He will take things from the countries he defeated. And he will give those things to his followers. He will plan to defeat and destroy strong cities. He will be successful, but only for a short time.

²⁵"That very cruel and hated ruler will have a large army. He will use it to stir up his strength and courage. He will attack the king of the South. The king of the South will get a large and very powerful army and get ready for war. But the people who are against him will make secret plans. And the king of the South will be defeated. ²⁶There were people who were supposed to be good friends of the king of the South.

But they will try to destroy him. His army will be swept away in defeat. Many of his soldiers will be killed in battle. ²⁷ Those two kings will want to hurt each other. They will sit at the same table and lie to each other. But it will not do either one any good. This is because God has set a time for their end to come. ²⁸ The king of the North will go back to his own country with much wealth. Then he will decide to go against the holy agreement. He will do what he planned. Then he will go back to his own country.

²⁹"At the right time the king of the North will attack the king of the South again. But this time he will not be successful as he was before. ³⁰ Ships from the west will come and fight against the king of the North. He will see those ships coming and be afraid. Then he will return and show his anger against God's people who obey the holy agreement. He will be good to those who have stopped obeying the holy agreement.

³¹"The king of the North will send his army. They will make the Temple in Jerusalem unclean. They will stop the people from offering the daily sacrifice. Then they will set up the horrible thing that destroys. ³² The king of the North will tell lies to God's people. Those who have not obeyed God will be ruined. But there will be some who know God and obey him. They will be strong and fight back.

³³"Those who are wise will help the others understand what is happening. But some of them will be killed with swords. Some will be burned or taken captive. Some of them will have their homes and things taken away. These things will continue for many days. ³⁴ When the wise ones are suffering, they will get a little help. Many who join the wise ones will not love God. ³⁵ Some of the wise ones will be killed. But the hard times must come. This is so they can be made stronger and purer. They will be without faults until the time of the end comes. Then, at the right time the end will come.

THE KING WHO PRAISES HIMSELF

³⁶"The king of the North will do whatever he wants. He will brag about himself. He will praise himself and think he is even better than a god. He will say things against the God of gods that no one has ever heard. He will be successful until all the bad things have happened. What God has planned to happen will happen. ³⁷ That king of the North will not care about the gods his ancestors worshiped. He won't care about the god that women worship. He won't care about any god. Instead, he will make himself more important than any god. ³⁸ The king of the North will worship power and strength. His ancestors did not love power as he will. He will honor the god of power with gold and silver, expensive jewels and gifts. ³⁹ That king will attack strong, walled cities. He will do it with the help of a foreign god. He will give much honor to the people who join him. He will make them rulers in charge of many other people. He will make those rulers pay him for the land they rule.

⁴⁰"At the time of the end, the king of the South will fight a battle against the king of the North. The king of the North will attack him. He will attack with chariots and soldiers on horses and many large ships. He will invade many countries and sweep through their lands like a flood. ⁴¹ The king of the North will attack the beautiful land of Judah. He will defeat many countries. But Edom, Moab and the leaders of Ammon will be saved from him. ⁴² The king of the North will show his power in many countries. Egypt will not escape. ⁴³ The king will get treasures of gold and silver. And he will get all the riches of Egypt. The Libyan and Nubian people will obey him. ⁴⁴ But the king of the North will hear news from the east and the north. And it will make him afraid and angry. He will go to destroy

completely many nations. ⁴⁵He will set up his royal tents. They will be between the sea and the beautiful mountain where the Temple is built. But, finally, his end will come. There will not be anyone to help him when he dies.

THE TIME OF THE END

12 "Daniel, at that time Michael, the great prince, will stand up. (He is the one who protects your people.) There will be a time of much trouble. It will be the worst time since nations have been on earth. But your people will be saved. Everyone whose name is written in God's book will be saved. ²Many people who have already died will live again. Some of them will wake up to have life forever. But some will wake up to find shame and disgrace forever. ³The wise people will shine like the brightness of the sky. Those who teach others to live right will shine like stars forever and ever.

⁴"But you, Daniel, close up the book and seal it. These things will happen at

☆ Daniel 12:3

God sent a messenger to Daniel and showed him things that would happen in the future. And not just his future, but our future too. This messenger told him that people who had once been dead would live again. This message encourages people to follow God's wisdom and to help others find that wisdom.

God is the smartest person you will ever know. And he loves us a whole lot. He will never try to get us to do anything that will hurt us. He teaches us the right things to do because he knows what will keep us out of danger.

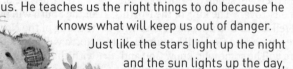

Just like the stars light up the night and the sun lights up the day, God says that people can be like that. The person who teaches others what God teaches will shine like the sun and the stars.

· · · · · · · · · · · · · ·

You can help your friends do the right thing. You might be the only light they will see.

the time of the end. Many people will go here and there to find true knowledge."

⁵Then I, Daniel, looked, and I saw two other men. One was standing on my side of the river. And the other was standing on the far side. ⁶The man who was dressed in linen was standing over the water in the river. One of the two men spoke to him. He asked, "How long will it be before these amazing things come true?"

⁷The man dressed in linen who stood over the water raised his hands toward heaven. And I heard him make a promise. He used the name of God who lives forever. He said, "It will be for three and one-half years. The power of the holy people will finally be broken. Then all these things will come true."

⁸I heard the answer, but I did not really understand. So I asked, "Master, what will happen after all these things come true?"

⁹He answered, "Go your way, Daniel. The message is closed up and sealed until the time of the end. ¹⁰Many people will be made clean, pure and spotless. But the wicked will continue to be wicked. And those wicked people will

not understand these things. But the wise people will understand them.

¹¹"The daily sacrifice will be stopped. There will be 1,290 days from that time. Then the horrible thing that destroys will be set up. ¹²Those who wait for the end of the 1,335 days will be happy.

¹³"As for you, Daniel, go your way till the end. You will get your rest when you die. And at the end you will rise from the dead to get your reward."

FROM TEARS TO HOPE

God told Abraham that his descendants would become a great nation called Israel, and they did. God gave them the land he promised them, and they lived there happily for many years. But they had a hard time remembering the good things God had done for them. They forgot that he wanted to be a Father to them.

The people of Israel wanted to be like the other nations who did not follow God, because those nations seemed happier. After a long time of trying to be like the other nations, Israel looked and acted like people who didn't know God.

As God's people moved further away from him, they were no longer safe. Their soldiers went to war all the time, and enemies came through their country. Prophets warned them that one day another nation would force them to leave the land God had given them.

For many years, God tried to call his people back to him. He even cried over them.* God sent prophets to his people to remind them that he loved them and wanted to be their Father. The prophets also warned them of the bad things coming if they did not turn back to God.

But even in all the sadness, God still gave them hope. He reminded them that his Son was coming, and he would be a new kind of king. This is called God's mercy. The people did bad things, but God still had good plans for them.**

*[God said,] "Let my eyes be filled with tears. I will cry night and day, without stopping. I will cry for my people. They have received a terrible blow. They have been hurt very badly."
JEREMIAH 14:17

**"I say this because I know what I have planned for you," says the Lord. "I have good plans for you. I don't plan to hurt you. I plan to give you hope and a good future."
JEREMIAH 29:11

Lamentations

JERUSALEM CRIES OVER HER DESTRUCTION

1 Jerusalem once was full of people.
  But now the city is empty.
Jerusalem once was a great city
  among the nations.
  But now she[n] has become like a
  widow.
She was like a queen of all the other
  cities.
  But now she is a slave.

2 She cries loudly at night.
  Tears are on her cheeks.
There is no one to comfort her.
  All her lovers are gone.
All her friends have turned against
  her.
  They have become her enemies.

3 Judah has gone into captivity.
  She has suffered and worked hard.
She lives among other nations.
  But she has found no rest.
Those who chased her caught her.
  They caught her when she was in
  trouble.

4 The roads to Jerusalem are sad.
  No one comes to Jerusalem for the
  feasts.
No one passes through her gates.
  And her priests groan.
Her young women are suffering.
  And Jerusalem suffers terribly.

5 Her enemies have become her
  masters.
  Her enemies enjoy the wealth they
  have won.
The Lord is punishing her
  for her many sins.
Her children have gone away.
  They are captives of the enemy in a
  foreign land.

6 The beauty of Jerusalem
  has gone away.
Her rulers are like deer
  that cannot find food.
They are weak and have run away
  from those who chased them.

7 Jerusalem is suffering and homeless.
  She remembers all the precious
  things
  she had in the past.
She remembers when her people
  were defeated by the enemy.
  There was no one to help her.
When her enemies saw her,
  they laughed to see her ruined.

8 Jerusalem sinned terribly.
  So she has become unclean.
Those who honored her hate her now
  because they have seen her
  nakedness.
Jerusalem groans
  and turns away.

9 Jerusalem made herself unclean by
  her sins.
  She did not think about what
  would happen to her.
Her defeat was surprising.
  There was no one to comfort her.
She says, "Lord, see how I suffer.
  The enemy has won."

10 The enemy reached out and took
  all her precious things.
She even saw foreigners
  enter her Temple.
Lord, you had commanded
  that they should not enter the
  meeting of your people.

11 All of Jerusalem's people are
  groaning.
  They are looking for bread.

1:1 she In this poem the city of Jerusalem is described as a woman.

They are giving away their precious
  things for food
   so they can stay alive.
The city says, "Look, Lord, and see.
  I am hated."

¹² Jerusalem says, "You who pass by on
   the road don't seem to care.
  Come, look at me and see.
Is there any pain like mine?
  Is there any pain like that he has
   caused me?
The Lord has punished me
  on the day of his great anger.

¹³ "The Lord sent fire from above.
  It went down into my bones.
He stretched out a net for my feet.
  He turned me back.
He made me sad and lonely.
  I am weak all day.

¹⁴ "He has noticed my sins.
  They are tied together by his hands.
They hang around my neck.
  He has turned my strength into
   weakness.
The Lord has let me be defeated
  by those who are stronger than I am.

¹⁵ "The Lord has rejected
  all my mighty men inside my walls.
He brought an army against me
  to destroy my young men.
As if in a winepress, the Lord has
   crushed
  the capital city of Judah.

¹⁶ "I cry about these things.
  My eyes overflow with tears.
There is no one near to comfort me.
  There is no one who can give me
   strength again.
My children are left sad and lonely
  because the enemy has won."

¹⁷ Jerusalem reaches out her hands,
  but there is no one to comfort her.
The Lord has commanded for the
   people of Jacob
  that their enemies surround them.

Jerusalem has become unclean
  like those around her.

¹⁸ Jerusalem says, "The Lord is right.
  But I refused to obey him.
Listen, all you people.
  Look at my pain.
My young women and men
  have gone into captivity.

¹⁹ "I called out to my friends,
  but they turned against me.
My priests and my elders
  have died in the city.
They were looking for food
  so they could stay alive.

²⁰ "Look at me, Lord. I am upset.
  I am troubled.
My heart is troubled
  because I have been so stubborn.
Out in the streets, the sword kills.
  Inside the houses, death destroys.

²¹ "People have heard my groaning.
  There is no one to comfort me.
All my enemies have heard of my
   trouble.
  They are happy that you have done
   this to me.
Now bring that day you have
   announced.
  Let my enemies be like me.

²² "Look at all their evil.
  Do to them what you have done
   to me
  because of all my sins.
I groan over and over again,
  and I am afraid."

THE LORD DESTROYED JERUSALEM

2 Look how the Lord in his anger
  has brought Jerusalem to shame.
He has thrown down the greatness
   of Israel
  from the sky to the earth.
He did not remember the Temple, his
   footstool,
  on the day of his anger.

2 The Lord swallowed up without
  mercy
    all the houses of the people of
    Jacob.
In his anger he pulled down
  the strong places of Judah.
He threw her kingdom and its rulers
  down to the ground in dishonor.

3 In his anger the Lord has removed
  all the strength of Israel.
He took away his power from Israel
  when the enemy came.
He burned against the people of
  Jacob like a flaming fire
  that burns up everything around it.

4 Like an enemy, the Lord prepared to
  shoot his bow.
    He took hold of his sword.
Like an enemy, he killed
  all the good-looking people.
He poured out his anger like fire
  on the tents of Jerusalem.

5 The Lord has become like an enemy.
  He has swallowed up Israel.
He has swallowed up all her palaces.
  He has destroyed all her strong
  places.
He has caused more moaning and
  groaning
  for Judah.

6 He has destroyed his Temple as if it
  were a garden tent.
  He has destroyed the place where
  he met with his people.
The Lord has made Jerusalem forget
  the set feasts and Sabbath days.
He has rejected the king and the
  priest
  in his great anger.

7 The Lord has rejected his altar
  and abandoned his Temple.
He has given to the enemy
  the walls of Jerusalem's palaces.
The enemy shouted in the Lord's
  Temple
  as if it were a feast day.

8 The Lord planned to destroy
  the wall around Jerusalem.
He marked the wall off with a
  measuring line.
  He did not stop himself from
  destroying it.
He made the walls and defenses sad.
  Together they have fallen.

9 Jerusalem's gates have fallen to the
  ground.
    He destroyed and smashed the
    bars of the gates.
Her king and her princes are sent
  away among the nations.
    The teaching of the Lord has
    stopped.
The prophets have not had
  any visions from the Lord.

10 The elders of Jerusalem
  sit on the ground and are silent.
They pour dust on their heads
  and put on rough cloth to show
  how sad they are.
The young women of Jerusalem
  bow their heads to the ground in
  sorrow.

11 My eyes are weak from crying.
  I am troubled.

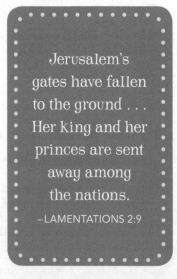

Jerusalem's gates have fallen to the ground . . . Her king and her princes are sent away among the nations.

–LAMENTATIONS 2:9

I feel as if I have been poured out on
 the ground
 because my people have been
  destroyed.
Children and babies are fainting
 in the streets of the city.

12 They say to their mothers,
 "Where is some bread and wine?"
They faint like wounded soldiers
 in the streets of the city.
 They die in their mothers' arms.

13 What can I say about you, Jerusalem?
 What can I compare you to?
What can I say you are like?
 How can I comfort you, Jerusalem?
Your ruin is as big as the sea.
 No one can heal you.

14 Your prophets saw visions about you.
 But they were false and worth
  nothing.
They did not expose your sins.
 They did not keep you from being
  captured.
The messages they preached to you
 were false.
 They fooled you.

15 All who pass by on the road
 clap their hands at you.
They make fun and shake their heads
 at Jerusalem.
They ask, "Is this the city that people
 called
 the most beautiful city,
 the happiest city on earth?"

16 All your enemies open their mouths
 to say things against you.
They make fun and grind their teeth
 in anger.
 They say, "We have swallowed
  her up.
This is the day we were waiting for.
 We have finally seen it happen."

17 The Lord has done what he planned.
 He has carried out the order
 that he commanded long ago.

He has destroyed without mercy.
 He has made your enemies happy
  because of what happened to
  you.
 He has strengthened your enemies.

18 The people
 cry out to the Lord.
Wall of Jerusalem,
 let your tears flow
 like a river day and night.
Do not stop.
 Do not let your eyes rest.

19 Get up, cry out in the night.
 Cry all through the night.
Pour out your heart like water
 in prayer to the Lord.
Lift up your hands in prayer to him.
 Pray for the life of your children.
They are fainting with hunger
 on every street corner.

20 Jerusalem says: "Look, Lord,
 and see.
 You have never done this to anyone
  else.
Women eat their own babies,
 the children they have cared for.
Priests and prophets
 are killed in the Temple of the
  Lord.

21 "Young men and old men
 lie on the ground in the streets of
  the city.
My young women and young men
 have been killed by the sword.
You, Lord, killed them on the day of
 your anger.
 You killed them without mercy.

22 "You invited terrors to come against
 me on every side.
 It was as if you were inviting them
  to a feast.
No one escaped or remained alive
 on the day of the Lord's anger.
My enemy has killed
 those whom I gave birth to and
  brought up."

THE MEANING OF SUFFERING

3 I am a man who has seen the
    suffering
    that comes from the rod of the
      Lord's anger.
2 He led me
    into darkness, not light.
3 He turned his hand against me
    again and again, all day long.

4 He caused my flesh and skin to wear
    out.
    He broke my bones.
5 He surrounded me and attacked me
    with sadness and grief.
6 He made me sit in the dark,
    like someone who has been dead a
      long time.

7 He shut me in so I could not get out.
    He put heavy chains on me.
8 I cry out and beg for help.
    But he ignores my prayer.
9 He has blocked my way with stones.
    He has made my life difficult.

10 The Lord is like a bear ready to
    attack me.
    He is like a lion in hiding.
11 He led me the wrong way and tore
    me to pieces.
    He left me without help.
12 He prepared to shoot his bow.
    He made me the target for his
      arrows.

13 He shot me in the kidneys
    with the arrows from his arrow
      bag.
14 I have become a joke to all my
    people.
    All day long they make fun of me
      with songs.
15 The Lord filled me with misery.
    He filled me with suffering.

16 The Lord broke my teeth with gravel.
    He crushed me into the dirt.
17 I have no more peace.
    I have forgotten what happiness is.
18 I said, "My strength is gone.

I have no more hope that the Lord
    will help me."

19 Lord, remember my suffering and
    how I have no home.
    Remember the misery and
      suffering.
20 I remember them well.
    And I am very sad.
21 But I have hope
    when I think of this:

22 The Lord's love never ends.
    His mercies never stop.
23 They are new every morning.
    Lord, your loyalty is great.
24 I say to myself, "The Lord is what I
    have left.
    So I have hope."

25 The Lord is good to those who put
    their hope in him.
    He is good to those who look to
      him for help.
26 It is good to wait quietly
    for the Lord to save.
27 It is good for a man to work hard
    while he is young.

28 He should sit alone and be quiet
    because the Lord has given him
      hard work to do.
29 He should bow to the Lord with his
    face to the ground.
    Maybe there is still hope.
30 He should offer his cheek if someone
    wants to hit him.
    He should be filled with shame.

31 The Lord will not reject
    his people forever.
32 Although the Lord brings sorrow, he
    also has mercy.
    His love is great.
33 The Lord does not like to punish
    people
    or make them sad.

34 The Lord sees if any prisoner of the
    earth
    is crushed under his feet.

☆ Lamentations 3:22–24

Remember Psalms, that book full of songs that praise God? There were lines like "Shout for joy to the Lord" (Psalm 98:6) and "Sing praises to the Lord who is king" (Psalm 9:11). These were happy songs. But there is a whole book of songs in the Bible that is full of tears. It is a short book with a long name: Lamentations. The word lamentation actually means "crying." And this book is all about crying.

The beautiful story of God's family seemed to end in tears as the nation he built fell apart. But God had a plan from the beginning. We can read Lamentations and be sad with his people. But when the sadness is over, there will be joy. In a few more pages, we get to meet God's Son, Jesus—the hope for Israel and the hope of the world!

Psalm 34:1 says, "I will praise the Lord at all times." Do you ever feel yucky? Maybe you feel sick or sad in your heart. Maybe you said something unkind to your friend, and now you feel sad. Do you feel sad when you have to go to bed and don't want to? You may feel yucky when you have to eat food you don't like. You can talk to Jesus when you are feeling yucky. He will listen to you. The Bible tells us to thank the Lord always, no matter how yucky we feel or how bad things may be.

· ·

When you're sad, it's okay to tell Jesus your problems. Like the people in Lamentations, you might even cry a little. But remember, God will always be there to comfort you.

---

³⁵ He sees if someone is treated unfairly
 before the Most High God.
³⁶ The Lord sees
 if someone is cheated in his case in court.

³⁷ Nobody can speak and have it happen
 unless the Lord commands it.

³⁸ Both bad and good things
 come by the command of the Most High God.
³⁹ No man should complain
 when he is punished for his sins.

⁴⁰ Let us examine and look at what we have done.

Then let us return to the Lord.
⁴¹ Let us lift up our hands and pray
   from our hearts.
Let us say to God in heaven,
⁴² "We have sinned and turned against
   you.
   And you have not forgiven us.

⁴³ "You wrapped yourself in anger and
   chased us.
   You killed us without mercy.
⁴⁴ You wrapped yourself in a cloud.
   No prayer could get through.
⁴⁵ You made us like scum and trash
   among the other nations.

⁴⁶ "All of our enemies
   open their mouths and say things
   against us.
⁴⁷ We have been frightened and fearful.
   We have been ruined and
   destroyed."
⁴⁸ Streams of tears flow from my eyes
   because my people are destroyed.

⁴⁹ My tears flow continually,
   without stopping,
⁵⁰ until the Lord looks down
   and sees from heaven.
⁵¹ I am sad when I see
   what has happened to all the
   women of my city.

⁵² Those who are my enemies for no
   reason
   hunted me like a bird.
⁵³ They threw me alive into a pit.
   They threw stones at me.
⁵⁴ Water came up over my head.
   I said to myself, "I am going to die."
⁵⁵ I called out to you, Lord,
   from the bottom of the pit.
⁵⁶ You heard me calling, "Do not close
   your ears.
   Do not ignore my cry for help."
⁵⁷ You came close when I called out
   to you.
   You said, "Don't be afraid."

⁵⁸ Lord, you have taken my case.
   You have given me back my life.

⁵⁹ Lord, you have seen how I have been
   wronged.
   Now judge my case for me.
⁶⁰ You have seen how my enemies took
   revenge on me.
   You have seen all their evil plans
   against me.

⁶¹ Lord, you have heard their insults
   and all their evil plans against me.
⁶² The words and thoughts of my
   enemies
   are against me all the time.
⁶³ Look! In everything they do
   they make fun of me with songs.

⁶⁴ Punish them as they should be
   punished, Lord.
   Pay them back for what they have
   done.
⁶⁵ Make them stubborn.
   Put your curse on them.
⁶⁶ Chase them in anger.
   Destroy them from the Lord's earth.

THE ATTACK ON JERUSALEM

4 See how the gold has lost its
   shine!
   See how the good gold has
   changed!
   The stones of the Temple are
   scattered
   at every street corner.

² The precious people of Jerusalem
   were more valuable than gold.
   But now they are thought of as clay
   jars
   made by the hands of a potter.

³ Even wild dogs give their milk
   to feed their young.
   But my people are cruel
   like ostriches in the desert.

⁴ The baby is so thirsty
   that his tongue sticks to the roof of
   his mouth.
   Children beg for bread.
   But no one breaks off a piece to
   share with them.

5 Those who once ate fine foods
   are now starving in the streets.
   The people who grew up wearing
      nice clothes
   now pick through trash piles.

6 My people have been punished
      more than Sodom was.
   Sodom was destroyed suddenly.
      No hands reached out to help her.

7 Our princes were purer than snow.
      They were whiter than milk.
   Their bodies were redder than rubies.
      Their faces shined like sapphires.

8 But now they are blacker than coal.
      No one even recognizes them in
         the streets.
   Their skin is stretched over their
         bones.
      It is as dry as wood.

9 Those people who were killed by the
         sword had it better
      than those killed by hunger.
   They starved in pain and died
      because there was no food from
         the field.

10 With their own hands kind women
      cooked their own children.
   The children became food for their
         parents.
      This happened when my people
         were destroyed.

11 The Lord turned loose all of his anger.
      He poured out his strong anger.
   He set fire to Jerusalem.
      It burned down to the foundations.

12 Kings of the earth and people of the
         world
      could not believe it.
   They could not believe that enemies
      could come through the gates of
         Jerusalem.

13 But it happened because her prophets
      had sinned.

And her priests had done evil.
   They killed in the city
      the people who did what was right.

14 They wandered in the streets
      like blind men.
   They became dirty with blood.
      So no one could touch their clothes.

15 "Go away! You are unclean," people
         shouted at them.
      "Get away! Get away! Do not touch
         us!"
   So they left and wandered around.
      The other nations said, "Don't stay
         here."

16 The Lord himself scattered them.
      He did not look after them anymore.
   He did not respect the priests.
      He showed no mercy to the elders.

17 Also, our eyes grew tired
      looking for help that never came.
   We kept watch from our towers
      for a nation to save us.

18 Our enemies hunted us
      so we could not even walk in the
         streets.
   Our end came near. Our time was up.
      Our end came.

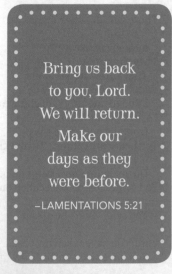

Bring us back
to you, Lord.
We will return.
Make our
days as they
were before.

–LAMENTATIONS 5:21

19 The men who chased us
    were faster than eagles in the sky.
They ran us into the mountains.
    They ambushed us in the desert.

20 The Lord's appointed king, who was
    our very breath,
    was caught in their traps.
We had said about him, "We will be
    protected by him
    among the nations."

21 Be happy and glad, people of Edom,
    you who live in the land of Uz.
But the Lord's anger is like a cup of
    wine that you also will have to
    drink.
    Then you will get drunk on it and
    make yourselves naked.

22 Your punishment is complete,
    Jerusalem.
    He will not keep you in captivity
    any longer.
But the Lord will punish your
    wrongs, people of Edom.
    He will uncover your sins.

A PRAYER TO THE LORD

5 Remember, Lord, what happened
    to us.
    Look and see our disgrace.
2 Our land has been turned over to
    strangers.
    Our houses have been given to
    foreigners.
3 We have become orphans with no
    father.
    Our mothers have become like
    widows.
4 We have to buy the water we drink.
    We must pay for the wood for our
    fires.
5 They work us hard as if we were
    animals with a yoke on our necks.
    We get tired and have no rest.
6 We made an agreement with Egypt
    and with Assyria to get enough
    food.

7 Our ancestors sinned against you.
    But they are gone.
    Now we must suffer because of
    their sins.
8 Slaves have become our rulers.
    There is no one who can save us
    from them.
9 We risk our lives to get our food
    because there are men with swords
    in the desert.
10 Our skin is hot like an oven.
    We burn with fever because of the
    terrible hunger.
11 The enemy raped the women of
    Jerusalem
    and the girls in the cities of Judah.
12 The enemy hung our princes by the
    hands.
    They do not honor our elders.
13 The young men grind grain at the
    mill.
    Boys stumble while carrying loads
    of wood.
14 The elders no longer sit at the city
    gates.
    The young men no longer make
    music.
15 We have no more joy in our hearts.
    Our dancing has turned into
    sadness.
16 The glory has gone from Jerusalem.
    How terrible it is for us because we
    have sinned.
17 Because of this we are afraid.
    Because of these things our eyes
    are dim.
18 Mount Zion is empty.
    Now wild dogs wander around it.

19 But you rule forever, Lord.
    You will be King from now on.
20 Why have you forgotten us for so
    long?
    Why have you left us for so long?
21 Bring us back to you, Lord. We will
    return.
    Make our days as they were before.
22 Or have you completely rejected us?
    Will your anger never end?

NEW TESTAMENT

THE SON AND THE SNAKE

Way back in Genesis, the first man and woman had a real problem. At first, they were best friends with God and didn't have a care in the world. But then the devil—in the form of a snake—tempted them to do something God told them not to do. They sinned and were no longer close to God like they were before. It was a very sad day for everybody: Adam, Eve, and everyone born after them.

God told all three of them that Eve's descendants and the snake's descendants would be enemies. If you have ever seen a snake cross your path and you got scared, well, that's why. But then God said something interesting. He said, "Her child will crush your head. And you will bite his heel" (Genesis 3:15).

God said child. And he said the snake would bite his heel. Eve was the first mom, so everyone who has ever lived is her descendant—millions and billions of us! So, why would God say just one child?

It's because he was talking about Jesus. Even though Jesus is God's Son, he had to be born through a woman like us. Jesus had a mom, just like you and I do. From the very first parents and the very first sin, God had planned to send his Son to defeat sin and the devil.

When things got sad in Israel and Judah and the people forgot to follow God, he never gave up on them. He sent Jesus to save Israel. But God's promise to Eve happened way before Abraham (Israel's grandfather) was born. God's promise to send his Son was for all of us—all of Eve's descendants. Jesus came to save us all.

Matthew

THE FAMILY HISTORY OF JESUS

1 This is the family history of Jesus Christ. He came from the family of David. David came from the family of Abraham.

2 Abraham was the father[n] of Isaac.
Isaac was the father of Jacob.
Jacob was the father of Judah and his brothers.
3 Judah was the father of Perez and Zerah.
   (Their mother was Tamar.)
Perez was the father of Hezron.
Hezron was the father of Ram.
4 Ram was the father of Amminadab.
Amminadab was the father of Nahshon.
Nahshon was the father of Salmon.
5 Salmon was the father of Boaz.
   (Boaz's mother was Rahab.)
Boaz was the father of Obed.
   (Obed's mother was Ruth.)
Obed was the father of Jesse.
6 Jesse was the father of King David.
David was the father of Solomon.
   (Solomon's mother had been Uriah's wife.)
7 Solomon was the father of Rehoboam.
Rehoboam was the father of Abijah.
Abijah was the father of Asa.[n]
8 Asa was the father of Jehoshaphat.
Jehoshaphat was the father of Jehoram.
Jehoram was the ancestor of Uzziah.
9 Uzziah was the father of Jotham.
Jotham was the father of Ahaz.
Ahaz was the father of Hezekiah.
10 Hezekiah was the father of Manasseh.
Manasseh was the father of Amon.
Amon was the father of Josiah.
11 Josiah was the grandfather of Jehoiachin[n] and his brothers.
   (This was at the time that the people were taken to Babylon.)
12 After they were taken to Babylon:
Jehoiachin was the father of Shealtiel.
Shealtiel was the grandfather of Zerubbabel.
13 Zerubbabel was the father of Abiud.
Abiud was the father of Eliakim.
Eliakim was the father of Azor.
14 Azor was the father of Zadok.
Zadok was the father of Akim.
Akim was the father of Eliud.
15 Eliud was the father of Eleazar.
Eleazar was the father of Matthan.
Matthan was the father of Jacob.
16 Jacob was the father of Joseph.
Joseph was the husband of Mary, and Mary was the mother of Jesus.
Jesus is called the Christ.

17 So there were 14 generations from Abraham to David. And there were 14 generations from David until the time when the people were taken to Babylon. And there were 14 generations from the time when the people were taken to Babylon until Christ was born.

THE BIRTH OF JESUS CHRIST

18 The mother of Jesus Christ was Mary. And this is how the birth of Jesus came about. Mary was engaged to marry Joseph. But before they married, she learned that she was going to have a baby. She was pregnant by the power of the Holy Spirit. 19 Mary's husband, Joseph, was a good man. He did not want to disgrace her in public, so he planned to divorce her secretly.

20 While Joseph thought about this, an angel of the Lord came to him in a dream. The angel said, "Joseph, descendant of David, don't be afraid to take Mary as your wife. The baby in her is from the Holy Spirit. 21 She will give

---

1:2 **father** "Father" in Jewish lists of ancestors can sometimes mean grandfather or more distant relative.
1:7 **Asa** Some Greek copies read "Asaph," another name for Asa (see 1 Chronicles 3:10).
1:11 **Jehoiachin** The Greek reads "Jeconiah," another name for Jehoiachin (see 2 Kings 24:6 and 1 Chronicles 3:16).

☆ Matthew 1:21

Mary and Joseph were chosen to be parents to God's Son, Jesus. But Jesus' Father was still God, not Joseph. Part of a father's job was to name their baby. But Joseph didn't choose the name. God did. God told Joseph to name the baby Jesus because Jesus means "salvation." Jesus would save his people from their sins!

What do you picture when you hear the word *red*? Apple? Fire truck? Think about the word *sparkle*. What do you think of? Have you ever touched something *sticky*? Your fingers keep sticking together, and the only thing that stops it is washing your hands. Words make us see different things in our minds. Back in Bible times, what a parent named a baby had a lot of meaning. Jesus was named *Salvation*. So just like the words *red*, *sparkle*, and *sticky* give us pictures in our minds, every time Jesus' mom or dad called his name, they were making a word picture: "He saves!" They were always reminding people that Jesus was born to save the world.

. . . .

There is a lot of power wrapped up in that name: Jesus. When you are scared or hurt, remember "he saves!" Call out his name.

birth to a son. You will name the son Jesus."[n] Give him that name because he will save his people from their sins."

22All this happened to make clear the full meaning of what the Lord had said through the prophet: 23"The virgin will be pregnant. She will have a son, and they will name him Immanuel."[n] This name means "God is with us."

24When Joseph woke up, he did what the Lord's angel had told him to do. Joseph married Mary. 25But he did not have intimate relations with her until she gave birth to the son. And Joseph named the son Jesus.

WISE MEN COME TO VISIT JESUS

2 Jesus was born in the town of Bethlehem in Judea during the time when Herod was king. After Jesus was born, some wise men from the east came to Jerusalem. 2They asked, "Where is the baby who was born to be the king of the Jews? We saw his star in the east. We came to worship him."

3When King Herod heard about this new king of the Jews, he was troubled. And all the people in Jerusalem were worried too. 4Herod called a meeting of all the leading priests and teachers of the law. He asked them where the Christ would be born. 5They answered, "In the town of Bethlehem in Judea. The prophet wrote about this in the Scriptures:

6 'But you, Bethlehem, in the land of Judah,
    you are important among the rulers of Judah.
  A ruler will come from you.
    He will be like a shepherd for my people, the Israelites.'" *Micah 5:2*

7Then Herod had a secret meeting with the wise men from the east. He learned from them the exact time they first saw the star. 8Then Herod sent the wise men to Bethlehem. He said to them, "Go and look carefully to find the child. When you find him, come tell me. Then I can go worship him too."

9The wise men heard the king and then left. They saw the same star they had seen in the east. It went before them until it stopped above the place where the child was. 10When the wise men saw the star, they were filled with joy. 11They went to the house where the child was and saw him with his mother, Mary. They bowed down and worshiped the child. They opened the gifts they brought for him. They gave him treasures of gold, frankincense, and myrrh. 12But God warned the wise men in a dream not to go back to Herod. So they went home to their own country by a different way.

JESUS' PARENTS TAKE HIM TO EGYPT

13After they left, an angel of the Lord came to Joseph in a dream. The angel said, "Get up! Take the child and his mother and escape to Egypt. Herod will start looking for the child to kill him. Stay in Egypt until I tell you to return."

14So Joseph got up and left for Egypt during the night with the child and his mother. 15Joseph stayed in Egypt until Herod died. This was to make clear the full meaning of what the Lord had said through the prophet. The Lord said, "I called my son out of Egypt."[n]

HEROD KILLS THE BABY BOYS

16When Herod saw that the wise men had tricked him, he was very angry. So he gave an order to kill all the baby boys in Bethlehem and in all the area around Bethlehem who were two years old or younger. This was in keeping with the time he learned from the wise men. 17So what God had said through the prophet Jeremiah came true:

1:21 **Jesus** The name Jesus means "salvation."
1:23 **"The virgin...Immanuel."** Quotation from Isaiah 7:14.
2:15 **"I called...Egypt."** Quotation from Hosea 11:1.

[18] "A sound was heard in Ramah.
    It was painful crying and much
        sadness.
Rachel cries for her children,
    and she cannot be comforted,
    because her children are dead."
Jeremiah 31:15

JOSEPH AND MARY RETURN

[19] After Herod died, an angel of the Lord came to Joseph in a dream. This happened while Joseph was in Egypt. [20] The angel said, "Get up! Take the child and his mother and go to Israel. The people who were trying to kill the child are now dead."

[21] So Joseph took the child and his mother and went to Israel. [22] But he heard that Archelaus was now king in Judea. Archelaus became king when his father Herod died. So Joseph was afraid to go there. After being warned in a dream, he went to the area of Galilee. [23] He went to a town called Nazareth and lived there. And so what God had said through the prophets came true: "He will be called a Nazarene." [n]

THE WORK OF JOHN THE BAPTIST

3 About that time John the Baptist came and began preaching in the desert area of Judea. [2] John said, "Change your hearts and lives because the kingdom of heaven is coming soon." [3] John the Baptist is the one Isaiah the prophet was talking about. Isaiah said:

    "This is a voice of a man
        who calls out in the desert:
    'Prepare the way for the Lord.
        Make the road straight for him.'"
Isaiah 40:3

[4] John's clothes were made from camel's hair. He wore a leather belt around his waist. For food, he ate locusts and wild honey. [5] Many people went to hear John preach. They came from Jerusalem and all Judea and all the area around the Jordan River. [6] They told of the sins they had done, and John baptized them in the Jordan River.

[7] Many of the Pharisees and Sadducees came to the place where John was baptizing people. When John saw them, he said: "You are snakes! Who warned you to run away from God's anger that is coming? [8] You must do the things that show that you have really changed your hearts and lives. [9] And don't think that you can say to yourselves, 'Abraham is our father.' I tell you that God could make children for Abraham from these rocks. [10] The ax is now ready to cut down the trees. Every tree that does not produce good fruit will be cut down and thrown into the fire. [n]

[11] "I baptize you with water to show that your hearts and lives have changed. But there is one coming later who is greater than I am. I am not good enough to carry his sandals. He will baptize you with the Holy Spirit and with fire. [12] He will come ready to clean the grain. He will separate the good grain from the chaff. He will put the good part of the grain into his barn. And he will burn the chaff with a fire that cannot be put out." [n]

JESUS IS BAPTIZED BY JOHN

[13] At that time Jesus came from Galilee to the Jordan River. He came to John and wanted John to baptize him. [14] But John tried to stop him. John said, "Why do you come to me to be baptized? I should be baptized by you!"

[15] Jesus answered, "Let it be this way for now. We should do all things that are right." So John agreed to baptize Jesus.

[16] Jesus was baptized and came up out of the water. Heaven opened, and he saw

---

2:23 Nazarene A person from the town of Nazareth. Matthew may be referring to Isaiah 11:1, where the Hebrew word translated "branch" sounds like "Nazarene."
3:10 The ax . . . fire. This means that God is ready to punish his people who do not obey him.
3:12 He will . . . out. This means that Jesus will come to separate the good people from the bad people, saving the good and punishing the bad.

God's Spirit coming down on him like a dove. [17]And a voice spoke from heaven. The voice said, "This is my Son and I love him. I am very pleased with him."

THE TEMPTATION OF JESUS

4 Then the Spirit led Jesus into the desert to be tempted by the devil. [2]Jesus ate nothing for 40 days and nights. After this, he was very hungry. [3]The devil came to Jesus to tempt him. The devil said, "If you are the Son of God, tell these rocks to become bread."

[4]Jesus answered, "It is written in the Scriptures, 'A person does not live only by eating bread. But a person lives by everything the Lord says.'" [n]

[5]Then the devil led Jesus to the holy city of Jerusalem. He put Jesus on a very high place of the Temple. [6]The devil said, "If you are the Son of God, jump off. It is written in the Scriptures,

'He has put his angels in charge of
    you.
    They will catch you with their
        hands.
And you will not hit your foot on a
    rock.'" *Psalm 91:11–12*

[7]Jesus answered him, "It also says in the Scriptures, 'Do not test the Lord your God.'" [n]

[8]Then the devil led Jesus to the top of a very high mountain. He showed Jesus all the kingdoms of the world and all the great things that are in those kingdoms. [9]The devil said, "If you will bow down and worship me, I will give you all these things."

[10]Jesus said to the devil, "Go away from me, Satan! It is written in the Scriptures, 'You must worship the Lord your God. Serve only him!'" [n]

[11]So the devil left Jesus. And then some angels came to Jesus and helped him.

JESUS BEGINS WORK IN GALILEE

[12]Jesus heard that John had been put in prison. So Jesus went back to Galilee. [13]He left Nazareth and went and lived in Capernaum, a town near Lake Galilee. Capernaum is in the area near Zebulun and Naphtali. [14]Jesus did this to make true what the prophet Isaiah said:

[15] "Land of Zebulun and land of
        Naphtali
    are on the way to the sea.
    They are along the Jordan River.
        This is Galilee where the non-
            Jewish people live.
[16] These people who live in darkness
        will see a great light.
    They live in a place that is very dark.
    But a light will shine on them."
                            Isaiah 9:1–2

JESUS CHOOSES SOME FOLLOWERS

[17]From that time Jesus began to preach, saying, "Change your hearts and lives, because the kingdom of heaven is coming soon."

[18]Jesus was walking by Lake Galilee. He saw two brothers, Simon (called Peter) and Simon's brother Andrew. The brothers were fishermen, and they were fishing in the lake with a net. [19]Jesus said, "Come follow me. I will make you fishermen for men." [20]At once Simon and Andrew left their nets and followed him.

[21]Jesus continued walking by Lake Galilee. He saw two other brothers, James and John, the sons of Zebedee. They were in a boat with their father Zebedee, preparing their nets to catch fish. Jesus told them to come with him. [22]At once they left the boat and their father, and they followed Jesus.

JESUS TEACHES AND HEALS PEOPLE

[23]Jesus went everywhere in Galilee. He taught in the synagogues and preached

---

4:4 'A person . . . says.' Quotation from Deuteronomy 8:3.
4:7 'Do . . . God.' Quotation from Deuteronomy 6:16.
4:10 'You . . . him!' Quotation from Deuteronomy 6:13.

the Good News about the kingdom of heaven. And he healed all the people's diseases and sicknesses. ²⁴The news about Jesus spread all over Syria, and people brought all the sick to him. These sick people were suffering from different kinds of diseases and pain. Some were suffering very great pain, some had demons, some were epileptics,[n] and some were paralyzed. Jesus healed all of them. ²⁵Many people followed him. They came from Galilee, the Ten Towns,[n] Jerusalem, Judea, and the land across the Jordan River.

JESUS TEACHES THE PEOPLE

5 Jesus saw the crowds who were there. He went up on a hill and sat down. His followers came to him. ²Jesus taught the people and said:

³ "Those people who know they have
    great spiritual needs are happy.
    The kingdom of heaven belongs to
    them.
⁴ Those who are sad now are happy.
    God will comfort them.
⁵ Those who are humble are happy.
    The earth will belong to them.
⁶ Those who want to do right more
    than anything else are happy.
    God will fully satisfy them.
⁷ Those who give mercy to others are
    happy.
    Mercy will be given to them.
⁸ Those who are pure in their thinking
    are happy.
    They will be with God.
⁹ Those who work to bring peace are
    happy.
    God will call them his sons.
¹⁰ Those who are treated badly for
    doing good are happy.
    The kingdom of heaven belongs to
    them.

¹¹"People will say bad things about you and hurt you. They will lie and say all kinds of evil things about you because you follow me. But when they do these things to you, you are happy. ¹²Rejoice and be glad. You have a great reward waiting for you in heaven. People did the same evil things to the prophets who lived before you.

YOU ARE LIKE SALT AND LIGHT

¹³"You are the salt of the earth. But if the salt loses its salty taste, it cannot be made salty again. It is good for nothing. It must be thrown out for people to walk on.

¹⁴"You are the light that gives light to the world. A city that is built on a hill cannot be hidden. ¹⁵And people don't hide a light under a bowl. They put the light on a lampstand. Then the light shines for all the people in the house. ¹⁶In the same way, you should be a light for other people. Live so that they will see the good things you do. Live so that they will praise your Father in heaven.

THE IMPORTANCE OF THE LAW

¹⁷"Don't think that I have come to destroy the law of Moses or the teaching of the prophets. I have not come to destroy their teachings but to do what they said. ¹⁸I tell you the truth. Nothing will disappear from the law until heaven and earth are gone. The law will not lose even the smallest letter or the smallest part of a letter until all has happened. ¹⁹Whoever refuses to obey any command and teaches other people not to obey that command will be the least important in the kingdom of heaven. But whoever obeys the law and teaches other people to obey the law will be great in the kingdom of heaven. ²⁰I tell you that you must do better than the teachers of the law and the Pharisees. If you are not better than they are, you will not enter the kingdom of heaven.

4:24 epileptics People with a disease that causes them sometimes to lose control of their bodies, and maybe faint, shake strongly, or not be able to move.
4:25 Ten Towns In Greek, called "Decapolis." It was an area east of Lake Galilee that once had ten main towns.

JESUS TEACHES ABOUT ANGER

[21]"You have heard that it was said to our people long ago, 'You must not murder anyone.'[n] Anyone who murders another will be judged.' [22]But I tell you, if you are angry with your brother,[n] you will be judged. And if you say bad things to your brother, you will be judged by the Jewish council. And if you call your brother a fool, then you will be in danger of the fire of hell.

[23]"So when you offer your gift to God at the altar, and you remember that your brother has something against you, [24]leave your gift there at the altar. Go and make peace with him. Then come and offer your gift.

[25]"If your enemy is taking you to court, become friends with him quickly. You should do that before you go to court. If you don't become his friend, he might turn you over to the judge. And the judge might give you to a guard to put you in jail. [26]I tell you that you will not leave that jail until you have paid everything you owe.

JESUS TEACHES ABOUT ADULTERY

[27]"You have heard that it was said, 'You must not be guilty of adultery.'[n] [28]But I tell you that if anyone looks at a woman with lust, he has already committed adultery with her in his mind. [29]If your right eye causes you to sin, then take it out and throw it away. It is better to lose one part of your body than to have your whole body thrown into hell. [30]If your right hand causes you to sin, then cut it off and throw it away. It is better to lose one part of your body than for your whole body to go into hell.

JESUS TEACHES ABOUT DIVORCE

[31]"It was also said, 'Anyone who divorces his wife must give her a written divorce paper.'[n] [32]But I tell you that anyone who divorces his wife is causing his wife to be guilty of adultery. The only reason for a man to divorce his wife is if she has been unfaithful to him. And anyone who marries that divorced woman is guilty of adultery.

MAKE PROMISES CAREFULLY

[33]"You have heard that it was said to our people long ago, 'When you make a promise, don't break your promise. Keep the promises that you make to the Lord.'[n] [34]But I tell you, never make an oath. Don't make an oath using the name of heaven, because heaven is God's throne. [35]Don't make an oath using the name of the earth, because the earth belongs to God. Don't make an oath using the name of Jerusalem, because that is the city of the great King. [36]And don't even say that your own head is proof that you will keep your oath. You cannot make one hair on your head become white or black. [37]Say only 'yes' if you mean 'yes,' and say only 'no' if you mean 'no.' If you must say more than 'yes' or 'no,' it is from the Evil One.

DON'T FIGHT BACK

[38]"You have heard that it was said, 'An eye for an eye, and a tooth for a tooth.'[n] [39]But I tell you, don't stand up against an evil person. If someone slaps you on the right cheek, then turn and let him slap the other cheek too. [40]If someone wants to sue you in court and take your shirt, then let him have your coat too. [41]If a soldier forces you to go with him one mile, then go with him two miles. [42]If a person asks you for something, then give it to him. Don't refuse to give to a person who wants to borrow from you.

5:21 **You . . . anyone.** Quotation from Exodus 20:13; Deuteronomy 5:17.
5:22 **brother** Some Greek copies continue, "without a reason."
5:27 **'You . . . adultery.'** Quotation from Exodus 20:14; Deuteronomy 5:18.
5:31 **'Anyone . . . divorce paper.'** Quotation from Deuteronomy 24:1.
5:33 **'When . . . Lord.'** Quotation from Leviticus 19:12; Numbers 30:2; Deuteronomy 23:21.
5:38 **'An eye . . . tooth.'** Quotation from Exodus 21:24; Leviticus 24:20; Deuteronomy 19:21.

LOVE ALL PEOPLE

⁴³"You have heard that it was said, 'Love your neighbor" and hate your enemies.' ⁴⁴But I tell you, love your enemies. Pray for those who hurt you." ⁴⁵If you do this, then you will be true sons of your Father in heaven. Your Father causes the sun to rise on good people and on bad people. Your Father sends rain to those who do good and to those who do wrong. ⁴⁶If you love only the people who love you, then you will get no reward. Even the tax collectors do that. ⁴⁷And if you are nice only to your friends, then you are no better than other people. Even people without God are nice to their friends. ⁴⁸So you must be perfect, just as your Father in heaven is perfect.

JESUS TEACHES ABOUT GIVING

6 "Be careful! When you do good things, don't do them in front of people to be seen by them. If you do that, then you will have no reward from your Father in heaven.

²"When you give to the poor, don't be like the hypocrites. They blow trumpets before they give so that people will see them. They do that in the synagogues and on the streets. They want other people to honor them. I tell you the truth. Those hypocrites already have their full reward. ³So when you give to the poor, give very secretly. Don't let anyone know what you are doing. ⁴Your giving should be done in secret. Your Father can see what is done in secret, and he will reward you.

JESUS TEACHES ABOUT PRAYER

⁵"When you pray, don't be like the hypocrites. They love to stand in the synagogues and on the street corners and pray loudly. They want people to see them pray. I tell you the truth. They

already have their full reward. ⁶When you pray, you should go into your room and close the door. Then pray to your Father who cannot be seen. Your Father can see what is done in secret, and he will reward you.

⁷"And when you pray, don't be like those people who don't know God. They continue saying things that mean nothing. They think that God will hear them because of the many things they say. ⁸Don't be like them. Your Father knows the things you need before you ask him. ⁹So when you pray, you should pray like this:

'Our Father in heaven,
 we pray that your name will always
  be kept holy.
¹⁰ We pray that your kingdom will come.
 We pray that what you want will be
  done,
  here on earth as it is in heaven.
¹¹ Give us the food we need for each day.
¹² Forgive the sins we have done,
  just as we have forgiven those who
   did wrong to us.
¹³ And do not cause us to be tested;
 but save us from the Evil One.'
  [The kingdom, the power, and the
   glory are yours forever. Amen.]"

¹⁴Yes, if you forgive others for the things they do wrong, then your Father in heaven will also forgive you for the things you do wrong. ¹⁵But if you don't forgive the wrongs of others, then your Father in heaven will not forgive the wrong things you do.

JESUS TEACHES ABOUT WORSHIP

¹⁶"When you give up eating," don't put on a sad face like the hypocrites. They make their faces look strange to show people that they are giving up eating. I

5:43 Love your neighbor Quotation from Leviticus 19:18.
5:44 you Some Greek copies continue, "Bless those who curse you, do good to those who hate you." Compare Luke 6:28.
6:13 The . . . Amen. Some Greek copies do not contain the bracketed text.
6:16 give up eating This is called "fasting." The people would give up eating for a special time of prayer and worship to God. It was also done to show sadness.

tell you the truth, those hypocrites already have their full reward. ¹⁷So when you give up eating, comb your hair and wash your face. ¹⁸Then people will not know that you are giving up eating. But your Father, whom you cannot see, will see you. Your Father sees what is done in secret, and he will reward you.

GOD IS MORE IMPORTANT THAN MONEY

¹⁹"Don't store treasures for yourselves here on earth. Moths and rust will destroy treasures here on earth. And thieves can break into your house and steal the things you have. ²⁰So store your treasure in heaven. The treasures in heaven cannot be destroyed by moths or rust. And thieves cannot break in and steal that treasure. ²¹Your heart will be where your treasure is.

²²"The eye is a light for the body. If your eyes are good, then your whole body will be full of light. ²³But if your eyes are evil, then your whole body will be full of darkness. And if the only light

☆ Matthew 6:25–34

Jesus taught his followers many things about God. One of the lessons he taught them is that they don't need to worry. God will provide everything we need. Just like he does for animals and plants, God provides what we need to eat and wear.

God cares about you. He helps you feel calm when you are worried. What makes you worry? When your mom leaves you with a babysitter, do you wonder when she will be home? On the first day of school, do you worry if you will like your teacher? Philippians 4:6 says, "Do not worry about anything. But pray and ask God for everything you need." God does not want you to worry. He wants you to talk to him. He will help you feel better.

* *

Read the verses in this section and remember that we can't solve anything by worrying about it. Give all your worries to Jesus.

you have is really darkness, then you have the worst darkness.

²⁴"No one can be a slave to two masters. He will hate one master and love the other. Or he will follow one master and refuse to follow the other. So you cannot serve God and money at the same time.

DON'T WORRY

²⁵"So I tell you, don't worry about the food you need to live. And don't worry about the clothes you need for your body. Life is more important than food. And the body is more important than clothes. ²⁶Look at the birds in the air. They don't plant or harvest or store food in barns. But your heavenly Father feeds the birds. And you know that you are worth much more than the birds. ²⁷You cannot add any time to your life by worrying about it.

²⁸"And why do you worry about clothes? Look at the flowers in the field. See how they grow. They don't work or make clothes for themselves. ²⁹But I tell you that even Solomon with his riches was not dressed as beautifully as one of these flowers. ³⁰God clothes the grass in the field like that. The grass is living today, but tomorrow it is thrown into the fire to be burned. So you can be even more sure that God will clothe you. Don't have so little faith! ³¹Don't worry and say, 'What will we eat?' or 'What will we drink?' or 'What will we wear?' ³²All the people who don't know God keep trying to get these things. And your Father in heaven knows that you need them. ³³The thing you should want most is God's kingdom and doing what God wants. Then all these other things you need will be given to you. ³⁴So don't worry about tomorrow. Each day has enough trouble of its own. Tomorrow will have its own worries.

BE CAREFUL ABOUT JUDGING OTHERS

7 "Don't judge other people, and you will not be judged. ²You will be judged in the same way that you judge others. And the forgiveness you give to others will be given to you. ³"Why do you notice the little piece of dust that is in your brother's eye, but you don't notice the big piece of wood that is in your own eye? ⁴Why do you say to your brother, 'Let me take that little piece of dust out of your eye'? Look at yourself first! You still have that big piece of wood in your own eye. ⁵You are a hypocrite! First, take the wood out of your own eye. Then you will see clearly enough to take the dust out of your brother's eye.

⁶"Don't give holy things to dogs. Don't throw your pearls before pigs. Pigs will only trample on them. And the dogs will only turn to attack you.

ASK GOD FOR WHAT YOU NEED

⁷"Continue to ask, and God will give to you. Continue to search, and you will find. Continue to knock, and the door will open for you. ⁸Yes, everyone who continues asking will receive. He who continues searching will find. And he who continues knocking will have the door opened for him.

⁹"What would you do if your son asks for bread? Which of you would give him a stone? ¹⁰Or if your son asks for a fish, would you give him a snake? ¹¹Even though you are bad, you know how to give good gifts to your children. So surely your heavenly Father will give good things to those who ask him.

THE MOST IMPORTANT RULE

¹²"Do for other people the same things you want them to do for you. This is the meaning of the law of Moses and the teaching of the prophets.

THE WAY TO HEAVEN IS HARD

¹³"Enter through the narrow gate. The road that leads to hell is a very easy road. And the gate to hell is very wide. Many people enter through that gate. ¹⁴But the gate that opens the way to true life is very small. And the road to true

life is very hard. Only a few people find that road.

PEOPLE KNOW YOU BY YOUR ACTIONS

¹⁵"Be careful of false prophets. They come to you and look gentle like sheep. But they are really dangerous like wolves. ¹⁶You will know these people because of the things they do. Good things don't come from bad people, just as grapes don't come from thornbushes. And figs don't come from thorny weeds. ¹⁷In the same way, every good tree produces good fruit. And bad trees produce bad fruit. ¹⁸A good tree cannot produce bad fruit. And a bad tree cannot produce good fruit. ¹⁹Every tree that does not produce good fruit is cut down and thrown into the fire. ²⁰You will know these false prophets by what they produce.

²¹"Not everyone who says 'You are my Lord' will enter the kingdom of heaven. The only people who will enter the kingdom of heaven are those who do the things that my Father in heaven wants. ²²On the last day many people will say to me, 'You are our Lord! We spoke for you. And through you we forced out demons and did many miracles.' ²³Then I will tell them clearly, 'Get away from me, you who do evil. I never knew you.'

TWO KINDS OF PEOPLE

²⁴"Everyone who hears these things I say and obeys them is like a wise man. The wise man built his house on rock. ²⁵It rained hard and the water rose. The winds blew and hit that house. But the house did not fall, because the house was built on rock. ²⁶But the person who hears the things I teach and does not obey them is like a foolish man. The foolish man built his house on sand. ²⁷It rained hard, the water rose, and the winds blew and hit that house. And the house fell with a big crash."

²⁸When Jesus finished saying these things, the people were amazed at his teaching. ²⁹Jesus did not teach like their teachers of the law. He taught like a person who had authority.

JESUS HEALS A SICK MAN

8 When Jesus came down from the hill, great crowds followed him. ²Then a man sick with a harmful skin disease came to Jesus. The man bowed down before him and said, "Lord, you have the power to heal me if you want."

³Jesus touched the man and said, "I want to heal you. Be healed!" And immediately the man was healed from his skin disease. ⁴Then Jesus said to him, "Don't tell anyone about what happened. But go and show yourself to the priest.^{n} And offer the gift that Moses commanded^n for people who are made well. This will show people that you are healed."

JESUS HEALS A SOLDIER'S SERVANT

⁵Jesus went to the city of Capernaum. When he entered the city, an army officer came to Jesus and begged for help. ⁶The officer said, "Lord, my servant is at home in bed. He can't move his body and is in much pain."

⁷Jesus said to the officer, "I will go and heal him."

⁸The officer answered, "Lord, I am not good enough for you to come into my house. All you need to do is command that my servant be healed, and he will be healed. ⁹I myself am a man under the authority of other men. And I have soldiers under my command. I tell one soldier, 'Go,' and he goes. I tell another soldier, 'Come,' and he comes. I say to my servant, 'Do this,' and my servant obeys me.

¹⁰When Jesus heard this, he was amazed. He said to those who were with him, "I tell you the truth. This man

---

8:4 **show . . . priest** The law of Moses said a priest must say when a Jew who had a harmful skin disease was well.
8:4 **Moses commanded** Read about this in Leviticus 14:1–32.

has more faith than any other person I have found, even in Israel. [11]Many people will come from the east and from the west. They will sit and eat with Abraham, Isaac, and Jacob in the kingdom of heaven. [12]And those people who should have the kingdom will be thrown outside into the darkness. In that place people will cry and grind their teeth with pain."

[13]Then Jesus said to the officer, "Go home. Your servant will be healed just as you believed he would." And at that same time his servant was healed.

JESUS HEALS MANY PEOPLE

[14]Jesus went to Peter's house. There Jesus saw that Peter's mother-in-law was in bed with a high fever. [15]Jesus touched her hand, and the fever left her. Then she stood up and began to serve Jesus.

[16]That evening people brought to Jesus many who had demons. Jesus spoke and the demons left them. Jesus healed all the sick. [17]He did these things to make come true what Isaiah the prophet said:

> "He took our suffering on him.
>   And he felt our pain for us."
>   Isaiah 53:4

PEOPLE WANT TO FOLLOW JESUS

[18]When Jesus saw the crowd around him, he told his followers to go to the other side of the lake. [19]Then a teacher of the law came to Jesus and said, "Teacher, I will follow you any place you go."

[20]Jesus said to him, "The foxes have holes to live in. The birds have nests to live in. But the Son of Man has no place where he can rest his head."

[21]Another man, one of Jesus' followers, said to Jesus, "Lord, let me go and bury my father first."

[22]But Jesus said to him, "Follow me, and let the people who are dead bury their own dead."

JESUS STOPS A STORM

[23]Jesus got into a boat, and his followers went with him. [24]A very bad storm arose on the lake. The waves covered the boat. But Jesus was sleeping. [25]The followers went to Jesus and woke him. They said, "Lord, save us! We will drown!"

[26]Jesus answered, "Why are you afraid? You don't have enough faith." Then Jesus got up and gave a command to the wind and the sea. The wind stopped, and the sea became very calm.

[27]The men were amazed. They said, "What kind of man is this? Even the wind and the sea obey him!"

> Jesus touched the man and said, "I want to heal you. Be healed!"
> –MATTHEW 8:3

JESUS HEALS TWO MEN WITH DEMONS

[28]Jesus arrived at the other side of the lake in the country of the Gadarene[n] people. There, two men came to Jesus. They had demons in them. These men lived in the burial caves. They were so dangerous that people could not use the road by those caves. [29]The two men came to Jesus and shouted, "What do you want with us, Son of God? Did you come here to punish us before the right time?"

[30]Near that place there was a large

8:28 Gadarene From Gadara, an area southeast of Lake Galilee. The exact location is uncertain and some Greek copies read "Gergesene"; others read "Gerasene."

herd of pigs feeding. [31]The demons begged Jesus, "If you make us leave these men, please send us into that herd of pigs."

[32]Jesus said to them, "Go!" So the demons left the men and went into the pigs. Then the whole herd of pigs ran down the hill into the lake and were drowned. [33]The men who were caring for the pigs ran away and went into town. They told about all of this and what had happened to the men who had demons. [34]Then the whole town went out to see Jesus. When they saw him, they begged him to leave their area.

JESUS HEALS A PARALYZED MAN

9 Jesus got into a boat and went back across the lake to his own town. [2]Some people brought to Jesus a man who was paralyzed. The man was lying on his mat. Jesus saw that these people had great faith, so he said to the paralyzed man, "Be happy, young man. Your sins are forgiven."

[3]Some of the teachers of the law heard this. They said to themselves, "This man speaks as if he were God— that is blasphemy!" [n]

[4]Jesus knew what they were thinking. So he said, "Why are you thinking evil thoughts? [5]Which is easier: to tell this paralyzed man, 'Your sins are forgiven,' or to tell him, 'Stand up and walk'? [6]But I will prove to you that the Son of Man has power on earth to forgive sins." Then Jesus said to the paralyzed man, "Stand up. Take your mat and go home." [7]And the man stood up and went home. [8]The people saw this and were amazed. They praised God for giving power like this to men.

JESUS CHOOSES MATTHEW

[9]When Jesus was leaving, he saw a man named Matthew. Matthew was sitting in the tax office. Jesus said to him, "Follow me." And Matthew stood up and followed Jesus.

[10]Jesus had dinner at Matthew's house. Many tax collectors and "sinners" came and ate with Jesus and his followers. [11]The Pharisees saw this and asked Jesus' followers, "Why does your teacher eat with tax collectors and 'sinners'?"

[12]Jesus heard the Pharisees ask this. So he said, "Healthy people don't need a doctor. Only the sick need a doctor. [13]Go and learn what this means: 'I want faithful love more than I want animal sacrifices.' [n] I did not come to invite good people. I came to invite sinners."

JESUS IS NOT LIKE OTHER JEWS

[14]Then the followers of John[n] came to Jesus. They said to Jesus, "We and the Pharisees often give up eating.[n] But your followers don't. Why?"

[15]Jesus answered, "The friends of the bridegroom are not sad while he is with them. But the time will come when the bridegroom will leave them. Then his friends are sad, and they will give up eating.

[16]"When someone sews a patch over a hole in an old coat, he never uses a piece of cloth that is not yet shrunk. If he does, the patch will shrink and pull away from the coat. Then the hole will be worse. [17]Also, people never pour new wine into old leather bags for holding wine. If they do, the old bags will break. The wine will spill, and the wine bags will be ruined. But people always pour new wine into new wine bags. Then the wine and the wine bags will continue to be good."

JESUS GIVES LIFE TO A DEAD GIRL AND HEALS A SICK WOMAN

[18]While Jesus was saying these things, a ruler of the synagogue came to him.

9:3 **blasphemy** Saying things against God.
9:13 **'I want . . . sacrifices.'** Quotation from Hosea 6:6.
9:14 **John** John the Baptist, who preached to people about Christ's coming (Matthew 3; Luke 3).
9:14 **give up eating** This is called "fasting." The people would give up eating for a special time of prayer and worship to God. It was also done to show sadness.

The ruler bowed down before Jesus and said, "My daughter has just died. But come and touch her with your hand, and she will live again."

¹⁹So Jesus stood up and went with the ruler. Jesus' followers went too.

²⁰Then a woman who had been bleeding for 12 years came behind Jesus and touched the edge of his coat. ²¹She was thinking, "If I can touch his coat, then I will be healed."

²²Jesus turned and saw the woman. He said, "Be happy, dear woman. You are made well because you believed." And the woman was healed at once.

²³Jesus continued along with the ruler and went into the ruler's house. Jesus saw people there who play music for funerals. And he saw many people there crying. ²⁴Jesus said, "Go away. The girl is not dead. She is only asleep." But the people laughed at Jesus. ²⁵After the crowd had been put outside, Jesus went into the girl's room. He took her hand, and she stood up. ²⁶The news about this spread all around the area.

JESUS HEALS MORE PEOPLE

²⁷When Jesus was leaving there, two blind men followed him. They cried out, "Show kindness to us, Son of David!"

²⁸Jesus went inside, and the blind men went with him. He asked the men, "Do you believe that I can make you see again?"

They answered, "Yes, Lord."

²⁹Then Jesus touched their eyes and said, "You believe that I can make you see again. So this will happen." ³⁰Then the men were able to see. But Jesus warned them very strongly, saying, "Don't tell anyone about this." ³¹But the blind men left and spread the news about Jesus all around that area.

³²When the two men were leaving, some people brought another man to Jesus. This man could not talk because he had a demon in him. ³³Jesus forced the demon to leave the man. Then the man who couldn't talk was able to speak. The crowd was amazed and said, "We have never seen anything like this in Israel."

³⁴But the Pharisees said, "The leader of demons is the one that gives him power to force demons out."

³⁵Jesus traveled through all the towns and villages. He taught in their synagogues and told people the Good News about the kingdom. And he healed all kinds of diseases and sicknesses. ³⁶He saw the crowds of people and felt sorry for them because they were worried and helpless. They were like sheep without a shepherd. ³⁷Jesus said to his followers, "There are many people to harvest, but there are only a few workers to help harvest them. ³⁸God owns the harvest. Pray to him that he will send more workers to help gather his harvest." [n]

JESUS SENDS OUT HIS APOSTLES

10 Jesus called his 12 followers together. He gave them power to drive out evil spirits and to heal every kind of disease and sickness. ²These are the names of the 12 apostles: Simon (also called Peter) and his brother Andrew; James son of Zebedee, and his brother John; ³Philip and Bartholomew; Thomas and Matthew, the tax collector; James son of Alphaeus, and Thaddaeus; ⁴Simon the Zealot and Judas Iscariot. Judas is the one who turned against Jesus.

⁵These 12 men he sent out with the following order: "Don't go to the non-Jewish people. And don't go into any town where the Samaritans live. ⁶But go to the people of Israel. They are like sheep that are lost. ⁷When you go, preach this: 'The kingdom of heaven is coming soon.' ⁸Heal the sick. Give dead people life again. Heal those who have harmful skin diseases. Force demons to leave people. I give you these powers

---

9:37–38 "There are . . . harvest." As a farmer sends workers to harvest the grain, Jesus sends his followers to bring people to God.

freely. So help other people freely.
⁹Don't carry any money with you—gold or silver or copper. ¹⁰Don't carry a bag. Take for your trip only the clothes and sandals you are wearing. Don't take a walking stick. A worker should be given the things he needs.

¹¹"When you enter a city or town, find some worthy person there and stay in his home until you leave. ¹²When you enter that home, say, 'Peace be with you.' ¹³If the people there welcome you, let your peace stay there. But if they don't welcome you, take back the peace you wished for them. ¹⁴And if a home or town refuses to welcome you or listen to you, then leave that place. Shake its dust off your feet.ⁿ ¹⁵I tell you the truth. On the Judgment Day it will be worse for that town than for the towns of Sodom and Gomorrah.ⁿ

JESUS WARNS HIS APOSTLES

¹⁶"Listen! I am sending you out, and you will be like sheep among wolves. So be as smart as snakes. But also be like doves and do nothing wrong. ¹⁷Be careful of people. They will arrest you and take you to court. They will whip you in their synagogues. ¹⁸Because of me you will be taken to stand before governors and kings. You will tell them and the non-Jewish people about me. ¹⁹When you are arrested, don't worry about what to say or how you should say it. At that time you will be given the things to say. ²⁰It will not really be you speaking. The Spirit of your Father will be speaking through you.

²¹"Brothers will turn against their own brothers and give them over to be killed. Fathers will turn against their own children and give them to be killed. Children will fight against their own parents and have them killed. ²²All people will hate you because you follow me. But the person who continues strong until the end will be saved. ²³When you are treated badly in one city, go to another city. I tell you the truth. You will not finish going through all the cities of Israel before the Son of Man comes.

²⁴"A student is not better than his teacher. A servant is not better than his master. ²⁵A student should be satisfied to become like his teacher. A servant should be satisfied to become like his master. If the head of the family is called Beelzebul, then the other members of the family will be called worse names!

FEAR GOD, NOT PEOPLE

²⁶"So don't be afraid of those people. Everything that is hidden will be shown. Everything that is secret will be made known. ²⁷I tell you these things in the dark, but I want you to tell them in the light. I speak these things only to you, but you should tell them to everyone. ²⁸Don't be afraid of people. They can only kill the body. They cannot kill the soul. The only one you should fear is the One who can destroy the body and the soul in hell. ²⁹When birds are sold, two small birds cost only a penny. But not even one of the little birds can die without your Father's knowing it. ³⁰God even knows how many hairs are on your head. ³¹So don't be afraid. You are worth much more than many birds.

> The blind can see . . . The deaf can hear. The dead are raised to life.
>
> –MATTHEW 11:5

10:14 **Shake . . . feet.** A warning. It showed that they were finished talking to these people.
10:15 **Sodom and Gomorrah** Two cities that God destroyed because the people were so evil.

TELL PEOPLE ABOUT YOUR FAITH

[32]"If anyone stands before other people and says he believes in me, then I will say that he belongs to me. I will say this before my Father in heaven. [33]But if anyone stands before people and says he does not believe in me, then I will say that he does not belong to me. I will say this before my Father in heaven.

[34]"Don't think that I have come to bring peace to the earth. I did not come to bring peace, but a sword. [35]I have come to make this happen:

'A son will be against his father,
    a daughter will be against her
        mother,
a daughter-in-law will be against her
        mother-in-law.
[36]   A person's enemies will be
        members of his own family.'
                            Micah 7:6

[37]"Whoever loves his father or mother more than he loves me is not worthy to be my follower. Whoever loves his son or daughter more than he loves me is not worthy to be my follower. [38]Whoever is not willing to die on a cross and follow me is not worthy of me. [39]Whoever tries to hold on to his life will give up true life. Whoever gives up his life for me will hold on to true life. [40]Whoever accepts you also accepts me. And whoever accepts me also accepts the One who sent me. [41]Whoever meets a prophet and accepts him will receive the reward of a prophet. And whoever accepts a good man because that man is good will receive the reward of a good man. [42]Whoever helps one of these little ones because they are my followers will truly get his reward. He will get his reward even if he only gave my follower a cup of cold water."

JESUS AND JOHN THE BAPTIST

11 Jesus finished telling these things to his 12 followers. Then he left there and went to the towns in Galilee to teach and preach.

[2]John the Baptist was in prison, but he heard about the things the Christ was doing. So John sent some of his followers to Jesus. [3]They asked Jesus, "Are you the man who John said was coming, or should we wait for another one?"

[4]Jesus answered, "Go back to John and tell him about the things you hear and see: [5]The blind can see. The crippled can walk. People with harmful skin diseases are healed. The deaf can hear. The dead are raised to life. And the Good News is told to the poor. [6]The person who does not lose faith because of me is blessed."

[7]As John's followers were leaving, Jesus began talking to the people about John. Jesus said, "What did you go out to the desert to see? A reed[n] blown by the wind? No. [8]Really, what did you go out to see? A man dressed in fine clothes? No. Those people who wear fine clothes live in kings' palaces. [9]So what did you go out to see? A prophet? Yes, and I tell you, John is more than a prophet. [10]This was written about John in the Scriptures:

'I will send my messenger ahead of
        you.
    He will prepare the way for you.'
                            Malachi 3:1

[11]I tell you the truth: John the Baptist is greater than any other man who has ever lived. But even the least important person in the kingdom of heaven is greater than John. [12]Since the time John the Baptist came until now, the kingdom of heaven has been going forward in strength. People using force have been trying to take the kingdom. [13]All the prophets and the law of Moses spoke until the time John came. They told about the things that would happen. [14]And if you will believe the things the law and the prophets said, then you will

---

11:7 reed It means that John was not weak like grass blown by the wind.

believe that John is Elijah. The law and the prophets said he would come. [15]Let those with ears use them and listen!

[16]"What can I say about the people who live today? What are they like? They are like children sitting in the marketplace. One group calls to the other,

[17] 'We played music for you, but you did not dance;
  we sang a sad song, but you did not cry.'

[18]John came, and he did not eat like other people or drink wine. And people say, 'He has a demon.' [19]The Son of Man came, eating and drinking wine, and people say, 'Look at him! He eats too much and drinks too much. He is a friend of tax collectors and "sinners."' But wisdom is proved to be right by the things it does."

JESUS WARNS UNBELIEVERS

[20]Then Jesus criticized the cities where he did most of his miracles. He criticized them because the people there did not change their lives and stop sinning. [21]Jesus said, "How terrible for you, Korazin! How terrible for you, Bethsaida! I did many miracles in you. If those same miracles had happened in Tyre and Sidon,[n] then the people there would have changed their lives a long time ago. They would have worn rough cloth and put ashes on themselves to show that they had changed. [22]But I tell you, on the Judgment Day it will be worse for you than for Tyre and Sidon. [23]And you, Capernaum,[n] will you be lifted up to heaven? No. You will be thrown down to the depths. I did many miracles in you. If those same miracles had happened in Sodom,[n] its people would have stopped sinning, and it would still be a city today. [24]But I tell you it will be worse for you on the Judgment Day than for Sodom."

JESUS OFFERS REST TO PEOPLE

[25]Then Jesus said, "I thank you, Father, Lord of heaven and earth. I praise you because you have hidden these things from the people who are wise and smart. But you have shown them to those who are like little children. [26]Yes, Father, this is what you really wanted.

[27]"My Father has given me all things. No one knows the Son—only the Father knows the Son. And no one knows the Father—only the Son knows the Father. And the only people who will know about the Father are those whom the Son chooses to tell.

[28]"Come to me, all of you who are tired and have heavy loads. I will give you rest. [29]Accept my work and learn from me. I am gentle and humble in spirit. And you will find rest for your souls. [30]The work that I ask you to accept is easy. The load I give you to carry is not heavy."

JESUS IS LORD OF THE SABBATH

12 About that same time, Jesus was walking through some fields of grain on a Sabbath day. His followers were with him, and they were hungry. So they began to pick the grain and eat it. [2]The Pharisees saw this, and they said to Jesus, "Look! Your followers are doing something that is against the Jewish law to do on the Sabbath day."

[3]Jesus answered, "Have you not read what David did when he and the people with him were hungry? [4]David went into God's house. He and those with him ate the bread that was made holy for God. It was against the law for them to eat that bread. Only the priests were allowed to eat it. [5]And have you not read in the law of Moses that on every Sabbath day the priests in the Temple break this law about the Sabbath day? But the priests are not wrong for doing that. [6]I tell you that there is something

---

11:21 **Tyre and Sidon** Towns where wicked people lived.
11:21–23 **Korazin...Bethsaida...Capernaum** Towns by Lake Galilee where Jesus preached to the people.
11:23 **Sodom** City that God destroyed because the people were so evil.

here that is greater than the Temple. [7]The Scripture says, 'I want faithful love more than I want animal sacrifices.' [n] You don't really know what those words mean. If you understood them, you would not judge those who have done nothing wrong.

[8]"The Son of Man is Lord of the Sabbath day."

JESUS HEALS A MAN'S CRIPPLED HAND

[9]Jesus left there and went into their synagogue. [10]In the synagogue, there was a man with a crippled hand. Some Jews there were looking for a reason to accuse Jesus of doing wrong. So they asked him, "Is it right to heal on the Sabbath day?" [n]

[11]Jesus answered, "If any of you has a sheep, and it falls into a ditch on the Sabbath day, then you will take the sheep and help it out of the ditch. [12]Surely a man is more important than a sheep. So the law of Moses allows people to do good things on the Sabbath day."

[13]Then Jesus said to the man with the crippled hand, "Let me see your hand." The man put his hand out, and the hand became well again, the same as the other hand. [14]But the Pharisees left and made plans to kill Jesus.

JESUS IS GOD'S CHOSEN SERVANT

[15]Jesus knew what the Pharisees were doing, so he left that place. Many people followed him, and he healed all who were sick. [16]But Jesus warned the people not to tell who he was. [17]He did these things to make come true what Isaiah the prophet had said:

[18] "Here is my servant whom I have chosen.
　　I love him, and I am pleased with him.
　　I will put my Spirit in him.
　　Then he will tell how I will judge all people fairly.
[19] He will not argue or shout.
　　No one will hear his voice in the streets.
[20] He will not break a crushed blade of grass.
　　He will not put out even a weak flame.
　　He will continue until he makes fair judgment win the victory.
[21]　In him will the nations find hope."
Isaiah 42:1–4

JESUS' POWER IS FROM GOD

[22]Then some people brought a man to Jesus. This man was blind and could not talk, because he had a demon. Jesus healed the man, and the man could talk and see. [23]All the people were amazed. They said, "Perhaps this man is the Son of David!"

[24]The Pharisees heard the people saying this. The Pharisees said, "Jesus uses the power of Beelzebul to force demons out of people. Beelzebul is the ruler of demons."

[25]Jesus knew what the Pharisees were thinking. So he said to them, "Every kingdom that is fighting against itself will be destroyed. And every city that is divided will fall. And every family that is divided cannot succeed. [26]So if Satan forces out his own demons, then Satan is divided, and his kingdom will not continue. [27]You say that I use the power of Satan when I force out demons. If that is true, then what power do your people use when they force out demons? So your own people prove that you are wrong. [28]But if I use the power of God's Spirit to force out demons, this shows that the kingdom of God has come to you.

[29]"If anyone wants to enter a strong man's house and steal his things, first he must tie up the strong man. Then he can steal the things from the strong man's house.

12:7 'I...sacrifices.' Quotation from Hosea 6:6.
12:10 "Is it right...day?" It was against Jewish law to work on the Sabbath day.

[30]"If anyone is not with me, then he is against me. He who does not work with me is working against me. [31]So I tell you, people can be forgiven for every sin they do. And people can be forgiven for every bad thing they say. But if anyone speaks against the Holy Spirit, then he will not be forgiven. [32]Anyone who says things against the Son of Man can be forgiven. But anyone who says things against the Holy Spirit will not be forgiven. He will not be forgiven now or in the future.

PEOPLE KNOW YOU BY YOUR WORDS

[33]"If you want good fruit, you must make the tree good. If your tree is not good, then it will have bad fruit. A tree is known by the kind of fruit it produces. [34]You snakes! You are evil people! How can you say anything good? The mouth speaks the things that are in the heart. [35]A good person has good things in his heart. And so he speaks the good things that come from his heart. But an evil person has evil in his heart. So he speaks the evil things that come from his heart. [36]And I tell you that people will have to explain about every careless thing they have said. This will happen on the Judgment Day. [37]The words you have said will be used to judge you. Some of your words will prove you right, but some of your words will prove you guilty."

THE LEADERS ASK FOR A MIRACLE

[38]Then some of the Pharisees and teachers of the law answered Jesus. They said, "Teacher, we want to see you work a miracle as a sign."

[39]Jesus answered, "Evil and sinful people are the ones who want to see a miracle for a sign. But no sign will be given to them. The only sign will be what happened to the prophet Jonah. [40]Jonah was in the stomach of the big fish for three days and three nights. In the same way, the Son of Man will be in the grave three days and three nights. [41]And on the Judgment Day the men from Nineveh[n] will stand up with you people who live today. They will show that you are guilty because when Jonah preached to them, they were sorry and changed their lives. And I tell you that someone greater than Jonah is here! [42]On the Judgment Day, the Queen of the South[n] will stand up with you people who live today. She will show that you are guilty because she came from far away to listen to Solomon's wise teaching. And I tell you that someone greater than Solomon is here!

PEOPLE TODAY ARE FULL OF EVIL

[43]"When an evil spirit comes out of a man, it travels through dry places looking for a place to rest. But it finds no place to rest. [44]So the spirit says, 'I will go back to the home I left.' When the spirit comes back to the man, the spirit finds the home still empty. The home is swept clean and made neat. [45]Then the evil spirit goes out and brings seven other spirits even more evil than it is. Then all the spirits go into the man and live there. And that man has even more trouble than he had before. It is the same way with the evil people who live today."

JESUS' TRUE FAMILY

[46]While Jesus was talking to the people, his mother and brothers stood outside. They wanted to talk to him. [47]Someone told Jesus, "Your mother and brothers are waiting for you outside. They want to talk to you."[n]

[48]He answered, "Who is my mother? Who are my brothers?" [49]Then he pointed to his followers and said, "See!

12:41 Nineveh The city where Jonah preached to warn the people. Read Jonah 3.
12:42 Queen of the South The Queen of Sheba. She traveled 1,000 miles to learn God's wisdom from Solomon. Read 1 Kings 10:1–13.
12:47 Someone . . . you. Some Greek copies do not have verse 47.

One of the ways Jesus taught people lessons was through telling stories. One of his stories was about how God's word is like a seed that gets planted in the ground.

Danny loved spending time with his grandmother. She worked in her garden almost every day, planting seeds, watering the seeds, and pulling weeds. She taught Danny how to plant seeds. She would dig in the dirt and let him drop the seeds into the ground. He would then cover them with dirt. Over the weeks and months, Danny would check on the plants that grew from those seeds. It was fun watching them grow. And then one day, Danny saw food growing where the seeds used to be. His grandmother showed him how to pick the food and cook it. But nobody had to tell Danny how to eat the food. It was always so good! The stories that Jesus told and the stories in the Bible are like those seeds. They get planted in our hearts, and then they grow. They make us healthy and strong!

. . . .

God's words are like seeds. The only way to plant them in your heart is to read them and hear them. Then God does the rest.

These people are my mother and my brothers. [50]My true brothers and sisters and mother are those who do the things that my Father in heaven wants."

A STORY ABOUT PLANTING SEED

13 That same day Jesus went out of the house and sat by the lake. [2]Large crowds gathered around him. So Jesus got into a boat and sat, while the people stayed on the shore. [3]Then Jesus used stories to teach them many things.

He said: "A farmer went out to plant his seed. [4]While he was planting, some seed fell by the road. The birds came and ate all that seed. [5]Some seed fell on rocky ground, where there wasn't enough dirt. That seed grew very fast, because the ground was not deep. [6]But when the sun rose, the plants dried up because they did not have deep roots. [7]Some other seed fell among thorny weeds. The weeds grew and choked the good plants. [8]Some other seed fell on good ground where it grew and became grain. Some plants made 100 times more grain. Other plants made 60 times more grain, and some made 30 times more grain. ⁹Let those with ears use them and listen!"

WHY JESUS USED STORIES TO TEACH

¹⁰The followers came to Jesus and asked, "Why do you use stories to teach the people?"

¹¹Jesus answered, "Only you can know the secret truths about the kingdom of heaven. Other people cannot know these secret truths. ¹²The person who has something will be given more. And he will have all he needs. But the person who does not have much, even what he has will be taken from him. ¹³This is why I use stories to teach the people: They see, but they don't really see. They hear, but they don't really understand. ¹⁴So they show that the things Isaiah said about them are true:

'You will listen and listen, but you
        will not understand.
    You will look and look, but you will
        not learn.
¹⁵ For these people have become
        stubborn.
    They do not hear with their ears.
    And they have closed their eyes.
Otherwise they might really
        understand
    what they see with their eyes
    and hear with their ears.
They might really understand in
        their minds.
    If they did this, they would come
        back to me and be forgiven.'
            Isaiah 6:9–10

¹⁶But you are blessed. You understand the things you see with your eyes. And you understand the things you hear with your ears. ¹⁷I tell you the truth. Many prophets and good people wanted to see the things that you now see. But they did not see them. And many prophets and good people wanted to hear the things that you now hear. But they did not hear them.

JESUS EXPLAINS THE SEED STORY

¹⁸"So listen to the meaning of that story about the farmer. ¹⁹What is the seed that fell by the road? That seed is like the person who hears the teaching about the kingdom but does not understand it. The Evil One comes and takes away the things that were planted in that person's heart. ²⁰And what is the seed that fell on rocky ground? That seed is like the person who hears the teaching and quickly accepts it with joy. ²¹But he does not let the teaching go deep into his life. He keeps it only a short time. When trouble or persecution comes because of the teaching he accepted, then he quickly gives up. ²²And what is the seed that fell among the thorny weeds? That seed is like the person who hears the teaching but lets worries about this life and love of money stop that teaching from growing. So the teaching does not produce fruit[n] in that person's life. ²³But what is the seed that fell on the good ground? That seed is like the person who hears the teaching and understands it. That person grows and produces fruit, sometimes 100 times more, sometimes 60 times more, and sometimes 30 times more."

A STORY ABOUT WHEAT AND WEEDS

²⁴Then Jesus told them another story. He said, "The kingdom of heaven is like a man who planted good seed in his field. ²⁵That night, when everyone was asleep, his enemy came and planted weeds among the wheat. Then the enemy went away. ²⁶Later, the wheat grew and heads of grain grew on the wheat plants. But at the same time the weeds also grew. ²⁷Then the man's servants came to him and said, 'You

---

13:22 **produce fruit** To produce fruit means to have in your life the good things God wants.

planted good seed in your field. Where did the weeds come from?' ²⁸The man answered, 'An enemy planted weeds.' The servants asked, 'Do you want us to pull up the weeds?' ²⁹The man answered, 'No, because when you pull up the weeds, you might also pull up the wheat. ³⁰Let the weeds and the wheat grow together until the harvest time. At harvest time I will tell the workers this: First gather the weeds and tie them together to be burned. Then gather the wheat and bring it to my barn.'"

STORIES OF MUSTARD SEED AND YEAST

³¹Then Jesus told another story: "The kingdom of heaven is like a mustard seed. A man plants the seed in his field. ³²That seed is the smallest of all seeds. But when it grows, it is one of the largest garden plants. It becomes a tree, big enough for the wild birds to come and make nests in its branches."

³³Then Jesus told another story: "The kingdom of heaven is like yeast that a woman mixes into a big bowl of flour. The yeast makes all the dough rise."

³⁴Jesus used stories to tell all these things to the people. He always used stories to teach people. ³⁵This is as the prophet said:

"I will speak using stories;
I will tell things that have been secret since the world was made." *Psalm 78:2*

JESUS EXPLAINS ABOUT THE WHEAT AND WEEDS

³⁶Then Jesus left the crowd and went into the house. His followers came to him and said, "Explain to us the meaning of the story about the weeds in the field."

³⁷Jesus answered, "The man who planted the good seed in the field is the Son of Man. ³⁸The field is the world. And the good seed are all of God's children in the kingdom. The weeds are those people who belong to the Evil One. ³⁹And the enemy who planted the bad seed is the devil. The harvest time is the end of the age. And the workers who gather are God's angels.

⁴⁰"The weeds are pulled up and burned in the fire. It will be this way at the end of the age. ⁴¹The Son of Man will send out his angels. They will gather out of his kingdom all who cause sin and all who do evil. ⁴²The angels will throw them into the blazing furnace. There the people will cry and grind their teeth with pain. ⁴³Then the good people will shine like the sun in the kingdom of their Father. Let those with ears use them and listen!

> That seed is like the person who hears the teaching and understands it. That person grows and produces fruit.
>
> –MATTHEW 13:23

STORIES OF A TREASURE AND A PEARL

⁴⁴"The kingdom of heaven is like a treasure hidden in a field. One day a man found the treasure, and then he hid it in the field again. The man was very happy to find the treasure. He went and sold everything that he owned to buy that field.

⁴⁵"Also, the kingdom of heaven is like a man looking for fine pearls. ⁴⁶One day he found a very valuable pearl. The man went and sold everything he had to buy that pearl.

A STORY OF A FISHING NET

⁴⁷"Also, the kingdom of heaven is like a net that was put into the lake. The net caught many different kinds of fish. ⁴⁸When it was full, the fishermen pulled the net to the shore. They sat down and

put all the good fish in baskets. Then they threw away the bad fish. ⁴⁹It will be this way at the end of the age. The angels will come and separate the evil people from the good people. ⁵⁰The angels will throw the evil people into the blazing furnace. In that place the people will cry and grind their teeth with pain."

⁵¹Jesus asked his followers, "Do you understand all these things?"

They answered, "Yes, we understand."

⁵²Then Jesus said to them, "So every teacher of the law who has been taught about the kingdom of heaven is like the owner of a house. He has both new things and old things saved in his house. And he brings out both those new things and old things."

JESUS GOES TO HIS HOMETOWN

⁵³When Jesus finished teaching with these stories, he left there. ⁵⁴He went to the town where he grew up. He taught the people in the synagogue, and they were amazed. They said, "Where did this man get this wisdom and this power to do miracles? ⁵⁵He is only the son of the carpenter. And his mother is Mary. His brothers are James, Joseph, Simon and Judas. ⁵⁶And all his sisters are here with us. So where does this man get all these things?" ⁵⁷And the people refused to accept Jesus.

But Jesus said to them, "A prophet is honored everywhere except in his own town or in his own home."

⁵⁸The people there did not believe in Jesus. So Jesus did not do many miracles there.

HOW JOHN THE BAPTIST WAS KILLED

14 At that time Herod, the ruler of Galilee, heard the reports about Jesus. ²So Herod said to his servants, "Jesus is really John the Baptist. He has risen from death. That is why he is able to do these miracles."

³Sometime before this, Herod had arrested John, tied him up, and put him into prison. Herod did this because of Herodias. Herodias was the wife of Philip, Herod's brother. ⁴Herod arrested John because he told Herod: "It is not right for you to have Herodias." ⁵Herod wanted to kill John, but he was afraid of the people. They believed that John was a prophet.

⁶On Herod's birthday, the daughter of Herodias danced for Herod and his guests. Herod was very pleased with her, ⁷so he promised he would give her anything she wanted. ⁸Herodias told her daughter what to ask for. So she said to Herod, "Give me the head of John the Baptist here on a platter." ⁹King Herod was very sad. But he had promised to give her anything she wanted, and the people eating with him had heard his promise. So Herod ordered that what she asked for be done. ¹⁰He sent men to the prison to cut off John's head. ¹¹And the men brought John's head on a platter and gave it to the girl. She took it to her mother, Herodias. ¹²John's followers came and got his body and buried it. Then they went and told Jesus what happened.

MORE THAN 5,000 PEOPLE FED

¹³When Jesus heard what happened to John, Jesus left in a boat. He went to a lonely place by himself. But when the crowds heard about it, they followed him on foot from the towns. ¹⁴When Jesus arrived, he saw a large crowd. He felt sorry for them and healed those who were sick.

¹⁵Late that afternoon, his followers came to Jesus and said, "No one lives in this place. And it is already late. Send the people away so they can go to the towns and buy food for themselves."

¹⁶Jesus answered, "They don't need to go away. You give them some food to eat."

¹⁷The followers answered, "But we have only five loaves of bread and two fish."

¹⁸Jesus said, "Bring the bread and the fish to me." ¹⁹Then he told the people to

sit down on the grass. He took the five loaves of bread and the two fish. Then he looked to heaven and thanked God for the food. Jesus divided the loaves of bread. He gave them to his followers, and they gave the bread to the people. ²⁰All the people ate and were satisfied. After they finished eating, the followers filled 12 baskets with the pieces of food that were not eaten. ²¹There were about 5,000 men there who ate, as well as women and children.

JESUS WALKS ON THE WATER

²²Then Jesus made his followers get into the boat. He told them to go ahead of him to the other side of the lake. Jesus stayed there to tell the people they could go home. ²³After he said goodbye to them, he went alone up into the hills to pray. It was late, and Jesus was there alone. ²⁴By this time, the boat was already far away on the lake. The boat was having trouble because of the waves, and the wind was blowing against it.

²⁵Between three and six o'clock in the morning, Jesus' followers were still in the boat. Jesus came to them. He was walking on the water. ²⁶When the followers saw him walking on the water, they were afraid. They said, "It's a ghost!" and cried out in fear.

²⁷But Jesus quickly spoke to them. He said, "Have courage! It is I! Don't be afraid."

²⁸Peter said, "Lord, if that is really you, then tell me to come to you on the water."

²⁹Jesus said, "Come."

And Peter left the boat and walked on the water to Jesus. ³⁰But when Peter saw the wind and the waves, he became afraid and began to sink. He shouted, "Lord, save me!"

³¹Then Jesus reached out his hand and caught Peter. Jesus said, "Your faith is small. Why did you doubt?"

³²After Peter and Jesus were in the boat, the wind became calm. ³³Then those who were in the boat worshiped Jesus and said, "Truly you are the Son of God!"

³⁴After they crossed the lake, they came to the shore at Gennesaret. ³⁵The people there saw Jesus and knew who he was. So they told people all around there that Jesus had come. They brought all their sick to him. ³⁶They begged Jesus to let them just touch the edge of his coat to be healed. And all the sick people who touched it were healed.

OBEY GOD'S LAW NOT MEN'S

15 Then some Pharisees and teachers of the law came to Jesus from Jerusalem. They asked him, ²"Why do your followers not obey the rules given to us by the great people who lived before us? Your followers don't wash their hands before they eat!"

³Jesus answered, "And why do you refuse to obey God's command so that you can follow those rules you have? ⁴God said, 'Honor your father and mother.' ⁿ And God also said, 'Anyone who says cruel things to his father or mother must be put to death.' ⁿ ⁵But you say that a person can tell his father or mother, 'I have something I could use to help you. But I will not use it for you. I will give it to God.' ⁶You teach that person not to honor his father. You teach that it is not important to do what God said. You think that it is more important to follow the rules you have. ⁷You are hypocrites! Isaiah was right when he spoke about you:

⁸ 'These people show honor to me with words.
But their hearts are far from me.
⁹ Their worship of me is worthless.
The things they teach are nothing but human rules they have memorized.'" *Isaiah 29:13*

15:4 'Honor . . . mother.' Quotation from Exodus 20:12; Deuteronomy 5:16.
15:4 'Anyone . . . death.' Quotation from Exodus 21:17.

[10]Jesus called the crowd to him. He said, "Listen and understand what I am saying. [11]It is not what a person puts into his mouth that makes him unclean. It is what comes out of his mouth that makes him unclean."

[12]Then his followers came to Jesus and asked, "Do you know that the Pharisees are angry because of what you said?"

[13]Jesus answered, "Every plant that my Father in heaven has not planted himself will be pulled up by the roots. [14]Stay away from the Pharisees. They are blind leaders.[n] And if a blind man leads another blind man, then both men will fall into a ditch."

[15]Peter said, "Explain the story to us."

[16]Jesus said, "You still have trouble under-standing? [17]Surely you know that all the food that enters the mouth goes into the stomach. Then that food goes out of the body. [18]But what a person says with his mouth comes from the way he thinks. And these are the things that make him unclean. [19]Out of the mind come evil thoughts, murder, adultery, sexual immorality, stealing, lying, and saying bad things against other people. [20]These things make a person unclean. But eating with unwashed hands does not make him unclean."

JESUS HELPS A NON-JEWISH WOMAN

[21]Jesus left that place and went to the area of Tyre and Sidon. [22]A Canaanite woman from that area came to Jesus. The woman cried out, "Lord, Son of David, please help me! My daughter has a demon, and she is suffering very much."

[23]But Jesus did not answer the woman. So the followers came to Jesus and begged him, "Tell the woman to go away. She is following us and shouting."

[24]Jesus answered, "God sent me only to the lost sheep, the people of Israel."

[25]Then the woman came to Jesus again. She bowed before him and said, "Lord, help me!"

[26]Jesus answered, "It is not right to take the children's bread and give it to the dogs."

[27]The woman said, "Yes, Lord, but even the dogs eat the pieces of food that fall from their masters' table."

[28]Then Jesus answered, "Woman, you have great faith! I will do what you asked me to do." And at that moment the woman's daughter was healed.

JESUS HEALS MANY PEOPLE

[29]Then Jesus left that place and went to the shore of Lake Galilee. He went up on a hill and sat there.

[30]Great crowds came to Jesus. They brought their sick with them: the lame, the blind, the crippled, the dumb and many others. They put them at Jesus' feet, and he healed them. [31]The crowd was amazed when they saw that people who could not speak were able to speak again. The crippled were made strong again. Those who could not walk were able to walk again. The blind were able to see again. And they praised the God of Israel for this.

MORE THAN 4,000 PEOPLE FED

[32]Jesus called his followers to him and said, "I feel sorry for these people. They have been with me three days, and now they have nothing to eat. I don't want

> Then Jesus answered, "Woman, you have great faith! I will do what you asked me to do."
>
> —MATTHEW 15:28

15:14 **leaders** Some Greek copies continue, "of blind people."

to send them away hungry. They might faint while going home."

³³His followers asked him, "Where can we get enough bread to feed all these people? We are far away from any town."

³⁴Jesus asked, "How many loaves of bread do you have?"

They answered, "We have seven loaves and a few small fish."

³⁵Jesus told the people to sit on the ground. ³⁶He took the seven loaves of bread and the fish and gave thanks to God for the food. Then Jesus divided the food and gave it to his followers. They gave the food to the people. ³⁷All the people ate and were satisfied. After this, the followers filled seven baskets with the pieces of food that were not eaten. ³⁸There were about 4,000 men there who ate, besides women and children. ³⁹After they ate, Jesus told the people to go home. He got into the boat and went to the area of Magadan.

THE LEADERS ASK FOR A MIRACLE

16 The Pharisees and Sadducees came to Jesus. They wanted to trap him. So they asked him to show them a miracle to prove that he was from God.

²Jesus answered,ⁿ "When you see the sunset, you know what the weather will be. If the sky is red, then you say we will have good weather. ³And in the morning if the sky is dark and red, then you say that it will be a rainy day. You see these signs in the sky, and you know what they mean. In the same way, you see the things that are happening now. But you don't know their meaning. ⁴Evil and sinful people ask for a miracle as a sign. But they will have no sign—only the sign of Jonah."ⁿ Then Jesus left them and went away.

GUARD AGAINST WRONG TEACHINGS

⁵Jesus and his followers went across the lake. But the followers forgot to bring bread. ⁶Jesus said to them, "Be careful! Guard against the yeast of the Pharisees and the Sadducees."

⁷The followers discussed the meaning of this. They said, "Did Jesus say this because we forgot to bring bread?"

⁸Jesus knew that they were talking about this. So he asked them, "Why are you talking about not having bread? Your faith is small. ⁹You still don't understand? Remember the five loaves of bread that fed the 5,000 people? And remember that you filled many baskets with bread after the people finished eating? ¹⁰And remember the seven loaves of bread that fed the 4,000 people? Remember that you filled many baskets then also? ¹¹So I was not talking to you about bread. Why don't you understand that? I am telling you to be careful and guard against the yeast of the Pharisees and the Sadducees."

¹²Then the followers understood what Jesus meant. He was not telling them to guard against the yeast used in bread. He was telling them to guard against the teaching of the Pharisees and the Sadducees.

PETER SAYS JESUS IS THE CHRIST

¹³Jesus went to the area of Caesarea Philippi. He said to his followers, "I am the Son of Man. Who do the people say I am?"

¹⁴They answered, "Some people say you are John the Baptist. Others say you are Elijah. And others say that you are Jeremiah or one of the prophets."

¹⁵Then Jesus asked them, "And who do you say I am?"

¹⁶Simon Peter answered, "You are the Christ, the Son of the living God."

16:2 answered Some Greek copies do not have the rest of verse 2 and verse 3.
16:4 sign of Jonah Jonah's three days in the big fish are like Jesus' three days in the tomb. The story about Jonah is in the book of Jonah.

[17]Jesus answered, "You are blessed, Simon son of Jonah. No person taught you that. My Father in heaven showed you who I am. [18]So I tell you, you are Peter.[n] And I will build my church on this rock. The power of death will not be able to defeat my church. [19]I will give you the keys of the kingdom of heaven. The things you don't allow on earth will be the things that God does not allow. The things you allow on earth will be the things that God allows." [20]Then Jesus warned his followers not to tell anyone that he was the Christ.

JESUS SAYS THAT HE MUST DIE

[21]From that time on Jesus began telling his followers that he must go to Jerusalem. He explained that the Jewish elders, the leading priests, and the teachers of the law would make him suffer many things. And he told them that he must be killed. Then, on the third day, he would be raised from death.

[22]Peter took Jesus aside and began to criticize him. Peter said, "God save you from those things, Lord! Those things will never happen to you!"

[23]Then Jesus said to Peter, "Go away from me, Satan![n] You are not helping me! You don't care about the things of God. You care only about things that men think are important."

[24]Then Jesus said to his followers, "If anyone wants to follow me, he must say 'no' to the things he wants. He must be willing even to die on a cross, and he must follow me. [25]Whoever wants to save his life will give up true life. And whoever gives up his life for me will have true life. [26]It is worth nothing for a man to have the whole world if he loses his soul. He could never pay enough to buy back his soul. [27]The Son of Man will come again with his Father's glory and with his angels. At that time, he will reward everyone for what he has done.

[28]I tell you the truth. There are some people standing here who, before they die, will see the Son of Man coming with his kingdom."

JESUS WITH MOSES AND ELIJAH

17 Six days later, Jesus took Peter, James, and John the brother of James up on a high mountain. They were all alone there. [2]While they watched, Jesus was changed. His face became bright like the sun. And his clothes became white as light. [3]Then two men were there, talking with him. The men were Moses and Elijah.[n]

[4]Peter said to Jesus, "Lord, it is good that we are here. If you want, I will put three tents here—one for you, one for Moses, and one for Elijah."

[5]While Peter was talking, a bright cloud covered them. A voice came from the cloud. The voice said, "This is my Son and I love him. I am very pleased with him. Obey him!"

[6]The followers with Jesus heard the voice. They were so frightened that they fell to the ground. [7]But Jesus went to them and touched them. He said, "Stand up. Don't be afraid." [8]When the followers looked up, they saw Jesus was now alone.

[9]When Jesus and the followers were coming down the mountain, Jesus commanded them, "Don't tell anyone about the things you saw on the mountain. Wait until the Son of Man has been raised from death. Then you may tell."

[10]The followers asked Jesus, "Why do the teachers of the law say that Elijah must come first, before the Christ comes?"

[11]Jesus answered, "They are right to say that Elijah is coming. And it is true that Elijah will make everything the way it should be. [12]But I tell you, Elijah has already come. People did not know who he was. They did to him everything they wanted to do. It will be the

---

16:18 Peter The Greek name "Peter," like the Aramaic name "Cephas," means "rock."
16:23 Satan Name for the devil, meaning "the enemy." Jesus means that Peter was talking like Satan.
17:3 Moses and Elijah Two of the most important Jewish leaders in the past.

☆ Matthew 17:14–20

Jesus told his followers that they could heal sick people just like Jesus did. So, one day, a man brought his sick boy to Jesus' followers to be healed. But they couldn't heal the boy. The man then brought his boy to Jesus. When Jesus commanded the boy to be well, he was instantly well. The followers were confused. They didn't understand why they couldn't heal the boy like Jesus said they should. Jesus told them it was because they had no faith. If they even had a little bit of faith—the size of a tiny seed—they could have healed the boy.

Jesus wanted his disciples to have faith in his power. He told them that all they needed was faith the size of a mustard seed. Have you ever seen a mustard seed? It is one of the smallest seeds there is. It is so small, you can barely see it. But when it is planted, it can grow into a tree that is nine feet tall! So, remember that tiny, tiny mustard seed—even if your faith seems small, God can still do big things through you.

. . . .

Jesus said that with God, anything is possible. Because he said it, you can have faith that he means it.

same with the Son of Man. Those same people will make the Son of Man suffer." [13]Then the followers understood that Jesus was talking about John the Baptist.

JESUS HEALS A SICK BOY

[14]Jesus and his followers went back to the crowd. A man came to Jesus and bowed before him. [15]The man said, "Lord, please help my son. He has epilepsy[n] and is suffering very much. He often falls into the fire or into the water. [16]I brought him to your followers, but they could not cure him."

[17]Jesus answered, "You people have no faith. Your lives are all wrong. How long must I stay with you? How long

17:15 epilepsy A disease that causes a person sometimes to lose control of his body, and maybe faint, shake strongly, or not be able to move.

must I continue to be patient with you? Bring the boy here." [18]Jesus gave a strong command to the demon inside the boy. Then the demon came out, and the boy was healed.

[19]The followers came to Jesus when he was alone. They said, "Why couldn't we force the demon out?"

[20]Jesus answered, "You were not able to drive out the demon because your faith is too small. I tell you the truth. If your faith is as big as a mustard seed,[n] you can say to this mountain, 'Move from here to there.' And the mountain will move. All things will be possible for you. [21][That kind of spirit comes out only if you use prayer and give up eating.]" [n]

JESUS TALKS ABOUT HIS DEATH

[22]Later, the followers met together in Galilee. Jesus said to them, "The Son of Man will be given into the control of some men. [23]They will kill him, but on the third day he will be raised from death." And the followers were filled with sadness.

JESUS TALKS ABOUT PAYING TAXES

[24]Jesus and his followers went to Capernaum. There some men came to Peter. They were the men who collected the Temple tax. They asked, "Does your teacher pay the Temple tax?"

[25]Peter answered, "Yes, Jesus pays the tax."

Peter went into the house where Jesus was. Before Peter could speak, Jesus said to him, "The kings on the earth collect different kinds of taxes. But who are the people who pay the taxes? Are they the king's children? Or do others pay the taxes? What do you think?"

[26]Peter answered, "Other people pay the taxes."

Jesus said to Peter, "Then the children of the king don't have to pay taxes.

[27]But we don't want to make these tax collectors angry. So go to the lake and fish. After you catch the first fish, open its mouth. Inside its mouth you will find a coin. Take that coin and give it to the tax collectors. That will pay the tax for you and me."

WHO IS THE GREATEST?

18 At that time the followers came to Jesus and asked, "Who is greatest in the kingdom of heaven?"

[2]Jesus called a little child to him. He stood the child before the followers. [3]Then he said, "I tell you the truth. You must change and become like little children. If you don't do this, you will never enter the kingdom of heaven. [4]The greatest person in the kingdom of heaven is the one who makes himself humble like this child.

[5]"Whoever accepts a little child in my name accepts me. [6]If one of these little children believes in me, and someone causes that child to sin, then it will be very bad for that person. It would be better for him to have a large stone tied around his neck and be drowned in the sea. [7]How terrible for the people of the world because of the things that cause them to sin. Such things will happen. But how terrible for the one who causes them to happen. [8]If your hand or your foot causes you to sin, cut it off and throw it away. It is better for you to have only part of your body but have life forever. That is much better than to have two hands and two feet but be thrown into the fire that burns forever. [9]If your eye causes you to sin, take it out and throw it away. It is better for you to have only one eye but have life forever. That is much better than to have two eyes but be thrown into the fire of hell.

A LOST SHEEP

[10]"Be careful. Don't think these little children are worth nothing. I tell you

---

17:20 **mustard seed** This seed is very small, but the plant grows taller than a man.
17:21 **That ... eating.** Some Greek copies do not contain the bracketed text.

that they have angels in heaven who are always with my Father in heaven. [11][The Son of Man came to save lost people.][n]

[12]"If a man has 100 sheep, but 1 of the sheep gets lost, he will leave the other 99 sheep on the hill. He will go to look for the lost sheep. [13]And if he finds it, he is happier about that 1 sheep than about the 99 that were never lost. I tell you the truth. [14]In the same way, your Father in heaven does not want any of these little children to be lost.

WHEN A PERSON SINS AGAINST YOU

[15]"If your brother sins against you,[n] go and tell him what he did wrong. Do this in private. If he listens to you, then you have helped him to be your brother again. [16]But if he refuses to listen, then go to him again and take one or two other people with you. 'Every case may be proved by two or three witnesses.'[n] [17]If he refuses to listen to them, then tell it to the church. If he refuses to listen to the church, then treat him as you would one who does not believe in God. Treat him as if he were a tax collector.

[18]"I tell you the truth. The things you don't allow on earth will be the things God does not allow. The things you allow on earth will be the things that God allows.

[19]"Also, I tell you that if two of you on earth agree about something, then you can pray for it. And the thing you ask for will be done for you by my Father in heaven. [20]This is true because if two or three people come together in my name, I am there with them."

AN UNFORGIVING SERVANT

[21]Then Peter came to Jesus and asked, "Lord, when my brother sins against me, how many times must I forgive him? Should I forgive him as many as 7 times?"

[22]Jesus answered, "I tell you, you must forgive him more than 7 times. You must forgive him even if he does wrong to you 70 times 7.

[23]"The kingdom of heaven is like a king who decided to collect the money his servants owed him. [24]So the king began to collect his money. One servant owed him several million dollars. [25]But the servant did not have enough money to pay his master, the king. So the master ordered that everything the servant owned should be sold, even the servant's wife and children. The money would be used to pay the king what the servant owed.

[26]"But the servant fell on his knees and begged, 'Be patient with me. I will pay you everything I owe.' [27]The master felt sorry for his servant. So the master told the servant he did not have to pay. He let the servant go free.

[28]"Later, that same servant found another servant who owed him a few dollars. The servant grabbed the other servant around the neck and said, 'Pay me the money you owe me!'

[29]"The other servant fell on his knees and begged him, 'Be patient with me. I will pay you everything I owe.'

[30]"But the first servant refused to be patient. He threw the other servant into prison until he could pay everything he owed. [31]All the other servants saw what happened. They were very sorry. So they went and told their master all that had happened.

[32]"Then the master called his servant in and said, 'You evil servant! You begged me to forget what you owed. So I told you that you did not have to pay anything. [33]I had mercy on you. You should have had the same mercy on that other servant.' [34]The master was very angry, and he put the servant in prison to be punished. The servant had to stay in prison until he could pay everything he owed.

18:11 **The . . . people.** Some Greek copies do not contain the bracketed text.
18:15 **against you** Some Greek copies do not have this phrase.
18:16 **'Every . . . witnesses.'** Quotation from Deuteronomy 19:15.

[35]"This king did what my heavenly Father will do to you if you do not forgive your brother from your heart."

JESUS TEACHES ABOUT DIVORCE

19 After Jesus said all these things, he left Galilee. He went into the area of Judea on the other side of the Jordan River. [2]Large crowds followed Jesus, and he healed them there.

[3]Some Pharisees came to Jesus and tried to trick him. They asked, "Is it right for a man to divorce his wife for any reason he chooses?"

[4]Jesus answered, "Surely you have read in the Scriptures: When God made the world, 'he made them male and female.'[n] [5]And God said, 'So a man will leave his father and mother and be united with his wife. And the two people will become one body.'[n] [6]So the two are not two, but one. God joined the two people together. No person should separate them."

[7]The Pharisees asked, "Why then did Moses give a command for a man to divorce his wife by giving her divorce papers?"

[8]Jesus answered, "Moses allowed you to divorce your wives because you refused to accept God's teaching. But divorce was not allowed in the beginning. [9]I tell you that anyone who divorces his wife and marries another woman is guilty of adultery.[n] The only reason for a man to divorce and marry again is if his first wife has been unfaithful to him."

[10]The followers said to him, "If that is the only reason a man can divorce his wife, then it is better not to marry."

[11]Jesus answered, "Not everyone can accept this truth about marriage. But God has made some able to accept it. [12]There are different reasons why some men cannot marry. Some men were born without the ability to become fathers. Others were made that way later in life by other people. And other men have given up marriage because of the kingdom of heaven. But the person who can marry should accept this teaching about marriage."[n]

JESUS WELCOMES CHILDREN

[13]Then the people brought their little children to Jesus so that he could put his hands on them[n] and pray for them. When his followers saw this, they told the people to stop bringing their children to Jesus. [14]But Jesus said, "Let the little children come to me. Don't stop them, because the kingdom of heaven belongs to people who are like these children." [15]After Jesus put his hands on the children, he left there.

A RICH YOUNG MAN'S QUESTION

[16]A man came to Jesus and asked, "Teacher, what good thing must I do to have life forever?"

[17]Jesus answered, "Why do you ask me about what is good? Only God is good. But if you want to have life forever, obey the commands."

[18]The man asked, "Which commands?"

Jesus answered, "'You must not murder anyone. You must not be guilty of adultery. You must not steal. You must not tell lies about your neighbor in court. [19]Honor your father and mother.[n] Love your neighbor as you love yourself.'"[n]

[20]The young man said, "I have

19:4 'he made . . . female.' Quotation from Genesis 1:27 or 5:2.
19:5 'So . . . body.' Quotation from Genesis 2:24.
19:9 adultery Some Greek copies continue, "And anyone who marries a divorced woman is guilty of adultery." Compare Matthew 5:32.
19:12 But . . . marriage. This may also mean, "The person who can accept this teaching about not marrying should accept it."
19:13 put his hands on them Showing that Jesus gave special blessings to these children.
19:18–19 'You . . . mother.' Quotation from Exodus 20:12–16; Deuteronomy 5:16–20.
19:19 'Love . . . yourself.' Quotation from Leviticus 19:18.

obeyed all these things. What else do I need to do?"

²¹Jesus answered, "If you want to be perfect, then go and sell all the things you own. Give the money to the poor. If you do this, you will have a treasure in heaven. Then come and follow me!"

²²But when the young man heard this, he became very sad because he was very rich. So he left Jesus.

²³Then Jesus said to his followers, "I tell you the truth. It will be very hard for a rich person to enter the kingdom of heaven. ²⁴Yes, I tell you that it is easier for a camel to go through the eye of a needle than for a rich person to enter the kingdom of God."

²⁵When the followers heard this, they were very surprised. They asked, "Then who can be saved?"

²⁶Jesus looked at them and said, "For men this is impossible. But for God all things are possible."

²⁷Peter said to Jesus, "We left everything we had and followed you. So what will we have?"

²⁸Jesus said to them, "I tell you the truth. When the new age comes, the Son of Man will sit on his great throne. And all of you who followed me will also sit on 12 thrones. And you will judge the 12 tribes of Israel. ²⁹And everyone who has left houses, brothers, sisters, father, mother,ⁿ children, or farms to follow me will get much more than he left. And he will have life forever. ³⁰Many who are first now will be last in the future. And many who are last now will be first in the future.

A STORY ABOUT VINEYARD WORKERS

20 "The kingdom of heaven is like a man who owned some land. One morning, he went out very early to hire some people to work in his vineyard. ²The man agreed to pay the workers one silver coinⁿ for working that day. Then he sent them into the vineyard to work. ³About nine o'clock the man went to the marketplace and saw some other people standing there, doing nothing. ⁴So he said to them, 'If you go and work in my vineyard, I will pay you what your work is worth.' ⁵So they went to work in the vineyard. The man went out again about twelve o'clock and again at three o'clock. Both times he hired people to work in his vineyard. ⁶About five o'clock the man went to the marketplace again. He saw others standing there. He asked them, 'Why did you stand here all day doing nothing?' ⁷They answered, 'No one gave us a job.' The man said to them, 'Then you can go and work in my vineyard.'

⁸"At the end of the day, the owner of the vineyard said to the boss of all the workers, 'Call the workers and pay them. Start by paying the last people I hired. Then pay all of them, ending with the workers I hired first.'

⁹"The workers who were hired at five o'clock came to get their pay. Each worker received one silver coin. ¹⁰Then the workers who were hired first came to get their pay. They thought they would be paid more than the others. But each one of them also received one silver coin. ¹¹When they got their silver coin, they complained to the man who

> The people brought their little children to Jesus so that he could . . . pray for them.
>
> –MATTHEW 19:13

19:29 mother Some Greek copies continue, "or wife."
20:2 silver coin A Roman denarius. One coin was the average pay for one day's work.

owned the land. [12]They said, 'Those people were hired last and worked only one hour. But you paid them the same as you paid us. And we worked hard all day in the hot sun.' [13]But the man who owned the vineyard said to one of those workers, 'Friend, I am being fair to you. You agreed to work for one silver coin. [14]So take your pay and go. I want to give the man who was hired last the same pay that I gave you. [15]I can do what I want with my own money. Are you jealous because I am good to those people?'

[16]"So those who are last now will someday be first. And those who are first now will someday be last."

JESUS TALKS ABOUT HIS OWN DEATH

[17]Jesus was going to Jerusalem. His 12 followers were with him. While they were on the way, Jesus gathered the followers together and spoke to them privately. He said to them, [18]"We are going to Jerusalem. The Son of Man will be turned over to the leading priests and the teachers of the law. They will say that he must die. [19]They will give the Son of Man to the non-Jewish people. They will laugh at him and beat him with whips, and then they will kill him on a cross. But on the third day after his death, he will be raised to life again."

A MOTHER ASKS JESUS A FAVOR

[20]Then the wife of Zebedee came to Jesus. Her sons were with her. The mother bowed before Jesus and asked him to do something for her.

[21]Jesus asked, "What do you want?"

She said, "Promise that one of my sons will sit at your right side in your kingdom. And promise that the other son will sit at your left side."

[22]But Jesus said, "You don't understand what you are asking. Can you

accept the kind of suffering that I must suffer?"[n]

The sons answered, "Yes, we can!"

[23]Jesus said to them, "Truly you will suffer the same things that I will suffer. But I cannot choose who will sit at my right side or my left side. Those places belong to those for whom my Father has prepared them."

[24]The other ten followers heard this and were angry with the two brothers.

[25]Jesus called all the followers together. He said, "You know that the rulers of the non-Jewish people love to show their power over the people. And their important leaders love to use all their authority. [26]But it should not be that way among you. If one of you wants to become great, then he must serve the rest of you like a servant. [27]If one of you wants to become first, then he must serve the rest of you like a slave. [28]So it is with the Son of Man. The Son of Man did not come for other people to serve him. He came to serve others. The Son of Man came to give his life to save many people."

JESUS HEALS TWO BLIND MEN

[29]When Jesus and his followers were leaving Jericho, a great many people followed Jesus. [30]There were two blind men sitting by the road. The blind men heard that Jesus was going by, so they shouted, "Lord, Son of David, please help us!"

[31]All the people criticized the blind men. They told them to be quiet. But the blind men shouted more and more, "Lord, Son of David, please help us!"

[32]Jesus stopped and said to the blind men, "What do you want me to do for you?"

[33]They answered, "Lord, we want to be able to see."

[34]Jesus felt sorry for the blind men. He touched their eyes, and at once they were able to see. Then the men followed Jesus.

20:22 accept . . . suffer Literally, "drink the cup that I must drink." Jesus used the idea of drinking from a cup to mean accepting the terrible things that would happen to him.

JESUS ENTERS JERUSALEM AS A KING

21 Jesus and his followers were coming closer to Jerusalem. But first they stopped at Bethphage at the hill called the Mount of Olives. From there Jesus sent two of his followers into the town. ²He said to them, "Go to the town you can see there. When you enter it, you will find a donkey tied there with its colt. Untie them and bring them to me. ³If anyone asks you why you are taking the donkeys, tell him, 'The Master needs them. He will send them back soon.'" ⁴This was to make clear the full meaning of what the prophet said:

⁵ "Tell the people of Jerusalem,
　'Your king is coming to you.
He is gentle and riding on a donkey.
　He is on the colt of a donkey.'"
　　　　Isaiah 62:11; Zechariah 9:9

⁶The followers went and did what Jesus told them to do. ⁷They brought the donkey and the colt to Jesus. They laid their coats on the donkeys, and

---

☆ Matthew 21:5–7

Hundreds of years before Jesus was born, one of Israel's prophets spoke of the coming King. It was the Good News Israel and Judah had been waiting for. But then he explained how he would show up in Jerusalem, the capital city. Instead of riding a big white horse, he would be riding on a donkey . . . a young donkey even!

In Jesus' day, important people rode in chariots or on big horses. Today, they ride in big, fancy cars. When some people walk onto a stage, they like a spotlight to shine on them. And they like when people clap. Most people like to be noticed. But not Jesus. Instead of riding in a chariot so people would think he was important, he rode what ordinary people rode, a donkey. He wanted God to be in the spotlight. Instead of people clapping for him, he wanted them to know his heavenly Father as their own Father.

. . . .

Like Jesus, we can live so people notice God and not us.

Jesus sat on them. [8]Many people spread their coats on the road before Jesus. Others cut branches from the trees and spread them on the road. [9]Some of the people were walking ahead of Jesus. Others were walking behind him. All the people were shouting,

> "Praise[n] to the Son of David!
> God bless the One who comes in the name of the Lord!   *Psalm 118:26*
> Praise to God in heaven!"

[10]Then Jesus went into Jerusalem. The city was filled with excitement. The people asked, "Who is this man?"

[11]The crowd answered, "This man is Jesus. He is the prophet from the town of Nazareth in Galilee."

JESUS GOES TO THE TEMPLE

[12]Jesus went into the Temple. He threw out all the people who were buying and selling there. He turned over the tables that belonged to the men who were exchanging different kinds of money. And he upset the benches of those who were selling doves. [13]Jesus said to all the people there, "It is written in the Scriptures, 'My Temple will be a house where people will pray.'[n] But you are changing God's house into a 'hideout for robbers.'"[n]

[14]The blind and crippled people came to Jesus in the Temple, and Jesus healed them. [15]The leading priests and the teachers of the law saw that Jesus was doing wonderful things. They saw the children praising him in the Temple. The children were saying, "Praise[n]

to the Son of David." All these things made the priests and the teachers of the law very angry.

[16]They asked Jesus, "Do you hear the things these children are saying?"

Jesus answered, "Yes. Haven't you read in the Scriptures, 'You have taught children and babies to sing praises'?"[n]

[17]Then Jesus left and went out of the city to Bethany, where he spent the night.

THE POWER OF FAITH

[18]Early the next morning, Jesus was going back to the city. He was very hungry. [19]He saw a fig tree beside the road. Jesus went to it, but there were no figs on the tree. There were only leaves. So Jesus said to the tree, "You will never again have fruit!" The tree immediately dried up.

[20]His followers saw this and were amazed. They asked, "How did the fig tree dry up so quickly?"

[21]Jesus answered, "I tell you the truth. If you have faith and do not doubt, you will be able to do what I did to this tree. And you will be able to do more. You will be able to say to this mountain, 'Go, mountain, fall into the sea.' And if you have faith, it will happen. [22]If you believe, you will get anything you ask for in prayer."

LEADERS DOUBT JESUS' AUTHORITY

[23]Jesus went to the Temple. While he was teaching there, the leading priests and the elders of the people came to Jesus. They said to him, "Tell us! What

> All the people were shouting, "Praise to the Son of David! God bless the One who comes in the name of the Lord!"
>
> —MATTHEW 21:9

21:9, 15 Praise Literally, "Hosanna," a Hebrew word used at first in praying to God for help. At this time it was probably a shout of joy used in praising God or his Messiah.
21:13 'My Temple . . . pray.' Quotation from Isaiah 56:7.
21:13 'hideout for robbers.' Quotation from Jeremiah 7:11.
21:16 'You . . . praises' Quotation from the Septuagint (Greek) version of Psalm 8:2.

authority do you have to do these things? Who gave you this authority?"

²⁴Jesus answered, "I will ask you a question, too. If you answer me, then I will tell you what authority I have to do these things. ²⁵Tell me: When John baptized people, did that come from God or from man?"

The priests and the leaders argued about Jesus' question. They said to each other, "If we answer, 'John's baptism was from God,' then Jesus will say, 'Then why didn't you believe John?' ²⁶But if we say, 'It was from man,' we are afraid of what the people will do because they all believe that John was a prophet."

²⁷So they answered Jesus, "We don't know."

Then Jesus said, "Then I won't tell you what authority I have to do these things!

A STORY ABOUT TWO SONS

²⁸"Tell me what you think about this: There was a man who had two sons. He went to the first son and said, 'Son, go and work today in my vineyard.' ²⁹The son answered, 'I will not go.' But later the son decided he should go, and he went. ³⁰Then the father went to the other son and said, 'Son, go and work today in my vineyard.' The son answered, 'Yes, sir, I will go and work.' But he did not go. ³¹Which of the two sons obeyed his father?"

The priests and leaders answered, "The first son."

Jesus said to them, "I tell you the truth. The tax collectors and the prostitutes will enter the kingdom of God before you do. ³²John came to show you the right way to live. And you did not believe him. But the tax collectors and prostitutes believed John. You saw this, but you still refused to change and believe him.

GOD SENDS HIS SON

³³"Listen to this story: There was a man who owned a vineyard. He put a wall around the vineyard and dug a hole for a winepress. Then he built a tower. He leased the land to some farmers and left for a trip. ³⁴Later, it was time for the grapes to be picked. So the man sent his servants to the farmers to get his share of the grapes. ³⁵But the farmers grabbed the servants, beat one, killed another, and then killed a third servant with stones. ³⁶So the man sent some other servants to the farmers. He sent more servants than he sent the first time. But the farmers did the same thing to the servants that they had done before. ³⁷So the man decided to send his son to the farmers. He said, 'The farmers will respect my son.' ³⁸But when the farmers saw the son, they said to each other, 'This is the owner's son. This vineyard will be his. If we kill him, then his vineyard will be ours!' ³⁹So the farmers grabbed the son, threw him out of the vineyard, and killed him. ⁴⁰So what will the owner of the vineyard do to these farmers when he comes?"

⁴¹The priests and leaders said, "He will surely kill those evil men. Then he will lease the vineyard to some other farmers. They will give him his share of the crop at harvest time."

⁴²Jesus said to them, "Surely you have read this in the Scriptures:

'The stone that the builders did not
    want
  became the cornerstone.
The Lord did this,
  and it is wonderful to us.'
                Psalm 118:22–23

⁴³"So I tell you that the kingdom of God will be taken away from you. It will be given to people who do the things God wants in his kingdom. ⁴⁴The person who falls on this stone will be broken. But if the stone falls on him, he will be crushed." [n]

⁴⁵The leading priests and the Pharisees heard these stories that Jesus

---

21:44 The . . . crushed. Some Greek copies do not have verse 44.

told. They knew he was talking about them. [46]They wanted to arrest him. But they were afraid of the people, because the people believed that Jesus was a prophet.

A STORY ABOUT A WEDDING FEAST

22 Jesus used stories to tell other things to the people. He said, [2]"The kingdom of heaven is like a king who prepared a wedding feast for his son. [3]The king invited some people to the feast. When the feast was ready, the king sent his servants to tell the people to come. But they refused to come to the feast.

[4]"Then the king sent other servants. He said to them, 'Tell those who have been invited that my feast is ready. I have killed my best bulls and calves for the dinner. Everything is ready. Come to the wedding feast.'

[5]"But the people refused to listen to the servants. They went to do other things. One went to work in his field, and another went to his business. [6]Some of the other people grabbed the servants, beat them, and killed them. [7]The king was very angry. He sent his army to kill the people who had killed his servants. And the army burned their city.

[8]"After that, the king said to his servants, 'The wedding feast is ready. I invited those people, but they were not worthy to come. [9]So go to the street corners and invite everyone you see. Tell them to come to my feast.' [10]So the servants went into the streets. They gathered all the people they could find, both good and bad. And the wedding hall was filled with guests.

[11]"Then the king came in to see all the guests. He saw a man there who was not dressed in the right clothes for a wedding. [12]The king said, 'Friend, how were you allowed to come in here? You

are not wearing the right clothes for a wedding.' But the man said nothing. [13]So the king told some servants, 'Tie this man's hands and feet. Throw him out into the darkness. In that place, people will cry and grind their teeth with pain.'

[14]"Yes, many are invited. But only a few are chosen."

THE PHARISEES TRY TO TRAP JESUS

[15]Then the Pharisees left the place where Jesus was teaching. They made plans to trap Jesus with a question. [16]They sent some of their own followers and some men from the group called Herodians.[n] These men said, "Teacher, we know that you are an honest man. We know that you teach the truth about God's way. You are not afraid of what other people think about you. All men are the same to you. [17]So tell us what you think. Is it right to pay taxes to Caesar or not?"

[18]But Jesus knew that these men were trying to trick him. So he said, "You hypocrites! Why are you trying to trap me? [19]Show me a coin used for paying the tax." The men showed him a silver coin.[n] [20]Then Jesus asked, "Whose picture is on the coin? And whose name is written on the coin?"

[21]The men answered, "Caesar's."

Then Jesus said to them, "Give to Caesar the things that are Caesar's. And give to God the things that are God's."

[22]The men heard what Jesus said, and they were amazed. They left him and went away.

SADDUCEES TRY TO TRICK JESUS

[23]That same day some Sadducees came to Jesus. (Sadducees believe that no person will rise from death.) The Sadducees asked Jesus a question. [24]They said, "Teacher, Moses told us that a married man might die without

---

22:16 Herodians A political group that followed Herod and his family.
22:19 silver coin A Roman denarius. One coin was the average pay for one day's work.

having children. Then his brother must marry the widow and have children for him. [25]There were seven brothers among us. The first one married but died. He had no children. So his brother married the widow. [26]Then the second brother also died. The same thing happened to the third brother and all the other brothers. [27]The woman was last to die. [28]But all seven men had married her. So when people rise from death, whose wife will she be?"

[29]Jesus answered, "You don't understand because you don't know what the Scriptures say. And you don't know about the power of God. [30]When people rise from death, there will be no marriage. People will not be married to each other. They will be like the angels in heaven. [31]Surely you have read what God said to you about the rising from death? [32]God said, 'I am the God of Abraham, the God of Isaac, and the God of Jacob.'[n] God is the God of living people, not dead people."

[33]All the people heard this. They were amazed at Jesus' teaching.

THE MOST IMPORTANT COMMAND

[34]The Pharisees learned that the Sadducees could not argue with Jesus' answers to them. So the Pharisees met together. [35]One Pharisee was an expert in the law of Moses. That Pharisee asked Jesus a question to test him. [36]The Pharisee asked, "Teacher, which command in the law is the most important?"

[37]Jesus answered, "'Love the Lord your God with all your heart, soul and mind.'[n] [38]This is the first and most important command. [39]And the second command is like the first: 'Love your neighbor as you love yourself.'[n] [40]All the law and the writings of the prophets depend on these two commands."

JESUS QUESTIONS THE PHARISEES

[41]While the Pharisees were together, Jesus asked them a question. [42]He asked, "What do you think about the Christ? Whose son is he?"

The Pharisees answered, "The Christ is the Son of David."

[43]Then Jesus said to them, "Then why did David call him 'Lord'? David was speaking by the power of the Holy Spirit. David said,

[44] 'The Lord said to my Lord:
>   Sit by me at my right side,
>   until I put your enemies under your
>   control.'   *Psalm 110:1*

[45]David calls the Christ 'Lord.' So how can he be David's son?"

[46]None of the Pharisees could answer Jesus' question. And after that day no one was brave enough to ask Jesus any more questions.

JESUS ACCUSES THE LEADERS

23 Then Jesus spoke to the crowds and to his followers. Jesus said, [2]"The teachers of the law and the Pharisees have the authority to tell you what the law of Moses says. [3]So you should obey and follow whatever they tell you. But their lives are not good examples for you to follow. They tell you to do things, but they don't do the things themselves. [4]They make strict rules and try to force people to obey them. But they themselves will not try to follow any of those rules.

[5]"The reason they do good things is so other people will see them. They make the boxes[n] of Scriptures that they wear bigger and bigger. And they make their special prayer clothes very long so that people will notice them. [6]Those Pharisees and teachers of the law love

---

22:32 'I am . . . Jacob.' Quotation from Exodus 3:6.
22:37 'Love . . . mind.' Quotation from Deuteronomy 6:5.
22:39 'Love . . . yourself.' Quotation from Leviticus 19:18.
23:5 boxes Small leather boxes containing four important Scriptures. Some Jews tied these to the forehead and left arm, probably to show they were very religious.

to have the most important seats at the feasts. And they love to have the most important seats in the synagogues. [7]They love people to show respect to them in the marketplaces. And they love to have people call them 'Teacher.'

[8]"But you must not be called 'Teacher.' You are all brothers and sisters together. You have only one Teacher. [9]And don't call any person on earth 'Father.' You have one Father. He is in heaven. [10]And you should not be called 'Master.' You have only one Master, the Christ. [11]He who serves you as a servant is the greatest among you. [12]Whoever makes himself great will be made humble. Whoever makes himself humble will be made great.

[13]"How terrible for you, teachers of the law and Pharisees! You are hypocrites! You close the door for people to enter the kingdom of heaven. You yourselves don't enter, and you stop others who are trying to enter. [14][How terrible for you, teachers of the law and Pharisees. You are hypocrites. You take away widows' houses, and you make long prayers so that people can see you. So you will have a worse punishment.][n]

[15]"How terrible for you, teachers of the law and Pharisees! You are hypocrites! You travel across land and sea to find one person who will follow your ways. When you find that person, you make him more fit for hell than you are.

[16]"How terrible for you, teachers of the law and Pharisees! You guide the people, but you are blind. You say, 'If anyone swears by the Temple when he makes a promise, that means nothing. But if anyone swears by the gold that is in the Temple, then he must keep that promise.' [17]You are blind fools! Which is greater: the gold or the Temple? The Temple makes that gold holy. [18]And you say, 'If anyone swears by the altar when he makes a promise, that means nothing.

But if he swears by the gift on the altar, then he must keep his promise.' [19]You are blind! Which is greater: the gift or the altar? The altar makes the gift holy. [20]The person who swears by the altar is really using the altar and also everything on the altar. [21]And the person who uses the Temple to make a promise is really using the Temple and also everything in the Temple. [22]The person who uses heaven to make a promise is also using God's throne and the One who sits on that throne.

[23]"How terrible for you, teachers of the law and Pharisees! You are hypocrites! You give to God one-tenth of everything you earn—even your mint, dill, and cummin.[n] But you don't obey the really important teachings of the law—being fair, showing mercy, and being loyal. These are the things you should do, as well as those other things. [24]You guide the people, but you are blind! You are like a person who picks a fly out of his drink and then swallows a camel![n]

[25]"How terrible for you, teachers of the law and Pharisees! You are hypocrites! You wash the outside of your cups and dishes. But inside they are full of things that you got by cheating others and pleasing only yourselves. [26]Pharisees, you are blind! First make the inside of the cup clean and good. Then the outside of the cup can be truly clean.

[27]"How terrible for you, teachers of the law and Pharisees. You are hypocrites! You are like tombs that are painted white. Outside, those tombs look fine. But inside, they are full of the bones of dead people, and all kinds of unclean things are there. [28]It is the same with you. People look at you and think you are good. But on the inside you are full of hypocrisy and evil.

[29]"How terrible for you, teachers of

23:14 How . . . punishment. Some Greek copies do not contain the bracketed text.
23:23 mint, dill, and cummin Small plants grown in gardens and used for spices. Only very religious people would be careful enough to give a tenth of these plants.
23:24 You . . . camel! Meaning, "You worry about the smallest mistakes but commit the biggest sin."

the law and Pharisees! You are hypocrites! You build tombs for the prophets. You show honor to the graves of people who lived good lives. 30And you say, 'If we had lived during the time of our fathers, we would not have helped them kill the prophets.' 31But you give proof that you are children of those people who murdered the prophets. 32And you will complete the sin that your fathers started!

33"You are snakes! A family of poisonous snakes! You will not escape God. You will all be judged guilty and be sent to hell! 34So I tell you this: I am sending to you prophets and wise men and teachers. You will kill some of these people. You will nail some of them to crosses. You will beat some of them in your synagogues. You will chase them from town to town. 35So you will be guilty for the death of all the good people who have been killed on earth. You will be guilty for the murder of that good man Abel. And you will be guilty for the murder of Zechariah[n] son of Berakiah. He was murdered when he was between the Temple and the altar. 36I tell you the truth. All of these things will happen to you people who are living now.

JESUS FEELS SORRY FOR JERUSALEM

37"Jerusalem, Jerusalem! You kill the prophets and kill with stones those men God sent to you. Many times I wanted to help your people! I wanted to gather them together as a hen gathers her chicks under her wings. But you did not let me. 38Now your home will be left completely empty. 39I tell you, you will not see me again until that time when you will say, 'God bless the One who comes in the name of the Lord.'" [n]

THE TEMPLE WILL BE DESTROYED

24 Jesus left the Temple and was walking away. But his followers came to show him the Temple's buildings. 2Jesus asked, "Do you see all these buildings? I tell you the truth. Every stone will be thrown down to the ground. Not one stone will be left on another."

3Later, Jesus was sitting on the Mount of Olives. His followers came to be alone with him. They said, "Tell us when these things will happen. And what will happen to show us that it is time for you to come again and for the world to end?"

4Jesus answered: "Be careful that no one fools you. 5Many people will come in my name. They will say, 'I am the Christ.' And they will fool many people. 6You will hear about wars and stories of wars that are coming. But don't be afraid. These things must happen before the end comes. 7Nations will fight against other nations. Kingdoms will fight against other kingdoms. There will be times when there is no food for people to eat. And there will be earthquakes in different places. 8These things are like the first pains when something new is about to be born.

9"Then men will arrest you and hand you over to be hurt and kill you. They will hate you because you believe in me. 10At that time, many who believe will lose their faith. They will turn

> Jerusalem, Jerusalem! . . . Many times I wanted to help your people! . . . But you did not let me.
> —MATTHEW 23:37

23:35 **Abel . . . Zechariah** In the Hebrew Old Testament, the first and last men to be murdered.
23:39 **'God . . . Lord.'** Quotation from Psalm 118:26.

against each other and hate each other. [11]Many false prophets will come and cause many people to believe false things. [12]There will be more and more evil in the world. So most people will stop showing their love for each other. [13]But the person who continues to be strong until the end will be saved. [14]The Good News about God's kingdom will be preached in all the world, to every nation. Then the end will come.

[15]"Daniel the prophet spoke about 'the horrible thing that destroys.'[n] You will see this terrible thing standing in the holy place." (You who read this should understand what it means.) [16]"At that time, the people in Judea should run away to the mountains. [17]If a person is on the roof[n] of his house, he must not go down to get anything out of his house. [18]If a person is in the field, he must not go back to get his coat. [19]At that time, it will be hard for women who are pregnant or have nursing babies! [20]Pray that it will not be winter or a Sabbath day when these things happen and you have to run away. [21]This is because at that time there will be much trouble. There will be more trouble than has ever happened since the beginning of the world. And nothing as bad as that will ever happen again. [22]God has decided to make that terrible time short. If that time were not made short, then no one would go on living. But God will make that time short to help the people he has chosen. [23]At that time, someone might say to you, 'Look, there is the Christ!' Or another person might say, 'There he is!' But don't believe them. [24]False Christs and false prophets will come and perform great things and miracles. They will do these things to the people God has chosen. They will fool them, if that is possible. [25]Now I have warned you about this before it happens.

[26]"If people tell you, 'The Christ is in the desert'—don't go there. If they say, 'The Christ is in the inner room'—don't believe it. [27]When the Son of Man comes, he will be seen by everyone. It will be like lightning flashing in the sky that can be seen everywhere. [28]Wherever there is a dead body, there the vultures will gather.

[29]"Soon after the trouble of those days, this will happen:

'The sun will grow dark.
    And the moon will not give its
        light.
The stars will fall from the sky.
    And everything in the sky will be
        changed.'   *Isaiah 13:10; 34:4*

[30]"At that time, there will be something in the sky that shows the Son of Man is coming. All the peoples of the world will cry. They will see the Son of Man coming on clouds in the sky. He will come with great power and glory. [31]He will use a loud trumpet to send his angels all around the earth. They will gather his chosen people from every part of the world.

[32]"The fig tree teaches us a lesson: When its branches become green and soft, and new leaves begin to grow, then you know that summer is near. [33]So also, when you see all these things happening, you will know that the time is near, ready to come. [34]I tell you the truth. All these things will happen while the people of this time are still living! [35]The whole world, earth and sky, will be destroyed, but the words I have said will never be destroyed!

WHEN WILL JESUS COME AGAIN?

[36]"No one knows when that day or time will be. Even the Son[n] and the angels in heaven don't know. Only the Father knows. [37]When the Son of Man comes, it will be the same as what happened

---

24:15 **'the horrible . . . destroys.'** Mentioned in Daniel 9:27; 12:11 (cf. Daniel 11:31).
24:17 **roof** In Bible times houses were built with flat roofs. The roof was used for drying things such as flax and fruit. And it was used as an extra room, as a place for worship and as a place to sleep in the summer.
24:36 **Even the Son** Some Greek copies do not have this phrase.

during Noah's time. [38]In those days before the flood, people were eating and drinking. They were marrying and giving their children to be married. They were still doing those things until the day Noah entered the boat. [39]They knew nothing about what was happening. But then the flood came, and all those people were destroyed. It will be the same when the Son of Man comes. [40]Two men will be working together in the field. One man will be taken and the other left. [41]Two women will be grinding grain with a hand mill.[n] One woman will be taken and the other will be left.

[42]"So always be ready. You don't know the day your Lord will come. [43]Remember this: If the owner of the house knew what time a thief was coming, then the owner would be ready for him. The owner would watch and not let the thief enter his house. [44]So you also must be ready. The Son of Man will come at a time you don't expect him.

[45]"Who is the wise and trusted servant? The master trusts one servant to give the other servants their food at the right time. [46]When the master comes and finds the servant doing his work, the servant will be very happy. [47]I tell you the truth. The master will choose that servant to take care of everything the master owns. [48]But what will happen if the servant is evil and thinks his master will not come back soon? [49]Then that servant will begin to beat the other servants. He will feast and get drunk with others like him. [50]And the master will come when the servant is not ready and is not expecting him. [51]Then the master will punish that servant. He will send him away to be among the hypocrites. There people will cry and grind their teeth with pain.

A STORY ABOUT TEN GIRLS

25 "At that time the kingdom of heaven will be like ten girls who went to wait for the bridegroom. They took their lamps with them. [2]Five of the girls were foolish and five were wise. [3]The five foolish girls took their lamps, but they did not take more oil for the lamps to burn. [4]The wise girls took their lamps and more oil in jars. [5]The bridegroom was very late. All the girls became sleepy and went to sleep.

[6]"At midnight someone cried out, 'The bridegroom is coming! Come and meet him!' [7]Then all the girls woke up and got their lamps ready. [8]But the foolish girls said to the wise, 'Give us some of your oil. Our lamps are going out.' [9]The wise girls answered, 'No! The oil we have might not be enough for all of us. Go to the people who sell oil and buy some for yourselves.'

[10]"So the five foolish girls went to buy oil. While they were gone, the bridegroom came. The girls who were ready went in with the bridegroom to the wedding feast. Then the door was closed and locked.

[11]"Later the others came back. They called, 'Sir, sir, open the door to let us in.' [12]But the bridegroom answered, 'I tell you the truth, I don't know you.'

[13]"So always be ready. You don't know the day or the time the Son of Man will come.

A STORY ABOUT THREE SERVANTS

[14]"The kingdom of heaven is like a man who was going to another place for a visit. Before he left, he talked with his servants. The man told them to take care of his things while he was gone. [15]He decided how much each servant would be able to care for. He gave one servant five bags of money. He gave another servant two bags of money. And he gave a third servant one bag of money. Then the man left. [16]The servant who got five bags went quickly to invest the money. The five bags of money earned five more. [17]It was the same with the servant who had two bags of money. He invested the money

24:41 **mill** Two large, round, flat rocks used for grinding grain to make flour.

and earned two more. ¹⁸But the servant who got one bag of money went out and dug a hole in the ground. Then he hid his master's money in the hole.

¹⁹"After a long time the master came home. He asked the servants what they did with his money. ²⁰The servant who got five bags of money brought five more bags to the master. The servant said, 'Master, you trusted me to care for five bags of money. So I used your five bags to earn five more.' ²¹The master answered, 'You did well. You are a good servant who can be trusted. You did well with small things. So I will let you care for much greater things. Come and share my happiness with me.'

²²"Then the servant who got two bags of money came to the master. The servant said, 'Master, you gave me two bags of money to care for. So I used your two bags to earn two more.' ²³The master answered, 'You did well. You are a good servant who can be trusted. You did well with small things. So I will let you care for much greater things. Come and share my happiness with me.'

²⁴"Then the servant who got one bag of money came to the master. The servant said, 'Master, I knew that you were a hard man. You harvest things you did not plant. You gather crops where you did not sow any seed. ²⁵So I was afraid. I went and hid your money in the ground. Here is the bag of money you gave me.' ²⁶The master answered, 'You are a bad and lazy servant! You say you knew that I harvest things I did not plant, and that I gather crops where I did not sow any seed? ²⁷So you should have put my money in the bank. Then, when I came home, I would get my money back with interest.'

²⁸"So the master told his other servants, 'Take the bag of money from that servant and give it to the servant who has ten bags of money. ²⁹Everyone who uses what he has will get more. He will have much more than he needs. But the one who does not use what he has will have everything taken away from him.' ³⁰Then the master said, 'Throw that useless servant outside, into the darkness! There people will cry and grind their teeth with pain.'

THE KING WILL JUDGE ALL PEOPLE

³¹"The Son of Man will come again in his great glory. All his angels will come with him. He will be King and sit on his great throne. ³²All the people of the world will be gathered before him. Then he will separate them into two groups as a shepherd separates the sheep from the goats. ³³The Son of Man will put the sheep, the good people, on his right and the goats, the bad people, on his left.

³⁴"Then the King will say to the good people on his right, 'Come. My Father has given you his blessing. Come and receive the kingdom God has prepared for you since the world was made. ³⁵I was hungry, and you gave me food. I was thirsty, and you gave me something to drink. I was alone and away from home, and you invited me into your house. ³⁶I was without clothes, and you gave me something to wear. I was sick, and you cared for me. I was in prison, and you visited me.'

³⁷"Then the good people will answer, 'Lord, when did we see you hungry and give you food? When did we see you thirsty and give you something to drink? ³⁸When did we see you alone and away from home and invite

> I tell you the truth. Anything you did for any of my people here, you also did for me.
> —MATTHEW 25:40

you into our house? When did we see you without clothes and give you something to wear? ³⁹When did we see you sick or in prison and care for you?'

⁴⁰"Then the King will answer, 'I tell you the truth. Anything you did for any of my people here, you also did for me.'

⁴¹"Then the King will say to those on his left, 'Go away from me. God has said that you will be punished. Go into the fire that burns forever. That fire was prepared for the devil and his helpers. ⁴²I was hungry, and you gave me nothing to eat. I was thirsty, and you gave me nothing to drink. ⁴³I was alone and away from home, and you did not invite me into your house. I was without clothes, and you gave me nothing to wear. I was sick and in prison, and you did not care for me.'

⁴⁴"Then those people will answer, 'Lord, when did we see you hungry or thirsty? When did we see you alone and away from home? Or when did we see you without clothes or sick or in prison? When did we see these things and not help you?'

⁴⁵"Then the King will answer, 'I tell you the truth. Anything you refused to do for any of my people here, you refused to do for me.'

⁴⁶"These people will go off to be punished forever. But the good people will go to live forever."

THE PLAN TO KILL JESUS

26 After Jesus finished saying all these things, he told his followers, ²"You know that the day after tomorrow is the day of the Passover Feast. On that day the Son of Man will be given to his enemies to be killed on a cross."

³Then the leading priests and the Jewish elders had a meeting at the palace of the high priest. The high priest's name was Caiaphas. ⁴At the meeting, they planned to set a trap to arrest Jesus and kill him. ⁵But they said, "We must not do it during the feast. The people might cause a riot."

A WOMAN WITH PERFUME FOR JESUS

⁶Jesus was in Bethany. He was at the house of Simon, who had a harmful skin disease. ⁷While Jesus was there, a woman came to him. She had an alabaster jar filled with expensive perfume. She poured this perfume on Jesus' head while he was eating.

⁸His followers saw the woman do this and were upset. They asked, "Why waste that perfume? ⁹It could be sold for a great deal of money, and the money could be given to the poor."

¹⁰But Jesus knew what happened. He said, "Why are you troubling this woman? She did a very beautiful thing for me. ¹¹You will always have the poor with you. But you will not always have me. ¹²This woman poured perfume on my body to prepare me for burial. ¹³I tell you the truth. The Good News will be told to people in all the world. And in every place where it is preached, what this woman has done will be told. And people will remember her."

JUDAS BECOMES AN ENEMY OF JESUS

¹⁴Then 1 of the 12 followers went to talk to the leading priests. This was the follower named Judas Iscariot. ¹⁵He said, "I will give Jesus to you. What will you pay me for doing this?" The priests gave Judas 30 silver coins. ¹⁶After that, Judas waited for the best time to give Jesus to the priests.

JESUS EATS THE PASSOVER FEAST

¹⁷On the first day of the Feast of Unleavened Bread, the followers came to Jesus. They said, "We will prepare everything for you to eat the Passover Feast. Where do you want to have the feast?"

¹⁸Jesus answered, "Go into the city to a certain man. Tell him that the Teacher says, 'The chosen time is near. I will have the Passover Feast with

my followers at your house.'" [19]The followers did what Jesus told them to do, and they prepared the Passover Feast.

[20]In the evening Jesus was sitting at the table with his 12 followers. [21]They were all eating. Then Jesus said, "I tell you the truth. One of you 12 will turn against me."

[22]This made the followers very sad. Each one said to Jesus, "Surely, Lord, I am not the one who will turn against you. Am I?"

[23]Jesus answered, "The man who has dipped his hand with me into the bowl is the one who will turn against me. [24]The Son of Man will die. The Scriptures say this will happen. But how terrible it will be for the person who gives the Son of Man to be killed. It would be better for him if he had never been born."

[25]Then Judas said to Jesus, "Teacher, surely I am not the one. Am I?" (Judas is the one who would give Jesus to his enemies.)

Jesus answered, "Yes, it is you."

THE LORD'S SUPPER

[26]While they were eating, Jesus took some bread. He thanked God for it and broke it. Then he gave it to his followers and said, "Take this bread and eat it. This bread is my body."

[27]Then Jesus took a cup. He thanked God for it and gave it to the followers. He said, "Every one of you drink this. [28]This is my blood which begins the new[n] agreement that God makes with his people. This blood is poured out for many to forgive their sins. [29]I tell you this: I will not drink of this fruit of the vine[n] again until that day when I drink it new with you in my Father's kingdom."

[30]They sang a hymn. Then they went out to the Mount of Olives.

JESUS' FOLLOWERS WILL ALL LEAVE HIM

[31]Jesus told the followers, "Tonight you will lose your faith because of me. It is written in the Scriptures:

> 'I will kill the shepherd,
>   and the sheep will scatter.'
> *Zechariah 13:7*

[32]But after I rise from death, I will go ahead of you into Galilee."

[33]Peter said, "All the other followers may lose their faith because of you. But I will never lose my faith."

[34]Jesus said, "I tell you the truth. Tonight you will say you don't know me. You will say this three times before the rooster crows."

[35]But Peter said, "I will never say that I don't know you! I will even die with you!" And all the other followers said the same thing.

JESUS PRAYS ALONE

[36]Then Jesus went with his followers to a place called Gethsemane. He said to them, "Sit here while I go over there and pray." [37]He told Peter and the two sons of Zebedee to come with him. Then Jesus began to be very sad and troubled. [38]He said to Peter and the two sons of Zebedee, "My heart is full of sorrow and breaking with sadness. Stay here with me and watch."

[39]Then Jesus walked a little farther away from them. He fell to the ground and prayed, "My Father, if it is possible, do not give me this cup[n] of suffering. But do what you want, not what I want." [40]Then Jesus went back to his followers and found them asleep. Jesus said to Peter, "You men could not stay awake with me for one hour? [41]Stay awake and pray for strength against temptation. Your spirit wants to do what is right. But your body is weak."

26:28 **new** Some Greek copies do not have this word. Compare Luke 22:20.
26:29 **fruit of the vine** Product of the grapevine; this may also be translated "wine."
26:39 **cup** Jesus is talking about the bad things that will happen to him. Accepting these things will be very hard, like drinking a cup of something that tastes very bitter.

[42]Then Jesus went away a second time. He prayed, "My Father, if it is not possible for this painful thing to be taken from me, and if I must do it, then I pray that what you want will be done."

[43]Then Jesus went back to the followers. Again he found them asleep, because their eyes were heavy. [44]So Jesus left them and went away one more time and prayed. This third time he prayed, he said the same thing.

[45]Then Jesus went back to the followers and said, "You are still sleeping and resting? The time has come for the Son of Man to be given to sinful people. [46]Get up. We must go. Here comes the man who has turned against me."

JESUS IS ARRESTED

[47]While Jesus was still speaking, Judas came up. Judas was 1 of the 12 followers. He had many people with him. They had been sent from the leading priests and the elders of the people. They carried swords and clubs. [48]Judas had planned to give them a signal. He had said, "The man I kiss is Jesus. Arrest him." [49]At once Judas went to Jesus and said, "Greetings, Teacher!" Then Judas kissed him.

[50]Jesus answered, "Friend, do the thing you came to do."

Then the men came and grabbed Jesus and arrested him. [51]When that happened, one of Jesus' followers reached for his sword and pulled it out. The follower struck the servant of the high priest with the sword and cut off his ear.

[52]Jesus said to the man, "Put your sword back in its place. All who use swords will be killed with swords. [53]Surely you know I could ask my Father, and he would give me more than 12 armies of angels. [54]But this thing must happen this way so that it will be as the Scriptures say."

[55]Then Jesus said to the crowd, "You came to get me with swords and clubs as if I were a criminal. Every day I sat in the Temple teaching. You did not arrest me there. [56]But all these things have happened so that it will be as the prophets wrote." Then all of Jesus' followers left him and ran away.

JESUS BEFORE THE LEADERS

[57]Those men who arrested Jesus led him to the house of Caiaphas, the high priest. The teachers of the law and the Jewish elders were gathered there. [58]Peter followed Jesus but did not go near him. He followed Jesus to the courtyard of the high priest's house. He sat down with the guards to see what would happen to Jesus.

[59]The leading priests and the Jewish council tried to find something false against Jesus so that they could kill him. [60]Many people came and told lies about him. But the council could find no real reason to kill Jesus. Then two people came and said, [61]"This man said, 'I can destroy the Temple of God and build it again in three days.'"

[62]Then the high priest stood up and said to Jesus, "Aren't you going to answer? Don't you have something to say about their charges against you?" [63]But Jesus said nothing.

Again the high priest said to Jesus, "You must swear to this. I command you by the power of the living God to tell us the truth. Tell us, are you the Christ, the Son of God?"

[64]Jesus answered, "Yes, I am. But I tell you, in the future you will see the Son of Man sitting at the right hand of God, the Powerful One. And you will see him coming in clouds in the sky."

[65]When the high priest heard this, he was very angry. He tore his clothes and said, "This man has said things that are against God! We don't need any more witnesses. You all heard him say these things against God. [66]What do you think?"

The people answered, "He is guilty, and he must die."

[67]Then the people there spit in Jesus' face and beat him with their fists. Others slapped Jesus. [68]They said,

"Prove to us that you are a prophet, you Christ! Tell us who hit you!"

PETER SAYS HE DOESN'T KNOW JESUS

⁶⁹At that time, Peter was sitting in the courtyard. A servant girl came to him and said, "You were with Jesus, that man from Galilee."

⁷⁰But Peter said that he was never with Jesus. He said this to all the people there. Peter said, "I don't know what you are talking about."

⁷¹Then he left the courtyard. At the gate, another girl saw him. She said to the people there, "This man was with Jesus of Nazareth."

⁷²Again, Peter said that he was never with Jesus. Peter said, "I swear that I don't know this man Jesus!"

⁷³A short time later, some people standing there went to Peter. They said, "We know you are one of those men who followed Jesus. We know this because of the way you talk."

⁷⁴Then Peter began to curse. He said, "May a curse fall on me if I'm not telling the truth. I don't know the man." After Peter said this, a rooster crowed. ⁷⁵Then he remembered what Jesus had told him: "Before the rooster crows, you will say three times that you don't know me." Then Peter went outside and cried painfully.

JESUS IS TAKEN TO PILATE

27 Early the next morning, all the leading priests and elders of the people decided to kill Jesus. ²They tied him, led him away, and turned him over to Pilate, the governor.

JUDAS KILLS HIMSELF

³Judas saw that they had decided to kill Jesus. Judas was the one who gave Jesus to his enemies. When Judas saw what happened, he was very sorry for what he had done. So he took the 30 silver coins back to the priests and the leaders. ⁴Judas said, "I sinned. I gave you an innocent man to be killed."

The leaders answered, "What is that to us? That's your problem, not ours."

⁵So Judas threw the money into the Temple. Then he went off and hanged himself.

⁶The leading priests picked up the silver coins in the Temple. They said, "Our law does not allow us to keep this money with the Temple money. This money has paid for a man's death." ⁷So they decided to use the coins to buy a field called Potter's Field. This field would be a place to bury strangers who died while visiting Jerusalem. ⁸That is why that field is still called the Field of Blood. ⁹So the thing came true that Jeremiah the prophet had said: "They took 30 silver coins. That is how little the Israelites thought he was worth. ¹⁰They used those 30 silver coins to buy Potter's Field, as the Lord commanded me."ⁿ

PILATE QUESTIONS JESUS

¹¹Jesus stood before Pilate the governor. Pilate asked him, "Are you the King of the Jews?"

Jesus answered, "Yes, I am."

¹²When the leading priests and the elders accused Jesus, he said nothing.

¹³So Pilate said to Jesus, "Don't you hear these people accusing you of all these things?"

¹⁴But Jesus said nothing in answer to Pilate. Pilate was very surprised at this.

PILATE TRIES TO FREE JESUS

¹⁵Every year at the time of Passover the governor would free one person from prison. This was always a person the people wanted to be set free. ¹⁶At that time there was a man in prison who was known to be very bad. His name was Barabbas.ⁿ ¹⁷All the people gathered at Pilate's house. Pilate said, "Which man do you want me to free: Barabbas,ⁿ or

---

27:10 **"They . . . commanded me."** See Zechariah 11:12–13 and Jeremiah 32:6–9.
27:16, 17 **Barabbas** Some Greek copies read "Jesus Barabbas."

Jesus who is called the Christ?" [18]Pilate knew that they gave Jesus to him because they were jealous.

[19]Pilate said these things while he was sitting on the judge's seat. While he was sitting there, his wife sent a message to him. The message said, "Don't do anything to that man. He is not guilty. Today I had a dream about him, and it troubled me very much."

[20]But the leading priests and elders told the crowd to ask for Barabbas to be freed and for Jesus to be killed.

[21]Pilate said, "I have Barabbas and Jesus. Which do you want me to set free for you?"

The people answered, "Barabbas!"

[22]Pilate asked, "What should I do with Jesus, the one called the Christ?"

They all answered, "Kill him on a cross!"

[23]Pilate asked, "Why do you want me to kill him? What wrong has he done?"

But they shouted louder, "Kill him on a cross!"

[24]Pilate saw that he could do nothing about this, and a riot was starting. So he took some water and washed his hands[n] in front of the crowd. Then he said, "I am not guilty of this man's death. You are the ones who are causing it!"

[25]All the people answered, "We will be responsible. We accept for ourselves and for our children any punishment for his death."

[26]Then Pilate freed Barabbas. Pilate told some of the soldiers to beat Jesus with whips. Then he gave Jesus to the soldiers to be killed on a cross.

[27]Pilate's soldiers took Jesus into the governor's palace. All the soldiers gathered around Jesus. [28]They took off his clothes and put a red robe on him. [29]Then the soldiers used thorny branches to make a crown. They put this crown of thorns on Jesus' head. They put a stick in his right hand. Then the soldiers bowed before Jesus and made fun of him. They said, "Hail, King of the Jews!" [30]They spit on Jesus. Then they took his stick and hit him on the head many times. [31]After they finished making fun of Jesus, the soldiers took off the robe and put his own clothes on him again. Then they led Jesus away to be killed on a cross.

> They put a sign above Jesus' head . . . The sign read:
> "THIS IS JESUS THE KING OF THE JEWS."
> –MATTHEW 27:37

JESUS IS KILLED ON A CROSS

[32]The soldiers were going out of the city with Jesus. They forced another man to carry the cross to be used for Jesus. This man was Simon, from Cyrene. [33]They all came to the place called Golgotha. (Golgotha means the Place of the Skull.) [34]At Golgotha, the soldiers gave Jesus wine to drink. This wine was mixed with gall.[n] He tasted the wine but refused to drink it. [35]The soldiers nailed Jesus to a cross. They threw lots to decide who would get his clothes.[n] [36]The soldiers sat there and continued watching him. [37]They put a sign above Jesus' head with the charge against him written on it. The sign read: "THIS IS JESUS THE KING OF THE JEWS." [38]Two robbers were nailed to crosses beside Jesus, one on the right and the other on the left. [39]People walked by and insulted Jesus. They shook their heads, [40]saying, "You said you could destroy the Temple and build it again in three days. So save

---

27:24 **washed his hands** He did this as a sign to show that he wanted no part in what the people did.
27:34 **gall** Probably a drink of wine mixed with drugs to help a person feel less pain.
27:35 **clothes** Some Greek copies continue, "So what God said through the prophet came true, 'They divided my clothes among them, and they threw lots for my clothing.'"

yourself! Come down from that cross, if you are really the Son of God!"

⁴¹The leading priests, the teachers of the law, and the Jewish elders were also there. These men made fun of Jesus ⁴²and said, "He saved other people, but he can't save himself! People say he is the King of Israel! If he is the King, then let him come down now from the cross. Then we will believe in him. ⁴³He trusts in God. So let God save him now, if God really wants him. He himself said, 'I am the Son of God.'" ⁴⁴And in the same way, the robbers who were being killed on crosses beside Jesus also insulted him.

JESUS DIES

⁴⁵At noon the whole country became dark. This darkness lasted for three hours. ⁴⁶About three o'clock Jesus cried out in a loud voice, "Eli, Eli, lama sabachthani?" This means, "My God, my God, why have you left me alone?"

⁴⁷Some of the people standing there heard this. They said, "He is calling Elijah."

⁴⁸Quickly one of them ran and got a sponge. He filled the sponge with vinegar and tied it to a stick. Then he used the stick to give the sponge to Jesus to drink from it. ⁴⁹But the others said, "Don't bother him. We want to see if Elijah will come to save him."

⁵⁰Again Jesus cried out in a loud voice. Then he died.

⁵¹Then the curtain in the Templeⁿ split into two pieces. The tear started at the top and tore all the way down to the bottom. Also, the earth shook and rocks broke apart. ⁵²The graves opened, and many of God's people who had died were raised from death. ⁵³They came out of the graves after Jesus was raised from death. They went into the holy city, and many people saw them.

⁵⁴The army officer and the soldiers guarding Jesus saw this earthquake and everything else that happened. They were very frightened and said, "He really was the Son of God!"

⁵⁵Many women were standing at a distance from the cross, watching. These were women who had followed Jesus from Galilee to care for him. ⁵⁶Mary Magdalene, and Mary the mother of James and Joseph, and the mother of James and John were there.

JESUS IS BURIED

⁵⁷That evening a rich man named Joseph came to Jerusalem. He was a follower of Jesus from the town of Arimathea. ⁵⁸Joseph went to Pilate and asked to have Jesus' body. Pilate gave orders for the soldiers to give it to Joseph. ⁵⁹Then Joseph took the body and wrapped it in a clean linen cloth. ⁶⁰He put Jesus' body in a new tomb that he had cut in a wall of rock. He rolled a very large stone to block the entrance of the tomb. Then Joseph went away. ⁶¹Mary Magdalene and the other woman named Mary were sitting near the tomb.

THE TOMB OF JESUS IS GUARDED

⁶²That day was the day called Preparation Day. The next day, the leading priests and the Pharisees went to Pilate. ⁶³They said, "Sir, we remember that while that liar was still alive he said, 'After three days I will rise from death.' ⁶⁴So give the order for the tomb to be guarded closely till the third day. His followers might come and steal the body. Then they could tell the people that he has risen from death. That lie would be even worse than the first one."

⁶⁵Pilate said, "Take some soldiers and go guard the tomb the best way you know." ⁶⁶So they all went to the tomb and made it safe from thieves. They did this by sealing the stone in the entrance and then putting soldiers there to guard it.

27:51 curtain in the Temple A curtain divided the Most Holy Place from the other part of the Temple. That was the special building in Jerusalem where God commanded the Jews to worship him.

JESUS RISES FROM DEATH

28 The day after the Sabbath day was the first day of the week. At dawn on the first day, Mary Magdalene and another woman named Mary went to look at the tomb.

²At that time there was a strong earthquake. An angel of the Lord came down from heaven. The angel went to the tomb and rolled the stone away from the entrance. Then he sat on the stone. ³He was shining as bright as lightning. His clothes were white as snow. ⁴The soldiers guarding the tomb were very frightened of the angel. They shook with fear and then became like dead men.

⁵The angel said to the women, "Don't be afraid. I know that you are looking for Jesus, the one who was killed on the cross. ⁶But he is not here. He has risen from death as he said he would. Come and see the place where his body was. ⁷And go quickly and tell his followers. Say to them: 'Jesus has risen from death. He is going into Galilee. He will

---

☆ Matthew 28:20

Jesus died and was buried. But God raised him from the dead! He led his followers to the top of a mountain and gave them instructions. Jesus told his followers to tell others about him. He told them to teach them everything he taught them while he was on the earth. And then he made a huge promise. He said, "You can be sure that I will be with you always. I will continue with you until the end of the world."

Jesus knows us inside and out. He even knows what we think and feel. We might be able to hide our feelings from friends and family, but not from Jesus. Jesus knows all about you because he loves you. He told his followers that he would be with them and all his new followers forever. That means you! And that means forever. Each morning, you can thank Jesus for his promise that he is always with you. And you can talk to Jesus about anything—anytime. He is with you.

· · · · · · · · · · · · · ·

Jesus told his followers to tell others about him. That's why you know about Jesus now. His promise is for you. He will never leave you. Ever!

be there before you. You will see him there.'" Then the angel said, "Now I have told you."

⁸The women left the tomb quickly. They were afraid, but they were also very happy. They ran to tell Jesus' followers what had happened. ⁹Suddenly, Jesus met them and said, "Greetings." The women came up to Jesus, took hold of his feet, and worshiped him. ¹⁰Then Jesus said to them, "Don't be afraid. Go and tell my brothers to go on to Galilee. They will see me there."

THE SOLDIERS REPORT TO THE JEWISH LEADERS

¹¹The women went to tell Jesus' followers. At the same time, some of the soldiers who had been guarding the tomb went into the city. They went to tell the leading priests everything that had happened. ¹²Then the priests met with the Jewish elders and made a plan. They paid the soldiers a large amount of money. ¹³They said to the soldiers, "Tell the people that Jesus' followers came during the night and stole the body while you were asleep. ¹⁴If the governor hears about this, we will satisfy him and save you from trouble." ¹⁵So the soldiers kept the money and obeyed the priests. And that story is still spread among the Jews even today.

JESUS TALKS TO HIS FOLLOWERS

¹⁶The 11 followers went to Galilee. They went to the mountain where Jesus told them to go. ¹⁷On the mountain they saw Jesus and worshiped him. But some of them did not believe that it was really Jesus. ¹⁸Then Jesus came to them and said, "All power in heaven and on earth is given to me. ¹⁹So go and make followers of all people in the world. Baptize them in the name of the Father and the Son and the Holy Spirit. ²⁰Teach them to obey everything that I have told you. You can be sure that I will be with you always. I will continue with you until the end of the world."

Luke

LUKE WRITES ABOUT JESUS' LIFE

1 To Theophilus:
   Many have tried to give a history of the things that happened among us. [2]They have written the same things that we learned from others—the people who saw those things from the beginning and served God by telling people his message. [3]I myself studied everything carefully from the beginning, your Excellency.[n] I thought I should write it out for you. So I put it in order in a book. [4]I write these things so that you can know that what you have been taught is true.

ZECHARIAH AND ELIZABETH

[5]During the time Herod ruled Judea, there was a priest named Zechariah. He belonged to Abijah's group.[n] Zechariah's wife came from the family of Aaron. Her name was Elizabeth. [6]Zechariah and Elizabeth truly did what God said was good. They did everything the Lord commanded and told people to do. They were without fault in keeping his law. [7]But Zechariah and Elizabeth had no children. Elizabeth could not have a baby; and both of them were very old.

[8]Zechariah was serving as a priest before God for his group. It was his group's time to serve. [9]According to the custom of the priests, he was chosen to go into the Temple of the Lord and burn incense. [10]There were a great many people outside praying at the time the incense was offered. [11]Then, on the right side of the incense table, an angel of the Lord came and stood before Zechariah. [12]When he saw the angel, Zechariah was confused and frightened. [13]But the angel said to him, "Zechariah, don't be afraid. Your prayer has been heard by God. Your wife, Elizabeth, will give birth to a son. You will name him John. [14]You will be very happy. Many people will be happy because of his birth. [15]John will be a great man for the Lord. He will never drink wine or beer. Even at the time John is born, he will be filled with the Holy Spirit. [16]He will help many people of Israel return to the Lord their God. [17]He himself will go first before the Lord. John will be powerful in spirit like Elijah. He will make peace between fathers and their children. He will bring those who are not obeying God back to the right way of thinking. He will make people ready for the coming of the Lord."

[18]Zechariah said to the angel, "How can I know that what you say is true? I am an old man, and my wife is old, too."

[19]The angel answered him, "I am Gabriel. I stand before God. God sent me to talk to you and to tell you this good news. [20]Now, listen! You will not be able to talk until the day these things happen. You will lose your speech because you did not believe what I told you. But these things will really happen."

[21]Outside, the people were still waiting for Zechariah. They were surprised that he was staying so long in the Temple. [22]Then Zechariah came outside, but he could not speak to them. So they knew that he had seen a vision in the Temple. Zechariah could not speak. He could only make signs to them. [23]When his time of service as a priest was finished, he went home.

[24]Later, Zechariah's wife, Elizabeth, became pregnant. She did not go out of her house for five months. Elizabeth said, [25]"Look what the Lord has done for me! My people were ashamed[n] of me,

---

1:3 **Excellency** This word was used to show respect to an important person like a king or ruler.
1:5 **Abijah's group** The Jewish priests were divided into 24 groups. See 1 Chronicles 24.
1:25 **ashamed** The Jews thought it was a disgrace for women not to have children.

but now the Lord has taken away that shame."

THE VIRGIN MARY

²⁶⁻²⁷During Elizabeth's sixth month of pregnancy, God sent the angel Gabriel to a virgin who lived in Nazareth, a town in Galilee. She was engaged to marry a man named Joseph from the family of David. Her name was Mary. ²⁸The angel came to her and said, "Greetings! The Lord has blessed you and is with you."

²⁹But Mary was very confused by what the angel said. Mary wondered, "What does this mean?"

³⁰The angel said to her, "Don't be afraid, Mary, because God is pleased with you. ³¹Listen! You will become pregnant. You will give birth to a son, and you will name him Jesus. ³²He will be great, and people will call him the Son of the Most High. The Lord God will give him the throne of King David, his ancestor. ³³He will rule over the people of Jacob forever. His kingdom will never end."

☆ Luke 1:46

After Mary found out she was going to have a baby, she visited Elizabeth, who was also expecting a baby. When Mary greeted her, Elizabeth's unborn baby tumbled around inside her. Elizabeth said Mary was blessed because she believed what God had told her. Mary was so filled with joy, she began to praise God.

Praising is the same thing as saying, "You are awesome!" or "What you did was so cool!" God loves it when we tell him how much we love him. One of the ways we can praise God is by singing songs to him. Jesus came to save us. And that should make us very happy! Sing a song or do a happy dance for God today. And thank him for loving you and saving you. Your heart will be happy when you are praising God.

· · · · · · · · · · · · · · · · ·

Even an unborn baby jumped for joy when Jesus was near. You can too because Jesus is always near. He can make your heart feel good.

³⁴Mary said to the angel, "How will this happen? I am a virgin!"

³⁵The angel said to Mary, "The Holy Spirit will come upon you, and the power of the Most High will cover you. The baby will be holy. He will be called the Son of God. ³⁶Now listen! Elizabeth, your relative, is very old. But she is also pregnant with a son. Everyone thought she could not have a baby, but she has been pregnant for six months. ³⁷God can do everything!"

³⁸Mary said, "I am the servant girl of the Lord. Let this happen to me as you say!" Then the angel went away.

MARY'S VISIT

³⁹Mary got up and went quickly to a town in the mountains of Judea. ⁴⁰She went to Zechariah's house and greeted Elizabeth. ⁴¹When Elizabeth heard Mary's greeting, the unborn baby inside Elizabeth jumped. Then Elizabeth was filled with the Holy Spirit. ⁴²She cried out in a loud voice, "God has blessed you more than any other woman. And God has blessed the baby which you will give birth to. ⁴³You are the mother of my Lord, and you have come to me! Why has something so good happened to me? ⁴⁴When I heard your voice, the baby inside me jumped with joy. ⁴⁵You are blessed because you believed what the Lord said to you would really happen."

MARY PRAISES GOD

⁴⁶Then Mary said,

"My soul praises the Lord;
⁴⁷   my heart is happy because God is
        my Savior.
⁴⁸ I am not important, but God has
        shown his care for me, his
        servant girl.
    From now on, all people will say that
        I am blessed,
⁴⁹   because the Powerful One has
        done great things for me.
    His name is holy.
⁵⁰ God will always give mercy
        to those who worship him.

⁵¹ God's arm is strong.
    He scatters the people who are
        proud
    and think great things about
        themselves.
⁵² God brings down rulers from their
        thrones,
    and he raises up the humble.
⁵³ God fills the hungry with good
        things,
    but he sends the rich away with
        nothing.
⁵⁴ God has helped his people Israel who
        serve him.
    He gave them his mercy.
⁵⁵ God has done what he promised to
        our ancestors,
    to Abraham and to his children
        forever."

⁵⁶Mary stayed with Elizabeth for about three months and then returned home.

THE BIRTH OF JOHN

⁵⁷When it was time for Elizabeth to give birth, she had a boy. ⁵⁸Her neighbors and relatives heard how good the Lord was to her, and they rejoiced.

⁵⁹When the baby was eight days old, they came to circumcise him. They wanted to name him Zechariah because this was his father's name. ⁶⁰But his mother said, "No! He will be named John."

⁶¹The people said to Elizabeth, "But no one in your family has this name!" ⁶²Then they made signs to his father, "What would you like to name him?"

⁶³Zechariah asked for something to write on. Then he wrote, "His name is John." Everyone was surprised. ⁶⁴Then Zechariah could talk again. He began to praise God. ⁶⁵And all their neighbors became alarmed. In all the mountains of Judea people continued talking about all these things. ⁶⁶The people who heard about these things wondered about them. They thought, "What will this child be?" They said this because the Lord was with him.

ZECHARIAH PRAISES GOD

[67] Then Zechariah, John's father, was filled with the Holy Spirit. He told the people what would happen:

[68] "Let us thank the Lord, the God of Israel.
God has come to help his people
and has given them freedom.
[69] God has given us a powerful Savior
from the family of God's servant David.
[70] God said that he would do this.
He said it through his holy prophets who lived long ago.
[71] God will save us from our enemies
and from the power of all those who hate us.
[72] God said he would give mercy to our ancestors.
And he remembered his holy promise.
[73] God promised Abraham, our father,
[74] that he would free us from the power of our enemies,
so that we could serve him without fear.
[75] We will be righteous and holy before God as long as we live.

[76] "Now you, child, will be called a prophet of the Most High God.
You will go first before the Lord
to prepare the people for his coming.
[77] You will make his people know that they will be saved.
They will be saved by having their sins forgiven.
[78] With the loving mercy of our God,
a new day from heaven will shine upon us.
[79] God will help those who live in darkness,
in the fear of death.
He will guide us into the path that goes toward peace."

[80] And so the child grew up and became strong in spirit. John lived away from other people until the time when he came out to preach to Israel.

THE BIRTH OF JESUS

2 At that time, Augustus Caesar sent an order to all people in the countries that were under Roman rule. The order said that they must list their names in a register. [2] This was the first registration[n] taken while Quirinius was governor of Syria. [3] And everyone went to their own towns to be registered.

[4] So Joseph left Nazareth, a town in Galilee. He went to the town of Bethlehem in Judea. This town was known as the town of David. Joseph went there because he was from the family of David. [5] Joseph registered with Mary because she was engaged to marry him. (Mary was now pregnant.) [6] While Joseph and Mary were in Bethlehem, the time came for her to have the baby. [7] She gave birth to her first son. There were no rooms left in the inn. So she wrapped the baby with cloths and laid him in a box where animals are fed.

SOME SHEPHERDS HEAR ABOUT JESUS

[8] That night, some shepherds were in the fields nearby watching their sheep. [9] An angel of the Lord stood before them. The glory of the Lord was shining around them, and suddenly they became very frightened. [10] The angel said to them, "Don't be afraid, because I am bringing you some good news. It will be a joy to all the people. [11] Today your Savior was born in David's town. He is Christ, the Lord. [12] This is how you will know him: You will find a baby wrapped in cloths and lying in a feeding box." [13] Then a very large group of angels from heaven joined the first angel. All the angels were praising God, saying:

2:2 **registration** Census. A counting of all the people and the things they own.

14 "Give glory to God in heaven,
    and on earth let there be peace to
        the people who please God."[n]

15 Then the angels left the shepherds and went back to heaven. The shepherds said to each other, "Let us go to Bethlehem and see this thing that has happened. We will see this thing the Lord told us about."

16 So the shepherds went quickly and found Mary and Joseph. 17 And the shepherds saw the baby lying in a feeding box. Then they told what the angels had said about this child. 18 Everyone was amazed when they heard what the shepherds said to them. 19 Mary hid these things in her heart; she continued to think about them. 20 Then the shepherds went back to their sheep, praising God and thanking him for everything that they had seen and heard. It was just as the angel had told them.

21 When the baby was eight days old, he was circumcised, and he was named Jesus. This name had been given by the angel before the baby began to grow inside Mary.

JESUS IS PRESENTED IN THE TEMPLE

22 The time came for Mary and Joseph to do what the law of Moses taught about being made pure.[n] They took Jesus to Jerusalem to present him to the Lord. 23 It is written in the law of the Lord: "Give every firstborn male to the Lord."[n] 24 Mary and Joseph also went to offer a sacrifice, as the law of the Lord says: "You must sacrifice two doves or two young pigeons."[n]

SIMEON SEES JESUS

25 A man named Simeon lived in Jerusalem. He was a good man and very religious. He was waiting for the time when God would help Israel. The Holy Spirit was in him. 26 The Holy Spirit told Simeon that he would not die before he saw the Christ promised by the Lord. 27 The Spirit led Simeon to the Temple. Mary and Joseph brought the baby Jesus to the Temple to do what the law said they must do. 28 Then Simeon took the baby in his arms and thanked God:

29 "Now, Lord, you can let me, your servant,
    die in peace as you said.
30 I have seen your Salvation[n] with my own eyes.
31   You prepared him before all people.
32 He is a light for the non-Jewish people to see.
    He will bring honor to your people, the Israelites."

33 Jesus' father and mother were amazed at what Simeon had said about him. 34 Then Simeon blessed them and said to Mary, "Many in Israel will fall and many will rise because of this child. He will be a sign from God that many people will not accept. 35 The things they think in secret will be made known. And the things that will happen will make your heart sad, too."

ANNA SEES JESUS

36 Anna, a prophetess, was there at the Temple. She was from the family of Phanuel in the tribe of Asher. Anna was very old. She had once been married for seven years. 37 Then her husband died and she lived alone. She was now 84 years old. Anna never left the Temple. She worshiped God by going without food and praying day and night.

2:14 and . . . God Some Greek copies read "and on earth let there be peace and goodwill among people."
2:22 pure The law of Moses said that 40 days after a Jewish woman gave birth to a baby, she must be cleansed by a ceremony at the Temple. Read Leviticus 12:2–8.
2:23 "Give . . . Lord." Quotation from Exodus 13:2.
2:24 "You . . . pigeons." Quotation from Leviticus 12:8.
2:30 Salvation Simeon was talking about Jesus. The name Jesus means "salvation."

[38]She was standing there at that time, thanking God. She talked about Jesus to all who were waiting for God to free Jerusalem.

JOSEPH AND MARY RETURN HOME

[39]Joseph and Mary finished doing everything that the law of the Lord commanded. Then they went home to Nazareth, their own town in Galilee. [40]The little child began to grow up. He became stronger and wiser, and God's blessings were with him.

JESUS AS A BOY

[41]Every year Jesus' parents went to Jerusalem for the Passover Feast. [42]When Jesus was 12 years old, they went to the feast as they always did. [43]When the feast days were over, they went home. The boy Jesus stayed behind in Jerusalem, but his parents did not know it. [44]Joseph and Mary traveled for a whole day. They thought that Jesus was with them in the group. Then they began to look for him among their family and friends, [45]but they did not find him. So they went back to Jerusalem to look for him there. [46]After three days they found him. Jesus was sitting in the Temple with the religious teachers, listening to them and asking them questions. [47]All who heard him were amazed at his understanding and wise answers. [48]When Jesus' parents saw him, they were amazed. His mother said to him, "Son, why did you do this to us? Your father and I were very worried about you. We have been looking for you."

[49]Jesus asked, "Why did you have to look for me? You should have known that I must be where my Father's work

> Jesus continued to learn more and more . . . People liked him, and he pleased God.
>
> –LUKE 2:52

is!" [50]But they did not understand the meaning of what he said.

[51]Jesus went with them to Nazareth and obeyed them. His mother was still thinking about all that had happened. [52]Jesus continued to learn more and more and to grow physically. People liked him, and he pleased God.

THE PREACHING OF JOHN

3 It was the fifteenth year of the rule of Tiberius Caesar. These men were under Caesar: Pontius Pilate was the ruler of Judea. Herod was the ruler of Galilee. Philip, Herod's brother, was the ruler of Iturea and Trachonitis. And Lysanias was the ruler of Abilene. [2]Annas and Caiaphas were the high priests. At this time, a command from God came to John son of Zechariah. John was living in the desert. [3]He went all over the area around the Jordan River and preached to the people. He preached a baptism of changed hearts and lives for the forgiveness of their sins. [4]As it is written in the book of Isaiah the prophet:

"This is a voice of a man
  who calls out in the desert:
'Prepare the way for the Lord.
  Make the road straight for him.
[5] Every valley should be filled in.
  Every mountain and hill should be made flat.
Roads with turns should be made straight,
  and rough roads should be made smooth.
[6] And all people will know about the salvation of God!'" *Isaiah 40:3–5*

[7]Crowds of people came to be baptized by John. He said to them, "You poisonous snakes! Who warned you to

run away from God's anger that is coming? [8] You must do the things that will show that you really have changed your hearts. Don't say, 'Abraham is our father.' I tell you that God can make children for Abraham from these rocks here. [9] The ax is now ready to cut down the trees. Every tree that does not produce good fruit will be cut down and thrown into the fire." [n]

[10] The people asked John, "What should we do?"

[11] John answered, "If you have two shirts, share with the person who does not have one. If you have food, share that too."

[12] Even tax collectors came to John to be baptized. They said to John, "Teacher, what should we do?"

[13] John said to them, "Don't take more taxes from people than you have been ordered to take."

[14] The soldiers asked John, "What about us? What should we do?"

John said to them, "Don't force people to give you money. Don't lie about them. Be satisfied with the pay you get."

[15] All the people were hoping for the Christ to come, and they wondered about John. They thought, "Maybe he is the Christ."

[16] John answered everyone, "I baptize you with water, but there is one coming later who can do more than I can. I am not good enough to untie his sandals. He will baptize you with the Holy Spirit and with fire. [17] He will come ready to clean the grain. He will separate the good grain from the chaff. He will put the good part of the grain into his barn. Then he will burn the chaff with a fire that cannot be put out." [n] [18] And John continued to preach the Good News, saying many other things to encourage the people.

[19] But John spoke against Herod, the governor, because of his sin with Herodias, the wife of Herod's brother. John also criticized Herod for the many other evil things Herod did. [20] So Herod did another evil thing: He put John in prison.

JESUS IS BAPTIZED BY JOHN

[21] When all the people were being baptized by John, Jesus also was baptized. While Jesus was praying, heaven opened and [22] the Holy Spirit came down on him. The Spirit was in the form of a dove. Then a voice came from heaven and said, "You are my Son and I love you. I am very pleased with you."

THE FAMILY HISTORY OF JESUS

[23] When Jesus began to teach, he was about 30 years old. People thought that Jesus was Joseph's son.

Joseph was the son [n] of Heli.
[24] Heli was the son of Matthat.
Matthat was the son of Levi.
Levi was the son of Melki.
Melki was the son of Jannai.
Jannai was the son of Joseph.
[25] Joseph was the son of Mattathias.
Mattathias was the son of Amos.
Amos was the son of Nahum.
Nahum was the son of Esli.
Esli was the son of Naggai.
[26] Naggai was the son of Maath.
Maath was the son of Mattathias.
Mattathias was the son of Semein.
Semein was the son of Josech.
Josech was the son of Joda.
[27] Joda was the son of Joanan.
Joanan was the son of Rhesa.
Rhesa was the son of Zerubbabel.
Zerubbabel was the grandson of Shealtiel.
Shealtiel was the son of Neri.
[28] Neri was the son of Melchi.
Melchi was the son of Addi.
Addi was the son of Cosam.
Cosam was the son of Elmadam.
Elmadam was the son of Er.
[29] Er was the son of Joshua.

3:9 The ax . . . fire. This means that God is ready to punish his people who do not obey him.
3:17 He will . . . out. This means that Jesus will come to separate the good people from the bad people, saving the good and punishing the bad.
3:23 son "Son" in Jewish lists of ancestors can sometimes mean grandson or more distant relative.

Joshua was the son of Eliezer.
Eliezer was the son of Jorim.
Jorim was the son of Matthat.
Matthat was the son of Levi.
30 Levi was the son of Simeon.
Simeon was the son of Judah.
Judah was the son of Joseph.
Joseph was the son of Jonam.
Jonam was the son of Eliakim.
31 Eliakim was the son of Melea.
Melea was the son of Menna.
Menna was the son of Mattatha.
Mattatha was the son of Nathan.
Nathan was the son of David.
32 David was the son of Jesse.
Jesse was the son of Obed.
Obed was the son of Boaz.
Boaz was the son of Salmon.[n]
Salmon was the son of Nahshon.
33 Nahshon was the son of Amminadab.
Amminadab was the son of Admin.
Admin was the son of Arni.
Arni was the son of Hezron.
Hezron was the son of Perez.
Perez was the son of Judah.
34 Judah was the son of Jacob.
Jacob was the son of Isaac.
Isaac was the son of Abraham.
Abraham was the son of Terah.
Terah was the son of Nahor.
35 Nahor was the son of Serug.
Serug was the son of Reu.
Reu was the son of Peleg.
Peleg was the son of Eber.
Eber was the son of Shelah.
36 Shelah was the son of Cainan.
Cainan was the son of Arphaxad.
Arphaxad was the son of Shem.
Shem was the son of Noah.
Noah was the son of Lamech.
37 Lamech was the son of Methuselah.
Methuselah was the son of Enoch.
Enoch was the son of Jared.
Jared was the son of Mahalalel.
Mahalalel was the son of Kenan.
38 Kenan was the son of Enosh.
Enosh was the son of Seth.

Seth was the son of Adam.
Adam was the son of God.

JESUS IS TEMPTED BY THE DEVIL

4 Jesus, filled with the Holy Spirit, returned from the Jordan River. The Spirit led Jesus into the desert 2 where the devil tempted Jesus for 40 days. Jesus ate nothing during that time. When those days were ended, he was very hungry.

3 The devil said to Jesus, "If you are the Son of God, tell this rock to become bread."

4 Jesus answered, "It is written in the Scriptures: 'A person does not live only by eating bread.'"[n]

5 Then the devil took Jesus and showed him all the kingdoms of the world in a moment of time. 6 The devil said to Jesus, "I will give you all these kingdoms and all their power and glory. It has all been given to me, and I can give it to anyone I wish. 7 If you worship me, all will be yours."

8 Jesus answered, "It is written in the Scriptures: 'You must worship the Lord your God. Serve only him!'"[n]

9 Then the devil led Jesus to Jerusalem and put him on a high place of the Temple. He said to Jesus, "If you are the Son of God, jump off! 10 It is written in the Scriptures:

'He has put his angels in charge of
    you.
    They will watch over you.'
                                    Psalm 91:11
11 'They will catch you with their hands.
    And you will not hit your foot on a
        rock.'"   *Psalm 91:12*
12 Jesus answered, "But it also says in the Scriptures: 'Do not test the Lord your God.'"[n]

13 After the devil had tempted Jesus in every way, he went away to wait until a better time.

3:32 **Salmon** Some Greek copies read "Sala."
4:4 **'A person . . . bread.'** Quotation from Deuteronomy 8:3.
4:8 **'You . . . him!'** Quotation from Deuteronomy 6:13.
4:12 **'Do . . . God.'** Quotation from Deuteronomy 6:16.

JESUS TEACHES THE PEOPLE

[14]Jesus went back to Galilee with the power of the Holy Spirit. Stories about Jesus spread all through the area. [15]He began to teach in the synagogues, and all the people praised him.

[16]Jesus traveled to Nazareth, where he had grown up. On the Sabbath day he went to the synagogue as he always did. Jesus stood up to read. [17]The book of Isaiah the prophet was given to him. He opened the book and found the place where this is written:

[18] "The Spirit of the Lord is in me.
   This is because God chose me
      to tell the Good News to
      the poor.
God sent me to tell the prisoners of
      sin that they are free,

☆ Luke 4:20–30

Jesus taught and traveled all over the place. But when he went back to his hometown to help people, things got bad. The people kept saying, "Isn't this Joseph's son?" (They did not know he was really God's Son.) The people became so angry, they pushed Jesus to the edge of a cliff. They were about to kill him, but Jesus just walked through the crowd and went on his way.

Jesus was the most loving person to ever live. He healed people who were sick. He fed people who were hungry. He made friends with the people others would not touch. Jesus did many great things, but not everyone liked him. One day, when Jesus was teaching, some evil people got mad at him. They tried to hurt him. It looked like there was no way out of trouble for Jesus, but God made a way of escape for him. It is strange to think that not everybody liked Jesus. But it's true. And just as God protected Jesus, he will protect us when others may not like us.

. . . .

Jesus lived his life unafraid because he knew his Father would protect him. You can too because you have the same Father!

and to tell the blind that they can
   see again.   *Isaiah 61:1*
God sent me to free those who have
   been treated unfairly,
                           Isaiah 58:6
19 and to announce the time when
      the Lord will show kindness
      to his people."   *Isaiah 61:2*

 20Jesus closed the book, gave it back, and sat down. Everyone in the synagogue was watching Jesus closely. 21He began to speak to them. He said, "While you heard these words just now, they were coming true!"

22All the people praised Jesus. They were amazed at the beautiful words he spoke. They asked, "Isn't this Joseph's son?"

23Jesus said to them, "I know that you will tell me the old saying: 'Doctor, heal yourself.' You want to say, 'We heard about the things you did in Capernaum. Do those things here in your own town!'" 24Then Jesus said, "I tell you the truth. A prophet is not accepted in his own town. 25What I say is true. During the time of Elijah it did not rain in Israel for three and a half years. There was no food anywhere in the whole country. And there were many widows in Israel during that time. 26But Elijah was sent to none of those widows. He was sent only to a widow in Zarephath, a town in Sidon. 27And there were many with a harmful skin disease living in Israel during the time of the prophet Elisha. But none of them were healed except Naaman, who was from the country of Syria."

28When all the people in the synagogue heard these things, they became very angry. 29They got up and forced Jesus out of town. The town was built on a hill. They took Jesus to the edge of the hill and wanted to throw him off. 30But Jesus walked through the crowd and went on his way.

JESUS REMOVES AN EVIL SPIRIT

31Jesus went to Capernaum, a city in Galilee. On the Sabbath day, Jesus taught the people. 32They were amazed at his teaching, because he spoke with authority. 33In the synagogue there was a man who had an evil spirit from the devil inside him. The man shouted in a loud voice, 34"Jesus of Nazareth! What do you want with us? Did you come here to destroy us? I know who you are— God's Holy One!"

35But Jesus warned the evil spirit to stop. He said, "Be quiet! Come out of the man!" The evil spirit threw the man down to the ground before all the people. Then the evil spirit left the man and did not hurt him.

36The people were amazed. They said to each other, "What does this mean? With authority and power he commands evil spirits, and they come out." 37And so the news about Jesus spread to every place in the whole area.

JESUS HEALS MANY PEOPLE

38Jesus left the synagogue and went to Simon's[n] house. Simon's mother-in-law was very sick with a high fever. They asked Jesus to do something to help her. 39He stood very close to her and commanded the fever to leave. It left her immediately, and she got up and began serving them.

40When the sun went down, the people brought their sick to Jesus. They had many different diseases. Jesus put his hands on each sick person and healed every one of them. 41Demons came out of many people. The demons would shout, "You are the Son of God." But Jesus gave a strong command for the demons not to speak. They knew Jesus was the Christ.

42At daybreak, Jesus went to a place to be alone, but the people looked for him. When they found him, they tried to keep him from leaving. 43But Jesus said to them, "I must tell the Good

---

4:38 **Simon** Simon's other name was Peter.

News about God's kingdom to other towns, too. This is why I was sent." [44]Then Jesus kept on preaching in the synagogues of Judea.[n]

JESUS' FIRST FOLLOWERS

5 One day Jesus was standing beside Lake Galilee. Many people were pressing all around him. They wanted to hear the word of God. [2]Jesus saw two boats at the shore of the lake. The fishermen had left them and were washing their nets. [3]Jesus got into one of the boats, the one which belonged to Simon.[n] Jesus asked Simon to push off a little from the land. Then Jesus sat down in the boat and continued to teach the people on the shore.

[4]When Jesus had finished speaking, he said to Simon, "Take the boat into deep water. If you will put your nets in the water, you will catch some fish."

[5]Simon answered, "Master, we worked hard all night trying to catch fish, but we caught nothing. But you say to put the nets in the water; so I will." [6]The fishermen did as Jesus told them. And they caught so many fish that the nets began to break. [7]They called to their friends in the other boat to come and help them. The friends came, and both boats were filled so full that they were almost sinking.

[8-9]The fishermen were all amazed at the many fish they caught. When Simon Peter saw what had happened, he bowed down before Jesus and said, "Go away from me, Lord. I am a sinful man!" [10]James and John, the sons of Zebedee, were amazed too. (James and John were Simon's partners.)

Jesus said to Simon, "Don't be afraid. From now on you will be fishermen for men." [11]When the men brought their boats to the shore, they left everything and followed Jesus.

JESUS HEALS A SICK MAN

[12]One time Jesus was in a town where a very sick man lived. The man was covered with a harmful skin disease. When he saw Jesus, he bowed before Jesus and begged him, "Lord, heal me. I know you can if you want to."

[13]Jesus said, "I want to. Be healed!" And Jesus touched the man. Immediately the disease disappeared. [14]Then Jesus said, "Don't tell anyone about what happened. But go show yourself to the priest.[n] And offer a gift to God for your healing as Moses commanded.[n] This will prove to everyone that you are healed."

[15]But the news about Jesus was spreading more and more. Many people came to hear Jesus and to be healed of their sicknesses. [16]But Jesus often slipped away to other places to be alone so that he could pray.

JESUS HEALS A PARALYZED MAN

[17]One day Jesus was teaching the people. The Pharisees and teachers of the law were there, too. They had come from every town in Galilee and from Judea and Jerusalem. The Lord was giving Jesus the power to heal people. [18]There was a man who was paralyzed. Some men were carrying him on a mat. They tried to bring him in and put him down before Jesus. [19]But because there were so many people there, they could not find a way to Jesus. So the men went up on the roof and made a hole in the ceiling. They lowered the mat so that the paralyzed man was lying right before Jesus. [20]Jesus saw that these men believed. So he said to the sick man, "Friend, your sins are forgiven."

[21]The Jewish teachers of the law and the Pharisees thought to themselves, "Who is this man? He is saying things that are against God! Only God can forgive sins."

4:44 **Judea** Some Greek copies read "Galilee."
5:3 **Simon** Simon's other name was Peter.
5:14 **show . . . priest** The law of Moses said a priest must say when a Jew with a harmful skin disease was well.
5:14 **Moses commanded** Read about this in Leviticus 14:1–32.

[22]But Jesus knew what they were thinking. He said, "Why do you have thoughts like that in your hearts? [23]Which is easier: to tell this paralyzed man, 'Your sins are forgiven,' or to tell him, 'Stand up and walk'? [24]But I will prove to you that the Son of Man has authority on earth to forgive sins." So Jesus said to the paralyzed man, "I tell you, stand up! Take your mat and go home."

[25]Then the man stood up before the people there. He picked up his mat and went home, praising God. [26]All the people were fully amazed and began to praise God. They were filled with much respect and said, "Today we have seen amazing things!"

LEVI FOLLOWS JESUS

[27]After this, Jesus went out and saw a tax collector named Levi sitting in the tax office. Jesus said to him, "Follow me!" [28]Levi got up, left everything, and followed Jesus.

[29]Then Levi gave a big dinner for Jesus. The dinner was at Levi's house. At the table there were many tax collectors and other people, too. [30]But the Pharisees and the men who taught the law for the Pharisees began to complain to the followers of Jesus. They said, "Why do you eat and drink with tax collectors and 'sinners'?"

[31]Jesus answered them, "Healthy people don't need a doctor. It is the sick who need a doctor. [32]I have not come to invite good people. I have come to invite sinners to change their hearts and lives!"

JESUS ANSWERS A QUESTION

[33]They said to Jesus, "John's followers often give up eating[n] and pray, just as the Pharisees do. But your followers eat and drink all the time."

[34]Jesus said to them, "When there is a wedding, you cannot make the friends of the bridegroom give up eating while he is still with them. [35]But the time will come when he will be taken away from them. Then his friends will give up eating."

[36]Jesus told them this story: "No one takes cloth off a new coat to cover a hole in an old coat. If he does, he ruins the new coat, and the cloth from the new coat will not be the same as the old cloth. [37]People never pour new wine into old leather bags for holding wine. If they do, the new wine will break the bags, and the wine will spill out. Then the leather bags for holding wine will be ruined. [38]People always put new wine into new leather bags. [39]No one after drinking old wine wants new wine because he says, 'The old wine is better.'"

> I have not come to invite good people. I have come to invite sinners to change their hearts and lives!
>
> –LUKE 5:32

JESUS IS LORD OVER THE SABBATH

6 One Sabbath day Jesus was walking through some grainfields. His followers picked the heads of grain, rubbed them in their hands, and ate them. [2]Some Pharisees said, "Why are you doing that? It is against the law of Moses to do that on the Sabbath day."

[3]Jesus answered, "Haven't you read about what David did when he and those with him were hungry? [4]David went into God's house. He took the bread that was made holy for God and ate it. And he gave some of the bread to the people with him. This was against the law of Moses. It says that only priests can eat that bread." [5]Then Jesus

---

5:33 give up eating This is called "fasting." The people would give up eating for a special time of prayer and worship to God. It was also done to show sadness.

said to the Pharisees, "The Son of Man is Lord of the Sabbath day."

JESUS HEALS A MAN'S CRIPPLED HAND

⁶On another Sabbath day Jesus went into the synagogue and was teaching. A man with a crippled right hand was there. ⁷The teachers of the law and the Pharisees were watching to see if Jesus would heal on the Sabbath day. They wanted to see Jesus do something wrong so that they could accuse him. ⁸But he knew what they were thinking. He said to the man with the crippled hand, "Get up and stand before these people." The man got up and stood there. ⁹Then Jesus said to them, "I ask you, which is it right to do on the Sabbath day: to do good, or to do evil? Is it right to save a life or to destroy one?" ¹⁰Jesus looked around at all of them. He said to the man, "Let me see your hand." The man stretched out his hand, and it was completely healed.

¹¹The Pharisees and the teachers of the law became very angry. They said to each other, "What can we do to Jesus?"

JESUS CHOOSES HIS APOSTLES

¹²At that time Jesus went off to a mountain to pray. He stayed there all night, praying to God. ¹³The next morning, Jesus called his followers to him. He chose 12 of them, whom he named "apostles." They were ¹⁴Simon (Jesus named him Peter) and Andrew, Peter's brother; James and John, Philip and Bartholomew; ¹⁵Matthew, Thomas, James son of Alphaeus, and Simon (called the Zealot), ¹⁶Judas son of James and Judas Iscariot. This Judas was the one who gave Jesus to his enemies.

JESUS TEACHES AND HEALS

¹⁷Jesus and the apostles came down from the mountain. Jesus stood on level ground where there was a large group of his followers. Also, there were many people from all around Judea, Jerusalem, and the seacoast cities of Tyre and Sidon. ¹⁸They all came to hear Jesus teach and to be healed of their sicknesses. He healed those who were troubled by evil spirits. ¹⁹All the people were trying to touch Jesus, because power was coming from him and healing them all!

²⁰Jesus looked at his followers and said,

"Poor people, you are happy,
  because God's kingdom belongs to
    you.
²¹ You people who are now hungry are
    happy,
  because you will be satisfied.
You people who are now crying are
    happy,
  because you will laugh with joy.

²²"You are happy when people hate you and are cruel to you. You are happy when they say that you are evil because you belong to the Son of Man. ²³At that time be full of joy, because you have a great reward in heaven. Their fathers were cruel to the prophets in the same way these people are cruel to you.

²⁴ "But how terrible it will be for you
    who are rich,
  because you have had your easy
    life.
²⁵ How terrible it will be for you who
    are full now,
  because you will be hungry.
How terrible it will be for you who
    are laughing now,
  because you will be sad and cry.

²⁶"How terrible when all people say only good things about you. Their fathers always said good things about the false prophets.

LOVE YOUR ENEMIES

²⁷"I say to you who are listening to me, love your enemies. Do good to those who hate you. ²⁸Ask God to bless those who say bad things to you. Pray for those who are cruel to you. ²⁹If anyone

slaps you on one cheek, let him slap the other cheek too. If someone takes your coat, do not stop him from taking your shirt. ³⁰Give to everyone who asks you. When a person takes something that is yours, don't ask for it back. ³¹Do for other people what you want them to do for you. ³²If you love only those who love you, should you get some special praise for doing that? No! Even sinners love the people who love them! ³³If you do good only to those who do good to you, should you get some special praise for doing that? No! Even sinners do that! ³⁴If you lend things to people, always hoping to get something back, should you get some special praise for that? No! Even sinners lend to other sinners so that they can get back the same amount! ³⁵So love your enemies. Do good to them, and lend to them without hoping to get anything back. If you do these things, you will have a great reward. You will be sons of the Most High God. Yes, because God is kind even to people who are ungrateful and full of sin. ³⁶Show mercy just as your father shows mercy.

LOOK AT YOURSELVES

³⁷"Don't judge other people, and you will not be judged. Don't accuse others of being guilty, and you will not be accused of being guilty. Forgive other people, and you will be forgiven. ³⁸Give, and you will receive. You will be given much. It will be poured into your hands—more than you can hold. You will be given so much that it will spill into your lap. The way you give to others is the way God will give to you."

³⁹Jesus told them this story: "Can a blind man lead another blind man? No! Both of them will fall into a ditch. ⁴⁰A student is not better than his teacher. But when the student has fully learned all that he has been taught, then he will be like his teacher.

⁴¹"Why do you notice the little piece of dust that is in your brother's eye, but you don't see the big piece of wood that is in your own eye? ⁴²You say to your brother, 'Brother, let me take that little piece of dust out of your eye.' Why do you say this? You cannot see that big piece of wood in your own eye! You are a hypocrite! First, take the piece of wood out of your own eye. Then you will see clearly to take the dust out of your brother's eye.

TWO KINDS OF FRUIT

⁴³"A good tree does not produce bad fruit. Also, a bad tree does not produce good fruit. ⁴⁴Each tree is known by its fruit. People don't gather figs from thornbushes. And they don't get grapes from bushes. ⁴⁵A good person has good things saved up in his heart. And so he brings good things out of his heart. But an evil person has evil things saved up in his heart. So he brings out bad things. A person speaks the things that are in his heart.

TWO KINDS OF PEOPLE

⁴⁶"Why do you call me, 'Lord, Lord,' but do not do what I say? ⁴⁷Everyone who comes to me and listens to my words and obeys ⁴⁸is like a man building a house. He digs deep and lays his foundation on rock. The floods come, and the water tries to wash the house away. But the flood cannot move the house, because the house was built well. ⁴⁹But the one who hears my words and does not obey is like a man who builds his house on the ground without a foundation. When the floods come, the house quickly falls down. And that house is completely destroyed."

JESUS HEALS A SOLDIER'S SERVANT

7 When Jesus finished saying all these things to the people, he went to Capernaum. ²In Capernaum there was an army officer. He had a servant who was so sick he was nearly dead. The officer loved the servant very much. ³When the officer heard about Jesus, he sent some Jewish elders to

him. The officer wanted the leaders to ask Jesus to come and heal his servant. [4]The men went to Jesus and begged him saying, "This officer is worthy of your help. [5]He loves our people, and he built us a synagogue."

[6]So Jesus went with the men. He was getting near the officer's house when the officer sent friends to say, "Lord, you don't need to come into my house. I am not good enough for you to be under my roof. [7]That is why I did not come to you myself. You only need to say the word, and my servant will be healed. [8]I, too, am a man under the authority of other men. And I have soldiers under my command. I tell one soldier, 'Go,' and he goes. And I tell another soldier, 'Come,' and he comes. And I say to my servant, 'Do this,' and my servant obeys me."

[9]When Jesus heard this, he was amazed. He turned to the crowd following him and said, "I tell you, this is the greatest faith I have seen anywhere, even in Israel."

[10]The men who had been sent to Jesus went back to the house. There they found that the servant was healed.

JESUS BRINGS A MAN BACK TO LIFE

[11]The next day Jesus went to a town called Nain. His followers and a large crowd were traveling with him. [12]When he came near the town gate, he saw a funeral. A mother, who was a widow, had lost her only son. A large crowd from the town was with the mother while her son was being carried out. [13]When the Lord saw her, he felt very sorry for her. Jesus said to her, "Don't cry." [14]He went up to the coffin and touched it. The men who were carrying it stopped. Jesus said, "Young man, I tell you, get up!" [15]And the son sat up and began to talk. Then Jesus gave him back to his mother.

[16]All the people were amazed. They began praising God. They said, "A great prophet has come to us! God is taking care of his people."

[17]This news about Jesus spread through all Judea and into all the places around there.

JOHN ASKS A QUESTION

[18]John's followers told him about all these things. He called for two of his followers. [19]He sent them to the Lord to ask, "Are you the One who is coming, or should we wait for another?"

[20]So the men came to Jesus. They said, "John the Baptist sent us to you with this question: 'Are you the One who is coming, or should we wait for another?'"

[21]At that time, Jesus healed many people of their sicknesses, diseases, and evil spirits. He healed many blind people so that they could see again. [22]Then Jesus said to John's followers, "Go tell John the things that you saw and heard here. The blind can see. The crippled can walk. People with a harmful skin disease are healed. The deaf can hear, and the dead are given life. And the Good News is told to the poor. [23]The person who does not lose faith is blessed!"

[24]When John's followers left, Jesus began to tell the people about John: "What did you go out into the desert to see? A reed[n] blown by the wind? [25]What did you go out to see? A man dressed in fine clothes? No. People who have fine clothes live in kings' palaces. [26]But what did you go out to see? A prophet? Yes, and I tell you, John is more than a prophet. [27]This was written about John:

'I will send my messenger ahead of you.
He will prepare the way for you.'
Malachi 3:1

[28]I tell you, John is greater than any other man ever born. But even the least

---

7:24 **reed** It means that John was not weak like grass blown by the wind.

important person in the kingdom of God is greater than John."

²⁹(When the people heard this, they all agreed that God's teaching was good. Even the tax collectors agreed. These were people who were already baptized by John. ³⁰But the Pharisees and teachers of the law refused to accept God's plan for themselves; they did not let John baptize them.)

³¹Then Jesus said, "What shall I say about the people of this time? What are they like? ³²They are like children sitting in the marketplace. One group of children calls to the other group and says,

'We played music for
  you, but you did not
  dance.
We sang a sad song,
  but you did not
  cry.'

³³John the Baptist came and did not eat like other people or drink wine. And you say, 'He has a demon in him.' ³⁴The Son of Man came eating like other people and drinking wine. And you say, 'Look at him! He eats too much and drinks too much wine! He is a friend of the tax collectors and "sinners"!' ³⁵But wisdom is shown to be right by the things it does."

SIMON THE PHARISEE

³⁶One of the Pharisees asked Jesus to eat with him. Jesus went into the Pharisee's house and sat at the table. ³⁷A sinful woman in the town learned that Jesus was eating at the Pharisee's house. So she brought an alabaster jar of perfume. ³⁸She stood at Jesus' feet, crying, and began to wash his feet with her tears. She dried his feet with

her hair, kissed them many times and rubbed them with the perfume. ³⁹The Pharisee who asked Jesus to come to his house saw this. He thought to himself, "If Jesus were a prophet, he would know that the woman who is touching him is a sinner!"

⁴⁰Jesus said to the Pharisee, "Simon, I have something to say to you."

Simon said, "Teacher, tell me."

⁴¹Jesus said, "There were two men. Both men owed money to the same banker. One man owed the banker 500 silver coins.ⁿ The other man owed the banker 50 silver coins. ⁴²The men had no money; so they could not pay what they owed. But the banker told the men that they did not have to pay him. Which one of the two men will love the banker more?"

⁴³Simon, the Pharisee, answered, "I think it would be the one who owed him the most money."

Jesus said to Simon, "You are right." ⁴⁴Then Jesus turned toward the woman and said to Simon, "Do you see this woman? When I came into your house, you gave me no water for my feet. But she washed my feet with her tears and dried my feet with her hair. ⁴⁵You did not kiss me, but she has been kissing my feet since I came in! ⁴⁶You did not rub my head with oil, but she rubbed my feet with perfume. ⁴⁷I tell you that her many sins are forgiven. This is clear because she showed great love. But the person who has only a little to be forgiven will feel only a little love."

⁴⁸Then Jesus said to her, "Your sins are forgiven."

⁴⁹The people sitting at the table began to think to themselves, "Who is this man? How can he forgive sins?"

> Jesus said to the woman, "Because you believed, you are saved from your sins. Go in peace."
> –LUKE 7:50

7:41 **silver coins** A Roman denarius. One coin was the average pay for one day's work.

[50]Jesus said to the woman, "Because you believed, you are saved from your sins. Go in peace."

THE GROUP WITH JESUS

8 The next day, while Jesus was traveling through some cities and small towns, he preached and told the Good News about God's kingdom. The 12 apostles were with him. [2]There were also some women with him who had been healed of sicknesses and evil spirits. One of the women was Mary, called Magdalene, from whom seven demons had gone out. [3]Also among the women were Joanna, the wife of Chuza (Herod's helper), Susanna, and many other women. These women used their own money to help Jesus and his apostles.

A STORY ABOUT PLANTING SEED

[4]A great crowd gathered. People were coming to Jesus from every town. He told them this story:

[5]"A farmer went out to plant his seed. While he was planting, some seed fell beside the road. People walked on the seed, and the birds ate all this seed. [6]Some seed fell on rock. It began to grow but then died because it had no water. [7]Some seed fell among thorny weeds. This seed grew, but later the weeds choked the good plants. [8]And some seed fell on good ground. This seed grew and made 100 times more grain."

Jesus finished the story. Then he called out, "Let those with ears use them and listen!"

[9]Jesus' followers asked him, "What does this story mean?"

[10]Jesus said, "You have been chosen to know the secret truths of the kingdom of God. But I use stories to speak to other people. I do this so that:

'They will look, but they may not see.
    They will listen, but they may not
        understand.'   *Isaiah 6:9*

[11]"This is what the story means: The seed is God's teaching. [12]What is the seed that fell beside the road? It is like the people who hear God's teaching, but then the devil comes and takes it away from their hearts. So they cannot believe the teaching and be saved. [13]What is the seed that fell on rock? It is like those who hear God's teaching and accept it gladly. But they don't have deep roots. They believe for a while, but then trouble comes. They stop believing and turn away from God. [14]What is the seed that fell among the thorny weeds? It is like those who hear God's teaching, but they let the worries, riches, and pleasures of this life keep them from growing. So they never produce good fruit. [15]And what is the seed that fell on the good ground? That is like those who hear God's teaching with a good, honest heart. They obey God's teaching and patiently produce good fruit.

USE WHAT YOU HAVE

[16]"No one lights a lamp and then covers it with a bowl or hides it under a bed. Instead, he puts the lamp on a lampstand so that those who come in will have enough light to see. [17]Everything that is hidden will become clear. Every secret thing will be made known. [18]So be careful how you listen. The person who has something will be given more. But to the person who has nothing, this will happen: Even what he thinks he has will be taken away from him."

JESUS' TRUE FAMILY

[19]Jesus' mother and brothers came to see him. There was such a crowd that they could not get to him. [20]Someone said to Jesus, "Your mother and your brothers are standing outside. They want to see you."

[21]Jesus answered them, "My mother and my brothers are those who listen to God's teaching and obey it!"

JESUS STOPS A STORM

[22]One day Jesus and his followers got into a boat. He said to them, "Come

⭐ Luke 8:24–25

*Jesus and his followers got in
a boat and started across a
lake the size of an ocean.
Suddenly a storm blew
in and knocked the boat
around. The people in the
boat thought they were
going to drown, but Jesus was
not afraid. He even took a nap
during the storm!*

There are many things that can cause us to be afraid. The wind can be scary when it makes howling sounds. Waves can be scary when they get big. Jesus' disciples were scared because of the strong wind and the huge waves. They thought their boat was going to sink. But Jesus was sleeping through it because he was not afraid. They woke Jesus up and cried, "Help us!" Jesus spoke to the wind and waves. And suddenly it all stopped. Everything was okay. Jesus asked them, "Where is your faith?" He was right there with them. They needed to believe he would not let the storm hurt them.

. . . .

*Do not forget that Jesus is always with you, even when
you cannot see him. You do not need to be afraid.*

with me across the lake." And so they started across. 23 While they were sailing, Jesus fell asleep. A big storm blew up on the lake. The boat began to fill with water, and they were in danger.

24 The followers went to Jesus and woke him. They said, "Master! Master! We will drown!"

Jesus got up and gave a command to the wind and the waves. The wind stopped, and the lake became calm.

25 Jesus said to his followers, "Where is your faith?"

The followers were afraid and amazed. They said to each other, "What kind of man is this? He commands the wind and the water, and they obey him!"

A MAN WITH DEMONS INSIDE HIM

26 Jesus and his followers sailed across the lake from Galilee to the area where the Gerasene[n] people live. 27 When

8:26 Gerasene From Gerasa, an area southeast of Lake Galilee. The exact location is uncertain and some Greek copies read "Gadarene"; others read "Gergesene."

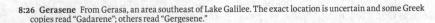

Jesus got out of the boat, a man from the town came to Jesus. This man had demons inside him. For a long time he had worn no clothes. He lived in the burial caves, not in a house. [28]When he saw Jesus, he cried out and fell down before him. The man said with a loud voice, "What do you want with me, Jesus, Son of the Most High God? Please don't punish me!" [29]He said this because Jesus had commanded the evil spirit to come out of him. Many times it had taken hold of him. He had been kept under guard and chained hand and foot. But he had broken his chains and had been driven by the demon out into the desert.

[30]Jesus asked him, "What is your name?"

The man answered, "Legion." [n] (He said his name was "Legion" because many demons were in him.) [31]The demons begged Jesus not to send them into eternal darkness.[n] [32]On the hill there was a large herd of pigs eating. The demons begged Jesus to allow them to go into the pigs. So Jesus allowed them to do this. [33]Then the demons came out of the man and went into the pigs. The herd of pigs ran down the hill and into the lake. All the pigs drowned.

[34]The men who took care of the pigs ran away. They told about this in the town and the countryside. [35]And people went to see what had happened. They came to Jesus and found the man sitting there at Jesus' feet. The man was clothed and in his right mind because the demons were gone. But the people were frightened. [36]The men who saw these things happen told the others all about how Jesus had made the man well. [37]All the people of the Gerasene country asked Jesus to go away. They were all very afraid. So Jesus got into the boat and went back across the lake.

[38]The man that Jesus had healed begged to go with him. But Jesus sent him away, saying, [39]"Go back home and tell people what God did for you." So the man went all over town telling how much Jesus had done for him.

JESUS GIVES LIFE TO A DEAD GIRL AND HEALS A SICK WOMAN

[40]When Jesus got back to the other side of the lake, a crowd welcomed him. Everyone was waiting for him. [41]A man named Jairus came to Jesus. Jairus was a ruler of the synagogue. He bowed down at Jesus' feet and begged him to come to his house. [42]Jairus had only one daughter. She was 12 years old, and she was dying.

While Jesus was on his way to Jairus' house, the people were crowding all around him. [43]A woman was there who had been bleeding for 12 years. She had spent all her money on doctors, but no doctor was able to heal her. [44]The woman came up behind Jesus and touched the edge of his coat. At that moment, her bleeding stopped. [45]Then Jesus said, "Who touched me?"

All the people said they had not touched Jesus. Peter said, "Master, the people are all around you and are pushing against you."

[46]But Jesus said, "Someone did touch me! I felt power go out from me." [47]When the woman saw that she could not hide, she came forward, shaking. She bowed down before Jesus. While all the people listened, she told why she had touched him. Then, she said, she was healed immediately. [48]Jesus said to her, "Dear woman, you are healed because you believed. Go in peace."

[49]While Jesus was still speaking, someone came from the house of the synagogue ruler and said to the ruler, "Your daughter has died! Don't bother the teacher now."

[50]When Jesus heard this, he said to

8:30 **"Legion"** Means very many. A legion was about 5,000 men in the Roman army.
8:31 **eternal darkness** Literally, "the abyss," something like a pit or a hole that has no end.

Jairus, "Don't be afraid. Just believe, and your daughter will be well."

⁵¹Jesus went to the house. He let only Peter, John, James, and the girl's father and mother go inside with him. ⁵²All the people were crying and feeling sad because the girl was dead. But Jesus said, "Don't cry. She is not dead; she is only sleeping."

⁵³The people laughed at Jesus because they knew that the girl was dead. ⁵⁴But Jesus took her by the hand and called to her, "My child, stand up!" ⁵⁵Her spirit came back into her, and she stood up immediately. Jesus said, "Give her something to eat." ⁵⁶The girl's parents were amazed. Jesus told them not to tell anyone about what happened.

JESUS SENDS OUT THE APOSTLES

9 Jesus called the 12 apostles together. He gave them power to heal sicknesses and power over all demons. ²Jesus sent the apostles out to tell about God's kingdom and to heal the sick. ³He said to them, "When you travel, don't take a walking stick. Also, don't carry a bag, or food, or money. Take for your trip only the clothes you are wearing. ⁴When you go into a house, stay there until it is time to leave. ⁵If the people in the town will not welcome you, go outside the town and shake the dust off of your feet.ⁿ This will be a warning to them."

⁶So the apostles went out. They traveled through all the towns. They told the Good News and healed people everywhere.

HEROD IS CONFUSED ABOUT JESUS

⁷Herod, the governor, heard about all these things that were happening. He was confused because some people said, "John the Baptist is risen from death." ⁸Others said, "Elijah has come to us." And still others said, "One of the prophets from long ago has risen from death." ⁹Herod said, "I cut off John's head. So who is this man I hear these things about?" And Herod kept trying to see Jesus.

MORE THAN 5,000 PEOPLE FED

¹⁰When the apostles returned, they told Jesus all the things they had done on their trip. Then Jesus took them away to a town called Bethsaida. There, Jesus and his apostles could be alone together. ¹¹But the people learned where Jesus went and followed him. Jesus welcomed them and talked with them about God's kingdom. He healed those who needed to be healed.

¹²Late in the afternoon, the 12 apostles came to Jesus and said, "No one lives in this place. Send the people away. They need to find food and places to sleep in the towns and countryside around here."

¹³But Jesus said to them, "You give them something to eat."

They said, "We have only five loaves of bread and two fish. Do you want us to go buy food for all these people?" ¹⁴(There were about 5,000 men there.)

Jesus said to his followers, "Tell the people to sit in groups of about 50 people."

¹⁵So the followers did this, and all the people sat down. ¹⁶Then Jesus took the five loaves of bread and two fish. He looked up to heaven and thanked God for the food. Then Jesus divided the food and gave it to the followers to give to the people. ¹⁷All the people ate and were satisfied. And there was much food left. Twelve baskets were filled with pieces of food that were not eaten.

JESUS IS THE CHRIST

¹⁸One time when Jesus was praying alone, his followers came together there. Jesus asked them, "Who do the people say I am?"

¹⁹They answered, "Some say you are

9:5 shake . . . feet A warning. It showed that they were finished talking to these people.

John the Baptist. Others say you are Elijah.[n] And others say you are one of the prophets from long ago who has come back to life."

²⁰Then Jesus asked, "And who do you say I am?"

Peter answered, "You are the Christ from God."

²¹Jesus warned them not to tell anyone. Then he said, ²²"The Son of Man must suffer many things. He will be rejected by the Jewish elders, the leading priests, and the teachers of the law. The Son of Man will be killed. But after three days he will be raised from death."

²³Jesus went on to say to all of them, "If anyone wants to follow me, he must say 'no' to the things he wants. Every day he must be willing even to die on a cross, and he must follow me. ²⁴Whoever wants to save his life will lose it. And whoever gives his life for me will save it. ²⁵It is worth nothing for a man to have the whole world, if he himself is destroyed or lost. ²⁶If anyone is ashamed of me and my teaching, then I[n] will be ashamed of him. I will be ashamed of him at the time I come with my glory and with the glory of the Father and the holy angels. ²⁷I tell you the truth. Some of you people standing here will see the kingdom of God before you die."

JESUS WITH MOSES AND ELIJAH

²⁸About eight days after Jesus said these things, he took Peter, James, and John and went up on a mountain to pray. ²⁹While Jesus was praying, his face was changed, and his clothes became shining white. ³⁰Then two men were talking with Jesus. The men were Moses and Elijah.[n] ³¹They appeared in heavenly glory, talking with Jesus about his death which would happen in Jerusalem. ³²Peter and the others were asleep. But they woke up and saw the glory of Jesus. They also saw the two men who were standing with him. ³³When Moses and Elijah were about to leave, Peter said, "Master, it is good that we are here. We will put three tents here— one for you, one for Moses, and one for Elijah." (Peter did not know what he was saying.)

³⁴While Peter was saying these things, a cloud came down all around them. Peter, James, and John became afraid when the cloud covered them. ³⁵A voice came from the cloud. The voice said, "This is my Son. He is the One I have chosen. Obey him."

³⁶When the voice finished speaking, only Jesus was there. Peter, James, and John said nothing. At that time they told no one about what they had seen.

JESUS HEALS A SICK BOY

³⁷The next day, Jesus, Peter, James, and John came down from the mountain. A large crowd met Jesus. ³⁸A man in the crowd shouted to Jesus, "Teacher, please come and look at my son. He is the only child I have. ³⁹An evil spirit comes into my son, and then he shouts. He loses control of himself, and he foams at the mouth. The evil spirit keeps on hurting him and almost never leaves him. ⁴⁰I begged your followers to make the evil spirit leave my son, but they could not do it."

⁴¹Jesus answered, "You people who live now have no faith. Your lives are all wrong. How long must I be with you and be patient with you?" Then Jesus said to the man, "Bring your son here."

⁴²While the boy was coming, the demon threw him on the ground. The boy lost control of himself. But Jesus gave a strong command to the evil spirit. Then the boy was healed, and Jesus gave him back to his father. ⁴³All the people were amazed at the great power of God.

9:19 **Elijah** A man who spoke for God. He lived hundreds of years before Christ.
9:26 **I** Literally, "the Son of Man."
9:30 **Moses and Elijah** Two of the most important Jewish leaders in the past.

JESUS TALKS ABOUT HIS DEATH

The people were all wondering about the things Jesus did. But he said to his followers, 44"Don't forget the things I tell you now: The Son of Man will be handed over into the control of men." 45But the followers did not understand what Jesus meant. The meaning was hidden from them so that they could not understand it. But they were afraid to ask Jesus about what he said.

THE MOST IMPORTANT PERSON

46Jesus' followers began to have an argument about which one of them was the greatest. 47Jesus knew what they were thinking. So he took a little child and stood the child beside him. 48Then Jesus said, "If anyone accepts a little child like this in my name, then he accepts me. And when he accepts me, he accepts the One who sent me. He who is least among you all—he is the greatest."

ANYONE NOT AGAINST US IS FOR US

49John answered, "Master, we saw someone using your name to force demons out of people. We told him to stop because he does not belong to our group."

50Jesus said to him, "Don't stop him. If a person is not against you, then he is for you."

A SAMARITAN TOWN

51The time was coming near when Jesus would leave and be taken to heaven. He was determined to go to Jerusalem 52and sent some men ahead of him. The men went into a town in Samaria to make everything ready for Jesus. 53But the people there would not welcome him because he was going toward Jerusalem. 54James and John, the followers of Jesus, saw this. They said, "Lord, do you want us to call fire down from heaven and destroy those people?"[n]

55But Jesus turned and scolded them. [And Jesus said, "You don't know what kind of spirit you belong to. 56The Son of Man did not come to destroy the souls of men but to save them."][n] Then he and his followers went to another town.

FOLLOWING JESUS

57They were all going along the road. Someone said to Jesus, "I will follow you any place you go."

58Jesus answered, "The foxes have holes to live in. The birds have nests to live in. But the Son of Man has no place to rest his head."

59Jesus said to another man, "Follow me!"

But the man said, "Lord, first let me go and bury my father."

60But Jesus said to him, "Let the people who are dead bury their own dead! You must go and tell about the kingdom of God."

61Another man said, "I will follow you, Lord, but first let me go and say good-bye to my family."

62Jesus said, "Anyone who begins to plow a field but keeps looking back is of no use in the kingdom of God."

JESUS SENDS THE 72 MEN

10 After this, the Lord chose 72[n] others. He sent them out in pairs. He sent them ahead of him into every town and place where he planned to go. 2He said to them, "There are a great many people to harvest. But there are only a few workers to harvest them. God owns the harvest. Pray to God that he will send more workers to help gather his harvest. 3You can go now. But listen! I am sending you, and you will be like sheep among wolves. 4Don't carry a purse, a bag, or sandals. Don't stop to talk with people on the road. 5Before you go into a house, say, 'Peace be with this house.' 6If a peaceful man

---

9:54 **people** Some Greek copies add: " ... as Elijah did."
9:55–56 **And . . . them.** Some Greek copies do not contain the bracketed text.
10:1 **72** Some Greek copies read "70."

lives there, your blessing of peace will stay with him. If the man is not peaceful, then your blessing of peace will come back to you. ⁷Stay in the same house. Eat and drink what the people there give you. A worker should be given his pay. Don't move from house to house. ⁸If you go into a town and the people welcome you, eat what they give you. ⁹Heal the sick who live there. Tell them, 'The kingdom of God is soon coming to you!' ¹⁰But if you go into a town, and the people don't welcome you, then go out into the streets of that town. Say to them, ¹¹"Even the dirt from your town that sticks to our feet we wipe off against you.ⁿ But remember that the kingdom of God is coming soon.' ¹²I tell you, on the Judgment Day it will be worse for the people of that town than for the people of Sodom.ⁿ

JESUS WARNS UNBELIEVERS

¹³"How terrible for you, Korazin! How terrible for you, Bethsaida! I did many miracles in you. If those same miracles had happened in Tyre and Sidon,ⁿ those people would have changed their lives and stopped sinning long ago. They would have worn rough cloth and put ashes on themselves to show that they had changed. ¹⁴But on the Judgment Day it will be worse for you than for Tyre and Sidon. ¹⁵And you, Capernaum,ⁿ will you be lifted up to heaven? No! You will be thrown down to the depths!

¹⁶"He who listens to you is really listening to me. He who refuses to accept you is really refusing to accept me. And he who refuses to accept me is refusing to accept the One who sent me."

SATAN FALLS

¹⁷When the 72ⁿ men came back from their trip, they were very happy. They said, "Lord, even the demons obeyed us when we used your name!"

¹⁸Jesus said to the men, "I saw Satan falling like lightning from the sky. ¹⁹Listen! I gave you power to walk on snakes and scorpions. I gave you more power than the Enemy has. Nothing will hurt you. ²⁰You should be happy, but not because the spirits obey you. You should be happy because your names are written in heaven."

> You should be happy because your names are written in heaven.
>
> –LUKE 10:20

JESUS PRAYS TO THE FATHER

²¹Then the Holy Spirit made Jesus rejoice. He said, "I thank you, Father, Lord of heaven and earth, because you have hidden these things from the people who are wise and smart. But you have shown them to those who are like little children. Yes, Father, you did this because this is what you really wanted.

²²"My Father has given me all things. No one knows the Son—only the Father knows. And only the Son knows the Father. The only people who will know about the Father are those whom the Son chooses to tell."

²³Then Jesus turned to his followers and said privately, "You are blessed to see what you now see! ²⁴I tell you, many prophets and kings wanted to see what you now see. But they did not see these things. And many prophets and kings

---

10:11 **dirt . . . you** A warning. It showed that they were finished talking to these people.
10:12 **Sodom** City that God destroyed because the people were so evil.
10:13 **Tyre and Sidon** Towns where wicked people lived.
10:13–15 **Korazin . . . Bethsaida . . . Capernaum** Towns by Lake Galilee where Jesus preached to the people.
10:17 **72** Some Greek copies read "70."

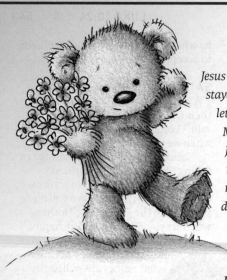

☆ Luke 10:39

Jesus and his followers traveled a lot and stayed in people's homes. Mary and Martha let Jesus stay in their home. While Martha made dinner, Mary listened to Jesus tell stories. She sat with all the men—right at Jesus' feet! Martha got mad because Mary wasn't helping with dinner. So she complained to Jesus. He told her she was upset about too many things. All that mattered was following him. And that is what Mary had chosen to do.

This Mary was a friend of Jesus, and she loved to hear him teach. She had never heard anyone teach like Jesus did. Even though Jesus was speaking to a crowd of people, she felt like he was speaking just to her. Did you know that Jesus speaks to us? He speaks to us when we read the Bible. He speaks to us when we pray. Sometimes he speaks to us through other people. When we listen, he speaks to us and tells us what we should do next.

• •

One of the best things Jesus likes to tell us is how much he loves us. Listen. You just might hear him say, "I love you!"

---

wanted to hear what you now hear. But they did not hear these things."

THE GOOD SAMARITAN
25 Then a teacher of the law stood up. He was trying to test Jesus. He said, "Teacher, what must I do to get life forever?"

26 Jesus said to him, "What is written in the law? What do you read there?"

27 The man answered, "Love the Lord your God. Love him with all your heart, all your soul, all your strength, and all your mind." [n] Also, "You must love your neighbor as you love yourself." [n]

28 Jesus said to him, "Your answer is right. Do this and you will have life forever."

29 But the man wanted to show that the way he was living was right.

10:27 **"Love . . . mind."** Quotation from Deuteronomy 6:5.
10:27 **"You . . . yourself."** Quotation from Leviticus 19:18.

So he said to Jesus, "And who is my neighbor?"

[30] To answer this question, Jesus said, "A man was going down the road from Jerusalem to Jericho. Some robbers attacked him. They tore off his clothes and beat him. Then they left him lying there, almost dead. [31] It happened that a Jewish priest was going down that road. When the priest saw the man, he walked by on the other side of the road. [32] Next, a Levite[n] came there. He went over and looked at the man. Then he walked by on the other side of the road. [33] Then a Samaritan[n] traveling down the road came to where the hurt man was lying. He saw the man and felt very sorry for him. [34] The Samaritan went to him and poured olive oil and wine[n] on his wounds and bandaged them. He put the hurt man on his own donkey and took him to an inn. At the inn, the Samaritan took care of him. [35] The next day, the Samaritan brought out two silver coins[n] and gave them to the inn-keeper. The Samaritan said, 'Take care of this man. If you spend more money on him, I will pay it back to you when I come again.'"

[36] Then Jesus said, "Which one of these three men do you think was a neighbor to the man who was attacked by the robbers?"

[37] The teacher of the law answered, "The one who helped him."

Jesus said to him, "Then go and do the same thing he did!"

MARY AND MARTHA

[38] While Jesus and his followers were traveling, Jesus went into a town. A woman named Martha let Jesus stay at her house. [39] Martha had a sister named Mary. Mary was sitting at Jesus' feet and listening to him teach. [40] Martha became angry because she had so much work to do. She went in and said, "Lord, don't you care that my sister has left me alone to do all the work? Tell her to help me!"

[41] But the Lord answered her, "Martha, Martha, you are getting worried and upset about too many things. [42] Only one thing is important. Mary has chosen the right thing, and it will never be taken away from her."

JESUS TEACHES ABOUT PRAYER

11 One time Jesus was praying in a place. When he finished, one of his followers said to him, "John taught his followers how to pray. Lord, please teach us how to pray, too."

[2] Jesus said to them, "When you pray, say:

'Father, we pray that your name will
     always be kept holy.
We pray that your kingdom will
     come.
[3] Give us the food we need for each
     day.
[4] Forgive us the sins we have done,
     because we forgive every person
          who has done wrong to us.
And do not cause us to be tested.'" [n]

CONTINUE TO ASK

[5-6] Then Jesus said to them, "Suppose one of you went to your friend's house at midnight and said to him, 'A friend of mine has come into town to visit me. But I have nothing for him to eat. Please loan me three loaves of bread.' [7] Your friend inside the house answers, 'Don't bother me! The door is already locked. My children and I are in bed. I cannot get up and give you the bread

---

10:32 **Levite** Levites were men from the tribe of Levi who helped the Jewish priests with their work in the Temple. Read 1 Chronicles 23:24–32.
10:33 **Samaritan** Samaritans were people from Samaria. These people were part Jewish, but the Jews did not accept them as true Jews. Samaritans and Jews hated each other.
10:34 **olive oil and wine** Oil and wine were used like medicine to soften and clean wounds.
10:35 **silver coins** A Roman denarius. One coin was the average pay for one day's work.
11:2–4 **'Father . . . tested.'** Some Greek copies include phrases from Matthew's version of this prayer (Matthew 6:9–13).

now.' [8]I tell you, maybe friendship is not enough to make him get up to give you the bread. But he will surely get up to give you what you need if you continue to ask. [9]So I tell you, continue to ask, and God will give to you. Continue to search, and you will find. Continue to knock, and the door will open for you. [10]Yes, if a person continues asking, he will receive. If he continues searching, he will find. And if he continues knocking, the door will open for him. [11]What would you fathers do if your son asks you for[n] a fish? Would any of you give him a snake? [12]Or, if your son asks for an egg, would you give him a scorpion? [13]Even though you are bad, you know how to give good things to your children. So surely your heavenly Father knows how to give the Holy Spirit to those who ask him."

JESUS' POWER IS FROM GOD

[14]One time Jesus was sending a demon out of a man who could not talk. When the demon came out, the man was able to speak. The people were amazed. [15]But some of them said, "Jesus uses the power of Beelzebul to force demons out of people. Beelzebul is the ruler of demons."

[16]Other people wanted to test Jesus. They asked him to give them a sign from heaven. [17]But Jesus knew what they were thinking. So he said to them, "Every kingdom that is divided and fights against itself will be destroyed. And a family that fights against itself will break apart. [18]So if Satan is fighting against himself, then how will his kingdom last? You say that I use the power of Beelzebul to force out demons. [19]But if I use the power of Beelzebul to force out demons, then by what power do your people force out demons? So your own people prove that you are wrong. [20]But if I use the power of God to force

out demons, the kingdom of God has come to you!

[21]"When a strong man with many weapons guards his own house, then the things in his house are safe. [22]But suppose a stronger man comes and defeats him. The stronger man will take away the weapons that the first man trusted to keep his house safe. Then the stronger man will do what he wants with the first man's things.

[23]"If anyone is not with me, he is against me. He who does not work with me is working against me.

THE EMPTY MAN

[24]"When an evil spirit comes out of a person, it travels through dry places, looking for a place to rest. But that spirit finds no place to rest. So it says, 'I will go back to the home I left.' [25]When the spirit comes back to that person, it finds that home swept clean and made neat. [26]Then the evil spirit goes out and brings seven other spirits more evil than itself. Then all the evil spirits go into that person and live there. And he has even more trouble than he had before."

PEOPLE WHO ARE TRULY BLESSED

[27]When Jesus was saying these things, a woman in the crowd spoke out. She said to Jesus, "Your mother is blessed because she gave birth to you and nursed you."

[28]But Jesus said, "Those who hear the teaching of God and obey it—they are the ones who are truly blessed."

GIVE US PROOF!

[29]The crowd grew larger. Jesus said, "The people who live today are evil. They ask for a miracle as a sign from God. But they will have no sign—only the sign of Jonah.[n] [30]Jonah was a sign for those people who lived in Nineveh.

11:11 for Some Greek copies include the phrase "for bread? Would any of you give him a stone? Or if he asks you for . . . " and continue to verse 12.
11:29 sign of Jonah Jonah's three days in the big fish are like Jesus' three days in the tomb.

In the same way the Son of Man will be a sign for the people of this time. [31]On the Judgment Day the Queen of the South[n] will stand up with the men who live now. She will show that they are guilty because she came from far away to listen to Solomon's wise teaching. And I tell you that someone greater than Solomon is here! [32]On the Judgment Day the men of Nineveh will stand up with the people who live now. And they will show that you are guilty, because when Jonah preached to those people, they changed their hearts and lives. And I tell you that someone greater than Jonah is here!

BE A LIGHT TO THE WORLD

[33]"No one takes a light and puts it under a bowl or hides it. Instead, he puts the light on a lampstand so that the people who come in can see. [34]Your eye is a light for the body. If your eyes are good, then your whole body will be full of light. But if your eyes are evil, then your whole body will be full of darkness. [35]So be careful! Don't let the light in you become darkness. [36]If your whole body is full of light, and none of it is dark, then you will shine bright, as when a lamp shines on you."

JESUS ACCUSES THE PHARISEES

[37]After Jesus had finished speaking, a Pharisee asked Jesus to eat with him. So Jesus went in and sat at the table. [38]But the Pharisee was surprised when he saw that Jesus did not wash his hands[n] before the meal. [39]The Lord said to him, "You Pharisees clean the outside of the cup and the dish. But inside you are full of greed and evil. [40]You are foolish. The same One who made what is outside also made what is inside. [41]So give what is in your cups and dishes to the poor. Then you will be fully clean.

[42]But how terrible for you Pharisees! You give God one-tenth of even your mint, your rue, and every other plant in your garden. But you forget to be fair to other people and to love God. These are the things you should do. And you should also continue to do those other things—like giving one-tenth. [43]How terrible for you Pharisees, because you love to get the most important seats in the synagogues. And you love people to show respect to you in the marketplaces. [44]How terrible for you, because you are like hidden graves. People walk on them without knowing it."

JESUS TALKS TO TEACHERS OF THE LAW

[45]One of the teachers of the law said to Jesus, "Teacher, when you say these things, you are insulting us, too."

[46]Jesus answered, "How terrible for you, you teachers of the law! You make strict rules that are very hard for people to obey. But you yourselves don't even try to follow those rules. [47]How terrible for you, because you build tombs for the prophets. But these are the prophets that your fathers killed! [48]And now you show that you approve of what your fathers did. They killed the prophets, and you build tombs for the prophets! [49]This is why in his wisdom God said, 'I will send prophets and apostles to them. Some of my prophets and apostles will be killed, and others will be treated cruelly.' [50]So you who live now will be punished for the deaths of all the prophets who were killed since the beginning of the world. [51]You will be punished for the killing of Abel and for the killing of Zechariah.[n] Zechariah was killed between the altar and the Temple. Yes, I tell you that you people who live now will be punished for them all.

11:31 **Queen of the South** The Queen of Sheba. She traveled 1,000 miles to learn God's wisdom from Solomon. Read 1 Kings 10:1–3.
11:38 **wash his hands** This was a Jewish religious custom that the Pharisees thought was very important.
11:51 **Abel . . . Zechariah** In the Hebrew Old Testament, the first and last men to be murdered.

⁵²"How terrible for you, you teachers of the law. You have hidden the key to learning about God. You yourselves would not learn, and you stopped others from learning, too."

⁵³When Jesus was leaving, the teachers of the law and the Pharisees began to give him trouble, asking him questions about many things. ⁵⁴They were trying to catch Jesus saying something wrong.

DON'T BE LIKE THE PHARISEES

12 Many thousands of people had gathered. There were so many people that they were stepping on each other. Before Jesus spoke to them, he said to his followers, "Be careful of the yeast of the Pharisees. They are hypocrites. ²Everything that is hidden will be shown. Everything that is secret will be made known. ³The things you say in the dark will be told in the light. The things you have whispered in an inner room will be shouted from the top of the house."

FEAR ONLY GOD

⁴Then Jesus said to the people, "I tell you, my friends, don't be afraid of people. People can kill the body, but after that they can do nothing more to hurt you. ⁵I will show you the One to fear. You should fear him who has the power to kill you and also to throw you into hell. Yes, he is the One you should fear.

⁶"When five sparrows are sold, they cost only two pennies. But God does not forget any of them. ⁷Yes, God even knows how many hairs you have on your head. Don't be afraid. You are worth much more than many sparrows.

DON'T BE ASHAMED OF JESUS

⁸"I tell you, if anyone stands before others and says that he believes in me, then I will say that he belongs to me. I will say this before the angels of God. ⁹But if anyone stands before others and says he does not believe in me, then I will say that he does not belong to me. I will say this before the angels of God.

¹⁰"If a person says something against the Son of Man, he can be forgiven. But a person who says bad things against the Holy Spirit will not be forgiven.

¹¹"When men bring you into the synagogues before the leaders and other important men, don't worry about how to defend yourself or what to say. ¹²At that time the Holy Spirit will teach you what you must say."

JESUS WARNS AGAINST SELFISHNESS

¹³One of the men in the crowd said to Jesus, "Teacher, tell my brother to divide with me the property our father left us."

¹⁴But Jesus said to him, "Who said that I should be your judge or decide how to divide the property between you two?" ¹⁵Then Jesus said to them, "Be careful and guard against all kinds of greed. A man's life is not measured by the many things he owns."

¹⁶Then Jesus used this story: "There was a rich man who had some land, which grew a good crop of food. ¹⁷The rich man thought to himself, 'What will I do? I have no place to keep all my crops.' ¹⁸Then he said, 'I know what I will do. I will tear down my barns and build bigger ones! I will put all my grain and other goods together in my new barns. ¹⁹Then I can say to myself, I have enough good things stored to last for

> (What) you should seek is God's kingdom. Then all the other things you need will be given to you.
> —LUKE 12:31

many years. Rest, eat, drink, and enjoy life!'

²⁰"But God said to that man, 'Foolish man! Tonight you will die. So who will get those things you have prepared for yourself?'

²¹"This is how it will be for anyone who stores things up only for himself and is not rich toward God."

DON'T WORRY

²²Jesus said to his followers, "So I tell you, don't worry about the food you need to live. Don't worry about the clothes you need for your body. ²³Life is more important than food. And the body is more important than clothes. ²⁴Look at the birds. They don't plant or harvest. They don't save food in houses or barns. But God takes care of them. And you are worth much more than birds. ²⁵None of you can add any time to your life by worrying about it. ²⁶If you cannot do even the little things, then why worry about the big things? ²⁷Look at the wild flowers. See how they grow. They don't work or make clothes for themselves. But I tell you that even Solomon, the great and rich king, was not dressed as beautifully as one of these flowers. ²⁸God clothes the grass in the field like that. That grass is living today, but tomorrow it will be thrown into the fire. So you know how much more God will clothe you. Don't have so little faith! ²⁹Don't always think about what you will eat or what you will drink. Don't worry about it. ³⁰All the people in the world are trying to get those things. Your Father knows that you need them. ³¹The thing you should seek is God's kingdom. Then all the other things you need will be given to you.

DON'T TRUST IN MONEY

³²"Don't fear, little flock. Your Father wants to give you the kingdom. ³³Sell the things you have and give to the poor. Get for yourselves purses that don't wear out. Get the treasure in heaven that never runs out. Thieves can't steal it in heaven, and moths can't destroy it. ³⁴Your heart will be where your treasure is.

ALWAYS BE READY

³⁵"Be ready! Be dressed for service and have your lamps shining. ³⁶Be like servants who are waiting for their master to come home from a wedding party. The master comes and knocks. The servants immediately open the door for him. ³⁷Those servants will be blessed when their master comes home, because he sees that his servants are ready and waiting for him. I tell you the truth. The master will dress himself to serve and tell the servants to sit at the table. Then the master will serve them. ³⁸Those servants might have to wait until midnight or later for their master. But they will be happy when he comes in and finds them still waiting.

³⁹"Remember this: If the owner of the house knew what time a thief was coming, then the owner would not allow the thief to enter his house. ⁴⁰So you also must be ready! The Son of Man will come at a time when you don't expect him!"

WHO IS THE TRUSTED SERVANT?

⁴¹Peter said, "Lord, did you tell this story for us or for all people?"

⁴²The Lord said, "Who is the wise and trusted servant? Who is the servant the master trusts to give the other servants their food at the right time? ⁴³When the master comes and finds his servant doing the work he gave him, that servant will be very happy. ⁴⁴I tell you the truth. The master will choose that servant to take care of everything the master owns. ⁴⁵But what will happen if the servant is evil and thinks that his master will not come back soon? That servant will begin to beat the other servants, men and women. He will eat and drink and get drunk. ⁴⁶Then the master will come when that servant is not ready. It will be a time when the servant is not expecting him.

Then the master will cut him in pieces and send him away to be with the others who don't obey.

[47]"The servant who knows what his master wants but is not ready or does not do what the master wants will be beaten with many blows! [48]But the servant who does not know what his master wants and does things that should be punished will be beaten with few blows. Everyone who has been given much will be responsible for much. Much more will be expected from the one who has been given more."

JESUS CAUSES DIVISION

[49]Jesus continued speaking, "I came to set fire to the world. I wish it were already burning! [50]I must be baptized with a different kind of baptism.[n] I feel very troubled until it is over. [51]Do you think that I came to give peace to the world? No! I came to divide the world! [52]From now on, a family with five people will be divided, three against two, and two against three. [53]A father and son will be divided: The son will be against his father. The father will be against his son. A mother and her daughter will be divided: The daughter will be against her mother. The mother will be against her daughter. A mother-in-law and her daughter-in-law will be divided: The daughter-in-law will be against her mother-in-law. The mother-in-law will be against her daughter-in-law."

UNDERSTANDING THE TIMES

[54]Then Jesus said to the people, "When you see clouds coming up in the west, you say, 'It's going to rain.' And soon it begins to rain. [55]When you feel the wind begin to blow from the south, you say, 'It will be a hot day.' And you are right. [56]Hypocrites! You can understand the weather. Why don't you understand what is happening now?

SETTLE YOUR PROBLEMS

[57]"Why can't you decide for yourselves what is right? [58]When someone is suing you, and you are going with him to court, try hard to settle it on the way. If you don't settle it, he may take you to the judge. The judge might turn you over to the officer. And the officer might throw you into jail. [59]You will not get out of there until they have taken everything you have."

CHANGE YOUR HEARTS

13 At that time some people were there with Jesus. They told him about what had happened to some people from Galilee. Pilate[n] killed those people while they were worshiping. He mixed their blood with the blood of the animals they were sacrificing to God. [2]Jesus answered, "Do you think this happened to them because they were more sinful than all others from Galilee? [3]No, they were not! But if all of you don't change your hearts and lives, then you will be destroyed as they were! [4]What about those 18 people who died when the tower of Siloam fell on them? Do you think they were more sinful than all the others who live in Jerusalem? [5]They were not! But I tell you, if you don't change your hearts and lives, then you will all be destroyed too!"

THE USELESS TREE

[6]Jesus told this story: "A man had a fig tree planted in his vineyard. He came looking for some fruit on the tree, but he found none. [7]So the man said to his servant who took care of his vineyard, 'I have been looking for fruit on this tree for three years, but I never find any. Cut it down! Why should it waste the ground?' [8]But the servant answered, 'Master, let the tree have one more year to produce fruit. Let me dig up the dirt around it and put on some fertilizer.

12:50 I...baptism. Jesus was talking about the suffering he would soon go through.
13:1 Pilate Pontius Pilate was the Roman governor of Judea from A.D. 26 to A.D. 36.

9Maybe the tree will produce fruit next year. If the tree still doesn't produce fruit, then you can cut it down.'"

JESUS HEALS ON THE SABBATH

10Jesus was teaching in one of the synagogues on the Sabbath day. 11In the synagogue there was a woman who had an evil spirit in her. This spirit had made the woman a cripple for 18 years. Her back was always bent; she could not stand up straight. 12When Jesus saw her, he called her over and said, "Woman, your sickness has left you!" 13Jesus put his hands on her. Immediately she was able to stand up straight and began praising God.

14The synagogue leader was angry because Jesus healed on the Sabbath day. He said to the people, "There are six days for work. So come to be healed on one of those days. Don't come for healing on the Sabbath day."

15The Lord answered, "You people are hypocrites! All of you untie your work animals and lead them to drink water every day—even on the Sabbath day! 16This woman that I healed is our Jewish sister. But Satan has held her for 18 years. Surely it is not wrong for her to be freed from her sickness on a Sabbath day!" 17When Jesus said this, all the men who were criticizing him were ashamed. And all the people were happy for the wonderful things Jesus was doing.

STORIES OF MUSTARD SEED AND YEAST

18Then Jesus said, "What is God's kingdom like? What can I compare it with? 19God's kingdom is like the seed of the mustard plant.[n] A man plants this seed in his garden. The seed grows and becomes a tree. The wild birds build nests on its branches."

20Jesus said again, "What can I compare God's kingdom with? 21It is like yeast that a woman mixes into a big bowl of flour. The yeast makes all the dough rise."

THE NARROW DOOR

22Jesus was teaching in every town and village. He continued to travel toward Jerusalem. 23Someone said to Jesus, "Lord, how many people will be saved? Only a few?"

Jesus said, 24"Try hard to enter through the narrow door that opens the way to heaven! Many people will try to enter there, but they will not be able. 25A man gets up and closes the door of his house. You can stand outside and knock on the door. You can say, 'Sir, open the door for us!' But he will answer, 'I don't know you! Where did you come from?' 26Then you will say, 'We ate and drank with you. You taught in the streets of our town.' 27But he will say to you, 'I don't know you! Where did you come from? Go away from me! All of you do evil!' 28You will see Abraham, Isaac, Jacob, and all the prophets in God's kingdom. But you will be thrown outside. Then you will cry and grind your teeth with pain. 29People will come from the east, west, north, and south. They will sit down at the table in the kingdom of God. 30Those who are last now will be first in the future. And those who are first now will be last in the future."

JESUS WILL DIE IN JERUSALEM

31At that time some Pharisees came to Jesus and said, "Go away from here! Herod wants to kill you!"

32Jesus said to them, "Go tell that fox Herod, 'Today and tomorrow I am forcing demons out of people and finishing my work of healing. Then, on the third day, I will reach my goal.' 33Yet I must be on my way today and tomorrow and the next day. Surely it cannot be right for a prophet to be killed anywhere except in Jerusalem.

34"Jerusalem, Jerusalem! You kill the

13:19 mustard plant The seed is very small, but the plant grows taller than a man.

prophets. You kill with stones those men that God has sent you. Many times I wanted to help your people. I wanted to gather them together as a hen gathers her chicks under her wings. But you did not let me. [35]Now your home will be left completely empty. I tell you, you will not see me again until that time when you will say, 'God bless the One who comes in the name of the Lord.'" [n]

IS IT RIGHT TO HEAL ON THE SABBATH?

14 On a Sabbath day, Jesus went to the home of a leading Pharisee to eat with him. The people there were all watching Jesus very closely. [2]A man with dropsy[n] was brought before Jesus. [3]Jesus said to the Pharisees and teachers of the law, "Is it right or wrong to heal on the Sabbath day?" [4]But they would not answer his question. So Jesus took the man, healed him, and sent him away. [5]Jesus said to the Pharisees and teachers of the law, "If your son[n] or ox falls into a well on the Sabbath day, will you not pull him out quickly?" [6]And they could not answer him.

DON'T MAKE YOURSELF IMPORTANT

[7]Then Jesus noticed that some of the guests were choosing the best places to sit. So Jesus told this story: [8]"When someone invites you to a wedding feast, don't take the most important seat. The host may have invited someone more important than you. [9]And if you are sitting in the most important seat, the host will come to you and say, 'Give this man your seat.' Then you will begin to move down to the last place. And you will be very embarrassed. [10]So when you are invited, go sit in a seat that is not important. Then the host will come to you and say, 'Friend, move up here to a more important place!' Then all the other guests

will respect you. [11]Everyone who makes himself great will be made humble. But the person who makes himself humble will be made great."

YOU WILL BE REWARDED

[12]Then Jesus said to the man who had invited him, "When you give a lunch or a dinner, don't invite only your friends, brothers, relatives, and rich neighbors. At another time they will invite you to eat with them. Then you will have your reward. [13]Instead, when you give a feast, invite the poor, the crippled, the lame and the blind. [14]Then you will be blessed, because they cannot pay you back. They have nothing. But you will be rewarded when the good people rise from death."

A STORY ABOUT A BIG BANQUET

[15]One of the men sitting at the table with Jesus heard these things. The man said to Jesus, "The people who will eat a meal in God's kingdom are blessed."

[16]Jesus said to him, "A man gave a big banquet and invited many people. [17]When it was time to eat, the man sent his servant to tell the guests, 'Come! Everything is ready!'

[18]"But all the guests said they could not come. Each man made an excuse. The first one said, 'I have just bought a field, and I must go look at it. Please excuse me.' [19]Another man said, 'I have just bought five pairs of oxen; I must go and try them. Please excuse me.' [20]A third man said, 'I just got married; I can't come.' [21]So the servant returned. He told his master what had happened. Then the master became angry and said, 'Go at once into the streets and alleys of the town. Bring in the poor, the crippled, the blind, and the lame.' [22]Later the servant said to him, 'Master, I did what you told me to do, but we still have places for more people.' [23]The

---

13:35 'God . . . Lord.' Quotation from Psalm 118:26.
14:2 dropsy A sickness that causes the body to swell larger and larger.
14:5 son Some Greek copies read "donkey."

master said to the servant, 'Go out to the roads and country lanes. Tell the people there to come. I want my house to be full! ²⁴None of those men that I invited first will ever eat with me!'"

YOU MUST FIRST PLAN

²⁵Large crowds were traveling with Jesus. He turned and said to them, ²⁶"If anyone comes to me but loves his father, mother, wife, children, brothers, or sisters more than he loves me, then he cannot be my follower. A person must love me more than he loves himself! ²⁷If anyone is not willing to die on a cross when he follows me, then he cannot be my follower. ²⁸If you wanted to build a tower, you would first sit down and decide how much it would cost. You must see if you have enough money to finish the job. ²⁹If you don't do that, you might begin the work, but you would not be able to finish. And if you could not finish it, then all who would see it would laugh at you. ³⁰They would say, 'This man began to build but was not able to finish!'

³¹"If a king is going to fight against another king, first he will sit down and plan. If the king has only 10,000 men, he will plan to see if he is able to defeat the other king who has 20,000 men. ³²If he cannot defeat the other king, then he will send some men to speak to the other king and ask for peace. ³³In the same way, you must give up everything you have to follow me. If you don't, you cannot be my follower!

DON'T LOSE YOUR INFLUENCE

³⁴"Salt is a good thing. But if the salt loses its salty taste, then it is worth nothing. You cannot make it salty again. ³⁵It is no good for the soil or for manure. People throw it away.

"Let those with ears use them and listen!"

A LOST SHEEP AND A LOST COIN

15 Many tax collectors and "sinners" came to listen to Jesus. ²The Pharisees and the teachers of the law began to complain: "Look! This man welcomes sinners and even eats with them!"

³Then Jesus told them this story: ⁴"Suppose one of you has 100 sheep, but he loses 1 of them. Then he will leave the other 99 sheep alone and go out and look for the lost sheep. The man will keep on searching for the lost sheep until he finds it. ⁵And when he finds it, the man is very happy. He puts it on his shoulders ⁶and goes home. He calls to his friends and neighbors and says, 'Be happy with me because I found my lost sheep!' ⁷In the same way, I tell you there is much joy in heaven when 1 sinner changes his heart. There is more joy for that 1 sinner than there is for 99 good people who don't need to change.

⁸"Suppose a woman has ten silver coins,ⁿ but she loses one of them. She will light a lamp and clean the house. She will look carefully for the coin until she finds it. ⁹And when she finds it, she will call her friends and neighbors and say, 'Be happy with me because I have found the coin that I lost!' ¹⁰In the same way, there is joy before the angels of God when 1 sinner changes his heart."

THE SON WHO LEFT HOME

¹¹Then Jesus said, "A man had two sons. ¹²The younger son said to his father,

> I tell you there is much joy in heaven when 1 sinner changes his heart.
> –LUKE 15:7

15:8 **silver coins** A Roman denarius. One coin was the average pay for one day's work.

'Give me my share of the property.' So the father divided the property between his two sons. ¹³Then the younger son gathered up all that was his and left. He traveled far away to another country. There he wasted his money in foolish living. ¹⁴He spent everything that he had. Soon after that, the land became very dry, and there was no rain. There was not enough food to eat anywhere in the country. The son was hungry and needed money. ¹⁵So he got a job with one of the citizens there. The man sent the son into the fields to feed pigs. ¹⁶The son was so hungry that he was willing to eat the food the pigs were eating. But no one gave him anything. ¹⁷The son realized that he had been very foolish. He thought, 'All of my father's servants have plenty of food. But I am here, almost dying with hunger. ¹⁸I will leave and return to my father. I'll say to him: Father, I have sinned against God and against you. ¹⁹I am not good enough to be called your son. But let me be like one of your servants.' ²⁰So the son left and went to his father.

"While the son was still a long way off, his father saw him coming. He felt sorry for his son. So the father ran to him, and hugged and kissed him. ²¹The son said, 'Father, I have sinned against God and against you. I am not good enough to be called your son.'ⁿ ²²But the father said to his servants, 'Hurry! Bring the best clothes and put them on him. Also, put a ring on his finger and sandals on his feet. ²³And get our fat calf and kill it. Then we can have a feast and celebrate! ²⁴My son was dead, but now he is alive again! He was lost, but now he is found!' So they began to celebrate.

²⁵"The older son was in the field. As he came closer to the house, he heard the sound of music and dancing. ²⁶So he called to one of the servants and asked, 'What does all this mean?' ²⁷The servant said, 'Your brother has come

back. Your father killed the fat calf to eat because your brother came home safely!' ²⁸The older son was angry and would not go in to the feast. So his father went out and begged him to come in. ²⁹The son said to his father, 'I have served you like a slave for many years! I have always obeyed your commands. But you never even killed a young goat for me to have a feast with my friends. ³⁰But your other son has wasted all your money on prostitutes. Then he comes home, and you kill the fat calf for him!' ³¹The father said to him, 'Son, you are always with me. All that I have is yours. ³²We had to celebrate and be happy because your brother was dead, but now he is alive. He was lost, but now he is found.'"

TRUE WEALTH

16 Jesus also said to his followers, "Once there was a rich man. He had a manager to take care of his business. Later, the rich man learned that his manager was cheating him. ²So he called the manager in and said to him, 'I have heard bad things about you. Give me a report of what you have done with my money. You can't be my manager any longer!' ³Later, the manager thought to himself, 'What will I do? My master is taking my job away from me! I am not strong enough to dig ditches. I am too proud to beg. ⁴I know! I'll do something so that when I lose my job, people will welcome me into their homes.'

⁵"So the manager called in everyone who owed the master any money. He said to the first man, 'How much do you owe my master?' ⁶The man answered, 'I owe him 800 gallons of olive oil.' The manager said to him, 'Here is your bill; sit down quickly and make the bill less. Write 400 gallons.' ⁷Then the manager said to another man, 'How much do you owe my master?' The man answered, 'I owe him 1,000 bushels of wheat.' Then

---

15:21 son Some Greek copies continue, "But let me be like one of your servants" (see verse 19).

the manager said to him, 'Here is your bill; you can make it less. Write 800 bushels.' [8]Later, the master praised the dishonest manager for being smart. Yes, worldly people are smarter with their own kind than spiritual people are.

[9]"I tell you, make friends for yourselves using worldly riches. Then, when those things are gone, you will be welcomed in that home that continues forever. [10]Whoever can be trusted with small things can also be trusted with large things. Whoever is dishonest in little things will be dishonest in large things too. [11]If you cannot be trusted with worldly riches, then you will not be trusted with the true riches. [12]And if you cannot be trusted with the things that belong to someone else, then you will not be given things of your own.

[13]"No servant can serve two masters. He will hate one master and love the other. Or he will follow one master and refuse to follow the other. You cannot serve both God and money."

GOD'S LAW CANNOT BE CHANGED

[14]The Pharisees were listening to all these things. They made fun of Jesus because they all loved money. [15]Jesus said to them, "You make yourselves look good in front of people. But God knows what is really in your hearts. The things that are important to people are worth nothing to God.

[16]"God wanted the people to live by the law of Moses and the writings of the prophets. But ever since John[n] came, the Good News about the kingdom of God is being told. Now everyone is trying hard to get into the kingdom. [17]Even the smallest part of a letter in the law cannot be changed. It would be easier for heaven and earth to pass away.

DIVORCE AND REMARRIAGE

[18]"If a man divorces his wife and marries another woman, he is guilty of adultery. And the man who marries a divorced woman is also guilty of adultery."

THE RICH MAN AND LAZARUS

[19]Jesus said, "There was a rich man who always dressed in the finest clothes. He lived in luxury every day. [20]There was also a very poor man named Lazarus, whose body was covered with sores. Lazarus was often placed at the rich man's gate. [21]He wanted to eat only the small pieces of food that fell from the rich man's table. And the dogs would come and lick his sores! [22]Later, Lazarus died. The angels took Lazarus and placed him in the arms of Abraham. The rich man died, too, and was buried. [23]But he was sent to where the dead are and had much pain. The rich man saw Abraham far away with Lazarus in his arms. [24]He called, 'Father Abraham, have mercy on me! Send Lazarus to me so that he can dip his finger in water and cool my tongue. I am suffering in this fire!' [25]But Abraham said, 'My child, remember when you lived? You had all the good things in life, but all the bad things happened to Lazarus. Now Lazarus is comforted here, and you are suffering. [26]Also, there is a big pit between you and us. No one can cross over to help you. And no one can leave there and come here.' [27]The rich man said, 'Then please send Lazarus to my father's house on earth! [28]I have five brothers. Lazarus could warn my brothers so that they will not come to this place of pain.' [29]But Abraham said, 'They have the law of Moses and the writings of the prophets to read; let them learn from them!' [30]The rich man said, 'No, father Abraham! If someone came to them from the dead, they would believe and change their hearts and lives.' [31]But Abraham said to him, 'No! If your brothers won't listen to Moses and the prophets, then they won't listen to someone who comes back from death.'"

16:16 **John** John the Baptist, who preached to people about Christ's coming (Matthew 3; Luke 3).

SIN AND FORGIVENESS

17 Jesus said to his followers, "Things will surely happen that cause people to sin. But how terrible for the one who causes them to happen. [2]It would be better for him to be thrown into the sea with a large stone around his neck than to cause one of these weak people to sin. [3]So be careful!

"If your brother sins, tell him he is wrong. But if he is sorry and stops sinning, forgive him. [4]If your brother sins against you seven times in one day, but he says that he is sorry each time, then forgive him."

HOW BIG IS YOUR FAITH?

[5]The apostles said to the Lord, "Give us more faith!"

[6]The Lord said, "If your faith is as big as a mustard seed,[n] then you can say to this mulberry tree, 'Dig yourself up and plant yourself in the sea!' And the tree will obey you.

BE GOOD SERVANTS

[7]"Suppose one of you has a servant who has been plowing the ground or caring for the sheep. When the servant comes in from working in the field, would you say, 'Come in and sit down to eat'? [8]No, you would say to your servant, 'Prepare something for me to eat. Then get yourself ready and serve me. When I finish eating and drinking, then you can eat and drink.' [9]The servant does not get any special thanks for doing what his master told him to do. [10]It is the same with you. When you do everything you are told to do, you should say, 'We don't deserve any special thanks. We have only done the work we should do.'"

BE THANKFUL

[11]Jesus was on his way to Jerusalem. Traveling from Galilee to Samaria, [12]he came into a small town. Ten men met him there. These men did not come close to Jesus, because they all had a harmful skin disease. [13]But they called to him, "Jesus! Master! Please help us!"

[14]When Jesus saw the men, he said, "Go and show yourselves to the priests."[n]

While the ten men were going, they were healed. [15]When one of them saw that he was healed, he went back to Jesus. He praised God in a loud voice. [16]Then he bowed down at Jesus' feet and thanked him. (This man was a Samaritan.) [17]Jesus asked, "Ten men were healed; where are the other nine? [18]Is this Samaritan the only one who came back to thank God?" [19]Then Jesus said to him, "Stand up and go on your way. You were healed because you believed."

> Then Jesus said to him, "Stand up and go on your way. You were healed because you believed."
>
> —LUKE 17:19

GOD'S KINGDOM IS WITHIN YOU

[20]Some of the Pharisees asked Jesus, "When will the kingdom of God come?"

Jesus answered, "God's kingdom is coming, but not in a way that you will be able to see with your eyes. [21]People will not say, 'Look, God's kingdom is here!' or, 'There it is!' No, God's kingdom is within you."

[22]Then Jesus said to his followers, "The time will come when you will want very much to see one of the days of the Son of Man. But you will not be able to see it. [23]People will say to you, 'Look, there he is!' or, 'Look, here he is!'

17:6 **mustard seed** This seed is very small, but the plant grows taller than a man.
17:14 **show . . . priests** The law of Moses said a priest must say when a Jew with a harmful skin disease became well.

Stay where you are; don't go away and search.

WHEN JESUS COMES AGAIN

24"The Son of Man will come again. On the day he comes he will shine like lightning, which flashes across the sky and lights it up from one side to the other. 25But first, the Son of Man must suffer many things and be rejected by the people of this time. 26When the Son of Man comes again, it will be as it was when Noah lived. 27In the time of Noah, people were eating, drinking, and getting married even on the day when Noah entered the boat. Then the flood came and killed all the people. 28It will be the same as during the time of Lot. Those people were eating, drinking, buying, selling, planting, and building. 29They were doing these things even on the day Lot left Sodom.n Then fire and sulfur rained down from the sky and killed them all. 30This is exactly how it will be when the Son of Man comes again.

31"On that day, if a man is on his roof, he will not have time to go inside and get his things. If a man is in the field, he cannot go back home. 32Remember what happened to Lot's wife?n 33Whoever tries to keep his life will give up true life. But whoever gives up his life will have true life. 34At the time when I come again, there may be two people sleeping in one bed. One will be taken and the other will be left. 35There may be two women grinding grain together. One will be taken and the other will be left. 36[Two men will be in the same field. One man will be taken, but the other man will be left behind.]"n

37The followers asked Jesus, "Where will this be, Lord?"

Jesus answered, "People can always find a dead body by looking for the vultures."

GOD WILL ANSWER HIS PEOPLE

18 Then Jesus used this story to teach his followers that they should always pray and never lose hope. 2"Once there was a judge in a town. He did not care about God. He also did not care what people thought about him. 3In that same town there was a widow who kept coming to this judge. She said, 'There is a man who is not being fair to me. Give me my rights!' 4But the judge did not want to help the widow. After a long time, he thought to himself, 'I don't care about God. And I don't care about what people think. 5But this widow is bothering me. I will see that she gets her rights, or she will bother me until I am worn out!'"

6The Lord said, "Listen to what the bad judge said. 7God's people cry to him night and day. God will always give them what is right, and he will not be slow to answer them. 8I tell you, God will help his people quickly! But when the Son of Man comes again, will he find those on earth who believe in him?"

BEING RIGHT WITH GOD

9There were some people who thought that they were very good and looked down on everyone else. Jesus used this story to teach them: 10"One day there was a Pharisee and a tax collector. Both went to the Temple to pray. 11The Pharisee stood alone, away from the tax collector. When the Pharisee prayed, he said, 'God, I thank you that I am not as bad as other people. I am not like men who steal, cheat, or take part in adultery. I thank you that I am better than this tax collector. 12I give up eatingn twice a week, and I give one-tenth of everything I earn!'

13"The tax collector stood at a distance. When he prayed, he would

---

17:29 **Sodom** City that God destroyed because the people were so evil.
17:32 **Lot's wife** A story about what happened to Lot's wife is found in Genesis 19:15–17, 26.
17:36 **Two . . . behind.** Some Greek copies do not have verse 36.
18:12 **give up eating** This is called "fasting." The people would give up eating for a special time of prayer and worship to God. It was also done to show sadness.

not even look up to heaven. He beat on his chest because he was so sad. He said, 'God, have mercy on me. I am a sinner!' [14]I tell you, when this man went home, he was right with God. But the Pharisee was not right with God. Everyone who makes himself great will be made humble. But everyone who makes himself humble will be made great."

WHO WILL ENTER GOD'S KINGDOM

[15]Some people brought their small children to Jesus so that he could touch them. When the followers saw this, they told the people not to do this. [16]But Jesus called the little children to him and said to his followers, "Let the little children come to me. Don't stop them, because the kingdom of God belongs to people who are like these little children. [17]I tell you the truth. You must accept God's kingdom like a little child, or you will never enter it!"

A RICH MAN'S QUESTION

[18]A Jewish leader asked Jesus, "Good Teacher, what must I do to get the life that continues forever?"

[19]Jesus said to him, "Why do you call me good? Only God is good. [20]You know the commands: 'You must not be guilty of adultery. You must not murder anyone. You must not steal. You must not tell lies about your neighbor in court. Honor your father and mother.'" [n]

[21]But the leader said, "I have obeyed all these commands since I was a boy!"

[22]When Jesus heard this, he said to him, "But there is still one more thing you need to do. Sell everything you have and give the money to the poor. You will have a reward in heaven. Then come and follow me!" [23]But when the man heard this, he became very sad because he was very rich.

[24]When Jesus saw that the man was sad, he said, "It will be very hard for rich people to enter the kingdom of God! [25]It would be easier for a camel to go through the eye of a needle than for a rich person to enter the kingdom of God!"

WHO CAN BE SAVED?

[26]When the people heard this, they asked, "Then who can be saved?"

[27]Jesus answered, "The things impossible for men are possible for God."

[28]Peter said, "Look, we left everything we had and followed you!"

[29]Jesus said, "I tell you the truth. Everyone who has left his house, wife, brothers, parents, or children for God's kingdom [30]will get much more than he left. He will receive many times more in this life. And after he dies, he will live with God forever."

JESUS WILL RISE FROM DEATH

[31]Then Jesus talked to the 12 apostles alone. He said to them, "Listen! We are going to Jerusalem. Everything that God told the prophets to write about the Son of Man will happen! [32]He will be turned over to the non-Jewish people. They will laugh at him, insult him, and spit on him. [33]They will beat him with whips and then kill him. But on the third day after his death, he will rise to life again." [34]The apostles tried to understand this, but they could not; the meaning was hidden from them.

JESUS HEALS A BLIND MAN

[35]Jesus was coming near the city of Jericho. There was a blind man sitting beside the road, begging for money. [36]When he heard the people coming down the road, he asked, "What is happening?"

[37]They told him, "Jesus, the one from Nazareth, is coming here."

[38]The blind man cried out, "Jesus, Son of David! Please help me!"

[39]The people who were in front, leading the group, told the blind man

---

18:20 'You . . . mother.' Quotation from Exodus 20:12–16; Deuteronomy 5:16–20.

☆ Luke 19:4–6

Zacchaeus was a very rich man because he was a tax collector. Many tax collectors took more money from people than they were supposed to. For that reason, many of them were not liked. And some were even hated. Zacchaeus probably did not have many true friends because of his job. But he wanted to see Jesus so much that even the huge crowds couldn't keep him away.

Zacchaeus was so excited! Jesus was coming to town! He joined a large crowd of people and waited to see Jesus. Because he was not very tall, Zacchaeus decided to climb a tree so he could see Jesus for himself. When Jesus saw Zacchaeus, he told him to come down from the tree and take him to his house. Jesus wanted to spend time with Zacchaeus and get to know him. He wanted to be Zacchaeus's friend.

• •

Just like Jesus wanted to know Zacchaeus, he wants to know you. You can tell him anything—and you don't have to climb a tree for him to see you!

to be quiet. But the blind man shouted more and more, "Son of David, please help me!"

⁴⁰Jesus stopped and said, "Bring the blind man to me!" When he came near, Jesus asked him, ⁴¹"What do you want me to do for you?"

He said, "Lord, I want to see again."

⁴²Jesus said to him, "Then see! You are healed because you believed."

⁴³At once the man was able to see, and he followed Jesus, thanking God. All the people who saw this praised God.

ZACCHAEUS

19 Jesus was going through the city of Jericho. ²In Jericho there was a man named Zacchaeus. He was a wealthy, very important tax collector. ³He wanted to see who Jesus was, but he was too short to see above the crowd. ⁴He ran ahead to a place where he knew Jesus would come. He climbed a syca- more tree so he could see Jesus. ⁵When Jesus came to that place, he looked up and saw Zacchaeus in the tree. He said to him, "Zacchaeus, hurry and come down! I must stay at your house today."

⁶Zacchaeus came down quickly. He was pleased to have Jesus in his house. ⁷All the people saw this and began to complain, "Look at the kind of man Jesus stays with. Zacchaeus is a sinner!"

⁸But Zacchaeus said to the Lord, "I

will give half of my money to the poor. If I have cheated anyone, I will pay that person back four times more!"

⁹Jesus said, "Salvation has come to this house today. This man truly belongs to the family of Abraham. ¹⁰The Son of Man came to find lost people and save them."

A STORY ABOUT THREE SERVANTS

¹¹Jesus traveled closer to Jerusalem. Some of the people thought that God's kingdom would appear soon. ¹²Jesus knew that the people thought this, so he told them this story: "A very important man was preparing to go to a country far away to be made a king. Then he planned to return home and rule his people. ¹³So the man called ten of his servants together. He gave a bag of money[n] to each servant. He said, 'Do business with this money till I get back.' ¹⁴But the people in the kingdom hated the man. So they sent a group to follow him and say, 'We don't want this man to be our king!'

¹⁵"But the man became king. When he came home, he said, 'Call those servants who have my money. I want to know how much they earned with it.'

¹⁶"The first servant came and said, 'Sir, I earned ten bags of money with the one bag you gave me!' ¹⁷The king said to the servant, 'Fine! You are a good servant. I see that I can trust you with small things. So now I will let you rule over ten of my cities.'

¹⁸"The second servant said, 'Sir, with your one bag of money I earned five bags!' ¹⁹The king said to this servant, 'You can rule over five cities.'

²⁰"Then another servant came in. The servant said to the king, 'Sir, here is your bag of money. I wrapped it in a piece of cloth and hid it. ²¹I was afraid of you because you are a hard man. You even take money that you didn't earn

and gather food that you didn't plant.' ²²Then the king said to the servant, 'You evil servant! I will use your own words to condemn you. You said that I am a hard man. You said that I even take money that I didn't earn and gather food that I didn't plant. ²³If that is true, then you should have put my money in the bank. Then, when I came back, my money would have earned some interest.'

²⁴"Then the king said to the men who were watching, 'Take the bag of money away from this servant and give it to the servant who earned ten bags of money.' ²⁵They said to the king, 'But sir, that servant already has ten bags of money!' ²⁶The king said, 'The one who uses what he has will get more. But the one who does not use what he has will have everything taken away from him. ²⁷Now where are my enemies who didn't want me to be king? Bring them here and kill them before me.'"

JESUS ENTERS JERUSALEM AS A KING

²⁸After Jesus said this, he went on toward Jerusalem. ²⁹Jesus came near Bethphage and Bethany, towns near the hill called the Mount of Olives. Then he sent out two of his followers. ³⁰He said, "Go into the town you can see there. When you enter it, you will find a colt tied there. No one has ever ridden this colt. Untie it, and bring it here to me. ³¹If anyone asks you why you are taking it, say, 'The Master needs it.'"

³²The two followers went into town. They found the colt just as Jesus told them. ³³The followers untied it, but the owners of the colt came out. They asked the followers, "Why are you untying our colt?"

³⁴The followers answered, "The Master needs it." ³⁵So they brought it to Jesus. They threw their coats on the colt's back and put Jesus on it. ³⁶As Jesus rode toward Jerusalem, the followers

---

19:13 bag of money One bag of money was a Greek "mina." One mina was enough money to pay a person for working three months.

spread their coats on the road before him.

[37]Jesus was coming close to Jerusalem. He was already near the bottom of the Mount of Olives. The whole crowd of followers was very happy. They began shouting praise to God for all the powerful works they had seen. They said,

[38] "God bless the king who comes in the name of the Lord!
    There is peace in heaven and glory to God!"   *Psalm 118:26*

[39]Some of the Pharisees said to Jesus, "Teacher, tell your followers not to say these things!"

[40]But Jesus answered, "I tell you, if my followers don't say these things, then the stones will cry out."

JESUS CRIES FOR JERUSALEM

[41]Jesus came near Jerusalem. He saw the city and began to cry for it. [42]Jesus said to Jerusalem, "I wish you knew today what would bring you peace! But you can't know it, because it is hidden from you. [43]A time is coming when your enemies will build a wall around you and will hold you in on all sides. [44]They will destroy you and all your people. Not one stone of your buildings will be left on another. All this will happen because you did not know the time when God came to save you."

JESUS GOES TO THE TEMPLE

[45]Jesus went into the Temple. He began to throw out the people who were selling things there. [46]He said, "It is written in the Scriptures, 'My Temple will be a house where people will pray.' [n] But you have changed it into a 'hideout for robbers'!" [n]

[47]Jesus taught in the Temple every day. The leading priests, the teachers of the law, and some of the leaders of the people wanted to kill Jesus. [48]But all the people were listening closely to him and were interested in all the things he said. So the leading priests, the teachers of the law, and the leaders did not know how they could kill him.

THE LEADERS QUESTION JESUS

20 One day Jesus was in the Temple, teaching the people and telling them the Good News. The leading priests, teachers of the law, and Jewish elders came up to talk with him. [2]They said, "Tell us! What authority do you have to do these things? Who gave you this authority?"

[3]Jesus answered, "I will ask you a question too. Tell me: [4]When John baptized people, did that come from God or from man?"

[5]The priests, the teachers of the law, and the Jewish leaders all talked about this. They said to each other, "If we answer, 'John's baptism was from God,' then Jesus will say, 'Then why did you not believe John?' [6]But if we say, 'John's baptism was from man,' then all the people will kill us with stones because they believe that John was a prophet." [7]So they answered, "We don't know the answer."

[8]So Jesus said to them, "Then I will not tell you by what authority I do these things!"

GOD SENDS HIS SON

[9]Then Jesus told the people this story: "A man planted a vineyard. The man leased the land to some farmers. Then he went away for a long time. [10]Later, it was time for the grapes to be picked. So the man sent a servant to those farmers to get his share of the grapes. But they beat the servant and sent him away with nothing. [11]Then he sent another servant. They beat this servant too. They showed no respect for him and sent him away with nothing. [12]So the man sent a third servant. The farmers hurt this servant badly and threw him out. [13]The owner of

---

19:46 'My Temple . . . pray.' Quotation from Isaiah 56:7.
19:46 'hideout for robbers' Quotation from Jeremiah 7:11.

the vineyard said, 'What will I do now? I will send my son whom I love very much. Maybe they will respect him!' [14]When they saw the son, they said to each other, 'This is the owner's son. This vineyard will be his. If we kill him, then it will be ours!' [15]So the farmers threw the son out of the vineyard and killed him.

"What will the owner of this vineyard do? [16]He will come and kill those farmers! Then he will give the vineyard to other farmers."

The people heard this story. They said, "No! Let this never happen!"

[17]But Jesus looked at them and said, "Then what does this verse mean:

'The stone that the builders did not
     want
   became the cornerstone'?
                         Psalm 118:22

[18]Everyone who falls on that stone will be broken. If that stone falls on you, it will crush you!"

[19]The teachers of the law and the priests heard this story that Jesus told. They knew the story was about them. So they wanted to arrest Jesus at once. But they were afraid of what the people would do.

THE LEADERS TRY TO TRAP JESUS

[20]So they waited for the right time to get Jesus. They sent some spies who acted as if they were good men. They wanted to trap Jesus in what he said so they could hand him over to the authority and power of the governor. [21]So the spies asked Jesus, "Teacher, we know that what you say and teach is true. You teach the same to all people. You always teach the truth about God's way. [22]Tell us, is it right that we pay taxes to Caesar or not?"

[23]But Jesus knew that these men were trying to trick him. He said, [24]"Show me a coin. Whose name is on the coin? And whose picture is on it?"

They said, "Caesar's."

[25]Jesus said to them, "Then give to Caesar the things that are Caesar's. And give to God the things that are God's."

[26]The men were amazed at his answer. They could say nothing. They were not able to trap Jesus in anything he said before the people.

SADDUCEES TRY TO TRICK JESUS

[27]Some Sadducees came to Jesus. (Sadducees believe that people will not rise from death.) They asked, [28]"Teacher, Moses wrote that a man's brother might die. He leaves a wife but no children. Then that man must marry the widow and have children for his dead brother. [29]One time there were seven brothers. The first brother married, but died. He had no children. [30]Then the second brother married the widow, and he died. [31]And the third brother married the widow, and he died. The same thing happened with all the other brothers. They all died and had no children. [32]The woman was the last to die. [33]But all seven brothers married her. So when people rise from death, whose wife will the woman be?"

[34]Jesus said to the Sadducees, "On earth, people marry each other. [35]But those who will be worthy to be raised from death and live again will not marry. [36]In that life they are like angels and cannot die. They are children of God, because they have been raised from death. [37]Moses clearly showed that the dead are raised to life. When Moses wrote about the burning bush,[n] he said that the Lord is 'the God of Abraham, the God of Isaac, and the God of Jacob.'[n] [38]God is the God of living people, not dead people. All people are alive to God."

[39]Some of the teachers of the law said, "Teacher, your answer was good."

20:37 **burning bush** Read Exodus 3:1–12 in the Old Testament.
20:37 **'the God of . . . Jacob'** These words are taken from Exodus 3:6.

[40] No one was brave enough to ask him another question.

IS THE CHRIST THE SON OF DAVID?

[41] Then Jesus said, "Why do people say that the Christ is the Son of David? [42] In the book of Psalms, David himself says:

'The Lord said to my Lord:
  Sit by me at my right side,
[43]   until I put your enemies under
    your control.' [n]   *Psalm 110:1*

[44] David calls the Christ 'Lord.' But the Christ is also the son of David. How can both these things be true?"

JESUS ACCUSES THE LEADERS

[45] While all the people were listening, Jesus said to his followers, [46] "Be careful of the teachers of the law. They like to walk around wearing clothes that look important. And they love for people to show respect to them in the marketplaces. They love to have the most important seats in the synagogues and at the feasts. [47] But they cheat widows and steal their houses. Then they try to make themselves look good by saying long prayers. God will punish these men very much."

TRUE GIVING

21 Jesus saw some rich people putting their gifts into the Temple money box. [n] [2] Then Jesus saw a poor widow. She put two small copper coins into the box. [3] He said, "I tell you the truth. This poor widow gave only two small coins. But she really gave more than all those rich people. [4] The rich have plenty; they gave only what they did not need. This woman is very poor, but she gave all she had. And she needed that money to live on."

THE TEMPLE WILL BE DESTROYED

[5] Some of the followers were talking about the Temple and how it was decorated with beautiful stones and gifts offered to God. [6] But Jesus said, "The time will come when all that you see here will be destroyed. Every stone will be thrown down to the ground. Not one stone will be left on another!"

[7] Some followers asked Jesus, "Teacher, when will these things happen? What will show us that it is time for them to take place?"

[8] Jesus said, "Be careful! Don't be fooled. Many people will come using my name. They will say, 'I am the Christ' and, 'The right time has come!' But don't follow them. [9] When you hear about wars and riots, don't be afraid. These things must happen first. Then the end will come later."

[10] Then he said to them, "Nations will fight against other nations. Kingdoms will fight against other kingdoms. [11] There will be great earthquakes, sicknesses, and other terrible things in many places. In some places there will be no food for the people to eat. Fearful events and great signs will come from heaven.

[12] "But before all these things happen, people will arrest you and treat you cruelly. They will judge you in their

> God is the God of living people, not dead people. All people are alive to God.
> —LUKE 20:38

20:43 **until . . . control** Literally, "until I make your enemies a footstool for your feet."
21:1 **money box** A special box in the Jewish place for worship where people put their gifts to God.

synagogues and put you in jail. You will be forced to stand before kings and governors. They will do all these things to you because you follow me. [13]But this will give you an opportunity to tell about me. [14]Don't worry about what you will say. [15]I will give you the wisdom to say things so that none of your enemies will be able to show that you are wrong. [16]Even your parents, brothers, relatives and friends will turn against you. They will kill some of you. [17]All people will hate you because you follow me. [18]But none of these things can really harm you. [19]You will save yourselves by continuing strong in your faith through all these things.

JERUSALEM WILL BE DESTROYED

[20]"When you see armies all around Jerusalem, then you will know that it will soon be destroyed. [21]At that time, the people in Judea should run away to the mountains. The people in Jerusalem must get out. If you are near the city, don't go in! [22]These are the days of punishment to make come true all that is written in the Scriptures. [23]At that time, it will be hard for women who are pregnant or have nursing babies! Great trouble will come upon this land, and God will be angry with these people. [24]Some will be killed by the sword and taken as prisoners to all nations. Jerusalem will be crushed by non-Jewish people until their time is over.

DON'T FEAR

[25]"Amazing things will happen to the sun, moon, and stars. On earth, nations will be afraid because of the roar and fury of the sea. They will not know what to do. [26]People will be so afraid they will faint. They will wonder what is happening to the whole world. Everything in the sky will be changed. [27]Then people will see the Son of Man coming in a cloud with power and great glory. [28]When these things begin to happen, don't fear. Look up and hold your heads high because the time when God will free you is near!"

MY WORDS WILL LIVE FOREVER

[29]Then Jesus told this story: "Look at the fig tree and all the other trees. [30]When their leaves appear, you know that summer is near. [31]In the same way, when you see all these things happening, then you will know that God's kingdom is coming very soon.

[32]"I tell you the truth. All these things will happen while the people of this time are still living! [33]The whole world, earth and sky, will be destroyed; but the words I have said will never be destroyed!

BE READY ALL THE TIME

[34]"Be careful! Don't spend your time feasting and drinking. Or don't be too busy with worldly things. If you do that, you will not be able to think straight. And then that day might come when you are not ready. [35]It will close like a trap on all people on earth. [36]So be ready all the time. Pray that you will be strong enough to escape all these things that will happen. And pray that you will be able to stand before the Son of Man."

[37]During the day, Jesus taught the people in the Temple. At night he went out of the city and stayed on the Mount of Olives. [38]Every morning all the people got up early to go to the Temple to listen to him.

PLANS TO KILL JESUS

22 It was almost time for the Jewish Feast of Unleavened Bread, called the Passover Feast. [2]The leading priests and teachers of the law were trying to find a way to kill Jesus. But they were afraid of the people.

[3]One of Jesus' 12 apostles was named Judas Iscariot. Satan entered Judas, and he went to [4]the leading priests and some of the soldiers who guarded the Temple. He talked to them about a way to give Jesus to them. [5]They were pleased and promised to give Judas money. [6]Judas agreed. Then he waited

for the best time to turn Jesus over to them without the crowd knowing it.

PREPARATION OF THE PASSOVER MEAL

[7] The Day of Unleavened Bread came. This was the day the Passover lambs had to be sacrificed. [8] Jesus said to Peter and John, "Go and prepare the Passover meal for us to eat."

[9] They asked, "Where do you want us to prepare it?"

Jesus said to them, [10] "Listen! After you go into the city, you will see a man carrying a jar of water. Follow him into the house that he enters. [11] Tell the person who owns that house, 'The Teacher asks that you please show us the room where he and his followers may eat the Passover meal.' [12] Then he will show you a large room upstairs. This room is ready for you. Prepare the Passover meal there."

[13] So Peter and John left. Everything happened as Jesus had said. So they prepared the Passover meal.

THE LORD'S SUPPER

[14] When the time came, Jesus and the apostles were sitting at the table. [15] He said to them, "I wanted very much to eat this Passover meal with you before I die. [16] I will never eat another Passover meal until it is given its true meaning in the kingdom of God."

[17] Then Jesus took a cup. He gave thanks to God for it and said, "Take this cup and give it to everyone here. [18] I will not drink again from the fruit of the vine[n] until God's kingdom comes."

[19] Then Jesus took some bread. He thanked God for it, broke it, and gave it to the apostles. Then Jesus said, "This bread is my body[n] that I am giving for you. Do this to remember me." [20] In the same way, after supper, Jesus took the cup and said, "This cup shows the new agreement that God makes with his people. This new agreement begins with my blood which is poured out for you."

WHO WILL TURN AGAINST JESUS?

[21] Jesus said, "One of you will turn against me. His hand is by my hand on the table. [22] The Son of Man will do what God has planned. But how terrible it will be for that man who gives the Son of Man to be killed."

[23] Then the apostles asked each other, "Which one of us would do that to Jesus?"

BE LIKE A SERVANT

[24] Then the apostles began to argue about which one of them was the most important. [25] But Jesus said to them, "The kings of the world rule over their people. Men who have authority over others are called 'very important.' [26] But you must not be like that. The greatest among you should be like the youngest, and the leader should be like the servant. [27] Who is more important: the one sitting at the table or the one serving him? You think the one at the table is more important. But I am like a servant among you!

[28] "You men have stayed with me through many struggles. [29] My Father has given me the power to rule. I also give you authority to rule with me. [30] You will eat and drink at my table in my kingdom. You will sit on thrones and judge the 12 tribes of Israel.

DON'T LOSE YOUR FAITH!

[31] "Satan has asked to test all of you as a farmer tests his wheat. Simon, Simon, [32] I have prayed that you will not lose your faith! Help your brothers be stronger when you come back to me."

[33] But Peter said to Jesus, "Lord, I am ready to go to prison with you. I will even die with you!"

[34] But Jesus said, "Peter, before the rooster crows tonight, you will say you

---

22:18 fruit of the vine Product of the grapevine; this may also be translated "wine."
22:19 body Some Greek copies do not have the rest of verse 19 or verse 20.

don't know me. You will say this three times!"

BE READY FOR TROUBLE

[35] Then Jesus said to the apostles, "When I sent you out without money, a bag, or sandals, did you need anything?"

They said, "No."

[36] He said to them, "But now if you have money or a bag, carry that with you. If you don't have a sword, sell your coat and buy one. [37] The Scripture says, 'He was treated like a criminal.'[n] This scripture must have its full meaning. It was written about me, and it is happening now."

[38] The followers said, "Look, Lord, here are two swords!"

He said to them, "That's enough."

JESUS PRAYS ALONE

[39-40] Jesus left the city and went to the Mount of Olives. His followers went with him. (Jesus went there often.) He said to his followers, "Pray for strength against temptation."

[41] Then Jesus went about a stone's throw away from them. He kneeled down and prayed, [42]"Father, if it is what you want, then let me not have this cup[n] of suffering. But do what you want, not what I want." [43] Then an angel from heaven appeared to him to help him. [44] Jesus was full of pain; he prayed even more. Sweat dripped from his face as if he were bleeding. [45] When he finished praying, he went to his followers. They were asleep. (Their sadness had made them very tired.) [46] Jesus said to them, "Why are you sleeping? Get up and pray for strength against temptation."

JESUS IS ARRESTED

[47] While Jesus was speaking, a crowd came up. One of the 12 apostles was leading them. He was Judas. He came close to Jesus so that he could kiss him.

[48] But Jesus said to him, "Judas, are you using the kiss to give the Son of Man to his enemies?"

[49] The followers of Jesus were standing there too. They saw what was happening. They said to Jesus, "Lord, should we use our swords?" [50] And one of them did use his sword. He cut off the right ear of the servant of the high priest.

[51] Jesus said, "Stop!" Then he touched the servant's ear and healed him.

[52] Those who came to arrest Jesus were the leading priests, the soldiers who guarded the Temple, and the Jewish elders. Jesus said to them, "Why did you come out here with swords and sticks? Do you think I am a criminal? [53] I was with you every day in the Temple. Why didn't you try to arrest me there? But this is your time— the time when darkness rules."

PETER SAYS HE DOESN'T KNOW JESUS

[54] They arrested Jesus and took him away. They brought him into the house of the high priest. Peter followed them, but he did not go near Jesus. [55] The soldiers started a fire in the middle of the courtyard and sat together. Peter sat with them. [56] A servant girl saw Peter sitting there near the light. She looked

> Beginning now, the Son of Man will sit at the right hand of the powerful God.
> –LUKE 22:69

22:37 'He . . . criminal.' Quotation from Isaiah 53:12.
22:42 cup Jesus is talking about the bad things that will happen to him. Accepting these things will be hard, like drinking a cup of something that tastes very bitter.

closely at Peter's face and said, "This man was also with him!"

⁵⁷But Peter said this was not true. He said, "Girl, I don't know him."

⁵⁸A short time later, another person saw Peter and said, "You are also one of them."

But Peter said, "Man, I am not!"

⁵⁹About an hour later, another man insisted, "It is true! This man was with him. He is from Galilee!"

⁶⁰But Peter said, "Man, I don't know what you are talking about!"

Immediately, while Peter was still speaking, a rooster crowed. ⁶¹Then the Lord turned and looked straight at Peter. And Peter remembered what the Lord had said: "Before the rooster crows tonight, you will say three times that you don't know me." ⁶²Then Peter went outside and cried with much pain in his heart.

THE PEOPLE LAUGH AT JESUS

⁶³⁻⁶⁴Some men were guarding Jesus. They made fun of him like this: They covered his eyes so that he could not see them. Then they hit him and said, "Prove that you are a prophet, and tell us who hit you!" ⁶⁵The men said many cruel things to Jesus.

JESUS BEFORE THE LEADERS

⁶⁶When day came, the elders of the people, the leading priests, and the teachers of the law came together. They led Jesus away to their highest court. ⁶⁷They said, "If you are the Christ, then tell us that you are!"

Jesus said to them, "If I tell you I am the Christ, you will not believe me. ⁶⁸And if I ask you, you will not answer. ⁶⁹But beginning now, the Son of Man will sit at the right hand of the powerful God."

⁷⁰They all said, "Then are you the Son of God?"

Jesus said to them, "Yes, you are right when you say that I am."

⁷¹They said, "Why do we need

witnesses now? We ourselves heard him say this!"

GOVERNOR PILATE QUESTIONS JESUS

23 Then the whole group stood up and led Jesus to Pilate.[n] ²They began to accuse Jesus. They told Pilate, "We caught this man telling things that were confusing our people. He says that we should not pay taxes to Caesar. He calls himself the Christ, a king."

³Pilate asked Jesus, "Are you the king of the Jews?"

Jesus answered, "Yes, that is right."

⁴Pilate said to the leading priests and the people, "I find nothing wrong with this man."

⁵They said again and again, "But Jesus is making trouble with the people! He teaches all around Judea. He began in Galilee, and now he is here!"

PILATE SENDS JESUS TO HEROD

⁶Pilate heard this and asked if Jesus was from Galilee. ⁷If so, Jesus was under Herod's authority. Herod was in Jerusalem at that time; so Pilate sent Jesus to him. ⁸When Herod saw Jesus, he was very glad. He had heard about Jesus and had wanted to meet him for a long time. Herod was hoping to see Jesus work a miracle. ⁹Herod asked Jesus many questions, but Jesus said nothing. ¹⁰The leading priests and teachers of the law were standing there. They were shouting things against Jesus. ¹¹Then Herod and his soldiers made fun of Jesus. They dressed him in a kingly robe and then sent him back to Pilate. ¹²In the past, Pilate and Herod had always been enemies. But on that day they became friends.

JESUS MUST DIE

¹³Pilate called all the people together with the leading priests and the Jewish leaders. ¹⁴He said to them, "You brought this man to me. You said that he was

23:1 **Pilate** Pontius Pilate was the Roman governor of Judea from A.D. 26 to A.D. 36.

making trouble among the people. But I have questioned him before you all, and I have not found him guilty of the things you say. [15]Also, Herod found nothing wrong with him; he sent him back to us. Look, he has done nothing for which he should die. [16]So, after I punish him, I will let him go free." [17][Every year at the Passover Feast, Pilate had to release one prisoner to the people.][n]

[18]But all the people shouted, "Kill him! Let Barabbas go free!" [19](Barabbas was a man who was in prison because he started a riot in the city. He was guilty of murder.)

[20]Pilate wanted to let Jesus go free. So he told this to the crowd. [21]But they shouted again, "Kill him! Kill him on a cross!"

[22]A third time Pilate said to them, "Why? What wrong has he done? I can find no reason to kill him. So I will have him punished and set him free."

[23]But they continued to shout. They demanded that Jesus be killed on the cross. Their yelling became so loud that [24]Pilate decided to give them what they wanted. [25]They wanted Barabbas to go free, the man who was in jail for starting a riot and for murder. Pilate let Barabbas go free and gave Jesus to them to be killed.

JESUS IS KILLED ON A CROSS

[26]The soldiers led Jesus away. At that time, there was a man coming into the city from the fields. His name was Simon, and he was from the city of Cyrene. The soldiers forced Simon to carry Jesus' cross and walk behind him.

[27]A large crowd of people was following Jesus. Some of the women were sad and crying. [28]But Jesus turned and said to them, "Women of Jerusalem, don't cry for me. Cry for yourselves and for your children too! [29]The time is coming when people will say, 'Happy are the women who cannot have children! Happy are the women who have no babies to nurse.' [30]Then people will say to the mountains, 'Fall on us!' And they will say to the hills, 'Cover us!' [31]If they act like this now when life is good, what will happen when bad times come?"[n]

[32]There were also two criminals led out with Jesus to be killed. [33]Jesus and the two criminals were taken to a place called the Skull. There the soldiers nailed Jesus to his cross. They also nailed the criminals to their crosses, one beside Jesus on the right and the other beside Jesus on the left. [34]Jesus said, "Father, forgive them. They don't know what they are doing."[n]

The soldiers threw lots to decide who would get his clothes. [35]The people stood there watching. The leaders made fun of Jesus. They said, "If he is God's Chosen One, the Christ, then let him save himself. He saved other people, didn't he?"

[36]Even the soldiers made fun of him. They came to Jesus and offered him some vinegar. [37]They said, "If you are the king of the Jews, save yourself!" [38](At the top of the cross these words were written: "THIS IS THE KING OF THE JEWS.")

[39]One of the criminals began to shout insults at Jesus: "Aren't you the Christ? Then save yourself! And save us too!"

[40]But the other criminal stopped him. He said, "You should fear God! You are getting the same punishment as he is. [41]We are punished justly; we should die. But this man has done nothing wrong!" [42]Then this criminal said to Jesus, "Jesus, remember me when you come into your kingdom!"

[43]Then Jesus said to him, "Listen! What I say is true: Today you will be with me in paradise!"[n]

JESUS DIES

[44]It was about noon, and the whole land became dark until three o'clock in the

---

23:17 **Every . . . people.** Some Greek copies do not contain the bracketed text.
23:31 **If . . . come?** Literally, "If they do these things in the green tree, what will happen in the dry?"
23:34 **Jesus . . . doing.** Some Greek copies do not have this part of verse 34.
23:43 **paradise** A place where good people go when they die.

afternoon. [45] There was no sun! The curtain in the Temple[n] was torn into two pieces. [46] Jesus cried out in a loud voice, "Father, I give you my life." After Jesus said this, he died.

[47] The army officer there saw what happened. He praised God, saying, "I know this was a good man!"

[48] Many people had gathered there to watch this thing. When they saw what happened, they returned home. They beat their chests because they were so sad. [49] Those who were close friends of Jesus were there. Some were women who had followed Jesus from Galilee. They all stood far away from the cross and watched.

JOSEPH OF ARIMATHEA

[50-51] A man from the Jewish town of Arimathea was there, too. His name was Joseph. He was a good, religious man. He wanted the kingdom of God to come. Joseph was a member of the Jewish council, but he had not agreed when the other leaders decided to kill Jesus. [52] Joseph went to Pilate to ask for the body of Jesus. [53] So Joseph took the body down from the cross and wrapped it in cloth. Then he put Jesus' body in a tomb that was cut in a wall of rock. This tomb had never been used before. [54] This was late on Preparation Day. When the sun went down, the Sabbath day would begin.

[55] The women who had come from Galilee with Jesus followed Joseph. They saw the tomb and saw inside where the body of Jesus was laid. [56] Then the women left to prepare perfumes and spices.

On the Sabbath day they rested, as the law of Moses commanded.

JESUS RISES FROM DEATH

24 Very early on the first day of the week, the women came to the tomb where Jesus' body was laid. They brought the spices they had prepared. [2] They found that the stone had been rolled away from the entrance of the tomb. [3] They went in, but they did not find the body of the Lord Jesus. [4] While they were wondering about this, two men in shining clothes suddenly stood beside them. [5] The women were very afraid; they bowed their heads to the ground. The men said to the women, "Why are you looking for a living person here? This is a place for the dead. [6] Jesus is not here. He has risen from death! Do you remember what he said in Galilee? [7] He said that the Son of Man must be given to evil men, be killed on a cross, and rise from death on the third day." [8] Then the women remembered what Jesus had said.

[9] The women left the tomb and told all these things to the 11 apostles and the other followers. [10] These women were Mary Magdalene, Joanna, Mary the mother of James, and some other women. The women told the apostles everything that had happened at the tomb. [11] But they did not believe the women. It sounded like nonsense. [12] But Peter got up and ran to the tomb. He looked in, but he saw only the cloth that Jesus' body had been wrapped in. Peter went away to be alone, wondering about what had happened.

ON THE ROAD TO EMMAUS

[13] That same day two of Jesus' followers were going to a town named Emmaus. It is about seven miles from Jerusalem. [14] They were talking about everything that had happened. [15] While they were discussing these things, Jesus himself came near and began walking with them. [16] (They were not allowed to recognize Jesus.) [17] Then he said, "What are these things you are talking about while you walk?"

The two followers stopped. Their faces were very sad. [18] The one named Cleopas answered, "You must be the

---

23:45 curtain in the Temple A curtain divided the Most Holy Place from the other part of the Temple. This was the special building in Jerusalem where God commanded the Jews to worship him.

only one in Jerusalem who does not know what just happened there."

¹⁹Jesus said to them, "What are you talking about?"

The followers said, "It is about Jesus of Nazareth. He was a prophet from God to all the people. He said and did many powerful things. ²⁰Our leaders and the leading priests gave him up to be judged and killed. They nailed him to a cross. ²¹But we were hoping that he would free the Jews. It is now the third day since this happened. ²²And today some women among us told us some amazing things. Early this morning they went to the tomb, ²³but they did not find his body there. They came and told us that they had seen a vision of angels. The angels said that Jesus was alive! ²⁴So some of our group went to the tomb, too. They found it just as the women said, but they did not see Jesus."

²⁵Then Jesus said to them, "You are foolish and slow to realize what is true. You should believe everything the prophets said. ²⁶They said that the

☆ Luke 24:47–48

Three days after Jesus was crucified, God raised him from the dead. Jesus appeared to many of his followers so they would know he was alive. When Jesus was getting ready to go back to heaven, he told his followers to tell everyone about him—that he is alive!

Have you ever been told to be quiet? Maybe you were talking loudly or too much. We talk about the things we like and that make us happy. We talk about going to an amusement park, getting a new toy, or going on vacation. When something is important to us, it is hard to stay quiet! That's why we want to tell our friends about Jesus. When we tell our friends and neighbors about what Jesus did in our lives, he can change their lives too. And then they can know about his love like we do.

. . . .

Think about all the good things Jesus has done for you, then tell others the Good News.

Christ must suffer these things before he enters his glory." 27 Then Jesus began to explain everything that had been written about himself in the Scriptures. He started with Moses, and then he talked about what all the prophets had said about him.

28 They came near the town of Emmaus, and Jesus acted as if he did not plan to stop there. 29 But they begged him, "Stay with us. It is late; it is almost night." So he went in to stay with them.

30 Jesus sat down with them and took some bread. He gave thanks for the food and divided it. Then he gave it to them. 31 And then, they were allowed to recognize Jesus. But when they saw who he was, he disappeared. 32 They said to each other, "When Jesus talked to us on the road, it felt like a fire burning in us. It was exciting when he explained the true meaning of the Scriptures."

33 So the two followers got up at once and went back to Jerusalem. There they found the 11 apostles and others gathered. 34 They were saying, "The Lord really has risen from death! He showed himself to Simon."

35 Then the two followers told what had happened on the road. They talked about how they recognized Jesus when he divided the bread.

JESUS APPEARS TO HIS FOLLOWERS

36 While the two followers were telling this, Jesus himself stood among those gathered. He said to them, "Peace be with you."

37 They were fearful and terrified. They thought they were seeing a ghost. 38 But Jesus said, "Why are you troubled? Why do you doubt what you see? 39 Look at my hands and my feet. It is I myself! Touch me. You can see that I have a living body; a ghost does not have a body like this."

40 After Jesus said this, he showed them his hands and feet. 41 The followers were amazed and very happy. They still could not believe it. Jesus said to them, "Do you have any food here?" 42 They gave him a piece of cooked fish. 43 While the followers watched, Jesus took the fish and ate it.

44 He said to them, "Remember when I was with you before? I said that everything written about me must happen— everything in the law of Moses, the books of the prophets, and the Psalms."

45 Then Jesus opened their minds so they could understand the Scriptures. 46 He said to them, "It is written that the Christ would be killed and rise from death on the third day. 47-48 You saw these things happen—you are witnesses. You must tell people to change their hearts and lives. If they do this, their sins will be forgiven. You must start at Jerusalem and preach these things in my name to all nations. 49 Listen! My Father has promised you something; I will send it to you. But you must stay in Jerusalem until you have received that power from heaven."

JESUS GOES BACK TO HEAVEN

50 Jesus led his followers out of Jerusalem almost to Bethany. He raised his hands and blessed them. 51 While he was blessing them, he was separated from them and carried into heaven. 52 They worshiped him and then went back to the city very happy. 53 They stayed in the Temple all the time, praising God.

John

CHRIST COMES TO THE WORLD

1 Before the world began, there was the Word.[n] The Word was with God, and the Word was God. [2]He was with God in the beginning. [3]All things were made through him. Nothing was made without him. [4]In him there was life. That life was light for the people of the world. [5]The Light shines in the darkness. And the darkness has not overpowered[n] the Light.

[6]There was a man named John[n] who was sent by God. [7]He came to tell people about the Light. Through him all people could hear about the Light and believe. [8]John was not the Light, but he came to tell people about the Light. [9]The true Light was coming into the world. The true Light gives light to all.

[10]The Word was in the world. The world was made through him, but the world did not know him. [11]He came to the world that was his own. But his own people did not accept him. [12]But some people did accept him. They believed in him. To them he gave the right to become children of God. [13]They did not become his children in the human way. They were not born because of the desire or wish of some man. They were born of God.

[14]The Word became a man and lived among us. We saw his glory—the glory that belongs to the only Son of the Father. The Word was full of grace and truth. [15]John told about him. He said, "This is the One I was talking about. I said, 'The One who comes after me is greater than I am. He was living before me.'"

[16]The Word was full of grace and truth. From him we all received more and more blessings. [17]The law was given through Moses, but grace and truth came through Jesus Christ. [18]No man has ever seen God. But God the only Son is very close to the Father.[n] And the Son has shown us what God is like.

JOHN TELLS PEOPLE ABOUT JESUS

[19]The Jews in Jerusalem sent some priests and Levites to John.[n] The Jews sent them to ask, "Who are you?"

[20]John spoke freely and did not refuse to answer. He said clearly, "I am not the Christ."

[21]So they asked him, "Then who are you? Are you Elijah?"[n]

He answered, "No, I am not Elijah."

Then they asked, "Are you the Prophet?"[n]

He answered, "No, I am not the Prophet."

[22]Then they said, "Who are you? Give us an answer to tell those who sent us. What do you say about yourself?"

[23]John told them in the words of the prophet Isaiah:

"I am the voice of a man
    calling out in the desert:
'Make the road straight for the
        Lord.'"   *Isaiah 40:3*

[24]In the group of Jews who were sent, there were some Pharisees. [25]They

---

1:1 **Word** The Greek word is "logos," meaning any kind of communication. It could be translated "message." Here, it means Christ. Christ was the way God told people about himself.
1:5 **overpowered** This can also be translated, "understood."
1:6, 19 **John** John the Baptist, who preached to people about Christ's coming (Matthew 3; Luke 3).
1:18 **But . . . Father.** This could be translated, "But the only God is very close to the Father." Also, some Greek copies read "But the only Son is very close to the Father."
1:21 **Elijah** A man who spoke for God. He lived hundreds of years before Christ.
1:21 **Prophet** They probably meant the prophet that God told Moses he would send (Deuteronomy 18:15–19).

☆ John 1:12

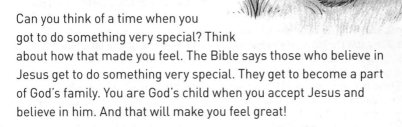

After Jesus died, rose from the dead, and went back up to heaven, some of his followers wrote books about him. John was one of those followers. John was very close to Jesus, and they became like brothers. In his book, John told people— and us—that if we believe in Jesus, we become real children of God.

Can you think of a time when you got to do something very special? Think about how that made you feel. The Bible says those who believe in Jesus get to do something very special. They get to become a part of God's family. You are God's child when you accept Jesus and believe in him. And that will make you feel great!

· ·

When we believe in Jesus, we get to be brothers and sisters of Jesus!

---

said to John: "You say you are not the Christ. You say you are not Elijah or the Prophet. Then why do you baptize people?"

²⁶John answered, "I baptize people with water. But there is one here with you that you don't know. ²⁷He is the One who comes after me. I am not good enough to untie the strings of his sandals."

²⁸This all happened at Bethany on the other side of the Jordan River. This is where John was baptizing people.

²⁹The next day John saw Jesus coming toward him. John said, "Look, the Lamb of God.ⁿ He takes away the sins of the world! ³⁰This is the One I was talking about. I said, 'A man will come after me, but he is greater than I am, because he was living before me.' ³¹Even I did not know who he was. But I came baptizing with water so that the people of Israel could know who he is."

³²⁻³³Then John said, "I did not know who the Christ was. But God sent me to baptize with water. And God told me, 'You will see the Spirit come down and rest on a man. That man is the One who will baptize with the Holy Spirit.'" John said, "I saw the Spirit come down from heaven. The Spirit looked like a dove and rested on him. ³⁴I have seen this

1:29 Lamb of God Name for Jesus. Jesus is like the lambs that were offered for a sacrifice to God.

happen. So I tell people: 'He is the Son of God.'" [n]

THE FIRST FOLLOWERS OF JESUS

[35] The next day John[n] was there again with two of his followers. [36] He saw Jesus walking by and said, "Look, the Lamb of God!" [n]

[37] The two followers heard John say this. So they followed Jesus. [38] Jesus turned and saw them following him. He asked, "What do you want?"

They said, "Rabbi, where are you staying?" ("Rabbi" means "Teacher.")

[39] Jesus answered, "Come with me and you will see." So the two men went with Jesus. They saw the place where Jesus was staying and stayed there with him that day. It was then about four o'clock.

[40] These two men followed Jesus after they heard about him from John. One of the men was Andrew. He was Simon Peter's brother. [41] The first thing Andrew did was to find his brother, Simon. He said to Simon, "We have found the Messiah." ("Messiah" means "Christ.")

[42] Then Andrew took Simon to Jesus. Jesus looked at Simon and said, "You are Simon son of John. You will be called Cephas." ("Cephas" means "Peter." [n])

[43] The next day Jesus decided to go to Galilee. He found Philip and said to him, "Follow me." [44] Philip was from the town of Bethsaida, where Andrew and Peter lived. [45] Philip found Nathanael and told him, "Remember that Moses wrote in the law about a man who was coming, and the prophets also wrote about him. We have found him. He is Jesus, the son of Joseph. He is from Nazareth."

[46] But Nathanael said to Philip, "Nazareth! Can anything good come from Nazareth?"

Philip answered, "Come and see."

[47] Jesus saw Nathanael coming toward him. He said, "Here is truly a person of Israel. There is nothing false in him."

[48] Nathanael asked, "How do you know me?"

Jesus answered, "I saw you when you were under the fig tree. That was before Philip told you about me."

[49] Then Nathanael said to Jesus, "Teacher, you are the Son of God. You are the King of Israel."

[50] Jesus said to Nathanael, "You believe in me because I told you I saw you under the fig tree. But you will see greater things than that!" [51] And Jesus said to them, "I tell you the truth. You will all see heaven open. You will see 'angels of God going up and coming down' [n] on the Son of Man."

THE WEDDING AT CANA

2 Two days later there was a wedding in the town of Cana in Galilee. Jesus' mother was there. [2] Jesus and his followers were also invited to the wedding. [3] When all the wine was gone, Jesus' mother said to him, "They have no more wine."

[4] Jesus answered, "Dear woman, why come to me? My time has not yet come."

[5] His mother said to the servants, "Do whatever he tells you to do."

[6] In that place there were six stone water jars. The Jews used jars like these in their washing ceremony. [n] Each jar held about 20 or 30 gallons.

[7] Jesus said to the servants, "Fill the jars with water." So they filled the jars to the top.

[8] Then he said to them, "Now take some out and give it to the master of the feast."

So the servants took the water to the master. [9] When he tasted it, the water had become wine. He did not know where the wine came from. But the

---

1:34 **the Son of God** Some Greek copies read "God's Chosen One."
1:35 **John** John the Baptist, who preached to people about Christ's coming (Matthew 3; Luke 3).
1:36 **Lamb of God** Name for Jesus. Jesus is like the lambs that were offered for a sacrifice to God.
1:42 **Peter** The Greek name "Peter," like the Aramaic name "Cephas," means "rock."
1:51 **'angels . . . down'** These words are from Genesis 28:12.
2:6 **washing ceremony** The Jews washed themselves in special ways before eating, before worshiping in the Temple, and at other special times.

servants who brought the water knew. The master of the wedding called the bridegroom [10]and said to him, "People always serve the best wine first. Later, after the guests have been drinking a lot, they serve the cheaper wine. But you have saved the best wine till now."

[11]So in Cana of Galilee, Jesus did his first miracle. There he showed his glory, and his followers believed in him.

JESUS IN THE TEMPLE

[12]Then Jesus went to the town of Capernaum with his mother, brothers and his followers. They all stayed in Capernaum for a few days. [13]But it was almost time for the Jewish Passover Feast. So Jesus went to Jerusalem. [14]In the Temple he found men selling cattle, sheep, and doves. He saw others sitting at tables, exchanging money. [15]Jesus made a whip out of cords. Then he forced all these men, with the sheep and cattle, to leave the Temple. He turned over the tables and scattered the money of the men who were exchanging it. [16]Then he said to those who were selling pigeons, "Take these things out of here! Don't make my Father's house a place for buying and selling!"

[17]When this happened the followers remembered what was written in the Scriptures: "My strong love for your Temple completely controls me." [n]

[18]The Jews said to Jesus, "Show us a miracle for a sign. Prove that you have the right to do these things."

[19]Jesus answered, "Destroy this temple, and I will build it again in three days."

[20]The Jews answered, "Men worked 46 years to build this Temple! Do you really believe you can build it again in three days?"

[21](But the temple Jesus meant was his own body. [22]After Jesus was raised from death, his followers remembered that Jesus had said this. Then they believed the Scripture and the words Jesus said.)

[23]Jesus was in Jerusalem for the Passover Feast. Many people believed in him because they saw the miracles he did. [24]But Jesus did not believe in them because he knew them all. [25]He did not need anyone to tell him about people. Jesus knew what was in a person's mind.

> [John the Baptist] saw Jesus walking by and said, "Look, the Lamb of God!"
> –JOHN 1:36

JESUS AND NICODEMUS

3 There was a man named Nicodemus who was one of the Pharisees. He was an important Jewish leader. [2]One night Nicodemus came to Jesus. He said, "Teacher, we know that you are a teacher sent from God. No one can do the miracles you do, unless God is with him."

[3]Jesus answered, "I tell you the truth. Unless you are born again, you cannot be in God's kingdom."

[4]Nicodemus said, "But if a man is already old, how can he be born again? He cannot enter his mother's body again. So how can he be born a second time?"

[5]But Jesus answered, "I tell you the truth. Unless you are born from water and the Spirit, you cannot enter God's kingdom. [6]A person's body is born from his human parents. But a person's spiritual life is born from the Spirit. [7]Don't be surprised when I tell you, 'You must all be born again.' [8]The wind blows where it wants to go. You hear the wind blow. But you don't know where the

2:17 "My . . . me." Quotation from Psalm 69:9.

wind comes from or where it is going. It is the same with every person who is born from the Spirit."

9Nicodemus asked, "How can all this be possible?"

10Jesus said, "You are an important teacher in Israel. But you still don't understand these things? 11I tell you the truth. We talk about what we know. We tell about what we have seen. But you don't accept what we tell you. 12I have told you about things here on earth, but you do not believe me. So surely you will not believe me if I tell you about the things of heaven! 13The only one who has ever gone up to heaven is the One who came down from heaven—the Son of Man.n

14"Moses lifted up the snake in the desert.n It is the same with the Son of Man. The Son of Man must be lifted up too. 15Then everyone who believes in him can have eternal life.

16"For God loved the world so much that he gave his only Son. God gave his Son so that whoever believes in him may not be lost, but have eternal life. 17God did not send his Son into the world to judge the world guilty, but to save the world through him. 18He who believes in God's Son is not judged guilty. He who does not believe has already been judged guilty, because he has not believed in God's only Son. 19People are judged by this fact: I am the Light from God that has come into the world. But men did not want light. They wanted darkness because they were doing evil things. 20Everyone who does evil hates the light. He will not come to the light because it will show all the evil things he has done. 21But he who follows the true way comes to the light. Then the light will show that the things he has done were done through God."

JESUS AND JOHN THE BAPTIST

22After this, Jesus and his followers went into the area of Judea. There Jesus stayed with his followers and baptized people. 23John was also baptizing in Aenon, near Salim, because there was plenty of water there. People were going there to be baptized. 24(This was before John was put into prison.)

25Some of John's followers had an argument with a Jew about religious washing.n 26So they came to John and said, "Teacher, remember the man who was with you on the other side of the Jordan River, the one you spoke about? He is baptizing, and everyone is going to him."

27John answered, "A man can get only what God gives him. 28You yourselves heard me say, 'I am not the Christ. I am only the one God sent to prepare the way for him.' 29The bride belongs only to the bridegroom. The friend who helps the bridegroom waits and listens for him. He is glad when he hears the bridegroom's voice. That is the same pleasure I have. And my time of joy is now here. 30He must become greater. And I must become less important.

THE ONE WHO COMES FROM HEAVEN

31"The One who comes from above is greater than all. He who is from the earth belongs to the earth and talks about things on the earth. But the One who comes from heaven is greater than all. 32He tells what he has seen and heard, but no one accepts what he says. 33The person who accepts what he says has proven that God is true. 34God sent him, and he tells the things that God says. God gives him the Spirit fully. 35The Father loves the Son and has given him power over everything. 36He

---

3:13 the Son of Man Some Greek copies continue, "who is in heaven."
3:14 Moses . . . desert. The people of Israel were dying from snake bites. God told Moses to put a bronze snake on a pole. The people who looked at the snake were healed (Numbers 21:4–9).
3:25 religious washing The Jews washed themselves in special ways before eating, before worshiping in the Temple, and at other special times.

who believes in the Son has eternal life. But he who does not obey the Son will never have that life. God's anger stays with him."

JESUS AND A SAMARITAN WOMAN

4 The Pharisees heard that Jesus was making and baptizing more followers than John. [2](But really Jesus himself did not baptize people. His followers did the baptizing.) Jesus knew that the Pharisees had heard about him. [3]So he left Judea and went back to Galilee. [4]On the way he had to go through the country of Samaria.

[5]In Samaria Jesus came to the town called Sychar. This town is near the field that Jacob gave to his son Joseph. [6]Jacob's well was there. Jesus was tired from his long trip. So he sat down beside the well. It was about noon. [7]A Samaritan woman came to the well to get some water. Jesus said to her, "Please give me a drink." [8](This happened while Jesus' followers were in town buying some food.)

[9]The woman said, "I am surprised that you ask me for a drink. You are a Jew and I am a Samaritan." (Jews are not friends with Samaritans.")

[10]Jesus said, "You don't know what God gives. And you don't know who asked you for a drink. If you knew, you would have asked me, and I would have given you living water."

[11]The woman said, "Sir, where will you get that living water? The well is very deep, and you have nothing to get water with. [12]Are you greater than Jacob, our father? Jacob is the one who gave us this well. He drank from it himself. Also, his sons and flocks drank from this well."

[13]Jesus answered, "Every person who drinks this water will be thirsty again. [14]But whoever drinks the water I give will never be thirsty again. The water I give will become a spring of water flowing inside him. It will give him eternal life."

[15]The woman said to him, "Sir, give me this water. Then I will never be thirsty again. And I will not have to come back here to get more water."

[16]Jesus told her, "Go get your husband and come back here."

[17]The woman answered, "But I have no husband."

Jesus said to her, "You are right to say you have no husband. [18]Really you have had five husbands. But the man you live with now is not your husband. You told the truth."

[19]The woman said, "Sir, I can see that you are a prophet. [20]Our fathers worshiped on this mountain. But you Jews say that Jerusalem is the place where people must worship."

[21]Jesus said, "Believe me, woman. The time is coming when you will not have to be in Jerusalem or on this mountain to worship the Father. [22]You Samaritans worship what you don't understand. We Jews understand what we worship. Salvation comes from the Jews. [23]The time is coming when the true worshipers will worship the Father in spirit and truth. That time is now here. And these are the kinds of worshipers the Father wants. [24]God is spirit. Those who worship God must worship in spirit and truth."

[25]The woman said, "I know that the Messiah is coming." (Messiah is the One called Christ.) "When the Messiah comes, he will explain everything to us."

[26]Then Jesus said, "He is talking to you now. I am he."

[27]Just then his followers came back from town. They were surprised because they saw Jesus talking with a woman. But none of them asked, "What do you want?" or "Why are you talking with her?"

[28]Then the woman left her water jar and went back to town. She said to the people, [29]"A man told me everything I

4:9 Jews . . . Samaritans. This can also be translated "Jews don't use things that Samaritans have used."

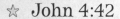

☆ John 4:42

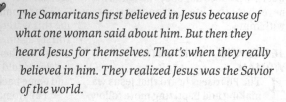

The Samaritans first believed in Jesus because of what one woman said about him. But then they heard Jesus for themselves. That's when they really believed in him. They realized Jesus was the Savior of the world.

Who are your favorite superheroes? Do they have special powers that they use to rescue people? Jesus is more amazing than the most amazing superhero. Jesus is God, and he came to earth to save the whole world! God is big and powerful, but he is also kind and gentle. God wants to save us. He rescues us from trouble! When we believe in Jesus, he will save us.

• •

Jesus is the super-est of superheroes. And even though you can't see him right now, know that he is with you. He is always watching out for you.

have ever done. Come see him. Maybe he is the Christ!" ³⁰So the people left the town and went to see Jesus.

³¹While the woman was away, the followers were begging him, "Teacher, eat something!"

³²But Jesus answered, "I have food to eat that you know nothing about."

³³So the followers asked themselves, "Did somebody already bring Jesus some food?"

³⁴Jesus said, "My food is to do what the One who sent me wants me to do. My food is to finish the work that he gave me to do. ³⁵You say, 'Four more months to wait before we gather the grain.' But I tell you, open your eyes. Look at the fields that are ready for harvesting now. ³⁶Even now, the one

who harvests the crop is being paid. He is gathering crops for eternal life. So now the one who plants can be happy along with the one who harvests. ³⁷It is true when we say, 'One person plants, but another harvests the crop.' ³⁸I sent you to harvest a crop that you did not work for. Others did the work, and you get the profit from their work." [n]

³⁹Many of the Samaritans in that town believed in Jesus. They believed because of what the woman said: "He told me everything I have ever done." ⁴⁰The Samaritans came to Jesus and begged him to stay with them. So he stayed there two days. ⁴¹Many more believed because of the things he said.

⁴²They said to the woman, "First we

4:35–38 **Look at . . . their work.** As a farmer sends workers to harvest grain, Jesus sends his followers out to bring people to God.

believed in Jesus because of what you told us. But now we believe because we heard him ourselves. We know that this man really is the Savior of the world."

JESUS HEALS AN OFFICER'S SON

[43] Two days later, Jesus left and went to Galilee. [44] (Jesus had said before that a prophet is not respected in his own country.) [45] When Jesus arrived in Galilee, the people there welcomed him. They had seen all the things he did at the Passover Feast in Jerusalem. They had been at the Passover Feast, too.

[46] Jesus went to visit Cana in Galilee again. This is where Jesus had changed the water into wine. One of the king's important officers lived in the city of Capernaum. This man's son was sick. [47] The man heard that Jesus had come from Judea and was now in Galilee. He went to Jesus and begged him to come to Capernaum and heal his son. His son was almost dead. [48] Jesus said to him, "You people must see signs and miracles before you will believe in me."

[49] The officer said, "Sir, come before my child dies."

[50] Jesus answered, "Go. Your son will live."

The man believed what Jesus told him and went home. [51] On the way the man's servants came and met him. They told him, "Your son is well."

[52] The man asked, "What time did my son begin to get well?"

They answered, "It was about one o'clock yesterday when the fever left him."

[53] The father knew that one o'clock was the exact time that Jesus had said, "Your son will live." So the man and all the people of his house believed in Jesus.

[54] That was the second miracle that Jesus did after coming from Judea to Galilee.

JESUS HEALS A MAN AT A POOL

5 Later Jesus went to Jerusalem for a special Jewish feast. [2] In Jerusalem there is a pool with five covered porches. In the Jewish language[n] it is called Bethzatha.[n] This pool is near the Sheep Gate. [3] Many sick people were lying on the porches beside the pool. Some were blind, some were crippled, and some were paralyzed [and they waited for the water to move. [4] Sometimes an angel of the Lord came down to the pool and stirred up the water. After the angel did this, the first person to go into the pool was healed from any sickness he had].[n] [5] There was a man lying there who had been sick for 38 years. [6] Jesus saw the man and knew that he had been sick for a very long time. So Jesus asked him, "Do you want to be well?"

[7] The sick man answered, "Sir, there is no one to help me get into the pool when the water starts moving. I try to be the first one into the water. But when I try, someone else always goes in before I can."

[8] Then Jesus said, "Stand up. Pick up your mat and walk." [9] And immediately the man was well. He picked up his mat and began to walk.

The day all this happened was a Sabbath day. [10] So the Jews said to the man who had been healed, "Today is the Sabbath. It is against our law for you to carry your mat on the Sabbath day."

[11] But he answered, "The man who made me well told me, 'Pick up your mat and walk.'"

[12] Then they asked him, "Who is the man who told you to pick up your mat and walk?"

[13] But the man who had been healed did not know who it was. There were many people in that place, and Jesus had left.

[14] Later, Jesus found the man at the

5:2 **Jewish language** Aramaic, the language of the Jews in the first century.
5:2 **Bethzatha** Also called Bethsaida or Bethesda, a pool of water north of the Temple in Jerusalem.
5:3–4 **and . . . had** Some Greek copies do not contain all or most of the bracketed text.

Temple. Jesus said to him, "See, you are well now. But stop sinning or something worse may happen to you!"

[15] Then the man left and went back to the Jews. He told them that Jesus was the one who had made him well.

[16] Jesus was doing this on the Sabbath day. So the Jews began to do bad things to him. [17] But Jesus said to them, "My Father never stops working. And so I work, too."

[18] This made the Jews try harder to kill him. They said, "First Jesus was breaking the law about the Sabbath day. Then he said that God is his own Father! He is making himself equal with God!"

JESUS HAS GOD'S AUTHORITY

[19] But Jesus said, "I tell you the truth. The Son can do nothing alone. The Son does only what he sees his Father doing. The Son does whatever the Father does. [20] The Father loves the Son, and the Father shows the Son all the things he himself does. But the Father will show the Son greater things than this to do. Then you will all be amazed. [21] The Father raises the dead and gives them life. In the same way, the Son gives life to those he wants to. [22] Also, the Father judges no one. But the Father has given the Son power to do all the judging. [23] God did this so that all people will respect the Son the same way they respect the Father. He who does not respect the Son does not respect the Father. The Father is the One who sent the Son.

[24] "I tell you the truth. Whoever hears what I say and believes in the One who sent me has eternal life. He will not be judged guilty. He has already left death and has entered into life. [25] I tell you the truth. The time is coming and is already here when the dead will hear the voice

of the Son of God. And those who hear will have life. [26] Life comes from the Father himself. So the Father has allowed the Son to give life. [27] And the Father has given the Son the approval to judge because he is the Son of Man. [28] Don't be surprised at this. A time is coming when all who are dead and in their graves will hear his voice. [29] Then they will come out of their graves. Those who did good will rise and have life forever. But those who did evil will rise to be judged guilty.

JESUS IS GOD'S SON

[30] "I can do nothing alone. I judge only the way I am told, so my judgment is right. I don't try to please myself. I try to please the One who sent me.

[31] "If I tell people about myself, then they will not accept what I say about myself. [32] But there is another who tells about me. And I know that the things he says about me are true.

[33] "You have sent men to John. And he has told you about the truth. [34] But I don't need a man to tell about me. I tell you this so that you can be saved. [35] John was like a burning and shining lamp. And you were happy to enjoy his light for a while.

[36] "But I have a proof about myself that is greater than that of John. The things I do are my proof. These are the things my Father gave me to do. They show that the Father sent me. [37] And the Father who sent me has given proof about me himself. You have never heard his voice. You have never seen what he looks like. [38] His teaching does not live in you because you don't believe in the One that the Father sent. [39] You carefully study the Scriptures because you think that they give you eternal life. Those are the same Scriptures that tell

> The Father loves the Son, and the Father shows the Son all the things he himself does.
>
> –JOHN 5:20

about me! ⁴⁰But you refuse to come to me to have that life.

⁴¹"I don't want praise from men. ⁴²But I know you—I know that you don't have God's love in you. ⁴³I have come from my Father—I speak for him. But you don't accept me. But when another person comes, speaking only for himself, you will accept him. ⁴⁴You like to have praise from each other. But you never try to get the praise that comes from the only God. So how can you believe? ⁴⁵Don't think that I will stand before the Father and say that you are wrong. Moses is the one who says that you are wrong. And he is the one that you hoped would save you. ⁴⁶If you really believed Moses, you would believe me because Moses wrote about me. ⁴⁷But you don't believe what Moses wrote. So how can you believe what I say?"

MORE THAN 5,000 PEOPLE FED

6 After this, Jesus went across Lake Galilee (or, Lake Tiberias). ²Many people followed him because they saw the miracles he did to heal the sick. ³Jesus went up on a hill and there sat down with his followers. ⁴It was almost the time for the Jewish Passover Feast.

⁵Jesus looked up and saw a large crowd coming toward him. He said to Philip, "Where can we buy bread for all these people to eat?" ⁶(Jesus asked Philip this question to test him. Jesus already knew what he planned to do.)

⁷Philip answered, "Someone would have to work almost a year to buy enough bread for each person here to have only a little piece."

⁸Another follower there was Andrew. He was Simon Peter's brother. Andrew said, ⁹"Here is a boy with five loaves of barley bread and two little fish. But that is not enough for so many people."

¹⁰Jesus said, "Tell the people to sit down." This was a very grassy place. There were about 5,000 men who sat down there. ¹¹Then Jesus took the loaves of bread. He thanked God for the bread and gave it to the people who were sitting there. He did the same with the fish. He gave them as much as they wanted.

¹²They all had enough to eat. When they had finished, Jesus said to his followers, "Gather the pieces of fish and bread that were not eaten. Don't waste anything." ¹³So they gathered up the pieces that were left. They filled 12 large baskets with the pieces that were left of the five barley loaves.

¹⁴The people saw this miracle that Jesus did. They said, "He must truly be the Prophet[n] who is coming into the world."

¹⁵Jesus knew that the people planned to come and take him by force and make him their king. So he left and went into the hills alone.

JESUS WALKS ON THE WATER

¹⁶That evening Jesus' followers went down to Lake Galilee. ¹⁷It was dark now and Jesus had not yet come to them. The followers got into a boat and started across the lake to Capernaum. ¹⁸By now a strong wind was blowing, and the waves on the lake were getting bigger. ¹⁹They rowed the boat about three or four miles. Then they saw Jesus walking on the water, coming toward the boat. The followers were afraid. ²⁰But Jesus said to them, "Don't be afraid. It is I." ²¹Then they were glad to take him into the boat. At once the boat came to land at the place where they wanted to go.

THE PEOPLE SEEK JESUS

²²The next day came. Some people had stayed on the other side of the lake. They knew that Jesus had not gone in the boat with his followers but that they had left without him. And they knew that only one boat had been there. ²³But then some boats came from Tiberias. They landed near the place where the people had eaten the bread after the

---

6:14 Prophet They probably meant the prophet that God told Moses he would send (Deuteronomy 18:15–19).

Lord had given thanks. 24The people saw that Jesus and his followers were not there now. So they got into boats and went to Capernaum. They wanted to find Jesus.

JESUS, THE BREAD OF LIFE

25The people found Jesus on the other side of the lake. They asked him, "Teacher, when did you come here?"

26Jesus answered, "Are you looking for me because you saw me do miracles? No! I tell you the truth. You are looking for me because you ate the bread and were satisfied. 27Earthly food spoils and ruins. So don't work to get that kind of food. But work to get the food that stays good always and gives you eternal life. The Son of Man will give you that food. God the Father has shown that he is with the Son of Man."

28The people asked Jesus, "What are the things God wants us to do?"

29Jesus answered, "The work God wants you to do is this: to believe in the One that God sent."

30So the people asked, "What miracle will you do? If we can see a miracle, then we will believe you. What will you do? 31Our ancestors ate the manna in the desert. This is written in the Scriptures: 'God gave them bread from heaven to eat.'" [n]

32Jesus said, "I tell you the truth. Moses was not the one who gave you bread from heaven. But my Father gives you the true bread from heaven. 33God's bread is the One who comes down from heaven and gives life to the world."

34The people said, "Sir, give us this bread always."

35Then Jesus said, "I am the bread that gives life. He who comes to me will never be hungry. He who believes in me will never be thirsty. 36But as I told you before, you have seen me, and still you don't believe. 37The Father gives me the people who are mine. Every one of them will come to me, and I will always accept them. 38I came down from heaven to do what God wants me to do. I did not come to do what I want to do. 39I must not lose even one of those that God has given me, but I must raise them up on the last day. This is what the One who sent me wants me to do. 40Everyone who sees the Son and believes in him has eternal life. I will raise him up on the last day. This is what my Father wants."

41The Jews began to complain about Jesus. They complained because he said, "I am the bread that comes down from heaven." 42The Jews said, "This is Jesus. We know his father and mother. He is only Joseph's son. How can he say, 'I came down from heaven'?"

43But Jesus answered, "Stop complaining to each other. 44The Father is the One who sent me. No one can come to me unless the Father draws him to me. And I will raise him up on the last day. 45It is written in the prophets, 'God will teach all the people.' [n] Everyone who listens to the Father and learns from him comes to me. 46No one has seen the Father except the One who is from God. Only he has seen the Father. 47I tell you the truth. He who believes has eternal life. 48I am the bread that gives life. 49Your ancestors ate the manna in the desert. But still they died. 50Here is the bread that comes down from heaven. If anyone eats this bread, he will never die. 51I am the living bread that came down from heaven. If anyone eats this bread, he will live forever. This bread is my flesh. I will give my flesh so that the people in the world may have life."

52Then the Jews began to argue among themselves. They said, "How can this man give us his flesh to eat?"

53Jesus said, "I tell you the truth. You must eat the flesh of the Son of Man. And you must drink his blood. If you don't do this, then you won't have real

---

6:31 'God gave . . . eat.' Quotation from Psalm 78:24.
6:45 'God . . . people.' Quotation from Isaiah 54:13.

life in you. ⁵⁴He who eats my flesh and drinks my blood has eternal life. I will raise him up on the last day. ⁵⁵My flesh is true food. My blood is true drink. ⁵⁶Whoever eats my flesh and drinks my blood lives in me, and I live in him. ⁵⁷The Father sent me. The Father lives, and I live because of the Father. So he who eats me will live because of me. ⁵⁸I am not like the bread our ancestors ate. They ate that bread, but still they died. I am the bread that came down from heaven. He who eats this bread will live forever." ⁵⁹Jesus said all these things while he was teaching in the synagogue in Capernaum.

THE WORDS OF ETERNAL LIFE

⁶⁰The followers of Jesus heard this. Many of them said, "This teaching is hard. Who can accept it?"

⁶¹Jesus knew that his followers were complaining about this. So he said, "Does this teaching bother you? ⁶²Then will it also bother you to see the Son of Man going back to the place where he came from? ⁶³It is not the flesh that gives a person life. It is the spirit that gives life. The words I told you are spirit, and so they give life. ⁶⁴But some of you don't believe." (Jesus knew who did not believe. He knew this from the beginning. And he knew who would turn against him.) ⁶⁵Jesus said, "That is the reason I said, 'If the Father does not let a person come to me, then he cannot come.'"

⁶⁶After Jesus said this, many of his followers left him. They stopped following him.

⁶⁷Jesus asked the 12 followers, "Do you want to leave, too?"

⁶⁸Simon Peter answered Jesus, "Lord, who would we go to? You have the words that give eternal life. ⁶⁹We believe in you. We know that you are the Holy One from God."

⁷⁰Then Jesus answered, "I chose all 12 of you. But 1 of you is a devil."

⁷¹Jesus was talking about Judas, the son of Simon Iscariot. Judas was 1 of the 12. But later he was going to turn against Jesus.

JESUS AND HIS BROTHERS

7 After this, Jesus traveled around Galilee. He did not want to travel in Judea, because the Jews there wanted to kill him. ²It was time for the Jewish Feast of Shelters. ³So Jesus' brothers said to him, "You should leave here and go to Judea. Then your followers there can see the miracles you do. ⁴Anyone who wants to be well known does not hide what he does. If you are doing these things, show yourself to the world." ⁵(Even Jesus' brothers did not believe in him.)

⁶Jesus said to his brothers, "The right time for me has not yet come. But any time is right for you. ⁷The world cannot hate you. But it hates me, because I tell about the evil things it does. ⁸So you go to the feast. I will not go now. The right time for me has not yet come." ⁹After saying this, Jesus stayed in Galilee.

¹⁰So Jesus' brothers left to go to the feast. When they had gone, Jesus went, too. But he did not let people see him. ¹¹At the feast the Jews were looking for him. They said, "Where is that man?"

¹²There was a large crowd of people there. Many of them were whispering to each other about Jesus. Some said, "He is a good man."

Others said, "No, he fools the people." ¹³But no one was brave enough to talk about Jesus openly. They were afraid of the Jews.

JESUS TEACHES AT THE FEAST

¹⁴The feast was about half over. Then Jesus went to the Temple and began to teach. ¹⁵The Jews were amazed. They said, "This man has never studied in school. How did he learn so much?"

¹⁶Jesus answered, "The things I teach are not my own. My teaching comes from him who sent me. ¹⁷If anyone chooses to do what God wants, then he will know that my teaching comes from God. He will know that this teaching is

not my own. [18]He who teaches his own ideas is trying to get honor for himself. But he who tries to bring honor to the one who sent him—that person speaks the truth. There is nothing false in him. [19]Moses gave you the law,[n] but none of you obey that law. Why are you trying to kill me?"

[20]The people answered, "A demon has come into you. We are not trying to kill you."

[21]Jesus said to them, "I did one miracle, and you are all amazed. [22]Moses gave you the law about circumcision. (But really Moses did not give you circumcision. Circumcision came from our ancestors.) And yet you circumcise a baby boy on a Sabbath day. [23]This shows that a baby boy can be circumcised on a Sabbath day to obey the law of Moses. So why are you angry at me for healing a person's whole body on the Sabbath day? [24]Stop judging by the way things look! Be fair, and judge by what is really right."

IS JESUS THE CHRIST?

[25]Then some of the people who lived in Jerusalem said, "This is the man they are trying to kill. [26]But he is teaching where everyone can see and hear him. And no one is trying to stop him. Maybe the leaders have decided that he really is the Christ. [27]But we know where this man is from. Yet when the real Christ comes, no one will know where he comes from."

[28]Jesus was still teaching in the Temple. He cried out, "Yes, you know me, and you know where I am from. But I have not come by my own authority. I was sent by the One who is true. You don't know him. [29]But I know him. I am from him, and he sent me."

[30]When Jesus said this, they tried to seize him. But no one was able to touch him. It was not yet the right time. [31]But many of the people believed in Jesus. They said, "When the Christ comes, will he do more miracles than this man has done?"

SOME LEADERS TRY TO ARREST JESUS

[32]The Pharisees heard the crowd whispering these things about Jesus. So the leading priests and the Pharisees sent some Temple guards to arrest him. [33]Then Jesus said, "I will be with you a little while longer. Then I will go back to the One who sent me. [34]You will look for me, but you will not find me. And you cannot come where I am."

[35]The Jews said to each other, "Where will this man go so we cannot find him? Will he go to the Greek cities where our people live? Will he teach the Greek people there? [36]This man says, 'You will look for me but you will not find me.' He also says, 'You cannot come where I am.' What does this mean?"

JESUS TALKS ABOUT THE SPIRIT

[37]The last day of the feast came. It was the most important day. On that day Jesus stood up and said in a loud voice, "If anyone is thirsty, let him come to me and drink. [38]If a person believes in me, rivers of living water will flow out from his heart. This is what the Scripture says." [39]Jesus was talking about the Holy Spirit. The Spirit had not yet been given because Jesus had not yet been raised to glory. But later, those who believed in Jesus would receive the Spirit.

THE PEOPLE ARGUE ABOUT JESUS

[40]The people heard these things that Jesus said. Some of them said, "This man really is the Prophet." [n]

[41]Others said, "He is the Christ."

Still others said, "The Christ will not come from Galilee. [42]The Scripture says that the Christ will come from David's family. And the Scripture says that the Christ will come from Bethlehem, the

---

7:19 law Moses gave God's people the law that God gave him on Mount Sinai (Exodus 34:29–32).
7:40 Prophet They probably meant the prophet that God told Moses he would send (Deuteronomy 18:15–19).

town where David lived." [43]So the people did not agree with each other about Jesus. [44]Some of them wanted to arrest him, but no one was able to touch him.

THE LEADERS WON'T BELIEVE

[45]The Temple guards went back to the leading priests and the Pharisees. The priests and the Pharisees asked, "Why didn't you bring Jesus?"

[46]The Temple guards answered, "The things he says are greater than the words of any man!"

[47]The Pharisees answered, "So Jesus has fooled you too! [48]Have any of the leaders or the Pharisees believed in him? No! [49]But those people, who know nothing about the law, are under God's curse!"

[50]But Nicodemus was there in that group. He was the one who had gone to see Jesus before.[n] Nicodemus said, [51]"Our law does not judge a man without hearing him. We cannot judge him until we know what he has done."

[52]They answered, "Are you from Galilee too? Study the Scriptures. You will learn that no prophet comes from Galilee."

[53]And everyone left and went home.[n]

THE WOMAN CAUGHT IN ADULTERY

8 Jesus went to the Mount of Olives. [2]But early in the morning he went back to the Temple. All the people came to Jesus, and he sat and taught them. [3]The teachers of the law and the Pharisees brought a woman there. She had been caught in adultery. They forced the woman to stand before the people. [4]They said to Jesus, "Teacher, this woman was caught having physical relations with a man who is not her husband. [5]The law of Moses commands that we kill with stones every woman who does this. What do you say we should do?" [6]They were asking this to trick Jesus so that they could have some charge against him.

But Jesus knelt down and started writing on the ground with his finger. [7]They continued to ask Jesus their question. So he stood up and said, "Is there anyone here who has never sinned? The person without sin can throw the first stone at this woman." [8]Then Jesus knelt down again and wrote on the ground.

[9]Those who heard Jesus began to leave one by one. The older men left first, and then the others. Jesus was left there alone with the woman. She was standing before him. [10]Jesus stood up again and asked her, "Woman, all of those people have gone. Has no one judged you guilty?"

[11]She answered, "No one has judged me, sir."

Then Jesus said, "So I also don't judge you. You may go now, but don't sin again."

> Jesus answered, "The things I teach are not my own. My teaching comes from him who sent me."
> —JOHN 7:16

JESUS IS THE LIGHT OF THE WORLD

[12]Later, Jesus talked to the people again. He said, "I am the light of the world. The person who follows me will never live in darkness. He will have the light that gives life."

[13]But the Pharisees said to Jesus, "When you talk about yourself, you are the only one to say these things are true. We cannot accept these things you say."

7:50 **But Nicodemus...before.** The story about Nicodemus going and talking to Jesus is in John 3:1–21.
7:53 Some of the earliest surviving Greek copies do not contain 7:53—8:11.

[14]Jesus answered, "Yes, I am saying these things about myself, but they are true. I know where I came from. And I know where I am going. You don't know where I came from or where I am going. [15]You judge me the way you would judge any man. I don't judge anyone. [16]But if I judge, I judge truthfully. When I judge, I am not alone. The Father who sent me is with me. [17]Your own law says that when two witnesses say the same thing, then you must accept what they say. [18]I am one of the witnesses who speaks about myself. And the Father who sent me is my other witness."

[19]They asked, "Where is your father?"

Jesus answered, "You don't know me or my Father. But if you knew me, then you would know my Father, too." [20]Jesus said these things while he was teaching in the Temple. He was near the place where the money that the people give is kept. But no one arrested him. The right time for Jesus had not yet come.

THE PEOPLE MISUNDERSTAND JESUS

[21]Again, Jesus said to the people, "I will leave you. You will look for me, but you

---

☆ John 8:12

Jesus said, "I am the light of the world." He told the people that anyone who follows him will never live in darkness. The people who follow Jesus "will have the light that gives life."

Have the lights ever gone out in your house at night during a storm? That can be kind of scary because you cannot see well. Your mom or dad probably got out a flashlight or lit some candles. The light chased the darkness away, and you could see things around you. Jesus came into the world to chase away things that make you afraid. He shines his light of love and forgiveness and makes everything better.

When you have Jesus in your heart, you don't have to be afraid or confused. He is a light inside you that makes everything clear.

will die in your sins. You cannot come where I am going."

²²So the Jews asked, "Will he kill himself? Is that why he said, 'You cannot come where I am going'?"

²³But Jesus said, "You people are from here below. But I am from above. You belong to this world, but I don't belong to this world. ²⁴So I told you that you would die in your sins. Yes, you will die in your sins if you don't believe that I am he."

²⁵They asked, "Then who are you?"

Jesus answered, "I am what I have told you from the beginning. ²⁶I have many things to say about you and to judge you for. But I tell people only the things I have heard from the One who sent me. And he speaks the truth."

²⁷The people did not understand that Jesus was talking to them about the Father. ²⁸So Jesus said to them, "You will lift up the Son of Man. Then you will know that I am he. You will know that these things I do are not by my own authority. You will know that I say only what the Father has taught me. ²⁹The One who sent me is with me. I always do what is pleasing to him. So he has not left me alone." ³⁰While Jesus was saying these things, many people believed in him.

FREEDOM FROM SIN

³¹So Jesus said to the Jews who believed in him, "If you continue to obey my teaching, you are truly my followers. ³²Then you will know the truth. And the truth will make you free."

³³They answered, "We are Abraham's children. And we have never been slaves. So why do you say that we will be free?"

³⁴Jesus answered, "I tell you the truth. Everyone who lives in sin is a slave to sin. ³⁵A slave does not stay with a family forever, but a son belongs to the family forever. ³⁶So if the Son makes you free, then you will be truly free. ³⁷I

know you are Abraham's children. But you want to kill me because you don't accept my teaching. ³⁸I am telling you what my Father has shown me. But you do what your father has told you."

³⁹They answered, "Our father is Abraham."

Jesus said, "If you were really Abraham's children, you would do[n] the things that Abraham did. ⁴⁰I am a man who has told you the truth which I heard from God. But you are trying to kill me. Abraham did nothing like that. ⁴¹So you are doing the things that your own father did."

But they said, "We are not like children who never knew who their father was. God is our Father. He is the only Father we have."

⁴²Jesus said to them, "If God were really your Father, you would love me. I came from God and now I am here. I did not come by my own authority. God sent me. ⁴³You don't understand what I say because you cannot accept my teaching. ⁴⁴Your father is the devil. You belong to him and want to do what he wants. He was a murderer from the beginning. He was against the truth, for there is no truth in him. He is a liar, and he is like the lies he tells. He is the father of lies. ⁴⁵But I speak the truth. That is why you don't believe me. ⁴⁶Can any of you prove that I am guilty of sin? If I am telling the truth, why don't you believe me? ⁴⁷He who belongs to God accepts what God says. But you don't accept what God says, because you don't belong to God."

JESUS AND ABRAHAM

⁴⁸The Jews answered, "We say you are a Samaritan! We say a demon has come into you. Are we not right?"

⁴⁹Jesus answered, "I have no demon in me. I give honor to my Father, but you dishonor me. ⁵⁰I am not trying to get honor for myself. There is One who wants this honor for me, and he is the

---

8:39 **If...do** Some Greek copies read "If you are really Abraham's children, you will do."

judge. [51]I tell you the truth. If anyone obeys my teaching, he will never die."

[52]The Jews said to Jesus, "Now we know that you have a demon in you! Even Abraham and the prophets died. But you say, 'Whoever obeys my teaching will never die.' [53]Do you think that you are greater than our father Abraham? Abraham died. And the prophets died, too. Who do you think you are?"

[54]Jesus answered, "If I give honor to myself, that honor is worth nothing. The One who gives me honor is my Father. And you say that he is your God. [55]But you don't really know him. I know him. If I said I did not know him, then I would be a liar as you are liars. But I do know him, and I obey what he says. [56]Your father Abraham was very happy that he would see my day. He saw that day and was glad."

[57]The Jews said to him, "What? You have never seen Abraham! You are not even 50 years old!"

[58]Jesus answered, "I tell you the truth. Before Abraham was born, I am!" [59]When Jesus said this, the people picked up stones to throw at him. But Jesus hid himself, and then he left the Temple.

JESUS HEALS A MAN BORN BLIND

9 As Jesus was walking along, he saw a man who had been born blind. [2]His followers asked him, "Teacher, whose sin caused this man to be born blind—his own sin or his parents' sin?"

[3]Jesus answered, "It is not this man's sin or his parents' sin that made him blind. This man was born blind so that God's power could be shown in him. [4]While it is daytime, we must continue doing the work of the One who sent me. The night is coming. And no one can work at night. [5]While I am in the world, I am the light of the world."

[6]After Jesus said this, he spit on the ground and made some mud with it. He put the mud on the man's eyes. [7]Then he told the man, "Go and wash

in the Pool of Siloam." (Siloam means Sent.) So the man went to the pool. He washed and came back. And he was able to see.

[8]Some people had seen this man begging before. They and the man's neighbors said, "Look! Is this the same man who always sits and begs?"

[9]Some said, "Yes! He is the one." But others said, "No, he's not the same man. He only looks like him."

So the man himself said, "I am the man."

[10]They asked, "What happened? How did you get your sight?"

[11]He answered, "The man named Jesus made some mud and put it on my eyes. Then he told me to go to Siloam and wash. So I went and washed and came back seeing."

[12]They asked him, "Where is this man?"

The man answered, "I don't know."

PHARISEES QUESTION THE HEALING

[13]Then the people took to the Pharisees the man who had been blind. [14]The day Jesus had made mud and healed his eyes was a Sabbath day. [15]So now the Pharisees asked the man, "How did you get your sight?"

He answered, "He put mud on my eyes. I washed, and now I can see."

[16]Some of the Pharisees were saying, "This man does not keep the Sabbath day. He is not from God!"

Others said, "But a man who is a sinner can't do miracles like these." So they could not agree with each other.

[17]They asked the man again, "What do you say about him? It was your eyes he opened."

The man answered, "He is a prophet."

[18]The Jews did not believe that he had been blind and could now see again. So they sent for the man's parents [19]and asked them, "Is this your son? You say that he was born blind. Then how does he see now?"

[20]His parents answered, "We know

that this is our son, and we know that he was born blind. ²¹But we don't know how he can see now. We don't know who opened his eyes. Ask him. He is old enough to answer for himself." ²²His parents said this because they were afraid of the Jews. The Jews had already decided that anyone who said that Jesus was the Christ would be put out of the synagogue. ²³That is why his parents said, "He is old enough. Ask him."

²⁴So for the second time, they called the man who had been blind. They said, "You should give God the glory by telling the truth. We know that this man is a sinner."

²⁵He answered, "I don't know if he is a sinner. But one thing I do know. I was blind, and now I can see."

²⁶They asked, "What did he do to you? How did he make you see again?"

²⁷He answered, "I have already told you that. But you would not listen to me. Why do you want to hear it again? Do you want to become his followers, too?"

²⁸Then they insulted him and said, "You are his follower. We are followers of Moses. ²⁹We know that God spoke to Moses. But we don't even know where this man comes from!"

³⁰The man answered, "This is a very strange thing. You don't know where he comes from, and yet he opened my eyes. ³¹We all know that God does not listen to sinners. But God listens to anyone who worships and obeys him. ³²Nobody has ever heard of anyone giving sight to a man born blind. ³³If this man were not from God, he could do nothing."

³⁴They answered, "You were born full of sin! Are you trying to teach us?" And they threw the man out.

SPIRITUAL BLINDNESS

³⁵Jesus heard that they had thrown him out. So Jesus found him and said, "Do you believe in the Son of Man?"

³⁶He asked, "Who is the Son of Man, sir? Tell me, so I can believe in him!"

³⁷Jesus said to him, "You have already seen him. The Son of Man is the one talking with you now."

³⁸He said, "Yes, Lord, I believe!" Then the man bowed and worshiped Jesus.

³⁹Jesus said, "I came into this world so that the world could be judged. I came so that the blind[n] could see and so that those who see will become blind."

⁴⁰Some of the Pharisees were near Jesus. When they heard him say this, they asked, "What? Are you saying that we are blind, too?"

⁴¹Jesus said, "If you were really blind, you would not be guilty of sin. But now that you say you can see, your guilt remains."

THE SHEPHERD AND HIS SHEEP

10 Jesus said, "I tell you the truth. The man who does not enter the sheepfold by the door, but climbs in some other way, is a thief and a robber. ²The one who enters by the door is the shepherd of the sheep. ³The man who guards the door opens it for him. And the sheep listen to the voice of the shepherd. He calls his own sheep, using their names, and he leads them out. ⁴He brings all of his sheep out. Then he goes ahead of them and leads them. They follow him because they know his voice. ⁵But they will never follow a stranger. They will run away from him because they don't know his voice." ⁶Jesus told the people this story, but they did not understand what it meant.

JESUS IS THE GOOD SHEPHERD

⁷So Jesus said again, "I tell you the truth. I am the door for the sheep. ⁸All the people who came before me were thieves and robbers. The sheep did not listen to them. ⁹I am the door. The person who enters through me will be saved. He will be able to come in and go out and find pasture. ¹⁰A thief comes to

---

9:39 **blind** Jesus is talking about people who are spiritually blind, not physically blind.

steal and kill and destroy. But I came to give life—life in all its fullness.

[11]"I am the good shepherd. The good shepherd gives his life for the sheep. [12]The worker who is paid to keep the sheep is different from the shepherd who owns them. So when the worker sees a wolf coming, he runs away and leaves the sheep alone. Then the wolf attacks the sheep and scatters them. [13]The man runs away because he is only a paid worker. He does not really care for the sheep.

[14]"I am the good shepherd. I know my sheep, and my sheep know me, [15]just as the Father knows me, and I know the Father. I give my life for the sheep. [16]I have other sheep that are not in this flock here. I must bring them also. They will listen to my voice, and there will be one flock and one shepherd. [17]The Father loves me because I give my life. I give my life so that I can take it back again. [18]No one takes it away from me. I give my own life freely. I have the right to give my life, and I have the right to take it back. This is what my Father commanded me to do."

[19]Again the Jews did not agree with each other because of these words Jesus said. [20]Many of them said, "A demon has come into him and made him crazy. Why listen to him?"

[21]But others said, "A man who is crazy with a demon does not say things like this. Can a demon open the eyes of the blind?"

[22]The time came for the Feast of Dedication at Jerusalem. This was during the winter. [23]Jesus was walking in the Temple in Solomon's Porch. [24]The Jews gathered around him and said, "How long will you make us wonder about you? If you are the Christ, then tell us plainly."

JESUS IS THE SON OF GOD

[25]Jesus answered, "I told you already, but you did not believe. I do miracles in my Father's name. Those miracles show who I am. [26]But you don't believe because you are not my sheep. [27]My sheep listen to my voice. I know them, and they follow me. [28]I give them eternal life, and they will never die. And no person can steal them out of my hand. [29]My Father gave my sheep to me. He is greater than all, and no person can steal my sheep out of my Father's hand. [30]The Father and I are one."

[31]Again the Jews picked up stones to kill Jesus. [32]But Jesus said to them, "I have done many good works from the Father. Which of these good works are you killing me for?"

[33]The Jews answered, "We are not killing you for any good work you did. But you say things that are against God. You are only a man, but you say you are the same as God!"

[34]Jesus answered, "It is written in your law that God said, 'I have said you are gods!' [n] [35]This Scripture called those people gods, the people who received God's message. And Scripture is always true. [36]So why do you say that I speak against God because I said, 'I am God's Son'? I am the one God chose and sent into the world. [37]If I don't do what my Father does, then don't believe me. [38]But if I do what my Father does, even though you don't believe in me, believe what I do. Then you will know and understand that the Father is in me and I am in the Father."

> My sheep listen to my voice. I know them, and they follow me . . . No person can steal them out of my hand.
>
> –JOHN 10:27–28

10:34 'I . . . gods.' Quotation from Psalm 82:6.

³⁹They tried to take Jesus again, but he escaped from them.

⁴⁰Then Jesus went back across the Jordan River to the place where John had first baptized. Jesus stayed there, ⁴¹and many people came to him. They said, "John never did a miracle. But everything John said about this man is true." ⁴²And in that place many believed in Jesus.

THE DEATH OF LAZARUS

11 There was a man named Lazarus who was sick. He lived in the town of Bethany, where Mary and her sister Martha lived. ²Mary is the woman who later put perfume on the Lord and wiped his feet with her hair. Mary's brother was Lazarus, the man who was now sick. ³So Mary and Martha sent someone to tell Jesus, "Lord, the one you love is sick."

⁴When Jesus heard this he said, "This sickness will not end in death. It is for the glory of God. This has happened to bring glory to the Son of God." ⁵Jesus loved Martha and her sister and Lazarus. ⁶But when he heard that Lazarus was sick, he stayed where he was for two more days. ⁷Then Jesus said to his followers, "Let us go back to Judea."

⁸The followers said, "But Teacher, the Jews there tried to kill you with stones. That was only a short time ago. Now you want to go back there?"

⁹Jesus answered, "Are there not 12 hours in the day? If anyone walks in the daylight, he will not stumble because he can see by this world's light. ¹⁰But if anyone walks at night he stumbles because there is no light to help him see."

¹¹After Jesus said this, he added, "Our friend Lazarus has fallen asleep. But I am going there to wake him."

¹²The followers said, "But Lord, if he can sleep, he will get well."

¹³Jesus meant that Lazarus was dead. But Jesus' followers thought that he meant Lazarus was really sleeping. ¹⁴So then Jesus said plainly, "Lazarus is dead. ¹⁵And I am glad for your sakes that I was not there so that you may believe. But let us go to him now."

¹⁶Then Thomas (the one called Didymus) said to the other followers, "Let us go, too. We will die with him."

JESUS IN BETHANY

¹⁷Jesus arrived in Bethany. There he learned that Lazarus had already been dead and in the tomb for four days. ¹⁸Bethany was about two miles from Jerusalem. ¹⁹Many Jews had come there to comfort Martha and Mary about their brother.

²⁰Martha heard that Jesus was coming, and she went out to meet him. But Mary stayed at home. ²¹Martha said to Jesus, "Lord, if you had been here, my brother would not have died. ²²But I know that even now God will give you anything you ask."

²³Jesus said, "Your brother will rise and live again."

²⁴Martha answered, "I know that he will rise and live again in the resurrection^n on the last day."

²⁵Jesus said to her, "I am the resurrection and the life. He who believes in me will have life even if he dies. ²⁶And he who lives and believes in me will never die. Martha, do you believe this?"

²⁷Martha answered, "Yes, Lord. I believe that you are the Christ, the Son of God. You are the One who was coming to the world."

JESUS CRIES

²⁸After Martha said this, she went back to her sister Mary. She talked to Mary alone. Martha said, "The Teacher is here and he is asking for you." ²⁹When Mary heard this, she got up quickly and went to Jesus. ³⁰Jesus had not yet come into the town. He was still at the place where Martha had met him. ³¹The Jews

11:24 resurrection Being raised from death to live again.

were with Mary in the house, comforting her. They saw Mary stand and leave quickly. They followed her, thinking that she was going to the tomb to cry there. ³²But Mary went to the place where Jesus was. When she saw him, she fell at his feet and said, "Lord, if you had been here, my brother would not have died."

³³Jesus saw that Mary was crying and that the Jews who came with her were crying, too. Jesus felt very sad in his heart and was deeply troubled. ³⁴He asked, "Where did you bury him?"

"Come and see, Lord," they said.

³⁵Jesus cried.

³⁶So the Jews said, "See how much he loved him."

³⁷But some of them said, "If Jesus healed the eyes of the blind man, why didn't he keep Lazarus from dying?"

JESUS RAISES LAZARUS

³⁸Again Jesus felt very sad in his heart. He came to the tomb. The tomb was a cave with a large stone covering the entrance. ³⁹Jesus said, "Move the stone away."

Martha said, "But, Lord, it has been four days since he died. There will be a bad smell." Martha was the sister of the dead man.

⁴⁰Then Jesus said to her, "Didn't I tell you that if you believed, you would see the glory of God?"

⁴¹So they moved the stone away from the entrance. Then Jesus looked up and said, "Father, I thank you that you heard me. ⁴²I know that you always hear me. But I said these things because of the people here around me. I want them to believe that you sent me." ⁴³After Jesus said this, he cried out in a loud voice, "Lazarus, come out!" ⁴⁴The dead man came out. His hands and feet were wrapped with pieces of cloth, and he had a cloth around his face.

Jesus said to them, "Take the cloth off of him and let him go."

THE LEADERS PLAN TO KILL JESUS

⁴⁵There were many Jews who had come to visit Mary. They saw what Jesus did. And many of them believed in him. ⁴⁶But some of them went to the Pharisees. They told the Pharisees what Jesus had done. ⁴⁷Then the leading priests and Pharisees called a meeting of the Jewish council. They asked, "What should we do? This man is doing many miracles. ⁴⁸If we let him continue doing these things, everyone will believe in him. Then the Romans will come and take away our Temple and our nation."

⁴⁹One of the men there was Caiaphas. He was the high priest that year. Caiaphas said, "You people know nothing! ⁵⁰It is better for one man to die for the people than for the whole nation to be destroyed. But you don't realize this."

⁵¹Caiaphas did not think of this himself. He was high priest that year. So he was really prophesying that Jesus would die for the Jewish nation ⁵²and for God's scattered children. This would bring them all together and make them one.

⁵³That day they started planning to kill Jesus. ⁵⁴So Jesus no longer traveled openly among the Jews. He left there and went to a place near the desert. He went to a town called Ephraim and stayed there with his followers.

⁵⁵It was almost time for the Jewish Passover Feast. Many from the country went up to Jerusalem before the Passover. They went to do the special things to make themselves pure. ⁵⁶The people looked for Jesus. They stood in the Temple and were asking each other, "Is he coming to the Feast? What do you think?" ⁵⁷But the leading priests and the Pharisees had given orders about Jesus. They said that if anyone knew where Jesus was, he must tell them. Then they could arrest Jesus.

JESUS WITH FRIENDS IN BETHANY

12 Six days before the Passover Feast, Jesus went to Bethany, where Lazarus lived. (Lazarus is the man Jesus raised from death.) ²There they had a dinner for Jesus. Martha served the food. Lazarus was one of the people eating with Jesus. ³Mary brought in a pint of very expensive perfume made from pure nard. She poured the perfume on Jesus' feet, and then she wiped his feet with her hair. And the sweet smell from the perfume filled the whole house.

⁴Judas Iscariot, one of Jesus' followers, was there. (He was the one who would later turn against Jesus.) Judas said, ⁵"This perfume was worth an entire year's wages. It should have been sold and the money given to the poor." ⁶But Judas did not really care about the poor. He said this because he was a thief. He was the one who kept the money box, and he often stole money from it.

⁷Jesus answered, "Let her alone. It was right for her to save this perfume for today—the day for me to be prepared for burial. ⁸The poor will always be with you, but you will not always have me."

THE PLOT AGAINST LAZARUS

⁹A large crowd of Jews heard that Jesus was in Bethany. So they went there to see not only Jesus but also Lazarus. Lazarus was the one Jesus raised from death. ¹⁰So the leading priests made plans to kill Lazarus, too. ¹¹Because of Lazarus many Jews were leaving them and believing in Jesus.

JESUS ENTERS JERUSALEM

¹²The next day a great crowd in Jerusalem heard that Jesus was coming there. These were the people who had come to the Passover Feast. ¹³They took branches of palm trees and went out to meet Jesus. They shouted,

"Praise* God!
God bless the One who comes in the name of the Lord!

God bless the King of Israel!"
Psalm 118:25–26

¹⁴Jesus found a colt and sat on it. This was as the Scripture says,

¹⁵ "Don't be afraid, people of Jerusalem!
Your king is coming.
He is sitting on the colt of a
donkey." *Zechariah 9:9*

¹⁶The followers of Jesus did not understand this at first. But after Jesus was raised to glory, they remembered that this had been written about him. And they remembered that they had done these things to him.

PEOPLE TELL ABOUT JESUS

¹⁷There had been many people with Jesus when he raised Lazarus from death and told him to come out of the tomb. Now they were telling others about what Jesus did. ¹⁸Many people went out to meet Jesus, because they had heard about this miracle. ¹⁹So the Pharisees said to each other, "You can see that nothing is going right for us. Look! The whole world is following him."

JESUS TALKS ABOUT HIS DEATH

²⁰There were some Greek people, too, who came to Jerusalem to worship at the Passover Feast. ²¹They went to Philip. (Philip was from Bethsaida, in Galilee.) They said, "Sir, we would like to see Jesus." ²²Philip told Andrew. Then Andrew and Philip told Jesus.

²³Jesus said to them, "The time has come for the Son of Man to receive his glory. ²⁴I tell you the truth. A grain of wheat must fall to the ground and die. Then it makes many seeds. But if it never dies, it remains only a single seed. ²⁵The person who loves his life will give up true life. But the person who hates his life in this world will keep true life

---

12:13 Praise Literally, "Hosanna," a Hebrew word used at first in praying to God for help, but at this time it was probably a shout of joy used in praising God or his Messiah.

forever. ²⁶Whoever serves me must follow me. Then my servant will be with me everywhere I am. My Father will honor anyone who serves me.

²⁷"Now I am very troubled. What should I say? Should I say, 'Father, save me from this time'? No, I came to this time so that I could suffer. ²⁸Father, bring glory to your name!"

Then a voice came from heaven, "I have brought glory to it, and I will do it again."

²⁹The crowd standing there heard the voice. They said it was thunder.

But others said, "An angel has spoken to him."

³⁰Jesus said, "That voice was for you, not for me. ³¹Now is the time for the world to be judged. Now the ruler of this world will be thrown down. ³²I will be lifted up from the earth. And when this happens, I will draw all people toward me." ³³Jesus said this to show how he would die.

³⁴The crowd said, "We have heard from the law that the Christ will live forever. So why do you say, 'The Son of Man must be lifted up'? Who is this 'Son of Man'?"

³⁵Then Jesus said, "The light will be with you for a little longer. So walk while you have the light. Then the darkness will not catch you. He who walks in the darkness does not know where he is going. ³⁶So believe in the light while you still have it. Then you will become sons of light." When Jesus had said this, he left and hid himself from them.

SOME DON'T BELIEVE IN JESUS

³⁷Though Jesus had done many miracles before the people, they still did not believe in him. ³⁸This was to make clear the full meaning of what Isaiah the prophet said:

"Lord, who believed the things we told them?
    Who has seen the Lord's power?"
                              Isaiah 53:1

³⁹This is why the people could not believe: Isaiah also said,

⁴⁰ "He has blinded their eyes.
    He has closed their minds.
    This is so that they will not see with their eyes
        nor understand in their minds.
    This is so they will not
        come back to me and be forgiven."
                              Isaiah 6:10

⁴¹Isaiah said this because he saw Jesus' glory and spoke about him.

⁴²But many people believed in Jesus, even many of the leaders. But because of the Pharisees, they did not say that they believed in him. They were afraid that they would be put out of the synagogue. ⁴³They loved praise from men more than praise from God.

⁴⁴Then Jesus cried out, "He who believes in me is really believing in the One who sent me. ⁴⁵He who sees me sees the One who sent me. ⁴⁶I have come as light into the world. I came so that whoever believes in me would not stay in darkness.

⁴⁷"If anyone hears my words and does not obey them, I do not judge him. For I did not come to judge the world, but to save the world. ⁴⁸There is a judge for the one who refuses to believe in me and does not accept my words. The word I have taught will be his judge on the last day. ⁴⁹The things I taught were not from myself. The Father who sent me told me what to say and what to teach. ⁵⁰And I know that eternal life comes from what the Father commands. So whatever I say is what the Father told me to say."

JESUS WASHES HIS FOLLOWERS' FEET

13 It was almost time for the Jewish Passover Feast. Jesus knew that it was time for him to leave this world and go back to the Father. He had always loved those who were his own in the world, and he loved them all the way to the end.

[2]Jesus and his followers were at the evening meal. The devil had already persuaded Judas Iscariot to turn against Jesus. (Judas was the son of Simon.) [3]Jesus knew that the Father had given him power over everything. He also knew that he had come from God and was going back to God. [4]So during the meal Jesus stood up and took off his outer clothing. Taking a towel, he wrapped it around his waist. [5]Then he poured water into a bowl and began to wash the followers' feet. He dried them with the towel that was wrapped around him.

[6]Jesus came to Simon Peter. But Peter said to Jesus, "Lord, are you going to wash my feet?"

[7]Jesus answered, "You don't understand what I am doing now. But you will understand later."

[8]Peter said, "No! You will never wash my feet."

Jesus answered, "If I don't wash your feet, then you are not one of my people."

[9]Simon Peter answered, "Lord, after you wash my feet, wash my hands and my head, too!"

[10]Jesus said, "After a person has had a bath, his whole body is clean. He needs only to wash his feet. And you men are clean, but not all of you." [11]Jesus knew who would turn against him. That is why Jesus said, "Not all of you are clean."

[12]When he had finished washing their feet, he put on his clothes and sat down again. Jesus asked, "Do you understand what I have just done for you? [13]You call me 'Teacher' and 'Lord.'

And this is right, because that is what I am. [14]I, your Lord and Teacher, have washed your feet. So you also should wash each other's feet. [15]I did this as an example for you. So you should do as I have done for you. [16]I tell you the truth. A servant is not greater than his master. A messenger is not greater than the one who sent him. [17]If you know these things, you will be happy if you do them.

[18]"I am not talking about all of you. I know those I have chosen. But what the Scripture said must happen: 'The man who ate at my table has now turned against me.'[n] [19]I am telling you this now before it happens. Then when it happens you will believe that I am he. [20]I tell you the truth. Whoever accepts anyone I send also accepts me. And whoever accepts me also accepts the One who sent me."

JESUS TALKS ABOUT HIS DEATH

[21]After Jesus said this, he was very troubled. He said openly, "I tell you the truth. One of you will turn against me."

[22]The followers all looked at each other. They did not know whom Jesus was talking about. [23]One of the followers was sitting[n] next to Jesus. This was the follower Jesus loved. [24]Simon Peter made signs to him to ask Jesus who it was that he was talking about.

[25]That follower leaned closer to Jesus and asked, "Lord, who is it that will turn against you?"

[26]Jesus answered, "I will dip this bread into the dish. The man I give it to is the man who will turn against

> Then Jesus cried out, "He who believes in me is really believing in the One who sent me."
>
> –JOHN 12:44

13:18 'The man...me.' Quotation from Psalm 41:9.
13:23 sitting Literally, "lying." The people of that time ate lying down and leaning on one arm.

me." So Jesus took a piece of bread. He dipped it and gave it to Judas Iscariot, the son of Simon. [27]As soon as Judas took the bread, Satan entered him. Jesus said to Judas, "The thing that you will do—do it quickly!" [28]None of the men at the table understood why Jesus said this to Judas. [29]He was the one who kept the money box. So some of the followers thought that Jesus was telling Judas to buy what was needed for the feast. Or they thought that Jesus wanted Judas to give something to the poor.

[30]Judas accepted the bread Jesus gave him and immediately went out. It was night.

[31]When Judas was gone, Jesus said, "Now the Son of Man receives his glory. And God receives glory through him. [32]If God receives glory through him,[n] then God will give glory to the Son through himself. And God will give him glory quickly."

[33]Jesus said, "My children, I will be with you only a little longer. You will look for me. And what I told the Jews, I tell you now: Where I am going you cannot come.

[34]"I give you a new command: Love each other. You must love each other as I have loved you. [35]All people will know that you are my followers if you love each other."

PETER WILL SAY HE DOESN'T KNOW JESUS

[36]Simon Peter asked Jesus, "Lord, where are you going?"

Jesus answered, "Where I am going you cannot follow now. But you will follow later."

[37]Peter asked, "Lord, why can't I follow you now? I am ready to die for you!"

[38]Jesus answered, "Will you really die for me? I tell you the truth. Before the rooster crows, you will say three times that you don't know me."

JESUS COMFORTS HIS FOLLOWERS

14 Jesus said, "Don't let your hearts be troubled. Trust in God. And trust in me. [2]There are many rooms in my Father's house. I would not tell you this if it were not true. I am going there to prepare a place for you. [3]After I go and prepare a place for you, I will come back. Then I will take you to be with me so that you may be where I am. [4]You know the way to the place where I am going."[n]

[5]Thomas said to Jesus, "Lord, we don't know where you are going. So how can we know the way?"

[6]Jesus answered, "I am the way. And I am the truth and the life. The only way to the Father is through me. [7]If you really knew me, then you would know my Father, too. But now you do know him, and you have seen him."

[8]Philip said to him, "Lord, show us the Father. That is all we need."

[9]Jesus answered, "I have been with you a long time now. Do you still not know me, Philip? He who has seen me has seen the Father. So why do you say, 'Show us the Father'? [10]Don't you believe that I am in the Father and the Father is in me? The words I say to you don't come from me. The Father lives in me, and he is doing his own work. [11]Believe me when I say that I am in the Father and the Father is in me. Or believe because of the miracles I have done. [12]I tell you the truth. He who believes in me will do the same things that I do. He will do even greater things than these because I am going to the Father. [13]And if you ask for anything in my name, I will do it for you. Then the Father's glory will be shown through the Son. [14]If you ask me for anything in my name, I will do it.

THE PROMISE OF THE HOLY SPIRIT

[15]"If you love me, you will do the things I command. [16]I will ask the Father, and

---

13:32 If . . . him Some Greek copies do not have this phrase.
14:4 You . . . going. Some Greek copies read "You know where I am going and the way to the place I am going."

he will give you another Helper.ⁿ He will give you this Helper to be with you forever. ¹⁷The Helper is the Spirit of truth. The world cannot accept him because it does not see him or know him. But you know him. He lives with you and he will be in you.

¹⁸"I will not leave you all alone like orphans. I will come back to you. ¹⁹In a little while the world will not see me anymore, but you will see me. Because I live, you will live, too. ²⁰On that day you will know that I am in my Father. You will know that you are in me and I am in you. ²¹He who knows my commands and obeys them is the one who loves me. And my Father will love him who loves me. I will love him and will show myself to him."

²²Then Judas (not Judas Iscariot) said, "But, Lord, why do you plan to show yourself to us, but not to the world?"

²³Jesus answered, "If anyone loves me, then he will obey my teaching. My Father will love him, and we will come to him and make our home with him. ²⁴He who does not love me does not obey my teaching. This teaching that you hear is not really mine. It is from my Father, who sent me.

14:16 **Helper** "Counselor," or "Comforter." Jesus is talking about the Holy Spirit.

⭐ John 14:15–17

Jesus promised his followers that God his Father would send the Helper to be with us forever. He is also called the Spirit of truth. He is the part of Jesus that lives in our hearts.

Jesus was not going to be on the earth much longer. He wanted his disciples to enjoy spending time with him. And he wanted them to know that even after he was gone, he would be with them. Jesus is always with us. We can talk to him anytime. His love makes us feel warm and happy. When we feel Jesus' love, it overflows. And others can see his love too!

· · · · · · · · · · · · · · · · · · ·

Remember, God is always with you. The Spirit of truth—God's Spirit—is there. He is your Helper and best friend.

²⁵"I have told you all these things while I am with you. ²⁶But the Helper will teach you everything. He will cause you to remember all the things I told you. This Helper is the Holy Spirit whom the Father will send in my name.

²⁷"I leave you peace. My peace I give you. I do not give it to you as the world does. So don't let your hearts be troubled. Don't be afraid. ²⁸You heard me say to you, 'I am going, but I am coming back to you.' If you loved me, you should be happy that I am going back to the Father because he is greater than I am. ²⁹I have told you this now, before it happens. Then when it happens, you will believe. ³⁰I will not talk with you much longer. The ruler of this world is coming. He has no power over me. ³¹But the world must know that I love the Father. So I do exactly what the Father told me to do.

"Come now, let us go.

JESUS IS LIKE A VINE

15 "I am the true vine; my Father is the gardener. ²He cuts off every branch of mine that does not produce fruit. And he trims and cleans every branch that produces fruit so that it will produce even more fruit. ³You are already clean because of the words I have spoken to you. ⁴Remain in me, and I will remain in you. No branch can produce fruit alone. It must remain in the vine. It is the same with you. You cannot produce fruit alone. You must remain in me.

⁵"I am the vine, and you are the branches. If a person remains in me and I remain in him, then he produces much fruit. But without me he can do nothing. ⁶If anyone does not remain in me, then he is like a branch that is thrown away. That branch dies. People pick up dead branches, throw them into the fire, and burn them. ⁷Remain in me and follow my teachings. If you do this, then you can ask for anything you want, and it will be given to you. ⁸You should produce much fruit and show that you are my followers. This brings glory to my Father. ⁹I loved you as the Father loved me. Now remain in my love. ¹⁰I have obeyed my Father's commands, and I remain in his love. In the same way, if you obey my commands, you will remain in my love. ¹¹I have told you these things so that you can have the same joy I have. I want your joy to be the fullest joy.

¹²"This is my command: Love each other as I have loved you. ¹³The greatest love a person can show is to die for his friends. ¹⁴You are my friends if you do what I command you. ¹⁵I don't call you servants now. A servant does not know what his master is doing. But now I call you friends because I have made known to you everything I heard from my Father. ¹⁶You did not choose me; I chose you. And I gave you this work, to go and produce fruit. I want you to produce fruit that will last. Then the Father will give you anything you ask for in my name. ¹⁷This is my command: Love each other.

JESUS WARNS HIS FOLLOWERS

¹⁸"If the world hates you, remember that it hated me first. ¹⁹If you belonged to the world, then it would love you as it loves its own. But I have chosen you out of the world. So you don't belong to it. That is why the world hates you. ²⁰Remember what I told you: A servant is not greater than his master. If people did wrong to me, they will do wrong to you, too. And if they obeyed my teaching, they will obey yours, too. ²¹They will do all this to you because of me. They don't know the One who sent me. ²²If I had not come and spoken to them, they would not be guilty of sin. But now they have no excuse for their sin. ²³He who hates me also hates my Father. ²⁴I did works among them that no one else has ever done. If I had not done those works, they would not be guilty of sin. But now they have seen what I did, and yet they have hated both me and my Father. ²⁵But this

happened so that what is written in their law would be true: 'They hated me for no reason.'[n]

²⁶"I will send you the Helper[n] from the Father. He is the Spirit of truth who comes from the Father. When he comes, he will tell about me. ²⁷And you also must tell people about me because you have been with me from the beginning.

16 "I have told you these things to keep you from giving up. ²People will put you out of their synagogues. Yes, the time is coming when whoever kills you will think that he is offering service to God. ³They will do this because they have not known the Father and they have not known me. ⁴I have told you these things now. So when the time comes, you will remember that I warned you.

THE WORK OF THE HOLY SPIRIT

"I did not tell you these things at the beginning, because I was with you then. ⁵Now I am going back to the One who sent me. But none of you asks me, 'Where are you going?' ⁶Your hearts are filled with sadness because I have told you these things. ⁷But I tell you the truth. It is better for you that I go away. When I go away I will send the Helper[n] to you. If I do not go away, then the Helper will not come. ⁸When the Helper comes, he will prove to the people of the world the truth about sin, about being right with God, and about judgment. ⁹He will prove to them about sin, because they don't believe in me. ¹⁰He will prove to them that I am right with God, because I am going to the Father. You will not see me anymore. ¹¹And the Helper will prove to them the truth about judgment, because the ruler of this world is already judged.

¹²"I have many more things to say to you, but they are too much for you now.

¹³But when the Spirit of truth comes he will lead you into all truth. He will not speak his own words. He will speak only what he hears and will tell you what is to come. ¹⁴The Spirit of truth will bring glory to me. He will take what I have to say and tell it to you. ¹⁵All that the Father has is mine. That is why I said that the Spirit will take what I have to say and tell it to you.

SADNESS WILL BECOME HAPPINESS

¹⁶"After a little while you will not see me. And then after a little while you will see me again."

¹⁷Some of the followers said to each other, "What does Jesus mean when he says, 'After a little while you will not see me, and then after a little while you will see me again'? And what does he mean when he says, 'Because I am going to the Father'?" ¹⁸They also asked, "What does he mean by 'a little while'? We don't understand what he is saying."

¹⁹Jesus saw that the followers wanted to ask him about this. So Jesus said to the followers, "Are you asking each other what I meant when I said, 'After a little while you will not see me. And then after a little while you will see me again'? ²⁰I tell you the truth. You will cry and be sad, but the world will be happy. You will be sad, but your sadness will become joy. ²¹When a woman gives birth to a baby, she has pain, because her time has come. But when her baby is born, she forgets the pain. She forgets because she is so happy that a child has been born into the world. ²²It is the same with you. Now you are sad. But I will see you again and you will be happy. And no one will take away your joy. ²³In that day you will not ask me for anything. I tell you the truth. My Father will give you anything you ask for in my name. ²⁴You have never asked for anything in my name. Ask and you will

---

15:25 'They . . . reason.' These words could be from Psalm 35:19 or Psalm 69:4.
15:26; 16:7 Helper "Counselor," or "Comforter." Jesus is talking about the Holy Spirit.

receive. And your joy will be the fullest joy.

VICTORY OVER THE WORLD

²⁵"I have told you these things, using words that hide the meaning. But the time will come when I will not use words like that to tell you things. I will speak to you in plain words about the Father. ²⁶In that day you will ask the Father for things in my name. I am saying that I will not need to ask the Father for you. ²⁷No! The Father himself loves you. He loves you because you have loved me. And he loves you because you have believed that I came from God. ²⁸I came from the Father into the world. Now I am leaving the world and going back to the Father."

²⁹Then the followers of Jesus said, "You are speaking clearly to us now. You are not using words that are hard to understand. ³⁰We can see now that you know all things. You can answer a person's question even before he asks it. This makes us believe that you came from God."

³¹Jesus answered, "So now you believe? ³²Listen to me. A time is coming when you will be scattered. Each of you will be scattered to your own home. That time is now here. You will leave me. I will be alone. But I am never really alone. Why? Because the Father is with me.

³³"I told you these things so that you can have peace in me. In this world you will have trouble. But be brave! I have defeated the world!"

JESUS PRAYS FOR HIS FOLLOWERS

17 After Jesus said these things he looked toward heaven. Jesus prayed, "Father, the time has come. Give glory to your Son so that the Son can give glory to you. ²You gave the Son power over all people so that the Son could give eternal life to all those people you have given to him. ³And this is eternal life: that men can know you, the only true God, and that men can know Jesus Christ, the One you sent. ⁴I finished the work you gave me to do. I brought you glory on earth. ⁵And now, Father, give me glory with you. Give me the glory I had with you before the world was made.

⁶"You gave me some men from the world. I have shown them what you are like. Those men belonged to you, and you gave them to me. They have obeyed your teaching. ⁷Now they know that everything you gave me comes from you. ⁸I gave these men the teachings that you gave me. They accepted those teachings. They know that I truly came from you. ⁹I pray for them now. I am not praying for the people in the world. But I am praying for those men you gave me, because they are yours. ¹⁰All I have is yours, and all you have is mine. And my glory is shown through these men.

¹¹Now I am coming to you. I will not stay in the world now. But these men are still in the world. Holy Father, keep them safe. Keep them safe by the power of your name (the name you gave me), so that they will be one, the same as you and I are one. ¹²While I was with them, I kept them safe. I kept them safe by the power of your name—the name you gave me. I protected them. And only one of them, the one who is going to hell, was lost. He was lost so that what was said in the Scripture would happen.

¹³"I am coming to you now. But I pray these things while I am still in the world. I say these things so that these men can have my joy. I want them to

> This is eternal life: (to) know you, the only true God, and . . . Jesus Christ, the One you sent.
>
> –JOHN 17:3

have all of my joy. [14]I have given them your teaching. And the world has hated them. The world hated these men, because they don't belong to the world, the same as I don't belong to the world. [15]I am not asking you to take them out of the world. But I am asking that you keep them safe from the Evil One. [16]They don't belong to the world, the same as I don't belong to the world. [17]Make them ready for your service through your truth. Your teaching is truth. [18]I have sent them into the world, the same as you sent me into the world. [19]I am making myself ready to serve. I do this for them so that they can truly be ready for your service.

[20]"I pray for these men. But I am also praying for all people who will believe in me because of the teaching of these men. [21]Father, I pray that all people who believe in me can be one. You are in me and I am in you. I pray that these people can also be one in us, so that the world will believe that you sent me. [22]I have given these people the glory that you gave me. I gave them this glory so that they can be one, the same as you and I are one. [23]I will be in them and you will be in me. So they will be completely one. Then the world will know that you sent me. And the world will know that you loved these people the same as you loved me.

[24]"Father, I want these people that you have given me to be with me in every place I am. I want them to see my glory. This is the glory you gave me because you loved me before the world was made. [25]Father, you are the One who is good. The world does not know you, but I know you. And these people know that you sent me. [26]I showed them what you are like. And again I will show them what you are like. Then they will have the same love that you have for me. And I will live in them."

JESUS IS ARRESTED

18 When Jesus finished praying, he left with his followers. They went across the Kidron Valley. On the other side there was a garden of olive trees. Jesus and his followers went there.

[2]Judas knew where this place was, because Jesus met there often with his followers. Judas was the one who turned against Jesus. [3]So Judas led a group of soldiers to the garden. Judas also brought some guards from the leading priests and the Pharisees. They were carrying torches, lanterns, and weapons.

[4]Jesus knew everything that would happen to him. Jesus went out and asked, "Who is it you are looking for?"

[5]The men answered, "Jesus from Nazareth."

Jesus said, "I am Jesus." (Judas, the one who turned against Jesus, was standing there with them.) [6]When Jesus said, "I am Jesus," the men moved back and fell to the ground.

[7]Jesus asked them again, "Who is it you are looking for?"

They said, "Jesus of Nazareth."

[8]Jesus said, "I told you that I am he. So if you are looking for me, then let these other men go." [9]This happened so that the words Jesus said before might come true: "I have not lost any of the men you gave me."

[10]Simon Peter had a sword. He took out the sword and struck the servant of the high priest, cutting off his right ear. (The servant's name was Malchus.) [11]Jesus said to Peter, "Put your sword back. Shall I not drink of the cup[n] the Father has given me?"

JESUS IS BROUGHT BEFORE ANNAS

[12]Then the soldiers with their commander and the Jewish guards arrested Jesus. They tied him [13]and led him first

---

18:11 cup Jesus is talking about the bad things that will happen to him. Accepting these things will be very hard, like drinking a cup of something that tastes very bitter.

to Annas. Annas was the father-in-law of Caiaphas, the high priest that year. [14]Caiaphas was the one who had told the Jews that it would be better if one man died for all the people.

PETER SAYS HE DOESN'T KNOW JESUS

[15]Simon Peter and another one of Jesus' followers went along after Jesus. This follower knew the high priest. So he went with Jesus into the high priest's courtyard. [16]But Peter waited outside near the door. The follower who knew the high priest came back outside. He spoke to the girl at the door and brought Peter inside. [17]The girl at the door said to Peter, "Aren't you also one of that man's followers?"

Peter answered, "No, I am not!"

[18]It was cold, so the servants and guards had built a fire. They were standing around it and warming themselves. Peter was standing with them, warming himself.

THE HIGH PRIEST QUESTIONS JESUS

[19]The high priest asked Jesus questions about his followers and his teaching. [20]Jesus answered, "I have spoken openly to everyone. I have always taught in synagogues and in the Temple, where all the Jews come together. I never said anything in secret. [21]So why do you question me? Ask the people who heard my teaching. They know what I said."

[22]When Jesus said this, one of the guards standing there hit him. The guard said, "Is that the way you answer the high priest?"

[23]Jesus answered him, "If I said something wrong, then say what was wrong. But if what I said is true, why do you hit me?"

[24]Then Annas sent Jesus to Caiaphas, the high priest. Jesus was still tied.

PETER SAYS AGAIN HE DOESN'T KNOW JESUS

[25]Simon Peter was standing and warming himself. They said to him, "Aren't you one of that man's followers?"

Peter denied it and said, "No, I am not."

[26]One of the servants of the high priest was there. This servant was a relative of the man whose ear Peter had cut off. The servant said, "Didn't I see you with him in the garden?"

[27]Again Peter said it wasn't true. Just then a rooster crowed.

JESUS IS BROUGHT BEFORE PILATE

[28]Then they led Jesus from Caiaphas' house to the Roman governor's palace. It was early in the morning. The Jews would not go inside the palace. They did not want to make themselves unclean,[n] because they wanted to eat the Passover meal. [29]So Pilate went outside to them. He asked, "What charges do you bring against this man?"

[30]They answered, "He is a criminal. That is why we brought him to you."

[31]Pilate said to them, "Take him yourselves and judge him by your own law."

They answered, "But we are not allowed to put anyone to death." [32](This happened so that what Jesus had said about how he would die would come true.)

[33]Then Pilate went back inside the palace. He called Jesus to him and asked, "Are you the king of the Jews?"

[34]Jesus said, "Is that your own question, or did others tell you about me?"

[35]Pilate answered, "I am not a Jew. It was your own people and their leading priests who brought you before me. What have you done wrong?"

[36]Jesus said, "My kingdom does not belong to this world. If it belonged to this world, my servants would have

---

18:28 unclean Going into a non-Jewish place would make them unfit to eat the Passover Feast, according to Jewish law.

fought to keep me from being given over to the Jewish leaders. But my kingdom is from another place."

37Pilate said, "So you are a king!"

Jesus answered, "You say that I am a king. That is true. I was born for this: to tell people about the truth. That is why I came into the world. And everyone who belongs to the truth listens to me."

38Pilate said, "What is truth?" After he said this, he went out to the Jews again. He said to them, "I can find nothing to charge against this man. 39But it is your custom that I free one prisoner to you at the time of the Passover. Do you want me to free this 'king of the Jews'?"

40They shouted back, "No, not him! Let Barabbas go free!" (Barabbas was a robber.)

19 Then Pilate ordered that Jesus be taken away and whipped. 2The soldiers used some thorny branches to make a crown. They put this crown on Jesus' head and put a purple robe around him. 3Then they came to Jesus many times and said, "Hail, King of the Jews!" They hit Jesus in the face.

4Again Pilate came out and said to them, "Look! I am bringing Jesus out to you. I want you to know that I find nothing I can charge against him." 5Then Jesus came out, wearing the crown of thorns and the purple robe. Pilate said to the Jews, "Here is the man!"

6When the leading priests and the guards saw Jesus they shouted, "Kill him on a cross! Kill him on a cross!"

But Pilate answered, "Take him and nail him to a cross yourselves. I find nothing I can charge against him."

7The Jews answered, "We have a law that says he should die, because he said he is the Son of God."

8When Pilate heard this, he was even more afraid. 9He went back inside the palace and asked Jesus, "Where are you from?" But Jesus did not answer him. 10Pilate said, "You refuse to speak to me? Don't you know that I have power to set you free and power to have you killed on a cross?"

11Jesus answered, "The only power you have over me is the power given to you by God. The man who gave me to you is guilty of a greater sin."

12After this, Pilate tried to let Jesus go free. But the Jews cried out, "Anyone who makes himself king is against Caesar. If you let this man go free, you are not Caesar's friend."

13Pilate heard what the Jews were saying. So he brought Jesus out to the place called The Stone Pavement. (In the Jewish language[n] the name is Gabbatha.) Pilate sat down on the judge's seat there. 14It was about six o'clock in the morning on Preparation Day of Passover week. Pilate said to the Jews, "Here is your king!"

15They shouted, "Take him away! Take him away! Kill him on a cross!"

Pilate asked them, "Do you want me to kill your king on a cross?"

The leading priests answered, "The only king we have is Caesar!"

16So Pilate gave Jesus to them to be killed on a cross.

JESUS IS KILLED ON A CROSS

The soldiers took charge of Jesus. 17Carrying his own cross, Jesus went out to a place called The Place of the Skull. (In the Jewish language[n] this place is called Golgotha.) 18There they nailed Jesus to the cross. They also put two other men on crosses, one on each side of Jesus with Jesus in the middle. 19Pilate wrote a sign and put it on the cross. It read: "JESUS OF NAZARETH, THE KING OF THE JEWS." 20The sign was written in the Jewish language, in Latin, and in Greek. Many of the Jews read the sign, because this place where Jesus was killed was near the city. 21The leading Jewish priests said to Pilate,

19:13, 17 **Jewish language** Aramaic, the language of the Jews in the first century.

"Don't write, 'The King of the Jews.' But write, 'This man said, I am the King of the Jews.'"

²²Pilate answered, "What I have written, I have written!"

²³After the soldiers nailed Jesus to the cross, they took his clothes. They divided them into four parts. Each soldier got one part. They also took his long shirt. It was all one piece of cloth, woven from top to bottom. ²⁴So the soldiers said to each other, "We should not tear this into parts. We should throw lots to see who will get it." This happened to give full meaning to the Scripture:

> "They divided my clothes among
> them.
> And they threw lots for my
> clothing." *Psalm 22:18*

So the soldiers did this.

²⁵Jesus' mother stood near his cross. His mother's sister was also standing there, with Mary the wife of Clopas, and Mary Magdalene. ²⁶Jesus saw his mother. He also saw the follower he loved standing there. He said to his mother, "Dear woman, here is your son." ²⁷Then he said to the follower, "Here is your mother." From that time on, this follower took her to live in his home.

JESUS DIES

²⁸After this, Jesus knew that everything had been done. To make the Scripture come true, he said, "I am thirsty." [n]

²⁹There was a jar full of vinegar there, so the soldiers soaked a sponge in it. Then they put the sponge on a branch of a hyssop plant and lifted it to Jesus' mouth. ³⁰Jesus tasted the vinegar. Then he said, "It is finished." He bowed his head and died.

³¹This day was Preparation Day. The next day was a special Sabbath day.

The Jews did not want the bodies to stay on the cross on the Sabbath day. So they asked Pilate to order that the legs of the men be broken [n] and the bodies be taken away. ³²So the soldiers came and broke the legs of the first man on the cross beside Jesus. Then they broke the legs of the man on the other cross beside Jesus. ³³But when the soldiers came to Jesus, they saw that he was already dead. So they did not break his legs. ³⁴But one of the soldiers stuck his spear into Jesus' side. At once blood and water came out. ³⁵(The one who saw this happen has told about it. The things he says are true. He knows that he tells the truth. He told about it so that you also can believe.) ³⁶These things happened to make the Scripture come true: "Not one of his bones will be broken." [n] ³⁷And another Scripture said, "They will look at the one they have stabbed." [n]

JESUS IS BURIED

³⁸Later, a man named Joseph from Arimathea asked Pilate if he could take the body of Jesus. (Joseph was a secret follower of Jesus, because he was afraid of the Jews.) Pilate gave his permission. So Joseph came and took Jesus' body away. ³⁹Nicodemus went with Joseph. Nicodemus was the man who earlier had come to Jesus at night. He brought about 75 pounds of spices. This was a mixture of myrrh and aloes. ⁴⁰These two men took Jesus' body and wrapped it with the spices in pieces of linen cloth. (This is how the Jews bury people.) ⁴¹In the place where Jesus was killed, there was a garden. In the garden was a new tomb where no one had ever been buried. ⁴²The men laid Jesus in that tomb because it was near, and the Jews were preparing to start their Sabbath day.

19:28 **"I am thirsty."** Read Psalms 22:15; 69:21.
19:31 **broken** The breaking of the men's bones would make them die sooner.
19:36 **"Not one . . . broken."** Quotation from Psalm 34:20. The idea is from Exodus 12:46; Numbers 9:12.
19:37 **"They . . . stabbed."** Quotation from Zechariah 12:10.

JESUS' TOMB IS EMPTY

20 Early on the first day of the week, Mary Magdalene went to the tomb. It was still dark. Mary saw that the large stone had been moved away from the tomb. [2]So Mary ran to Simon Peter and the other follower (the one Jesus loved). Mary said, "They have taken the Lord out of the tomb. We don't know where they have put him."

[3]So Peter and the other follower started for the tomb. [4]They were both running, but the other follower ran faster than Peter. So the other follower reached the tomb first. [5]He bent down and looked in. He saw the strips of linen cloth lying there, but he did not go in. [6]Then following him came Simon Peter. He went into the tomb and saw the strips of linen lying there. [7]He also saw the cloth that had been around Jesus' head. The cloth was folded up and laid in a different place from the strips of linen. [8]Then the other follower, who had reached the tomb first, also went in. He saw and believed. [9](These followers did not yet understand from the Scriptures that Jesus must rise from death.)

JESUS APPEARS TO MARY MAGDALENE

[10]Then the followers went back home. [11]But Mary stood outside the tomb, crying. While she was still crying, she bent down and looked inside the tomb. [12]She saw two angels dressed in white. They were sitting where Jesus' body had been, one at the head and one at the feet.

[13]They asked her, "Woman, why are you crying?"

She answered, "They have taken away my Lord. I don't know where they have put him." [14]When Mary said this, she turned around and saw Jesus standing there. But she did not know that it was Jesus.

[15]Jesus asked her, "Woman, why are you crying? Whom are you looking for?"

Mary thought he was the gardener. So she said to him, "Did you take him away, sir? Tell me where you put him, and I will get him."

[16]Jesus said to her, "Mary."

Mary turned toward Jesus and said in the Jewish language,[n] "Rabboni." (This means Teacher.)

[17]Jesus said to her, "Don't hold me. I have not yet gone up to the Father. But go to my brothers and tell them this: 'I am going back to my Father and your Father. I am going back to my God and your God.'"

[18]Mary Magdalene went and said to the followers, "I saw the Lord!" And she told them what Jesus had said to her.

JESUS APPEARS TO HIS FOLLOWERS

[19]It was the first day of the week. That evening Jesus' followers were together. The doors were locked, because they were afraid of the Jews. Then Jesus came and stood among them. He said, "Peace be with you!" [20]After he said this, he showed them his hands and his side. His followers were very happy when they saw the Lord.

[21]Then Jesus said again, "Peace be with you! As the Father sent me, I now send you." [22]After he said this, he breathed on them and said, "Receive

> Then Jesus said again, "Peace be with you! As the Father sent me, I now send you."
>
> –JOHN 20:21

20:16 **Jewish language** Aramaic, the language of the Jews in the first century.

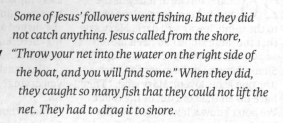

☆ John 21:6

Some of Jesus' followers went fishing. But they did not catch anything. Jesus called from the shore, "Throw your net into the water on the right side of the boat, and you will find some." When they did, they caught so many fish that they could not lift the net. They had to drag it to shore.

Obedience is doing what we are told to do and with a willing heart. It is important for us to obey parents, teachers, police officers, and other leaders. But it is more important to obey God. Sometimes it may not make sense to obey. You may not think you need to brush your teeth like your parents say. But you do. Bad breath or rotten teeth are gross! Jesus told his disciples to throw their net back into the water—but on the *right* side of the boat. Maybe they thought he didn't know what he was talking about. They were fisherman; he was not. But when they obeyed, they caught a lot of fish!

. . . .

Obedience always brings God's goodness into our lives!

---

the Holy Spirit. ²³If you forgive anyone his sins, they are forgiven. If you don't forgive them, they are not forgiven."

JESUS APPEARS TO THOMAS

²⁴Thomas (called Didymus) was not with the followers when Jesus came. Thomas was 1 of the 12. ²⁵The other followers told Thomas, "We saw the Lord."

But Thomas said, "I will not believe it until I see the nail marks in his hands. And I will not believe until I put my finger where the nails were and put my hand into his side."

²⁶A week later the followers were in the house again. Thomas was with them. The doors were locked, but Jesus came in and stood among them. He said, "Peace be with you!" ²⁷Then he said to Thomas, "Put your finger here. Look at my hands. Put your hand here in my side. Stop doubting and believe."

²⁸Thomas said to him, "My Lord and my God!"

²⁹Then Jesus told him, "You believe because you see me. Those who believe without seeing me will be truly happy."

WHY JOHN WROTE THIS BOOK

³⁰Jesus did many other miracles before his followers that are not written in this book. ³¹But these are written so that you can believe that Jesus is

the Christ, the Son of God. Then, by believing, you can have life through his name.

JESUS APPEARS TO SEVEN FOLLOWERS

21 Later, Jesus showed himself to his followers by Lake Galilee.[n] This is how it happened: [2]Some of the followers were together. They were Simon Peter, Thomas (called Didymus), Nathanael from Cana in Galilee, the two sons of Zebedee, and two other followers. [3]Simon Peter said, "I am going out to fish."

The other followers said, "We will go with you." So they went out and got into the boat. They fished that night but caught nothing.

[4]Early the next morning Jesus stood on the shore. But the followers did not know that it was Jesus. [5]Then he said to them, "Friends, have you caught any fish?"

They answered, "No."

[6]He said, "Throw your net into the water on the right side of the boat, and you will find some." So they did this. They caught so many fish that they could not pull the net back into the boat.

[7]The follower whom Jesus loved said to Peter, "It is the Lord!" When Peter heard him say this, he wrapped his coat around himself. (Peter had taken his clothes off.) Then he jumped into the water. [8]The other followers went to shore in the boat, dragging the net full of fish. They were not very far from shore, only about 100 yards. [9]When the followers stepped out of the boat and onto the shore, they saw a fire of hot coals. There were fish on the fire, and there was bread.

[10]Then Jesus said, "Bring some of the fish that you caught."

[11]Simon Peter went into the boat and pulled the net to the shore. It was full of big fish. There were 153. Even though there were so many, the net did not tear. [12]Jesus said to them, "Come and eat." None of the followers dared ask him, "Who are you?" They knew it was the Lord. [13]Jesus came and took the bread and gave it to them. He also gave them the fish.

[14]This was now the third time Jesus showed himself to his followers after he was raised from death.

JESUS TALKS TO PETER

[15]When they finished eating, Jesus said to Simon Peter, "Simon son of John do you love me more than these?"

He answered, "Yes, Lord, you know that I love you."

Jesus said, "Take care of my lambs."

[16]Again Jesus said, "Simon son of John do you love me?"

He answered, "Yes, Lord, you know that I love you."

Jesus said, "Take care of my sheep."

[17]A third time he said, "Simon son of John do you love me?"

Peter was hurt because Jesus asked him the third time, "Do you love me?" Peter said, "Lord, you know everything. You know that I love you!"

He said to him, "Take care of my sheep. [18]I tell you the truth. When you were younger, you tied your own belt and went where you wanted. But when you are old, you will put out your hands and someone else will tie them. They will take you where you don't want to go." [19](Jesus said this to show how Peter would die to give glory to God.) Then Jesus said to Peter, "Follow me!"

[20]Peter turned and saw that the follower Jesus loved was walking behind them. (This was the follower who had leaned against Jesus at the supper and had said, "Lord, who will turn against you?") [21]When Peter saw him behind them he asked Jesus, "Lord, what about him?"

[22]Jesus answered, "Perhaps I want

21:1 **Lake Galilee** Literally, "Sea of Tiberias."

him to live until I come back. That should not be important to you. You follow me!"

²³So a story spread among the brothers that this follower would not die. But Jesus did not say that he would not die. He only said, "Perhaps I want him to live until I come back. That should not be important to you."

²⁴That follower is the one who is telling these things. He is the one who has now written them down. We know that what he says is true.

²⁵There are many other things that Jesus did. If every one of them were written down, I think the whole world would not be big enough for all the books that would be written.

GOD'S FAMILY IS THE CHURCH

Have you ever seen a brand-new baby? Do you remember how tiny and soft the baby was? We all started out that way. We were weak and wobbly. We could not walk or stand up. We couldn't even feed ourselves. If you are reading this, then you have had people in your life who have taken care of you. We can thank God for giving us a family to care for us.

God loves families. That is why he made Adam and Eve and all their children. God has always wanted to be a Father to us. When Adam sinned, every person born after him carried that desire to sin. It took Jesus, God's own Son, to fix that. Jesus obeyed all of God's rules and never sinned. So when he died on the cross, he took everybody else's sins on him. And when he was buried, those sins were buried with him. It's not easy to understand how he did this. But thank God he did it anyway!

When we accept this gift, we can have a brand-new start. Actually, God calls it a brand-new heart. It's like we're babies in God's family.

God never forgot Israel. He still loved Abraham's family. But there are a lot of people in the world. And God wanted all of Adam and Eve's children to be in his family. Jesus lived, died, and then rose again to open the way for all of us. It was time for new babies to be born into God's family.

Fifty days after Jesus went back to heaven, his Spirit *whooshed* into the earth. The followers of Jesus who were waiting for it finally got that new heart. They were the first new babies in God's family. When one of those believers preached, three thousand people became part of God's family—on the first day! And the family grew more and more every day. This family is called the church. And you are part of it now thanks to Jesus!

Acts

LUKE WRITES ANOTHER BOOK

1 To Theophilus,
The first book I wrote was about everything that Jesus did and taught. [2]I wrote about the whole life of Jesus, from the beginning until the day he was taken up into heaven. Before this, Jesus talked to the apostles he had chosen. With the help of the Holy Spirit, Jesus told them what they should do. [3]After his death, he showed himself to them and proved in many ways that he was alive. The apostles saw Jesus during the 40 days after he was raised from death. He spoke to them about the kingdom of God. [4]Once when he was eating with them, he told them not to leave Jerusalem. He said, "The Father has made you a promise which I told you about before. Wait here to receive this promise. [5]John baptized people with water, but in a few days you will be baptized with the Holy Spirit."

JESUS IS TAKEN UP INTO HEAVEN

[6]The apostles were all together. They asked Jesus, "Lord, are you at this time going to give the kingdom back to Israel?"

[7]Jesus said to them, "The Father is the only One who has the authority to decide dates and times. These things are not for you to know. [8]But the Holy Spirit will come to you. Then you will receive power. You will be my witnesses—in Jerusalem, in all of Judea, in Samaria, and in every part of the world."

[9]After he said this, as they were watching, he was lifted up. A cloud hid him from their sight. [10]As he was going, they were looking into the sky. Suddenly, two men wearing white clothes stood beside them. [11]They said, "Men of Galilee, why are you standing here looking into the sky? You saw Jesus taken away from you into heaven. He will come back in the same way you saw him go."

A NEW APOSTLE IS CHOSEN

[12]Then they went back to Jerusalem from the Mount of Olives. (This mountain is about half a mile from Jerusalem.) [13]When they entered the city, they went to the upstairs room where they were staying. Peter, John, James, Andrew, Philip, Thomas, Bartholomew, Matthew, James son of Alphaeus, Simon (known as the Zealot), and Judas son of James were there. [14]They all continued praying together. Some women, including Mary the mother of Jesus, and Jesus' brothers were also there with the apostles.

[15]During this time there was a meeting of the believers. (There were about 120 of them.) Peter stood up and said, [16-17]"Brothers, in the Scriptures the Holy Spirit said through David that something must happen. The Spirit was talking about Judas, one of our own group, who served together with us. The Spirit said that Judas would lead men to arrest Jesus. [18](Judas bought a field with the money he got for his evil act. But Judas fell to his death, his body burst open, and all his intestines poured out.) [19]Everyone in Jerusalem learned about this. This is why they named the field Akeldama. In their language Akeldama means "field of blood.") [20]In the book of Psalms, this is written:

'May his place be empty.
   Leave no one to live in it.'
                    Psalm 69:25

And it is also written:

'Let another man replace him as
      leader.'   *Psalm 109:8*

²¹⁻²²"So now a man must join us and become a witness of Jesus' being raised from death. He must be one of the men who were part of our group during all the time the Lord Jesus was with us. He must have been with us from the time John began to baptize people until the day when Jesus was taken up from us to heaven."

²³They put the names of two men before the group. One was Joseph Barsabbas, who was also called Justus. The other was Matthias. ²⁴⁻²⁵The apostles prayed, "Lord, you know the minds of everyone. Show us which one of these two you have chosen to do this work. Judas turned away from it and went where he belongs. Lord, show us which one should take his place as an apostle!" ²⁶Then they used lots to choose between them, and the lots showed that Matthias was the one. So he became an apostle with the other 11.

THE COMING OF THE HOLY SPIRIT

2 When the day of Pentecost came, they were all together in one place. ²Suddenly a noise came from heaven. It sounded like a strong wind blowing. This noise filled the whole house where they were sitting. ³They saw something that looked like flames of fire. The flames were separated and stood over each person there. ⁴They were all filled with the Holy Spirit, and they began to speak different languages. The Holy Spirit was giving them the power to speak these languages.

⁵There were some religious Jews staying in Jerusalem who were from every country in the world. ⁶When they heard this noise, a crowd came together. They were all surprised, because each one heard them speaking in his own language. ⁷They were completely amazed at this. They said, "Look! Aren't all these men that we hear speaking from Galilee?ⁿ ⁸But each of us hears them in his own language.

How is this possible? We are from different places: ⁹Parthia, Media, Elam, Mesopotamia, Judea, Cappadocia, Pontus, Asia, ¹⁰Phrygia, Pamphylia, Egypt, the areas of Libya near Cyrene, Rome ¹¹(both Jews and those who had become Jews), Crete and Arabia. But we hear these men telling in our own languages about the great things God has done!" ¹²They were all amazed and confused. They asked each other, "What does this mean?"

¹³But others were making fun of them, saying, "They have had too much wine."

PETER SPEAKS TO THE PEOPLE

¹⁴But Peter stood up with the 11 apostles. In a loud voice he spoke to the crowd: "My fellow Jews, and all of you who are in Jerusalem, listen to me. Pay attention to what I have to say. ¹⁵These men are not drunk, as you think; it is only nine o'clock in the morning! ¹⁶But Joel the prophet wrote about what is happening here today:

¹⁷ 'God says: In the last days
   I will give my Spirit freely to all
      kinds of people.
   Your sons and daughters will
      prophesy.
   Your old men will dream dreams.
   Your young men will see visions.
¹⁸ At that time I will give my Spirit
      even to my servants, both men and
         women.
   And they will prophesy.
¹⁹ I will show miracles
      in the sky and on the earth:
      blood, fire and thick smoke.
²⁰ The sun will become dark.
   The moon will become red as
      blood.
   And then the great and glorious
      day of the Lord will come.
²¹ Then anyone who asks the Lord for
      help
   will be saved.'   *Joel 2:28–32*

2:7 from Galilee The people thought men from Galilee could speak only their own language.

²²"Men of Israel, listen to these words: Jesus from Nazareth was a very special man. God clearly showed this to you by the miracles, wonders, and signs God did through him. You all know this, because it happened right here among you. ²³Jesus was given to you, and you killed him. With the help of evil men you nailed him to a cross. But God knew all this would happen. This was God's plan which he had made long ago. ²⁴God raised Jesus from death. God set him free from the pain of death. Death could not hold him. ²⁵For David said this about him:

'I keep the Lord before me always.
    Because he is close by my side,
    I will not be hurt.
²⁶ So I am glad, and I rejoice.
    Even my body has hope.
²⁷ This is because you will not leave me
    in the grave.
    You will not let your Holy One rot.
²⁸ You will teach me God's way to live.
    Being with you will fill me with joy.'
Psalm 16:8–11

☆ Acts 2:17

Jesus had promised to send the Helper—the Spirit of truth—to his followers. When the Spirit showed up, a huge crowd of Jews noticed. Peter spoke up and reminded them what one of their prophets had said. He said that God would give his "Spirit freely to all kinds of people." God's promise of family wasn't just for the Jews anymore. It was for everybody!

Have you ever felt alone? Things can happen that make us feel that way. It is easy to forget that God is always with you. But God says, "I will never leave you; I will never abandon you" (Hebrews 13:5). You see, when we trust in Jesus we enter a friendship with God that never ends. But the news gets better! This isn't a regular friendship like we know it. God's Spirit lives inside us. His Holy Spirit comforts and helps us in many ways. One of those ways is that his Spirit can help you understand God's plans.

· ·

When you feel alone or confused, remember this: the God who knows can help you know!

[29]"Brothers, I can tell you truly about David, our ancestor. He died and was buried. His grave is still here with us today. [30]David was a prophet and knew what God had said. God had promised David that he would make a person from David's family a king just as he was.[n] [31]David knew this before it happened. That is why he said:

'He was not left in the grave.
His body did not rot.'

David was talking about the Christ rising from death. [32]So Jesus is the One who God raised from death! And we are all witnesses to this. [33]Jesus was lifted up to heaven and is now at God's right side. The Father has given the Holy Spirit to Jesus as he promised. So now Jesus has poured out that Spirit. This is what you see and hear. [34]David was not the one who was lifted up to heaven. But he said:

'The Lord said to my Lord:
    Sit by me at my right side,
[35]   until I put your enemies under your
        control.'[n]   Psalm 110:1

[36]"So, all the people of Israel should know this truly: God has made Jesus both Lord and Christ. He is the man you nailed to the cross!"

[37]When the people heard this, they were sick at heart. They asked Peter and the other apostles, "What shall we do?"

[38]Peter said to them, "Change your hearts and lives and be baptized, each one of you, in the name of Jesus Christ for the forgiveness of your sins. And you will receive the gift of the Holy Spirit. [39]This promise is for you. It is also for your children and for all who are far away. It is for everyone the Lord our God calls to himself."

[40]Peter warned them with many other words. He begged them, "Save yourselves from the evil of today's people!" [41]Then those people who accepted what Peter said were baptized. About 3,000 people were added to the number of believers that day. [42]They spent their time learning the apostles' teaching. And they continued to share, to break bread,[n] and to pray together.

THE BELIEVERS SHARE

[43]The apostles were doing many miracles and signs. And everyone felt great respect for God. [44]All the believers stayed together. They shared everything. [45]They sold their land and the things they owned. Then they divided the money and gave it to those people who needed it. [46]The believers met together in the Temple every day. They all had the same purpose. They broke bread in their homes, happy to share their food with joyful hearts. [47]They praised God, and all the people liked them. More and more people were being saved every day; the Lord was adding those people to the group of believers.

PETER HEALS A CRIPPLED MAN

3 One day Peter and John went to the Temple. It was three o'clock in the afternoon. This was the time for the daily prayer service. [2]There, at the Temple gate called Beautiful Gate, was a man who had been crippled all his life. Every day he was carried to this gate to beg. He would ask for money from the people going into the Temple. [3]The man saw Peter and John going into the Temple and asked them for money. [4]Peter and John looked straight at him and said, "Look at us!" [5]The man looked at them; he thought they were going to give him some money. [6]But Peter said, "I don't have any silver or gold,

---

2:30 **God . . . was.** See 2 Samuel 7:13; Psalm 132:11.
2:35 **until . . . control** Literally, "until I make your enemies a footstool for your feet."
2:42 **break bread** This may mean a meal as in verse 46, or the Lord's Supper, the special meal Jesus told his followers to eat to remember him (Luke 22:14–20).

but I do have something else I can give you: By the power of Jesus Christ from Nazareth—stand up and walk!" [7]Then Peter took the man's right hand and lifted him up. Immediately the man's feet and ankles became strong. [8]He jumped up, stood on his feet, and began to walk. He went into the Temple with them, walking and jumping, and praising God. [9-10]All the people recognized him. They knew he was the crippled man who always sat by the Beautiful Gate begging for money. Now they saw this same man walking and praising God. The people were amazed. They could not understand how this could happen.

PETER SPEAKS TO THE PEOPLE

[11]The man was holding on to Peter and John. All the people were amazed and ran to Peter and John at Solomon's Porch. [12]When Peter saw this, he said to them, "Men of Israel, why are you surprised? You are looking at us as if it were our own power that made this man walk. Do you think this happened because we are good? No! [13]The God of Abraham, Isaac and Jacob, the God of our ancestors, gave glory to Jesus, his servant. But you gave him up to be killed. Pilate decided to let him go free. But you told Pilate you did not want Jesus. [14]He was pure and good, but you said you did not want him. You told Pilate to give you a murderer[n] instead of Jesus. [15]And so you killed the One who gives life! But God raised him from death. We are witnesses to this. [16]It was the power of Jesus that made this crippled man well. This happened because we trusted in the power of Jesus. You can see this man, and you know him. He was made completely well because of trust in Jesus. You all saw it happen!

[17]"Brothers, I know you did those things to Jesus because you did not understand what you were doing. Your leaders did not understand either. [18]God said this would happen. He said through the prophets that his Christ would suffer and die. And now God has made these things come true in this way. [19]So you must change your hearts and lives! Come back to God, and he will forgive your sins. [20]Then the Lord will give you times of spiritual rest. He will give you Jesus, the One he chose to be the Christ. [21]But Jesus must stay in heaven until the time comes when all things will be made right again. God told about this time long ago when he spoke through his holy prophets. [22]Moses said, 'The Lord your God will give you a prophet like me. He will be one of your own people. You must obey everything he tells you. [23]Anyone who does not obey him will die, separated from God's people.' [n] [24]Samuel, and all the other prophets who spoke for God after Samuel, told about this time now. [25]You have received what the prophets talked about. You have received the agreement God made with your ancestors. He said to your father Abraham, 'Through your descendants all the nations on the earth will be blessed.' [n] [26]God has raised up his servant and sent him to you first. He sent Jesus to bless you by turning each of you away from doing evil things."

> Jesus is the only One who can save people. No one else in the world is able to save us.
>
> –ACTS 4:12

3:14 **murderer** Barabbas, the man the Jews asked Pilate to let go free instead of Jesus (Luke 23:18).
3:22–23 **'The Lord . . . people.'** Quotation from Deuteronomy 18:15, 19.
3:25 **'Through . . . blessed.'** Quotation from Genesis 22:18; 26:24.

PETER AND JOHN AT THE COUNCIL

4 While Peter and John were speaking to the people, a group of men came up to them. There were Jewish priests, the captain of the soldiers that guarded the Temple, and some Sadducees. ²They were upset because the two apostles were teaching the people. Peter and John were preaching that people will rise from death through the power of Jesus. ³The Jewish leaders grabbed Peter and John and put them in jail. It was already night, so they kept them in jail until the next day. ⁴But many of those who heard Peter and John preach believed the things they said. There were now about 5,000 men in the group of believers.

⁵The next day the Jewish rulers, the Jewish elders, and the teachers of the law met in Jerusalem. ⁶Annas the high priest, Caiaphas, John, and Alexander were there. Everyone from the high priest's family was there. ⁷They made Peter and John stand before them. The Jewish leaders asked them: "By what power or authority did you do this?"

⁸Then Peter was filled with the Holy Spirit. He said to them, "Rulers of the people and you elders, ⁹are you questioning us about a good thing that was done to a crippled man? Are you asking us who made him well? ¹⁰We want all of you and all the Jewish people to know that this man was made well by the power of Jesus Christ from Nazareth! You nailed him to a cross, but God raised him from death. This man was crippled, but he is now well and able to stand here before you because of the power of Jesus! ¹¹Jesus is

'the stone[n] that you builders did not want.

It has become the cornerstone.'

Psalm 118:22

¹²Jesus is the only One who can save

people. No one else in the world is able to save us."

¹³The Jewish leaders saw that Peter and John were not afraid to speak. They understood that these men had no special training or education. So they were amazed. Then they realized that Peter and John had been with Jesus. ¹⁴They saw the crippled man standing there beside the two apostles. They saw that the man was healed. So they could say nothing against them. ¹⁵The Jewish leaders told them to leave the meeting. Then the leaders talked to each other about what they should do. ¹⁶They said, "What shall we do with these men? Everyone in Jerusalem knows that they have done a great miracle! We cannot say it is not true. ¹⁷But we must warn them not to talk to people anymore using that name. Then this thing will not spread among the people."

¹⁸So they called Peter and John in again. They told them not to speak or to teach at all in the name of Jesus. ¹⁹But Peter and John answered them, "What do you think is right? What would God want? Should we obey you or God? ²⁰We cannot keep quiet. We must speak about what we have seen and heard." ²¹⁻²²The Jewish leaders could not find a way to punish them because all the people were praising God for what had been done. (This miracle was a proof from God. The man who was healed was more than 40 years old!) So the Jewish leaders warned the apostles again and let them go free.

THE BELIEVERS' PRAYER

²³Peter and John left the meeting of Jewish leaders and went to their own group. They told them everything that the leading priests and the Jewish elders had said to them. ²⁴When the believers heard this, they prayed to God with one purpose. They prayed, "Lord, you are the One who made the sky, the earth, the sea, and everything in the

4:11 stone A symbol meaning Jesus.

world. ²⁵Our father David was your servant. With the help of the Holy Spirit he said:

'Why are the nations so angry?
    Why are the people making useless plans?
²⁶ The kings of the earth prepare to fight.
    Their leaders make plans together against the Lord
    and against his Christ.' *Psalm 2:1–2*

²⁷These things really happened when Herod, Pontius Pilate, the non-Jewish people, and the Jewish people all came together against Jesus here in Jerusalem. Jesus is your holy Servant. He is the One you made to be the Christ. ²⁸These people made your plan happen; it happened because of your power and your will. ²⁹And now, Lord, listen to what they are saying. They are trying to make us afraid! Lord, we are your servants. Help us to speak your word without fear. ³⁰Help us to be brave by showing us your power; make sick people well, give proofs, and make miracles happen by the power of Jesus, your holy servant."

³¹After they had prayed, the place where they were meeting was shaken. They were all filled with the Holy Spirit, and they spoke God's word without fear.

THE BELIEVERS SHARE

³²The group of believers were joined in their hearts, and they had the same spirit. No person in the group said that the things he had were his own. Instead, they shared everything. ³³With great power the apostles were telling people that the Lord Jesus was truly raised from death. And God blessed all the believers very much. ³⁴They all received the things they needed. Everyone that owned fields or houses sold them. They brought the money ³⁵and gave it to the apostles. Then each person was given the things he needed.

³⁶One of the believers was named Joseph. The apostles called him Barnabas. (This name means "one who encourages.") He was a Levite, born in Cyprus. ³⁷Joseph owned a field. He sold it, brought the money, and gave it to the apostles.

ANANIAS AND SAPPHIRA

5 A man named Ananias and his wife Sapphira sold some land. ²But he gave only part of the money to the apostles. He secretly kept some of it for himself. His wife knew about this, and she agreed to it. ³Peter said, "Ananias, why did you let Satan rule your heart? You lied to the Holy Spirit. Why did you keep part of the money you received for the land for yourself? ⁴Before you sold the land, it belonged to you. And even after you sold it, you could have used the money any way you wanted. Why did you think of doing this? You lied to God, not to men!" ⁵⁻⁶When Ananias heard this, he fell down and died. Some young men came in, wrapped up his body, carried it out, and buried it. And everyone who heard about this was filled with fear.

⁷About three hours later his wife came in. She did not know what had happened. ⁸Peter said to her, "Tell me how much money you got for your field. Was it this much?"

Sapphira answered, "Yes, that was the price."

⁹Peter said to her, "Why did you and your husband agree to test the Spirit of the Lord? Look! The men who buried your husband are at the door! They will carry you out." ¹⁰At that moment Sapphira fell down by his feet and died. The young men came in and saw that she was dead. They carried her out and buried her beside her husband. ¹¹The whole church and all the others who heard about these things were filled with fear.

PROOFS FROM GOD

¹²The apostles did many signs and miracles among the people. And they would all meet together on Solomon's

Porch. ¹³None of the others dared to stand with them. All the people were saying good things about them. ¹⁴More and more men and women believed in the Lord and were added to the group of believers. ¹⁵As Peter was passing by, the people brought their sick into the streets. They put their sick on beds and mats so at least Peter's shadow might fall on them. ¹⁶Crowds came from all the towns around Jerusalem. They brought their sick and those who were bothered by evil spirits. All of them were healed.

THE APOSTLES OBEY GOD

¹⁷The high priest and all his friends (a group called the Sadducees) became very jealous. ¹⁸They took the apostles and put them in jail. ¹⁹But during the night, an angel of the Lord opened the doors of the jail. He led the apostles outside and said, ²⁰"Go and stand in the Temple. Tell the people everything about this new life." ²¹When the apostles heard this, they obeyed and went into the Temple. It was early in the morning, and they began to teach.

The high priest and his friends arrived. They called a meeting of the Jewish leaders and all the important older men of the Jews. They sent some men to the jail to bring the apostles to them. ²²When the men went to the jail, they could not find the apostles. So they went back and told the Jewish leaders about this. ²³They said, "The jail was closed and locked. The guards were standing at the doors. But when we opened the doors, the jail was empty!" ²⁴Hearing this, the captain of the Temple guards and the leading priests were confused. They wondered, "What will happen because of this?"

²⁵Then someone came and told them, "Listen! The men you put in jail are standing in the Temple. They are teaching the people!" ²⁶Then the captain and his men went out and brought the apostles back. But the soldiers did not use force, because they were afraid that the people would kill them with stones.

²⁷The soldiers brought the apostles to the meeting and made them stand before the Jewish leaders. The high priest questioned them. ²⁸He said, "We gave you strict orders not to go on teaching in that name. But look what you have done! You have filled Jerusalem with your teaching. You are trying to make us responsible for this man's death."

²⁹Peter and the other apostles answered, "We must obey God, not men! ³⁰You killed Jesus. You hung him on a cross. But God, the same God our ancestors had, raised Jesus up from death! ³¹Jesus is the One whom God raised to be on his right side. God made Jesus our Leader and Savior. God did this so that the people of Israel could change their hearts and lives and have their sins forgiven. ³²We saw all these things happen. The Holy Spirit also proves that these things are true. God has given the Spirit to all who obey him."

³³When the Jewish leaders heard this, they became very angry and wanted to kill them. ³⁴A Pharisee named Gamaliel stood up in the meeting. He was a teacher of the law, and all the people respected him. He ordered the apostles to leave the meeting for a little while. ³⁵Then he said to them, "Men of Israel, be careful of what you are planning to do to these men! ³⁶Remember when Theudas appeared? He said that he was a great man, and about 400 men joined him. But he was killed. And all his followers were scattered. They were able to do nothing. ³⁷Later, a man named Judas came from Galilee at the time of the registration.ⁿ He led a group of followers, too. He was also killed, and all his followers were scattered. ³⁸And so now

5:37 **registration** Census. A counting of all the people and the things they own.

I tell you: Stay away from these men. Leave them alone. If their plan comes from men, it will fail. [39]But if it is from God, you will not be able to stop them. You might even be fighting against God himself!"

The Jewish leaders agreed with what Gamaliel said. [40]They called the apostles in again. They beat the apostles and told them not to speak in the name of Jesus again. Then they let them go free. [41]The apostles left the meeting full of joy because they were given the honor of suffering disgrace for Jesus. [42]The apostles did not stop teaching people. Every day in the Temple and in people's homes they continued to tell the Good News—that Jesus is the Christ.

SEVEN MEN ARE CHOSEN

6 More and more people were becoming followers of Jesus. But during this same time, the Greek-speaking followers had an argument with the other Jewish followers. The Greek-speaking Jews said that their widows were not getting their share of the food that was given out every day. [2]The 12 apostles called the whole group of followers together. They said, "It is not right for us to stop our work of teaching God's word in order to serve tables. [3]So, brothers, choose seven of your own men. They must be men who are good. They must be full of wisdom and full of the Spirit. We will put them in charge of this work. [4]Then we can use all our time to pray and to teach the word of God."

[5]The whole group liked the idea. So they chose these seven men: Stephen (a man with great faith and full of the Holy Spirit), Philip,[n] Procorus, Nicanor, Timon, Parmenas, and Nicolas (a man from Antioch who had become a Jew). [6]Then they put these men before the apostles. The apostles prayed and laid their hands on[n] the men.

[7]The word of God was reaching more and more people. The group of followers in Jerusalem became larger and larger. A great number of the Jewish priests believed and obeyed.

STEPHEN IS ARRESTED

[8]Stephen was richly blessed by God. God gave him the power to do great miracles and signs among the people. [9]But some Jews were against him. They belonged to a synagogue of Free Men[n] (as it was called). (This synagogue was also for Jews from Cyrene and from Alexandria.) Jews from Cilicia and Asia were also with them. They all came and argued with Stephen.

[10]But the Spirit was helping him to speak with wisdom. His words were so strong that they could not argue with him. [11]So they paid some men to say, "We heard him say things against Moses and against God!"

[12]This upset the people, the Jewish elders, and the teachers of the law. They came to Stephen, grabbed him and brought him to a meeting of the Jewish leaders. [13]They brought in some men to tell lies about Stephen. They said, "This man is always saying things against this holy place and the law of Moses. [14]We heard him say that Jesus from Nazareth will destroy this place. He also said that Jesus will change the things that Moses told us to do." [15]All the people in the meeting were watching Stephen closely. His face looked like the face of an angel.

STEPHEN'S SPEECH

7 The high priest said to Stephen, "Are these things true?"

[2]Stephen answered, "Brothers and fathers, listen to me. Our glorious God appeared to Abraham, our ancestor. Abraham was in Mesopotamia

---

6:5 Philip Not the apostle named Philip.
6:6 laid their hands on Here, doing this showed that these men were given a special work of God.
6:9 Free Men Jews who had been slaves or whose fathers had been slaves, but were now free.

☆ Acts 6:10

The church grew. The 12 apostles were preaching to and helping thousands of people. So they chose some leaders to help them. A man named Stephen was chosen because he was full of the Holy Spirit. When people tried to argue with Stephen, the Spirit helped Stephen remember the word of God. The Spirit gave Stephen wisdom to know exactly what to say.

Have you ever wanted to help someone, but you did not know what to say? Maybe a friend was sad, or a classmate did not know Jesus. You wanted to share but struggled to find the words, so you chose to just be quiet. What you need to know is that God can help! You see, he made words. He spoke with words, and the world was created. God is so good with words that Jesus is called "the Word" (see John 1:14). So, if you are confused about what to say, God can give you the right words. Wise words! He knows them all.

· ·

Stephen was not the only person who could speak with God's wisdom. You can too!

---

before he lived in Haran. ³God said to Abraham, 'Leave your country and your relatives. Go to the land I will show you.'[n] ⁴So Abraham left the country of Chaldea and went to live in Haran. After Abraham's father died, God sent him to this place where you now live. ⁵God did not give Abraham any of this land, not even a foot of it. But God promised that he would give him and his descendants this land. (This was before Abraham had any descendants.) ⁶This is what God said to him: 'Your descendants will be strangers in a land they don't own. The people there will make them slaves. And they will do cruel things to them for 400 years. ⁷But I will punish the nation where they are slaves. Then your descendants will leave that land. Then they will worship me in this place.'[n] ⁸God made an agreement with Abraham; the sign for this agreement was circumcision. And so when Abraham had his son Isaac,

7:3 'Leave . . . you.' Quotation from Genesis 12:1.
7:6–7 'Your descendants . . . place.' Quotation from Genesis 15:13–14 and Exodus 3:12.

Abraham circumcised him when he was eight days old. Isaac also circumcised his son Jacob. And Jacob did the same for his sons, the 12 ancestors[n] of our people.

9"These sons became jealous of Joseph. They sold him to be a slave in Egypt. But God was with him. 10Joseph had many troubles there, but God saved him from all those troubles. The king of Egypt liked Joseph and respected him because of the wisdom that God gave him. The king made him governor of Egypt. He put Joseph in charge of all the people in his palace.

11"Then all the land of Egypt and of Canaan became so dry that nothing would grow there. This made the people suffer very much. The sons could not find anything to eat. 12But when Jacob heard that there was grain in Egypt, he sent his sons, our ancestors, there. This was their first trip to Egypt. 13Then they went there a second time. This time, Joseph told his brothers who he was. And the king learned about Joseph's family. 14Then Joseph sent some men to invite Jacob, his father, to come to Egypt. He also invited all his relatives (75 persons altogether). 15So Jacob went down to Egypt, where he and his sons died. 16Later their bodies were moved to Shechem and put in a grave there. (It was the same grave that Abraham had bought in Shechem from the sons of Hamor for a sum of money.)

17"The number of people in Egypt grew large. There were more and more of our people there. (The promise that God made to Abraham was soon to come true.) 18Then a new king began to rule Egypt. He did not know who Joseph was. 19This king tricked our people and was cruel to our ancestors. He forced them to put their babies outside to die. 20This was the time when Moses was born. He was a fine child. For three months Moses was cared for in his father's house. 21When they put Moses outside, the king's daughter took him. She raised him as if he were her own son. 22The Egyptians taught Moses all the things they knew. He was a powerful man in the things he said and did.

23"When Moses was about 40 years old, he thought it would be good to visit his brothers, the people of Israel. 24Moses saw an Egyptian doing wrong to a Jew. So he defended the Jew and punished the Egyptian for hurting him. Moses killed the Egyptian. 25Moses thought that his fellow Jews would understand that God was using him to save them. But they did not understand. 26The next day, Moses saw two Jewish men fighting. He tried to make peace between them. He said, 'Men, you are brothers! Why are you hurting each other?' 27The man who was hurting the other man pushed Moses away. He said, 'Who made you our ruler and judge? 28Are you going to kill me as you killed the Egyptian yesterday?'[n] 29When Moses heard him say this, he left Egypt. He went to live in the land of Midian where he was a stranger. While Moses lived in Midian, he had two sons.

30"After 40 years Moses was in the desert near Mount Sinai. An angel appeared to him in the flames of a burning bush. 31When Moses saw this, he was amazed. He went near to look closer at it. Moses heard the Lord's voice. 32The Lord said, 'I am the God of your ancestors. I am the God of Abraham, Isaac and Jacob.'[n] Moses began to shake with fear and was afraid to look. 33The Lord said to him, 'Take off your sandals. You are standing on holy ground. 34I have seen the troubles my people have suffered in Egypt. I have

---

7:8 **12 ancestors** Important ancestors of the Jews; the leaders of the 12 Jewish tribes.
7:27–28 **'Who . . . yesterday?'** Quotation from Exodus 2:14.
7:32 **'I am . . . Jacob.'** Quotation from Exodus 3:6.

heard their cries. I have come down to save them. And now, Moses, I am sending you back to Egypt.' [n]

35"This Moses was the same man the Jews said they did not want. They had said to him, 'Who made you our ruler and judge?' [n] Moses is the same man God sent to be a ruler and savior, with the help of an angel. This was the angel Moses saw in the burning bush. 36So Moses led the people out of Egypt. He worked miracles and signs in Egypt, at the Red Sea, and then in the desert for 40 years. 37This is the same Moses that said to the Jewish people: 'God will give you a prophet like me. He will be one of your own people.' [n] 38This is the same Moses who was with the gathering of the Jews in the desert. He was with the angel that spoke to him at Mount Sinai, and he was with our ancestors. He received commands from God that give life, and he gave those commands to us.

39But our fathers did not want to obey Moses. They rejected him. They wanted to go back to Egypt again. 40They said to Aaron, 'Moses led us out of Egypt. But we don't know what has happened to him. So make us gods who will lead us.' [n] 41So the people made an idol that looked like a calf. Then they brought sacrifices to it. The people were proud of what they had made with their own hands! 42But God turned against them. He did not try to stop them from worshiping the sun, moon and stars. This is what is written in the book of the prophets: God says,

'People of Israel, you did not bring me sacrifices and offerings
while you traveled in the desert for 40 years.
43 But now you will have to carry with you
the tent to worship the false god Molech
and the idols of the star god Rephan that you made to worship.
This is because I will send you away beyond Babylon.'   *Amos 5:25–27*

44"The Holy Tent where God spoke to our fathers was with the Jews in the desert. God told Moses how to make this Tent. He made it like the plan God showed him. 45Later, Joshua led our fathers to capture the lands of the other nations. Our people went in, and God drove the other people out. When our people went into this new land, they took with them this same Tent. They received this Tent from their fathers and kept it until the time of David. 46God was very pleased with David. He asked God to let him build a house for him, the God of Jacob. [n] 47But Solomon was the one who built the Temple.

48"But the Most High does not live in houses that men build with their hands. This is what the prophet says:

49 'Heaven is my throne.
The earth is my footstool.
So do you think you can build a house for me? says the Lord.

> But the Most High does not live in houses that men build with their hands.
> –ACTS 7:48

7:33–34 'Take . . . Egypt.' Quotation from Exodus 3:5–10.
7:35 'Who . . . judge?' Quotation from Exodus 2:14.
7:37 'God . . . people.' Quotation from Deuteronomy 18:15.
7:40 'Moses . . . us.' Quotation from Exodus 32:1.
7:46 the God of Jacob Some Greek copies read "the house of Jacob." This means the people of Israel.

There is no place where I need to
rest.
⁵⁰ Remember, I made all these things!'"
                                        Isaiah 66:1–2

⁵¹Stephen continued speaking: "You stubborn Jewish leaders! You have not given your hearts to God! You won't listen to him! You are always against what the Holy Spirit is trying to tell you. Your ancestors were like this, and you are just like them! ⁵²Your fathers tried to hurt every prophet who ever lived. Those prophets said long ago that the Righteous One would come. But your fathers killed them. And now you have turned against the Righteous One and killed him. ⁵³You received the law of Moses, which God gave you through his angels. But you don't obey it!"

STEPHEN IS KILLED

⁵⁴When the leaders heard Stephen saying all these things, they became very angry. They were so mad that they were grinding their teeth at Stephen. ⁵⁵But Stephen was full of the Holy Spirit. He looked up to heaven and saw the glory of God. He saw Jesus standing at God's right side. ⁵⁶He said, "Look! I see heaven open. And I see the Son of Man standing at God's right side!"

⁵⁷Then they all shouted loudly. They covered their ears with their hands and all ran at Stephen. ⁵⁸They took him out of the city and threw stones at him until he was dead. The men who told lies against Stephen left their coats with a young man named Saul. ⁵⁹While they were throwing stones, Stephen prayed, "Lord Jesus, receive my spirit!" ⁶⁰He fell on his knees and cried in a loud voice, "Lord, do not hold this sin against them!" After Stephen said this, he died.

8 Saul agreed that the killing of Stephen was a good thing.

TROUBLE FOR THE BELIEVERS

²⁻³Some religious men buried Stephen. They cried very loudly for him. On that day people began trying to hurt the church in Jerusalem and make it suffer. Saul was also trying to destroy the church. He went from house to house. He dragged out men and women and put them in jail. All the believers, except the apostles, went to different places in Judea and Samaria. ⁴And everywhere the believers were scattered, they told people the Good News.

PHILIP PREACHES IN SAMARIA

⁵Philipⁿ went to the cityⁿ of Samaria and preached about the Christ. ⁶The people there heard Philip and saw the miracles he was doing. They all listened carefully to the things he said. ⁷Many of these people had evil spirits in them. But Philip made the evil spirits leave them. The spirits made a loud noise when they came out. There were also many weak and crippled people there. Philip healed them, too. ⁸So the people in that city were very happy.

⁹But there was a man named Simon in that city. Before Philip came there, Simon had practiced magic. He amazed all the people of Samaria with his magic. He bragged and called himself a great man. ¹⁰All the people—the least important and the most important— paid attention to what Simon said. They said, "This man has the power of God, called 'the Great Power'!" ¹¹Simon had amazed them with his magic tricks so long that the people became his followers. ¹²But Philip told them the Good News about the kingdom of God and the power of Jesus Christ. Men and women believed Philip and were baptized. ¹³Simon himself believed and was baptized. He stayed very close to Philip. When he saw the miracles and the very powerful things that Philip did, Simon was amazed.

8:5 **Philip** Not the apostle named Philip.
8:5 **the city** Some Greek copies read "a city."

[14]The apostles were still in Jerusalem. They heard that the people of Samaria had accepted the word of God. So they sent Peter and John to them. [15]When Peter and John arrived, they prayed that the Samaritan believers might receive the Holy Spirit. [16]These people had been baptized in the name of the Lord Jesus. But the Holy Spirit had not yet entered any of them. [17]Then, when the two apostles began laying their hands on[n] the people, they received the Holy Spirit.

[18]Simon saw that the Spirit was given to people when the apostles laid their hands on them. So he offered the apostles money. [19]He said, "Give me also this power so that when I lay my hands on a person, he will receive the Holy Spirit."

[20]Peter said to him, "You and your money should both be destroyed! You thought you could buy God's gift with money. [21]You cannot share with us in this work. Your heart is not right before God. [22]Change your heart! Turn away from this evil thing you have done. Pray to the Lord. Maybe he will forgive you for thinking this. [23]I see that you are full of bitter jealousy and ruled by sin."

[24]Simon answered, "Both of you pray for me to the Lord. Pray that the things you have said will not happen to me!"

[25]Then the two apostles told the people the things they had seen Jesus do. And after the apostles had given the message of the Lord, they went back to Jerusalem. On the way, they went through many Samaritan towns and preached the Good News to the people.

PHILIP TEACHES AN ETHIOPIAN

[26]An angel of the Lord spoke to Philip.[n] The angel said, "Get ready and go south. Go to the road that leads down to Gaza from Jerusalem—the desert road." [27]So Philip got ready and went. On the road he saw a man from Ethiopia, a eunuch. He was an important officer in the service of Candace, the queen of the Ethiopians. He was responsible for taking care of all her money. He had gone to Jerusalem to worship, and [28]now he was on his way home. He was sitting in his chariot and reading from the book of Isaiah, the prophet. [29]The Spirit said to Philip, "Go to that chariot and stay near it."

[30]So Philip ran toward the chariot. He heard the man reading from Isaiah, the prophet. Philip asked, "Do you understand what you are reading?"

[31]He answered, "How can I understand? I need someone to explain it to me!" Then he invited Philip to climb in and sit with him. [32]The verse of Scripture that he was reading was this:

"He was like a sheep being led to be killed.
   He was quiet, as a sheep is quiet while its wool is being cut.
He said nothing.
[33]   He was shamed and was treated unfairly.
He died without children to continue his family.
   His life on earth has ended."

Isaiah 53:7–8

[34]The officer said to Philip, "Please tell me, who is the prophet talking about? Is he talking about himself or about someone else?" [35]Philip began to speak. He started with this same Scripture and told the man the Good News about Jesus.

[36]While they were traveling down the road, they came to some water. The officer said, "Look! Here is water! What is stopping me from being baptized?" [37][Philip answered, "If you believe with all your heart, you can." The officer said, "I believe that Jesus Christ is the Son of God."][n] [38]Then the officer commanded

8:17 **laying their hands on** Here, doing this showed that these men were given a special work of God.
8:26 **Philip** Not the apostle named Philip.
8:37 **Philip . . . God.** Some Greek copies do not contain the bracketed text.

the chariot to stop. Both Philip and the officer went down into the water, and Philip baptized him. [39] When they came up out of the water, the Spirit of the Lord took Philip away; the officer never saw him again. The officer continued on his way home, full of joy. [40] But Philip appeared in a city called Azotus and preached the Good News in all the towns on the way from Azotus to Caesarea.

SAUL IS CONVERTED

9 In Jerusalem Saul was still trying to frighten the followers of the Lord by saying he would kill them. So he went to the high priest [2] and asked him to write letters to the synagogues in the city of Damascus. Saul wanted the high priest to give him the authority to find people in Damascus who were followers of Christ's Way. If he found any there, men or women, he would arrest them and bring them back to Jerusalem.

[3] So Saul went to Damascus. As he came near the city, a bright light from heaven suddenly flashed around him. [4] Saul fell to the ground. He heard a voice saying to him, "Saul, Saul! Why are you doing things against me?"

[5] Saul said, "Who are you, Lord?"

The voice answered, "I am Jesus. I am the One you are trying to hurt. [6] Get up now and go into the city. Someone there will tell you what you must do."

[7] The men traveling with Saul stood there, but they said nothing. They heard the voice, but they saw no one. [8] Saul got up from the ground. He opened his eyes, but he could not see.

So the men with Saul took his hand and led him into Damascus. [9] For three days Saul could not see, and he did not eat or drink.

[10] There was a follower of Jesus in Damascus named Ananias. The Lord spoke to Ananias in a vision, "Ananias!"

Ananias answered, "Here I am, Lord."

[11] The Lord said to him, "Get up and go to the street called Straight Street. Find the house of Judas.[n] Ask for a man named Saul from the city of Tarsus. He is there now, praying. [12] Saul has seen a vision. In it a man named Ananias comes to him and lays his hands on him. Then he sees again."

[13] But Ananias answered, "Lord, many people have told me about this man and the terrible things he did to your people in Jerusalem. [14] Now he has come here to Damascus. The leading priests have given him the power to arrest everyone who worships you."

[15] But the Lord said to Ananias, "Go! I have chosen Saul for an important work. He must tell about me to non-Jews, to kings, and to the people of Israel. [16] I will show him how much he must suffer for my name."

[17] So Ananias went to the house of Judas. He laid his hands on Saul and said, "Brother Saul, the Lord Jesus sent me. He is the one you saw on the road on your way here. He sent me so that you can see again and be filled with the Holy Spirit." [18] Immediately, something that looked like fish scales fell from Saul's eyes. He was able to see again! Then Saul got up and was baptized. [19] After eating some food, his strength returned.

> With the help of the Holy Spirit, the group became stronger (and) grew larger and larger.
>
> –ACTS 9:31

9:11 Judas This is not either of the apostles named Judas.

SAUL PREACHES IN DAMASCUS

Saul stayed with the followers of Jesus in Damascus for a few days. ²⁰Soon he began to preach about Jesus in the synagogues, saying, "Jesus is the Son of God!"

²¹All the people who heard him were amazed. They said, "This is the man who was in Jerusalem. He was trying to destroy those who trust in this name! He came here to do the same thing. He came here to arrest the followers of Jesus and take them back to the leading priests."

²²But Saul became more and more powerful. His proofs that Jesus is the Christ were so strong that the Jews in Damascus could not argue with him.

SAUL ESCAPES FROM DAMASCUS

²³After many days, the Jews made plans to kill Saul. ²⁴They were watching the city gates day and night. They wanted to kill him, but Saul learned about their plan. ²⁵One night some followers of Saul helped him leave the city. They lowered him in a basket through an opening in the city wall.

SAUL IN JERUSALEM

²⁶Then Saul went to Jerusalem. He tried to join the group of followers, but they were all afraid of him. They did not believe that he was really a follower. ²⁷But Barnabas accepted Saul and took him to the apostles. Barnabas told them that Saul had seen the Lord on the road. He explained how the Lord had spoken to Saul. Then he told them how boldly Saul had preached in the name of Jesus in Damascus.

²⁸And so Saul stayed with the followers. He went everywhere in Jerusalem, preaching boldly in the name of Jesus. ²⁹He would often talk and argue with the Jews who spoke Greek. But they were trying to kill him. ³⁰When the brothers learned about this, they took Saul to Caesarea. From there they sent him to Tarsus.

³¹The church everywhere in Judea, Galilee, and Samaria had a time of peace. With the help of the Holy Spirit, the group became stronger. The believers showed that they respected the Lord by the way they lived. Because of this, the group of believers grew larger and larger.

PETER HEALS AENEAS

³²As Peter was traveling through all the area, he visited God's people who lived in Lydda. ³³There he met a paralyzed man named Aeneas. Aeneas had not been able to leave his bed for the past eight years. ³⁴Peter said to him, "Aeneas, Jesus Christ heals you. Stand up and make your bed!" Aeneas stood up immediately. ³⁵All the people living in Lydda and on the Plain of Sharon saw him. These people turned to the Lord.

PETER IN JOPPA

³⁶In the city of Joppa there was a follower named Tabitha. (Her Greek name, Dorcas, means "a deer.") She was always doing good and helping the poor. ³⁷While Peter was in Lydda, Tabitha became sick and died. Her body was washed and put in a room upstairs. ³⁸The followers in Joppa heard that Peter was in Lydda. (Lydda is near Joppa.) So they sent two men to Peter. They begged him, "Hurry, please come to us!" ³⁹Peter got ready and went with them. When he arrived, they took him to the upstairs room. All the widows stood around Peter, crying. They showed him the shirts and coats that Tabitha had made when she was still alive. ⁴⁰Peter sent everyone out of the room. He kneeled and prayed. Then he turned to the body and said, "Tabitha, stand up!" She opened her eyes, and when she saw Peter, she sat up. ⁴¹He gave her his hand and helped her up. Then he called the believers and the widows into the room. He showed them Tabitha; she was alive! ⁴²People everywhere in Joppa learned about this, and many believed in the Lord.

⁴³Peter stayed in Joppa for many days with a man named Simon who was a leatherworker.

PETER AND CORNELIUS

10 At Caesarea there was a man named Cornelius. He was an officer in the Italian group of the Roman army. ²Cornelius was a religious man. He and all the other people who lived in his house worshiped the true God. He gave much of his money to the poor and prayed to God often. ³One afternoon about three o'clock, Cornelius saw a vision clearly. In the vision an angel of God came to him and said, "Cornelius!"

⁴Cornelius stared at the angel. He became afraid and said, "What do you want, Lord?"

The angel said, "God has heard your prayers. He has seen what you give to the poor. And God remembers you. ⁵Send some men now to Joppa to bring back a man named Simon. Simon is also called Peter. ⁶Simon is staying with a man, also named Simon, who is a leatherworker. He has a house beside the sea." ⁷Then the angel who spoke to Cornelius left. Cornelius called two of his servants and a soldier. The soldier was a religious man who worked for Cornelius. ⁸Cornelius explained everything to these three men and sent them to Joppa.

⁹The next day as they came near Joppa, Peter was going up to the roof [n] to pray. It was about noon. ¹⁰Peter was hungry and wanted to eat. But while the food was being prepared, he had a vision. ¹¹He saw heaven opened and something coming down. It looked like a big sheet being lowered to earth by its four corners. ¹²In it were all kinds of animals, reptiles, and birds. ¹³Then a voice said to Peter, "Get up, Peter; kill and eat."

¹⁴But Peter said, "No, Lord! I have never eaten food that is unholy or unclean."

¹⁵But the voice said to him again, "God has made these things clean. Don't call them 'unholy'!" ¹⁶This happened three times. Then the sheet was taken back to heaven.

¹⁷While Peter was wondering what this vision meant, the men Cornelius sent had found Simon's house. They were standing at the gate. ¹⁸They asked, "Is Simon Peter staying here?"

¹⁹Peter was still thinking about the vision. But the Spirit said to him, "Listen! Three men are looking for you. ²⁰Get up and go downstairs. Go with them and don't ask questions. I have sent them to you."

²¹So Peter went down to the men. He said, "I am the man you are looking for. Why did you come here?"

²²They said, "A holy angel spoke to Cornelius, an army officer. He is a good man; he worships God. All the Jewish people respect him. The angel told Cornelius to ask you to his house so that he can hear what you have to say." ²³Peter asked the men to come in and spend the night.

The next day Peter got ready and went with them. Some of the brothers from Joppa joined him. ²⁴On the following day they came to Caesarea. Cornelius was waiting for them. He had called together his relatives and close friends. ²⁵When Peter entered, Cornelius met him. He fell at Peter's feet and worshiped him. ²⁶But Peter helped him up, saying, "Stand up! I too am only a man." ²⁷Peter went on talking with Cornelius as they went inside. There Peter saw many people together. ²⁸He said, "You people understand that it is against our Jewish law for a Jew to associate with or visit anyone who is not a Jew. But God has shown me that I should not call any person 'unholy' or 'unclean.' ²⁹That is why I did not argue

---

10:9 roof In Bible times houses were built with flat roofs. The roof was used for drying things such as flax and fruit. And it was used as an extra room, as a place for worship and as a place to sleep in the summer.

when I was asked to come here. Now, please tell me why you sent for me."

[30]Cornelius said, "Four days ago, I was praying in my house. It was at this same time—three o'clock in the afternoon. Suddenly, there was a man standing before me wearing shining clothes. [31]He said, 'Cornelius! God has heard your prayer. He has seen what you give to the poor. And God remembers you. [32]So send some men to Joppa and ask Simon Peter to come. Peter is staying in the house of a man, also named Simon, who is a leatherworker. His house is beside the sea.' [33]So I sent for you immediately, and it was very good of you to come. Now we are all here before God to hear everything the Lord has commanded you to tell us."

PETER'S SPEECH

[34]Peter began to speak: "I really understand now that to God every person is the same. [35]God accepts anyone who worships him and does what is right. It is not important what country a person comes from. [36]You know that God has sent his message to the people of Israel. That message is the Good News that peace has come through Jesus Christ. Jesus is the Lord of all people! [37]You know what has happened all over Judea. It began in Galilee after John[n] preached to the people about baptism. [38]You know about Jesus from Nazareth. God made him the Christ by giving him the Holy Spirit and power. You know how Jesus went everywhere doing good. He healed those who were ruled by the devil, for God was with Jesus. [39]We saw all the things that Jesus did in Judea and in Jerusalem. But they killed him by nailing him to a cross. [40]Yet, on the third day, God raised Jesus to life and caused him to be seen. [41]But he was not seen by all the people. Only the witnesses that God had already chosen saw him, and we are those witnesses. We ate and drank with him after he was raised

from death. [42]He told us to preach to the people and to tell them that he is the one whom God chose to be the judge of the living and the dead. [43]Everyone who believes in Jesus will be forgiven. God will forgive his sins through Jesus. All the prophets say this is true."

NON-JEWS RECEIVE THE HOLY SPIRIT

[44]While Peter was still saying this, the Holy Spirit came down on all those who were listening. [45]The Jewish believers who came with Peter were amazed that the gift of the Holy Spirit had been given even to the non-Jewish people. [46]These Jewish believers heard them speaking in different languages and praising God. Then Peter said, [47]"Can anyone keep these people from being baptized with water? They have received the Holy Spirit just as we did!" [48]So Peter ordered that they be baptized in the name of Jesus Christ. Then they asked Peter to stay with them for a few days.

PETER RETURNS TO JERUSALEM

11 The apostles and the believers in Judea heard that non-Jewish people had accepted God's teaching too. [2]But when Peter came to Jerusalem, some Jewish believers argued with him. [3]They said, "You went into the homes of people who are not Jews and are not circumcised! You even ate with them!"

[4]So Peter explained the whole story to them. [5]He said, "I was in the city of Joppa. While I was praying, I had a vision. In the vision, I saw something which looked like a big sheet coming down from heaven. It was being lowered to earth by its four corners. It came down very close to me, and [6]I looked inside it. I saw animals, wild beasts, reptiles, and birds. [7]I heard a voice say to me, 'Get up, Peter. Kill and eat.' [8]But I said, 'No, Lord! I have never eaten anything that is unholy or unclean.' [9]But

---

10:37 **John** John the Baptist, who preached to people about Christ's coming (Matthew 3; Luke 3).

the voice from heaven answered again, 'God has made these things clean. Don't call them unholy!' [10]This happened three times. Then the whole thing was taken back to heaven. [11]Right then three men came to the house where I was staying. They were sent to me from Caesarea. [12]The Spirit told me to go with them without doubting. These six believers here also went with me. We went to the house of Cornelius. [13]He told us about the angel he saw standing in his house. The angel said to him, 'Send some men to Joppa and invite Simon Peter to come. [14]He will speak to you. The things he will say will save you and all your family.' [15]When I began my speech, the Holy Spirit came on them just as he came on us at the beginning. [16]Then I remembered the words of the Lord. He said, 'John baptized in water, but you will be baptized in the Holy Spirit!' [17]God gave to them the same gift that he gave to us who believed in the Lord Jesus Christ. So could I stop the work of God? No!"

[18]When the Jewish believers heard this, they stopped arguing. They praised God and said, "So God is allowing the non-Jewish people also to turn to him and live."

THE GOOD NEWS COMES TO ANTIOCH

[19]Many of the believers were scattered by the terrible things that happened after Stephen was killed. Some of them went to places as far away as Phoenicia, Cyprus, and Antioch. They were telling the message to others, but only to Jews. [20]Some of these believers were men from Cyprus and Cyrene. When they came to Antioch, they spoke also to Greeks,[n] telling them the Good News about the Lord Jesus. [21]The Lord was helping the believers. And a large group of people believed and turned to the Lord.

[22]The church in Jerusalem heard about all of this, so they sent Barnabas to Antioch. [23-24]Barnabas was a good man, full of the Holy Spirit and full of faith. When he reached Antioch and saw how God had blessed the people, he was glad. He encouraged all the believers in Antioch. He told them, "Never lose your faith. Always obey the Lord with all your hearts." Many people became followers of the Lord.

[25]Then Barnabas went to the city of Tarsus to look for Saul. [26]When he found Saul, he brought him to Antioch. And for a whole year Saul and Barnabas met with the church. They taught many people there. In Antioch the followers were called Christians for the first time.

[27]About that time some prophets came from Jerusalem to Antioch. [28]One of them was named Agabus. He stood up and spoke with the help of the Holy Spirit. He said, "A very hard time is coming to the whole world. There will be no food for people to eat." (This happened when Claudius ruled.) [29]The followers all decided to help their brothers who lived in Judea. Each one planned to send them as much as he could. [30]They gathered the money and gave it to Barnabas and Saul, who brought it to the elders in Judea.

HEROD AGRIPPA HURTS THE CHURCH

12 During that same time King Herod began to do terrible things to some who belonged to the church. [2]He ordered James, the brother of John, to be killed by the sword. [3]Herod saw that the Jews liked this, so he decided to arrest Peter, too. (This happened during the time of the Feast of Unleavened Bread.) [4]After Herod arrested Peter, he put him in jail and handed him over to be guarded by 16 soldiers. Herod planned to bring Peter before the people for trial after the Passover Feast. [5]So Peter

11:20 **Greeks** Some Greek copies read "Hellenists," non-Greeks who spoke Greek.

The Holy Spirit helped a man named Agabus speak the right words. He warned the Christians that a very hard time was coming. There would be no food for people in Judea (where Jerusalem was). The believers gathered all the money they could to help the people in Judea.

Has anyone ever done something nice for you? Have *you* ever helped someone? God created us like him. He is a giver, so we are too. Just like God helps us when we need him, we can help others when they have a need. You can *tell* people that Jesus loves them. But when you do something nice for them, you *show* them Jesus loves them. Look for ways to help others whenever you can. It's all part of being in God's family.

· ·

You may not have money like the grown-ups who heard Agabus. But you can still do nice things for people. You can play with someone at school who seems lonely. Pray for someone who is sick. Make cookies for someone who is sad.

was kept in jail. But the church kept on praying to God for him.

PETER LEAVES THE JAIL

[6]The night before Herod was to bring him to trial, Peter was sleeping. He was between two soldiers, bound with two chains. Other soldiers were guarding the door of the jail. [7]Suddenly, an angel of the Lord stood there. A light shined in the room. The angel touched Peter on the side and woke him up. The angel said, "Hurry! Get up!" And the chains fell off Peter's hands. [8]The angel said to him, "Get dressed and put on your sandals." And so Peter did this. Then the angel said, "Put on your coat and follow me." [9]So the angel went out, and Peter followed him. Peter did not know if what the angel was doing was real. He thought he might be seeing a vision. [10]They went past the first and the second guard. They came to the iron gate that separated them from the city. The gate opened itself for them. They went through the gate and walked down a street. And the angel suddenly left him.

[11]Then Peter realized what had happened. He thought, "Now I know that the Lord really sent his angel to me. He rescued me from Herod and from all the

things the Jewish people thought would happen."

¹²When he realized this, he went to the home of Mary. She was the mother of John. (John was also called Mark.) Many people were gathered there, praying. ¹³Peter knocked on the outside door. A servant girl named Rhoda came to answer it. ¹⁴She recognized Peter's voice, and she was very happy. She even forgot to open the door. She ran inside and told the group, "Peter is at the door!"

¹⁵They said to her, "You are crazy!" But she kept on saying that it was true. So they said, "It must be Peter's angel."

¹⁶Peter continued to knock. When they opened the door, they saw him and were amazed. ¹⁷Peter made a sign with his hand to tell them to be quiet. He explained how the Lord led him out of the jail. And he said, "Tell James and the other believers what happened." Then he left to go to another place.

¹⁸The next day the soldiers were very upset. They wondered what had happened to Peter. ¹⁹Herod looked everywhere for Peter but could not find him. So he questioned the guards and ordered that they be killed.

THE DEATH OF HEROD AGRIPPA

Later Herod moved from Judea and went to the city of Caesarea, where he stayed for a while. ²⁰Herod was very angry with the people of Tyre and Sidon. But the people of those cities all came in a group to Herod. They were able to get Blastus, the king's personal servant, on their side. They asked Herod for peace because their country got its food from his country.

²¹On a chosen day Herod put on his royal robes. He sat on his throne and made a speech to the people. ²²They shouted, "This is the voice of a god, not a man!" ²³Herod did not give the glory to God. So an angel of the Lord caused

him to become sick. He was eaten by worms and died.

²⁴God's message continued to spread and reach more and more people.

²⁵After Barnabas and Saul finished their task in Jerusalem, they returned to Antioch. John, also called Mark, was with them.

BARNABAS AND SAUL ARE CHOSEN

13 In the church at Antioch there were these prophets and teachers: Barnabas, Simeon (also called Niger), Lucius (from the city of Cyrene), Manaen (who had grown up with Herod, the ruler) and Saul. ²They were all worshiping the Lord and giving up eating.ⁿ The Holy Spirit said to them, "Give Barnabas and Saul to me to do a special work. I have chosen them for it."

³So they gave up eating and prayed. They laid their hands onⁿ Barnabas and Saul and sent them out.

BARNABAS AND SAUL IN CYPRUS

⁴Barnabas and Saul were sent out by the Holy Spirit. They went to the city of Seleucia. From there they sailed to the island of Cyprus. ⁵When they came to Salamis, they preached the Good News of God in the Jewish synagogues. John Mark was with them to help.

⁶They went across the whole island to Paphos. In Paphos they met a Jew who was a magician. His name was Bar-Jesus. He was a false prophet, ⁷who always stayed close to Sergius Paulus, the governor. Sergius Paulus was a smart man. He asked Barnabas and Saul to come to him, because he wanted to hear the message of God. ⁸But Elymas, the magician (that is what his name means), was against them. He tried to stop the governor from believing in Jesus. ⁹But Saul was filled with the Holy Spirit. (Saul's other name was Paul.) He

---

13:2 giving up eating This is called "fasting." The people would give up eating for a special time of prayer and worship to God. It was also done to show sadness.
13:3 laid their hands on Here, this was a sign to show that these men were given a special work of God.

looked straight at Elymas [10]and said, "You son of the devil! You are an enemy of everything that is right! You are full of evil tricks and lies. You are always trying to change the Lord's truths into lies! [11]Now the Lord will touch you, and you will be blind. For a time you will not be able to see anything—not even the light from the sun."

Then everything became dark for Elymas. He walked around, trying to find someone to lead him by the hand. [12]When the governor saw this, he believed. He was amazed at the teaching about the Lord.

PAUL AND BARNABAS LEAVE CYPRUS

[13]Paul and those with him sailed away from Paphos. They came to Perga, in Pamphylia. But John Mark left them and returned to Jerusalem. [14]They continued their trip from Perga and went to Antioch, a city in Pisidia. On the Sabbath day they went into the synagogue and sat down. [15]The law of Moses and the writings of the prophets were read. Then the leaders of the synagogue sent a message to Paul and Barnabas: "Brothers, if you have any message that will encourage the people, please speak!"

[16]Paul stood up. He raised his hand and said, "Men of Israel and you other people who worship God, please listen! [17]The God of the people of Israel chose our ancestors. He made the people great during the time they lived in Egypt. He brought them out of that country with great power. [18]And he was patient with them[n] for 40 years in the desert. [19]God destroyed seven nations in the land of Canaan and gave the land to his people. [20]All this happened in about 450 years.

"After this, God gave them judges until the time of Samuel the prophet. [21]Then the people asked for a king. God gave them Saul son of Kish. Saul was from the tribe of Benjamin. He was king for 40 years. [22]After God took him away, God made David their king. This is what God said about him: 'I have found David son of Jesse. He is the kind of man I want. He will do all that I want him to do.' [23]So God has brought one of David's descendants to Israel to be their Savior. That descendant is Jesus. And God promised to do this. [24]Before Jesus came, John[n] preached to all the people of Israel. He told them about a baptism of changed hearts and lives. [25]When he was finishing his work, he said, 'Who do you think I am? I am not the Christ. He is coming later. I am not worthy to untie his sandals.'

[26]"Brothers, sons in the family of Abraham, and you non-Jews who worship God, listen! The news about this salvation has been sent to us. [27]Those who live in Jerusalem and their leaders did not realize that Jesus was the Savior. They did not understand the words that the prophets wrote, which are read every Sabbath day. But they made them come true when they said Jesus was guilty. [28]They could not find any real reason for Jesus to die, but they asked Pilate to have him killed. [29]They did to him all that the Scriptures had said. Then they took him down from the cross and

> The Holy Spirit said to them, "Give Barnabas and Saul to me to do a special work."
>
> –ACTS 13:2

13:18 **And . . . them** Some Greek copies read "And he cared for them."
13:24 **John** John the Baptist, who preached to people about Christ's coming (Matthew 3; Luke 3).

laid him in a tomb. [30]But God raised him up from death! [31]After this, for many days, the people who had gone with Jesus from Galilee to Jerusalem saw him. They are now his witnesses to the people. [32]We tell you the Good News about the promise God made to our ancestors. [33]We are their children, and God has made this promise come true for us. God did this by raising Jesus from death. We read about this also in Psalm 2:

'You are my Son.
  Today I have become your Father.'
  Psalm 2:7

[34]God raised Jesus from death. He will never go back to the grave and become dust. So God said:

'I will give you the holy and sure blessings
  that I promised to David.'
  Isaiah 55:3

[35]But in another place God says:

'You will not let your Holy One rot in the grave.'   *Psalm 16:10*

[36]David did God's will during his lifetime. Then he died and was buried with his fathers. And his body did rot in the grave! [37]But the One God raised from death did not rot in the grave. [38-39]Brothers, you must understand what we are telling you: You can have forgiveness of your sins through Jesus. The law of Moses could not free you from your sins. But everyone who believes is free from all sins through him. [40]Be careful! Don't let what the prophets said happen to you:

[41] 'Listen, you people who doubt!
  You can wonder, and then die.
  I will do something in your lifetime
    that will amaze you.

You won't believe it even when you are told about it!'   *Habakkuk 1:5*

[42]While Paul and Barnabas were leaving the synagogue, the people asked them to tell them more about these things on the next Sabbath. [43]After the meeting, many Jews followed Paul and Barnabas from that place. With the Jews there were many who had changed to the Jewish religion and worshiped God. Paul and Barnabas were persuading them to continue trusting in God's kindness.

[44]On the next Sabbath day, almost all the people in the city came to hear the word of the Lord. [45]Seeing the crowd, the Jews became very jealous. They said insulting things and argued against what Paul said. [46]But Paul and Barnabas spoke very boldly. They said, "We must speak the message of God to you first. But you refuse to listen. You are judging yourselves not worthy of having eternal life! So we will now go to the people of other nations! [47]This is what the Lord told us to do. The Lord said:

'I have made you a light for the non-Jewish nations.
  You will show people all over the world the way to be saved.'"
  Isaiah 49:6

[48]When the non-Jewish people heard Paul say this, they were happy. They gave honor to the message of the Lord. And many of the people believed the message. They were the ones chosen to have life forever.

[49]And so the message of the Lord was spreading through the whole country. [50]But the Jews stirred up some of the important religious women and the leaders of the city against Paul and Barnabas. They started trouble against Paul and Barnabas and drove them out of their area. [51]So Paul and Barnabas shook the dust off their feet[n] and went

13:51 shook . . . feet A warning. It showed that they were finished talking to these people.

to Iconium. [52]But the followers were filled with joy and the Holy Spirit.

PAUL AND BARNABAS IN ICONIUM

14 In Iconium, Paul and Barnabas went as usual to the Jewish synagogue. They spoke so well that a great many Jews and Greeks believed. [2]But some of the Jews who did not believe excited the non-Jewish people and turned them against the believers. [3]But Paul and Barnabas stayed in Iconium a long time and spoke bravely for the Lord. The Lord showed that their message about his grace was true by giving them the power to work miracles and signs. [4]But some of the people in the city agreed with the Jews. Others believed the apostles. So the city was divided.

[5]Some non-Jewish people, some Jews, and some of their rulers wanted to harm Paul and Barnabas by killing them with stones. [6]When Paul and Barnabas learned about this, they went to Lystra and Derbe, cities in Lycaonia, and to the areas around those cities. [7]They announced the Good News there, too.

PAUL IN LYSTRA AND DERBE

[8]In Lystra there sat a man who had been born crippled; he had never walked. [9]This man was listening to Paul speak. Paul looked straight at him and saw that the man believed God could heal him. [10]So he cried out, "Stand up on your feet!" The man jumped up and began walking around. [11]When the crowds saw what Paul did, they shouted in their own Lycaonian language. They said, "The gods have become like men! They have come down to us!" [12]And the people began to call Barnabas "Zeus."[n] They called Paul "Hermes,"[n] because he was the main speaker. [13]The temple of Zeus was near the city. The priest of this temple brought some bulls and flowers to the city gates. The priest and the people wanted to offer a sacrifice to Paul and Barnabas. [14]But when the apostles, Barnabas and Paul, understood what they were about to do, they tore their clothes in anger. Then they ran in among the people and shouted, [15]"Men, why are you doing these things? We are only men, human beings like you! We are bringing you the Good News. We are telling you to turn away from these worthless things and turn to the true living God. He is the One who made the sky, the earth, the sea, and everything that is in them. [16]In the past, God let all the nations do what they wanted. [17]Yet he did things to prove he is real: He shows kindness to you. He gives you rain from heaven and crops at the right times. He gives you food and fills your hearts with joy." [18]Even with these words, they were barely able to keep the crowd from offering sacrifices to them.

[19]Then some Jews came from Antioch and Iconium. They persuaded the people to turn against Paul. And so they threw stones at Paul and dragged him out of town. They thought that they had killed him. [20]But the followers gathered around him, and he got up and went back into the town. The next day, he and Barnabas left and went to the city of Derbe.

THE RETURN TO ANTIOCH IN SYRIA

[21]Paul and Barnabas told the Good News in Derbe and many became followers. Paul and Barnabas returned to Lystra, Iconium, and Antioch. [22]In those cities they made the followers of Jesus stronger. They helped them to stay in the faith. They said, "We must suffer many things to enter God's kingdom." [23]They chose elders for each church, by praying and giving up eating.[n] These elders were men who had trusted the

---

14:12 "Zeus" The Greeks believed in many gods. Zeus was their most important god.
14:12 "Hermes" The Greeks believed he was a messenger for the other gods.
14:23 giving up eating This is called "fasting." The people would give up eating for a special time of prayer and worship to God. It was also done to show sadness.

Lord. So Paul and Barnabas put them in the Lord's care.

²⁴Then they went through Pisidia and came to Pamphylia. ²⁵They preached the message in Perga, and then they went down to Attalia. ²⁶And from there they sailed away to Antioch. This is where the believers had put them into God's care and had sent them out to do this work. And now they had finished the work.

²⁷When they arrived in Antioch, they gathered the church together. Paul and Barnabas told them all about what God had done with them. They told how God had made it possible for the non-Jews to believe! ²⁸And they stayed there a long time with the followers.

THE MEETING AT JERUSALEM

15 Then some men came to Antioch from Judea. They began teaching the non-Jewish brothers: "You cannot be saved if you are not circumcised. Moses taught us to do this." ²Paul and Barnabas were against this teaching and argued with the men about it. So the group decided to send Paul, Barnabas, and some other men to Jerusalem. There they could talk more about this with the apostles and elders.

³The church helped the men leave on the trip. They went through the countries of Phoenicia and Samaria, telling all about how the non-Jewish people had turned to God. This made all the believers very happy. ⁴When they arrived in Jerusalem, the apostles, the elders, and the church welcomed them. Paul, Barnabas, and the others told about all the things that God had done with them. ⁵But some of the believers who had belonged to the Pharisee group came forward. They

said, "The non-Jewish believers must be circumcised. We must tell them to obey the law of Moses!"

⁶The apostles and the elders gathered to study this problem. ⁷There was a long debate. Then Peter stood up and said to them, "Brothers, you know what happened in the early days. God chose me from among you to preach the Good News to the non-Jewish people. They heard the Good News from me, and they believed. ⁸God, who knows the thoughts of all men, accepted them. He showed this to us by giving them the Holy Spirit, just as he did to us. ⁹To God, those people are not different from us. When they believed, he made their hearts pure. ¹⁰So now why are you testing God? You are putting a heavy load around the necks of the non-Jewish brothers. It is a load that neither we nor our fathers were able to carry. ¹¹But we believe that we and they too will be saved by the grace of the Lord Jesus!"

¹²Then the whole group became quiet. They listened to Paul and Barnabas speak. Paul and Barnabas told about all the miracles and signs that God did through them among the non-Jewish people. ¹³After they finished speaking, James spoke. He said, "Brothers, listen to me. ¹⁴Simon has told us how God showed his love for the non-Jewish people. For the first time he has accepted them and made them his people. ¹⁵The words of the prophets agree with this too:

¹⁶ 'After these things I will return.
    The kingdom of David is like a
        fallen tent.
    But I will rebuild it.
        And I will again build its ruins.
        And I will set it up.

> God showed his love for the non-Jewish people . . . He has accepted them and made them his people.
> —ACTS 15:14

17 Then those people who are left alive
        may ask the Lord for help.
    And all people from other nations
        may worship me,
    says the Lord.
    And he will make it happen.
18   And these things have been known
        for a long time.'   *Amos 9:11–12*

19 "So I think we should not bother the non-Jewish brothers who have turned to God. 20 Instead, we should write a letter to them. We should tell them these things: Do not eat food that has been offered to idols. (This makes the food unclean.) Do not take part in any kind of sexual sin. Do not taste blood. Do not eat animals that have been strangled. 21 They should not do these things, because there are still men in every city who teach the law of Moses. For a long time the words of Moses have been read in the synagogue every Sabbath day."

LETTER TO NON-JEWISH BELIEVERS

22 The apostles, the elders, and the whole church decided to send some of their men with Paul and Barnabas to Antioch. They chose Judas Barsabbas and Silas, who were respected by the believers. 23 They sent the following letter with them:

From the apostles and elders, your brothers.
    To all the non-Jewish brothers in Antioch, Syria and Cilicia:
    Dear Brothers,
    24 We have heard that some of our men have come to you and said things that trouble and upset you. But we did not tell them to do this! 25 We have all agreed to choose some men and send them to you. They will be with our dear friends Barnabas and Paul— 26 men who have given their lives to serve our Lord Jesus Christ. 27 So we have sent Judas and Silas with them. They will tell you the same things. 28 It has pleased the Holy Spirit that you should not have a heavy load to carry, and we agree. You need to do only these things: 29 Do not eat any food that has been offered to idols. Do not taste blood. Do not eat any animals that have been strangled. Do not take part in any kind of sexual sin. If you stay away from these things, you will do well.
    Good-bye.

30 So the men left Jerusalem and went to Antioch. There they gathered the church and gave them the letter. 31 When they read it, they were very happy because of the encouraging letter. 32 Judas and Silas were also prophets, who said many things to encourage the believers and make them stronger. 33 After some time Judas and Silas were sent off in peace by the believers. They went back to those who had sent them. 34 [But Silas decided to remain there.]*n*

35 But Paul and Barnabas stayed in Antioch. They and many others preached the Good News and taught the people the message of the Lord.

PAUL AND BARNABAS SEPARATE

36 After some time, Paul said to Barnabas, "We preached the message of the Lord in many towns. We should go back to all those towns to visit the believers and see how they are doing."

37 Barnabas wanted to take John Mark with them too. 38 But John Mark had left them at Pamphylia; he did not continue with them in the work. So Paul did not think it was a good idea to take him. 39 Paul and Barnabas had a serious argument about this. They separated and went different ways. Barnabas sailed to Cyprus and took Mark with him. 40 But Paul chose Silas and left. The believers in Antioch put Paul into the Lord's

---

15:34 **But . . . there.** Some Greek copies do not contain the bracketed text.

care. [41]And he went through Syria and Cilicia, giving strength to the churches.

TIMOTHY GOES WITH PAUL AND SILAS

16 Paul came to Derbe and Lystra. A follower named Timothy was there. Timothy's mother was Jewish and a believer. His father was a Greek.

[2]The brothers in Lystra and Iconium respected Timothy and said good things about him. [3]Paul wanted Timothy to travel with him. But all the Jews living in that area knew that Timothy's father was Greek. So Paul circumcised Timothy to please the Jews. [4]Paul and the men with him traveled from town to town. They gave the decisions made by the apostles and elders in Jerusalem for the people to obey. [5]So the churches became stronger in the faith and grew larger every day.

PAUL IS CALLED OUT OF ASIA

[6]Paul and the men with him went through the areas of Phrygia and Galatia. The Holy Spirit did not let them preach the Good News in Asia. [7]When they came near the country of Mysia, they tried to go into Bithynia. But the Spirit of Jesus did not let them. [8]So they passed by Mysia and went to Troas. [9]That night Paul had a vision. In the vision, a man from Macedonia came to him. The man stood there and begged, "Come over to Macedonia. Help us!" [10]After Paul had seen the vision, we immediately prepared to leave for Macedonia. We understood that God had called us to tell the Good News to those people.

LYDIA BECOMES A CHRISTIAN

[11]We left Troas in a ship, and we sailed straight to the island of Samothrace. The next day we sailed to Neapolis.[n] [12]Then we went by land to Philippi, the leading city in that part of Macedonia. It is also a Roman colony.[n] We stayed there for several days.

[13]On the Sabbath day we went outside the city gate to the river. There we thought we would find a special place for prayer. Some women had gathered there, so we sat down and talked with them. [14]There was a woman named Lydia from the city of Thyatira. Her job was selling purple cloth. She worshiped the true God. The Lord opened her mind to pay attention to what Paul was saying. [15]She and all the people in her house were baptized. Then Lydia invited us to her home. She said, "If you think I am truly a believer in the Lord, then come stay in my house." And she persuaded us to stay with her.

PAUL AND SILAS IN JAIL

[16]Once, while we were going to the place for prayer, a servant girl met us. She had a special spirit[n] in her. She earned a lot of money for her owners by telling fortunes. [17]This girl followed Paul and us. She said loudly, "These men are servants of the Most High God! They are telling you how you can be saved!"

[18]She kept this up for many days. This bothered Paul, so he turned and said to the spirit, "By the power of Jesus Christ, I command you to come out of her!" Immediately, the spirit came out.

[19]The owners of the servant girl saw this. These men knew that now they could not use her to make money. So they grabbed Paul and Silas and dragged them before the city rulers in the marketplace. [20]Here they brought Paul and Silas to the Roman rulers and said, "These men are Jews and are making trouble in our city. [21]They are teaching things that are not right for us as Romans to do."

[22]The crowd joined the attack against them. The Roman officers tore the

---

16:11 Neapolis City in Macedonia. It was the first city Paul visited on the continent of Europe.
16:12 Roman colony A town begun by Romans with Roman laws, customs and privileges.
16:16 spirit This was a spirit from the devil. It caused her to say she had special knowledge.

clothes of Paul and Silas and had them beaten with rods again and again. [23] After being severely beaten, Paul and Silas were thrown into jail. The jailer was ordered to guard them carefully. [24] When he heard this order, he put them far inside the jail. He pinned down their feet between large blocks of wood.

[25] About midnight Paul and Silas were praying and singing songs to God. The other prisoners were listening to them.

[26] Suddenly, there was a big earthquake. It was so strong that it shook the foundation of the jail. Then all the doors of the jail broke open. All the prisoners were freed from their chains. [27] The jailer woke up and saw that the jail doors were open. He thought that the prisoners had already escaped. So he got his sword and was about to kill himself.[n] [28] But Paul shouted, "Don't hurt yourself! We are all here!"

16:27 **kill himself** He thought the leaders would kill him for letting the prisoners escape.

☆ Acts 16:30–31

Paul and Silas were men who preached about Jesus. But not everybody liked hearing about Jesus. Some people got so mad they put chains on Paul and Silas and threw them into jail. Late that night Paul and Silas were singing songs to God. Suddenly there was a big earthquake. The cell doors opened, and the chains fell off the prisoners. The noise woke up the jailer who thought the prisoners had escaped. But they were all right there. Paul and Silas were just waiting to tell the jailer about Jesus.

By a miracle, God freed Paul and Silas from prison. The jailer who kept them locked up knew that Paul and Silas knew Jesus. He asked them, "What must I do to be saved?" He wanted to know God like Paul and Silas did. They told the jailer that he must believe in Jesus. He believed in Jesus and became a Christian. When he told his family about Jesus, they believed and became Christians too.

· · · · · · · · · · · · · · · · · · ·

It is so simple to become a Christian. It all starts with believing in Jesus.

[29]The jailer told someone to bring a light. Then he ran inside. Shaking with fear, he fell down before Paul and Silas. [30]Then he brought them outside and said, "Men, what must I do to be saved?"

[31]They said to him, "Believe in the Lord Jesus and you will be saved—you and all the people in your house." [32]So Paul and Silas told the message of the Lord to the jailer and all the people in his house. [33]At that hour of the night the jailer took Paul and Silas and washed their wounds. Then he and all his people were baptized immediately. [34]After this the jailer took Paul and Silas home and gave them food. He and his family were very happy because they now believed in God.

[35]The next morning, the Roman officers sent the police to tell the jailer, "Let these men go free!"

[36]The jailer said to Paul, "The officers have sent an order to let you go free. You can leave now. Go in peace."

[37]But Paul said to the police, "They beat us in public without a trial, even though we are Roman citizens.[n] And they threw us in jail. Now they want to make us go away quietly. No! Let them come themselves and bring us out!"

[38]The police told the Roman officers what Paul said. When the officers heard that Paul and Silas were Roman citizens, they were afraid. [39]So they came and told Paul and Silas they were sorry. They took Paul and Silas out of jail and asked them to leave the city. [40]So when they came out of the jail, they went to Lydia's house. There they saw some of the believers and encouraged them. Then they left.

PAUL AND SILAS IN THESSALONICA

17 Paul and Silas traveled through Amphipolis and Apollonia and came to Thessalonica. In that city there was a Jewish synagogue. [2]Paul went into the synagogue as he always did. On each Sabbath day for three weeks, Paul talked with the Jews about the Scriptures. [3]He explained and proved that the Christ must die and then rise from death. He said, "This Jesus I am telling you about is the Christ." [4]Some of the Jews were convinced and joined Paul and Silas. Many of the Greeks who worshiped the true God and many of the important women joined them.

[5]But the Jews became jealous. They got some evil men from the marketplace, formed a mob and started a riot. They ran to Jason's house, looking for Paul and Silas. The men wanted to bring Paul and Silas out to the people. [6]But they did not find them. So they dragged Jason and some other believers to the leaders of the city. The people were yelling, "These men have made trouble everywhere in the world. And now they have come here too! [7]Jason is keeping them in his house. All of them do things against the laws of Caesar. They say that there is another king called Jesus."

[8]When the people and the leaders of the city heard these things, they became very upset. [9]They made Jason and the others put up a sum of money. Then they let the believers go free.

PAUL AND SILAS GO TO BEREA

[10]That same night the believers sent Paul and Silas to Berea. There Paul and Silas went to the Jewish synagogue. [11]These Jews were better than the Jews in Thessalonica. They were eager to hear the things Paul and Silas said. These Jews in Berea studied the Scriptures every day to find out if these things were true. [12]So, many of them believed. Many important Greek men and women also believed. [13]But when the Jews in Thessalonica learned that Paul was preaching the word of God in Berea, they came there, too. They upset the people and made trouble. [14]So the believers quickly sent Paul away to the coast. But Silas and Timothy stayed in

---

16:37 **Roman citizens** Roman law said that Roman citizens must not be beaten before they had a trial.

Berea. [15]The men who took Paul went with him to Athens. Then they carried a message from Paul back to Silas and Timothy. It said, "Come to me as soon as you can."

PAUL IN ATHENS

[16]Paul was waiting for Silas and Timothy in Athens. He was troubled because he saw that the city was full of idols. [17]In the synagogue, he talked with the Jews and the Greeks who worshiped the true God. He also talked every day with people in the marketplace.

[18]Some of the Epicurean and Stoic philosophers[n] argued with him. Some of them said, "This man doesn't know what he is talking about. What is he trying to say?" Paul was telling them the Good News of Jesus' rising from death. They said, "He seems to be telling us about some other gods." [19]They got Paul and took him to a meeting of the Areopagus.[n] They said, "Please explain to us this new idea that you have been teaching. [20]The things you are saying are new to us. We want to know what this teaching means." [21](All the people of Athens and those from other countries always used their time talking about all the newest ideas.)

[22]Then Paul stood before the meeting of the Areopagus. He said, "Men of Athens, I can see that you are very religious in all things. [23]I was going through your city, and I saw the things you worship. I found an altar that had these words written on it: "TO A GOD WHO IS NOT KNOWN." You worship a god that you don't know. This is the God I am telling you about! [24]He is the God who made the whole world and everything in it. He is the Lord of the land and the sky. He does not live in temples that men build! [25]This God is the One who gives life, breath, and everything

else to people. He does not need any help from them. He has everything he needs. [26]God began by making one man. From him came all the different people who live everywhere in the world. He decided exactly when and where they must live. [27]God wanted them to look for him and perhaps search all around for him and find him. But he is not far from any of us: [28]'By his power we live and move and exist.' Some of your own poets have said: 'For we are his children.' [29]We are God's children. So, you must not think that God is like something that people imagine or make. He is not like gold, silver, or rock. [30]In the past, people did not understand God, but God ignored this. But now, God tells everyone in the world to change his heart and life. [31]God has decided on a day that he will judge all the world. He will be fair. He will use a man to do this. God chose that man long ago. And God has proved this to everyone by raising that man from death!"

[32]When the people heard about Jesus being raised from death, some of them laughed. They said, "We will hear more about this from you later." [33]So Paul went away from them. [34]But some of the people believed Paul and joined him. One of those who believed was Dionysius, a member of the Areopagus. Also a woman named Damaris and some others believed.

PAUL IN CORINTH

18 Later, Paul left Athens and went to Corinth. [2]Here he met a Jew named Aquila. Aquila was born in the country of Pontus. But Aquila and his wife, Priscilla, had recently moved to Corinth from Italy. They left Italy because Claudius[n] commanded that all Jews must leave Rome. Paul went to visit Aquila and Priscilla. [3]They were

---

17:18 Epicurean and Stoic philosophers Philosophers were those who searched for truth. Epicureans believed that pleasures, especially pleasures of the mind, were the goal of life. Stoics believed that life should be without feelings of joy or grief.
17:19 Areopagus A council or group of important leaders in Athens. They were like judges.
18:2 Claudius The emperor (ruler) of Rome, A.D. 41–54.

tentmakers, just as he was. He stayed with them and worked with them. [4]Every Sabbath day he talked with the Jews and Greeks in the synagogue. Paul tried to persuade these people to believe in Jesus.

[5]Silas and Timothy came from Macedonia and joined Paul in Corinth. After this, Paul used all his time telling people the Good News. He showed the Jews that Jesus is the Christ. [6]But they would not accept Paul's teaching and said some evil things. So he shook off the dust from his clothes.[n] He said to them, "If you are not saved, it will be your own fault! I have done all I can do! After this, I will go to non-Jewish people!" [7]Paul left the synagogue and moved into the home of Titius Justus. It was next to the synagogue. This man worshiped the true God. [8]Crispus was the leader of that synagogue. He and all the people living in his house believed in the Lord. Many others in Corinth also listened to Paul. They too believed and were baptized.

[9]During the night, Paul had a vision. The Lord said to him, "Don't be afraid! Continue talking to people and don't be quiet! [10]I am with you. No one will hurt you because many of my people are in this city." [11]Paul stayed there for a year and a half, teaching God's word to the people.

PAUL IS BROUGHT BEFORE GALLIO

[12]Gallio became the governor of the country of Southern Greece. At that time, some of the Jews came together against Paul and took him to the court. [13]They said to Gallio, "This man is teaching people to worship God in a way that is against our law!"

[14]Paul was about to say something, but Gallio spoke to the Jews. Gallio said, "I would listen to you Jews if you were complaining about a crime or some wrong. [15]But the things you are saying are only questions about words and names—arguments about your own law. So you must solve this problem yourselves. I don't want to be a judge of these things!" [16]Then Gallio made them leave the court.

[17]Then they all grabbed Sosthenes. (Sosthenes was now the leader of the synagogue.) They beat him there before the court. But this did not bother Gallio.

PAUL RETURNS TO ANTIOCH

[18]Paul stayed with the believers for many more days. Then he left and sailed for Syria. Priscilla and Aquila went with him. At Cenchrea, Paul cut off his hair.[n] This showed that he had made a promise to God. [19]Then they went to Ephesus, where Paul left Priscilla and Aquila. While Paul was there, he went into the synagogue and talked with the Jews. [20]When they asked him to stay with them longer, he refused. [21]He left them, but he said, "I will come back to you again if God wants me to." And so he sailed away from Ephesus.

[22]Paul landed at Caesarea. Then he went and gave greetings to the church in Jerusalem. After that, Paul went to Antioch. [23]He stayed there for a while and then left and went through the countries of Galatia and Phrygia. He traveled from town to town in these countries, giving strength to all the followers.

APOLLOS IN EPHESUS AND CORINTH

[24]A Jew named Apollos came to Ephesus. He was born in the city of Alexandria. He was an educated man who knew the Scriptures well. [25]He had been taught about the Lord. He was always very excited when he spoke and taught the truth about Jesus. But the only baptism that Apollos knew about was the baptism that John[n] taught.

18:6 shook . . . clothes This was a warning. It showed that Paul was finished talking to the Jews.
18:18 cut . . . hair Jews did this to show that the time of a special promise to God was finished.

[26]Apollos began to speak very boldly in the synagogue, and Priscilla and Aquila heard him. So they took him to their home and helped him better understand the way of God. [27]Now Apollos wanted to go to the country of Southern Greece, so the believers helped him. They wrote a letter to the followers there, asking them to accept him. These followers had believed in Jesus because of God's grace. When Apollos went there, he helped them very much. [28]He argued very strongly with the Jews before all the people. Apollos clearly proved that the Jews were wrong. Using the Scriptures, he proved that Jesus is the Christ.

PAUL IN EPHESUS

19 While Apollos was in Corinth, Paul was visiting some places on the way to Ephesus. There he found some followers. [2]Paul asked them, "Did you receive the Holy Spirit when you believed?"

They said, "We have never even heard of a Holy Spirit!"

[3]So he asked, "What kind of baptism did you have?"

They said, "It was the baptism that John[n] taught."

[4]Paul said, "John's baptism was a baptism of changed hearts and lives. He told people to believe in the One who would come after him. That One is Jesus."

[5]When they heard this, they were baptized in the name of the Lord Jesus. [6]Then Paul laid his hands on them,[n] and the Holy Spirit came upon them. They began speaking different languages and prophesying. [7]There were about 12 men in this group.

[8]Paul went into the synagogue and spoke out boldly for three months. He talked with the Jews and persuaded them to accept the things he said about the kingdom of God. [9]But some of the Jews became stubborn and refused to believe. These Jews said evil things about the Way of Jesus. All the people heard these things. So Paul left them and took the followers with him. He went to a place where a man named Tyrannus had a school. There Paul talked with people every day [10]for two years. Because of his work, every Jew and Greek in Asia heard the word of the Lord.

> Don't be afraid! Continue talking to people and don't be quiet! I am with you.
> —ACTS 18:9–10

THE SONS OF SCEVA

[11]God used Paul to do some very special miracles. [12]Some people took handkerchiefs and clothes that Paul had used and put them on the sick. When they did this, the sick were healed and evil spirits left them.

[13-14]But some Jews also were traveling around and making evil spirits go out of people. The seven sons of Sceva were doing this. (Sceva was a leading Jewish priest.) These Jews tried to use the name of the Lord Jesus to force the evil spirits out. They would say, "By the same Jesus that Paul talks about, I order you to come out!"

[15]But one time an evil spirit said to these Jews, "I know Jesus, and I know about Paul, but who are you?"

[16]Then the man, who had the evil spirit in him, jumped on these Jews. He was much stronger than all of them.

18:25; 19:3 **John** John the Baptist, who preached to people about Christ's coming (Matthew 3; Luke 3).
19:6 **laid his hands on them** Here, doing this was a sign to show that Paul had God's authority or power to give these people special powers of the Holy Spirit.

He beat them and tore their clothes off, so they ran away from the house. [17]All the people in Ephesus, Jews and Greeks, learned about this. They were filled with fear. And the people gave great honor to the Lord Jesus. [18]Many of the believers began to confess openly and tell all the evil things they had done. [19]Some of them had used magic. These believers brought their magic books and burned them before everyone. Those books were worth about 50,000 silver coins.[n]

[20]So in a powerful way the word of the Lord kept spreading and growing.

PAUL PLANS A TRIP

[21]After these things, Paul made plans to go to Jerusalem. He planned to go through the countries of Macedonia and Southern Greece, and then on to Jerusalem. He said, "After I have been to Jerusalem, I must also visit Rome." [22]Paul sent Timothy and Erastus, two of his helpers, ahead to Macedonia. He himself stayed in Asia for a while.

TROUBLE IN EPHESUS

[23]But during that time, there was some serious trouble in Ephesus about the Way of Jesus. [24]There was a man named Demetrius, who worked with silver. He made little silver models that looked like the temple of the goddess Artemis.[n] The men who did this work made much money. [25]Demetrius had a meeting with these men and some others who did the same kind of work. He told them, "Men, you know that we make a lot of money from our business. [26]But look at what this man Paul is doing! He has convinced and turned away many people in Ephesus and in almost all of Asia! He says the gods that men make are not real. [27]There is a danger that our business will lose its good name. But there is also another danger: People will begin to think that the temple of the great goddess Artemis is not important! Her greatness will be destroyed. And Artemis is the goddess that everyone in Asia and the whole world worships."

[28]When the men heard this, they became very angry. They shouted, "Great is Artemis of the Ephesians!" [29]The whole city became confused. The people grabbed Gaius and Aristarchus. (These two men were from Macedonia and were traveling with Paul.) Then all the people ran to the theater. [30]Paul wanted to go in and talk to the crowd, but the followers did not let him. [31]Also, some leaders of Asia were friends of Paul. They sent him a message, begging him not to go into the theater. [32]Some people were shouting one thing, and some were shouting another. The meeting was completely confused. Most of the people did not know why they had come together. [33]The Jews put a man named Alexander in front of the people. Some of them had told him what to do. Alexander waved his hand because he wanted to explain things to the people. [34]But when they saw that Alexander was a Jew, they all began shouting the same thing. They continued shouting for two hours: "Great is Artemis of the Ephesians!"

[35]Then the city clerk made the crowd be quiet. He said, "Men of Ephesus, everyone knows that Ephesus is the city that keeps the temple of the great goddess Artemis. All people know that we also keep her holy stone[n] that fell from heaven. [36]No one can say that this is not true. So you should be quiet. You must stop and think before you do anything. [37]You brought these men here, but they have not said anything evil against our goddess. They have not stolen anything from her temple. [38]We have courts of law, and there are judges. Do Demetrius and the men who work with him have a charge against anyone? They should

---

19:19 **50,000 silver coins** Probably drachmas. One coin was enough to pay a man for working one day.
19:24 **Artemis** A Greek goddess that the people of Asia Minor worshiped.
19:35 **holy stone** Probably a meteorite or stone that the people thought looked like Artemis.

go to the courts! That is where they can argue with each other! ³⁹Is there something else you want to talk about? It can be decided at the regular town meeting of the people. ⁴⁰I say this because some people might see this trouble today and say that we are rioting. We could not explain this because there is no real reason for this meeting." ⁴¹After the city clerk said these things, he told the people to go home.

PAUL IN MACEDONIA AND GREECE

20 When the trouble stopped, Paul sent for the followers to come to him. He encouraged them and then told them good-bye. Paul left and went to the country of Macedonia. ²He said many things to strengthen the followers in the different places on his way through Macedonia. Then he went to Southern Greece. ³He stayed there three months. He was ready to sail for Syria, but some Jews were planning something against him. So Paul decided to go back through Macedonia to Syria. ⁴Some men went with him. They were Sopater son of Pyrrhus, from the city of Berea; Aristarchus and Secundus, from the city of Thessalonica; Gaius, from Derbe; and Timothy; and Tychicus and Trophimus, two men from Asia. ⁵These men went first, ahead of Paul, and waited for us at Troas. ⁶We sailed from Philippi after the Feast of Unleavened Bread and we met them in Troas five days later. We stayed there seven days.

PAUL'S LAST VISIT TO TROAS

⁷On the first day of the week,ⁿ we all met together to break bread.ⁿ Paul spoke to the group. Because he was planning to leave the next day, he kept on talking till midnight. ⁸We were all together in a room upstairs, and there were many lamps in the room. ⁹A young man named Eutychus was sitting in the window. As Paul continued talking, Eutychus was falling into a deep sleep. Finally, he went sound asleep and fell to the ground from the third floor. When they picked him up, he was dead. ¹⁰Paul went down to Eutychus. He knelt down and put his arms around him. He said, "Don't worry. He is alive now." ¹¹Then Paul went upstairs again, broke bread, and ate. He spoke to them a long time, until it was early morning. Then he left. ¹²They took the young man home alive and were greatly comforted.

THE TRIP FROM TROAS TO MILETUS

¹³We sailed for the city of Assos. We went first, ahead of Paul. He wanted to join us on the ship there. Paul planned it this way because he wanted to go to Assos by land. ¹⁴When he met us at Assos, we took him aboard and went to Mitylene. ¹⁵The next day, we sailed from Mitylene and came to a place near Chios. The next day, we sailed to Samos. A day later, we reached Miletus. ¹⁶Paul had already decided not to stop at Ephesus. He did not want to stay too long in Asia. He was hurrying to be in Jerusalem on the day of Pentecost, if that was possible.

THE ELDERS FROM EPHESUS

¹⁷Now from Miletus Paul sent to Ephesus and called for the elders of the church. ¹⁸When they came to him, he said, "You know about my life from the first day I came to Asia. You know the way I lived all the time I was with you. ¹⁹The Jews plotted against me. This troubled me very much. But you know that I always served the Lord. I never thought of myself first, and I often cried. ²⁰You know I preached to you,

---

20:7 **first day of the week** Sunday, which for the Jews began at sunset on our Saturday. But if in this part of Asia a different system of time was used, then the meeting was on our Sunday night.
20:7 **break bread** Probably the Lord's Supper, the special meal that Jesus told his followers to eat to remember him (Luke 22:14–20).

and I did not hold back anything that would help you. You know that I taught you in public and in your homes. ²¹I warned both Jews and Greeks to change their lives and turn to God. And I told them all to believe in our Lord Jesus. ²²But now I must obey the Holy Spirit and go to Jerusalem. I don't know what will happen to me there. ²³I know only that in every city the Holy Spirit tells me that troubles and even jail wait for me. ²⁴I don't care about my own life. The most important thing is that I complete my mission. I want to finish the work that the Lord Jesus gave me—to tell people the Good News about God's grace.

²⁵"And now, I know that none of you will ever see me again. All the time I was with you, I was preaching the kingdom of God. ²⁶So today I can tell you one thing that I am sure of: If any of you should be lost, I am not responsible. ²⁷This is because I have told you everything God wants you to know. ²⁸Be careful for yourselves and for all the people God has given you. The Holy Spirit gave you the work of caring for this flock. You must be like shepherds to the church of God." This is the church that God bought with his own death. ²⁹I know that after I leave, some men will come like wild wolves and try to destroy the flock. ³⁰Also, men from your own group will rise up and twist the truth. They will lead away followers after them. ³¹So be careful! Always remember this: For three years I never stopped warning each of you. I taught you night and day. I often cried over you.

³²"Now I am putting you in the care of God and the message about his grace. That message is able to give you strength, and it will give you the blessings that God has for all his holy people. ³³When I was with you, I never wanted anyone's money or fine clothes. ³⁴You know that I always worked to take care of my own needs and the needs of those who were with me. ³⁵I showed you in all things that you should work as I did and help the weak. I taught you to remember the words of Jesus. He said, 'It is more blessed to give than to receive.'"

³⁶When Paul had said this, he knelt down with all of them and prayed. ³⁷⁻³⁸And they all cried because Paul had said that they would never see him again. They put their arms around him and kissed him. Then they went with him to the ship.

Paul . . . told them everything that God had done among the non-Jewish people through him.
–ACTS 21:19

PAUL GOES TO JERUSALEM

21 We all said good-bye to them and left. We sailed straight to Cos island. The next day, we reached Rhodes, and from Rhodes we went to Patara. ²There we found a ship that was going to Phoenicia. We went aboard and sailed away. ³We sailed near the island of Cyprus. We could see it to the north, but we sailed on to Syria. We stopped at Tyre because the ship needed to unload its cargo there. ⁴We found some followers in Tyre, and we stayed with them for seven days. Through the Holy Spirit they warned Paul not to go to Jerusalem. ⁵When we finished our visit, we left and continued our trip. All the followers, even the women and children, came outside the city with us. We all knelt down on the beach and prayed. ⁶Then we said good-bye and got on the ship. The followers went back home.

20:28 **of God** Some Greek copies read "of the Lord."

[7]We continued our trip from Tyre and arrived at Ptolemais. We greeted the believers there and stayed with them for a day. [8]We left Ptolemais and went to the city of Caesarea. There we went into the home of Philip and stayed with him. Philip had the work of telling the Good News. He was one of the seven helpers.[n] [9]He had four unmarried daughters who had the gift of prophesying. [10]After we had been there for some time, a prophet named Agabus arrived from Judea. [11]He came to us and borrowed Paul's belt. Then he used the belt to tie his own hands and feet. He said, "The Holy Spirit says, 'This is how the Jews in Jerusalem will tie up the man who wears this belt. Then they will give him to the non-Jewish people.'"

[12]We all heard these words. So we and the people there begged Paul not to go to Jerusalem. [13]But he said, "Why are you crying and making me so sad? I am ready to be tied up in Jerusalem. And I am ready to die for the Lord Jesus!"

[14]We could not persuade him to stay away from Jerusalem. So we stopped begging him and said, "We pray that what the Lord wants will be done."

[15]After this, we got ready and started on our way to Jerusalem. [16]Some of the followers from Caesarea went with us. They took us to the home of Mnason, a man from Cyprus. Mnason was one of the first followers. They took us to his home so that we could stay with him.

PAUL VISITS JAMES

[17]In Jerusalem the believers were glad to see us. [18]The next day, Paul went with us to visit James. All the elders were there, too. [19]Paul greeted them and told them everything that God had done among the non-Jewish people through him. [20]When they heard this, they praised God. Then they said to Paul, "Brother, you can see that many thousands of Jews have become believers. But they think it is very important to obey the law of Moses. [21]These Jews have heard about your teaching. They heard that you tell the Jews who live among non-Jews to leave the law of Moses. They heard that you tell them not to circumcise their children and not to obey Jewish customs. [22]What should we do? The Jewish believers here will learn that you have come. [23]So we will tell you what to do: Four of our men have made a promise to God. [24]Take these men with you and share in their cleansing ceremony.[n] Pay their expenses. Then they can shave their heads.[n] Do this and it will prove to everyone that what they have heard about you is not true. They will see that you follow the law of Moses in your own life. [25]We have already sent a letter to the non-Jewish believers. The letter said: 'Do not eat food that has been offered to idols. Do not taste blood. Do not eat animals that have been strangled. Do not take part in any kind of sexual sin.'"

[26]Then Paul took the four men with him. The next day, he shared in the cleansing ceremony. Then he went to the Temple. Paul announced the time when the days of the cleansing ceremony would be finished. On the last day an offering would be given for each of the men.

[27]The seven days were almost over. But some Jews from Asia saw Paul at the Temple. They caused all the people to be upset, and they grabbed Paul. [28]They shouted, "Men of Israel, help us! This is the man who goes everywhere teaching things that are against the law of Moses, against our people, and against this Temple. And now he has brought some Greek men into the Temple. He has made this holy place unclean!" [29](The Jews said this because they had

---

21:8 helpers The seven men chosen for a special work described in Acts 6:1–6.
21:24 cleansing ceremony The special things Jews did to end the Nazirite promise.
21:24 shave their heads The Jews did this to show that their promise was finished.

seen Trophimus with Paul in Jerusalem. Trophimus was a man from Ephesus. The Jews thought that Paul had brought him into the Temple.)

[30]All the people in Jerusalem became very upset. They ran and took Paul and dragged him out of the Temple. The Temple doors were closed immediately. [31]The people were about to kill Paul. Now the commander of the Roman army in Jerusalem learned that there was trouble in the whole city. [32]Immediately he ran to the place where the crowd was gathered. He brought officers and soldiers with him, and the people saw them. So they stopped beating Paul. [33]The commander went to Paul and arrested him. He told his soldiers to bind Paul with two chains. Then he asked, "Who is this man? What has he done wrong?" [34]Some in the crowd were yelling one thing, and some were yelling another. Because of all this confusion and shouting, the commander could not learn what had happened. So he ordered the soldiers to take Paul to the army building. [35-36]The whole mob was following them. When the soldiers came to the steps, they had to carry Paul. They did this because the people were ready to hurt him. They were shouting, "Kill him!"

[37]The soldiers were about to take Paul into the army building. But he spoke to the commander, "May I say something to you?"

The commander said, "Do you speak Greek? [38]I thought you were the Egyptian who started some trouble against the government not long ago. He led 4,000 killers out to the desert."

[39]Paul said, "No, I am a Jew from Tarsus in the country of Cilicia. I am a citizen of that important city. Please, let me speak to the people."

[40]The commander gave permission, so Paul stood on the steps. He waved with his hand so that the people would be quiet. When there was silence, Paul spoke to them in the Jewish language.[n]

PAUL SPEAKS TO THE PEOPLE

22 Paul said, "Brothers and fathers, listen to me! I will make my defense to you." [2]When the Jews heard him speaking the Jewish language,[n] they became very quiet. Paul said, [3]"I am a Jew. I was born in Tarsus in the country of Cilicia. I grew up in this city. I was a student of Gamaliel.[n] He carefully taught me everything about the law of our ancestors. I was very serious about serving God, just as are all of you here today. [4]I hurt the people who followed the Way of Jesus. Some of them were even killed. I arrested men and women and put them in jail. [5]The high priest and the whole council of Jewish elders can tell you that this is true. These leaders gave me letters to the Jewish brothers in Damascus. So I was going there to arrest these people and bring them back to Jerusalem to be punished.

[6]"But something happened to me on my way to Damascus. It was about noon when I came near Damascus. Suddenly a bright light from heaven flashed all around me. [7]I fell to the ground and heard a voice saying, 'Saul, Saul, why are you doing things against me?' [8]I asked, 'Who are you, Lord?' The voice said, 'I am Jesus from Nazareth. I am the One you are trying to hurt.' [9]The men who were with me did not understand the voice. But they saw the light. [10]I said, 'What shall I do, Lord?' The Lord answered, 'Get up and go to Damascus. There you will be told about all the things I have planned for you to do.' [11]I could not see, because the bright light had made me blind. So the men led me into Damascus.

[12]"There a man named Ananias came to me. He was a religious man; he obeyed the law of Moses. All the Jews who lived there respected him. [13]Ananias came to

---

21:40; 22:2 **Jewish language** Aramaic, the language of the Jews in the first century.
22:3 **Gamaliel** A very important teacher of the Pharisees, a Jewish religious group (Acts 5:34).

me, stood by me, and said, 'Brother Saul, see again!' Immediately I was able to see him. ¹⁴Ananias told me, 'The God of our fathers chose you long ago. He chose you to know his plan. He chose you to see the Righteous One and to hear words from him. ¹⁵You will be his witness to all people. You will tell them about the things you have seen and heard. ¹⁶Now, why wait any longer? Get up, be baptized, and wash your sins away. Do this, trusting in him to save you.'

¹⁷"Later, I returned to Jerusalem. I was praying in the Temple, and I saw a vision. ¹⁸I saw the Lord saying to me, 'Hurry! Leave Jerusalem now! The people here will not accept the truth about me.' ¹⁹But I said, 'Lord, they know that in every synagogue I put the believers in jail and beat them. ²⁰They also know that I was there when Stephen, your witness, was killed. I stood there and agreed that they should kill him. I even held the coats of the men who were killing him!' ²¹But the Lord said to me, 'Leave now. I will send you far away to the non-Jewish people.'"

²²The crowd listened to Paul until he said this. Then they began shouting, "Get rid of him! A man like this doesn't deserve to live!" ²³They shouted and threw off their coats.ⁿ They threw dust into the air.ⁿ

²⁴Then the commander ordered the soldiers to take Paul into the army building and beat him. The commander wanted to make Paul tell why the people were shouting against him like this. ²⁵So the soldiers were tying him up, preparing to beat him. But Paul said to an officer there, "Do you have the right to beat a Roman citizenⁿ who has not been proven guilty?"

²⁶When the officer heard this, he went to the commander and told him about it. The officer said, "Do you know what you are doing? This man is a Roman citizen!"

²⁷The commander came to Paul and said, "Tell me, are you really a Roman citizen?"

He answered, "Yes."

²⁸The commander said, "I paid a lot of money to become a Roman citizen."

But Paul said, "I was born a citizen."

²⁹The men who were preparing to question Paul moved away from him immediately. The commander was frightened because he had already tied Paul, and Paul was a Roman citizen.

PAUL SPEAKS TO JEWISH LEADERS

³⁰The next day the commander decided to learn why the Jews were accusing Paul. So he ordered the leading priests and the Jewish council to meet. The commander took Paul's chains off. Then he brought Paul out and stood him before their meeting.

23 Paul looked at the Jewish council and said, "Brothers, I have lived my life in a good way before God up to this day." ²Ananias,ⁿ the high priest, heard this and told the men who were standing near Paul to hit him on his mouth. ³Paul said to Ananias, "God will hit you too! You are like a wall that has been painted white! You sit there and judge me, using the law of Moses. But you are telling them to hit me, and that is against the law."

⁴The men standing near Paul said to him, "You cannot talk like that to God's high priest! You are insulting him!"

⁵Paul said, "Brothers, I did not know this man was the high priest. It is written in the Scriptures, 'You must not curse a leader of your people.'"ⁿ

⁶Some of the men in the meeting were Sadducees, and others were Pharisees. So Paul shouted to them,

---

22:23 threw off their coats This showed that the Jews were very angry at Paul.
22:23 threw dust into the air This showed even greater anger.
22:25 Roman citizen Roman law said that Roman citizens must not be beaten before they had a trial.
23:2 Ananias This is not the same man named Ananias in Acts 22:12.
23:5 'You . . . people.' Quotation from Exodus 22:28.

"My brothers, I am a Pharisee and my father was a Pharisee! I am on trial here because I hope that people will rise from death!"

⁷When Paul said this, there was an argument between the Pharisees and the Sadducees. The group was divided. ⁸(The Sadducees believe that after people die, they cannot live again. The Sadducees also teach that there are no angels or spirits. But the Pharisees believe in them all.) ⁹So there was a great uproar. Some of the teachers of the law, who were Pharisees, stood up and argued, "We find nothing wrong with this man! Maybe an angel or a spirit did speak to him."

¹⁰The argument was beginning to turn into a fight. The commander was afraid that the Jews would tear Paul to pieces. So the commander told the soldiers to go down and take Paul away and put him in the army building.

¹¹The next night the Lord came and stood by Paul. He said, "Be brave! You have told people in Jerusalem about me. You must do the same in Rome also."

¹²In the morning some of the Jews made a plan to kill Paul. They made a promise that they would not eat or drink anything until they had killed him. ¹³There were more than 40 Jews who made this plan. ¹⁴They went and talked to the leading priests and the Jewish elders. They said, "We have made a promise to ourselves that we will not eat or drink until we have killed Paul! ¹⁵So this is what we want you to do: Send a message to the commander to bring Paul out to you. Tell him you want to ask Paul more questions. We will be waiting to kill him while he is on the way here."

¹⁶But Paul's nephew heard about this plan. He went to the army building and told Paul about it. ¹⁷Then Paul called one of the officers and said, "Take this young man to the commander. He has a message for him."

¹⁸So the officer brought Paul's nephew to the commander. The officer said, "The prisoner, Paul, asked me to bring this young man to you. He wants to tell you something."

¹⁹The commander led the young man to a place where they could be alone. The commander asked, "What do you want to tell me?"

²⁰The young man said, "The Jews have decided to ask you to bring Paul down to their council meeting tomorrow. They want you to think that they are going to ask him more questions. ²¹But don't believe them! There are more than 40 men who are hiding and waiting to kill Paul. They have all made a promise not to eat or drink until they have killed him! Now they are waiting for you to agree."

²²The commander sent the young man away. He said to him, "Don't tell anyone that you have told me about their plan."

PAUL IS SENT TO CAESAREA

²³Then the commander called two officers. He said to them, "I need some men to go to Caesarea. Get 200 soldiers ready. Also, get 70 horsemen and 200 men with spears. Be ready to leave at nine o'clock tonight. ²⁴Get some horses for Paul to ride. He must be taken to Governor Felix safely." ²⁵And he wrote a letter that said:

²⁶From Claudius Lysias.

To the Most Excellent Governor Felix:

Greetings.
²⁷The Jews had taken this man, and they planned to kill him. But I learned that he is a Roman citizen, so I went with my soldiers and saved him. ²⁸I wanted to know why they were accusing him. So I brought him before their council meeting. ²⁹I learned that the Jews said Paul did some things that were wrong. But these charges were about their own laws. And no charge was worthy of jail or death. ³⁰I was told that some of

the Jews were planning to kill Paul. So I sent him to you at once. I also told those Jews to tell you what they have against him.

[31]So the soldiers did what they were told. They took Paul and brought him to the city of Antipatris that night. [32]The next day the horsemen went with Paul to Caesarea. But the other soldiers went back to the army building in Jerusalem. [33]The horsemen came to Caesarea and gave the letter to the governor. Then they turned Paul over to him. [34]The governor read the letter. Then he asked Paul, "What area are you from?" He learned that Paul was from Cilicia. [35]He said, "I will hear your case when those who are against you come here too." Then the governor gave orders for Paul to be kept under guard in the palace. (This building had been built by Herod.)

THE JEWS ACCUSE PAUL

24 Five days later Ananias, the high priest, went to the city of Caesarea. With him were some of the Jewish elders and a lawyer named Tertullus. They had come to make charges against Paul before the governor. [2]Paul was called into the meeting, and Tertullus began to accuse him, saying: "Most Excellent Felix! Our people enjoy much peace because of you, and many wrong things in our country are being made right through your wise help. [3]We accept these things always and in every place. And we are thankful for them. [4]But I do not want to take any more of your time. I beg you to be kind and listen to our few words. [5]This man is a troublemaker. He makes trouble among the Jews everywhere in the world. He is a leader of the Nazarene group. [6]Also, he was trying to make the Temple unclean, but we stopped him. [And we wanted to judge him by our own law. [7]But the officer Lysias came and used much force to take him from us. And Lysias commanded his people to come to you to accuse us.][n] [8]You can decide if all these things are true. Ask him some questions yourself." [9]The other Jews agreed and said that all of this was true.

[10]The governor made a sign for Paul to speak. So Paul said, "Governor Felix, I know that you have been a judge over this nation for a long time. So I am happy to defend myself before you. [11]I went to worship in Jerusalem only 12 days ago. You can learn for yourself that this is true. [12]Those who are accusing me did not find me arguing with anyone in the Temple. I was not stirring up the people. And I was not making trouble in the Temple or in the synagogues or in the city. [13]They cannot prove the things they are saying against me now. [14]But I will tell you this: I worship the God of our ancestors as a follower of the Way of Jesus. The Jews say that the Way of Jesus is not the right way. But I believe everything that is taught in the law of Moses and that is written in the books of the Prophets. [15]I have the same hope in God that they have—the hope that all people, good and bad, will be raised from death. [16]This is why I always try to do what I believe is right before God and men.

[17]"I was away from Jerusalem for several years. I went back there to bring money to my people and to offer

> The next night the Lord came and stood by Paul. He said, "Be brave!"
>
> –ACTS 23:11

24:6–7 **And . . . us.** Some Greek copies do not contain the bracketed text.

sacrifices. [18]I was doing this when they found me in the Temple. I had finished the cleansing ceremony. I had not made any trouble; no people were gathering around me. [19]But some Jews from Asia were there. They should be here, standing before you. If I have really done anything wrong, they are the ones who should accuse me. [20]Or ask these Jews here if they found any wrong in me when I stood before the Jewish council in Jerusalem. [21]But I did say one thing when I stood before them: 'You are judging me today because I believe that people will rise from death!'"

[22]Felix already understood much about the Way of Jesus. He stopped the trial and said, "When commander Lysias comes here, I will decide about your case." [23]Felix told the officer to keep Paul guarded. But he told the officer to give Paul some freedom and to let his friends bring what he needed.

PAUL SPEAKS TO FELIX AND HIS WIFE

[24]After some days Felix came with his wife, Drusilla, who was a Jew. He asked for Paul to be brought to him. He listened to Paul talk about believing in Christ Jesus. [25]But Felix became afraid when Paul spoke about things like right living, self-control, and the time when God will judge the world. He said, "Go away now. When I have more time, I will call for you." [26]At the same time Felix hoped that Paul would give him some money. So he sent for Paul often and talked with him.

[27]But after two years, Porcius Festus became governor. Felix was no longer governor, but he had left Paul in prison to please the Jews.

PAUL ASKS TO SEE CAESAR

25 Three days after Festus became governor, he went from Caesarea to Jerusalem. [2]There the leading priests and the important Jewish leaders made charges against Paul before Festus. [3]They asked Festus to do something for them; they wanted him to send Paul back to Jerusalem. (They had a plan to kill Paul on the way.) [4]But Festus answered, "No! Paul will be kept in Caesarea. I will return there soon myself. [5]Some of your leaders should go with me. They can accuse the man there in Caesarea, if he has really done something wrong."

[6]Festus stayed in Jerusalem another eight or ten days. Then he went back to Caesarea. The next day he told the soldiers to bring Paul before him. Festus was seated on the judge's seat [7]when Paul came into the room. The Jews who had come from Jerusalem stood around him. They started making serious charges against Paul. But they could not prove any of them. [8]This is what Paul said to defend himself: "I have done nothing wrong against the Jewish law, against the Temple, or against Caesar!"

[9]But Festus wanted to please the Jews. So he asked Paul, "Do you want to go to Jerusalem? Do you want me to judge you there on these charges?"

[10]Paul said, "I am standing at Caesar's judgment seat now. This is where I should be judged! I have done nothing wrong to the Jews; you know this is true. [11]If I have done something wrong and the law says I must die, I do not ask to be saved from death. But if these charges are not true, then no one can give me to them. No! I want Caesar to hear my case!"

[12]Festus talked about this with the people who advised him. Then he said, "You have asked to see Caesar; so you will go to Caesar!"

PAUL BEFORE KING AGRIPPA

[13]A few days later King Agrippa and Bernice came to Caesarea to visit Festus. [14]They stayed there for some time, and Festus told the king about Paul's case. Festus said, "There is a man that Felix left in prison. [15]When I went to Jerusalem, the leading priests and the Jewish elders there made charges against him. They wanted

me to sentence him to death. [16]But I answered, 'When a man is accused of a crime, Romans do not hand him over just to please someone. The man must be allowed to face his accusers and defend himself against their charges.' [17]So these Jews came here to Caesarea for the trial. And I did not waste time. The next day I sat on the judge's seat and commanded that the man be brought in. [18]The Jews stood up and accused him. But they did not accuse him of any serious crime as I thought they would. [19]The things they said were about their own religion and about a man named Jesus. Jesus died, but Paul said that he is still alive. [20]I did not know much about these things; so I did not ask questions. But I asked Paul, 'Do you want to go to Jerusalem and be judged there?' [21]But he asked to be kept in Caesarea. He wants a decision from the Emperor.[n] So I ordered that Paul be held until I could send him to Caesar in Rome."

[22]Agrippa said to Festus, "I would like to hear this man, too."

Festus said, "Tomorrow you will hear him!"

[23]The next day Agrippa and Bernice appeared. They dressed and acted like very important people. Agrippa and Bernice, the army leaders, and the important men of Caesarea went into the judgment room. Then Festus ordered the soldiers to bring Paul in. [24]Festus said, "King Agrippa and all who are gathered here with us, you see this man. All the Jewish people, here and in Jerusalem, have complained to me about him. They shout that he should not live any longer. [25]When I judged him, I could find nothing wrong. I found no reason to order his death. But he asked to be judged by Caesar. So I decided to send him. [26]But I have nothing definite to write the Emperor about him. So I have brought him before all of you—especially you, King Agrippa. I hope that you can question him and give me something to write. [27]I think it is foolish to send a prisoner to Caesar without telling what the charges are against him."

PAUL DEFENDS HIMSELF

26 Agrippa said to Paul, "You may now speak to defend yourself."

Then Paul raised his hand and began to speak. [2]He said, "King Agrippa, I will answer all the charges that the Jews make against me. I think it is a blessing that I can stand here before you today. [3]I am very happy to talk to you, because you know so much about all the Jewish customs and the things that the Jews argue about. Please listen to me patiently.

[4]"All the Jews know about my whole life. They know the way I lived from the beginning in my own country and later in Jerusalem. [5]They have known me for a long time. If they want to, they can tell you that I was a good Pharisee. And the Pharisees obey the laws of the Jewish religion more carefully than any other group of Jewish people. [6]Now I am on trial because I hope for the promise that God made to our ancestors. [7]This is the promise that the 12 tribes of our people hope to receive. For this hope the Jews serve God day and night. My king, the Jews have accused me because I hope for this same promise! [8]Why do any of you people think it is impossible for God to raise people from death?

[9]"I too thought I ought to do many things against Jesus from Nazareth. [10]And in Jerusalem I did many things against God's people. The leading priests gave me the power to put many of them in jail. When they were being killed, I agreed that it was a good thing. [11]In every synagogue, I often punished them. I tried to make them say evil things against Jesus. I was so angry against them that I even went to other cities to find them and punish them. [12]"One time the leading priests gave

25:21 **Emperor** The ruler of the Roman Empire, which was almost all the world.

me permission and the power to go to Damascus. [13]On the way there, at noon, I saw a light from heaven. The light was brighter than the sun. It flashed all around me and the men who were traveling with me. [14]We all fell to the ground. Then I heard a voice speaking to me in the Jewish language.[n] The voice said, 'Saul, Saul, why are you doing things against me? You are only hurting yourself by fighting me.' [15]I said, 'Who are you, Lord?' The Lord said, 'I am Jesus. I am the One you are trying to hurt. [16]Stand up! I have chosen you to be my servant. You will be my witness— you will tell people the things that you have seen and the things that I will show you. This is why I have come to you today. [17]I will not let your own people hurt you. And I will keep you safe from the non-Jewish people too. These are the people I am sending you to. [18]I send you to open their eyes that they may turn away from darkness to the light. I send you that they may turn away from the power of Satan and turn to God. Then their sins can be forgiven and they can have a place with those people who have been made holy by believing in me.'

[19]"King Agrippa, after I had this vision from heaven, I obeyed it. [20]I began telling people that they should change their hearts and lives and turn to God. I told them to do things to show that they really had changed. I told this first to those in Damascus, then in Jerusalem and in every part of Judea, and also to the non-Jewish people. [21]This is why the Jews took me and were trying to kill me in the Temple. [22]But God helped me and is still helping me today. With God's help I am standing here today and telling all people what I have seen. But I am saying nothing new. I am saying what Moses and the prophets said would happen. [23]They said that the Christ would die and be the first to rise from death. They said that the Christ would bring light to the Jewish and non-Jewish people."

PAUL TRIES TO PERSUADE AGRIPPA

[24]While Paul was saying these things to defend himself, Festus said loudly, "Paul, you are out of your mind! Too much study has driven you crazy!"

[25]Paul said, "Most Excellent Festus, I am not crazy. My words are true. They are not the words of a foolish man. [26]King Agrippa knows about these things. I can speak freely to him. I know that he has heard about all of these things. They did not happen off in a corner. [27]King Agrippa, do you believe what the prophets wrote? I know you believe!"

[28]King Agrippa said to Paul, "Do you think you can persuade me to become a Christian in such a short time?"

[29]Paul said, "Whether it is a short or a long time, I pray to God that not only you but every person listening to me today would be saved and be like me— except for these chains I have!"

[30]Then King Agrippa, Governor Festus, Bernice, and all the people sitting with them stood up [31]and left the room. They were talking to each other. They said, "There is no reason why this man should die or be put in jail." [32]And Agrippa said to Festus, "We could let this man go free, but he has asked Caesar to hear his case."

> With God's help I am standing here today and telling all people what I have seen.
>
> –ACTS 26:22

26:14 **Jewish language** Aramaic, the language of the Jews in the first century.

PAUL SAILS FOR ROME

27 It was decided that we would sail for Italy. An officer named Julius, who served in the Emperor's[n] army, guarded Paul and some other prisoners. [2]We got on a ship and left. The ship was from the city of Adramyttium and was about to sail to different ports in Asia. Aristarchus, a man from the city of Thessalonica in Macedonia, went with us. [3]The next day we came to Sidon. Julius was very good to Paul. He gave Paul freedom to go visit his friends, who took care of his needs. [4]We left Sidon and sailed close to the island of Cyprus because the wind was blowing against us. [5]We went across the sea by Cilicia and Pamphylia. Then we came to the city of Myra, in Lycia. [6]There the officer found a ship from Alexandria that was going to Italy. So he put us on it.

[7]We sailed slowly for many days. We had a hard time reaching Cnidus because the wind was blowing against us. We could not go any farther that way. So we sailed by the south side of the island of Crete near Salmone. [8]We sailed along the coast, but the sailing was hard. Then we came to a place called Safe Harbors, near the city of Lasea.

[9]But we had lost much time. It was now dangerous to sail, because it was already after the Day of Cleansing.[n] So Paul warned them, [10]"Men, I can see there will be a lot of trouble on this trip. The ship and the things in the ship will be lost. Even our lives may be lost!" [11]But the captain and the owner of the ship did not agree with Paul. So the officer did not believe Paul. Instead, the officer believed what the captain and owner of the ship said. [12]And that harbor was not a good place for the ship to stay for the winter. So most of the men decided that the ship should leave. The men hoped we could go to Phoenix. The ship could stay there for the winter. (Phoenix was a city on the island of Crete. It had a harbor which faced southwest and northwest.)

THE STORM

[13]Then a good wind began to blow from the south. The men on the ship thought, "This is the wind we wanted, and now we have it!" So they pulled up the anchor. We sailed very close to the island of Crete. [14]But then a very strong wind named the "Northeaster" came from the island. [15]This wind took the ship and carried it away. The ship could not sail against it. So we stopped trying and let the wind blow us. [16]We went below a small island named Cauda. Then we were able to bring in the lifeboat, but it was very hard to do. [17]After the men took the lifeboat in, they tied ropes around the ship to hold it together. The men were afraid that the ship would hit the sandbanks of Syrtis.[n] So they lowered the sail and let the wind carry the ship. [18]The next day the storm was blowing us so hard that the men threw out some of the cargo. [19]A day later they threw out the ship's equipment. [20]For many days we could not see the sun or the stars. The storm was very bad. We lost all hope of staying alive—we thought we would die.

[21]The men had gone without food for a long time. Then one day Paul stood up before them and said, "Men, I told you not to leave Crete. You should have listened to me. Then you would not have all this trouble and loss. [22]But now I tell you to cheer up. None of you will die! But the ship will be lost. [23]Last night an angel from God came to me. This is the God I worship. I am his. [24]God's angel said, 'Paul, do not be afraid! You must stand before Caesar. And God has given you this promise: He will save the lives of all

---

27:1 **Emperor** The ruler of the Roman Empire, which was almost all the world.
27:9 **Day of Cleansing** An important Jewish holy day in the fall of the year. This was the time of year that bad storms happened on the sea.
27:17 **Syrtis** Shallow area in the sea near the Libyan coast.

those men sailing with you.' ²⁵So men, be cheerful! I trust in God. Everything will happen as his angel told me. ²⁶But we will crash on an island."

²⁷On the fourteenth night we were floating around in the Adriatic Sea.ⁿ The sailors thought we were close to land. ²⁸They threw a rope into the water with a weight on the end of it. They found that the water was 120 feet deep. They went a little farther and threw the rope in again. It was 90 feet deep. ²⁹The sailors were afraid that we would hit the rocks, so they threw four anchors into the water. Then they prayed for daylight to come. ³⁰Some of the sailors wanted to leave the ship, and they lowered the lifeboat. These sailors wanted

27:27 **Adriatic Sea** The sea between Greece and Italy, including the central Mediterranean.

☆ Acts 27:24–25

Paul was a prisoner again, and it had been decided that he would sail to Italy. While he was out at sea, a huge storm appeared. Strong winds blew against the ship for many days. Everyone thought they were going to die. And they would have! But Paul told them an angel from God had visited him. The angel told Paul that God would save everyone on the ship. They just had to believe.

When God makes us a promise, we can always count on his keeping it. When he tells us something, we can believe he is telling us the truth. The Bible promises that if we believe in Jesus, we will be saved. He will be with us here on earth. And later we will be with him in heaven—forever. You can trust what God says in the Bible because he is perfect. And he always keeps his promises.

. . . .

God promised Paul that he and all the people on the ship would be safe. Just like Paul trusted God's promises, you can trust them too. God always speaks the truth.

the other men to think that they were throwing more anchors from the front of the ship. [31]But Paul told the officer and the other soldiers, "If these men do not stay in the ship, your lives cannot be saved!" [32]So the soldiers cut the ropes and let the lifeboat fall into the water.

[33]Just before dawn Paul began persuading all the people to eat something. He said, "For the past 14 days you have been waiting and watching. You have not eaten. [34]Now I beg you to eat something. You need it to stay alive. None of you will lose even one hair off your heads." [35]After he said this, Paul took some bread and thanked God for it before all of them. He broke off a piece and began eating. [36]All the men felt better. They all started eating too. [37](There were 276 people on the ship.) [38]We ate all we wanted. Then we began making the ship lighter by throwing the grain into the sea.

THE SHIP IS DESTROYED

[39]When daylight came, the sailors saw land. They did not know what land it was, but they saw a bay with a beach. They wanted to sail the ship to the beach, if they could. [40]So they cut the ropes to the anchors and left the anchors in the sea. At the same time, they untied the ropes that were holding the rudders. Then they raised the front sail into the wind and sailed toward the beach. [41]But the ship hit a sandbank. The front of the ship stuck there and could not move. Then the big waves began to break the back of the ship to pieces.

[42]The soldiers decided to kill the prisoners so that none of them could swim away and escape. [43]But Julius, the officer, wanted to let Paul live. He did not allow the soldiers to kill the prisoners. Instead he ordered everyone who could swim to jump into the water and swim to land. [44]The rest used wooden boards or pieces of the ship. And this is how all the people made it safely to land.

PAUL ON THE ISLAND OF MALTA

28 When we were safe on land, we learned that the island was called Malta. [2]It was raining and very cold. But the people who lived there were very good to us. They made us a fire and welcomed all of us. [3]Paul gathered a pile of sticks for the fire. He was putting them on the fire when a poisonous snake came out because of the heat and bit him on the hand. [4]The people living on the island saw the snake hanging from Paul's hand. They said to each other, "This man must be a murderer! He did not die in the sea, but Justice[n] does not want him to live." [5]But Paul shook the snake off into the fire. He was not hurt. [6]The people thought that Paul would swell up or fall down dead. The people waited and watched him for a long time, but nothing bad happened to him. So they changed their minds about Paul. Now they said, "He is a god!"

[7]There were some fields around there owned by a very important man on the island. His name was Publius. He welcomed us into his home and was very good to us. We stayed in his house for three days. [8]Publius' father was very sick with a fever and dysentery.[n] But Paul went to him and prayed. Then he put his hands on the man and healed him. [9]After this, all the other sick people on the island came to Paul, and he healed them, too. [10-11]The people on the island gave us many honors. We stayed there three months. When we were ready to leave, they gave us the things we needed.

PAUL GOES TO ROME

We got on a ship from Alexandria. The ship had stayed on the island during the winter. On the front of the ship was the sign of the twin gods." [12]We stopped at Syracuse for three days and then left. [13]From there we sailed to Rhegium. The next day a wind began to blow from the southwest, so we were able to leave. A day later we came to Puteoli. [14]We found some believers there, and they asked us to stay with them for a week. Finally, we came to Rome. [15]The believers in Rome heard that we were there. They came out as far as the Market of Appius" and the Three Inns" to meet us. When Paul saw them, he was encouraged and thanked God.

PAUL IN ROME

[16]Then we arrived at Rome. There, Paul was allowed to live alone. But a soldier stayed with him to guard him.

[17]Three days later Paul sent for the Jewish leaders there. When they came together, he said, "Brothers, I have done nothing against our people. I have done nothing against the customs of our fathers. But I was arrested in Jerusalem and given to the Romans. [18]The Romans asked me many questions. But they could find no reason why I should be killed. They wanted to let me go free, [19]but the Jews there did not want that. So I had to ask to come to Rome to have my trial before Caesar. But I have no charge to bring against my own people. [20]That is why I wanted to see you and talk with you. I am bound with this chain because I believe in the hope of Israel."

[21]The Jews answered Paul, "We have received no letters from Judea about you. None of our Jewish brothers who have come from there brought news about you or told us anything bad about you. [22]We want to hear your ideas. We know that people everywhere are speaking against this religious group."

[23]Paul and the Jews chose a day for a meeting. On that day many more of the Jews met with Paul at the place he was staying. Paul spoke to them all day long, explaining the kingdom of God to them. He tried to persuade them to believe these things about Jesus. He used the law of Moses and the writings of the prophets to do this. [24]Some of the Jews believed what Paul said, but others did not. [25]So they argued, and the Jews were ready to leave. But Paul said one more thing to them: "The Holy Spirit spoke the truth to your fathers through Isaiah the prophet. He said,

[26] 'Go to this people and say:
You will listen and listen, but you
    will not understand.
You will look and look, but you will
    not learn.
[27] For these people have become
    stubborn.
They don't hear with their ears.
And they have closed their eyes.
Otherwise, they might really
    understand
what they see with their eyes
and hear with their ears.
They might really understand in
    their minds.
If they did this, they would come
    back to me and be forgiven.'
                    Isaiah 6:9–10

[28]"I want you Jews to know that God has also sent his salvation to the non-Jewish people. They will listen!" [29][After Paul said this, the Jews left. They were arguing very much with each other.]"

[30]Paul stayed two full years in his own rented house. He welcomed all people who came and visited him. [31]He preached about the kingdom of God and taught about the Lord Jesus Christ. He was very bold, and no one stopped him.

28:10–11 **twin gods** Statues of Castor and Pollux, gods in old Greek tales.
28:15 **Market of Appius** A town about 40 miles from Rome.
28:15 **Three Inns** A town about 30 miles from Rome.
28:29 **After ... other.** Some Greek copies do not contain the bracketed text.

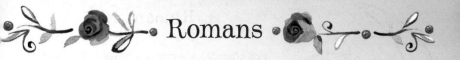

Romans

A PRAYER OF THANKS

1 From Paul, a servant of Christ Jesus. God called me to be an apostle and chose me to tell the Good News.

²God promised this Good News long ago through his prophets. That promise is written in the Holy Scriptures. ³⁻⁴The Good News is about God's Son, Jesus Christ our Lord. As a man, he was born from the family of David. But through the Spirit of holiness he was declared to be God's Son with great power by rising from death. ⁵Through Christ, God gave me the special work of an apostle. This was to lead people of all nations to believe and obey. I do this work for Christ. ⁶And you who are in Rome are also called to belong to Jesus Christ.

⁷This letter is to all of you in Rome whom God loves and has called to be his holy people.

May God our Father and the Lord Jesus Christ show you kindness and give you peace.

⁸First I want to say that I thank my God through Jesus Christ for all of you. I thank God because people everywhere in the world are talking about your great faith. ⁹⁻¹⁰God knows that every time I pray I always mention you. God is the One I serve with my whole heart by telling the Good News about his Son. I pray that I will be allowed to come to you, and this will happen if God wants it. ¹¹I want very much to see you, to give you some spiritual gift to make you strong. ¹²I mean that I want us to help each other with the faith that we have. Your faith will help me, and my faith will help you. ¹³Brothers, I want you to know that I planned many times to come to you. But this has not been possible. I wanted to come so that I could help you grow spiritually. I wanted to help you as I have helped the other non-Jewish people.

¹⁴I must serve all people—Greeks and non-Greeks, the wise and the foolish. ¹⁵That is why I want so much to preach the Good News to you in Rome.

¹⁶I am not ashamed of the Good News. It is the power God uses to save everyone who believes—to save the Jews first, and then to save the non-Jews. ¹⁷The Good News shows how God makes people right with himself. God's way of making people right with him begins and ends with faith. As the Scripture says, "The person who is made right with God by faith will live forever." ⁿ

ALL PEOPLE HAVE DONE WRONG

¹⁸God's anger is shown from heaven against all the evil and wrong things that people do. By their own evil lives they hide the truth. ¹⁹God shows his anger because everything that may be known about God has been made clear. Yes, God has clearly shown them everything that may be known about him. ²⁰There are things about God that people cannot see—his eternal power and all the things that make him God. But since the beginning of the world those things have been easy to understand. They are made clear by what God has made. So people have no excuse for the bad things they do. ²¹They knew God. But they did not give glory to God, and they did not thank him. Their thinking became useless. Their foolish minds were filled with darkness. ²²They said they were wise, but they became fools. ²³They gave up the glory of God who lives forever. They traded that glory for the worship of idols made to look like earthly people. They traded God's

---

1:17 **"The person . . . forever."** Quotation from Habakkuk 2:4.

☆ Romans 1:12

*God's family grew, and new believers lived and
traveled all over the world. To teach them God's
word, the apostles wrote letters. These letters
were full of lessons and later became books
in the Bible. The Book of Romans was written
by the apostle Paul. In it, he told the Jewish
Christians in Rome that he wanted to travel to
see them. He had things to share that would give
them strength. And Paul knew what they had to
share would also strengthen him.*

It makes God happy when we give our time and things to others to
help them. What can you do for people who might have less than
you? Maybe you can give some of your stuffed animals to a children's
hospital. Or maybe you can have a garage sale and send the money
to a country that had an earthquake or a hurricane. There are so
many ways you can help others. Giving pleases God, and it will make
your heart happy too!

· ·

It's good to help each other with whatever we have.

glory for things that look like birds,
animals, and snakes.

²⁴People were full of sin, wanting
only to do evil. So God left them to
follow their evil desires, and they made
one another's bodies impure by what
they did. ²⁵They traded the truth of
God for a lie and worshiped and served
things that were made by man. But
they did not worship and serve the God
who made those things. God should be
praised forever. Amen.

²⁶Because people did those things,
God left them and let them do the
shameful things they wanted to
do. Women stopped having natural

physical relations with men for what
is unnatural. ²⁷In the same way, men
stopped having natural physical relations with women and began wanting
each other. Men did shameful things
with other men. And in their bodies
they received the punishment for those
wrongs.

²⁸People did not think it was important to have a true knowledge of God.
So God left them and allowed them to
have their own worthless thinking.
And so those people do the things that
they should not do. ²⁹They are filled
with every kind of sin, evil, selfishness,
and hatred. They are full of jealousy,

murder, fighting, lying, and thinking the worst about each other. They gossip [30]and say evil things about each other. They hate God. They are rude and conceited and brag about themselves. They invent ways of doing evil. They do not obey their parents. [31]They are foolish, they do not keep their promises, and they show no kindness or mercy to other people. [32]They know God's law says that those who live like this should die. But they continue to do these evil things. And they also feel that those who do these things are doing right.

YOU PEOPLE ALSO ARE SINFUL

2 If you think that you can judge others, then you are wrong. You too are guilty of sin. You judge people, but you do the same bad things they do. So when you judge them, you are really judging yourself guilty. [2]God judges those who do wrong things. And we know that God's judging is right. [3]You judge those who do wrong, but you do wrong yourselves. Do you think you will be able to escape the judgment of God? [4]God has been very kind to you, and he has been patient with you. God has been waiting for you to change. But you think nothing of his kindness. Perhaps you do not understand that God is kind to you so that you will change your hearts and lives. [5]But you are hard and stubborn and refuse to change. So you are making your own punishment greater and greater on the day God shows his anger. On that day all people will see God's right judgments. [6]God will reward or punish every person for what he has done. [7]Some people live for God's glory, for honor, and for life that has no end. They live for those things by always continuing to do good. God will give life forever to them. [8]But other people are selfish and refuse to follow truth. They follow evil. God will give them his punishment and anger. [9]He will give trouble and suffering to everyone who does evil—to the Jews first and also to the non-Jews. [10]But

God will give glory, honor, and peace to everyone who does good—to the Jews first and also to the non-Jews. [11]For God judges all people in the same way.

[12]People who have God's law and those who have never heard of the law are all the same when they sin. Those who do not have the law and are sinners will be lost. And, in the same way, people who have the law and are sinners will be judged by the law. [13]Hearing the law does not make people right with God. The law makes people right with God only if they obey what the law says. [14](The non-Jews do not have the law. But when they freely do things that the law commands, then they are the law for themselves. This is true even though they do not have the law. [15]They show that in their hearts they know what is right and wrong, just as the law commands. And they also show this by the way they feel about right and wrong. Sometimes their thoughts tell them they did wrong. And sometimes their thoughts tell them they did right.) [16]All these things will happen on the day when God will judge the secret thoughts of people's hearts. The Good News that I preach says that God will judge everyone through Christ Jesus.

THE JEWS AND THE LAW

[17]What about you? You call yourself a Jew. You trust in the law of Moses and brag that you are close to God. [18]You know what God wants you to do. And you know the things that are important because you have learned the law. [19]You think you are a guide for the blind and a light for those who are in darkness. [20]You think you can show foolish people what is right and teach those who know nothing. You have the law; so you think you know everything and have all truth. [21]You teach other people. So why don't you teach yourself? You tell others not to steal. But you yourselves steal. [22]You say that others must not take part in adultery. But you yourselves are guilty of that sin. You

hate idols. But you steal from temples. [23] You brag about having God's law. But you bring shame to God by breaking his law. [24] It is written in the Scriptures: "The non-Jews speak against God's name because of you Jews." [n]

[25] If you follow the law, then your circumcision has meaning. But if you break the law, then it is as if you were never circumcised. [26] The non-Jews are not circumcised. But if they do what the law says, then it is as if they were circumcised. [27] You Jews have the written law and circumcision, but you break the law. So those who are not circumcised in their bodies, but still obey the law, will show that you are guilty.

[28] A person is not a true Jew if he is only a Jew in his physical body. True circumcision is not only on the outside of the body. [29] A person is a true Jew only if he is a Jew inside. True circumcision is done in the heart by the Spirit, not by the written law. Such a person gets praise from God, not from other people.

3 So, do Jews have anything that other people do not have? Is there anything special about being circumcised? [2] Yes, of course, there is in every way. The most important thing is this: God trusted the Jews with his teachings. [3] It is true that some Jews were not faithful to God. But will that stop God from doing what he promised? [4] No! God will continue to be true even when every person is false. As the Scriptures say:

"So your words may be shown to be right.
You are fair when you judge me."
Psalm 51:4

[5] When we do wrong, that shows more clearly that God is right. So can we say that God is wrong to punish us? (I am talking as men might talk.) [6] No! If God could not punish us, then God could not judge the world.

[7] A person might say, "When I lie, it really gives God glory, because my lie shows God's truth. So why am I judged a sinner?" [8] It would be the same to say, "We should do evil so that good will come." Some people find fault with us and say that we teach this. Those who say such things about us are wrong, and they should be punished.

ALL PEOPLE ARE GUILTY

[9] So are we Jews better than others? No! We have already said that Jews and non-Jews are the same. They are all guilty of sin. [10] As the Scriptures say:

"There is no one without sin.
    None!
[11]   There is no one who understands.
    There is no one who looks to God
        for help.
[12] All have turned away.
    Together, everyone has become
        evil.
    None of them does anything good."
Psalm 14:1–3
[13] "Their throats are like open graves.
    They use their tongues for telling
        lies."   *Psalm 5:9*
"Their words are like snake's poison."
Psalm 140:3
[14]   "Their mouths are full of cursing
        and hate."   *Psalm 10:7*
[15] "They are always ready to kill people.
[16]   Everywhere they go they cause
        ruin and misery.
[17] They don't know how to live in
        peace."   *Isaiah 59:7–8*
[18]   "They have no fear of or respect for
        God."   *Psalm 36:1*

[19] The law commands many things. We know that those commands are for those who are under the law. This stops all excuses and brings the whole world under God's judgment, [20] because no one can be made right with God by following the law. The law only shows us our sin.

2:24 "The non-Jews . . . Jews." Quotation from Isaiah 52:5; Ezekiel 36:20.

HOW GOD MAKES PEOPLE RIGHT

21But God has a way to make people right with him without the law. And God has now shown us that way which the law and the prophets told us about. 22God makes people right with himself through their faith in Jesus Christ. This is true for all who believe in Christ, because all are the same. 23All people have sinned and are not good enough for God's glory. 24People are made right with God by his grace, which is a free gift. They are made right with God by being made free from sin through Jesus Christ. 25God sent him to die in our place to take away our sins. We receive forgiveness through faith. And all of this is because of the blood of Jesus' death. This showed that God always does what is right and fair. God was right in the past when he was patient and did not punish people for their sins. 26And God gave Jesus to show today that God does what is right. God did this so that he could judge rightly and also make right any person who has faith in Jesus.

27So do we have a reason to brag about ourselves? No! And why not? It is the way of faith that stops all bragging, not the way of following the law. 28A person is made right with God through faith, not through what he does to follow the law. 29Is God only the God of the Jews? Is he not also the God of the non-Jews? 30Of course he is, for there is only one God. He will make Jews right with him by their faith. And he will also make non-Jews right with him through their faith. 31So do we destroy the law by following the way of faith? No! Faith causes us to be what the law truly wants.

THE EXAMPLE OF ABRAHAM

4 So what can we say about Abraham,[n] the father of our people? What did he learn about faith?

2If Abraham was made right by the things he did, then he had a reason to brag. But he could not brag before God. 3The Scripture says, "Abraham believed God. And that faith made him right with God."[n]

4When a person works, his pay is not given to him as a gift. He earns the pay he gets. 5But a person cannot do any work that will make him right with God. So he must trust in God. Then God accepts his faith, and that makes him right with God. God is the One who can make even those who are evil right in his sight. 6David said the same thing. He said that a person is truly blessed when God does not look at what he has done but accepts him as good:

7 "Happy are they
whose sins are forgiven,
whose wrongs are pardoned.
8 Happy is the person
whom the Lord does not consider
guilty."   *Psalm 32:1–2*

9Is this blessing only for those who are circumcised? Or is it also for those who are not circumcised? We have already said that God accepted Abraham's faith, and that faith made him right with God. 10So how did this happen? Did God accept Abraham before or after he was circumcised? God accepted him before his circumcision. 11Abraham was circumcised later to show that God accepted him. His circumcision was proof that he was right with God through faith before he was circumcised. So Abraham is the father of all those who believe but are not circumcised. He is the father of all believers who are accepted as being right with God. 12And Abraham is also the father of those who have been circumcised. But it is not their circumcision that makes him their father. He is

---

4:1 **Abraham** Most respected ancestor of the Jews. Every Jew hoped to see Abraham.
4:3 **"Abraham ... God."** Quotation from Genesis 15:6.

their father only if they live following the faith that our father Abraham had before he was circumcised.

GOD KEEPS HIS PROMISE

[13]Abraham[n] and his descendants received the promise that they would get the whole world. But Abraham did not receive that promise through the law. He received it because he was right with God through his faith. [14]If people could receive what God promised by following the law, then faith is worthless. And God's promise to Abraham is worthless, [15]because the law can only bring God's anger. But if there is no law, then there is nothing to disobey.

[16]So people receive God's promise by having faith. This happens so that the promise can be a free gift. And if the promise is a free gift, then all of Abraham's children can have that promise. The promise is not only for those people that live under the law of Moses. It is for anyone who lives with faith like Abraham. He is the father of us all. [17]As it is written in the Scriptures: "I am making you a father of many nations."[n] This is true before God. Abraham believed in God—the God who gives life to the dead and decides that things will happen that have not yet happened.

[18]There was no hope that Abraham would have children. But Abraham believed God and continued hoping. And that is why he became the father of many nations. As God told him, "Your descendants will also be too many to count."[n] [19]Abraham was almost 100 years old, much past the age for having children. Also, Sarah could not have children. Abraham thought about

all this. But his faith in God did not become weak. [20]He never doubted that God would keep his promise. Abraham never stopped believing. He grew stronger in his faith and gave praise to God. [21]Abraham felt sure that God was able to do the thing that God promised. [22]So, "God accepted Abraham's faith, and that made him right with God."[n] [23]Those words ("God accepted Abraham's faith") were written not only for Abraham. [24]They were written also for us. God will accept us also because we believe. We believe in the One who raised Jesus our Lord from death. [25]Jesus was given to die for our sins. And he was raised from death to make us right with God.

RIGHT WITH GOD

5 We have been made right with God because of our faith. So we have[n] peace with God through our Lord Jesus Christ. [2]Through our faith,[n] Christ has brought us into that blessing of God's grace that we now enjoy. And we are happy because of the hope we have of sharing God's glory. [3]And we also have joy with our troubles because we know that these troubles produce patience. [4]And patience produces character, and character produces hope. [5]And this hope will never disappoint us, because God has poured out his love to fill our hearts. God gave us his love through the Holy Spirit, whom God has given to us.

[6]Christ died for us while we were still weak. We were living against God, but at the right time, Christ died for us. [7]Very few people will die to save the life of someone else. Although perhaps for a good man someone might possibly die. [8]But Christ died for us while we were

---

4:13 **Abraham** Most respected ancestor of the Jews. Every Jew hoped to see Abraham.
4:17 **"I . . . nations."** Quotation from Genesis 17:5.
4:18 **"Your . . . count."** Quotation from Genesis 15:5.
4:22 **"God . . . God."** Quotation from Genesis 15:6.
5:1 **we have** Some Greek copies read "let us have."
5:2 **Through our faith** Some Greek copies do not include this phrase.

still sinners. In this way God shows his great love for us.

⁹We have been made right with God by the blood of Christ's death. So through Christ we will surely be saved from God's anger. ¹⁰I mean that while we were God's enemies, God made us his friends through the death of his Son. Surely, now that we are God's friends, God will save us through his Son's life. ¹¹And not only that, but now we are also very happy in God through our Lord Jesus Christ. Through Jesus we are now God's friends again.

ADAM AND CHRIST

¹²Sin came into the world because of what one man did. And with sin came death. And this is why all men must die—because all men sinned. ¹³Sin was in the world before the law of Moses. But God does not judge people guilty of sin if there is no law. ¹⁴But from the time of Adam to the time of Moses, everyone had to die. Adam died because he sinned by not obeying God's command. But even those who did not sin in the same way had to die.

Adam was like the One who was

☆ Romans 5:8

Paul told the Christians in Rome that God put his love in their hearts, and that God made them his friends. Even while people did not care about God, God cared about them. Jesus loves us so much. Even when we were sinners, he died for us to take away those sins.

The Bible calls the bad things we do sin. Things like disobeying our parents, telling a lie, or saying mean things. The good news is that God loves us even when we make bad choices. Nothing you do, no matter how bad, will ever change how much Jesus loves you. He died on the cross for your sins and wants to forgive you.

* * * * * * * * * * * * * * * * * * *

Paul's message was not just for Christians who lived a long time ago. The message is for us too. Jesus paid for our sins before we were even born. Now we can say, "Thank you, Jesus, for your great gift!"

coming in the future. [15]But God's free gift is not like Adam's sin. Many people died because of the sin of that one man. But the grace that they received from God was much greater. Many people received God's gift of life by the grace of the one man, Jesus Christ. [16]After Adam sinned once, he was judged guilty. But the gift of God is different. God's free gift came after many sins. And the gift makes people right with God. [17]One man sinned, and so death ruled all people because of that one man. But now some people accept God's full grace and the great gift of being made right with him. They will surely have true life and rule through the one man, Jesus Christ.

[18]So one sin of Adam brought the punishment of death to all people. But in the same way, one good act that Christ did makes all people right with God. And that brings true life for all. [19]One man disobeyed God, and many became sinners. But in the same way, one man obeyed God, and many will be made right. [20]The law came to make people have more sin. But when people had more sin, God gave them more of his grace. [21]Sin once used death to rule us. But God gave people more of his grace so that grace could rule by making people right with him. And this brings life forever through Jesus Christ our Lord.

DEAD TO SIN BUT ALIVE IN CHRIST

6 So do you think that we should continue sinning so that God will give us more and more grace? [2]No! We died to our old sinful lives. So how can we continue living with sin? [3]Did you forget that all of us became part of Christ when we were baptized? We shared his death in our baptism. [4]So when we were baptized, we were buried with Christ and shared his death. We were buried with him so that we could live a new life, just as Christ was raised from death by the wonderful power of the Father.

[5]Christ died, and we have been joined with Christ by dying too. So we will also be joined with him by rising from death as he did. [6]We know that our old life died with Christ on the cross. This was so that our sinful selves would have no power over us, and we would not be slaves to sin. [7]Anyone who has died is made free from sin's control.

[8]If we died with Christ, we know that we will also live with him. [9]Christ was raised from death. And we know that he cannot die again. Death has no power over him now. [10]Yes, when Christ died, he died to defeat the power of sin one time—enough for all time. He now has a new life, and his new life is with God. [11]In the same way, you should see yourselves as being dead to the power of sin and alive with God through Christ Jesus.

[12]So, do not let sin control you in your life here on earth. You must not be ruled by the things your sinful self makes you want to do. [13]Do not offer the parts of your body to serve sin. Do not use your bodies as things to do evil with, but offer yourselves to God. Be like people who have died and now live. Offer the parts of your body to God to be used for doing good. [14]Sin will not be your master, because you are not under law but under God's grace.

SLAVES OF RIGHTEOUSNESS

[15]So what should we do? Should we sin because we are under grace and not

> If we died with Christ, we know that we will also live with him.
>
> –ROMANS 6:8

under law? No! [16]Surely you know that when you give yourselves like slaves to obey someone, then you are really slaves of that person. The person you obey is your master. You can follow sin, or obey God. Sin brings spiritual death. But obeying God makes you right with him. [17]In the past you were slaves to sin—sin controlled you. But thank God, you fully obeyed the things that were taught to you. [18]You were made free from sin, and now you are slaves to goodness. [19]I use this example because this is hard for you to understand. In the past you offered the parts of your body to be slaves to sin and evil. You lived only for evil. In the same way now you must give yourselves to be slaves of goodness. Then you will live only for God.

[20]In the past you were slaves to sin, and goodness did not control you. [21]You did evil things, and now you are ashamed of them. Those things only bring death. [22]But now you are free from sin and have become slaves of God. This brings you a life that is only for God. And this gives you life forever. [23]The payment for sin is death. But God gives us the free gift of life forever in Christ Jesus our Lord.

AN EXAMPLE FROM MARRIAGE

7 Brothers, all of you understand the law of Moses. So surely you know that the law rules over a person only while he is alive. [2]For example, a woman must stay married to her husband as long as he is alive. But if her husband dies, then she is free from the law of marriage. [3]But if she marries another man while her husband is still alive, the law says she is guilty of adultery. But if her husband dies, then the woman is free from the law of marriage. So if she marries another man after her husband dies, she is not guilty of adultery.

[4]In the same way, my brothers, your old selves died, and you became free from the law through the body of Christ. Now you belong to someone else. You belong to the One who was raised from death. We belong to Christ so that we can be used in service to God. [5]In the past, we were ruled by our sinful selves. The law made us want to do sinful things. And those sinful things we wanted to do controlled our bodies, so that the things we did were only bringing us death. [6]In the past, the law held us like prisoners. But our old selves died, and we were made free from the law. So now we serve God in a new way, not in the old way with written rules. Now we serve God in the new way, with the Spirit.

OUR FIGHT AGAINST SIN

[7]You might think that I am saying that sin and the law are the same thing. That is not true. But the law was the only way I could learn what sin meant. I would never have known what it means to want something wrong if the law had not said, "You must not want to take your neighbor's things." [n] [8]And sin found a way to use that command and cause me to want every kind of wrong thing. So sin came to me because of that command. But without the law, sin has no power. [9]I was alive without the law before I knew the law. But when the law's command came to me, then sin began to live. [10]And I died because of sin. The command was meant to bring life, but for me that command brought death. [11]Sin found a way to fool me by using the command. Sin used the command to make me die.

[12]So the law is holy, and the command is holy and right and good. [13]Does this mean that something that is good brought death to me? No! Sin used something that is good to bring death to me. This happened so that I could see what sin is really like. The command was used to show that sin is something very evil.

7:7 "You . . . things." Quotation from Exodus 20:13, 15–17.

THE WAR WITHIN MAN

[14] We know that the law is spiritual. But I am not spiritual. Sin rules me as if I were its slave. [15] I do not understand the things I do. I do not do the good things I want to do. And I do the bad things I hate to do. [16] And if I do not want to do the bad things I do, then that means that I agree that the law is good. [17] But I am not really the one who is doing these bad things. It is sin living in me that does these things. [18] Yes, I know that nothing good lives in me—I mean nothing good lives in the part of me that is earthly and sinful. I want to do the things that are good. But I do not do them. [19] I do not do the good things that I want to do. I do the bad things that I do not want to do. [20] So if I do things I do not want to do, then I am not the one doing those things. It is sin living in me that does those bad things.

[21] So I have learned this rule: When I want to do good, evil is there with me. [22] In my mind, I am happy with God's law. [23] But I see another law working in my body. That law makes war against the law that my mind accepts. That other law working in my body is the law of sin, and that law makes me its prisoner. [24] What a miserable man I am! Who will save me from this body that brings me death? [25] God will. I thank him for saving me through Jesus Christ our Lord!

So in my mind I am a slave to God's law. But in my sinful self I am a slave to the law of sin.

LIFE IN THE SPIRIT

8 So now, those who are in Christ Jesus are not judged[n] guilty. [2] I am not judged guilty because in Christ Jesus the law of the Spirit that brings life made me free. It made me free from the law that brings sin and death. [3] The law was without power, because the law was made weak by our sinful selves. But God did what the law could not do. He sent his own Son to earth with the same human life that others use for sin. He sent his Son to be an offering to pay for sin. So God used a human life to destroy sin. [4] He did this so that we could be right as the law said we must be. Now we do not live following our sinful selves, but we live following the Spirit.

[5] Those who live following their sinful selves think only about things that their sinful selves want. But those who live following the Spirit are thinking about the things that the Spirit wants them to do. [6] If a person's thinking is controlled by his sinful self, then there is death. But if his thinking is controlled by the Spirit, then there is life and peace. [7] This is true because if a person's thinking is controlled by his sinful self, then he is against God. He refuses to obey God's law. And really he is not able to obey God's law. [8] Those people who are ruled by their sinful selves cannot please God.

[9] But you are not ruled by your sinful selves. You are ruled by the Spirit, if that Spirit of God really lives in you. But if anyone does not have the Spirit of Christ, then he does not belong to Christ. [10] Your body will always be dead because of sin. But if Christ is in you, then the Spirit gives you life, because Christ made you right with God. [11] God raised Jesus from death. And if God's Spirit is living in you, then he will also give life to your bodies that die. God is the One who raised Christ from death. And he will give life through[n] his Spirit that lives in you.

[12] So, my brothers, we must not be ruled by our sinful selves. We must not live the way our sinful selves want. [13] If you use your lives to do the wrong things your sinful selves want, then

---

8:1 **judged** Some Greek copies continue, "guilty, those who do not live in the power of their sinful selves, but in the power of the Spirit."
8:11 **through** Some Greek copies read "because of."

☆ Romans 8:9–10

Romans chapter 8 teaches Christians what it means to have the Spirit of God living in them. The Bible says we don't have to be ruled by sins. We can be ruled by the Spirit.

Do you like blowing bubbles? You put the stick in the liquid, hold it up, blow gently, and the bubble is formed. Your breath is inside the bubble. When you ask Jesus to come into your life, you become like that bubble. He comes into your life, and suddenly you have Jesus inside you. It is his Spirit living in you, which is how Jesus can always be with you.

. . . .

Jesus said, "You can be sure that I will be with you always" (Matthew 28:20). It is his Spirit living in each of us that makes this possible.

you will die spiritually. But if you use the Spirit's help to stop doing the wrong things you do with your body, then you will have true life.

[14]The true children of God are those who let God's Spirit lead them. [15]The Spirit that we received is not a spirit that makes us slaves again to fear. The Spirit that we have makes us children of God. And with that Spirit we say, "Father, dear Father." [n] [16]And the Spirit himself joins with our spirits to say that we are God's children. [17]If we are God's children, then we will receive the blessings God has for us. We will receive these things from God together with Christ. But we must suffer as Christ suffered, and then we will have glory as Christ has glory.

OUR FUTURE GLORY

[18]We have sufferings now. But the sufferings we have now are nothing compared to the great glory that will be given to us. [19]Everything that God made is waiting with excitement for the time when God will show the world who his children are. The whole world wants very much for that to happen. [20]Everything that God made was changed to become useless. This was not by its own wish. It happened because God wanted it. But there was this hope: [21]that everything God made would be set free from ruin. There was hope that everything God made would have the freedom and glory that belong to God's children. [22]We know that everything God

8:15 **"Father, dear Father."** Literally, "Abba, Father." Jewish children called their fathers "Abba."

made has been waiting until now in pain, like a woman ready to give birth. [23]Not only the world, but we also have been waiting with pain inside us. We have the Spirit as the first part of God's promise. So we are waiting for God to finish making us his own children. I mean we are waiting for our bodies to be made free. [24]We were saved, and we have this hope. If we see what we are waiting for, then that is not really hope. People do not hope for something they already have. [25]But we are hoping for something that we do not have yet. We are waiting for it patiently.

[26]Also, the Spirit helps us. We are very weak, but the Spirit helps us with our weakness. We do not know how to pray as we should. But the Spirit himself speaks to God for us, even begs God for us. The Spirit speaks to God with deep feelings that words cannot explain. [27]God can see what is in people's hearts. And he knows what is in the mind of the Spirit, because the Spirit speaks to God for his people in the way that God wants.

[28]We know that in everything God works for the good of those who love him.[n] They are the people God called, because that was his plan. [29]God knew them before he made the world. And God chose them to be like his Son. Then Jesus would be the firstborn[n] of many brothers. [30]God planned for them to be like his Son. And those he planned to be like his Son, he also called. And those he called, he also made right with him. And those he made right, he also glorified.

GOD'S LOVE IN CHRIST JESUS

[31]So what should we say about this? If God is for us, then no one can defeat us. [32]God let even his own Son suffer for us. God gave his Son for us all. So with Jesus, God will surely give us all things.

[33]Who can accuse the people that God has chosen? No one! God is the One who makes them right. [34]Who can say that God's people are guilty? No one! Christ Jesus died, but that is not all. He was also raised from death. And now he is on God's right side and is begging God for us. [35]Can anything separate us from the love Christ has for us? Can troubles or problems or sufferings? If we have no food or clothes, if we are in danger, or even if death comes—can any of these things separate us from Christ's love? [36]As it is written in the Scriptures:

> "For you we are in danger of death all the time.
> People think we are worth no more than sheep to be killed."
> *Psalm 44:22*

[37]But in all these things we have full victory through God who showed his love for us. [38-39]Yes, I am sure that nothing can separate us from the love God has for us. Not death, not life, not angels, not ruling spirits, nothing now, nothing in the future, no powers, nothing above us, nothing below us, or anything else in the whole world will ever be able to separate us from the love of God that is in Christ Jesus our Lord.

GOD AND THE JEWISH PEOPLE

9 I am in Christ, and I am telling you the truth. I do not lie. My feelings are ruled by the Holy Spirit, and they tell me that I am not lying. [2]I have great sorrow and always feel much sadness for the Jewish people. [3]I wish I could help my Jewish brothers, my people. I would even wish that I were cursed and cut off from Christ if that would help them. [4]They are the people of Israel. They were God's chosen children. They have the glory

---

8:28 We...him. Some Greek copies read "We know that everything works together for good for those who love God."

8:29 firstborn Here this probably means that Christ was the first in God's family to share God's glory.

of God and the agreements that God made between himself and his people. God gave them the law of Moses and the right way of worship. And God gave his promises to them. [5]They are the descendants of our great ancestors, and they are the earthly family of Christ. Christ is God over all. Praise him forever![n] Amen.

[6]I do not mean that God failed to keep his promise to them. But only some of the people of Israel are truly God's people.[n] [7]And only some of Abraham's[n] descendants are true children of Abraham. But God said to Abraham: "The descendants I promised you will be from Isaac."[n] [8]This means that not all of Abraham's descendants are God's true children. Abraham's true children are those who become God's children because of the promise God made to Abraham. [9]God's promise to Abraham was this: "At the right time I will return, and Sarah will have a son."[n] [10]And that is not all. Rebekah also had sons. And those sons had the same father, our father Isaac. [11-12]But before the two boys were born, God told Rebekah, "The older will serve the younger."[n] This was before the boys had done anything good or bad. God said this before they were born so that the one chosen would be chosen because of God's own plan. He was chosen because he was the one God wanted to call, not because of anything he did. [13]As the Scripture says, "I loved Jacob, but I hated Esau."[n]

[14]So what should we say about this? Is God unfair? In no way. [15]God said to Moses, "I will show kindness to anyone I want to show kindness. I will show mercy to anyone I want to show mercy."[n] [16]So God will choose the one he decides to show mercy to. And his choice does not depend on what people want or try to do. [17]The Scripture says to the king of Egypt: "I made you king so I might show my power in you. In this way my name will be talked about in all the earth."[n] [18]So God shows mercy where he wants to show mercy. And he makes stubborn the people he wants to make stubborn.

[19]So one of you will ask me: "If God controls the things we do, then why does he blame us for our sins? Who can fight his will?" [20]Do not ask that. You are only human. And human beings have no right to question God. An object cannot tell the person who made it, "Why did you make me like this?" [21]The man who makes a jar can make anything he wants to make. He can use the same clay to make different things. He can make one thing for special use and another thing for daily use.

[22]It is the same way with what God has done. God wanted to show his anger and to let people see his power. But God patiently stayed with those people he was angry with—people who were ready to be destroyed. [23]God waited with patience so that he could make known his rich glory. He wanted to give that glory to the people who receive his mercy. He has prepared these people to have his glory, and [24]we are those people whom God called. He called us from the Jews and from the non-Jews. [25]As the Scripture says in Hosea:

> "I will say, 'You are my people'
>   to those I had called 'not my
>   people.'

9:5 **Christ . . . forever!** This can also mean, "May God, who rules over all things, be praised forever!"
9:6 **God's people** Literally, "Israel," the people God chose to bring his blessings to the world.
9:7 **Abraham** Most respected ancestor of the Jews. Every Jew hoped to see Abraham.
9:7 **"The descendants . . . Isaac."** Quotation from Genesis 21:12.
9:9 **"At . . . son."** Quotation from Genesis 18:10, 14.
9:11–12 **"The older . . . younger."** Quotation from Genesis 25:23.
9:13 **"I . . . Esau."** Quotation from Malachi 1:2–3.
9:15 **"I . . . mercy."** Quotation from Exodus 33:19.
9:17 **"I . . . earth."** Quotation from Exodus 9:16.

And I will show my love
  to those people I did not love."
                              Hosea 2:1, 23
²⁶ "Now it is said to Israel,
  'You are not my people.'
But later they will be called
  'children of the living God.'"
                              Hosea 1:10

²⁷And Isaiah cries out about Israel:

"There are so many people of Israel.
  They are like the grains of sand by
    the sea.
But only a few of them will be
    saved.
²⁸ For the Lord will quickly
      and completely
      punish the people
      on the earth."
                              Isaiah 10:22–23

²⁹It is as Isaiah said:

"The Lord of
    heaven's armies
    allowed a few of
    our descendants
    to live.
Otherwise we
    would have been
    completely destroyed
    like the cities of Sodom
    and Gomorrah." *ⁿ*
                              Isaiah 1:9

³⁰So what does all this mean? It means this: the non-Jews were not trying to make themselves right with God. But they were made right with God because of their faith. ³¹And the people of Israel tried to follow a law to make themselves right with God. But they did not succeed, ³²because they tried to make themselves right by the things they did. They did not trust in God to make them right. They fell over the stone that causes people to fall. ³³As it is written in the Scripture:

"I will put in Jerusalem a stone that
    causes people to stumble.
  It is a rock that makes them fall.
Anyone who trusts in him will
    not be disappointed."
                              Isaiah 8:14; 28:16

10 Brothers, the thing I want most is for all the Jews to be saved. That is my prayer to God. ²I can say this about them: They really try to follow God. But they do not know the right way. ³They did not know the way that God makes people right with him. And they tried to make themselves right in their own way. So they did not accept God's way of making people right. ⁴Christ ended the law, so that everyone who believes in him may be right with God.

⁵Moses writes about being made right by following the law. He says, "A person who does these things will have life forever because of them." *ⁿ* ⁶But this is what the Scripture says about being made right through faith: "Don't say to yourself, 'Who will go up into heaven?'" (That means, "Who will go up to heaven to get Christ and bring him down to earth?") ⁷"And do not say, 'Who will go down into the world below?'" (That means, "Who will go down to get Christ and bring him up from death?") ⁸This is what the Scripture says: "God's teaching is near you; it is in your mouth and in your heart." *ⁿ* That is the teaching of faith that we tell. ⁹If you declare with your mouth, "Jesus is Lord," and if you

> The Scripture says, "Anyone who asks the Lord for help will be saved."
>
> –ROMANS 10:13

9:29 **Sodom and Gomorrah** Two cities that God destroyed because the people were so evil.
10:5 **"A person . . . them."** Quotation from Leviticus 18:5.
10:6–8 **Don't . . . heart.** Quotations from Deuteronomy 9:4; 30:12–14; Psalm 107:26.

believe in your heart that God raised Jesus from death, then you will be saved. [10]We believe with our hearts, and so we are made right with God. And we declare with our mouths to say that we believe, and so we are saved. [11]As the Scripture says, "Anyone who trusts in him will never be disappointed."[n] [12]That Scripture says "anyone" because there is no difference between Jew and non-Jew. The same Lord is the Lord of all and gives many blessings to all who trust in him. [13]The Scripture says, "Anyone who asks the Lord for help will be saved."[n]

[14]But before people can trust in the Lord for help, they must believe in him. And before they can believe in the Lord, they must hear about him. And for them to hear about the Lord, someone must tell them. [15]And before someone can go and tell them, he must be sent. It is written, "How beautiful is the person who comes to bring good news."[n]

[16]But not all the Jews accepted the good news. Isaiah said, "Lord, who believed what we told them?"[n] [17]So faith comes from hearing the Good News. And people hear the Good News when someone tells them about Christ.

[18]But I ask: Didn't people hear the Good News? Yes, they heard—as the Scripture says:

> "Their message went out through all
> the world.
> It goes everywhere on earth."
>
> *Psalm 19:4*

[19]Again I ask: Didn't the people of Israel understand? Yes, they did understand. First, Moses says:

> "I will use those who are not a nation
> to make you jealous.

> I will use a nation that does not
> understand to make you angry."
>
> *Deuteronomy 32:21*

[20]Then Isaiah is bold enough to say:

> "I was found by those who were not
> asking me for help.
> I made myself known to people
> who were not looking for me."
>
> *Isaiah 65:1*

[21]But about Israel God says,

> "All day long I stood ready to accept
> people who disobey and are
> stubborn." *Isaiah 65:2*

GOD SHOWS MERCY TO ALL PEOPLE

11 So I ask: Did God throw out his people? No! I myself am an Israelite. I am from the family of Abraham, from the tribe of Benjamin. [2]God chose the Israelites to be his people before they were born. And God did not leave his people. Surely you know what the Scripture says about Elijah, how he prayed to God against the people of Israel. Elijah said, [3]"They have killed your prophets, and they have destroyed your altars. I am the only prophet left. And now they are trying to kill me, too."[n] [4]But what answer did God give Elijah? He said, "But I have left 7,000 people in Israel. Those 7,000 have never bowed down before Baal."[n] [5]It is the same now. There are a few people that God has chosen by his grace. [6]And if God chose them by grace, then it is not for the things they have done. If they could be made God's people by what they did, then God's gift of grace would not really be a gift.

10:11 "Anyone...disappointed." Quotation from Isaiah 28:16.
10:13 "Anyone...saved." Quotation from Joel 2:32.
10:15 "How...news." Quotation from Isaiah 52:7.
10:16 "Lord...them?" Quotation from Isaiah 53:1.
11:3 "They...too." Quotation from 1 Kings 19:10, 14.
11:4 "But...Baal." Quotation from 1 Kings 19:18.

⁷So this is what has happened: The people of Israel tried to be right with God. But they did not succeed. But the ones God chose did become right with him. The others became hard and refused to listen to God. ⁸As it is written in the Scriptures:

"God gave the people a dull mind
    so they could not understand."
                        Isaiah 29:10
"God closed their eyes so they could
    not see,
    and God closed their ears so they
    could not hear.
This continues until today."
                    Deuteronomy 29:4

⁹And David says:

"Let their own feasts trap them and
    cause their ruin.
Let their feasts cause them to sin
    and be paid back.
¹⁰ Let their eyes be closed so they
    cannot see.
Let their backs be forever
    weak from troubles."
                        Psalm 69:22–23

¹¹So I ask: When the Jews fell, did that fall destroy them? No! But their failure brought salvation to the non-Jews. This took place to cause the Jews to be jealous. ¹²The Jews' failure brought rich blessings for the world. And what the Jews lost brought rich blessings for the non-Jewish people. So surely the world will get much richer blessings when enough Jews become the kind of people God wants.

¹³Now I am speaking to you who are not Jews. I am an apostle to the non-Jews. So while I have that work, I will do the best I can. ¹⁴I hope I can make my own people jealous. That way, maybe I can help some of them to be saved. ¹⁵God turned away from the Jews. When that happened, God became friends with the other people in the world. So when God accepts the Jews, then surely that will bring to them life after death.

¹⁶If the first piece of bread is offered to God, then the whole loaf is made holy. If the roots of a tree are holy, then the tree's branches are holy too.

¹⁷Some of the branches from an olive tree have been broken off, and the branch of a wild olive tree has been joined to that first tree. You non-Jews are the same as that wild branch, and you now share the strength and life of the first tree, the Jews. ¹⁸So do not brag about those branches that were broken off. You have no reason to brag. Why? You do not give life to the root. The root gives life to you. ¹⁹You will say, "Branches were broken off so that I could be joined to their tree." ²⁰That is true. But those branches were broken off because they did not believe. And you continue to be part of the tree only because you believe. Do not be proud, but be afraid. ²¹If God did not let the natural branches of that tree stay, then he will not let you stay if you don't believe.

²²So you see that God is kind, but he can also be very strict. God punishes those who stop following him. But God is kind to you, if you continue following in his kindness. If you do not continue following him, you will be cut off from the tree. ²³And if the Jews will believe in God again, then God will accept the Jews back again. God is able to put them back where they were. ²⁴It is not natural for a wild branch to be part of a good tree. But you non-Jews are like a branch cut from a wild olive tree. And you were joined to a good olive tree. But those Jews are like a branch that grew from the good tree. So surely they can be joined to their own tree again.

²⁵I want you to understand this secret truth, brothers. This truth will help you understand that you do not know everything. The truth is this: Part of Israel has been made stubborn. But that will change when many non-Jews

have come to God. ²⁶And that is how all Israel will be saved. It is written in the Scriptures:

> "The Savior will come from
> Jerusalem;
> he will take away all evil from the
> family of Jacob."ⁿ
> ²⁷ And I will make this agreement with
> those people
> when I take away their sins."
>
> *Isaiah 59:20–21; 27:9*

²⁸The Jews refuse to accept the Good News, so they are God's enemies. This has happened to help you non-Jews. But the Jews are still God's chosen people, and God loves them very much. He loves them because of the promises he made to their ancestors. ²⁹God never changes his mind about the people he calls and the things he gives them. ³⁰At one time you refused to obey God. But now you have received mercy, because those people refused to obey. ³¹And now the Jews refuse to obey, because God showed mercy to you. But this happened so that they also canⁿ receive mercy from God. ³²All people have refused to obey God. God has given them all over to their stubborn ways, so that God can show mercy to all.

PRAISE TO GOD

³³Yes, God's riches are very great! God's wisdom and knowledge have no end! No one can explain the things God decides. No one can understand God's ways. ³⁴As the Scripture says,

> "Who has known the mind of the
> Lord?
> Who has been able to give the Lord
> advice?" *Isaiah 40:13*
> ³⁵ "No one has ever given God anything
> that he must pay back." *Job 41:11*

³⁶Yes, God made all things. And everything continues through God and for God. To God be the glory forever! Amen.

GIVE YOUR LIVES TO GOD

12 So brothers, since God has shown us great mercy, I beg you to offer your lives as a living sacrifice to him. Your offering must be only for God and pleasing to him. This is the spiritual way for you to worship. ²Do not be shaped by this world. Instead be changed within by a new way of thinking. Then you will be able to decide what God wants for you. And you will be able to know what is good and pleasing to God and what is perfect. ³God has given me a special gift. That is why I have something to say to everyone among you. Do not think that you are better than you are. You must see yourself as you really are. Decide what you are by the amount of faith God has given you. ⁴Each one of us has a body, and that body has many parts. These parts all have different uses. ⁵In the same way, we are many, but in Christ we are all one body. Each one is a part of that body. And each part belongs to all the other parts. ⁶We all have different gifts. Each gift came because of the grace that God gave us. If one has the gift of prophecy, he should use that gift with the faith he has. ⁷If one has the gift of serving, he should serve. If one has the gift of teaching, he should teach. ⁸If one has the gift of encouraging others, he should encourage. If one has the gift of giving to others, he should give freely. If one has the gift of being a leader, he should try hard when he leads. If one has the gift of showing kindness to others, that person should do so with joy.

⁹Your love must be real. Hate what is evil. Hold on to what is good. ¹⁰Love each other like brothers and sisters. Give your brothers and sisters more

---

11:26 **Jacob** Father of the 12 family groups of Israel, the people God chose to be his people.
11:31 **can** Some Greek copies read "can now."

honor than you want for yourselves. [11]Do not be lazy but work hard. Serve the Lord with all your heart. [12]Be joyful because you have hope. Be patient when trouble comes. Pray at all times. [13]Share with God's people who need help. Bring strangers in need into your homes.

[14]Wish good for those who do bad things to you. Wish them well and do not curse them. [15]Be happy with those who are happy. Be sad with those who are sad. [16]Live together in peace with each other. Do not be proud, but make friends with those who seem unimportant. Do not think how smart you are.

[17]If someone does wrong to you, do not pay him back by doing wrong to him. Try to do what everyone thinks is right. [18]Do your best to live in peace with everyone. [19]My friends, do not try to punish others when they wrong you. Wait for God to punish them with his anger. It is written: "I am the One who punishes; I will pay people back," [n] says the Lord. [20]But you should do this:

"If your enemy is hungry, feed him;
    if your enemy is thirsty, give him a
    drink.
Doing this will be like pouring
    burning coals on his head."
Proverbs 25:21–22

[21]Do not let evil defeat you. Defeat evil by doing good.

CHRISTIANS SHOULD OBEY THE LAW

13 All of you must obey the government rulers. No one rules unless God has given him the power to rule. And no one rules now without that power from God. [2]So if anyone is against the government, he is really against what God has commanded. And so he brings punishment on himself. [3]Those who do right do not have to fear the rulers. But people who do wrong must fear them. Do you want to be unafraid of the rulers? Then do what is right, and the ruler will praise you. [4]He is God's servant to help you. But if you do wrong, then be afraid. The ruler has the power to punish; he is God's servant to punish those who do wrong. [5]So you must obey the government. You must obey not only because you might be punished, but because you know it is the right thing to do.

[6]And this is also why you pay taxes. Rulers are working for God and give their time to their work. [7]Pay everyone, then, what you owe him. If you owe any kind of tax, pay it. Show respect and honor to them all.

LOVING OTHERS

[8]Do not owe people anything. But you will always owe love to each other. The person who loves others has obeyed all the law. [9]The law says, "You must not be guilty of adultery. You must not murder anyone. You must not steal. You must not want to take your neighbor's things." [n] All these commands and all others are really only one rule: "Love your neighbor as you love yourself." [n] [10]Love never hurts a neighbor. So loving is obeying all the law.

[11]I say this because we live in an important time. Yes, it is now time for you to wake up from your sleep. Our salvation is nearer now than when we first believed. [12]The "night" [n] is almost finished. The "day" [n] is almost here. So we should stop doing things that belong to darkness and take up the weapons used for fighting in the

---

12:19 "I . . . back" Quotation from Deuteronomy 32:35.
13:9 "You . . . things." Quotation from Exodus 20:13–15, 17.
13:9 "Love . . . yourself." Quotation from Leviticus 19:18.
13:12 "night" This is used as a symbol of the sinful world we live in. This world will soon end.
13:12 "day" This is used as a symbol of the good time that is coming, when we will be with God.

light. [13]Let us live in a right way, as in the daytime. We should not have wild parties or get drunk. There should be no sexual immorality or evil conduct, no fighting or jealousy. [14]But clothe yourselves with the Lord Jesus Christ. Forget about satisfying your sinful self.

DO NOT CRITICIZE OTHER PEOPLE

14 Do not refuse to accept into your group someone who is weak in faith. And do not argue with him about opinions. [2]One person believes that he can eat all kinds of food.[n] But if another man's faith is weak, then he believes he can eat only vegetables. [3]The one who knows that he can eat any kind of food must not feel that he is better than the one who eats only vegetables. And the person who eats only vegetables must not think that the one who eats all foods is wrong. God has accepted him. [4]You cannot judge another man's servant. His own master decides if he is doing well or not. And the Lord's servant will do well because the Lord helps him do well.

[5]One person thinks that one day is more important than another. And someone else thinks that every day is the same. Each one should be sure in his own mind. [6]The person who thinks one day is more important than other days is doing that for the Lord. And the one who eats all kinds of food is doing that for the Lord. Yes, he gives thanks to God for that food. And the man who refuses to eat some foods does that for the Lord, and he gives thanks to God. [7]For we do not live or die for ourselves.

[8]If we live, we are living for the Lord. And if we die, we are dying for the Lord. So living or dying, we belong to the Lord.

[9]That is why Christ died and rose from death to live again. He did this so that he would be Lord over both the dead and the living. [10]So why do you judge your brother in Christ? And why do you think that you are better than he is? We will all stand before God, and he will judge us all. [11]Yes, it is written in the Scriptures:

"Everyone will bow before me; everyone will say that I am God. As surely as I live, these things will happen, says the Lord." *Isaiah 45:23*

[12]So each of us will have to answer to God for what he has done.

DO NOT CAUSE OTHERS TO SIN

[13]So we should stop judging each other. We must make up our minds not to do anything that will make a Christian brother sin. [14]I am in the Lord Jesus, and I know that there is no food that is wrong to eat. But if a person believes that something is wrong, then that thing is wrong for him. [15]If you hurt your brother's faith because of something you eat, then you are not really following the way of love. Do not destroy his faith by eating food that he thinks is wrong. Christ died for him. [16]Do not allow what you think is good to become what others say is evil. [17]In the kingdom of God, eating and drinking are not important. The important things are living right with God, peace, and joy in the Holy Spirit. [18]Anyone who serves

> Live together in peace with each other . . . Make friends with those who seem unimportant.
> —ROMANS 12:16

14:2 **all . . . food** The Jewish law said there were some foods Jews should not eat. When Jews became Christians, some of them did not understand they could now eat all foods.

Christ by living this way is pleasing God and will be accepted by other people.

¹⁹So let us try to do what makes peace and helps one another. ²⁰Do not let the eating of food destroy the work of God. All foods are all right to eat, but it is wrong to eat food that causes someone else to sin. ²¹It is better not to eat meat or drink wine or do anything that will cause your brother to sin.

²²Your beliefs about these things should be kept secret between you and God. A person is blessed if he can do what he thinks is right without feeling guilty. ²³But if he eats something without being sure that it is right, then he is wrong because he did not believe that it was right. And if he does anything without believing that it is right, then it is a sin.

15 We who are strong in faith should help those who are weak. We should help them with their weaknesses, and not please only ourselves. ²Let each of us please his neighbor for his good, to help him be stronger in faith. ³Even Christ did not live to please himself. It was as the Scriptures said: "When people insult you, it hurts me."ⁿ ⁴Everything that was written in the past was written to teach us, so that we could have hope. That hope comes from the patience and encouragement that the Scriptures give us. ⁵Patience and encouragement come from God. And I pray that God will help you all agree with each other the way Christ Jesus wants. ⁶Then you will all be joined together, and you will give glory to God the Father of our Lord Jesus Christ. ⁷Christ accepted you, so you should accept each other. This will bring glory to God. ⁸I tell you that Christ became a servant of the Jews. This was to show that God's promises to the Jewish ancestors are true. ⁹And he also did this so that the non-Jews could give glory to God for the mercy

he gives to them. It is written in the Scriptures:

> "So I will praise you among the non-Jewish people.
> I will sing praises to your name."
> *Psalm 18:49*

¹⁰The Scripture also says,

> "Be happy, you non-Jews,
> together with God's people."
> *Deuteronomy 32:43*

¹¹Again the Scripture says,

> "All you non-Jews, praise the Lord.
> All you people, sing praises to him." *Psalm 117:1*

¹²And Isaiah says,

> "A new king will come from Jesse's family.ⁿ
> He will come to rule over the non-Jews;
> and the non-Jews will have hope because of him." *Isaiah 11:10*

¹³I pray that the God who gives hope will fill you with much joy and peace while you trust in him. Then your hope will overflow by the power of the Holy Spirit.

PAUL TALKS ABOUT HIS WORK

¹⁴My brothers, I am sure that you are full of goodness. I know that you have all the knowledge you need and that you are able to teach each other. ¹⁵But I have written to you very openly about some things that I wanted you to remember. I did this because God gave me this special gift: ¹⁶to be a minister of Christ Jesus to the non-Jewish people. I served God by teaching his Good News, so that the non-Jewish people could be an offering that God would accept—an offering made holy by the Holy Spirit.

15:3 "When . . . me." Quotation from Psalm 69:9.
15:12 Jesse's family Jesse was the father of David, king of Israel. Jesus was from their family.

[17]So I am proud of what I have done for God in Christ Jesus. [18]I will not talk about anything I did myself. I will talk only about what Christ has done through me in leading the non-Jewish people to obey God. They have obeyed God because of what I have said and done. [19]And they have obeyed God because of the power of miracles and the great things they saw, and the power of the Holy Spirit. I preached the Good News from Jerusalem all the way around to Illyricum. And so I have finished that part of my work. [20]I always want to preach the Good News in places where people have never heard of Christ. I do this because I do not want to build on the work that someone else has already started. [21]But it is written in the Scriptures:

> "Those who were not told about him
>   will see,
>   and those who have not heard
>   about him will understand."
>
>   Isaiah 52:15

PAUL'S PLAN TO VISIT ROME

[22]That is why many times I was stopped from coming to you. [23]Now I have finished my work here. Since for many years I have wanted to come to you, [24]I hope to visit you on my way to Spain. I will enjoy being with you, and you can help me on my trip. [25]Now I am going to Jerusalem to help God's people. [26]The believers in Macedonia and Southern Greece were happy to give their money to help the poor among God's people at Jerusalem. [27]They were happy to do this, and really they owe it to them. These non-Jews have shared in the Jews' spiritual blessings. So they should use their material possessions to help the Jews. [28]I must be sure that the poor in Jerusalem get the money that has been given for them. After I do this, I will leave for Spain and stop and visit you. [29]I know that when I come to you, I will bring Christ's full blessing.

[30]Brothers, I beg you to help me in my work by praying for me to God. Do this because of our Lord Jesus and the love that the Holy Spirit gives us. [31]Pray that I will be saved from the non-believers in Judea. And pray that this help I bring to Jerusalem will please God's people there. [32]Then, if God wants me to, I will come to you. I will come with joy, and together you and I will have a time of rest. [33]The God who gives peace be with you all. Amen.

GREETINGS TO THE CHRISTIANS

16 I recommend to you our sister Phoebe. She is a helper[n] in the church in Cenchrea. [2]I ask you to accept her in the Lord in the way God's people should. Help her with anything she needs because she has helped me and many other people too.

[3]Give my greetings to Priscilla and Aquila, who work together with me in Christ Jesus. [4]They risked their own lives to save my life. I am thankful to them, and all the non-Jewish churches are thankful to them as well. [5]Also, greet for me the church that meets at their house.

Greetings to my dear friend Epenetus. He was the first person in Asia to follow Christ. [6]Greetings to Mary, who worked very hard for you. [7]Greetings to Andronicus and Junias, my relatives, who were in prison with me. The apostles feel they are very important. They were believers in Christ before I was. [8]Greetings to Ampliatus, my dear friend in the Lord. [9]Greetings to Urbanus. He is a worker together with me for Christ. And greetings to my dear friend Stachys. [10]Greetings to Apelles. He was tested and proved that he truly loves Christ. Greetings to all those who are in the family of Aristobulus.

16:1 helper Literally, "deaconess." This might mean the same as one of the special women helpers in 1 Timothy 3:11.

[11]Greetings to Herodion, my relative. Greetings to all those in the family of Narcissus who belong to the Lord. [12]Greetings to Tryphena and Tryphosa. Those women work very hard for the Lord. Greetings to my dear friend Persis. She also has worked very hard for the Lord. [13]Greetings to Rufus who is a special person in the Lord. Greetings to his mother, who has been a mother to me also. [14]Greetings to Asyncritus, Phlegon, Hermes, Patrobas, Hermas, and all the brothers who are with them. [15]Greetings to Philologus and Julia, Nereus and his sister, and Olympas. And greetings to all God's people with them. [16]Greet each other with a holy kiss. All of Christ's churches send greetings to you.

[17]Brothers, I ask you to look out for those who cause people to be against each other and who upset other people's faith. They are against the true teaching you learned. Stay away from them.

☆ Romans 16:25

Through the years, the people of Israel tried to follow God but failed. But God had a plan. He said he would send his Son who would save everyone from their sins. But they did not understand how this could work. In Romans 16, Paul explained that this had been a secret truth. But God is now sharing it with us. And this message about Jesus is really, really Good News!

Have you ever been so busy you forgot to eat? Then all of a sudden you feel weak and tired. When you get something to eat, you feel better. The way we get strong is by putting the right food into our bodies. The same is true about our spirits. God wants you to be strong. And there are some things you can do to make that happen. First, you can put God's word in you. That is what you do when you read your Bible. Second, you can pray. That just means talking to God like the friend and Father he is. Both of these will help make you strong.

• • • • • • • • • • • • • • • • • •

Reading the Bible and talking to God are also great ways to grow your friendship with God.

[18]For such people are not serving our Lord Christ. They are only doing what pleases themselves. They use fancy talk and fine words to fool the minds of those who do not know about evil. [19]All the believers have heard that you obey. So I am very happy because of you. But I want you to be wise in what is good and innocent in what is evil.

[20]The God who brings peace will soon defeat Satan and give you power over him.

The grace of our Lord Jesus be with you.

[21]Timothy, a worker together with me, sends greetings, as well as Lucius, Jason, and Sosipater, my relatives.

[22]I am Tertius, and I am writing this letter from Paul. I send greetings to you in the Lord.

[23]Gaius is letting me and the whole church here use his home. He also sends greetings to you, as do Erastus and our brother Quartus. Erastus is the city treasurer here. [24][The grace of our Lord Jesus Christ be with all of you. Amen.][n]

[25]Glory to God! God is the One who can make you strong in faith by the Good News that I tell people and by the message about Jesus Christ. The message about Christ is the secret truth that was hidden for long ages past, but is now made known. [26]It has been made clear through the writings of the prophets. And by the command of the eternal God it is made known to all nations, that they might believe and obey.

[27]To the only wise God be glory forever through Jesus Christ! Amen.

16:24 The . . . Amen. Some Greek copies do not contain the bracketed text.

1 Corinthians

PAUL GIVES THANKS TO GOD

1 From Paul. I was called to be an apostle of Christ Jesus because that is what God wanted. Also from Sosthenes, our brother in Christ.

²To the church of God in Corinth, to those people who have been made holy in Christ Jesus. You were called to be God's holy people with all people everywhere who trust in the name of the Lord Jesus Christ—their Lord and ours:

³Grace and peace to you from God our Father and the Lord Jesus Christ.

⁴I always thank my God for you because of the grace that God has given you in Christ Jesus. ⁵In Jesus you have been blessed in every way, in all your speaking and in all your knowledge. ⁶The truth about Christ has been proved in you. ⁷So you have every gift from God while you wait for our Lord Jesus Christ to come again. ⁸Jesus will keep you strong until the end. He will keep you strong, so that there will be no wrong in you on the day our Lord Jesus Christ comes again. ⁹God is faithful. He is the One who has called you to share life with his Son, Jesus Christ our Lord.

PROBLEMS IN THE CHURCH

¹⁰I beg you, brothers, in the name of our Lord Jesus Christ. I beg that all of you agree with each other, so that you will not be divided into groups. I beg that you be completely joined together by having the same kind of thinking and the same purpose. ¹¹My brothers, some people from Chloe's family have told me that there are arguments among you. ¹²This is what I mean: One of you says, "I follow Paul"; another says, "I follow Apollos"; another says, "I follow Peter"; and another says, "I follow Christ." ¹³Christ cannot be divided into different groups! Did Paul die on the cross for you? No! Were you baptized in the name of Paul? No! ¹⁴I am thankful that I did not baptize any of you except Crispus and Gaius. ¹⁵I am thankful, because now no one can say that you were baptized in my name. ¹⁶(I also baptized the family of Stephanas. But I do not remember that I myself baptized any others.) ¹⁷Christ did not give me the work of baptizing people. He gave me the work of preaching the Good News, and he sent me to preach the Good News without using words of worldly wisdom. If I used worldly wisdom to tell the Good News, the cross[n] of Christ would lose its power.

CHRIST IS GOD'S POWER AND WISDOM

¹⁸The teaching about the cross seems foolish to those who are lost. But to us who are being saved it is the power of God. ¹⁹It is written in the Scriptures:

> "I will cause the wise men to lose
> their wisdom.
> I will make the wise men unable to
> understand."   *Isaiah 29:14*

²⁰Where is the wise person? Where is the educated person? Where is the philosopher[n] of our times? God has made the wisdom of the world foolish. ²¹The world did not know God through its own wisdom. So God chose to use the message that sounds foolish to save those who believe it. ²²The Jews ask for miracles as proofs. The Greeks want wisdom. ²³But we preach Christ on the cross. This is a big problem to the Jews. And it seems foolish to the non-Jews.

1:17 cross Paul uses the cross as a picture of the gospel, the story of Christ's death and rising from death to pay for men's sins. The cross, or Christ's death, was God's way to save men.
1:20 philosopher Philosophers were those who searched for truth.

²⁴But Christ is the power of God and the wisdom of God to those people God has called—Jews and Greeks. ²⁵Even the foolishness of God is wiser than men. Even the weakness of God is stronger than men.

²⁶Brothers, look at what you were when God called you. Not many of you were wise in the way the world judges wisdom. Not many of you had great influence. Not many of you came from important families. ²⁷But God chose the foolish things of the world to shame the wise. He chose the weak things of the world to shame the strong. ²⁸And he chose what the world thinks is not important. He chose what the world hates and thinks is nothing. He chose these to destroy what the world thinks is important. ²⁹God did this so that no man can brag before him. ³⁰It is God who has made you part of Christ Jesus. Christ has become wisdom for us from God. Christ is the reason we are right with God and have freedom from sin; Christ is the reason we are holy. ³¹So, as the Scripture says, "If a person brags, he should brag only about the Lord." [n]

1:31 "If . . . Lord." Quotation from Jeremiah 9:24.

⭐ 1 Corinthians 1:30

Because of what Jesus did—giving up his life to pay for our sins—we are right with God. God made us part of Jesus, and Jesus made us right with God.

Have you watched your mom or dad make Kool-Aid? They take the packet of flavoring and pour it into a pitcher of water. Then they stir the flavoring and water together, and it becomes Kool-Aid! Two things actually become one. That's what happens when Jesus becomes our Savior. We become part of him, and nothing can ever separate us from him.

. . . .

Being "part of Christ Jesus" means more than you might realize. Read the whole verse. It says you have God's wisdom, you have freedom from sin, and you are holy.

THE MESSAGE OF CHRIST'S DEATH

2 Dear brothers, when I came to you, I did not come as a proud man. I preached God's truth, but not with fancy words or a show of great learning. ²I decided that while I was with you I would forget about everything except Jesus Christ and his death on the cross. ³When I came to you, I was weak and shook with fear. ⁴My teaching and my speaking were not with wise words that persuade people. But the proof of my teaching was the power that the Spirit gives. ⁵I did this so that your faith would be in God's power, not in the wisdom of a man.

GOD'S WISDOM

⁶Yet I speak wisdom to those who are mature. But this wisdom is not from this world or of the rulers of this world. (These rulers are losing their power.) ⁷But I speak God's secret wisdom, which he has kept hidden. God planned this wisdom for our glory, before the world began. ⁸None of the rulers of this world understood it. If they had, they would not have killed the Lord of glory on a cross. ⁹But as it is written in the Scriptures:

"No one has ever seen this.
   No one has ever heard about it.
No one has ever imagined
   what God has prepared for those
   who love him."   *Isaiah 64:4*

¹⁰But God has shown us these things through the Spirit.

The Spirit knows all things, even the deep secrets of God. ¹¹It is like this: No one knows the thoughts that another person has. Only a person's spirit that lives in him knows his thoughts. It is the same with God. No one knows the thoughts of God. Only the Spirit of God knows God's thoughts. ¹²We did not receive the spirit of the world, but we received the Spirit that is from God. We received this Spirit so that we can know all that God has given us. ¹³When we speak, we do not use words taught to us by the wisdom that men have. We use words taught to us by the Spirit. We use spiritual words to explain spiritual things. ¹⁴A person who is not spiritual does not accept the gifts that come from the Spirit of God. That person thinks they are foolish. He cannot understand the Spirit's gifts, because they can only be judged spiritually. ¹⁵But the spiritual person is able to judge all things. Yet no one can judge him. The Scripture says:

¹⁶ "Who has known the mind of the
      Lord?
   Who has been able to teach him?"
                          Isaiah 40:13

But we have the mind of Christ.

FOLLOWING MEN IS WRONG

3 Brothers, in the past I could not talk to you as I talk to spiritual people. I had to talk to you as I would to people of the world—babies in Christ. ²The teaching I gave you was like milk, not solid food. I did this because you were not ready for solid food. And even now you are not ready. ³You are still not spiritual. You have jealousy and arguing among you. This shows that you are not spiritual. You are acting like people of the world. ⁴One of you says, "I follow Paul," and another says, "I follow Apollos." When you say things like this, you are acting like worldly people.

⁵Is Apollos important? No! Is Paul important? No! We are only servants of God who helped you believe. Each one of us did the work God gave us to do. ⁶I planted the seed of the teaching in you, and Apollos watered it. But God is the One who made the seed grow. ⁷So the one who plants is not important, and the one who waters is not important. Only God is important, because he is the One who makes things grow. ⁸The one who plants and the one who waters have the same purpose. And each will

be rewarded for his own work. [9]We are workers together for God. And you are like a farm that belongs to God.

And you are a house that belongs to God. [10]Like an expert builder I built the foundation of that house. I used the gift that God gave me to do this. Others are building on that foundation. But everyone should be careful how he builds. [11]The foundation has already been built. No one can build any other foundation. The foundation that has already been laid is Jesus Christ. [12]Anyone can build on that foundation, using gold, silver, jewels, wood, grass, or straw. [13]But the work that each person does will be clearly seen, because the Day[n] will make it plain. That Day will appear with fire, and the fire will test every man's work. [14]If the building that a man puts on the foundation still stands, he will get his reward. [15]But if his building is burned up, he will suffer loss. The man will be saved, but it will be as if he escaped from a fire.

[16]You should know that you yourselves are God's temple. God's Spirit lives in you. [17]If anyone destroys God's temple, God will destroy him, because God's temple is holy. You yourselves are God's temple.

[18]Do not fool yourselves. If anyone among you thinks he is wise in this world, he should become a fool. Then he can become truly wise, [19]because the wisdom of this world is foolishness to God. It is written in the Scriptures, "He catches wise men in their own clever traps." [n] [20]It is also written in the Scriptures, "The Lord knows what people think. He knows they are just a puff of wind." [n] [21]So you should not brag about men. All things are yours: [22]Paul, Apollos and Peter; the world, life, death, the present, and the future—all these things are yours. [23]And you belong to Christ, and Christ belongs to God.

APOSTLES OF CHRIST

4 This is what people should think about us: We are servants of Christ. We are the ones God has trusted with his secret truths. [2]A person who is trusted with something must show that he is worthy of that trust. [3]I do not care if I am judged by you or if I am judged by any human court. I do not even judge myself. [4]I know of no wrong that I have done. But this does not make me innocent. The Lord is the One who judges me. [5]So do not judge before the right time; wait until the Lord comes. He will bring to light things that are now hidden in darkness. He will make known the secret purposes of people's hearts. Then God will give everyone the praise he should get.

[6]Brothers, I have used Apollos and myself as examples. I did this so that you could learn from us the meaning of the words, "Follow only what is written in the Scriptures." Then you will not be proud of one man and hate another. [7]Who says that you are better than others? Everything you have was given to you. And if this is so, why do you brag as if you got these things by your own power?

[8]You think you have everything you need. You think you are rich. You think you have become kings without us. I wish you really were kings! Then we could be kings together with you. [9]But it seems to me that God has given me and the other apostles the last place. We are like men sentenced to die. We are like a show for the whole world to see—angels and people. [10]We are fools for Christ's sake. But you think you are very wise in Christ. We are weak, but you think you are strong. You receive honor, but we are hated. [11]Even now we still do not have enough to eat or drink or enough clothes. We are often beaten. We have no homes. [12]We work

---

3:13 **Day** The day Christ will come to judge all people and take his people home to live with him.
3:19 **"He ... traps."** Quotation from Job 5:13.
3:20 **"The Lord ... wind."** Quotation from Psalm 94:11.

hard with our own hands for our food. People curse us, but we bless them. They hurt us, and we accept it. [13]They say evil things against us, but we say only kind things to them. Even today, we are treated as though we are the garbage of the world—the dirt of the earth.

[14]I am not trying to make you feel ashamed. I am writing this to give you a warning as if you were my own dear children. [15]For though you may have 10,000 teachers in Christ, you do not have many fathers. Through the Good News I became your father in Christ Jesus. [16]So I beg you, please be like me. [17]That is why I am sending Timothy to you. He is my son in the Lord. I love Timothy, and he is faithful. He will help you remember the way I live in Christ Jesus. This way of life is what I teach in all the churches everywhere.

[18]Some of you have become proud, thinking that I will not come to you again. [19]But I will come very soon if the Lord wants me to. Then I will see what those who are proud can do, not what they say. [20]I want to see this because the kingdom of God is not talk but power. [21]Which do you want: that I come to you with punishment, or that I come with love and gentleness?

WICKEDNESS IN THE CHURCH

5 Now, it is actually being said that there is sexual sin among you. And it is of such a bad kind that it does not happen even among those who do not know God. A man there is living sinfully with his stepmother. [2]And still you are proud of yourselves! You should have been filled with sadness. And the man who did that sin should be put out of your group. [3]My body is not there with you, but I am with you in spirit. And I have already judged the man who did that sin. I judged him just as I would if I were really there. [4]Meet together as the people of our Lord Jesus. I will be with you in spirit, and you will have the power of our Lord Jesus with you. [5]Then give this man to Satan, so that his sinful self [n] will be destroyed. And then his spirit can be saved on the day of the Lord.

[6]Your bragging is not good. You know the saying, "Just a little yeast makes the whole batch of dough rise." [7]Take out all the old yeast so that you will be a new batch of dough. And you really are new dough without yeast. For Christ, our Passover lamb, was killed to cleanse us. [8]So let us continue our feast, but not with the bread that has the old yeast. That old yeast is the yeast of sin and wickedness. But let us eat the bread that has no yeast. This is the bread of goodness and truth.

[9]I wrote to you in my letter that you should not associate with those who take part in sexual sin. [10]But I did not mean that you should not associate with the sinful people of this world. People of the world do take part in sexual sin, or they are selfish and they cheat each other, or they worship idols. But to get away from them you would have to leave this world. [11]I am writing to tell you that the person you must not associate with is this: anyone who calls himself a brother in Christ but who takes part in sexual sin, or is greedy, or worships idols, or lies about others, or gets drunk, or cheats people. Do not even eat with someone like that.

> But you were washed clean. You were made holy. And you were made right with God.
>
> –1 CORINTHIANS 6:11

5:5 **sinful self** Literally, "flesh." This could also mean his body.

12-13It is not my business to judge those who are not part of the church. God will judge them. But you must judge the people who are part of the church. The Scripture says, "You must get rid of the evil person among you." [n]

JUDGING PROBLEMS AMONG CHRISTIANS

6 When one of you has something against a brother in Christ, why do you go to the judges in the law courts? Those people are not right with God. So why do you let them decide who is right? You should be ashamed! Why do you not let God's people decide who is right? 2Surely you know that God's people will judge the world. So if you are to judge the world, then surely you are able to judge small things as well. 3You know that in the future we will judge angels. So surely we can judge things in this life. 4So if you have disagreements that must be judged, why do you take them to those who are not part of the church? They mean nothing to the church. 5I say this to shame you. Surely there is someone among you wise enough to judge a complaint between two brothers in Christ. 6But now one brother goes to court against another brother. And you let men who are not believers judge their case!

7The lawsuits that you have against each other show that you are already defeated. It would be better for you to let someone wrong you! It would be better for you to let someone cheat you! 8But you yourselves do wrong and cheat! And you do this to your own brothers in Christ!

9-10Surely you know that the people who do wrong will not receive God's kingdom. Do not be fooled. These people will not receive God's kingdom: those who are sexually immoral, or worship idols, or take part in adultery, or men who have physical relations with other men, or steal, or are selfish, or get drunk, or lie about others, or cheat. 11In the past, some of you were like that. But you were washed clean. You were made holy. And you were made right with God in the name of the Lord Jesus Christ and by the Spirit of our God.

USE YOUR BODIES FOR GOD'S GLORY

12"I am allowed to do all things." But not all things are good for me to do. "I am allowed to do all things." But I must not do those things that will make me their slave. 13"Food is for the stomach, and the stomach for food." Yes. But God will destroy them both. The body is not for sexual immorality. The body is for the Lord, and the Lord is for the body. 14By God's power God raised the Lord Jesus from death. And God will also raise us from death. 15Surely you know that your bodies are parts of Christ himself. So I must never take parts of Christ and join them to a prostitute! 16It is written in the Scriptures, "The two people will become one body." [n] So you should know that a man who joins himself with a prostitute becomes one with her in body. 17But the one who joins himself with the Lord is one with the Lord in spirit.

18So run away from sexual immorality. Every other sin that a person does is outside the body. But those who are sexually immoral sin against their own bodies. 19You should know that your body is a temple for the Holy Spirit. The Holy Spirit is in you. You have received the Holy Spirit from God. You do not own yourselves. 20You were bought by God for a price. So honor God with your bodies.

ABOUT MARRIAGE

7 Now I will discuss the things you wrote to me about. It is good for a

5:12–13 "You . . . you." Quotation from Deuteronomy 17:7; 19:19; 22:21, 24; 24:7.
6:16 "The two . . . body." Quotation from Genesis 2:24.

man not to marry. [2]But sexual immorality is a danger. So each man should have his own wife. And each woman should have her own husband. [3]The husband should give his wife all that she should have as his wife. And the wife should give her husband all that he should have as her husband. [4]The wife does not have power over her own body. Her husband has the power over her body. And the husband does not have power over his own body. His wife has the power over his body. [5]Do not refuse to give your bodies to each other. But you might both agree to stay away from intimate relations for a time. You might do this so that you can give your time to prayer. Then come together again. This is so that Satan cannot tempt you in your weakness. [6]I say this to give you permission. It is not a command. [7]I wish everyone were like me. But each person has his own gift from God. One has one gift, another has another gift.

[8]Now for those who are not married and for the widows I say this: It is good for them to stay single as I am. [9]But if they cannot control their bodies, then they should marry. It is better to marry than to burn with lust.

[10]Now I give this command for the married people. (The command is not from me; it is from the Lord.) A wife should not leave her husband. [11]But if she does leave, she must not marry again. Or she should go back to her husband. Also the husband should not divorce his wife.

[12]For all the others I say this (I am saying this, not the Lord): A brother in Christ might have a wife who is not a believer. If she will live with him, he must not divorce her. [13]And a woman might have a husband who is not a believer. If he will live with her, she must not divorce him. [14]The husband who is not a believer is made holy through his believing wife. And the wife who is not a believer is made holy through her believing husband. If this were not true, then your children would not be clean. But now your children are holy.

[15]But if the person who is not a believer decides to leave, let him leave. When this happens, the brother or sister in Christ is free. God called us[n] to a life of peace. [16]Wives, maybe you will save your husband; and husbands, maybe you will save your wife. You do not know now what will happen later.

LIVE AS GOD CALLED YOU

[17]But each one should continue to live the way God has given him to live—the way he was when God called him. This is a rule I make in all the churches. [18]If a man was already circumcised when he was called, he should not change his circumcision. If a man was without circumcision when he was called, he should not be circumcised. [19]It is not important if a man is circumcised or not circumcised. The important thing is obeying God's commands. [20]Each one should stay the way he was when God called him. [21]If you were a slave when God called you, do not let that bother you. But if you can be free, then become free. [22]The person who was a slave when the Lord called him is free in the Lord. He belongs to the Lord. In the same way, the one who was free when he was called is now Christ's slave. [23]You all were bought for a price. So do not become slaves of men. [24]Brothers, in your new life with God each one of you should continue the way you were when you were called.

QUESTIONS ABOUT GETTING MARRIED

[25]Now I write about people who are not married. I have no command from the Lord about this, but I give my opinion. And I can be trusted, because the Lord has given me mercy. [26]This is a time of trouble. So I think that it is good for you

7:15 **us** Some Greek copies read "you."

to stay the way you are. ²⁷If you have a wife, then do not try to become free from her. If you are not married, then do not try to find a wife. ²⁸But if you decide to marry, this is not a sin. And it is not a sin for a girl who has never married to get married. But those who marry will have trouble in this life. And I want you to be free from this trouble.

²⁹Brothers, this is what I mean: We do not have much time left. So starting now, those who have wives should use their time to serve the Lord as if they had no wives. ³⁰Those who are sad should live as if they are not sad. Those who are happy should live as if they are not happy. Those who buy things should live as if they own nothing. ³¹Those who use the things of the world should live as if those things are not important to them. You should live like this, because this world, the way it is now, will soon be gone.

³²I want you to be free from worry. A man who is not married is busy with the Lord's work. He is trying to please the Lord. ³³But a man who is married is busy with things of the world. He is trying to please his wife. ³⁴He must think about two things—pleasing his wife and pleasing the Lord. A woman who is not married or a girl who has never married is busy with the Lord's work. She wants to give herself fully—body and soul—to the Lord. But a married woman is busy with things of the world. She is trying to please her husband. ³⁵I am saying this to help you. I am not trying to limit you. But I want you to live in the right way. And I want you to give yourselves fully to the Lord without giving your time to other things.

³⁶A man might think that he is not doing the right thing with the girl he is engaged to. The girl might be almost past the best age to marry. So he might feel that he should marry her. He should do what he wants. They should get married. It is no sin. ³⁷But another man might be more sure in his mind. There may be no need for marriage, so he is free to do what he wants. If he has decided in his own heart not to marry, he is doing the right thing. ³⁸So the man who marries his girl does right. And the man who does not marry does even better.

³⁹A woman must stay with her husband as long as he lives. If the husband dies, she is free to marry any man she wants. But she must marry another believer. ⁴⁰The woman is happier if she does not marry again. This is my opinion, and I believe that I have God's Spirit.

ABOUT FOOD OFFERED TO IDOLS

8 Now I will write about meat that is sacrificed to idols. We know that "we all have knowledge." Knowledge puffs you up with pride, but love builds up. ²Whoever thinks he knows something does not yet know anything as he should. ³But he who loves God is known by God.

⁴So this is what I say about eating meat sacrificed to idols: We know that an idol is really nothing in the world. And we know that there is only one God. ⁵It is really not important if there are things called gods, in heaven or on earth. (And there are many things that people call "gods" and "lords.") ⁶But for us there is only one God. He is our Father. All things came from him, and we live for him. And there is only one Lord—Jesus Christ. All things were made through Jesus, and we also have life through him.

⁷But not all people know this. Until now, some people have had the habit of worshiping idols. So now when they eat meat, they still feel as if it belongs to an idol. They are not sure that it is right to eat this meat. When they eat it, they feel guilty. ⁸But food will not make us closer to God. Refusing to eat does not make us less pleasing to God. And eating does not make us better in God's sight.

⁹But be careful with your freedom. Your freedom may cause those who are

weak in faith to fall into sin. [10]Suppose one of you who has knowledge eats in an idol's temple.[n] Someone who is weak in faith might see you eating there. This would encourage him to eat meat sacrificed to idols. But he really thinks it is wrong. [11]So this weak brother is ruined because of your "knowledge." And Christ died for this brother. [12]When you sin against your brothers in Christ like this and cause them to do what they feel is wrong, you are also sinning against Christ. [13]So if the food I eat makes my brother fall into sin, I will never eat meat again. I will stop eating meat, so that I will not cause my brother to sin.

PAUL IS LIKE THE OTHER APOSTLES

9 I am a free man. I am an apostle. I have seen Jesus our Lord. You people are all an example of my work in the Lord. [2]Others may not accept me as an apostle, but surely you accept me. You are proof that I am an apostle in the Lord.

[3]Some people want to judge me. So this is the answer I give them: [4]Do we not have the right to eat and drink? [5]Do we not have the right to bring a believing wife with us when we travel? The other apostles, the Lord's brothers, and Peter all do this. [6]And are Barnabas and I the only ones who must work to earn our living? [7]No soldier ever serves in the army and pays his own salary. No one ever plants a vineyard without eating some of the grapes himself. No person takes care of a flock of sheep without drinking some of the milk himself.

[8]This is not only what men think. God's law says the same thing. [9]Yes, it is written in the law of Moses: "When an ox is working in the grain, do not cover its mouth and keep it from eating."[n] When God said this, was he thinking only about oxen? No. [10]He was really talking about us. Yes, that Scripture was written for us. The one who plows and the one who works in the grain should hope to get some of the grain for their work. [11]We planted spiritual seed among you. So we should be able to harvest from you some things for this life. Surely this is not asking too much. [12]Other men have the right to get something from you. So surely we have this right, too. But we do not use this right. No, we put up with everything ourselves so that we will not stop anyone from obeying the Good News of Christ. [13]Surely you know that those who work at the Temple get their food from the Temple. And those who serve at the altar get part of what is offered at the altar. [14]It is the same with those who tell the Good News. The Lord has commanded that those who tell the Good News should get their living from this work.

[15]But I have not used any of these rights. And I am not writing this now to get anything from you. I would rather die than to have my reason for bragging taken away. [16]Telling the Good News is not my reason for bragging. Telling the Good News is my duty—something I must do. And how bad it will be for me if I do not tell the Good News. [17]If I preach because it is my own choice, I should get a reward. But I have no choice. I must tell the Good News. I am only doing the duty that was given to me. [18]So what reward do I get? This is my reward: that when I tell the Good News I can offer it freely. In this way I do not use my right to be paid in my work for the Good News.

[19]I am free. I belong to no man. But I make myself a slave to all people. I do this to help save as many people as I can. [20]To the Jews I became like a Jew. I did this to help save the Jews. I myself am not ruled by the law. But to those

---

8:10 **idol's temple** Building where a false god is worshiped.
9:9 **"When an ox . . . eating."** Quotation from Deuteronomy 25:4.

who are ruled by the law I became like a person who is ruled by the law. I did this to help save those who are ruled by the law. [21] To those who are without the law I became like a person who is without the law. I did this to help save those people who are without the law. (But really, I am not without God's law—I am ruled by Christ's law.) [22] To those who are weak, I became weak so that I could help save them. I have become all things to all people. I did this so that I could save some of them in any way possible. [23] I do all this because of the Good News. I do it so that I can share in the blessings of the Good News.

[24] You know that in a race all the runners run. But only one gets the prize. So run like that. Run to win! [25] All those who compete in the games use strict training. They do this so that they can win a crown. That crown is an earthly thing that lasts only a short time. But our crown will continue forever. [26] So I do not run without a goal. I fight like a boxer who is hitting something—not just the air. [27] It is my own body that I hit. I make it my slave. I do this so that I myself will not be rejected after I have preached to others.

DON'T BE LIKE THE JEWS

10 Brothers, I want you to know what happened to our ancestors who followed Moses. They were all under the cloud, and they all went through the sea. [2] They were all baptized as followers of Moses in the cloud and in the sea. [3] They all ate the same spiritual food. [4] And they all drank the same spiritual drink. They drank from that spiritual rock that was with them. That rock was Christ. [5] But God was not pleased with most of them. They died in the desert.

[6] And these things that happened are examples for us. They should stop us from wanting evil things as those people did. [7] Do not worship idols, as some of them did. It is written in the Scriptures: "The people sat down to eat and drink. Then they got up and had wild parties."[n] [8] We should not take part in sexual sin, as some of them did. In one day 23,000 of them died because of their sins. [9] We should not test the Lord as some of them did. They were killed by snakes. [10] And do not complain as some of them did. They were killed by the angel that destroys.

[11] The things that happened to those people are examples. And they were written down to be warnings for us. For we live in a time when all these things of the past have reached their goal. [12] So anyone who thinks he is standing strong should be careful not to fall. [13] The only temptations that you have are the temptations that all people have. But you can trust God. He will not let you be tempted more than you can stand. But when you are tempted, God will also give you a way to escape that temptation. Then you will be able to stand it.

[14] So, my dear friends, stay away from worshiping idols. [15] I am speaking to you, as to reasonable people; judge for yourselves what I say. [16] We give thanks for the cup of blessing.[n] It is a sharing

> You know that in a race all the runners run. But only one gets the prize. So run like that. Run to win!
> – 1 CORINTHIANS 9:24

10:7 **"The people ... parties."** Quotation from Exodus 32:6.
10:16 **cup of blessing** The cup of the fruit of the vine that Christians thank God for and drink at the Lord's Supper.

in the blood of Christ's death. And the bread that we break is a sharing in the body of Christ. [17]There is one loaf of bread. And we are many people. But we all share from that one loaf. So we are really one body.

[18]Think about the people of Israel: Do not those who eat the sacrifices share in the altar? [19]I do not mean that the food sacrificed to an idol is something important. And I do not mean that an idol is anything at all. [20]But I say that what is sacrificed to idols is offered to demons, not to God. And I do not want you to share anything with demons. [21]You cannot drink the cup of the Lord and the cup of demons, too. You cannot share in the Lord's table and the table of demons, too. [22]Do we want to make the Lord jealous? We are not stronger than he is, are we?

HOW TO USE CHRISTIAN FREEDOM

[23]"We are allowed to do all things." Yes. But not all things are good for us to do. "We are allowed to do all things." Yes. But not all things help others grow stronger. [24]No one should try to do what will help only himself. He should try to do what is good for others.

[25]Eat any meat that is sold in the meat market. Do not ask questions about the meat to see if it is something you think is wrong to eat. [26]You can eat it, "because the earth and everything on it belong to the Lord." [n]

[27]Someone who is not a believer may invite you to eat with him. If you want to go, eat anything that is put before you. Do not ask questions about it. [28]But if anyone says to you, "That food was offered to idols," then do not eat it. Do not eat it because of that person who told you and because eating it would be something that might be thought wrong. [29]I don't mean that you think it is wrong. But the other person might

think it is wrong. My own freedom should not be judged by what someone else thinks. [30]I eat the meal with thankfulness. And I do not want to be criticized because of something I thank God for.

[31]So if you eat, or if you drink, or if you do anything, do everything for the glory of God. [32]Never do anything that might make others do wrong—Jews, Greeks, or God's church. [33]I do the same thing. I try to please everybody in every way. I am not trying to do what is good for me. I try to do what is good for the most people. I do this so that they can be saved.

11 Follow my example, as I follow the example of Christ.

BEING UNDER AUTHORITY

[2]I praise you because you remember me in everything. You follow closely the teachings that I gave you. [3]But I want you to understand this: The head of every man is Christ. And the head of a woman is the man.[n] And the head of Christ is God. [4]Every man who prophesies or prays with his head covered brings shame to his head. [5]But every woman who prays or prophesies should have her head covered. If her head is not covered, she brings shame to her head. She is the same as a woman who has her head shaved. [6]If a woman does not cover her head, it is the same as cutting off all her hair. But it is shameful for a woman to cut off her hair or to shave her head. So she should cover her head. [7]But a man should not cover his head, because he is made like God and is God's glory. But woman is man's glory. [8]Man did not come from woman, but woman came from man. [9]And man was not made for woman. Woman was made for man. [10]So that is why a woman should have her head covered with something to show that she is under authority. And

10:26 "because . . . Lord" Quotation from Psalms 24:1; 50:12; 89:11.
11:3 the man This could also mean "her husband."

also she should do this because of the angels.

[11]But in the Lord the woman is important to the man, and the man is important to the woman. [12]This is true because woman came from man, but also man is born from woman. Really, everything comes from God. [13]Decide this for yourselves: Is it right for a woman to pray to God without something on her head? [14]Even nature itself teaches you that wearing long hair is shameful for a man. [15]But wearing long hair is a woman's honor. Long hair is given to the woman to cover her head. [16]Some people may still want to argue about this. But I would add that neither we nor the churches of God accept any other practice.

THE LORD'S SUPPER

[17]In the things I tell you now I do not praise you. Your meetings hurt you more than they help you. [18]First, I hear that when you meet together as a church you are divided. And I believe some of this. [19](It is necessary for there to be differences among you. That is the way to make it clear which of you are really doing right.) [20]When you all come together, you are not really eating the Lord's Supper.[n] [21]This is because when you eat, each person eats without waiting for the others. Some people do not get enough to eat, while others have too much to drink. [22]You can eat and drink in your own homes! It seems that you think God's church is not important. You embarrass those who are poor. What should I tell you? Should I praise you for doing this? I do not praise you.

[23]The teaching that I gave you is the same teaching that I received from the Lord: On the night when Jesus was handed over to be killed, he took bread [24]and gave thanks for it. Then he broke the bread and said, "This is my body; it is[n] for you. Do this to remember me."

[25]In the same way, after they ate, Jesus took the cup. He said, "This cup shows the new agreement from God to his people. This new agreement begins with the blood of my death. When you drink this, do it to remember me." [26]Every time you eat this bread and drink this cup, you show others about the Lord's death until he comes.

[27]So a person should not eat the bread or drink the cup of the Lord in a way that is not worthy of it. If he does he is sinning against the body and the blood of the Lord. [28]Everyone should look into his own heart before he eats the bread and drinks the cup. [29]If someone eats the bread and drinks the cup without recognizing the body, then he is judged guilty by eating and drinking. [30]That is why many in your group are sick and weak. And some of you have died. [31]But if we judged ourselves in the right way, then God would not judge us. [32]But when the Lord judges us, he disciplines us to show us the right way. He does this so that we will not be destroyed along with the world.

[33]So my brothers, when you come together to eat, wait for each other. [34]If anyone is too hungry, he should eat at home. Do this so that your meeting together will not bring God's judgment on you. I will tell you what to do about the other things when I come.

GIFTS FROM THE HOLY SPIRIT

12 Now, brothers, I want you to understand about spiritual gifts. [2]You remember the lives you lived before you were believers. You let yourselves be influenced and led away to worship idols—things that have no life. [3]So I tell you that no one who is speaking with the help of God's Spirit says, "Jesus be cursed." And no one can say, "Jesus is Lord," without the help of the Holy Spirit.

[4]There are different kinds of gifts;

11:20 Lord's Supper The meal Jesus told his followers to eat to remember him (Luke 22:14–20).
11:24 it is Some Greek copies read "it is broken."

but they are all from the same Spirit. [5]There are different ways to serve; but all these ways are from the same Lord. [6]And there are different ways that God works in people; but all these ways are from the same God. God works in us all in everything we do. [7]Something from the Spirit can be seen in each person, to help everyone. [8]The Spirit gives one person the ability to speak with wisdom. And the same Spirit gives another the ability to speak with knowledge. [9]The same Spirit gives faith to one person. And that one Spirit gives another gifts of healing. [10]The Spirit gives to another person the power to do miracles, to another the ability to prophesy. And he gives to another the ability to know the difference between good and evil spirits. The Spirit gives one person the ability to speak in different kinds of languages and to another the ability to interpret those languages. [11]One Spirit, the same Spirit, does all these things. The Spirit decides what to give each person.

☆ 1 Corinthians 12:12–31

God's family is known as the church. The church is also called the body of Christ. The body of Christ is made up of many people with different gifts, talents, and strengths. But no gift is more important than any other. We are all one body with God's Spirit.

God made your body in such a way that every part is important. All parts work together, and no part is better than another part. Your brain tells your body what to do. Your eyes help you see. Your hands hold things. Even your little toes are important. Without them, you could fall over when you walk. God's family, the church, is described as a body. Just as our body needs every part to work the way it should, the church needs every member. Every person in the church plays a very important part to make a healthy church.

. . . .

The family of God is like one body, which means every part—including you—is important.

THE BODY OF CHRIST

¹²A person's body is one thing, but it has many parts. Yes, there are many parts to a body, but all those parts make only one body. Christ is like that too. ¹³Some of us are Jews, and some of us are Greeks. Some of us are slaves, and some of us are free. But we were all baptized into one body through one Spirit. And we were all made to share in the one Spirit.

¹⁴And a person's body has more than one part. It has many parts. ¹⁵The foot might say, "I am not a hand. So I am not part of the body." But saying this would not stop the foot from being a part of the body. ¹⁶The ear might say, "I am not an eye. So I am not part of the body." But saying this would not make the ear stop being a part of the body. ¹⁷If the whole body were an eye, the body would not be able to hear. If the whole body were an ear, the body would not be able to smell anything. ¹⁸⁻¹⁹If each part of the body were the same part, there would be no body. But truly God put the parts in the body as he wanted them. He made a place for each one of them. ²⁰And so there are many parts, but only one body.

²¹The eye cannot say to the hand, "I don't need you!" And the head cannot say to the foot, "I don't need you!" ²²No! Those parts of the body that seem to be weaker are really very important. ²³And the parts of the body that we think are not worth much are the parts that we give the most care to. And we give special care to the parts of the body that we want to hide. ²⁴The more beautiful parts of our body need no special care. But God put the body together and gave more honor to the parts that need it. ²⁵God did this so that our body would not be divided. God wanted the different parts to care the same for each other. ²⁶If one part of the body suffers, then all the other parts suffer with it. Or if one part of

our body is honored, then all the other parts share its honor.

²⁷All of you together are the body of Christ. Each one of you is a part of that body. ²⁸And in the church God has given a place first to apostles, second to prophets, and third to teachers. Then God has given a place to those who do miracles, those who have gifts of healing, those who can help others, those who are able to lead, and those who can speak in different languages. ²⁹Not all are apostles. Not all are prophets. Not all are teachers. Not all do miracles. ³⁰Not all have gifts of healing. Not all speak in different languages. Not all interpret those languages. ³¹But you should truly want to have the greater gifts.

LOVE

And now I will show you the best way of all.

13 I may speak in different languages of men or even angels. But if I do not have love, then I am only a noisy bell or a ringing cymbal. ²I may have the gift of prophecy; I may understand all the secret things of God and all knowledge; and I may have faith so great that I can move mountains. But even with all these things, if I do not have love, then I am nothing. ³I may give everything I have to feed the poor. And I may even give my body as an offering to be burned.ⁿ But I gain nothing by doing these things if I do not have love.

⁴Love is patient and kind. Love is not jealous, it does not brag, and it is not proud. ⁵Love is not rude, is not selfish, and does not become angry easily. Love does not remember wrongs done against it. ⁶Love takes no pleasure in evil, but rejoices over the truth. ⁷Love patiently accepts all things. It always trusts, always hopes, and always continues strong.

⁸Love never ends. There are gifts of

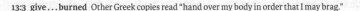

13:3 **give...burned** Other Greek copies read "hand over my body in order that I may brag."

The early church leaders talked a lot about love. One of them even wrote that "God is love" (1 John 4:8, 16). Paul used one of his letters to tell us what love—or God—is really like. "Love is patient and kind," and "Love never ends."

God tells us that love is important. Many verses in the Bible tell us to love others, to love our neighbors, to love our enemies! Yikes! But sometimes loving others is hard to do. Some people may be too hard to be around. Some people might seem weird. And some are just plain mean. So how do we love them like God wants us to? The Bible says, "God has poured out his love to fill our hearts" (Romans 5:5). It also says that "we love because God first loved us" (1 John 4:19). This means you don't have to try to love people with your own strength. The love of God is already in your heart. Ask God to help you let it out. He'll do it!

• •

God promises to be with you always. That means he will help you love people even when it's hard to do.

---

prophecy, but they will be ended. There are gifts of speaking in different languages, but those gifts will end. There is the gift of knowledge, but it will be ended. ⁹These things will end, because this knowledge and these prophecies we have are not complete. ¹⁰But when perfection comes, the things that are not complete will end. ¹¹When I was a child, I talked like a child; I thought like a child; I made plans like a child. When I became a man, I stopped those childish ways. ¹²It is the same with us. Now we see as if we are looking into a dark mirror. But at that time, in the future, we shall see clearly. Now I know only a part. But at that time I will know fully, as God has known me. ¹³So these three things continue forever: faith, hope and love. And the greatest of these is love.

SPIRITUAL GIFTS

14 Love, then, is what you should try for. And you should truly want to have the spiritual gifts. And the gift you should want most is to be able to prophesy. ²I will explain why. One who has the gift of speaking in a different language is not speaking to people. He is speaking to God. No one understands him—he is speaking secret things through the Spirit. ³But one who prophesies is speaking to people. He gives people strength, encouragement, and comfort. [4]The one who speaks in a different language is helping only himself. But the one who prophesies is helping the whole church. [5]I would like all of you to have the gift of speaking in different kinds of languages. But more, I want you to prophesy. The person who prophesies is greater than the one who can only speak in different languages—unless someone is there who can explain what he says. Then the whole church can be helped.

[6]Brothers, will it help you if I come to you speaking in different languages? No! It will help you only if I bring you a new truth or some knowledge, or some prophecy, or some teaching. [7]It is the same as with non-living things that make sounds—like a flute or a harp. If different musical notes are not made clear, you will not know what song is being played. Each note must be played clearly for you to be able to understand the tune. [8]And in a war, if the trumpet does not sound clearly, the soldiers will not know it is time to prepare for fighting. [9]It is the same with you. The words you speak with your tongue must be clear. Unless you speak clearly, no one can understand what you are saying. You will be talking in the air! [10]It is true that there are many kinds of speech in the world. And they all have meaning. [11]So unless I understand the meaning of what someone says to me, we will be like strangers to each other. [12]It is the same with you. You want spiritual gifts very much. So try most to have the gifts that help the church grow stronger.

[13]The one who has the gift of speaking in a different language should pray that he can also interpret what he says. [14]If I pray in a different language, my spirit is praying, but my mind does nothing. [15]So what should I do? I will pray with my spirit, but I will also pray with my mind. I will sing with my spirit, but I will also sing with my mind. [16]You might be praising God with your spirit. But a person there without understanding cannot say "Amen" [n] to your prayer of thanks. He does not know what you are saying. [17]You may be thanking God in a good way, but the other person is not helped.

[18]I thank God that my gift of speaking in different kinds of languages is greater than any of yours. [19]But in the church meetings I would rather speak five words that I understand than thousands of words in a different language. I would rather speak with my understanding, so that I can teach others.

[20]Brothers, do not think like children. In evil things be like babies. But in your thinking you should be like full-grown men. [21]It is written in the Scriptures:

> "I will use strange words and foreign languages
> to speak to these people.
> But even then they will not listen."
> *Isaiah 28:11–12*

That is what the Lord says. [22]So the gift of speaking in different kinds of languages is a sign for those who do not believe, not for those who believe. And prophecy is for people who believe, not for those who do not believe. [23]Suppose the whole church meets together and everyone speaks in different languages. If some people come in who are without understanding or do not believe, they will say you are crazy. [24]But suppose everyone is prophesying and someone comes in who does not believe or is without understanding. If everyone is prophesying, his sin will be shown to him, and he will be judged by all that he hears. [25]The secret things in his heart will be made known. So he will bow down and worship God. He will say, "Truly, God is with you."

14:16 "Amen" When a person says "Amen," it means he agrees with the things that were said.

MEETINGS SHOULD HELP THE CHURCH

26So, brothers, what should you do? When you meet together, one person has a song. Another has a teaching. Another has a new truth from God. Another speaks in a different language, and another person interprets that language. The purpose of all these things should be to help the church grow strong. 27When you meet together, if anyone speaks in a different language, then it should be only two, or not more than three, who speak. They should speak one after the other. And someone should interpret what they say. 28But if there is no interpreter, then anyone who speaks in a different language should be quiet in the church meeting. He should speak only to himself and to God.

29And only two or three prophets should speak. The others should judge what they say. 30And if a message from God comes to another person who is sitting, then the first speaker should stop. 31You can all prophesy one after the other. In this way all the people can be taught and encouraged. 32The spirits of prophets are under the control of the prophets themselves. 33God is not a God of confusion but a God of peace.

This is true in all the churches of God's people. 34Women should keep quiet in the church meetings. They are not allowed to speak. They must be under control. This is also what the law of Moses says. 35If there is something the women want to know, they should ask their own husbands at home. It is shameful for a woman to speak in the church meeting. 36Did God's teaching come from you? Or are you the only ones who have received that teaching?

37If anyone thinks that he is a prophet or that he has a spiritual gift, then he should understand that what I am writing to you is the Lord's command. 38If that person does not know this, then he is not known by God.

39So my brothers, you should truly want to prophesy. And do not stop people from using the gift of speaking in different kinds of languages. 40But let everything be done in a way that is right and orderly.

THE GOOD NEWS ABOUT CHRIST

15 Now, brothers, I want you to remember the Good News I brought to you. You received this Good News, and you continue strong in it. 2And you are saved by this Good News. But you must continue believing what I told you. If you do not, then you believed for nothing.

3I passed on to you what I received. And this was the most important: that Christ died for our sins, as the Scriptures say; 4that he was buried and was raised to life on the third day as the Scriptures say; 5and that he showed himself to Peter and then to the twelve apostles. 6After that, Jesus showed himself to more than 500 of the believers at the same time. Most of them are still living today. But some have died. 7Then Jesus showed himself to James and later to all the apostles. 8Last of all he showed himself to me— as to a person not born at the normal time. 9All the other apostles are greater than I am. This is because I persecuted the church of God. And this is why I am not even good enough to be called an apostle. 10But God's grace has made me what I am. And his grace to me was not wasted. I worked harder than all the other apostles. (But I was not really

> You received this Good News, and you continue strong in it. And you are saved by (it).
>
> – 1 CORINTHIANS 15:1–2

the one working. It was God's grace that was with me.) ¹¹So then it is not important if I preached to you or if the other apostles preached to you. We all preach the same thing, and this is what you believed.

WE WILL BE RAISED FROM DEATH

¹²It is preached that Christ was raised from death. So why do some of you say that people will not be raised from death? ¹³If no one will ever be raised from death, then Christ was not raised from death. ¹⁴And if Christ was not raised, then our preaching is worth nothing. And your faith is worth nothing. ¹⁵And also, we will be guilty of lying about God. Because we have preached about him by saying that he raised Christ from death. And if people are not raised from death, then God never raised Christ from death. ¹⁶If the dead are not raised, Christ has not been raised either. ¹⁷And if Christ has not been raised, then your faith is for nothing; you are still guilty of your sins. ¹⁸And also, those in Christ who have already died are lost. ¹⁹If our hope in Christ is for this life only, we should be pitied more than anyone else in the world.

²⁰But Christ has truly been raised from death—the first one and proof that those who are asleep in death will also be raised. ²¹Death comes to everyone because of what one man did. But the rising from death also happens because of one man. ²²In Adam all of us die. In the same way, in Christ all of us will be made alive again. ²³But everyone will be raised to life in the right order. Christ was first to be raised. When Christ comes again, those who belong to him will be raised to life. ²⁴Then the end will come. Christ will destroy all rulers, authorities, and powers. And he will give the kingdom to God the Father. ²⁵Christ must rule until God

puts all enemies under Christ's control. ²⁶The last enemy to be destroyed will be death. ²⁷The Scripture says, "God put all things under his control." [n] When it says that "all things" are put under him, it is clear that this does not include God himself. God is the one putting everything under Christ's control. ²⁸After everything has been put under Christ, then the Son himself will be put under God. God is the One who put all things under Christ. And Christ will be put under God, so that God will be the complete ruler over everything.

²⁹If the dead are never raised, then what will people do who are baptized for those who have died? If the dead are not raised at all, why are people baptized for them?

³⁰And what about us? Why do we put ourselves in danger every hour? ³¹I die every day. That is true, brothers, just as it is true that I brag about you in Christ Jesus our Lord. ³²If I fought wild animals in Ephesus only for human reasons, I have gained nothing. If the dead are not raised, then, "Let us eat and drink, because tomorrow we will die." [n]

³³Do not be fooled: "Bad friends will ruin good habits." ³⁴Come back to your right way of thinking and stop sinning. I say this to shame you—some of you do not know God.

WHAT KIND OF BODY WILL WE HAVE?

³⁵But someone may ask, "How are the dead raised? What kind of body will they have?" ³⁶Those are stupid questions. When you plant something, it must die in the ground before it can live and grow. ³⁷And when you plant it, what you plant does not have the same "body" that it will have later. What you plant is only a seed, maybe wheat or something else. ³⁸But God gives it a body that he has planned for it. And God gives each kind of seed its own

---

15:27 **"God put ... control."** Quotation from Psalm 8:6.
15:32 **"Let us ... die."** Quotation from Isaiah 22:13; 56:12.

body. [39]All things made of flesh are not the same kinds of flesh: People have one kind of flesh, animals have another kind, birds have another, and fish have another. [40]Also there are heavenly bodies and earthly bodies. But the beauty of the heavenly bodies is one kind. The beauty of the earthly bodies is another kind. [41]The sun has one kind of beauty. The moon has another beauty, and the stars have another. And each star is different in its beauty.

[42]It is the same with the dead who are raised to life. The body that is "planted" will ruin and decay. But that body is raised to a life that cannot be destroyed. [43]When the body is "planted," it is without honor. But it is raised in glory. When the body is "planted," it is weak. But when it is raised, it has power. [44]The body that is "planted" is a physical body. When it is raised, it is a spiritual body.

There is a physical body. And there is also a spiritual body. [45]It is written in the Scriptures: "The first man became a living person." [n] But the last Adam became a spirit that gives life. [46]The spiritual man did not come first. It was the physical man who came first; then came the spiritual. [47]The first man came from the dust of the earth. The second man came from heaven. [48]People belong to the earth. They are like the first man of earth. But those people who belong to heaven are like the man of heaven. [49]We were made like the man of earth. So we will[n] also be made like the man of heaven.

[50]I tell you this, brothers: Flesh and blood cannot have a part in the kingdom of God. A thing that will ruin cannot have a part in something that never ruins. [51]But listen, I tell you this secret: We will not all die, but we will all be changed. [52]It will only take a second. We will be changed as quickly as an eye blinks. This will happen when the last trumpet sounds. The trumpet will sound

and those who have died will be raised to live forever. And we will all be changed. [53]This body that will ruin must clothe itself with something that will never ruin. And this body that dies must clothe itself with something that will never die. [54]So this body that ruins will clothe itself with that which never ruins. And this body that dies will clothe itself with that which never dies. When this happens, then this Scripture will be made true:

> "Death is destroyed forever in victory." *Isaiah 25:8*
> [55] "Death, where is your victory? Death, where is your power to hurt?" *Hosea 13:14*

[56]Death's power to hurt is sin. The power of sin is the law. [57]But we thank God! He gives us the victory through our Lord Jesus Christ.

[58]So my dear brothers, stand strong. Do not let anything move you. Always give yourselves fully to the work of the Lord. You know that your work in the Lord is never wasted.

THE GIFT FOR OTHER BELIEVERS

16 Now I will write about the collection of money for God's people. Do the same thing that I told the Galatian churches to do: [2]On the first day of every week, each one of you should put aside as much money as you can from what you are blessed with. You should save it up, so that you will not have to collect money after I come. [3]When I arrive, I will send some men to take your gift to Jerusalem. These will be men who you all agree should go. I will send them with letters of introduction. [4]If it seems good for me to go also, these men will go along with me.

PAUL'S PLANS

[5]I plan to go through Macedonia. So I will come to you after I go through

---

15:45 **"The first . . . person."** Quotation from Genesis 2:7.
15:49 **So we will** Some Greek copies read "So let us."

there. ⁶Maybe I will stay with you for a time. I might even stay all winter. Then you can help me on my trip, wherever I go. ⁷I do not want to come to see you now, because I would have to leave to go other places. I hope to stay a longer time with you if the Lord allows it. ⁸But I will stay at Ephesus until Pentecost. ⁹I will stay, because a good opportunity for a great and growing work has been given to me now. And there are many people working against me.

¹⁰Timothy might come to you. Try to make him feel comfortable with you. He is working for the Lord just as I am. ¹¹So none of you should refuse to accept Timothy. Help him on his trip in peace, so that he can come back to me. I am expecting him to come back with the brothers.

¹²Now about our brother Apollos: I strongly encouraged him to visit you with the other brothers. But he was sure that he did not want to go now. But when he has the opportunity, he will go to you.

PAUL ENDS HIS LETTER

¹³Be careful. Continue strong in the faith. Have courage, and be strong. ¹⁴Do everything in love.

¹⁵You know that the family of Stephanas were the first believers in Southern Greece. They have given themselves to the service of God's people. I ask you, brothers, ¹⁶to follow the leading of people like these and anyone else who works and serves with them.

¹⁷I am happy that Stephanas, Fortunatus, and Achaicus have come. You are not here, but they have filled your place. ¹⁸They have given rest to my spirit and to yours. You should recognize the value of men like these.

¹⁹The churches in the country of Asia send greetings to you. Aquila and Priscilla greet you in the Lord. Also the church that meets in their house greets you. ²⁰All the brothers here send greetings. Give each other a holy kiss when you meet.

²¹I am Paul, and I am writing this greeting with my own hand.

²²If anyone does not love the Lord, then let him be separated from God— lost forever!

Come, O Lord!

²³The grace of the Lord Jesus be with you.

²⁴My love be with all of you in Christ Jesus.

2 Corinthians

PAUL ANSWERS THOSE WHO ACCUSE HIM

1 From Paul, an apostle of Christ Jesus. I am an apostle because that is what God wanted.

Also from Timothy our brother in Christ.

To the church of God in Corinth, and to all of God's people in the whole country of Southern Greece:

²Grace and peace to you from God our Father and the Lord Jesus Christ.

PAUL GIVES THANKS TO GOD

³Praise be to the God and Father of our Lord Jesus Christ. God is the Father who is full of mercy. And he is the God of all comfort. ⁴He comforts us every time we have trouble, so that we can comfort others when they have trouble. We can comfort them with the same comfort that God gives us. ⁵We share in the many sufferings of Christ. In the same way, much comfort comes to us through Christ. ⁶If we have troubles, it is for your comfort and salvation. If we have comfort, then you also have comfort. This helps you to accept patiently the same sufferings that we have. ⁷Our hope for you is strong. We know that you share in our sufferings. So we know that you also share in the comfort we receive.

⁸Brothers, we want you to know about the trouble we suffered in the country of Asia. We had great burdens there that were greater than our own strength. We even gave up hope for life. ⁹Truly, in our own hearts we believed that we would die. But this happened so that we would not trust in ourselves. It happened so that we would trust in God, who raises people from death. ¹⁰God saved us from these great dangers of death. And he will continue to save us. We have put our hope in him, and he will save us again. ¹¹And you can help us with your prayers. Then many people will give thanks for us—that God blessed us because of their many prayers.

THE CHANGE IN PAUL'S PLANS

¹²This is what we are proud of, and I can say with all my heart that it is true: In all the things we have done in the world, we have done everything with an honest[n] and pure heart from God. And this is even more true in what we have done with you. We did this by God's grace, not by the kind of wisdom the world has. ¹³For we write to you only what you can read and understand. And I hope that ¹⁴as you have understood some things about us, you may come to know everything about us. Then you can be proud of us, as we will be proud of you on the day our Lord Jesus Christ comes again.

¹⁵I was very sure of all this. That is why I made plans to visit you first. Then you could be blessed twice. ¹⁶I planned to visit you on my way to Macedonia. Then I planned to visit you again on my way back. I wanted to get help from you for my trip to Judea. ¹⁷Do you think that I made these plans without really thinking? Or maybe you think I make plans as the world does, so that I say "Yes, yes," and at the same time "No, no."

¹⁸But since you can believe God, then you can believe that what we tell you is never both "Yes" and "No." ¹⁹The Son of God, Jesus Christ, that Silas and Timothy and I preached to you, was not "Yes" and "No." In Christ it has always been "Yes." ²⁰The "Yes" to all of God's promises is in Christ. And that is why we say "Amen"[n] through Christ

---

1:12 **honest** Some Greek copies read "holy."
1:20 **"Amen"** When a person says "Amen," it means he agrees with the things that were said.

to the glory of God. ²¹And God is the One who makes you and us strong in Christ. God made us his chosen people. ²²He put his mark on us to show that we are his. And he put his Spirit in our hearts to be a guarantee for all he has promised.

²³I tell you this, and I ask God to be my witness that this is true: The reason I did not come back to Corinth was that I did not want to punish or hurt you. ²⁴I do not mean that we are trying to control your faith. You are strong in faith.

But we are workers with you for your own happiness.

2 So I decided that my next visit to you would not be another visit to make you sad. ²If I make you sad, who will make me happy? Only you can make me happy—you whom I made sad. ³I wrote you a letter for this reason: that when I came to you I would not be made sad by the people who should make me happy. I felt sure of all of you. I felt sure that you would share my joy. ⁴When I wrote to you before, I was very

---

☆ 2 Corinthians 1:21–22

Remember how God chose Abraham to be the ancestor of God's chosen people? Well, because of what Jesus did, we are all God's chosen people. He put "his mark on us" and "put his Spirit in our hearts" to show that we belong to him.

At recess one day some kids decided to play dodgeball. The two captains prepared to pick teams. Shawn hung his head. He was smaller than everybody else and was always picked last. Suddenly he heard, "I pick Shawn!" Shawn ran to his captain's side. "Why did you pick me?" Shawn asked. "Because you're small; you will be hard to hit." Shawn smiled from ear to ear. He was small, but he would be fast. He was chosen for this team!

. . . .

Life is bigger than dodgeball. Just know that God has chosen you for his team. And his team always wins!

troubled and unhappy in my heart. I wrote with many tears. I did not write to make you sad, but to let you know how much I love you.

FORGIVE THE SINNER

[5]Someone there among you has caused sadness. He caused this not to me, but to all of you—I mean he caused sadness to all in some way. (I do not want to make it sound worse than it really is.) [6]The punishment that most of you gave him is enough for him. [7]But now you should forgive him and comfort him. This will keep him from having too much sadness and giving up completely. [8]So I beg you to show him that you love him. [9]This is why I wrote to you. I wanted to test you and see if you obey in everything. [10]If you forgive someone, I also forgive him. And what I have forgiven—if I had anything to forgive—I forgave it for you, and Christ was with me. [11]I did this so that Satan would not win anything from us. We know very well what Satan's plans are.

PAUL'S CONCERN IN TROAS

[12]I went to Troas to preach the Good News of Christ. The Lord gave me a good opportunity there. [13]But I had no peace because I did not find my brother Titus there. So I said good-bye and went to Macedonia.

VICTORY THROUGH CHRIST

[14]But thanks be to God, who always leads us in victory through Christ. God uses us to spread his knowledge everywhere like a sweet-smelling perfume. [15]Our offering to God is this: We are the sweet smell of Christ among those who are being saved and among those who are being lost. [16]To those who are lost, we are the smell of death that brings death. But to those who are being saved, we are the smell of life that brings life. So who is able to do this work? [17]We do not sell the word of God for a profit as many other people do. But in Christ we speak the truth before God. We speak as men sent from God.

SERVANTS OF THE NEW AGREEMENT

3 Are we starting to brag about ourselves again? Do we need letters of introduction to you or from you, like some other people? [2]You yourselves are our letter, written on our hearts. It is known and read by everyone. [3]You show that you are a letter from Christ that he sent through us. This letter is not written with ink, but with the Spirit of the living God. It is not written on stone tablets.[n] It is written on human hearts.

[4]We can say this, because through Christ we feel sure before God. [5]I do not mean that we are able to say that we can do this work ourselves. It is God who makes us able to do all that we do. [6]God made us able to be servants of a new agreement from himself to his people. This new agreement is not a written law. It is of the Spirit. The written law brings death, but the Spirit gives life.

[7]The law that brought death was written in words on stone. It came with God's glory. Moses' face was so bright with glory that the people of Israel could not continue to look at his face. And that glory later disappeared. [8]So surely the new way that brings the Spirit has even more glory. [9]That law judged people guilty of sin, but it had glory. So surely the new way that makes people right with God has much greater glory. [10]That old law had glory. But it really loses its glory when it is compared to the much greater glory of this new way. [11]If that law which disappeared came with glory, then this new way which continues forever has much greater glory.

[12]We have this hope, so we are very brave. [13]We are not like Moses. He put

3:3 **stone tablets** Meaning the law of Moses that was written on stone tablets (Exodus 24:12; 25:16).

a covering over his face so that the people of Israel would not see it. The glory was disappearing, and Moses did not want them to see it end. [14]But their minds were closed. Even today that same covering hides the meaning when they read the old agreement. That covering is taken away only through Christ. [15]But even today, when they read the law of Moses, there is a covering over their minds. [16]But when a person changes and follows the Lord, that covering is taken away. [17]The Lord is the Spirit. And where the Spirit of the Lord is, there is freedom. [18]Our faces, then, are not covered. We all show the Lord's glory, and we are being changed to be like him. This change in us brings more and more glory. And it comes from the Lord, who is the Spirit.

PREACHING THE GOOD NEWS

4 God, with his mercy, gave us this work to do. So we don't give up. [2]But we have turned away from secret and shameful ways. We use no trickery, and we do not change the teaching of God. We teach the truth plainly. This is how we show everyone who we are. And this is how they can know in their hearts what kind of people we are before God. [3]The Good News that we preach may be hidden. But it is hidden only to those who are lost. [4]The devil who rules this world has blinded the minds of those who do not believe. They cannot see the light of the Good News—the Good News about the glory of Christ, who is exactly like God. [5]We do not preach about ourselves. But we preach that Jesus Christ is Lord; and we preach that we are your servants for Jesus. [6]God once said, "Let the light shine out of the darkness!" And this is the same God who made his light shine in our hearts. He gave us light by letting us know the glory of God that is in the face of Christ.

SPIRITUAL TREASURE IN CLAY JARS

[7]We have this treasure from God. But we are only like clay jars that hold the treasure. This shows that this great power is from God, not from us. [8]We have troubles all around us, but we are not defeated. We do not know what to do, but we do not give up. [9]We are persecuted, but God does not leave us. We are hurt sometimes, but we are not destroyed. [10]We carry the death of Jesus in our own bodies, so that the life of Jesus can also be seen in our bodies. [11]We are alive, but for Jesus we are always in danger of death. This is so that the life of Jesus can be seen in our bodies that die. [12]So death is working in us, but life is working in you.

[13]It is written in the Scriptures, "I believed, so I spoke." [n] Our faith is like this, too. We believe, and so we speak. [14]God raised the Lord Jesus from death. And we know that God will also raise us with Jesus. God will bring us together with you, and we will stand before him. [15]All these things are for you. And so the grace of God is being given to more and more people. This will bring more and more thanks to God for his glory.

LIVING BY FAITH

[16]So we do not give up. Our physical body is becoming older and weaker, but our spirit inside us is made new every day. [17]We have small troubles for a while now, but they are helping us gain an eternal glory. That glory is much greater than the troubles. [18]So we set our eyes not on what we see but on what we cannot see. What we see will last only a short time. But what we cannot see will last forever.

5 We know that our body—the tent we live in here on earth—will be destroyed. But when that happens, God will have a house for us to live in. It will not be a house made by men. It will be a home in heaven that will

---

4:13 "I . . . spoke." Quotation from Psalm 116:10.

last forever. ²But now we are tired of this body. We want God to give us our heavenly home. ³It will clothe us, and we will not be naked. ⁴While we live in this body, we have burdens, and we complain. We do not want to be naked. We want to be clothed with our heavenly home. Then this body that dies will be fully covered with life. ⁵This is what God made us for. And he has given us the Spirit to be a guarantee for this new life.

⁶So we always have courage. We know that while we live in this body, we are away from the Lord. ⁷We live by what we believe, not by what we can see. ⁸So I say that we have courage. And we really want to be away from this body and be at home with the Lord. ⁹Our only goal is to please God.

⭐ 2 Corinthians 5:17

This verse says, "If anyone belongs to Christ, then he is made new. The old things have gone; everything is made new!" The verse repeats "made new" and adds an exclamation point. That is how important this new life is!

Toys sometimes break. Arms fall off dolls. Tires pop off toy trucks. And teddy bear seams rip. When a toy breaks or rips, sometimes your mom or dad can fix it. They twist and turn the piece to get it back on. They thread a needle to sew the tear. They want to make it like new. Sometimes it works. But sometimes it doesn't. God fixes things too. And God's "fixes" always work. When you believed in Jesus, the Bible says God made you new! He didn't just fix your heart—the one that didn't know how to follow God. He gave you a new heart. And now you can follow him for the rest of your life.

When you believe in Jesus, you belong to Christ, and you are "made new."

We want to please him whether we live here or there. [10]For we must all stand before Christ to be judged. Each one will receive what he should get—good or bad—for the things he did when he lived in the earthly body.

BECOMING FRIENDS WITH GOD

[11]We know what it means to fear the Lord. So we try to help people accept the truth. God knows what we really are. And I hope that in your hearts you know, too. [12]We are not trying to prove ourselves to you again. But we are telling you about ourselves, so you will be proud of us. Then you will have an answer for those who are proud about things that can be seen. They do not care about what is in the heart. [13]If we are out of our minds, it is for God. If we have our right mind, then it is for you. [14]The love of Christ controls us. Because we know that One died for all. So all have died. [15]Christ died for all so that those who live would not continue to live for themselves. He died for them and was raised from death so that they would live for him.

[16]From this time on we do not think of anyone as the world does. It is true that in the past we thought of Christ as the world thinks. But we no longer think of him in that way. [17]If anyone belongs to Christ, then he is made new. The old things have gone; everything is made new! [18]All this is from God. Through Christ, God made peace between us and himself. And God gave us the work of bringing everyone into peace with him. [19]I mean that God was in Christ, making peace between the world and himself. In Christ, God did not hold the world guilty of its sins. And he gave us this message of peace. [20]So we have been sent to speak for Christ. It is as if God is calling to you through us. We speak for Christ when we beg you to be at peace with God. [21]Christ had no sin. But God made him become sin. God did this for us so that in Christ we could become right with God.

6 We are workers together with God. So we beg you: Do not let the grace that you received from God be for nothing. [2]God says,

"I heard your prayers at the right time,
and I gave you help on the day of salvation." *Isaiah 49:8*

I tell you that the "right time" is now. The "day of salvation" is now.

[3]We do not want anyone to find anything wrong with our work. So we do nothing that will be a problem for anyone. [4]But in every way we show that we are servants of God: in accepting many hard things, in troubles, in difficulties, and in great problems. [5]We are beaten and thrown into prison. Men become upset and fight us. We work hard, and sometimes we get no sleep or food. [6]We show that we are servants of God by living a pure life, by our understanding, by our patience, and by our kindness. We show this by the Holy Spirit, by true love, [7]by speaking the truth, and by God's power. We use our right living to defend ourselves against everything. [8]Some people honor us, but other people shame us. Some people say good things about us, but other people say bad things. Some people say we are liars, but we speak the truth. [9]We are not known, but we are well-known. We seem to be dying, but look—we continue to live. We are punished, but we are not killed. [10]We have much sadness, but we are always rejoicing. We are poor, but we are making many people rich in faith. We have nothing, but really we have everything.

[11]We have spoken freely to you in Corinth. We have opened our hearts to you. [12]Our feelings of love for you have not stopped. It is you that have stopped your feelings of love for us. [13]I speak to you as if you were my children. Do to us as we have done—open your hearts to us.

WARNING ABOUT NON-CHRISTIANS

[14]You are not the same as those who do not believe. So do not join yourselves to them. Good and bad do not belong together. Light and darkness cannot share together. [15]How can Christ and Belial, the devil, have any agreement? What can a believer have together with a non-believer? [16]The temple of God cannot have any agreement with idols. And we are the temple of the living God. As God said: "I will live with them and walk with them. And I will be their God. And they will be my people."[n]

[17] "Leave those people,
and make yourselves pure, says the Lord.
Touch nothing that is unclean,
and I will accept you."
Isaiah 52:11; Ezekiel 20:34, 41

[18] "I will be your father,
and you will be my sons and daughters,
says the Lord All-Powerful."
2 Samuel 7:14; 7:8

7 Dear friends, we have these promises from God. So we should make ourselves pure—free from anything that makes body or soul unclean. We should try to become perfect in the way we live, because we respect God.

PAUL'S JOY

[2]Open your hearts to us. We have not done wrong to anyone. We have not ruined the faith of any person, and we have cheated no one. [3]I do not say this to blame you. I told you before that we love you so much that we would live or die with you. [4]I feel very sure of you. I am very proud of you. You give me much comfort. And in all of our troubles I have great joy.

[5]When we came into Macedonia, we had no rest. We found trouble all around us. We had fighting on the outside and fear on the inside. [6]But God comforts those who are troubled. And God comforted us when Titus came. [7]We were comforted by his coming and also by the comfort that you gave him. Titus told us about your wish to see me. He told us that you are very sorry for what you did. And he told me about your great care for me. When I heard this, I was much happier.

[8]Even if the letter I wrote you made you sad, I am not sorry I wrote it. I know it made you sad, and I was sorry for that. But it made you sad only for a short time. [9]Now I am happy, but not because you were made sad. I am happy because your sorrow made you change your hearts. You became sad in the way God wanted you to. So you were not hurt by us in any way. [10]Being sorry in the way God wants makes a person change his heart and life. This leads to salvation, and we cannot be sorry for that. But the kind of sorrow the world has will bring death. [11]You had the kind of sorrow God wanted you to have. Now see what this sorrow has brought you: It has made you very serious. It made you want to prove that you were not wrong. It made you angry and afraid. It made you want to see me. It made you care. It made you want the right thing to be done. You proved that you were not guilty in any part of the problem. [12]I wrote that letter, but not because of the one who did the wrong. And it was not written because of the person who was hurt. But I wrote the letter so that you could see, before God, the great care that you have for us. [13]That is why we were comforted.

We were very comforted. And we were even happier to see that Titus was so happy. All of you made him feel much better. [14]I bragged to Titus about you. And you showed that I was right. Everything that we said to you was true. And you have proved that what we

The early Christians faced many hard times.
Leaders like Paul and the believers who read his
letters faced danger, hunger, and fear. But Paul told
them—and us—that God promised to comfort his
people.

We all have days when we feel sad. And sometimes
life seems unfair. You fall and skin your knee.
You do badly on your spelling test. It rains on
the day of the big game. But sometimes small
things can bring comfort, like a Band-Aid, a
nice note from your teacher, or a friend coming
over to play. But even better than a Band-Aid,
Jesus promised to comfort us when life is
hard. He promised that he will never leave
you or forget about you. He will give peace to
your heart when you feel sad.

· ·

When things are bad, talk to Jesus. He is always listening.
And he is always ready to bring you comfort.

---

bragged about to Titus is true. [15]And his
love for you is stronger when he remembers that you were all ready to obey. You
welcomed him with respect and fear. [16]I
am very happy that I can trust you fully.

CHRISTIAN GIVING

8 And now, brothers, we want you
to know about the grace that God
gave the churches in Macedonia. [2]They
have been tested by great troubles. And
they are very poor. But they gave much
because of their great joy. [3]I can tell you
that they gave as much as they were
able. They gave even more than they
could afford. No one told them to do it.
[4]But they asked us again and again—
they begged us to let them share in this
service for God's people. [5]And they
gave in a way that we did not expect:
They first gave themselves to the Lord
and to us. This is what God wants. [6]So
we asked Titus to help you finish this
special work of grace. He is the one
who started this work. [7]You are rich in
everything—in faith, in speaking, in
knowledge, in truly wanting to help,
and in the love you learned from us.[n]
And so we want you to be rich also in
this gift of giving.

8:7 in . . . us Some Greek copies read "in your love for us."

[8]I am not commanding you to give. But I want to see if your love is true love. I do this by showing you that others really want to help. [9]You know the grace of our Lord Jesus Christ. You know that Christ was rich, but for you he became poor. Christ did this so that by his being poor you might become rich.

[10]This is what I think you should do: Last year you were the first to want to give. And you were the first who gave. [11]So now finish the work that you started. Then your "doing" will be equal to your "wanting to do." Give from what you have. [12]If you want to give, your gift will be accepted. Your gift will be judged by what you have, not by what you do not have. [13]We do not want you to have troubles while other people are at ease. We want everything to be equal. [14]At this time you have plenty. What you have can help others who are in need. Then later, when they have plenty, they can help you when you are in need. Then all will be equal. [15]As it is written in the Scriptures, "The person who gathered more did not have too much. The person who gathered less did not have too little."[n]

TITUS AND HIS COMPANIONS

[16]I thank God because he gave Titus the same love for you that I have. [17]Titus accepted what we asked him to do. He wanted very much to go to you. This was his own idea. [18]We are sending with him the brother who is praised by all the churches. This brother is praised because of his service in preaching the Good News. [19]Also, this brother was chosen by the churches to go with us when we deliver this gift of money. We are doing this service to bring glory to the Lord and to show that we really want to help.

[20]We are being careful so that no one will criticize us about the way we are handling this large gift. [21]We are trying to do what is right. We want to do what the Lord accepts as right and also what people think is right.

[22]Also, we are sending with them our brother who is always ready to help. He has proved this to us in many ways. And he wants to help even more now because he has much faith in you.

[23]Now about Titus—he is my partner who is working with me to help you. And about the other brothers—they are sent from the churches, and they bring glory to Christ. [24]So show these men that you really have love. Show them why we are proud of you. Then all the churches can see it.

HELP FOR FELLOW CHRISTIANS

9 I really do not need to write to you about this help for God's people. [2]I know that you want to help. I have been bragging about this to the people in Macedonia. I have told them that you in Southern Greece have been ready to give since last year. And your wanting to give has made most of them here ready to give also. [3]But I am sending the brothers to you. I do not want our bragging about you in this to be for nothing. I want you to be ready, as I said you would be. [4]If any of the people from Macedonia come with me and find that you are not ready, we will be ashamed. We will be ashamed that we were so sure of you. (And you will be ashamed, too!) [5]So I thought that I should ask these brothers to go to you before we come. They will finish getting in order the gift you promised. Then the gift will be ready when we come, and it will be a gift you wanted to give—not a gift that you hated to give.

[6]Remember this: The person who plants a little will have a small harvest. But the person who plants a lot will have a big harvest. [7]Each one should give, then, what he has decided in his heart to give. He should not give if it makes him sad. And he should not give if he thinks he is forced to give. God

---

8:15 **"The person . . . little."** Quotation from Exodus 16:18.

loves the person who gives happily. [8]And God can give you more blessings than you need. Then you will always have plenty of everything. You will have enough to give to every good work. [9]It is written in the Scriptures:

"He gives freely to the poor.
    The things he does are right
        and will continue forever."
                            Psalm 112:9

[10]God is the One who gives seed to the farmer. And he gives bread for food. And God will give you all the seed you need and make it grow. He will make a great harvest from your goodness. [11]God will make you rich in every way so that you can always give freely. And your giving through us will cause many to give thanks to God. [12]This service that you do helps the needs of God's people. It is also bringing more and more thanks to God. [13]This service you do is a proof of your faith. Many people will praise God because of it. They will praise God because you follow the Good News of Christ—the gospel you say you believe. They will praise God because you freely share with them and with all others. [14]And when they pray, they will wish they could be with you. They will feel this because of the great grace that God has given you. [15]Thanks be to God for his gift that is too wonderful to explain.

PAUL DEFENDS HIS MINISTRY

10 I, Paul, am begging you with the gentleness and the kindness of Christ. Some people say that I am easy on you when I am with you and strict when I am away. [2]They think that we live in a worldly way. I plan to be very strict against them when I come. I beg you that when I come I will not need to use that same strictness with you. [3]We do live in the world. But we do not fight in the same way that the world fights. [4]We fight with weapons that are different from those the world uses. Our weapons have power from God. These weapons can destroy the enemy's strong places. We destroy men's arguments. [5]And we destroy every proud thing that raises itself against the knowledge of God. We capture every thought and make it give up and obey Christ. [6]We are ready to punish anyone there who does not obey. But first we want you to obey fully.

[7]You must look at the facts before you. If anyone feels sure that he belongs to Christ, then he must remember that we belong to Christ just as he does. [8]It is true that we brag freely about the authority the Lord gave us. But he gave us this authority to strengthen you, not to hurt you. So I will not be ashamed of the bragging we do. [9]I don't want you to think that I am trying to scare you with my letters. [10]Some people say, "Paul's letters are powerful and sound important. But when he is with us, he is weak. And his speaking is nothing." [11]They should know this: We are not there with you now, so we say these things in letters. But when we are there with you, we will show the same authority that we show in our letters.

[12]We do not dare to put ourselves in the same group with those who think that they are very important. We do not compare ourselves to them. They use themselves to measure themselves, and they judge themselves by what they themselves are. This shows that they know nothing. [13]But we will not

> God can give you more blessings than you need . . . You will have enough to give to every good work.
>
> —2 CORINTHIANS 9:8

brag about things outside the work that was given us to do. We will limit our bragging to the work that God gave us. And this work includes our work with you. [14]We are not bragging too much. We would be bragging too much if we had not already come to you. But we have come to you with the Good News of Christ. [15]We limit our bragging to the work that is ours. We do not brag in the work other men have done. We hope that your faith will continue to grow. And we hope that you will help our work to grow much larger. [16]We want to tell the Good News in the areas beyond your city. We do not want to brag about work that has already been done in another man's area. [17]But, "If a person brags, he should brag only about the Lord." [n] [18]It is not the one who says he is good who is accepted but the one that the Lord thinks is good.

PAUL AND THE FALSE APOSTLES

11 I wish you would be patient with me even when I am a little foolish. But you are already doing that. [2]I am jealous over you. And this jealousy comes from God. I promised to give you to Christ. He must be your only husband. I want to give you to Christ to be his pure bride. [3]But I am afraid that your minds will be led away from your true and pure following of Christ. This might happen just as Eve was tricked by the snake with his evil ways. [4]You are very patient with anyone who comes to you and preaches a different Jesus than the one we preached. You are very willing to accept a spirit or Good News that is different from the Spirit and Good News that you received from us.

[5]I do not think that those "great apostles" are any better than I am. [6]I may not be a trained speaker, but I do have knowledge. We have shown this to you clearly in every way.

[7]I preached God's Good News to you without pay. I made myself unimportant to make you important. Do you think that was wrong? [8]I accepted pay from other churches. I took their money so that I could serve you. [9]If I needed something when I was with you, I did not trouble any of you. The brothers who came from Macedonia gave me all that I needed. I did not allow myself to depend on you in any way. And I will never depend on you. [10]No one in Southern Greece will stop me from bragging about that. I say this with the truth of Christ in me. [11]And why do I not depend on you? Do you think it is because I do not love you? No. God knows that I love you.

[12]And I will keep on doing what I am doing now. I will continue because I want to stop those people from having a reason to brag. They would like to say that the work they brag about is the same as ours. [13]Such men are not true apostles. They are workers who lie. And they change themselves to look like apostles of Christ. [14]This does not surprise us. Even Satan changes himself to look like an angel of light. [n] [15]So it does not surprise us if Satan's servants also make themselves look like servants who work for what is right. But in the end they will be punished for the things they do.

PAUL TELLS ABOUT HIS SUFFERINGS

[16]I tell you again: No one should think that I am a fool. But if you think that I am a fool, then accept me as you would accept a fool. Then I can brag a little, too. [17]I brag because I feel sure of myself. But I am not talking as the Lord would talk. I am bragging like a fool. [18]Many people are bragging about their lives in the world. So I will brag, too. [19]You are wise, so you will gladly be patient with fools! [20]You are even patient with someone who orders you

---

10:17 **"If a person . . . Lord."** Quotation from Jeremiah 9:24.
11:14 **angel of light** Messenger from God. The devil fools people so that they think he is from God.

around and uses you! You are patient with those who trick you, or think they are better than you, or hit you in the face! ²¹It is shameful to me to say this, but we were too "weak" to do those things to you!

But if anyone else is brave enough to brag, then I also will be brave and brag. (I am talking like a fool.) ²²Are they Hebrews?ⁿ So am I. Are they Israelites? So am I. Are they from Abraham's family? So am I. ²³Are they serving Christ? I am serving him more. (I am crazy to talk like this.) I have worked much harder than they. I have been in prison more often. I have been hurt more in beatings. I have been near death many times. ²⁴Five times the Jews have given me their punishment of 39 lashes with a whip. ²⁵Three different times I was beaten with rods. One time they tried to kill me with stones. Three times I was in ships that were wrecked, and one of those times I spent the night and the next day in the sea. ²⁶I have gone on many travels. And I have been in danger from rivers, from thieves, from my own people, the Jews, and from those who are not Jews. I have been in danger in cities, in places where no one lives, and on the sea. And I have been in danger with false brothers. ²⁷I have done hard and tiring work, and many times I did not sleep. I have been hungry and thirsty. Many times I have been without food. I have been cold and without clothes. ²⁸Besides all this, there is on me every day the load of my concern for all the churches. ²⁹I feel weak every time someone is weak. I feel upset every time someone is led into sin.

³⁰If I must brag, I will brag about the things that show I am weak. ³¹God knows that I am not lying. He is the God and Father of the Lord Jesus Christ, and he is to be praised forever. ³²When I was in Damascus, the governor under King Aretas wanted to arrest me. So he put guards around the city. ³³But my friends put me in a basket. Then they put the basket through a hole in the wall and lowered me down. So I escaped from the governor.

A SPECIAL BLESSING IN PAUL'S LIFE

12 I must continue to brag. It will do no good, but I will talk now about visions and revelationsⁿ from the Lord. ²I know a man in Christ who was taken up to the third heaven. This happened 14 years ago. I do not know whether the man was in his body or out of his body. But God knows. ³⁻⁴And I know that this man was taken up to paradise.ⁿ I don't know if he was in his body or away from his body. But he heard things he is not able to explain. He heard things that no man is allowed to tell. ⁵I will brag about a man like that. But I will not brag about myself, except about my weaknesses. ⁶But if I wanted to brag about myself, I would not be a fool. I would not be a fool, because I would be telling the truth. But I will not brag about myself. I do not want people to think more of me than what they see me do or hear me say.

⁷But I must not become too proud of the wonderful things that were shown to me. So a painful problemⁿ was given to me. This problem is a messenger from Satan. It is sent to beat me and keep me from being too proud. ⁸I begged the Lord three times to take this problem away from me. ⁹But the Lord said to me, "My grace is enough for you. When you are weak, then my power is made perfect in you." So I am very happy to brag about my weaknesses. Then Christ's power can live in me. ¹⁰So I am happy when I have weaknesses,

11:22 **Hebrews** A name for the Jews that some Jews were very proud of.
12:1 **revelations** Revelation is making known a truth that was hidden.
12:3–4 **paradise** A place where good people go when they die.
12:7 **painful problem** Literally, "thorn in the flesh."

insults, hard times, sufferings, and all kinds of troubles. All these things are for Christ. And I am happy, because when I am weak, then I am truly strong.

PAUL'S LOVE FOR THE CHRISTIANS

[11]I have been talking like a fool. But you made me do it. You are the ones who should say good things about me. I am worth nothing, but those "great apostles" are not worth any more than I am! [12]When I was with you, I did what proves that I am an apostle—signs, wonders, and miracles. And I did these things with much patience. [13]So you received everything that the other churches have received. Only one thing was different: I was not a burden to you. Forgive me for this!

[14]I am now ready to visit you the third time. And I will not be a burden to you. I want nothing from you, I only want you. Children should not have to save up to give to their parents. Parents should save to give to their children. [15]So I am happy to give everything I have for you. I will even give myself for you. If I love you more, will you love me less?

[16]It is clear that I was not a burden to you. But you think that I was tricky and used lies to catch you. [17]Did I cheat you by using any of the men I sent to you? No, you know I did not. [18]I asked Titus to go to you. And I sent our brother with him. Titus did not cheat you, did he? No, you know that Titus and I did the same thing and with the same spirit.

[19]Do you think that we have been defending ourselves to you all this time? We have been speaking in Christ and before God. You are our dear friends. And everything that we do is to make you stronger. [20]I do this because I am afraid that when I come, you will not be what I want you to be. And I am afraid that I will not be what you want me to be. I am afraid that among you there may be arguing, jealousy, anger, selfish fighting, evil talk, gossip, pride, and confusion. [21]I am afraid that when I come to you again, my God will make me ashamed before you. I may be saddened by many of those who have sinned. I may be saddened because they have not changed their hearts and have not turned away from their impurity and their sexual immorality.

> I am happy, because when I am weak, then I am truly strong.
>
> –2 CORINTHIANS 12:10

FINAL WARNINGS AND GREETINGS

13 I will come to you for the third time. And remember, "Every case must be proved by two or three witnesses."[n] [2]When I was with you the second time, I gave a warning to those who had sinned. Now I am away from you, and I give a warning to all the others. When I come to you again, I will not be easy with them. [3]You want proof that Christ is speaking through me. My proof is that he is not weak among you, but he is powerful. [4]It is true that he was weak when he was killed on the cross. But he lives now by God's power. It is true that we are weak in Christ. But for you we will be alive in Christ by God's power.

[5]Look closely at yourselves. Test yourselves to see if you are living in the faith. You know that Christ Jesus is in you—unless you fail the test. [6]But I hope you will see that we ourselves have not failed the test. [7]We pray to

13:1 "Every . . . witnesses." Quotation from Deuteronomy 19:15.

God that you will not do anything wrong. It is not important to see that we have passed the test. But it is important that you do what is right, even if it seems that we have failed. [8]We cannot do anything against the truth, but only for the truth. [9]We are happy to be weak, if you are strong. And we pray that you will grow stronger and stronger. [10]I am writing this while I am away from you. I am writing so that when I come I will not have to be harsh in my use of authority. The Lord gave me this authority to use to make you stronger, not to destroy you.

[11]Now, brothers, I say good-bye. Live in harmony. Do what I have asked you to do. Agree with each other, and live in peace. Then the God of love and peace will be with you.

[12]Give each other a holy kiss when you greet each other. [13]All of God's holy people send greetings to you.

[14]The grace of the Lord Jesus Christ, the love of God, and the fellowship of the Holy Spirit be with you all.

Galatians

THE ONLY GOOD NEWS

1 From Paul, an apostle.
I was not chosen to be an apostle by men. I was not sent from men. It was Jesus Christ and God the Father who made me an apostle. God is the One who raised Jesus from death.

[2] This letter is also from all the brothers who are with me.

To the churches in Galatia.[n]

[3] I pray that God our Father and the Lord Jesus Christ will be good to you and give you peace. [4] Jesus gave himself for our sins to free us from this evil world we live in. This is what God the Father wanted. [5] The glory belongs to God forever and ever. Amen.

[6] A short time ago God called you to follow him. He called you by his grace that came through Christ. But now I am amazed at you! You are already turning away and believing something different than the Good News. [7] Really, there is no other Good News. But some people are confusing you and want to change the Good News of Christ. [8] We preached to you the Good News. So if we ourselves, or even an angel from heaven, preach to you something different than the Good News, he should be condemned! [9] I said this before. Now I say it again: You have already accepted the Good News. If anyone tells you another way to be saved, he should be condemned!

[10] Do you think I am trying to make people accept me? No! God is the One I am trying to please. Am I trying to please men? If I wanted to please men, I would not be a servant of Christ.

PAUL'S AUTHORITY IS FROM GOD

[11] Brothers, I want you to know that the Good News I preached to you was not made by men. [12] I did not get it from men, nor did any man teach it to me. Jesus Christ showed it to me.

[13] You have heard about my past life. I belonged to the Jewish religion. I hurt the church of God very much and tried to destroy it. [14] I was becoming a leader in the Jewish religion. I did better than most other Jews of my age. I tried harder than anyone else to follow the old rules. These rules were the customs handed down by our ancestors.

[15] But God had special plans for me even before I was born. So he called me through his grace that I might [16] tell the Good News about his Son to the non-Jewish people. So God showed me about his Son. When God called me, I did not get advice or help from any man. [17] I did not go to Jerusalem to see those who were apostles before I was. But, without waiting, I went away to Arabia and later went back to Damascus.

[18] After three years I went to Jerusalem to meet Peter and stayed with him for 15 days. [19] I met no other apostles, except James, the brother of the Lord. [20] God knows that these things I write are not lies. [21] Later, I went to the areas of Syria and Cilicia.

[22] In Judea the churches in Christ had never met me. [23] They had only heard this about me: "This man was trying to hurt us. But now he is preaching the same faith that he once tried to destroy." [24] And these believers praised God because of me.

OTHER APOSTLES ACCEPTED PAUL

2 After 14 years, I went to Jerusalem again, this time with Barnabas. I also took Titus with me. [2] I went because

---

1:2 Galatia Probably the same country where Paul preached and began churches on his first missionary trip. Read the book of Acts, chapters 13 and 14.

God showed me that I should go. I met with those men who were the leaders of the believers. When we were alone, I told them the Good News that I preach to the non-Jewish people. I did not want my past work and the work I am now doing to be wasted. ³Titus was with me. But Titus was not forced to be circumcised, even though he was a Greek. ⁴We talked about this problem because some false brothers had come into our group secretly. They came in like spies to find out about the freedom we have in Christ Jesus. They wanted to make us slaves. ⁵But we did not agree with anything those false brothers wanted! We wanted the truth of the Good News to continue for you.

⁶Those men who seemed to be important did not change the Good News that I preach. (It doesn't matter to me if they were "important" or not. To God all men are the same.) ⁷But these leaders saw that God had given me special work, just as he had to Peter. God gave Peter the work of telling the Good News to the Jews. But God gave me the work of telling the Good News to the non-Jewish people. ⁸God gave Peter the power to work as an apostle for the Jewish people. But he also gave me the power to work as an apostle for those who are not Jews. ⁹James, Peter, and John, who seemed to be the leaders, saw that God had given me this special grace. So they accepted Barnabas and me. They said, "Paul and Barnabas, we agree that you should go to the people who are not Jews. We will go to the Jews." ¹⁰They asked us to do only one thing—to remember to help the poor. And this was something that I really wanted to do.

PAUL SHOWS THAT PETER WAS WRONG

¹¹When Peter came to Antioch, I was against him because he was wrong. ¹²This is what happened: When Peter first came to Antioch, he ate with the non-Jewish people. But then some Jewish men were sent from James. When they arrived, Peter stopped eating with the non-Jewish people and separated himself from them. He was afraid of the Jews who believe that all non-Jewish people must be circumcised. ¹³So Peter was a hypocrite. The other Jewish believers joined with him and were hypocrites, too. Even Barnabas was influenced by what these Jewish believers did. ¹⁴I saw what they did. They were not following the truth of the Good News. So I spoke to Peter in front of them all. I said: "Peter, you are a Jew, but you are not living like a Jew. You are living like the non-Jewish people. So why do you now try to force the non-Jewish people to live like Jews?"

¹⁵We were not born as non-Jewish "sinners," but we were born as Jews. ¹⁶Yet we know that a person is not made right with God by following the law. No! It is trusting in Jesus Christ that makes a person right with God. So we, too, have put our faith in Christ Jesus, that we might be made right with God. And we are right with God because we trusted in Christ—not because we followed the law. For no one can be made right with God by following the law.

¹⁷We Jews came to Christ to be made right with God. So it is clear that we were sinners too. Does this mean that Christ makes us sinners? No! ¹⁸But I would really be wrong to begin teaching again those things of the Law of Moses that I gave up. ¹⁹I stopped living for the law. It was the law that put me to death. I died to the law so that I can now live for God. I was put to death on the cross with Christ. ²⁰I do not live anymore—it is Christ living in me. I still live in my body, but I live by faith in the Son of God. He loved me and gave himself to save me. ²¹This gift is from God, and it is very important to me. If the law could make us right with God, then Christ did not have to die.

BLESSING COMES THROUGH FAITH

3 You people in Galatia were told very clearly about the death of Jesus Christ on the cross. But you were very foolish. You let someone trick you. [2]Tell me this one thing: How did you receive the Holy Spirit? Did you receive the Spirit by following the law? No! You received the Spirit because you heard the Good News and believed it. [3]You began your life in Christ by the Spirit. Now do you try to continue it by your own power? That is foolish. [4]You have experienced many things. Were all those experiences wasted? I hope not! [5]Does God give you the Spirit because you follow the law? No! Does God work miracles among you because you follow the law? No! God gives you his Spirit and works miracles among you because you heard the Good News and believed it.

[6]The Scriptures say the same thing about Abraham: "Abraham believed God, and God accepted Abraham's faith, and that faith made him right with God."[n] [7]So you should know that the true children of Abraham are those who have faith. [8]The Scriptures told what would happen in the future. They said that God would make the non-Jewish people right through their faith. This Good News was told to Abraham beforehand, as the Scripture says: "All nations will be blessed through you."[n] [9]Abraham believed this, and because he believed, he was blessed. It is the same today. All who believe today are blessed just as Abraham was blessed. [10]But those who depend on following the law to make them right are under a curse because the Scriptures say, "Anyone will be cursed who does not always obey what is written in the Book of the Law!"[n] [11]So it is clear that no one can be made right with God by the law. The Scriptures say, "He who is right with God by faith will live."[n] [12]The law does not use faith. It says, "A person who does these things will live forever because of them."[n] [13]So the law put a curse on us, but Christ took away that curse. He changed places with us and put himself under that curse. It is written in the Scriptures, "Everyone whose body is displayed on a tree[n] is cursed." [14]Christ did this so that God's blessing promised to Abraham might come to the non-Jews. This blessing comes through Jesus Christ. Jesus died so that we could have the Spirit that God promised and receive this promise by believing.

THE LAW AND THE PROMISE

[15]Brothers, let me give you an example: Think about an agreement that a person makes with another person. After that agreement is accepted by both people, no one can stop that agreement or add anything to it. [16]God made promises to Abraham and his descendant. God did not say, "and to your descendants." That would mean many people. But God said, "and to your descendant." That means only one person; that person is Christ. [17]This is what I mean: God had an agreement with Abraham and promised to keep it. The law, which came 430 years later, cannot change God's promise to Abraham. [18]Can following the law give us what God promised? No! If this is so, it is not God's promise that brings us the blessings. Instead God freely gave his blessings to Abraham through the promise he had made.

[19]So what was the law for? The law was given to show the wrong things

3:6 "Abraham...God." Quotation from Genesis 15:6.
3:8 "All...you." Quotation from Genesis 12:3.
3:10 "Anyone...Law!" Quotation from Deuteronomy 27:26.
3:11 "He...live." Quotation from Habakkuk 2:4.
3:12 "A person...them." Quotation from Leviticus 18:5.
3:13 displayed on a tree Deuteronomy 21:22–23 says that when a person was killed for doing wrong, his body was hung on a tree to show shame. Paul means that the cross of Jesus was like that.

☆ Galatians 4:6–7

We are God's children, so we are part of his family. He sent his Spirit to fill our hearts, which means he is always with us. And because we're his children, God will give us everything he promised us.

Have you ever woken up from a bad dream? It is the middle of the night, your eyes fly open, and you yell . . . What do you yell? Mommy? Daddy? Whoever you call to, they are there in an instant. A hug, a prayer, and you are ready to go back to sleep. That's what it's like to be part of a family. As a Christian, you are a part of a great big family with brothers and sisters all over the world. But we have just one heavenly Father. He put his Spirit in each of us and made us his very own children. And just like your parent, God wants you to talk to him when you are afraid or happy or anywhere in between.

. . . .

God knows everything about you. But he still loves to hear you talk. Tell him about your day. Ask him about his. He is always ready to bring you comfort.

---

people do. It continued until the special descendant of Abraham came. God's promise was about this descendant. The law was given through angels who used Moses for a mediator[n] to give the law to men. [20]But a mediator is not needed when there is only one side. And God is only one.

THE PURPOSE OF THE LAW OF MOSES

[21]Does this mean that the law is against God's promises? Never! If there were a law that could give men life, then we could be made right by following that law. [22]But this is not true, because the Scriptures showed that the whole world is bound by sin. This was so that the promise would be given through faith. And it is given to people who believe in Jesus Christ.

[23]Before this faith came, we were all held prisoners by the law. We had no freedom until God showed us the way of faith that was coming. [24]So the law was our master until Christ came. After

3:19 mediator A person who helps one person talk to or give something to another person.

Christ came, we could be made right with God through faith. ²⁵Now the way of faith has come, and we no longer live under the law.

²⁶⁻²⁷You were all baptized into Christ, and so you were all clothed with Christ. This shows that you are all children of God through faith in Christ Jesus. ²⁸Now, in Christ, there is no difference between Jew and Greek. There is no difference between slaves and free men. There is no difference between male and female. You are all the same in Christ Jesus. ²⁹You belong to Christ. So you are Abraham's descendants. You get all of God's blessings because of the promise that God made to Abraham.

4 I want to tell you this: While the one who will inherit his father's property is still a child, he is no different from a slave. It does not matter that the child owns everything. ²While he is a child, he must obey those who are chosen to care for him. But when the child reaches the age set by his father, he is free. ³It is the same for us. We were once like children. We were slaves to the useless rules of this world. ⁴But when the right time came, God sent his Son. His Son was born of a woman and lived under the law. ⁵God did this so that he could buy freedom for those who were under the law. His purpose was to make us his children.

⁶And you are God's children. That is why God sent the Spirit of his Son into your hearts. The Spirit cries out, "Father, dear Father."ⁿ ⁷So now you are not a slave; you are God's child, and God will give you what he promised, because you are his child.

PAUL'S LOVE FOR THE CHRISTIANS

⁸In the past you did not know God. You were slaves to gods that were not real. ⁹But now you know the true God. Really,

it is God who knows you. So why do you turn back to those weak and useless rules you followed before? Do you want to be slaves to those things again? ¹⁰You still follow teachings about special days, months, seasons, and years. ¹¹I am afraid for you. I fear that my work for you has been wasted.

¹²Brothers, I was like you; so I beg you to become like me. You were very good to me before. ¹³You remember that I came to you the first time because I was sick. That was when I preached the Good News to you. ¹⁴Though my sickness was a trouble for you, you did not hate me or make me leave. But you welcomed me as an angel from God, as if I were Jesus Christ himself! ¹⁵You were very happy then. Where is that joy now? I remember that you would have taken out your eyes and given them to me if that were possible. ¹⁶Now am I your enemy because I tell you the truth?

¹⁷Those peopleⁿ are working hard to persuade you. But this is not good for you. They want to persuade you to turn against us. They want you to follow only them. ¹⁸It is good for people to show interest in you, but only if their purpose is good. This is always true. It is true when I am with you and when I am away. ¹⁹My little children, again I feel pain for you as a mother feels when she gives birth. I will feel this until you truly become like Christ. ²⁰I wish I could be with you now. Then maybe I could change the way I am talking to you. Now I do not know what to do about you.

THE EXAMPLE OF HAGAR AND SARAH

²¹Some of you people still want to be under the law of Moses. Tell me, do you know what the law says? ²²The Scriptures say that Abraham had two sons. The mother of one son was a slave woman. The mother of the other son

---

4:6 "Father, dear Father" Literally, "Abba, Father." Jewish children called their fathers "Abba."
4:17 Those people They are the false teachers who were bothering the believers in Galatia (Galatians 1:7).

was a free woman. [23]Abraham's son from the slave woman was born in the normal human way. But the son from the free woman was born because of the promise God made to Abraham.

[24]This makes a picture for us. The two women are like the two agreements between God and men. One agreement is the law that God made on Mount Sinai.[n] The people who are under this agreement are like slaves. The mother named Hagar is like that agreement. [25]She is like Mount Sinai in Arabia and is a picture of the earthly Jewish city of Jerusalem. This city is a slave, and all its people are slaves to the law. [26]But the heavenly Jerusalem which is above is like the free woman. She is our mother. [27]It is written in the Scriptures:

> "Be happy,
>   Jerusalem.
>   You are like a
>   woman who
>   never gave birth
>   to children.
>   Start singing and
>   shout for joy.
>   You never felt the pain
>   of giving birth to
>   children.
>   But you will have more
>   children
>   than the woman who has a
>   husband."   *Isaiah 54:1*

[28]My brothers, you are God's children because of his promise, as Isaac was then. [29]The son who was born in the normal way treated the other son badly. It is the same today. [30]But what does the Scripture say? "Throw out the slave woman and her son! The son of the free woman will receive everything his father has. But the son of the slave woman will receive nothing."[n] [31]So,

my brothers, we are not children of the slave woman. We are children of the free woman.

KEEP YOUR FREEDOM

5 We have freedom now because Christ made us free. So stand strong. Do not change and go back into the slavery of the law. [2]Listen! I am Paul. I tell you that if you go back to the law by being circumcised, then Christ is no good for you. [3]Again, I warn every man: If you allow yourselves to be circumcised, then you must follow all the law. [4]If you try to be made right with God through the law, then your life with Christ is over—you have left God's grace. [5]But we hope to be made right with God through faith, and we wait for this hope anxiously with the Spirit's help. [6]When we are in Christ Jesus, it is not important if we are circumcised or not. The important thing is faith—the kind of faith that works through love. [7]You were running a good race. You were obeying the truth. Who stopped you from following the true way? [8]Whatever way he used did not come from the One who chose you. [9]Be careful! "Just a little yeast makes the whole batch of dough rise." [10]But I trust in the Lord that you will not believe those different ideas. Someone is confusing you with such ideas. And he will be punished, whoever he is.

[11]My brothers, I do not teach that a man must be circumcised. If I teach circumcision, then why am I still being treated badly? If I still taught circumcision, my preaching about the cross

> You belong to Christ . . . You get all of God's blessings because of the promise that God made to Abraham.
>
> –GALATIANS 3:29

4:24 **Mount Sinai** Mountain in Arabia where God gave his laws to Moses (Exodus 19 and 20).
4:30 **"Throw . . . nothing."** Quotation from Genesis 21:10.

would not be a problem. [12]I wish the people who are bothering you would castrate[n] themselves!

[13]My brothers, God called you to be free. But do not use your freedom as an excuse to do the things that please your sinful self. Serve each other with love. [14]The whole law is made complete in this one command: "Love your neighbor as you love yourself."[n] [15]If you go on hurting each other and tearing each other apart, be careful! You will completely destroy each other.

THE SPIRIT AND HUMAN NATURE

[16]So I tell you: Live by following the Spirit. Then you will not do what your sinful selves want. [17]Our sinful selves want what is against the Spirit. The Spirit wants what is against our sinful selves. The two are against each other. So you must not do just what you please. [18]But if you let the Spirit lead you, you are not under the law.

[19]The result of sin's control in our lives is clear. It includes sexual immorality, impurity and wild living,

---

5:12 castrate To cut off part of the male sex organ. Paul uses this word because it is similar to "circumcision." Paul wanted to show that he is very upset with the false teachers.
5:14 "Love...yourself." Quotation from Leviticus 19:18.

☆ Galatians 6:2

Because we're part of God's family, God wants us to look out for each other. When our brothers and sisters are in trouble, we should try to help. This is how we show God's love.

God made us to be family. But he also wants us to be friends—with him and with others. It is easy to think only about ourselves, our home, our toys, or our best friends. Sometimes we don't see the troubles other people are having. Start looking around. If you see someone lonely, ask them to play with you. If someone is struggling to tie their shoes, help them. Walk a neighbor's dog. Help your teacher clean the classroom. How else can you help someone this week?

When we help others with their troubles, we show God's love to them. And we feel better too.

²⁰worshiping false gods, doing witch-craft, hating, making trouble, being jealous, being angry, being selfish, making people angry with each other, causing divisions among people, ²¹having envy, being drunk, having wild and wasteful parties, and doing other things like this. I warn you now as I warned you before: Those who do these things will not be in God's kingdom. ²²But the Spirit gives love, joy, peace, patience, kindness, goodness, faithful-ness, ²³gentleness, self-control. There is no law that says these things are wrong. ²⁴Those who belong to Christ Jesus have crucified their own sinful selves. They have given up their old selfish feelings and the evil things they wanted to do. ²⁵We get our new life from the Spirit. So we should follow the Spirit. ²⁶We must not be proud. We must not make trouble with each other. And we must not be jealous of each other.

HELP EACH OTHER

6 Brothers, someone in your group might do something wrong. You who are spiritual should go to him and help make him right again. You should do this in a gentle way. But be care-ful! You might be tempted to sin, too. ²Help each other with your troubles. When you do this, you truly obey the law of Christ. ³If anyone thinks that he is important when he is really not important, he is only fooling himself. ⁴He should not compare himself with others. Each person should judge his own actions. Then he can be proud for what he himself has done. ⁵Each person must be responsible for himself.

⁶Anyone who is learning the teaching of God should share all the good things he has with his teacher.

LIFE IS LIKE PLANTING A FIELD

⁷Do not be fooled: You cannot cheat God. A person harvests only what he plants. ⁸If he plants to satisfy his sinful self, his sinful self will bring him eternal death. But if he plants to please the Spirit, he will receive eternal life from the Spirit. ⁹We must not become tired of doing good. We will receive our harvest of eternal life at the right time. We must not give up! ¹⁰When we have the opportunity to help anyone, we should do it. But we should give special attention to those who are in the family of believers.

PAUL ENDS HIS LETTER

¹¹I am writing this myself. See what large letters I use. ¹²Some men are try-ing to force you to be circumcised. They do these things so that the Jews will accept them. They are afraid that they will be treated badly if they follow only the cross of Christ.ⁿ ¹³Those who are circumcised do not obey the law them-selves, but they want you to be circum-cised. Then they can brag about what they forced you to do. ¹⁴I hope I will never brag about things like that. The cross of our Lord Jesus Christ is my only reason for bragging. Through the cross of Jesus my world was crucified and I died to the world. ¹⁵It is not important if a man is circumcised or not circum-cised. The important thing is being the new people God has made. ¹⁶Peace and mercy to those who follow this rule—to all of God's people.

¹⁷So do not give me any more trouble. I have scars on my body. These showⁿ I belong to Christ Jesus.

¹⁸My brothers, I pray that the grace of our Lord Jesus Christ will be with your spirit. Amen.

6:12 **cross of Christ** Paul uses the cross as a picture of the gospel, the story of Christ's death and rising from death to pay for men's sins. The cross, or Christ's death, was God's way to save men.
6:17 **These show** Many times Paul was beaten and whipped by people who were against him because he was teaching about Christ. The scars were from these beatings.

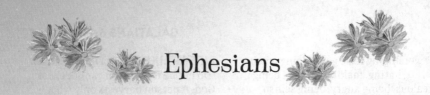

Ephesians

SPIRITUAL BLESSINGS IN CHRIST

1 From Paul, an apostle of Christ Jesus. I am an apostle because that is what God wanted.

To God's holy people living in Ephesus,[n] believers in Christ Jesus.

²Grace and peace to you from God our Father and the Lord Jesus Christ. ³Praise be to the God and Father of our Lord Jesus Christ. In Christ, God has given us every spiritual blessing in heaven. ⁴In Christ, he chose us before the world was made. In his love he chose us to be his holy people—people without blame before him. ⁵And before the world was made, God decided to make us his own children through Jesus Christ. That was what he wanted and what pleased him. ⁶This brings praise to God because of his wonderful grace. God gave that grace to us freely, in Christ, the One he loves. ⁷In Christ we are set free by the blood of his death. And so we have forgiveness of sins because of God's rich grace. ⁸God gave us that grace fully and freely. God, with full wisdom and understanding, ⁹let us know his secret purpose. This was what God wanted, and he planned to do it through Christ. ¹⁰His goal was to carry out his plan when the right time came. He planned that all things in heaven and on earth would be joined together in Christ as the head.

¹¹In Christ we were chosen to be God's people. God had already chosen us to be his people, because that is what he wanted. And God is the One who makes everything agree with what he decides and wants. ¹²We are the first people who hoped in Christ. And we were chosen so that we would bring praise to God's glory. ¹³So it is with you. You heard the true teaching—the Good News about your salvation. When you heard it, you believed in Christ. And in Christ, God put his special mark on you by giving you the Holy Spirit that he had promised. ¹⁴That Holy Spirit is the guarantee that we will get what God promised for his people. This will bring full freedom to the people who belong to God, to bring praise to God's glory.

PAUL'S PRAYER

¹⁵⁻¹⁶That is why I always remember you in my prayers and always thank God for you. I have always done this since the time I heard about your faith in the Lord Jesus and your love for all God's people. ¹⁷I always pray to the God of our Lord Jesus Christ—to the glorious Father. I pray that he will give you a spirit that will make you wise in the knowledge of God—the knowledge that he has shown you. ¹⁸I pray that you will have greater understanding in your heart. Then you will know the hope that God has chosen to give us. I pray that you will know that the blessings God has promised his holy people are rich and glorious. ¹⁹And you will know that God's power is very great for us who believe. That power is the same as the great strength ²⁰God used to raise Christ from death and put him at his right side in heaven. ²¹God made Christ more important than all rulers, authorities, powers, and kings. Christ is more important than anything in this world or in the next world. ²²God put everything under his power. And God made him the head over everything for the church. ²³The church is Christ's body. The church is filled with Christ, and Christ fills everything in every way.

FROM DEATH TO LIFE

2 In the past your spiritual lives were dead because of your sins and the

---

1:1 **in Ephesus** Some Greek copies do not have this phrase.

things you did wrong against God. ²Yes, in the past you lived the way the world lives. You followed the ruler of the evil powers that are above the earth. That same spirit is now working in those who refuse to obey God. ³In the past all of us lived like them. We lived trying to please our sinful selves. We did all the things our bodies and minds wanted. We should have suffered God's anger because we were sinful by nature. We were the same as all other people.

⁴But God's mercy is great, and he loved us very much. ⁵We were spiritually dead because of the things we did wrong against God. But God gave us new life with Christ. You have been saved by God's grace. ⁶And he raised us up with Christ and gave us a seat with him in the heavens. He did this for those of us who are in Christ Jesus. ⁷He did this so that for all future time he could show the very great riches of his grace. He shows that grace by being kind to us in Christ Jesus. ⁸I mean that you have been saved by grace because you believe. You did not save yourselves. It was a gift from God. ⁹You cannot brag that you are saved by the work you have done. ¹⁰God has made us what we are. In Christ Jesus, God made us new people so that we would

---

☆ Ephesians 1:4

God chose you to be part of his family even before the world was made. The Bible says you are one of "his holy people."

Did you know God knew you before you were even born? He knew your name and what you would like and not like. He knew everything about you then. And he knows everything about you now. Pretty cool, huh? Did you know that God chose to love you before the world was made? He chose to love you before the moon, stars, and sun were created. God chose to love you a long time ago. And he still loves you today! What a great Father he is!

· · · · · · · · · · · · · · · · ·

Way back when God made Adam and Eve, he was thinking about you. When you were born, God smiled so big. He was just waiting for you to get here!

do good works. God had planned in advance those good works for us. He had planned for us to live our lives doing them.

ONE IN CHRIST

[11] You were born non-Jews. You are the people the Jews call "uncircumcised."[n] Those who call you "uncircumcised" call themselves "circumcised." (Their circumcision is only something they themselves do on their bodies.) [12] Remember that in the past you were without Christ. You were not citizens of Israel. And you had no part in the agreements[n] with the promise that God made to his people. You had no hope, and you did not know God. [13] Yes, at one time you were far away from God. But now in Christ Jesus you are brought near to God through the blood of Christ's death. [14] Because of Christ we now have peace. Christ made both Jews and non-Jews one people. They were separated as if there were a wall between them. But Christ broke down that wall of hate by giving his own body. [15] The Jewish law had many commands and rules. But Christ ended that law. Christ's purpose was to make the two groups of people become one new people in him. By doing this Christ would make peace. [16] Through the cross Christ ended the hatred between the two groups. And after Christ made the two groups to be one body, he wanted to bring them back to God. Christ did this with his death on the cross. [17] Christ came and preached peace to you non-Jews who were far away from God. And he preached peace to those Jews who were near to God. [18] Yes, through Christ we all have the right to come to the Father in one Spirit.

[19] So now you non-Jews are not visitors or strangers. Now you are citizens together with God's holy people. You belong to God's family. [20] You believers are like a building that God owns. That building was built on the foundation of the apostles and prophets. Christ Jesus himself is the most important stone[n] in that building. [21] That whole building is joined together in Christ. And Christ makes it grow and become a holy temple in the Lord. [22] And in Christ you, too, are being built together with the Jews. You are being built into a place where God lives through the Spirit.

> You are joined together with peace through the Spirit. Do all you can to continue together in this way.
>
> –EPHESIANS 4:3

PAUL'S WORK FOR THE NON-JEWS

3 So I, Paul, am a prisoner of Christ Jesus. I am a prisoner for you who are not Jews. [2] Surely you know that God gave me this work to tell you about his grace. [3] God let me know his secret plan. He showed it to me. I have already written a little about this. [4] And if you read what I wrote, then you can see that I truly understand the secret truth about the Christ. [5] People who lived in other times were not told that secret truth. But now, through the Spirit, God has shown that secret truth to his holy apostles and prophets. [6] This is that secret truth: that the non-Jews will receive what God has for his people, just as the Jews will. The non-Jews are together with the Jews as part of the same body. And they share together in the promise that God made

---

2:11 "uncircumcised" People not having the mark of circumcision as the Jews have.
2:12 agreements The agreements that God gave to his people in the Old Testament.
2:20 most important stone Literally, "cornerstone." The first and most important stone in a building.

in Christ Jesus. The non-Jews have all of this because of the Good News.

⁷By God's special gift of grace, I became a servant to tell that Good News. God gave me that grace through his power. ⁸I am the least important of all God's people. But God gave me this gift—to tell the non-Jewish people the Good News about the riches of Christ. Those riches are too great to understand fully. ⁹And God gave me the work of telling all people about the plan for God's secret truth. That secret truth has been hidden in God since the beginning of time. God is the One who created everything. ¹⁰His purpose was that through the church all the rulers and powers in the heavenly world will now know God's wisdom, which has so many forms. ¹¹This agrees with the purpose God had since the beginning of time. And God carried out his plan through Christ Jesus our Lord. ¹²In Christ we can come before God with freedom and without fear. We can do this through faith in Christ. ¹³So I ask you not to become discouraged because of the sufferings I am having for you. My sufferings bring honor to you.

THE LOVE OF CHRIST

¹⁴So I bow in prayer before the Father. ¹⁵Every family in heaven and on earth gets its true name from him. ¹⁶I ask the Father in his great glory to give you the power to be strong in spirit. He will give you that strength through his Spirit. ¹⁷I pray that Christ will live in your hearts because of your faith. I pray that your life will be strong in love and be built on love. ¹⁸And I pray that you and all God's holy people will have the power to understand the greatness of Christ's love. I pray that you can understand how wide and how long and how high and how deep that love is. ¹⁹Christ's love is greater than any person can ever know. But I pray that you will be able to know that love. Then you can be filled with the fullness of God.

²⁰With God's power working in us,

God can do much, much more than anything we can ask or think of. ²¹To him be glory in the church and in Christ Jesus for all time, forever and ever. Amen.

THE UNITY OF THE BODY

4 I am in prison because I belong to the Lord. God chose you to be his people. I tell you now to live the way God's people should live. ²Always be humble and gentle. Be patient and accept each other with love. ³You are joined together with peace through the Spirit. Do all you can to continue together in this way. Let peace hold you together. ⁴There is one body and one Spirit. And God called you to have one hope. ⁵There is one Lord, one faith, and one baptism. ⁶There is one God and Father of everything. He rules everything. He is everywhere and in everything.

⁷Christ gave each one of us a special gift. Each one received what Christ wanted to give him. ⁸That is why it says in the Scriptures,

"When he went up to the heights,
  he led a parade of captives.
  And he gave gifts to people."
  Psalm 68:18

⁹When it says, "He went up," what does it mean? It means that he first came down to the earth. ¹⁰So Jesus came down, and he is the same One who went up. He went up above all the heavens. Christ did that to fill everything with himself. ¹¹And Christ gave gifts to men—he made some to be apostles, some to be prophets, some to go and tell the Good News, and some to have the work of caring for and teaching God's people. ¹²Christ gave those gifts to prepare God's holy people for the work of serving. He gave those gifts to make the body of Christ stronger. ¹³This work must continue until we are all joined together in the same faith and in the same knowledge about the

Son of God. We must become like a mature person—we must grow until we become like Christ and have all his perfection.

[14] Then we will no longer be babies. We will not be tossed about like a ship that the waves carry one way and then another. We will not be influenced by every new teaching we hear from men who are trying to fool us. Those men make plans and try any kind of trick to fool people into following the wrong path. [15] No! We will speak the truth with love. We will grow up in every way to be like Christ, who is the head. [16] The whole body depends on Christ. And all the parts of the body are joined and held together. Each part of the body does its own work. And this makes the whole body grow and be strong with love.

THE WAY YOU SHOULD LIVE

[17] In the Lord's name, I tell you this. I warn you: Do not continue living like those who do not believe. Their thoughts are worth nothing. [18] They do not understand. They know nothing, because they refuse to listen. So they cannot have the life that God gives. [19] They have lost their feeling of shame. And they use their lives for doing evil. More and more they want to do all kinds of evil things. [20] But the things you learned in Christ were not like this. [21] I know that you heard about him, and you are in him; so you were taught the truth. Yes, the truth is in Jesus. [22] You were taught to leave your old self—to stop living the evil way you lived before. That old self becomes worse and worse because people are fooled by the evil things they want to do. [23] But you were taught to be made new in your hearts. [24] You were taught to become a new person. That new person is made to be like God—made to be truly good and holy.

[25] So you must stop telling lies. Tell each other the truth because we all belong to each other in the same body.[n] [26] When you are angry, do not sin. And do not go on being angry all day. [27] Do not give the devil a way to defeat you. [28] If a person is stealing, he must stop stealing and start working. He must use his hands for doing something good. Then he will have something to share with those who are poor.

[29] When you talk, do not say harmful things. But say what people need—words that will help others become stronger. Then what you say will help those who listen to you. [30] And do not make the Holy Spirit sad. The Spirit is God's proof that you belong to him. God gave you the Spirit to show that God will make you free when the time comes. [31] Do not be bitter or angry or mad. Never shout angrily or say things to hurt others. Never do anything evil. [32] Be kind and loving to each other. Forgive each other just as God forgave you in Christ.

LIVING IN THE LIGHT

5 You are God's children whom he loves. So try to be like God. [2] Live a life of love. Love other people just as Christ loved us. Christ gave himself for us—he was a sweet-smelling offering and sacrifice to God.

[3] But there must be no sexual immorality among you. There must not be any kind of evil or greed. Those things are not right for God's holy people. [4] Also, there must be no evil talk among you. You must not speak foolishly or tell evil jokes. These things are not right for you. But you should be giving thanks to God. [5] You can be sure of this: No one will have a place in the kingdom of Christ and of God who engages in sexual sin, or does evil things, or is greedy. Anyone who is greedy is serving a false god.

[6] Do not let anyone fool you by telling you things that are not true. These things will bring God's anger on those

---

4:25 Tell...body. Quotation from Zechariah 8:16.

who do not obey him. [7]So have no part with them. [8]In the past you were full of darkness, but now you are full of light in the Lord. So live like children who belong to the light. [9]Light brings every kind of goodness, right living, and truth. [10]Try to learn what pleases the Lord. [11]Do not do the things that people in darkness do. That brings nothing good. But do good things to show that the things done in darkness are wrong. [12]It is shameful even to talk about what those people do in secret. [13]But the light makes all things easy to see. [14]And everything that is made easy to see can become light. This is why it is said:

> "Wake up, sleeper!
>   Rise from death,
> and Christ will shine on you."

[15]So be very careful how you live. Do not live like those who are not wise. Live wisely. [16]I mean that you should use every chance you have for doing good, because these are evil times. [17]So do not be foolish with your lives. But learn what the Lord wants you to do. [18]Do not be drunk with wine. That will ruin you spiritually. But be filled with the Spirit. [19]Speak to each other with psalms, hymns, and spiritual songs. Sing and make music in your hearts to the Lord. [20]Always give thanks to God the Father for everything, in the name of our Lord Jesus Christ.

WIVES AND HUSBANDS

[21]Be willing to obey each other. Do this because you respect Christ.

[22]Wives, be under the authority of your husbands, as of the Lord. [23]The husband is the head of the wife, as Christ is the head of the church. The church is Christ's body—Christ is the Savior of the body. [24]The church is under the authority of Christ. So it is the same with you wives. You should be under the authority of your husbands in everything.

[25]Husbands, love your wives as Christ loved the church. Christ died for the church [26]to make it belong to God. Christ used the word to make the church clean by washing it with water. [27]Christ died so that he could give the church to himself like a bride in all her beauty. He died so that the church could be pure and without fault, with no evil or sin or any other wrong thing in it. [28]And husbands should love their wives in the same way. They should love their wives as they love their own bodies. The man who loves his wife loves himself. [29]No person ever hates his own body, but feeds and takes care of it. And that is what Christ does for the church, [30]because we are parts of his body. [31]The Scripture says, "So a man will leave his father and mother and be united with his wife. And the two people will become one body." [n] [32]That secret truth is very important—I am talking about Christ and the church. [33]But each one of you must love his wife as he loves himself. And a wife must respect her husband.

CHILDREN AND PARENTS

6 Children, obey your parents the way the Lord wants. This is the right thing to do. [2]The command says, "Honor your father and mother." [n] This is the first command that has a promise with it. [3]The promise is: "Then everything will be well with you, and you will have a long life on the earth." [n]

[4]Fathers, do not make your children angry, but raise them with the training and teaching of the Lord.

SLAVES AND MASTERS

[5]Slaves, obey your masters here on earth with fear and respect. And do that with a heart that is true, just as you

---

5:31 "So . . . body." Quotation from Genesis 2:24.
6:2 "Honor . . . mother." Quotation from Exodus 20:12; Deuteronomy 5:16.
6:3 "Then . . . earth." Quotation from Exodus 20:12; Deuteronomy 5:16.

☆ Ephesians 6:1

The Book of Ephesians is one of the letters Paul wrote to believers. In it, Paul taught a lesson just for children. He told kids that they should obey their parents. Obeying leads to a long and happy life.

Think about a cold winter day. When you get ready for school, your mom says, "Wear a warm coat." When you are eating breakfast, she says it again: "Wear a warm coat today." She tells you more than once because she knows it is important. When God tells us something more than one time, it is really important. God says again and again that he wants children to obey their parents. He gave your parents wisdom to help you. They can help you make good choices. Listen to them. They want what is best for you.

. . . .

It is not always easy to obey everything our parents tell us. But if God asked you to do it, it means he will help you.

obey Christ. ⁶You must do more than obey your masters to please them only while they are watching you. You must obey them as you are obeying Christ. With all your heart you must do what God wants. ⁷Do your work, and be happy to do it. Work as if you were serving the Lord, not as if you were serving only men. ⁸Remember that the Lord will give a reward to everyone, slave or free, for doing good.

⁹Masters, in the same way, be good to your slaves. Do not say things to scare them. You know that the One who is your Master and their Master is in heaven. And that Master treats everyone alike.

WEAR THE FULL ARMOR OF GOD
¹⁰Finally, be strong in the Lord and in his great power. ¹¹Wear the full armor of God. Wear God's armor so that you can fight against the devil's evil tricks. ¹²Our fight is not against people on earth. We are fighting against the rulers and authorities and the powers of this world's darkness. We are fighting against the spiritual powers of evil in the heavenly world. ¹³That is why you need to get God's full armor. Then on the day of evil you will be able to stand strong. And when you have finished the whole fight, you will still be standing. ¹⁴So stand strong, with the belt of truth tied around your

waist. And on your chest wear the protection of right living. ¹⁵And on your feet wear the Good News of peace to help you stand strong. ¹⁶And also use the shield of faith. With that you can stop all the burning arrows of the Evil One. ¹⁷Accept God's salvation to be your helmet. And take the sword of the Spirit—that sword is the teaching of God. ¹⁸Pray in the Spirit at all times. Pray with all kinds of prayers, and ask for everything you need. To do this you must always be ready. Never give up. Always pray for all God's people.

¹⁹Also pray for me. Pray that when I speak, God will give me words so that I can tell the secret truth of the Good News without fear. ²⁰I have the work of speaking that Good News. I am doing that now, here in prison. Pray that when I preach the Good News I will speak without fear, as I should.

FINAL GREETINGS

²¹I am sending to you Tychicus, our brother whom we love. He is a faithful servant of the Lord's work. He will tell you everything that is happening with me. Then you will know how I am and what I am doing. ²²That is why I am sending him. I want you to know how we are. I am sending him to encourage you.

²³Peace and love with faith to you from God the Father and the Lord Jesus Christ. ²⁴God's grace to all of you who love our Lord Jesus Christ with love that never ends.

Philippians

SERVE OTHERS WITH JOY

1 From Paul and Timothy, servants of Jesus Christ.

To all of God's holy people in Christ Jesus who live in Philippi. And to your overseers and deacons.

²Grace and peace to you from God our Father and the Lord Jesus Christ.

PAUL'S PRAYER

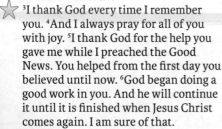

³I thank God every time I remember you. ⁴And I always pray for all of you with joy. ⁵I thank God for the help you gave me while I preached the Good News. You helped from the first day you believed until now. ⁶God began doing a good work in you. And he will continue it until it is finished when Jesus Christ comes again. I am sure of that.

⁷And I know that I am right to think like this about all of you. I am sure because I have you in my heart. All of you share in God's grace with me. You share in God's grace with me while I am in prison, while I am defending the Good News, and while I am proving the truth of the Good News. ⁸God knows that I want to see you very much. I love all of you with the love of Christ Jesus.

⁹This is my prayer for you: that your love will grow more and more; that you will have knowledge and understanding with your love; ¹⁰that you will see the difference between good and bad and choose the good; that you will be pure and without wrong for the coming of Christ; ¹¹that you will be filled with the good things produced in your life by Christ to bring glory and praise to God.

PAUL'S TROUBLES HELP THE WORK

¹²Brothers, I want you to know that what has happened to me has helped to spread the Good News. ¹³I am in prison because I am a believer in Christ. All the palace guards and everyone else knows this. ¹⁴I am still in prison, but most of the believers feel better about it now. And so they are much braver about telling the Good News about Christ.

¹⁵It is true that some preach about Christ because they are jealous and bitter. But others preach about Christ because they want to help. ¹⁶They preach because they have love, and they know that God gave me the work of defending the Good News. ¹⁷But others preach about Christ because they are selfish. Their reason for preaching is wrong. They want to make trouble for me in prison.

¹⁸But I do not care if they make trouble for me. The important thing is that they are preaching about Christ. They should do it for the right reasons. But I am happy even if they do it for wrong reasons. And I will continue to be happy. ¹⁹You are praying for me, and the Spirit of Jesus Christ helps me. So I know that this trouble will bring my freedom. ²⁰The thing I want and hope for is that I will not fail Christ in anything. I hope that I will have the courage now, as always, to show the greatness of Christ in my life here on earth. I want to do that if I die or if I live. ²¹To me the only important thing about living is Christ. And even death would be profit for me. ²²If I continue living in the body, I will be able to work for the Lord. But what should I choose—living or dying? I do not know. ²³It is hard to choose between the two. I want to leave this life and be with Christ. That is much better. ²⁴But you need me here in my body. ²⁵I know that you need me, and so I know that I will stay with you. I will help you grow and have joy in your faith. ²⁶You will be very happy in Christ Jesus when I am with you again.

²⁷Be sure that you live in a way that brings honor to the Good News of

☆ Philippians 1:3–6

The Bible tells us that even though we are Christians, God still works in us. He has only just begun. We have a whole lifetime to grow and to know him better.

Have you ever watched someone paint a picture? Maybe they start with a pencil outline. Then they add a few more lines to give it shape. It looks good enough to you, but they're not done. They get out their paints and they start adding color. They fill in the places inside the outline. Now it's done. Nope. They keep going. They add more color, shadows, shading—they just won't stop. You wonder if they will ever be done with the picture. That's how it is with God. He is our Creator. And when we decide to follow Jesus, he gives us a new heart. But he doesn't stop there. Like an artist, he adds color and shading and depth, and he keeps adding to us for the rest of our lives.

• •

If we every stopped growing and learning, life would be boring. Enjoy the color God adds to your life

---

Christ. Then whether I come and visit you or am away from you, I will hear good things about you. I will hear that you continue strong with one purpose and that you work together as a team for the faith of the Good News. ²⁸And you will not be afraid of those who are against you. All of these things are proof from God that you will be saved and that your enemies will be lost. ²⁹God gave you the honor both of believing in Christ and suffering for Christ. Both these things bring glory to Christ. ³⁰When I was with you, you saw the struggles I had. And you hear about the struggles I am having now. You yourselves are having the same kind of struggles.

2 Does your life in Christ give you strength? Does his love comfort you? Do we share together in the Spirit? Do you have mercy and kindness? ²If so, make me very happy by having the same thoughts, sharing the same love,

and having one mind and purpose. ³When you do things, do not let selfishness or pride be your guide. Be humble and give more honor to others than to yourselves. ⁴Do not be interested only in your own life, but be interested in the lives of others.

BE UNSELFISH LIKE CHRIST

⁵In your lives you must think and act like Christ Jesus.

⁶ Christ himself was like God in
everything.
He was equal with God.
But he did not think that being
equal with God was something
to be held on to.
⁷ He gave up his place with God and
made himself nothing.
He was born as a man
and became like a servant.
⁸ And when he was living as a man,
he humbled himself and was fully
obedient to God.
He obeyed even when that caused
his death—death on a cross.
⁹ So God raised Christ to the highest
place.
God made the name of Christ
greater than every other name.
¹⁰ God wants every knee to bow to
Jesus—
everyone in heaven, on earth, and
under the earth.
¹¹ Everyone will say, "Jesus Christ is
Lord"
and bring glory to God the Father.

BE THE PEOPLE GOD WANTS YOU TO BE

¹²My dear friends, you have always obeyed. You obeyed God when I was with you. It is even more important that you obey now while I am not with you. Keep on working to complete your salvation, and do it with fear and trembling. ¹³Yes, God is working in you to help you want to do what pleases him. Then he gives you the power to do it.

¹⁴Do everything without complaining or arguing. ¹⁵Then you will be innocent and without anything wrong in you. You will be God's children without fault. But you are living with crooked and mean people all around you. Among them you shine like stars in the dark world. ¹⁶You offer to them the teaching that gives life. So when Christ comes again, I can be happy because my work was not wasted. I ran in the race and won.

¹⁷Your faith makes you offer your lives as a sacrifice in serving God. Perhaps I will have to offer my own blood with your sacrifice. But if that happens, I will be happy and full of joy with all of you. ¹⁸You also should be happy and full of joy with me.

TIMOTHY AND EPAPHRODITUS

¹⁹I hope in the Lord Jesus to send Timothy to you soon. I will be happy to learn how you are. ²⁰I have no other person like Timothy. He truly cares for you. ²¹Other people are interested only in their own lives. They are not interested in the work of Christ Jesus. ²²You know the kind of person Timothy is. You know that he has served with me in telling the Good News, as a son serves his father. ²³I plan to send him to you quickly when I know what will happen to me. ²⁴I am sure that the Lord will help me to come to you soon.

²⁵Epaphroditus is my brother in Christ. He works and serves with me in the army of Christ. When I needed help, you sent him to me. I think now that I must send him back to you ²⁶because he wants very much to see all of you. He is worried because you heard that he was sick. ²⁷Yes, he was sick, and nearly died. But God helped him and me too, so that I would not have more sadness. ²⁸So I want very much to send him to you. When you see him, you can be happy. And I can stop worrying about you. ²⁹Welcome him in the Lord with much joy. Give honor to people like Epaphroditus.

30He should be honored because he almost died for the work of Christ. He put his life in danger so that he could help me. This was help that you could not give me.

THE IMPORTANCE OF CHRIST

3 My brothers, be full of joy in the Lord. It is no trouble for me to write the same things to you again, and it will help you to be more ready. 2Be careful of those who do evil. They are like dogs. They demand to cut[n] the body. 3But we are the ones who are truly circumcised. We worship God through his Spirit. We are proud to be in Christ Jesus. And we do not trust in ourselves or anything we can do. 4Even if I am able to trust in myself, still I do not. If anyone thinks that he has a reason to trust in himself, he should know that I have greater reason for trusting in myself. 5I was circumcised eight days after my birth. I am from the people of Israel and the tribe of Benjamin. I am a Hebrew, and my parents were Hebrews. The law of Moses was very important to me. That is why I became a Pharisee. 6I was so enthusiastic that I tried to hurt the church. No one could find fault with the way I obeyed the law of Moses. 7At one time all these things were important to me. But now I think those things are worth nothing because of Christ. 8Not only those things, but I think that all things are worth nothing compared with the greatness of knowing Christ Jesus my Lord. Because of Christ, I have lost all those things. And now I know that all those things are worthless trash. This allows me to have Christ 9and to belong to him. Now that I belong to Christ, I am right with God and this being right does not come from my following the law. It comes from God through faith. God uses my faith in Christ to make me right with him. 10All I want is to know Christ and the power of his rising from death. I want to share in Christ's sufferings and become like him in his death. 11If I have those things, then I have hope that I myself will be raised from death.

> All I want is to know Christ and the power of his rising from death.
> –PHILIPPIANS 3:10

CONTINUING TOWARD OUR GOAL

12I do not mean that I am already as God wants me to be. I have not yet reached that goal. But I continue trying to reach it and to make it mine. Christ wants me to do that. That is the reason Christ made me his. 13Brothers, I know that I have not yet reached that goal. But there is one thing I always do: I forget the things that are past. I try as hard as I can to reach the goal that is before me. 14I keep trying to reach the goal and get the prize. That prize is mine because God called me through Christ to the life above. 15All of us who have grown spiritually to be mature should think this way, too. And if there are things you do not agree with, God will make them clear to you. 16But we should continue following the truth we already have.

17Brothers, all of you should try to follow my example and to copy those who live the way we showed you. 18Many people live like enemies of the cross of Christ. I have often told you about them, and it makes me cry to tell you about them now. 19The way they live is leading them to destruction. Instead of serving God,

---

3:2 cut The word in Greek is like the word "circumcise," but it means "to cut completely off."

they do whatever their bodies want. They do shameful things, and they are proud of it. They think only about earthly things. ²⁰But our homeland is in heaven, and we are waiting for our Savior, the Lord Jesus Christ, to come from heaven. ²¹He will change our humble bodies and make them like his own glorious body. Christ can do this by his power. With that power he is able to rule all things.

WHAT THE CHRISTIANS ARE TO DO

4 My dear brothers, I love you and want to see you. You bring me joy and make me proud of you. Continue following the Lord as I have told you.

²I ask Euodia and Syntyche to agree in the Lord. ³And because you serve faithfully with me, my friend, I ask you to help these women to do this. They served with me in telling people the

☆ Philippians 4:13

The apostle Paul had a very hard life once he started telling people about Jesus. He never knew what the next day would bring: storms, shipwreck, hunger, cold—prison! He was in prison when he wrote a letter to a group of believers and thanked them for caring about him. Paul said that even when he didn't have everything he needed, God still took care of him. It was God who gave Paul strength.

Have you ever felt weak, scared, or not strong enough to do something? The Bible reminds us that sometimes we are not strong enough or big enough to do things on our own. Jesus wants us to ask him for help. You may be having trouble with homework. Ask Jesus for help. Do you argue with your brother or sister? Jesus can help you. Maybe you're starting a new school or learning a new sport. You are never alone. Whatever you need help with, Jesus will give you his strength to do all things.

. . . .

God's Spirit is in you. And because of that, you can do all things through him!

Good News. They served together with Clement and others who worked with me. Their names are written in the book of life.[n]

[4]Be full of joy in the Lord always. I will say again, be full of joy.

[5]Let all men see that you are gentle and kind. The Lord is coming soon. [6]Do not worry about anything. But pray and ask God for everything you need. And when you pray, always give thanks. [7]And God's peace will keep your hearts and minds in Christ Jesus. The peace that God gives is so great that we cannot understand it.

[8]Brothers, continue to think about the things that are good and worthy of praise. Think about the things that are true and honorable and right and pure and beautiful and respected. [9]And do what you learned and received from me. Do what I told you and what you saw me do. And the God who gives peace will be with you.

PAUL THANKS THE CHRISTIANS

[10]I am very happy in the Lord that you have shown your care for me again. You continued to care about me, but there was no way for you to show it. [11]I am telling you this, but it is not because I need anything. I have learned to be satisfied with the things I have and with everything that happens. [12]I know how to live when I am poor. And I know how to live when I have plenty. I have learned the secret of being happy at any time in everything that happens. I have learned to be happy when I have enough to eat and when I do not have enough to eat. I have learned to be happy when I have all that I need and when I do not have the things I need. [13]I can do all things through Christ because he gives me strength.

[14]But it was good that you helped me when I needed help. [15]You people in Philippi remember when I first preached the Good News there. When I left Macedonia, you were the only church that gave me help. [16]Several times you sent me things I needed when I was in Thessalonica. [17]Really, it is not that I want to receive gifts from you. But I want you to have the good that comes from giving. [18]And now I have everything, and more. I have all I need because Epaphroditus brought your gift to me. Your gift is like a sweet-smelling sacrifice offered to God. God accepts that sacrifice, and it pleases him. [19]My God will use his wonderful riches in Christ Jesus to give you everything you need. [20]Glory to our God and Father forever and ever! Amen.

[21]Greet each of God's people in Christ. God's people who are with me send greetings to you. [22]All of God's people greet you. And those believers from the palace of Caesar greet you, too.

[23]The grace of the Lord Jesus Christ be with you all.

4:3 **book of life** God's book that has the names of all God's chosen people (Revelation 3:5; 21:27).

Colossians

ONLY CHRIST CAN SAVE PEOPLE

1 From Paul, an apostle of Christ Jesus. I am an apostle because that is what God wanted.

Also from Timothy, our brother.

[2]To the holy and faithful brothers in Christ that live in Colosse. Grace and peace from God our Father.[n]

[3]In our prayers for you we always thank God, the Father of our Lord Jesus Christ. [4]We thank God because we have heard about the faith you have in Christ Jesus and the love you have for all of God's people. [5]You have this faith and love because of your hope, and what you hope for is saved for you in heaven. You learned about this hope when you heard the true teaching, the Good News [6]that was told to you. Everywhere in the world that Good News is bringing blessings and is growing. This has happened with you, too, since you heard the Good News and understood the truth about the grace of God. [7]You learned about God's grace from Epaphras, whom we love. Epaphras works together with us and is a faithful servant of Christ for us.[n] [8]He also told us about the love you have from the Holy Spirit.

[9]Since the day we heard this about you, we have continued praying for you. We ask God that you will know fully what God wants. We pray that you will also have great wisdom and understanding in spiritual things. [10]Then you will live the kind of life that honors and pleases the Lord in every way. You will produce fruit in every good work and grow in the knowledge of God. [11]Then God will strengthen you with his own great power. And you will not give up when troubles come, but you will be patient. [12]Then you will joyfully give thanks to the Father. He has made you[n] able to have all that he has prepared for his people who live in the light. [13]God made us free from the power of darkness, and he brought us into the kingdom of his dear Son. [14]The Son paid for our sins,[n] and in him we have forgiveness.

THE IMPORTANCE OF CHRIST

[15]No one has seen God, but Jesus is exactly like him. Christ ranks higher than all the things that have been made. [16]Through his power all things were made—things in heaven and on earth, things seen and unseen, all powers, authorities, lords, and rulers. All things were made through Christ and for Christ. [17]Christ was there before anything was made. And all things continue because of him. [18]He is the head of the body. (The body is the church.) Everything comes from him. And he is the first one who was raised from death. So in all things Jesus is most important. [19]God was pleased for all of himself to live in Christ. [20]And through Christ, God decided to bring all things back to himself again—things on earth and things in heaven. God made peace by using the blood of Christ's death on the cross.

[21]At one time you were separated from God. You were God's enemies in your minds because the evil deeds you did were against God. [22]But now Christ has made you God's friends again. He did this by his death while he was in the body, that he might bring you into God's presence. He brings you before God as people who are holy, with no wrong in you, and with nothing that God can

---

1:2 **Father** Some Greek copies continue, "and the Lord Jesus Christ."
1:7 **for us** Some Greek copies read "for you."
1:12 **you** Some Greek copies read "us."
1:14 **sins** Some Greek copies continue, "with his blood."

judge you guilty of. [23] And Christ will do this if you continue to believe in the Good News you heard. You must continue strong and sure in your faith. You must not be moved away from the hope that Good News gave you. That same Good News has been told to everyone in the world. I, Paul, help in preaching that Good News.

PAUL'S WORK FOR THE CHURCH

[24] I am happy in my sufferings for you. There are many things that Christ must still suffer through his body, the church. I am accepting my part of these things that must be suffered. I accept these sufferings in my body. I suffer for his body, the church. [25] I became a servant of the church because God gave me a special work to do that helps you. My work is to tell fully the teaching of God. [26] This teaching is the secret truth that was hidden since the beginning of time. It was hidden from everyone, but now it is made known to God's holy people. [27] God decided to let his people know this rich and glorious truth which he has for all people. This truth is Christ himself, who is in you. He is our only hope for glory. [28] So we

☆ Colossians 1:16

Jesus Christ is the Son of God the Father, but he is also God. If people know Jesus, they know God. The Bible says, "All things were made through Christ and for Christ."

Do you like to play in the grass? Do you ever play in the sand? Have you ever played in the rain or in the snow? It is fun to go outside and play. Did you know God wants us to have fun outside? God made everything. He made the sun, the clouds, and even the snow. Do you know why God made everything? He made it all for Jesus! Jesus is God's Son, and the world is God's present to Jesus! And because Jesus loves us so much, we get to enjoy his present too!

It doesn't have to be confusing. When you talk to Jesus, you are talking to God himself.

continue to preach Christ to all men. We use all wisdom to warn and to teach everyone. We are trying to bring each one into God's presence as a mature person in Christ. ²⁹To do this, I work and struggle, using Christ's great strength that works so powerfully in me.

2 I want you to know that I am trying very hard to help you. And I am trying to help those in Laodicea and others who have never seen me. ²I want them to be strengthened and joined together with love. I want them to be rich in the strong belief that comes from understanding. I mean I want you to know fully God's secret truth. That truth is Christ himself. ³And in him all the treasures of wisdom and knowledge are safely kept.

⁴I say this so that no one can fool you by arguments that seem good, but are false. ⁵I am not there with you, but my heart is with you. I am happy to see your good lives and your strong faith in Christ.

CONTINUE TO LIVE IN CHRIST

⁶As you received Christ Jesus the Lord, so continue to live in him. ⁷Keep your roots deep in him and have your lives built on him. Be strong in the faith, just as you were taught. And always be thankful.

⁸Be sure that no one leads you away with false ideas and words that mean nothing. Those ideas come from men. They are the worthless ideas of this world. They are not from Christ. ⁹All of God lives fully in Christ (even when Christ was on earth). ¹⁰And in him you have a full and true life. He is ruler over all rulers and powers.

¹¹In Christ you had a different kind of circumcision. That circumcision was not done by hands. I mean, you were made free from the power of your sinful self. That is the kind of circumcision Christ does. ¹²When you were baptized, you were buried with Christ and you were raised up with Christ because of your faith in God's power. That power was shown when he raised Christ from death. ¹³You were spiritually dead because of your sins and because you were not free from the power of your sinful self. But God made you alive with Christ. And God forgave all our sins. ¹⁴We owed a debt because we broke God's laws. That debt listed all the rules we failed to follow. But God forgave us that debt. He took away that debt and nailed it to the cross. ¹⁵God defeated the spiritual rulers and powers. With the cross God won the victory and defeated them. He showed the world that they were powerless.

DON'T FOLLOW PEOPLE'S RULES

¹⁶So do not let anyone make rules for you about eating and drinking or about a religious feast, a New Moon Festival, or a Sabbath day. ¹⁷In the past, these things were like a shadow of what was to come. But the new things that were coming are found in Christ. ¹⁸Some enjoy acting as if they were humble and love to worship angels. They are always talking about the visions they have seen. Do not let them tell you that you are wrong. They are full of foolish pride because of their human way of thinking. ¹⁹They do not keep themselves under the control of Christ, the head. The whole body depends on Christ. Because of him all the parts of the body care for each other and help each other. This strengthens the body and holds it together. And so the body grows in the way God wants.

> Your old sinful self has died, and your new life is kept with Christ in God. Christ is your life.
>
> —COLOSSIANS 3:3–4

[20]You died with Christ and were made free from the worthless rules of the world. So why do you act as if you still belong to this world? I mean, why do you follow rules like these: [21]"Don't handle this," "Don't taste that," "Don't touch that thing"? [22]These rules are talking about earthly things that are gone as soon as they are used. They are only human commands and teachings. [23]These rules seem to be wise. But they are only part of a human religion. They make people pretend not to be proud and make them punish their bodies. But they do not really control the evil desires of the sinful self.

YOUR NEW LIFE IN CHRIST

3 You were raised from death with Christ. So aim at what is in heaven, where Christ is sitting at the right hand of God. [2]Think only about the things in heaven, not the things on earth. [3]Your old sinful self has died, and your new life is kept with Christ in God. [4]Christ is your[n] life. When he comes again, you will share in his glory.

[5]So put all evil things out of your life. Get rid of sexual immorality and impure acts. Don't let your feelings get out of control. Remove from your life all evil desires. Stop always wanting more and more. This really means living to serve a false god. [6]These things make God angry.[n] [7]In your evil life in the past, you also did these things.

[8]But now put these things out of your life: anger, bad temper, doing or saying things to hurt others, and using evil words when you talk. [9]Do not lie to each other. You have left your old sinful life and the things you did before. [10]You have begun to live the new life. In your new life you are being made new. You are becoming like the One who made you. This new life brings you the true knowledge of God.

[11]In the new life there is no difference between Greeks and Jews. There is no difference between those who are circumcised and those who are not circumcised, or people that are foreigners, or Scythians.[n] There is no difference between slaves and free people. But Christ is in all believers. And Christ is all that is important.

[12]God has chosen you and made you his holy people. He loves you. So always do these things: Show mercy to others; be kind, humble, gentle, and patient. [13]Do not be angry with each other, but forgive each other. If someone does wrong to you, then forgive him. Forgive each other because the Lord forgave you. [14]Do all these things; but most important, love each other. Love is what holds you all together in perfect unity. [15]Let the peace that Christ gives control your thinking. You were all called together in one body[n] to have peace. Always be thankful. [16]Let the teaching of Christ live in you richly. Use all wisdom to teach and strengthen each other. Sing psalms, hymns, and spiritual songs with thankfulness in your hearts to God. [17]Everything you say and everything you do should all be done for Jesus your Lord. And in all you do, give thanks to God the Father through Jesus.

YOUR NEW LIFE WITH OTHER PEOPLE

[18]Wives, be under the authority of your husbands. This is the right thing to do in the Lord.

[19]Husbands, love your wives, and be gentle to them.

[20]Children, obey your parents in all things. This pleases the Lord.

[21]Fathers, do not nag your children. If you are too hard to please, they may want to stop trying.

[22]Slaves, obey your masters in all

3:4 **your** Some Greek copies read "our."
3:6 **These . . . angry.** Some Greek copies continue, "against the people who do not obey God."
3:11 **Scythians** The Scythians were known as very wild and cruel people.
3:15 **body** The spiritual body of Christ, meaning the church or his people.

things. Do not obey just when they are watching you, to gain their favor. But serve them honestly, because you respect the Lord. [23]In all the work you are doing, work the best you can. Work as if you were working for the Lord, not for men. [24]Remember that you will receive your reward from the Lord, which he promised to his people. You are serving the Lord Christ. [25]But remember that anyone who does wrong will be punished for that wrong. And the Lord treats everyone the same.

4 Masters, give the things that are good and fair to your slaves. Remember that you have a Master in heaven.

WHAT THE CHRISTIANS ARE TO DO

[2]Continue praying and keep alert. And when you pray, always thank God. [3]Also pray for us. Pray that God will give us an opportunity to tell people his message. Pray that we can preach the secret truth that God has made known about Christ. I am in prison because I preach this truth. [4]Pray that I can speak in a way that will make it clear as I should.

[5]Be wise in the way you act with people who are not believers. Use your time in the best way you can. [6]When you talk, you should always be kind and wise. Then you will be able to answer everyone in the way you should.

NEWS ABOUT THE PEOPLE WITH PAUL

[7]Tychicus is my dear brother in Christ. He is a faithful minister and servant with me in the Lord. He will tell you all the things that are happening to me. [8]That is why I am sending him. I want you to know how we are. I am sending him to encourage you. [9]I send him with Onesimus. Onesimus is a faithful and dear brother in Christ. He is one of your group. They will tell you all that has happened here.

[10]Aristarchus greets you. He is a prisoner with me. And Mark, the cousin of Barnabas, also greets you. (I have already told you what to do about Mark. If he comes, welcome him.) [11]Jesus, who is called Justus, also greets you. These are the only Jewish believers who work with me for the kingdom of God. They have been a comfort to me.

[12]Epaphras also greets you. He is a servant of Jesus Christ. And he is from your group. He always prays for you. He prays that you will grow to be spiritually mature and have everything that God wants for you. [13]I know that he has worked hard for you and the people in Laodicea and in Hierapolis. [14]Demas and our dear friend Luke, the doctor, greet you.

[15]Greet the brothers in Laodicea. And greet Nympha and the church that meets in her house. [16]After this letter is read to you, be sure that it is also read to the church in Laodicea. And you read the letter that I wrote to Laodicea. [17]Tell Archippus, "Be sure to do the work the Lord gave you."

[18]I, Paul, greet you and write this with my own hand. Remember me in prison. God's grace be with you.

JESUS IS THE NEW AND LIVING WAY

Jesus the Savior showed up just as God had promised. Some of the people of Israel, the Jews, were upset that Jesus did not look or act like a king. Some turned their backs on him. Many of the Jews, though, did believe in Jesus. But they had a problem.

The Jews who believed in Jesus were still Jews. They had been taught to obey the law of Moses since they were babies. Some of them thought they had followed the law of Moses perfectly. And many were proud of their religious work. But there were some things in their new belief that did not follow the traditions they had learned. Some people were confused about the Good News of Jesus. They thought the new message would weaken their belief in God.

The Book of Hebrews was written to help the Jews understand the Good News. It cleared some things up like—

1. The Jews thought the Savior was sent only to them. But Jesus died for all of us—Jewish people and non-Jewish people.
2. The Jews knew the Savior was supposed to be a king like David. But Jesus' earthly dad was a carpenter, not a king.
3. The Jews thought the Son of God would be like the angels. But Jesus came as a baby and grew up to be a regular man.
4. The Jews were taught to sacrifice animals to cover their sins. But when Jesus died on the cross, he became the only sacrifice we will ever need—forever.
5. The Jews were taught to worship at the Temple. But Jesus changed that; now people's own bodies are the temple of God's Spirit.

The Book of Hebrews was meant to show the Jews why they needed a Savior. And to show them that their works were useless. They were free to stop trusting in their own efforts. Now they could trust only what Jesus had done for them.

Hebrews

GOD SPOKE THROUGH HIS SON

1 In the past God spoke to our ancestors through the prophets. He spoke to them many times and in many different ways. ²And now in these last days God has spoken to us through his Son. God has chosen his Son to own all things. And he made the world through the Son. ³The Son reflects the glory of God. He is an exact copy of God's nature. He holds everything together with his powerful word. The Son made people clean from their sins. Then he sat down at the right side of God, the Great One in heaven. ⁴The Son became much greater than the angels. And God gave him a name that is much greater than theirs.

⁵This is because God never said to any of the angels,

"You are my Son.
   Today I have become your Father."
   Psalm 2:7

Nor did God say of any angel,

"I will be his Father,
   and he will be my Son."
   2 Samuel 7:14

⁶And when God brings his firstborn Son into the world, he says,

"Let all God's angels worship him." *[n]*
   Psalm 97:7

⁷This is what God said about the angels:

"God makes his angels become like winds.
   He makes his servants become like flames of fire." *Psalm 104:4*

⁸But God said this about his Son:

"God, your throne will last forever and ever.
   You will rule your kingdom with fairness.
⁹ You love what is right and hate evil.
   So God has chosen you to rule those with you.
   Your God has given you much joy."
   Psalm 45:6–7

¹⁰God also says,

"Lord, in the beginning you made the earth.
   And your hands made the skies.
¹¹ They will be destroyed, but you will remain.
   They will all wear out like clothes.
¹² You will fold them like a coat.
   And, like clothes, you will change them.
   But you never change.
   And your life will never end."
   Psalm 102:25–27

¹³And God never said this to an angel:

"Sit by me at my right side
until I put your enemies under your control." *[n]*   *Psalm 110:1*

¹⁴All the angels are spirits who serve God and are sent to help those who will receive salvation.

OUR SALVATION IS GREAT

2 So we must be more careful to follow what we were taught. Then we will not be pulled away from the truth. ²The teaching that God spoke through angels was shown to be true.

1:6 "Let . . . him." These words are found in Deuteronomy 32:43 in the Septuagint, the Greek version of the Old Testament, and in a Hebrew copy among the Dead Sea Scrolls.
1:13 until . . . control Literally, "until I make your enemies a footstool for your feet."

And anyone who did not follow it or obey it received the punishment he earned. [3]The salvation that was given to us is very great. So surely we also will be punished if we live as if this salvation were not important. It was the Lord himself who first told about this salvation. And those who heard him proved to us that this salvation is true. [4]God also proved it by using wonders, great signs, and many kinds of miracles. And he proved it by giving people gifts through the Holy Spirit, just as he wanted.

CHRIST BECAME LIKE MEN

[5]God did not choose angels to be the rulers of the new world that was coming. It is that future world we have been talking about. [6]It is written somewhere in the Scriptures,

> "Why is man important to you?
>   Why do you take care of the son of man?[n]
> [7] For a short time you made him lower
>   than the angels.
>   But you crowned him with glory
>   and honor.
> [8]   You put all things under his
>   control."   Psalm 8:4–6

If God put everything under his control, there was nothing left that he did not rule. But we do not yet see him ruling over everything. [9]But we see Jesus! For a short time he was made lower than the angels. But now we see him wearing a crown of glory and honor because he suffered and died. Because of God's grace, he died for everyone. [10]God is the One who made all things. And all things are for his glory. God wanted to have many sons share his glory. So God made perfect the One who leads people to salvation. He made Jesus a perfect Savior through Jesus' suffering. [11]Jesus, who makes people holy, and those who are made holy are from the same family. So he is not ashamed to call them his brothers. [12]He says,

> "Then, I will tell my fellow Israelites
>   about you.
>   I will praise you when your
>   people meet to worship you."
>   Psalm 22:22

[13]He also says,

> "I will trust in God."   Isaiah 8:17

And he also says,

> "I am here. And with me are the
>   children that God has given me."
>   Isaiah 8:18

[14]These children are people with physical bodies. So Jesus himself became like them and had the same experiences they have. He did this so that, by dying, he could destroy the one who has the power of death. That one is the devil. [15]Jesus became like men and died so that he could free them. They were like slaves all their lives because of their fear of death. [16]Clearly, it is not angels that Jesus helps, but the people who are from Abraham.[n] [17]For this reason Jesus had to be made like his brothers in every way. He became like men so that he could be their merciful and faithful high priest in service to God. Then Jesus could bring forgiveness for their sins. [18]And now he can help those who are tempted. He is able to help because he himself suffered and was tempted.

JESUS IS GREATER THAN MOSES

3 So all of you, holy brothers, should think about Jesus. You were all called by God. God sent Jesus to us, and he is the high priest of our faith. [2]And Jesus was faithful to God as Moses was.

2:6 son of man This can mean any, but the name "Son of Man" is often used to mean Jesus. When Jesus became a man, he showed what God planned for all people to be.

2:16 Abraham Most respected ancestor of the Jews. Every Jew hoped to see Abraham.

Moses did everything God wanted him to do in God's family. ³A man who is the head of a family receives more honor than others in the family. It is the same with Jesus. Jesus should have more honor than Moses. ⁴Every family has its head, but God is the head of everything. ⁵Moses was faithful in God's family as a servant. He told what God would say in the future. ☆ ⁶But Christ is faithful as a Son who is the head of God's family. And we are God's family if we hold on to our faith and are proud of the great hope we have.

WE MUST CONTINUE TO FOLLOW GOD

⁷So it is as the Holy Spirit says:

"Today listen to what he says.
⁸ Do not be stubborn as in the past
    when you turned against God.
There you tested God in the desert.
⁹ For 40 years in the desert your
    ancestors saw the things I did.
    But they tested me and my patience.
¹⁰ I was angry with them.
    I said, 'They are not loyal to me.
    They have not understood my
    ways.'
¹¹ So I was angry and made a promise.
    'They will never enter my land of
        rest.'" ⁿ   *Psalm 95:7–11*

¹²So brothers, be careful that none of you has an evil, unbelieving heart.

3:11 rest A place of rest God promised to give his people.

☆ Hebrews 3:6

Moses was a very important person to the Hebrew people. God considered him a faithful servant. But the Bible says Jesus is even greater than Moses. Jesus is a faithful Son and head of the family of God.

Jesus is God's Son. We become part of God's family by believing in Jesus. God loves you so much. He wants to call you his own son or daughter. Everyone who loves Jesus is part of God's family too. Isn't it great that we can be a part of the family of God!

. . . .

Moses was a servant of God. But because of Jesus, you get to be God's child. That is way better than being a servant!

This will stop you from following the living God. [13]But encourage each other every day. Do this while it is "today." [n] Help each other so that none of you will become hardened because of sin and its tricks. [14]We all share in Christ. This is true if we keep till the end the sure faith we had in the beginning. [15]This is what the Scripture says:

> "Today listen to what he says.
>   Do not be stubborn as in the past
>   when you turned against God."
>
> *Psalm 95:7–8*

[16]Who heard God's voice and was against him? It was all those people Moses led out of Egypt. [17]And whom was God angry with for 40 years? He was angry with those who sinned, who died in the desert. [18]And whom was God talking to when he promised that they would never enter and have his rest? He was talking to those who did not obey him. [19]So we see that they were not allowed to enter and have God's rest because they did not believe.

4 Now God has left us that promise that we may enter and have his rest. Let us be very careful, then, so that none of you will fail to get that rest. [2]The Good News was preached to us just as it was to them. But the teaching they heard did not help them. They heard it but did not accept it with faith. [n] [3]We who have believed are able to enter and have God's rest. As God has said,

> "So I was angry and made a promise.
>   'They will never enter my land of
>   rest.'" *Psalm 95:11*

But God's work was finished from the time he made the world. [4]Somewhere in the Scriptures he talked about the seventh day of the week: "And on the seventh day God rested from all his work." [n] [5]And again in the Scripture God said, "They will never enter my land of rest."

[6]It is still true that some people will enter and have God's rest. But those who first heard the way to be saved did not enter. They did not enter because they did not obey. [7]So God planned another day, called "today." He spoke about that day through David a long time later. It is the same Scripture used before:

> "Today listen to what he says.
>   Do not be stubborn."
>
> *Psalm 95:7–8*

[8]We know that Joshua[n] did not lead the people into that rest. We know this because God spoke later about another day. [9]This shows that the seventh-day rest[n] for God's people is still coming. [10]For anyone who enters and has God's rest will rest from his work as God did. [11]So let us try as hard as we can to enter God's rest. We must try hard so that no one will be lost by following the example of those who refused to obey.

[12]God's word is alive and working. It is sharper than a sword sharpened on both sides. It cuts all the way into us, where the soul and the spirit are joined. It cuts to the center of our joints and our bones. And God's word judges the thoughts and feelings in our hearts. [13]Nothing in all the world can be hidden from God. Everything is clear and lies open before him. And to him we must explain the way we have lived.

3:13 **"today"** This word is taken from verse 7. It means that it is important to do these things now.
4:2 **They . . . faith.** Some Greek copies read "They did not share the faith of those who heard it."
4:4 **"And . . . work."** Quotation from Genesis 2:2.
4:8 **Joshua** After Moses died, Joshua became leader of the Jewish people. Joshua led them into the land that God promised to give them.
4:9 **seventh-day rest** Literally, "sabbath rest," meaning a sharing in the rest that God began after he created the world.

★ Hebrews 4:16

Jesus understands our weaknesses. He faced some of the same problems we do. That is why we can talk to him when we need help. He is always ready to help us.

Grace had done a bad thing. She disobeyed her mom and knew she was in big trouble. She was scared! But she was in for a surprise. When her mom came to tuck her in that night, they had a serious talk about disobeying. Then, instead of being punished, Grace's mom gave her a big hug and a kiss and told her she loved her. Grace didn't get what she deserved. Grace got grace!

. . . .

God loves you no matter what you do. You don't ever have to be afraid to talk to him.

JESUS IS OUR HIGH PRIEST

¹⁴We have a great high priest who has gone into heaven. He is Jesus the Son of God. So let us hold on to the faith we have. ¹⁵For our high priest is able to understand our weaknesses. He was tempted in every way that we are, but he did not sin. ¹⁶Let us, then, feel free to come before God's throne. Here there is grace. And we can receive mercy and grace to help us when we need it.

5 Every high priest is chosen from among men. He is given the work of going before God for them. He must offer gifts and sacrifices for sins. ²He himself is weak. So he is able to be gentle with those who do not understand and who are doing wrong things. ³Because he is weak the high priest must offer sacrifices for his own sins. And then he offers sacrifices for the sins of the people.

⁴To be a high priest is an honor. But no one chooses himself for this work. He must be called by God as Aaron[n] was. ⁵So also Christ did not choose himself to have the honor of being a high priest. But God chose him. God said to him,

"You are my Son;
    today I have become your Father."
Psalm 2:7

⁶And in another Scripture God says,

5:4 **Aaron** Moses' brother and the first Jewish high priest.

"You are a priest forever,
 a priest like Melchizedek." [n]

Psalm 110:4

[7] While Jesus lived on earth, he prayed to God and asked God for help. He prayed with loud cries and tears to the One who could save him from death. And his prayer was heard because he left it all up to God. [8] Even though Jesus was the Son of God, he learned to obey by what he suffered. [9] And he became our perfect high priest. He gives eternal salvation to all who obey him. [10] And God made Jesus high priest, a priest like Melchizedek.

WARNING AGAINST FALLING AWAY

[11] We have much to say about this. But it is hard to explain because you are so slow to understand. [12] You have had enough time so that by now you should be teachers. But you need someone to teach you again the first lessons of God's message. You still need the teaching that is like milk. You are not ready for solid food. [13] Anyone who lives on milk is still a baby. He knows nothing about right teaching. [14] But solid food is for those who are grown up. They are mature enough to know the difference between good and evil.

6 So let us go on to grown-up teaching. Let us not go back over the beginning lessons we learned about Christ. We should not start over again with teaching about turning from acts that lead to death and about believing in God. [2] We should not return to the teaching of baptisms,[n] of laying on of hands,[n] of the raising of the dead and eternal judgment. [3] And we will go on to grown-up teaching if God allows.

[4] Some people cannot be brought back again to a changed life. They were once in God's light. They enjoyed heaven's gift, and they shared in the Holy Spirit. [5] They found out how good God's word is, and they received the powers of his new world. [6] And then they fell away from Christ! It is not possible to keep on bringing them back to a changed life again. For they are nailing the Son of God to a cross again and are shaming him in front of others.

[7] Some people are like land that gets plenty of rain. The land produces a good crop for those who work it, and it receives God's blessings. [8] Other people are like land that grows thorns and weeds and is worthless. It is about to be cursed by God. It will be destroyed by fire.

[9] Dear friends, we are saying this to you. But we really expect better things from you that will lead to your salvation. [10] God is fair. He will not forget the work you did and the love you showed for him by helping his people. And he will remember that you are still helping them. [11] We want each of you to go on with the same hard work all your lives. Then you will surely get what you hope for. [12] We do not want you to become lazy. Be like those who have faith and patience. They will receive what God has promised.

[13] God made a promise to Abraham. And as there is no one greater than God, he used himself when he swore to Abraham. [14] He said, "I will surely bless you and give you many descendants." [n] [15] Abraham waited patiently for this to happen. And he received what God promised.

[16] People always use the name of someone greater than themselves when they swear. The oath proves that what they say is true. And this ends

---

5:6 Melchizedek A priest and king who lived in the time of Abraham. (Read Genesis 14:17–24.)
6:2 baptisms The word here may refer to Christian baptism, or it may refer to the Jewish ceremonial washings.
6:2 laying on of hands Putting the hands on people showed that they were being given some special work or some spiritual gift or blessing.
6:14 "I...descendants." Quotation from Genesis 22:17.

all arguing about what they say. [17]God wanted to prove that his promise was true. He wanted to prove this to those who would get what he promised. He wanted them to understand clearly that his purposes never change. So God proved his promise by also making an oath. [18]These two things cannot change. God cannot lie when he makes a promise, and he cannot lie when he makes an oath. These things encourage us who came to God for safety. They give us strength to hold on to the hope we have been given. [19]We have this hope as an anchor for the soul, sure and strong. It enters behind the curtain in the Most Holy Place in heaven. [20]Jesus has gone in there ahead of us and for us. He has become the high priest forever, a priest like Melchizedek.[n]

THE PRIEST MELCHIZEDEK

7 Melchizedek[n] was the king of Salem and a priest for the Most High God. He met Abraham when Abraham was coming back after defeating the kings. When they met, Melchizedek blessed Abraham. [2]And Abraham gave Melchizedek a tenth of everything he had brought back from the battle. First, Melchizedek's name means "king of goodness." Also, he is king of Salem, which means "king of peace." [3]No one knows who Melchizedek's father or mother was.[n] No one knows where he came from. And no one knows when he was born or when he died. Melchizedek is like the Son of God; he continues being a priest forever.

[4]You can see that Melchizedek was very great. Abraham, the great father, gave Melchizedek a tenth of everything that Abraham won in battle. [5]Now the law says that those in the tribe of Levi who become priests must get a tenth from the people. The priests collect it from their own people, even though the priests and the people are both from the family of Abraham. [6]Melchizedek was not from the tribe of Levi. But he got a tenth from Abraham. And he blessed Abraham, the man who had God's promises. [7]And everyone knows that the more important person blesses the less important person. [8]Those priests get a tenth, but they are only men who live and then die. But Melchizedek, who got a tenth from Abraham, continues living, as the Scripture says. [9]It is Levi who gets a tenth from the people. But we might even say that when Abraham paid Melchizedek a tenth, then Levi also paid it. [10]Levi was not yet born. But Levi was in the body of his ancestor Abraham when Melchizedek met Abraham.

[11]The people were given the law[n] concerning the system of priests from the tribe of Levi. But they could not be made spiritually perfect through that system of priests. So there was a need for another priest to come. I mean a priest like Melchizedek, not Aaron. [12]And when a different kind of priest comes, the law must be changed, too. [13]We are saying these things about Christ. He belonged to a different tribe. No one from that tribe ever served as a priest at the altar. [14]It is clear that our Lord came from the tribe of Judah. And Moses said nothing about priests belonging to that tribe.

JESUS IS LIKE MELCHIZEDEK

[15]And this becomes even more clear. We see that another priest comes, who is like Melchizedek.[n] [16]He was not made a priest by human rules and laws. He became a priest through the power of his life, which continues forever. [17]In the Scriptures, this is said about him:

> "You are a priest forever,
>   a priest like Melchizedek."
>
> *Psalm 110:4*

6:20; 7:1, 15 **Melchizedek** A priest and king who lived in the time of Abraham. (Read Genesis 14:17–24.)
7:3 **No . . . was.** Literally, "Melchizedek was without father, without mother, without genealogy."
7:11 **The . . . law** This refers to the people of Israel who were given the law of Moses.

¹⁸The old rule is now set aside because it was weak and useless. ¹⁹The law of Moses could not make anything perfect. But now a better hope has been given to us. And with this hope we can come near to God.

²⁰Also, it is important that God made an oath when he made Jesus high priest. When the others became priests, there was no oath. ²¹But Christ became a priest with God's oath. God said:

> "The Lord has made a promise
>   and will not change his mind.
>   'You are a priest forever.'"
>
>   *Psalm 110:4*

²²So this means that Jesus is the guarantee of a better agreement[n] from God to his people.

²³Also, when one of the other priests died, he could not continue being a priest. So there were many priests. ²⁴But Jesus lives forever. He will never stop serving as priest. ²⁵So he is always able to save those who come to God through him. He can do this, because he always lives, ready to help those who come before God.

²⁶So Jesus is the kind of high priest that we need. He is holy; he has no sin in him. He is pure and not influenced by sinners. And he is raised above the heavens. ²⁷He is not like the other priests. They had to offer sacrifices every day, first for their own sins, and then for the sins of the people. But Christ does not need to do that. He offered his sacrifice only once and for all time. Christ offered himself! ²⁸The law chooses high priests who are men with all their weaknesses.

But the word of God's oath came later than the law. It made God's Son to be the high priest. And that Son has been made perfect forever.

JESUS IS OUR HIGH PRIEST

8 Here is the point of what we are saying: We do have a high priest who sits on the right side of God's throne in heaven. ²Our high priest serves in the Most Holy Place. He serves in the true place of worship that was made by God, not by men.

³Every high priest has the work of offering gifts and sacrifices to God. So our high priest must also offer something to God. ⁴If our high priest were now living on earth, he would not be a priest. I say this because there are already priests here who follow the law by offering gifts to God. ⁵The work that they do as priests is only a dim copy of what is in heaven. For when Moses was ready to build the Holy Tent, God warned him: "Be very careful to make everything by the plan I showed you on the mountain."[n] ⁶But the priestly work that has been given to Jesus is much greater than the work that was given to the other priests. In the same way, the new agreement that Jesus brought from God to his people is much greater than the old one. And the new agreement is based on promises of better things.

⁷If there was nothing wrong with the first agreement,[n] there would be no need for a second agreement. ⁸But God found something wrong with his people. He says:[n]

> Hold on to the hope we have been given. We have this hope as an anchor for the soul, sure and strong.
>
> —HEBREWS 6:18–19

7:22 agreement God gives a contract or agreement to his people. For the Jews, this agreement was the law of Moses. But now God has given a better agreement to his people through Christ.

8:5 "Be . . . mountain." Quotation from Exodus 25:40.

8:7 first agreement The contract God gave the Jewish people when he gave them the law of Moses.

8:8 But . . . says Some Greek copies read "But God found something wrong and says to his people."

"The time is coming, says the Lord,
　　when I will make a new agreement.
It will be with the people of Israel
　　and the people of Judah.
⁹ It will not be like the agreement
　　I made with their ancestors.
That was when I took them by the
　　hand
　　to bring them out of Egypt.
But they broke that agreement,
　　and I turned away from them, says
　　the Lord.
¹⁰ In the future I will make this
　　agreement
　　with the people of Israel, says the
　　Lord.
I will put my teachings in their
　　minds.
　　And I will write them on their
　　hearts.
I will be their God,
　　and they will be my people.
¹¹ People will no longer have to teach
　　their neighbors and relatives to
　　know the Lord.
This is because all will know me,
　　from the least to the most
　　important.
¹² I will forgive them for the wicked
　　things they did.
I will not remember their sins
　　anymore."　　*Jeremiah 31:31–34*

¹³God called this a new agreement, so he has made the first agreement old. And anything that is old and worn out is ready to disappear.

WORSHIP UNDER THE OLD AGREEMENT

9 The first agreement[n] had rules for worship. And it had a place on earth for worship. ²The Holy Tent was set up for this. The first area in the Tent was called the Holy Place. In it were the lamp and the table with the bread that was made holy for God. ³Behind the second curtain was a room called the Most Holy Place. ⁴In it was a golden altar for burning incense. Also there was the Ark of the Covenant that held the old agreement. The Ark of the Covenant was covered with gold. Inside this Ark of the Covenant was a golden jar of manna and Aaron's rod— the rod that once grew leaves. Also in it were the stone tablets of the old agreement. ⁵Above the Ark of the Covenant were the creatures with wings that showed God's glory. The wings of the creatures reached over the lid. But we cannot tell everything about these things now.

⁶Everything in the Tent was made ready in this way. Then the priests went into the first room every day to do their worship. ⁷But only the high priest could go into the second room, and he did that only once a year. He could never enter the inner room without taking blood with him. He offered that blood to God for himself and for the people's sins. These were sins people did without knowing that they were sinning. ⁸The Holy Spirit uses this to show that the way into the Most Holy Place was not open. This was while the system of the old Holy Tent was still being used. ⁹This is an example for the present time. It shows that the gifts and sacrifices offered cannot make the worshiper perfect in his heart. ¹⁰These gifts and sacrifices were only about food and drink and special washings. They were rules for the body, to be followed until the time of God's new way.

WORSHIP UNDER THE NEW AGREEMENT

¹¹But Christ has come as the high priest of the good things we now have.[n] The tent he entered is greater and more perfect. It is not made by men. It does not belong to this world. ¹²Christ entered the Most Holy Place only once—and for

---

9:1 **first agreement** The contract God gave the Jewish people when he gave them the law of Moses.
9:11 **good . . . have** Some Greek copies read "good things that are to come."

all time. He did not take with him the blood of goats and calves. His sacrifice was his own blood. He entered the Most Holy Place and set us free from sin forever. [13]The blood of goats and bulls and the ashes of a cow are sprinkled on the people who are unclean and this makes their bodies clean again.

[14]How much more is done by the blood of Christ. He offered himself through the eternal Spirit[n] as a perfect sacrifice to God. His blood will make our hearts clean from useless acts. We are made pure so that we may serve the living God.

[15]So Christ brings a new agreement from God to his people. Those who are called by God can now receive the blessings that God has promised. These blessings will last forever. They can have those things because Christ died so that the people who lived under the first agreement could be set free from sin.

[16]When there is a will,[n] it must be proven that the man who wrote that will is dead. [17]A will means nothing while the man is alive. It can be used only after he dies. [18]This is why even the first agreement could not begin without blood to show death. [19]First, Moses told all the people every command in the law. Next he took the blood of calves and mixed it with water. Then he used red wool and a branch of the hyssop plant to sprinkle the blood and water on the book of the law and on all the people. [20]He said, "This is the blood which begins the agreement that God commanded you to obey."[n] [21]In the same way, Moses sprinkled the blood on the Holy Tent and over all the things used in worship. [22]The law says that almost everything must be made clean by blood. And sins cannot be forgiven without blood to show death.

CHRIST'S DEATH TAKES AWAY SINS

[23]So the copies of the real things in heaven had to be made clean by animal sacrifices. But the real things in heaven need much better sacrifices. [24]For Christ did not go into the Most Holy Place made by men. It is only a copy of the real one. He went into heaven itself. He is there now before God to help us. [25]The high priest enters the Most Holy Place once every year. He takes with him blood that is not his own blood. But Christ did not go into heaven to offer himself many times. [26]Then he would have had to suffer many times since the world was made. But Christ came only once and for all time. He came at just the right time to take away all sin by sacrificing himself. [27]Everyone must die once. After a person dies, he is judged. [28]So Christ was offered as a sacrifice one time to take away the sins of many people. And he will come a second time, but not to offer himself for sin. He will come again to bring salvation to those who are waiting for him.

10 The law is only an unclear picture of the good things coming in the future. It is not a perfect picture of the real things. The people under the law offered the same sacrifices every year. These sacrifices can never make perfect those who come near to worship God. [2]If the law could make them perfect, the sacrifices would have already stopped. The worshipers would be made clean, and they would no longer feel guilty for their sins. [3]These sacrifices remind them of their sins every year, [4]because it is not possible for the blood of bulls and goats to take away sins.

[5]So when Christ came into the world, he said:

9:14 **Spirit** This refers to the Holy Spirit; to Christ's own spirit; or to the spiritual and eternal nature of his sacrifice.
9:16 **will** A legal document that shows how a person's money and property are to be distributed at the time of his death. This is the same word in Greek as "agreement" in verse 15.
9:20 **"This . . . obey."** Quotation from Exodus 24:8.

"You do not want sacrifices and
offerings.
But you have prepared a body for
me.
⁶ You do not ask for burnt offerings
and offerings to take away sins.
⁷ Then I said, 'Look, I have come.
It is written about me in the book.
My God, I have come to do what
you want.'" *Psalm 40:6–8*

⁸In this Scripture he first said, "You
do not want sacrifices and offerings.
You do not ask for burnt offerings and
offerings to take away sins." (These are
all sacrifices that the law commands.)
⁹Then he said, "Here I am. I have come
to do what you want." So God ends
the first system of sacrifices so that
he can set up the new system. ¹⁰Jesus
Christ did what God wanted him to do.
And because of this, we are made holy
through the sacrifice of his body. Christ
made this sacrifice only once, and for
all time.

¹¹Every day the priests stand and
do their religious service. Again and
again they offer the same sacrifices. But
those sacrifices can never take away
sins. ¹²But Christ offered one sacrifice
for sins, and it is good forever. Then he
sat down at the right side of God. ¹³And
now Christ waits there for his enemies
to be put under his power. ¹⁴With one
sacrifice he made perfect forever those
who are being made holy.

¹⁵The Holy Spirit also tells us about
this. First he says:

¹⁶ "In the future I will make this
agreement[n]
with the people of Israel, says the
Lord.
I will put my teachings in their
hearts.
And I will write them on their
minds." *Jeremiah 31:33*

¹⁷Then he says:

"Their sins and the evil things they
do—
I will not remember anymore."
Jeremiah 31:34

¹⁸And when these have been forgiven,
there is no more need for a sacrifice for
sins.

CONTINUE TO TRUST GOD

¹⁹So, brothers, we are completely free
to enter the Most Holy Place. We can do
this without fear because of the blood
of Jesus' death. ²⁰We can enter through
a new way that Jesus opened for us.
It is a living way. It leads through the
curtain—Christ's body. ²¹And we have a
great priest over God's house. ²²So let us
come near to God with a sincere heart
and a sure faith. We have been cleansed
and made free from feelings of guilt.
And our bodies have been washed with
pure water. ²³Let us hold firmly to the
hope that we have confessed. We can
trust God to do what he promised.

²⁴Let us think about each other and
help each other to show love and do
good deeds. ²⁵You should not stay away
from the church meetings, as some are
doing. But you should meet together
and encourage each other. Do this even
more as you see the Day[n] coming.

²⁶If we decide to go on sinning after
we have learned the truth, there is no
longer any sacrifice for sins. ²⁷There
is nothing but fear in waiting for the
judgment and the angry fire that will
destroy all those who live against God.
²⁸Any person who refused to obey the
law of Moses was found guilty from the
proof given by two or three witnesses.
He was put to death without mercy. ²⁹So
what do you think should be done to a
person who does not respect the Son
of God? He looks at the blood of the

10:16 **agreement** God gives a contract or agreement to his people. For the Jews, this agreement was the law of
Moses. But now God has given a better agreement to his people through Christ.
10:25 **Day** The day Christ will come to judge all people and take his people to live with him.

☆ Hebrews 10:23

The Jewish Christians were learning that believing in Jesus was a new—and better—way to follow God. They could go directly to God now instead of standing on the outside of the Temple. Christians then and now need to trust God's promises. And we should not forget the great thing Jesus did for us by dying and then being raised from the dead.

Has a friend ever lied to you? Has a family member ever broken a promise to you? They may not have meant to hurt you. But the lie makes it hard to trust that person again. People are not perfect. But God is! God never tells lies. And every promise God makes, he keeps—which seems like a big job because there are thousands of them in the Bible! But keeping promises isn't hard for God. It's what he does best.

. . . .

God promises good things to his kids. And you can trust him to do what he says.

agreement, the blood that made him holy, as no different from other men's blood. He insults the Spirit of God's grace. Surely he should have a much worse punishment. [30] We know that God said, "I will punish those who do wrong. I will repay them." [n] And he also said, "The Lord will judge his people." [n] [31] It is a terrible thing to fall into the hands of the living God.

[32] Remember those days in the past when you first learned the truth. You had a hard struggle with many sufferings, but you continued strong. [33] Sometimes you were hurt and persecuted before crowds of people. And sometimes you shared with those who were being treated that way. [34] You helped the prisoners. And you even had joy when all that you owned was taken

10:30 "I . . . them." Quotation from Deuteronomy 32:35.
10:30 "The Lord . . . people." Quotation from Deuteronomy 32:36; Psalm 135:14.

from you. You were joyful because you knew that you had something better and more lasting.

35 So do not lose the courage that you had in the past. It has a great reward. 36 You must hold on, so you can do what God wants and receive what he has promised. 37 For in a very short time,

> "The One who is coming will come.
>   He will not be late.
> 38 The person who is right with me
>   will have life because of his faith.
> But if he turns back with fear,
>   I will not be pleased with him."
>
> *Habakkuk 2:3–4*

39 But we are not those who turn back and are lost. We are people who have faith and are saved.

FAITH

11 Faith means being sure of the things we hope for. And faith means knowing that something is real even if we do not see it. 2 People who lived in the past became famous because of faith.

3 It is by faith we understand that the whole world was made by God's command. This means that what we see was made by something that cannot be seen.

4 It was by faith that Abel offered God a better sacrifice than Cain did. God said he was pleased with the gifts Abel offered. So God called Abel a good man because of his faith. Abel died, but through his faith he is still speaking.

5 It was by faith that Enoch was taken to heaven. He never died. He could not be found, because God had taken him away. Before he was taken, the Scripture says that he was a man who truly pleased God. 6 Without faith no one can please God. Anyone who comes to God must believe that he is real and that he rewards those who truly want to find him.

7 It was by faith Noah heard God's warnings about things that he could not yet see. He obeyed God and built a large boat to save his family. By his faith, Noah showed that the world was wrong. And he became one of those who are made right with God through faith.

8 It was by faith Abraham obeyed God's call to go to another place that God promised to give him. He left his own country, not knowing where he was to go. 9 It was by faith that he lived in the country God promised to give him. He lived there like a visitor who did not belong. He lived in tents with Isaac and Jacob, who had received that same promise from God. 10 Abraham was waiting for the city[n] that has real foundations—the city planned and built by God.

11 He was too old to have children, and Sarah was not able to have children. It was by faith that Abraham was made able to become a father. Abraham trusted God to do what he had promised.[n] 12 This man was so old that he was almost dead. But from him came as many descendants as there are stars in the sky. They are as many as the grains of sand on the seashore that cannot be counted.

13 All these great men died in faith. They did not get the things that God promised his people. But they saw them

> But we are not those who turn back and are lost. We are people who have faith and are saved.
>
> –HEBREWS 10:39

11:10 **city** The spiritual "city" where God's people live with him. Also called "the heavenly Jerusalem." (See Hebrews 12:22.)
11:11 **It . . . promised.** Some Greek copies refer to Sarah's faith, rather than Abraham's.

coming far in the future and were glad. They said that they were like visitors and strangers on earth. [14]When people say such things, then they show that they are looking for a country that will be their own country. [15]If they had been thinking about that country they had left, they could have gone back. [16]But those men were waiting for a better country—a heavenly country. So God is not ashamed to be called their God. For he has prepared a city for them.

[17]It was by faith that Abraham offered his son Isaac as a sacrifice. God made the promises to Abraham. But God tested him. And Abraham was ready to offer his own son as a sacrifice. [18]God had said, "The descendants I promised you will be from Isaac." [n] [19]Abraham believed that God could raise the dead. And really, it was as if Abraham got Isaac back from death.

[20]It was by faith that Isaac blessed the future of Jacob and Esau. [21]It was by faith that Jacob blessed each one of Joseph's sons. He did this while he was dying. Then he worshiped as he leaned on the top of his walking stick.

[22]It was by faith that Joseph spoke about the Israelites leaving Egypt while he was dying. He told them what to do with his body.

[23]It was by faith that Moses' parents hid him for three months after he was born. They saw that Moses was a beautiful baby. And they were not afraid to disobey the king's order.

[24]It was by faith that Moses, when he grew up, refused to be called the son of the king of Egypt's daughter. [25]He chose to suffer with God's people instead of enjoying sin for a short time. [26]He thought that it was better to suffer for the Christ than to have all the treasures of Egypt. He was looking only for God's reward. [27]It was by faith that Moses left Egypt. He was not afraid of the king's anger. Moses continued strong as if he could see the God that no one can see. [28]It was by faith that Moses prepared the Passover and spread the blood on the doors. It was spread so that the one who brings death would not kill the firstborn sons of Israel.

[29]It was by faith that the people crossed the Red Sea as if it were dry land. The Egyptians also tried to do it, but they were drowned.

[30]It was by faith that the walls of Jericho fell. They fell after the people had marched around the walls of Jericho for seven days.

[31]It was by faith that Rahab, the prostitute, welcomed the spies and was not killed with those who refused to obey God.

[32]Do I need to give more examples? I do not have time to tell you about Gideon, Barak, Samson, Jephthah, David, Samuel, and the prophets. [33]Through their faith they defeated kingdoms. They did what was right and received what God promised. They shut the mouths of lions, [34]stopped great fires and were saved from being killed with swords. They were weak, and yet were made strong. They were powerful in battle and defeated other armies. [35]Women received their dead relatives raised back to life. Others were tortured and refused to accept their freedom. They did this so that they could be raised from death to a better life. [36]Some were laughed at and beaten. Others were tied and put into prison. [37]They were killed with stones and they were cut in half.[n] They were killed with swords. Some wore the skins of sheep and goats. They were poor, abused, and treated badly. [38]The world was not good enough for them! They wandered in deserts and mountains, living in caves and holes in the earth.

[39]All these people are known for their faith. But none of them received what God had promised. [40]God planned to give us something better. Then

---

11:18 "The descendants . . . Isaac." Quotation from Genesis 21:12.
11:37 they were cut in half Some Greek copies also include, "and they were tested."

they would be made perfect, but only together with us.

FOLLOW JESUS' EXAMPLE

12 So we have many people of faith around us. Their lives tell us what faith means. So let us run the race that is before us and never give up. We should remove from our lives anything that would get in the way. And we should remove the sin that so easily catches us. ²Let us look only to Jesus. He is the one who began our faith, and he makes our faith perfect. Jesus suffered death on the cross. But he accepted the shame of the cross as if it were nothing. He did this because of the joy that God put before him. And now he is sitting at the right side of God's throne. ³Think about Jesus. He held on patiently while sinful men were doing evil things against him. Look at Jesus' example so that you will not get tired and stop trying.

GOD IS LIKE A FATHER

⁴You are struggling against sin, but your struggles have not yet caused you to be killed. ⁵You have forgotten his encouraging words for his sons:

"My son, don't think the Lord's
    discipline of you is worth
    nothing.
And don't stop trying when the
    Lord corrects you.
⁶ The Lord corrects those he loves.
And he punishes everyone
    he accepts as his child."
                    Proverbs 3:11–12

⁷So accept your sufferings as if they were a father's punishment. God does these things to you as a father punishing his sons. All sons are punished by their fathers. ⁸If you are never punished (and every son must be punished), you are not true children and not really sons. ⁹We have all had fathers here on earth who punished us. And we respected our fathers. So it is even more important that we accept punishment from the Father of our spirits. If we do this, we will have life. ¹⁰Our fathers on earth punished us for a short time. They punished us the way they thought was best. But God punishes us to help us, so that we can become holy as he is. ¹¹We do not enjoy punishment. Being punished is painful at the time. But later, after we have learned from being punished, we have peace, because we start living in the right way.

BE CAREFUL HOW YOU LIVE

¹²You have become weak. So make yourselves strong again. ¹³Keep on the right path so the weak will not stumble but rather be strengthened.

¹⁴Try to live in peace with all people. And try to live lives free from sin. If anyone's life is not holy, he will never see the Lord. ¹⁵Be careful that no one fails to get God's grace. Be careful that no one becomes like a bitter weed growing among you. A person like that can ruin all of you. ¹⁶Be careful that no one takes part in sexual sin. And be careful that no person is unholy like Esau. He sold all his rights as the oldest son for a single meal. ¹⁷You remember that after Esau did this, he wanted to get his father's blessing. He wanted this blessing so much that he cried. But his father refused to give him the blessing, because Esau could find no way to change what he had done.

¹⁸You have not come to a mountain that can be touched and that is burning with fire. You have not come to darkness, sadness and storms. ¹⁹You have not come to the noise of a trumpet or to the sound of a voice. When the people of Israel heard the voice, they begged not to have to hear another word. ²⁰They did not want to hear the command: "If anything, even an animal, touches the mountain, it must be put to death with stones." ⁿ ²¹What they saw

---

12:20 "If... stones." Quotation from Exodus 19:12–13.

was so terrible that Moses said, "I am shaking with fear." [n]

²²But you have not come to that kind of place. The new place you have come to is Mount Zion. [n] You have come to the city of the living God, the heavenly Jerusalem. You have come to thousands of angels gathered together with joy. ²³You have come to the meeting of God's firstborn [n] children. Their names are written in heaven. You have come to God, the judge of all people. And you have come to the spirits of good people who have been made perfect. ²⁴You have come to Jesus, the One who brought the new agreement from God to his people. You have come to the sprinkled blood [n] that has a better message than the blood of Abel. [n]

²⁵So be careful and do not refuse to listen when God speaks. They refused to listen to him when he warned them on earth. And they did not escape. Now God is warning us from heaven. So it will be worse for us if we refuse to listen to him. ²⁶When he spoke before, his voice shook the earth. But now he has promised, "Once again I will shake not only the earth but also the heavens." [n] ²⁷The words "once again" clearly show us that everything that was made will be destroyed. These are the things that can be shaken. And only the things that cannot be shaken will remain.

²⁸So let us be thankful because we have a kingdom that cannot be shaken. We should worship God in a way that pleases him. So let us worship him with respect and fear, ²⁹because our God is like a fire that burns things up.

13 Keep on loving each other as brothers in Christ. ²Remember to welcome strangers into your homes. Some people have done this and have welcomed angels without knowing it.

³Do not forget those who are in prison. Remember them as if you were in prison with them. Remember those who are suffering as if you were suffering with them.

⁴Marriage should be honored by everyone. Husband and wife should keep their marriage pure. God will judge guilty those who are sexually immoral and commit adultery. ⁵Keep your lives free from the love of money. And be satisfied with what you have. God has said,

"I will never leave you;
    I will never abandon you."
                    Deuteronomy 31:6

⁶So we can feel sure and say,

"I will not be afraid because the Lord
    is my helper.
People can't do anything to me."
                    Psalm 118:6

⁷Remember your leaders. They taught God's message to you. Remember how they lived and died, and copy their faith. ⁸Jesus Christ is the same yesterday, today, and forever.

⁹Do not let all kinds of strange teachings lead you into the wrong way. Your hearts should be strengthened by God's grace, not by obeying rules about foods. Obeying such rules does not help anyone.

¹⁰We have a sacrifice. But the priests who serve in the Holy Tent cannot eat from it. ¹¹The high priest carries the blood of animals into the Most Holy Place. There he offers this blood for sins. But the bodies of the animals are burned outside the camp. ¹²So Jesus also suffered outside the city. He died to make his people holy with his own

12:21 **"I . . . fear."** Quotation from Deuteronomy 9:19.
12:22 **Mount Zion** Another name for Jerusalem, here meaning the spiritual city of God's people.
12:23 **firstborn** The first son born in a Jewish family was given the most important place in the family and received special blessings. All of God's children are like that.
12:24 **sprinkled blood** The blood of Jesus' death.
12:24 **Abel** The son of Adam and Eve, who was killed by his brother Cain (Genesis 4:8).
12:26 **"Once . . . heavens."** Quotation from Haggai 2:6, 21.

blood. ¹³So let us go to Jesus outside the camp. We should accept the same shame that Jesus had.

¹⁴Here on earth we do not have a city that lasts forever. But we are looking for the city that we will have in the future. ¹⁵So through Jesus let us always offer our sacrifice to God. This sacrifice is our praise, coming from lips that speak his name. ¹⁶Do not forget to do good to others. And share with them what you have. These are the sacrifices that please God.

¹⁷Obey your leaders and be under their authority. These men are watching you because they are responsible for your souls. Obey them so that they will do this work with joy, not sadness. It will not help you to make their work hard.

¹⁸Continue praying for us. We feel sure about what we are doing, because we always want to do the right thing. ¹⁹And I beg you to pray that God will send me back to you soon.

²⁰⁻²¹I pray that the God of peace will give you every good thing you need so that you can do what he wants. God is the One who raised from death our Lord Jesus, the Great Shepherd of the sheep. God raised him because of the blood of his death. His blood began the agreement that God made with his people. And this agreement is eternal. I pray that God, through Christ, will do in us what pleases him. And to Jesus Christ be glory forever and ever. Amen.

²²My brothers, I beg you to listen patiently to this message I have written to encourage you. This letter is not very long. ²³I want you to know that our brother Timothy has been let out of prison. If he arrives soon, we will both come to see you.

²⁴Greet all your leaders and all of God's people. Those from Italy send greetings to you.

²⁵God's grace be with you all.

James

FAITH AND WISDOM

1 From James, a servant of God and of the Lord Jesus Christ. To all of God's people who are scattered everywhere in the world:

Greetings.

²My brothers, you will have many kinds of troubles. But when these things happen, you should be very happy. ³You know that these things are testing your faith. And this will give you patience. ⁴Let your patience show itself perfectly in what you do. Then you will be perfect and complete. You will have everything you need. ⁵But if any of you needs wisdom, you should ask God for it. God is generous. He enjoys giving to all people, so God will give you wisdom. ⁶But when you ask God, you must believe. Do not doubt God. Anyone who doubts is like a wave in the sea. The wind blows the wave up and down. ⁷⁻⁸He who doubts is thinking two different things at the same time. He cannot decide about anything he does. A person like that should not think that he will receive anything from the Lord.

TRUE RICHES

⁹If a believer is poor, he should take pride that God has made him spiritually rich. ¹⁰If he is rich, he should take pride that God has shown him that he is spiritually poor. The rich person will die like a wild flower in the grass. ¹¹The sun rises and becomes hotter and hotter. The heat makes the plants very dry, and the flower falls off. The flower was beautiful, but now it is dead. It is the same with a rich person. While he is still taking care of his business, he will die.

TEMPTATION IS NOT FROM GOD

¹²When a person is tempted and still continues strong, he should be happy. After he has proved his faith, God will reward him with life forever. God promised this to all people who love him. ¹³When someone is being tempted, he should not say, "God is tempting me." Evil cannot tempt God, and God himself does not tempt anyone. ¹⁴It is the evil that a person wants that tempts him. His own evil desire leads him away and holds him. ¹⁵This desire causes sin. Then the sin grows and brings death.

¹⁶My dear brothers, do not be fooled about this. ¹⁷Every good action and every perfect gift is from God. These good gifts come down from the Creator of the sun, moon, and stars. God does not change like their shifting shadows. ¹⁸God decided to give us life through the word of truth. He wanted us to be the most important of all the things he made.

LISTENING AND OBEYING

¹⁹My dear brothers, always be willing to listen and slow to speak. Do not become angry easily. ²⁰Anger will not help you live a good life as God wants. ²¹So put out of your life every evil thing and every kind of wrong you do. Don't be proud but accept God's teaching that is planted in your hearts. This teaching can save your souls.

²²Do what God's teaching says; do not just listen and do nothing. When you only sit and listen, you are fooling yourselves. ²³A person who hears God's teaching and does nothing is like a man looking in a mirror. ²⁴He sees his face, then goes away and quickly forgets what he looked like. ²⁵But the truly happy person is the one who carefully

studies God's perfect law that makes people free. He continues to study it. He listens to God's teaching and does not forget what he heard. Then he obeys what God's teaching says. When he does this, it makes him happy.

THE TRUE WAY TO WORSHIP GOD

[26] A person might think he is religious. But if he says things he should not say, then he is just fooling himself. His "religion" is worth nothing. [27] Religion that God the Father accepts is this: caring for orphans or widows who need help; and keeping yourself free from the world's evil influence. This is the kind of religion that God accepts as pure and good.

LOVE ALL PEOPLE

2 My dear brothers, you are believers in our glorious Lord Jesus Christ. So never think that some people are more important than others. [2] Suppose someone comes into your church meeting wearing very nice clothes and a gold ring. At the same time a poor man comes in wearing old, dirty clothes. [3] You show special attention to the one wearing nice clothes. You say, "Please, sit here in this good seat." But you say to the poor man, "Stand over there," or "Sit on the floor by my feet!" [4] What are you doing? You are making some people more important than others. With evil thoughts you are deciding which person is better.

[5] Listen, my dear brothers! God chose the poor in the world to be rich with faith. He chose them to receive the kingdom God promised to people who love him. [6] But you show no respect to the poor man. And you know that it is the rich who are always trying to control your lives. And they are the ones who take you to court. [7] They are the ones who say bad things against Jesus, who owns you.

[8] One law rules over all other laws.

This royal law is found in the Scriptures: "Love your neighbor as you love yourself." [n] If you obey this law, then you are doing right. [9] But if you are treating one person as if he were more important than another, then you are sinning. That royal law proves that you are guilty of breaking God's law. [10] A person might follow all of God's law. But if he fails to obey even one command, he is guilty of breaking all the commands in that law. [11] God said, "You must not be guilty of adultery." [n] The same God also said, "You must not murder anyone." [n] So if you do not take part in adultery, but you murder someone, then you are guilty of breaking all of God's law. [12] You will be judged by the law that makes people free. You should remember this in everything you say and do. [13] Yes, you must show mercy to others, or God will not show mercy to you when he judges you. But the person who shows mercy can stand without fear when he is judged.

FAITH AND GOOD WORKS

[14] My brothers, if someone says he has faith, but does nothing, his faith is worth nothing. Can faith like that save him? [15] A brother or sister in Christ might need clothes or might need food. [16] And you say to him, "God be with you! I hope you stay warm and get plenty to eat." You say this, but you do not give that person the things he needs. Unless you help him, your words are worth nothing. [17] It is the same with faith. If faith does nothing, then that faith is dead, because it is alone.

[18] Someone might say, "You have faith, but I do things. Show me your faith! Your faith does nothing. I will show you my faith by the things I do." [19] You believe there is one God. Good! But the demons believe that, too! And they shake with fear.

[20] You foolish person! Must you be

2:8 **"Love . . . yourself."** Quotation from Leviticus 19:18.
2:11 **"You . . . adultery."** Quotation from Exodus 20:14 and Deuteronomy 5:18.
2:11 **"You . . . anyone."** Quotation from Exodus 20:13 and Deuteronomy 5:17.

shown that faith that does nothing is worth nothing? [21]Abraham is our father. He was made right with God by the things he did. He offered his son Isaac to God on the altar. [22]So you see that Abraham's faith and the things he did worked together. His faith was made perfect by what he did. [23]This shows the full meaning of the Scripture that says: "Abraham believed God, and God accepted Abraham's faith, and that faith made him right with God." [n] And Abraham was called "God's friend." [n] [24]So you see that a person is made right with God by the things he does. He cannot be made right by faith only.

[25]Another example is Rahab, who was a prostitute. But she was made right with God by something she did: She helped the spies for God's people. She welcomed them into her home and helped them escape by a different road.

[26]A person's body that does not have a spirit is dead. It is the same with faith. Faith that does nothing is dead!

CONTROLLING THE THINGS WE SAY

3 My brothers, not many of you should become teachers. You know that we who teach will be judged more strictly than others. [2]We all make many mistakes. If there were a person who never said anything wrong, he would be perfect. He would be able to control his whole body, too. [3]We put bits into the mouths of horses to make them obey us. We can control their whole bodies. [4]It is the same with ships. A ship is very big, and it is pushed by strong winds.

But a very small rudder controls that big ship. The man who controls the rudder decides where the ship will go. The ship goes where the man wants. [5]It is the same with the tongue. It is a small part of the body, but it brags about doing great things.

A big forest fire can be started with only a little flame. [6]And the tongue is like a fire. It is a whole world of evil among the parts of our bodies. The tongue spreads its evil through the whole body. It starts a fire that influences all of life. The tongue gets this fire from hell. [7]People can tame every kind of wild animal, bird, reptile, and fish, and they have tamed them. [8]But no one can tame the tongue. It is wild and evil. It is full of poison that can kill. [9]We use our tongues to praise our Lord and Father, but then we curse people. And God made them like himself. [10]Praises and curses come from the same mouth! My brothers, this should not happen. [11]Do good and bad water flow from the same spring? [12]My brothers, can a fig tree make olives? Can a grapevine make figs? No! And a well full of salty water cannot give good water.

TRUE WISDOM

[13]Is there anyone among you who is truly wise and understanding? Then he should show his wisdom by living right. He should do good things without being proud. A wise person does not brag. [14]But if you are selfish and have bitter jealousy in your hearts, you have no reason to brag. Your bragging is a lie that hides the truth. [15]That kind of "wisdom" does not come from God.

> Religion that God the Father accepts is this: caring for orphans or widows who need help.
> –JAMES 1:27

2:23 **"Abraham ... God."** Quotation from Genesis 15:6.
2:23 **"God's friend."** These words about Abraham are found in 2 Chronicles 20:7 and Isaiah 41:8.

That "wisdom" comes from the world. It is not spiritual. It is from the devil. [16]Where there is jealousy and selfishness, there will be confusion and every kind of evil. [17]But the wisdom that comes from God is like this: First, it is pure. Then it is also peaceful, gentle, and easy to please. This wisdom is always ready to help those who are troubled and to do good for others. This wisdom is always fair and honest. [18]When people work for peace in a peaceful way, they receive the good result of their right living.

GIVE YOURSELVES TO GOD

4 Do you know where your fights and arguments come from? They come from the selfish desires that make war inside you. [2]You want things, but you do not have them. So you are ready to kill and are jealous of other people. But you still cannot get what you want. So you argue and fight. You do not get what you want because you do not ask God. [3]Or when you ask, you do not receive because the reason you ask is wrong. You want things only so that you can use them for your own pleasures.

[4]So, you people are not loyal to God! You should know that loving the world is the same as hating God. So if a person wants to be a friend of the world, he makes himself God's enemy. [5]Do you think the Scripture means nothing? It says, "The Spirit that God made to live in us wants us for himself alone." [n] [6]But God gives us even more grace, as the Scripture says,

"God is against the proud,
    but he gives grace to the humble."
                            Proverbs 3:34

[7]So give yourselves to God. Stand against the devil, and the devil will run away from you. [8]Come near to God, and God will come near to you. You are sinners. So clean sin out of your lives. You are trying to follow God and the world at the same time. Make your thinking pure. [9]Be sad, cry, and weep! Change your laughter into crying. Change your joy into sadness. [10]Humble yourself before the Lord, and he will honor you.

YOU ARE NOT THE JUDGE

[11]Brothers, do not say bad things about each other. If you say bad things about your brother in Christ or judge him, then you are saying bad things about the law he follows. You are also judging the law he follows. And when you are judging the law, you are not a follower of the law. You have become a judge! [12]God is the only One who makes laws, and he is the only Judge. He is the only One who can save and destroy. So it is not right for you to judge your neighbor.

LET GOD PLAN YOUR LIFE

[13]Some of you say, "Today or tomorrow we will go to some city. We will stay there a year, do business, and make money." [14]But you do not know what will happen tomorrow! Your life is like a mist. You can see it for a short time, but then it goes away. [15]So you should say, "If the Lord wants, we will live and do this or that." [16]But now you are proud and you brag. All of this bragging is wrong. [17]And when a person knows the right thing to do, but does not do it, then he is sinning.

A WARNING TO THE RICH

5 You rich people, listen! Cry and be very sad because of the trouble that will come to you. [2]Your riches will rot, and your clothes will be eaten by moths. [3]Your gold and silver will rust, and rust will be a proof that you were wrong. It will eat your bodies like fire. You saved your treasure for the last days. [4]Men worked in your fields, but you did not pay them. They harvested your crops and are crying out against you. Now the Lord of heaven's armies has heard

4:5 "The Spirit . . . alone." These words may be from Exodus 20:5.

their cries. [5]Your life on earth was full of rich living. You pleased yourselves with everything you wanted. You made yourselves fat, like an animal ready to be killed. [6]You showed no mercy to the innocent man. You murdered him. He cannot stand against you.

BE PATIENT

[7]Brothers, be patient until the Lord comes again. A farmer is patient. He waits for his valuable crop to grow from the earth. He waits patiently for it to receive the first rain and the last rain. [8]You, too, must be patient. Do not give up hope. The Lord is coming soon. [9]Brothers, do not complain against each other. If you do not stop complaining, you will be judged guilty. And the Judge is ready to come! [10]Brothers, follow the example of the prophets who spoke for the Lord. They suffered many hard things, but they were patient. [11]We say they are happy because they were able to do this. You have heard about Job's patience. You know that after all his trouble, the Lord helped him. This shows that the Lord is full of mercy and is kind.

BE CAREFUL WHAT YOU SAY

[12]My brothers, it is very important that you not use an oath when you make a promise. Don't use the name of heaven,

---

☆ James 5:8

Some believers in the church were getting impatient about many things. One of those things was when Jesus was coming back. Life was hard for them, and they wanted Jesus to rescue them and take them straight to heaven. The leader who wrote the Book of James told the people to be patient. Don't stop hoping. Jesus is kind and full of mercy. He will come back soon.

Do you have a hard time waiting? Do you say things like, "I want it right now"? Sometimes it is hard to wait for what we want. We need to trust that God will give us what we need. We should not give up hope. Even when we do not understand why we have to wait, we need to remember that God knows what is best for us. Trust God and believe that he will take care of you.

God always wants what is best for you. But he will help you be patient when the good things take more time to show up than you expect.

earth, or anything else to prove what you say. When you mean yes, say only "yes." When you mean no, say only "no." Do this so that you will not be judged guilty.

THE POWER OF PRAYER

¹³If one of you is having troubles, he should pray. If one of you is happy, he should sing praises. ¹⁴If one of you is sick, he should call the church's elders. The elders should pour oil on him[n] in the name of the Lord and pray for him. ¹⁵And the prayer that is said with faith will make the sick person well. The Lord will heal him. And if he has sinned, God will forgive him. ¹⁶Confess your sins to each other and pray for each other. Do this so that God can heal you. When a good man prays, great things happen. ¹⁷Elijah was a man just like us. He prayed that it would not rain. And it did not rain on the land for three and a half years! ¹⁸Then Elijah prayed again. And the rain came down from the sky, and the land grew crops again.

SAVING A SOUL

¹⁹My brothers, one of you may wander away from the truth. And someone may help him come back. ²⁰Remember this: Anyone who brings a sinner back from the wrong way will save that sinner's soul from death. By doing this, that person will cause many sins to be forgiven.

5:14 **pour oil on him** Oil was used like medicine, so that is probably how the believers used it.

1 Peter

ENCOURAGEMENT FOR SUFFERING CHRISTIANS

1 From Peter, an apostle of Jesus Christ.

To God's chosen people who are away from their homes. You are scattered all around Pontus, Galatia, Cappadocia, Asia, and Bithynia. [2]God the Father planned long ago to choose you by making you his holy people. Making you holy is the Spirit's work. God wanted you to obey him and to be made clean by the blood of the death of Jesus Christ. Grace and peace be yours more and more.

A LIVING HOPE

[3]Praise be to the God and Father of our Lord Jesus Christ. God has great mercy, and because of his mercy he gave us a new life. He gave us a living hope because Jesus Christ rose from death. [4]Now we hope for the blessings God has for his children. These blessings are kept for you in heaven. They cannot be destroyed or be spoiled or lose their beauty. [5]God's power protects you through your faith, and it keeps you safe until your salvation comes. That salvation is ready to be given to you at the end of time. [6]This makes you very happy. But now for a short time different kinds of troubles may make you sad. [7]These troubles come to prove that your faith is pure. This purity of faith is worth more than gold. Gold can be proved to be pure by fire, but gold can be destroyed. But the purity of your faith will bring you praise and glory and honor when Jesus Christ comes again. [8]You have not seen Christ, but still you love him. You cannot see him now, but you believe in him. You are filled with a joy that cannot be explained. And that joy is full of glory. [9]Your faith has a goal, to save your souls. And you are receiving that goal—your salvation.

[10]The prophets searched carefully and tried to learn about this salvation. They spoke about the grace that was coming to you. [11]The Spirit of Christ was in the prophets. And the Spirit was telling about the sufferings that would happen to Christ and about the glory that would come after those sufferings. The prophets tried to learn about what the Spirit was showing them. They tried to learn when those things would happen and what the world would be like at that time. [12]It was shown to them that their service was not for themselves. It was for you. They were serving you when they told about the truths you have now heard. The men who preached the Good News to you told you those things. They did it with the help of the Holy Spirit that was sent from heaven. These are truths that even the angels want very much to know about.

A CALL TO HOLY LIVING

[13]So prepare your minds for service and have self-control. All your hope should be for the gift of grace that will be yours when Jesus Christ comes again. [14]In the past you did not understand, so you did the evil things you wanted. But now you are children of God who obey. So do not live as you lived in the past. [15]But be holy in all that you do, just as God is holy. God is the One who called you. [16]It is written in the Scriptures: "You must be holy, because I am holy." [n]

[17]You pray to God and call him Father. And this Father judges each man's work equally. So while you are here on earth, you should live with respect for God. [18]You know that in the past you were living in a worthless way. You got that way of living from the

☆ 1 Peter 1:22

Peter, one of Jesus' twelve followers, also wrote letters to the believers. In his first letter, he reminded Christians that they were pure because they accepted Jesus. And because they had Jesus, they had the love of God in them. For that reason, they could love others like God loved them.

Do you obey your parents when they give you chores? Do you clean your room, put your clothes away, or help set the table? Sometimes we forget to do what we are told. And sometimes obeying is just plain hard. But obeying God is easy! If you believe in Jesus, then you have already obeyed God. The Bible says, "Now you have made yourselves pure by obeying the truth." And Jesus is the truth. Do you know what happens when you obey the truth? You can love others like God loves you.

* * *

When you know you belong to God, you can have "true love" for other people in God's family.

---

people who lived before you. But you were saved from that useless life. You were bought, but not with something that ruins like gold or silver. ¹⁹You were bought with the precious blood of the death of Christ, who was like a pure and perfect lamb. ²⁰Christ was chosen before the world was made. But he was shown to the world in these last times for you. ²¹You believe in God through Christ. God raised Christ from death and gave him glory. So your faith and your hope are in God.

²²Now you have made yourselves pure by obeying the truth. Now you can have true love for your brothers. So love each other deeply with all your heart. ²³You have been born again. This new life did not come from something that dies, but from something that cannot die. You were born again through God's living message that continues forever. ²⁴The Scripture says,

"All people are like the grass.
 And all their strength is like the
  flowers of the field.
The grass dies and the flowers fall.
²⁵ But the word of the Lord will live
  forever."   *Isaiah 40:6–8*

And this is the word that was preached to you.

JESUS IS THE LIVING STONE

2 So then, get rid of all evil and all lying. Do not be a hypocrite. Do not be jealous or speak evil of others. Put all these things out of your life. ²As newborn babies want milk, you should want the pure and simple teaching. By it you can mature in your salvation. ³For you have already examined and seen how good the Lord is.

⁴The Lord Jesus is the "stone" [n] that lives. The people of the world did not want this stone. But he was the stone God chose. To God he was worth much. So come to him. ⁵You also are like living stones. Let yourselves be used to build a spiritual temple—to be holy priests who offer spiritual sacrifices to God. He will accept those sacrifices through Jesus Christ. ⁶The Scripture says:

"I will put a stone in the ground in
        Jerusalem.
Everything will be built on this
        important and precious rock.
Anyone who trusts in him
    will never be disappointed."
                                    Isaiah 28:16

⁷This stone is worth much to you who believe. But to the people who do not believe, he is

"the stone that the builders did not
        want.
It has become the cornerstone."
                                    Psalm 118:22

⁸To people who do not believe, he is

"a stone that causes people to
        stumble.
It is a rock that makes them fall."
                                    Isaiah 8:14

They stumble because they do not obey what God says. This is what God planned to happen to them.

⁹But you are chosen people. You are the King's priests. You are a holy nation. You are a nation that belongs to God alone. God chose you to tell about the wonderful things he has done. He called you out of darkness into his wonderful light. ¹⁰At one time you were not God's people. But now you are his people. In the past you had never received mercy. But now you have received God's mercy.

LIVE FOR GOD

¹¹Dear friends, you are like visitors and strangers in this world. So I beg you to stay away from the evil things your bodies want to do. These things fight against your soul. ¹²People who do not believe are living all around you. They might say that you are doing wrong. So live good lives. Then they will see the good things you do, and they will give glory to God on the day when Christ comes again.

OBEY EVERY HUMAN AUTHORITY

¹³Obey the people who have authority in this world. Do this for the Lord. Obey the king, who is the highest authority. ¹⁴And obey the leaders who are sent by the king. They are sent to punish those who do wrong and to praise those who do right. ¹⁵So when you do good, you stop foolish people from saying stupid things about you. This is what God wants. ¹⁶Live as free men. But do not use your freedom as an excuse to do evil. Live as servants of God. ¹⁷Show respect for all people. Love the brothers and sisters of God's family. Respect God. Honor the king.

FOLLOW CHRIST'S EXAMPLE

¹⁸Slaves, accept the authority of your masters. Do this with all respect. You should obey masters who are good and kind, and you should obey masters who are bad. ¹⁹A person might have to suffer even when he has done nothing wrong.

2:4 "stone" The most important stone in God's spiritual temple or house (his people).

But if he thinks of God and bears the pain, this pleases God. [20]If you are punished for doing wrong, there is no reason to praise you for bearing punishment. But if you suffer for doing good, and you are patient, then that pleases God. [21]That is what you were called to do. Christ suffered for you. He gave you an example to follow. So you should do as he did.

[22] "He did no sin.
    He never lied."   *Isaiah 53:9*

[23]People insulted Christ, but he did not insult them in return. Christ suffered, but he did not threaten. He let God take care of him. God is the One who judges rightly. [24]Christ carried our sins in his body on the cross. He did this so that we would stop living for sin and start living for what is right. And we are healed because of his wounds. [25]You were like sheep that went the wrong way. But now you have come back to the Shepherd and Overseer of your souls.

WIVES AND HUSBANDS

3 In the same way, you wives should accept the authority of your husbands. Then, if some husbands have not obeyed God's teaching, they will be persuaded to believe. You will not need to say a word to them. They will be persuaded by the way their wives live. [2]Your husbands will see the pure lives that you live with your respect for God. [3]It is not fancy hair, gold jewelry, or fine clothes that should make you beautiful. [4]No, your beauty should come from within you—the beauty of a gentle and quiet spirit. This beauty will never disappear, and it is worth very much to God. [5]It was the same with the holy women who lived long ago and followed God. They made themselves beautiful in this way. They accepted the authority of their husbands. [6]Sarah obeyed Abraham, her husband, and called him her master. And you women are true children of Sarah if you always do what is right and are not afraid.

[7]In the same way, you husbands should live with your wives in an understanding way. You should show respect to them. They are weaker than you. But God gives them the same blessing that he gives you—the grace that gives true life. Do this so that nothing will stop your prayers.

SUFFERING FOR DOING RIGHT

[8]Finally, all of you should live together in peace. Try to understand each other. Love each other as brothers. Be kind and humble. [9]Do not do wrong to a person to pay him back for doing wrong to you. Or do not insult someone to pay him back for insulting you. But ask God to bless that person. Do this, because you yourselves were called to receive a blessing. [10]The Scripture says,

"A person must do these things
    to enjoy life and have many, happy
        days.
He must not say evil things.
    He must not tell lies.
[11] He must stop doing evil and do good.
    He must look for peace and work
        for it.
[12] The Lord sees the good people.
    He listens to their prayers.
But the Lord is against
    those who do evil."

                    Psalm 34:12–16

[13]If you are always trying to do good,

> You were like sheep that went the wrong way. But now you have come back to the Shepherd and Overseer of your souls.
>
> –1 PETER 2:25

no one can really hurt you. [14]But you may suffer for doing right. Even if that happens, you are blessed.

> "Don't be afraid of the things they fear.
> Do not dread those things.
> [15] But respect Christ as the holy Lord in your hearts." *Isaiah 8:12–13*

Always be ready to answer everyone who asks you to explain about the hope you have. [16]But answer in a gentle way and with respect. Always feel that you are doing right. Then, those who speak evil of your good life in Christ will be made ashamed. [17]It is better to suffer for doing good than for doing wrong. Yes, it is better, if that is what God wants. [18]Christ himself died for you. And that one death paid for your sins. He was not guilty, but he died for those who are guilty. He did this to bring you all to God. His body was killed, but he was made alive in the spirit. [19]And in the spirit he went and preached to the spirits in prison. [20]These were the spirits who refused to obey God long ago in the time of Noah. God was waiting patiently for them while Noah was building the boat. Only a few people—eight in all— were saved by water. [21]That water is like baptism that now saves you—not the washing of dirt from the body, but the promise made to God from a good heart. And this is because Jesus Christ was raised from death. [22]Now Jesus has gone into heaven and is at God's right side. He rules over angels, authorities, and powers.

CHANGED LIVES

4 Christ suffered while he was in his body. So you should strengthen yourselves with the same way of thinking Christ had. The person who has suffered in his body is finished with sin. [2]Strengthen yourselves so that you will live your lives here on earth doing what God wants, not doing the evil things that people want. [3]In the past you wasted too much time doing what the non-believers like to do. You lived for the body and evil desires. You were getting drunk, you had wild and drunken parties, and you did wrong by worshiping idols. [4]Non-believers think it is strange that you do not do the many wild and wasteful things that they do. And so they insult you. [5]But they will have to explain about what they have done. They must explain to God who is ready to judge the living and the dead. [6]The Good News was preached to those who are now dead. By their dying, they were judged like all men. But the Good News was preached to them so that they could live in the spirit as God lives.

USE GOD'S GIFTS WISELY

[7]The time is near when all things will end. So keep your minds clear, and control yourselves. Then you will be able to pray. [8]Most importantly, love each other deeply. Love has a way of not looking at others' sins. [9]Open your homes to each other, without complaining. [10]Each of you received a spiritual gift. God has shown you his grace in giving you different gifts. And you are like servants who are responsible for using God's gifts. So be good servants and use your gifts to serve each other. [11]Anyone who speaks should speak words from God. The person who serves should serve with the strength that God gives. You should do these things so that in everything God will be praised through Jesus Christ. Power and glory belong to him forever and ever. Amen.

SUFFERING AS A CHRISTIAN

[12]My friends, do not be surprised at the painful things you are now suffering. These things are testing your faith. So do not think that something strange is happening to you. [13]But you should be happy that you are sharing in Christ's sufferings. You will be happy and full of joy when Christ comes again in glory.

[14]When people insult you because you follow Christ, then you are blessed. You are blessed because the glorious Spirit, the Spirit of God, is with you. [15]Do not suffer for murder, theft, or any other crime, nor because you trouble other people. [16]But if you suffer because you are a Christian, then do not be ashamed. You should praise God because you wear that name. [17]It is time for judgment to begin, and it will begin with God's family. If that judging begins with us, what will happen to those people who do not obey the Good News of God?

[18] "It is very hard for a good person to
be saved.
Then the wicked person and
the sinner will surely be lost!" [n]

[19]So then those who suffer as God wants them to should trust their souls to him. God is the One who made them, and they can trust him. So they should continue to do what is right.

THE FLOCK OF GOD

5 Now I have something to say to the elders in your group. I am also

---

4:18 "It ... lost!" Quotation from Proverbs 11:31 in the Septuagint, the Greek version of the Old Testament.

⭐ 1 Peter 5:7

Tell God everything you're worried about and then let it go. We are God's children and he cares for us.

Abby's mom was sick. Her mom took some medicine and went to bed for the night. Her dad said that God was going to help her mom feel better. Abby loved her mom and was worried about her. Abby was even a little bit afraid. What if her mom didn't get better? Abby went to her room and talked to God. She started to lose the worry, and she was not afraid anymore. And best of all—her mom was better by the next morning! Jesus does not want us to worry. He is strong enough to take care of us. He wants us to tell him when things bother us because he cares about us.

When you feel worried, talk to Jesus. He can take your worry away and give you peace.

an elder. I myself have seen Christ's sufferings. And I will share in the glory that will be shown to us. I beg you to ²take care of God's flock, his people, that you are responsible for. Watch over it because you want to, not because you are forced to do it. That is how God wants it. Do it because you are happy to serve, not because you want money. ³Do not be like a ruler over people you are responsible for. Be good examples to them. ⁴Then when Christ, the Head Shepherd, comes, you will get a crown. This crown will be glorious, and it will never lose its beauty.

⁵In the same way, younger men should be willing to be under older men. And all of you should be very humble with each other.

> "God is against the proud,
>   but he gives grace to the humble."
> *Proverbs 3:34*

⁶So be humble under God's powerful hand. Then he will lift you up when the right time comes. ⁷Give all your worries to him, because he cares for you.

⁸Control yourselves and be careful! The devil is your enemy. And he goes around like a roaring lion looking for someone to eat. ⁹Refuse to give in to the devil. Stand strong in your faith. You know that your Christian brothers and sisters all over the world are having the same sufferings you have.

¹⁰Yes, you will suffer for a short time. But after that, God will make everything right. He will make you strong. He will support you and keep you from falling. He is the God who gives all grace. He called you to share in his glory in Christ. That glory will continue forever. ¹¹All power is his forever and ever. Amen.

FINAL GREETINGS

¹²I wrote this short letter with the help of Silas. I know that he is a faithful brother in Christ. I wrote to comfort and encourage you. I wanted to tell you that this is the true grace of God. Stand strong in that grace.

¹³The church in Babylon sends you greetings. They were chosen the same as you. Mark, my son in Christ, also greets you. ¹⁴Give each other a kiss of Christian love when you meet.

Peace to all of you who are in Christ.

2 Peter

CORRECTING FALSE TEACHINGS

1 From Simon Peter, a servant and apostle of Jesus Christ.

To you who have received a faith as valuable as ours. You received that faith because our God and Savior Jesus Christ is fair and does what is right. [2]Grace and peace be given to you more and more. You will have grace and peace because you truly know God and Jesus our Lord.

GOD HAS GIVEN US BLESSINGS

[3]Jesus has the power of God. His power has given us everything we need to live and to serve God. We have these things because we know him. Jesus called us by his glory and goodness. [4]Through his glory and goodness, he gave us the very great and rich gifts he promised us. With those gifts you can share in God's nature. And so the world will not ruin you with its evil desires.

[5]Because you have these blessings, you should try as much as you can to add these things to your lives: to your faith, add goodness; and to your goodness, add knowledge; [6]and to your knowledge, add self-control; and to your self-control, add the ability to hold on; and to your ability to hold on, add service for God; [7]and to your service for God, add kindness for your brothers and sisters in Christ; and to this kindness, add love. [8]If all these things are in you and are growing, they will help you never to be useless. They will help your knowledge of our Lord Jesus Christ make your lives better. [9]But if anyone does not have these things, he cannot see clearly. He is blind. He has forgotten that he was made clean from his past sins.

[10]My brothers, God called you and chose you to be his. Try hard to show that you really are God's chosen people. If you do all these things, you will never fall. [11]And you will be given a very great welcome into the kingdom of our Lord and Savior Jesus Christ. That kingdom continues forever.

[12]You know these things, and you are very strong in the truth. But I will always help you to remember these things. [13]I think it is right for me to help you remember while I am still living here on earth. [14]I know that I must soon leave this body. Our Lord Jesus Christ has shown me that. [15]I will try the best I can to help you remember these things always. I want you to be able to remember them even after I am gone.

WE SAW CHRIST'S GLORY

[16]We have told you about the powerful coming of our Lord Jesus Christ. What we told you were not just smart stories that someone invented. But we saw the greatness of Jesus with our own eyes. [17]Jesus heard the voice of God, the Greatest Glory. That was when Jesus received honor and glory from God the Father. The voice said, "This is my Son, and I love him. I am very pleased with him." [18]We heard that voice. It came from heaven while we were with Jesus on the holy mountain.

[19]This makes us more sure about the message the prophets gave. And it is good for you to follow closely what they said. Their message is like a light shining in a dark place. That light shines until the day begins and the morning star rises in your hearts. [20]Most of all, you must understand this: No prophecy in the Scriptures ever comes from the prophet's own interpretation. [21]No prophecy ever came from what a man wanted to say. But men led by the Holy Spirit spoke words from God.

FALSE TEACHERS

2 There used to be false prophets among God's people, just as there

☆ 2 Peter 1:5–9

God has given us everything we need to live godly lives. So to be more and more like Jesus, we should use the gifts he gave us. Some of these gifts are goodness, knowledge, self-control, kindness, and love. But if we don't let these things show up, it means we forgot that our hearts were made clean through Jesus.

When you were born, you became part of your family. But babies don't do very much except eat, sleep, and dirty up diapers. Babies grow and become children. Children grow and become teenagers. Teens grow and become adults. This is just like being a Christian. Getting God's forgiveness is awesome. But there is so much more! We can add good things to our faith, which will help us grow up. Adding things like patience, kindness, and love for others makes our lives better. And it makes our families happy too.

. . . .

God already put some great gifts in you. Get them working and become the great person he made you to be!

---

are now. And you will have some false teachers in your group. They will secretly teach things that are wrong—teachings that will cause people to be lost. They will even refuse to accept the Master, Jesus, who bought their freedom. And so they will quickly destroy themselves. [2] Many will follow their evil ways and say evil things about the Way of truth. [3] Those false teachers only want your money. So they will use you by telling you what is not true. But God has already judged them guilty. And they will not escape the One who will destroy them.

[4] When angels sinned, God did not let them go free without punishment. God sent them to hell and put them in caves[n] of darkness. They are being held there to be judged. [5] And God punished the evil people who lived long ago. He brought a flood to the world that was full of people who were against him. But God saved Noah and seven other people with him. Noah was a man who preached about being right with God. [6] And God also punished the evil cities of Sodom and Gomorrah.[n] He burned those cities until there was nothing left but ashes. He made those cities

---

2:4 caves Some Greek copies read "chains."
2:6 Sodom and Gomorrah Two cities God destroyed because the people were so evil.

an example to show what will happen to those who are against God. [7]But God saved Lot from those cities. Lot, a good man, was troubled because of the sinful behavior of evil people. [8](Lot was a good man, but he lived with evil people every day. His good heart was hurt by the evil things that he saw and heard.) [9]And so the Lord knows how to save those who serve him. He will save them when troubles come. And the Lord will hold evil people and punish them, while waiting for the Judgment Day. [10]That punishment is especially for those who live by doing the evil things their sinful selves want, and for those who hate the Lord's authority.

These false teachers do anything they want and brag about it. They are not afraid to say bad things about the glorious angels. [11]The angels are much stronger and more powerful than false teachers. But even the angels do not accuse them with insults before[n] the Lord. [12]But these men say bad things about what they do not understand. They are like animals that act without thinking. These animals are born to be caught and killed. And, like wild animals, these false teachers will be destroyed. [13]They have caused many people to suffer; so they themselves will suffer. That is their pay for what they have done. They take pleasure in doing evil things openly. So they are like dirty spots and stains among you. They bring shame to you in the meals that you eat together. [14]Every time they look at a woman they want her. Their desire for sin is never satisfied. They lead weak people into the trap

of sin. They have taught their hearts to be selfish. God will punish them. [15]These false teachers left the right road and lost their way. They followed the way that Balaam went. Balaam was the son of Beor, who loved being paid for doing wrong. [16]But a donkey told Balaam that he was sinning. And the donkey is an animal that cannot talk. But the donkey spoke with a man's voice and stopped the prophet's crazy thinking.

[17]Those false teachers are like rivers that have no water. They are like clouds blown by a storm. A place in the blackest darkness has been kept for them. [18]They brag with words that mean nothing. By their evil desires they lead people into the trap of sin. They lead away people who are just beginning to escape from other people who live in error. [19]They promise them freedom, but they themselves are not free. They are slaves of things that will be destroyed. For a person is a slave of anything that controls him. [20]They were made free from the evil in the world by knowing our Lord and Savior Jesus Christ. But if they return to evil things and those things control them, then it is worse for them than it was before. [21]Yes, it would be better for them to have never known the right way. That would be better than to know the right way and then to turn away from the holy teaching that was given to them. [22]What they did is like this true saying: "A dog eats what it throws up."[n] And, "After a pig is washed, it goes back and rolls in the mud."

> We are waiting for what he promised—a new heaven and a new earth where goodness lives.
>
> —2 PETER 3:13

2:11 **before** Some Greek copies read "from."
2:22 **"A dog...up."** Quotation from Proverbs 26:11.

JESUS WILL COME AGAIN

3 My friends, this is the second letter I have written to you. I wrote both letters to you to help your honest minds remember something. ²I want you to remember the words that the holy prophets spoke in the past. And remember the command that our Lord and Savior gave us through your apostles. ³It is important for you to understand what will happen in the last days. People will laugh at you. They will live doing the evil things they want to do. ⁴They will say, "Jesus promised to come again. Where is he? Our fathers have died. But the world continues the way it has been since it was made." ⁵But they do not want to remember what happened long ago. God spoke and made heaven and earth. He made the earth from water and with water. ⁶Then the world was flooded and destroyed with water. ⁷And that same word of God is keeping heaven and earth that we have now. They are being kept to be destroyed by fire. They are being kept for the Judgment Day and the destruction of all who are against God.

⁸But do not forget this one thing, dear friends: To the Lord one day is like a thousand years, and a thousand years is like one day. ⁹The Lord is not slow in doing what he promised—the way some people understand slowness. But God is being patient with you. He does not want anyone to be lost. He wants everyone to change his heart and life.

¹⁰But the day the Lord comes again will be a surprise, like a thief. The skies will disappear with a loud noise. Everything in the skies will be destroyed by fire. And the earth and everything in it will be exposed.ⁿ ¹¹In that way everything will be destroyed. So what kind of people should you be? You should live holy lives and serve God. ¹²You should wait for the day of God and look forward to its coming. When that day comes, the skies will be destroyed with fire, and everything in the skies will melt with heat. ¹³But God made a promise to us. And we are waiting for what he promised—a new heaven and a new earth where goodness lives.

¹⁴Dear friends, we are waiting for this to happen. So try as hard as you can to be without sin and without fault. Try to be at peace with God. ¹⁵Remember that we are saved because our Lord is patient. Our dear brother Paul told you the same thing when he wrote to you with the wisdom that God gave him. ¹⁶Paul writes about this in all his letters. Sometimes there are things in Paul's letters that are hard to understand. And some people explain these things falsely. They are ignorant and weak in faith. They also falsely explain the other Scriptures. But they are destroying themselves by doing that.

¹⁷Dear friends, you already know about this. So be careful. Do not let those evil people lead you away by the wrong they do. Be careful so that you will not fall from your own strong faith. ¹⁸But grow in the grace and knowledge of our Lord and Savior Jesus Christ. Glory be to him now and forever! Amen.

3:10 **And . . . exposed.** Some Greek copies read "And everything in it will be burned up."

1 John

GOD FORGIVES OUR SINS

1 We write you now about something
that has always existed.
We have heard.
We have seen with our own eyes.
We have watched,
and we have touched with our hands.

We write to you about the Word[n] that
gives life. [2]He who gives life was shown
to us. We saw him, and we can give
proof about it. And now we tell you
that he has life that continues forever.
The one who gives this life was with
God the Father. God showed him to us.
[3]Now we tell you what we have seen
and heard because we want you to
have fellowship with us. The fellowship we share together is with God the
Father and his Son, Jesus Christ. [4]We
write this to you so that we may be full
of joy.[n]

[5]Here is the message we have heard
from God and now tell to you: God is
light,[n] and in him there is no darkness
at all. [6]So if we say that we have fellowship with God, but we continue living
in darkness, then we are liars. We do
not follow the truth. [7]God is in the
light. We should live in the light, too. If
we live in the light, we share fellowship with each other. And when we live
in the light, the blood of the death of
Jesus, God's Son, is making us clean
from every sin.

[8]If we say that we have no sin, we
are fooling ourselves, and the truth is
not in us. [9]But if we confess our sins, he
will forgive our sins. We can trust God.
He does what is right. He will make us
clean from all the wrongs we have done.
[10]If we say that we have not sinned,
then we make God a liar. We do not
accept God's true teaching.

JESUS IS OUR HELPER

2 My dear children, I write this
letter to you so that you will not
sin. But if anyone does sin, we have
Jesus Christ to help us. He is the
Righteous One. He defends us before
God the Father. [2]Jesus died in our place
to take away our sins. And Jesus is the
way that all people can have their sins
taken away, too.

[3]If we obey what God has told us to
do, then we are sure that we truly know
God. [4]If someone says, "I know God!"
but does not obey God's commands,
then he is a liar. The truth is not in him.
[5]But if someone obeys God's teaching,
then God's love has truly arrived at its
goal in him. This is how we know that
we are following God: [6]Whoever says
that God lives in him must live as Jesus
lived.

THE COMMAND TO LOVE OTHERS

[7]My dear friends, I am not writing a
new command to you. It is the same
command you have had since the
beginning. It is the teaching you have
already heard. [8]But I am writing a new
command to you. This command is
true; you can see its truth in Jesus and
in yourselves. The darkness is passing away, and the true light is already
shining.

[9]Someone says, "I am in the light."[n]
But if he hates his brother, he is still
in the darkness. [10]Whoever loves his
brother lives in the light, and there
is nothing in him that will cause him
to do wrong. [11]But whoever hates his

1:1 **Word** The Greek word is "logos," meaning any kind of communication. It could be translated "message." Here,
it means Christ. Christ was the way God told people about himself.
1:4 **so . . . joy** Some Greek copies read "so that you may be full of joy."
1:5; 2:9 **light** This word is used to show what God is like. It means goodness or truth.

brother is in darkness. He lives in darkness and does not know where he is going. The darkness has made him blind.

[12] I write to you, dear children,
because your sins are forgiven
through Christ.
[13] I write to you, fathers,
because you know the One who
existed from the beginning.
I write to you, young men,
because you have defeated the Evil
One.
[14] I write to you, children,
because you know the Father.
I write to you, fathers,
because you know the One who
existed from the beginning.
I write to you, young men,
because you are strong;
the word of God lives in you,
and you have defeated the Evil One.

[15] Do not love the world or the things in the world. If anyone loves the world, the love of the Father is not in him. [16] These are the evil things in the world: wanting things to please our sinful selves, wanting the sinful things we see, being too proud of the things we have. But none of those things comes from the Father. All of them come from the world. [17] The world is passing away. And everything that people want in the world is passing away. But the person who does what God wants lives forever.

REJECT THE ENEMIES OF CHRIST

[18] My dear children, the end is near! You have heard that the Enemy of Christ is coming. And now many enemies of Christ are already here. So we know that the end is near. [19] Those enemies of Christ were in our group. But they left us. They did not really belong with us. If they were really part of our group, then they would have stayed with us. But they left. This shows that none of them really belonged with us.

[20] You have the gift[n] that the Holy One gave you. So you all know the truth.[n] [21] Why do I write to you? Do I write because you do not know the truth? No, I write this letter because you do know the truth. And you know that no lie comes from the truth.

[22] So who is the liar? It is the person who says Jesus is not the Christ. A person who says Jesus is not the Christ is the enemy of Christ. He does not believe in the Father or in his Son. [23] If anyone does not believe in the Son, he does not have the Father. But whoever accepts the Son has the Father, too. [24] Be sure that you continue to follow the teaching that you heard from the beginning. If you continue in that teaching, you will stay in the Son and in the Father. [25] And this is what the Son promised to us—life forever.

[26] I am writing this letter about those people who are trying to lead you the wrong way. [27] Christ gave you a special gift. You still have this gift in you. So you do not need any other teacher. The gift he gave you teaches you about everything. This gift is true, not false. So continue to live in Christ, as his gift taught you.

[28] Yes, my dear children, live in him. If we do this, we can be without fear on the day when Christ comes back. We will not need to hide and be ashamed when he comes. [29] You know that Christ is righteous. So you know that all who do what is right are God's children.

WE ARE GOD'S CHILDREN

3 The Father has loved us so much! He loved us so much that we are called children of God. And we really

---

2:20 **gift** This might mean the Holy Spirit. Or it might mean teaching or truth as in verse 24.
2:20 **So...truth.** Some Greek copies read "So you know all things."

are his children. But the people in the world do not understand that we are God's children, because they have not known him. [2]Dear friends, now we are children of God. We have not yet been shown what we will be in the future. But we know that when Christ comes again, we will be like him. We will see him as he really is. [3]Christ is pure. And every person who has this hope in Christ keeps himself pure like Christ.

[4]When a person sins, he breaks God's law. Yes, sinning is the same as living against God's law. [5]You know that Christ came to take away sins. There is no sin in Christ. [6]So the person who lives in Christ does not go on sinning. If he goes on sinning, he has never really understood Christ and has never known him.

[7]Dear children, do not let any person lead you the wrong way. Christ is righteous. To be like Christ, a person must do what is right. [8]The devil has been sinning since the beginning. Anyone who continues to sin belongs to the devil. The Son of God came for this purpose: to destroy the devil's work.

[9]When God makes someone his child, that person does not go on sinning. The new life God gave that person stays in him. So he is not able to go on sinning, because he has become a child of God. [10]So we can see who God's children are and who the devil's children are. Those who do not do what is right are not children of God. And anyone who does not love his brother is not a child of God.

WE MUST LOVE EACH OTHER

[11]This is the teaching you have heard from the beginning: We must love each other. [12]Do not be like Cain who belonged to the Evil One. Cain killed his brother. He killed his brother because the things Cain did were evil, and the things his brother did were good.

[13]Brothers, do not be surprised when the people of this world hate you. [14]We know that we have left death and have come into life. We know this because we love our brothers in Christ. Whoever does not love is still in death. [15]Everyone who hates his brother is a murderer.[n] And you know that no murderer has eternal life in him. [16]This is how we know what real love is: Jesus gave his life for us. So we should give our lives for our brothers. [17]Suppose a believer is rich enough to have all that he needs. He sees his brother in Christ who is poor and does not have what he needs. What if the believer does not help the poor brother? Then the believer does not have God's love in his heart. [18]My children, our love should not be only words and talk. Our love must be true love. And we should show that love by what we do.

[19-20]This is the way we know that we belong to the way of truth. When our hearts make us feel guilty, we can still have peace before God. God is greater than our hearts, and he knows everything.

[21]My dear friends, if we do not feel that we are doing wrong, we can be without fear when we come to God. [22]And God gives us the things we ask for. We receive these things because we obey God's commands, and we do what pleases him. [23]This is what God commands: that we believe in his Son, Jesus Christ, and that we love each other, just as he commanded. [24]The person who obeys God's commands lives in God. And God lives in him. How do we know that God lives in us? We know because of the Spirit whom God gave us.

3:15 Everyone . . . murderer. If a person hates his brother in Christ, then in his mind he has killed his brother. Jesus taught about this sin to his followers (Matthew 5:21–26).

WARNING AGAINST FALSE TEACHERS

4 My dear friends, many false prophets are in the world now. So do not believe every spirit. But test the spirits to see if they are from God. [2] This is how you can know God's Spirit: One spirit says, "I believe that Jesus is the Christ who came to earth and became a man." That Spirit is from God. [3] Another spirit refuses to say this about Jesus. That spirit is not from God but is the spirit of the Enemy of Christ. You have heard that the Enemy of Christ is coming. And now he is already in the world.

[4] My dear children, you belong to God. So you have defeated them because God's Spirit, who is in you, is greater than the devil, who is in the world. [5] And they belong to the world. What they say is from the world, and the world listens to them. [6] But we are from God, and those who know God listen to us. But those who are not from God do not listen to us. That is how we know the Spirit that is true and the spirit that is false.

LOVE COMES FROM GOD

[7] Dear friends, we should love each other, because love comes from God. The person who loves has become God's child and knows God. [8] Whoever does not love does not know God, because God is love. [9] This is how God showed his love to us: He sent his only Son into the world to give us life through him. [10] True love is God's love for us, not our love for God. God sent his Son to die in our place to take away our sins.

[11] That is how much God loved us, dear friends! So we also must love each other. [12] No one has ever seen God. But if we love each other, God lives in us.

If we love each other, God's love has reached its goal. It is made perfect in us.

[13] We know that we live in God and God lives in us. We know this because God gave us his Spirit. [14] We have seen that the Father sent his Son to be the Savior of the world. That is what we teach. [15] If someone says, "I believe that Jesus is the Son of God," then God lives in him. And he lives in God. [16] And so we know the love that God has for us, and we trust that love.

God is love. Whoever lives in love lives in God, and God lives in him. [17] If God's love is made perfect in us, then we can be without fear on the day God judges us. We will be without fear, because in this world we are like him. [18] Where God's love is, there is no fear, because God's perfect love takes away fear. It is punishment that makes a person fear. So love is not made perfect in the person who has fear. [19] We love because God first loved us. [20] If someone says, "I love God," but hates his brother, he is a liar. He can see his brother, but he hates him. So he cannot love God, whom he has never seen. [21] And God gave us this command: Whoever loves God must also love his brother.

We love
because God
first loved us.
−1 JOHN 4:19

FAITH IN THE SON OF GOD

5 Everyone who believes that Jesus is the Christ is God's child. The person who loves the Father also loves the Father's children. [2] How do we know that we love God's children? We know because we love God and we obey his commands. [3] Loving God means obeying his commands. And God's commands are not too hard for us. [4] Everyone who is a child of God has the power to win against the world. It is our faith that wins the victory against the

world. ⁵So the one who conquers the world is the person who believes that Jesus is the Son of God.

⁶Jesus Christ is the One who came with water[n] and with blood.[n] He did not come by water only. He came by both water and blood. And the Spirit says that this is true. The Spirit is the truth. ⁷So there are three witnesses:[n] ⁸the Spirit, the water, and the blood. These three witnesses agree. ⁹We believe people when they say something is true.

But what God says is more important. And he has told us the truth about his own Son. ¹⁰Anyone who believes in the Son of God has the truth that God told us. Anyone who does not believe makes God a liar. He does not believe what God told us about his Son. ¹¹This is what God told us: God has given us eternal life, and this life is in his Son. ¹²Whoever has the Son has life. But the person who does not have the Son of God does not have life.

5:6 **water** This probably means the water of Jesus' baptism.
5:6 **blood** This probably means the blood of Jesus' death.
5:7 **So . . . witnesses** A few very late Greek copies and the Latin Vulgate read "in heaven: the Father, the Word, and the Holy Spirit, and these three witnesses agree. ⁸And there are three witnesses on earth."

☆ 1 John 5:13–15

John the apostle wrote a letter to believers to tell them how much God loves them. John told them and us that when we pray, God will hear us. He cares for us and knows what we need.

Kyle has three brothers and two sisters. Things get busy—and noisy—at home. And sometimes Kyle feels ignored. But then his mom or dad does something amazing. His mom takes him out for lunch or his dad takes him to play mini golf. Kyle talks and talks. And his parents listen to everything he says. God is like that. He loves you, and he wants you to talk to him. And he is never distracted by others. You have his complete attention. He listens to you. Every time.

. . . .

Prayer is just another word for "talking to God." God hears you every time you pray. And he will answer you.

WE HAVE ETERNAL LIFE NOW

[13] I write this letter to you who believe in the Son of God. I write so that you will know that you have eternal life now. [14] We can come to God with no doubts. This means that when we ask God for things (and those things agree with what God wants for us), then God cares about what we say. [15] God listens to us every time we ask him. So we know that he gives us the things that we ask from him.

[16] Suppose someone sees his brother in Christ sinning (sin that does not lead to eternal death). That person should pray for his brother who is sinning. Then God will give the brother life. I am talking about people whose sin does not lead to eternal death. There is sin that leads to death. I do not mean that a person should pray about that sin. [17] Doing wrong is always sin. But there is sin that does not lead to eternal death.

[18] We know that anyone who is God's child does not continue to sin. The Son of God keeps him safe, and the Evil One cannot hurt him. [19] We know that we belong to God. But the Evil One controls the whole world. [20] And we know that the Son of God has come and has given us understanding. Now we can know God, the One who is true. And our lives are in that true God and in his Son, Jesus Christ. He is the true God, and he is eternal life. [21] So, dear children, keep yourselves away from false gods.

Revelation

JOHN TELLS ABOUT THIS BOOK

1 This is the revelation[n] of Jesus Christ. God gave this revelation to Jesus, to show his servants what must soon happen. And Jesus sent his angel to show it to his servant John. [2]John has told everything that he has seen. It is the truth that Jesus Christ told him; it is the message from God. [3]The one who reads the words of God's message is happy. And the people who hear this message and do what is written in it are happy. The time is near when all of this will happen.

JESUS' MESSAGE TO THE CHURCHES

[4]From John,

To the seven churches in Asia:

Grace and peace to you from the One who is and was and is coming, and from the seven spirits before his throne, [5]and from Jesus Christ. Jesus is the faithful witness. He is first among those raised from death. He is the ruler of the kings of the earth.

He is the One who loves us. And he is the One who made us free from our sins with the blood of his death. [6]He made us to be a kingdom of priests who serve God his Father. To Jesus Christ be glory and power forever and ever! Amen.

[7]Look, Jesus is coming with the clouds! Everyone will see him, even those who stabbed him. And all peoples of the earth will cry loudly because of him. Yes, this will happen! Amen.

[8]The Lord God says, "I am the Alpha and the Omega.[n] I am the One who is and was and is coming. I am the All-Powerful."

[9]I am John, and I am your brother in Christ. We are together in Jesus, and we share in these things: in suffering, in the kingdom, and in patience. I was on the island of Patmos[n] because I had preached God's message and the truth about Jesus. [10]On the Lord's day the Spirit took control of me. I heard a loud voice behind me that sounded like a trumpet. [11]The voice said, "Write what you see and send that book to the seven churches: to Ephesus, Smyrna, Pergamum, Thyatira, Sardis, Philadelphia, and Laodicea."

[12]I turned to see who was talking to me. When I turned, I saw seven golden lampstands. [13]I saw someone among the lampstands who was "like a Son of Man."[n] He was dressed in a long robe. He had a gold band around his chest. [14]His head and hair were white like wool, as white as snow. His eyes were like flames of fire. [15]His feet were like bronze that glows hot in a furnace. His voice was like the noise of flooding water. [16]He held seven stars in his right hand. A sharp two-edged sword came out of his mouth. He looked like the sun shining at its brightest time.

[17]When I saw him, I fell down at his feet like a dead man. He put his right hand on me and said, "Do not be afraid! I am the First and the Last. [18]I am the One who lives. I was dead, but look: I am alive forever and ever! And I hold the keys of death and where the dead are. [19]So write the things you see, what is now and what will happen later. [20]Here is the hidden meaning of the seven stars that you saw in my right hand and the seven golden lampstands that you saw: The seven lampstands are the

---

1:1 **revelation** A making known of truth that has been hidden.
1:8 **the Alpha and the Omega** The first and last letters in the Greek alphabet. This means "the beginning and the end."
1:9 **Patmos** A small island in the Aegean Sea, near the coast of Asia Minor (modern Turkey).
1:13 **"like ... Man"** "Son of Man" is a name Jesus called himself. It showed he was God's Son, but he was also a man. See dictionary.

☆ Revelation 1:3

Revelation is the last book in the Bible. It describes things that will happen in the future. Jesus comes back to earth on a huge white horse. A sparkling city comes down from the sky. But more than that, Revelation tells Christians that they should read God's message—the Bible. Reading, understanding, and following God's word makes us happy.

Most of us love to hear stories, especially stories from the Bible. You might have read about Joseph and his colorful coat. You saw baby Moses get rescued from the river and then grow up to lead the people of Israel out of Egypt. And do you remember the boy David knocking down a giant with one small rock?

The best story of all, though, is about God's love for you and me! He loved us so much that he sent Jesus to save us from our sins. If you have not asked Jesus to come into your life yet, do it now. You are never too young or too old. Having Jesus in your heart is the secret to a happy life!

. . . .

The Bible is God's special message to us. It's like a love letter straight from him. Read on!

seven churches. The seven stars are the angels of the seven churches.

TO THE CHURCH IN EPHESUS

2 "Write this to the angel of the church in Ephesus:

"The One who holds the seven stars in his right hand and walks among the seven golden lampstands says this to you. [2]I know what you do. You work hard, and you never give up. I know that you do not accept evil people. You have tested those who say that they are apostles but really are not. You found that they are liars. [3]You continue to serve me. You have suffered troubles for my name, and you have not given up.

[4]"But I have this against you: You have left the love you had in the beginning. [5]So remember where you were

before you fell. Change your hearts and do what you did at first. If you do not change, I will come to you. I will take away your lampstand from its place. [6]But there is something you do that is right: You hate what the Nicolaitans[n] do, as much as I.

[7]"Every person who has ears should listen to what the Spirit says to the churches. To him who wins the victory I will give the right to eat the fruit from the tree of life. This tree is in the garden of God.

TO THE CHURCH IN SMYRNA

[8]"Write this to the angel of the church in Smyrna:

"The One who is the First and the Last says this to you. He is the One who died and came to life again. [9]I know your troubles. I know that you are poor, but really you are rich! I know the bad things that some people say about you. They say they are Jews, but they are not true Jews. They are a synagogue that belongs to Satan. [10]Do not be afraid of what will happen to you. I tell you, the devil will put some of you in prison to test you. You will suffer for ten days. But be faithful, even if you have to die. If you are faithful, I will give you the crown of life.

[11]"Everyone who has ears should listen to what the Spirit says to the churches. He who wins the victory will not be hurt by the second death.

TO THE CHURCH IN PERGAMUM

[12]"Write this to the angel of the church in Pergamum:

"The One who has the sharp two-edged sword says this to you. [13]I know where you live. You live where Satan has his throne. But you are true to me. You did not refuse to tell about your faith in me even during the time of Antipas. Antipas was my faithful witness who was killed in your city. Your city is where Satan lives.

[14]"But I have a few things against you: You have some there who follow the teaching of Balaam. Balaam taught Balak how to cause the people of Israel to sin. They sinned by eating food offered to idols and by taking part in sexual sins. [15]You also have some who follow the teaching of the Nicolaitans.[n] [16]So change your hearts and lives! If you do not, I will come to you quickly and fight against them with the sword that comes out of my mouth. [17]Everyone who has ears should listen to what the Spirit says to the churches!

"I will give the hidden manna to everyone who wins the victory. I will also give him a white stone with a new name written on it. No one knows this new name except the one who receives it.

> When (Jesus) opens something, it cannot be closed. And when he closes something, it cannot be opened.
> —REVELATION 3:7

TO THE CHURCH IN THYATIRA

[18]"Write this to the angel of the church in Thyatira:

"The Son of God is saying these things. He is the One who has eyes that blaze like fire and feet like shining bronze. He says this to you: [19]I know what you do. I know about your love, your faith, your service, and your patience. I know that you are doing more now than you did at first. [20]But I have this against you: You let that woman Jezebel do what she wants. She says that she is a prophetess. But she is leading my servants away with her

---

2:6, 15 **Nicolaitans** This is the name of a religious group that followed false beliefs and ideas.

teaching. Jezebel leads them to take part in sexual sins and to eat food that is offered to idols. ²¹I have given her time to change her heart and turn away from her sin. But she does not want to change. ²²And so I will throw her on a bed of suffering. And all those who take part in adultery with her will suffer greatly. I will do this now if they do not turn away from the wrongs she does. ²³I will also kill her followers. Then all the churches will know that I am the One who knows what people feel and think. And I will repay each of you for what you have done.

²⁴"But others of you in Thyatira have not followed her teaching. You have not learned what some call Satan's deep secrets. This is what I say to you: I will not put any other load on you. ²⁵Only continue the way you are until I come.

²⁶"I will give power to everyone who wins the victory and continues to the end to do what I want. I will give him power over the nations:

²⁷ 'You will make them obey you by
    punishing them with an iron
    rod.
  You will break them into pieces like
    pottery.'   *Psalm 2:9*

²⁸This is the same power I received from my Father. I will also give him the morning star. ²⁹Everyone who has ears should listen to what the Spirit says to the churches.

TO THE CHURCH IN SARDIS

3 "Write this to the angel of the church in Sardis:

"The One who has the seven spirits and the seven stars says this to you. I know what you do. People say that you are alive, but really you are dead. ²Wake up! Make yourselves stronger while you still have something left and before it dies completely. I have found that what you are doing is not good enough for my God. ³So do not forget what you have received and heard. Obey it. Change your hearts and lives! You must wake up, or I will come to you and surprise you like a thief. And you will not know when I will come. ⁴But you have a few there in Sardis who have kept themselves clean. They will walk with me. They will wear white clothes, because they are worthy. ⁵He who wins the victory will be dressed in white clothes like them. I will not take away his name from the book of life. I will say that he belongs to me before my Father and before his angels. ⁶Everyone who has ears should listen to what the Spirit says to the churches.

TO THE CHURCH IN PHILADELPHIA

⁷"Write this to the angel of the church in Philadelphia:

"The One who is holy and true says this to you. He holds the key of David. When he opens something, it cannot be closed. And when he closes something, it cannot be opened. ⁸I know what you do. I have put an open door before you, and no one can close it. I know that you have a little strength. But you have followed my teaching. And you were not afraid to speak my name. ⁹Listen! There is a synagogue that belongs to Satan. Those in this synagogue say they are Jews, but they are liars. They are not true Jews. I will make them come before you and bow at your feet. They will know that I have loved you. ¹⁰You have followed my teaching about not giving up. So I will keep you from the time of trouble that will come to the whole world. This trouble will test those who live on earth.

¹¹"I am coming soon. Continue the way you are now. Then no one will take away your crown. ¹²I will make the one who wins the victory a pillar in the temple of my God. He will never have to leave it. I will write on him the name of my God and the name of the city of my God. This city is the new Jerusalem."

3:12 Jerusalem This name is used to mean the spiritual city God built for his people.

☆ Revelation 4:8

One of the pictures described in Revelation is of God's throne in heaven. Around the throne are four creatures with wings and lots of eyes. They never stop praising God. Day and night, they say, "Holy, holy, holy is the Lord God All-Powerful. He was, he is, and he is coming."

Have you ever lost something you cared about—your favorite toy, a pet, or maybe even someone in your family? How did it make you feel when it wasn't there anymore? It probably made you feel sad. We don't like it when we lose things. It's good to know that Jesus can't be lost. You see, Jesus is always there. He always was. And he always will be. He is right there with you when you feel sad or mad, happy or glad. Because he is always with you, you can talk to him. Telling Jesus how awesome he is actually makes you feel better.

. . . .

Like the singing creatures in heaven, you can praise Jesus anytime. Even something simple like, "You're here with me!" is praise.

It comes down out of heaven from my God. I will also write on him my new name. [13]Every person who has ears should listen to what the Spirit says to the churches.

TO THE CHURCH IN LAODICEA

[14]"Write this to the angel of the church in Laodicea:

"The Amen[n] is the One who is the faithful and true witness. He is the ruler of all that God has made. He says this to you: [15]I know what you do. You are not hot or cold. I wish that you were hot or cold! [16]But you are only warm—not hot, not cold. So I am ready to spit you out of my mouth. [17]You say you are rich. You think you have become wealthy and do not need anything. But you do not know that you are really miserable, pitiful, poor, blind, and naked. [18]I advise you to buy gold from me—gold made pure in fire. Then you can be truly rich. Buy from me clothes that are white. Then you can cover your shameful nakedness.

3:14 **Amen** Used here as a name for Jesus, it means to agree fully that something is true.

Buy from me medicine to put on your eyes. Then you can truly see.

[19]"I correct and punish those whom I love. So be eager to do right. Change your hearts and lives. [20]Here I am! I stand at the door and knock. If anyone hears my voice and opens the door, I will come in and eat with him. And he will eat with me.

[21]"He who wins the victory will sit with me on my throne. It was the same with me. I won the victory and sat down with my Father on his throne. [22]Everyone who has ears should listen to what the Spirit says to the churches."

JOHN SEES HEAVEN

4 After this I looked, and there before me was an open door in heaven. And I heard the same voice that spoke to me before. It was the voice that sounded like a trumpet. The voice said, "Come up here, and I will show you what must happen after this." [2]Then the Spirit took control of me. There before me was a throne in heaven. Someone was sitting on the throne. [3]The One who sat on the throne looked like precious stones, like jasper and carnelian. All around the throne was a rainbow the color of an emerald. [4]Around the throne there were 24 other thrones. There were 24 elders[n] sitting on the 24 thrones. The elders were dressed in white, and they had golden crowns on their heads. [5]Lightning flashes and noises of thunder came from the throne. Before the throne there were seven lamps burning. These lamps are the seven spirits of God. [6]Also before the throne there was something that looked like a sea of glass. It was clear like crystal.

Around the throne, on each side, there were four living things. These living things had eyes all over them, in front and in back. [7]The first living thing was like a lion. The second was like a calf. The third had a face like a man. The fourth was like a flying eagle. [8]Each of these four living things had six wings. The living things were covered all over with eyes, inside and out. Day and night they never stop saying:

> "Holy, holy, holy is the Lord God
> All-Powerful.
> He was, he is, and he is coming."

[9]These living things give glory and honor and thanks to the One who sits on the throne. He is the One who lives forever and ever. And every time the living things do this, [10]the 24 elders bow down before the One who sits on the throne. The elders worship him who lives forever and ever. They put their crowns down before the throne and say:

> [11] "Our Lord and God! You are worthy
> to receive glory and honor and
> power.
> You made all things.
> Everything existed and was made
> because you wanted it."

5 Then I saw a scroll in the right hand of the One sitting on the throne. The scroll had writing on both sides. It was kept closed with seven seals. [2]And I saw a powerful angel. He called in a loud voice, "Who is worthy to break the seals and open the scroll?" [3]But there was no one in heaven or on earth or under the earth who could open the scroll or look inside it. [4]I cried and cried because there was no one who was worthy to open the scroll or look inside. [5]But one of the elders said to me, "Do not cry! The Lion[n] from the tribe of Judah has won the victory. He is David's descendant. He is able to open the scroll and its seven seals."

[6]Then I saw a Lamb standing in the center of the throne with the four living things around it. The elders were also

---

4:4 24 elders Elder means "older." Here the elders probably represent God's people.
5:5 Lion Here refers to Christ.

around the Lamb. The Lamb looked as if he had been killed. He had seven horns and seven eyes. These are the seven spirits of God that were sent into all the world. [7] The Lamb came and took the scroll from the right hand of the One sitting on the throne. [8] After he took the scroll, the four living things and the 24 elders bowed down before the Lamb. Each one of them had a harp. Also, they were holding golden bowls full of incense. These bowls of incense are the prayers of God's holy people. [9] And they all sang a new song to the Lamb:

"You are worthy to take the scroll
and to open its seals,
because you were killed;
and with the blood of your death
you bought men for God
from every tribe, language, people,
and nation.
[10] You made them to be a kingdom of
priests for our God.
And they will rule on the earth."

[11] Then I looked, and I heard the voices of many angels. The angels were around the throne, the four living things, and the elders. There were thousands and thousands of angels—there were 10,000 times 10,000. [12] The angels said in a loud voice:

"The Lamb who was killed is worthy
to receive power, wealth, wisdom and
strength,
honor, glory, and praise!"

[13] Then I heard every living thing in heaven and on earth and under the earth and in the sea. I heard every thing in all these places, saying:

"All praise and honor and glory and
power
forever and ever
to the One who sits on the throne
and to the Lamb!"

[14] The four living things said, "Amen!" And the elders bowed down and worshiped.

6 Then I watched while the Lamb opened the first of the seven seals. I heard one of the four living things speak with a voice like thunder. It said, "Come!" [2] I looked and there before me was a white horse. The rider on the horse held a bow, and he was given a crown. And he rode out, defeating the enemy. He rode out to win the victory.

[3] The Lamb opened the second seal. Then I heard the second living thing say, "Come!" [4] Then another horse came out. This was a red horse. Its rider was given power to take away peace from the earth. He was given power to make people kill each other. And he was given a big sword.

[5] The Lamb opened the third seal. Then I heard the third living thing say, "Come!" I looked, and there before me was a black horse. Its rider held a pair of scales in his hand. [6] Then I heard something that sounded like a voice. It came from where the four living things were. The voice said, "A quart of wheat for a day's pay. And three quarts of barley for a day's pay. And do not damage the olive oil and wine!"

[7] The Lamb opened the fourth seal. Then I heard the voice of the fourth living thing say, "Come!" [8] I looked, and there before me was a pale horse. Its rider was named death. Hades[n] was following close behind him. They were given power over a fourth of the earth. They were given power to kill people by war, by starving them, by disease, and by the wild animals of the earth.

[9] The Lamb opened the fifth seal. Then I saw some souls under the altar. They were the souls of those who had been killed because they were faithful to God's message and to the truth they had received. [10] These souls shouted in a loud voice, "Holy and true Lord, how long until you judge the people of

6:8 Hades The unseen world where the dead are.

the earth and punish them for killing us?" ¹¹Then each one of these souls was given a white robe. They were told to wait a short time longer. There were still some of their brothers in the service of Christ who must be killed as they were. They were told to wait until all of this killing was finished.

¹²Then I watched while the Lamb opened the sixth seal. There was a great earthquake. The sun became black like rough black cloth. The full moon became red like blood. ¹³The stars in the sky fell to the earth like figs falling from a fig tree when the wind blows. ¹⁴The sky disappeared. It was rolled up like a scroll. And every mountain and island was moved from its place.

¹⁵Then all people hid in caves and behind the rocks on the mountains. There were the kings of the earth, the rulers, the generals, the rich people and the powerful people. Everyone, slave and free, hid himself. ¹⁶They called to the mountains and the rocks, "Fall on us. Hide us from the face of the One who sits on the throne. Hide us from the anger of the Lamb! ¹⁷The great day for their anger has come. Who can stand against it?"

THE 144,000 PEOPLE OF ISRAEL

7 After this I saw four angels standing at the four corners of the earth. The angels were holding the four winds of the earth. They were stopping the wind from blowing on the land or on the sea or on any tree. ²Then I saw another angel coming from the east. This angel had the seal of the living God. He called out in a loud voice to the four angels. These were the four angels that God had given power to harm the earth and the sea. He said to the four angels, ³"Do not harm the land or the sea or the trees before we put the sign on the people who serve our God. We must put the sign on their foreheads." ⁴Then I heard how many people were marked with the sign. There were 144,000. They were from every tribe of the people of Israel.

⁵ From the tribe of Judah 12,000 were
    marked with the sign,
 from the tribe of Reuben 12,000,
 from the tribe of Gad 12,000,
⁶ from the tribe of Asher 12,000,
 from the tribe of Naphtali 12,000,
 from the tribe of Manasseh 12,000,
⁷ from the tribe of Simeon 12,000,
 from the tribe of Levi 12,000,
 from the tribe of Issachar 12,000,
⁸ from the tribe of Zebulun 12,000,
 from the tribe of Joseph 12,000,
 from the tribe of Benjamin 12,000.

THE GREAT CROWD

⁹Then I looked, and there was a great number of people. There were so many people that no one could count them. They were from every nation, tribe, people, and language of the earth. They were all standing before the throne and before the Lamb. They wore white robes and had palm branches in their hands. ¹⁰They were shouting in a loud voice, "Salvation belongs to our God, who sits on the throne, and to the Lamb." ¹¹The elders ⁿ and the four living things were there. All the angels were standing around them and the throne. The angels bowed down on their faces before the throne and worshiped God. ¹²They were saying, "Amen! Praise, glory, wisdom, thanks, honor, power, and strength belong to our God forever and ever. Amen!"

¹³Then one of the elders asked me, "Who are these people in white robes? Where did they come from?"

¹⁴I answered, "You know who they are, sir."

And the elder said, "These are the people who have come out of the great

---

7:11 **elders** Elder means "older." Here the elders probably represent God's people.

suffering. They have washed their robes[n] with the blood of the Lamb. Now they are clean and white. [15]And they are before the throne of God. They worship God day and night in his temple. And the One who sits on the throne will protect them. [16]Those people will never be hungry again. They will never be thirsty again. The sun will not hurt them. No heat will burn them. [17]For the Lamb at the center of the throne will be their shepherd. He will lead them to springs of water that give life. And God will wipe away every tear from their eyes."

THE SEVENTH SEAL

8 The Lamb opened the seventh seal. Then there was silence in heaven for about half an hour. [2]And I saw the seven angels who stand before God. They were given seven trumpets.

[3]Another angel came and stood at the altar. This angel had a golden pan for incense. The angel was given much incense to offer with the prayers of all God's holy people. The angel put this offering on the golden altar before the throne. [4]The smoke from the incense went up from the angel's hand to God. It went up with the prayers of God's people. [5]Then the angel filled the incense pan with fire from the altar and threw it on the earth. There were flashes of lightning, thunder and loud noises, and an earthquake.

THE SEVEN ANGELS AND TRUMPETS

[6]Then the seven angels who had the seven trumpets prepared to blow them.

[7]The first angel blew his trumpet. Then hail and fire mixed with blood was poured down on the earth. And a third of the earth and all the green grass and a third of the trees were burned up.

[8]The second angel blew his trumpet. Then something that looked like a big mountain burning with fire was thrown into the sea. And a third of the sea became blood. [9]And a third of the living things in the sea died, and a third of the ships were destroyed.

[10]The third angel blew his trumpet. Then a large star, burning like a torch, fell from the sky. It fell on a third of the rivers and on the springs of water. [11]The name of the star is Wormwood.[n] And a third of all the water became bitter. Many people died from drinking the water that was bitter.

[12]The fourth angel blew his trumpet. Then a third of the sun and a third of the moon and a third of the stars were hit. So a third of them became dark. A third of the day was without light.

[13]While I watched, I heard an eagle that was flying high in the air. The eagle said with a loud voice, "Trouble! Trouble! Trouble for those who live on the earth! The trouble will begin with the sounds of the trumpets that the other three angels are about to blow."

9 Then the fifth angel blew his trumpet. And I saw a star fall from the sky to the earth. The star was given the key to the deep hole that leads down to the bottomless pit. [2]Then it opened the bottomless pit. Smoke came up from the hole like smoke from a big furnace. The sun and sky became dark because of the smoke from the hole. [3]Then locusts came down to the earth out of the smoke. They were given the power to sting like scorpions.[n] [4]They were told not to harm the grass on the earth or any plant or tree. They could harm only the people who did not have the sign of God on their foreheads. [5]These locusts were given the power to cause pain to the people for five months. But they were not given the power to kill anyone. And the pain they felt was like the pain that a scorpion gives when it stings a

---

7:14 **washed their robes** This means they believed in Jesus so that their sins could be forgiven by Christ's blood.
8:11 **Wormwood** Name of a very bitter plant, used here to give the idea of bitter sorrow.
9:3 **scorpions** A scorpion is an insect that stings with a bad poison.

person. ⁶During those days people will look for a way to die, but they will not find it. They will want to die, but death will run away from them.

⁷The locusts looked like horses prepared for battle. On their heads they wore things that looked like crowns of gold. Their faces looked like human faces. ⁸Their hair was like women's hair, and their teeth were like lions' teeth. ⁹Their chests looked like iron breastplates. The sound their wings made was like the noise of many horses and chariots hurrying into battle. ¹⁰The locusts had tails with stingers like scorpions. The power they had to hurt people for five months was in their tails. ¹¹The locusts had a king who was the angel of the bottomless pit. His name in the Hebrew language is Abaddon. In the Greek language his name is Apollyon.ⁿ

¹²The first great trouble is past. There are still two other great troubles that will come.

¹³The sixth angel blew his trumpet. Then I heard a voice coming from the horns on the golden altar that is before God. ¹⁴The voice said to the sixth angel who had the trumpet, "Free the four angels who are tied at the great river Euphrates." ¹⁵These four angels had been kept ready for this hour and day and month and year. They were freed to kill a third of all people on the earth. ¹⁶I heard how many troops on horses were in their army. There were 200,000,000.

¹⁷In my vision I saw the horses and their riders. They looked like this: They had breastplates that were fiery red, dark blue, and yellow like sulfur. The heads of the horses looked like heads of lions. The horses had fire, smoke, and sulfur coming out of their mouths. ¹⁸A third of all the people on earth were killed by these three terrible things coming out of the horses' mouths: the fire, the smoke, and the sulfur. ¹⁹The horses' power was in their mouths and also in their tails. Their tails were like snakes that have heads to bite and hurt people.

²⁰The other people on the earth were not killed by these terrible things. But they still did not change their hearts and turn away from what they had made with their own hands. They did not stop worshiping demons and idols made of gold, silver, bronze, stone, and wood— things that cannot see or hear or walk. ²¹These people did not change their hearts and turn away from murder or evil magic, from their sexual immorality or stealing.

THE ANGEL AND THE LITTLE SCROLL

10 Then I saw another powerful angel coming down from heaven. He was dressed in a cloud and had a rainbow around his head. His face was like the sun, and his legs were like poles of fire. ²The angel was holding a small scroll open in his hand. He put his right foot on the sea and his left foot on the land. ³He shouted loudly like the roaring of a lion. When he shouted, the voices of seven thunders spoke. ⁴The seven thunders spoke, and I started to write. But then I heard a voice from heaven. The voice said, "Do not write what the seven thunders said. Keep these things secret."

⁵Then the angel I saw standing on the sea and on the land raised his right hand to heaven. ⁶He made a promise by

> He will lead them to springs of water that give life. And God will wipe away every tear from their eyes.
>
> –REVELATION 7:17

9:11 Abaddon...Apollyon Both names mean "Destroyer."

the power of the One who lives forever and ever. He is the One who made the skies and all that is in them. He made the earth and all that is in it, and he made the sea and all that is in it. The angel said, "There will be no more waiting! [7]In the days when the seventh angel is ready to blow his trumpet, God's secret plan will be finished. This plan is the Good News God told to his servants, the prophets."

[8]Then I heard the same voice from heaven again. The voice said to me, "Go and take the open scroll that is in the angel's hand. This is the angel that is standing on the sea and on the land."

[9]So I went to the angel and asked him to give me the little scroll. He said to me, "Take the scroll and eat it. It will be sour in your stomach. But in your mouth it will be sweet as honey." [10]So I took the little scroll from the angel's hand and I ate it. In my mouth it tasted sweet as honey. But after I ate it, it was sour in my stomach. [11]Then I was told, "You must prophesy again about many peoples, nations, languages, and kings."

THE TWO WITNESSES

11 Then I was given a measuring stick like a rod. I was told, "Go and measure the temple[n] of God and the altar, and count the number of people worshiping there. [2]But do not measure the yard outside the temple. Leave it alone. It has been given to the people who are not Jews. They will walk on the holy city for 42 months. [3]And I will give power to my two witnesses to prophesy for 1,260 days. They will be dressed in rough cloth to show how sad they are."

[4]These two witnesses are the two olive trees and the two lampstands that stand before the Lord of the earth. [5]If anyone tries to hurt the witnesses,

fire comes from their mouths and kills their enemies. Anyone who tries to hurt them will die like this. [6]These witnesses have the power to stop the sky from raining during the time they are prophesying. They have power to make the waters become blood. They have power to send every kind of trouble to the earth. They can do this as many times as they want.

[7]When the two witnesses have finished telling their message, the beast will fight against them. This is the beast that comes up from the bottomless pit. He will defeat them and kill them. [8]The bodies of the two witnesses will lie in the street of the great city. This city is named Sodom[n] and Egypt. These names for the city have a special meaning. It is the city where the Lord was killed. [9]Men from every race of people, tribe, language, and nation will look at the bodies of the two witnesses for three and a half days. They will refuse to bury them. [10]People who live on the earth will be happy because these two are dead. They will have parties and send each other gifts. They will do these things because these two prophets brought much suffering to those who live on the earth.

[11]But after three and a half days, God put the breath of life into the two prophets again. They stood on their feet. Everyone who saw them was filled with fear. [12]Then the two prophets heard a loud voice from heaven say, "Come up here!" And they went up into heaven in a cloud. Their enemies watched them go.

[13]At that same time there was a great earthquake. A tenth of the city was destroyed. And 7,000 people were killed in the earthquake. Those who did not die were very afraid. They gave glory to the God of heaven.

[14]The second great trouble is

11:1 **temple** God's house—the place where God's people worship and serve him. Here, John sees it pictured as the special building in Jerusalem where God commanded the Jews to worship him.
11:8 **Sodom** City that God destroyed because the people were so evil.

finished. The third great trouble is coming soon.

THE SEVENTH TRUMPET

[15] Then the seventh angel blew his trumpet. And there were loud voices in heaven. The voices said:

> "The power to rule the world
>   now belongs to our Lord and his
>   Christ.
> And he will rule forever and ever."

[16] Then the 24 elders[n] bowed down on their faces and worshiped God. These are the elders who sit on their thrones before God. [17] They said:

> "We give thanks to you, Lord God
>   All-Powerful.
> You are the One who is and who was.
> We thank you because you have used
>   your great power
>   and have begun to rule!
> [18] The people of the world were angry;
>   but now is the time for your anger.
> Now is the time for the dead to be
>   judged.
> It is time to reward your servants the
>   prophets
>   and to reward your holy people,
>   all who respect you, great and small.
> It is time to destroy those who
>   destroy the earth!"

[19] Then God's temple[n] in heaven was opened. The Ark of the Covenant that holds the agreement that God gave to his people could be seen in his temple. Then there were flashes of lightning, noises, thunder, an earthquake, and a great hailstorm.

THE WOMAN AND THE DRAGON

12 And then a great wonder appeared in heaven: There was a woman who was clothed with the sun. The moon was under her feet. She had a crown of 12 stars on her head. [2] The woman was pregnant. She cried out with pain because she was about to give birth. [3] Then another wonder appeared in heaven: There was a giant red dragon. He had seven heads with seven crowns on each head. He also had ten horns. [4] The dragon's tail swept a third of the stars out of the sky and threw them down to the earth. The dragon stood in front of the woman who was ready to give birth to a baby. He wanted to eat the woman's baby as soon as it was born. [5] The woman gave birth to a son. He will rule all the nations with an iron scepter. But her child was taken up to God and to his throne. [6] The woman ran away into the desert to a place God prepared for her. There she would be taken care of for 1,260 days.

[7] Then there was a war in heaven. Michael[n] and his angels fought against the dragon. The dragon and his angels fought back. [8] But the dragon was not strong enough. He and his angels lost their place in heaven. [9] He was thrown down out of heaven. (The giant dragon is that old snake called the devil or Satan. He leads the whole world the wrong way.) The dragon with his angels was thrown down to the earth.

[10] Then I heard a loud voice in heaven say:

> "The salvation and the power and the
>   kingdom of our God
>   and the authority of his Christ
>   have now come.
> They have come because the accuser
>   of our brothers has been thrown
>   out.
> He accused our brothers day and
>   night before our God.
> [11] And our brothers defeated him

11:16 **24 elders** Elder means "older." Here the elders probably represent God's people.
11:19 **temple** God's house—the place where God's people worship and serve him. John sees the heavenly temple pictured to be like the Temple of God's people in the Old Testament.
12:7 **Michael** The archangel—leader among God's angels or messengers (Jude 9).

by the blood of the Lamb's death
and by the truth they preached.
They did not love their lives so much
that they were afraid of death.
¹² So be happy, you heavens
and all who live there!
But it will be terrible for the earth
and the sea,
because the devil has come down
to you!
He is filled with anger.
He knows that he does not have
much time."

¹³The dragon saw that he had been thrown down to the earth. So he hunted down the woman who had given birth to the son. ¹⁴But the woman was given the two wings of a great eagle. Then she could fly to the place that was prepared for her in the desert. There she would be taken care of for three and a half years. There she would be away from the snake. ¹⁵Then the snake poured water out of its mouth like a river. He poured the water toward the woman, so that the flood would carry her away. ¹⁶But the earth helped her. The earth opened its mouth and swallowed the river that came from the mouth of the dragon. ¹⁷Then the dragon was very angry at the woman. He went off to make war against all her other children. Her children are those who obey God's commands and have the truth that Jesus taught.

¹⁸And the dragon[n] stood on the seashore.

THE TWO BEASTS

13 Then I saw a beast coming up out of the sea. It had ten horns

and seven heads. There was a crown on each horn. A name against God was written on each head. ²This beast looked like a leopard, with feet like a bear's feet. He had a mouth like a lion's mouth. The dragon gave the beast all of his power and his throne and great authority. ³One of the heads of the beast looked as if it had been wounded and killed. But this death wound was healed. The whole world was amazed and followed the beast. ⁴People worshiped the dragon because he had given his power to the beast. And they also worshiped the beast. They asked, "Who is as powerful as the beast? Who can make war against him?"

⁵The beast was allowed to say proud words and words against God. He was allowed to use his power for 42 months. ⁶He used his mouth to speak against God. He spoke against God's name, against the place where God lives, and against all those who live in heaven. ⁷He was given power to make war against God's holy people and to defeat them. He was given power over every tribe, people, language, and nation. ⁸All who live on earth will worship the beast. These are all the people since the beginning of the world whose names are not written in the Lamb's book of life. The Lamb is the One who was killed.

⁹If anyone has ears, he should listen:

¹⁰ If anyone is to be a prisoner,
then he will be a prisoner.
If anyone is to be killed with the
sword,
then he will be killed with the
sword.

> Worship God. He made the heavens, the earth, the sea, and the springs of water.
> —REVELATION 14:7

12:18 **the dragon** Some Greek copies read "I."

This means that God's holy people must have patience and faith.

[11] Then I saw another beast coming up out of the earth. He had two horns like a lamb, but he talked like a dragon. [12] This beast stands before the first beast and uses the same power that the first beast has. He uses this power to make everyone living on earth worship the first beast. The first beast was the one that had the death wound that was healed. [13] The second one does great miracles. He even makes fire come down from heaven to earth while people are watching. [14] This second beast fools those who live on earth. He fools them by the miracles he has been given the power to do. He does these miracles to serve the first beast. The second beast ordered people to make an idol to honor the first beast. This was the one that was wounded by the sword but did not die. [15] The second beast was given power to give life to the idol of the first one. Then the idol could speak and order all who did not worship it to be killed. [16] The second animal also forced all people, small and great, rich and poor, free and slave, to have a mark on their right hand or on their forehead. [17] No one could buy or sell without this mark. This mark is the name of the beast or the number of his name. [18] Whoever has understanding can find the meaning of the number. This requires wisdom. This number is the number of a man. His number is 666.[n]

THE SONG OF THE SAVED

14 Then I looked, and there before me was the Lamb. He was standing on Mount Zion.[n] There were 144,000 people with him. They all had his name and his Father's name written on their foreheads. [2] And I heard a sound from heaven like the noise of flooding water and like the sound of loud thunder. The sound I heard was like people playing harps. [3] And they sang a new song before the throne and before the four living things and the elders.[n] The only ones who could learn the new song were the 144,000 who had been saved from the earth. No one else could learn the song. [4] These 144,000 are the ones who did not do sinful things with women. They kept themselves pure. They follow the Lamb every place he goes. These 144,000 were saved from among the people of the earth. They are the first people to be offered to God and the Lamb. [5] They were not guilty of telling lies. They are without fault.

THE THREE ANGELS

[6] Then I saw another angel flying high in the air. The angel had the eternal Good News to preach to those who live on earth—to every nation, tribe, language, and people. [7] The angel said in a loud voice, "Fear God and give him praise. The time has come for God to judge all people. Worship God. He made the heavens, the earth, the sea, and the springs of water."

[8] Then the second angel followed the first angel and said, "She is destroyed! The great city of Babylon is destroyed! She made all the nations drink the wine of her adultery and of God's anger."

[9] A third angel followed the first two angels. This third angel said in a loud voice: "It will be bad for the person who worships the beast and his idol and gets the beast's mark on the forehead or on the hand. [10] He will drink the wine of God's anger. This wine is prepared with all its strength in the cup of God's anger. He will be put in pain with burning sulfur before the holy angels and the Lamb. [11] And the smoke from their burning pain will

---

13:18 666 Some Greek copies read "616."
14:1 Mount Zion Another name for Jerusalem, here meaning the spiritual city of God's people.
14:3 elders Elder means "older." Here the elders probably represent God's people.

rise forever and ever. There will be no rest, day or night, for those who worship the beast and his idol or who get the mark of his name." [12]This means that God's holy people must be patient. They must obey God's commands and keep their faith in Jesus.

[13]Then I heard a voice from heaven. It said, "Write this: From now on, the dead who were in the Lord when they died are happy."

The Spirit says, "Yes, that is true. They will rest from their hard work. The reward of all they have done stays with them."

THE EARTH IS HARVESTED

[14]I looked and there before me was a white cloud. Sitting on the white cloud was One who looked like a Son of Man.[n] He had a gold crown on his head and a sharp sickle[n] in his hand. [15]Then another angel came out of the temple. This angel called to the One who was sitting on the cloud, "Take your sickle and gather from the earth. The time to harvest has come. The fruit of the earth is ripe." [16]So the One that was sitting on the cloud swung his sickle over the earth. And the earth was harvested.

[17]Then another angel came out of the temple in heaven. This angel also had a sharp sickle. [18]And then another angel came from the altar. This angel has power over the fire. This angel called to the angel with the sharp sickle. He said, "Take your sharp sickle and gather the bunches of grapes from the earth's vine. The earth's grapes are ripe." [19]The angel swung his sickle over the earth. He gathered the earth's grapes and threw them into the great winepress of God's anger. [20]The grapes were crushed in the winepress outside the city. And blood flowed out of the winepress. It rose as high as the heads of the horses for a distance of 200 miles.

THE LAST TROUBLES

15 Then I saw another wonder in heaven. It was great and amazing. There were seven angels bringing seven troubles. These are the last troubles, because after these troubles God's anger is finished.

[2]I saw what looked like a sea of glass mixed with fire. All of those who had won the victory over the beast and his idol and over the number of his name were standing by the sea. They had harps that God had given them. [3]They sang the song of Moses, the servant of God, and the song of the Lamb:

"You do great and wonderful things,
　　　　　　　　　　　　Psalm 111:2
Lord God, the God of heaven's armies.　　　　　　*Amos 3:13*
Everything the Lord does is right and true,　　　　　*Psalm 145:17*
King of the nations."[n]
[4] Everyone will respect you, Lord.
　　　　　　　　　　　　Jeremiah 10:7
They will honor you.
Only you are holy.
All people will come and worship you.　　*Psalm 86:9–10*
This is because he is a faithful God who does no wrong.
He is right and fair."
　　　　　　　　　　　Deuteronomy 32:4

[5]After this I saw the temple (the Tent of the Agreement) in heaven. The temple was opened. [6]And the seven angels bringing the seven troubles came out of the temple. They were dressed in clean, shining linen. They wore golden bands tied around their chests. [7]Then one of the four living things gave seven golden bowls to the seven angels. The bowls were filled with

---

14:14 Son of Man "Son of Man" is a name Jesus called himself. It showed he was God's Son, but he was also a man. See dictionary.
14:14 sickle A farming tool with a curved blade. It was used to harvest grain.
15:3 King...nations. Some Greek copies read "King of the ages."

the anger of God, who lives forever and ever. [8]The temple was filled with smoke from the glory and the power of God. No one could enter the temple until the seven troubles of the seven angels were finished.

THE BOWLS OF GOD'S ANGER

16 Then I heard a loud voice from the temple. The voice said to the seven angels, "Go and pour out the seven bowls of God's anger on the earth."

[2]The first angel left. He poured out his bowl on the land. Then ugly and painful sores came upon all those who had the mark of the beast and who worshiped his idol.

[3]The second angel poured out his bowl on the sea. Then the sea became blood like that of a dead man. Every living thing in the sea died.

[4]The third angel poured out his bowl on the rivers and the springs of water. And they became blood. [5]Then I heard the angel of the waters say to God:

"Holy One, you are the One who is
   and who was.
   You are right to decide to punish
      these evil people.
[6] They have spilled the blood of your
      holy people and your prophets.
   Now you have given them blood to
      drink as they deserve."

[7] And I heard the altar say:
"Yes, Lord God All-Powerful,
   the way you punish evil people is
      right and fair."

[8]The fourth angel poured out his bowl on the sun. The sun was given power to burn the people with fire. [9]They were burned by the great heat, and they cursed the name of God. God is the One who had control over these troubles. But the people refused to change their hearts and lives and give glory to God.

[10]The fifth angel poured out his bowl on the throne of the beast. And darkness covered the beast's kingdom. People bit their tongues because of the pain. [11]They cursed the God of heaven because of their pain and the sores they had. But they refused to change their hearts and turn away from the evil things they did.

[12]The sixth angel poured out his bowl on the great river Euphrates. The water in the river was dried up. This prepared the way for the kings from the east to come. [13]Then I saw three evil spirits that looked like frogs. They came out of the mouth of the dragon, out of the mouth of the beast, and out of the mouth of the false prophet. [14]These evil spirits are the spirits of demons. They have power to do miracles. They go out to the kings of the whole world. They go out to gather the kings for battle on the great day of God All-Powerful.

[15]"Listen! I will come as a thief comes! Happy is the person who stays awake and keeps his clothes with him. Then he will not have to go without clothes and be ashamed because he is naked."

[16]Then the evil spirits gathered the kings together to the place that is called Armageddon[n] in the Hebrew language.

[17]The seventh angel poured out his bowl into the air. Then a loud voice came out of the temple from the throne. The voice said, "It is finished!" [18]Then there were flashes of lightning, noises, thunder, and a big earthquake. This was the worst earthquake that has ever happened since people have been on earth. [19]The great city split into three parts. The cities of the nations were destroyed. And God did not forget to punish Babylon the Great. He gave that city the cup filled with the wine of his terrible anger. [20]Every island disappeared, and there were no more mountains. [21]Giant hailstones fell on people from the sky. The hailstones

---

16:16 Armageddon This word means "Hill of Megiddo," where many battles were fought long ago.

weighed about 100 pounds each. People cursed God because of the hail. This trouble was a terrible thing.

THE WOMAN ON THE ANIMAL

17 One of the seven angels came and spoke to me. This was one of the angels that had the seven bowls. He said, "Come, and I will show you the punishment that will be given to the famous prostitute. She is the one sitting over many waters. ²The kings of the earth sinned sexually with her. And the people of the earth became drunk from the wine of her sexual immorality."

³Then the angel carried me away by the Spirit to the desert. There I saw a woman sitting on a red beast. He was covered with names against God written on him. He had seven heads and ten horns. ⁴The woman was dressed in purple and red. She was shining with the gold, jewels, and pearls she was wearing. She had a golden cup in her hand. This cup was filled with evil things and the uncleanness of her sexual immorality. ⁵She had a title written on her forehead. This title has a hidden meaning. This is what was written:

THE GREAT BABYLON
MOTHER OF PROSTITUTES
AND THE EVIL THINGS OF THE EARTH.

⁶I saw that the woman was drunk. She was drunk with the blood of God's holy people. She was drunk with the blood of those who were killed because of their faith in Jesus.

When I saw the woman, I was fully amazed. ⁷Then the angel said to me, "Why are you amazed? I will tell you the hidden meaning of this woman and the beast she rides—the one with seven heads and ten horns. ⁸The beast that you saw was once alive. He is not alive now. But he will be alive and come up out of the bottomless pit and go away to be destroyed. The people who live on earth will be amazed when they see the beast. They will be amazed because he was once alive, is not alive now, but will come again. These are the people whose names have never been written in the book of life since the beginning of the world.

⁹"You need a wise mind to understand this. The seven heads on the beast are the seven hills where the woman sits. They are also seven kings. ¹⁰Five of the kings have already died. One of the kings lives now. And the last king is coming. When he comes, he will stay only a short time. ¹¹The beast that was once alive but is not alive now is an eighth king. This eighth king also belongs to the first seven kings. And he will go away to be destroyed.

¹²"The ten horns you saw are ten kings. These ten kings have not yet begun to rule. But they will receive power to rule with the beast for one hour. ¹³All ten of these kings have the same purpose. And they will give their power and authority to the beast. ¹⁴They will make war against the Lamb. But the Lamb will defeat them, because he is Lord of lords and King of kings. He will defeat them with his chosen and faithful followers—the people that he has called."

¹⁵Then the angel said to me, "You saw the water where the prostitute sits. These waters are the many peoples, the different races, nations, and languages. ¹⁶The beast and the ten horns you saw will hate the prostitute. They will take everything she has and leave her naked. They will eat her body and burn her with fire. ¹⁷God made the ten horns want to carry out his purpose: They agreed to give the beast their power to rule. They will rule until what God has said is completed. ¹⁸The woman you saw is the great city that rules over the kings of the earth."

BABYLON IS DESTROYED

18 Then I saw another angel coming down from heaven.

This angel had great power. The angel's glory made the earth bright. ²The angel shouted in a powerful voice:

"The great city of Babylon is
  destroyed!
She has become a home for
  demons.
She has become a city for every evil
  spirit,
  a city for every unclean and hated
  bird.
³ All the peoples of the earth have
  drunk
  the strong wine of her sexual
  immorality.
The kings of the earth have sinned
  sexually with her,
  and the businessmen of the world
  have grown rich from the great
  wealth of her luxury."

⁴Then I heard another voice from heaven say:

"Come out of that city, my people,
  so that you will not share in her
  sins.
Then you will not receive the
  terrible things that will happen
  to her.
⁵ The city's sins are piled up as high as
  the sky.
God has not forgotten the wrongs
  she has done.
⁶ Give that city the same as she gave to
  others.
Pay her back twice as much as she
  did.
Prepare wine for her that is twice as
  strong
  as the wine she prepared for
  others.
⁷ She gave herself much glory and rich
  living.
Give her that much suffering and
  sadness.
She says to herself, 'I am a queen
  sitting on my throne.
I am not a widow; I will never be
  sad.'

⁸ So these terrible things will come to
  her in one day:
  death, crying, and great hunger.
She will be destroyed by fire,
  because the Lord God who judges
  her is powerful."

⁹The kings of the earth who sinned sexually with her and shared her wealth will see the smoke from her burning. Then they will cry and weep because of her death. ¹⁰They will be afraid of her suffering and stand far away. They will say:

"Terrible! How terrible, great city,
  powerful city of Babylon!
Your punishment has come in one
  hour!"

¹¹And the businessmen of the earth will cry and weep for her. They will be sad because now there is no one to buy the things they sell. ¹²They sell gold, silver, jewels, pearls, fine linen cloth, purple cloth, silk, and red cloth. They sell all kinds of citron wood and all kinds of things made from ivory, expensive wood, bronze, iron, and marble. ¹³They also sell cinnamon, spice, incense, myrrh, frankincense, wine, and olive oil; fine flour, wheat, cattle, sheep, horses, and carriages. They sell the bodies and souls of men. ¹⁴They will say,

"Babylon, the good things you
  wanted are gone from you.
All your rich and fancy things have
  disappeared.
You will never have them again."

¹⁵The businessmen will be afraid of her suffering and stand far away from her. These are the men who became rich from selling those things to her. The men will cry and be sad. ¹⁶They will say:

"Terrible! How terrible for the great
  city!

> She was dressed in fine linen,
> purple and red cloth.
> She was shining with gold, jewels,
> and pearls!
>
> [17] All these riches have been destroyed
> in one hour!"

Every sea captain, all those who travel on ships, the sailors, and all the people who earn money from the sea stood far away from Babylon. [18] They saw the smoke from her burning. They said loudly, "There was never a city like this great city!" [19] They threw dust on their heads and cried to show how sad they were. They said:

> "Terrible! How terrible for the great
> city!
> All the people who had ships on the
> sea
> became rich because of her wealth!
> But she has been destroyed in one
> hour!
>
> [20] Be happy because of this, heaven!
> Be happy, God's holy people and
> apostles and prophets!
> God has punished her because of
> what she did to you."

[21] Then a powerful angel picked up a stone like a large stone for grinding grain. The angel threw the stone into the sea and said:

> "That is how the great city of Babylon
> will be thrown down.
> The city will never be found again.
> [22] The music of people playing harps
> and other instruments, flutes
> and trumpets,
> will never be heard in you again.
> No workman doing any job
> will ever be found in you again.
> The sound of grinding grain
> will never be heard in you again.
> [23] The light of a lamp
> will never shine in you again.

> The voices of a bridegroom and bride
> will never be heard in you again.
> Your businessmen were the world's
> great men.
> All the nations were tricked by
> your magic.
> [24] She is guilty of the death
> of the prophets and God's holy
> people
> and of all who have been killed on
> earth."

PEOPLE IN HEAVEN PRAISE GOD

19 After this I heard what sounded like a great many people in heaven. They were saying:

> "Hallelujah![n]
> Salvation, glory, and power belong to
> our God.
> [2]   His judgments are true and right.
> Our God has punished the prostitute.
> She is the one who made the earth
> evil with her sexual immorality.
> God has punished the prostitute to
> pay her back for the death of his
> servants."

[3] Again they said:

> "Hallelujah!
> She is burning, and her smoke will
> rise forever and ever."

[4] Then the 24 elders[n] and the four living things bowed down. They worshiped God, who sits on the throne. They said:

> "Amen, Hallelujah!"

[5] Then a voice came from the throne:

> "Praise our God, all you who serve
> him!
> Praise our God, all you who honor
> him, both small and great!"

19:1 **Hallelujah** This means "Praise God!"
19:4 **24 elders** Elder means "older." Here the elders probably represent God's people.

⁶Then I heard what sounded like a great many people. It sounded like the noise of flooding water and like loud thunder. The people were saying:

"Hallelujah!
    Our Lord God rules. He is the All-Powerful.
⁷ Let us rejoice and be happy
    and give God glory!
Give God glory, because the wedding
    of the Lamb has come.
And the Lamb's bride has made
    herself ready.
⁸ Fine linen was given to the bride
    for her to wear.
The linen was bright and
    clean."

(The fine linen means the good things done by God's holy people.)

⁹Then the angel said to me, "Write this: Those who are invited to the wedding meal of the Lamb are happy!" Then the angel said, "These are the true words of God."

¹⁰Then I bowed down at the angel's feet to worship him. But he said to me, "Do not worship me! I am a servant like you and your brothers who have the truth of Jesus. Worship God! Because the truth about Jesus is the spirit that gives all prophecy."

THE RIDER ON THE WHITE HORSE

¹¹Then I saw heaven open. There before me was a white horse. The rider on the horse is called Faithful and True. He is right when he judges and makes war. ¹²His eyes are like burning fire, and on his head are many crowns. He has a name written on him, but he is the only one who knows the name. No other person knows the name. ¹³He is dressed in a robe dipped in blood. His name is the Word of God. ¹⁴The armies of heaven were following him on white horses. They were dressed in fine linen, white and clean. ¹⁵A sharp sword comes out of the rider's mouth. He will use this sword to defeat the nations. He will rule them with a scepter of iron. He will crush out the wine in the winepress of the terrible anger of God All-Powerful. ¹⁶On his robe and on his leg was written this name: "KING OF KINGS AND LORD OF LORDS."

¹⁷Then I saw an angel standing in the sun. The angel called with a loud voice to all the birds flying in the sky, "Come together for the great feast of God. ¹⁸Come together so that you can eat the bodies of kings and generals and famous men. Come to eat the bodies of the horses and their riders and the bodies of all people—free, slave, small, and great."

¹⁹Then I saw the beast and the kings of the earth. Their armies were gathered together to make war against the rider on the horse and his army. ²⁰But the beast was captured and with him the false prophet. This false prophet was the one who did the miracles for the beast. The false prophet had used these miracles to trick those who had the mark of the beast and worshiped his idol. The false prophet and the beast were thrown alive into the lake of fire that burns with sulfur. ²¹Their armies were killed with the sword that came out of the mouth of the rider on the horse. All the birds ate the bodies until they were full.

THE 1,000 YEARS

20 I saw an angel coming down from heaven. He had the key to the bottomless pit. He also held a large chain in his hand. ²The angel grabbed the dragon, that old snake who is the devil. The angel tied him up for 1,000 years. ³Then he threw him into

> Then I saw heaven open. There before me was a white horse. The rider on the horse is called Faithful and True.
> —REVELATION 19:11

the bottomless pit and closed it and locked it over him. The angel did this so that he could not trick the people of the earth anymore until the 1,000 years were ended. After 1,000 years he must be set free for a short time.

[4]Then I saw some thrones and people sitting on them. They had been given the power to judge. And I saw the souls of those who had been killed because they were faithful to the truth of Jesus and the message from God. They had not worshiped the beast or his idol. They had not received the mark of the beast on their foreheads or on their hands. They came back to life and ruled with Christ for 1,000 years. [5](The others that were dead did not live again until the 1,000 years were ended.) This is the first raising of the dead. [6]Blessed and holy are those who share in this first raising of the dead. The second death has no power over them. They will be priests for God and for Christ. They will rule with him for 1,000 years.

[7]When the 1,000 years are over, Satan will be set free from his prison. [8]He will go out to trick the nations in all the earth—Gog and Magog. Satan will gather them for battle. There will be so many people that they will be like sand on the seashore. [9]And Satan's army marched across the earth and gathered around the camp of God's people and the city that God loves. But fire came down from heaven and burned them up. [10]And Satan, who tricked them, was thrown into the lake of burning sulfur with the beast and the false prophet. There they will be punished day and night forever and ever.

PEOPLE OF THE WORLD ARE JUDGED

[11]Then I saw a great white throne and the One who was sitting on it. Earth and sky ran away from him and disappeared. [12]And I saw the dead, great and small, standing before the throne. And the book of life was opened. There were also other books opened. The dead were judged by what they had done, which was written in the books. [13]The sea gave up the dead who were in it. Death and Hades[n] gave up the dead who were in them. Each person was judged by what he had done. [14]And Death and Hades were thrown into the lake of fire. This lake of fire is the second death. [15]And if anyone's name was not found written in the book of life, he was thrown into the lake of fire.

THE NEW JERUSALEM

21 Then I saw a new heaven and a new earth. The first heaven and the first earth had disappeared. Now there was no sea. [2]And I saw the holy city coming down out of heaven from God. This holy city is the new Jerusalem.[n] It was prepared like a bride dressed for her husband. [3]I heard a loud voice from the throne. The voice said, "Now God's home is with men. He will live with them, and they will be his people. God himself will be with them and will be their God.[n] [4]He will wipe away every tear from their eyes. There will be no more death, sadness, crying, or pain. All the old ways are gone."

[5]The One who was sitting on the throne said, "Look! I am making everything new!" Then he said, "Write this, because these words are true and can be trusted."

[6]The One on the throne said to me: "It is finished! I am the Alpha and the Omega,[n] the Beginning and the End. I will give free water from the spring of the water of life to anyone who is thirsty. [7]Anyone who wins the victory will receive this. And I will be his God,

---

20:13 **Hades** Where the dead are.
21:2 **new Jerusalem** The spiritual city where God's people live with him.
21:3 **and . . . God** Some Greek copies do not have this phrase.
21:6 **the Alpha and the Omega** The first and last letters in the Greek alphabet. This means "the beginning and the end."

☆ Revelation 21:1-4

At the end of Revelation, we are told there will be "a new heaven and a new earth." When that happens, there will be no more sad things, no more crying, and nobody will ever die.

One day God will make a new place for us to live with him. It will be a perfect and beautiful place! No one will say mean words, and nobody will make fun of others. There will be no stealing or cheating. No one will get sick, and no one will die. There will be no sadness or tears. There will be pretty, green trees and calm, clear rivers. There will be a big, bright, shiny city where Jesus will live. We will be able to see him in person and hang out with him! It sounds exciting, doesn't it?

• •

If you're a child of God, you will get to live in this new place with Jesus forever and ever.

---

and he will be my son. ⁸But those who are cowards, who refuse to believe, who do evil things, who kill, who are sexually immoral, who do evil magic, who worship idols, and who tell lies—all these will have a place in the lake of burning sulfur. This is the second death."

⁹One of the seven angels came to me. This was one of the angels who had the seven bowls full of the seven last troubles. He said, "Come with me. I will show you the bride, the wife of the Lamb." ¹⁰The angel carried me away by the Spirit to a very large and high mountain. He showed me the holy city, Jerusalem. It was coming down out of heaven from God. ¹¹It was shining with the glory of God. It was shining bright like a very expensive jewel, like a jasper. It was clear as crystal. ¹²The city had a great high wall with 12 gates. There were 12 angels at the gates. On each gate was written the name of 1 of the 12 tribes of Israel. ¹³There were three gates on the east, three on the north, three on the south, and three on the west. ¹⁴The walls of the city were built on 12 foundation stones. On the stones were written the names of the 12 apostles of the Lamb.

¹⁵The angel who talked with me had a measuring rod made of gold. He had this rod to measure the city, its gates, and its wall. ¹⁶The city was built in a square. Its length was equal to its width. The angel measured the city with the rod. The city was 1,500

miles long, 1,500 miles wide, and 1,500 miles high. ¹⁷The angel also measured the wall. It was 216 feet high, by man's measurement. That was the measurement the angel was using. ¹⁸The wall was made of jasper. The city was made of pure gold, as pure as glass. ¹⁹The foundation stones of the city walls had every kind of jewel in them. The first cornerstone was jasper, the second was sapphire, the third was chalce-dony, the fourth was emerald, ²⁰the fifth was onyx, the sixth was carnelian, the seventh was chrysolite, the eighth was beryl, the ninth was topaz, the tenth was chrysoprase, the eleventh was jacinth, and the twelfth was amethyst. ²¹The 12 gates were 12 pearls. Each gate was made from a single pearl. The street of the city was made of pure gold. The gold was clear as glass.

²²I did not see a temple in the city. The Lord God All-Powerful and the Lamb are the city's temple. ²³The city does not need the sun or the moon to shine on it. The glory of God is its light, and the Lamb is the city's lamp. ²⁴By its light the people of the world will walk. The kings of the earth will bring their glory into it. ²⁵The city's gates will never be shut on any day, because there is no night there. ²⁶The greatness and the honor of the nations will be brought into it. ²⁷Nothing unclean will ever enter the city. No one who does shameful things or tells lies will ever go into it. Only those whose names are written in the Lamb's book of life will enter the city.

22 Then the angel showed me the river of the water of life. The river was shining like crystal. It flows from the throne of God and of the Lamb ²down the middle of the street of the city. The tree of life was on each side of the river. It produces fruit 12 times a year, once each month. The leaves of the tree are for the healing of all people. ³Nothing that God judges guilty will be in that city. The throne of God and of the Lamb will be there. And God's servants will worship him. ⁴They will see his face, and his name will be written on their foreheads. ⁵There will never be night again. They will not need the light of a lamp or the light of the sun. The Lord God will give them light. And they will rule like kings forever and ever.

⁶The angel said to me, "These words are true and can be trusted. The Lord is the God of the spirits of the prophets. He sent his angel to show his servants the things that must happen soon."

⁷"Listen! I am coming soon! He who obeys the words of prophecy in this book will be happy."

⁸I am John. I am the one who heard and saw these things. When I heard and saw them, I bowed down to worship at the feet of the angel who showed these things to me. ⁹But the angel said to me, "Do not worship me! I am a servant like you and your brothers the prophets. I am a servant like all those who obey the words in this book. Worship God!"

¹⁰Then the angel told me, "Do not keep secret the words of prophecy in this book. The time is near for all this to happen. ¹¹Whoever is doing evil, let him continue to do evil. Whoever is unclean, let him continue to be unclean. Whoever is doing right, let him continue to do right. Whoever is holy, let him continue to be holy."

¹²"Listen! I am coming soon! I will bring rewards with me. I will repay

> I am the Alpha and the Omega, the First and the Last, the Beginning and the End.
>
> —REVELATION 22:13

each one for what he has done. [13]I am the Alpha and the Omega,[n] the First and the Last, the Beginning and the End.

[14]"Those who wash their robes[n] will be blessed. They will have the right to eat the fruit from the tree of life. They may go through the gates into the city. [15]Outside the city are the evil people, those who do evil magic, who are sexually immoral, who murder, who worship idols, and who love lies and tell lies.

[16]"I, Jesus, have sent my angel to tell you these things for the churches. I am the descendant from the family of David. I am the bright morning star."

[17]The Spirit and the bride say, "Come!" Everyone who hears this should also say, "Come!" If anyone is thirsty, let him come; whoever wishes it may have the water of life as a free gift.

[18]I warn everyone who hears the words of the prophecy of this book: If anyone adds anything to these words, God will give him the troubles written about in this book. [19]And if anyone takes away from the words of this book of prophecy, God will take away his share of the tree of life and of the holy city, which are written about in this book.

[20]Jesus is the One who says that these things are true. Now he says, "Yes, I am coming soon."

Amen. Come, Lord Jesus!

[21]The grace of the Lord Jesus be with all. Amen.

22:13 the Alpha and the Omega The first and last letters in the Greek alphabet. This means "the beginning and the end."
22:14 wash their robes This means they believed in Jesus so that their sins could be forgiven by Christ's blood.

Contributors

Additional Contributions

Between-the-book summaries and additional devotions written by Jill M. Smith. Feature summaries written by Jill M. Smith and Bri Loomis.

Books of the Bible

OLD TESTAMENT

Genesis
Exodus
Leviticus
Numbers
Deuteronomy
Joshua
Judges
Ruth
1 Samuel
2 Samuel
1 Kings
2 Kings
1 Chronicles
2 Chronicles
Ezra
Nehemiah
Esther
Job
Psalms
Proverbs
Ecclesiastes
Song of Songs
Isaiah
Jeremiah
Lamentations
Ezekiel
Daniel
Hosea
Joel
Amos
Obadiah
Jonah
Micah
Nahum
Habakkuk
Zephaniah
Haggai
Zechariah
Malachi

NEW TESTAMENT

Matthew
Mark
Luke
John
Acts
Romans
1 Corinthians
2 Corinthians
Galatians
Ephesians
Philippians
Colossians
1 Thessalonians
2 Thessalonians
1 Timothy
2 Timothy
Titus
Philemon
Hebrews
James
1 Peter
2 Peter
1 John
2 John
3 John
Jude
Revelation

Callout Verses Index